The Intellectual World of Late Antique Christianity

Reshaping Classical Traditions

Edited by LEWIS AYRES
University of Durham & Australian Catholic University, Melbourne

MICHAEL W. CHAMPION
Australian Catholic University, Melbourne

MATTHEW R. CRAWFORD
Australian Catholic University, Melbourne

Shaftesbury Road, Cambridge CB2 8EA, United Kingdom

One Liberty Plaza, 20th Floor, New York, NY 10006, USA

477 Williamstown Road, Port Melbourne, VIC 3207, Australia

314–321, 3rd Floor, Plot 3, Splendor Forum, Jasola District Centre, New Delhi – 110025, India

103 Penang Road, #05–06/07, Visioncrest Commercial, Singapore 238467

Cambridge University Press is part of Cambridge University Press & Assessment, a department of the University of Cambridge.

We share the University's mission to contribute to society through the pursuit of education, learning and research at the highest international levels of excellence.

www.cambridge.org
Information on this title: www.cambridge.org/9781108835299

DOI: 10.1017/9781108883559

© Cambridge University Press & Assessment 2023

This publication is in copyright. Subject to statutory exception and to the provisions of relevant collective licensing agreements, no reproduction of any part may take place without the written permission of Cambridge University Press & Assessment.

First published 2023

Printed in the United Kingdom by TJ Books Limited, Padstow Cornwall

A catalogue record for this publication is available from the British Library

Library of Congress Cataloging-in-Publication Data
Names: Ayres, Lewis, author. | Champion, Michael W., author. |
Crawford, Matthew R., author.
Title: The intellectual world of late antique Christianity : reshaping classical traditions / edited by Lewis Ayres, University of Durham, Michael W. Champion, Australian Catholic University, Melbourne, Matthew R. Crawford, Australian Catholic University, Melbourne.
Description: Cambridge, United Kingdom ; New York, NY, USA :
Cambridge University Press, [2023] | Includes bibliographical references and index.
Identifiers: LCCN 2022028962 | ISBN 9781108835299 (hardback) |
ISBN 9781108883559 (ebook)
Subjects: LCSH: Church history – Primitive and early church, ca. 30–600 |
Knowledge, Theory of (Religion) – History. | Intellectual life – History – To 1500. |
Learning and scholarship – History – To 1500.
Classification: LCC BR162.3 .A97 2023 | DDC 270.1–dc23/eng/20230126
LC record available at https://lccn.loc.gov/2022028962

ISBN 978-1-108-83529-9 Hardback

Cambridge University Press & Assessment has no responsibility for the persistence or accuracy of URLs for external or third-party internet websites referred to in this publication and does not guarantee that any content on such websites is, or will remain, accurate or appropriate.

Contents

List of Plates   [*page* ix]
Notes on Contributors   [x]
Preface   [xv]
List of Abbreviations   [xvii]

1 Modes of Knowing and Ordering Knowledge
   in Early Christianity   [1]
   LEWIS AYRES, MICHAEL W. CHAMPION, AND MATTHEW R. CRAWFORD

2 The Beginnings of a Christian Doctrine of the Spiritual
   Senses before Origen   [21]
   JANE HEATH

3 Health, Medicine, and Philosophy in the School of Justin
   Martyr   [47]
   JARED SECORD

4 Learning Through Experience: The Structure of Asceticism in
   Irenaeus of Lyons   [66]
   PAUL SAIEG

5 The Order of Education and Knowledge in Clement
   of Alexandria   [89]
   MATYÁŠ HAVRDA

6 Origen's Institutions and the Shape of Biblical
   Scholarship   [100]
   PETER W. MARTENS

7 Dialogue and Catalogue: Fate, Free Will, and Belief
   in the *Book of the Laws of the Countries*   [118]
   SCOTT FITZGERALD JOHNSON

8 Iamblichus on Divination and Prophecy   [134]
   PETER T. STRUCK

9 Cyprian, Scripture, and Socialisation: Forming Faith in the Catechumenate and Beyond [153]
EDWINA MURPHY

10 Sacrificial Knowing: Cyprian and Early Christian Ritual Knowledge [166]
ANDREW McGOWAN

11 Learning the Language of God: Tables in Early Christian Texts [185]
ANDREW M. RIGGSBY

12 The Aëtian *Placita* and the Church Fathers: Creative Use of a Distinctive Mode of Ordering Knowledge [198]
DAVID T. RUNIA

13 Nicaea's Frame: The Organisation of Creedal Knowledge in Late Antiquity and Modernity [221]
ANDREW RADDE-GALLWITZ

14 The Arian Controversy and the Problem of Image(s) [246]
REBECCA LYMAN

15 Imagining Ephrem the Author [261]
JEFFREY WICKES

16 Homilies as 'Modes of Knowing': An Exploration on the Basis of Greek Patristic Festal Sermons (*c.* 350–*c.* 450 CE) [282]
JOHAN LEEMANS

17 Dissemination of Biblical Narratives, Motifs, and Figures through Early Christian Inscriptions and Homilies [303]
CILLIERS BREYTENBACH

18 How to Make Use of Pagan Knowledge without Separating Oneself from the Church's Milk: The Function of Otherness in Gregory of Nyssa's Theory of Self-Perfection [328]
JAN R. STENGER

19 Female Characters as Modes of Knowing in Late Imperial Dialogues: The Body, Desire, and the Intellectual Life [347]
DAWN LAVALLE NORMAN

Contents   vii

20 The Christianity of Latin Christian Poetry   [366]
    MARK EDWARDS

21 Ambrose's Hymns as Modes of Knowing the 'Real'   [388]
    BRIAN DUNKLE, SJ

22 Confused Voices: Sound and Sense in the Later Augustine   [404]
    CAROL HARRISON

23 Precision and the Limits of Autopsy in Augustine's
    Critique of Pagan Divination   [426]
    MICHAEL HANAGHAN

24 The Duplex Via: Authority and Reason at Cassiciacum   [443]
    GERALD P. BOERSMA

25 The Object of Our Gaze: Visual Perception as a Mode
    of Knowing   [466]
    ROBIN M. JENSEN

26 Reconsidering the *Tholos* Image in the Eusebian Canon
    Tables: Symbols, Space, and Books in the Late Antique
    Christian Imagination   [484]
    MATTHEW R. CRAWFORD

27 Condemning the Glutton of the Monastery:
    Rhetorical Strategies and the Epistemology of
    Philoxenos of Mabbug   [516]
    JEANNE-NICOLE MELLON SAINT-LAURENT

28 Evagrius of Pontus on Λύπη: Distress and Cognition
    between Philosophy, Medicine, and Monasticism   [530]
    JONATHAN L. ZECHER

29 Liturgical Modes of Knowing: Coming to
    Know God (and Oneself) in Sixth-Century
    Hymns and Homilies   [548]
    SARAH GADOR-WHYTE

30 Prolegomena to Philosophy and the Ascetic Ordering
    of Knowledge   [569]
    MICHAEL W. CHAMPION

31 Bureaucratic Modes of Knowing in the Late Roman Empire   [590]
    SARA AHBEL-RAPPE

32 The Dissemination and Appropriation of Legal
   Knowledge in the Age of Justinian   [608]
   PETER SARRIS

33 The Ordering of Knowledge in Four Late Patristic
   Christological Handbooks   [626]
   DIRK KRAUSMÜLLER

34 World and Empire: Contrasting the Cosmopolitan
   Visions of George of Pisidia and Maximus the
   Confessor in Seventh-Century Byzantium   [644]
   PAUL M. BLOWERS

35 Boethius on the Ordering of Knowledge   [663]
   JOHN MAGEE

36 Ordering Emotional Communities: Modes
   of Knowing in Gregory the Great   [690]
   BRONWEN NEIL

37 Creating Knowledge and Knowing Creation
   in Theological and Scientific Writing in Late Antique
   Western Christendom   [705]
   HELEN FOXHALL FORBES

38 Hierarchies of Knowledge in the Works of Bede   [729]
   ZACHARY GUILIANO

39 Epilogue   [752]
   TERESA MORGAN

Bibliography   [758]
Index Locorum   [853]
General Index   [884]

A plate section will be found between pages 498 and 499

Plates

2.1 Baptism. Fresco. Catacomb of Saints Marcellinus and Peter. Rome, Italy. 3rd century (Archivah / Alamy Stock Photo)
17.1 Apse mosaic, Anemurium (Photo: Campbell 1998: plate xv)
26.1 *Tholos* image in Abba Garima I (6th–7th century). Ethiopia, Abba Garima Monastery, AG II, fol. 258v (Photo © Michael Gervers, 2004)
26.2 Fountain of life image in the Gospels of St Médard de Soissons (before 827 CE). Paris, Bibliothèque nationale de France, MS lat. 8850, fol. 6v.
26.3 *Tholos* with a *hypothesis* inscription, serving as the frontispiece for the sequence of Canon Tables that follow in a Greek gospel-book (9th century). Venice, Biblioteca Nazionale Marciana, MS gr. I 8, fol. 3r.
26.4 *Tholos* image in Etchmiadzin Gospels (989). Erevan, Matenadaran, MS 2374, fol. 5v.
26.5 Taybat al-Imam near Hama, Syria, Church of the Holy Martyrs, floor mosaic (441 CE) (Photo © Judith McKenzie)
26.6 Mosaic in the Dome of the Rotunda of Thessaloniki. © Ephorate of Antiquities of Thessaloniki, Hellenic Ministry of Culture & Sports – Archaeological Resources Fund

Notes on Contributors

SARA AHBEL-RAPPE is Professor of Classical Studies at the University of Michigan and author of *Reading Neoplatonism* (Cambridge, 2000); a translation of Damascius' *Problems and Solutions Concerning First Principles* (Oxford, 2010); and several books on Socrates.

LEWIS AYRES is Professor of Catholic and Historical Theology at Durham University and Professorial Fellow in the Australian Catholic University's Institute for Religion and Critical Inquiry (IRCI).

PAUL M. BLOWERS (PhD University of Notre Dame, 1988) is Dean E. Walker Professor of Church History at Emmanuel Christian Seminary in Milligan University (Tennessee).

GERALD P. BOERSMA is Associate Professor of Theology at Ave Maria University where he also serves as Director of the MA Program in Theology. His research focuses on Patristic theology, especially fourth- and fifth-century Latin Christianity and the thought of Augustine. He is the author of *Augustine's Early Theology of Image* (Oxford, 2016).

CILLIERS BREYTENBACH taught in Pretoria and Munich before holding a chair for New Testament at Humboldt-Universität Berlin (1993–2019). He is Professor Extraordinary at Stellenbosch University.

MICHAEL W. CHAMPION is Associate Professor in Early Christian and Late Antique Studies at the IRCI, Australian Catholic University.

MATTHEW R. CRAWFORD completed his PhD and an AHRC-funded postdoc at Durham University before joining the Institute for Religion and Critical Inquiry at Australian Catholic University, Melbourne in 2015, where he is Associate Professor and currently serves as Director of the Biblical and Early Christian Studies Program.

BRIAN DUNKLE, SJ, is Associate Professor of Historical Theology at Boston College School of Theology and Ministry. He is the author of *Enchantment and Creed in the Hymns of Ambrose of Milan* (Oxford, 2016) and *Ambrose of Milan: Treatises on Noah and David* (Catholic University of America, 2020).

MARK EDWARDS has been tutor in Theology at Christ Church, Oxford, and University Lecturer (now Associate Professor) in Patristics at the University of Oxford since 1993. Since 2014 he has held the title Professor of Early Christian Studies.

HELEN FOXHALL FORBES is Professoressa Ordinaria of Medieval History at Università Ca' Foscari, Venice. Her research focuses on the meeting points between intellectual culture and social and environmental history in late antiquity and the early Middle Ages, and covers the disciplines of theology, history, and archaeology.

SARAH GADOR-WHYTE is a research fellow in Biblical and Early Christian Studies at the Institute for Religion and Critical Inquiry at the Australian Catholic University. She is the author of *Theology and Poetry in Early Byzantium: The Kontakia of Romanos the Melodist* (Cambridge, 2017).

ZACHARY GUILIANO The Rev. Dr Zachary Guiliano is chaplain and career development research fellow in early medieval history at St Edmund Hall, Oxford. He is the author of *The Homiliary of Paul the Deacon: Religious and Cultural Reform in Carolingian Europe* (Turnhout, 2021), which won the 2022 Ecclesiastical History Book Prize for best first monograph.

MICHAEL HANAGHAN is Research Fellow (Latin Christianity in Late Antiquity) at the Institute for Religion and Critical Inquiry, Australian Catholic University, Melbourne.

CAROL HARRISON is Lady Margaret Professor of Divinity in the Faculty of Theology and Religion, Oxford University, and a canon of Christ Church Cathedral, Oxford.

MATYÁŠ HAVRDA is Research Professor at the Institute of Philosophy, Czech Academy of Sciences. His publications include *The So-Called Eighth Stromateus by Clement of Alexandria: Early Christian Reception of Greek Scientific Methodology* (Brill, 2016) and *Galen's Epistemology: Experience, Reason, and Method in Ancient Medicine* (co-edited with R.J. Hankinson, Cambridge University Press, 2022).

JANE HEATH is an associate professor in the Department of Theology and Religion at Durham University.

ROBIN M. JENSEN is the Patrick O'Brien Professor of Theology at the University of Notre Dame (USA), where she is also a concurrent professor in Art History and in Classics and a Fellow of the Medieval Institute. Her most recent, single-authored books include *The Cross: History, Art, and Controversy* (Harvard University Press, 2015); and *From Idols to Icons: The Emergence of Christian Art in Late Antiquity* (University of California Press, 2022).

SCOTT FITZGERALD JOHNSON is Associate Professor and Chair of Classics and Letters at the University of Oklahoma. He studies the literary, cultural, and intellectual history of the late antique world.

DIRK KRAUSMÜLLER is currently employed by the University of Vienna. His research is focused on late patristic theology and Byzantine monasticism.

DAWN LAVALLE NORMAN is a research fellow in Early Christianity at Australian Catholic University. She works on the history of the philosophical dialogue, with a particular interest in gender. Her first book, *The Aesthetics of Hope in Later Greek Literature: Methodius of Olympus'* Symposium *and the Crisis of the Third Century* (Cambridge University Press, 2019), demonstrated how Methodius of Olympus' *Symposium* was central to the literary revolutions of the third century CE in the transitional period between the Second Sophistic and late antiquity.

JOHAN LEEMANS is Professor of Christianity in Late Antiquity at the Faculty of Theology and Religious Studies, Catholic University of Louvain (KU Leuven), Belgium.

REBECCA LYMAN is the Samuel Garrett Professor of Church History emerita at The Church Divinity School of the Pacific, Berkeley, California.

JOHN MAGEE is Professor of Classics and of Medieval Studies at the University of Toronto. His publications have focused on Boethius, Calcidius, and other later ancient commentators and philosophers.

PETER W. MARTENS is Professor of Early Christianity at Saint Louis University. His books include *Origen and Scripture: Contours of the Exegetical Life* (Oxford University Press, 2012), *Adrian's Introduction to the Divine Scriptures: An Antiochene Handbook for Scriptural Interpretation* (Oxford University Press, 2017), and, with Paul M. Blowers, *The Oxford Handbook of Early Christian Biblical Interpretation* (Oxford University Press, 2019).

ANDREW MCGOWAN is Dean of the Berkeley Divinity School and McFaddin Professor of Anglican Studies at Yale, and former Warden of

Trinity College, The University of Melbourne. His publications include *Ascetic Eucharists* (Oxford, 1999) and *Ancient Christian Worship* (Grand Rapids, 2014).

JEANNE-NICOLE MELLON SAINT-LAURENT is Associate Professor of Historical Theology and Syriac Patristics at Marquette University, Milwaukee, WI, USA.

TERESA MORGAN is McDonald-Agape Professor of New Testament and Early Christianity at Yale Divinity School.

EDWINA MURPHY is Deputy Dean and Director of Research at the Australian College of Theology.

BRONWEN NEIL is Professor of Ancient History at Macquarie University (Sydney) and a research associate of the Department of Biblical and Ancient Studies, UNISA (Pretoria).

ANDREW RADDE-GALLWITZ is Professor in the Program of Liberal Studies at the University of Notre Dame. His most recent monograph is *Gregory of Nyssa's Doctrinal Works: A Literary Study* (Oxford University Press, 2018), and he edits the series The Cambridge Edition of Early Christian Writings.

ANDREW M. RIGGSBY is Lucy Shoe Meritt Professor in Classics at the University of Texas at Austin. His current work focuses on information technology in the ancient world and the application of modern cognitive theory to antiquity.

DAVID T. RUNIA is an honorary professor at the Australian Catholic University and a professorial fellow at the University of Melbourne.

PAUL SAIEG is a PhD candidate at the University of Notre Dame. His dissertation examines the connection between asceticism and theology in John Chrysostom.

PETER SARRIS studied late antique and Byzantine history at the University of Oxford, where he was elected to a Prize Fellowship at All Souls College. He is currently Professor of Late Antique, Medieval, and Byzantine Studies at the University of Cambridge and a Fellow of Trinity College.

JARED SECORD works as a student advisor at the University of Calgary. He is the author of *Christian Intellectuals and the Roman Empire: From Justin Martyr to Origen* (Pennsylvania State University Press, 2020).

JAN R. STENGER is Professor of Classics at the Julius-Maximilians-Universität Würzburg, Germany. From 2012 to 2019 he was MacDowell Professor of Greek at the University of Glasgow.

PETER T. STRUCK is Professor and Chair of the Department of Classical Studies at the University of Pennsylvania.

JEFFREY WICKES is Associate Professor in the Department of Theology at the University of Notre Dame. His work studies the role of Syriac poetry in the religious and literary landscape of late antiquity.

JONATHAN L. ZECHER is a senior research fellow in the Institute for Religion and Critical Inquiry at the Australian Catholic University and a researcher on the Modes of Knowing project.

Preface

This book is the result of a multi-year project generously funded by the Australian Catholic University (ACU), titled 'Modes of Knowing and the Ordering of Knowledge in Early Christianity' (2017–22). We thank the University for the material and institutional support that made the project possible. Housed in ACU's Institute for Religion and Critical Inquiry, the Modes of Knowing project was led by Chief Investigators Lewis Ayres (Durham University/ACU), Michael Champion (ACU), Matthew Crawford (ACU), Jane Heath (Durham University), and Andrew Radde-Gallwitz (University of Notre Dame). Sarah Gador-Whyte, Michael Hanaghan, Dawn LaValle Norman, and Jonathan Zecher (ACU) made substantial intellectual contributions throughout, including participating in fortnightly research meetings in Melbourne, taking lead roles in the project's annual international seminars, commenting on draft essays, and helping to shape this volume in a myriad of other ways. Jonatan Simons also enriched our discussions as he completed a PhD dissertation funded by the project. The project's annual seminars, held at ACU's Rome Campus 2017–19, offered an opportunity to debate key ideas and develop and refine many of the essays included in this book. (Others were specially commissioned; all contributions were subject to peer review, and we thank those involved in this process.). The Rome Seminars were enjoyable occasions of lively and friendly scholarly debate, and we record our deep gratitude to all the participants for their stimulating contributions. The Modes of Knowing project also sponsored sessions and workshops at the 2017 annual meeting of the North American Patristics Society and the XVIII International Conference on Patristic Studies at Oxford (2019), the latter in partnership with Jeremiah Coogan and Philip Forness. We thank all presenters and audience members at those events for their insightful contributions, which broadened and deepened the conversations that have resulted in this volume. Jeremiah Coogan assisted ably in preparing the manuscript for submission, including checking references, compiling the bibliography, and formatting the chapters. We thank the team at Cambridge University Press, led by Beatrice Rehl, for their efficient support and their patience with our pandemic-induced delays, and we are grateful to the five anonymous readers for the Press, whose feedback helped to improve the volume. We hope that this collection of case studies may stimulate further investigation of how early Christian epistemologies affected individual and communal norms and shaped discourses, institutions, and embodied practices in late antiquity.

Abbreviations

ACO	*Acta conciliorum oecumenicorum*
ACT	Ancient Christian Texts
ACW	Ancient Christian Writers
Aev	*Aevum: Rassegna de scienze, storiche, linguistiche, e filologiche*
AfR	*Archiv für Religionsgeschichte*
AJP	*American Journal of Philology*
AKGWG.PHK	Abhandlungen der Königlichen Gesellschaft der Wissenschaften zu Göttingen. Philologisch-Historische Klasse
AnBoll	*Analecta Bollandiana*
ANF	Ante-Nicene Fathers
ANRW	*Aufstieg und Niedergang der römischen Welt: Geschichte und Kultur Roms im Spiegel der neueren Forschung*
ASE	*Annali di Storia dell'Esegesi*
Aug	*Augustinianum*
AugStud	*Augustinian Studies*
BAug	Bibliothèque augustinienne
BBR	*Bulletin for Biblical Research*
BHT	Beiträge zur historischen Theologie
BL	British Library
BLE	*Bulletin de littérature ecclésiastique*
BSGRT	Bibliotheca Scriptorum Graecorum et Romanorum Teubneriana
Budé	Collection des universités de France, publiée sous le patronage de l'Association Guillaume Budé
ByzZ	*Byzantinische Zeitschrift*
BZ	*Biblische Zeitschrift*
CAG	Commentaria in Aristotelem Graeca
CCCM	Corpus Christianorum Continuatio Mediaevalis
CCSG	*Corpus Christianorum: Series Graeca*
CCSL	*Corpus Christianorum: Series Latina*

CGL	Coptic Gnostic Library
CH	*Church History*
CIL	Corpus Inscriptionum Latinarum
ClAnt	*Classical Antiquity*
CMG	Corpus Medicorum Graecorum
CNS	*Cristianesimo nella storia*
CP	*Classical Philology*
CPG	*Clavis Patrum Graecorum*, ed. M. Geerard. 5 vols. Turnhout (1974–87)
CQ	*Classical Quarterly*
CSCO	Corpus Scriptorum Christianorum Orientalium
CSEL	Corpus Scriptorum Ecclesiasticorum Latinorum
CSS	Cistercian Studies Series
DOP	*Dumbarton Oaks Papers*
DRev	*Downside Review*
EC	*Early Christianity*
EIr	*Encyclopaedia Iranica*, ed. E. Yarshater. London (1982–)
ETL	*Ephemerides Theologicae Lovanienses*
FC	Fathers of the Church
FMSt	*Frühmittelalterliche Studien*
GCS	Die griechischen christlichen Schriftsteller der ersten [drei] Jahrhunderte
GEDSH	*The Gorgias Encyclopedic Dictionary of the Syriac Heritage.*, ed. Sebastian P. Brock, Aaron M. Butts, George A. Kiraz, and Lucas van Rompay. Piscataway, NJ, 2011.
GNO	Gregorii Nysseni Opera
GR	*Greece and Rome*
GRBS	*Greek, Roman, and Byzantine Studies*
HBT	*Horizons in Biblical Theology*
Herm	*Hermathena*
HTR	*Harvard Theological Review*
Hug	*Hugoye: Journal of Syriac Studies*
ICG	*Inscriptiones Christianae Graecae*
IJST	*International Journal of Systematic Theology*
ITQ	*Irish Theological Quarterly*
JAJ	*Journal of Ancient Judaism*
JbAC	*Jahrbuch für Antike und Christentum*
JBRec	*Journal of the Bible and Its Reception*
JCSCS	*Journal of the Canadian Society for Coptic Studies*

JCSSS	*Journal of the Canadian Society for Syriac Studies*
JECH	*Journal of Early Christian History*
JECS	*Journal of Early Christian Studies*
JEH	*Journal of Ecclesiastical History*
JHS	*Journal of Hellenic Studies*
JLA	*Journal of Late Antiquity*
JLARC	*Journal for Late Antique Religion and Culture*
JML	*Journal of Medieval Latin*
JÖB	*Jahrbuch der österreichischen Byzantinistik*
JQR	*Jewish Quarterly Review*
JRS	*Journal of Roman Studies*
JTI	*Journal of Theological Interpretation*
JTS	*Journal of Theological Studies*
KlPauly	*Der kleine Pauly*
LCL	Loeb Classical Library
LTK	*Lexikon für Theologie und Kirche*
LTP	*Laval théologique et philosophique*
MGH	Monumenta Germaniae Historica
MH	*Museum Helveticum*
MS	*Mediaeval Studies*
MTZ	*Münchener theologische Zeitschrift*
Mus	*Muséon: Revue d'études orientales*
NAWG	*Nachrichten (von) der Akademie der Wissenschaften in Göttingen*
NBA	Nuova Biblioteca Agostiniana
NPNF[2]	Nicene and Post Nicene Fathers, Second Series
NRSV	New Revised Standard Version
NTS	*New Testament Studies*
OCA	Orientalia Christiana Analecta
OCP	*Orientalia Christiana Periodica*
OCT	Oxford Classical Texts / Scriptorum Classicorum Bibliotheca Oxoniensis
OECS	Oxford Early Christian Studies
OECT	Oxford Early Christian Texts
OLP	*Orientalia Lovaniensia Periodica*
OrChrAn	Orientalia Christiana Analecta
OrSyr	*L'Orient syrien*
OW	Origenes: Werke mit deutscher Übersetzung
P&P	*Past & Present*
ParOr	*Parole de l'orient*

List of Abbreviations

PG	*Patrologia Graeca*, ed. J.-P. Migne. Paris (1857–86)
PGL	*Patristic Greek Lexicon*, ed. G. W. H. Lampe. Cambridge (1969)
PhA	Philosophia Antiqua
PL	*Patrologia Latina*, ed. J.-P. Migne. Paris (1844–64)
PO	*Patrologia Orientalis*
PTS	Patristische Texte und Studien
PW	*Paulys Real-Encyclopädie der classischen Altertumswissenschaft*, ed. G. Wissowa and W. Kroll. Stuttgart (1894–1980)
RA	*Recherches augustiniennes et patristiques*
RAC	*Reallexikon für Antike und Christentum*, ed. T. Klauser et al. Stuttgart (1950–)
RB	*Revue biblique*
RBén	*Revue bénédictine*
REAug	*Revue des études augustiniennes*
RevPhil	*Revue de philologie*
RPP	*Religion Past and Present: Encyclopedia of Theology and Religion*, ed. H. D. Betz. Leiden (2007–13)
RRE	*Religion in the Roman Empire*
RSPT	*Revue des sciences philosophiques et théologiques*
RSR	*Recherches de science religieuse*
SA	*Studia Anselmiana*
SAPERE	Scripta Antiquitatis Posterioris ad Ethicam Religionemque pertinentia
SC	Sources chrétiennes
SCH	*Studies in Church History*
SEG	*Supplementum epigraphicum Graecum* (1923–)
SGLG	Sammlung griechischer und lateinischer Grammatike
SLA	*Studies in Late Antiquity*
SMSR	*Studi e materiali di storia delle religioni*
SO	Symbolae Osloenses
Spec	*Speculum*
SPhiloA	*Studia Philonica Annual*
StPatr	Studia Patristica
SVF	*Stoicorum Veterum Fragmenta*, H. von Arnim. Leipzig (1903–05)
SVTQ	*St Vladimir's Theological Quarterly*
TAPA	*Transactions of the American Philological Association*
TJT	*Toronto Journal of Theology*
TLG	Thesaurus Linguae Graecae
TLZ	*Theologische Literaturzeitung*
TP	*Theologie und Philosophie*

TRE	*Theologische Realenzyklopädie*, ed. G. Krause and G. Müller. Berlin (1977–)
TSK	*Theologische Studien und Kritiken*
TTH	Translated Texts for Historians
TU	Texte und Untersuchungen
USQR	*Union Seminary Quarterly Review*
VC	*Vigiliae Christianae*
WGRW	Writings from the Greco-Roman World
WSA	Works of Saint Augustine: A Translation for the 21st Century
YCS	*Yale Classical Studies*
ZAC	*Zeitschrift für Antikes Christentum*
ZKG	*Zeitschrift für Kirchengeschichte*
ZKunstG	*Zeitschrift für Kunstgeschichte*
ZNW	*Zeitschrift für die neutestamentliche Wissenschaft*

1 | Modes of Knowing and Ordering Knowledge in Early Christianity

LEWIS AYRES, MICHAEL W. CHAMPION,
AND MATTHEW R. CRAWFORD

For nothing is / sweeter than to know everything.

οὐδέν ⟨ἐστι⟩ γὰρ / γλυκύτερον ἢ πάντ' εἰδέναι.

Menander, *Epit.* fr. 2

But since 'it is sweet to know everything', for this reason we, quite sensibly, also devote ourselves to studying the opinions of the Greeks which they have collected on each of the subjects.

Ἐπειδὴ δέ ἐστι γλυκὺ τὸ πάντα εἰδέναι, ταύτῃ τοι, καὶ μάλα ἐμφρόνως, καὶ τὰς τῶν Ἑλλήνων πολυπραγμονοῦμεν δόξας, ἃς δὴ καὶ ἐφ' ἑκάστῳ συνειλόχασι τῶν πραγμάτων.

Cyril of Alexandria, *Against Julian* 7.17

Between the second and the seventh century CE, Christianity expanded throughout the Mediterranean basin and beyond. Throughout this expansion, Christian thinkers were imbued with the intellectual currents of the Greco-Roman world even as they at times critiqued them. Believing that Christian faith pressed them to reinterpret history and divide true from false wisdom in other philosophical and religious traditions, Christians encompassed, reorganised, and reoriented existing bodies of knowledge and conceptions of the process of knowing. Appropriating earlier traditions, they integrated bodily practices, ethics, and political identities with conceptions of reasoning informed by Christian theological claims. Christian perspectives thus provided a basis for rethinking earlier notions while classical and Jewish ideas and practices nurtured and shaped Christian intellectual traditions at the very deepest levels. In this process, Christians developed cultures of interpretation and argument, defining what it meant for them to be a textually oriented religious community

---

The editors thank Sarah Gador-Whyte, Michael Hanaghan, Dawn LaValle Norman, and Jonathan Zecher for stimulating discussion and debate throughout the project that contributed significantly to the arguments presented in this introduction. Their feedback on contributors' chapters also helped to sharpen and bring coherence to the overall volume. We also thank Jeremiah Coogan for his perceptive comments.

within the Roman empire, and thereby laid an intellectual foundation that would be built upon and modified in a variety of different later contexts, stretching from deep within the continents of Africa and Asia to the furthest limits of Europe.[1]

Questions of epistemology – what can be known? how can things be known? who has access to truth? is access to truth possible for sinful humans? – were highly contested in this formative period. Texts such as Matthew's 'no one has known the Father except the Son and those to whom the Son has revealed him' (Matt 11:27) placed Christ the revealer of truth at the centre of Christian intellectual endeavour and forced Christian thinkers into multifaceted, creative, generative, sometimes tense, engagements with established epistemic schemes and standards of classical philosophy, grammar, rhetoric, and medicine. Contests over theories of knowledge were, in turn, shaped by the institutional and economic realities of empire, educational establishments, and emerging Christian ecclesial communities, which together gave expression to Christian identity and transmitted it from one generation to the next. In the context of these institutional structures, Christian practices of pilgrimage, liturgy, asceticism, art and architecture, and use of sacred objects such as relics and holy books enacted and formed epistemic commitments by ordering the entire person towards the goal of becoming godlike (*theosis*).

Central to this intellectual and religious project was the notion of 'order', itself adapted from Greco-Roman philosophical and rhetorical sources. By following the divine Logos made known in Jesus Christ, Christians believed themselves to be restored to the original lost 'order', which enabled them to recognise and evaluate all other claims to knowledge. This bold stance is already staked out in the second-century *Oration to the Greeks* composed by Tatian the Assyrian[2] and would eventually result in ambitious encyclopaedic efforts such as Isidore of Seville's massive *Etymologiae*, one of the most influential works of the Middle Ages which attempted to 'order' all human knowledge. Similarly, the adaptation by early Christians of Platonic traditions of the 'ascent' of the intellect towards the intelligible world shaped ways of conceiving the activity of knowing and contemplation that would persist long into the modern period. The development of Christian thought and practice moulded patterns of ordering knowledge and modes of knowing which produced a distinct way of being in the world and flowed over into the formation of Christian communities.

---

[1] For Brian Stock's notion of a 'textual community', picked up by other contributors to this volume, see Stock 1983. See also caveats and discussion in Heath 2018.

[2] See Crawford 2015c.

Many lines of investigation pursued in this volume were first traversed in recent classical scholarship, which has explored how imperial power structures and communal practices affected the ordering of knowledge in the ancient world, but without considering Christian material in any great detail. Such scholarship has, for example, considered how the Roman empire's universalising grasp is interrelated with the development of encyclopaedic tendencies in literature. Michel Foucault's insight that each society nurtures its own 'mode' or 'modes of knowing' – those discourses taken to describe that which is true, mechanisms for distinguishing truth from falsehood, institutional structures that identify particular persons as able to speak truth – was a fundamental influence for this tradition of scholarship.[3] More recently, scholarship on late antiquity has demonstrated the fruitfulness of such questions for this later period while leaving scope for further work on the entanglement of Christian theology in epistemological schemes. For example, Michael Chin and Moulie Vidas have drawn together a collection of studies, amply demonstrating that the manner in which late antique people went about knowing is bound up with questions of how they negotiated and constructed structures of power, social relationships, and intersecting imaginative universes.[4]

Although Foucault is thus a point of departure here, we also hope to move debate in new directions in our attitude towards theological discourse and in our methodological variety. In common with Foucault and other cultural historians, we maintain that early Christian ideas were deeply embedded in the cultural, political, and social worlds of the Roman empire in which they evolved. A number of contributions to the volume engage Pierre Hadot's notion of philosophy as a 'way of life', which foregrounds the ethical consequences of epistemological commitments and the ways in which thought, instantiated in forms of practice and power relations, helps to shape action.[5] But we also claim that such ideas cannot be reduced to matrices of cultural and social power, since traditions of rationality have an internal dynamic force that impels them forward with wider historical consequences beyond the strictly epistemological. We are therefore convinced that understanding early Christian thought (in all its diversity and fuzzy boundaries) requires careful attention to its internal logics and theological assumptions, which in turn inflect the wider cultural and intellectual world of the empire and changing political realities of the period. Despite, and partly because of, the endless ways in which

---

[3] Foucault 1966/1973, 1969/1972; König and Whitmarsh 2007b.
[4] Chin and Vidas 2015a. [5] Hadot 1995b, 1995a/2002.

Christians participate in the wider epistemological landscape, Christianity remains identifiable as a distinct set of more and less coherent traditions: sometimes by the expression of unique Christian ideas; sometimes by the rejection of other views or practices as inconsistent with Christian faith; at other times by distinct ways of assembling or orienting those discourses, institutions, and practices that are shared with non-Christians of the period. Thus, we seek to understand how Christians attempted to order knowledge and knowing in the multiple contexts of Roman imperial culture (and ideology), Christian and non-Christian institutions and social practices and the particular *foci* of Christian beliefs about the world, its history and purpose.

This volume is intended to provide points of departure across a wide field for those who want to take forward this opportunity. The collection of case studies could never be exhaustive, and we are aware of several gaps and areas – thematic and linguistic – that could easily have been given greater prominence.[6] We hope, though, that others may find approaches and guiding questions in the individual essays productive and may be motivated to contribute to an ongoing discussion from the perspective of other scholarly specialisms.

Our original project took as its title and focus the twin themes 'modes of knowing' and 'ordering knowledge'. We understand these heuristic categories to mark out, first, the means by which knowledge is accessed or attained and, second, how one handles, processes, or arranges the knowledge thus gained. Of course, these two often overlap, since the act of knowing is contingent upon both the knowing subject and the known object. Consequently, the way in which knowledge is ordered inevitably shapes how subsequent knowers engage with it, since it delimits the modes of knowing able to be employed, opening up certain possibilities and discouraging others or even making them impossible. Nevertheless, we have found that distinguishing these two themes is useful insofar as they bring into sharper focus different aspects of the epistemological process and allow closer scrutiny of each in turn. Furthermore, our aim was to examine these twin themes across the three domains of (a) discourses, (b) the institutions that perpetuated discourses over time, and (c) the material forms that affect discourses and institutional practices. These domains likewise overlap and readers will find that frequently two or even all three are in play in the treatment of a given topic.

---

[6] Some of these gaps were the consequence of the Covid-19 pandemic, and we thank all who worked on the project in these difficult circumstances.

Although this volume is not structured around these two themes or the three domains of investigation, the collection of case studies our authors have contributed addresses all these issues at one point or another. What follows here is an attempt to draw out common threads across the collection. By so doing, our intention is to provide an alternate 'ordering' scheme for this volume, to complement the roughly chronological sequence of the chapters. We provide two maps of the collection, first tracing the intersecting contours of modes of knowing and the ordering of knowledge, and then charting the connections between discourses, institutions, and materiality by drawing on theoretical approaches to structure and agency to connect these phenomena.

Modes of Knowing

The question of whether the five bodily senses provide sound and trustworthy knowledge or something less certain was a long-running topic of philosophical debate. These classical debates continued throughout late antiquity and were reshaped in light of Christian concerns. The capacities of the human body understood as 'in Christ' inspired the development of the notion of analogous 'spiritual senses' modelled on the five corporeal modes of sensation. Scholars have typically gone to Origen as the source of this idea, and, although his robust elaboration of it is justly famous, Jane Heath shows that Origen was building upon an even older tradition evident in Clement of Alexandria and reaching back all the way to the apostle Paul, which emphasised the transformation of the human person effected by the Christ-event. For these authors, sight, hearing, taste, smell, and touch became evocative metaphors for describing the new epistemological capacities created by undergoing the waters of baptism, being united with Christ, and joining the Christian community established by him.

Divination – a well-established and theorised mode of knowing in antiquity – depended in large part on a distinction between attaining knowledge through discursive reason and gaining insight through intuition and the senses. It is thus an important case study for thinking through bodily cognition and the relation of the embodied knower to the wider order of the material cosmos. As Peter Struck notes, Iamblichus' defence of theurgical practice against the criticisms of Porphyry was influential for later Neoplatonic philosophers and helped to establish liturgical practice as a way of knowing for Neoplatonists, as it would also be for Christians. Yet some forms of divination remained problematic for Platonists. Struck highlights compelling parallels between Iamblichus' notion of 'divine divination' and the explication of biblical prophecy among Christian authors like Origen, who also were highly critical of the way in which traditional divinatory practices were implicated in matter, making them epistemologically insecure. It is possible that Iamblichus was responding to such criticisms by reshaping the classical notion of divination to avoid their bite. Iamblichus comes to regard divination as capable of revealing not mundane details, such as whom to marry or whether to engage in a business transaction, but the deepest truths of reality, in a manner akin to the Christian belief that the meaning of history is unveiled in the scriptures and the person of Jesus foretold by the prophets.

This notion of 'seeing through' textually configured material things to disclose reality fundamentally shapes early Christian modes of knowing. As in the case of the wider Platonic tradition, Christians closely associated sight and knowledge in their thinking about the transformed and embodied spiritual senses. For example, Robin Jensen explores how Christian theologians regarded vision not merely as a metaphor for a non-bodily mode of knowing but also as itself a means of gaining access to invisible and transcendent realities. If meditation on Christ's incarnation led to the belief that material reality has an intrinsic potential to become the bearer of divine presence and action, then this line of reflection could be extended to other material objects, which, Jensen argues, accords with the preference for scenes of biblical narrative in surviving Christian art from the period. It was not merely that images could teach for some audiences more effectively than extended discourse – although leaders like Augustine and Paulinus recognised that they could be just as pedagogically effective as words and texts, if not even more so. At a deeper level, images could disclose truth because material creation, understood in the light of Christian narratives, could be taken to provide access to divine reality. Such a view extended from nature to claims about the revelatory potential of cultural production. Matthew Crawford takes up such themes by analysing a specific image from late antique Christian art which had a long medieval afterlife. The so-called *tholos* image that accompanies many copies of the Eusebian Canon Tables has traditionally been understood as a depiction of Constantine's *aedicula* over Christ's tomb at the Church of the Holy Sepulchre. Crawford argues, on the contrary, that the image is designedly abstract and undefined in order to invite an imaginative response from the viewer. Eusebius' own corpus provides evidence of Christians beginning to use sacred architecture as a sort of cognitive machine or mode of knowing, which suggests that architectural images like the *tholos* page, when activated by a biblically inspired *ekphrasis*, could similarly function in a symbolic and constructive fashion.

Such epistemological practices are congruent with the wider phenomenon of Christian worship becoming a key site for developing and inculcating early Christian modes of knowing. Johan Leemans examines surviving festal sermons to illustrate how preachers trained in Greek rhetoric drew upon the sacred scriptures as an authoritative archive to create an immersive world that drew the listener in and united past, present, and future in one overarching divine plan to redeem humanity. Moreover, even though we typically hear only the voice of the preacher in our surviving sources, there is compelling evidence that the sermon was, to some extent, a dialogical mode of knowing in which the preacher had to respond in the moment to his congregation's reaction. Brian Dunkle examines the hymns composed by Ambrose which construct a compelling world for the congregant through the use of evocative imagery. Ambrose's sermons presented biblical material in an 'abstract, narrative, and conceptual' manner, while his hymns repackaged the same content in terms of 'personal, concrete and actualising *exempla*', illustrating how multiple modes of knowing could be applied to the same stock of information to produce different effects. Dunkle follows John Henry Newman's development of Ambrose's epistemology to argue that the hymns were designed to effect the 'real assent' that could not be produced solely through the dialectic of a sermon. Sarah Gador-Whyte picks up similar themes in her study of hymns and homilies in sixth-century Byzantium. She broadens the scope to explore the liturgy as a whole, arguing that its various components provided participants with an all-embracing and truth-disclosing experience. This experience did not merely involve the discursive reason of the individual but aimed to produce an embodied, emotional reaction involving the whole person and the worshipping community. Gador-Whyte's analysis of the function of the hymns of Romanos and the homilies of Leontius suggests that lay communities in sixth-century Constantinople came to know what it meant in that time and place to be a Christian and were consciously and unconsciously formed, as individuals and coherent communities, in accordance with that ideal.

Ordering Knowledge

Because effective pedagogy depends upon some kind of intelligible curriculum, the classroom is a significant social location for ordering knowledge. Various ordering schemes were employed in ancient educational contexts, and several of our contributors highlight ways in which these were adopted, adapted, and transformed by Christians for their own purposes. One of the most common Platonic schemes was the threefold division of philosophy into ethics, physics, and epoptics (theology or contemplation of divine mysteries).[7] We see this scheme among Christian authors as early as Clement of Alexandria who, as Matyáš Havrda argues, used it to structure his own corpus. Given that Clement probably employed this division of topics in an ecclesially affiliated educational institution in Alexandria, Clement exemplifies the way existing epistemological schemes could be used for distinctly Christian ends.[8] The most striking difference between Clement and his non-Christian philosophical peers is his claim that these branches of learning mapped onto Christian sacred texts which were henceforth to serve as the foundation of the curriculum. (On this point Philo of Alexandria serves as a partial precedent in his prioritisation of the Hebrew Bible.)

The tripartite Platonic division of philosophy would be picked up in the next generation by Origen, and we see it still exerting influence three centuries later in more elaborate schemes in Boethius and Cassiodorus, as explored by John Magee. Magee traces how Boethius' understanding of this ordering scheme developed over the course of his career, as well as how the differing institutional settings of Boethius and Cassiodorus resulted in altered curricula to meet the needs of their respective communities. Such transformations would eventually crystallise in the quadrivium and trivium comprising the seven liberal arts that became a staple of the epistemological landscape of the Middle Ages. Michael Champion probes similar questions in the Eastern traditions of philosophy and asceticism, exploring how epistemological assumptions shared by Neoplatonists and the sixth-century monk Dorotheus of Gaza are transformed in Dorotheus' case by working through consequences of taking humility as an epistemic virtue within ascetic education. Platonic ordering of philosophical knowledge would be taken up into the Byzantine tradition by commentators on both Aristotle and John of Damascus. Thus, through a variety of institutional settings over the entire span of time covered by our volume, we can observe both continuity and change in the epistemological regimes represented in our case studies, as educators reshaped received traditions to meet the needs of the moment and differing pedagogical contexts.

A key problem across this collection is how to conceptualise Christian epistemological schemes in relation to other modes of ordering knowledge.

---

[7] Dillon 1996; Boys-Stones 2018.   [8] van den Hoek 1997.

Different authors adopt diverse approaches, characterising Christian epistemology as the adoption of philosophical or Jewish categories or their appropriation and transformation for Christian purposes. While much is taken over especially from Platonism, sometimes no doubt largely unconsciously, new institutional contexts (for example asceticism, catechetical schools), a concern to induct a large group of people from differing social classes into Christian truth claims, and the need to interpret different and newly authoritative texts often put pressure on Christian thinkers from different traditions to adapt earlier schemes and reflect on their utility. For example, Scott Johnson examines one of our earliest surviving Syriac texts, Bardaisan's *Book of the Laws of the Countries*, and highlights its innovative juxtaposition of two established genres, the Platonic dialogue and the ethnographic catalogue. The latter was, of course, a classic form used by authors since Herodotus to order the world and render its diversity intelligible. Yet Bardaisan uniquely deployed this genre within an argument against determinism and in favour of the universalising belief that all humanity can be transformed by the Christian message, no matter where they were located or what ancestral customs they practised. The fact that Bardaisan was using these well-known genres of Greek literature while writing in the dialect of Aramaic spoken in Edessa is a further innovative aspect of his literary and, most likely, educational undertaking which has otherwise almost entirely perished. Much conceptual innovation in our period was achieved through translation of intellectual traditions into new linguistic categories, as Johnson's chapter makes plain.[9]

The reconfiguring of classical traditions is also apparent in David Runia's chapter on the *Placita* composed by the shadowy figure of Aëtius who, within the tripartite division of philosophy, focused in detail on physics, compiling the views of dozens of ancient philosophers on a wide range of questions related to the natural world. Aëtius' *vademecum* of philosophical opinions perhaps originally stemmed from an educational context, though we have no way of knowing its *Sitz im Leben* with certainty. Whatever the case, its reception history runs almost entirely through the hands of Christian authors who transformed its presentation of 'structured disorder' into a deconstructive argument against non-Christian philosophy itself. As this demonstrates, attempts at ordering knowledge in one context could be put to very different uses in the hands of later pedagogues with unforeseen intellectual commitments.

---

[9] A parallel case is the translation of Aristotelian thought through the commentary tradition from Greek into Syriac and Arabic. See D'Ancona Costa 2002; Adamson, Baltussen, and Stone 2004; Sorabji 2004; Becker 2006; King 2010.

The development of new information technologies also enabled the formation of distinctive schemes for ordering knowledge. Drawing upon his extensive research on information technology in classical antiquity, Andrew Riggsby considers the innovative way tabular organisation was repurposed as a knowledge-ordering device by the Christian scholars Origen of Alexandria and Eusebius of Caesarea. While Origen's massive *Hexapla* is well known, Riggsby offers a new theory of its origins by positing that Origen was adapting and expanding an existing genre of bilingual texts used for language instruction which presented corresponding words in parallel columns, for example Latin to Greek, Greek to Coptic, and so on. Because these bilingual texts were used at a fairly rudimentary level of educational instruction, they do not appear in the elite discourses captured by surviving literary sources. Origen, however, recognised that presenting information in parallel columns could be further exploited, and he produced a text, or more accurately a collection of texts, that ordered multilingual knowledge on an unprecedented scale. Eusebius, Origen's enthusiastic follower, would later adapt this information technology yet again by combining it with numerical representation to elucidate the complex relationships of similarity and difference that exist within the church's four canonical gospels.[10]

Origen's *Hexapla* and Eusebius's Canon Tables are both examples of attempts to order knowledge that is distinctly Christian in content, focused on Christian sacred texts.[11] Other attempts at ordering knowledge by Christians were also driven by specifically Christian concerns, including the needs of specific audiences. Edwina Murphy's chapter provides one such case study, examining how Cyprian of Carthage distilled the knowledge of the Christian scriptures into a memorable format that could be readily employed for the purposes of catechetical instruction. The *testimonia* collections he produced utilised classical rhetorical insights about human memory, such as the use of keywords as ordering devices, but were aimed at producing a community transformed by its adherence to the distinct ethical precepts expressed in this body of texts.

Andrew Radde-Gallwitz shines a spotlight on another Christian genre with no clear parallel in the classical world, the conciliar creed. Radde-Gallwitz argues, first, that modern scholarly attempts at organising

---

[10] Crawford 2019.

[11] Of course, Origen's *Hexapla* focused on the Hebrew scriptures and thus overlapped in terms of content with Jewish sacred texts. However, the existence of multiple Greek translations and their correspondence to the Hebrew version(s) seems to have been a problem felt acutely by Christians, though Rabbinic literature also demonstrates some concern with it.

the surviving body of creedal literature from the ancient world have, in fact, hindered our understanding of them, since creeds composed for different purposes are often lumped together without appropriate differentiation. Examining the quasi-legal role played by creeds with appended anathemas, Radde-Gallwitz proposes that, in late antiquity, the anathemas were often regarded as the most important component of a creedal document and that they are a location where one can witness innovation, as bishops added new anathemas to existing creeds to address fresh doctrinal problems. Creedal formulae and their attached anathemas were thus a key mechanism by which Christians in our period ordered the body of knowledge represented by their received faith and rendered that knowledge serviceable to meet contemporary challenges.

The attempt to order Christian doctrinal knowledge remains a key concern of Christian thinkers. Dirk Krausmüller highlights four texts produced in Palestine and Egypt between the late sixth and early seventh centuries, a period when the christological debates between Miaphysites and Chalcedonians had stopped producing fresh arguments. This was instead a period of consolidation, when existing stockpiles of positions and arguments were digested and arranged in forms and structures amenable to shoring up one's base and clarifying the boundaries of one's community. In a manner similar to Aëtius' collection of philosophical opinions about the cosmos, these authors produced handbooks for non-specialists designed to enable them to understand and defend the christological position of their own community while also deconstructing the position of their opponents. The attempt to provide a clear path through competing truth claims sets these handbooks apart from Aëtius' non-partisan work, but even these texts sometimes reveal a desire to be encyclopaedic and exhaustive rather than polemical, and to treat their opponents in as fair a manner as possible.

Structures of Knowing

This volume thus approaches modes of knowing and ordering of knowledge in early Christianity through soundings from multiple sites of cultural production. Discursive structures, including translation between languages and rules for reasoning, offer modes of knowing that also limit how knowledge can be ordered. Diverse genres – including creeds, anathemas, dialogues, lives, historiography, hymnody, homiletics, narratives, mirrors to princes and advice literature, and technical writing – shape knowledge production and provide mechanisms for ordering knowledge. Information technologies offer ways of knowing that order knowledge in productive ways. Institutions of education, law, liturgy, and imperial administration form processes of thought and mental schemas. Theorisation of the senses themselves and evaluation of the role of sense data in the acquisition of knowledge prioritise particular ways of knowing and establish epistemic hierarchies.

This volume elucidates this dialectic between modes of knowing and ordering knowledge by thinking through the epistemic role of discourses, institutions, and materiality. Built into this account is the claim that how one goes about knowing is formed by and simultaneously configures social action. In this connection, the American historian and social scientist William Sewell's conceptualisation of structure offers one productive analytical framework.[12] For Sewell, in dialogue with Anthony Giddens and Pierre Bourdieu, structures may be defined as 'schemas and resources that empower and constrain social action and that tend to be reproduced by that action'.[13] Schemas are rules, norms, conventions, or expectations. Resources are unevenly distributed objects or capacities that can be used to establish, sustain, and increase power.[14] Structure is thus understood (with Giddens) as both material and discursive.[15] The discursive element is most clearly taken up in the notion of schemas, which are at least partially transposable between cultural domains but are limited by diverse material factors.[16] Resources are similarly dual – as objects and physical capacities that set material limits on interactions and ideas and as entities which themselves carry and shape meaning. Given that rules, norms, and the evaluation and distribution of resources are each difficult to change, this account of structure is consistent with the observation that cultures tend to reproduce established patterns of social interaction, embodied practices, institutional forms, and thought. It can help to explain the striking continuities between Jewish and classical epistemologies and associated ethical practices into early Christianity. But Sewell's notion of structure also makes room for cultural and intellectual changes such as the developments in early Christian epistemologies that are traced in this book. People have agency to the extent that they can manipulate schemas and access and deploy resources in new ways or in novel contexts. Such cultural reproduction and transformation through utilising schemas and resources is risky and contingent, always dependent

---

[12] Sewell 1992, 2005.   [13] Sewell 1992: 19. See also Bourdieu 1977; Giddens 1984.
[14] Sewell 1992: 19–20.   [15] Sewell 1992: 4.
[16] In Marshall Sahlins' terms, they are 'burdened by the world' (1985: 138). See Sewell 1992: 18.

on multiple factors and never merely on single actors. In contrast to more homogenous accounts of structure, Sewell's account also foregrounds its multiplicity in various areas of life. Such multiplicity enables actors to apply incompatible structures in different domains. This is one mechanism by which cultural change can take place: structures from one local culture can shift the established conventions or distribution of resources in another. Intersections between different local cultures are particularly crucial for understanding the establishment of Christian epistemology and associated communal norms, given that Christians in late antiquity – as today – inhabited, influenced, and were formed by multiple institutions and domains of social life.

This collection does not adopt a single analytical framework for exploring modes of knowing and the ordering of knowledge in early Christianity. But it does insist that there is a complex interaction between tradition and innovation in early Christian epistemology. Elucidating this complex interaction requires the consideration of discursive, institutional, and material factors, since structures generate and are moulded by these phenomena. The chapters in this volume can test theorisations like Sewell's, partly by mapping the mechanics of continuity and change in epistemological commitments and their associated social practices through exploring discursive, institutional, and material constraints and affordances. The book thus explores the manifold and contingent ways in which early Christian knowers were implicated in discourses, institutions, and materiality – both as these were put into practice and as they shaped practice and thought. We also explore (unlike earlier social science theories of structure) how early Christians changed structures of knowledge – in their discursive, institutional, and material forms. Key questions, then, across the volume, include: what were the sites of cultural and intellectual reproduction and change; what attempts were made to refashion discourses, institutions, and the material world to embody and open up new schemas of knowledge and ways of knowing; and the extent to which the result was a transformation of structures of knowledge instead of a reproduction of Greco-Roman or Jewish schemas and resources.

Discourses

With the claim that God is the Word, Christians had distinctive reasons to care about discourse. As they developed ways of knowing, early Christian thinkers paid careful attention to grammatical categories. Carol Harrison focuses on Augustine's intricate and evolving account of language across his career. She probes the function in Augustine's thought of the grammatical distinction between the *vox confusa* and the *vox articulata*, finding theological significance in non-verbal voices. Her chapter explores just one example of early Christian thought on the relationship between thought and discourse, word and sound, and words and the Word. Augustine's startling claim that language – discourse itself – is mere sound unless it points towards and is given meaning by the Word illumines a fundamental aspect of early Christian epistemology. In engaging with the intellectual traditions of grammar, rhetoric, philosophy, medicine, and law, Christians often sought to incorporate established discourses into a larger set of claims about discourse itself, what Averil Cameron has called a 'totalising discourse', setting Christian truth claims at the heart of any work of meaning-making.[17]

Practising and engaging with the discourses of grammar, rhetoric, law, philosophy, and medicine partly legitimised early Christian ways of knowing and ordering knowledge by grounding them in established discourses. Christian use and adaptation of these elite discourses was shaped by institutional and material factors discussed below, while also being influenced by questions of literary form and tradition. Several contributors focus on one or more of these discourses and their generic contours. In different contexts, Cilliers Breytenbach and Johan Leemans investigate how homilies and biblical commentaries may be formed by the discursive power of commentary evident in late antiquity across the domains of grammar, rhetoric, law, medicine, and philosophy. In the area of genre, Dawn LaValle Norman argues that competing generic expectations enabled knowledge to be configured – and gendered – in different ways in lives and philosophical dialogues, while Bronwen Neil analyses how genres of epistolography, homiletics, commentaries, rules, and dialogues generate different forms of knowledge across Gregory the Great's oeuvre. Mark Edwards argues that Christian Latin poetry, for all its continuation of earlier discursive traditions, enabled forms of expression which increased the cultural and political power of the church. Michael Hanaghan teases apart Christian and classical literary and philosophical presentations of divination to explore Augustine's epistemological criticisms of the practice. Gerald Boersma explores the construction of epistemological authority in Augustine's Cassiciacum dialogues through interaction with philosophical traditions. Jonathan Zecher studies grammatical, philosophical, and medical lists

[17] Cameron 1994.

to explore how they established discursive possibilities, drawing on earlier schemas from different domains of knowledge and shifting them by rearranging key terms, adding new ones and introducing revised conceptual schemes derived from the Christian scriptures. Paul Blowers traces how Christians developed a totalising cosmology by drawing on Platonic discursive constructions of *theoria* and the performance of the *theoros*, attending carefully to the different political ramifications of competing accounts. The exploration of the natural world alongside scrutiny of the biblical text is also the topic of the chapter by Helen Foxhall Forbes, which focuses on commentaries and educational texts produced in the British Isles and neighbouring regions. Jan Stenger interrogates the discourse of education; schemas of otherness, ethnicity, and kinship; and the philosophical ideal of *morphosis* in his chapter on Gregory of Nyssa's pedagogy. As in other areas of late antique education, mimesis plays a key role. It reproduces established discourses, while Moses as the object of imitation offers a radical configuration of possibilities of knowledge and ways of knowing. Across contributions like these, ways in which elite discourses generate and are shaped by multiple intersecting genres come to the fore, as do mechanisms for the appropriation, reproduction, and transformation of earlier discourses in the development of early Christian epistemologies.

In thinking about the Christian reproduction and reconfiguration of earlier discourses, the chapters in this volume explore how the assumptions, axioms, and conventions of earlier knowledge systems affected early Christian thought. This phenomenon also highlights ways in which the epistemological presuppositions and conventional knowledge hierarchies of contemporary scholars affect their treatment of early Christian ways of organising knowledge and knowing. Our own scholarly discourses and discursive categories affect *our* knowledge about early Christian knowing, as we already observed above with respect to the chapter by Radde-Gallwitz. Jeffrey Wickes' chapter on Ephrem the Syrian also explores these issues, arguing that modern claims about authorship and authenticity and the unique epistemological insight of the so-called literary genius have negatively affected understanding of the Ephraemic corpus.[18] He uses this case study to suggest that epistemological assumptions in the history of scholarship create models for organising the past which often conceal as much as they illumine. The mechanisms by which early Christians ordered their own knowledge and interacted with other ways of knowing may themselves be held up as a mirror to modern scholarship, helping contemporary

---

[18] On questions of classifications of early Christian literature and their effects, see Martens 2022.

historians, literary scholars, and theologians reflect on their own methodologies and epistemological commitments. Teresa Morgan's Epilogue returns to some of these questions.

A recurring claim across this volume is that discourse affects social formations and individual human actions. In investigating the 'intellectual world' of early Christianity, the contributors aim to get at Yeats's 'lasting song' of those who 'think in the marrow bone'. As Andrew McGowan argues in his chapter on sacrificial knowing, citing the anthropologist Clifford Geertz, discourses are not immaterial (Geertz's 'unobservable mental stuff'). Sacrifice is given all manner of discursive meanings that are in part limited by material affordances and in part generated by them. This reminds us that the discursive is bound up with the institutional and the material, that knowing affects how people act, and that Christian epistemological claims shape religious practice, ethical behaviour, and communal norms. One claim of this volume is that understanding these wider domains of late antique life requires richly characterising the diverse ways in which Christians interacted with earlier discourses from other religious and intellectual traditions in forming their own epistemologies.

Institutions

Discourses are embodied in institutions. Institutions organise knowledge, affecting how it is generated, rendered powerful, and transmitted across time. They establish hierarchies by differentiating between expert and non-expert knowledge and by authorising roles that give people capacity to exercise knowledge in particular ways while constraining other ways of knowing.[19] Key sites of the institutional production of knowledge explored in this volume are education (classical and Christian), liturgy, asceticism, law, the church and its structures of governance, and imperial government and bureaucracy.[20] Three brief examples from education, law, and imperial administration may elucidate aspects of the institutional formation of early Christian epistemologies.

Taking education first, Peter Martens focuses on Origen, exploring how pedagogical institutions influenced how the Bible was interpreted and used.

---

[19] See the essays in Ayres and Ward 2020.
[20] Asceticism: Champion, Guiliano, Mellon Saint-Laurent, Zecher. Education: Champion, Havrda, Magee, Martens, Murphy, Stenger. Church: Havrda, Krausmüller, McGowan, Murphy, Neil, Radde-Gallwitz. Empire and administration: Blowers, Ahbel-Rappe. Liturgy: Gador-Whyte, Leemans, Breytenbach, Dunkle, McGowan, Murphy. Law: Sarris.

As Martens argues, the diversity of institutional contexts for Christian knowledge production is crucial. Christians moved between different institutional domains. Their epistemologies were shaped by classical schools (especially of grammar, rhetoric, and philosophy) and by the institutional requirements of the Christian community, as it sought to educate both lay Christians with differing educational backgrounds and also ascetics and those who would take on leadership roles in the church. Martens argues that in Origen's case, we see much reproduction of powerful institutional forms and associated knowledge structures. But agency is exercised within established institutional parameters and results in a new curriculum, that is, in power given to a new set of cultural and intellectual resources and to the experts who preside over them. Knowledge is ordered through prioritising one institution over another, as the demands of catechetical schools trump those of classical rhetorical education.

In the case of law, Peter Sarris explores how legal systems – and the social and political institutions which they license – organised knowledge near the end of late antiquity under the emperor Justinian. Law is bound up in and structures discourses of morality and epistemology and, as such, is crucial for the formation of knowers' minds and habits as well as communal norms. As in the case of epistemology affected by imperial institutions, ascent through the legal *cursus* can be likened to the progress of the soul and the grasping of higher order truths; institutionalised legal knowledge becomes embodied in the practitioners it forms. The institution of the law also provides multiple mechanisms for transmitting knowledge which shapes individual minds and communities, for example through legal judgments, through public proclamations in civic or religious contexts, or through encyclopaedic collections and commentaries. This determined what people knew about imperial and ecclesiastical law, and about a range of related areas, across a broad swathe of society. Sarris shows that legal institutions transmitted knowledge to the peasantry in ways that gave lower social groups some measure of agency, although where peasants sought to take advantage of legal frameworks, legislators could be quick to close down legal avenues for redistributing power. The law thus established epistemic power differentials which, in turn, solidified powerful discursive oppositions, leading to the persecution and disenfranchisement of outsider groups, such as schismatics, Jews, pagans, and ethnic minorities. The social function of the law had always been tied to moral demands; under Christian emperors, there is an increasing connection between legal institutions and the maintenance of religious order.

Our final example of interrelationships between epistemology and institutions comes from Sara Ahbel-Rappe's chapter on the relationship between imperial bureaucracy and philosophical epistemology. Ahbel-Rappe draws attention to similar assumptions that underpin the cascading hierarchies of imperial bureaucracy and late antique Platonism. Eric Osborn long ago identified the 'bureaucratic fallacy' of some gnosticisms (also found in Plotinus and later Platonism), where multiplying levels between humans and the One provide a means of ascent by analogy with government departments, where, it is spuriously claimed, adding levels of bureaucracy makes it possible for citizens to communicate with the exalted Minister.[21] The epistemic claim is that bureaucrats can represent, enforce, and make the emperor's *imperium* accessible at different levels of specificity and abstraction; just so, lower orders of the metaphysical hierarchy, which operate as one travels down the ladder with increasingly limited but more concrete power, can relate philosophers to the One. The later Platonic ontological hierarchy seems persuasive, on this view, because the bureaucracy to which it is so similar is taken to be unproblematic. Ahbel-Rappe does not make an argument about influence but draws out close coincidences between literature describing institutions of imperial bureaucracy and the fine metaphysical distinctions of the fifth-century Neoplatonist Proclus. She argues that there are important epistemological implications generated by Proclus' 'proliferative' account of metaphysical hierarchy which are shared in some Christian literature, especially Pseudo-Dionysius. Ahbel-Rappe postulates a 'bureaucratic way of knowing' that is totalising both in its domain of applicability and in its authorisation of vertical hierarchies of power and knowledge, although there are also points of resistance. Within this epistemology, reason plays a central role, but there is also a need for the knower to be united to the one truth through faith and love. This may threaten to undermine the place of reason in Proclus' system and provides a potential parallel with Christianity.

Materiality

As we have argued, the reality of material existence and human embodiment similarly both generates and constrains epistemic schemes. Most basically, material resources are required for knowledge production: money for providing time and space for education, resources and technologies for

---

[21] Osborn 1993.

inscribing and transmitting knowledge. Zachary Guiliano's chapter on Bede explores in detail how wealth and social status undergirded Bede's ordering of knowledge and privileged ways of knowing, establishing and maintaining an 'inequality regime' (in Piketty's formulation). The function and affordances of materiality itself open a way into complex epistemic schemes, as we have already seen, for example, in Jensen's exploration of early Christian vision and Crawford's discussion of architecture. Material embodiment also shapes knowing and helps to order knowledge as, for example, Nicole Mellon Saint-Laurent argues in her investigation of knowing and gluttony, Harrison traces in the case of sound and senses, or Gador-Whyte, Neil, and Zecher explore in the case of emotions. Paul Saieg argues that Irenaeus of Lyons has left us the earliest fully developed Christian account of embodiment, which grants a prominent role to an empirical epistemology and emphasises the need for all Christians to practise self-control and disciplined attention to enable the true perception of the world and their place within it – themes that reverberate in later authors. Rebecca Lyman also foregrounds the epistemic implications and pitfalls of materiality in her chapter on the early Arian controversy, lived religion in Alexandria, and debates over visuality and materialism.

Inscriptions illuminate how material objects can serve as modes of knowing and how objects interact with and generate discursive constructions of knowledge. Cilliers Breytenbach investigates how inscriptions in churches, in cemeteries, and on mosaics transmit knowledge and shape other knowledge-producing practices, including liturgical performances. The difficulty of deciding what constitutes a Christian inscription is an instance of a general question across the volume about the distinctiveness of 'Christian' forms of knowing. His chapter also charts significant interactions between the material and the discursive by comparing homilies and inscriptions.

Most generally, the 'scriptural universe' of which Guy Strousma writes and which provided significant epistemic parameters for early Christianity is impoverished without dedicated attention to the material productions of Christian communities and to how they affected what could be thought or imagined.[22] Inscriptional evidence suggests ways of thinking about scripture and its role in constructing Christian minds that are sometimes overlooked in merely textual histories. Scripture was heard, memorised, and performed in liturgical contexts, and inscriptions record benedictions, supplications, invocations, and a variety of other prayers, foregrounding

---

[22] Stroumsa 2016.

how liturgical experience of scripture influenced people's lives. The lived experience of scripture, embodied in liturgy or chiselled into sacred objects, is thus entangled with a variety of practices implicating the whole person. Again, the discursive is shaped by material contexts even as it gives meaning to significant objects.

Investigating early Christian ways of knowing and ordering of knowledge, then, offers stimulating perspectives on intriguing and persistent questions about how epistemology affects social action and agency, about how Christians interacted with other cultural groups in their discursive, institutional, and material formations, about how knowing generates individual and communal practices and norms, and about the mechanics of the reproduction, reconfiguration, and transformation of traditions. The chapters in this volume grapple with case studies of phenomena like these, foregrounding how Christian ways of knowing and ordering of knowledge were embedded in a range of different traditions while offering a distinctive account inflected by theological commitments. They seek to open up new avenues of research into the intellectual world of late antique Christianity and its cultural forms.

2 | The Beginnings of a Christian Doctrine of the Spiritual Senses before Origen

JANE HEATH

What Are 'Spiritual Senses'? Starting with Origen

When Origen wrote his response to Celsus' attack on Christianity, one of the challenges that he had to deal with was: Did Jesus *really* see 'the apparition of a bird' (φάσμα ὄρνιθος) flying out of the air onto him at his baptism, and did he *really* hear a voice from heaven making him to be the Son of God?[1] (*Cels.* 1.41) It was a challenge, essentially, to Christians' appeal to sense perception as a mode of knowing, both for Christ and, implicitly, for those baptised in his name.

Origen suggests that this line of argument might have carried some force in the mouth of an Epicurean or some other kind of materialist philosopher. Such people might well doubt the story about the apparition (φάσμα) of the Holy Spirit in the form of a dove. But Celsus placed it in the mouth of a Jew. And Jews, as Origen points out, believe all sorts of miraculous things. Ezekiel and Isaiah are great visionaries, and Jesus is surely more credible than they, since he is known to have done a great many more good things. In any case, the doctrine of providence relies on trust that true impressions come in dreams – so why not waking also?[2] If Ezekiel said that he saw the heaven opened, we are not to envisage that the sky actually was rent apart rather than that Ezekiel had the experience of an impression of that kind. To interpret biblical visions as if they were describing events in the physical, material realm rather than apparitions is simple-minded naivety (*Cels.* 1.43–48).

It is at this point in the argument that Origen introduces what has come to be treated in modern scholarship as a *locus classicus* for his doctrine of the spiritual senses as a distinctively Christian mode of knowing.

---

[1] ἔστι δ' ὁ Ἰουδαῖος αὐτῷ ἔτι ταῦτα λέγων, πρὸς ὃν ὁμολογοῦμεν εἶναι κύριον ἡμῶν τὸν Ἰησοῦν· Λουομένῳ, φησί, σοὶ παρὰ τῷ Ἰωάννῃ φάσμα ὄρνιθος ἐξ ἀέρος λέγεις ἐπιπτῆναι. Εἶτα πυνθανόμενος ὁ παρ' αὐτῷ Ἰουδαῖός φησι· Τίς τοῦτο εἶδεν ἀξιόχρεως μάρτυς τὸ φάσμα, ἢ τίς ἤκουσεν ἐξ οὐρανοῦ φωνῆς εἰσποιούσης σε υἱὸν τῷ θεῷ; Πλὴν ὅτι σὺ φῂς καί τινα ἕνα ἐπάγῃ τῶν μετὰ σοῦ κεκολασμένων.

[2] Dillon (1986: 444) points out the Stoic origins of this account of oneiromancy.

I give Chadwick's translation, which is often quoted in English-language discussions of the issue. The passage reads:

> Anyone who looks into this subject more deeply will say that there is, as the scripture calls it, a certain generic divine sense (θείας τινὸς γενικῆς αἰσθήσεως) which only the man who is blessed finds on this earth. Thus Solomon says (Prov 2:5): 'Thou shalt find a divine sense' (ὅτι αἴσθησιν θείαν εὑρήσεις). There are many forms of this sense: a sight (ὁράσεως) which can see things superior to corporeal beings, the cherubim or seraphim being obvious instances, and a hearing (ἀκοῆς) which can receive impressions of sounds that have no objective existence in the air, and a taste (γεύσεως) which feeds on living bread that has come down from heaven and gives life to the world (John 6:33). So also there is a sense of smell (ὀσφρήσεως) which smells spiritual things, as Paul speaks of 'a sweet savour of Christ unto God' (2 Cor 2:15) and a sense of touch (ἁφῆς) in accordance with which John says that he has handled with his hands 'of the Word of life' (1 John 1:1). (*Contra Celsum*, 1.48 (PG 11.749A–B, trans. Chadwick 1953: 44))

In this passage, Origen outlines an idea of the human being as able to discover a form of sense perception that is more divine than the ordinary kind and that structures people's experience of spiritual realities in five different sensory modalities.

In making this argument, Origen has shifted away from the more obviously visionary narratives of Ezekiel and Isaiah. Vision and hearing are treated somewhat vaguely, as too well known to need discussion. Taste, smell, and touch are backed up with examples from the New Testament, but Origen's attitude to the materiality of the New Testament texts is unclear. Is he using New Testament language to characterise immaterial, visionary experience, or does he intend us to think also of the material encounters with bread at the feeding of the five thousand (John 6:33), with apostles who are the savour of Christ unto God (2 Cor 2:15), and with the incarnate Word, whom John recollects (1 John 1:1)? Later in *Contra Celsum*, defending the doctrine of the resurrection, Origen suggests that the human being is capable of acquiring a full set of five sensory organs, which are analogous to those of the body, but differ from them, as superior and more divine. They can apprehend spiritual realities in five different sensory modes, though they do not need the body in order to do so (e.g., *Cels.* 7.33–34).

These passages in the *Contra Celsum* evoke ways of thinking and writing about Christian somatology and sanctification that recur across Origen's work.[3] However, he never writes a treatise to systematise something that he would call 'a doctrine of the spiritual senses'. His presentation depends on the exegesis of a handful of biblical passages, which he hooks onto his Greek

---

[3] Rahner 1932: 113–36.

reading of Prov 2:5 (αἴσθησιν θείαν εὑρήσεις).[4] He employs the language and the concept in diverse ways. He never finally resolves the ambiguity as to whether or how the more divine sense perception may integrate experiences mediated through the body, such as eating the bread that came down from heaven or listening to the words spoken by Jesus. He envisages the possibility of people being able to attain to a single divine sense without being able to exercise all five.[5] It is only the truly blessed person, as indicated in the passage quoted, who enjoys the use of the full sensorium on this earth. Holy people such as Ezekiel, Isaiah, and Paul were of such a kind.[6] It is in commenting on Canticles that Origen makes most extensive use of the language spiritual sense perception.[7] In Origen's scheme of Christian development, Canticles belongs to the most advanced stage, for the most fully purified readers, who are most ready for encounter with God. Even they will only acquire use of the spiritual senses if God also grants it to them.[8]

I have begun with Origen because he is a crucial figure in the modern debate about 'the doctrine of the spiritual senses'. In that discussion, it has been influentially asserted that the doctrine *originated* with him, and this has shaped how scholars have approached the language of the spiritual senses in early Christian sources. In particular, it has led them to exclude all sources earlier than Origen, even the Bible itself. The next part of this chapter will show how and why this emphasis has arisen, and will argue that it is both historically and theologically problematic. The remainder of the chapter will turn to sources earlier than Origen, including both Clement, who was his predecessor in Alexandria, and selected portions of the Bible, from Paul, John, and Revelation. On the basis of these texts, I will seek to show how the study of the spiritual senses prior to Origen could give us a richer account of the origin and function of the early Christians' emphasis on spiritual senses as a mode of knowing.

Origen as the Originator of the Doctrine of the Spiritual Senses: From Karl Rahner to Paul Gavrilyuk and Sarah Coakley

Origen's centrality to the modern debate was established by Karl Rahner (1904–84) in an essay that was first published in French in 1932. Rahner's

---

[4] *Cels.* 1.48; 7.34; *Princ.* 1.1.9; *Fr. Luc.* 186.40–45; *Fr. Ps. ad* Ps 134:15–18. Rahner 1932: 116–17 notes Prov 2:5 and Heb 5:14 as crucial.
[5] Rahner 1932: 119–20, 125.   [6] Rahner 1932: 120, 136.   [7] Rahner 1932: 118.
[8] Rahner 1932: 132. Rahner's account of Origen is in Rahner 1932: 114–36. As the notes above show, I have substantially relied on his work in my account of Origen above.

title, 'Le début d'une doctrine des cinq sens spirituels chez Origène', gave prominence to the idea that Origen introduced something new.[9] That something Rahner called a 'doctrine of the five spiritual senses'. He explained that religious experience, especially mystical experience, defies description, and so mystics have recourse to the language of sense perception. They speak of seeing, hearing, and touching spiritual realities. The Bible already uses the language of sense perception metaphorically – Rahner cites as examples Eph 1:18; 2 Cor 2:18 (*sic*[10]); Ps 33:9[11]; Acts 17:27; and Ps 84:9.[12] However, he suggested that we should speak of a 'doctrine of the spiritual senses only when these partly figurative, partly literal ('mi-figuratives, mi-réelles') expressions (to touch God, the eyes of the heart, etc.) are found integrated into a complete system of the five instruments of the spiritual perception of supra-sensible religious realities'. According to this definition, Origen seems to be the first to formulate a doctrine of the five spiritual senses. Rahner's seminal article is devoted to clarifying Origen's thought and its reception.[13] I have already drawn on it in my account of Origen above.

In recent years, there has been something of a renaissance of interest in the 'spiritual senses'.[14] The most ambitious architect of this renewed discussion has been Paul Gavrilyuk of the University of St Thomas in St Paul, Minnesota. He has organised a large-scale collaborative project around the spiritual senses, which is intended to produce a series of essay collections. The first of these, co-edited with Sarah Coakley, appeared in 2012 under the title *The Spiritual Senses: Perceiving God in Western Christianity*.[15] That first book aimed to give a historical overview of the theological tradition

---

[9] In this chapter, I focus on Rahner's original French publication. He later published an abridged form in German (in 1975); this was eventually translated loosely into English (in 1979).

[10] Rahner undoubtedly meant 2 Cor 3:18.   [11] Rahner must be citing the LXX or Vulgate.

[12] Eph 1:18: πεφωτισμένους τοὺς ὀφθαλμοὺς τῆς καρδίας [ὑμῶν] εἰς τὸ εἰδέναι ὑμᾶς τίς ἐστιν ἡ ἐλπὶς τῆς κλήσεως αὐτοῦ; 2 Cor 3:18, ἡμεῖς δὲ πάντες ἀνακεκαλυμμένῳ προσώπῳ τὴν δόξαν κυρίου κατοπτριζόμενοι τὴν αὐτὴν εἰκόνα μεταμορφούμεθα ἀπὸ δόξης εἰς δόξαν καθάπερ ἀπὸ κυρίου πνεύματος; LXX Ps 33:9, γεύσασθε καὶ ἴδετε ὅτι χρηστὸς ὁ κύριος μακάριος ἀνὴρ ὃς ἐλπίζει ἐπ' αὐτόν; Acts 17:27, ζητεῖν τὸν θεόν, εἰ ἄρα γε ψηλαφήσειαν αὐτὸν καὶ εὕροιεν, καί γε οὐ μακρὰν ἀπὸ ἑνὸς ἑκάστου ἡμῶν ὑπάρχοντα; Ps 84:9, ἀκούσομαι τί λαλήσει ἐν ἐμοὶ κύριος ὁ θεός ὅτι λαλήσει εἰρήνην ἐπὶ τὸν λαὸν αὐτοῦ καὶ ἐπὶ τοὺς ὁσίους αὐτοῦ καὶ ἐπὶ τοὺς ἐπιστρέφοντας πρὸς αὐτὸν καρδίαν.

[13] Rahner 1932: esp. 113–14.   [14] McInroy 2014; Coolman 2016; Michaud 2017.

[15] Gavrilyuk and Coakley 2012a. The next essay collection, *Sensing Things Divine: Towards a Constructive Account of Spiritual Perception* (ed. Frederick D. Aquino and Paul L. Gavrilyuk) is announced on Aquino and Gavrilyuk's academia.edu pages (accessed 1 August 2018). See also https://spiritualperceptionproject.wordpress.com (accessed 18 October 2022).

from its beginnings to the modern day. Following Rahner, they defined it as 'beginning' with Origen.

However, they did not follow Rahner in much else, and this is significant for how they steered a new course for the debate. One of their key moves in introducing the project was to open up the definition of the spiritual senses. Whereas Rahner had initially insisted on an integrated account of a *fivefold sensorium*,[16] Gavrilyuk and Coakley allowed that many theologians have something interesting to say about the spiritual senses even if they do not treat all five, indeed even if they only treat one or two, and unsystematically at that. They acknowledged that the sources have no uniform terminology; they may not use the word 'spiritual' at all; they may use the language of sense perception to describe the encounter with God, but without connecting it explicitly with soul, mind, or heart. By 'spiritual senses', Gavrilyuk and Coakley thus wanted to suggest no more than a 'non-physical mode of perception' by which the human encounters the divine. This is not dependent on a particular anthropology, pneumatology, or theology:

> The qualifier 'spiritual' before 'senses' is intended to indicate non-physical mode of perception, rather than to prioritize an anthropology in which 'spirit' is consistently differentiated from the other aspects of the self, such as body, soul, intellect or affect. A further variant is that some Christian authors link the language of spiritual senses explicitly to pneumatology, and thence to their trinitarianism, while others do not, or do so only very implicitly.[17]

With such a broad definition and flexible approach to spiritual senses, the way is open for the inclusion of many more theologians than Rahner had considered.

We might therefore begin to wonder why no sources *prior* to Origen were discussed. My reading of Gavrilyuk and Coakley is that they return to a restrictive definition of the spiritual senses when they consider the earlier material, and that this is at least partly because they understand the doctrine of spiritual senses as exegetical rather than as original to the biblical authors. The implication is that it is the province of systematicians rather than scriptural scholars. Gavrilyuk and Coakley acknowledge that meditation upon the scriptural text was crucial to the development of accounts

---

[16] Gavrilyuk and Coakley (2012b: 5) point out that Rahner did not in fact hold to this definition in his later work (or even in the later parts of the initial article) but moved towards interest in the 'unitive character' of spiritual perception.

[17] Gavrilyuk and Coakley 2012b: 2–5, quotation at 3–4.

of the spiritual senses, and that there are many expressions and even theologies in scripture that resonate with the doctrine. However, they declare that:

> Despite this wealth of material gleaned from scripture, it should be emphasised that *the Bible as such* offers no 'doctrine of the spiritual senses'. Most patristic authors attuned to our theme commonly offer their insights about spiritual perception when prompted by their favorite biblical passages. But for some early Christian theologians – and Origen is perhaps the first of them – the spiritual senses came to occupy *a distinct place in their theological anthropology*. This being the *systematic focus* of our volume, our collection necessarily starts with Origen.[18]

Two things are remarkable about this comment. Firstly, the notion of 'the Bible as such' and what doctrines are contained in it is difficult at the best of times. Secondly, the relative simplicity of this definition of spiritual senses stands in contrast to the earlier discussion: the doctrine of the spiritual senses is now defined in relation to an author's 'theological anthropology'. This sounds far more restrictive than before, when they were willing to include many authorities whose notion of the spiritual senses was unsystematic, diverse, and *not bound to a particular terminology, anthropology, pneumatology, or theology.*

If Origen were cited simply as an arbitrary starting point, then the question of where the doctrine began would be of no significance. But Gavrilyuk and Coakley are making him into a systematic starting point, as if he defined the *theological* beginnings of the doctrine, as well as connecting this with the grounds for programmatically excluding the Bible from consideration. To understand this move better, we need to look first at the treatment of Origen in the opening essay of Gavrilyuk and Coakley's volume (2012b), and then at the way its programme is realised within the larger discussion of the book.

Mark McInroy's piece on Origen begins the collection. It deserves close attention because if Origen is to be regarded as the first to articulate a real doctrine of the spiritual senses, then we need to understand what that means in terms of the Gavrilyuk and Coakley project. A key feature of McInroy's treatment is that he operates with a distinction between *metaphor* and *analogy* that became common in twentieth-century discussions of the spiritual senses. It should be noted at once that the language of 'metaphor' and 'analogy' is not being used in the way that we might expect within a rhetorical frame: in the spiritual senses debate, these terms

---

[18] Gavrilyuk and Coakley 2012b: 12 (emphasis mine).

are not identifying rhetorical tropes. Rather, they are used to distinguish occasions when Origen (or others) use the language of sense perception to mean 'understanding', such that it can be translated into the language of 'understanding' without losing anything significant in that translation. This is counted as a 'metaphor'; a commonly cited example is *Princ.* 1.1.9, where Origen explains that 'to see God in the heart' is 'to understand and know him with the mind'. 'Analogy', on the other hand, is used when there is a strong idea of organs of sense perception analogous to the corporeal ones, which are therefore part of a kind of spiritual somatology. An example would be *Contra Celsum* 1.48 (quoted above).[19]

In this context, the terms 'metaphor' and 'analogy' drive a wedge between rhetorical usage of the language of the spiritual senses and anthropological claims, where the spiritual senses are part of a theological anthropology. They underscore the possibility of a non-physical physiognomy and to discount language of spiritual sense perception that does not conform to this concept. They also tend to ossify the functions of comparative tropes, such that both 'metaphor' and 'analogy' cease to have the open-endedness that usually characterises them; 'analogy' acquires a specific referent; 'metaphor' becomes limited to essentially *dead* metaphors, where 'spiritual senses' simply *mean* understanding without remainder.[20]

This proves problematic. Origen uses the language of spiritual sensation in both ways and often intertwines them.[21] McInroy's chief interlocutor, John Dillon, explained this by positing a difference between early and late Origen: he thought that the spiritual sensorium was an offspring of the saint's senile mind and that his account of the spiritual senses was driven by the need to explain away awkward anthropomorphic passages of the Bible, which he would have done much better simply to describe as figurative.[22] McInroy disputes the evidence for a significant difference between early and late Origen; the distinction between metaphor and analogy he finds useful but insufficient, and he seeks to sharpen it by the addition of a further criterion. He turns to Augustin Poulain's descriptive manual of mystical experience, which was influential in the early twentieth century,

---

[19] McInroy 2012: 22–24.
[20] Gavrilyuk and Coakley (2012b: 6–7) point out that the preoccupation of distinguishing 'metaphorical' from 'analogical' language of spiritual perception is rooted in Aquinas' differentiation between 'analogical statements that are literally (*proprie*) true', and 'metaphorical statements that are not'. But this is not a conceptual distinction that Origen or other patristic authors were using.
[21] See McInroy 2012: 29–30, 34.   [22] Dillon 1986: 444–49.

and which was cited by Rahner.[23] Following Poulain, he suggests that it is when the spiritual senses perceive God as *present* to them that they emerge as part of *theological anthropology*. By accentuating the difference between 'metaphor' and 'analogy' through a criterion of 'presence', McInroy indicates that the spiritual senses are primarily a problem of *theological anthropology experienced in direct mystical encounter.*

As the essay on Origen in a volume that makes Origen the programmatic starting point for the history of the theology of the spiritual senses, we might expect the rest of the essays to build on this opening definition. A perusal of the others, however, will swiftly show that this is not an account of the spiritual senses that they rigorously maintain.

Several contributors explicitly differentiate their subjects from Origen, because the analogy with the corporeal sensorium is transcended or rejected in their case.[24] For some, what is really at stake is the perfection of the corporeal senses to perceive more spiritually (e.g., Gregory of Nyssa, Maximus); for others, it is the perfection of the spiritual senses across a continuum (Pseudo-Dionysius); some theologians prioritise a single spiritual sense over the others (Maximus, Pseudo-Dionysius, Alexander of Hales, Nicholas of Cusa) and may envisage its function in ways that are not properly analogous to corporeal sense perception (Maximus, Pseudo-Dionysius). For some, Aristotle is as important as Origen in interpreting the spiritual senses (Nicholas of Cusa); for others, spiritual sensation is a thoroughly biblical discourse (Gregory the Great, John Wesley). Some doctrines of the spiritual senses accentuate the difference between body and spirit, but often the purpose is quite the opposite: The oxymoron of the 'spiritual senses' is intended to refuse that dichotomy, and to evoke how encounter with the divine overwhelms our usual categories of language and experience.[25]

---

[23] McInroy is more different from Rahner than he acknowledges. I find his gloss on Rahner 1932: 114 particularly misleading: Rahner writes, 'Il nous semble prudent de ne parler d'une doctrine des sens spirituels que lorsque ces expressions mi-figuratives, mi-réelles (toucher Dieu, les yeux du coeur, etc. …) se trouvent intégrées dans un système complet de cinq instruments de perception spirituelle pour les réalités suprasensibles religieuses.' McInroy (2012: 22) glosses, 'Karl Rahner writes that one may speak "properly" of a "doctrine of the spiritual senses" when one finds (1) a non-metaphorical use of sensory language in which (2) all five senses are used in "the spiritual perception of immaterial realities".' The second part of this is accurate, but to represent Rahner's comments on biblical expressions that are 'mi-figuratives, mi-réelles' as a criterion of non-metaphoricity I find misleading.

[24] Coakley 2012: 42–43 (Gregory of Nyssa); Gavrilyuk 2012: 99 (Pseudo-Dionysius); Aquino 2012: 107 (Maximus); Green 2012: 210–23 (Nicholas of Cusa).

[25] Coolman 2012b: 157.

In fact, the essays in the volume confirm plurality in accounts of the spiritual senses much more than a consistent systematic core to any such 'doctrine'. The issues that structure thought about the spiritual senses are diverse: attaining the beatific vision (e.g., Thomas Gallus, Bonaventure); asceticism to purify the senses and reform the self (Maximus, Gregory the Great); the *corpus mysticum* of the ecclesia, especially the perfection of senses in Christ the 'head' (Alexander of Hales); sacraments, especially baptism to initiate spiritual sense perception (Pseudo-Dionysius) or the Eucharist to maintain it (Alexander of Hales); the nature of the resurrected body (Augustine) or of the post-mortem body (Gregory the Great); or some combination of these. Some of the authors included in the volume treat the spiritual senses systematically as part of their 'doctrine' (e.g., Bonaventure); others simply mention them in ways that suggest their significance, but without systematising them (e.g., Gregory of Nyssa). Aquinas is included even though the point of the chapter is that Aquinas' 'more fully developed theological anthropology allows him to dispense with spiritual senses'.[26]

My purpose in emphasising this is not to denigrate the work in this book. On the contrary, the breadth is central to its purpose of mapping out the significance of the spiritual senses in Christian tradition. It also underpins the next stage in the project, where Gavrilyuk and Aquino will introduce a collection of studies that take a range of different disciplinary approaches.[27] Without such breadth, our understanding of the tradition would be utterly impoverished.

My point is rather that this breadth renders particularly inapposite the insistence on starting with Origen and on excluding the Bible as a relevant source in its own right. Origen cannot be a programmatic starting point if the tradition that is outlined so often departs from Origen's approach. And if what we are really looking at is often 'not ... a consciously enunciated "spiritual senses *doctrine*" as such, but rather certain key phrases which signal ... wrestling with the manifold epistemological issues of sensuality and its relation to the mind (*nous*) and soul (*psychê*)',[28] then it is surely

---

[26] Cross 2012: 177. [27] See n. 15 above.
[28] Coakley 2012: 45, on Gregory of Nyssa. Cf. Abraham 2012: 278, 'I take the spiritual senses tradition to be minimally constituted by the thesis that perception of the divine can be a legitimate ground for theological assertion. It is nicely captured in the beatitude "Blessed are the pure in heart for they shall see God" (Matt 5:8). More generally it posits that the reality, activity and nature of God are visible in, say, creation, the life of Jesus of Nazareth and the lives of the saints. So the core claim hinges on the possibility of perception of the divine. This

appropriate to consider the Bible as the earliest stage in the *Christian* history of this tradition. The way the tradition draws on (at least) Jewish and classical patterns of language and thought would be a further layer of study beyond that.

In the scope of this chapter, it is only possible to scrape the surface of this expansive field, but a small number of case studies can suffice to establish it as a part of the tradition of spiritual senses that would be worthy of further research. The aim is to do more than just show that there is further relevant material than has been taken into account before: simply having greater bulk of material is not in itself very useful unless the further sources change our perspective on the tradition itself. I want to indicate that they probably would do so if they received extended study. The discussion is in two parts. Firstly, I give a case study from Clement of Alexandria in order to show that there is a church father prior to Origen who is taking notice of the spiritual senses in a way that resonates strongly with some of the more established figures of the later tradition. However, Clement's emphases are also distinctive in interesting ways. Secondly, I give three examples from three different parts of the New Testament (Paul, the Fourth Gospel, and Revelation). This material is very different from Clement, Origen, and the medieval tradition. But it highlights something that is often lost in studies of the later tradition: At its historical and scriptural source, Christian thinking about the spiritual senses is thoroughly christological, and (I suggest) intimately bound up with faith in the incarnation and its consequences for humanity.

Before Origen: Spiritual Senses in Clement of Alexandria – The Case of Baptism

It has often been noted that Clement of Alexandria has the same peculiar Greek rendering of Prov 2:5 as Origen does: 'you shall find a divine sense perception' (αἴσθησιν θείαν εὑρήσεις).[29] For Origen, this phrase became the hook in his memory for storing an array of other texts that are the backbone of his so-called 'doctrine of the five spiritual senses'. Little has been made of its prior appearance in Clement, so this might

---

can then be extended to the denser claim that human agents are equipped by appropriate senses that discern the truth about God accurately.' The 'core claim' in Abraham's summary is far from the Origenist approach and is even articulated explicitly in biblical terms.

[29] *Strom.* 1.4.27.2.

seem an obvious way into studying the spiritual senses earlier than Origen. Indeed, it would be possible to hypothesise that Origen developed his account on the basis of a meditative reading of Clement.[30] However, if we are to understand Clement's approach to spiritual senses, we need to start with what is important to Clement, rather than approaching him via what matters to Origen. In this way, we can also hope to appreciate why studying spiritual senses before Origen is theologically as well as historically important.

Unlike in Origen, Prov 2:5 did not become a proof-text or a formula for Clement. If there is a single verse that most frequently drives his reflection on spiritual senses, it is probably St Paul's words about 'what eye has not seen, nor ear heard, nor has it entered into the heart of a human being' (1 Cor 2:9).[31] However, Clement's attention to the spiritual senses goes beyond any one verse or even collection of verses. He often notices the eyes and ears in particular – either separately or together – as organs with a special role in the economy of salvation. They may be primarily instruments of cognition, affect, ethical agency, or discernment. They are picked out at moments that are critical in a person's Christian formation. Sometimes that coincides with structurally significant points in Clement's own literary work. Sometimes it appears in close conjunction with the idea of Christians as a new creation.

I focus on Clement's account of baptism in *Paed.* 1.6, since this is where he develops an extended account of how the eyes and ears are activated for gnostic vision and audition. If ever there were a passage where Clement might seem to have something like a *doctrine* of the spiritual senses, this would be it. That said, I do not agree with the approach to Clement that treats his work as if the way to the 'real

---

[30] In *Strom.* 1.4, Clement compares different kinds of wisdom, including those that have to do with sense perception and those that are more intellectual. His taxonomy is difficult to follow, since it involves a differentiation between *aisthêsis* and *synaisthêsis*, which, however, is complicated by Clement's attempt to align his analytic vocabulary with the somewhat different mode of expression in scripture. However, like Origen, he makes Prov 2:5 an important point of reflection; Clement even considers it in its wider context (Prov 2:3–7 and 3:23). Like Origen, he finds an analogy between sensual and intellectual perception, and he is able to use *pneuma aisthêseôs* in relation to both, and to find ways of qualifying or modifying *aisthêsis* that allow him to associate it closely with knowledge of immaterial realities, e.g., συναίσθησις, ἡ κατὰ φιλοσοφίαν αἴσθησις, ἡ ἐν θεοσεβείᾳ αἴσθησις, ἡ εἰς θεοσέβειαν συναίσθησις. Clement explicitly invites his readers to search for hidden seeds in his 'notes' and farm them for gnostic insight. This complicated passage on the spirit of perception could plausibly have been well farmed by Origen so as to bear richer exegetical and theological fruit through Prov 2:5.

[31] *Protr.* 10.94.4; 11.118.4; *Paed.* 1.4.37.1; 2.12.129.4; 3.12.86.2; *Strom.* 2.4.15.3; 4.18.114.1; 4.22.135.3; 5.4.25.4; 5.6.40.1; 6.8.68.1; *Exc.* 10.5; *Quis div.* 23.3. References found with the help of Stählin's *Register*. Dubious 'allusions' omitted.

Clement' were through systematising the hints that he has left scattered. I do not think that the parts of his work that are incipiently systematic are more significant than the incidental things that come up again and again in passing.

However, baptism *is* a scenario where Clement gives special attention to the origins of what we might call the spiritual senses. He not only mentions the eye of the spirit but also explains the process by which it is activated for vision:

> Just as those who have shaken off sleep have immediately woken up on the inside, or rather just as those who try to draw the mist away from the eyes, do not supply themselves with light from the outside, which they do not have, but by (clearing away) the obstacle from the eyes they leave the pupil free, so too we who are being baptised – when we have rubbed away the sins that were casting the holy spirit in darkness in the manner of a mist – we have the eye of the spirit (ὄμμα τοῦ πνεύματος) unobstructed and bright, with which alone we see the divine (τὸ θεῖον ἐποπτεύομεν), when the holy spirit flows onto and into us from heaven (ᾧ δὴ μόνῳ τὸ θεῖον ἐποπτεύομεν, οὐρανόθεν ἐπεισρέοντος ἡμῖν τοῦ ἁγίου πνεύματος). This admixture of eternal radiance able to see the everlasting light, since like is dear to like, and what is holy is dear to that from which it is holy, which is properly called light, 'for you were once darkness, but now light in the lord' (cf. John 1:5).[32] (*Paed.* 1.6.28.1)

The 'eye of the spirit', then, has sins cleared away from it so that it can entertain the vision of the divine. Clement uses the emotionally charged mystery vocabulary of ἐποπτεύειν to suggest an epiphanic encounter. The sanctity of the vision is further marked out by the way it occurs: It depends first on the intromission of the Holy Spirit flowing onto and into the baptisand from heaven. Clement's complicated compound verb ἐπεισρέω for the Holy Spirit suggests an attempt to harmonise the gospel accounts of the spirit descending *onto* (ἐπ' αὐτόν, Matt 3:16 // Luke 3:22 // John 1:32) or *into* (εἰς αὐτόν, Mark 1:10) Jesus, who is the explicit paradigm for the Christian's baptism.[33] Next, the vision is enabled through 'likeness'. The phrase τὸ ὅμοιον τῷ ὁμοίῳ φίλον ('like is dear to like') was a commonplace of Greek philosophical argument;[34] Clement reorients it through the scriptural vocabulary of divine 'holiness'. In baptism, likeness between

---

[32] Translation is my own, but with an eye on Choufrine 2002: 41, 82. Choufrine offers an excellent, detailed exegesis of this passage and its relationship to gnostic, Philonic, and Platonic material, as well as to the understudied works of Clement (the 'other Clement', as Bucur calls him).

[33] The curious Markan version was recently the subject of an excellent short study by Botner 2015.

[34] Rankin 1964: 59–61.

'what is holy' and 'what makes it holy' gives rise to the possibilities of perception.

This passage emphasises the 'eyes' alone. The preference for the eyes depends on the imagery of baptism as 'illumination', which is found in the New Testament and was already traditional by Clement's day. Nonetheless, the ears are sufficiently important that it is not long before Clement introduces how illumination is experienced in two ways, both as vision and as hearing. He writes first, 'gnosis is illumination, which makes ignorance disappear and inserts the ability to see clearly' (29.4).[35] Shortly afterward, he adds: 'gnosis rises up and flashes round the mind with illumination, and at once we hear as disciples, we who are without learning' (30.1).[36] His point is the same in both instances, namely that baptism brings about a way of knowing that is best understood as a form of sense perception. Like the miracles in the gospels, where Jesus' messianic role was to give sight to the blind and hearing to the deaf, so here vision and hearing are granted all at once. There is no process of learning: the jingle μαθηταὶ οἱ ἀμαθεῖς underscores this. Perception is immediate apprehension; it neither requires nor entails discursive reason; it is grounded in experience. Where there is light, there is no darkness (29.4).

This emphasis on a particular Christian mode of knowing, which is best articulated as perceptual, is important for Clement's apologetic purpose. He wants to argue against the claim that there are different grades of Christian after baptism, some of them childish, others distinguished by superior gnosis. Clement holds that there is a real transformation and perfection in baptism itself. The gift of the Holy Spirit marks a new creation, parallel to God's initial act of 'breathing in something of his own' when he first made man (cf. *Paed.* 1.3.7.2). This is experienced as a renewal of embodied life, including an illumination to see and hear as disciples.

However, Clement also maintains that baptism is not the final end of the Christian life. The language of sense perception can articulate this experience of the 'not yet' as well. Paul says, 'Now we see through a glass darkly, but then we shall see face to face.' Clement explains that after purifying ourselves of fleshly thoughts, eventually we will have faces equal to the angels, and then shall see face to face. The text that he so often quotes, 'what eye has not seen, nor ear heard, nor has it entered into the mind of a human

---

[35] φωτισμὸς ἄρα ἡ γνῶσίς ἐστιν, ὁ ἐξαφανίζων τὴν ἄγνοιαν καὶ τὸ διορατικὸν ἐντιθείς.
[36] ὅτι δὲ ἡ γνῶσις συνανατέλλει τῷ φωτίσματι περιστράπτουσα τὸν νοῦν, καὶ εὐθέως ἀκούομεν μαθηταὶ οἱ ἀμαθεῖς.

being', can underscore precisely the 'not yet' aspect of the Christians' current situation. There is only one ear that has heard it, Clement observes sagely, namely the one that was snatched up into the third heaven. But even that one was bidden to keep mum.[37]

The fact that baptism is the moment for contemplating the activation of the spiritual senses is consistent with the longer Christian tradition, where liturgical practice and material culture continually interacted with and influenced emergent epistemologies. Even prior to Clement, the senses were sometimes given special notice at baptism – Hebrews understands baptism as illumination and tasting the heavenly gift (Heb 6:4–5); Tertullian associates it with having the sins of our original blindness washed away (*Bapt.* 1.1);[38] some scholars have suggested that the Gospel of Truth may be a baptismal homily, in which case its list of *five* senses in this context is particularly striking.[39] The passage of Origen with which this chapter began also arose in discussion of Jesus' baptism, and the vision and audition of the spirit that he perceived there. Jesus' baptism was perceived as the type and pattern for all his disciples.

In later meditation on baptism, the doctrine of the spiritual senses is more fully developed. Gavrilyuk's essay on Pseudo-Dionysius the Areopagite underscores the role of baptism in Dionysius' reflection on spiritual senses.[40] Consider also the fresco from the Catacomb of Saints Marcellinus and Peter, dated to the fourth century (see Plate 2.1). The baptisand stands stark naked with a dove pouring water over him from a shell. His eyes and ears are particularly prominent, as if we were intended to recognise their significance in the baptismal rite. The hand placed on his head evokes the sense of touch, and the nose and mouth are also firmly outlined.[41] The motif of nudity suggests the experience of re-creation, as well as transition from one mode of corporeal life to another.[42]

---

[37] *Paed.* 1.6.37.1: «ὃ οὖς οὐκ ἤκουσέν ποτε» ἢ μόνον ἐκεῖνο τὸ ἐν τρίτῳ ἁρπασθὲν οὐρανῷ; Ἀλλὰ κἀκεῖνο ἐχεμυθεῖν ἐκελεύετο τότε. Pythagorean teaching on keeping silent characteristically used the term ἐχεμυθία. Clement cites Pythagorean practices of silence in *Strom.* 5.11.67.4, discussed in Mortley 1973: 201.

[38] Noted in Jensen 2012a: 113.

[39] Gos. Truth 30.17–30: 'And the Spirit ran after him, hastening from waking him up. Having extended his hand to him who lay upon the ground, he set him up on his feet, for he had not yet risen. He gave them the means of knowing the knowledge of the Father and the revelation of his Son. For, when they had seen him and had heard him, he granted them to taste him and to smell him and to touch the beloved Son' (trans. Attridge and MacRae, p. 101 in CGL 1). On the relationship between Gos. Truth and Clement's account of baptism, see Choufrine 2002: 27–68. On this passage in particular, see Choufrine 2002: 29–30.

[40] Gavrilyuk 2012: 91–101.   [41] Jensen 2011: 19–20, 112–15.

[42] Jensen 2011: 158–68; 2012b: 311–12.

The emphasis on the senses in art and text may remind us that the liturgy itself eventually came to incorporate ways of stimulating all the senses: vision, through the choreography of movement from dark to light and the use of torches; touch and smell through the laying on of hands and the anointing with scented oils; hearing, through the words of the liturgy and scripture; and taste, by the milk and honey that were given after emerging from the water. Baptism was a full-body experience of re-creation.[43]

Clement's interest in the senses at baptism, then, appears to be an early witness to a concern that became increasingly prominent in Christian tradition. His account of the spiritual illumination of eyes and ears is not just a figure of speech. It has a ritual context in ecclesial life; it is underpinned by a theology of new creation, a typology of Jesus' baptism, and a pneumatology of the bestowal of the Holy Spirit. From this arises a Christian somatology that is grounded in experience. The experiential ground does not stop Clement from giving a philosophical account of it, based in a phenomenology of perception; nor does its Christian character stop him from articulating it in a way that appropriates and transforms Greek discourse of mystery initiation, which also involved rites of sudden illumination, epoptic vision of the divine, and the reception of a verbal revelation at the same time.

This account of the passage on baptism, however, is one-sided unless we also take into account the imagery of the mother with which it is intertwined. In addition to the illumination of the spiritual senses, Clement also engages extensively with the idea of baptism as regeneration, and he dwells at length on the image of mother church suckling her Christian children; he pays close attention to the substance of the milk that nourishes them. This both contextualises and relativises the discourse of illumination of the spiritual senses. If anything, the image of the mother church and her suckling children seems to absorb Clement more than the image of the baptisand's newfound ability to see and hear. He seems to find it more emotively and rhetorically powerful, more compelling for detailed medical analysis, and to be closer to the heart of his personal experience of mystic wonder and adoration.

This juxtaposition with the imagery of the spiritual senses throws into relief some things that might otherwise pass unnoticed. Firstly, the spiritual senses tradition tends to emphasise the individual, whereas the image of mother church and her children, and the milky logos-mush that

---

[43] Jensen 2012a, 2012b.

nourishes them,[44] emphasises the community. Thus, it spotlights the role of institutional structures and their embodied ritual practices in the construction of epistemological discourse. Secondly, the image of the mother and her children relates to material reality in a different way from the imagery of the spiritual senses. There may be child-bearing women in church, but the church as an institution is not a maternal body. By contrast, every able-bodied baptisand has physical eyes and ears, which provide a direct corporeal correlate to the imagery of the spiritual sensorium. This difference is important for the way we understand the early Christian corporeal imagination. The image of mother church and her breast-milk is no less *real* to Clement than the image of the spiritual senses interwoven with it, even though it has no direct, isomorphic, material counterpart, and they do.[45] The modern discussion of the spiritual senses is often closely concerned with the relationship between material and immaterial realities; the terms of 'metaphor', 'analogy', and 'mysticism' each strive to frame that relationship in different ways. However, the corporeal realism of the mother church in Clement, which is juxtaposed and intertwined with the imagery of the spiritual senses, cautions us to be prepared for a more complex account of the significance of materiality in the tradition of the spiritual senses as well.

This brief study of Clement's interest in the spiritual senses, as it appears in his passage on baptism, is enough to underscore that the spiritual senses were important to Clement, in ways that are analogous to what developed in later Christian tradition. If one does not insist on a fivefold spiritual sensorium, then we definitely ought to begin earlier than Origen (and even if one does, then the Gospel of Truth should be taken into account). But more than that, we have seen that Clement draws our attention to the significance of the participatory, ritual experience of baptism at the heart of the tradition, its close association with the personal experience of illumination, and the communal experience of incorporation into the body of the church, nourished by *mater ecclesia*. This is a Christian reception and transformation of Greco-Roman experiences of mystery initiation and Platonic categories of intellectual illumination, which was already articulated in terms drawn from the mysteries by Plato himself. In the next section, we will turn to the New Testament to learn how some of the earliest sources in the Christian tradition reflected on

---

[44] ἀγαπητικὴ δὲ ὡς μήτηρ, καὶ τὰ αὑτῆς παιδία προσκαλουμένη ἁγίῳ τιθηνεῖται γάλακτι, τῷ βρεφώδει λόγῳ, 42.1.

[45] Christians came to understand the baptismal font as the womb of mother church: Jensen 2008.

non-physical dimensions of sensory perception – and, conversely, on sensory dimensions of perception of Christ.

Starting with Scripture: Spiritual Sensation and the New Testament Witness to Christ

The material in the New Testament has a different character from Clement's work. The purpose in this part of my paper is not to argue that the New Testament uses language in a way that is closely similar to the way Clement, Origen, or later theologians write of the spiritual senses. However, the biblical authors do show intentional engagement with the role of sense perception in response to experiences of God's work through Christ and/or the Spirit. The christological formation of their mode of knowing God involves new modes of thinking and talking about sensory experience. I shall give three brief case studies, drawn from three different genres in the New Testament.

Paul's Letter to the Philippians: Love Abounding in Recognition (Epignôsis) and Sense Perception (Aisthêsis)

Paul writes to the Philippians from prison. His opening address is very moving, as he portrays the love that he and his community share, and his own situation in bondage. In 1:9, he writes that he prays that their love might abound yet more and more in 'insight and all sense perception' (ἐν ἐπιγνώσει καὶ πάσῃ αἰσθήσει). The coupling of ἐπίγνωσις with αἴσθησις is striking, and closely relevant to our theme.[46]

Αἴσθησις is a standard term for sense perception: it was the term that featured in Origen's (and Clement's) version of Prov 2:5 (αἴσθησιν θείαν εὑρήσεις, 'you shall find a divine sense') – whereas the LXX as we know it has ἐπίγνωσιν instead (ἐπίγνωσιν θείαν εὑρήσεις, LXX Prov 2:5). Αἴσθησις occurs nowhere else in the New Testament; and the only other αισθ- stem is found in Heb 5:14, which refers to 'the perfect, who have their organs of sense perception (τὰ αἰσθητήρια) exercised by habit for distinguishing good from bad' (τελείων δέ ... τῶν διὰ τὴν ἕξιν τὰ αἰσθητήρια γεγυμνασμένα ἐχόντων πρὸς διάκρισιν καλοῦ τε καὶ κακοῦ). This was Origen's other key

---

[46] Wainwright (2012: 225) mentions that Thomas Brooks (c. 1608–86) took special notice of *aisthêsis* here as signifying 'sense, not a corporal, but a spiritual sense and taste, an inward experimental knowledge of holy and heavenly things', which he called 'heart knowledge'.

scriptural text, along with Prov 2:5, in developing his so-called 'doctrine' of the spiritual senses.[47] At a lexical level, then, Paul's use of αἴσθησις resonates closely with what we know of Origen's texts for meditation on the role of the senses in knowledge of Christ. This makes it particularly interesting to ask whether Paul's choice of terminology is merely incidental, or whether he, too, is meditating on the role of sense perception in knowing Christ? On the basis of a contextual reading of Philippians, I suggest the latter is strongly probable.

Let us begin with the immediate context:

⁸ μάρτυς γάρ μου ὁ θεὸς ὡς ἐπιποθῶ πάντας ὑμᾶς ἐν σπλάγχνοις Χριστοῦ Ἰησοῦ. ⁹ Καὶ τοῦτο προσεύχομαι, ἵνα ἡ ἀγάπη ὑμῶν ἔτι μᾶλλον καὶ μᾶλλον περισσεύῃ ἐν ἐπιγνώσει καὶ πάσῃ αἰσθήσει ¹⁰ εἰς τὸ δοκιμάζειν ὑμᾶς τὰ διαφέροντα, ἵνα ἦτε εἰλικρινεῖς καὶ ἀπρόσκοποι εἰς ἡμέραν Χριστοῦ.

God is my witness how I long for you all in the bowels of Christ Jesus. And this I pray, that your love may abound still more and more in knowledge[48] and all sense perception, to the end that you test things that differ, so that you may be pure and without stumbling till the day of Christ. (Phil 1:4–10)

By combining αἴσθησις with ἐπίγνωσις, Paul suggests that he is praying that the Philippians' love might abound in a form of knowledge that is *both* cognitive *and* perceptual. This mode of knowing is presented as a way of loving (may your *love abound in* epignôsis *and* aisthêsis). It is grounded in the experience of the Philippians and Paul bound in love for one another, even while Paul is in a situation of suffering (1:6–8). Paul hopes that it will be practised as a pattern of discernment until the day of Christ (1:10–11).

The incorporation of *sense perception* into this vision of love, insight, and practical discrimination, is significant in the context of Paul's epistle to the Philippians, because this epistle is marked by a concern for experiencing Christ in the body and through the body.[49] Already in the opening address, Paul portrays himself 'longing' (ἐπιποθῶ) for the Philippians 'in the bowels of Christ' (ἐν σπλάγχνοις Χριστοῦ Ἰησοῦ, 1:8). This is a strikingly physical

---

[47] Rahner 1932: 116–17.

[48] ἐπίγνωσις is not a common word, and was not part of the Greek philosophical tradition, which favoured vocabulary of ἐπιστήμη for 'knowledge'. It suggests personal 'recognition' involved in 'knowing'; the Pauline epistles use it elsewhere in close connection with a way of knowing God and what pertains to knowledge of God (cf. Rom 1:28; 3:20; 10:2; 1 Cor 13:12; 2 Cor 1:13; Eph 1:17; 4:13; etc.).

[49] E.g., Fowl 2011 (though I think he overemphasises the category of 'witness'; the language of μαρτυρία is absent from Philippians).

inflection of his common phrase, 'in Christ' (ἐν Χριστῷ). Nowhere else does he use this form of that expression, or anything like it. It is arresting, and bold. It encourages us to think of Paul experiencing Christ's emotions of human longing for the community, and feeling it in his very bowels, as if they were Christ's own.[50]

In the next part of the letter, Paul wants the Philippians to know that what is affecting him has turned out for the advancement of the gospel, with the result that 'my chains have become manifest in Christ (φανερούς ἐν Χριστῷ) in the whole praetorium and among all the rest' (1:13). The adjective φανερός indicates manifestation to senses;[51] here it is applied to the chains. Paul is not stating the unremarkable fact that the chains are visible to bodily eyes, but the remarkable one, that they have become a site of revelation, for they are now 'manifest in Christ'. The tag 'in Christ' is as potent as it is widespread in Paul's oeuvre; here it points up how the chains are caught up in the economy of salvation. Paul is modelling a way of perceiving his chains in joy because they prompt everyone to speak about the gospel. He evokes the pain of his own situation – not only is he in chains, but some of the brothers put on a false front in the way they speak the gospel, since their underlying motivation is to stir up suffering for his chains (1:17). Paul's focus on the chains themselves suggests his own detachment from the experience of pain as he takes the part of an interested observer, seeing Christ proclaimed and rejoicing in that (1:12–18).

He portrays, too, his joyful confidence that Christ will be magnified in his body (μεγαλυνθήσεται Χριστὸς ἐν τῷ σώματί μου, 1:20). Here, he models another exercise of discernment concerning how this will happen – whether through life or death. Again, this requires sensitivity both to understand and to perceive the situation aright: he grounds his judgement in the experience of loving relationship and the desire for presence – his desire for presence with Christ and the Philippians' need for his presence to them for their advancement and joy in the faith. The discriminating exercise of love once again depends both on ἐπίγνωσις (personal understanding of God's work in Christ) and on αἴσθησις (perception of the body as the site where Christ is magnified, and sensitivity to the importance

---

[50] There has been extensive discussion of 'union with Christ' in Paul and the wider New Testament in recent years, but Phil 1:8 has received little attention. For example, it is not cited in either Campbell 2012 or Macaskill 2013. The σπλάγχνα were the part of the victim that were opened up in Greek and Roman sacrifice, but it is not used in this way in the LXX. Paul portrays himself and the Philippians as elements of a sacrifice later in the letter (2:17), though here he is focused on the emotion of longing.
[51] Bockmuehl 1988.

of perceptibility to the Philippians). It involves cognitive and perceptual awareness in Christian love.

In a fuller study, we could examine how Paul portrays further ways in which he is co-formed with Christ's experience of embodiment (3:10–11, 20), and how he uses the vocabulary of initiation in the mysteries to describe his breadth of experience of the material world (4:12). We could discuss how his life in the body is grounded in Christ's experience of embodiment from the divine form to the pattern of human life unto death, and then exaltation for the glory of God the father (2:6–11). We could explore how the Philippians are drawn into this economy of embodiment, where they are called upon to be Paul's fellow-imitators (3:17) and to put into practise what they have *seen* or *heard* in him (4:9; cf. 1:30). The letter offers considerable scope to develop a Christian ideal of embodiment grounded in discernment of God's activity in Christ, which presents itself to the mind as ἐπίγνωσις, to the senses as αἴσθησις, all within the frame of relationship as ἀγάπη. This is similar to the pattern of purification of spiritual sense perception to work in a proper relationship with the mind, which Frederick Aquino discerned in Maximus the Confessor.[52] The emphasis on interpersonal love in Christ is an important counterbalance to the emphasis on attraction to the divine lover in the medieval tradition of the spiritual senses, which leans heavily on the Song of Songs and the aspiration to beatific vision.[53]

Paul's treatment of sense perception in Philippians is not isolated in early Christianity. Its motifs are picked up in Heb 5:14, whose influence on the spiritual senses tradition is more widely recognised; here we find again not only the language of sense perception but also the idea of a Christian training in the use of the sensory organs until they become habituated to a right pattern of discerning good and bad. Paul's chains, so important in the sensual manifestation of the gospel in Philippians, became a widespread focus of meditation in Christian piety, and the material form – even in the imagination – anchored the Christian experience of hope and trust in relationship to Paul.[54]

By including Paul in our study of the origins of the spiritual senses, then, we can better perceive the significance of embodied, sensually perceptible experiences of suffering 'in Christ' at the start of Christian meditation on sensory modes of knowing.

---

[52] Aquino 2012.
[53] E.g., Coolman 2012b (Thomas Gallus); McGinn 2012: esp. 192–95 (Bernard of Clairvaux, William of St-Thierry).
[54] Heath 2016: 231–33.

The Fourth Gospel: Spiritual Senses in the Evangelical Curriculum

When Paul was in prison, he rejoiced that his chains were 'manifest' in Christ unto the advancement of the 'gospel' (Phil 1:12–18). The bodily facts might look like chains, but Christ was proclaimed insofar as they emerged as 'manifest in Christ'. The relation between bodily facts and spiritual insight here takes the form of an evangelical paradox. When we turn to the Fourth Gospel, we find a different kind of invitation to view bodily facts from a spiritual perspective.

According to John's Gospel, no one has ever seen God and yet the one who was in the bosom of the Father has made him known (John 1:18). The Logos was made flesh as Jesus Christ; he performed on earth what he saw his father doing, he spoke on earth what he heard his father saying, and so he made God visible, audible, and present to the sense of those about him (5:19–20; 12:49–50).[55] Blindness and vision took on a new meaning in this setting: those who had eyes were blind if they did not perceive God in Jesus (cf. 9:39–41). They might *see* Jesus corporeally, but a different kind of vision was needed, and if they lacked it, they were still blind.

The *Spirit* in John's Gospel abides with Jesus from the very start of his ministry (1:32) and he bestows it on his closest disciples after his resurrection (20:22). The role of the Spirit in enabling his disciples' better apprehension of him – sensually, cognitively, and affectively – is underscored in his special teaching on the Spirit in the farewell discourses. The whole section is prefaced by Philip's egregious failure to discern God in Jesus while he is present with them (14:8–11); it is only when he goes away that Jesus anticipates that the 'Spirit of Truth' will abide with them, and they will gain a fuller apprehension that is experienced at once as contemplative vision (θεωρεῖτε), cognition (γνώσεσθε), and as self-involving through life (ζήσετε), obedience (ἔχων τὰς ἐντολάς μου καὶ τηρῶν), and love (ἀγαπῶν ἀγαπηθήσεται, 14:19–21). John does not use the term 'spiritual senses', but his teaching on perception in the Spirit, and the contrast between that and perceiving Jesus without it, suggests that he has the concept of spiritual sense perception.

John emphasises vision and hearing most of all, but as Rainer Hirsch-Luipold has underscored, he also draws special attention to *taste, smell, and touch* at crucial points in the narrative. The *taste* of good wine at the wedding of Cana is at the very beginning of the public ministry (John 2);

---

[55] Wang 2017.

the *smell* of Lazarus' corpse marks the centre of the Gospel, as the public ministry gives way to the story of the passion (John 11–12); the *touch* that Thomas asked for and Jesus offered concludes his account of the commission of the disciples after the resurrection, at what seems to be the original ending of the Gospel (John 20). Hirsch-Luipold elucidates the function of this rhetorical emphasis on the senses by arguing that the Fourth Gospel is written from the perspective of those who came too late: hence its blessing is on those who have not seen and yet have believed (John 20:29).[56] The Gospel invites readers to enter imaginatively into the experience of Jesus' ministry, where God was made present to all the senses, and so to cultivate the art of sense perception that enabled the first witnesses to the resurrection also to believe.

This interpretation of John's emphasis on sense perception helps make sense of Clement's understanding of the relation between the gospels: Clement wrote of John the Evangelist that, 'when he saw that *the bodily facts* (τὰ σωματικά) had been revealed in the gospels, urged on by his acquaintances, God-borne by the spirit (πνεύματι), he composed a spiritual gospel (πνευματικὸν εὐαγγέλιον)' (Clement *apud* Eusebius, *Hist. eccl.* 3.24.7).[57] I suggest that Clement (like Origen after him) envisaged the Fourth Gospel as a later stage in the curriculum, giving a spiritual perspective on the 'bodily facts' that had been conveyed by the other three.[58] This highlights the way John gives insight into the manifestation of God through revelation to the senses. What is intended here is not that sense perception is left behind, but that it is now transformed through the Spirit, as the learner too transitions to a more spiritual stage of progress.[59]

John's Gospel, then, develops a Christian theology of narrative epiphany that makes sense perception central. As with Paul, his focus on spiritual sense perception is christologically oriented; John grounds it in his understanding of the incarnation and the gift of the Spirit. Unlike in Philippians, this mode of perceiving is cultivated primarily through imaginative reading about the life of Christ rather than through focused attention to the material conditions of a contemporary saint.

---

[56] Hirsch-Luipold 2017.

[57] τὸν μέντοι Ἰωάννην ἔσχατον, συνιδόντα ὅτι τὰ σωματικὰ ἐν τοῖς εὐαγγελίοις δεδήλωται, προτραπέντα ὑπὸ τῶν γνωρίμων, πνεύματι θεοφορηθέντα πνευματικὸν ποιῆσαι εὐαγγέλιον (Clement of Alexandria, quoted in Eusebius, *Hist. eccl.* 3.24.7).

[58] Origen, *Comm. Jo.* 1.8.44–45; Hirsch-Luipold 2017: 42; see also Niculescu 2007. Clement himself, similarly, structured a curriculum that first trained baptised Christians in the habits of the body, sometimes with exempla drawn from the gospels (in the *Paedagogus*) and subsequently developed an ardently scholarly search for hidden wisdom (in the *Stromateis*).

[59] For grades of progress in Clement: Bucur 2006.

Alexandrian readers such as Clement and Origen recognised John's 'spirituality' as playing a crucial role in developing a reading programme for Christian formation: it assisted at the point of transition from recognition of the sense-perceptible realities to attaining a spiritual way of encountering those realities. When we consider this alongside Clement's and Origen's shared reading of Prov 2:5, we begin to discern that Origen's emphasis on the spiritual senses emerged in a distinctively Alexandrian tradition of Christian spirituality.[60]

Revelation 2–3: An Ear to Hear What the Spirit Says to the Churches

Paul and John, in different ways, both evoked the evangelical paradox of immanent revelation of God to the senses through or in Jesus Christ within the everyday material world. In Rev 2–3, we encounter a different kind of appeal to 'spiritual sensation', which resonates with the gospel tradition but engages more explicitly with the experience of transcending the material realm in a visionary encounter with the risen Christ. Revelation 2–3 contains seven letters to seven churches. The heavenly Jesus instructs John the Seer about what to write for the 'angel' of each church. Each letter closes with the formula, 'he who has an ear, let him hear what the Spirit says to the churches' (2:7, 11, 17, 29; 3:6, 13, 22), and then a promise is made 'for the one who conquers'. The *Spirit* speaks, but special notice is given to the organ of sense perception as necessary for hearing: '*he who has an ear*, let *him* hear'.

Commentators point out that this formula, 'he who has an ear, let him hear', is found in six variant versions across different strands of the early Jesus tradition. There is no verbally identical parallel to the formula in Revelation 2–3, but variants are found in the Synoptics, where it is closely linked with the parables, and in a range of apocryphal texts.[61] Scholars have debated its purpose, but focused especially on its *esoteric* or *paraenetic* function.[62] A few have rightly pointed out that it does not have the same function in every context in which it is used.[63] I focus here specifically on its use in Revelation 2–3, which is not identical to the Synoptics.

---

[60] Was Clement's and Origen's reading of Prov 2:5 distinctively Alexandrian, or should we think of the Septuagint as the truly 'Alexandrian' reading (ἐπίγνωσιν), and Clement and Origen's (αἴσθησιν) as an alternative? The provenance of LXX Proverbs has been debated; many scholars locate it in Alexandria, but Palestine has also been defended: van der Louw 2007: 335.
[61] In Gos. Thom. (six times), Acts of Thomas (once), Gos. Mary (twice), *Pistis Sophia* (ten times), and *Sophia of Jesus Christ* (four times): Aune 1997: 150–51.
[62] Esotericism: Dibelius 1910: 47; paraenesis: Räisänen 1973: 85–86. Both cited in Enroth 1990: 598.
[63] Enroth 1990.

Unlike in the Synoptic parables, what we are witnessing is the substance of visionary experience. John the Seer has described how he was himself in the Spirit on the Lord's day when he heard a voice behind him, turned to see the voice, and there was one like the Son of Man amid the lampstands (Rev 1:10–12). What John is hearing and writing down is the message from this exalted figure of the First and the Last, for the angel of each church. Whether the angel is a spiritual inhabitant of heaven, or a figure of authority on earth, remains debated,[64] but in either case what John is writing down is the substance of a message from heaven, received in the spirit, in a vision. The readers are invited into this imagination and asked to hear – if they have an ear to do so. The phrasing 'he who has an ear, let him hear' picks out the sensory organ. This is distinctively Christian. The Old Testament prophets cry to their audiences to 'hear the word of the Lord!'[65] but it belongs to Jesus' tradition to single out recurrently the ear that must play its part.

Furthermore, the *person* to be heard is explicitly designated 'the Spirit'. Exegetes suppose that this means Jesus himself, or else that Jesus is speaking through the Spirit to the churches.[66] In either case, the 'ear' by which they hear is cocked to the voice of the Spirit. This is not a form of listening that wholly abandons corporeal, bodily life, since what they hear concerns, in the first instance, their day-to-day life in their churches. Rather, it is a form of listening that is attentive to the Spirit's perspective on that life and thereby opens up the possibility of 'conquering' even within their embodied existence. We may recall the macarism at the start of Revelation, which was pronounced on 'the one who reads *and* on the one who hears the words of the prophecy and keeps the things written in it' (1:3). Such a person is blessed (μακάριος). The book of Revelation is thus written for a people whose blessedness is characterised by reading and hearing; it is no wonder that they are expected to have especially saintly ears. The 'ear' that hears the 'Spirit' is far from being a dead metaphor. The lack of precision in defining just what kind of ear and what kind of spirit points up unresolved tensions that characterise early Christian modes of knowing. Like Paul and John, the author of Revelation is grappling with the way Christian experience involves heightened sensory awareness of the Spirit; for John the seer, this starts out as a vision, but it has its *telos* in the daily life of the churches.

---

[64] Ferguson 2011. [65] Amos 7:16; Isa 1:10; Jer 2:4; 22:2; Ezek 6:3; 16:35; 21:3; etc.
[66] Aune 1997: 151.

Conclusion

This chapter offered a modest corrective to the monumental study of the spiritual senses by Paul Gavrilyuk and Sarah Coakley, concerning the beginning of the Christian 'doctrine' of spiritual sense perception. While they have done wonderful work in opening up the definition of the 'spiritual senses' in order to include a wider range of material from Origen onwards, I argued that they provided inadequate grounds for beginning only with Origen. The significance of this is not just that there is earlier material to consider (though it includes that). More importantly, the tradition is historically and even theologically misconstrued if the beginning is misidentified. Gavrilyuk and Coakley, like Rahner before them, treated Origen as normative, because he was perceived as first. But in their work, this only threw into relief how often other case studies in the tradition differed from Origen. It even drew attention to the way Origen himself failed to live up to the normatively Origenist account of the spiritual senses as a distinctive theological anthropology: parts of his language of spiritual sense perception had to be explained away as 'merely' metaphorical, but this was not satisfactory to any of his interpreters.

Our investigation of Clement as well as three biblical authors suggests a much broader perspective on the tradition from the first. Clement draws attention to the significance of baptism as the moment of activating the spiritual senses of vision and hearing through regeneration; Jesus' baptism was the type for Christian baptism, but the consequences of the ritual shifted attention to the 'body' of *mater ecclesia* who suckled her children, the baptised Christians. Paul noticed the language of αἴσθησις, and John developed a whole narrative theology of epiphany perceived through all five sensory organs. Both were acutely aware of the evangelical paradox of the manifestation to the senses of God's work in Christ: perceptible not to the *mere* physical senses, but rather to the sense perception that operated in conjunction with rational personal knowledge (*epignôsis* in Paul) or spiritual insight (*pneuma* in John), to involve people in a transformative mode of knowing, to abound in love (cf. Phil 1:8–9). In a visionary context, Revelation 2–3 noticed the ears of hearers, which alone can hear what the Spirit says to the churches. In all cases, the relation between spiritual and sensual is integral to how these authors apprehend Christ.

The significance of the incarnation and resurrection is particularly apparent in this early layer of the tradition: it is Jesus himself who manifests God's work to the senses in John, but it is the Spirit granted after the resurrection that enables people to perceive it; it is Christ who is magnified in Paul's body, but it is the exaltation of Christ after his death that makes that meaningful; in Revelation, the Spirit that speaks to the churches is, if not Christ himself, still closely associated with the risen Christ who speaks to John the seer. This christological emphasis is at risk of receding if we study the spiritual senses tradition only from later sources and treat theological *anthropology* as the normative. It is not, fundamentally, anthropology but *christology* that grounds this doctrine, and the union with Christ that is made possible through the incarnation and resurrection and/or exaltation.

3 | Health, Medicine, and Philosophy in the School of Justin Martyr

JARED SECORD

Introduction

When the philosopher Seneca was forced by Nero to end his life, he chose a method informed by medical knowledge, first having incisions made in his legs and arms so he might bleed to death, and then asking his personal physician Statius Annaeus to give him poison.[1] Other elite Romans in this period found death in similar ways, seeking assistance from physicians if they were suffering from an illness deemed incurable or if they were forced to commit suicide.[2] This common task undertaken by physicians in the Roman empire, however, makes little appearance in the works of its medical writers.[3] Medical assistance in dying was evidently not something that ancient physicians wished to emphasise, in keeping with the general aversion that they had to discussing patients who died in their care.[4] Helping someone die in this way served as a reminder to physicians of the subservient status that their profession often had in the Roman empire, where many physicians, including Seneca's Statius Annaeus, were slaves or freedmen.[5] Philosophers like Seneca, in contrast, prided themselves on helping people prepare themselves for death, in keeping with Socrates' claim that 'those who philosophise correctly practice dying'.[6] Seneca's death, in this sense, encapsulated a basic difference in the popular images of philosophers and physicians in the Roman empire. A philosopher would die with the right state of mind and help others achieve this state, while a physician might simply hasten someone's death. Philosophers therefore cast themselves as something like mental health specialists, whereas physicians were often dismissed as simple craftsmen, concerned only with the bodily health of their patients.[7]

---

[1] See Tacitus, *Ann.* 15.63–64.
[2] See Tacitus, *Ann.* 15.69; Suetonius, *Life of Lucan*; Flemming 2005: 303–6.
[3] For two partial exceptions, both discussing circumstances when medical assistance in dying was inappropriate, see Scribonius Largus, *Compounds* ep. 4–5 and Aretaeus, *Cur. Acut.* 2.5 with Flemming 2005: 311–14.
[4] See Mattern 2008: 92–94 with discussion below.   [5] See Nutton 1992: 39.
[6] Plato, *Phaed.* 67e: οἱ ὀρθῶς φιλοσοφοῦντες ἀποθνῄσκειν μελετῶσι.
[7] See Nutton 1985: 28.

The contrasting images of philosophers and physicians formed part of the Roman empire's medical marketplace, a term used to describe the competing specialists who offered therapy and treatment in various forms.[8] Physicians and philosophers were among the most prominent members of this marketplace, especially in the second century, when many philosophers claimed for themselves the ability to heal their pupils.[9] The claims they made went beyond the metaphorical, inasmuch as they did offer to pupils advice in the area of regimen, one of the three branches of ancient medicine, alongside surgery and pharmacology.[10] Regimen focused on eating, drinking, sexual activity, bathing, massage, and other areas that might help people preserve and maintain good health.[11] Physicians could claim expertise in these areas, but philosophers focused special attention on appetitive desires, meaning that they were able not only to tell people what to eat or drink but also to help them overcome their urges for excessive consumption.[12] As Brooke Holmes shows, appetitive desires receive little attention in the Hippocratic corpus, making this something of a vulnerable area for physicians, though Galen and others in the Roman empire sought to make up for this lack.[13] As such, Galen and other physicians of his time developed conceptions of health, illness, and treatment that moved beyond the somatic emphasis of earlier physicians, leading them to compete more directly with philosophers as mental health specialists.[14] Health of the body and of the mind consequently were overlapping fields, with a range of specialists offering their own types of expertise to provide treatment. The older disciplinary boundaries between philosophers and physicians were breaking down in the second century, with physicians claiming for themselves the status held by philosophers even as philosophers asserted their expertise in bodily and mental health.

Competition in these areas has significant bearing on the claims that early Christian intellectuals made regarding their expertise in health and medicine. This has been a difficult point in scholarship on early Christians and medicine, which has offered substantially different claims about how much Christianity functioned as a healing religion. A major part of the issue has to do with different approaches to the medical marketplace of the Roman empire, and how Christians related to it. Studies focusing on Christian engagement with medicine as practised by physicians have come

---

[8] See Israelowich 2015: 30–35. [9] See Trapp 2017: 33–34.
[10] E.g., Musonius Rufus 3.7; 4.2; 16.8, with Celsus, *On Medicine* praef. 9 on the three divisions of medicine.
[11] See Beer 2010; Jouanna 2012. [12] See Holmes 2013b: 19–20.
[13] Holmes 2013b: 22–23. [14] See Boudon-Millot 2013; Gill 2018.

to different conclusions than studies whose focus on health and healing includes exorcism and magic.[15] A missing factor in much of this work has been consideration of how the claims or silences of Christian intellectuals on health and medicine were shaped by the norms of Roman intellectual culture. Christian intellectuals seeking to be taken seriously might not wish to associate themselves closely with physicians, given their lingering reputation as slaves or craftsmen. Similar hesitancy informed how Christian intellectuals might present exorcists and other ritual experts, given the associations that this group had with magic and a consequent lack of legitimacy.[16] The desire for intellectual legitimacy shaped how Christian intellectuals portrayed themselves and their coreligionists, leading them in some instances to emphasise philosophy rather than other areas of intellectual and healing activity. The larger context of Roman intellectual culture and its medical marketplace informs the claims of expertise made by Christian writers about health and medicine.[17]

My aim in this chapter is to explore a range of Christian claims to intellectual expertise in health and medicine by focusing on Justin Martyr and his school. I use the word 'school' as shorthand to describe the impact that Justin had on Christian writers in the late second century who were influenced by his works, rather than as a reference to the location in Rome where he may have taught a small group of pupils.[18] As such, the chapter covers Tatian, who was taught by Justin, but also Pseudo-Justin, the unknown author of a Greek work *On the Resurrection* that was subsequently attributed to Justin Martyr.[19] Like Tatian, Pseudo-Justin shows familiarity with Justin's works, and he also seems to have been active in the late second century, qualifying him as a member of Justin's 'school'.[20] These three authors demonstrate some of the choices that Christian intellectuals of this period had in portraying themselves as experts with respect to health, medicine, and philosophy. In the chapter's first part, I argue that Justin's self-presentation as a philosopher limited and shaped his claims of expertise in health and medicine. His emphasis on a philosophical approach to death

---

[15] Contrast Twelftree 2007; Daunton-Fear 2009; and Jefferson 2014 with Ferngren 2009: 1–4 and Temkin 1991: xii.
[16] See Sorensen 2002: 5.
[17] Compare Wendt 2016 on the efforts of Christians to portray themselves as – and compete with – freelance religious experts in the Roman empire.
[18] For Justin's school, see Pouderon 1998: 239–41; Georges 2012: 75–87; Ulrich 2012: 62–74.
[19] Tatian as Justin's pupil: Trelenberg 2012: 195–203.
[20] See D'Anna 2001: esp. 282–87. Contrast Heimgartner 2001 for the argument that Pseudo-Justin should be identified with Athenagoras. Petrey (2016: 32 n. 3) reviews competing scholarly claims on all these points.

led him to portray himself and other Christians more like Seneca, rather than like an attending physician who might help people end their lives. In the process, Justin displays a dismissive attitude towards physicians, segregating the health of the body from the health of the mind, and focusing nearly all of his attention on the latter subject. In the chapter's second part, I show that Tatian and Pseudo-Justin engaged more directly than Justin with medicine and bodily health in their works, demonstrating increased awareness of the role that physicians were playing in the intellectual culture of the second century. Tatian and Pseudo-Justin display expertise in the fields of health and medicine even as they reject the status and authority held by physicians. They also emphasise that Christianity provided a better way to good health, especially by following an ascetic form of regimen. Unlike Justin, Pseudo-Justin and Tatian both acknowledge that the health of the body and the health of the mind were overlapping fields, and that intellectuals of all sorts might be concerned with both. The examples of all three authors show that the claims of Christian intellectuals about health and medicine need to be approached in the larger context of the Roman medical marketplace and of the competing claims of physicians and philosophers to present themselves as experts. Justin joined this marketplace almost exclusively as a philosopher unconcerned with physicians and bodily health, while Tatian and Pseudo-Justin demonstrate how the health of the body and that of the mind could be integrated into their self-portraits as Christian intellectuals.

Death and Christian Philosophy

According to Tertullian, Justin was a 'philosopher and martyr'.[21] These two titles were fundamental to Justin's presentation of himself and of his fellow Christians, something that I have argued at length in an earlier publication.[22] There I compared Justin with some of his non-Christian intellectual contemporaries, showing that he had many things in common with them, particularly in his efforts to promote himself and the Christian philosophical school that he was representing. I here offer an extension and counterpoint to my earlier arguments, focusing on the limited place that bodily health and medicine have in Justin's claims to intellectual expertise. This subject has received limited scholarly attention, although it is something that makes Justin stand out from other philosophers of

---

[21] Tertullian, *Val.* 5.1.   [22] See Secord 2020: 46–76.

his time, including Epictetus, who told his students that a 'philosopher's school is a doctor's office'.[23] A partial explanation of why Justin says so little about bodily health and medicine may simply be his limited education, a point that he makes about himself in his *Dialogue with Trypho*.[24] But an emphasis on health and medicine also seems to be at odds with his conception of an ideal philosopher. In Justin's view, people proved themselves to be philosophers by how they faced death, in keeping with the emphasis that Seneca and other philosophers of the Roman empire placed on this point.[25] This focus on the connections between death and philosophy restricted how much bodily health and medicine could enter Justin's portrayal of the ideal philosopher, given the different roles that physicians and philosophers had traditionally held in matters relating to death. In Justin's view, philosophers were distinguished by their excellent mental control when they faced death, but the health of their bodies while they were alive was basically irrelevant, as were the physicians who concerned themselves with this subject. In this sense, Justin's portrait of the ideal Christian philosopher makes no allowance for the increasingly crowded medical marketplace of the Roman empire in his time.

Justin's scattered references to bodily health and medicine across his extant works reveal how little both topics featured in his self-presentation and claims to expertise. Justin clearly shows his familiarity with earlier Christian stories about miraculous healings, but he mentions these briefly and without any clear connections to his presentation of Christian philosophy. Justin offers little more than a general comparison between Christ and Asclepius, along with the claim that Christ 'will heal all diseases (θεραπεύσειν πάσας νόσους)'.[26] Justin likewise suggests that Christians could expect to live again after death, when they would be made 'corruptionless, passionless, and deathless (ἀφθάρτους καὶ ἀπαθεῖς καὶ ἀθανάτους)'.[27] But Justin offers no explanation of how Christians in his time, much less how he himself, might provide treatment or therapy to others. In this regard, the only reference that Justin makes to Christian healing among his contemporaries is to the activities of exorcists. His concern here, though, seems to be focused on answering the objections that non-Christian readers might have about the legitimacy of exorcism. Marcus Aurelius, one

---

[23] Epictetus, *Diatr.* 3.23.30: ἰατρεῖόν ἐστιν … τὸ τοῦ φιλοσόφου σχολεῖον. For brief discussions of Justin on healing, see Daunton-Fear 2009: 48–51; Jefferson 2014: 58–63.
[24] See Justin, *Dial.* 2.4–5 with Secord 2020: 63–65.   [25] See Edwards 2007: 78–112.
[26] Justin, *1 Apol.* 48.1; cf. 31.7; 54.10. For the comparison between Christ and Asclepius, see *Dial.* 69.3.
[27] Justin, *Dial.* 46.7.

of the addressees of Justin's apologetic works, suggests that he had been taught to put 'no faith in the claims of miracle-workers and sorcerers concerning enchantments and the sending away of demons and such things'.[28] Justin appears to be answering this type of objection when he says that Christian exorcists were able to 'heal [the demon-possessed people who] had not been healed by all the others – exorcists and enchanters and sorcerers'.[29] Justin's claim here is simply to suggest that Christians were not practitioners of magic.[30] But there is no connection between the activities of these unidentified Christian exorcists and Justin himself or the martyred Christian philosophers he describes. The ability of some Christians to heal is disconnected from Justin's image of himself and of the ideal Christian philosopher.

Healing forms no part of Justin's claims to expertise, even when he addresses a situation that many of his contemporaries would have deemed treatable by changes in regimen. This situation is the only reference Justin makes to a physician in his extant works. It concerns a Christian youth who sought medical assistance to help him give up sex completely:

> And recently one of us, to persuade you that licentious sex is not a mystery rite for us, delivered a petition in Alexandria to the governor Felix, praying that he would allow a physician to remove his testicles. For, without the authorisation of the governor, the physicians there were saying that it was forbidden to do this. When Felix was not at all willing to subscribe [the petition], the youth remained on his own, satisfied with his own conscience and of those like-minded.[31]

The argumentative point of the story appears in its first sentence, demonstrating that Justin was responding to rumours about Christian sexual rites.[32] Emphasis on this point shapes Justin's treatment of the story, leading him to offer implicit approval of the Christian youth's desire to be castrated. This approval is at odds with how other authors of Justin's time treat pharmacological or surgical methods for libido regulation. Origen

---

[28] Marcus Aurelius, *Med.* 1.6: τὸ ἀπιστητικὸν τοῖς ὑπὸ τῶν τερατευομένων καὶ γοήτων περὶ ἐπῳδῶν καὶ [περὶ] δαιμόνων ἀποπομπῆς καὶ τῶν τοιούτων λεγομένοις.

[29] *2 Apol.* 5.6: ὑπὸ τῶν ἄλλων πάντων ἐπορκιστῶν καὶ ἐπᾳστῶν καὶ φαρμακευτῶν μὴ ἰαθέντας, ἰάσαντο.

[30] See *Dial.* 69.7 for Justin's concern on this point.

[31] Justin, *2 Apol.* 29.2–3: καὶ ἤδη τις τῶν ἡμετέρων – ὑπὲρ τοῦ πεῖσαι ὑμᾶς ὅτι οὐκ ἔστιν ἡμῖν μυστήριον ἡ ἀνέδην μίξις – βιβλίδιον ἀνέδωκεν ἐν Ἀλεξανδρείᾳ Φήλικι ἡγεμονεύοντι ἀξιῶν ἐπιτρέψαι ἰατρῷ τοὺς διδύμους αὐτοῦ ἀφελεῖν· ἄνευ γὰρ τῆς τοῦ ἡγεμόνος ἐπιτροπῆς τοῦτο πράττειν ἀπειρῆσθαι οἱ ἐκεῖ ἰατροὶ ἔλεγον. καὶ μηδόλως βουληθέντος Φήλικος ὑπογράψαι, ἐφ' ἑαυτοῦ μείνας ὁ νεανίσκος ἠρκέσθη τῇ ἑαυτοῦ καὶ τῶν ὁμογνωμόνων συνειδήσει.

[32] For more regarding such rumours, see Justin, *1 Apol.* 3.1.

and Pseudo-Hippolytus both cite with disapproval the example of an Athenian cult official who applied hemlock to his genitals to control his sexual desires.[33] Surgical solutions were likewise not generally approved, something apparent from the Roman legislation that Justin references and from the rumours and innuendo about Origen's alleged self-castration.[34] In his own work, Origen suggested that it was possible for Christians to 'drive all lust from their mind' with prayer, rather than by seeking pharmacological or surgical help.[35] The solution Origen proposed involved regimen and the control of appetitive desires, in keeping with the methods favoured by philosophers. Even Galen, from his perspective as a physician who also claimed to be a philosopher, preferred regimen as a solution for sexual control.[36] When a friend asked for advice about how to give up sex completely, Galen suggested that he should simply 'shut himself off completely from spectacles, and from stories and memories with the potential for rousing him to desire'.[37] The consistent disapproval of pharmacological and surgical solutions for sexual regulation is at odds with Justin's perspective. Justin's Christian youth evidently turned to prayer and his 'own conscience' after his petition was denied. But Justin makes no suggestion that this was what the youth should have done at the outset and he says nothing about the ability of Christian philosophers to help the youth regulate his appetitive sexual desires. Justin seems disinterested in the potential of regimen to regulate appetitive desires and bodily health, giving this no role in his presentation of Christian philosophers.

Justin's focus, instead, is on the mental state Christian philosophers have when they face death, speaking directly to the major concerns of philosophers. How much Justin may have known about the philosophical interests of his imperial addressees is unclear, but he does refer to Marcus Aurelius as a philosopher on multiple occasions.[38] This philosophical focus is especially apparent through the vocabulary and themes that Justin uses in his discussion of the recent deaths by execution of three Christians in Rome.[39] Justin anticipates the objection that these deaths may have been little more than suicide, given that two of the three Christians involved volunteered

---

[33] See Pseudo-Hippolytus, *Haer.* 5.8.40 and Origen, *Cels.* 7.48, with Secord 2018: 484.
[34] Origen's alleged castration: Eusebius, *Hist. eccl.* 6.8.1; Epiphanius, *Pan.* 64.3.12–13. Roman legislation against castration: Caner 1997: 398.
[35] Origen, *Cels.* 7.48: πᾶσαν ἐπιθυμίαν ἀπὸ τῆς διανοίας αὐτῶν ἐξελάσαντες.
[36] On Galen as a physician and philosopher, see Boudon-Millot 2019.
[37] Galen, *Affected Places* 6.6 (8.451 K): θεαμάτων καὶ διηγήσεως καὶ μνήμης ἐπεγείρειν δυναμένης εἰς ἀφροδίσια παντάπασιν εἴργειν ἑαυτόν.
[38] For examples, see *1 Apol.* 1.1; 2.2; *2 Apol.* 2.16.   [39] Justin, *2 Apol.* 2.1–20.

the information that led to their deaths.⁴⁰ In response, Justin explains that these Christians made the choices that led to their deaths 'without fear (ἀφόβως)'.⁴¹ Justin adds elsewhere that Christians were 'fearless towards death and all the other things judged to be frightening'.⁴² This lack of fear for death was a sign that Christians were able to master their passions (*pathē*) and that they consequently had the excellent mental control of a philosopher.⁴³ Justin's claim that Christians lived a 'pure and passionless life (καθαρὸν καὶ ἀπαθῆ βίον)' corresponds closely to one of the chief goals that Marcus Aurelius set for himself, 'not to be overthrown by any passion (τοῦ ὑπὸ μηδενὸς πάθους καταβληθῆναι)'.⁴⁴ Following Stoic doctrine, Marcus set himself with the task of regularly contemplating death in order to master his fears of it.⁴⁵ Marcus was also interested in the health of his body, as any reader of his correspondence with Fronto will know, but this was not a subject Justin explored in his presentation of the deaths of Christian philosophers.⁴⁶ The fearless way in which they approached death was the philosophical point that Justin emphasised.

With death as his focus, Justin seems to have realised that any discussion of the bodily health of his Christian philosophers might have seemed incongruous, and even unintentionally humorous. This impression comes from prevailing attitudes about death, health, and suicide in the Roman empire, especially as depicted in satirical literature. The best demonstration of this comes from Lucian's account of Peregrinus, the philosopher and charlatan whose self-immolation following the Olympic Games in 165 CE was the final step in his lifelong goal of becoming famous.⁴⁷ According to Lucian, Peregrinus still feared death even after he announced his intention to jump into the flames. He demonstrated this by remaining concerned about his bodily health in the days leading up to his suicide, writhing in pain and demanding a drink of water from a physician when he was suffering from a fever.⁴⁸ The narrator of Lucian's story adds a further point about Peregrinus' continuing focus on bodily health, this time relating to some sort of eye ailment: 'And I myself saw him not many days ago anointed, so that he might be made to weep by the pungent drug.'⁴⁹ As

---

[40] Justin, *2 Apol.* 2.15–20. [41] Justin, *2 Apol.* 3.1.
[42] Justin, *2 Apol.* 12.1: ἀφόβους πρὸς θάνατον καὶ πάντα τὰ ἄλλα νομιζόμενα φοβερά. Cf. Justin, *1 Apol.* 57.2: 'We do not fear death (οὐ γὰρ δεδοίκαμεν θάνατον)'.
[43] On *pathē*, see Singer 2018: 383–85. [44] Marcus Aurelius, *Med.* 3.4.3.
[45] See Marcus Aurelius, *Med.* 10.36, with Newman 1989: 1506–12.
[46] Marcus Aurelius, Fronto, and their interest in bodily health: Mazzini 2001 and Freisenbruch 2007.
[47] Peregrinus: Jones 1986: 117–32. [48] Lucian, *Peregr.* 44.
[49] Lucian, *Peregr.* 45: ἐγὼ δὲ οὐδ᾽ αὐτὸς πρὸ πολλῶν ἡμερῶν εἶδον αὐτὸν ἐγκεχρισμένον, ὡς ἀποδακρύσειε τῷ δριμεῖ φαρμάκῳ.

Lucian says, with a likely allusion to Christianity, Peregrinus' concern with bodily health under these circumstances was 'the same as if a man about to be put up on the cross should treat the bump on his finger'.[50] The same theme shows up in the *Philogelos*, a late antique jokebook, about a suicidal man from the city of Abdera: 'An Abderite who wanted to hang himself bumped his head when the rope broke. He got a bandage from the doctor, put it on the wound, and went back and hanged himself.'[51] This joke, along with Lucian's stories, suggests that a concern with bodily health was laughable in someone who was about to die, especially by suicide. This fits with a general pattern in ancient sources whereby people with illnesses deemed terminal would seek no further treatment and instead choose suicide.[52] Though Justin insisted that there was nothing suicidal in the choices of his executed Christian philosophers, he must have known that any mention of their bodily health in the moments leading up to their deaths would have seemed irrelevant and potentially even funny. In matters relating to death, it was the philosopher rather than the physician who mattered, and this comes through clearly in Justin's work.

Justin's limited claims to expertise in health and medicine make him stand out among other philosophers of the second century but nonetheless fit well with his presentation of himself and his fellow Christians. He and they were philosophers, something that they proved by how they faced death. Their lack of fear demonstrated their control over their passions, which Justin connected to the mind rather than the body. Any claims about the bodily health of Christian philosophers in the moments leading up to their death were trivial in comparison, and something that might have subjected Justin to criticism and ridicule from observers who viewed Christian martyrdom as akin to suicide. Justin may have lacked the knowledge of health and medicine that some of his better-educated contemporaries had, but he constructed his claims to expertise in such a way that his relative ignorance was irrelevant. If more of Justin's works were extant, we might have a different view of his self-presentation, particularly if we had access to his lost work of heresiology, a genre that often gave Christian authors the chance to offer encyclopaedic displays of erudition.[53] But, as it is, our

---

[50] Lucian, *Peregr.* 45: ὅμοιον ὡς εἴ τις ἐπὶ σταυρὸν ἀναβήσεσθαι μέλλων τὸ ἐν τῷ δακτύλῳ πρόσπταισμα θεραπεύοι. For Lucian's knowledge of Christianity, see Bremmer 2007.

[51] *Philogelos* 110: Ἀβδηρίτης ἀπάγξασθαι βουλόμενος καὶ τοῦ σχοινίου διαρραγέντος τὴν κεφαλὴν ἐπλήγη. λαβὼν οὖν ἔμπλαστρον παρὰ τοῦ ἰατροῦ καὶ θεὶς κατὰ τοῦ τραύματος, ἀπελθὼν πάλιν ἀπήγξατο. On the reputation of Abderites for stupidity, see Tschiedel 1986.

[52] See Gourevitch 1969.

[53] Justin's work of heresiology: *1 Apol.* 26.8 with den Dulk 2018. Encyclopaedic elements in heresiology: Maldonado Rivera 2017.

portrait of Justin derives from works that construct his self-image and expertise in terms of death and philosophy, leaving him little opportunity to discuss bodily health and medicine. For different images of Christian intellectuals, we must turn to Justin's successors, who built from his example while also finding ways to incorporate bodily health and medicine into their self-presentation and claims to expertise.

Christian Health and the Medical Marketplace

With Justin's successors, we move into a different world of Christian engagement with the Roman empire's medical marketplace. Pseudo-Justin and Tatian display greater erudition than Justin and put this to use in wider-ranging treatments of Greek intellectual culture in the late second century. Both authors shared some of Justin's concern with death, but their works gave them greater latitude to explore topics relating to health and medicine outside of the context of death and persecution. Pseudo-Justin deploys his knowledge of health and medicine to defend the literal reality of bodily resurrection, while Tatian critiques Greek medical practices in his *Against the Greeks*.[54] Tatian's critique has received much attention, with a growing trend of scholars challenging past attempts to minimise the extent of his rejection of medicine.[55] I follow this trend, but my aim here is to take a different approach than past work, shifting attention from Tatian's rejection of medicine to his views on bodily and mental health, subjects that have mostly been ignored even in scholarship discussing the ascetic practices attributed to Tatian by heresiologists.[56] The relative disinterest in this topic reflects a larger tendency to assume that good health was irrelevant or even antithetical to Christian asceticism, an idea that I challenge.[57] My argument is that Tatian's perspective on health depends largely on regimen and on the control of appetitive desires, features that come out more clearly when his work is compared with Pseudo-Justin's. Together, the two authors demonstrate how medical and philosophical approaches to health in the second century impacted emerging forms of Christian asceticism. Tatian and Pseudo-Justin position themselves as rejecting the Greek world, with Tatian offering a substantial critique of the Roman empire's medical marketplace. But the perspectives on health of both authors still have demonstrable similarities to

---

[54] Tatian's attack: Secord 2020: 77–119. Pseudo-Justin's argument: Petrey 2016: 19–34.
[55] See Crosignani 2017: 188–89 and Crawford 2021 *contra* Temkin 1991: 119–25; Amundsen 1995; Ferngren 2009: 52.
[56] See Hunt 2003: 144–75; Crawford 2016: 556–63.   [57] See Secord 2018: 468.

those of their non-Christian contemporaries. An emphasis on good health forms a basic part of how Tatian and Pseudo-Justin attempted to demonstrate their expertise as intellectuals, taking places of their own in the Roman empire's competitive medical marketplace.

Tatian's critique of Greek healing and medicine hinges on the malicious influence he believes that demons have had on humanity.[58] This argument draws from stories of the Greek gods and from Jewish and Christian traditions about fallen angels, with Tatian equating the two groups and calling them demons.[59] Some of the demons, Tatian claims, became 'intemperate and luxurious (ἄσωτοι καὶ λίχνοι)', a suggestion based on how the Greek gods behaved in the works of Homer and other poets.[60] There was consequently much evidence for Tatian to suggest that Zeus and the other demons called gods by the Greeks were 'ruled by the same passions that also rule men'.[61] By this argument, the uncontrolled appetites of the 'frenzied (παραφόρων)' demons provided a negative example for Greeks to emulate, while also ensuring that Greek 'customs border on madness'.[62] Demons made this situation worse by making it seem that they possessed the ability to heal. Tatian cites his teacher Justin for this point, likening demons to bandits who 'kidnap men, then return them to their families for a ransom'.[63] This image underlies Tatian's suggestion that the supposed healing abilities of demons derived only from removing the illnesses that they had themselves caused. The reward that demons received from the people they 'kidnapped' came in the form of laudatory speeches like those offered to Asclepius by Aelius Aristides.[64] Demons apparently formed an appreciative audience for these sorts of speeches. 'When', Tatian explains, '[the demons] have derived enjoyment from the praise, they fly away from the sick, remove the sickness that they have contrived, and return the men to their previous [condition]'.[65] The people who were thus deceived by demons thought that they were healthy and that they had received divine healing. Tatian thereby attempts to undercut one major component of the medical marketplace of his time, arguing that cults of healing were baseless, part of the negative impact that demons had on human health. The

---

[58] On the epistemological capabilities of demons in relation to divination, see also Chapter 23 by Michael Hanaghan, this volume.
[59] See Tatian, *Or. Graec.* 7 with Crawford 2021.   [60] Tatian, *Or. Graec.* 12.5.
[61] Tatian, *Or. Graec.* 8.2: τοῖς αὐτοῖς πάθεσιν οἷσπερ καὶ οἱ ἄνθρωποι κρατηθέντες.
[62] Tatian, *Or. Graec.* 12.10 and 33.1: ἔθη μανίας ἔχεται πολλῆς.
[63] Tatian, *Or. Graec.* 18.6: ζωγρεῖν τινας, εἶτα τοὺς αὐτοὺς μισθοῦ τοῖς οἰκείοις ἀποκαθιστᾶν.
[64] See Secord 2020: 89–90.
[65] Tatian, *Or. Graec.* 18.6: ἐπειδὰν τῶν ἐγκωμίων ἀπολαύσωσιν, ἀποπτάμενοι τῶν καμνόντων, ἣν ἐπραγματεύσαντο νόσον περιγράφοντες, τοὺς ἀνθρώπους εἰς τὸ ἀρχαῖον ἀποκαθιστῶσιν.

uncontrolled passions of demons provided a poor basis for Greeks seeking divine help for bodily and mental health.

Tatian attacks another major aspect of the medical marketplace with his critique of Greek philosophers, focusing on how they failed to keep their appetitive desires under control, leading to poor bodily health. Tatian supports this argument with a collection of anecdotes drawn from the biographical traditions of Greek philosophers, emphasising stories that relate to uncontrolled desires and poor health. As such, Tatian includes a story that emphasises Plato's 'gluttony (γαστριμαργίαν)', a character trait that he also identifies in philosophers of his own time.[66] Gluttony features in discussions by Musonius Rufus and Galen, with the former suggesting that it leads to 'harm for the body (βλάβην ... τὴν τοῦ σώματος)' and the latter identifying it as something associated with the 'appetitive function (ἐπιθυμητικῆς ἐστι δυνάμεως)' of the soul.[67] Tatian therefore presents Plato as decidedly unphilosophical in his bodily health and self-control. A similar theme appears in Tatian's discussion of Diogenes the Cynic: 'Diogenes, who boasted about his self-sufficiency (αὐτάρκειαν) because of the jar [where he lived], was seized with pain from eating raw octopus and died of an intestinal obstruction because of his lack of self-control'.[68] The doxographer Pseudo-Plutarch, Tatian's contemporary, equated health (ὑγείαν) with 'moderation in diet and self-sufficiency (εὐταξίαν καὶ αὐτάρκειαν)', leading to the obvious conclusion that Diogenes' lack of self-control was unhealthy.[69] A climax to Tatian's stories about the ill health of philosophers comes with his account of the death of Heraclitus: '[Heraclitus] was afflicted with dropsy and practiced medicine as he did philosophy, smearing himself with ox dung. When the filth hardened, it caused cramps over his entire body, and he died in convulsions'.[70] Though this story was told by many other authors, none of them emphasised Heraclitus' medical failings as much as Tatian did.[71] This hints at the expanded interest that philosophers of Tatian's time tended to have in health and regimen. Tatian

---

[66] Tatian, *Or. Graec.* 2.1; 25.1. For the motif of Plato's gluttony, see Riginos 1976: 71 n. 3.
[67] Musonius Rufus 18b.1; Galen, *Affections and Errors* 1.6 (5.27 K).
[68] Tatian, *Or. Graec.* 2.1: Διογένης πιθάκνης καυχήματι τὴν αὐτάρκειαν σεμνυνόμενος πολύποδος ὠμοβορίᾳ πάθει συσχεθεὶς εἰλεῷ διὰ τὴν ἀκρασίαν ἀποτέθνηκεν. Compare Athenaeus, *Deipn.* 8.341E; Lucian, *Vit. auct.* 10; Diogenes Laertius, *Lives* 6.23 and 6.76; Plutarch, *De esu* 995C–D.
[69] Pseudo-Plutarch, *Plac. philos.* 911B.
[70] Tatian, *Or. Graec.* 3.2: ὕδρωπι γὰρ συσχεθεὶς καὶ τὴν ἰατρικὴν ὡς φιλοσοφίαν ἐπιτηδεύσας βολβίτοις τε περιπλάσας ἑαυτὸν τῆς κόπρου κρατυνθείσης συνολκάς τε τοῦ παντὸς ἀπεργασαμένης σώματος σπασθεὶς ἐτελεύτησεν. For the use of ox dung as a remedy for dropsy, see Galen, *Simple Drugs* 10.23 (12.301 K).
[71] For other stories of Heraclitus' death, see Fairweather 1973.

responds to this trend by emphasising the poor self-control of Greek philosophers, challenging their authority in matters relating to health.

Tatian also subjected physicians to criticism, implicating them as contributors in the malevolent efforts of demons against humanity. Tatian's critique includes a straightforward objection to the recognition and praise that physicians might receive: 'Why are you called a benefactor for healing your neighbour?'[72] This question responds to the common Greek suggestion that health was a great benefaction to humanity.[73] Tatian seems to grant that physicians might sometimes be successful in the treatment they provide, but he emphasises that this came at a cost. The argument he offers focuses on pharmacology, an area of medicine that Tatian brands as demonic. Demons, Tatian claims, 'turn people away from the worship of God with their cunning and contrive that they are won over by herbs and roots'.[74] These types of remedies might sometimes work, Tatian acknowledges. But, as Tatian says, 'even if you are healed by drugs (I yield this to you as an excuse), you still ought to offer witness to God'.[75] Tatian's point here seems to be that pharmacological remedies were an inferior method of treatment, fitting with the efforts of demons to divert humanity's 'thoughts, [which are] already inclined to lower regions, so that people are quite unable to rise up on their journey to the heavens'.[76] This was part of a demonic effort to keep people at the level of animals, rather than having them continue upward on their journey to the heavens. Pharmacological remedies contributed to this process because they were accessible even to animals, leading Tatian to a simple question: '[Why] do you heal yourself just as a dog does with grass, a deer with a snake, a hog with river crabs, or a lion with monkeys?'[77] In Tatian's view, pharmacology was not worth the associated costs. It made physicians co-conspirators with the demons they worshipped. Pharmacology might sometimes provide healing, but it also fit with the plans that demons had for humanity.

Faced with a medical marketplace dependent on the false claims of demons, Tatian offered a portrait of Christianity that emphasised its ability

---

[72] Tatian, *Or. Graec.* 18.5: τί δὲ θεραπεύων τὸν πλησίον εὐεργέτης ἀποκαλῇ;
[73] See Samama 2003: index s.vv. εὐεργεσία, εὐεργετέω, εὐεργέτημα, and εὐεργέτης.
[74] Tatian, *Or. Graec.* 17.5: τέχνῃ γὰρ τῆς θεοσεβείας τοὺς ἀνθρώπους παρατρέπουσι, πόαις αὐτοὺς καὶ ῥίζαις πείθεσθαι παρασκευάζοντες.
[75] Tatian, *Or. Graec.* 20.1: Κἂν θεραπεύησθε φαρμάκοις (κατὰ συγγνώμην ἐπιτρέπω σοι), τὴν μαρτυρίαν προσάπτειν σε δεῖ τῷ θεῷ.
[76] Tatian, *Or. Graec.* 16.3: τὰς γνώμας αὐτῶν παρατρέπουσι κάτω νενευκυίας, ὅπως μεταρσιοῦσθαι πρὸς τὴν ἐν οὐρανοῖς πορείαν ἐξαδυνατῶσιν.
[77] Tatian, *Or. Graec.* 18.4: θεραπεύεις δὲ μᾶλλον αὐτὸν ὥσπερ ὁ μὲν κύων διὰ πόας, ὁ δὲ ἔλαφος δι'ἐχίδνης, ὁ δὲ σῦς διὰ τῶν ἐν ποταμοῖς καρκίνων, ὁ δὲ λέων διὰ τῶν πιθήκων;

to heal. Like Justin, Tatian drew on stories of miraculous healings, presenting these as a way to counter the false claims of demons about their healing powers. Tatian takes up Paul's image of a 'breastplate (θώρακι)' with which Christians are armed, claiming that they had a 'heavenly spirit (πνεύματος ἐπουρανίου)' to protect them against demons.[78] This protection underlies Tatian's description of a miraculous healing: '[Demons] are struck by the power of God and go away in terror, and the sick person is healed'.[79] People should consequently regard as inferior the methods of physicians and the pharmacological substances they use, which Tatian dismisses as 'matter (ὕλη)'. As Tatian says, 'if a person is healed by matter by trusting in it, he will be healed all the more by relying on the power of God'.[80] The same applies to mental health: 'How is it good to attribute to matter and not to God a cure for the mad?'[81] With divine support for both body and mind, Christians can expect to be healthier than Greeks. As Tatian says, Christians have risen 'above the passions (παθῶν ... ἀνώτερος)', a state that Tatian himself claims to have achieved: 'I rise above (ἀνώτερος) every type of disease; grief does not destroy my soul'.[82] The methods of Greek medicine might sometimes work or seem to work, but they were no match for what Christians could achieve with the power of God.

Tatian's view on Christian good health is complicated, however, by the emphasis he places on what is best described as an ascetic mode of regimen.[83] As Tatian surely knew, regimen was a basic component of Greek medicine, alongside pharmacology and surgery. But he neglected to mention this in his attack on Greek medical methods, focusing his attention on pharmacology and ignoring surgery completely, while acting as if control of the appetitive desires was entirely antithetical to Greek customs. This emphasis comes through in the one-sided view that Tatian offers of Greeks and in his consistent effort to claim that he, as a barbarian and a Christian, rejects their lifestyle. As such, Tatian's presentation of Greek regimen serves throughout his work as a sign of what he has repudiated. Based on this principle, Tatian emerges as someone who follows a moderate and restricted diet, objecting

---

[78] Tatian, *Or. Graec.* 16.7 with Eph 6:14 and 1 Thess 5:8. Cf. *Or. Graec.* 15.7.
[79] Tatian, *Or. Graec.* 16.8: οἳ λόγῳ θεοῦ δυνάμεως πληττόμενοι δεδιότες ἀπίασιν, καὶ ὁ κάμνων θεραπεύεται.
[80] Tatian, *Or. Graec.* 18.1: εἰ γάρ τις ὑπὸ τῆς ὕλης θεραπεύεται πιστεύων αὐτῇ, θεραπευθήσεται μᾶλλον αὐτὸς δυνάμει θεοῦ προσανέχων.
[81] Tatian, *Or. Graec.* 17.5: πῶς ὕλη καλὸν προσάπτειν τὴν εἰς τοὺς μεμηνότας βοήθειαν καὶ μὴ τῷ θεῷ;
[82] Tatian, *Or. Graec.* 11.1: νόσου παντοδαπῆς ἀνώτερος γίνομαι, λύπη μου τὴν ψυχὴν οὐκ ἀναλίσκει.
[83] See Trelenberg 2012: 217–18.

to the training undertaken by Greek athletes: 'I saw men weighed down by bodily exercise, carrying around the burden of their flesh'.[84] Tatian also implies that he is a vegetarian, objecting to the carnivorous habits of his Greek addressees: 'You slaughter animals for the purpose of eating their flesh'.[85] Tatian never makes this point, but eating meat was commonly linked in antiquity with an increased sex drive, another subject that he treats in his critique of Greek culture.[86] In this respect, Tatian objects particularly to paederasty, claiming that his philosophical rival Crescens practised it.[87] Tatian says nothing about his own sexual habits, but he observes that 'any trace of licentiousness is kept far away' in Christian gatherings.[88] He adds that Christian habits are marked by 'chastity (σωφρονεῖ)', and that 'all our women are chaste (πᾶσαι δὲ αἱ παρ' ἡμῖν σωφρονοῦσιν)'.[89] The portrait that Tatian offers of himself and other Christians partially aligns with the charges made against him by Irenaeus and other heresiologists, who suggest that he rejected marriage completely and was part of a group that advocated 'abstinence from what is called among them ensouled [flesh]'.[90] But, more significantly for the present argument, Tatian ignores completely any interest in vegetarianism and sexual abstinence among his non-Christian contemporaries.[91] Acknowledging this would have undercut Tatian's consistent emphasis on the poor bodily and mental health of his Greek addressees. He thereby claimed for himself and other Christians exclusive access to an ascetic regimen as a means to maintain health.

Read alongside Tatian, Pseudo-Justin makes more explicit the connections between ascetic regimen and health. This comes out especially in Pseudo-Justin's treatment of sexual abstinence, a point that comes up almost incidentally as part of an attempt to refute objections to the literal resurrection of the body. His unnamed rivals evidently suggested that resurrected human bodies would still possess sexual functions, a point that disturbed them.[92] Pseudo-Justin offers a long response to this objection, citing the examples of people and animals who were incapable or unwilling to have offspring.[93] His argument includes a defence of the claim that sexual activity was unnecessary

---

[84] Tatian, *Or. Graec.* 23.1: Εἶδον ἀνθρώπους ὑπὸ τῆς σωμασκίας βεβαρημένους καὶ φορτίον τῶν ἐν αὐτοῖς κρεῶν περιφέροντας.
[85] Tatian, *Or. Graec.* 23.5: θύετε ζῶα διὰ τὴν κρεωφαγίαν.
[86] Meat and increased sex drive: e.g., Clement of Alexandria, *Strom.* 7.6.33.6.
[87] Tatian, *Or. Graec.* 8.2; 19.2; 28.3.   [88] Tatian, *Or. Graec.* 32.2.
[89] Tatian, *Or. Graec.* 33.1, 5.
[90] Irenaeus, *Haer.* 1.28.1: τῶν λεγομένων παρ' αὐτοῖς ἐμψύχων ἀποχήν.
[91] Vegetarianism: e.g., Seneca, *Ep.* 108. Sexual abstinence: Secord 2018: 469–74.
[92] See Pseudo-Justin, *On the Resurrection* 3.1–2.
[93] See Pseudo-Justin, *On the Resurrection* 3.4–12.

for good health. This comes through in a discussion of the life of Jesus: 'And when he had been born and was living the life of the flesh (I mean eating, drinking, and wearing clothing), he did not exercise only one feature of fleshly life, that of sexual intercourse'.[94] Pseudo-Justin offers a rationale for this choice: 'For if the flesh lacked food, drink, and clothing, it would be destroyed. But if it were deprived of lawless sexual intercourse, it would suffer no harm'.[95] The immediate point is to demonstrate that resurrected human bodies could exist without having sex. But Pseudo-Justin's claim regarding Jesus' life also serves to validate the healthiness of total sexual abstinence. Medical authors of the second century had much to say on this topic, challenging suggestions in the Hippocratic corpus that sexual activity was necessary for a healthy life.[96] Among these authors, Soranus stands out as a great defender of abstinence, suggesting that 'sexual intercourse was harmful in its own right'.[97] But other physicians of this period made similar points, hinting that a larger shift was taking place in attitudes towards the role of sexual activity in human health.[98] Pseudo-Justin's claims about sex fit into this context. By his argument, Christians who gave up sex completely were making a healthy choice, in keeping with a growing emphasis on regimen and the control of appetitive desires among philosophers and physicians.

Pseudo-Justin has more to say about regimen, demonstrating that it was fundamental for his views on a healthy life for Christians. This comes across in a critique of physicians, but a very different type of critique from the one that Tatian offers. Pseudo-Justin's critique begins with a standard claim made about physicians in the Greco-Roman world, namely that they would abandon patients suffering from conditions deemed incurable.[99] This was something that Pseudo-Justin could have encountered in medical literature, but he was more likely familiar with the theme from its frequent appearance in the rhetorical exercises used in ancient education.[100] Pseudo-Justin contrasts this type of physician with the care that Christians show even for people suffering from incurable conditions: 'Why do we not imitate physicians, who, when they have a person who is despaired for and cannot

---

[94] Pseudo-Justin, *On the Resurrection* 3.14: Καὶ γεννηθεὶς δὲ καὶ πολιτευσάμενος τὴν λοιπὴν τῆς σαρκὸς πολιτείαν, λέγω δὴ ἐν τροφαῖς καὶ ποτοῖς καὶ ἐνδύμασι, ταύτην δὲ τὴν διὰ συνουσίας μόνον οὐκ εἰργάσατο.

[95] Pseudo-Justin, *On the Resurrection* 3.15: Τροφῆς μὲν γὰρ καὶ ποτοῦ καὶ ἐνδύματος ὑστερουμένη σὰρξ καὶ διαφθαρείη ἄν, συνουσίας δὲ στερουμένη ἀνόμου οὐδὲν ὅ τι πάσχει κακόν.

[96] See Pinault 1992: 127–30. [97] Soranus, *Gyn.* 1.32.1: βλαβερὰ κατὰ γένος ἡ συνουσία.

[98] See Secord 2018. [99] See Staden 1990: 75–112; Rosen and Horstmanshoff 2003: 95–114.

[100] See Seneca, *Controv.* 4.5; Lucian, *Abdic.* 2 with Gibson 2013: 538.

be saved, allow him to be a slave to his desires?'[101] This was a watered-down version of Tatian's suggestion that all Greeks were controlled by their passions and consequently slaves to their desires. But Pseudo-Justin takes his argument in a different direction, choosing not to reject Greek medicine and physicians completely, as Tatian does. Instead, Pseudo-Justin co-opts for Christians the image of a good physician, focusing on the benefit that physicians hold for people with curable conditions. He applies this image to Jesus, in keeping with the practice of some other Christian authors in referring to 'our physician Jesus Christ'.[102] The language that Pseudo-Justin uses, however, shows that he had a particular type of medicine in mind. The physician Christ, Pseudo-Justin says, 'rescues us from our desires, and regiments (διαιτᾶται) our flesh according to his own chaste and temperate regimen (διαίτῃ)'.[103] According to this image, the physician Christ specialises in regimen, with no hint that he has anything to do with surgery or pharmacology. He helps people to control their appetitive desires, which is a sign that Pseudo-Justin has some awareness of the attention that physicians in the second century were devoting to this area. This represents a significant difference from Tatian, who completely segregated ascetic regimen from the practice of Greek physicians. Pseudo-Justin, in contrast, acknowledges that physicians might help Christians to follow an ascetic regimen, one that evidently involved no sexual activity. Regimen was of basic importance for both Tatian and Pseudo-Justin, but only the latter was willing to treat it as part of the medicine practised by physicians.

Together, Tatian and Pseudo-Justin offer substantially different perspectives on health and medicine than Justin did just decades earlier. While bodily health was an irrelevant consideration for Justin's portrait of Christian philosophers, it became a fundamental part in the claims to expertise made by Tatian and Pseudo-Justin. In Tatian's case, bodily and mental health were ways in which Christians could separate themselves from the negative influence of demons on the world. Medicine as practised by physicians was something to be rejected, even if this meant offering a highly selective and partial account of Greek medicine and the emphasis it placed on regimen. For Pseudo-Justin as well, Greek medicine was something to be criticised,

---

[101] Pseudo-Justin, *On the Resurrection* 10.14: καὶ οὐ μιμούμεθα τοὺς ἰατρούς, οἵτινες, ἐπειδὰν ἀπεγνωσμένον ἔχωσιν ἄνθρωπον σώζεσθαι μὴ δυνάμενον, ἐπιτρέπουσιν αὐτῷ ταῖς ἐπιθυμίαις ὑπηρετεῖν;

[102] Pseudo-Justin, *On the Resurrection* 10.17: ὁ ἡμέτερος ἰατρὸς Ἰησοῦς ὁ Χριστός. For discussion of the 'Christ as Physician' theme, see See Fichtner 1982: 7.

[103] Pseudo-Justin, *On the Resurrection* 10.17: ἀπὸ τῶν ἐπιθυμιῶν ἡμῶν ἀποσπάσας, διαιτᾶται τῇ κατ' αὐτὸν σώφρονι καὶ ἐγκρατεῖ διαίτῃ τὴν σάρκα ἡμῶν.

though largely in terms of how physicians treated patients suffering from terminal conditions. Some of Greek medicine's methods, however, were worth saving. Pseudo-Justin co-opted its emphasis on regimen and arguments about the healthiness of total sexual abstinence. For both Tatian and Pseudo-Justin, knowledge of health and medicine was key to their self-presentation as intellectuals. Tatian used this to mark himself off as a Christian and barbarian from the Greek world, while Pseudo-Justin employed it in the context of a debate about bodily resurrection that was of no interest to non-Christians. Despite their differences, Tatian and Pseudo-Justin had both moved far beyond Justin's portrait of Christian philosophers facing death fearlessly with no consideration of bodily health. In different contexts and with different goals, Tatian and Pseudo-Justin show how Christian intellectuals were entering the competitive medical marketplace of the Roman empire rather than simply calling themselves philosophers.

Conclusion

When early Christian intellectuals engaged with issues relating to bodily and mental health, they were entering territory already occupied with competing specialists and approaches. There were philosophers like Seneca, who displayed considerable expertise in medical subjects and terminology while at the same time claiming more authority than physicians because of their interests in death and appetitive desires.[104] There were also physicians like Galen, who challenged older images of their profession by emphasising their philosophical expertise and ability to treat conditions of both the body and the mind. We can add many other types of specialists to this list, including athletic trainers, exorcists, and ritual experts of all sorts. All these specialists claimed to offer something unique with respect to bodily or mental health, demonstrating just how crowded the Roman empire's medical marketplace already was. It was also a place with overlap and interactions between different specialists, something especially evident from the makeup of intellectual gatherings depicted in the works of second-century authors.[105] The medical marketplace was a complicated place to navigate, especially for intellectuals who lacked connections to an established philosophical or medical school.

This was the reality for Justin, Tatian, and Pseudo-Justin when they attempted to demonstrate expertise in the fields of bodily and mental

---

[104] See Nutton 1992: 38–39.   [105] See Boulogne 1996: 2764–65; Flemming 2000.

health. As such, all three authors need to be read alongside a larger context of intellectual activity relating to these areas. Justin emerges as a figure attuned to prevailing attitudes about bodily health and death, even as he offers an image of his Christian philosophers that was out of touch with the blurred boundaries between physicians and philosophers in his time. A few decades later, Tatian shows greater awareness of bodily health and medicine, while offering what seems to be a deliberately selective image of Greek physicians, ignoring their interest in regimen as a key factor for bodily health and the control of appetitive desires. Pseudo-Justin, meanwhile, redeploys popular images of physicians almost incidentally within an argument about bodily resurrection, suggesting that Christians were following the best regimen of all under the care of their physician Christ. What emerges across all three authors is a concern to demonstrate the excellent bodily or mental health of Christians and a willingness to engage creatively with prevailing views and arguments about health and medicine. Justin, Tatian, and Pseudo-Justin entered the medical marketplace as Christians, but a full appreciation of their contributions requires engagement with these figures as intellectuals seeking to demonstrate their expertise in a crowded and competitive field.

4 | Learning Through Experience: The Structure of Asceticism in Irenaeus of Lyons

PAUL SAIEG

Introduction

Irenaeus made significant contributions to the intellectual life of late antiquity when he developed his radical vision of the human being as a creature made to grow into the likeness of the Uncreated God.[1] This chapter will examine how Irenaeus ordered the knowledge of late antique physics, epistemology, and psychology into an ascetic framework of daily practice for participating in the process of being formed by the hands of God. To do this, Irenaeus made three ascetic disciplines an intrinsic part of his 'theology of growth'. Accordingly, Irenaeus' theological vision was not simply a dogmatic concept, but a 'lived' framework of self-transformation that, perhaps for the first time, defined the theory and practice of Christian asceticism with philosophical sophistication.[2] This chapter provides a preliminary sketch of this framework.

Irenaeus argued that the goal of human existence, the *telos* of creation, is to make never-ending progress towards being made into 'the image and likeness of God'.[3] This is a process of growth[4] and accustoming[5] that begins at birth and progresses through preliminary ethical training,[6] receiving the Spirit in baptism, being formed by it through the experiences of life, death, and bodily resurrection, and continuing to new heights through the permanent union of the body and soul with the Spirit of God[7] and the vision of God the Father, which bestows eternal life.[8] This entire pattern is made possible, revealed, demonstrated, and recapitulated by the work of Jesus Christ.[9]

To realise this *telos*, God provides the human being with 'a complete course of education' (τελείαν ἀγωγή) by revealing himself to us through his 'good counsel' (*consilium bonum*),[10] his providential direction of

---

[1] *Haer.* 4.38.4. [2] See Saieg 2019. [3] Orbe 1969; de Andia 1986; Fantino 1986; Behr 2000.
[4] Bacq 1978: 363–88. [5] Évieux 1967. [6] *Haer.* 4.38.1.
[7] *Haer.* 5.8.1; 4.9–11; Briggman 2012: 173–81; Smit 2011.
[8] de Andia 1986: 321–47; Behr 2013: 185–98.
[9] On this question, see Saieg 2019: 307–16. [10] *Haer.* 4.37.1; 3.25.1.

the world (including through scripture),[11] and our lived experiences.[12] Irenaeus' asceticism – as I will demonstrate – is not based in permanent voluntary abstention from bodily comforts,[13] like the encratite disciplines he rejects,[14] but rather consists in the practices that a human being must use to participate in the divine pedagogy. These daily disciplines provide training (γυμνασία / ἄσκησις) designed to work together with God's providence to cultivate true beliefs and perceptions in order to harmonise the thoughts, emotions, and actions of the human being with the skilful work of the Creator. By participating with God in this divine training, both the individual human being and the human race as a whole are able to make 'daily progress' (ἡμέρα προκόπτοντος), 'little by little, becoming accustomed to receive and bear God'.[15] Because Irenaeus' 'theology of growth' has been well studied as a soteriological theory, while its intrinsic connection to ascetic training has drawn little attention, we should start with a short outline of the disciplines and concrete criteria Irenaeus used to cultivate and measure holiness.[16]

Holiness: The Single and Ascending Road to God

The goal of Irenaeus' asceticism is to train people to become 'mature' or 'complete' (τέλειος / *perfectos*). Irenaeus describes the mature as people who have two key characteristics: they '**both** keep the Spirit of God continually (*semper*) abiding in them **and** have guarded their bodies and souls from blame, **that is**, by guarding their faith in God and paying attention to their righteousness (τὴν δικαιοσύνην) towards their neighbour'.[17] Ascetic training is necessary because 'keeping the Spirit' requires a person to keep the commandments consistently through a *habitus* of faith and righteousness. If falsehoods enter the soul or if injustice mars the body, Irenaeus says, the human being 'spits out the Spirit',[18] and 'casts it off', like a robe.[19] This is a problem because the Spirit is not only an essential element of the 'mature' person, and the human being's source of life, but also the very 'Ladder of Ascent' that enables her to be made ever more like God.[20] Therefore,

---

[11] *Haer.* 4.38.3.   [12] *Haer.* 4.38.3; 2.27.1; Behr 2013: 144–61; Saieg 2019.
[13] Behr 1993; 2000: 117–19; cf. Finn 2009: 1.   [14] *Haer.* 1.28.1; cf. Guffy 2014: 518.
[15] *Haer.* 4.38.3; 5.8.1; Évieux 1967.
[16] Saieg 2016, 2019; Berthouzoz 1980: 236–37 nn. 146–47. Behr 1993 and Behr 2000 do not analyse the ascetic practices that Irenaeus *does* endorse.
[17] *Haer.* 5.6.1; cf. 5.9.3.   [18] *Haer.* 5.8.3; cf. 3.23.5.   [19] *Haer.* 5.10.1.
[20] *Haer.* 3.24.1, 4.39.2, 5.36.2; See Behr 2000: 50–68, but also Briggman 2012: 151–64.

Irenaeus defines the true good (*bonum*) of the human being as those practices that enable her to keep the Spirit: 'to obey God: to believe in him, and keep his precepts, for this is the life of the human being'.[21] Likewise, the true evil (*malum*) for the human being is that which expels the Spirit: 'not to obey God is evil and the death of the human being'.[22] Therefore, Irenaeus' ascetic practices build a person's capacity to consistently keep truth and faith in the soul and righteousness in the body. Irenaeus called this state of practising the highest human good 'holiness' for body and soul or, simply, 'piety'.[23]

Irenaeus outlines the ascetic path of ascent – the 'single and ascending road' – to 'holiness' and 'maturity' in the opening chapters of his concise handbook for teaching the faith.[24] He lays out the ascent as a way of life by adapting the well-known 'two ways' tradition.[25]

> One, single and ascending, is the road for all those who keep watch, because it is illuminated by light from heaven, but many and dark are the roads of those who are not keeping watch. The one leads the human being to the kingdom of heaven by uniting (s: ἕνων) her with God, but the others lead down to death by separating the human being from God. Because of this, it is necessary for you and for all those who are using deliberation (r: τοῖς φρόνουσι) for their own salvation to make their journey without swerving (r: ἀκλινῶς) and with a sure step (r: ἑδραίως) by means of faith; because, otherwise, by slacking, you continue in material desires or, by swerving, you slip off the right (road). Yet, because the human being is an animal composed of a body and a soul, it is necessary to make this journey by means of each of these. Since each of them is susceptible to false steps, there is on the one hand holiness for the body ... and on the other holiness for the soul ... for these rejoice together and fight as allies to offer the human being to God.[26]

Irenaeus uses the fork between the 'two ways' to identify the foundational discipline of ascetic progress: the use of vigilant attention to 'see' or 'watch' over the activities of both soul and body 'illuminated by the light from heaven'.[27] Although they both require watchfulness and deliberation (r: φρονήσις), the body and soul make 'false steps' in different ways. We can 'slack' by ceasing to make progress towards freedom from material desires in the body through a sheer inertia and lack of ascetic effort or by transgressing the commandments,[28] whereas, much more seriously, we can 'swerve' off the path to God entirely by accepting false beliefs in the soul.

---

[21] *Haer.* 4.39.1; cf. Briggman 2012: 176–77. [22] *Haer.* 4.39.1. [23] *Epid.* 2.
[24] Rousseau 1995: 406; Graham 2001: 220 n. 42. [25] Cf. *Didache* 1; *Ep. Barn.* 18–20.
[26] *Epid.* 1–2. For the Greek, see Rousseau 1995: 228–30, C.1 nn. 8–9. For ἕνων (r: *unissant*), cf. *Haer.* 5.28.1: διὰ τῆς πίστεως ἑνοῦσιν ἑαυτοὺς τῷ Θεῷ.
[27] Cf. *Haer.* 4.14.1; 4.37.7; 5.10.1.
[28] Cf. *Haer.* 4.39.1: *nunquam segnis neque neglegens praecepti fiat Dei*.

Therefore, the first step in the ascent to God is the decision to 'see' – to maintain constant watchfulness over each 'step' or movement the soul and body make towards (or away from) God.

Holiness for the Body

Unlike the Platonic-Aristotelian pattern of asceticism, which provided separate kinds of training for the 'rational' and 'irrational' parts of the self, Irenaeus does not train the body and soul separately. Rather, he centres his askesis on the soul (making progress 'by means of faith') and insists that holiness for both body and soul 'fight together as allies' and 'rejoice together' to sanctify the united human being.[29]

Irenaeus defines 'holiness for the body' as his second basic form of ascetic training: 'the self-mastery of patient endurance (s: ἡ ἐγκράτεια τῆς ὑπομονῆς) in the face of every shameful situation and every unrighteous act'.[30] *Egkrateia* is the 'disposition (διάθεσις) that does not act against right reason (ὀρθὸν λόγον), or the virtue that enables us to resist things that *seem hard* to abstain from'.[31] Irenaeus describes bodily holiness as *egkrateia* and 'endurance', not 'abstinence', because it requires both watchfulness and effort. For example, to really grasp the truth about God and the human being requires that we learn 'our own weakness through [the] patient endurance (*per sustinentiam*)' of experiencing our own death and resurrection.[32] Endurance makes learning through difficult experiences possible, transforming even death into a human good that helps secure our faith against 'wandering' from the truth.[33] Endurance allows us, like Adam, to undergo the fear (*timor*) of God, shame (*confusus*), unworthiness (*indignus*), and the painful choice of repentance (*paenitentiam*) in the wake of our apostasy, so that through this experience we can learn to perceive the 'bitterness' of disobedience and the magnitude of God's love for humankind.[34]

---

[29] See Gill 2010: 243–329; Saieg 2019. Irenaeus' cognitive focus in asceticism is similar to that of the Stoics; cf. Musonius, *Diss.* 6; Epictetus, *Diatr.* 3.12. See Hijmans 1959; Newman 1989.

[30] *Epid.* 2: ՍրբութիւՆ մարմնոյ համբերութեամբ, pace Rousseau's ἀποχή (= Behr's 'abstention'). Abstemiousness, as such, is an impediment to holiness for Irenaeus (*Haer.* 4.39.1; Berthouzoz 1980: 236). Cf. *Ep. Barn.* 2.1–3, where φόβος, ὑπομονή, μακροθυμία, and ἐγκράτεια 'fight together' (συμμαχοῦντα) as 'helpers' of faith, and, when they remain 'holy' vis-à-vis the δικαιώματα, the virtues of σοφία, σύνεσις, ἐπιστήμη and γνῶσις 'rejoice together' (συνευφραίνονται) with them. On *Barnabas* in the *Epid.*, see Blanchard 1993; Smith 1952, Index s.v. Barnabas (Epistle of).

[31] Sextus Empiricus, *Math.* 9.153 (emphasis added); cf. Arius Didymus, *Epit. Sto. Eth.* 5b24.

[32] *Haer.* 5.3.1.   [33] *Haer.* 5.3.1.   [34] *Haer.* 3.23.5, treated below.

Just as Adam and Eve took up 'the bridle of self-mastery' (*frenum continentiae*) after their apostasy because (*quoniam*) it was only then that they needed to *resist* the 'uneducated impulse of the flesh', the same need to practise self-mastery (*egkrateia*) exists now, in the wake of our own apostasy, for everyone who desires holiness for the body.[35] Unlike being abstemious, *egkrateia* requires a confrontation with resistance; it requires a temptation, a risk of *akrasia*.[36] *Egkrateia* is essential for learning the difference between good and evil, because it enables us to stand firm and exert the 'violent' ascetic effort of 'keeping watch' (*vigilantes*) that is needed to emerge victorious from the *agōne* ('struggle') of temptation and 'take the kingdom by force'.[37]

These disciplines are illuminated by the light of the 'natural precepts' aimed at bodily holiness,[38] such as the prohibitions against murder and adultery, which Irenaeus sums up as 'abstaining from injustice towards one's neighbour'.[39] The 'natural precepts' are especially helpful for beginners to use with watchfulness and *egkrateia* as first 'steps' in being formed into the likeness of God.[40] The actions they proscribe are easy to notice and prevent and, moreover, require watchfulness precisely where the beginner's attention is naturally focused: on 'external' (*foris*) and 'bodily things' (*corporalia*).[41] By prohibiting visible actions, they use the body to 'educate the soul, drawing it, almost by a chain, to obey the precepts (*praeceptorum*), so that the human being would learn how to give assent (*assentire*) to God'.[42] By 'drawing' the soul into *willing* obedience through the body's natural attention to the visible world, over time these precepts remove the human being's 'bonds of slavery': its attachment to *corporalia*. For example, they eliminate the desire for material wealth by prescribing 'good works' in the body that retrain the soul, such as distributing unjustly gotten money to the poor, as Zacchaeus did.[43] The freedom of detachment from *corporalia* that is won by practising 'all the natural precepts' (*naturalia omnia praecepta*) in the 'law of bondage' through wakefulness and *egkrateia* forms a foundation for practising the more extensive and inward 'teachings of freedom' (*decreta libertatis*) that liberate the soul's thoughts and emotions from falsehood and vice.[44]

---

[35] *Haer.* 3.23.5. On the impulse, see Saieg 2019 and below.
[36] Note the difference from the Platonic-Peripatetic view of *egkrateia* as the *victory* of reason over the non-rational parts of the self (Arius Didymus, *Epit. Peri. Eth.* 128.21–22). On *akrasia*, see below.
[37] *Haer.* 4.37.7. See below.
[38] *Haer.* 4.13.1; 4.13.4; 4.16.3; later commemorated in the Decalogue (4.15.1). See Hasler 1953: 48–57.
[39] *Haer.* 4.16.5.   [40] Cf. *Haer.* 4.9.3; 4.12.5: *velut gradus proponens praecepta legis*.
[41] *Haer.* 5.8.2.   [42] *Haer.* 4.13.2.
[43] *Haer.* 4.12.5, 4.13.2; cf. Luke 19:8.   [44] *Haer.* 4.13.1–3.

Holiness for the Soul

Just as one must continually watch the body's actions, one must also keep constant vigilance over the soul's thoughts and emotions to support Irenaeus' third core ascetic discipline: *meletē*.[45] Like γυμνάζειν and ἀσκεῖν, the basic meaning of μελετᾶν is to expend effort for a purpose ('to exercise', 'to practise'), and, in intellectual or ethical contexts, denotes training the mind through repetition ('to rehearse', 'to meditate on').[46] Its purpose as a daily ascetic practice was to 'digest'[47] the central teachings of one's school to fundamentally transform one's patterns of thought, emotion, and behaviour.[48] *Meletē* was widely regarded as a *sine qua non* of the *vita beata*.[49]

For Irenaeus, *meletē* is essential for guarding the soul's holiness, which consists of three parts: 'keeping the faith in God whole, neither adding, nor subtracting from it', preventing 'falsehoods from entering the soul', and, most importantly, keeping 'truth continually in the soul'.[50] *Meletē* is an indispensable tool for cultivating holiness for the soul because it teaches the soul how to love God according to reason by solidifying and deepening the integrity of faith, as well as how not to desire what the law forbids or think evil thoughts by rejecting falsehoods and keeping truth constantly in the mind.[51] *Meletē* aids progress through the divine *praecepta* and the *decreta libertatis* because it can use the words themselves to 'free the soul' from evil desires and to teach the body 'to be purified through [the soul] by voluntary actions (*voluntarie*)'.[52] Thus, only those who practise *meletē* 'in the necessary way' (καθ' ὃν δεῖ τρόπον), Irenaeus tells us, can keep the faith whole, are 'adorned with good works', and remain united with the Spirit.[53]

To describe the essential role *meletē* plays in cultivating holiness, Irenaeus allegorises the dietary laws in Leviticus 11:3.[54] Irenaeus uses the image of 'pure' and 'impure' animals to distinguish those who practise the discipline properly from those who do not. Those who neglect the discipline are 'impure' animals ('carnal people', unable to bear the Spirit). Those who practise *meletē* diligently are the 'pure' animals ('spiritual

---

[45] For the classic studies, see Rabbow 1954: esp. 24; Hijmans 1959; Hadot 1974; Newman 1989. In Irenaeus, see Saieg 2016.
[46] Newman 1989: 1474. *LSJ* s.v. μελετάω; s.v. μελέτη.
[47] Epictetus, *Diatr.* 3.21.1–3; Seneca, *Ep.* 84.5–7. [48] Newman 1989: 1475.
[49] Newman 1989: 1488; cf. Epicurus, *Ep. Men.* 135; Seneca, *Ep.* 16.1; LXX-Ps 1:1–2; *Haer.* 5.8.3; *Epid.* 2.
[50] *Epid.* 2. [51] See below. [52] *Haer.* 4.13.2. [53] *Haer.* 5.8.2–3; Saieg 2016.
[54] *Haer.* 5.8.3; Saieg 2016.

people', able to bear the Spirit).[55] Recalling his words from *Epid.* 1–2 almost verbatim, Irenaeus uses the animals to describe *meletē* as the ascetic discipline that defines those who are making progress up the 'single and ascending road'.

Who are the pure animals? They are those who both make their journey with a sure step (r: ἑδραίως) by means of faith in the Father and the Son, for this is the stability (*firmitas*) of those who are 'double hoofed', and who practise *meletē* on the oracles of God day and night with the result that they are adorned with good works,[56] for this is the power of those who 'chew the cud'.[57]

Only those who practise *meletē* 'in the necessary way'[58] – meditating 'day and night' and 'by means of faith in the Father and the Son'[59] – are able to become and stay 'spiritual' people. Because *meletē* solidifies faith, prevents the soul from making a 'false step' in thought or from 'swerving' off the path, and adorns the body with righteous actions, those who practise it are able to demonstrate holiness of both body and soul. Because of this, they are able to consistently 'keep' (κατέχειν) the Spirit of God – the life of the 'mature' human being. However, all those who fail to practise *meletē* correctly or often enough, according to Irenaeus, will be unable to keep the faith whole or practise the commandments and therefore will also 'throw off' (r: ἀποβαλλόντας) the Life-giving Spirit.[60]

Irenaeus taught two distinct methods for practising *meletē*. The first is a form of daily, extended meditation on the phenomena of perceptual experience and the clear passages of scripture by using the clear 'pattern' (*characterem*) of the rule of truth to organise our investigations,[61] and 'to adapt' (*adaptari*) what is unclear to what is clear:[62]

As many things as God has given to the power (ἐξουσίᾳ) of human beings and assigned to our ability to know (γνώσει), [the healthy mind (νοῦς)] will practise *meletē* on these things with care and desire (προθύμως ἐκμελετήσει), and it will make progress (προκόψε) with them through daily askesis (διὰ τῆς καθημερινῆς ἀσκήσεως), easily learning the lesson for its benefit (ῥᾳδίαν τὴν μάθησιν ἑαυτῷ ποιούμενος).[63]

The immediate purpose of contemplative *meletē* is to benefit the mind and keep 'the body of truth whole'[64] and cause us to 'grow in love for God'[65] by progressively internalising the rule of truth as the underlying order of

---

[55] *Haer.* 5.8.2. On the identity of the terms, see *Haer.* 5.9.1 and Orbe 1985: 388.
[56] Cf. LXX-Ps. 1:1–2; Rom 3:2, 8:5.   [57] *Haer.* 5.8.3.   [58] *Haer.* 5.8.3.
[59] I.e., 'the double hoof' (= using the rule of truth); see Saieg 2016: 79.
[60] *Haer.* 5.8.3; cf. *Haer.* 3.23.5; 5.10.1; *Epid.* 12.   [61] *Haer.* 2.28.1; see below.
[62] *Haer.* 2.27.1.   [63] *Haer.* 2.27.1.   [64] *Haer.* 2.27.1.   [65] *Haer.* 2.28.3; also see below.

the perceptual phenomena of life and scripture it organises in one's memory. As one learns each day's lesson, *meletē* builds confidence that the rule represents the true, symphonic order of things as they are.[66] Ultimately, the purpose of 'chewing the cud' of *meletē* is the total transformation of perception so that the mind can grasp the true essence of phenomena in faith, adorn the body with good works, and keep the continuous, palpable presence of the Spirit.[67]

The second strategy of *meletē* that Irenaeus teaches is an early form of what Evagrius would famously call *antirrhēsis* or 'refutation'.[68] Antirrhetic *meletē* relies on constant watchfulness to discern one's thoughts and emotions as they arise and then on *egkrateia* to patiently endure the effort of the fight (*agōne*) of refuting them.[69] If the thought is vicious or false, *meletē* disperses it by recalling a powerful phrase or image that opposes it.[70]

To practise this effectively, a person would likely first use contemplative *meletē* to internalise a rich network of images and phrases from life experiences or the scriptures that were emotionally charged, rhetorically persuasive, and organised in the mind according to the rule. 'Meditating on the commandments' (*meditantibus praecepta*)[71] and 'training' (*exerciti*) 'through the investigation of the mystery and economy' of God[72] as well as with Irenaeus' own 'refutations' are a few important examples.[73] The most powerful images or phrases would then be re-indexed in memory according to the particular thoughts or passions they oppose.[74] With practice, these thoughts would become 'ready to hand' (*prae manu habere*) as principles of action, like weapons ready for battle.[75]

Irenaeus uses the temptation of Christ as his *exemplum* of antirrhetic *meletē* par excellence.[76] Immediately after he presents Jesus as recapitulating Adam's failure to reject the falsehoods of the Devil, Irenaeus exhorts his readers to imitate Christ's practice. They should memorise the same striking *sententiae* that Jesus Christ used against Satan and keep them 'ready to hand (*prae manu habere*)' by indexing them to the same temptations, so that they can call them to mind immediately whenever those temptations

---

[66] See below. [67] *Haer.* 5.8.3 and below.
[68] Brakke 2009. Cf. *Haer.* 4.37.7; 5.10.1; and below. [69] Cf. *Haer.* 4.37.7; 4.39.1.
[70] *Haer.* 4.18.3; 4.37.7. The *carnis impetum* is cognitive (Saieg 2019: 324, *pace* Rousseau, SC 100 t.1: 243, P. 603 n. 1).
[71] *Haer.* 5.20.1. [72] *Haer.* 2.28.1.
[73] *Haer.* 4.41.1: *nos ipsos et te ad contradictionem omnium haereticorum in quinque exercentes libris.*
[74] See examples below.
[75] Foucault 2005: 357; on 'ready to hand' as a technical term in *meletē*, see Newman 1989.
[76] *Haer.* 5.20–22.

arise.[77] For example, when readers notice an inducement to pride, they should recall Rom 12:16, recast in the form of a powerful *sententia*: *non alta sentiens, sed humilibus consentiens*. If they notice a desire for wealth, they should recall: *Dominum Deum tuum adorare oportet et ipsi soli servire*.[78] Antirrhetic *meletē* protects holiness, first by using vigilance to detect deceptive thoughts and passions in the soul, and then overturning them by recalling the powerful weapons of persuasion it has 'ready to hand'.[79] Through *meletē*, the *gradus* of the divine *praecepta* and *decreta*, ascending from 'bondage' of the desire for visible things to 'freedom' even from invisible thoughts and emotions, provides Irenaeus with a concrete scale for measuring progress towards the likeness of God.

Now that we have a rough sketch of his ascetic disciplines, we can turn to see how Irenaeus, prompted by the questions of his opponents, worked up from the first principles of physics and epistemology to develop the ethical principles that grounded his asceticism. These questions set Irenaeus on a path to answering why asceticism was necessary and what part of the human being needed to be trained by its disciplines.

Empirical Epistemology: Growth in Knowledge

The Ptolemeans' question was this: 'Why couldn't God have made the human being 'mature' (τέλειον) from the beginning?'[80] What made a human being 'mature' was a common question about the human *telos* and forms of askesis needed to reach it.[81] For most philosophers, the *telos* was an image of the ideal of virtue: someone with a knowledge of the truth that they demonstrated in ethical practice.[82] For Irenaeus the *telos* was a 'mature' person: a human being in the very 'likeness of God'.[83] Yet, physics presented a challenge to this. All created (γεννητός) beings are, by definition, 'unlike' the Uncreated (ἀγένητος) God, who has no beginning or end in time.[84] The eternal does not admit of change, but anything that has

---

[77] *Haer.* 5.22.2; on the phrase 'ready to hand' as a technical term in *meletē*, see Newman 1989.
[78] Deut 6:13 *apud* Matt 4:10; the implication being to serve God, not Mammon (Matt 6:24).
[79] *Haer.* 5.21–22.1.   [80] *Haer.* 4.38.1.
[81] Mansfeld and Runia 2020: 141; Mansfeld 2020; cf. Galen, *Pecc. Dig.* 5.14.9–10 (Kühn). 'Each of us needs training (ἀσκήσεως) ... to become a complete man (τέλειος ἀνήρ)'; Musonius Rufus, *Diss.* 6.1; Aristotle, *Pol.* 7.17; Wis 9:1–18, esp. 6.
[82] Ps-Plutarch, *Plac. philos.* 1.*pr*.3.3; cf. Eph 4:13; Seneca, *Dial.* 2.6.8; Clement of Alexandria, *Strom.* 7.88.5.
[83] ὁμοίωσις is a *process*, not a *state* (Fantino 1994: 113).
[84] *Haer.* 4.38.1; 4.11.2; Fantino 1994: 276–79.

received a beginning in time (a γένεσις) must admit of growth, corruption, and change.[85] While the Uncreated is unchangeable and 'mature' or 'complete' (τέλειος) by nature, whatever is created must be 'immature' or 'incomplete' relative to it (ὑστερεῖται τοῦ τελείου), since it comes to be at the beginning of its existence.[86] To overcome this problem, Irenaeus reasons, the eternal God created a temporal universe *ex nihilo*,[87] in order to use its natural capacity for growth to *train* the human being so that what had a beginning and was mortal could, over long ages, *become one* with the Life-giving Spirit, and *become like* the God Who Is.[88]

Irenaeus also considered the epistemic dimension of the question. The very fact of being created with a beginning in time prevented the creature from having any innate knowledge of God – only the natural *capacity* to develop it.[89] Since human beings come into existence at birth, Irenaeus argues, they have no prior knowledge or experience from past lives or visions of the Forms, the Pleroma, or anything else.[90] Therefore, rather than acquiring 'perfect knowledge' through recollection or direct contemplation of the Forms, Irenaeus argued that our ability to acquire knowledge is always limited by the finite, temporal nature of our embodied experience – the human being will never be able to have the 'experience (*experientiam*) and understanding (*cogitationem*) of all things, like God'.[91] Because it lacks both prior knowledge and experience, Irenaeus saw that every human being must be born as an 'infant' or 'child' (νήπιος), in the sense that their mind and faculty of judgement is still immature and, like a child's, is easily deceived.[92]

From epistemology, Irenaeus turned to ethics. The human being is born without experience (ἀσυνήθη) and in need of ascetic training (ἀγύμναστα) to teach it how to discern the truth and choose the good.[93] Therefore, to develop our capacity for holiness, God provides a structured ascetic programme – a 'complete course of education' (τὴν τελείαν ἀγωγὴν)[94] – in which God is 'always teaching, and the human being always learning',[95] as we make 'daily progress' (ἡμέρα προκόπτοντος) in our likeness to God.[96]

---

[85] *Haer.* 2.34.2; 3.9.3; Fantino 1994: 309–37.   [86] *Haer.* 4.38.1.
[87] *Haer.* 5.36.1; 4.38.3; cf. Aristotle, *Gen. et cor.* 2.10 (336b–37a).
[88] *Haer.* 4.38.3; Aubineau 1956; de Andia 1986: 127–38.
[89] Vis-à-vis *ratio infixa* (*Haer.* 2.6.1). See Briggman 2019: 52–70.
[90] *Haer.* 2.33–34; cf. van Unnik 1976; Norris 1980. For Irenaeus, the Ophites and Sethians (*Haer.* 1.30–31), Simon and Carpocrates (*Haer.* 2.33–34), and the Gnostics (*Haer.* 1.29.3) all belong to the same Platonic 'innatist' family of epistemologies as the Valentinians, which he roundly rejects (*Haer.* 2.14.3).
[91] *Haer.* 2.25.3.   [92] Saieg 2019: 319.   [93] *Haer.* 4.38.1.   [94] *Haer.* 4.38.1.
[95] *Haer.* 2.28.3.   [96] *Haer.* 4.38.3; cf. 2.27.1.

Learning through Experience: How to Grasp the Truth

The need for learning through experience was another fact his opponents forced Irenaeus to grapple with. In a way, it motivates his entire project. Taking up the problem in the opening paragraphs of *Against Heresies*, Irenaeus says that the *nous* of those who lack experience (τὸν νοῦν τῶν ἀπειροτέρων) with the texts, teachings, and way of life of the church are vulnerable to being deceived by the 'plausible' (πιθανόν), but 'false', teachings of his opponents.[97] These teachings are deceptive because they *seem* familiar. They use recognisable names and phrases from scripture, but they are false because they organise these familiar phrases around a radically different underlying order – making, for example, 'the Word' and 'Jesus' refer to different beings.

Inexperienced minds are deceived by these apparent similarities because they are only able to perceive the familiar, outer surface of the teachings (τῆς ἔξωθεν φαντασίας) but are unable to grasp its deeper order or to think critically about it. Without the experience required to perceive the underlying order, Irenaeus saw that it was simply impossible for people 'to distinguish falsehood from truth (μὴ διακρίνειν δυναμένων τὸ ψεῦδος ἀπὸ τοῦ ἀληθοῦς)'.[98] Irenaeus saw the same epistemological problem in ethics. The inexperienced human being's 'faculty of judgement' (τὰ αἰσθητήρια / *sensum*), which judges the difference between good and evil, is still in a 'weak and untrained state' that is not able to reliably choose the good.[99] The result is an 'inconsistent way of life' (ἀσθενὲς τῆς πολιτείας) that is incapable of keeping the Spirit.[100]

To remedy the problem of inexperience, Irenaeus saw that ascetic training had to provide structured experiences that teach a person to grasp the underlying order of the truth and the desirability of the good. Throughout his surviving corpus, Irenaeus identifies three qualities of experience that are necessary to train the mind to discern the truth: *katalepsis*, the rule of truth, and repetition. Although *katalepsis* was originally a Stoic term, by the second century CE it had become part of the philosophical *koine*.[101] Irenaeus uses it to mean grasping the 'essential properties' (*subjacentium*)[102] or essences of 'things that exist as they exist' (τῶν ὄντων ὡς ἔστιν) with the *nous* by perceiving properties or essences of phenomena, through embodied experience (πεῖρα / *experimento*), in a structured, cognitive relationship with prior perceptions.[103] For Irenaeus, what we learn

---

[97] *Haer.* 1.pr.1. [98] *Haer.* 1.pr.1. [99] *Haer.* 4.38.2; Saieg 2019: 322–23. [100] *Haer.* 4.38.2.
[101] Cf. Sextus Empiricus, *Math.* 7.248; 7.257–58. See Frede 1983; Nawar 2014.
[102] *Haer.* 4.39.1. See below. [103] *Haer.* 5.2.3; cf. Saieg 2016.

through *katalepsis* is 'indubitable' in comparison to learning from theoretical reasoning alone[104] and can 'prevent us from erring' in our perception of those essences.[105] *Kataleptic* experiences *reveal* the essence of phenomena 'as they are' in relation to both one another and to the holistic order of the creation.

Irenaeus requires three elements for *katalepsis* to occur. The first are the raw data of sensory experience (τά τε ὑπ' ὄψιν πίπτοντα τὴν ἡμετέραν) and all the things that have been said clearly and unambiguously at the lexical level of scripture (καὶ ὅσα φανερῶς καὶ ἀναμφιβόλως αὐτολεξεὶ ἐν ταῖς θείαις γραφαῖς λέλεκται).[106] The second is an *'underlying hypothesis or relationship'* (*subiacenti ... argumento siue rationi*) that the mind uses as a cognitive framework to 'join' (*copulare*) these perceptions together in an ordered way.[107] A *hypothesis* is a kind of *thesis*: a question open to doubt and demonstration.[108] For Irenaeus, this includes both literary *hypotheses* concerning the 'plot' of scripture,[109] such as whether 'Jesus' and the 'Word' refer to the same being in John 1,[110] and 'theoretical' hypotheses such as philosophers are accustomed to ask,[111] such as whether life comes from God or from ourselves.[112] Irenaeus also used more general logical relationships (*rationi*), such as *contraria*[113] and *symphonia*,[114] to provide the cognitive structure for *katalepseis*.[115] The last criterion is a 'healthy' *nous*, which is humble and loving, and has faith and a knowledge of the good.[116] The healthy *nous* 'guards the order' of its knowledge by using a coherent cognitive framework to guide it in asking and investigating answerable questions.[117]

The most important cognitive framework for Irenaeus is the 'rule of truth' (κανὼν τῆς ἀληθείας) or 'rule of faith'[118] because it captures the logic connecting the 'many and various' created things (including the scriptures) that have been 'well fitted and harmonised' together to form a single, wisely constructed whole – a *kosmos*.[119] The rule is 'the order of the faith'[120] that organises the phenomena of experience in the mind and allows faith to

---

[104] *Haer.* 4.39.1.   [105] *Haer.* 5.2.3.   [106] *Haer.* 2.27.1.   [107] *Haer.* 2.27.1.
[108] Ps-Hermogenes, *Progym.* 11.25; cf. Theon, *Progym.* 11; Aphthonius, *Progym.* 13. On Irenaeus' rhetorical training, see Ayres 2015b; Briggman 2019: 32–33.
[109] Ps-Hermogenes, *Progym.* 11.24; Meijering 1987: 99–133; Behr 2013: 110–20; Ayres 2015b; Briggman 2015; 2019: 11–23.
[110] *Haer.* 1.9.2.   [111] Ps-Hermogenes, *Progym.* 11.25.
[112] *Haer.* 5.2.3. Irenaeus' *hypotheses* are not limited to scripture: *ea quae facta sunt aptare debent subiacenti ueritatis argumento* (*Haer.* 2.25.1).
[113] *Haer.* 4.39.1.   [114] Morlet 2019: 209–36.   [115] *Haer.* 2.27.1.
[116] *Haer.* 2.25.4; 2.26.1; 5.20.1–2.   [117] *Haer.* 2.25.4; 2.27.1–28.1.
[118] Fantino 1994: 15–21; cf. Osborn 1989; Vinzent and Kinzig 1999.
[119] *Haer.* 2.25.2.   [120] *Epid.* 6.

attain a *kataleptic* grasp of things as they are.[121] Thus, the rule is not simply a *summary* of the *content* of the faith,[122] as it is often treated, but a tool for training perception and organising memory.[123] Because it captures the underlying 'order' (τάξις)[124] of God's activity, the rule structures *meletē* so that it trains (*exerceri*) the mind to perceive the *kosmos* 'as it is' in order to reveal a true perception of the God who made it, which, in turn, causes us to grow in love for the One 'who has done, and still does, such great things for us' and joyously obey his commandments.[125]

To grasp this underlying order, the eye of the mind needs training through repeated experience. 'The inexperienced' (τοὺς ἀπειροτέρους) are those 'who have not had a *katalepsis*' of the shape (μορφῆς), underlying form (ὑποκειμένην ἰδέαν), or order (τάξιν) which organises the true image in Irenaeus' well-known 'mosaic of the king'.[126] The more often we confirm the rule through successful *katalepsis*, the more confidence we have that the rule reveals the true underlying *symphonia* of the created world and the wisdom of its Creator.[127]

Responding to the same problem of inexperience he used to open *Against Heresies*, Irenaeus lays out this principle in his famous metaphor of the Homeric *cento*.[128] Those who are 'inexperienced' in reading Homer are easily deceived by the familiar appearance of Homeric-sounding verses into thinking a *cento* is a genuine work of the poet.[129] Experienced people who have meditated on many verses of Homer in the order laid out by the poet, on the other hand, are not so easily fooled. Studying Homer deeply – which normally began with copying and memorising large parts of the poems along with repeated reading and recitation[130] – builds experience by familiarising one with the particularities or identifying marks (ἐπισήμων) of the materials being examined at the lexical level of the poems (e.g., = the λέξεις, ὀνόματα, and παραβολάς), and, over time, provides a clear vision (cf. εἰδῶς) of the deep order (τάξιν) of the relationship that those materials bear to one another in the poem's *hypothesis* (e.g., who says what words to whom, under what circumstances, and for what reasons).[131]

The implications of Irenaeus' epistemology of experience are clear for his asceticism. Since the mind (νοῦς) grows in experience through repeated *katalepsis*, the daily practice of contemplative *meletē* on the clear

---

[121] *Epid.* 3b (trans. below). [122] See Ayres 2020.
[123] E.g., Young 1990: 45–60; Blowers 1997. [124] *Haer.* 1.8.1; *Epid.* 6. [125] *Haer.* 2.28.1.
[126] *Haer.* 1.8.1. [127] Cf. *Haer.* 2.25.1. [128] *Haer.* 1.9.4.
[129] *Haer.* 1.9.4; on the *cento*, see Wilken 1967 and Le Boulluec 2021.
[130] Hock 2001; Marrou 1964: 210–42; Cribiore 2001: 127–85.
[131] *Haer.* 1.9.4; cf. Meijering 1987: 99–133.

phenomena of creation (including scripture) is the way to develop it. In this way, the mind acquires the ability both to 'identify' (γνωρίσει) raw materials or the 'outer surface' of its perceptions and to 'recognise' (ἐπιγνώσεται) the underlying order (τάξιν) connecting them with confidence. Thus, in harmony with the epistemological principles he developed in responding to his opponents, Irenaeus saw that *meletē* provides the mind that trains with it the repeated *kataleptic* perceptions it needs to differentiate between a true *hypothesis* and a false one with accuracy and consistency, thereby enabling it to cultivate and maintain 'holiness for the soul'.

Learning through Experience: How to Choose the Good

Even after people have 'been instructed (ἐμαθητεύθητε) regarding the advent of the Lord as a human being', their 'faculties for perceiving (τὰ αἰσθητήρια)' the difference between good and evil are still weak and untrained.[132] This lack of training causes them to be 'inconsistent (ἀσθενὲς) in their way of life (τῆς πολιτείας)', which makes it impossible for them to maintain holiness in the body or receive the Spirit.[133]

To learn to choose the good, the mind needs *kataleptic* perceptions of a different set of experiences.[134] To recognise the true good and life of the human being as faith and obedience to God, the 'eye of the mind' must receive its education (*disciplinam*) 'through the experience of both' good and evil.[135] For the mind needs to have 'a *katalepsis* of [its] essential properties (*subjacentium apprehensio*)' through the experience of its opposite, not merely to 'reason by analogy from a preconception (*ex suspicione conjectura*)'.[136] However, this *katalepsis* is not revealed through the experience of doing evil (disobedience), nor even by experiencing the punishment for evil (death).[137] After all, Cain, for all his experience of sin and mortality, never learned this lesson.[138]

The experience the mind must learn through is *repentance*. Adam *first* (*primum*) had to 'spit out disobedience through repentance because it is bitter and evil', and only *then* (*deinde*) could his inexperienced mind

---

[132] *Haer.* 4.38.2; cf. Saieg 2019: 322–23.   [133] *Haer.* 4.38.2.   [134] *Haer.* 5.2.3.
[135] *Haer.* 4.39.1.
[136] For *suspicio* as ὑπόληψις, see Orbe 1985: 163–64. Cf. *ex suspicione conjectura* here with *collatione rationis* in Cicero, *Fin.* 3.33, and κατ' ἀναλογίαν in Diogenes Laertius 7.53 (= *SVF* 2.87). Irenaeus seems to be describing something like the Stoic account of educating the natural 'preconceptions' (ὑπολήψεις) of good and evil into mature 'concepts' (ἔννοιαι) through experience and reflection (*intellectus*) in oikeiosis.
[137] *Haer.* 3.23.5.   [138] *Haer.* 3.23.4; 4.18.3.

learn 'by *katalepsis* (*ex comprehensione*) what kind of thing (*quale*) the contrary of the good and sweet is'.[139] Only *after* he repented could Adam understand the difference between the 'bitterness' – the fear, shame, and indignity of his sin that separated him from the Life-giving Spirit – and the sweet 'loving-kindness' of the God who forgave him.[140] The contrast between these two opposing experiences – between moving away from God and towards death through apostasy and returning to him and to life through repentance – provided Adam with the *kataleptic* perception of good and evil that gave him his 'concept (*cognitionem* / s: ἔννοιαν) of both'.[141]

In addition to recognising the good, Irenaeus says that the mind must learn to value the good through experience.[142] The mind learns the *cost* (*pretiosa*) of the good through the experience of ascetic struggle: 'by practising intense vigilance with violence and struggle' to acquire the kingdom.[143] Without the effort of our own free thoughts and actions (*suo proprio motu*), our careful attention (*cura*), and askesis (*studio*),[144] the mind cannot love the good consistently, since it cannot perceive its value.[145] As long as the good remains 'without the exertion of askesis' (*inexercitatum*), it is invisible (*insensatum*) to the *nous* as a good. The mind learns how much more desirable (*honorabilius*) one thing is than another by perceiving pairs of experiences with differential value, like seeing and then becoming blind or knowing earthly life and then life in the kingdom of heaven.[146] Again, without these experiences, the mind is unable to see the good as valuable and therefore will not desire or choose it consistently.

God's course of education provides us with these often painful experiences and 'bears us through them' to teach us to have an aversion to losing the good[147] and a desire to keep it, even through adversity.[148] Experiencing these contrasts in light of the rule that reveals their purpose and order reveals the goodness of God, teaches us to 'love God with reason' (*rationabiliter edocti*

---

[139] *Haer.* 4.39.1; cf. 3.23.5: '*timor autem Domini initium intellegentiae,*' *intellectus uero transgressionis fecit paenitentiam, paenitentibus autem largitur benignitatem suam Deus.*

[140] *Haer.* 3.23.5; cf. 4.36.6; *Epid.* 12–14.   [141] See below; cf. nn. 129, 135.

[142] Cf. the Stoic Cato's distinction between the good (*bonum*) and the valuable (*aestimabile*) in Cicero, *Fin.* 3.44. Irenaeus may be adapting the notion of *oikeiosis* (Hebing 1922: 320–21) to his definition of the *summum bonum* in *Haer.* 4.39.1.

[143] *Haer.* 4.37.7: *cum vi et agone vigilantes instanter diripiunt* [*regnum caelorum*]; Berthouzoz 1980: 212.

[144] *Haer.* 4.37.6.

[145] *Haer.* 4.37.7: *quanto autem pretiosior, tanto **semper** eam diligamus.*

[146] *Haer.* 4.37.7: *quanto autem honorabilius, tanto **magis** diligimus illud.*

[147] *Haer.* 4.37.6: *in omnibus in futurum simus cauti.*

[148] *Haer.* 4.37.6: *perseveremus in omni ejus dilectione.*

diligere Deum), and trains the mind to perceive (*intellegentes*) that the good is sweet (*suave*), beautiful (*pulchrum*), glorious (*gloriam*), costly (*pretiosa*), and desirable (*appetendum*), and enables it to enjoy (*fruentes*) possessing it.[149] Without these contrasts, Irenaeus says, even real goods appear 'irrational' to the mind, since it has no way to value them.[150] With such an education, Irenaeus says, the mind will 'never (*umquam*) be tempted to taste disobedience to God' and will easily maintain holiness in the body.[151]

Irenaeus defines the ethical need for asceticism on the basis of his physics of creation *ex nihilo* and the logic of his epistemology. Irenaeus' epistemology starts from the physical hypothesis that the human being comes into the world as a kind of *tabula rasa*, ready to learn through experience. We could say in fairness that Irenaeus has a 'working theory' of knowledge that fits into the family of broadly 'empirical'[152] (not 'empiricist')[153] epistemological theories that have their roots in Aristotle's rejection of Plato's Forms,[154] and that therefore oppose 'innatist' epistemologies that approach learning as 'recollecting' the Forms.[155]

Holistic Psychology: Ordering the Self

If Irenaeus used the physics of creation to ground his epistemology, he used the physics of embodiment to ground his psychology. Although the question of what exactly Irenaeus thought constitutes a human being has been something of a quagmire,[156] it is safe to say that he thought of the 'immature' human being as mortal, rational, free, and composed of body and soul, and the 'mature' as also united with the Spirit.[157] Irenaeus models the relationship between body and soul using the Stoic theory of mixture (κρᾶσις).[158] He sees the soul as composed of a very fine material that has a definite shape and can exist apart from the body.[159] This fine material 'mixes' with the denser stuff of the passive body and becomes the active principle that governs and directs it by allowing the body to 'participate' in its qualities (like life, growth, self-motion, and thought), while the body tempers those qualities with its own.[160] Irenaeus ascribed no independent

---

[149] *Haer.* 4.37.6–7.   [150] *Haer.* 4.37.6–7.   [151] *Haer.* 4.39.2.
[152] 'Derived from sense-perception', not 'anti-metaphysical' (Helmig 2012: 2, 29).
[153] Briggman 2017; 2019: 33–51.
[154] Aristotle, *An. post.* 2.19 (100a); *Metaph.* 1.1–2 (980a); cf. Audet 1943: 26–29.
[155] Helmig 2012: 29–35.   [156] Cf. Briggman 2012: 149 n. 4.
[157] E.g., *Haer.* 4.37.1; 4.37.6; 5.1.3; 5.6.1; 5.8.1; cf. Briggman 2017: 164–81.
[158] Briggman 2013.   [159] *Haer.* 2.33.4.   [160] *Haer.* 2.33.4.

agency to the body, but thought that the body and the soul affected one another.[161] Irenaeus rejects the idea that the soul is composed of separate 'substances' and never describes it either as having distinct 'parts' that could conflict with one another, like Plato's *logistikon, thumoeides*, and *epithumetikon*, or as an insulated 'core' self, like the divine Valentinian 'seed'.[162] Irenaeus' view aligns with what Gill has called 'psychological holism', similar to that of the Stoics and Epicureans.[163]

Irenaeus' psychological holism has two major implications for his asceticism. First, because it implies a cognitive psychology of action, his asceticism focuses on cultivating the soul's faith in the things 'as they are' and keeping it 'whole' to create lasting emotional and behavioural change. Second, because *akrasia* or 'inner conflict' for Irenaeus takes place in a non-composite soul, his strategies against it are fundamentally cognitive and centre on 'keeping truth continually in the soul' and 'rejecting falsehood' through *meletē*. Let's turn now to look at how he integrated his psychology of action with his asceticism to create change over time.

The Psychology of Action: Creating Lasting Change

> Therefore (lest we fail in holiness of body or soul) we must keep the rule (r: κανών) of faith without swerving (r: ἀκλινῶς) and perform the commandments of God by believing in God – both fearing him because he is Lord and loving him because he is Father. Action, then comes from faith, as Isaiah says, 'if you do not believe, you will not have understanding', and the truth brings about faith, for faith truly grasps (s: καταλαμβάνω) the things that exist, so that we may believe in things that exist as they exist, and by believing in things as they are, we should always maintain our firm conviction (r: πεισμονή). And because faith is what holds our salvation together (r: συνεκτικός), we must take great care (r: ἐπιμέλεια) of it, in order to possess a true comprehension (r: κατάληψις) of what is.[164]

Here, Irenaeus illuminates two key principles of his asceticism that arise from his holistic psychology. The first is that 'action comes about by faith' (r: τὸ μὲν οὖν ποιεῖν ἐκ τῆς πίστεως περιγίνεται). Irenaeus supports this claim by citing Isaiah 7:9, where the sense of 'have understanding' (r: συνῆτε) means to be able to act according to reason,[165] which Irenaeus seamlessly blends into the idea that a belief-set (faith) built on the 'order' of the rule is both

---

[161] Briggman 2013: 519–20.   [162] *Haer.* 1.6–7; 2.29.3.   [163] Gill 2006: 16.
[164] *Epid.* 3b; *pace* Rousseau's plausible separation of հ վերայ ... կաս into ἐπὶ ... ἵσταται. Reading it as an idiom for καταλαμβάνω yields better sense in Irenaeus' argument that faith is necessary for κατάληψις. Miskjian 1966 s.v. կաս; cf. *Haer.* 5.2.3.
[165] Rousseau 1995: 232–33.

necessary for a *kataleptic* grasp of the essence of phenomena and that with each successful grasp, we 'care for' our faith by reinforcing the 'firm conviction' of our beliefs.[166] The 'order' of the rule founds a way of life in accord with the truth by structuring faith, which in turn organises emotions and actions: because a person *believes* God is Father, she *loves* God, and because she loves God, she *performs* his commandments willingly and in gratitude; likewise, if a person *believes* God is Lord, she *fears* him, and because she fears God, she *obeys* him.[167] Likewise, when we learn through the experience of our own death and resurrection that we are mortal and that God has truly liberated us from death, our 'true *katalepsis* of things as they are' will make us *always* love God and be grateful him.[168] Thus, 'unswerving' (r: ἀκλινῶς)[169] faith leads directly to truth for the soul and righteousness for the body.[170] Likewise, if our faith 'swerves', so too do our emotions and actions. For example, if someone, failing to practise *antirrhetic meletē*, accepts (*accipiat*) a thought contrary to God (*sensum contrarium*), like judging (*arbitrans*) that he is like God by nature, then 'by not keeping the truth, he becomes agitated by vainglory', which makes him 'more ungrateful (*ingratum*) to God'.[171]

These two passions (vainglory and ingratitude), in turn, affect his mind.[172] They make the love God has for us invisible to him – they 'blind his mind' (*sensum*) to what is valuable (*dignum*) about God, thus impairing his ability to recognise, value, or choose the good.[173] The effect of these two passions on the mind illuminates our second principle: the mutual influence of thought and emotion. Emotions and passions arise from beliefs in relation to experiences, and our emotions affect our beliefs and perceptions of experience.[174] In light of these principles, we can see that when the rule is put into practice through daily *meletē* (as the 'divided hoof'), it becomes both the 'order of our faith' and 'the support of our way of life (r: *conversationis*)'.[175]

Finally, because faith provides the coherence necessary for *katalepsis* and *katalepsis* increases the 'firm conviction' of faith, 'caring for our faith' through *meletē* is essential for creating long-term cognitive and ethical change. The more we meditate on all the wonderful works of God in the divine economy and all the good he has done us, the more we grow to love him. And the more we love God, Irenaeus says, the more grateful and willing we are to obey him.[176] Thus, 'through faith in him, he causes us to grow

---

[166] *Pace* Rousseau 1995: 232–33. [167] Cf. *Haer.* 4.11.2; 4.12.2; 4.39.2–3.
[168] *Haer.* 3.20.2; 5.2.3–3.1: μὴ σφαλῶμέν ποτε τῆς ἀληθοῦς περὶ τῶν ὄντων ὡς ἔστι καταλήψεως.
[169] *Haer.* 1.9.4; *Epid.* 3b.   [170] *Haer.* 4.12.
[171] *Haer.* 3.20.1: *non tenens ueritatem, inani supercilio iactaretur*.
[172] Cf. *Haer.* 3.23.4.   [173] *Haer.* 3.20.1; cf., e.g., 2.28.1–3; 4.39.2–3.
[174] For belief and experience, see *Epid.* 8.   [175] *Epid.* 6.   [176] *Haer.* 4.12.2.

in love towards God and our neighbour, rendering us godly, righteous, and good'.[177] Therefore, whatever else it may be, the rule is a powerful tool of askesis designed to structure experience through the discipline *meletē*, and thereby, to shape one's cognitive, affective, and ethical life into the very likeness of God.[178]

The Psychology of Akrasia: *Creating Immediate Change*

It remains for us to consider what was perhaps *the* ethical question that drove psychology in antiquity from Plato forward: how to explain and overcome *akrasia* or 'inner conflict'.[179] Irenaeus models *akrasia* as the dynamic relationship of three aspects of the 'mature' or 'complete' human being: The soul is a single entity 'mixed' with the body and in 'union' with the Spirit.[180] The soul is a unified whole: it has no 'parts' and is not composed of different substances. The mind (*nous*) itself is a 'movement' or 'activity' of the soul and 'has no substance apart from the soul'.[181] The *nous* is the 'the origin and source of all thought (r: νοήσεως)'.[182] Its activities seem to be structured by natural reason (*ratio mentibus infixa* / r: ἔμφυτος τοῖς νοῖς λόγος);[183] it acts both as 'the controlling power' (r: ἡγεμονικόν)[184] that creates, directs, and governs thoughts with free will and power over itself[185] and as the 'eye of the mind' that perceives experience and learns from *katalepsis*.[186] The *nous* produces all thought, including interior discourse (r: ἐνδιάθετος λόγος / διαλογισμός) and the deliberative judgements (arm: φρόνησις, lat: *sensum*) that result in bodily actions.[187] If the *nous* is like a whirlpool ceaselessly spinning in the water of the soul, then thoughts are merely the 'motions and activities' rippling out from its centre and, in that sense, are 'nothing other than the *nous* itself'.[188] In Irenaeus' psychology,

---

[177] *Epid.* 87; Behr 2013: 136–38. [178] Saieg 2016: 78.
[179] Sorabji 2002: 303–18. [180] Briggman 2013.
[181] *Haer.* 2.29.3: *Sensus* (r: νοῦς) *enim hominis et cogitatio et intentio mentis et ea quae sunt huiusmodi non aliud quid praeter animam sunt, sed ipsius animae motus et operationes, nullam sine anima substantiam habentes.*
[182] *Haer.* 2.13.1: *Nus est ... uelut principium et fons uniuersi sensus.* Also, Rousseau SC 293: 111.
[183] *Haer.* 2.6.1; see Briggman 2019: 60–70.
[184] *Haer.* 2.13.1. The Greek reconstruction is 'largement assurée' (Rousseau SC 293: 233–34 P. 111 nn. 1–2).
[185] *Haer.* 2.13.2: *condente et administrante et gubernante libere et ex sua potestate.*
[186] *Haer.* 4.39.1: *oculus mentis* (r: νοῦ) *... accipiens experimentum* [...] *Quemadmodum ... lingua ... et oculus ... et auris ... sic et mens ... ex comprehensione discernis.*
[187] *Haer.* 2.13.1. Context supports the Armenian witness to φρονήσις. (Rousseau SC 293: 233–34 P. 111 nn. 1–2).
[188] *Haer.* 2.13.1.

akrasia occurs as a kind of interference between contrary motions in the soul – like waves crashing into each other on the water – which can be created by disordered beliefs (faith)[189] in one's 'mindset' (γνώμη) or by the turbulent thoughts, emotions, or judgements produced by the *nous*.[190] Thus, Irenaeus explains all temptations as forms of disordered cognition or 'motions' of the soul.[191]

The sins of Cain and Adam demonstrate how emotions and thoughts, respectively, can affect the *nous* to create *akratic* situations. When God offered Cain 'counsel' to keep him from fratricide, Cain's emotional state was 'jealousy and malice' towards his brother. This disposition created a potential conflict in him between accepting the 'counsel' God gave him – which would 'quiet' his vicious impulse – or rejecting it, killing his brother as he intended.[192] For Adam, it was not his emotional state, but his cognitive inexperience that created the opportunity for *akrasia*. Adam could choose either to believe what God had said and keep his commandment or to accept Satan's false counsel and break it. Without knowing how either to discern the truth or to choose the good because of his inexperience, despite having no prior false beliefs (i.e., still having kept the 'order and strength' of his soul), Adam, like a child, was easily deceived.[193] Once he accepted his first false belief, he had his own 'thought of worse things' which, in turn, created an 'uneducated impulse of the flesh' in him that impelled him to break the commandment.[194] In each case, the souls' own emotions, thoughts, and perceptions are the sources of *akratic* disorder and conflict. The flesh itself is never a source of deception or sin for Irenaeus.

Irenaeus' holism helps us understand why he taught his students to combat *akrasia* 'by keeping truth continually in the mind' and 'rejecting falsehood' with *antirrhetic meletē*. Since thoughts and passions are motions in the soul, they differ from one another in time and cause, but are otherwise identical.[195] Therefore, just as these motions can disturb the mind, the mind can destroy a disturbing motion by generating an opposing one.[196] Although Irenaeus upholds his holistic psychology and the unity of the 'I' across all three aspects of the self, he models the relationship between the soul, the flesh, and the Spirit by adapting a picture from *Hermas* of angels producing 'suggestions' (ἐνθυμήσεις), which, if one 'enters the heart', will perforce result in bodily action.[197]

---

[189] *Haer.* 4.37.5: *propriam fidem hominis ostendens quoniam propriam suam habet sententiam* (r: γνώμη).
[190] *Haer.* 4.37.1. See Laird 2012; Karavites 1990.   [191] Saieg 2019.   [192] *Haer.* 3.23.4–5.
[193] *Epid.* 12–14; Saieg 2019.   [194] *Haer.* 3.23.4–5; *Epid.* 12–14. See above.
[195] *Haer.* 2.18.1.   [196] *Haer.* 2.18.2.   [197] *Herm. Mand.* 6.2 (36).

The Spirit preserves and forms, but the flesh is preserved and formed; there is another between these, the soul, which, when it follows the Spirit, is elevated by it, but when it agrees with the flesh, it falls into earthly desires.[198]

In Irenaeus' model, there is a hierarchy of activity. While the Spirit is a totally active principle and the flesh basically passive, the soul is free to choose what the 'complete' human being ('I') will do in response to its perceptions. As we saw above, when the soul does not 'reject falsehood', it experiences a cognitive impulse (that is, a kind of aversion or desire) from the flesh towards some 'irrational' course of action.[199] Instead, it must practise constant vigilance and practical judgement (φρόνησις). The Spirit, on the other hand, gives the soul the opportunity to be formed by God's course of education, providing counsels (*concilii*) and commands (*praecepta*), which the soul can choose to 'follow' or 'reject'.[200] If the soul accepts the Spirit's advice, the Spirit shocks it with a powerful desire (*promptum* / r: τὸ πρόθυμον) – a goad (*stimulum*) – to act.[201] This desire is the phenomenological manifestation of the 'strength (ἰσχύος) of the Spirit' that 'mixes with the weakness (ἀσθένειαν) of the flesh' and 'absorbs' it, overpowering any *akratic* impulses or slackness that might resist.[202]

A 'mature' person who enacts the Spirit's desire is 'spiritual' – they demonstrate that they are not 'enslaved by the desires of the flesh, but obey the Spirit and practise a way of life that follows reason in every situation'.[203] They bear the 'fruits of the Spirit', which are 'the spiritual actions which vivify the human being', and enable them to inherit the Kingdom of God.[204] If, on the other hand, a person wishes to be 'carnal' and chooses to 'reject the counsel of the Spirit', they will 'have no desire (ἐπιθυμίαν) of the Spirit' and 'lack any restraint' to guide them (ἀχαλιναγωγήτους).[205] Such people 'only think about carnal things (*carnalia*)',[206] then get 'dragged down into their own desires', become 'slaves to the pleasures (ἡδοναῖς) of the flesh', and ultimately practise 'a way of life without reason' (*irrationalem conversationem*), becoming more like animals instead of like God.[207]

Apart from the soul's own disorder, the sources of temptation lie *outside* the self. Much as the Spirit offers good advice to all, the devil (and

---

[198] *Haer.* 5.9.2 (trans. condensed for space).
[199] Irrational: 'against reason', not 'a-rational'; cf. Seneca, *Ep.* 113.18; Inwood 1985: 80, 175–76.
[200] *Haer.* 4.37.1.   [201] *Haer.* 5.9.2.   [202] *Haer.* 5.10.1.
[203] *Haer.* 5.8.2.   [204] *Haer.* 5.11.1.
[205] *Haer.* 5.8.2. For Basil's ἐπιθυμίαν, r: ἐπίπνοιαν, but προθυμίαν may be more likely (cf. 5.1.3; 5.10.1). Cf. Adam's *frenum continentiae* (= *egkrateia*) in 3.23.5 vs. ἀχαλιναγωγήτους (= lack of *egkrateia*).
[206] Cf. Rom 8:5.   [207] *Haer.* 5.8.2.

his 'children', who are Irenaeus' opponents, 'the heretics') attempt to *persuade* people using plausible-sounding forgeries. Irenaeus sometimes calls these deceptions 'tares' that are sown 'secretly' (λάθρα).[208] Although Adam accepted Satan's lie because he was inexperienced and 'careless, but without a real understanding of evil',[209] this was still enough to disrupt the epistemic 'order and strength' of his soul,[210] and to drive both the Spirit and its 'powerful desire' from him. Irenaeus exhorts his readers to practise 'vigilant attention' (*vigilare*) because the devil sows these deceptions 'when people are asleep'.[211] To keep falsehood out of the mind, and retain the anti-akratic power of the Spirit, the human being must pay attention to her self – body and soul. If she fails to exert herself, as one of the 'violent who take the kingdom by force' through the *agōne* of attention, *egkrateia*, and *meletē*,[212] the 'tares' of deception will accumulate and grow into a 'forest' of false belief inside of her. In the end, she will lose the graft of the Spirit and become 'lost among the brambles' of a mind and a faith overgrown with lies.[213] Yet, if she remains vigilant and 'makes progress through faith towards what is better' by practising *meletē*, she will 'be inherited by the Spirit' and bear the fruits of the Spirit in the paradise of the Church.[214]

Conclusion

This chapter has offered a preliminary sketch of Irenaeus' theology as the oldest surviving, fully developed Christian framework for ascetic training. In response to his opponents, Irenaeus created this framework by organising the branches of human knowledge in a sophisticated, but practical, way. He argued from the physics of creation and of embodiment to ground his empirical epistemology and holistic psychology, respectively. He directed these, in turn, towards the *telos* of his ethics – by understanding how 'God makes', Irenaeus could describe the ascetic disciplines the human being had to practise in order to participate in 'being made'.

Through his theology of growth, Irenaeus was perhaps the first to establish philosophically rigorous, foundational principles of Christian askesis. He showed that the fundamental purpose of Christian asceticism was to train the inexperienced mind how to consistently discern the true and choose the good in order to remain united with the Spirit in holiness. To achieve this goal, his asceticism trained the mind. In the present, it

---

[208] *Haer.* 4.40.2–3; 5.10.1–2.   [209] *Haer.* 4.30.2.   [210] *Epid.* 14.   [211] *Haer.* 5.10.1.
[212] Cf. the need to 'watch' in *Haer.* 4.37.7.   [213] *Haer.* 5.10.1.   [214] *Haer.* 5.10.1.

developed the powers of attention and self-control to keep truth continually in the mind, reject falsehoods, cultivate virtuous emotions, destroy passions, and follow the desires of the Spirit towards righteous actions. Over time, askesis created a foundation of faith, a basic belief-set, that was capable of grasping the essence of phenomena 'as they are', reliably revealing both the true and the good, thus ever increasing our gratitude and love for God and righteousness towards our neighbour.

To embody these principles and make visible progress in becoming like God, Irenaeus taught that it was essential to train every day using three ascetic disciplines: watchfulness, the *egkrateia* of patient endurance, and *meletē*. Watchful attention to the movements of body and soul was the foundation of Irenaeus' askesis. What attention exposed, *egkrateia* endured while it provided the mind with the strength to choose. With the force of *egkrateia* and the Spirit's goad, the mind could use *antirrhetic meletē* to refute false thoughts and destroy passions by recalling the persuasive thoughts it kept 'ready to hand' or use contemplative *meletē* to train itself to discern the true and choose the good by structuring perceptual experiences through the rule of truth. These practices could restructure perception itself by developing a faith able to grasp the essence of phenomena, cultivate virtuous patterns of living, and build the human capacity to receive and keep the Holy Spirit. These ascetic disciplines are an *intrinsic* part of Irenaeus' theology – they are how it is *used*. They are the everyday effort, the concrete practices, that the human being must employ to make visible progress in her climb up 'the single and ascending road' to God. They are our active contribution to *learning* through the experience of our struggle in 'the *agōne* for incorruptibility' and *growing* through the 'complete course' of our 'education'. Ultimately, for Irenaeus, asceticism is how *we participate* in being formed into the image and likeness of God.

5 | The Order of Education and Knowledge in Clement of Alexandria

MATYÁŠ HAVRDA

Introduction

In his prologue to the *Commentary on the Song of Songs*, Origen broaches the question of where in the order of Solomon's writings the commented text should be placed. He introduces his answer by the following distinction:

> The branches of learning by means of which men generally attain to knowledge of things are the three which the Greeks called *ethics*, *physics*, and *epoptics*. These we may call respectively moral, natural, and inspective. Some among the Greeks, of course, add a fourth branch, logic, which we may describe as rational. Others have said that logic does not stand by itself, but it is connected and intertwined throughout with the three studies that we mentioned earlier.[1]

What does this have to do with the Song of Songs? According to Origen, each of the three branches of learning is represented by one work in the collection of Solomon's writings adopted by the church: ethics by Proverbs, physics by *Ecclesiastes*, and epoptics by the Song of Songs. Origen even suggests that the threefold division was originally Solomon's idea, which was later copied by the Greeks.[2] As far as logic is concerned, Origen sides with those who believe that it 'requires not so much to be separated from the other studies as to be mingled and intertwined with them'. For, in his view, logic 'deals with the meanings of words and statements, their proper and improper use, their genera and species, and teaches about the

---

The first draft of this chapter was presented at the Eighteenth International Conference on Patristic Studies in Oxford on August 23, 2019, within the workshop 'Modes of Knowing and Ordering of Knowledge', organised by Michael Champion and Dawn LaValle Norman. I am grateful to the editors of the present volume for their incisive comments on that draft, which helped me revise it substantially.

[1] Origen, *Comm. Cant.* pr. 3.1–2 (SC 375: 128): *Generales disciplinae quibus ad rerum scientiam pervenitur tres sunt, quas Graeci ethicam, physicam, epopticen appellarunt; has nos dicere possumus moralem, naturalem, inspectivam. Nonnulli sane apud Graecos etiam logicen, quam nos rationalem possumus dicere, quarto in numero posuere. Alii non extrinsecus eam, sed per has tres, quas supra memoravimus, disciplinas innexam consertamque per omne corpus esse dixerunt.*

[2] See Fürst and Strutwolf 2016: 92 n. 62. See also the discussion of this passage in Chapter 6 by Peter Martens, this volume.

form of any particular statement'.[3] Insofar as every branch of learning is mediated by words and statements, logic is obviously intertwined with all of them.[4]

Origen presents the threefold division of learning into ethics, physics, and epoptics (henceforth referred to as the 'EPHE scheme') as if it were commonly accepted by the Greeks. He does not associate it with a particular school of philosophy. Moreover, by suggesting its biblical origin, he insinuates that it is very ancient. Historically speaking, this cannot be true. But it could reflect the position of the philosophical circles with which Origen was most familiar.

Not surprisingly, this position appears to be one of contemporary Platonism. There is debate on whether the EPHE scheme is of Platonist origin, as Pierre Hadot once thought, or whether it builds on the order of study developed by second-century CE Peripatetics, as has been recently argued by Matthias Perkams.[5] In any case, Porphyry adopts a variant of it in his division of Plotinus' *Enneads* (*Vit. Plot.* 24–26), just as Origen does before him with regard to the books of Solomon.[6] This could be taken as an indication pointing to the common source of Porphyry's and Origen's Platonism. If we accept the ancient tradition postulating a link between Origen and Plotinus' teacher Ammonius Saccas, we could speculate that this source was Ammonius.[7] However, the scheme could not have been invented by Ammonius; for, as Perkams has pointed out, it is already found in Aspasius, a Peripatetic commentator on Aristotle who was active sometime in the first half of the second century.[8]

Moreover, there is an important witness in Clement of Alexandria, which suggests that in his time – roughly one generation before Ammonius – the scheme had already been adapted to the needs of a Platonist curriculum.[9] In *Strom.* 1.28.176, Clement distinguishes four parts of 'the philosophy according to Moses', that is to say, of the Torah: one part is 'historical',

---

[3] *Comm. Cant.* pr. 3.2 (SC 375: 128–30): *Est enim logice haec vel, ut nos dicimus, rationalis, quae verborum dictorumque videtur continere rationes proprietatesque et improprietates, generaque et species, et figuras singulorum quorumque edocere dictorum, quam utique disciplinam non tam separari quam inseri ceteris convenit et intexi.*

[4] Origen seems to associate the study of logic, too, with Proverbs; see Harl 1987: 252 n. 17; Martens 2012: 80. Unfortunately, Origen's statements on the nature of logic and its place in the programme of education are scarce and brief, and do not seem to be entirely consistent; see the thorough examination by Somos 2015: 20–30.

[5] Hadot 1982; Perkams 2015.   [6] Cf. Hadot 1982: 440.

[7] For the *status quaestionis*, see Riedweg, Horn, and Wyrwa 2018: 1.959–60.

[8] Perkams 2015: 154–56.

[9] For the antecedents and parallels of the EPHE scheme in the post-Hellenistic Platonist curriculum, see Bonazzi and Petrucci 2020: 151–53, 160–62.

another 'legislative' (in the strict sense),[10] another 'liturgical', and the last Clement calls the 'theological kind' (θεολογικὸν εἶδος). The first three labels are already found in Philo, whereas the fourth replaces Philo's 'prophetic' part of the Torah.[11] But the most important innovation is this: according to Clement, the historic and legislative parts 'properly belong to the study of ethics', the liturgical part 'is already a matter of natural science', whereas 'the theological kind' is 'the epoptic vision (ἐποπτεία) which, as Plato puts it, belongs to the truly great mysteries, while Aristotle calls this kind [of philosophy] metaphysics'.[12] Clement goes on to explain the role of dialectic in the Platonist sense in reaching the goal of philosophy as a whole, and of its third part in particular – namely 'the knowledge of that which is divine and heavenly, followed also by the appropriate use of that which is human, both with regard to speeches and to actions'.[13] The fact that Aristotle's metaphysics is mentioned within a curriculum whose description is, at least on the verbal level, distinctly Platonic suggests that, whatever its origin, the EPHE scheme had already been in use within Platonist circles before Clement, circles characterised by a 'harmonising' view of the relation between Plato's and Aristotle's philosophy.[14] At any rate, in this passage, Clement organises the Torah according to the same scheme that Origen recognises in the order of the books of Solomon.[15]

This similarity could be attributed to literary influence. We could suppose that Origen read the first book of the *Stromateis* and, while accepting the idea that the division of philosophy into ethics, physics, and epoptics – which he knew from contemporary Platonism – is found already in scripture, he chose to support this claim with other biblical texts.[16] Yet it must

---

[10] The qualification 'in the strict sense' distinguishes the legislative part of the Mosaic philosophy from the 'Law', i.e., Torah, as a whole.

[11] Cf. van den Hoek 1988: 60–62.

[12] *Strom.* 1.28.176.1–2 (GCS 108.24–30): Ἡ μὲν οὖν κατὰ Μωυσέα φιλοσοφία τετραχῇ τέμνεται, εἴς τε τὸ ἱστορικὸν καὶ τὸ κυρίως λεγόμενον νομοθετικόν, ἅπερ ἂν εἴη τῆς ἠθικῆς πραγματείας ἴδια, τὸ τρίτον δὲ εἰς τὸ ἱερουργικόν, ὅ ἐστιν ἤδη τῆς φυσικῆς θεωρίας· καὶ τέταρτον ἐπὶ πᾶσι τὸ θεολογικὸν εἶδος, ἡ ἐποπτεία, ἥν φησιν ὁ Πλάτων τῶν μεγάλων ὄντως εἶναι μυστηρίων, Ἀριστοτέλης δὲ τὸ εἶδος τοῦτο μετὰ τὰ φυσικὰ καλεῖ.

[13] *Strom.* 1.28.177.1 (GCS 109.9–11).

[14] For early attempts to integrate Aristotle's metaphysics into the Platonist framework, see Chiaradonna 2017: 143–57.

[15] Apart from the books of Solomon, Origen applies the same scheme to scripture more generally; see Fürst 2011: 29.

[16] For this option, see Fürst 2011: 29, mentioning (after Kobusch 2006: 173 n. 4) a scholion on Ps 76:21, attributed to Origen (ed. Pitra, *Analecta sacra spicilegio Solesmensi parata*, Vol. III (Veneto: Mekhitarist Monastery of San Lazzaro, 1883), 109), which contains a literal quotation from Clement, *Strom.* 1.18.176.1 and 3 (GCS 108.24–28 and 110.4–7). See also Fürst and Strutwolf 2016: 93 n. 63. However, this scholion cannot be taken as evidence of Origen's acquaintance with

not be forgotten that both authors belonged to the same intellectual milieu and even, most likely, to the same educational institution, the so-called catechetical school attached to the Christian community in Alexandria.[17] Even though we know very little about the programme of study within this institution, it is tempting to assume that it is somehow reflected in the EPHE scheme.

This is supported by the following consideration: it is often believed – and it can, in my view, be firmly established – that Clement's major writings – the *Protrepticus*, the *Paedagogus*, and the *Stromateis* – are subordinated to a programme of Christian education, understood as a progress towards and within a particular type of knowledge.[18] Moreover, there are reasons to think that this programme is, by and large, informed by the aforementioned scheme of the 'Mosaic philosophy' outlined in *Strom.* 1.28.176.[19] But if this is the case, it seems plausible that the scheme also informed the programme of teaching within the institutional context of Clement's writings.

The main goal of this chapter is to lend credence to this assumption by showing how the EPHE scheme is adapted for Christian use in Clement's programme of Christian philosophy. However, I will also argue that the programme does not overlap with the order of Christian education in Clement's view but only corresponds to its higher, theoretical part. While opening space for philosophy in the sense of a theoretical study within the Christian tradition, Clement insists on its continuity with the ethical requirements for a good life and the confessional presuppositions of Christian identity. In the last part of the chapter, I will elaborate on this point, setting it in the wider context of Clement's cultural environment.

Strom. 1.18.176, since it was not written by Origen, but by Evagrius; see Rondeau 1960. (I am grateful to Lorenzo Perrone for enlightening me on this issue.) The second option mentioned by Fürst is that both Clement and Origen drew on a common philosophical tradition.

[17] The existence of an institutional backdrop to Clement's literary activity in second-century Alexandria is now generally accepted by scholars; cf. van den Hoek 1997: 59–87; Wyrwa 2005: 271–306; Le Boulluec 2019: 24–33.

[18] This is indisputably true of *Protr.* and *Paed.*, as Clement himself points out in the prologue to the latter treatise. See further below, pp. 96–97. Whether or not *Strom.* reflects another stage of the educational programme outlined in the *Paed.* has been a matter of controversy; see Lilla 1971: 189–90 n. 4; for a full summary of the debate, see Le Boulluec 2019: 91–95. For a recent argument in the affirmative, building on Méhat 1966 and Le Boulluec 1987, see Havrda 2019.

[19] This observation, which provides a key to understanding Clement's programme of Christian philosophy, has not attracted the attention it deserves in Clementine scholarship. See, however, Bucur 2009: 18–21 with references. See now also Le Boulluec 2019: 94–95. In this chapter, I largely draw on the investigations in Havrda 2019 and Havrda 2021.

The Evidence

A clear reference to the EPHE scheme is found in *Strom.* 4.1.1.1–2.3, a passage in which Clement outlines his immediate and more distant agenda.[20] He points out that his immediate agenda belongs to 'the ethical account', to be succeeded later by 'gnostic physiology, even epoptic vision', as it ascends from the account about cosmogony to 'the theological kind'. It is true that between the 'ethical account' and 'gnostic physiology', Clement was planning to deal with other issues: (1) 'a brief exposition of scriptures against the Greeks and the Jews' (probably addressing specific objections against Christian faith on their part); (2) an inquiry of 'the physiological views about the first principles held by the Greeks and other [i.e. non-Christian] barbarians' and polemics against the most important views (still presumably those pertaining to the first principles) that the philosophers have invented; (3) an outline of theology followed by an account of the tradition concerning prophecy,

which will enable us to show, by means of their interconnection, that scriptures, believed to be 'lordly' by us, proceed from the almighty authority, and to prove from that fact to all the schools that God and almighty Lord, who is genuinely proclaimed through the Law and the prophets, as well as through the blessed gospel, is one.[21]

In connection with these topics, Clement prepares his readers for numerous polemics against the 'heterodox' views and their refutations on the basis of scripture. It is only after these polemics and refutations that Clement promises to proceed to 'gnostic physiology' and 'theology'.[22] Yet, the EPHE structure of the programme is unmistakable: the issues to be dealt with after 'the ethical account' are clearly relevant to, and preparatory for, the upcoming two parts – either dealing with objections against Christian faith, or inquiring into various views about the principles of nature, or establishing the divine origin of scripture and the unity of God.

Another passage indicative of the EPHE scheme, albeit less manifestly, occurs near the beginning of the second book of *Stromateis* (2.2.4.1–6.4).[23] Here, Clement outlines the stages of education according to the providential dispensation of God, also called παιδεία σοφίας ('education by Wisdom': GCS 115.7f.). Two descriptions of divine education are offered.[24] The first

---

[20] Cf. Rizzerio 1996: 161, recognising the EPHE scheme at the background of this passage.
[21] *Strom.* 4.1.2.2 (GCS 248.21–25).   [22] Cf. Nautin 1976: 286–89; Havrda 2016: 50–54.
[23] For a detailed analysis of this passage, see Havrda 2019: 133–37.
[24] For the passage, see Osborn 2005: 183–84, who, however, does not distinguish between the two types of education adumbrated there.

is based on Prov 3:5–12: ways of wisdom lead to 'the way of truth', namely faith. It is a way of education by means of 'the fear of God' (θεῖος φόβος), which is the same thing as 'the rejection of evil' (ἔκκλισις κακοῦ). Educating those he loves, God 'causes them pain, which leads to understanding, and restores them to peace and incorruptibility'.[25] The second description takes its starting point from Wis 7:17–20, a passage which, as Clement puts it, encompasses 'the natural science (τὴν φυσικὴν θεωρίαν) of all things that have come into being in the sensible world'. The next verse, then, deals with intelligible matters, says Clement: 'I have learned all that is hidden and manifest; for wisdom, which is the crafter of all things, has taught me' (Wis 7:21). Clement comments:

> Here you have the promise of our philosophy in few words. The learning about these matters, practised together with the right way of life, leads us through wisdom, 'the crafter of all things' (Wis 7:21), to the ruler of the universe – a thing hard to get hold of, hard to capture, as it always recedes and keeps remote from those who pursue it. But, despite being far, he has been very close – an unspeakable wonder. ... For though he is distant in being, he is near in his power, with which he encompasses everything. ... Indeed, the power of God is always present, touching us with its overseeing, beneficent, and educative power.[26]

Thus, in Clement's second description, 'our' (i.e., Christian) philosophy starts with natural science and culminates in theology, in accordance with the second and third stages of the EPHE scheme. The ethical stage is not mentioned by name. Nonetheless, divine education according to the first description based on Proverbs clearly operates on the ethical level.

This is confirmed by the following: in the Proverbs passage, divine education is characterised as one which operates by means of faith and fear of God. Now faith and fear of God belong among the topics discussed extensively in the second book of *Stromateis*, alongside other 'virtues of truth', as Clement calls them.[27] The list of these virtues, drafted at the outset of the second book, is the following: 'faith, wisdom, knowledge, science, hope, love, repentance, self-control, fear of God'.[28] Clement indicates that the list is not exhaustive and that he will deal with everything else that the 'rough outline in the area lying before us will require'.[29] The expression 'area lying before us' (προκείμενος τόπος) probably refers to the part of Christian

---

[25] *Strom.* 2.2.4.2–4 (GCS 114.29–115.9).
[26] *Strom.* 2.2.5.3 (GCS 115.17–21); cf. Philo, *Post.* 18.
[27] For the role of fear in Clement's project of Christian education, see Ashwin-Siejkowski 2008: 68–78. For faith, see Lilla 1971: 118–42; Osborn 2005: 159–96.
[28] *Strom.* 2.1.1.1 (GCS 113.9–11).   [29] *Strom.* 2.1.1.2 (GCS 113.12).

philosophy that Clement identifies as the 'ethical area' (ἠθικὸς τόπος) or 'ethical account' (ἠθικὸς λόγος). Clement is clear that the second book and almost all the rest of the *Stromateis* also belongs to the 'ethical area', dealing as it does with 'the virtues of truth' already mentioned, as well as with other virtues and issues related thereto.[30] Thus, when pointing out on the basis of the Proverbs passage that divine education operates by means of faith and fear of God, Clement accentuates aspects of divine education he identifies as ethical. In contrast, in his interpretation of the passage from the Book of Wisdom, he gestures beyond ethical issues towards physics and theology.

Virtues of Truth

Clement's treatment of the virtues of truth extends throughout the extant *Stromateis*, starting with Book 2, but it may be divided roughly into three sections. In the first section (*Strom.* 2.2.7.1–17.77.6), Clement articulates the cognitive or volitional conditions of participating in divine education: faith, fear, and repentance are the chief among them, being based on divine love and mercy on the one hand, and human will and love for wisdom on the other, together opening the hope of salvation and knowledge.

The second section, which covers the latter half of Book 2 and the whole of Books 3 and 4, explores the virtues characterising the goal of divine education and the notion of this goal as such. First, Clement shows how all the ethical virtues known to Greek philosophers are encapsulated in the Mosaic law. This pertains to the four cardinal virtues – courage, temperance, prudence, and justice – to which Clement further adds perseverance and endurance, shyness, self-control, and piety (*Strom.* 2.18.78.1). The person who exhibits all these virtues reaches the limit of human perfection, becoming like God, that is to say, like the Christ-Logos, himself, as far as is possible for a human being.[31] The life of a perfect Christian, represented by the martyr, is characterised by 'temperance' (σωφροσύνη), the ability to control one's passions even in the face of death (cf. *Strom.* 4.8.58.2–59.3).

The third section, covering Books 5, 6, and 7, focuses on the virtues of knowledge and piety, and culminates in a passage where the notion of perfection is revisited again on a new level, beyond the level of temperance (*Strom.* 7.10.55.1–14.88.7). Here the epitome of human perfection is no

---

[30] The 'ethical part' ends at *Strom.* 7.14.88.7; cf. Havrda 2019: 132.
[31] *Strom.* 2.19.97.1 and up to 2.20.104.3; the topic continues in 2.21.127–22.136. For the motif of the assimilation to God in Clement's ethics, see Lilla 1971: 106–17; Wyrwa 1983: 173–89; Ashwin-Siejkowski 2008: 13–15, 176–86; see also Havrda 2011: 35–39, with further references.

longer the martyr, but rather 'the real presbyter of the church', 'the true deacon of God's will', capable of 'doing and teaching that which belongs to the Lord' (*Strom.* 6.13.106.2).

The Order of Education

So much – very briefly – for the ethical part of Christian philosophy. Clement shows how the whole of Christian teaching on virtues and the goal of life is contained in scripture and the tradition of the church and how this tradition includes and surpasses the best ethical doctrines of Greek philosophy. In the continuation of the *Stromateis*, ethics was supposed to be followed by physics and theology, not immediately, as we have seen, but after some preliminary discussions. Of this continuation, lost or never fulfilled, Clement gives us merely a glimpse here and there in his extant writings. We know, for instance, that he was planning to start his exposition on physics with 'the account on cosmogony' (ὁ περὶ κοσμογονίας λόγος) based on Genesis (*Strom.* 4.1.3.2–3), and he also describes eschatological doctrines as pertaining to this area of study.[32] Clement's theological views of the ungenerated and unknowable Father, the generated and intelligible Son-Logos, and the Holy Spirit – whom Clement seems to identify with the first-created angels – can also be partly reconstructed from occasional remarks.[33] It is likely that the highest, theological part of his teaching was planned to deal with these issues, whose starting point is the confessional formula accepted by all Christians in faith.[34]

However, this order of knowledge does not overlap with the order of education. Clement does not propose that Christian education should start with the study of ethics or, for that matter, with any theoretical study at all. His vision of Christian education is reflected in the prologue to his *Paedagogus*. There, Clement famously distinguishes three modes of activities of the Logos: first, the Logos 'urges' or 'exhorts' (προτρέπων), then, it guides as a paedagogue (παιδαγωγῶν), and finally, it teaches (ἐκδιδάσκων). These three modes represent three stages of divine education, which constitute what Clement describes as a 'beautiful dispensation' (καλὴ οἰκονομία).[35] Each of the three modes has

---

[32] *Strom.* 2.18.87.1; 4.25.162.2, referring back to 4.25.161.2–162.
[33] See Lilla 1971: 189–99; Wyrwa 1983: 305–16. For Clement's angelology, see Bucur 2009.
[34] For Clement's hints of a trinitarian confession, see *Strom.* 5.11.73.2 and *Exc.* 80.3; see also *Strom.* 1.5.31.5; van den Hoek 1988: 39–40. For 'confession', see further *Paed.* 2.2.36.2; *Strom.* 4.9.70–73; 5.11.71.2; 7.11.67.1; 7.15.90.1–2. For faith in this sense as the basis of knowledge, see Havrda 2012.
[35] *Paed.* 1.1.3.3.

a different aim: the exhortative 'takes hold of our character, making us to renounce old beliefs and grow young again for salvation'. It does so by laying the foundation of truth in our soul, namely, the 'desire for eternal life through rational obedience'. The pedagogical mode, then, has a double focus: it heals us from passions; and it presides over our actions. The healing from passions is performed by means of images, used either as models to imitate or as deterrent examples. Actions, in turn, are directed by means of precepts and advice, telling us what to do in particular circumstances. This mode, based on obedience, is further distinguished from the mode of teaching, which is 'clarificatory and revelatory in matters of doctrine' (ἐν τοῖς δογματικοῖς δηλωτικὸς καὶ ἀποκαλυπτικός).[36] Clement makes clear that in his *Paedagogus*, he will follow the pedagogical mode, whereas teaching will come on a later occasion. His task in the *Paedagogus* is 'to lead forward, not to provide a method … to improve the soul, not to teach it, to introduce it to a temperate life, not to the life of knowledge'.[37] Its contents, then, correspond to an earlier phase of Christian education than the one represented by the *Stromateis*, a phase which does not teach any doctrines but provides practical guidance to believers by means of captivating images and pieces of advice.[38]

Once again, it is tempting to think that the distinction between the pedagogical and teaching modes of education was paralleled in the practice of Clement's institutional setting, whether before his time, or through his own efforts.[39] We could imagine, for example, that the catechetical school in Alexandria provided one sort of education to prospective teachers of Christian doctrine, and another sort to students who were either less advanced or less theoretically inclined, seeking merely practical instruction on how to live a good life.[40] Clement emphasises that even an illiterate person can become a perfect Christian.[41] Yet only an educated person can give an account of Christian virtues based on solid biblical grounds, explain how and why Christian ethics is superior to Greek ethics, and expose the errors of heterodox teachings.[42] Whereas the *Paedagogus* reaches a wider audience, the *Stromateis* is arguably intended for those who have the talent, resources, and

---

[36] *Paed.* 1.1.1.1–2.1.

[37] *Paed.* 1.1.1.4: προακτικός, οὐ μεθοδικὸς ὢν ὁ παιδαγωγός, ᾗ καὶ τὸ τέλος αὐτοῦ βελτιῶσαι τὴν ψυχήν ἐστιν, οὐ διδάξαι, σώφρονός τε, οὐκ ἐπιστημονικοῦ καθηγήσασθαι βίου.

[38] Again, in this distinction between practical and theoretical instruction, Clement follows a philosophical model. See Mühlenberg 2006: 45–52; Havrda 2019: 125–32.

[39] See Wyrwa 2005: 297.

[40] Similar divisions are mentioned in connection with Origen's teaching practice, and it seems plausible that they go back to Clement in some form; see Eusebius, *Hist. eccl.* 6.15.1; van den Hoek 1997: passim and esp. 70–71. For Clement's intended audience in *Paed.*, see Le Boulluec 2019: 71–74.

[41] Cf. *Strom.* 4.8.58.3, 62.4, 67.1, 69.4.   [42] See, e.g., *Strom.* 1.6.35.2.

time to seek this theoretical expertise. Within this framework of Christian 'philosophy', ethical considerations come first, followed by the instructions about the world, its beginning and end, and, finally, about matters divine.

Conclusion: The Bigger Picture

Pierre Hadot famously distinguishes three types of division of philosophy in antiquity – hierarchical, organic, and pedagogical – and identifies three different ideals of wisdom associated with them. For the first type, exemplified by Aristotelianism, wisdom is 'a universal knowledge which embraces the architecture of the system of sciences, their methods, and the diversity of their objects'; for the second, represented by Stoicism, wisdom is 'a concentrated attention on the presence of the *logos* within all things'. The third, pedagogical type, in turn, describes 'an itinerary or concrete method which leads to wisdom'. The parts of philosophy according to this type are conceived as 'stages of an inner path which one must traverse'; 'the phases of an evolution and of a transformation which one must realise'; 'an effort, a search, an exercise which leads to wisdom'.[43]

As Hadot points out, the EPHE scheme obviously belongs to the third type of division.[44] Indeed, Clement's programme of Christian philosophy, as outlined in the *Stromateis*, is one of the best-documented examples of an attempt to develop an entire curriculum of study around the idea of a spiritual progress.[45] As already mentioned, Clement frames this curriculum within a larger programme of education, in which the study of ethics is preceded by the formation of character by means of precepts and images. This integration of practical ethical instruction and theoretical study in a single educational programme – although it builds on distinctions from earlier sources – does not have a precise parallel in the second century, certainly not within an institutional setting.[46] Of course, for Clement, this whole programme is further framed by a specifically Christian context,

---

[43] Hadot 1982: 443–44; English translation: Hadot 2020: 126.
[44] Hadot 1982: 439–40 = Hadot 2020: 122–23.
[45] Closely connected to this is Clement's predilection for the terminology of initiation. See esp. *Strom.* 4.1.3.1, where Clement divides the EPHE scheme into the 'lesser mysteries' (corresponding to ethics) and the 'greater' ones, corresponding to physics and theology. For other instances, see Ramelli 2017a: 82. Once again, this is a common feature of the pedagogical division of philosophy, going back to Plato himself; see, e.g., Wyrwa 1983: 123–24; Bonazzi and Petrucci 2020: 160–61.
[46] The closest parallel is witnessed in later Neoplatonism; see Hadot 1982: 442 = Hadot 2020: 124, referring to Hadot 1978: 160–64.

defined by the institution of the church on the one hand, and by the set of beliefs expressed in the confession formula on the other.[47] This context, which encompasses the whole of a person's existence, not only safeguards a remarkable cohesion between all stages of education and learning but also determines, every step of the way, their specific content.

Hadot also makes an important observation regarding the function of the division of philosophy for the pedagogical purpose. Since, as Hadot points out, philosophical teaching around Clement's time largely consisted in reading of and commentary on the works of the founders of the school, the divisions of philosophy served mainly to establish the order of reading and commenting on these and other relevant texts.[48] For Clement the founding texts are the scriptures, and the 'ethical account' of the *Stromateis* consists, to a large extent, of exegetical notes on scriptural passages relevant to particular themes.[49] It is true that Clement frequently deals with philosophical sources as well. But his reason for doing so is, on the one hand, to show the superiority of biblical wisdom over Greek philosophy and, on the other, to help his readers, prospective experts on Christian doctrine, to grasp, through the veil of Greek philosophical doctrines (*dogmata*), the doctrinal contents of scriptures themselves.[50] In this way, Greek philosophy is merely an instrument in the hands of the λόγος διδασκαλικός, whose function, as Clement puts it in the *Paedagogus*, is 'clarificatory and revelatory in matters of doctrine'.[51]

Even though Clement's writings have directly influenced subsequent generations of Christian thinkers only rarely and always remained in the shadow of Origen and the Cappadocians, his programme of education and knowledge, set out as a coherent and powerful alternative to other similar programmes on the religious-intellectual market of his time, deserves attention not only for its rigour and ingenuity, but also because it invites us to reflect on the very foundations of Christian intellectual culture.

---

[47] For the confession formula see above, note 34.
[48] Hadot 1982: 441–42 = Hadot 2020: 124.
[49] The best study on the literary form of *Strom.* remains Méhat 1966: 179–279. For Clement's scriptural exegesis, see Kovacs 2017.
[50] For the superiority of biblical wisdom, as expressed in the idea of 'the theft of the Greeks', see, e.g., Lilla 1971: 31–41; Wyrwa 1983: 298–316. For Clement's appropriation of Greek philosophy as an instrument of teaching, see esp. the subtle analyses by Wyrwa 1983 and Le Boulluec 1987, 1989, 2012.
[51] *Paed.* 1.1.2.1.

6 | Origen's Institutions and the Shape of Biblical Scholarship

PETER W. MARTENS

Introduction

In this chapter, I examine how late ancient educational institutions configured biblical scholarship. Origen, the first prolific interpreter of Christian scripture, was affiliated with a number of such institutions over his lifetime. Yet accounts of his exegetical project have often underplayed, if not ignored altogether, the roles that these institutional settings played in his engagement with scripture. This oversight is significant since it underestimates, as I will argue, the extent to which these institutions exercised power over the Bible, the lives of its readers, and their interpretative techniques. I suspect that this oversight is also a missed opportunity for the wider re-examination of early Christian biblical interpretation. What new light could we shed on the ever-shifting profile of scriptural exegesis in late ancient Christianity if our narratives acknowledged how institutions shaped, and not simply sponsored, engagements with scripture? And how might the diversity of late ancient educational institutions help account for the different, and sometimes competing, ways in which scripture was examined? This chapter seeks to contribute to the organising theme of this volume by asking how institutions ordered the knowledge and ways of knowing that were associated with one of the central artefacts of the Christian community: its collection of sacred writings.[1]

Eusebius reports that Origen became a grammarian when he was around eighteen years of age (*Hist. eccl.* 6.2.12–3.3).[2] Several decades ago, Bernhard Neuschäfer took up this biographical cue and through extensive comparison with the Homeric scholia demonstrated what had long been overlooked: that Origen's later commentaries and homilies on Christian

---

[1] For orientation (with bibliography) to late ancient institutions and their relationship to Christian theology, see Markschies 2015. For the purposes of this chapter, 'institution' will refer to 'organized social structures that show the same enduring characteristics as governing bodies – namely, explicit norm structures, regular membership, transpersonal goals of action, and corporate power' (Markschies 2015: 23).

[2] The preceding years of instruction in the field might have lasted ten years. Cf. *Hom. Ps. 74*, sect. 6 (GCS NF 19 [OW 13], 279.11–13).

scripture were decisively shaped by the training he both received and provided in grammatical schools.[3] Neuschäfer's argument took the important step of highlighting an institutional context for Origen's biblical scholarship. Yet Origen was affiliated with other institutions, not just, or even primarily, grammatical schools. From the time he was eighteen years of age in Alexandria, through his later years in Caesarea Maritima, he was principally associated with institutions that looked very much like philosophical schools. Indeed, his scriptural commentaries were *not* produced in his grammatical school, but in his philosophical schools.[4]

By making this distinction between the grammarian's and philosopher's schools, I do not mean to suggest that when Origen eventually stepped down as a *grammatikos* in Alexandria that he simultaneously abandoned the textual skills he had hitherto acquired and, in turn, developed a whole new suite of reading strategies as a *philosophos*. It might, instead, be helpful to think of Origen as an 'internal plurality' of individuals, a 'bearer of heterogeneous habits, schemes, or dispositions',[5] since the case can be made that the mature Origen was not only a *grammatikos* and *philosophos*, but also an *ekklesiastikos*.[6] Each of these roles, themselves not always easily distinguished from one another, informed his scriptural project. In this chapter, I will foreground how Origen's philosophical schools gave shape and style to his exegetical project. I will also briefly reflect on the other institution with which he was affiliated: the church in Caesarea, where he was ordained as a priest. The homilies delivered in its liturgy bear, at times, a very close relationship to his commentaries that were produced in his philosophical schools and thus raise provocative questions about what Origen thought he was doing in his homilies. After providing an overview

---

[3] Neuschäfer 1987.
[4] In the Roman imperial period, the main vehicle for teaching and writing philosophy was textual commentary on past authorities. For more on this theme, see Praechter 1909; Hahn 1989; Lamberton 2001; I. Hadot 2003; Baltussen 2008; Sorabji 2019.
[5] Lahire 2003: 346, 344. The references come from Rebillard 2012: 3–4.
[6] I agree with L. Perrone's observation that in the concluding lines of Origen's *Hom. Ps. 74*, sect. 6, we find an oblique autobiographical reference to Origen's dual identity as a grammarian and philosopher – his 'identity card', as Perrone puts it. Origen comments on Ps 74:10 ('I will explain forever, I will make music to the God of Jacob') as follows: 'Our teacher and master is in possession of so many teachings that he explains not for ten years, as the grammarian explains … nor as the philosopher who hands on traditions explains, but then no longer has anything new to say. But the teachings of Christ are of such a number that he explains for all eternity' (Perrone 2013: 79). For Origen as an *ekklesiastikos*, consider the following passage: 'For this reason, it seems to me necessary that one able to genuinely serve as ambassador for the church's teaching [τὸν δυνάμενον πρεσβεύειν ὑπὲρ τοῦ ἐκκλησιαστικοῦ λόγου ἀπαραχαράκτως] …' (*Comm. Jo.* 5.8 [GCS 105.10–11]). Similar affiliation with the church is announced at *Dial.* 15; *Hom. Lev.* 10.1; and the self-designation as 'man of the church' at *Hom. Luc.* 16.6.

of Origen's school affiliations, I will examine three facets of his exegetical project that were shaped by the philosopher's schoolroom: how he framed the subject matter of scripture, the exegetical tools he thought were necessary for discovering its message, and the profile of the biblical scholar he hoped to train. While the discussion below is not exhaustive, it will hopefully demonstrate how a particular institutional setting left its signature on Origen's scriptural exegesis.

Origen's Grammatical and Philosophical Schools

In the sixth book of his *Ecclesiastical History*, Eusebius portrays Origen as a precocious student of the Greek language and its literature who quickly became a lecturer in a grammatical school (*Hist. eccl.* 6.2.15–3.1). But as we continue with Eusebius' narrative, Origen's later, and much longer-lasting, institutional affiliations come to light. While still earning his living as a grammarian, the eighteen-year-old Origen was given the additional responsibility of leading 'the school of instruction [τοῦ τῆς κατηχήσεως ... διδασκαλείου]' in Alexandria (*Hist. eccl.* 6.3.3).[7] The impetus for this development was that students, including 'some unbelievers', were coming to Origen to receive 'instruction in the faith' because there were no competent instructors in Alexandria (*Hist. eccl.* 6.3.1). Eventually Origen's dual career came to an end after his bishop, Demetrius, charged him with sole responsibility for the church's increasingly sought-after instruction. Origen gave up his first job as a grammarian, funded his living through the sale of his library, and turned his energies exclusively to instruction for the church (*Hist. eccl.* 6.3.8–9).

But even the singular appointment to the church's school proved too demanding. We are told that Origen – now likely several years later – did

---

[7] Translations of the *Church History* are from McGiffert 1995. There is a large literature on the so-called 'catechetical school' of Origen in Alexandria. S.v. κατήχησις (*PGL*) distinguishes between '*instruction*; esp. in the faith' and the use of this term in a technical sense, '*instruction*, of those preparing for baptism, *catechetical instruction*'. The older literature interpreted Eusebius' use of κατήχησις here in the latter sense: a school that was run by Origen that prepared candidates for baptism. This interpretation, however, seems unlikely for a number of reasons, not least of which is that Origen's early writings that come from this school (e.g., *On First Principles*, the first five books of the *Commentary on John*, and the *Stromata* in which he compared Christian views with those of the philosophers) are clearly addressed to advanced pupils with significant philosophical training. These works do not seem to have baptismal candidates in view. I am more inclined to hear Eusebius using κατήχησις in the former sense: Origen ran a 'school of (Christian) *instruction*' (see esp. Scholten 1995: 29–31). For literature on the Alexandrian and Caesarea schools, see Bardy 1937; Hornschuh 1960; Knauber 1968; Crouzel 1970; Scholten 1995; van den Broek 1995; van den Hoek 1997; Markschies 2015: 80–91.

not have time 'for the investigation and interpretation of the sacred scriptures, and also for the instruction of those who came to him' (*Hist. eccl.* 6.15). So he divided his students into two groups and split instructional duties between himself and his star pupil Heraclas: 'He entrusted to him [Heraclas] the elementary training of beginners, but reserved for himself the teaching of those who were farther advanced' (*Hist. eccl.* 6.15).[8] What curriculum did Origen offer in his wing of the school? Eusebius tells us that Origen taught his students 'divine things' – a sweeping gesture to his lectures on scripture, which were subsequently polished into commentaries, as well as thematically organised works like *On First Principles*.[9] But the curriculum offered more. Origen also taught his pupils 'foreign philosophy'.

For when he perceived that any persons had superior intelligence he instructed them also in philosophic branches – in geometry, arithmetic, and other preparatory studies – and then advanced to the schools of the philosophers and explained their writings. And he made observations and comments upon each of them, so that he became celebrated as a great philosopher even among the Greeks themselves. (*Hist. eccl.* 6.18.2–3, modified)

This portrait of Origen the philosopher, the student of philosophical texts, and teacher of the disciplines that prepare for philosophy, is bolstered at other moments in Eusebius' biography of Origen. He underscores how, when Origen gave up his grammatical school, he embarked upon the 'philosophical life' through rigorous ascetic practices, including fasting and poverty, and intensive scriptural study through the night (*Hist. eccl.* 6.3.9–13). Eusebius also quotes from one of Origen's few surviving letters, in which he justifies his continued education as a hearer of an anonymous philosopher.[10] Origen invokes the precedent of Pantaenus and Heraclas, both of whom were well acquainted with philosophy, as

---

[8] Note here that even Heraclas was 'not ignorant of philosophy', which tells us something about the orientation of training in Alexandria. Note as well that Ammonius, under whom perhaps our Origen studied, was said to divide his students into two groups, beginners and more advanced (Watts 2006: 156–57).

[9] Heine 1993.

[10] Perhaps under Ammonius Saccas. Recall the testimony of Porphyry in his treatise *Against the Christians* that an Origen who allegorised scripture was a hearer of Ammonius in Alexandria. This Origen was familiar with a wide range of philosophers, including Plato, Pythagoreans, and Stoics (testimony preserved in Eusebius, *Hist. eccl.* 6.19.5–8). This note by Porphyry, the fragment of Origen's letter cited by Eusebius (*Hist. eccl.* 6.19.12–14), and the two other references to Ammonius in Porphyry's *Life of Plotinus* raise a host of questions about the identity of Origen. Some have argued for two Origens, one the philosopher and the other the Christian, whereas others have argued for only one, most notably Böhm 2002 and Ramelli 2009c. For an overview of the debate and a rebuttal of these two essays in favour of the two Ammonii and two Origens hypothesis, see Edwards 2015a. Most recently, see Bäbler and Nesselrath 2018.

well as his professional responsibility to stay informed, since philosophers were increasingly numbered among his pupils (*Hist. eccl.* 6.19.12-14; cf. 6.3.13; 6.18.2).[11]

The picture that emerges of this Alexandrian school, or at least of the wing under Origen's direct supervision, is of an ecclesiastical institution strongly coloured by philosophy: philosophers are in attendance, gifted students are studying fields preparatory of philosophy, and they are eventually reading and commenting upon philosophical texts – as well as the Christian scriptures – and all this transpires under the tutelage of a philosopher par excellence whose doctrine harmonises with his 'philosophic life' (*Hist. eccl.* 6.3.7). Book Six of the *Ecclesiastical History*, Arthur Urbano writes, 'was about much more than the life of Origen. It is, in a sense, the *bios* of a Christian philosophical tradition.'[12]

After Origen moved to Caesarea Maritima in 232 CE, he set up a school whose curriculum appears to have shared many similarities with his educational programme in Alexandria.[13] In the heavily stylised *Panegyric* delivered by one of Origen's students traditionally identified as Gregory Thaumaturgus, we learn that pupils in this school 'embraced the good philosophy' (*Orat. paneg.* 1.3). Origen led his Caesarean students from logic (7) through physics, geometry, astronomy (8), ethics (9), and a wide reading of philosophical writings (13) before, finally, interpreting with them the divine words of scripture (15). The breadth of philosophical knowledge indicated by this description echoes Origen's earlier days in Alexandria when he worked through a similar curriculum with advanced students – a curriculum widely shared among Greek philosophical schools in the imperial period.[14] The *Panegyric* also strongly resembles some of the language in

---

[11] On the plausibility of students, Christian and non-Christian, sharing the same teachers and curriculum in third-century Alexandria, see Watts 2006: 155-68.

[12] Urbano 2013: 74, following Barnes 1981: 128. Among recent studies on Origen, the philosophical orientation of Origen's Alexandrian and Caesarean schools is most strongly emphasised by Watts 2006: 162-63; Heine 2010: 48-51, 60-64; Urbano 2013: 41-42, 70-79, 141-46; Fürst 2017: 5-8, 12-13.

[13] Important here is not only that the descriptions of the Alexandrian and Caesarean schools strongly overlap with one another, but that they also strikingly resemble Origen's remarks in *Ep. Greg.* and *Cels.* 3.58. Scholars who see similarities between both of these schools include Grant 1986: 185 and van den Broek 1995: 45-47.

[14] The division of philosophy into three parts – logic, ethics, and physics – was already characteristic of the Stoic philosophical curriculum (see Long 1986: 118-20, as well as source texts in Long/Sedley 26A-H). These are the three main themes under which John Dillon organises the thinking of 'Middle Platonism' (1996: 43-51). Philo too has a similar version, dividing philosophy in four parts: logic, ethics, physics, and praxis (*Leg.* 1.57). The notion that encyclical *paideia* is preparatory for philosophy is also in the Stoics (e.g., Seneca, *Ep.* 88.25-28) and Philo (*Congr.* 145).

Origen's *Letter to Gregory* where he recommends the study of philosophy as preparatory for the study of Christianity. 'For just as the servants of philosophers say concerning geometry, music, grammar, rhetoric, and astronomy that they are adjuncts to philosophy, we say this very thing about philosophy itself with regard to Christianity' (*Ep. Greg.* 2.1). Philosophy prepared the student for the examination of Christianity, which for Origen was chiefly the study of its scriptures (*Ep. Greg.* 2.4).[15]

Origen's Exegetical Project and Philosophy

The new kind of philosophical school that Origen introduced into the late ancient educational landscape was a competitor from the Christian ranks whose central innovation appears to have been curricular: the addition of Christian scripture to a syllabus of philosophical writings. The question I am posing in this chapter is how the location of the Bible in the philosophical classroom might have shaped Origen's approach to the Bible. My contention is that this institution – the characteristics of its teachers, students, curricula, and aims – ordered his exegetical project in a number of ways.

Subject of Scripture

Already in Origen's earliest writings we find clear statements about the subject matter of scripture that reflect the concerns of the Greek philosophical tradition. While this collection of writings is diverse – it includes precepts, stories, poems, and so on – what pulls it together is its singular aim: it is the textual expression of God's *sophia*. '[T]he Wisdom of God', Origen writes in the preface to his *Commentary on Psalms 1–25*, 'has permeated the whole of scripture even to the individual letter'. Just as divine providence is evident in the creation, '[s]o with regard to everything recorded by the inspiration of the Holy Spirit we accept that, since divine providence has endowed the human race with a superhuman wisdom by means of the scriptures, he has, so to speak, sowed traces of wisdom as saving oracles, in so far as possible, in each letter' (*Comm. Ps.* pref. 4).[16] In another early writing, *On First Principles*, Origen elaborates on the contents of this 'superhuman wisdom'. '[T]he aim of the Spirit who, by the providence of God through the Word …

---

[15] To what extent this letter describes Origen's Alexandrian or Caesarean schools (or perhaps both) is not clear. See Dorival 2004: 21–22. There is perhaps more than an allusion to an institution in this letter (and in *Cels*. 3.58, discussed below).
[16] Trans. Trigg 1998: 71.

enlightened the servants of the truth, that is, the prophets and apostles, was pre-eminently concerned with the unspeakable mysteries connected with the affairs of men.' These mysteries, Origen says shortly thereafter, are 'the rich and wise truth about God' (*Princ.* 4.2.7).[17] The main subject matter of scripture – wisdom – strongly echoes the stated aim of Hellenistic and Middle Platonic philosophers. Seneca, for instance, writes that 'philosophy is the love and pursuit of wisdom' (*Ep.* 89.4). Sextus Empiricus reports that 'philosophy is the cultivation of wisdom, and wisdom is the knowledge of divine and human things' (*Math.* 9.13). This Stoic definition of wisdom as the 'knowledge of divine and human things', and often with the added remark 'and their causes', circulated widely. We find it in Cicero (*Off.* 2.2.5) and Seneca (*Ep.* 89.5), but also Philo (*Congr.* 79–80), Clement (*Strom.* 1.5.31), and Origen himself (e.g., *Cels.* 3.72; *Hom. Jer.* 8.2).[18]

After the above-cited passage from *On First Principles*, Origen catalogues the scriptural topics that make up the 'wise truth about God':

We attach of necessity pre-eminent importance to the doctrines concerning God and His only-begotten Son; of what nature the Son is, and in what manner he can be the Son of God, and what are the causes of his descending to the level of human flesh and completely assuming humanity; and what, also, is the nature of his activity, and towards whom and at what times it is exercised. It was necessary, too, that the doctrines concerning beings akin to man and the rest of the rational creatures, both those that are nearer the divine and those that have fallen from blessedness, and the causes of the fall of these later, should be included in the accounts of the divine teaching; and the question of the differences between souls and how these differences arose, and what the world is and why it exists, and further, how it comes about that evil is so widespread and so terrible on earth, and whether it is not only to be found on earth but also in other places – all this it was necessary that we should learn.[19] (*Princ.* 4.2.7)

Many of the themes enumerated here dovetail with the recurring themes in the Middle Platonic philosophical curriculum with which Origen was certainly familiar. John Dillon identifies these main themes as the first principles, God and the Dyad, the range of intermediate beings ('daemons'), and the human soul, especially its freedom and how this links with divine providence.[20] The resemblance between the themes Origen saw in his scriptures and the themes these philosophers saw in their authoritative writings is palpable.

---

[17] Trans. Butterworth 1973: 282–83.
[18] This conception of philosophy was also echoed in Middle Platonic authors. Alcinous defines philosophy as 'a striving for wisdom' (*Didask.* 1, with reference perhaps to Plato, *Resp.* 5.475b).
[19] Trans. Butterworth 1973: 283–84.   [20] Dillon 1996: 43–51.

Origen's prologue to his *Commentary on the Song of Songs* offers his most explicit statement on the philosophical themes in scripture. Discussing the rationale behind the church's adoption of the three Solomonic books in the order of Proverbs, Ecclesiastes, and Song of Songs, his proposal runs as follows. There are three broad fields by which people attain true knowledge: ethics, physics, and enoptics (or epoptics).[21] The Greek wise men, Origen continued, 'borrowed these ideas from Solomon, who had learnt them by the Spirit of God at an age and time long before their own. ... Solomon discovered and taught these things by the wisdom that he received from God, before anyone' (*Comm. Cant.* pr. 3.4).[22] Solomon wished to distinguish these three branches of learning from one another, and so he relegated each to its own book, and sequenced them appropriately so that readers began with ethics, moved to natural studies, and finally turned to the inspective science where they learned to commune with God through knowledge and love. And so, Origen concludes, Solomon established 'these basic principles of true philosophy [*haec ... verae philosophiae fundamenta*]' in his writings (*Comm. Cant.* pr. 3.8).[23] And even more strongly a few lines later: Solomon 'was the first to teach men divine philosophy [*qui primus homines divinam philosophiam docet*]' (*Comm. Cant.* pr. 3.14).[24]

For Origen, scripture was the philosophical text par excellence, teaching its readers the deepest mysteries about God, the universe, and its rational inhabitants.[25] But this hermeneutical conviction had institutional roots. Teachers and students had expectations about the texts they would study in the philosopher's classroom. By putting Christian scripture onto the reading lists of his philosophical curricula, Origen helped create expectations that his students would find doctrines leading to wisdom when they began

---

[21] Parallels to this division of philosophy can be found in Plutarch, Theon of Smyrna, and Clement of Alexandria. See I. Hadot 1987: 117. See also the discussion of this passage by Matyáš Havrda, Chapter 5, this volume.

[22] Trans. Lawson 1957: 40–41.   [23] Trans. Lawson 1957: 41.

[24] Trans. Lawson 1957: 43.

[25] There are many other places where Origen finds philosophical themes in scripture: the incorporeality of God, which he admits is only a latent theme in scripture, but one openly discussed by 'Greek philosophers' (*Princ.* pr. 8–9); the philosophical theme of freedom is 'the meaning of the whole scripture' (*Comm. Rom.* pr. 2; see Koch 1932: 289–91); in his treatise *On Prayer*, Origen raises a series of objections to prayer, similar to those found in the fifth oration of the second-century philosopher, Maximus of Tyre (*Or.* 5–7; see Perrone 2011: 79–90 and compare with P. W. van der Horst 1996: esp. 336); in his *Commentary on the Song of Songs*, in response to the passage, 'Unless thou know thyself' (1:8), Origen provides his readers with a long list of disputed questions on the topic of the soul (e.g., is the soul corporeal or incorporeal? composite or simple?) (*Comm. Cant.* 2.5.22–23; for similar lists, see *Princ.* pr. 5; *Cels.* 4.30; *Comm. Jo.* 6.14). The parallels to the lists in Seneca (*Ep.* 88.34) and others suggested to Henry Chadwick 'that there was a standard list of questions in philosophical schools' (1999: 75–76).

to examine it. And of course, scripture did not just offer *more* philosophy; it offered a *better* philosophy, signified by adjectives like 'true' and 'divine', the sort of philosophy that merited its place at the apex of a late ancient philosophical curriculum.

Studying Scripture

Origen's conviction that the entire message of scripture was configured by the concerns of philosophy had a number of implications for how he studied it. I highlight two of these below.

Problems and Solutions

Where principles, doctrines, or themes beneficial for life were openly taught in scripture, the reader could proceed in a relatively quick and straightforward manner. Much in scripture, however, did not conform to these expectations. And many passages, even if thought to be straightforward, had engendered alternative interpretations in rival communities that required special attention on the part of the reader. The ability to identify problems and propose solutions (προβλήματα καὶ λύσεις) was a widespread feature of late ancient textual scholarship and was especially prominent among philosophers.[26] It likely went back to the study of Homer's poems and the variety of difficulties detected therein: Aristotle wrote a work (now lost) entitled, *Homeric Problems*, as did others, including Zeno, the founder of the Stoic school. A number of closer contemporaries to Origen, including Philo, Tatian, Heraclitus, and Porphyry also wrote treatises of this sort.[27] Origen likely never produced a commentary that had problems and solutions as its overarching structure, although other authors in the Christian tradition did. However, as Gustave Bardy has already observed, throughout his surviving writings we see Origen tackling individual problems and presenting his readers with solutions.[28] Some of these problems were thematic, such as the question of whether one should pray.[29] Many more problems were specific to a particular text. In a fragment from book 3 of the *Commentary on Genesis*, Origen identifies four problems raised by Gen 1:14 ('And let them [stars] be for signs') that he will tackle in subsequent paragraphs:

These, then, are the problems [προβλήματα] which confront us – (α) How, if God knows from all eternity what we regard as done by the individual, Free

---

[26] Neuschäfer 1987: 340–42; Perrone 1995.   [27] Gudeman 1927; Dreyer 1968–69.
[28] Bardy 1932. See now Perrone 1994; Bendinelli 1997: 141–242.   [29] See n. 25 above.

Will is to be maintained; (β) in what way the stars are not productive of human affairs, but only indicate them; (γ) that men cannot have an accurate knowledge of these things, but the signs are shown to Powers superior to men; (δ) why it is that God has made the signs for the Powers to know, shall be the fourth point of investigation.[30] (*Philoc.* 23)

Perhaps the *locus classicus* for questions and answers in early Christian literature was the hardening of Pharaoh's heart (e.g., Exod 4:21), which Origen discusses at length in *Princ.* 3.1.8–14 and which drew him into lengthy reflections on a topic widely discussed in Stoic circles, the capacity of humans to make decisions for which they were responsible (τὸ αὐτεξούσιον, τὸ ἐφ᾽ἡμῖν).[31] What is particularly interesting for our purposes is that Origen explicitly paralleled the practice of discussing problems in the philosophical schools with solving problems in scripture. In one of the newly discovered homilies on Psalm 77[78] he comments on verse 2 ('I will utter problems from of old') as follows: 'For just as among the Greek philosophers there are certain problems which they propose to those about to study ... so there are certain problems in scripture' (*Hom. 1 in Ps. 77*, sect. 5).[32] He then lists a number of scriptural difficulties that should be discussed by his listeners if they are to approach scripture with the same sort of rigour as that found in the philosophical schools.

Allegory

In Origen's hands, allegory was a privileged means for dealing with some of the aforementioned difficulties in scripture. But allegory could also be invoked when approaching narratives that were pleasing and beautiful, yet whose granularity – detailed stories, concrete individuals, specific actions, and so on – did not point immediately to the deeper doctrines and precepts which he thought constituted scripture's fundamental subject matter. Allegorical interpretation, like problems-and-solutions, was another interpretative strategy adopted by Origen with clear precedent in philosophical

---

[30] Trans. Lewis 1911: 179–80.
[31] See also *Princ.* 4.3.1–5, where Origen provides an impressive catalogue of difficulties – 'irrationalities' and 'impossibilities' – in scripture. E.g., who could believe that God, 'after the manner of a farmer', planted a garden in Eden (Gen 2:8–9)? Was it not irrational to prohibit the eating of vultures when in the worst of famines no one would do such a thing (Lev 11:14)? From what 'high mountain' did the devil show Jesus all the kingdoms of the world (Matt 4:8)? These questions echo Aristotle's discussion of the types of problems readers encountered in texts: 'So then, people make criticisms of types [of problems]: that things are impossible, irrational, harmful, contradictory, or contrary to artistic standards' (*Poet.* 25; trans. Halliwell 1995: 135).
[32] GCS OW 13, 361.18–363.1.

circles.[33] While allegory was never practised exclusively by philosophers in antiquity, it was prevalent among them, especially among Stoics and later Platonists who sought out their teachings within the Greek myths. In Porphyry's famous critique of Origen, precisely this link between allegorising and philosophy is established:

> For he [Origen] was continually studying Plato, and he busied himself with the writings of Numenius and Cronius, Apollophanes, Longinus, Moderatus, and Nicomachus, and those famous among the Pythagoreans. And he used the books of Chaeremon the Stoic, and of Cornutus. Becoming acquainted through them with the figurative interpretation of the Grecian mysteries, he applied it to the Jewish scriptures.[34] (Eusebius, *Hist. eccl.* 6.19.8)

Of course, Origen himself made links between his allegorical exegesis and philosophy. In *Against Celsus*, for instance, he defends the allegorical reading of the passage in Genesis where God made Adam fall into a trance, took a rib from him, and out of the rib made a woman (Gen 2:21–22). In response to Celsus' ridicule of this passage, Origen wonders how it can be reasonable to allegorise the myths of Hesiod in order to discover the 'philosophical truths contained' in them, but then to deny such a move when it comes to Christian scripture. 'In reply to the man who gives a profound allegorical interpretation [τὸν ταῦτα σεμνῶς ἀλληγοροῦντα] of these verses [from Hesiod], whether his allegory is successful or not, we will say this: Are the Greeks alone allowed to find philosophical truths in a hidden form [ἐν ὑπονοίᾳ ἔξεστι φιλοσοφεῖν], and the Egyptians too, and all barbarians whose pride is in mysteries and in the truth which they contain' (*Cels.* 4.38)?[35] This rhetorical question nicely conveys how Origen understood scripture as a collection of writings that contained philosophical truths and that, when cloaked in the language of myth, called for the same allegorical exegesis as the Greek myths did.

This close relationship between philosophy and allegory is even encoded in the term φιλοσοφεῖν whose lexical range – 'to investigate philosophically' –

---

[33] The literature here is large. For an overview, Joosen and Waszink 1950 is still useful. For a more recent treatment, see Struck 2004.

[34] This report seems to be very much about our Origen: he mentions Chrysippus by name and knows his allegorical interpretation of Homer, as well as those by Pherecydes and Heraclitus (*Cels.* 4.48; 6.42); he knows of allegorical interpretations of Hesiod (*Cels.* 4.38) and the Dionysian mysteries (*Cels.* 3.23; 4.17); and he indicates familiarity with the allegories of the Old Testament by Aristobulus, Philo, and Numenius (*Cels.* 4.51).

[35] Trans. Chadwick 1953: 214. See also *Cels.* 4.17 for a similar juxtaposition of allegorical interpretation and philosophical inquiry. This sentiment can also be found in Philo, *Contempl.* 3.28, where reading the Bible allegorically allows one to discover philosophical wisdom.

sometimes specifically meant 'to interpret allegorically'.[36] We see this usage of the term in Origen's defence of his treatment of the opening chapters of Genesis. He argues that these must be read philosophically; from the literary context, it is clear that he means: 'interpreted allegorically'. '[T]he story of Adam and his sin will be interpreted philosophically [φιλοσοφήσουσιν] by those who know that Adam means *anthropos* (man) in the Greek language, and that in what appears to be concerned with Adam Moses is speaking of the nature of man' (*Cels.* 4.40).[37] The Bible, Origen continues, is not simply talking about one man, but about the whole human race. And the reference to the 'coats of skins' (Gen 3:21) with which God clothed the first couple after it sinned 'has a certain secret and mysterious meaning', which we know from other places in Origen's corpus concerns the embodiment of souls who fell in the primordial realm.[38]

The Ideal Reader of Scripture

The philosopher's schoolroom also corresponded to a kind of reader. As we have already seen from the biographical reports about his Alexandrian and Caesarea schools, Origen oriented his scriptural instruction to higher-level students whom he frequently distinguished from the simpler (*simpliciores*) Christians. In a thinly veiled autobiographical passage from *Against Celsus*, he explains how, after 'young men' 'had first been trained in a general education and in philosophical thought I would try to lead them on to the exalted height, unknown to the multitude, of the profoundest doctrines of the Christians, who discourse about the greatest and most advanced truths, proving and showing that this philosophy was taught by the prophets of God and the apostles of Jesus'.[39] These words echo the advice Origen penned in his *Letter to Gregory* and mirror Eusebius' and Gregory's accounts of Origen's school curricula in Alexandria and Caesarea: students advanced through a sequence of study that began with the general education, led to philosophy, and culminated in the supreme philosophy, the 'greatest and most advanced truths' communicated through Christian scripture.[40]

Pierre Hadot's work on late ancient philosophy draws out additional implications about the kinds of advanced students Origen taught. Hadot has argued that philosophy in this period was increasingly practised as a

---

[36] S.v. φιλοσοφέω 4 *PGL*.   [37] Trans. Chadwick 1953: 216.   [38] See Martens 2013.
[39] *Cels.* 3.58 (trans. Chadwick 1953: 168).
[40] See also *Princ.* pr. 3; *Exp. Prov.* 1.6 (PG 13.24D–25A); *Comm. Rom.* pr. 2.

'way of life and existential option which demand[ed] from the individual a total change of lifestyle, a conversion of one's entire being, and ultimately a certain desire to be and to live in a certain way'.[41] Illustrative of his thesis is a mid-second-century manual introducing students to Plato's thought and writings. In his *Didaskalikos*, Alcinous sketches a portrait of the ideal philosopher. This person

> must be enamoured of the truth, and in no way tolerate falsehood. Furthermore, he must also be endowed with a temperate nature, and, in relation to the passionate part of the soul, he must be naturally restrained …. The prospective philosopher must also be endowed with liberality of mind, for nothing is so inimical as small-mindedness to a soul which is proposing to contemplate things divine and human. He must also possess natural affinity for justice, just as he must towards truth and liberality and temperance; and he should also be endowed with a ready capacity to learn and a good memory, for these too contribute to the formation of the philosopher.[42] (Alcinous, *Didask.* 1.2–3)

Alcinous highlights a range of desired, personal characteristics that illustrates how philosophising was not just about technical skill, education, or ability. It also required a commitment to a particular way of life that conditioned the activity and results of philosophical inquiry.[43] Arguably the main activity of the late ancient philosophical way of life was textual commentary on an authority's writings. This spiritual exercise, Hadot contends, was cultivated by philosophers, 'not only because the search for the meaning of a text really d[id] demand the moral qualities of modesty and love for the truth, but also because the reading of each philosophical text was supposed to produce a transformation in the person reading or listening to the commentary'.[44] 'To learn philosophy, even by reading and commenting upon texts, meant both to learn a way of life and to practice it.'[45]

One might argue that Origen is as exemplary of Hadot's thesis as any non-Christian philosopher that falls within his purview. For Origen, biblical interpretation was pursued with a view to promoting, as well as practising, a Christian way of life. In his writings we find a robust emphasis

---

[41] Hadot 2002: 3. For more recent treatments on philosophy as a pursuit of both intellectual and ethical ideals, see Cooper 2012 and Trapp 2017: 31–33. See also Watts 2012: 470.

[42] Trans. Dillon 1993: 3. For comparison, Eusebius reports how Origen adopted a range of ascetic practices when he embarked upon the 'philosophical life' (*Hist. eccl.* 6.3.9–13). For the moral resonance of the term 'philosophy' in Greek patristic literature, s.v. φιλοσοφία *PGL*, 4, 5, and 8.

[43] See also the list of introductory topics before embarking upon the study of a philosopher. Invariably on this list is a discussion of the qualities required of the would-be student. See Westerink 1962: xxvi; Mansfeld 1994: 4–5.

[44] Hadot 2002: 155.   [45] Hadot 2002: 153.

on the interpreter's abilities, education, beliefs, practices, aims, and dispositions – in short, the exegete's way of life – and an insistence that such a way of life played an important and complex role in shaping exegetical activity.[46] Ideal interpreters hold to the church's rule of faith (e.g., *Princ.* pr.), follow apostolic precedent in handling particular passages (*Cels.* 4.49), practise a range of reading virtues, such as attentiveness and curiosity, pray to God for divine help, and aim through their interpretative work to know and become like God (see *Princ.* 3.6.1 where Plato is approvingly invoked: 'that the highest good is to become as far as possible like God' (*Theaet.* 176b)). Origen depicted ideal interpreters, then, as variously implicated in the Christian way of life: their exegesis presupposed this life, continually sought to reinforce it, and was often shaped by its leading convictions. Yet this conception of the ideal interpreter was entirely in keeping with the expectations of contemporary philosophers who sought pupils in whom excellence of character and the quest for wisdom shone forth.

Origen's Exegetical Project and the Liturgy

I have argued that Origen's exegetical project both reflected and reinforced his decision to embed Christian scripture into the philosophical curriculum. Yet the philosophical schools in Alexandria and Caesarea were not the only institutions with which Origen had an affiliation. He was also ordained to the priesthood in Caesarea around 232 and several years thereafter was commissioned by the city's bishop, Theoctistus, to deliver homilies on the Old Testament and gospels.[47] It was in the Caesarean liturgies that Origen's homilies – a sizeable percentage of his surviving writings – were delivered. What impact might this different institution have had on his approach to scripture?

The temptation from a contemporary perspective is to assume a significant difference between a commentary and homily. For many today, there is 'the gut feeling that, at bottom, "going to school" and "going to church" are two entirely different kinds of activity'.[48] Yet Origen's homilies were delivered at an 'amazingly high' level.[49] The evidence for this assertion abounds: in

---

[46] This is the argument in Martens 2012.
[47] According to Pierre Nautin, Origen was commissioned by Theoctistus in 239 to deliver homilies during the three-year liturgical cycle of the church during which the Old Testament and gospels were apparently read in their entirety (1977: 389–409).
[48] Alexander 2004: 65.
[49] Heine 2010: 179. The high level of his sermons is also confirmed by the challenges Origen experienced in the pulpit. He heard criticisms from some quarters about his more sophisticated

his homilies he discusses variant biblical readings and engages in textual criticism;[50] the polemical remarks against the heterodox, a common and sometimes occasioning feature of the commentaries, surface extensively in the homilies;[51] sophisticated textual analysis, such as the identification of problems and solutions[52] and allegory (*passim*), occur throughout, as do esoteric doctrines such as the pre-existence of souls.[53] The differences between Origen's homilies and commentaries are not particularly striking. The homilies tend to be less exhaustive than the commentaries, but this is hardly surprising given the time constraints facing the preacher. Origen picked his spots, focusing on the material that was most obviously edifying for his audiences.[54] But in most other matters, there was significant overlap of technique and concern between his established mode of commentary writing and his homilies. The evidence suggests, then, that we ought not to push for too great a difference between Origen's scriptural instruction in the philosophical school and in the liturgical homily.

One of the reasons for this phenomenon was the overlapping educational mission of Origen's philosophical schoolroom and the church. On the one hand, his homilies had a scholastic orientation, since many of these were apparently delivered in daily, morning non-eucharistic services where the focus was explicitly on the teaching of scripture.[55] On the other hand,

---

textual strategies, including the use of allegory and reliance on Jewish translations of the law and prophets (*Hom. Gen.* 13.3; *Hom. Lev.* 1.1; *Comm. Rom.* 8.8; Nautin 1977: 405). People walked out of church before he could preach on the scriptural passage that had been read (*Hom. Exod.* 12.2). Ronald Heine has remarked how one homily in particular illustrates Origen's frustrations with the laxity of his congregation (Heine 2010: 183 on *Hom. Gen.* 10). Nautin has even suggested that these difficulties might have led Theoctistus to remove Origen from the pulpit in Caesarea (1977: 405, 408, 434). It appears that Origen's homilies often went over the heads of a large number of his hearers.

[50] *Hom. Judic.* 1.1; *Hom. Jer.* 14.3.1; 15.5.2; 16.10.1; *Hom. 1 in Ps. 77*, sect. 1.

[51] *Hom. Lev.* 1.1.4–6; *Hom. Num.* 9.1.1–7; *Hom. Jos.* 7.6, 9.8; *Hom. 2 in Ps. 77*, sect. 4; *Hom. Isa.* 7.3; *Hom. Jer.* 5.14.1; *Hom. Ezech.* 2.2; *Hom. Luc.* 16.6.

[52] *Hom. 1 in Ps. 77*, sect. 6; *Cels.* 6.49.

[53] On this theme in the *Homilies on Genesis*, see Martens 2013.

[54] *Hom. Lev.* 7.1.1; 7.4.3; *Hom. Num.* 14.1.1. In a number of places, Origen distinguishes between homilies and commentaries in this way: homilies do not have the luxury of an exhaustive, word-for-word interpretation of the biblical text but rather focus on passages that edify. In *Hom. Num.* 14.1.1 Origen remarks that commentaries provide word-for-word analysis and that homilies cannot address all points in detail because of the constraints of time. 'But because the sermon [*tractatus*] that is being given in the church for the sake of edification is of limited duration, there was not enough time for us to set forth in detail the words of scripture, so that nothing at all would remain unconsidered, and to present an explanation of each detail. For indeed the latter method would be more in the style of a commentary [*commentarii*]' (trans. Scheck 2009: 79). See also *Hom. Lev.* 1.1.5; 7.1.1; Klostermann 1947; Junod 1994.

[55] Nautin 1977: 391–401.

Origen's philosophical schools had an ecclesial orientation. In the passage below, he juxtaposes the 'schools' of the heterodox with the 'church' of the orthodox but, tellingly, does not locate these institutions in different spheres of cultural activity:

For in our youth the heresies really blossomed and there seemed to be many who were gathered among them. For they were all ravenous for the teachings of Christ but did not find resources of sufficient teachings in the church [ἐν τῇ ἐκκλησίᾳ διδασκάλων ἱκανῶν], and so, because of hunger, they imitated those who eat human flesh in a famine, and deserting the healthy teaching they turned their minds to teachings of whatever kind, and their schools [τὰ διδασκαλεῖα] were formed. But when the grace of God shone a superior teaching [διδασκαλίαν πλείονα], with each passing day the heresies disbanded, and their apparent esoterica were exposed for mockery and their impious and godless teachings were demonstrated to be irreverent.[56] (*Hom. 2 in Ps. 77*, sect. 4)

The schools of the heterodox and the church rival one another for establishing the true teachings of Christ – Origen envisions them as competitors in the same educational space. It seems reasonable to conclude that he would have considered his own philosophical schools as also operating in this same field of ecclesial activity, which would further explain the striking similarities between his commentaries and homilies.

In addition to school and church sharing an educational mission, they also shared a membership. Origen's congregations were diverse. He preached before a wide range of listeners, from pre-catechumens, catechumens, and baptised members of the church, to priests and bishops.[57] Within his congregations there was also a wide range of abilities, interests, and education. Remarks from his homilies indicate that some of his hearers enjoyed a high level of education.[58] There are also scattered remarks where Origen emphasises the importance of his hearers engaging in their own research and independent inquiry into biblical texts.[59] Comments like these presuppose levels of wealth and education among his hearers that we would more readily associate with Origen's advanced students. It is entirely likely that pupils in his philosophical classroom

---

[56] GCS OW 13 371.15–372.6 (trans. mine). For a very similar passage, see *Comm. Jo.* 5.8. Note as well Galen, who labelled a variety of philosophical groups, along with Jews and Christians, as 'sects' (*haireseis*) and 'schools' (*diatribai*), not reserving special labels for one community or the other (Snyder 2000: 6).
[57] Junod 1994: 78.
[58] *Hom. Gen.* 10.1; 13.3; *Hom. Exod.* 13.3; *Hom. Jos.* 1.7. See Castagno 2014: 242.
[59] *Hom. Gen.* 10.5; 12.5; 13.3; *Hom. 7 in Ps. 77*, sect. 4.

or other readers of his commentaries also came to hear his sermons.[60] So while we could be forgiven for assuming that lectures delivered in a philosophical school would be of a fundamentally different category from homilies preached in a church, in the case of Origen the evidence suggests precisely the opposite: he handled scriptural exposition in the liturgy much as he did in his schools.

For Origen, then, the homily was made to look like his philosophy lectures, which he had begun to deliver a full two decades before he started preaching regularly. When he did eventually fold preaching into his duties, only minimal modifications to his long-standing routine were initiated. He consistently mentioned a single adaptation, as already noted above: the need to keep within the time constraints of the liturgy, which he tried to do by focusing on passages which yielded an edifying message. The homily became an abbreviated philosophy lecture. It is interesting, in this light, to follow Pierre Nautin's observation that there was no particular term to designate a 'preacher' in the third century CE. Instead, Origen designated himself in his homilies as a διδάσκαλος: 'instructor, schoolmaster, teacher'.[61] It is a striking self-designation, since it shows how he 'assimilated' his later role as preacher into his long-standing position as an educator.[62] Thus, the liturgy appears to have made few new demands on the conventions of scriptural commentary that Origen had been practising in his schools. His scriptural exposition in the liturgical homilies was almost entirely configured by his decades-long engagement with scripture in the philosophical schools over which he presided in Alexandria and Caesarea.[63]

***

Many studies on Origen over the last century have located philosophy in some binary: this discipline is opposed to orthodox Christian teaching, to the pure simplicity of the Hebraic spirit, or in the case of the topic of this chapter, to the Bible.[64] I hope I have demonstrated that such a neat

---

[60] Frequent first-person plural references in the homilies when discussing schoolroom activities like textual editing also suggest that students attended his homilies (Solheid 2020: 109–11). Solheid argues that Origen's *Homilies on the Psalms* have so many features in common with his commentaries from his Caesarean period that the 'entire purpose in these homilies was either to persuade his audience to join him and his students in their scholarly pursuits, or to at least cultivate similar reading habits in his audience' (2020: 132–33).

[61] *Hom. Jer.* 5.13.2; 14.3.2.   [62] Trans. Nautin 1976: 152.

[63] So too Nautin: 'Sa spiritualité n'est pas celle d'un prêtre fondée sur une fonction liturgique, mais celle d'un "didascale"' (1976: 157).

[64] E.g., Vermes 2013. For a critique, see Martens 2015.

distinction between philosophy and the Bible fails to do justice to how pervasively late ancient philosophical schooling ordered Origen's perspective on, and approach to, the Christian scriptures. And of course, this was not the only institution that early Christians affiliated with the Bible. As time went on, increasingly diverse options within the church's evolving structures, including the later emergence of monasteries, presented different settings within which the Bible was studied and taught. A wider examination of early Christian biblical interpretation with a view to its diverse institutional locations will help clarify important differences in how the Bible was envisioned and engaged.

7 Dialogue and Catalogue: Fate, Free Will, and Belief in the *Book of the Laws of the Countries*

SCOTT FITZGERALD JOHNSON

Introduction

Were there distinctive modes of knowledge in the Syriac world? Certainly at the beginning of Syriac literary history we see authors wrestling with how to combine different intellectual traditions – Greek, Mesopotamian, Roman – into new frameworks suited to their language and geographical setting. The province of Osrhoene in northern Mesopotamia, with its centre of Edessa, was the setting in which several Syriac works of different character emerged. This intellectual world communicated its ideas through two primary media: hymnic poetry and philosophical prose. Bardaisan of Edessa (154–c. 222 CE), courtier to King Abgar VIII, employed these modes in Syriac and, from the surviving evidence, was very much a pioneer in both of them. This chapter investigates his *Book of the Laws of the Countries*, the first prose work in Syriac attributed to a known, contemporary author. This is the only Syriac composition of the period that can be reliably placed in Edessa itself, though there is no question that Edessa's political and religious distinctiveness affected much early Syriac writing. The *Book of the Laws of the Countries* does not demonstrate a wholly different approach to knowledge, unconnected to received patterns of writing and argument in the Greco-Roman world. At the same time, the work is highly original and responds to specific concerns stemming from the unique intellectual and cultural scene of Roman Edessa.

The principal question addressed in this chapter, therefore, is how Bardaisan innovatively addresses the issues of his day within the intellectual traditions he received. Later Syriac tradition considered Bardaisan to have innovated in both poetry and prose, and he is regarded today as a foundational figure in the history of Syriac. Demonstrating why this is so is more complicated and requires close attention to how he ordered knowledge through language and literary form. In the context of the present volume and the growing scholarly literature on the organisation of knowledge, Bardaisan's contribution to late Roman thought and literature is an important comparandum from a nascent literary tradition.[1] Syriac thereafter emerged as a vibrant intellectual medium with a significant corpus of writings and, from the fourth century on, became crucial to the maturation of Christian thought in the East.

Bardaisan of Edessa lived in a tumultuous period for northern Mesopotamia.[2] His adult life largely coincided with King Abgar VIII's reign in Edessa (r. 177–212 CE). It was during his reign that the Roman empire, under Septimius Severus, took special notice of the kingdom of Edessa and made Osrhoene a province of the empire.[3] Edessa had been founded by Seleucus I Nicator, the Hellenistic king, in 303/2 BCE. Osrhoene was subsequently acknowledged as an independent province by the Parthians, who had taken it from the Greeks. The Abgarids thus inherited their rule both from the successors of Alexander the Great and from the Persians.[4] A small kingdom by comparison with those great empires, Osrhoene was both deeply Hellenised and fundamentally Aramaic.[5] (Aramaic having been the imperial language of the Achaemenid Persians.) During the early Roman empire, Osrhoene remained on the border between Rome and Parthian Persia and acted as a buffer province. The location of Edessa was a benefit to the Abgarids in that it allowed them to maintain independence for a long time. The Abgarid royal line ruled in Edessa, more or less continuously, from *c.* 132 BCE to 212 CE.[6] Soon after Abgar VIII's reign, Edessa became a Roman *colonia*, and, except for one possible attempt to reassert the kingdom in 239 CE, the city and province remained fully within the later Roman empire.[7]

The Greek historian and miscellanist Julius Africanus (*c.* 160–240 CE) visited the court of Abgar VIII in the retinue of Septimius Severus. He provides a vivid picture of the courtly and intellectual life of the place at

---

[1] While many studies of individual Syriac works or authors have appeared in recent years, there is little current scholarship on the organisation of knowledge as a broader concept in Syriac. See, however, Muriel Debié's (2015) study of Syriac historiography from a thematic and structural point of view, with the review by Peter Brown (2018) on the book's significance. The discussion of this subject for Greek and, especially, Latin literature in Late Antiquity is more robust. Among others, see Asper 2007; Bausi et al. 2018; Formisano 2001, 2013, 2018; Formisano and Van der Eijk 2017; Johnson 2016.

[2] On the dates of his life, see Drijvers 1966: 185–88. The date of death is much less secure. The name Bar Daisan, 'son of the river Daisan [in Edessa]', signifies his native home.

[3] The authoritative account of the Roman movements in this region can be found in Millar 1993. See also Butcher 2003; Ross 2001.

[4] See Ross 2001: 5–11, 22–28; Segal 1970: 1–8.

[5] For a survey of the topic and its scholarly fault lines, see Healey 2011.

[6] On the last half century of Edessan independence, see Possekel 2016; Ross 2001: 46–82.

[7] Millar 1993: 475–77. The history of Osrhoene/Edessa in this period is intricate and depends on a variety of types of evidence. For a list of sources, see 'Appendix C' in Millar 1993: 553–62.

this time.[8] He accompanied the king's son on a royal hunt during which Maʿnu (*Mannos*) shot an attacking bear with two arrows, one in each of its eyes. Indeed, archery seems to have been the preferred pastime.[9] Africanus witnessed Bardaisan himself perform artistic feats with a bow and arrow, drawing the image of a man on a shield with his shots: '[Bardaisan] took pride in having combined the art of painting with the use of the bow, an artist who paints with arrows, and an archer who shoots pictures.'[10]

Early testimonies in Syriac, Greek, and Armenian describe a royal or public archive at the centre of Edessa, where pronouncements and legal and historical documents were deposited.[11] Julius Africanus consulted these archives while there, according to the Armenian historian Moses of Khoren: '[Africanus] transcribed everything from the charters of the archive of Edessa, that is Urha, which concerned the history of our [Armenian] kings. These books had been transported there from Nisibis and from the temple histories of Sinope in Pontus. Let no one doubt this, for we have seen that archive with our own eyes.'[12] Eusebius of Caesarea claims he had access to the archive via a Greek translation of the famous Jesus–Abgar correspondence in Syriac.[13] The *Chronicle of Edessa to 540* mentions the archive and was perhaps based on earlier patriographical chronicles with access to the archive.[14] Overall the archive attests a certain self-awareness in Edessa, the pride of the dynasty, and intellectual traditions, partly Mesopotamian in origin, that privileged the accumulation and preservation of knowledge. Perhaps the clearest example of the Edessan archive as an institution, in memory as much as in fact, is its central role in the *Doctrina Addai*, a legendary fifth-century account of the conversion of Edessa (in the first century CE). Not only does this text describe its own deposition in the archive, but its stated 'witness', Hanan (Ananias), was himself the chief archivist of the city.[15] Thus, the archive as an institution, and institutionalised practice in Syriac Edessa, becomes enmeshed with the Christian framework of the city's embellished history.

---

[8] On Africanus and Edessa, see Adler 2017.

[9] The names of Edessa's kings (Abgar, Waʾel, Maʿnu, etc.) are of Iranian, Arab, and Nabatean origin; see Segal 1982.

[10] Julius Africanus, *Kesti* F12.20.35–47 (Wallraff et al. 2012: 102–3).

[11] On the archives of Edessa, see Debié 2015: 166–73; Debié 2000.

[12] Julius Africanus, *Chronographiae* T88 (Wallraff et al. 2007: 260–61).

[13] This was Abgar V Ukkama 'the Black' (r. 4 BC–7 CE and 13–50 CE). Elsewhere, Eusebius shows little awareness of Syriac Christianity; see Brock 1992. Ramelli makes the suggestion that Bardaisan himself was responsible for the consolidation of the Abgar–Jesus legend as later reported by Eusebius (2009b: 263–73 and passim).

[14] See Debié 2015: 527–29; Witakowski 1984.

[15] Ed. and trans. Howard 1981. See *GEDSH* 9–10 (s.v. 'Addai, Teaching of', by T. S. Wardle).

Bardaisan's *Book of the Laws of the Countries*

Bardaisan of Edessa was the pre-eminent Syriac author in the early period.[16] He was acknowledged as a major intellect by later Christian writers, even though they were all hostile to him in varying degrees.[17] Ephrem the Syrian wrote against him in his *Prose Refutations* and in his *Hymns against Heresies*.[18] Many reports of his life and thought survive and extend well into the medieval period in Greek, Latin, Syriac, Armenian, and Arabic.[19] As noted, he wrote in both prose and verse.[20] In addition to the *Book of the Laws of the Countries*, he is assigned the following works by later accounts: a treatise 'Against Fate' (Κατὰ εἱμαρμένης) addressed to the emperor Antoninus (probably Marcus Aurelius),[21] 150 Hymns/Psalms (in imitation of David),[22] a treatise against the Marcionites,[23] a 'Book of the Mysteries' that was later used by Mani for his work of the same name,[24] a work 'On Domnus' against the Platonists (against which Ephrem wrote a treatise of his own),[25] a work on India (derived from an embassy to the emperor Elagabalus *c.* 220 CE),[26] and a history of the Armenians (drawing on Armenian archives at Ani).[27] According to Epiphanius of Salamis in the fourth century, Bardaisan knew both Syriac and Greek, though most scholars today agree that his writings began in Syriac.[28]

---

[16] The scholarship on Bardaisan is substantial. For authoritative modern treatments, of diverse interpretation, see Drijvers 1966; Teixidor 1992; Possekel 2007; 2018; Camplani 1998a; 1998b; 2003; Skjaervø 1988; Ramelli 2009a. An excellent succinct survey of scholarship and ancient *testimonia* can be found in Possekel 2012: 515–21.

[17] A good overview of the reception of Bardaisan in Syriac is offered in Possekel 2018.

[18] *Prose Refutations*: standard edition and translation by Mitchell 1912–21; *Hymns against Heresies*: new translation and study by Ruani 2018.

[19] See Drijvers 1966: 166–212; Camplani 1998b; Ramelli 2009a.

[20] The basic scope of his corpus is given in Brock et al. 2011: 56–57 (s.v. 'Bardaiṣan of Edessa', by S. P. Brock), but the evidence for each of these works, sometimes meagre, is analysed in detail in Drijvers 1966; Ramelli 2009a. Medieval Arabic writers knew the names of works which do not appear elsewhere and claimed that Bardesanites survived into their times along the Silk Road: Skjaervø 1988. See the succinct account of evidence for individual works, esp. prose, in Andrade 2020.

[21] See Ramelli 2009b.

[22] See Drijvers 1966: 165; Teixidor 1992: 112–13; Ruani 2018: xxix–xxx.

[23] See Drijvers 1966: 170; Briquel-Chatonnet and Debié 2017: 51.

[24] See Drijvers 1966: 163; Teixidor 1992: 102–5.   [25] See Drijvers 1966: 163–65.

[26] See Ramelli 2009a: 58–59, 108–9; Drijvers 1966: 173–75; Biffi 2011; Winter 1999. Cf. Andrade 2020: 296–97.

[27] See Drijvers 1966: 15–16, 207–9; and Ramelli 2009a: 253–87, where she attempts to connect Moses of Khoren's account of Bardaisan to the Abgar Legend, the *Acts of Thomas*, and the *Doctrina Addai*.

[28] Epiphanius: Drijvers 1966: 177–78.

His works were translated into Greek by his students according to the testimonies of Eusebius and others. Later tradition claimed that he was ordained, either as a deacon or priest, and that he apostatised either to paganism or to the Valentinians later in life.[29] The later reports about his biography, while intriguing, should nevertheless be considered spurious given his infamy as a heretic, a reputation which was already current by the fourth century.

The *Book of the Laws of the Countries* is the only work attributed to Bardaisan to have survived in full.[30] It survives whole in a single manuscript of the seventh century, combined with a number of other philosophical works.[31] The title represents the second half of this two-part work. The first half is a literary dialogue in the Platonic mode, debating whether human lives are determined by the stars.[32] The second half is a semi-ethnography or anthropological survey of foreign customs, anecdotal evidence which Bardaisan uses to prove the philosophical argument that human lives are not fully determined.

At the beginning of the work, initiating the dialogue, Bardaisan's interlocutor, Awida, asks, why God did not create humans so that they could not sin?[33] Bardaisan responds with a long argument to the following effect. If man were created not to sin, he would merely be an instrument. Man is created after the image of God. God's goodness is displayed in giving humanity more liberty than all other created things, except for the angels, who also have free will. Those who have carried out the will of their Lord in their free will 'have been raised up and sanctified and have received great gifts. For everyone who exists, needs God in everything, nor is there any limit to his gifts.'[34] Man is not accused because of how he is created but

---

[29] Brock 1971.
[30] See the new French translation and commentary by Poirier and Créghur 2020. As noted below, the work was written by his student Philip, who appears in the dialogue. Most recent scholarship affirms that it is representative of his thought, while allowing room for revisions made by later followers (Camplani 1998a; 2003; cf. Ehlers 1970).
[31] BL, Add. MS 14,658: Wright 1870–72: 3.1154–60. Daniel King associates this manuscript with so-called Origenists of the sixth century, for whom these pagan philosophical texts – including the work of the Syriac philosopher Sergius of Resh'ayna – served to support their school of cosmology: King 2011.
[32] For the literary context of late antique dialogues in Greek and Syriac, see Rigolio 2019: esp. 51–57.
[33] Ramelli (2009a: 59) observes that the emperor Elagabalus' original Roman name was Varius Avitus and suggests that 'Awida' may be a transliteration of Avitus into Syriac. There are no other indications that this is the case, and a reference to Elagabalus (r. 218–22) would place the *Book of the Laws of the Countries* at the very end of Bardaisan's life. Regardless, Awida is a literary device, a philosophy student who serves the dramatic situation for Bardaisan (= Socrates), the master.
[34] Drijvers 1965: 14–15.

through his actions. Riches, honour, pain, poverty, etc., all depend on Fate and things happen against human desire. But just as Fate disorders nature, human liberty 'forces back and disorders Fate'.

The second half of the work, an investigation of the habits of different cultures, proves this philosophical conclusion to be true, in Bardaisan's mind. In broad strokes, Bardaisan says 'Chaldean astronomers' claimed that human lives are determined by the seven stars (i.e., seven planets, including the sun and moon) and their horoscopes. Bardaisan describes the customs of around twenty different societies, offering evidence that people behave contrary to astrological or climatological expectations. He claims that the Chaldeans invented the climates to bolster their own fallacy. There is a long-standing East–West dialectic at work here. The original Eastern view is (taken to be) that stars determine human lives. The Platonic retort, present already in Carneades (second century BCE), is the conflict between foreign customs (the venerable νόμιμα βαρβαρικά argument). The Chaldean response is the system of climates (κλίματα). Bardaisan's response, in turn, is that even cultures in the same climates have different customs and laws.[35]

Proceeding from the East and moving West towards Edessa, he discusses the Seres ('the people of silk', i.e., the Chinese), the Indians, the Persians, the Geli, and the Bactrians.[36] When he comes to Edessa, the tone of the catalogue shifts, and he discusses individual places, in his region, rather than peoples per se, Edessa and Hatra in particular. He then treats the various punishments for theft among the Romans, the peoples 'East of the Euphrates', and then the distinctive marriage customs of, in turn, 'the Orientals', the Britons, the Parthians, and the Amazonians. He then surveys, from the so-called Book of the Chaldeans, the various people-groups who 'lack the Muses'.

In the whole region of the Tayites, of the Saracens, in Upper Libya, among the Mauretanians, in the country of the Numidians, which lies at the mouth of the Oceanus, in Outer Germany, in Upper Sarmatia, in Spain, in all the countries to the North of Pontus, in the whole region of the Alanians, among the Albanians, and among the Sasaye in Brusa, which lies across the Duru, no one see sculptors, or painters, or perfumers, or money-changers, or poets.[37]

---

[35] Ramelli 2009a: 56 and passim.
[36] See the excellent article by Nathanael Andrade (2020) for an assessment of Bardaisan's ethnographic knowledge, which he esteems as quite minimal but nevertheless connected in interesting ways to broader East–West pathways of knowledge transmission in the second and third centuries CE.
[37] Drijvers 1965: 50–51.

The *Book of the Laws of the Countries* is usually cited as an example of ancient ethnography, but it is not a standard, distanced ethnographical treatise. Bardaisan's primary interest is in what stars can do to people, that is, in the concept of astral determinism, which he rejects. Nevertheless, he is not unaware of theories of geography and he claims that the Chaldeans invented the seven climates to bolster their fallacy of astral determinism. This quote about the peoples who 'lack the Muses' is, for him, proof of this theory because, even in their own books, the Chaldeans claim that people in different climates lack an acquaintance with the arts. In other words, the stars would have produced more consistent patterns of culture across the *oikoumenê*. This is not to say that Bardaisan believes in patterns of culture, just that he claims the Chaldeans were self-contradictory. While the search for knowledge is, in part, the search for causes of phenomena, true knowledge transcends phenomena, and God's law is the only true cause.

At the end of the second half of the *Book of the Laws of the Countries*, Bardaisan offers the strongest argument against determinism he can muster, that is, the Jews: 'They keep to the law laid upon them by their fathers.'

> Everywhere they are, they do not worship the idols and on one day in the week they and their children let all work rest, they do not build and do not travel, they do not buy and do not sell. Neither do they kill any animal on the sabbath, light any fire, or give judgment. And among them there is found no one who is charged by Fate to go to law and gain his suit on the sabbath or to do the same and have it against him, or to pull down his house or build it up again, or to do a single one of those things which all people do who have not received this law. They have other precepts also, through which they lead a life different from that of other people, although on this day they too beget children, are born, fall ill and die, for over these things man has no power.[38]

He appears to know the basic tenets of the Jewish faith and approves of them. This may reflect a personal interaction with Jews in Edessa, which were by most accounts numerous.[39]

In between his discussion of Jews and Christians, Bardaisan turns to local affairs in Edessa. He notes that Abgar VIII, 'when he had come to the faith', forbade self-castration by citizens who worshipped the Syrian goddess Atargatis.

---

[38] Drijvers 1965: 58–59.

[39] Jews may have constituted as much as 10 per cent of the population of Edessa around 100 CE and probably increased in number through the second century: Briquel-Chatonnet and Debié 2017: 34. Cf. Segal 1970: 41–43; Drijvers 1984b.

In Syria and Edessa there was the custom of self-emasculation in honor of Tar'ata [i.e., Atargatis], but when king Abgar had come to the faith, he ordered that every man who emasculated himself should have his hand chopped off. And from that day to this no one emasculates himself in the territory of Edessa.[40]

Abgar's 'faith' has sometimes been read as implying a conversion to Christianity, but this is not manifest in the text, as will be discussed further below. Suffice it to say that, whatever Abgar's belief was, Bardaisan considers it to be a positive change and it serves his greater purpose of showing the mutability of local law and customs.

Before closing the treatise, Bardaisan points to the Christians, among whom he places himself.

What shall we say of the new people of us Christians, that the Messiah has caused to arise in every place and in all climates by his coming. For behold, we all, wherever we may be, are called Christians after the one name of the Messiah ... The local laws cannot force them to give up the law of their Messiah, nor does the Fate of the Guiding Signs force them to do things that are unclean for them.[41]

Bardaisan is a firm monotheist and aligns himself with the Christians, over, for instance, the Marcionites (against whom, as mentioned, he wrote a whole treatise, now lost).

The idea of horoscopes as determinative is obviously not new in the Roman period, nor limited to Chaldeans or Persians. Nor, indeed, is the idea of free will. Bardaisan's arguments for free will are aimed at the astrologers but could also relate to an anti-gnostic agenda, which is shared by other early Syriac texts, notably the *Acts of Thomas*.[42] Nevertheless, the compromise Bardaisan offers is interesting, if anecdotal: circumstances are determined by Fate but human actions can disrupt the negative outcomes of Fate or mitigate their effects. Bardaisan shows acquaintance with Hellenistic thought and at times favours a Stoic ethic. However, overall he is anti-Stoic in the sense that he applauds active resistance to evil or negative circumstances.[43] Narratively, his disagreement is specifically with local 'magians', Chaldean astronomers, who were seemingly competing with the followers of Bardaisan in Edessa.

Bardaisan's ethical arguments cannot be divorced from his metaphysics. Indeed, in that sense he sits squarely in the field of Platonic philosophy. Unfortunately, the *Book of the Laws of the Countries* gives us precious

---

[40] Drijvers 1965: 58–59.   [41] Drijvers 1965: 58–61.

[42] Drijvers (1966) insists that Bardaisan is anti-gnostic, but this conclusion is disputed: see Ehlers 1970.

[43] There is ambiguity on this point in Stoic thought, which comes through in Bardaisan: see Teixidor 1992: 90.

little concrete detail. It does not represent a *summa* of his thought. To gain any purchase, we must sift the hostile witnesses from later centuries who had more of his works than we do and who engaged his followers.[44] Without doubt his cosmology was not dogmatically Christian, taking cues instead from Greco-Roman and Mesopotamian traditions. He claims four elements: earth, water, fire, and light; light is mixed with darkness, but darkness (equated with evil) is not an active force. In opposition to the Marcionite and Gnostic systems, God is not at all responsible for the existence of evil, even indirectly or through a secondary god. Matter was originally pure and under the control of God, and its corruption was due to an accident, 'the cosmic fall'.[45] The seven stars are beings created by God, though they do not have the free will that humans and angels have, because they run their course as determined. Ephrem acknowledged Bardaisan's arguments about evil and on this basis made a distinction between Bardaisan and Mani, though he still condemned Bardaisan as an astrologer.[46] (For himself, Bardaisan in the *Book of the Laws of the Countries* claims to have rejected astrology.) Nevertheless, the differentiation between these groups even in a hostile writer like Ephrem is telling – it shows Ephrem's discretion, but it also shows there were recognisable differences between Bardaisan and others in the religious marketplace of third-century (and fourth-century) Edessa.[47] The Greek tradition generally lumps Bardaisan

---

[44] Systematising Bardaisan's cosmology on the basis of later hostile sources is fraught, but the attempt has been made several times. Skjaervø (1988) offers a useful and succinct overview, though views him as a gnostic (in line with Ehlers 1970). For an attempt to distinguish between what is Bardaisan's thought and what belongs to his followers, see Camplani 2003. In many cases, it seems that ideas negatively attributed to Bardaisan were subsequent elaborations, including perhaps, according to Camplani, parts of the *Book of the Laws of the Countries* itself. Ephrem recognised that a distinction needed to be made between Bardaisan and Bardesanites: Drijvers 1966: 143.

[45] Camplani 2003: esp. 49.

[46] There is an unnecessary conflation between Bardaisan and Mani in later sources, though not in Ephrem. Mani used Bardaisan but also criticised him as not being dualistic enough. As Manichaeism became more of an opponent in Christian circles, Bardaisan became tainted by it: see Ramelli 2009a: 53–54. Ephrem is adamant that the word 'being' (*'ityā*), which Bardaisan uses for the stars and other created things, should be reserved for God alone (Drijvers 1966: 134). *Ousia* is one Greek equivalent of the word, so perhaps the influence of Nicaea is at play; the plural *ousiai* would have been highly problematic. On the terminology of 'beings' in the *Book of the Laws of the Countries*, see below. See also Johnson 2021.

[47] It is still debated whether Ephrem presents an accurate picture of Bardaisan, despite the fact that he describes Bardaisan's ideas in some detail. Ephrem certainly had books attributed to Bardaisan in front of him and he quotes from them, especially the hymns. What these books were and how they relate to the *Book of the Laws of the Countries* remain open questions. Some of these works were undoubtedly by his followers: see Camplani 2003. The Greek tradition is much less informed than Ephrem: see Drijvers 1966: 183–85.

in with other heretics, Mani and Valentinus among them, and does not have a clear understanding of his teaching, even though Eusebius (among others) had Greek translations of some of Bardaisan's works in front of him.

Recent scholarship sees Bardaisan as effectively Christian: for instance, Ramelli via his connections to Origen's thought, Camplani through a (probable but unattested) Christian school at Edessa which Bardaisan may have led (apart from the church), and Possekel because of his demonstrable acquaintance with Christian theology.[48] Above all, Bardaisan's self-identification as a Christian suggests two things: first, a Christian presence in Edessa around 200 CE and, second, a flexibility with regard to that label. An important element often disregarded by scholars is that this work, like some other early Syriac texts, is directed to a literate elite interested in speculative questions expressed in Hellenistic genres. Africanus' portrait of Bardaisan at the court of Abgar VIII is a reminder of this setting.[49] Later critics, notably Ephrem, were not a part of that social world, were not invested in these topics or genres, and, understandably, saw the whole package as foreign to their scriptural and liturgical Christianity. In other words, locating Christianity in the *Book of the Laws of the Countries* may be a problem hinging less on doctrine than on audience, tone, and language.

Belief, Argument, and Free Will

At the beginning of the *Book of the Laws of the Countries*, Bardaisan makes statements about how and why people remain convinced or unconvinced by his argument. As the dialogue progresses, these reflections become intertwined with the cosmology in the background of his treatise. (As noted above, his cosmology is never systematically presented in the *Book of the Laws of the Countries*.) In form, Bardaisan's reflections appear in the guise of similar arguments over philosophical warrant in Plato's dialogues. The theological terminology and philosophical mode he employs thus mingle with the cosmological background and, consequently, the anthropological evidence he marshals in the second half of the treatise is framed by a religious model of creation and belief. This corresponds to the two genres chosen: the dialogue and the catalogue. While we can see clearly the division

---

[48] E.g., Ramelli 2009a; Camplani 1998b (with Camplani 2009); Possekel 2007, 2012.
[49] On the question of 'elite' Christians in Edessa and what that term might entail for their specific historical context, see Adler 2017.

of labour in content, it must be remembered that these genres arrive with their own expectations for writer and reader alike.

In his opening engagement with Awida and the other students, Bardaisan makes clear that most of his interlocutors already believe what he is about to argue – including Philip, who signals through the use of the first person that he is the author (or compiler) of the dialogue.[50] His chief interlocutor, Awida, is the 'one who will not believe (ܠܡܗܝܡܢܘ ܠܐ ܨ ܕ)', but, out of apparent generosity to his student, Bardaisan says there are many others for whom 'faith (ܗܝܡܢܘܬܐ) is not in them'.[51] He continues, 'There are many people who have no faith (ܗܝܡܢܘܬܐ) and so have not obtained the knowledge of true wisdom (ܚܟܡܬܐ)', and further, 'nor have they hope (ܬܘܟܠܢܐ) as a basis on which to cherish hope (ܡܣܒܪܝܢ)'.[52] Regarding Awida's opening question about why God did not create humanity so as not to sin, Bardaisan says, 'Not so did God in his goodness will to create man, but through liberty he raised him above many creatures and made him equal to the angels.'[53] The created things that lack liberty are 'instruments of God's infallible wisdom' (i.e., the sun, the moon, the ocean, the mountains, the winds). 'Instruments' here should be read as 'mere instruments' because they are placed lower than free beings.

Wisdom is the creative force, and humans, some themselves possessing wisdom, are created in the 'image of God'.[54] There is, therefore, already a connection at the beginning of the dialogue between human knowledge, creation, and God's sovereign will. Bardaisan immediately then makes the distinction between those parts of creation who are given the ability to believe, in their freedom or 'liberty' (ܚܐܪܘܬܐ), and those that are not.

---

[50] Drijvers 1965: 14–15. Besides Awida and Philip the only other individuals mentioned are Bar Jamma (Drijvers 1965: 26–27), a fellow student with Philip, and 'our brother' Shemashgram in whose house the dialogue is set (Drijvers 1965: 4–5). Drijvers suggests that Bar Jamma could be a reference to Marcion as 'Son of the Sea' (1966: 82–83).

[51] Drijvers 1965: 8–9. Poirier 2002 makes a semantic distinction in such passages between 'belief' and 'to believe' in Syriac, based upon the Greek πίστις and πιστεύειν. The suggestion is attractive on the background of the literature of 'persuasion' that he cites, but it does not hold within the internal logic of the text, which depends on the semantic equivalence of these words.

[52] 'Hope' (ܬܘܟܠܢܐ) – really, 'trust' or 'confidence' – paired with the root sbr, the standard root for 'hope'.

[53] Drijvers 1965: 10–11. Cf. pp. 14–15: 'We understand well, that if angels had not possessed free will, they would not have had intercourse with the daughters of men, they would not have sinned, and would not have fallen from their state' (cf. Gen 6:4).

[54] Image of God: Drijvers 1965: 24–25. It is not surprising that wisdom (ܚܟܡܬܐ = σοφία) is the creative force. Not only are there deep Jewish roots for the idea but it shows up in, among other places, Middle Platonism, Gnosticism, and Manichaeism, and it becomes a christological dogma in later trinitarian thought. Its importance here is in relation to the specific image of God's sovereignty that Bardaisan presents.

Humans and angels both have the freedom to believe, but this is purely a gift from God to certain created things:

> It will be made clear to you, therefore, that God's goodness (ܛܒܘܬܗ) to man is great in giving him more liberty than to all those natural objects (ܐܣܛܘܟܣܐ) we have spoken of. Through this liberty he justifies himself, leads his life divinely, and is associated with the angels, who also possess a free will of their own.[55]

The turn in the argument here is from the freedom to believe in his philosophical demonstration to the freedom to act justly according to God's law.

Bardaisan says that the 'natural objects' are servants of humanity because they lack liberty. These are called various things throughout the treatise. The Syriac words are as follows: ܪܝܫܐ, ܡܕܒܪܢܐ, ܐܝܬܐ, ܐܣܛܘܟܣܐ. The standard modern translation, that of H. J. W. Drijvers, translates them using different English words depending on the context, sometimes using the same English word or phrase for two in Syriac: thus, 'substances' or 'elemental substances' (ܐܝܬܐ); 'components of nature' or 'natural objects' or 'elements' (ܐܣܛܘܟܣܐ = the Syriac transliteration of Greek στοιχεῖα, 'elements'); 'guiding signs' (ܡܕܒܪܢܐ and ܐܣܛܘܟܣܐ); and 'rulers' (ܪܝܫܐ and ܫܠܝܛܐ). Scholars have attempted to make distinctions between these concepts in analysing Bardaisan's cosmology, based in part on reports of Bardaisan's thought in later hostile refutations (Ephrem above all).[56] However, on the sole basis of the *Book of the Laws of the Countries* it is difficult to find any nuance between them.

It should be emphasised that the basic principle underlying the concepts is shared: unlike humanity, the 'natural objects' do not have free will, but they nevertheless have direct and active effects on human lives. The (delimited) power that these substances have over humanity is what Bardaisan calls Fate. 'For that which is called Fate [by the Chaldeans] (ܚܠܩܐ) is really the fixed course determined by God for the rulers (ܫܠܝܛܐ) and the Guiding Signs (ܐܣܛܘܟܣܐ).'[57] The 'fixed course' does not completely determine the lives of humans and angels because the latter have been given the gift of freedom. The sovereign ability to make distinct these two categories of creation is the power of the one God: 'For he who has power

---

[55] Drijvers 1965: 12–13.
[56] E.g., Teixidor 1992: 80–81, 106–7. Teixidor is more negative than others on Ephrem's comprehension of Bardaisan's thought. For the context of these terms in Ephrem's critique of Bardaisan, see Possekel 1999: 117–26.
[57] Drijvers 1965: 32–33. In this passage, Bardaisan claims that fate is responsible for 'whenever nature is deflected from her true course', i.e., for negative experiences in life, though that observation does not bear itself out through his whole argument, in which, for the most part, Fate simply produces the natural circumstances of life, whether good or bad.

over everything is One.'[58] Fate is a real thing that has real effects principally because God, who has perfect freedom and power, has ordained it to be so, acting through the medium of these 'natural objects' which run in fixed courses. Their fixity is their limitation. Fate thus has its role in determining the course of human life, but humans are not absolutely constrained by it because they are 'free beings' (ܒܢܝ ܚܐܪܐ) with power of their own (ܫܘܠܛܢܐ).[59]

The language in the *Book of the Laws of the Countries* is not as precise as we would like. Bardaisan uses different terms for concepts that are effectively the same. This results in Drijvers' translation, for example, attempting to distinguish them in context through various renderings. The key element, as stated above, is that the connection is established at the beginning between first principles – here, the will to believe (or have 'faith') – and the freedom granted by God to act justly according to his commandments. For certain, there is an admixture of Stoicism here, that is, to respond to the (limited) constraints of Fate through right action and 'hope'.[60]

The proof of this argument, which buoys the trust of those with the will to believe, is the second half of the treatise, where the anthropological evidence of the laws and customs of various peoples is laid out. Awida interjects that he is convinced from 'the exposition you [Bardaisan] have given' that humans do not sin because they are constrained to do so by their own natures. But he asks for proof that they do not do so 'under the influence of Fate and destiny'.[61] This is a significant shift by Bardaisan's interlocutor because it refocuses his initial question towards the 'ability to believe' argument that Bardaisan has maintained from the beginning. Once again, in a Platonic mode, Bardaisan is tasked with specifically combatting the views of the Chaldean astrologers. This time he shifts genres and turns to the catalogue.

The basic outlines of the catalogue have been given above. It will be enough to show that the language of belief is continued through this section. Above all, the statement about Abgar's changes to the local laws of Edessa is highly significant. Abgar 'came to the faith' (ܗܝܡܢ) and changed the local custom of emasculation – which is specifically assigned to religious observance of the goddess Tar'ata (Atargatis) – and instituted a law

---

[58] Drijvers 1965: 28–29. [59] Drijvers 1965: 24–25.
[60] See especially the comments on how individuals' evil actions trouble their minds, souls, and bodies: Drijvers 1965: 18–21. By contrast, 'The peace that is in a good conscience, founded on good hope, is one thing, and the impassivity belonging to the debility of disease, based on unsound hope [i.e., unbelief], is another' (Drijvers 1965: 20–21).
[61] Drijvers 1965: 38–39.

against it.[62] The root of 'believed' (*hmn*) is the same as what was used in the opening of the dialogue and throughout to signal the free will of humanity, first to believe his argument against fate and, by logical extension, to act freely in upholding the commandments of God.

The question of whether this means Abgar became a Christian is secondary. Instead, the point is that he is a living example of someone who acted upon the gift of God and effected change in the dominant culture around him. It is not a stretch to say that Bardaisan is offering a reverse *speculum principis* and thereby encouraging his students to act freely, and to 'believe', in the way that Abgar has done. Abgar, the only ruler singled out in the entire treatise, becomes the paradigm of Bardaisan's demonstration on behalf of free will, which began as a reflection on first principles. The ability to believe in rational argument – at least in Bardaisan's schema – is made visceral by appeal to a living figure who acted in accordance with belief and, in the end, worked against the dominant (as in 'fated', according to the Chaldeans) custom of the locality.

That Abgar, when he instituted a law against Atargatis' emasculation, is acting in accordance with the 'wisdom of God', the 'image of God', and the 'goodness of God' (in making humans free) should not be in doubt. This is the culmination of the entire treatise and reiterates Bardaisan's language throughout. Whether Abgar was or was not personally a Christian is not a question that is answered by this 'belief' alone – after all, 'belief' or 'faith' here is the assent to the proposition that God gave free will and then, by extension, the free acting upon that will in choosing God's commands. The specific religious background of those commands is not given. Nevertheless, a hint towards Abgar's Christianity is the fact that Bardaisan places him between the Jews and the Christians, among whom he also (significantly) locates himself. Narratively, the Christians are the culmination of the treatise because Bardaisan ends the *Book of the Laws of the Countries* with them. But, structurally and epistemologically, the culmination of the treatise is Abgar VIII, who is a living example between the two groups Bardaisan praises most highly. Bardaisan agrees with the king's local

---

[62] Drijvers 1965: 58–59. Atargatis, the famous Dea Syria, a Mesopotamian goddess of fertility, was mainly associated with Hierapolis/Mabbug but was also worshipped in Edessa. On her cult, see Drijvers 1980: 76–121, esp. 121: 'She was the goddess of the life-giving springs near the citadel [of Edessa], where she had her temple. She was the Tyche of the city, where she had her priests and begging *galli* and was worshipped with ecstatic music and tremendous noise. Although her cult at Edessa may have been influenced by her center at Hierapolis, it certainly belonged to the most authentic traditions of the city, which was founded close to her life-giving wells at a safe place in Northern Mesopotamia.'

intervention and associates it with the pinnacle examples of his anthropological catalogue, the Jews and Christians.

Conclusion

As a means for organising knowledge, the *Book of the Laws of the Countries* shows familiarity with the ancient literary modes of the dialogue and the catalogue. Bardaisan does not catalogue the nations of the earth as a geographical exercise or to fill out a mental map, and in that sense it hardly matters whether his mental cartography is complete or not. The anecdotal customs of various peoples serve as examples of the philosophical assertion, from the first part of the treatise, that humanity is ultimately not determined by anything, whether that be a sinful nature or horoscopy.

The question arises then, why use a catalogue of nations to prove the point? A general answer would be that lists and catalogues, particularly of the cartographical realm, were part and parcel of literature in this period.[63] Poems such as Aratus' *Phaenomena*, from the Hellenistic period, and that of Dionysius Periegetes, from the Roman, were widely read and imitated during the Second Sophistic and late antiquity. Pausanias' prose survey of all of Greece is roughly contemporary with Bardaisan and shows a defined structure of movement over the Greek mainland based around hub cities. As noted, Bardaisan organises his catalogue around cities when he gets to his own region. Later, more loosely structured geographical works, such as pilgrimage texts or Cosmas Indicopleustes' *Christian Topography*, survey the *oikoumenê* through journeys, imitating classical *itineraria* and *periploi*.[64] Open-ended fictional works such as the *Alexander Romance* or *Barlaam and Joasaph*, which were recycled in various languages, religions, and cultures, retain an even looser geographical structure.

A more specific, functional answer as to why use a catalogue would perhaps be that it is flexible enough to allow him to include variegated data with no apparent narrative structure.[65] This literary device is common in compilatory literature. The subject matter discussed in the second half of

---

[63] I explore this realm of literature in Johnson 2016.

[64] On this point, see the detailed discussion in Johnson 2016: chs. 1–2.

[65] Ramelli (2009a: 96–101) argues that the second half of the *Book of the Laws of the Countries* imitates a cross, proceeding east to west. She adduces the fragments of Bardaisan's *de India* in Porphyry, which describe an Indian statue in a cave with a cruciform pose. The statue is a combination macro- and micro-cosmos in which the whole of creation and human endeavour are depicted. She detects echoes of Plato's *Timaeus*.

the *Book of the Laws of the Countries* varies considerably, from general descriptions of peoples, to specific marriage laws, to larger legal systems, to the vicissitudes of circumcision depending on the ruling culture, and, in the Jews' case, the refusal to abide by local laws at all when in conflict with their own God-given law. The catalogue form serves as a container that in itself becomes an argument for the relatedness and reliability of this disparate information. The mass of examples is the bulwark, regardless of their internal structure.

The two halves of the work are strange bedfellows, and, to my knowledge, no other example of this combination exists in ancient literature.[66] The *Book of the Laws of the Countries* is unique in the canon of Syriac literature and is at least highly innovative, if not equally unique, within the canon of surviving Greco-Roman literature. As argued above, the catalogue as deployed – and as a literary form on its own – is in many ways the culmination of the argument against fatalism and astrology.[67] This is most evident in the person of Abgar whose logical prominence in the catalogue is demonstrated by the language of belief and by his placement between the descriptions of the Jews and Christians. The catalogue offers proof through its compilation that many different and varied examples can be adduced to support Bardaisan's position. While Bardaisan's cosmology is not explained in a systematic manner, he is adept at connecting the language of belief with observation, and his meditation on creation and free will at the beginning of the treatise is maintained and manipulated throughout, in order to lead his interlocutor, Awida, towards asking the right questions about why exactly astral determinism is incorrect. Modern readers often prefer the dialogue half because it offers insight into Bardaisan's metaphysical terminology and larger system of thought. However, the treatise is a whole and is clearly meant to be read as a single work. The uniqueness of the *Book of the Laws of the Countries* is found in its organisation of knowledge across two different modes of writing joined together to perform the task of a unified argument about fate, free will, and belief.

---

[66] Outside of, at a stretch, Plato's *Timaeus*, where anthropological examples bolster the creation narrative. Later hexaemeral ('six-day creation') texts serve both exegetical and cataloguing purposes. On hexaemeral literature in Syriac, see ten Napel 1987 and Jansma 1959.

[67] Even within the first part of the *Book of the Laws of the Countries*, shorter and more generalised anthropological catalogues are offered: Drijvers 1965: 24–25, 30–31.

8 | Iamblichus on Divination and Prophecy

PETER T. STRUCK

Introduction

Scholars have worked on links between Christians and Neoplatonists with some care. Often these studies look at questions of influence, and when they do, they are mostly positioned to uncover influences in one direction, from the Neoplatonists and other philosophical schools towards Christian thinkers – whether a scholar sees a Greek idea shaping a Christian one, or being remade by Christians for their own ends. I myself have claimed that accounts of the Eucharist were influenced by theories of pagan theurgy, and a figure like Pseudo-Dionysius the Areopagite seems positively to invite consideration of how Neoplatonists set terms of thinking for some pivotal figures in the history of Christian theology.[1] But rarer is a study that looks for influences from Christian thinkers on pagan philosophers. For starters, there seems to be a chronological impediment, first comes paganism, then comes Christianity. But this concern is of course specious, given that a half millennium of intellectual ferment intercedes between Paul and Olympiodorus and that none of the figures from this period operates from our vantage and the teleology it might assume. When one starts to look, it seems reasonable to think that one will find possible avenues, maybe many of them. For example, I am not aware of a good explanation for why the *Timaeus* vaults into prime importance for later Platonists. Could it be in answer to the raised salience of the intellectual question of creation, a Christian focal point that rarely engaged earlier Greek philosophers?

In this chapter, I would like to follow up on a suggestion that I made in a recent book that traces the history of ideas about divination in classical antiquity.[2] There, in looking at the Neoplatonist Iamblichus, I was struck by the innovations he brought to the topic, as compared with his classical antecedents. Parallels to Christian thinkers were striking. I will take up that

I thank Lewis Ayres, Matthew Crawford, and the participants of the Rome Seminar on 'Modes of Knowing and the Ordering of Knowledge in Early Christianity' for stimulating conversation in the summer of 2018, and David Runia for very helpful observations.

[1] Struck 2001.   [2] Struck 2016.

topic again here, proceeding in three parts: some background on classical divination; consideration of Origen; and then consideration of Iamblichus. This debate brings to the fore a distinctive quality of late antique epistemology. Classical philosophers were strict in placing claims for knowledge within the domain of rationality alone. Though they allowed a para-rational capacity for hunches about what awaits one in the near future, there is no embrace of a transrational mode of knowledge acquisition. The late-antique thinkers considered here had a more robust expectation of modes of knowing outside of rationality, even expecting that it could yield the most profound insights it is possible for humans to have.

Greek Divination

Since classical divination is not widely discussed beyond specialist circles, some background will be useful. Divination is a name for a disparate group of modes by which knowledge otherwise impossible to gain is precipitated in a human subject. This knowledge, which could be of the past, present, or future, derives from the interpretation of signs. They may be external signs, that are either chanced upon (like the flights of birds) or purposefully produced (like sacrificial entrails), or internal, in which case the human subject becomes the medium through which a sign is delivered, in the form of sneezes (and other behaviours not consciously controlled), speech acts (cledonomancy, oracles), or visions passively received when asleep or awake. Both internal and external signs then become targets of hermeneutics. In the classical tradition, the information yielded by divination pertains to a proximate future in the form of tactical advice about procuring a discrete outcome. It was not a source of insight on broader questions of theology or cosmology.

The phenomenon has provoked many studies over the years, two types of which are common. One sees scholars build a context for it in social history. The oracle of Delphi and others of high stature had vast cultural authority which extended even beyond the Greeks. They played an important role in advising in affairs of great interest to states, including in matters of war, peace, and colonisation. In these scholarly studies, divination is typically seen as a means for the elite to harness the power of the divine voice to manipulate the masses for their own ends. This positioning neglects the fact that nearly all ancients, elites and masses alike, thought divination worked. And it also neglects the fact that divination was thought to be just as useful in matters of personal and even intimate concern – providing advice to both meek and powerful on the likely success of business deals, personal travel, or alliances in marriage – in none of which cases is the question of manipulation pertinent.

The other type of study places divination in the history of magic. Magic was a common practice in Greek and Roman antiquity. It was at the same time highly socially stigmatised and marginalised. Magic was an occult and underhanded business that brought shame to those involved. That said, our best estimate is that everyone, at least once in their lives, and maybe more often, would find themselves in a situation difficult enough to warrant employing the services of a magician, even though it was not something one admitted in polite company.[3] Just on these grounds the problem with the pairing 'magic and divination' – to be found in the titles of articles, books, and conference papers – becomes apparent. While we may think they belong to the same family of practices, this was not the ancient view at all. Divination was never on the fringes of classical society and was not socially stigmatised. It allowed for offices high in social standing and was not considered an occult activity. While it is true that we find many divinatory spells among practising magicians, this does not mean divination has particularly to do with magic. We also find magicians offering cures for headaches, techniques to improve one's chariot racing, methods of performing well in law courts, and countless other results that would otherwise be obtainable only through the mastery of a complex and difficult *technê*. Magicians offer shortcuts in an indiscriminate range of endeavours. That they claim to have a specialty in divination does not mean that divination has particularly to do with magic. Rather, it puts divination in a category of things like rhetoric, medicine, athletics, and other specialist domains of technical knowledge on which magicians encroach in their drive to satisfy their clients. All of this suggests that the pairing of magic and divination rests on not much more than a modern sense that they both seem to be irrational behaviours, but it would mostly be jarring for a classical observer to hear the two lumped together. One can see the consequences of such an error by imagining a similar mistake more obvious to us. A reasonable outsider might take the view that the killing of live animals in honour of a divinity is also an irrational or superstitious behaviour, add to that the further observation that magical texts make extensive use of sacrifice as a technique, and so set out on a study of 'magic and sacrifice'. But as a guiding approach, that way would hardly give us the most productive lens fully to understand sacrifice, a practice that sits at the core of religious praxis across the Mediterranean and beyond. Finally, this particular error carries

---

[3] See the introduction to Gager 1999.

a further liability in the present context. The characterisation of classical diviners as magicians is a polemical position that comes into the conversation in late antiquity. More on this follows below.

In turning to the texts of ancient philosophers, I have worked on building a different history of divination, one that positions it not as a mode of social manipulation or superstition, but rather as a way of knowing.[4] When the likes of Plato, Aristotle, the Stoics, and the Neoplatonists examine divination (and all the philosophers, except for the Epicureans, do, with varying degrees of interest), the topic raises questions of epistemology. They reckon with the possibility of charlatans, of course, but none of them dismisses the idea that some people, sometimes, are good at seeing around corners and sensing what might come next, in ways that are difficult to explain. The possibility of foresight beyond self-aware inference is, as Aristotle puts it, not easy to embrace nor easy to dismiss.[5] When they take it seriously, Plato and Aristotle mostly consider it in the context of prescient dreams, while the Stoics and Neoplatonists study the wide range of possible divinatory vehicles. It is even more interesting that, while the philosophical schools weigh in on the topic from vastly different premises, not only in epistemology but in many fundamental areas, they converge on certain salient points when they try to unravel the puzzle. They generally see the appearance of these signs as engaging in a twitchy kind of knowledge, which arrives not via stretching our normal self-conscious apparatus for knowing things, but rather along a separate track that aligns with what you and I might call our faculty of intuition. Across their many differences, these thinkers converge on considering divination as a materially embedded and physiologically based means to gain insight, which is non-conscious and non-discursive.

The divine does not play a role in the mechanics of these explanations, and the idea that a divine sign is an intentional act of communication from a god to a human recipient is never embraced. These are physiological explanations for uncanny insight and not a means to imagine hierophanies. The insight expected via these systems is incremental and no match for the insights reachable via reason. Plato sees it as a function of the appetitive soul, the part most enmeshed in the body, typically tragically so. The *Timaeus* tells us that the gods, wishing to make even the lowly appetitive soul as good as possible, gave it a shadow of reasoning (divination) which operates during sleep when the rational soul is out of operation. Aristotle also sees prescient dreams as embedded in the lowest orders of his taxonomy of the soul. They are an epiphenomenon of non-conscious impulses towards motion

---

[4] Struck 2016.   [5] Aristotle, *Prophesying by Dreams* 462b12–14.

in the nutritive soul (the only part active during sleep) that reach towards what is good for us, since even our physical nature reaches for the good, always or for the most part. The Stoics also see divination as attached to the workings of a physiology, but here the pertinent physiology is that of the entire universe, which for them is a single living thing. A human sometimes operates like a receptor internal to the body of the cosmos, non-consciously picking up signals that course through it. As we will see, this *grosso modo* consistency in classical ways of positioning divination – setting its operation within the context of the organism and the material world – endures past the classical and Hellenistic periods. It remains consistent in both of the late antique observers, Origen and Iamblichus, to whom we now turn.

Origen

The subject of divination came to the notice of early Christian thinkers. We have dozens of considerations of it in the works of Clement of Alexandria, Tertullian, Augustine, and others. The typical context is alongside a Christian notion of prophecy, in comparison with which classical divination is found lacking. These Christian ideas were in circulation during centuries of Neoplatonic thinking and were at least in a position to be known by the philosophers. While it is typically difficult to speak of specific Christian texts read by specific pagan philosophers, Porphyry presents a proof of concept. His knowledge of Christianity was sufficient for him to write his tract critiquing it, which shows extensive and detailed knowledge of scripture and of interpretative traditions that grew up around it.[6] On the side of circumstantial evidence, Origen (*c.* 185–*c.* 253), on whom I will focus, set up his extensive library in Caesarea, about 300 miles to the south of Apamea, where Iamblichus (*c.* 250–330), the Neoplatonist on whom I will concentrate, later established his school. Origen is a particularly rich source on the topic, and whether or not one concludes that the Christian Origen is the same one that studied with Ammonius Saccus as a peer of Plotinus, it is nevertheless observable that he is rather deeply engaged with the philosophers.[7] I focus here on the *Contra Celsum*, which presents much low-hanging fruit.[8]

---

[6] Becker 2016.
[7] On this question recently, see the helpful overview of Edwards 2015a. See also Bäbler and Nesselrath 2018.
[8] The *Homilies on Numbers* holds promise as well; see the fascinating discussion of Balaam in Baskin 1983. For a wide treatment of the evidence in Origen, see Ramelli 2017b.

Two sections of the *Contra Celsum*, a tract written as a rebuttal to an attack on Christianity by the pagan Celsus, are of particular interest for present purposes. In Book 4, Origen considers Celsus' statements regarding divination that are provoked by a consideration of the place of animals vis-à-vis humans in the hierarchy of living things. In Book 7, he considers classical oracles and Christian prophecy at length. In Book 4, Origen objects to some of Celsus' statements regarding animals. That divination comes up in this context is a first indicator of the classical habit of mind that sees divination as having to do with physiology, which the Greek philosophers construed as a dimension of humanity adjacent to the non-human class of animals. The central issue at stake is that Celsus does not cede dominion over nature to humans and instead takes what is likely a more Aristotelian position of a gradient among living things, with less complex forms of life exhibiting something like, or at least analogous to, the sensible behaviour that results from human rationality.[9] (This is not Platonic.) Origen quotes Celsus pointing to the divine knowledge conveyed by birds, and other animals thought by Greeks to be prophetic, as proof that they have specific knowledge of divine will, and so on this score are even higher in station than humans. Origen answers by observing that there is disagreement, even among pagan thinkers, regarding the status of such divination, an observation that is surely true. Plato and Aristotle, as mentioned above, are uninterested in augury, confining their most trenchant remarks to dreams, while the Stoics endorse such techniques but do not come to a consensus on how they work.[10] After registering his scepticism that these practices could produce any knowledge of value, Origen is willing to entertain the claim that birds and other animals exhibit predictive behaviours: 'Let the principal point of investigation, however, be this: whether there actually is or is not an art of divination, by means of birds and other living things believed to have such power.' He continues in a sentiment that echoes Aristotle: 'For the arguments which tend to establish either view are not to be despised' (4.90).[11]

Origen's entertaining of the idea that there might be signs in nature soon turns to considering that demons (*daimones*) are the sources behind them.[12] Bringing them up in the context of divination would be unsurprising to pagan thinkers. From Homer forward to Proclus, *daimones* are thought of as intermediate divinities, and as such, demons and 'the demonic' are

---

[9] On this aspect of the debate, see Gilhus 2006: 57–61.
[10] For more on this, see Struck 2016: 171–214.
[11] Translations draw from Crombie in the *Ante-Nicene Christian Library*.
[12] On the role of demons in divination, see also Chapter 23 by Michael Hanaghan, this volume.

categories commonly appealed to in classical thinking on divination.[13] To take one example, when Plato makes his famous and provocative claim to have a sort of guardian angel, he playfully positions it as a kind of divination and says that a 'demonic' voice warns him from taking incorrect action.[14] Later Platonists begin to think of demons as attached to the tiers of denser material – air, water, earth – that are found below the heavens.[15] So, up to this point, the fact that Origen would think demons are linked with divination aligns with classical thinking, but he adds a further specification that is the dominant one among Christian thinkers. Origen reckons that demons are fallen angels and that, as a class, they are evil. This has no analogue in the classical tradition, in which demons could be evil and could also be good. As a class, they are defined by their intermediate position and not by their ethical orientation. Origen allows that, because they are lacking bodies of earthly material, they have a certain limited power to discern the future (ἔχοντές τι περὶ τῶν μελλόντων διορατικόν, ἅτε γυμνοὶ τῶν γηΐνων σωμάτων τυγχάνοντες, 4.92). But they are also pernicious, presenting a distraction from the true, transcendent god. They cause humans to grovel on the earth among the lowly animals. Demons have a connection to the material world and manipulate the unsuspecting with their limited power as a purposeful means to corrupt souls downward. They, and not the transcendent god, are responsible for producing such signs.[16]

With the topic of divination having arisen in the context of animal intelligence, Origen takes his consideration a next step, looking at cases of cledonomancy, wherein an omen is thought to reside in overheard words or in sneezing, a traditional mark of divine affirmation. Discussion of these is mainly a chance for Origen to point out an incoherence in Celsus' reasoning: if animal signs indicate that animals have knowledge of gods of higher quality than humans, would not Celsus also have to admit that humans sometimes are similarly the vehicles of such signs, and so there is no basis for saying that animals are higher on this score than humans (4.95)? At this point, Origen pulls back a bit to emphasise his overall point. Knowledge derived from these types of signs is produced not by the true God, but by pernicious demons:

This information is imparted to men by demons by means of signs, with the view of having men deceived by demons, and having their understanding dragged down from God and heaven to earth, and to places lower still. (4.97)[17]

---

[13] Struck 2016: 68–71, 112–22, 164–68.
[14] Plato, *Apol.* 36d, 40a–b; *Resp.* 496c; *Euthyphr.* 3e; *Phaedr.* 242b–d.
[15] On the topic, see Brisson, O'Neill, and Timotin 2018.   [16] *Cels.* 4.92.
[17] Text from Borret 1967–69.

τοῦτ' ἐροῦμεν ἀπὸ τῶν δαιμόνων συμβολικῶς ἀνθρώποις δεδηλῶσθαι κατὰ σκοπὸν τὸν περὶ τοῦ ἀπατηθῆναι ὑπὸ τῶν δαιμόνων τὸν ἄνθρωπον καὶ κατασπασθῆναι αὐτοῦ τὸν νοῦν ἀπ' οὐρανοῦ καὶ θεοῦ ἐπὶ γῆν καὶ τὰ ἔτι κατωτέρω.

Of further interest, Origen claims that animals' forward-looking behaviours are on par with natural instinct, and so, by his reckoning, could not be counted as divination. After considering how demons manipulate animals to send signs to humans, he considers other analogous behaviours in which animals appear to exhibit sensible action. When storks tend for their parents, for example, this is 'not from a regard to what is proper, nor from reflection, but from a natural instinct' (λεκτέον ὅτι καὶ τοῦτ' οὐκ ἀπὸ θεωρήματος τοῦ περὶ τοῦ καθήκοντος ποιοῦσιν οἱ πελαργοὶ οὐδ' ἀπὸ λογισμοῦ ἀλλ' ἀπὸ φύσεως, 4.98). He claims that such salutary behaviours are built into nature by the divine as a prod to push humans to emulate them. So, Origen agrees that the divine communicates to us via the natural world but disagrees with Celsus over what information is communicated and how.

Next, Origen has a long discussion in Book 7 in which he treats classical oracles. Several familiar themes arise. Also, a new and powerful context greatly amplifies distinctions between classical and Christian perspectives. Origen's main line of argument is to 'defend the prophets' (περὶ τῶν προφητῶν ἀπολογησώμεθα, 7.2) of the Hebrew Bible. This will mean shoring up the authority of those in the biblical texts who are looked to for prophecies pointing to Christ, and denigrating their counterparts in the classical tradition, including the Pythia at Delphi and the officials at Dodona, Claros, etc. This is a consequential positioning. It takes the classical tradition I framed at the beginning, in which cultural authorities gave advice regarding political alliances, business relationships, military strategy, personal travel, and programmes of colonisation, and sets it in parallel with a very different cultural formation that seeks to understand the basic structure of the divine. Origen construes prophecy as a core of Christian theology. It is a means to reveal, via a correct reading of the Hebrew Bible, the divine status of Jesus of Nazareth and so the nature of the divine itself, and the underlying structure of history to boot. These are kinds of questions on which the Pythia, wise though she may have been, had no purchase. Further, Christian prophecy does not provide tactical advice on what to do the next day or week; it does not focus on an insight about what to do next in a discrete situation, which might be thought of as analogous to intuition.

In his treatment, Origen claims, rightly again, that he could enlist writings of Aristotle and Epicurus against the authority of these classical figures.[18] He

---

[18] *Cels.* 7.3.

then moves to his main objection, which strikes a familiar chord with what we have already seen. The Greek oracles are embedded in the material world, and what successful forecasting they do produce is solely the result of their being inhabited and steered by demons who are themselves attached to the material world. He begins with the Pythia, referencing an idea well attested among pagan writers, claiming that from the ground of Delphi a frenzy-inspiring vapour issued, which was a catalyst of the state that resulted in an oracle. Chthonic vapours mean earthly origin in this analysis, and Origen puts this mechanism in opposition to wisdom truly gained from the divine. He also passes on an idea, which circulated in anti-pagan polemic, that this vapour entered through the Pythia's genitals. While not endorsed in the classical period, this does, in a way, carry forward, into the form of a *reductio*, the idea that the trance state is linked to bodily perturbance. Origen and his interlocutors both would have assessed the sexual act as more earthy than just inhaling. However it is achieved, Origen positions the ecstatic madness for which the Pythia was known as antithetical to a state of true inspiration: 'That should especially be a time of even clearer perception, when a person is in close contact with the Deity' (καὶ διορατικώτερον παρ' ἐκεῖνο μάλιστα καιροῦ τυγχάνειν, ὅτε σύνεστιν αὐτῷ τὸ θεῖον, 7.3). He continues, questioning how a true divinity could be restricted to a certain location, attached for entire ages to a particular place. Further, that such prophesying spirits take delight in the blood of sacrifice, and take sustenance in it, is a further indication that they are attached to earthly and bodily pleasures (7.5).

To illuminate his objections, he forwards contrasting accounts of the mechanism by which true prophecy, including prophecy in the Hebrew Bible, operates. A statement of such thinking early in Book 7 is characteristic:

Accordingly, we can show from an examination of the sacred scriptures, that the Jewish prophets, who were enlightened as far as was necessary for their prophetic work by the Spirit of God, were the first to enjoy the benefit of the inspiration; and by the contact – if I may so say – of the Holy Spirit they became clearer in mind, and their souls were filled with a brighter light. And the body no longer served as a hindrance to a virtuous life; for to that which we call the lust of the flesh, it was deadened (7.4).

Ὅθεν ἡμεῖς ἀποδείκνυμεν συνάγοντες ἀπὸ τῶν ἱερῶν γραμμάτων ὅτι οἱ ἐν Ἰουδαίοις προφῆται, ἐλλαμπόμενοι ὑπὸ τοῦ θείου πνεύματος τοσοῦτον, ὅσον ἦν καὶ αὐτοῖς τοῖς προφητεύουσι χρήσιμον, προαπέλαυον τῆς τοῦ κρείττονος εἰς αὐτοὺς ἐπιδημίας· καὶ διὰ τῆς πρὸς τὴν ψυχὴν αὐτῶν, ἵν' οὕτως ὀνομάσω, ἁφῆς τοῦ καλουμένου ἁγίου πνεύματος διορατικώτεροί τε τὸν νοῦν ἐγίνοντο καὶ τὴν ψυχὴν λαμπρότεροι ἀλλὰ καὶ τὸ σῶμα, οὐδαμῶς ἔτι ἀντιπρᾶττον τῷ κατ' ἀρετὴν βίῳ, ἅτε κατὰ τὸ παρ' ἡμῖν καλούμενον «φρόνημα τῆς σαρκὸς» νεκρούμενον.

Their prophesying state is not a frenzy, but a serenity brought on by a clearing of the mind, the brighter light that fills them, and a separation from bodily sensation. Origen's position is a standard Christian one by this time, which had developed in reaction to Montanism in the second century.[19] In this state, these figures are connected with actual wisdom, the kind that resides in the invisible and non-corporeal realm. The true divinity in the form of the Holy Spirit, and not a local demon attached to vapours or sacrifices, inhabits them. This line of argument accesses a deeply held Platonic idea that strongly opposes the material and immaterial, and situates true knowledge and higher realms of being definitively with the latter.

Before moving on to Iamblichus, a general point is worthy of emphasis. Origen's criticisms of divination as particularly attached to the material world and of limited scope are quite in keeping with classical philosophers on the topic. As mentioned above, despite their many differences, Greek philosophers generally assess what insights can be gained from divination to be connected particularly to the material and to emerge from the physiological character of the human being.

Iamblichus

While Origen's statements are, in their way, stern criticisms of pagan practices in favour of a very different Christian notion of the divine and of how to access knowledge of it, they align in surprising ways with a series of arguments put forward by the pagan Neoplatonist Iamblichus a half century or so later. The specifics will have to wait for a moment since a few words of context, again, will be helpful. Iamblichus is in the line of the prominent followers of Plotinus (204/5–70 CE). He most likely did not study with Plotinus himself, but with his student Porphyry (234?–305? CE), the editor of the Plotinian corpus.[20] Plotinus founded the school we know as Neoplatonism by positing a transcendent One over and above the worlds of matter (*hulê*), Soul (*psychê*), and Intellect (*nous*). In alignment with Plato's reference in *Republic* 6 to the Good as a kind of uber-form, beyond even being itself, Plotinus posits the supreme principle of the One (*to hen*) above everything. He is emphatic regarding its absolute transcendence, and even the few words used here to describe it are strictly speaking incorrect. Since it sits beyond intellect, and beyond even being itself, there is no way for

---

[19] I thank Matthew Crawford for this insight.
[20] For detailed consideration of the evidence, see Clarke, Dillon, and Hershbell 2003: xxi–xxiii.

us to describe the One using concepts conveyed by human language. It is a perfectly simple unity, and from it all the rest of the universe descends. Plotinus embraces from his predecessors the idea that philosophy is a way of life, and he adds an even stronger commitment to the idea that it has a soteriological dimension.[21] All of reality, including each human, is energised by an upward-pulling impulse to return to the perfect One from which it descended. But at the same time, the distraction of the material world produces an opposite pull downward towards its shadowy realm. On the question of how a human should achieve upward movement, Plotinus is a strict contemplationist. He recommends against engagement with the material world, which would include almost all of traditional Greek religious praxis, and would surely include divination. Instead, an individual needs to lead a disciplined life of intellectual examination and meditation in order to reach back up towards the One. Plotinus' immediate successor, Porphyry, is in line with this view. Iamblichus strikes out on his own and proposes a radical change. He advocates for a praxis to accompany the contemplation of Plotinus. Remaking traditional Greek religious rites and fashioning new ones, he proposes a programme he calls (coining a new term) '*theourgia*', typically rendered 'theurgy' in English, in which divination has an important place. Iamblichus' innovations provoked a spirited debate about the status of these rites and whether and how theurgy was beyond reason, and, therefore, whether access to the divine transcends rationality.

Most of what we know about Iamblichus' views on the subject of theurgy generally, and divination in particular (which Iamblichus construes as a subset of theurgy), survives in his *De mysteriis*, a tract written in a polemical context that will strike some oddly familiar chords with what we saw in Origen's *Contra Celsum*. Like Origen's, Iamblichus' tract is an extended rebuttal of a critique by a Greek philosopher. And like Origen, he was responding to a philosopher hostile to his religious views. Porphyry, disagreeing with Iamblichus' turn towards the rites embodied in theurgy, had criticised his pupil's commitments in his 'Letter to Anebo'.[22] The *De mysteriis*, which could just as easily be called the *Contra Porphyrium*, is Iamblichus' extended answer.[23] I will look at Iamblichus' text in order to evaluate not so

---

[21] See Hadot 1993.

[22] That Porphyry also wrote a treatise *Against the Christians*, which survives only in fragments, raises the interesting prospect that we might characterise Porphyry as an anti-ritualist just as much as an anti-Christian, as he tends to be known in the history of Christianity.

[23] As part of the critique, Porphyry calls theurgy 'magic' (*goêteia*), which is clearly polemical since Iamblichus' programme of praxis mostly does not resemble what we see consistently exhibited in our ancient sources on magic, in the *Papyri Graecae Magicae* and the surviving lead tablets, for example.

much what it does to the legacy of Plotinian rationalism, as has been typical of treatments of it since at least E. R. Dodds' time, but what it adds to our understanding of ideas about religious praxis in late antiquity.[24] It is, after all, our most extended surviving discussion of ideas on ritual from the whole of the classical tradition. Iamblichus likely embraced praxis because of an intention to add a social dimension to the contemplative work that Plotinus advocates, and so to help bring to a wider world the salvific power that the Neoplatonists thought was embedded in their philosophy.[25] Perhaps he had in mind something like a social movement, which may also show the influence of Christianity (but this is another large question).[26] It is worth noting that Iamblichus decisively won the debate. Most Neoplatonists for the next thousand years, down to at least Ficino's day, understood theurgy to be an efficacious part of the Neoplatonists' programme.[27]

For the present purposes, most pertinent is *De mysteriis* Book 3, the longest book in the treatise, in which divination is the topic. Iamblichus begins each section by quoting Porphyry's criticisms, and then follows with rebuttals in a lemmatic arrangement (again similar to Origen's work). Porphyry claimed that the divination in Iamblichus' theurgy simply perpetuated what in his mind were antiquated rites, based on entrails and bird flights, or stimulated by intoxicating vapours or waters in places like Delphi, Claros, and Delos. His criticisms are not dissimilar to the criticisms we have already seen from Origen. Following Plotinian logic, which in this case is not so different from Origen's logic, Porphyry denigrates traditional Greek *mantikê*, on the grounds that it is enmeshed in the material world, connected to animal instinct, relies on narrow divine powers (demons not gods), and pulls us away from the divine and towards the world of matter. While, according to the Neoplatonists, demons are not evil, nor are they fallen angels, they are lesser deities, closer to the material world, some of whom are tied to particular locations. On all these grounds, Porphyry advocates that divination be abandoned in favour of inward-turning contemplation as a more effective means of facilitating return to the highest divinity.

Not only does Porphyry's critique align with Origen's arguments, but the observations presented by each, in this context as criticisms, hardly deviate from the broad currents of classical thinking on divination sketched

---

[24] Dodds 1951: 283–312. [25] Dodds 1951: 287–88.
[26] That Iamblichus' writings were warmly embraced by Julian the Apostate in his revival of paganism is a testimony to the congeniality of Iamblichus' thinking with the possibility of a larger social movement. On questions like these, a wide range of scholarly terrain has opened up. For this conversation, Fowden 1982 has served as an inflection point.
[27] See Vanhaelen 2013: II.438–44.

above. Like Plato, Aristotle, and the Stoics, these later figures see divination as a form of gaining information from the material world via physiologically embedded capacities (both animal behaviours and human bodies in contact with the forces of nature). What differs over the centuries is how they value this aspect of it. Plato and Aristotle allowed there may be something to insights derived from such sources, extracted from the material world of nature. And for the Stoics, matter is not a problem, since they are committed materialists. For the Neoplatonists, and for Origen too, by contrast, the connection with the material now carries higher stakes and bigger problems. It is probably fair to say that no major school is as vehement in its distrust of the material as the Neoplatonists are, perhaps even more so than Plato himself, who, despite his trenchant critiques of matter, did after all produce the *Timaeus*.[28] Porphyry, Iamblichus, and Origen, each in his own way, now inhabit a cosmos in which the salvation of souls, through aspiration for the divine and *away from* the material, has become an even more urgent imperative. For Plato, an over-attachment to matter meant risking ignorance (and possibly ontological demotion during reincarnation); for the later thinkers, it is an offence against the divine order of the cosmos. In this context, the endorsement of insight through divination, construed as emerging from the *physis* by the classical philosophers, faces the more severe impediments that first Origen, then Porphyry, set out in their challenges.

Iamblichus' answer to Porphyry is striking and results in several innovations vis-à-vis the thinking that preceded them. As a way to defend divination, Iamblichus jettisons some of it. He denigrates some traditional rites, those which he thinks are embedded in the material, and proposes a new form of it, which he calls 'divine divination', that transcends the material and comes into direct contact with the highest god.[29] This inspiration does not come from demons but from the divine itself.[30] The new form, in my

---

[28] It is important to note, as is well known, that while Plotinus severely distrusts matter, he definitively separates himself from the Gnostics (*Enn*. II.9). They claimed that matter was such a problem as to be a locus of active evil, and a residue of an evil demiurge. This is a step that Plotinus could not take, and against them he insists that even matter itself must come from the supremely transcendent One and therefore must contain at least a scintilla of the divine. In the language of Christianity, it is a kind of mystery, congruent in its evocative power for the Neoplatonists, to at least some extent, to mystery of the incarnation for the Christians.

[29] For 'divine divination', see *Myst*. 3.4.2; 3.10.2; 3.17.51; 3.27.6, 9, 12, 37, 45, 56; 3.31.41, 58; 9.3.33; 9.5.19; 10.4.1; 10.5.2; 10.8.2. He also sometimes calls it 'true divination'; see *Myst*. 3.3.25; 3.8.3; 3.26.23; 3.27.2.

[30] 'But it is also necessary to know what divine possession is, and how it happens. So, then, it is falsely believed to be a transport of the mind by daemonic inspiration. For the human intellect

view, resembles Origen's characterisations of Christian prophecy. Making wide concessions to Porphyry's criticisms, Iamblichus is ready to agree that traditional divination does indeed result in only a lowly form of knowing, attached to the material world. But these techniques belong only to the unenlightened. In contrast to traditional divination, the true, divine form transcends the modes by which the lower forms operate. This contrast is Iamblichus' most common theme, and it has no precedent among the Greek philosophers that come before him.

Further to the specifics, according to Iamblichus, the lower forms of prescience embedded in the material world are connected to animal instinct, rely on demons, and produce only tentative insights. The true or divine form, on the other hand, belongs entirely to the divine and sits wholly beyond what could be contained in materials, vapours, animals, or specific locations. Again, such a claim is unknown to the philosophical tradition. Iamblichus opens Book 3 by pushing aside almost all previous accounts of how divination works. He says that the origin and principle (ἀρχή) of divination

neither originated from bodies, nor from bodily affections, nor from any nature, nor from powers that have to do with nature, nor from human disposition, nor from the conditions that have to do with a human disposition, but neither is it from any acquired external technical practice, performed for some part of the human way of life.[31] (*Myst.* 3.1)

οὔτε ἀπὸ σωμάτων ἐστὶν ὁρμωμένη οὔτε ἀπὸ τῶν περὶ τοῖς σώμασι παθημάτων, οὔτε ἀπὸ φύσεώς τινος καὶ τῶν περὶ τὴν φύσιν δυνάμεων, οὔτε ἀπὸ τῆς ἀνθρωπίνης παρασκευῆς ἢ τῶν περὶ αὐτὴν ἕξεων, ἀλλ' οὐδ' ἀπὸ τέχνης τινὸς ἔξωθεν ἐπικτήτου περί τι μέρος τῶν ἐν τῷ βίῳ διαπραγματευομένης.

In place of this edifice of classical thinking, Iamblichus forwards the following in the lines that are immediately adjacent:

Rather, all of its supreme power belongs to the gods, and is bestowed by the gods. … All the rest is subordinate, instrumental to the gift of foreknowledge sent down by the gods: everything that concerns our soul, our body, everything that is inherent in the nature of the universe, and in the particular constitution of each thing. (3.1)

is neither carried away if it is really possessed, nor does inspiration come from daemons, but from the gods.' Ἀλλὰ χρὴ γνῶναι καὶ τίς ὁ ἐνθουσιασμός ἐστι καὶ ὅπως γίγνεται. Φορὰ μὲν οὖν τῆς διανοίας μετὰ δαιμονίας ἐπιπνοίας ψευδῶς δοξάζεται. Οὔτε γὰρ ἡ διάνοια ἡ ἀνθρωπίνη φέρεται, εἴ γε ὄντως κατέχεται, οὔτε δαιμόνων, θεῶν δὲ γίγνεται ἐπίπνοια (*Myst.* 3.7.3–7; trans. Clarke, Dillon, and Hershbell 2003).

[31] Translations draw from Clarke, Dillon, and Hershbell 2003. Text from des Places 1966.

τὸ δὲ πᾶν κῦρος αὐτῆς ἀνήκει εἰς τοὺς θεοὺς καὶ ἀπὸ τῶν θεῶν ἐνδίδοται. ... τὰ δ' ἄλλα πάντα ὡς ὄργανα ὑπόκειται τῇ ἐκ θεῶν καταπεμπομένῃ τῆς προγνώσεως δόσει, ὅσα τε περὶ τὴν ψυχὴν ἡμῶν ἐστι καὶ τὸ σῶμα καὶ ὅσα ἐν τῇ φύσει τοῦ παντὸς ἢ ταῖς ἰδίαις ἑκάστων φύσεσιν ἐνυπάρχει.

His treatment of divination proceeds from here. He starts with those kinds in which the human subject is the medium for the appearance of the divine sign – daytime visions, dreams, and inspired oracles. With each kind, he proposes that there is a lesser form that belongs to material layers of reality, and a higher, divine kind, which is only the result of the gift of the divine. In the case of dreams, the lesser form, in keeping with previous Platonic and Aristotelian thinking on the matter, emerges from physiological phenomena and the capacities of the human soul in contact with a sleeping body attuned to the environment. The lower form of daytime visions and oracles are traceable to mental states triggered by bodily disturbance. But the state a person reaches during divine divination is wholly different from these traditionally understood forms of frenzy or possession. During divine divination, a person is at peace and filled with light. They 'receive the divine fire' (3.6) and their power to divine comes only from the god, not from the surrounding physical environment:

> For such a power [sc. divine divination] if inseparable from the nature of places and of bodies subject to it ... cannot know beforehand things everywhere and always in the same manner. But if separate and free from places and times ... since it is superior to things happening in time and held in place, it is equally present with beings wherever they are, and is always at the same time present with those growing in time, and embraces in one the truth of all existing things because of its own separate and superior essence. (3.12)

Ἀχώριστος μὲν γὰρ οὖσα τῆς φύσεως τῶν τόπων καὶ τῶν ὑποκειμένων αὐτῇ σωμάτων ἡ τοιαύτη δύναμις ... οὐ δύναται τὰ πανταχοῦ καὶ ἀεὶ προγιγνώσκειν ὡσαύτως· ἀφειμένη δ' ἀπόλυτος τῶν τόπων καὶ τῶν ... χρόνων (ἅτε δὴ κρείττων οὖσα τῶν γιγνομένων κατὰ χρόνον καὶ τῶν ὑπὸ τόπου κατεχομένων) τοῖς πανταχοῦ οὖσιν ἐξ ἴσου πάρεστι, καὶ τοῖς κατὰ χρόνον φυομένοις πάντοτε ἅμα σύνεστιν, ἐν ἑνί τε συνείληφε τῶν ὅλων τὴν ἀλήθειαν διὰ τὴν χωριστὴν ἑαυτῆς καὶ ὑπερέχουσαν οὐσίαν.

Those who divine when linked with this transcendent power are to be contrasted with those in a state of frenzy or ecstasy which is brought on by physical perturbations deriving from the lowly material world:

> It is not a simple ecstasy, but an ascent to what is superior and a transformation, whereas frenzy and ecstasy actually reveal a perversion towards what is inferior. (3.7)

οὐδ' ἔκστασις ἁπλῶς οὕτως ἐστίν, ἀλλ' ἐπὶ τὸ κρεῖττον ἀναγωγὴ καὶ μετάστασις, ἡ δὲ παραφορὰ καὶ ἔκστασις ἐμφαίνει καὶ τὴν ἐπὶ τὸ χεῖρον ἀνατροπήν.

The lower kind is tentative, and relies on demons, here referred to as spirits (*pneumata*):

But those who conjure up the spirits secretly, without these blessed visions, grope, as it were, in darkness, and know nothing of what they do, except for some very small signs which appear through the body of the one in an ecstatic trance, and some other signs that manifest themselves; but they are ignorant of the whole of divine inspiration, which is hidden in obscurity. (3.6)

Οἱ δ' ἄνευ τῶν μακαρίων τούτων θεαμάτων ἀφανῶς ποιούμενοι τὰς ἀγωγὰς τῶν πνευμάτων ὥσπερ ἐν σκότῳ ἀφάσσουσι καὶ οὐδὲν ἴσασιν ὧν ποιοῦσι, πλὴν πάνυ σμικρῶν τῶν διὰ τοῦ σώματος φαινομένων σημείων τοῦ ἐνθουσιῶντος καὶ τῶν ἄλλων τῶν ἐναργῶς ὁρωμένων, τὰ ὅλα τῆς θείας ἐπιπνοίας ἐν ἀφανεῖ κεκρυμμένα ἀγνοοῦντες.

As for Neoplatonists generally, so for Iamblichus, demons are not all bad and they are not fallen angels, but they are lowly and get their hands dirty with the material world. They are intermediaries acting from a vantage that sits higher than typical humans, but they do get things wrong. And it is also true that they act on their own volition, and separate from the highest divinity, and their intentions may deviate from the gods'. It is wiser, then, to turn to the transcendent in an unmediated way, and to receive divine illumination from it.

Given the bifurcation Iamblichus makes between divination that is divine (true) and material (unsure), one could surmise that traditional forms embedded in external signs in the material world of nature might not fare well, and indeed they do not. When his consideration reaches signs embedded in the behaviour of birds, in entrails, and the like, he is generally dismissive:

Come, then, let us turn to the mode of divination, accomplished by human skill, which partakes largely of guessing and supposition. About this you say the following: 'some have indeed established a technique for pursuing the future by means of entrails, birds, and stars'. There are also many other such techniques, but these are sufficient for illustrating every technical kind of divination. To speak generally, this kind uses certain divine signs brought to be by the gods in various ways ... The technique somehow draws conclusions and guesses at the divination, inferring it from certain probabilities. The gods produce the signs either by means of nature, which is subservient to them for the creation of each thing, both universal and particular, or through the agency of demons concerned with creation, who, presiding over the elements of the universe and individual bodies, indeed over all living beings in the cosmos, guide the phenomena with ease in a manner pleasing to the gods. (3.15)

Φέρε δὴ οὖν ἐπὶ τὸν διὰ τέχνης ἀνθρωπίνης ἐπιτελούμενον τρόπον μετέλθωμεν, ὅστις στοχασμοῦ καὶ οἰήσεως πλείονος εἴληφε· λέγεις δὲ καὶ περὶ τούτου τοιαῦτα· οἱ δ' ἤδη καὶ διὰ σπλάγχνων καὶ δι' ὀρνίθων καὶ δι' ἀστέρων τέχνην συνεστήσαντο τῆς θήρας τοῦ μέλλοντος. Εἰσὶ μὲν καὶ ἄλλαι πλείονες τέχναι τοιαῦται, πλὴν ἀλλὰ καὶ αὗταί γε ἀποχρῶσιν ἐνδείξασθαι πᾶν τὸ τεχνικὸν εἶδος τῆς μαντικῆς. Ὡς μὲν οὖν τὸ ὅλον εἰπεῖν, σημείοις τισὶ τοῦτο θείοις χρῆται ἐκ θεῶν ἐπιτελουμένοις κατὰ ποικίλους τρόπους ... πως ἡ τέχνη καὶ στοχάζεται τὴν μαντείαν, ἐξ εἰκότων τινῶν αὐτὴν συλλογιζομένη. Τὰ μὲν οὖν σημεῖα οἱ θεοὶ ποιοῦσι διὰ τῆς φύσεως τῆς δουλευούσης αὐτοῖς πρὸς τὴν γένεσιν, τῆς τε κοινῆς καὶ τῆς ἰδίας ἑκάστων, ἢ διὰ τῶν γενεσιουργῶν δαιμόνων οἵτινες τοῖς στοιχείοις τοῦ παντὸς καὶ τοῖς μερικοῖς σώμασι ζῴοις τε καὶ τοῖς ἐν τῷ κόσμῳ πᾶσιν ἐπιβεβηκότες ἄγουσι τὰ φαινόμενα μετὰ ῥᾳστώνης ὅπηπερ ἂν δοκῇ τοῖς θεοῖς.

Again, Iamblichus characterises a mode of divination reliant on nature as a tentative and unreliable projection, connected with the demons that govern natural processes. Most interesting for the present purposes is the degree to which Iamblichus' approach is in agreement with what we have already seen from Origen. Each relies on separating out truly divine divination or prophecy from practices based on bodily frenzy and the material world. For both thinkers, lower divination depends on the material, involves demons, and is tied to a certain location, atmosphere, or bodily disposition of the diviner.

Of course, there are many important differences. The demons that superintend the lower material world are evil in Origen's estimation. They are intentionally mendacious and filled with subterfuge. While Origen allows that animal instinct may be operative, the main purpose of such animal behaviours is to provide encouragement to humans to behave in naturally salutary ways, not to provide signs. In addition to these differences, it is important to note that Origen's Christian god is no Neoplatonic One. The two thinkers share a commitment to seeing it as a transcendent principle, sitting wholly beyond the material world, that facilitates and inspires a wholly separate way of knowing, but the biblical deity is capable of decisive intervention in human history via discrete, conscious, and volitional acts. This is something the Neoplatonic One never does. This difference in theology leaves open the possibility that divine signs will be traceable, in the Christian case, to a divine intention to communicate to humans; whereas for the Neoplatonists, it will be a readable register of a meaningful cosmos. Even without papering over these important differences, the similarities stated above remain.

As a final point, it is worth bringing up once again a further characteristic on which Iamblichus' divine divination differs markedly from what we see in the classical period, and how surprisingly well it accords with Origen's ideas. Whereas classical figures only ever expect incremental knowledge from their oracles, Iamblichus anticipates something quite different from his divine, highest form of divination. He expects a soteriological communion with the divine. The knowledge conveyed will be transformative, welcoming the participant to a higher form of existence. It is a 'liberating' from the material world and makes participants 'united' with the gods (3.2); by participating in it they 'exchange their human life for the divine' (3.4). This has more in common with the expansive outcomes for prophecy to which Origen is committed than it does with classical thinking. While the classical *mantis* could enter a trancelike state, the transformation is typically temporary and lacks a soteriological dimension. For Christians, prophecy is capable of nothing less than discerning the nature of the divine. It is a vehicle that needs to be able, in this sense, to convey the entire Truth about the structure of the divine, humanity, history, and eschatology. That too is quite different from the kind of advice Greeks and Romans sought out from their oracles. Should I marry this woman? Should we found a colony on Melos? Should we launch the attack this morning? It is important to emphasise this, in my view, since comparative studies tend to gloss it over. Oracles in the classical world were simply not expected to know the secrets of the universe. While they yield information about a divine attitude, they were, interestingly, not thought to be sources for wisdom about the nature of the gods – or the universe or the human place in it. They were an early warning mechanism, steering a person away from trouble over the horizon by aiding in a decision being made in the here and now. In this sense, Origen is right to characterise the classical oracles as being a little narrow-minded in comparison with the expansive wisdom he thinks to be contained in what he knows as the Old Testament, now positioned as an extensive oracular pronouncement on the coming of a New Age of human and divine history. Iamblichus is closer to Origen's view of what an oracle might offer than he is to the classical one. There are, of course, further important differences in this line of comparison too, beginning with Iamblichus' commitment to the idea that a continuum of divine divination is and has been available in history, whereas for Origen, while prophetic powers may still be active, the most important divine prophecy is historically located. These positions are consonant with the difference in theology mentioned above. It would be inconceivable, from a Neoplatonic perspective, that some divine activity or power would be limited within one or the other finite time horizon. What knowledge could be gained from the gods would be equally capable of being gained irrespective of time. The Christian conception of divinity, as acting in discrete ways, allows for variance in its powers and activities. The human power to know, at least on this score, will be invariant over time for Iamblichus, whereas for Origen humans after biblical times face a more constrained epistemological domain. There are other consequential nuances as well. But again the main point in my view remains.

It is difficult to make a definitive statement of influence. It is surely possible that the consonant views on divination exhibited by Origen and Iamblichus are the results of independent intellectual work from premises that have, in one sense, comparable starting points regarding the nature of the divine. Both Origen and Iamblichus have strong commitments to the absolute transcendence of the divinity, have deeper suspicions about the material world than classical thinkers, and have an interest in producing a wider public connection for their ideas. It could be that a person who begins from such points, when turning to thinking about classical divination and the cluster of thought regarding embodiment that had surrounded it for centuries, will arrive at the structure of thinking at which both Iamblichus and Origen arrive.

9 | Cyprian, Scripture, and Socialisation: Forming Faith in the Catechumenate and Beyond

EDWINA MURPHY

Introduction

In *One True Life*, Kavin Rowe presents Stoicism and Christianity as two opposing ways of living based on different underlying apprehensions of truth.[1] Cyprian of Carthage (*c.* 200–258 CE) certainly shares that perspective.[2] But whereas philosophy was restricted to a privileged (mostly male) few, Christians claimed their intention was to shape men, women, and children of every class into the likeness of Christ.[3] The basis of the curriculum underpinning this endeavour was scripture: *testimonia* collections ordered and summarised this knowledge, enabling it to be transmitted to future generations; the catechumenate provided the setting in which it was memorised and applied. The practice of Cyprian's North African community therefore supports Averil Cameron's assertion that Christian reality is constructed by text and practice;[4] ideally, the biblical truths shape the *habitus* of believers.[5]

In order to understand this process of attempting to turn pious Romans into fully devoted followers of Jesus Christ, I will consider a number of works by Cyprian of Carthage, whose own life is evidence of just such a transformation. A wealthy rhetor who became an influential bishop, Cyprian was convinced that he had left behind worldly wisdom and embraced divine truth. In order to enable others to do the same, he wrote three

---

[1] Rowe 2016.
[2] See, for example, *Ep.* 55.16.1, citing Col 2:8a: 'But the fact is that a vast difference separates Christians and philosophers, and we are warned by the Apostle: "Beware lest you fall prey to the empty wiles of philosophy"' (*inter Christianos autem et philosophos plurimum distat. Et cum apostolus dicat: 'uidete ne quis uos depraedetur per philosophiam et inanem fallaciam'*). English translations of the letters are from Clarke 1984–89.
[3] See, for example, *Dom. orat.* 28: 'Our Lord Jesus Christ came unto all, and gathering alike the learned and unlearned, published to every sex and every age the precepts of salvation' (*Dominus noster Iesus Christus omnibus uenerit et colligens doctos pariter et indoctos omni sexu atque aetati praecepta salutis ediderit*). English translations of the treatises are modified from ANF.
[4] Cameron 1991: 21. For the way in which scripture can also shape the physical environment, see Chapter 17 by Cilliers Breytenbach, this volume.
[5] Kreider 2016: 165–66. Kreider uses Bourdieu's concept of *habitus* (2000: 130–46).

foundational texts: *Ad Donatum*, which depicts the process of conversion; *Ad Quirinum*, a *testimonia* collection compiled as a helpful summary of divine truths (here abbreviated *Test.*); and *De dominica oratione*, a commentary on the Lord's Prayer, possibly directed at catechumens. These works reveal both the content and the method by which Christians are, in Cyprian's view, formed. They also provide the opportunity to consider the role of the bishop in communicating and upholding divine truth, as well as the part played by catechists, presbyters, and private prayer and study of scripture. This chapter therefore focuses on how truths are ordered through the educational and institutional practices of the church – and the personal devotional practices encouraged in its members – which have the goal of believers imitating the perfection of Christ.[6]

Ad Donatum: The Case for Transformation

In *Ad Donatum*,[7] Cyprian takes his friend Donatus to the top of a metaphorical mountain in order to view the world from which the Christian has been freed.[8] In portraying the transition from the earthly to the heavenly realm, Cyprian emphasises the pouring out of the Holy Spirit in baptism. He gives the impression that the movement from darkness to light is accomplished in a moment.[9] We might compare this account with that given by Pontius in the *Vita Cypriani*,[10] which relates that even before Cyprian was born again (baptised), he relinquished his possessions and adopted continence.[11] Of course, the two recollections have different purposes: Cyprian's to point to heavenly grace;[12] Pontius' to highlight Cyprian's rapid growth to maturity, attempting to defuse criticism of Cyprian's status as a neophyte when appointed bishop.[13] And yet, Pontius' account also fits with the direction in *Test.* 3.98 that 'The catechumen should no

---

[6] For sacrificial knowledge, see Chapter 10 by Andrew McGowan, this volume.
[7] For an introduction to this work, see Molager 1982: 9–72. On its literary qualities, see Gassman 2017: 247–57.
[8] For this literary technique in antiquity, see Fredouille 2010: 445–55.
[9] *Don.* 3–4. This movement from darkness to light is also present in *Test.* 1.*pr.*; *Dom. orat.* 1.
[10] Adopting the attribution of Jerome, *Vir. ill.* 68.
[11] Pontius, *Vit. Cypr.* 2.
[12] For the paradigmatic nature of *Ad Donatum* as a conversion experience, see Engberg 2012: 129–44.
[13] Mattias Gassman (2019: 15–17) suggests that *Ad Donatum* may also have a role in countering opposition from the presbyters on Cyprian's election.

longer sin.'[14] Tertullian had already said something similar in his work *De paenitentia*: 'That baptismal washing is a sealing of faith, faith which is begun and is commended by the faith of repentance. We are not washed in order that we may cease sinning, but because we have ceased, since in heart we have been bathed already.'[15] A demonstration of repentance, evidence of an amended life, is required in order to receive baptism, the beginning of a new life.

Paul Bradshaw is certainly correct in emphasising the role that this right behaviour has in the catechumenate, but he goes too far in his claim that, in the third century, the gospels were restricted to those who had been (or were on the cusp of being) baptised.[16] He refers to some early church orders[17] but makes no mention of Tertullian or Cyprian, thereby extrapolating what might be happening in the third century from later periods, but ignoring the evidence from the third century itself.[18] As Alistair Stewart-Sykes has argued, the *disciplina arcani* was most likely a later development when the church's social position vis-à-vis the rest of society changed.[19] And as Bradshaw himself acknowledges, 'pagans' knew about Jesus and his teachings.[20] Indeed Cyprian concludes his apology to Demetrian[21] with a brief summary of Christian teaching. This is not restricted to ethics but specifically mentions Christ bestowing grace and mercy, 'by overcoming death in the trophy of the cross, by redeeming the believer with the price of his blood, by reconciling man to God the Father, by quickening our mortal nature with a heavenly regeneration'.[22] There is, at this stage at least, no great mystery – at heart, the gospel message is a simple one.[23] Christian knowledge, or doctrine, is therefore not a matter of secondary or minor importance in

---

[14] *Catecuminum peccare iam non debere* (*Test.* 3.98). This is supported by Rom 3:8: *In epistulis Pauli ad Romanos*: '*Faciamus mala, dum ueniunt bona: quorum condemnatio iusta est*' (*Test.* 3.98). Cyprian's text, 'Let us do evil while good is coming: their condemnation is just', differs from the Greek which translates as 'Why not do evil so that good may come?' (Fahey 1971: 427). See also Schelkle 1959, 1st edn, 1956: 101.

[15] *Lauacrum illud obsignatio est fidei, quae fides a paenitentiae fide incipitur et commendatur. Non ideo abluimur ut delinquere desinamus sed quia desiimus, quoniam iam corde loti sumus* (Tertullian, *Paen.* 6.16–17).

[16] Bradshaw 1999: 150–52. For a detailed response, see Kreider 2016: 179–81.

[17] Bradshaw 1999: 143–44, 152.

[18] Similarly, although Cyprian's name is mentioned several times, there is no engagement with *Ad Quirinum* or any of the bishop's other works in Gavrilyuk 2007.

[19] Stewart-Sykes 2003: 301–4.   [20] Bradshaw 1999: 151.

[21] Possibly a local magistrate. See Sage 1975: 276.

[22] *Subigendo mortem trophaeo crucis, redimendo credentem pretio sui sanguinis, reconciliando hominem Deo patri, uiuificando mortalem regeneratione caelesti* (*Demetr.* 26).

[23] Cf. *Dom. orat.* 28.

conversion. But knowing about something and committing oneself to it are two different things – conversion of life is evidence that the truth has been heard. How, then, were people initiated into this new way of living?

Ad Quirinum: The Foundation is Scripture

The reading of scripture played an important role in Cyprian's own conversion, according to Pontius,[24] and it is no surprise that he soon turns his attention to compiling a *testimonia* collection.[25] As Mattias Gassman says, 'Cyprian seems to have meant *Ad Quirinum* as a primer for precisely the sort of scripture-based piety that he exhorts Donatus to adopt.'[26] The identity and status of Quirinus is unknown.[27] However, a number of testimonies, including the one mentioned above, that 'the catechumen should no longer sin',[28] point to the possibility of a catechetical use, even if, as Everett Ferguson suggests, it has uses beyond the catechumenate as well.[29] Of course, the goal of catechesis is to form a person, not to learn a certain amount of material in order to pass an exam. It lays the foundation for Christian life, but such instruction is useful beyond the period of initiation.

Ordering Knowledge

How, then, is *Ad Quirinum* structured? The three books of biblical texts have different emphases: The first comprises twenty-four proofs against the Jews, the second focuses on the person of Christ (30),[30] and the third, which has a separate preface, addresses Christian living. Not only do the

---

[24] 'When he had learned from the reading of scripture certain things not according to the condition of his novitiate, but in proportion to the earliness of his faith, he immediately laid hold of what he had discovered' (*cum de lectione diuina quaedam iam non pro condicione nouitatis sed pro fidei festinatione didicisset, statim rapuit quod inuenit*, Vit. Cypr. 2).

[25] This ascription has been contested, most recently by Bobertz 1992: 112–28. See my argument in favour of Cyprian in Murphy 2014a: 533–50.

[26] Gassman 2019: 12.

[27] Perhaps a catechist (Kreider 2016: 161), a fictive catechumen (Stewart-Sykes 2003: 294), or a younger high-status convert akin to Donatus or Cyprian himself. For further references, see Gassman 2019: 11.

[28] *Catecuminum peccare iam non debere* (*Test*. 3.98). Cyprian also uses the term 'catechumenus' in *Ep*. 73.22.1–2. Elsewhere, he prefers 'audiens' (hearer). See, for example, *Ep*. 18.2.2; 29.2.

[29] Other texts suggestive of a catechetical context are *Test*. 3.25–27, 97, 114, 116, 119. Ferguson 2001: 241–42.

[30] One shows that the Jews *a Deo recessisse et indulgentiam Domini ... perdidisse, successisse uero in eorum locum Christianos ... Item libellus alius continet Christi sacramentum, quod idem uenerit, qui secundum scripturas adnuntiatus est* (*Test*. 1.pr.).

first two books of *Ad Quirinum* deal with matters of belief, framed apologetically, but so does the more practical Book 3. According to Kreider's calculations, 48 of the 120 testimonies in Book 3 could be categorised this way.[31] Thus knowing and doing are intertwined for Cyprian.

The preface to Book 1 indicates Cyprian's intentions: 'This treatise has been ordered in an abridged compendium, so that I ... might collect all that was necessary in selected and connected heads.'[32] That ordering is much more evident in Books 1 and 2 than it is in Book 3,[33] but I agree with Andy Alexis-Baker that Book 3 is not 'random and chaotic'.[34] He has tried too hard, however, to fit the texts into a system.[35] A more satisfactory explanation can be found by following his suggestion that attention to key words or phrases in the Latin text might be fruitful.[36] I will explore this in more detail elsewhere; for our purposes here, a few comments will suffice.

As John O'Keefe and Russell Reno demonstrate, verbal echoes and patterns play a significant role in how patristic writers organise their thoughts.[37] I have previously pointed out this phenomenon in the case of individual supporting texts in *Ad Quirinum*,[38] but here I apply it more broadly. In Book 3, Cyprian generally uses associative strategies to determine the next topic to be addressed, rather than systematically planning

---

[31] Kreider 2016: 164.

[32] *Libellus conpendio breuiante digestus est, ut quae ... excerptis capitulis et adnexis necessaria quaeque colligerem* (*Test.* 1.pr. Cf. *Fort.* pr.3).

[33] As Ferguson notes, Book 1 moves from the faithlessness of the Jews, to the loss of their privileges, and finally their replacement by the church; Book 2 follows the order of Irenaeus' *Demonstration of the Apostolic Preaching*, from Christ's pre-existence to his earthly life, death and resurrection, finishing with his return (Ferguson 2001: 241).

[34] Alexis-Baker 2009: 375.

[35] For example, he claims that the 'initial four precepts form the first discernible unit, teaching economic sharing' (Alexis-Baker 2009: 363). The first two certainly do, but regarding the third, 'That love and fraternal affection ought to be religiously and steadfastly practiced' (*agapem et dilectionem fraternam religiose et firmiter exercendam*), he says: 'Cyprian quotes passages that concern love – such as John 15.12-13 or Matt 18.19-20 – and he also cites the apostles who shared their possessions. Thus love and economic sharing are related' (Alexis-Baker 2009: 365). Love and economic sharing may be related, but that does not mean that a testimony (*Test.* 3.3) supported by fifteen distinct passages, only one of which even mentions care for the poor (Acts 4:32, which begins by emphasising the believers' unity), can be subsumed under the category of economic sharing.

[36] Alexis-Baker 2009: 362.   [37] O'Keefe and Reno 2005: 63-68.

[38] See, for example, the use of Matt 10:25, 'If they have called the master of the house Beelzebub, how much more those of his household!' (*Si patremfamilias dixerunt Belzebul, quanto magis domesticos eius*) in a testimony entitled, 'that every person ought to have care rather of their own people, and especially of believers' (*Suorum et maxime fidelum curam plus unumquemque habere debere*). All three supporting texts (the other two, more relevant, texts being 1 Tim 5:8 and Isa 58:7) include the word *domesticos* (*Test.* 3.75). For discussion, see Murphy 2017: 71-72.

them all out in advance. This is because, I believe, he is largely drawing which texts he will use from memory.[39]

If we begin with *Test.* 3.1, 'on the good of works and mercy',[40] it is easy to see how this might lead to the qualification in the heading of *Test.* 3.2, 'in works and alms, even if by smallness of power less be done, the will itself is sufficient'.[41] There is also bad news followed by good news. In *Test.* 3.63, for example, we are taught 'the sin of fornication is serious'.[42] This is followed by, 'what the carnal things are which breed death, and what the spiritual things are which lead to life'.[43] Then Cyprian returns to 1 Corinthians in the following testimony, 'all sins are put away in baptism',[44] which covers much the same ground as the previous testimony, but in which freedom from sin is found through baptism.

Some testimonies seem to have little connection between them. For example, *Test.* 3.80, 'the devil has no power against man unless God has allowed it',[45] is followed by, 'wages are to be quickly paid to the hireling'.[46] In these cases, attention to the specific words used in the supporting texts may pay dividends. Included under the first heading is the direction to Judas, 'what you are doing, do quickly'.[47] This may have brought to mind other things to be done swiftly, like paying wages to those whom one has employed. Subsequently, Cyprian lists several testimonies drawn from Leviticus. A number of these 'book stud[ies]' appear,[48] particularly in the latter part of the collection.[49]

---

[39] If not citing from memory. See examples in Murphy 2014a: 543–44. Memorisation was a key aspect of a rhetor's education, beginning in childhood. See for example, Quintilian, *Inst.* 2.7.3–4; Cicero, *De or.* 2.86–88. For a discussion of classical techniques for training memory, see Yates 1966: 1–49. For the continuation of such techniques, see Carruthers 1998. As discussed below written texts provided the 'solidified reference points' for these practices. Carr 2005: 6.

[40] *De bono operis et misericordiae* (*Test.* 3.1).

[41] *In opere et elemosynis, etiamsi per mediocritatem minus fiat, ipsam uoluntatem satis esse* (*Test.* 3.2).

[42] *Grauius delictum esse fornicationis* (*Test.* 3.63, supported by 1 Cor 6:18).

[43] *Quae sint carnalia quae mortem pariant et quae spiritalia quae ad uitam ducant* (*Test.* 3.64, supported by Gal 5:17, 19–24; Note the omission of Gal 5:18 as discussed in Murphy 2014b: 93–94, 100–101).

[44] *Omnia delicta in baptism deponi* (*Test.* 3.65, supported by 1 Cor 6:9–11).

[45] *Nihil licere diabolo in homine, nisi Deus permiserit* (*Test.* 3.80).

[46] *Mercedem mercennario cito reddendam* (*Test.* 3.81, supported by Lev 19:13).

[47] *Quod facis fac uelocius* (*Test.* 3.80).

[48] Alexis-Baker 2009: 376. Although some (but not all) of these were previously noted by Fahey 1971: 79, 156, 481, 502–3, 506.

[49] Cyprian may have consulted the written text to which he had access for these, or, more probably, the title of a book was another organising principle which he applied to the texts he had memorised.

The structure of Book 3 of *Ad Quirinum* may appear disorganised to modern readers, but the largely oral culture of antiquity led people to organise their thoughts in different ways. Even the numbering of the individual testimonies assisted in the memorisation process, as Mary Carruthers has shown.[50] Cyprian therefore appropriates the common means of organising knowledge in his society and applies it to the scriptures in order to shape believers. His success is seen in the influence that the texts he compiled in Book 3 had on North African Christians, particularly as portrayed in the martyrdom accounts.[51]

Memorisation of Scripture

Memory plays an important role in Cyprian's compilation of *Ad Quirinum*; it likewise plays an important role in its reception. In antiquity, as Carr states, 'The focus was on inscribing a culture's most precious traditions on the insides of people. Within this context, copies of texts served as solidified reference points for recitation and memorization of the tradition.'[52] This attitude is evident in the prefaces to both Book 1 and Book 3 which emphasise the advantages of brevity in allowing the reader to memorise the heavenly precepts.[53] Book 1 differs from Book 3, however: in Book 1, Cyprian encourages Quirinus to 'examine more fully the scriptures, old and new, and read through the complete volumes of the spiritual books'.[54] In Book 3, however, rather than this exhortation to search the scriptures thoroughly, we have instead, at Quirinus' request, a collection of precepts 'bearing on the religious teaching of our school'[55] so that he would not be 'wearied with long or numerous volumes of books'.[56] While, as a number of scholars have noted, the preface to Book 3 does not mention Books 1 and 2,[57] the similarity of language creates a scenario which portrays Quirinus as

---

[50] Carruthers 1990: 63.
[51] As Alexis-Baker (2009: 375) notes, it is the source of approximately half the scriptures cited in the *Passio sanctorum Montani et Lucii* and those used by Petilian as recorded by Augustine.
[52] Carr 2005: 6. For the shaping of such a 'textual community', even when many within it are illiterate, see Stock 1983: 88–240. For the applicability of Stock's concept to antiquity, see Heath 2018.
[53] *Test.* 1.*pr.*; *Test.* 3.*pr.*
[54] *Scrutanti scripturas ueteres ac nouas plenius et uniuersa librorum spiritalium uolumina perlegenti* (*Test.* 1.*pr.*).
[55] *Ad religiosam sectae nostrae disciplinam pertinentia.*
[56] *Non longis aut multis librorum uoluminibus fatigetur* (*Test.* 3.*pr.*). Here again it is said to be for Quirinus' instruction.
[57] See Bobertz 1992: 124 n. 18.

having asked for further resources (so that he does not have to do the hard work himself) and Cyprian as responding with this collection.[58]

Structures for Transmitting Knowledge

By the mid-third century, the catechumenate was well established. We do not know its exact length in third-century North Africa,[59] but it would appear to be a matter of years rather than of months.[60] It provided ample time for a person of Cyprian's education and devotion to absorb the biblical tradition and doctrinal emphases of the North African church.[61] Cyprian's own conversion, socialisation, and training took place under the auspices of Caecilianus, 'a presbyter in age as well as in honour'.[62] Caecilianus later entrusted his wife and children to his protégé's care.[63]

Perhaps Caecilianus was one of a class of teacher-presbyters that we hear of in *Ep.* 29.[64] In justifying his appointment of two new clergy, Cyprian is at pains to point out that he is only following through on a decision that had already been taken. In the case of Optatus, the confessor and newly minted subdeacon, he had previously been admitted to 'a rank next to the clergy':[65] 'When we were recently putting under careful examination readers for the teacher-presbyters we appointed him one of the readers for the teachers of catechumens'.[66] Graeme Clarke suggests that these *presbyteri doctores*

---

[58] Ferguson (2001: 241) also notes a connection between *Test.* 2.30 and *Test.* 3.1, both of which cite Matt 25:31–46 on the judgement of the sheep and the goats.

[59] Stewart-Sykes 2003: 294.

[60] The three-year catechumenate of the *Apostolic Tradition* (17.1) may not have applied to every community in Rome (Stewart-Sykes 2001: 40). The Roman clergy in *Ep.* 8 assume similar procedures in Carthage to those in Rome (Clarke 1984–89: I.216).

[61] This is also seen in Perpetua, whose Christian commitment and maturity is evident despite being a catechumen when arrested. *Perp.* 2. For further discussion, see DeVore 2017: 237–47.

[62] *Vit. Cypr.* 4. Stewart-Sykes (2003: 294) divides this into an informal period and a comparatively brief formal catechumenate.

[63] *Vit. Cypr.* 4. I read the passage this way, rather than Kreider's understanding that it was Cyprian who left his wife and children to his mentor when he was martyred (2016: 159). If Caecilianus had outlived Cyprian, he would surely have been named in Cyprian's letters as a senior and loyal presbyter at a time when Cyprian was in definite need of such support. Also, Christians were not permitted to appoint members of the clergy as guardians (*Ep.* 1.2.1). This further suggests that Caecilianus died before Cyprian was appointed bishop.

[64] Aspasius is referred to in the same way (*vidimus ... Aspasium presbyterum doctorem*) in *Perp.* 13.

[65] *Clero proximos*. Perhaps, as Clarke suggests, 'proximus' may be used in the sense of 'assistant to' (Clarke 1984–89: II.110 n. 9).

[66] *Cum presbyteris doctoribus lectores diligenter probaremus, Optatum inter lectores doctorum audientium constituimus* (*Ep.* 29.2). See also the reference to teachers (*doctori*) of former heretics in *Ep.* 73.3.2 – those coming to the church must first be catechised before being baptised.

may have been 'the leaders of the general class of catechists (*doctores audientium*), clerical and lay'.[67] It is not clear whether or not these mentions of *doctores* without the qualifier *presbyteri* are indeed lay teachers, although the inclusion of laity among the teachers is suggested a generation or two earlier – in the *Martyrdom of Perpetua and Felicitas*, Saturus, of no named clerical rank, instructed the catechumens.[68] In any case, by the mid-third century, we see a considerable level of organisation in the catechumenate, with various kinds of teachers and readers involved. In addition, exorcists were part of ensuring that the devil was renounced, not only verbally, but physically.[69]

So while the bishop is primarily responsible for teaching the congregation,[70] he does not carry the burden alone. As the preface to Book 1 indicates, Cyprian collects the biblical quotations so that others may expand upon them,[71] as he himself does in a number of his other works.[72] Although Cyprian argues over the interpretation of scripture, particularly in the rebaptismal controversy, he does not seek to control its interpretation.[73] His main concern is that people are shaped by the biblical text. So, in his letter to Donatus, for example, Cyprian speaks of the place of personal, rather than corporate, Bible reading and prayer: 'Keep a discipline uncorrupted and sober in the virtues of religion. Be constant both in prayer and in reading. Now speak with God, now God with you. He instructs you in his precepts, he directs.'[74] Personal Bible reading (albeit by the wealthier members of the congregation) is also suggested when Cyprian imagines the defence of someone who had gained a certificate of sacrifice when the opportunity presented itself: 'I had previously read and I had learnt from my bishop's preaching that we should not offer sacrifice to idols'.[75]

---

[67] Clarke 1984–89: II.112–13 n. 12.

[68] *Ascendit autem Saturus prior, qui postea se propter nos ultro tradiderat (quia ipse nos aedificaverat), et tunc cum adducti sumus, praesens non fuerat (Perp. 4).*

[69] *Ep.* 69.15.2. The devil is then completely vanquished in baptism.

[70] For a discussion of the bishop as *doctor*, see Seagraves 1993: 267–73. On Cyprian's construction of his identity as teacher and upholder of scripture, see Wilhite 2010: 81.

[71] *Quibus non tam tractasse quam tractantibus materiam praebuisse uideamur (Test.* 1.*pr.*; cf. *Fort. pr.*3).

[72] Bobertz 1992: 115.

[73] As Fahey says, 'Cyprian accepted Scriptural texts with self-assured confidence and naïve optimism that their meaning would be crystal clear to the unprejudiced reader' (1971: 52).

[74] *Tene incorruptam, tene sobriam religiosis uirtutibus disciplinam. Sit tibi uel oratio adsidua uel lectio. Nunc cum Deo loquere, nunc Deus tecum. Ille te praeceptis suis instruat, ille disponat* (*Don.* 15).

[75] *Ego prius legeram et episcopo tractante cognoueram non sacrificandum idolis nec simulacra seruum dei adorare debere* (*Ep.* 55.14.1).

And in *Ad Fortunatum*, Cyprian refers to the scriptures he has provided as the 'very wool and purple' (*lanam ipsam et purpuram*) of the Lamb, the raw material from which Fortunatus and others may fashion garments for themselves.[76] Scripture, then, is the ultimate authority, to be applied thoughtfully to one's own circumstances.

Modelling the Christian Life

One of the ways in which Cyprian appropriates scripture is by using characters which appear in it as models. Certainly, as Kreider says, catechumens 'learned to be Christians by watching believers whom they admired',[77] but equally worthy of imitation, if not more so, were the saints who had gone before. The use of exemplars was a cornerstone of Greco-Roman *paideia*,[78] and Cyprian exploits this method which had first impacted his own spiritual development.[79] He differs from other Latin apologists, however, by renouncing classical models and drawing only from scripture.[80] His primary model is, unsurprisingly, Christ,[81] but many other characters appear from both testaments as examples of how (or how not) to live.[82] These are most common in his letters and treatises[83] but are still present in *Ad Quirinum*. The first testimony of Book 3, for example, includes Job, Tobit, the pearl merchant, the rich young ruler, the sheep and the goats, and Zacchaeus.[84]

De dominica oratione: The Content and Practice of Prayer

Just as there is a link between *Ad Donatum* and *Ad Quirinum*, so too are these works connected with *De dominica oratione*.[85] The constant prayer

---

[76] *Fort. pr.*3. [77] Kreider 2016: 159.

[78] On the whole, Cyprian prefers illustrative rather than logical *exempla*. For examples of classical models, see Smit 2013: 16–30. On this 'moral exegesis', see Daniélou 1977: 321.

[79] Job is a particular example given by Pontius, *Vit. Cypr.* 3.

[80] See Carlson 1948: 93–104. In fact, he rejects all classical allusions: see Clarke 1984–89: I.17.

[81] As indicated by the testimony, 'an example of how to live has been given to us in Christ' (*datum nobis exemplum uiuendi in Christo*, *Test.* 3.39).

[82] A list of some (but not all) of these 'biblical figures' is in Fahey 1971: 555–611. For the use of biblical exemplars in Greek patristic sermons, see Chapter 16 by Johan Leemans, this volume.

[83] For some examples from *De zelo et liuore* and *Ad Fortunatum*, see Murphy 2018a: 75–91; 2020: 123–31.

[84] *Test.* 3.1.

[85] Most scholars date *De dominica oratione* to late 251 or 252 CE. For example, Sage, *Cyprian*, 381–83. Réveillaud, however, dates it to 250 (1964: 39). For the link between *De dominica oratione* and *De opere et eleemosynis*, see Murphy 2016: 427–28.

that Cyprian recommends to Donatus is found in the final testimony of Book 3 of *Ad Quirinum*: 'We must be urgent in prayer', supported by Col 4:2, 'Be urgent and watchful in prayer',[86] and Ps 1:2, 'But his desire is in the law of the Lord and he will meditate on his law day and night.'[87] In his treatise on the Lord's Prayer, Cyprian notes that scripture teaches us how to pray; the Lord teaches us what we should pray.[88]

Cyprian does not explicitly tell us the audience to which *De dominica oratione* was directed, although Stewart-Sykes suggests that it (along with Tertullian's work *De oratione*) reflects the instruction given in the final stage of the catechumenate.[89] Later, Augustine preached on the Lord's Prayer to those who were about to be baptised.[90] They had already learned what to believe, having heard and repeated the Creed; now they were learning how to call on the one in whom they believed.[91] Ambrose preferred to reveal the mysteries of the church after baptism. Moorhead suggests this is the reason that the bishop of Milan did not deal with the Lord's Prayer in his commentary on Luke,[92] although Réveillaud thinks it may be because Cyprian's treatise had become the pre-eminent work on the topic.[93]

In any case, for Cyprian, the Lord's Prayer encapsulates the gospel.[94] The treatise contains his clearest exposition of grace,[95] and all his characteristic emphases are evident here: the contrast between the earthly and the heavenly; the importance of love and unity; discipline and repentance; and the

---

[86] *In epistula Pauli ad Colosenses*: '*Instate orationi uigilantes in ea*' (*Test.* 3.120). This verse is also used in *Ep.* 11.5.1 and *Dom. or.* 31. Each time, the direction to be thankful is omitted (Murphy 2018b: 129). Fahey does not comment on this omission (1971: 502).

[87] *In psalmo I*: '*Sed in lege Domini uoluntas eius est et in lege eius meditabitur die et nocte*' (*Test.* 3.120).

[88] *Quae nos, fratres dilectissimi, de diuina lectione discentes, postquam cognouimus ad orationem qualiter accedere debeamus, cognoscamus docente Domino et quid oremus* (*Dom. orat.* 7).

[89] Stewart-Sykes 2003: 296–97.

[90] *Ecce baptizabimini, omnia ibi vestra peccata delebuntur: nullum omnino ibi remanebit* (Augustine, *Serm.* 57.8).

[91] Augustine, *Serm.* 57.1–2.   [92] Moorhead 1999.

[93] Réveillaud 1964: 3. He also cites Hilary of Poitiers, who does not comment on the Lord's Prayer in his commentary on Matthew's Gospel as Cyprian has already done the work: *De orationis autem sacramento necessitate nos commentaudi Cyprianus vir sanctae memoria liberavit* (*Comm. Matt.* 5.1).

[94] Jesus Christ, the Word of God, 'made a large compendium of his precepts, that the memory of the scholars might not be burdened in the celestial learning, but might quickly learn what was necessary to a simple faith' (*praeceptorum suorum fecit grande compendium, ut in disciplina caelesti discentium memoria non laboraret, sed quod esset simplici fidei necessarium uelociter discreet*, *Dom. orat.* 28).

[95] Han-luen Kantzer Komline argues that the work may have been an important influence on Augustine, demonstrating that Cyprian here anticipates the Doctor of Grace in four key areas of his thought (2014: 274–78). As Réveillaud notes, Augustine suggested the reading of the treatise in order to combat the Pelagians (1964: 57–62). See Augustine, *Ep.* 215.3.

right use of wealth.[96] He also draws widely on scripture to demonstrate the correct attitude to prayer and to explicate the meaning of the Lord's Prayer. Furthermore, prayer is central to the Christian life and must be conducted in accordance with that life: God does not hear the prayers of those who hate their brothers and sisters, nor of those who neglect the needs of the poor.[97]

The Christian life is also marked by rhythms of prayer. The third, sixth, and ninth hours should be observed as in the Hebrew Scriptures; symbolically they represent three trinities.[98] But believers should also pray in the morning, celebrating the resurrection, and in the evening, praying for the advent of the true sun at the setting of the physical one.[99] Ultimately, Christians should model themselves on the widow Anna who prayed and watched without ceasing.[100] Since in eternity they will pray continuously, they should imitate now what they will one day be.[101]

Conclusion

The goal of catechesis in the early church was to form people whose primary identity could be summed up with the words 'I am a Christian.'[102] Loyalty to Christ was to override every other social tie.[103] The extent to which this was successful is debatable.[104] As Harmless says, 'The third-century catechumenate should neither be romanticized nor underestimated.'[105] The rush, as Cyprian portrayed it,[106] of some Christians to sacrifice under Decius led him to believe that their loyalty, and thus their transformation, was incomplete. But the catechumenate did shape a distinctive community, one in which even most of the lapsed were eager to be included, marked by allegiance to an authority greater than Caesar, practising non-violence and care for the poor and needy.

---

[96] Murphy 2018b: 30–31.   [97] *Dom. orat.* 23–24, 32.
[98] *Dom. orat.* 34.   [99] *Dom. orat.* 35.   [100] Luke 2:37.
[101] *Dom. orat.* 35–36. As Hamman (1991: 172–73) says, by praying day and night 'nous répétons dès ici-bas notre rôle d'éternité. La vigilance donne à la prière sa dimension eschatologique' ('we repeat here below our role in eternity. Vigilance gives prayer its eschatological dimension').
[102] *Christianus/a sum* (*Acts of the Scillitan Martyrs* 9–10; cf. *Perp.* 3). Note Cyprian's variation: *Christianus sum et episcopus* ('I am a Christian and a bishop', *Acta* 1).
[103] See, for example, Cyprian's citation of Matt 10:26 in *De opere et eleemosynis* (*Eleem.*) 16. This kind of piety is in continuity with the Jewish determination to follow God's law rather than that of empire (hence Cyprian's frequent use of exemplars like the three youths, Daniel, and the Maccabean martyrs), but at odds with the Greco-Roman understanding.
[104] See, for example, Rebillard 2012.   [105] Harmless 2014, 1st edn. 1995: 56.
[106] *Laps.* 8.

For Cyprian, then, scripture must shape the thought and practice of Christians, leading them to renounce the ways of the world and embrace the way of Christ. To this end, he compiles *testimonia* collections like *Ad Quirinum* and the later exhortation to martyrdom, *Ad Fortunatum*, organising knowledge in culturally intelligible ways. This knowledge is likewise transmitted by standard means – the memorisation of texts, in this case, scriptural passages or, at least, the headings under which they are collected. Much of this training is initially undertaken through the institution of the catechumenate. But being able merely to recite scripture is insufficient; it must be lived out, in imitation of Christ and the believers of old, as embodied knowledge. The other fundamental element of Christian life, according to Cyprian, is prayer which, as he explains in *De dominica oratione*, is only effective when one practises harmony and generosity. Through these disciplines, the one in whom God dwells will be perfected, as *Ad Donatum* suggests.[107] In Cyprian's life and work, the shift from the classical knowledge of antiquity to the scriptural knowledge of late antiquity is made manifest.

---

[107] *Don.* 15.

10 | Sacrificial Knowing: Cyprian and Early Christian Ritual Knowledge

ANDREW McGOWAN

Introduction: Sacrificial Knowing

People know what 'sacrifice' is. Sacrifice is an altruistic act, in which the agent gives something of importance, perhaps even the gift of self, for a greater good. The sacrifices daily made by parents, lovers, sports stars, and soldiers alike bear witness to a shared logic that is deeply ingrained and widely observed. To sacrifice is to act well, at great cost; it is deadly altruism. Sacrifice in this common sense now requires no religious motive or ritual setting but is a form of shared knowledge and discourse. Michael Chwe has called this sort of shared idea 'common knowledge', which 'depends not only on me knowing that you receive a message but also on the existence of a shared symbolic system which allows me to know how you understand it'.[1] Such 'knowledge', however, is not authenticated in all ways by its commonality; as Clifford Geertz observes, the closely related idea of 'common sense' presents itself as plain fact but actually reflects specific cultural systems, variable between periods and between places, and is not necessarily uncontested even in the moment.[2] What we assume sacrifice to be need not be what it always was.

The resonance of such modern understandings of sacrifice with themes in Christian theology is obvious. Contemporary theologians tend to share a similar basic 'knowledge' that sacrifice means something like self-giving love or *kenosis*,[3] i.e., that it involves violence and self-abnegation. Debates about sacrifice in recent theological discourse tend, then, to centre on whether those themes can be tolerated or redeemed. Feminist theologians have often noted the gendered application of sacrifice as a means of establishing power.[4] For some others, Rene Girard's view of sacrifice offers a historicised and supersessionist critique; once inevitable, sacrifice is now

---

My thanks to the Institute for Religion and Critical Inquiry at ACU and to Lewis Ayres for the invitation to participate in the Rome Seminar where a first version of this chapter was given, to Jonathan Zecher who responded at the time, and to Matthew Crawford, Michael Champion, and Felicity Harley for subsequent careful readings.

[1] Chwe 2001: 7.   [2] Geertz 2000: 73–93.
[3] Recently, for instance, Ward 2005; Coakley 2011.
[4] See the discussions of Ward and Coakley in Tonstad 2016: 82, 108, and so on.

unnecessary or presumptuous.[5] Others again see competition between Christian sacrifice and violent practices pretending to redemptive power. Stanley Hauerwas thus criticises the 'sacrificial' ideologies of warfare:

> The sacrifices of war are undeniable, but in the cross of Christ the Father has forever ended our attempts to sacrifice to God in terms set by the city of man [sic]. Christians have now been incorporated into Christ's sacrifice for the world so that the world no longer needs to make sacrifices for tribe or state, or even humanity.[6]

A common idea is evident here, even across different assessments of sacrifice and different accounts of its origins. Sacrifice means sacralised violence. Yet sacrificial ritual, once somehow the centre of or source for these reflections, is mostly absent in these discourses.

Sacrifice as actual ritual has nevertheless concurrently been of interest to religious and social theory,[7] including in recent studies of ancient Mediterranean religion that include or impinge upon biblical and ancient Jewish and Christian ideas and practices.[8] The meanings attributed to these rituals by historians and anthropologists contrast markedly with most 'common' ideas of sacrifice, as well as those employed in systematic theology. Offerings to deities have functioned in the varied ways that (other) gifts do, to establish or maintain relationship, to acknowledge needs or occasions for thanks. Granted the unhappy fate of animal victims, ritual sacrifice does not begin with violence, or death, nor is it particularly altruistic.[9] Sacrifice as ritual practice thus turns out not to be 'sacrificial' in the now-assumed sense,[10] and so two or more quite different forms of common knowledge or common sense are at issue.

That words change their meanings over time is obvious, but here the problem lies in how the change in the referent of 'sacrifice' has not been accounted for. The modern and common notion of sacrifice as deadly altruism constitutes an inescapable starting point for thinking about early Christian sacrificial discourse, not because it is accurate but because the false obviousness of this 'sacrifice' continues in theological discourse and in some scholarly interpretation of ancient texts and traditions. Yet the modern 'common sense' of sacrifice does have roots in how cultic ideas and images developed in late antiquity; sacrifice was changed, not ended. To explore what ancient Christians knew about sacrifice is thus also to trace

---

[5] See, for instance, Alison 1996; Heim 2006. [6] Hauerwas 2011: 69.
[7] See, for extracts from most of these and for useful commentary, Carter 2003.
[8] On Greek sacrifice in particular, see Detienne and Vernant 1989.
[9] See further McClymond 2008.
[10] Social-theoretical discourse and other historical forms of inquiry are not immune from the criticism of a sort of crypto-Christian rationale; see Detienne and Vernant 1989: 20.

the origins of what is known, or assumed, about the quite different thing that is called sacrifice now.

Implicit Meanings and Ritual Knowledge

Ideas are not ... unobservable mental stuff. They are envehicled meanings, the vehicles being symbols (or in some usages, signs), a symbol being anything that denotes, describes, represents, exemplifies, labels, indicates, evokes, depicts, expresses – anything that somehow or other signifies.[11]

Geertz' comments point to the significance of symbol and ritual for ideas, but also place ideas about ritual itself in that realm of the 'common' (as Chwe uses it), not merely as the subject or product of specialised discourse, but as constantly produced and in use in social relations generally. Given the ubiquity of what moderns would call 'religion', implicit and explicit ritual knowledge was formed in the households, other workplaces, and in the more public spheres of commerce and politics.[12] In particular, the ancient Mediterranean was suffused with sacrifices; not with altruism, that is, but with the performance of offerings, and with the logic these rituals implied. Sacrificial cultus constituted the heart of ancient Mediterranean devotional or religious practice, and hence the logic of offering, present in the forum and in the bedroom, would inevitably be used to interpret emergent Christian ritual performance but would in turn be reinterpreted by it.

If existing Greek and Roman sensibilities were inevitable points of reference, there were also more specific and overlapping traditions concerned with the memory of the Jerusalem temple, but given first the distance and then the destruction of this sacrificial centre, these amounted to a different and more specialised form of knowledge, learned and deployed particularly through acts of speech and reading. Yet there was a commonality of sacrificial assumptions across all these that could be reflected, for instance, in the arguments of Paul to the Corinthians about meals and sacrifices:

I speak as to sensible people; judge for yourselves what I say. The cup of blessing that we bless, is it not a sharing in the blood of Christ? The bread that we break, is it not a sharing in the body of Christ? Because there is one bread, we who are many are one body, for we all partake of the one bread. Consider the people of Israel; are not those who eat the sacrifices partners in the altar? What do I imply then? That

---

[11] Geertz 1980: 135.
[12] On the difficulty of ancient Roman and other 'religion', see Beard, North, and Price 1998; Nongbri 2013.

food sacrificed to idols is anything, or that an idol is anything? No, I imply that what pagans sacrifice, they sacrifice to demons and not to God. I do not want you to be partners with demons. You cannot drink the cup of the Lord and the cup of demons. You cannot partake of the table of the Lord and the table of demons. (1 Cor 10:15–21 NRSV)

Paul assumes that the three types of activity – the Christian eucharistic meal, the sacrifices of the Jerusalem temple, and feasts based on Greek temple offerings – are comparable, and hence to an extent mutually exclusive.[13] Participation in all of them effects a sort of communion; without the common knowledge that sacrifices create solidarity, Paul's argument about the slightly different issue of compatibility would have no force. Paul relies here on a kind of sacrificial knowing, grounded not in ideas such as suffering or expiation but in the shared understanding that profound bonds are made through cultic participation. His readers might not have agreed with his conclusion about exclusivity, but they understood his assumption about solidarity. Such common ritual knowledge was required to negotiate the invitations, demands, and exclusions of sacrificial cultus which extended through ancient Mediterranean life. That knowledge was neither stable nor universal in its details, but those who took part in the ritual life of Christian communities, as well as their detractors, shared certain assumptions about what offerings and sacrifices were for, and how they worked. Participation (and non-participation) in these rituals as a part of daily life meant drawing on and recreating such meanings. While ideas about the earliest Christian gatherings have often foregrounded their relationship to textual and oral performance, with these forms of discourse went various implicit meanings assumed or formed in ritual practice centred on meals; the dispositions of bodies, substances, objects, places, and of time itself constituted not merely a set of media for the communication of ideas, but a different type of knowledge, a collective if not invariable *habitus* which both proclaimed and embodied their being in Christ.

Cultural Production and Early Christian Intellectuals

The relationship between discursive considerations of sacrifice by ancient authors and the implicit ritual knowledge shared by participants is not straightforward. Daniel Ullucci has rightly made a significant distinction

---

[13] This is not to say Paul regarded the Levitical cult and the Eucharist as mutually exclusive for Jews who were also Christians; these two were porous, but both incompatible with the Greek sacrifices and associated banquets.

between the views expressed in literary works by ancient intellectuals on the one hand, and attitudes attached to actual participation in ritual practice on the other.[14] Borrowing from Pierre Bourdieu and following Stanley Stowers, Ullucci suggests ancient theologians are 'cultural producers' whose distance from typical (but largely unknown) attitudes comes from their being members of a small literate minority.[15] Their entry into existing debates about sacrificial practice are probably distant from the surrounding ritual reality.[16]

This disjuncture between theory and practice is inescapable, although Ullucci's particular account results in a sort of agnosticism about common ritual knowledge. His cultural producers posture and play, but their relationship to the wider reality of culture and practice is obscure. However, the autonomy of these intellectuals may not be as complete as this model assumes. The notion of the cultural producer in this attenuated sense was for Bourdieu an outgrowth of capitalism; prior to the Renaissance, the equivalent artist or writer was in thrall to aristocratic and ecclesiastical demands.[17] Whether or not Bourdieu was quite right, even about the autonomy of modern cultural production, ancient discourses about sacrifice need not be read in this particular form of isolation. If the elite status of ancient sacrificial theorists was in some ways more extreme than that of modern artists, given the extent of social stratification and the limits of literacy, they made claims that depended on a sacrificial common sense. Ullucci's warning should be revised, then, to acknowledge that these connections need to be found and interrogated, rather than assumed. Paul's admonition to the Corinthians already provides one example where common knowledge and actual practice seem to intersect, even if not without conflict. Paul is not writing merely to theorise sacrifice but in hope of encouraging particular practices. In what follows, I pursue this leverage of the assumed, where ritual knowledge and aspects of sacrificial knowing can be discerned in the course of their use to make other points – and perhaps in attempts to change them.

A related difficulty for interpretation of early Christian discourse and practice is how what is arguably a communal offering practice in that tradition – that of eucharistic meals – has typically been seen by scholars either as an activity essentially unlike sacrifice[18] or as rendered sacrificial

---

[14] Ullucci 2012. [15] Ullucci 2012: 152–53 n. 9; Stowers 2011.
[16] Ullucci 2012: 5; see also Klawans 2006.
[17] Bourdieu 1985: 14; Ullucci acknowledges some of these difficulties but retains the notion of cultural production as autonomous (2012: 5 n. 9).
[18] On some important indications that early Christian understandings were concrete and cultic, see Frank 1978; on meal practice and sacrifice, see now also Öhler 2014.

only via metaphor, in relation to the death of Jesus.[19] Such omission or misapprehension arises because of assumptions in the theorising of sacrifices as violent, and because the relationship between dining ritual and ancient Mediterranean sacrifices has been given insufficient attention. The association of meal and sacrifice, based on meal practice more than on Jesus' death, is made by Paul and then by numerous others, but Cyprian of Carthage makes it more fulsomely than any prior author or text.[20]

Cyprian and Sacrifice

Cyprian has often been acknowledged as an important contributor to Christian discourse about sacrifice, not least in placing the Eucharist and the ministers of the church in the realm of sacrifice and priesthood more explicitly than in any earlier Christian author.[21] Historical theology has nevertheless tended to place Cyprian's theorising in works such as *De lapsis* in a trajectory of Christian 'spiritualisation' and rejection of sacrifice.[22] For some, Cyprian's fulsome uses of cultic language made him only a more generous, or less subtle, user of cultic metaphor.[23] Cyprian's language has occasionally, however, been acknowledged at something closer to face value, as theorising Christian practices as actually sacrificial. Nancy Jay, in her cross-cultural study of sacrifice and patriarchy, sees Cyprian's appropriation of cult as quite literal but emphasises its discontinuity with earlier understandings of Christian meal and ministry.[24] More recently, Allen Brent includes cultic ideas and images in presenting Cyprian's robust appropriation of Roman jurisprudence and notions of the political.[25]

Cyprian's willingness to speak so directly and concretely of sacrifice in Christian contexts can be taken (as by both Jay and Brent, in different ways) as a creative imposition or appropriation. Yet, even if innovative in his specific construction of links with Roman civic cult, Cyprian's thinking relies on an existing tradition of Christian sacrificial theory about the Eucharist. Such eucharistic sacrificial knowing was available for his use, rather than

---

[19] A criticism that can be directed at the premise of what is a brief but nevertheless the best study of the question of eucharist and sacrifice so far, Williams 1982.
[20] McGowan 2012. [21] Bévenot 1979.
[22] Daly 1978; Young 1979; Ferguson 1980.
[23] Cyprian does also use the imagery of sacrifice in ways closer to the 'spiritualised' form noted by such as Daly and Young; for a discussion of one instance, see Murphy 2016.
[24] Jay 1992: 166. [25] Brent 2010.

being his invention.[26] Cyprian's particular value as a case study for this kind of ritual knowledge lies in the particular ways and occasions in which this interest appears, and in his leverage of assumed common knowledge to make more specific points. As Ullucci puts it, 'Cyprian takes a position on sacrifice only when doing so advances his argument on other issues.'[27] While thus using sacrifice as something 'good to think with', Cyprian does not imagine – or at least does not admit – that he is innovating about the core significance of ritual, but appeals to understandings shared with his audiences in order to make points about faith, church, and authority, which are his real interests.[28] These discourses may then disclose implied and shared ancient sacrificial knowing, as well as aspects of its Christian adaptation.

It is the more remarkable, though, that Cyprian's boldly cultic theorisation of Christian practice takes place against the background of the 'Decian persecution', better described as the Decian decree of universal sacrifice.[29] What was traditional in this exercise, based on common ritual knowledge, was how verbal profession (on which see further below) and physical performance of sacrifice together represented an embodied knowledge that instantiated not mere belief in the modern sense but *religio*, the entirety of pious practice. Yet this imperial initiative was highly innovative also. Under the guise of supporting immemorial custom, the decree demanded participants perform a ritual fantasy of past fidelity in word and deed as they all sacrificed to the gods. Such universal participation in any particular cult was of course not traditional, relative to what had largely been a network of local cults, and its imposition even less so.[30]

In what follows I consider what may be Cyprian's two most significant writings on these topics, the treatise *De lapsis* and his *Letter* 63. In the first there are important indications of implicit ritual knowledge involved in sacrifice and solidarity, brought to the fore in the persecution. In the second, Cyprian uses shared understandings of the relationship between tradition and sacrifice, and common understandings of sacrificial food and drink, to address a specific controversy.[31] As Ullucci would remind us, Cyprian's own discursive treatments are hardly direct windows onto these processes. They may, however, be relevant to changing conceptions beyond the narrow realm of the ancient 'cultural producer'.

---

[26] See further Frank 1978; McGowan 2012; Öhler 2014.   [27] Ullucci 2012: 115.
[28] I take a slightly different approach to the discussion of *Laps.* in McGowan 2014.
[29] Rives 1999.   [30] Knipfing 1923: 367; Rives 1999: 144.
[31] Other writings of course are also relevant, not least the set of letters (5–43) from during the Decian persecution. See the translations and commentary in Clarke 1984–89.

Sacrifice, Community, and Identity: Cyprian, *De lapsis*

In his treatise on the lapsed, Cyprian considers the end of the Decian persecution and the pastoral challenges it presented, not least the readmission to communion of some who had performed the required civic sacrifices.[32] The treatise begins not with the failed, however, but with those who had succeeded, or even triumphed. An elaborate word picture compares the release of imprisoned Christians, ironically enough, to a Roman triumphal procession. Some of this *ekphrasis* is purely metaphorical, but there are more literal aspects of practice woven into the picture also:

Honourable hands, which were used only to divine works (*opera divina*), have resisted the sacrilegious sacrifices. Lips sanctified by heavenly food, after the body and blood of the Lord, have rejected profane contamination and the leftovers of idols. Your heads were free from the impious and wicked veil with which those captive heads of the sacrificers were veiled. Your brows, pure with the sign of God, could not bear the crown of the devil, but kept itself for the Lord's crown. (*Laps.* 2)[33]

Veils, garlands, and wreaths were commonly used in sacrificial ritual, although the point here is their refusal.[34] In the case of food, however, two material systems are juxtaposed. As in Paul's older discussion, the competing meals fill a similar place in implicit pictures of how divine service and communal practice connect. While the language of sacrifice is perhaps applied more literally to the idol offerings eschewed by the prisoners than to the Eucharist here, the *opera divina* of the confessors' hands are clearly parallel forms of worship. The concrete language of taste and touch used by Cyprian even echoes the Decian decree, which required supplicants to swear to the effect that 'I have sacrificed, poured a libation, and tasted of the sacred victim.'[35]

Cyprian turns to the situation of the less staunch Christians, whose failures are presented as a wound to the church as a whole (4). This he laments but interprets as a test of faith (5–6) and as correction (7). The extent of the failure is admitted in striking terms:

nor did they leave it so that they seemed to sacrifice to idols unwillingly. They ran to the forum of their own accord; they hurried freely to death, as if they already wanted it, as if they would grasp an opportunity now given, but previously hoped for. How many were delayed by the magistrates, when evening was coming on; how many even asked that their destruction not be deferred! (8)

---

[32] Dated to 251 CE; see Bévenot 1957: 74. [33] Translations mine, except as noted.
[34] See examples in Rives 1999: 145–46; cf. Tertullian, *Cor.* [35] See Knipfing 1923: 364.

Allowing for dramatic effect, the willingness of some Carthaginian Christians to sacrifice seems undeniable and reflects the ease or even alacrity with which they could step (back?) into observance of civic and religious duties, whose omission hitherto was perhaps overlooked in the diversity and ubiquity of cultic observance.

While fear of punishment was important, numerous Carthaginian Christians may indeed have been keen to answer a clear call to civic solidarity. Despite a possible 'intellectual disjunction', as Allen Brent puts it, this performance was the normal action at least of free male citizens, the logical expression of their innate sacrificial knowledge in its civic form.[36] We need not assume that even sincere Christians were all deeply convicted of the need to abstain. It is quite possible that the issue had been habitually avoided up to this point. In requiring a positive and individual enactment of what could otherwise have remained a collective but nevertheless not universal practice, the decree brought to the surface a tension between wider Roman assumptions about full (but not assiduous) participation in a non-exclusive ritual life, and Christian claims that eucharistic ritual and civic sacrifices were incompatible, partly because they were similar types of activity. The Christian insistence on exclusivity, inherited from Judaism, was of course a form of knowledge in tension with the wider common knowledge found in the Roman colony. While this clash could then or now be articulated in terms of conflicting propositions about the existence or legitimacy of the divine beings with or for whom the competing meals were celebrated, practice was in fact both the locus of tension prior to the decree and the arbiter of its resolution.

The decree seems to have articulated a sort of revisionist history for the participant in sacrifice, who affirmed that 'I have always and without interruption sacrificed to the gods and now in your presence in accordance with the edict's decree I have sacrificed.'[37] Not uniquely, innovation was draped in tradition. The alacrity of the sacrificial participant described by Cyprian was a race to this imagined past. The religious failure of the Christian sacrificers was not so much propositional as intuitive, a failure to negotiate the competing demands of systems based on implicit ritual knowledge, where the logic not only of the *civitas* but also of the *familia* stood on the side of

---

[36] Brent also sees this as a matter of world view, more specifically of 'form of life' and 'construction of reality'. The specifics of his argument about *potestas*, *auctoritas*, and *imperium* may give too much direct emphasis to elite political concepts, the concerns of the 'cultural producers'; see Brent 2010: 225–29.

[37] Knipfing 1923: 347, cf. 363.

the emperor and his decree.[38] When Cyprian goes on to argue the necessity of the Christian losing *patria* and *patrimonium* if this is demanded (10), he is not speaking narrowly of the loss of territory or property, even though he criticises those motivated by financial security (11–12), but of an identity formed by ritual, next to which the Christian *ecclesia* offers an alternative reality, political as well as religious. The clash of common senses is not about sacrifice but about the community with which ritual knowledge is interdependent. While Romans could accept considerable plurality of offerings within an authorised *religio*, the church constituted itself in the same place as the *imperium*, not merely as one cult, but as a political community that performed and claimed cult as its own.

Strikingly, Cyprian also introduces the notion that these sacrificers were themselves *sacrificati*, 'sacrificed':

Could a servant of God stand there, and speak and deny Christ, when he had already denied the devil and the world? Was that altar, which he approached to die, not his funeral pyre? Should he not cringe and flee from the devil's altar, which he had observed smoking and stinking with a foul odour, as if it were the funeral and cemetery of his life? Why bring a sacrifice with you, wretch, why bring a victim? You have come to the altar as a sacrifice, you have come as a victim; you have offered there your salvation, your hope; you have cremated your faith there in those funereal fires. (8)

This idea is part of his own word picture, rather than a piece of common knowledge; but it is worth noting that the idea of 'being sacrificed' has no immediate positive or redemptive notion in this context such as the modern idea of self-sacrifice would entail, even though it has a sense of destruction attached.

Although his account involves literary and theoretical artifice well beyond common understandings, Cyprian's caution on restoring the lapsed is grounded in a more concrete and shared sense of the power of sacred banquets. Returning to the theme of comparison and exclusion struck at the beginning of the treatise, and again picking up the gustatory sensuality of the decree and its requirements, he continues:

Returning from the altars of the devil, they approached the holy place of the Lord, with hands filthy and reeking with odour, still almost breathing the pestilent

---

[38] The same logic, of altar and sacrifice as a single and exclusive whole, is applied by Cyprian to the contemporary struggle between him and his loyalists and the supporters of Felicissimus, who is said to have erected another altar and founded another priesthood (*Ep.* 41). These discussions draw on both biblical and Roman ideas without clear separation.

idol-food; and with jowls still exhaling their crime, and reeking with the fatal contact, they intrude on the body of the Lord, even though the sacred scripture stands in their way and calls out 'Every one that is clean shall eat of the flesh; and whatever soul eats of the flesh of the saving sacrifice, which is the Lord's, having his uncleanness on him, that soul shall be cut off from his people.' (15, citing Lev 7:20)

Cyprian extends the cultic parallels from Christian meal to ministerial office for the participants; these transgressions take place 'before their conscience has been purged by sacrifice (*sacrificio*) and by the hand of the priest (*sacerdotis*)' (16).[39] Warnings about this incompatibility of sacred foods are extended into gruesome supernatural anecdotes including more sacrificial parallels. A child who vomited spectacularly at the Eucharist – a case where other experience suggests specific moments of divine wrath are not always required – had, it turned out, been taken to participate in the imperial cultus by a wetnurse (25). Another man 'dared to receive secretly with the rest a part of the sacrifice celebrated by the priest; he could neither eat nor handle the Lord's sacred [body] but found in his opened hands that he had a cinder' (26).

Cyprian's discourse addresses a particular situation of crisis and disruption, and involves creative identifications, but it reveals an implicit understanding of what sacrifice does and how it works, a knowledge which is not his actual point, but a requisite assumption for it to be made. This understanding is shared with the sponsors and participants in the imperial cult, and with Decius. Sacrifice is offered to a particular god or gods, but it creates community both between gods and humans and between the humans themselves. First, then, the Eucharist thus does for participants something analogous to (other) sacrifices by connecting them. Cyprian's laments and lambastings of the fallen Carthaginian Christians thus give not much emphasis to the real or supposed demons and deities of Rome and its empire, and much more to the human relations and allegiances involved. Wrong sacrifice is a communal disorder; positively speaking, the treatise confirms again and again that sacrifice creates and expresses community both vertically and horizontally; to sacrifice is not merely to signal allegiance, but to effect the allegiance it signifies. Yet this shared logic undergirds a different sense of community, what might deserve even to be termed an ecclesiology. Cyprian deflects the implied demand of civic sacrifice for social cohesion because the society for which he is concerned is his own Christian community.

---

[39] The cups of libation and Eucharist are also juxtaposed, as John Penniman (2015a) points out, as poison and medicine.

The second issue, that of sacrificial incompatibility, is more complex. Cyprian's argument is not merely a rebranding of existing Roman or other ancient understandings as Christian, even though it depends on them. Christian practice, like Jewish, refused idolatry and was exclusive in character. Just as Jewish sacrificial knowing and its Greek equivalent had clashed earlier in the Maccabean era, now Christian and traditional Roman forms of ritual knowledge were in deep conflict even while sharing common ground. For Cyprian, his flock should have acknowledged distinct sacrificial realms, even under pressure of violence; the *lapsi* were not so clear about the distinction. This exclusivity Cyprian sought was not an agreed part of the general sacrificial knowing of the Roman world, while the principle of sacrificial solidarity was. Just as Decius was innovating under the guise of tradition, Cyprian was synthesising aspects of Roman tradition with the exclusivity of deity and cult brought into Christianity from its Jewish origins. The lapsed were thus not necessarily greedy or cowardly but were caught between two ways of knowing the world and belonging to it which were increasingly diverging, and so seeking to have their Roman sacrifice and eat it too. This was therefore a competition between emerging kinds of ritual knowledge, not, however, merely the preserve of theorists, but a clash with practical or even deadly consequences.

Sacrifice, Authenticity, and Tradition: Cyprian, *Letter* 63

Although its date is uncertain,[40] the immediate occasion of Cyprian's *Letter* 63 is clear. A pastoral and liturgical problem had arisen concerning the use of water, rather than wine, at the celebration of the Eucharist. Cyprian's answer to this problem depends largely on forms of sacrificial knowing. In this case, the key knowledge is about tradition, and understanding of ritual authority in the strict sense, i.e., of authorship or origin. Complementing this is the assumption that wine is an element proper to sacrificial offerings, as the Decian decree of sacrifice had itself assumed.[41]

The reason this particular ritual curiosity arose is not completely clear. There are numerous cases, mostly a little earlier in date, where water rather than wine was used in Christian meals, whose commonality seems to lie in squeamishness about the place of wine in sacrifice.[42] Such avoidances were

---

[40] See Clarke 1984–89: III.287–88.
[41] See the parallels drawn by Rives 1999 with *supplicationes*.
[42] For more detail, see McGowan 1999: 204ff.

also known in Jewish and philosophical circles, where the dietary avoidance stood for a kind of dissent or dissociation from the wider norms of cult and dining. Cyprian seems to be aware that this teetotal practice is a tradition of sorts and not just a recent innovation, although some more specific pastoral context may be involved.[43] The Decian decree and a resulting heightened aversion to practices bound up with sacrifice may have played a part.[44]

There may also have been some uncertainty in African communities about proper ritual practice at the Eucharist, arising from the relatively recent shift from Christian evening meals to morning eucharistic gatherings, when wine was less apt.[45] This is another point, then, at which common knowledge about meals overlaps with that concerning sacrifices. Morning distributions of eucharistic food (in addition to, rather than instead of, at the evening *agape*) had already been known in Carthage half a century before,[46] but the shift to early gatherings as the normal venue for the Eucharist may not have everywhere been recent or smooth; for that matter, this letter seems to refer to settings beyond Carthage.

Cyprian insists that any remaining evening Christian events are (now) private, but in smaller towns the problem of community scale, which may have been a factor in the change away from banquets in major centres, will not have seemed so pressing. The fact of a morning Eucharist was not necessarily obvious or easy for communities still observing a common sympotic practice, and without the framework of the banquet – which involved a different ritual knowledge, even if one closely related to sacrifice – there was probably some confusion about the proprieties of ritual, including drinking. If the ritual knowledge applicable for a *cena* was now not available for application to the Eucharist, Cyprian still saw this morning event as a kind of *sacrificium*. This is the key assumption of the letter, which is worked out in a variety of ways, but above all in an emphasis on tradition and continuity, and in relation to the use of wine as a necessary element of sacrifice.

---

[43] 'There is then no reason, dearest brother, for anyone to think that the custom of some is to be followed, if they thought in the past that water alone should be offered in the cup of the Lord' (*Ep.* 63.14).

[44] The argument to be made below can be added to the factors that lead Graeme Clarke to favour a date after the Decian decree also (1984–89: III.287–88).

[45] On the preference for water, see McGowan 1999: 204–10; on the date and reasons for the change in time, see McGowan 2004; Leonhard 2015.

[46] See Tertullian, *Cor.* 3.

The centrality of this sacrifice, and of a set of ideas about the origins of the rite such as *traditio*, *doctrina*, and *auctoritas*, is presented by Cyprian from the beginning of the letter:

some, either out of ignorance or naivete, when sanctifying the cup of the Lord and ministering to the people do not do what Jesus Christ our Lord and God, the founder and teacher of this sacrifice (*sacrificii huius auctor et doctor*), did and taught ... (*Ep.* 63.1)

The term 'the Lord's tradition' (*dominica traditio*; cf. 1 Cor 11:23) appears six times in the relatively brief document, whose rhetorical foundation is a contrast between what was instituted by the Lord and maintained in the catholic church and the alternative, which is to innovate, choose human tradition – or rather 'custom', since Cyprian seems to treat 'bad' tradition as *consuetudo* and 'good' tradition as *traditio* – and thus fall into error.

Cyprian constructs a *traditio* for the Christian sacrifice that is more than just a chain from Jesus to the African church, but a primordial tradition going back to Genesis, based on the form of the rite including wine. He starts with Noah – where wine itself begins, in biblical tradition – then to Melchizedek (at some length, on which more below), to Solomon (meaning the sapiential tradition of wisdom's banquet in Prov 9), the blessing of Judah (Gen 49), and to Isaiah (63:2), presenting all these texts and their references to wine not only as types of the Eucharist, but as together constituting a tradition, a biblical version of the acknowledged use of wine in sacrifice 'always and without interruption'. Cyprian's examples concerning the use of wine are all biblical, but the logic about tradition is generic. Central to these scriptural prefigurings of eucharistic wine, and the most directly cultic in significance, is the case of Melchizedek, the biblical priest par excellence:

in the priest Melchizedek we see prefigured the sacrament of the sacrifice of the Lord, according to what divine scripture testifies and says, 'and Melchizedek, king of Salem, brought forth bread and wine'. For he was a priest of the most high God, and blessed Abraham. And in the Psalms, the Holy Spirit declares that Melchizedek bore the image of Christ, saying in the person of the Father to the Son: 'Before the morning star I begot you; you are a priest forever, after the order of Melchizedek.' The order at issue is of course this one, coming from that sacrifice and descending from it, in that Melchizedek was a priest of the most high God, that he offered wine and bread, and that he blessed Abraham. For who is more a priest of the most high God than our Lord Jesus Christ, who offered a sacrifice to God the Father, and offered the same thing which Melchizedek had offered, that is, bread and wine, to be understood as his body and blood? (63.4)

Cyprian thus traces a sort of logical and historical genealogy of the *ordo* of Melchizedek, not so much (or not only) as a group of priests, but as a way of practice and of understanding. For Cyprian, the *ordo* of Melchizedek is not an invisible and mysterious one that leaps into history again only with Christ, but is bestowed with the blessing of Abraham and thus genuinely historical, the present members being the descendants (leaning here on Paul's use of Abrahamic descent in Gal 3), who are now the followers of Christ.

The considerable emphasis upon the very concrete issue of the appropriate drink for cultic practice, which is another element of implicit knowledge carried by ritual practitioners and participants, complements this emphasis on tradition.[47] As Clarke points out, while Cyprian defends the use of a mixed cup he avoids reference to this ubiquitous meal custom as a mere issue of conviviality. Mixture is basically a way of talking about the necessary use of wine, invoking it as cultic substance as much or more than as customary adjunct to banqueting.[48] Thus, instead of referring to meal practice itself as a model, Cyprian emphasises the same sacrificial knowledge manifested negatively in the wineless eucharistic tradition, namely the understanding that wine is particularly an accoutrement of cultus.

Part of Cyprian's *traditio* is a brief foray into the Psalms, which allows something more like a 'natural theology' of wine; citing Ps 22(23):5 in the form 'your intoxicating cup' (*calix tuus inebrians*), Cyprian makes something of the innate properties of the fruit of the vine. While careful to distance himself and the Eucharist from 'the world's wine', he notes the change in perspective and consciousness brought by ordinary wine, by which 'the mind is dissolved, and the soul relaxed, and all sadness is laid aside'. With the wine of the Eucharist, however, 'the memory of the old man is laid aside [with] oblivion of the former worldly conversation … [and] the joy of the divine mercy' (11). Yet he also insists that the 'sacrifice' to be maintained is made with bread and wine, an offering of food and drink – specifically of wine – as might have been expected in other sacrifices in Roman Africa:[49]

So in Genesis, in order that the benediction in respect of Abraham by Melchizedek the priest might be duly celebrated, it came first as the image of Christ's sacrifice,

---

[47] On the significance of wine and of meat, see Detienne and Vernant 1989. On Christian eucharistic practice, including the scope of the water-drinking tendency, see McGowan 1999.

[48] Clarke 1984–89: III.289–90.

[49] We should refrain from assuming that the identification of Eucharist and sacrifice relies on the metaphorisation of the meal in terms of Jesus' death rather than its form; see McGowan 2012.

as constituted in bread and wine. The Lord, completing and fulfilling this, offered bread and mixed cup of wine, and so he who is the fullness of truth fulfilled the truth of the prefigured image. (63.4)

Although there is obviously a real difference between this pattern and sacrificial banquets centred on meat as well as wine, we should not assume that this identification of eucharistic eating as sacrificial on the basis of cuisine is tendentious. The difficulty for his implied readers was more likely to be the more tenuous connection between the morning event and its token foodstuffs, and their common ritual knowledge that (also) linked wine, banqueting, and sacrifice.

After a brief counter-narrative about water, which Cyprian takes always to be a type of baptism in scripture, he returns to the theme of authority and continuity with Paul, reading the narrative in 1 Cor 11 together with what is perhaps a less obvious text, about apostolic authority in Galatians (1:6–9). In the last third or so of the text, Cyprian shifts to more christological ground. Cyprian speaks frequently of 'the Lord's sacrifice' and similarly. These terms always refer, intriguingly, to the Eucharist itself. It would be going too far to say that this language does not (also) refer to the passion and death of Jesus, because at some points Cyprian seems to imply a sort of synecdoche between the Christian meal (and/or the Last Supper) and the whole of Christ's passion, and because at one point he identifies the two.[50] Yet the main focus of his discourse about Christ's 'sacrifice' is certainly the sacramental meal itself. The passion–Eucharist–sacrifice connection had also been made in chapter 14:

For if Jesus Christ, our Lord and God, is himself the high priest of God the Father, and has first offered himself as a sacrifice to the Father, and has ordered this to be done in commemoration of himself, certainly that priest truly discharges the office of Christ who imitates what Christ did; and he then offers a true and full sacrifice in the church to God the Father, if he goes on to offer it according to what he sees Christ himself offered.

What is offered and repeated of course is the eucharistic action of the Last Supper, not the giving of self in death. It would be a mistake, then, to assume that Cyprian's idea of the cultic reality of the Eucharist derives from its metaphorisation as a sign of Jesus' death; rather, the meal has the nature of a sacrifice because of its dominical origins and form, and so the relationship with the *passio* as a whole is synecdochic rather than metaphorical.

---

[50] *passio est enim Domini sacrificium quod offerimus* (63.17).

If Cyprian's argument in *De lapsis* is about community and participation, that in *Letter* 63 is about tradition and about cultic substances. The validity of sacrifice consists in fidelity to the tradition of its founder, and the ritual enactment of an unbroken tradition, as well as in the use of the elements proper to sacrifice. This is another fundamental piece of sacrificial common knowledge, a premise on which Cyprian builds his point about the concrete question of using wine in the eucharistic cup. Sacrifice (here, and typically elsewhere, too) is not an autonomous or innovative exercise – where innovation does occur, it tends to be presented as the renewal of tradition. In any case, when Cyprian says that 'every practice of piety and truth is overturned' (*omnis religionis et veritatis disciplina subvertitur*) in the wineless Eucharist (15.1), he is appealing to a sacrificial knowledge wider than that of the church. The same emphasis on an unchanging tradition, or even on its fictional construction, was of course also present in the contrivance of the Decian decree – the sacrificer's claim that they had 'always and without interruption sacrificed to the gods'.

Conclusions

Cyprian's appeals to sacrificial knowing help to reveal something of the shared understandings, not only of ancient 'cultural producers', but of typical participants in Christian and other sacrifices, such as the *sacrificati* of the Decian persecution and the abstemious water-drinkers of his eucharistic letter. We need not and should not restrict the significance of disputes over reconciliation of the lapsed or over the matter of the Eucharist to Cyprian's ecclesiology or sacramental theology. The different positions reflect concrete experiences and decisions by many Christians and reflect the awkward negotiation by these of changing understandings of what sacrifice was, and how it was to be practised. While Cyprian's arguments involve niceties that may have gone beyond the interest or knowledge of ancient Christians and others, he relies on shared understandings of solidarity and of tradition, as well as of proper sacrificial elements, to make his specific points.

As we have seen, ancient Mediterranean sacrificial knowing is a set of understandings associated with ritual practice itself, while modern western sacrificial knowing is an ethical tool. The latter is a way of interpreting behaviour that has no specific ritual context, although it can be reapplied to ritual via metaphor, so that ritualised actions as divergent as baseball and military service can both be termed 'sacrificial'. Ancient sacrificial knowing, however, is both transactional and reciprocal; gods and humans are variously linked (and distinguished) by roles in cultus. Ancient sacrifice is not altruistic, nor is it particularly deadly for the practitioner (although failures of practice, not sacrifice itself, could themselves incur divine wrath). And the use of sacrifice for expiation or propitiation is not as central in ancient settings, including early Christian ones, as later understandings more closely tied to 'religious' purposes have tended to make it. A commonality of sorts, however, emerges in the way ancient 'sacrifice' provides understandings that create society itself via reciprocity and tradition. Sacrificial knowing in both ancient and modern cases concerns how the self, other, and community relate by means of gift.

The two kinds of sacrificial knowing, ancient and modern, are linked genealogically. It is via Christian and Jewish reflection in late antiquity on human life and divine service, to which Cyprian's discussion of the *passio* of Christ can be seen to contribute, that the notion of sacrifice will shift into the familiar emphasis on suffering and self-abnegation.[51] The way the nascent church used cultic imagery to interpret its experience of a suffering Messiah, and how such images became more readily available after the end of the Jerusalem temple, is more fundamental to modern sacrificial knowing than any inherent or universal characteristic of ancient cultus or of sacrifice as a cross-cultural phenomenon. Yet this process was not very far advanced in Cyprian's time. Most of what he contributes to that broader narrative in these two works is the assertion that the new and proper sacrifice was the sacrifice of Jesus, centred on the Last Supper and the Eucharist, but incorporating his offering to the Father. This idea and its implications, including the understanding that true sacrifice is the gift of self, were only later to become the starting point of sacrificial knowing. Cyprian's connection of the Christian meal as sacrificial with the death of Jesus as itself a sacrifice is the strongest such identification made in early Christian literature up to this point, but is overtaken by the more fulsome constructions of fourth-century texts and theories.

Just as important, though, is how both Decius and Cyprian engaged existing common sacrificial knowledge, based not on altruism or violence but on the centrality of religious offerings as a system of gifts, to new ends, both practical and theoretical. Each of them constructs a form of tradition dependent on existing common sense and which appeals to it, but

---

[51] Before the early Christian experience of Jesus, Jewish reflection on martyrdom had already given rise to potent identifications of suffering as expiatory (4 Macc 6:27–28; 17:22). It is still commonplace, however, to misread other Old Testament references to voluntary and/or vicarious suffering as 'sacrificial', despite lack of cultic reference.

which in the process changes it. Of course, these changes were mutually incompatible in practice, just as the theological propositions attached were incompatible; but it was in ritual that this clash found its most important expression. The fact that these theological ideas about food and drink, tradition, and community draw on and contribute to a common sacrificial knowledge reminds us that specialised discourse can have impact beyond salon cultures and classrooms, and that it is always in conversation with that wider common sense wherein meanings are made.

11 Learning the Language of God: Tables in Early Christian Texts

ANDREW M. RIGGSBY

Introduction

This chapter begins from the ordering of knowledge in a literal, material sense – the use of tabular organisation in a loose-knit family of early Christian texts. Its question is then how the physical *mise-en-page* of those texts affords specific ways of 'knowing' in a more cognitive sense. My subject matter is a set of third- and fourth-century scholarly texts that, though not particularly well known in the broader world, will be familiar to most readers of this volume. These are Eusebius of Caesarea's (*c.* 260–339 CE) *Chronicle*, *Canon Tables*, and *Pinax* of the Psalms, and, above all, Origen of Alexandria's (*c.* 185–254 CE) *Hexapla*. My approach to these texts can be described as the combination of two vectors, one a larger project of my own, the other Anthony Grafton and Megan Williams' *Christianity and the Transformation of the Book*.[1] While the latter book has been invaluable to me (as will be clear from what follows), it will be clarifying to sketch my differences first. While both scholars contributed to the specific substance of the book, it seems to me that their goals were shaped by Grafton's larger project, carried out across many works (including other collaborations), in at least two related ways. First, though the book offers a narrative that ranges over something like a century, the view remains to my mind one from subsequent times. Second, it is centred around historiography and (more generally) scholarly methods for capturing and organising the past. What we are getting, then, is a glimpse of an important bit of the pre-history of the early modern scholarship that is at the centre of Grafton's work. In both respects, this seems to me to restrict the scope of the inquiry and of possible comparanda. In at least one case, I argue that this may have caused them to miss an important causal mechanism; in others, it means that the authors were perhaps more right than they knew. Moreover, Grafton and Williams are focused on the material role of the codex in the intellectual developments they trace. I am generally sympathetic to that line of thinking, but for the most part it is not what I will be discussing.

[1] Grafton and Williams 2006; Riggsby 2019.

My own project brought me to these texts more or less at the end of a longer study of information technologies in the classical Roman world. In looking at technologies such as lists, tables, and maps, my first-order sorting criteria have been broadly formal, not substantive. As a result, I have found that there is much important development and therefore evidence to be found not in the elite or scholarly world of antiquity, but in documentary texts of ordinary business-persons and soldiers. Also, though this is in some respects coincidental, I come at the texts in question essentially from an earlier period (though Origen is just within the outer edge of my work). Thus, my perspective on origins versus outcomes is somewhat different from that of Grafton and Williams.

With that preface, I make two main points in two sections, one about this set of texts as whole and one more specifically about *Hexapla*. On the first point, these texts are all – on information technological grounds – more startling than has been realised. On the second point, I argue for a specific generic origin for *Hexapla* (language-learning manuals) and consider the implications of that fact for Origen's project and for the horizon of expectations of ancient readers.

Tables and Other Organisational Devices

The main argument I make in this section concerns most of the works I referred to above – *Hexapla, Chronicle, Canon Tables, Pinax* – but let me start by making a more specific point about the latter two that illustrates my broader concerns.

Eusebius of course had each of the gospels divided into numbered sections, and then devised a series of tables to indicate which passages represented material more or less shared among various combinations of the evangelists – all four, the various sets of three, and so on.[2] The division of a text into numbered sections smaller than the book is not unprecedented at this period, but it is extremely rare.[3] As far as I have been able to determine, it occurs intermittently in Roman statutes, Scribonius Largus' medical formulary, and just possibly a couple of now-lost Greek philosophical texts. Moreover, these all seem to be authorial interventions rather than editorial ones. There is also another, more subtle innovation here, that goes a step further than simply

---

[2] For the *Canons*, Eusebius explicitly describes the method in his *Letter to Carpianus* (PG 22.1276c–77b); cf. Coogan 2017; Crawford 2019: 2–5. For the *Pinax* of the Psalms, see Wallraff 2013; Crawford 2019: 79–80, 90.

[3] The rest of this paragraph summarises material from Riggsby 2019: ch. 1.

adding section numbers. Let me illustrate with a pair of excerpts related to Roman law. The first is in a town charter from first-century Spain.

> if there is no judgment within the time which is foreseen by chapter 12 of the recent *lex Iulia* on civil trials or the decrees of the Senate pertaining to this chapter … (*Lex Irnitana* 91)[4]

Versus the following from a speech of Cicero's:

> Why does it matter in chapter 3 you require the ratification of officials by the passage of a law by the curiae [a somewhat obscure procedure], when in chapter 4 the elected are given the same powers even without such a law. (*Leg. Agr.* 2.29)[5]

In the Cicero passage, we seemingly already know everything we need to know about the draft statute he is critiquing; the reference to a numerical section only offers reassurance. We can go look it up to make sure it says what it is supposed to. This is the normal state of affairs when Romans make these kinds of numerical references. Contrast the first passage. You simply cannot understand the required timetable if you do not have access to (among other things) a text of the *lex Iulia* with numbered chapters. I have described this elsewhere as 'obligatory' cross-reference. The former case, where the citing text already incorporates the salient information from the cited text, could be called 'authorising cross-reference'. The example I just offered of *obligatory* cross-reference to an external text is in fact the only clear pre-Eusebian example I have been able to find. The whole premise of the *Canon Tables* is, of course, obligatory cross-reference. Thus, Eusebius' work is doubly radical.[6]

My claim about the whole set of works, then, is of a similar order. In a different way, they are all remarkable from the point of view of information technology. In particular, what three (though not the *Pinax*[7]) probably share (and the Eusebian ones certainly do) is a tabular structure. The reason I hesitate about including the *Hexapla* has to do with a point I need to introduce immediately anyway, and that has to do with the definition of 'table'.[8] The English word 'table' has many meanings. I am going to use it not just in one of its narrower senses, but frankly as a term of art. The sense I am going to introduce is based both on observation of actual cases

---

[4] *si intra it tempus quod legis Iuli/ae quae de iudici(i)s privatis proxime lata est kapite XII // senatusve consultis [[ad it kaput]] ad it kaput legis pertine/ntibus conpr(e)hensum est iudicatum non sit.*

[5] *quid attinet tertio capite legem curiatam ferre iubere, cum quarto permittas ut sine lege curiata idem iuris habeant quod haberent, si optima lege a populo essent creati?*

[6] On obligatory cross-reference using the Eusebian canons in the sixth-century Codex Fuldensis, see Crawford 2020.

[7] Crawford 2019: 79.

[8] The rest of this paragraph and the next two lean heavily on material in Riggsby 2019: ch. 2.

and on a survey of modern literature in information design and cognitive psychology on how tables work.

Tables break data up into distinct units, arrange those units along two (or more) axes, and (most distinctively) coordinate those two axes or variables. So when I say table, I mean a document with identifiable and meaningful columns which is used to access the stored data from multiple perspectives. In this sense, a filled-in crossword puzzle is not a table; the rows and columns are not meaningful. Nor is a graphically spaced list of Roman names such as the following inscription (CIL 11.3613, Caere, second century CE):

L	•	Arruntius	L	•	L	Helenus
C	•	Titinius	C	•	L	Adiutor
M	•	Visinius	M	•	L	Philadelphus
Q	•	Pomponius	Q	•	L	Urbanus
C	•	Sulpicius	C	•	L	Cthetus
C	•	Calumeius	C	•	L	Erastus
L	•	Otius	L	•	L	Communis
C	•	Oppius	C	•	L	Secundus

The columns are arguably meaningful (though the purely redundant ones are a problem), but the rows are not. Moreover, it is hard to believe that such a text was meant to be read any way but left-to-right, top-to-bottom. It is essentially just a linear list in aesthetically pleasing form.

One step further, I do not think the structure of an old-fashioned telephone directory normally makes for a table in this sense. While it might qualify, if only minimally, on the formal criteria, it also seems to invite access in one way only. So I think this structure again amounts to just a list, albeit in this case one whose entries have some complexity of structure. That may seem somewhat arbitrary, and in one sense it is. As I said, I am stipulating a definition of the sort of object I want to talk about. That said, I think that the distinction should have some real analytic purchase, and for two reasons. First, precisely this same list/table distinction has been arrived at independently by scholars working on similar material in fields as diverse as cuneiform studies, cognitive psychology, and mathematics pedagogy. Second, what I have described as the telephone-book type is reasonably common in the classical world, while tables in my narrowly defined sense are not; there is a real distinction there, however one wishes to label it.

So given all that definition, I can state three substantive claims from my broader research. (1) Tables, as I just said, are extremely rare in the classical Greco-Roman world. (2) The ones that do exist are largely restricted to narrow use contexts such as Roman military duty rosters and Greek astronomical tables of various sorts. In this general context of absence, it is all the more striking that Eusebius' *Chronicle* is made up of what is clearly a series of tables. The *Canon Tables* are also tabular even in my narrow sense. The columns represent (and are in fact labelled in a header as) the various evangelists.[9] The rows are not so labelled, but they are clearly meaningful as thematic units.[10] Moreover, depending on what text a reader is starting from, access will take place in a number of different directions. The case of the *Hexapla* is slightly more complicated, and in fact it parallels a borderline case in broader culture. I come down in favour of the view that it is in fact tabular, but the issue is closely tied to the subject of my second section, so I suspend discussion until then.

On this set of facts, the works of Origen and Eusebius are highly unusual on one level and less so on two others. One the one hand, Eusebius' *Chronicle* is not only an innovation in the study of chronology, as Grafton and Williams note; it is highly unusual in any context, as are the others here. On the other hand, where tables did exist in the broader world, they arose in limited cultural, literary, and social contexts. The several tabular devices in question here follow that pattern. They are produced by a very limited number of people, engaged in an interlocking set of projects. Unlike the classical tables, these were projected widely beyond the context of their original production, and I suspect this may have had long-term consequences in the broader culture. The pool of table-readers who could potentially become table-authors in other contexts was exponentially larger.

Burgess and Kulikowski, also operating in a historiographical context, have recently summarised a variety of ideological reasons that drove Eusebius' novel project in the *Chronicle*.[11] Synchronism, already important to ancient chronological thinking, became a first principle for the following reasons:

1. Priority: demonstrating the priority of, and so in some sense the superiority, of Christianity, broadly construed, in comparison to seemingly older traditions.
2. Eschatology: addressing the theory that the world would end 6,000 years after creation, that is, fairly soon.
3. Teleology: illustrating the divine plan for the world by showing the convergence of the manifold past into the single narrative of the (Christian) Roman empire.

---

[9] Crawford 2019: 35.
[10] Some later receptions of the canons label the rows with incipits or summaries of content; see Coogan 2020.
[11] Burgess and Kulikowski 2013: 124–25.

I think most of this applies *mutatis mutandis* to the other texts we are speaking of here. Still, having a good reason for a technology does not make that technology appear. The classical contexts in which tables arise are not only limited, but I have argued elsewhere that they are characterised by a high level of what students of distributed cognition call 'scaffolding'.[12] That is, material objects and social practices which take up some of the burden of thinking. To oversimplify considerably, it is possible to come up with a table by introspection, but it is easier with a pen and paper, and easier still in an environment in which different people are adding information to a given document at different times. In fact, this seems to be the case for our tables as well. Though they do not frame it this way, I would suggest that Grafton and Williams' account of the likely working methods of their scholars fits the notion of 'scaffolding' extremely well.

I close this section with a few words on a text I have not discussed so far, not least because it is now seemingly lost in its entirety. Crawford has argued that Ammonius' *dia tessaron* text of the gospels anticipated Origen's columnar organisation for similar comparative purposes.[13] If this is the case, it moves the most striking innovation earlier and makes it slightly more common, although without opening up the use context at all. This is certainly possible (and Crawford's broader case that Ammonius' scholarly contributions have been undervalued seems extremely strong to the eyes of this outsider), but I have my suspicions about the tabular organisation. One of these suspicions will have to be reserved for my next section, but most of the argument can be made now. We are essentially operating on the basis of two sentences in Eusebius' *Letter to Carpianus* (PG 22.1276c). Eusebius prefaces an explanation of his *Canon Tables* with a couple of sentences about his relationship to his predecessor:

Ammonius of Alexandria, with the expense of much industry and zeal – as was proper – left us the Diatessaron Gospel, in which he had placed the similar excerpts of the rest of the Evangelists next to Matthew, with the inevitable result that the coherent sequence of the three was destroyed in terms of the coherence of the readings.[14] (Trans. Oliver, slightly modified)

---

[12] Cf. Riggsby 2018.
[13] Crawford 2015b (revised and expanded as Crawford 2019: ch. 2).
[14] Ἀμμώνιος μὲν ὁ Ἀλεξανδρεὺς πολλὴν ὡς εἰκὸς φιλοπονίαν καὶ σπουδὴν εἰσαγηοχὼς τὸ διὰ τεσσάρων ἡμῖν καταλέλοιπεν εὐαγγέλιον, τῷ κατὰ Ματθαῖον τὰς ὁμοφώνους τῶν λοιπῶν εὐαγγελιστῶν περικοπὰς παραθείς, ὡς ἐξ ἀνάγκης συμβῆναι τὸν τῆς ἀκολουθίας εἱρμὸν τῶν τριῶν διαφθαρῆναι ὅσον ἐπὶ τῷ ὕφει τῆς ἀναγνώσεως·

Crawford (following Zahn) must be right that παραθείς points, in broad terms, to a synopsis rather than a harmony, but that does not quite get us to the Eusebian form.[15]

Setting next to (παρα-) is presumably horizontal in some sense, but it does not strictly exclude a continuous text (that is, going from the end of one excerpt to the beginning of the next on the same line). More significantly, it in no way implies the blank spaces that would be necessary to put the gospels into tabular form.[16] If anything, 'setting' passages 'next to' one another might better suggest to the ancient imagination the form taken by Roman *fasti* (perpetual calendars), lining up one parallel after another until you are done, not setting a blank space next to anything else.[17] The choice of Matthew as the key text is also not table-friendly. The issue is not Matthew as such, but the fact that three of the gospels are organised around any single other. It is not impossible to construct a table in this manner, but it is contrary to the spirit of multiple access. Even if constructed in columnar form with blank spaces, the ordering problem means it is vastly easier to find a parallel from Matthew than from anyone else. Nor can you necessarily interpret the context of the non-Matthew passages by moving up and down as you could with those from Matthew. Finally, there is the question, discussed at length by Crawford, of material in the other gospels that has no parallel in Matthew.[18] This could simply have been lumped together at the end, but I wonder if it might not have been interleaved more haphazardly in typical classical fashion.

As I suggested, I cannot prove that my view of Ammonius is correct, and even if I am wrong, it expands the range of tabular works only slightly. In either case, these Christian innovations are intellectually radical compared to their pagan predecessors. Now, I turn to my second section, which focuses more narrowly on Origen's *Hexapla*.

Hexapla and Language Learning

Some decades ago, in an article on approaches to translation generally in the ancient world, Brock suggested in passing that the form of *Hexapla*

---

[15] Crawford 2015b: 8 n. 12, but note that the parallel with Epiphanius, *Pan.* 64.3.5–7 (proposed at pp. 9–10) is inexact, since Epiphanius specifies *selides* as his unit, while Eusebius speaks of *perikopai*. As Crawford shows (pp. 8–10), διὰ τεσσάρων itself is too ambiguous to be of help.

[16] I am among those who doubt the use of critical sigla in the Septuagint column of *Hexapla*. See Schironi 2015: 194–97, with bibliography.

[17] On this type of calendar, see Riggsby 2019: 55–57.   [18] Crawford 2015b: 7–8, 19.

might be related to that of bilingual texts of Vergil.[19] Elsewhere in the article he noted that these were part of a larger category of bilingual texts apparently used for pedagogical purposes.[20] More recently, Law has picked up this suggestion, though even more passingly and referring only to the Vergil texts.[21] I think this suggestion is very near the truth, and I advance it in two ways in this section of my chapter. First, I argue that Origen had a slightly different, though closely related model in mind. Second, I suggest that this model is not only causally significant – that is, that it helps explain how *Hexapla* came to be – but that it was likely salient to how the work was understood in its own time, and therefore that it would affect our interpretation of Origen's project more broadly.

I suspect that Brock slid from Vergil *qua* representative of a larger category to simply Vergil for a couple of reasons. First, the general tendency of his paper is to value 'artistic' texts and disvalue 'functional' ones. Vergil, even if the object of a disvalued translation, is still the most 'artistic' possible author and therefore most prominent member of the category. Secondly, Brock could not have had access to Eleanor Dickey's vital 2015 study of, to quote her title, 'Columnar Translation: An Ancient Interpretive Tool that the Romans Gave the Greeks'. She gathers a wide range of bilingual translations on papyrus from the ancient Mediterranean including various pairings of Latin, Greek, and Coptic. This corpus includes not just Vergil, but Cicero, Aeschines, Aesop, student dialogues about daily life, and glossaries. A columnar format, that is two columns of brief phrases translating each other, is overwhelmingly correlated with texts in which the original was in Latin. She is almost certainly correct then to infer that:

> the columnar translation format originated in the Latin-speaking areas of the empire. Latin speakers had been learning Greek for centuries before Greek speakers began to learn Latin on any comprehensive scale; therefore, it is inherently likely that some of the Latin–Greek bilingual materials (especially glossaries and colloquia) originated in the West for use by Latin speakers and were later adapted for use by Greek speakers.[22]

Thus, the instructional context that Brock mentions briefly seems in fact to be the heart of the salient category. Columnar translation is a recognisable technology of language pedagogy.

As far as we can reconstruct it, *Hexapla* must have looked a lot like these pedagogical texts. It shares (1) a continuous text, broken down into (2) very short units, and (3) translated. A fourth feature, one that Dickey does

---

[19] Brock 1979: 78.   [20] Brock 1979: 73.   [21] Law 2008: 8.   [22] Dickey 2015: 820–21.

not bring up in this context, strengthens the parallel but may also be of particular importance for Origen's work in another respect. Not a few of the bilingual texts give the Latin words in Greek transliteration.[23] *Hexapla*, then, looks very much like this kind of text, given the presence of its column of (transliterated) Hebrew. The type is one that would have been well known among the educated classes. And, finally, the general idea of tabular organisation was, as I have previously stressed, not one that was generally in the air. The point presumably cannot be proven, but it seems likely to me that this genre provided inspiration for Origen. (The case is clearer if I was correct to suggest above that Ammonius did not work in columns. Since he has only one language to work with, he would have taken an even more dramatic leap than Origen in adopting such a form.)

Assuming for the sake of argument that this is correct, or at least plausible enough to be worth pursuing, I think about three possible kinds of consequences. One has to do with my own argument in the previous section about what counts as a table; one has to do with the value of transliteration; and the last (in this case a set of issues) has to do with implications for Origen's project and its reception more generally.

(1) *Tabularity*: A couple of features of the bilingual texts that Dickey does not dwell on will nonetheless be important for our purposes. First, in at least some cases, it can be shown that individual texts – and not just the general idea of how to make them – spread from Latin West to Greek East. That is, an individual reader would have read mainly or entirely in one direction (that is, right to left for native speakers of one language or left to right for speakers of the other), but as a group they must have done both. Secondly, except for the glossaries, all of these texts have a substantive or logical sequence. Thus, though they were presumably read originally from the top down, it would be relatively easy to find one's way back up to check on a particular word or phrase. Thus, we would expect fairly free access in the second dimension as well. All this is true for *Hexapla*, and indeed we would expect considerable and unordered scanning back and forth (i.e., right and left). While it is a rather speculative attempt, I would suggest the following scenario makes sense. These literally pedagogical texts may not have been designed with tabular intentions, and many users may have treated them in essentially 'phone book' fashion, but other users may have traversed them in more flexible ways. In *Hexapla*, Origen captured that potential and deliberately put it to work from the beginning; the six

---

[23] For instance (the earliest examples): BKT 9.150; O.Max. 356; P.Oxy. 33.2660, 2660a; 46.3315; 49.3452; P.Lund. 1.5; P.Mich. 2458; P.Laur. 4.147.

columns make the second dimension unmistakable. (For what it is worth, I have argued that when tables arose elsewhere, the scaffolding involved often included a similar 'intentionalisation' of table-like objects produced by local, mechanical forces.[24])

(2) *Transliteration*: Though not in itself decisive, considering the model of the pedagogical texts may cast some new light on the vexed issues of the origin and purpose of Origen's second column giving a Greek transliteration of the Hebrew text in the first column. The first question, to my mind, is whether this was produced as part of Origen's project (whether by himself or by collaborators more knowledgeable of Hebrew does not much matter here), or whether it was adopted wholesale from a pre-existing source, presumably from the same source as the plain Hebrew text. While there are certainly other attested instances of transliteration in the general milieu, no one has been able to produce direct evidence for such a systematic reworking – the equivalent of columns 1 and 2 of *Hexapla* – circulating within Jewish communities.[25] Moreover, such a text would be monolingual, whereas this kind of systematic transliteration is attested rather as a bilingual phenomenon. Absent, as I say, direct evidence to the contrary, I would prefer to see the transliteration as part of Origen's project, again whether his own work or a collaborator's.

So what would its purpose be? If the theory just advanced is correct, it would almost automatically rule out the view expressed by Jellicoe that Origen included the transliteration simply to illustrate the exhaustiveness of his research.[26] Conversely, my view might suggest a parallel with Orlinsky's old theory that *Hexapla* was, in the first instance, an instrument of language pedagogy, but I think that allows the tail to wag the dog.[27] There is simply too much else going on for this to be the principal goal. Other possibilities are more complicated. The main explanations have been at root auditory. Emerton suggested the practicality of using Greek characters to spell out vocalisations for those with little or no Hebrew of their own.[28] Martin more radically suggests an attempt to recuperate the supposed non-referential power of the very sounds of the Hebrew in the mouths of those with, again, little or no Hebrew of their own.[29] I think both mis-identify the likely audience for the transliterations. The pedagogical parallels suggest not the Hebrew-less, but rather Hellenophones

---

[24] Riggsby 2018: 63–68.   [25] Emerton 1970; 1971: 26–28; Norton 1998: 113–14.
[26] Jellicoe 1978: 110.
[27] Orlinsky 1936. In fact, I assume all the purposes canvassed in Law 2008: 9–19 are correct.
[28] Emerton 1956.   [29] Martin 2004.

who have some genuine grasp of the other language but find reading in the alien script (be it Latin or Hebrew) taxing. So what would I prefer? In essence, I would like to downplay the importance of the second column altogether. I think it is essentially a finding aid, helping the (already progressing) language learner connect the Greek and Hebrew parts of the text. Strictly speaking, an origin in pedagogical translation would not rule out several of the 'deep' interpretations canvassed above. It is possible that Origen found in the genre a ready resource to solve one or another of the problems that scholars have suggested the second column is meant to address. It does, however, mean that any such explanation must fend off Occam's Razor.

(3) *Genre and reader expectations*: As I suggested above, the pedagogical genre of columnar translation was likely recognisable, for the distinctiveness of tables and of its specific form and because many of the educated classes will probably have used just such things. In fact, all of that must be true even if I am wrong about the role of such texts in the creation of *Hexapla*. The question I close on, then, is what effect(s) might the casting-in-recognisable-form of *Hexapla* have had on users (including in that category its composer)?

One possible implication has to do with tabularity again. A lot of ink has been spilled on the order of the columns, and even more specific arguments hinge on the presumption that the initial position of the Hebrew text implies logical priority (I would concede that it probably does show compositional priority). But that may be an over- or misreading from the point of view of the reader. If Origen is adopting and adapting a form that already has at least tabular tendencies (the instructional texts), and then expands it in a way that enhances those tendencies (six columns instead of two), then the order of columns becomes less important. The point of the structure is precisely to allow free movement, and so we cannot assume much about supposedly privileged positions in the array.[30]

Two other implications are more ideological and arise from the pedagogical context rather than from the specifics of the form. First of all, the kinds of pedagogical texts that adopt the columnar translation form vary considerably, and the broader structure of ancient education was not precisely articulated, but my sense is that these texts run from a fairly early stage (though after learning alphabet and syllables) to perhaps an 'intermediate' one. (The use of transliterations particularly seems to indicate a

---

[30] We might compare here Johnson's observation (2007: n. 6) that the even number of columns means that there is no central one.

middling audience.) Origen is then asserting considerable authority over the audience of *Hexapla* by putting them in a subordinate, probably adolescent position. Now, the identity of any such 'audience', given reasonable doubts about how often, if at all, it was copied in its entirety, is unclear.[31] On the other hand, there were clearly at least a number of partial copies, any one of which would naturally have preserved the relevant structure to make its pedigree clear. Moreover, the most important audience in this respect may have been for the monumental original itself.

Secondly, as many scholars have noted, there is an inherent tension in having multiple versions of what is supposed to be a divinely inspired text. As they have also noted, Origen aggravates the problem by, in essence, drawing on at least two distinct stages of the evolution of the Hebrew text.[32] And indeed one of the seemingly avowed purposes of his work is text-critical: to attempt to 'heal' the differences between versions (*Comm. Matt.* 15.14 *ad* 19:18). Whatever philological *cure* to those problems Origen has in mind – and I do not intend to step into that debate – I suggest that the form itself of *Hexapla* offers a complementary, more symptomatic approach. Instructional materials were not home to antiquity's deep thinking on the philosophy of language. They simply asserted the equivalence of particular phrases without concern for the possibilities of only partial matching or of alternative versions. And they do not even genuinely address the additional layer of problems created in this case by transmission issues. But that means that the form presupposes away all the problems that Origen presumably did mean to address. It offers comfort in advance of all that work whether or not the labour is successful.

I conclude with a thought that touches on both methodology and ancient information technology. In a thoughtful review of Grafton and Williams' monograph, Scott Fitzgerald Johnson speaks of their array of

> comparanda for the [chronological] *Canons*, from historiographical tables mentioned by Herodotus and Thucydides, to the Parian Chronicle, and the *Liber annalis* of T. Pomponius Atticus (170–177). This survey is more evocative than source-critical and (notably) does not include a discussion of Greek and Roman calendrical tables, which could have served (even indirectly) to inspire later chronography.[33]

As I have mentioned in passing already, those 'tables' are not tables and so could not have been an 'inspiration' on the key point, but I do want to make more general claims here. I hope, on the one hand, that I have shown

---

[31] Doubts on recopying: Field 1875: xcix.
[32] E.g., Orlinsky 1936: 138–39; Jellicoe 1978: 102–3; Law 2008: 12.
[33] Johnson 2007.

that many of the salient comparanda are not 'sources' per se, but parallels, tables that arose independently of each other in similar circumstances. And this relative isolation of each context from the others is, I have argued, a general feature of the use and diffusion of Roman information technology. On the other hand, I did argue that an existing genre may well have served as a model or inspiration for Origen's *Hexapla*. And Crawford's recent argument that the parallels between Eusebius' *Chronicle* and the tradition of astronomical tables are much deeper than they first appear may suggest a second instance of borrowing or influence.[34] This, I would argue, is yet another distinctive feature of the informational environment along this axis, not just the rise of individual new devices, but the vision to repurpose old ones for new ends.

---

[34] Crawford 2019: 43–53.

12 | The Aëtian *Placita* and the Church Fathers: Creative Use of a Distinctive Mode of Ordering Knowledge

DAVID T. RUNIA

The 'Genre' of Doxography and the *Placita* of Aëtius

It is well known that 'doxography', the recording of opinions on philosophical topics, was not a recognised literary genre in the ancient world.[1] The word itself is a neologism, coined by the great nineteenth-century German philologist Herman Diels. In his celebrated *Doxographi graeci*, published in 1879, he collected a number of texts which recorded such opinions, naming their authors as *doxographi*.[2] The corresponding noun for this kind of text followed a little later and its use soon became widespread. The main work in Diels' collection was the Περὶ ἀρεσκόντων or *Placita*, which, on the basis of evidence in the church father Theodoret of Cyrrhus, he was able to attribute to an otherwise unknown author Aëtius, dated to the first century CE.[3]

Aëtius' *Placita* is not extant in its original form. It has to be reconstructed from the extensive use made of it by later authors, in particular by the author of the pseudo-Plutarchean *Epitome* of the work in the second century and by Ioannes Stobaeus and the aforementioned Theodoret in the fifth century. The reconstruction made by Diels has held sway for 140 years. Recently, however, my Dutch colleague Jaap Mansfeld and I have published a new reconstruction.[4] Not only does it offer an improved version of the text, accompanied by a full commentary, but it also provides a more complete account of all the witnesses to the original work. From this analysis, it is apparent what an important role patristic authors played in the preservation of the work. Indeed, well over half of these witnesses had a Christian allegiance, as can be seen in a diagram of the complex tradition of the work's transmission.[5]

In the present chapter, I wish to introduce a reversal of perspective. Instead of examining how important the patristic tradition has been for

---

[1] On ancient doxography, see the overview in Mansfeld 2012. [2] Diels 1879.
[3] The *Placita* are edited in Diels 1879: 273–444.
[4] Mansfeld and Runia 2020. On the relation to Diels' edition see 1.28–42.
[5] See the diagram in Mansfeld and Runia 2020: 1.98. See further the analysis of the tradition in the General Introduction on 1.42–69.

our knowledge of the *Placita*, I will now investigate what motivated the church fathers themselves to use it so extensively. Drawing on the wider theme of the present volume, I shall first briefly outline the distinctive mode of ordering knowledge employed in the *Placita*. This will be followed by an analysis of the usage made by patristic authors, beginning with early authors up to the third century, then moving to the heyday of patristic literature in the fourth and fifth centuries. This overview will make it possible to reach conclusions about how early Christian authors appropriated and adapted features of the *Placita* tradition as exemplified in Aëtius' compendium. It should be emphasised that in this chapter the main focus will not be so much on the extent of the appropriation – some authors make much more use of the *Placita* than others – but rather on the context in which the appropriation takes place, its objectives, and the way that it is carried out.

A Distinctive Mode of Ordering Knowledge

One of the objectives of the research programme which has resulted in the publication of this volume was to 'investigate and evaluate early Christian appropriations of dominant Classical discourses of knowledge from traditions of literary theory, rhetoric, philosophy, medicine and imperial ideology, focusing on how these appropriations shaped Christian conceptions of knowledge … and were themselves driven by particular Christian cultural and theological claims'.[6] There can be little doubt that the *Placita* of Aëtius belongs to the 'dominant classical discourses of knowledge' referred to above. As a summary of philosophical doctrines, it shared in the high prestige enjoyed by the pursuit of philosophy in the imperial period, universally recognised by the ruling elites and by society at large as the pre-eminent form of knowledge.[7] We commence our investigation, therefore, by first examining the *Placita* itself and outlining the chief characteristics that typify it as a distinctive mode of ordering knowledge within the much wider field of ancient philosophical discourse and practice.

Regrettably, there are few explicit statements in the work itself that can shed light on its aims and methods. Its opening words state no more than that its intention is 'to hand down the φυσικὸς λόγος', which we might translate as the 'account of physics' or the 'discourse on nature', and a little later, that 'our proposal is to examine τὰ φυσικά', what belongs to nature

---

[6] Australian Catholic University 2016.
[7] On the standing of philosophy at the time of the emergence of Christianity, see Hahn 1989.

or the natural realm.[8] It is thus by no means an easy task to determine the work's mode of ordering knowledge, and in order to achieve it there is no alternative but to base it on what it actually does.[9] From such an analysis I propose the following six characteristics.

(1) The *Placita* draws exclusively on the Hellenic tradition. In the opening sentence it refers to the 'business of philosophy' and simply assumes that this is a Hellenic enterprise.[10] The first philosopher to be mentioned in the early chapter on the first principles, ch. 1.3, is Thales, introduced as the 'man who started off philosophy'.[11] The statement that 'he philosophised in Egypt' is perhaps a hint that there was a non-Hellenic tradition before him, but if so, it is not developed. The only non-Hellenic thinker to be included is Berosus with his idiosyncratic theory about the moon.[12] He is treated no differently from any other purveyor of opinions. It is worth noting that by far the majority of *doxai* are attributed to individual philosophers (sometimes joined together as groups) and, to a lesser extent, schools, but that scientists and doctors are also included, both as individuals and as a group. They are all part of the one Hellenic tradition.

(2) It focuses exclusively on the realm of physics. In the proem, two views are given on the scope of philosophy.[13] According to the Stoics, philosophy is divided into physics, ethics, and logic, with physics stated to be the investigation of the cosmos and what it contains. Aristotle and his followers adopt a different approach: 'the complete human being', who of course must be a philosopher, 'needs to theorise about the things that are and perform the actions that must be done'. This involves investigation of both realms – of existents and of actions – and examples are given of questions pursued in relation to each of them. It is of course the former to which the *Placita* directs its attention.

(3) It offers an overview of the doctrines of physics that is both comprehensive and compact. The five books cover a vast terrain. Each of its 135 chapters treats a separate question or topic, from first principles and the structure of the macrocosm to the characteristics of the soul and body of the human microcosm. Because the work is so well organised, it

---

[8] Aëtius, *Plac.* 1.proem.1.1–3: μέλλοντες τὸν φυσικὸν παραδώσειν λόγον ἀναγκαῖον ἡγούμεθα εὐθὺς ἐν ἀρχαῖς διελέσθαι τὴν τῆς φιλοσοφίας πραγματείαν, ἵν' εἰδῶμεν τί ἐστι καὶ πόστον μέρος αὐτῆς ἡ φυσικὴ διέξοδος. 1.1.1.2–3: ἐπειδὴ πρόκειται ἡμῖν τὰ φυσικὰ θεωρῆσαι, ἀναγκαῖον ἡγοῦμαι δηλῶσαι, τί ποτ' ἐστὶν ἡ φύσις. We cite the text of Mansfeld and Runia 2020.
[9] Based primarily on Mansfeld and Runia 1997–2020; see esp. vol. 2.1 (2009), and the General Introduction in vol. 5.1 (2020: 2–28).
[10] τὴν τῆς φιλοσοφίας πραγματείαν, 1.proem.1.2, cited above in n. 8.
[11] Aëtius, *Plac.* 1.3.1.4–5.   [12] Aëtius, *Plac.* 2.25.13; 2.28.1; 2.29.2.
[13] Aëtius, *Plac.* 1.proem.3.13–14: ἀναγκαῖον τὸν τέλειον ἄνδρα καὶ θεωρητικὸν εἶναι τῶν ὄντων καὶ πρακτικὸν τῶν δεόντων.

is easily consulted as a source of philosophical doctrine. And all of this is made available in a work that, if it had been completely preserved, would have comprised about 25,000 words, no more than 150 pages of Greek text. Such concision, however, allows little room for argument. Only the *doxai* are presented, almost never the arguments used to support them.

(4) It practises a method which can best be described as dialectical. The opinions which form the contents of each chapter interact with each other, whether forming a division of views (*diaeresis*) or an opposition (*diaphonia*), or less often a sequence amounting to a list. Almost never does our compiler intervene with an evaluative meta-comment (exceptions are most likely taken over from a source).[14] Basically his attitude is one of strict neutrality, though of course he is aware that some opinions are more authoritative than others, i.e., those that belong to certain philosophers or schools, or those that refer to widely accepted scientific theories. What is astounding is the breadth of views that the work contains, including some that are quite esoteric and far removed from the *communis opinio* of the compiler's day.

(5) It does not wholly eschew historical aspects of the Greek philosophical tradition. Philosophers are introduced by their patronymic and ethnikon, account is taken of the chief *diadochai* of intellectual movements and schools, and attention is given to the discoverers of theories and terms. The order of the *doxai*, though primarily systematic, does sometimes take chronology into account. But the *Placita* are far from being a history of philosophy.

(6) Lastly, it adopts a markedly 'secular' attitude to the doctrines it presents. Gods and the divine realm are part of the domain of physics and are included as such.[15] The chapter on 'who the Deity is' is one of the longest.[16] But theological aspects of cosmology and anthropology are for the most part avoided. For example, in the chapter on providence, it is not qualified as 'divine' and there is no reference to divinity.[17] The question of divine providence *is* raised in the unusually long *doxa* on the question of whether God exists which commences the chapter on theology. Setting out the negative view, i.e., atheism, it argues against the theology of Anaxagoras and Plato,[18] a view that is taken over from an originally Epicurean source. Here, too, it is more likely that our compiler wishes to be even-handed than that he is taking a position himself.

Strange as it may seem, we are completely in the dark as to the actual *Sitz im Leben* of the *Placita*. Fully dependent on a tradition that goes back

---

[14] Rare criticisms using the verb 'be mistaken' (ἁμαρτάνω) at *Plac.* 1.2.1.11 (Thales), 1.3.2.19 (Anaximander), 1.3.3.27 (Anaximenes), 1.7.1.35 (Anaxagoras, Plato).

[15] Mansfeld 2013 speaks of 'detheologization'.   [16] Aëtius, *Plac.* 1.7, Τίς ὁ θεός.

[17] Aëtius, *Plac.* 2.3, Εἰ ἔμψυχος ὁ κόσμος καὶ προνοίᾳ διοικούμενος.

[18] Aëtius, *Plac.* 1.7.1.27–41.

at least to Aristotle, Theophrastus, and the Peripatetic school and then was further developed in the Hellenistic period, it is clearly a kind of manual or *vademecum*, setting out answers that philosophers had given to all the main questions relating to the physical world.[19] Because of the way it is organised and set out, it could have had a mnemonic function, enabling its users to recall the chief topics of physics and the diversity of answers given to them in the tradition. We have no information on any geographical or institutional context for the work.[20] What we do know is that it was available, whether in the original version or in a reduced form,[21] to generations of writers working in the Judaeo-Christian tradition. How they put it to use in developing their own modes of ordering knowledge is the subject that will occupy us in the remainder of this chapter.

Beginnings: Philo of Alexandria, Athenagoras, Hermias

My first author may come as a surprise, for he is not a Christian, and it is unlikely that he knew the *Placita*, since that work was most likely compiled at about the time of his death, c. 50 CE. But his writings reveal that he knew and used a collection of *doxai* similar to that of Aëtius.[22] Since he was consciously working within the tradition of biblical interpretation which was also of fundamental importance for the early Christian theologians, his evidence is essential for our topic.

Philo uses his familiarity with the questions of philosophy treated in doxographical works such as the *Placita* to indicate and structure the main subjects of philosophical investigation, mainly in physics, but also in ethics and occasionally in epistemology. In explaining the Platonic – but also, according to Philo, scriptural – theme of the origin of philosophy through the gift of sight, Philo sets out key philosophical questions, often citing them in opposed pairs, such as whether the physical world has always existed or whether it was created, whether there is one cosmos or many, and so on.[23] His philosophical treatise *De aeternitate mundi* treats

---

[19] See Mansfeld and Runia 2020: Part 1, General Introduction, p. 22 and passim, with full references to the scholarly literature.

[20] It has been suggested that it was produced in an Alexandrian context, but this must be regarded as no more than an educated guess; see Mansfeld and Runia 2020: 1.17.

[21] In what follows, I will not for the most part distinguish between the use of Aëtius or the derivative *Epitome* of Pseudo-Plutarch. The term *Placita*, used as book title, covers both.

[22] On Philo and ancient doxography, see Runia 2008; on his relation to the *Placita* and its tradition, see esp. 24–29.

[23] Various examples are given in Runia 2008: 22–24.

the first of these questions using exactly the same formulation as a chapter heading in Aëtius.[24] They agree in also including the question of the cosmos' origin, but Philo greatly expands his treatment with a plethora of arguments, whereas the *Placita* only gives names and views. In Philo's allegorical system, wells symbolise knowledge. So why is the well mentioned in Gen 28:10 the 'fourth'? The solution is that both in the cosmos and in us human beings there are four constituents, of which three can be known, but the fourth not. A whole bevy of questions is then raised on the heavens and the human mind (or rational soul).[25] The close parallels with Books 2 and 4 of the *Placita* show that Philo used a work that was a key source for the later work. How do these questions demonstrate that these subjects are unknowable? This occurs through the evident fact that all the opinions, and the philosophers who hold them, disagree with each other. In summarising the tenth trope of Aenesidemus, Philo concludes that the philosophers in their platoons posit doctrines that are discordant and opposed to each other.[26] In a little-known fragment of his *Quaestiones in Exodum* preserved in the *Catenae*, he writes:[27]

All the philosophies which have flourished in Greece and foreign countries, when investigating the world of nature, have not been able to clearly see even the smallest matter. A clear proof is the disagreements (διαφωνίαι) and conflicts (διαμάχιαι) and divergences of opinion (ἑτεροδοξίαι) on the part of those belonging to each school of thought, refuting and being refuted by each other in turn. And for all of them, their own *doxai* that these partisan schools defend are starting-points of conflict, with their controversial quarrels blinding the human mind, which has the potential to see but is unable to discern which theories to accept and which to reject.

Here the sceptical strand in Philo's thought appears to come strongly to the fore.

But it would be a mistake to conclude that Philo is a true sceptic. In a noteworthy passage giving an allegorical interpretation of Abraham sitting among the vultures, Philo says they symbolise enemies of the soul.[28] Inasmuch as they pursue the single goal of investigating the facts of nature, they could be regarded as friends. But because they reach differing conclusions, illustrated with a sequence of opposite views on philosophical

---

[24] Philo, *Aet.* 3: εἰ ἄφθαρτος ὁ κόσμος; cf. *Plac.* 2.4 tit.
[25] Philo, *Somn.* 1.21–32 and further texts; see above n. 22.
[26] Philo, *Ebr.* 193–202; see Runia 2008: 29–31.
[27] Philo, *QE* frag. 4, text in Petit 1978: 284. The passage is part of a larger sequence which appears to take its starting-point in God's statement at Exod 33:13 that Moses and human beings in general cannot see his face.
[28] Philo, *Her.* 243–48 on Gen 15:11.

questions, they must be regarded as sophists.[29] The situation remains one of conflict:

> until such time as the man who is both midwife and judge at the same time, takes his place in their midst, examines the products of each soul, rejects those which do not deserve to be nurtured, and preserves those that are suitable and which he thinks deserving of the appropriate care. (§247)

There is an allusion to Socrates here, who tests the thoughts of philosophical souls,[30] but what Philo has in mind above all is the role of the wise person or prophet who is divinely enlightened and inspired. In this text it is Abraham; more often it is the Jewish lawgiver Moses. In the doxography in *De aeternitate mundi*, the latter is actually included together with biblical texts as validating the view that represents the truth.[31] It is significant that Philo regards the birds as potentially friends. Philosophical investigation can be a positive exercise on the condition that it is focused on the right questions and leads to the truth. The context is exegetical, as it is nearly always the case in Philo. But there is an apologetic subtext: Jewish scripture, if properly explained and understood, gives answers to philosophical questions that in Greek culture have been sources of dispute and dissension. It will emerge in what follows that Philo's approach to the variety of Greek philosophical doctrines recorded in earlier versions of the *Placita* sets the scene (and in some cases may have directly influenced patristic authors),[32] though most will have a less positive view of Greek learning than he does.

The first Christian writer whom we know to have made use of the *Placita* is the apologist Athenagoras. His address to the emperor Marcus Aurelius entitled *An Embassy on Behalf of the Christians* (c. 176 CE) defends the Christians against various charges, the most important of which is atheism.[33] They should not be defamed, Athenagoras argues, when their views are seen in the light of what the philosophers have taught.[34] Of course he hardly wishes to teach the learned emperor about the doctrines of the philosophers, but he has to mention names, so he turns to 'the *doxai*' (*Leg.* 6.2),

---

[29] The importance of this passage was well seen by Mansfeld 1988, who emphasises its sceptical terminology; note esp. *Her.* 248: 'Philosophical subjects have become full of disagreement (διαφωνία) because the credulous (πιθανός) mind which proceeds by conjecture (στοχασμός) flees from the truth'; see also Runia 2008: 31–33.

[30] See Plato, *Theaet.* 150a–151b.

[31] Philo, *Aet.* 19; on the difficulties of interpreting this incompletely preserved work, see Runia 1981.

[32] For a survey of Philo's influence on the church fathers, see Runia 1993. With regard to the use of doxography, his influence will have been strongest in the case of Eusebius.

[33] For the date of the work and a sound introduction to its contents, see Schoedel 1972: xi–xxv.

[34] Athenagoras, *Leg.* 4.2–5.1.

a covert reference to the *Placita*. A little later (*Leg.* 7.2), in mentioning the differing doctrines of the Greek thinkers, he refers to the topics of God, matter, forms, and the cosmos, all chapter headings from the first part of the work.[35] There may be another mention when he refers to the φυσικὸς καὶ θεολογικὸς λόγος of which most of those accusing the Christians are ignorant.[36] But he does not exploit the huge diversity of names furnished in the *Placita*. The only ones to be cited are Plato, Aristotle, the Stoa (*Leg.* 6.2–4), and, later on, Thales (*Leg.* 23.4), where some words on the distinction between God, demons, and heroes are quoted.[37] Plato is favoured with a double treatment. His theology is summarised, but two key texts from the *Timaeus* (28c, 41a) are also quoted verbatim. These philosophers are cited as 'witnesses' for the truth of Christian theological views (cf. *Leg.* 23.3). In addition, he makes two brief allusions (*Leg.* 4.2; 16.1) to the beauty of the cosmos based on features outlined in *Plac.* 1.6, where Stoic arguments are presented showing how human beings obtain a conception of God. But the second of these comes with a warning: it is not the cosmos with all its beautiful arrangement that should be worshipped, but rather God its maker. This theme was already prominent in Hellenistic Judaism and the writings of Philo.[38]

Athenagoras thus makes a limited use of the *Placita* to suit the purposes of his apologetics. His usage is for the most part positive, using famous names as witnesses to support Christian doctrine. Admittedly, the poets and philosophers have reached their views through guesswork (στοχασμός, cf. *Leg.* 7.2), seeking the truth through an affinity of their souls with the divine spirit (an allusion to Gen 2:7). They were relying on their own powers and reached differing doctrines on key issues, instead of learning directly from God via his prophets. Athenagoras is being careful. As an apologist for a minority culture who is addressing the emperor (and perhaps beyond him a learned Greek audience), he wishes to persuade rather than to attack and disparage. The *Placita* is a useful work because it supplies compact and uncontroversial material. He needs a widely accepted source to act as a witness for philosophical doctrines that approximate revealed truth, and this is what the *Placita* can provide him with.

A brief discussion should also be devoted to the attractive little essay *Ridicule of the Outside Philosophers*, ascribed to an obscure author named

---

[35] *Plac.* 1.7, 1.9, 1.10, 2.1, cf. 1.4–5.
[36] See the self-description of the *Placita* in the text cited above in n. 8.
[37] Athenagoras here conflates *Plac.* 1.7.2.59 and 1.8.2.4–6 and, ignoring the three other name-labels in the second text, adds of his own accord, it seems, that Thales was the first to make this distinction (the well-known 'first discoverer' motif).
[38] Philo, *Opif.* 7; Wisd 13:1–9; Rom 1:20–25.

Hermias at a date probably prior to the fourth century. We cannot prove that Hermias used the *Placita* directly, but he certainly drew either on it or on very similar works within the same tradition.[39] How different is his approach compared to that of Athenagoras. He immediately goes on the attack, starting with the Pauline statement that 'the wisdom of this world is foolishness in the eyes of God' (1 Cor 3:19). Such wisdom has its origin in the apostasy of the angels and is the reason that the philosophers put forward doctrines that are neither in agreement nor consistent with each other (§1). A first example is their doctrines on the soul, utilising themes treated in *Plac.* 4.2–7. These views are 'either nonsense or ignorance or madness or strife or all of the above' (§4). He applies them to himself: 'if I am immortal, I am happy; if I am born mortal, I weep'. But if philosophers do not know who they themselves are, how are they able to declare the truth about the gods or the cosmos? There follows a longer section on the first principles of nature as set out in *Plac.* 1.3. At first, Anaxagoras with his doctrine that mind is the cause of the universe is Hermias' friend, but that philosopher is opposed by Parmenides and Melissus who say that being is one and eternal, and so he inclines to that doctrine (§6). Many others follow, from Anaximenes to Epicurus, including 'big mouth' Plato.[40] Like Philo, Hermias goes beyond the scope of the *Placita* and includes academics and sceptics among the disagreeing philosophers.[41] If we believe them, then truth disappears from humanity entirely and much-vaunted philosophy is just an exercise in shadow-boxing (§15). He ends by moving from principles to the theme of measurement. Pythagoras with his doctrine of the elements (cf. *Plac.* 2.6.5) measures the cosmos, but why stop there when, according to Epicurus, there are multiple and unlimited kosmoi (cf. *Plac.* 2.1.3)? But then, he states, I have to count all those atoms ... None of this will help me with what is essential for the flourishing of my household and city (§18).

Hermias and Athenagoras are writing for different audiences. Hermias' audience consists of insiders, not Greeks on the outside. His main theme is the *dissensio philosophorum* that was already prominent in Philo, though he does not use the former's more technical vocabulary.[42] Because of all these disagreements and contradictions, it is useless to pursue the investigations

---

[39] See Hanson et al. 1993 and the analysis in Mansfeld and Runia 1997: 315–17. Diels (1879: 651–56) included it in his collection of doxographical writings.

[40] The epithet μεγαλόφωνος is used of Plato at §11. The same application is also found in Pseudo-Justin, *Coh. ad Graec.* 31 and at *Plac.* 1.7.1.27, a sure sign of a shared tradition.

[41] See Philo, *Her.* 246: 'and in general terms those who argue that all things are beyond comprehension are opposed to those who affirm that very many things are known'. This is part of the passage discussed above at n. 28 and text thereto.

[42] One misses in particular the term διαφωνία.

of the philosophers. But the *doxai* of the *Placita* tradition have in themselves proved useful, precisely because they demonstrate that uselessness.

The Fourth Century: Eusebius, Pseudo-Justin, Nemesius

Of the church fathers no one – not even Theodoret – cites the *Placita* more than Eusebius, the bishop of Caesarea. In his *Praeparatio evangelica* (composed after 313 CE), citing Pseudo-Plutarch's *Epitome* rather than the Aëtian original, Eusebius writes out as much as a quarter of all its extant *doxai*.[43]

The opening words explain why the work is called a preparation for the gospel. It is intended as a guide in the manner of an elementary manual (στοιχείωσις) or introduction (εἰσαγωγή) for gentiles who have recently converted to Christianity. Eusebius' aim is to present a demonstration or proof of the gospel (the title of the sequel in ten books), but before he does so it will be worthwhile first to provide brief explanations on the questions which have been put to the Christians by Greeks and Jews and by everyone who engages in an exact examination of their views (*Praep. ev.* 1.1.12). For the former group, Eusebius devises a distinctive method in order to achieve his aim. He cites the words of the Greek authors themselves so that they can serve as witnesses to the errors and falsehoods of their own thought and culture, making good use of the resources of the episcopal library of Caesarea, which contained substantial holdings of Greek historical, literary, ethnographic, and philosophical writings.[44] Among these were at least three doxographical works, the Περὶ αἱρέσεων of Arius Didymus, the *Stromateis* also attributed to Plutarch (a brief collection of the main doctrines of the early Greek philosophers), and the *Epitome* of the *Placita*.[45]

The *Praeparatio* thus has a double aspect. The bulk of its text consists of hundreds of excerpts from Greek literature. The philosophical material is sometimes taken from original works (e.g., Plato, Plotinus), but more often from handbooks, such as Arius Didymus and Aristocles, or polemical writings such as Atticus against Aristotle. These excerpts are then placed within a highly structured framework, organised into books and chapters,

---

[43] He cites forty-one chapters (not all completely) with 187 *doxai*, which is 33 per cent of the *doxai* in the *Epitome* and 24 per cent of what remains in the reconstructed original; see further Mansfeld and Runia 2020: 1.46–48.

[44] On Eusebius' innovative method and the *Praeparatio evangelica*, see Grant 1980; Inowlocki 2006. On his library, see Carriker 2003.

[45] Diels 1879 contains the text of all three works, the *Epitome* complete, the other two fragmentary.

and accompanied by a kind of running commentary.[46] There is an obvious tension between these two aspects. The former conveys objectivity in recording actual words devoid of interpretation, but the framework in which they are placed is wholly the work of their compiler. There are at least two dangers. The excerpts can be used out of context and they can be tampered with in order to increase their applicability. We shall see that Eusebius succumbs to both temptations.

In his apologetic aims and methods, Eusebius continues along well-established paths. Like Athenagoras, he is prepared to say that some philosophers, notably Plato, have seen elements of revealed truth. Indeed, he admits to an admiration for the Greeks who have obtained fame through their philosophising (*Praep. ev.* 14.1.2). Through the witness of their own words, however, it is apparent that they have slid away from the truth. Eusebius follows Philo and Hermias in taking the theme of doctrinal disagreement as his main argumentative weapon. His survey of Greek philosophers will reveal their constant battles of words or arguments (λογομαχίαι), their rivalry (φιλοτιμία) and doctrinal oppositions (ἀντικαταστάσεις, 14.2.1). This strategy is already invoked at the outset when, in Book 1, he presents 'the *doxai* of the Greek philosophers on first principles and their dissensions (διαστάσεις) and disagreements (διαφωνίαι) with each other based on conjectures (στοχασμοί) and not on understanding' (1.7.16), but there he does not use the *Placita*, instead citing extended extracts from the pseudo-Plutarchean *Stromateis* to make his point (1.8).

Some books later, when presenting Hebrew *doxai* on God as the first cause (*Praep. ev.* 7.11), Eusebius compares them with the theologies of the Greek sages. For this purpose, he compiles two small centos of citations from the *Placita*, the first on theology, the second on the principles of reality, but does not mention his source. These brief extracts show how his knowledge of the work not only gives him the material but also enables him to organise it in a logical sequence, moving from atheism to cosmic theology and then on to providence and the origin of the cosmos, as well as allowing a comparison between Greek and Jewish theology, in which for the former he tendentiously cites only materialist and mathematical views.

It is not until midway through Book 14 that the bishop formally introduces the *Placita*. In Books 11–13 he had set out Plato's philosophy, giving him the privileged position he had by this time acquired in patristic theology. It is now time, Eusebius says, to examine the other Hellenic schools

---

[46] We use the edition of Mras 1982–83, which usefully distinguishes between quotations and Eusebius' own words by printing the latter in italic type.

of thought (αἱρέσεις, 13.21.14). Their disagreement (διαφωνία) and strife are in marked contrast to the unity and harmony of thought (συμφωνία) shown by Moses and the other Hebrew writers (14.3). Ten chapters are devoted to illustrating these controversies, with special attention to Plato's successors in the academic tradition. Eusebius then continues:

> Let us finally make a new start and examine the doctrinal contradictions (ἀντιδοξίαι) against each other of the physical philosophers who have been mentioned. Now Plutarch has collected together the opinions (δόξαι) of all the Platonists and Pythagoreans alike and also the reputed earlier physical philosophers, together with the more recent Peripatetics and Stoics and Epicureans and written them in a work which he gave the title 'On the physical doctrines held by the philosophers', from which I shall present the following.[47] (*Praep. ev.* 14.13.9)

In introducing the *Epitome*,[48] Eusebius indicates its chronological scope, placing the Platonic tradition at the centre, with the early Greek philosophers (i.e. Pre-Socratics) before them and the chief Hellenistic schools following thereafter. This is a recognition of the role of chronology in the work but also involves a slight distortion since, although Plato's views are prominent in the compendium,[49] no favoured role is granted to his school. There then follow two blocks of quotations from the *Placita*, each block using a quite different approach and method.[50]

The first block, in *Praep. ev.* 14.14 and 14.16, makes a selective use of material from the long chapters on the *archai* and theology in *Plac.* 1.3 and 1.7, respectively. From the former, as in 7.12.1, Eusebius selects just those *doxai* which put forward a materialist first principle, emphasising their disagreement and the fact that they make no reference to any god or any being beyond what is an object of sense perception. It was only Anaxagoras, whose *doxa* he had omitted earlier, who introduced an intellect (νοῦς) and so recognised a true first principle. From the latter, when he turns to the list of philosophers beginning with Thales, there seems little doubt that he tendentiously modifies the text he found in Pseudo-Plutarch, in which both Thales and Democritus are credited – dubiously of course – with the view that their god was an intellect.[51] It

---

[47] My translations are based on Gifford 1903 with modifications.
[48] Its epitomising character is mentioned in a secondary introduction at *Praep. ev.* 15.22.68.
[49] In what remains of the *Placita*, Plato is the second-most cited author (61x) after the Stoics (70x); see Jeremiah 2018: 328.
[50] On what follows, see the extended analysis in Mansfeld and Runia 1997: 132–39. I cannot discuss all the details here.
[51] *Praep. ev.* 14.16.6 Thales τὸν κόσμον τὸν θεόν (*Epit.* νοῦν τοῦ κόσμου); Democritus θεὸν ἐν πυρὶ σφαιροειδῆ τὴν κόσμου ψυχήν (*Epit.* νοῦν τὸν θεὸν ἐν πυρὶ σφαιροειδεῖ).

is theoretically possible, of course, that he had a different text in front of him, but given how neatly the alteration fits his theory about the prominent role of Anaxagoras as initiator, via his pupil Socrates, of the Platonic tradition, one has to be suspicious.

In the final book of the *Praeparatio*, we encounter a different strategy in the use of the *Placita*. After setting out the structure of his argument for the entire work and then various excerpts showing how Aristotle and the Stoics deviated from Plato, he returns to the *doxai*, stating that:

> it is time to ... examine the marvellous physical theories of the whole gathering of noble philosophers, especially from the time that all the Greeks in common regarded the sun and moon and remaining heavenly bodies, as well as the other parts of the cosmos, as visible gods and worshipped them, and transferred the mythical and nonsensical recitations of their polytheistic error by means of more respectful physical explanations to the elements and the divisions of the entire cosmos. (*Praep. ev.* 15.22.68)

There follows the verbatim quotation of no less than thirty-nine chapters from the *Epitome*, starting with the sun and moon, cosmos, and heavenly bodies (Book 2 with a few chapters from Book 1), then moving on to the earth (Book 3), and ending with just two chapters on the soul from Book 4. The chapters are all written out in full without any further abridgement. But even here it is possible to detect modifications in the interests of the larger project. Why, for example, does Eusebius depart from the logical sequence of topics in Book 2 and commence with the sun and moon? This can only be because he wishes to foreground the Greeks' astral theology, as seen in the text quoted above. Another example is found at 15.34, when he cites the chapter on cosmic ensoulment and providence (*Plac.* 2.3).[52] Eusebius omits the first *doxa* which states that 'all the others (i.e. philosophers) affirm that the cosmos is ensouled and administered by providence'. This almost universal recognition of divine providence is, it would appear, too great a concession to Greek philosophy, so it is better to leave it out and begin the chapter with the materialist atomists.

Only one chapter remains and it delivers a *coup de grâce*. Surveying all these opinions, Eusebius argues, do we not show sound judgement in staying away from all such astray-leading futile activity (ματαιοπονία, 15.61.11)? In so doing, we are actually agreeing with the example of Socrates, the wisest of all the Greeks, who according to Xenophon accused the crazy investigators of the sky of striving for what is unattainable and wasting time on matters that are unprofitable for human life. Only ethics,

---

[52] See above text at n. 17 on its lack of explicit reference to theology.

not physics, is the proper subject of philosophy.[53] This is the final excerpt of the work.

The *Placita* thus allow Eusebius to set up the climactic moment of his massive treatise. Like Hermias, he finds them useful because they offer him a most effective weapon to demonstrate the futility of the knowledge which they purport to record. He is able to exploit various features of their method of ordering knowledge, such as a well-organised sequence of topics, a chronological framework, a compact manner of presentation, and above all the great diversity of views that they summarise. However, his predominant focus on theology leads him to use them for a purpose that runs counter to their secular tendency and their even-handedness.[54] And so he cannot resist tinkering with subtle details of their content, which once noticed undermines his claim that he is refuting the Greeks with the witness of their own words. It should be noted, too, that many of Eusebius' cherished themes – such as the diversity and conflict of opinions, the restricted scope of true philosophy, the championship of Socrates, and the praise of barbarian philosophy – are *topoi* that have deep roots in the Greek philosophy and culture that is the focus of his polemic.[55]

The brief citations from the *Placita* in the treatise of Pseudo-Justin generally referred to under the title of *Cohortatio ad Graecos* need not delay us long, since it very much follows in the footsteps of the works we have studied so far. The pseudonymous work was long dated to the third century, but the research of Christoph Riedweg, based on TLG data, has shown that stylistic features support its attribution to Marcellus, bishop of Ancyra, a younger contemporary of Eusebius.[56] It is quite likely, therefore, that it was written at about the same time as the *Praeparatio*, when Christian intellectuals were gaining confidence. Riedweg argues that its title was not the traditional Λόγος παραινετικὸς πρὸς Ἕλληνας, but rather Πρὸς Ἕλληνας περὶ τῆς ἀληθοῦς θεοσεβείας λόγος, as indicated in its exordium (§1.2). Since the philosophers are the teachers of piety (θεοσέβεια), it is their views that need to be examined. For this purpose, he will expound the *doxa* of each of them on the subject, commencing with extracts from the chapter on the *archai* in *Plac*. 1.3 (§§3.2–4.1), and later briefly using *Plac*. 4.6 for a subsequent discussion on

---

[53] *Praep. ev.* 15.62.1–6 = Xenophon, *Mem.* 1.1.11–16. In his final summation, Eusebius also quotes poetic lines on philosophers' strife and combat from the *Silloi* of the Hellenistic poet Timon.
[54] See above n. 15 and text thereto.
[55] Compare for example the texts of Diodorus Siculus and Galen discussed in Mansfeld and Runia 1997: 139–41.
[56] Riedweg 1994: 167–84. He hesitates to attribute the work definitively to Marcellus (hence the question mark in the title of his book), but the evidence is strong.

Plato's and Aristotle's views on the soul (§6.1).[57] The mode of citation differs from that of Eusebius, not using direct quotation, but rather paraphrase in the manner that Theodoret will later use. But the conclusions are similar. The philosophers, by reaching opposed conclusions, refute each other's opinions (§7.1). They are in conflict with each other (§35.2, στασιάζουσι) and cannot possibly be accepted as teachers of true piety. The philosopher that one should follow in the first instance is again Socrates (§36.1–2). When he said he knew nothing, he was not being ironic, for as he was led away he said that he was going to 'the better state hidden to all but God' (*Apol.* 42a). But the true piety, Pseudo-Justin concludes, has been revealed through the prophets, including the ancient sybil (§37). Like Eusebius, therefore, he is less positive in using the *Placita* than Athenagoras a century or more earlier.

The next Christian author to use the *Placita* is also a bishop, but one who took a very different approach from his predecessors. Nothing is known about Nemesius except that he was the bishop of Emesa (now Homs) in Syria and what can be gleaned from his treatise, which shows him to be someone with at least a good layman's knowledge of philosophy and medicine.[58] Various indications point to a date towards the end of the fourth century. By this time, Christianity had become the dominant force in the Greco-Roman world, and the church was starting to channel more energy into determining doctrinal orthodoxy than into countering the influence of Greek philosophy. Recently Mark Edwards has claimed that Nemesius was 'the first Christian who openly made use of pagan thought as a corrective to errors in dogma', the purpose of the work being to refute the christologies of Apollinarius and Eunomius, for which he needed to present an account of the nature of the human being.[59] So his treatise has this subject as its title, Περὶ φύσεως ἀνθρώπου, and, more than virtually any other patristic work, it adopts the style and method of a philosophical handbook.

In setting out and organising his presentation of the nature of the human being, Nemesius makes extensive use of doxographical material and it can be shown that much of it is derived from a tradition closely related to the *Placita*, though not directly from either Aëtius or the *Epitome*.[60] The texts are mostly parallel to Book 4 on the soul, but there are also brief extracts similar to Book 1 on first principles, including the chapters towards the

---

[57] For the details, see now Mansfeld and Runia 2020: 1.48–49, replacing the discussion in 1997: 165–66.
[58] See the introduction in the translation of Sharples and Van der Eijk 2008, which summarises previous scholarship.
[59] Edwards 2019: 131.
[60] See now Mansfeld and Runia 2020: 1.67–68, with further references to the edition of Aëtius; this account revises the listing and analysis in Mansfeld and Runia 1997: 291–99.

end on necessity and fate (1.25–28). The most interesting text is found at the beginning of chapter 2, entitled Περὶ ψυχῆς (the same title as *Plac.* 4.2). Nemesius opens with the statement: 'The account of the soul shows disagreement (διαφωνεῖται) on the part of almost all the ancients' (p. 16.12).[61] He first summarises the list of philosophers who have a corporeal view of the soul (cf. *Plac.* 4.3), and then presents a similar list of those who say it is incorporeal (cf. *Plac.* 4.2), emphasising here too the ἄπειρος διαφωνία of those who espouse this view and adding another diaeresis on its substance which involves a tendentious understanding of the Aristotelian *doxa* (17.9–10).[62] A further diaeresis foreign to the *Placita* is added (17.10–14), which interestingly includes the view of the Manicheans. This detail was no doubt the work of Nemesius himself.[63] He is happy to include heretical views in the doxography, but – unlike Philo[64] – does not include scripture itself. There follows an examination of all the positions outlined in the three diaereses, all of them being refuted with one significant exception. Plato and others have developed many proofs of the soul's immortality, he concludes, but these are difficult to understand. For Christians the teaching of the sacred books, which is divinely inspired (θεόπνευστος, 1 Tim 3:16), will suffice. But for those who do not accept the sacred books, it will be enough to demonstrate that the soul is immortal (38.2–10).

Nemesius plainly delights in the structural clarity of the method of the *Placita*, which helps him to organise his presentation in a lucid and purposeful fashion. He recognises the role of the diaeresis and builds upon it, adding further divisions and supplying argumentation from other sources. The technical term διαφωνία is used to record disagreement, though with less polemical intent than in Eusebius and Pseudo-Justin.[65] His evaluative approach to the *doxai* and diaereses which he records, and his acceptance of doctrine on the basis of revelation of course differ from the *Placita*. Nevertheless, his respectful and constructive use of the views of the philosophers is unusual in the patristic context and makes for refreshing reading. It is no wonder that his work was popular during the Middle Ages, when it was translated into five different languages.[66]

---

[61] I cite the text of Morani 1987.
[62] See the comment of Sharples and Van der Eijk 2008: 53 n. 263.
[63] Mansfeld 1990: 3081 n. 89, cited by Sharples and Van der Eijk 2008: *ad loc.*
[64] See above text to n. 31.
[65] In addition to the two texts already discussed, see ch. 6, p. 56.1, where the term is used to describe the difference between Nemesius' own description of the imagination (τὸ φανταστικόν) and the Stoic analysis parallel to *Plac.* 4.12.
[66] Sharples and Van der Eijk 2008: 1–2.

The Fifth Century: Cyril, Theodoret

In this chapter, I will not discuss the contribution of Ioannes Stobaeus, who apart from the *Epitome* is the most important witness to Aëtius' compendium. As his first name indicates, he must have been a Christian, or at least came from a Christian (or Jewish) background.[67] His massive anthology, however, dated to the early fifth century, remains wholly within the Hellenic tradition, without a single reference to Christianity. Although it is certainly evidence of the wide range of intellectual activity on the part of Christian authors in late antiquity, Stobaeus himself can hardly be regarded as a patristic author. Despite its great interest, therefore, for reasons of space it will have to be set aside.

The next work we encounter is the *Contra Iulianum* of Cyril, bishop of Alexandria. Composed in the early fifth century,[68] on three occasions it makes use of material from Pseudo-Plutarch's *Epitome* as part of its elaborate and vitriolic refutation of the Emperor Julian's attack on the Galileans (as he called the Christians). This usage is highly contextual and not all the interesting details can be examined in the present discussion. Cyril knows the works of Pseudo-Justin (Marcellus) and Eusebius well, and takes over from them a central theme in his first two books,[69] the antithesis between the ancient unitary truth of scripture, particularly as seen in the writings of Moses, and the more recent stochastic and contradictory views of the Greek philosophers so admired by Julian.

At the outset, there is already mention of 'diverse opinions rising up as if against each other' (*Jul.* 1.4.10), together with a random selection of name-labels from the *Placita*, contemptuously used in the plural (*Jul.* 1.4.5–13),[70] but there is no explicit mention of them until later in the book (1.38), when the Greek sages are introduced. Just like Eusebius, Cyril cites views from *Plac.* 1.7 on who or what God is. He is more accurate than Eusebius in presenting the views of Thales and Democritus,[71] but for Anaximander he finds the *doxa* in 1.3 on first principles more suitable for his purpose

---

[67] This deduction, postulated in Mansfeld and Runia 1997: 197, is gaining acceptance among scholars.

[68] On the dating, see now the new edition of Riedweg and Kinzig 2015, which we cite. In the introduction (p. cxv), Kinzig argues for a time of writing between 416 and 428 CE.

[69] But Cyril did have independent access to the *Epitome*; see Mansfeld and Runia 2020: 1.51–52.

[70] Cyril, *Jul.* 1.4.7 (Riedweg and Kinzig 2015: 16): Ἀναξιμάνδρους ... καὶ Ἐμπεδοκλεῖς Πρωταγόρας τε καὶ Πλάτωνας.

[71] For Thales, God is the νοῦς τοῦ κόσμου; for Democritus, God is νοῦς ἐν πυρὶ σφαιροειδεῖ: contrast Eusebius above at n. 51.

and cites it instead.[72] The views of Aristotle and the Stoics are then cited from 1.7 (*Jul.* 1.39), but not Pythagoras or Plato. The reason for this soon becomes apparent. These two had spent time in Egypt and were aware of Moses' excellence (1.40.18–21), as evidenced by their recognition of God's uniqueness.[73] In Book 2, the *Placita* are again called upon in response to Julian's attack on the Mosaic creation account. Citing Plutarch by name as a distinguished Hellene, Cyril quotes verbatim *Plac.* 2.1–4 on the cosmos, its shape, whether it is ensouled and providentially administered (2.3 again), and whether it has a temporal origin and will come to an end (*Jul.* 2.14–15). In the evaluative comments that follow (2.16), he interestingly points out the contradictory nature of these views – all based on guesswork in his view – by summarising the series of oppositions that Aëtius has used in order to structure these chapters, although he does not actually use the technical term διαφωνία. Finally, at *Jul.* 2.20, Cyril returns to Moses and claims that when writing his creation account he was not motivated by ambition or the desire to engage in the niceties of natural philosophy, but because he wished to contribute a necessary and beneficial doctrine for people's lives (distantly reminiscent of Xenophon's Socrates). This is followed by the theme we already encountered in Philo and Athenagoras (and continued by Eusebius), the departure from true piety through the admiration and worship of the cosmos and its parts.[74] Like the apologist, Cyril recalls *Plac.* 1.6 and cites three passages on how people came to an erroneous conception of the deity (2.22).[75]

Cyril's use of the *Placita* in association with particular apologetic themes is hardly original and stands in the tradition that extends from Athenagoras to Eusebius and Pseudo-Justin. He knows the theme of the dissension of the philosophers well and relates it cleverly to the structure of the chapters he quotes. But when citing the *Placita*, he dwells on it less, preferring to attack its contents with defamatory terms and expressions such as 'nonsense', 'trivial prattle', and being 'drunk with weird opinions'.[76] What

---

[72] Deriving the 'infinite kosmoi' (ἀπείρους κόσμους) as gods from *Plac.* 1.3, a *doxa* which is clearly more bizarre than the 'heavenly stars' (ἀστέρας οὐρανίους) from *Plac.* 1.7 retained by Eusebius.

[73] Based on the *doxai* of Pythagoras and Plato in *Plac.* 1.7. Cyril does not follow Eusebius in emphasising the Anaxagorean *nous* because he has no interest in introducing the *doxa* of a creator god in this context.

[74] See above n. 38 and text preceding n. 52.

[75] The earlier and parallel use in Athenagoras is not noted by Riedweg and Kinzig 2015 in their apparatus *ad loc.*, but on pp. clix and clxxiv it is noted that Cyril knew the Apologist and his work. Cyril twice modifies the text of *Plac.* 1.6, not attributing the *doxa* to the Stoics and changing the first person ἐλάβομεν to the third person ἔλαβον at *Jul.* 2.22.8.

[76] λῆρος (*Jul.* 2.14.9; 2.16.2); στενολεσχία (2.14.9, a subtle allusion to Aristophanes' parody of Socrates in *Nub.* 320); ἀλλοκότοις δόξαις καταμεθυομένους (1.20.12; cf. 1.39.11; 2.16.13).

impels him then, we might ask, to quote the *doxai*? We may get a hint when he describes their compiler Plutarch as 'excessively subtle' (ἰσχνὸς ἄγαν, 2.22.7). The same term is repeatedly used to describe what Moses does *not* do in his creation account, to 'subtly discourse on physics', to present ideas of 'such subtlety', and so on.[77] The *Placita* are useful, it seems, for the compact yet subtle way that they summarise a diversity of views that actually serve no good purpose.

It is fitting to end our analysis of the patristic works that made use of the *Placita* with the treatise of bishop Theodoret of Cyrrhus, *Healing of the Hellenic Illnesses*, which is so crucial for our knowledge of Aëtius and his compendium.[78] Unlike Cyril's work, it does not respond to a specific treatise and the circumstances of its composition are not clear. Clemens Scholten argues that it was most likely written after Theodoret's election as bishop in 423 and after the Council of Ephesus in 431.[79] Writing in the hinterland of the city of Antioch where he had received his education, Theodoret assumes a readership that consists of both pagans and Christians.[80] As he tells us in the introduction (§§16–17), the former, who are ill, he wishes to heal; the latter, who are in good health, he wishes to assist. The book is thus not only a work of apologetics, standing in the tradition we have been studying, but also a work of instruction. Earlier in the same section, when outlining the contents of the twelve books, Theodoret twice mentions that he will be presenting the *doxai* of the Greek philosophers and will use them to demonstrate the difference between truth and falsehood and between light and darkness (§5 on Book 2, §8 on Book 5). By speaking of the δόξαι here, together with the subsequent more detailed references (2.95; 4.31; 5.16), he acknowledges the use of works of philosophical doxography, prime among which was Aëtius' compendium.[81]

Theodoret's treatise can be regarded as the climax of the early Christian apologetic tradition which had its earliest beginnings in the Acts of the

---

[77] *Jul.* 2.20.4: φυσιολογεῖν ἰσχνῶς; 2.21.7: συνιέναι τὰ οὕτως ἰσχνά; cf. 2.20.22: λίαν ἰσχνομυθεῖν. But for a more positive use of the term for the quest to see God, see 1.20.27.

[78] See above text at n. 3; also Mansfeld 2016; and more briefly Mansfeld and Runia 2020: 1.9–15. For recent translations with introductions, see Halton 2013; Scholten 2015. The standard text is still Raeder 1904.

[79] Scholten 2015: 89–103. This would mean he could make use of Cyril's work. But Scholten was unable to take into account the earlier date for that work which Kinzig has now proposed, on which see above n. 68.

[80] As noted by Scholten 2015: 48–49.

[81] He also names Pseudo-Plutarch's *Epitome*, but fortunately for posterity preferred to use the original. In total he cites 109 *doxai*, which amounts to 14 per cent of the extant remains of Aëtius' compendium.

Apostles and in writings such as Athenagoras' *Embassy* in the second century. Theodoret was conscious of standing in that tradition and, as scholars have noted, in preparing for his task he must have carefully studied earlier writings, notably those of Clement, Eusebius, and Pseudo-Justin, making excerpts and organising them into a tightly argued didactic structure. Because many of these writings are still extant, it is possible to follow this process much more closely and in greater detail than is usually the case.[82]

Against this background, it emerges that Theodoret appropriates all the main features of the patristic use of the Aëtian *doxai* identified so far. The *doxai* are used to set out the great diversity of philosophical views on theology (including first principles), cosmology, and anthropology. He is conscious of their diaeretic and diaphonic structure. He delights in pointing out how this confirms the incessant strife and contradictions of the Greek philosophers, consistently using the theme to introduce their views on the succession of topics.[83] It proves the falsehood of philosophy in contrast to the truth of scripture. An exception to this negativity and condemnation is Theodoret's view of Platonic philosophy, which is partly praised and partly refuted. Among other things, Aëtian *doxai* demonstrate how philosophers try to answer questions, e.g., on matters such as cosmic distances (*Cur.* 4.22), that are of no use to human life. The pointlessness of such efforts was already recognised by Socrates, as recorded in Xenophon's *Memorabilia* (4.27–29). It will be recognised that these themes follow well-established paths.

But, for all his debts to his predecessors, Theodoret also adds his own personal notes. The most interesting is an epistemological discussion in Book 1 which highlights the role of πίστις (faith, trust, conviction).[84] Those who follow the *doxai* of the philosophers, he argues, use faith as their guide, some welcoming these doctrines, other opting for different ones (1.62). As an illustration, he gives a potted summary of the main themes of the *Placita* in a few lines, with general examples from psychology, cosmology, and first principles (1.63). Despite these fundamental differences, the thinkers involved have followers who believe them on trust. A little later, Theodoret gives a brief doxography of Greek views on faith,[85] concluding that faith needs knowledge, but knowledge also needs faith, and in fact faith leads

---

[82] On his method see Scholten 2015: 103–22, building on earlier research including Mansfeld and Runia 1997: 272–90.
[83] For example, at 1.63; 1.97; 4.15; 4.22; 5.15; 5.19; etc. The favourite terms are διαμάχη and διαφωνία; see Mansfeld and Runia 1997: 276.
[84] Much indebted to Clement's doctrine of *pistis*, on which see Osborn 2005: 155–96.
[85] Based on Clement, *Strom.* 2.4.15–17; see previous note.

the way (*Cur.* 1.90–92). Another example from the *Placita* follows in §96. The pupils of astronomers place trust in their teachings, which reach quite different conclusions on astronomical measurements such as the size of the sun (*Plac.* 2.21), a disagreement which reaches ridiculous proportions. Why do the Greeks go beyond their own faith, which is so unreasonable, and criticise only our faith, which offers release from such mythical nonsense and grasps intelligibly what is divine and noetic (1.99)? The academic and sceptical elements which form part of the background of the doxographical tradition[86] belong to the distant past by Theodoret's time, and he is probably unaware of them. Instead, he connects them with the concept of faith which had become increasingly important in Christian apologetics from the time of Clement and Origen onwards.

One of the hallmarks of Theodoret's method, as noted above,[87] is the way that he seamlessly incorporates earlier material into his treatise. This also applies to his use of the *Placita*. They are much better integrated into his work than was the case in Eusebius' *Praeparatio*. Whereas Eusebius simply writes out large chunks of the *doxai*, Theodoret integrates their contents into the flow of his argument, paraphrasing rather than quoting verbatim (which of course makes them less useful for textual purposes). Like Eusebius he makes use of the motif of the relation between macrocosm and microcosm. But whereas Eusebius does this in a quite perfunctory fashion, citing only two chapters from the *Epitome* (15.60–61), Theodoret devotes an entire book to the 'nature of human beings'[88] and includes material from six chapters from the original work of Aëtius. In this book he also includes a section claiming that there is strife and rivalry between teachers and pupils (5.44–47), citing not only the celebrated case of Plato and Aristotle, but also the succession of the early Ionian philosophers which has a prominent place in the *Placita* (esp. 1.3), in contrast to the harmony of the authors of scripture (5.49–50). The first half of the work devoted to the views of the philosophers ends with a book on the subject of providence. Here, too, he will examine the *doxai* of the Greeks, including limited material from the *Placita*. This central theme cleverly brings together the theological, cosmological, and anthropological views that he has treated so far, since God, in taking care of the cosmos of which he is the creator, also positively affects the lives of the human beings who live in it. It also allows him to introduce the theme of the relative admiration of God and cosmos,

---

[86] See the discussion on Philo above at n. 26 and esp. Mansfeld 1988.
[87] Text above at n. 82.
[88] *Cur.* Book 5, Περὶ φύσεως ἀνθρώπου, exactly the same title used by Nemesius for his treatise.

which is so prominent in the apologetic treatises that we have examined in our survey.[89]

As Scholten has rightly emphasised, Theodoret is a consciously didactic writer. His work is at least partly directed at a Christian readership, particularly those who are less well educated, for whom it can be a useful compendium in support of their faith. For such a programme, the *Placita* could serve as a highly suitable didactic instrument. It not only enabled him to introduce a great deal of illustrative material in a compact fashion but also assisted him in organising it in a way that made it easy to follow and understand, as Jörg Ulrich has well summarised:[90] 'The whole material is arranged in clear and strictly ordered sequences – and that seems to be the new thing about Christian apologetics in Theodoret's *Curatio*. The text established a kind of medium genre between an *apologetic summa* and a "systematic theology".'

Concluding Remarks

The patristic appropriation of the method of ordering knowledge offered by the *Placita* takes place almost exclusively in an apologetic context, when Christian thinkers confront and attack the legacy of Greek philosophy in the course of defending their own views. We have been able to observe a striking continuity of usage from the Hellenistic-Jewish exegete and philosopher Philo – so often a precursor of later thought – in the first century CE to Cyril and Theodoret in the fifth. Many characteristics of the *doxai* are favourable for use. Their well-organised and comprehensive coverage of the *physikos logos* provides a compact and representative array of *doxai* which can be used selectively or presented in full force, depending on the argumentative strategy followed. There is an undeniable tendency to focus on the better-known names, with little use of the relatively scanty chronological details which the *Placita* contains. But the fathers are clearly in agreement with the *Placita* that it is the *doxai* that are central to the method and the argument, not the individual philosophers who hold these views (with the exception of Plato and Socrates, who both saw something of the truth).

It is the diversity of *doxai* that appeals to the fathers, not for the reason that they were assembled in the first place, but because this demonstrates the deplorable dissension, contradiction, rivalry, and conflict of the Greek

---

[89] See above n. 74 with further cross-references.
[90] Ulrich 2009: 113–30 at 1.27, cited by Scholten 2015: 52.

philosophical enterprise. This theme has proved to be the main connecting thread of all of the authors studied, from Philo to Theodoret. In the case of Philo, we may be certain that he was acquainted with the philosophical antecedents of this theme in Greek philosophy itself, but this awareness falls away, with a resultant decline in epistemological depth. Another point of differentiation comes to the fore in theology. In the *Placita*, theology has a place as an integral part of physics, but it is somewhat downplayed, for example in its treatment of the heavenly bodies, the divinity of which does not receive any emphasis. Predictably, the fathers take a quite different approach, as illustrated by Eusebius, who starts his long extract of *doxai* from Book 2 not with the cosmos, but with the sun and moon and other heavenly bodies that are the object of polytheistic worship.[91]

In sum, the *Placita* is a resource and an instrument to be utilised, selectively appropriated and adapted to purpose. Its distinctive mode of knowing assisted in the development of early Christians' own mode of ordering knowledge. In that work a kind of structured disorder prevails, in emphatic contrast with the secure ordering of Christian knowledge. The appropriation, it has to be said, served a primarily negative purpose, showing how one should not think. Philo was the only writer to integrate a scriptural author in a doxography, with Nemesius also happy to include heretical thinkers among the proponents of false views. As we saw at the end in Theodoret's work, however, the clear method of organisation of the *Placita* may have contributed to the development of more systematic forms of theological discourse. All the writings that we have examined combine apologetics with a didactic purpose, for which the material supplied by the *Placita* proved to be highly suitable.

---

[91] See above text preceding n. 52.

13 Nicaea's Frame: The Organisation of Creedal Knowledge in Late Antiquity and Modernity

ANDREW RADDE-GALLWITZ

Introduction

A chapter on creeds might seem out of place in a discussion of the ordering of knowledge, but the modern study of early Christian creeds has given rise to a distinctive genre, the anthology or library of creeds, which has proven to be a highly influential organisation of knowledge. This chapter sketches how this encyclopaedic genre has organised its material and argues that such anthologies, driven as they are by the twin emphases on literary form and organic development, tend to homogenise diverse types of creed. In particular, I will attend to the difference between creeds such as the Nicene, which ends with an anathema, and others such as the Apostles' Creed, which does not. I will ask whether fourth- and early fifth-century Christians had alternative ways to transmit and organise their knowledge of creeds, particularly the Nicene. While there was nothing in the fourth century comparable to a library of creeds, the sources we have do reflect a distinct understanding of how doctrinal confessions might be not only documented but also supplemented over time. The method, we will see, focused especially on creedal anathemas, which the late antique sources treated as integral parts of conciliar creeds. Thus, most of our time will be spent unearthing how our late antique sources created and interpreted anathemas. The present chapter focuses on Greek examples, which are the earliest and most abundant evidence, and pursues a series of questions: how did the authorship of creeds occur, how were the documents transmitted, and how did the fourth century Christians organise, interpret, and supplement these texts? As we will see, synods adopted some elements of both senatorial parliamentary procedures and trials, and these models shaped the production and reception of creeds. To lay out my approach to these questions, it will help to begin with a sketch of the modern anthological tradition. As we will see, not only did modern anthologists assemble diverse creeds in their volumes, they also produced a genealogical method to link diverse *types* of creed in a single family tree.

Faith in Fragments: Modern Creedal Anthologies

Since the fifteenth century, the study of creeds has been dominated by the question of the Apostles' Creed. Doubts about its authenticity arose in Latin Christendom through dialogue with the Greeks at the Council of Ferrara-Florence, who did not recognise it, and through humanist scholarship. The resultant confusion launched centuries of research into its origins. Out of this vexed question came the genre of the creedal anthology, which came into its own with J. G. F. Walch's *Bibliotheca symbolica vetus*, published in 1770, a work that reflected the era's encyclopaedic vision.[1] In 1842, the confessionalist Lutheran August Hahn sought to correct Walch's collection and to show the existence of an early 'apostolic-catholic church' culminating in Protestantism; his *Bibliothek der Symbole und Glaubensregeln der apostolisch-katholischen Kirche* would appear in two successive editions edited by his son; the third edition remains a standard work of reference. In 1854, the German Catholic Heinrich Denzinger produced his *Enchiridion symbolorum et definitionum*, which became an institution in its own right, having recently appeared in its forty-third edition.[2] In 1858, Charles A. Heurtley came out with *Harmonia Symbolica: A Collection of Creeds Belonging to the Ancient Western Church, and to the Mediaeval English Church Arranged in Chronological Order, and After the Manner of a Harmony*. Further anthologies were produced to supplement or condense Hahn.[3] A host of studies followed.[4] The impulse to collect creedal documents has continued into the twenty-first century, which has witnessed the publication of two multi-volume English-language compilations.[5]

If we look synoptically at the nineteenth- and early twentieth-century anthologies, we see that, while the organising principles of the collections vary, each seeks above all to explain the Apostles' Creed. Our earliest witness to this creed as such is Rufinus' *Commentary on the Apostles' Creed* from AD 404, though he claims it is apostolic and the creed, as cited, has some textual precedents. Scholars therefore asked how far back it goes and how it relates to other professions. The observation driving their work is that this text – which is so important for modern Western liturgies in various traditions, although entirely unknown to the East – looks somewhat

---

[1] Walch 1770. For the history of collections, see Kattenbusch 1894: 1.1–37; Kinzig 2017: 1.18–28. On Walch, see Markschies 2013: 160–63.

[2] Denzinger 1854.   [3] Supplement: Caspari 1866–75; condense: Lietzmann 1906.

[4] Hort 1876; Kattenbusch 1894; Harnack 1896; Burn 1899; Sanday 1899; Turner 1910; Lietzmann 1922.

[5] Pelikan and Hotchkiss 2003; Kinzig 2017.

like the profession of faith in the Nicene Creed and many other creedal and creed-like documents, from early 'rules of faith' to conciliar creeds of the fourth century. The still-regnant English term for the form – 'declarative creed' – was supplied by Heurtley.[6] The title was meant to distinguish such creeds from 'interrogative' baptismal formulae. On Heurtley's account, Irenaeus' 'rule of truth', the Nicene Creed, and the Apostles' Creed are equally examples of the declarative creed, and the aim of his book is not only to document their formal similarity but also, rather outlandishly, to produce a single harmonised creed out of these diverse exemplars of the common form, in particular out of the Apostles' and the Nicene. Other modern anthologies attempt merely to display this similarity by setting forth the documents, though in all cases the texts are completely shorn of context. Thus, the editors' concern with the Apostles' Creed frames their account of the Nicene, and it is the verbal parallels that justify the procedure.

How, then, to explain the variations among the samples? To answer this, the nineteenth- and early twentieth-century anthologisers brought an assumption of organic or genetic growth. The idea was that an original creed must have been adapted in diverse ways by local churches to suit their baptismal liturgy. To demonstrate this phenomenon, the editors placed the documents in a genealogical order. The documents would show variations of form, which were typically explained by reference to local custom, and out of these remnants scholarly ingenuity could reconstruct the lost original; following the scholarly habit of using single letter abbreviations for reconstructed texts, Hans Lietzmann dubbed the lost text 'O'.[7] On this model, both rules of faith and conciliar creeds were taken as publications of pre-existing baptismal creeds. Denzinger stated that 'rule of faith' was simply the early term for the Apostles' Creed; for him this creed took diverse local forms and in his book all extant creeds, save those of the ecumenical councils, are fitted into this story: for example, Arius' creeds are exemplars of the *Forma Alexandrina*; Eusebius' is the lone exemplar of the *Forma Caesarensis* – after printing the text, Denzinger merely notes *caetera desunt*.[8] Various collections and studies included the ecumenical councils in the narrative of descent: Nicaea (now 'N') was taken to be a revision of

---

[6] Heurtley first drew the distinction between 'the Interrogative Creeds used at baptism and the Declarative Creeds'. For him, rules of truth are examples of the latter: Heurtley 1858: vii, 4, 7. Heurtley's term is still used by Wolfram Kinzig in his four-volume anthology (Kinzig 2017).
[7] Lietzmann 1922; see also A. E. Burn's reconstruction of the two primitive Greek creeds – dating, he supposes, to the first decade of the second century – the one roughly representing what was used by Jewish Christians and the other the primitive creed of Gentile Christians: Burn 1899: 31–32.
[8] Denzinger 1854: 7.

the Caesarean creed, Constantinople 381 ('NC' or 'C') a version of the Jerusalem creed ('J'), and so on.[9] It was J. N. D. Kelly who laid much of this particular kind of speculation to rest with his epochal *Early Christian Creeds*.[10]

Each of the modern collections aimed to characterise early Christian history in a way that leads continuously to modern confessions. In its 1854 edition, Denzinger's anthology extended to Pope Pius IX's allocution on civil marriage from September 27, 1852; Heurtley's ended with the baptismal confession used during the reign of Edward VI; Hahn's traced the baptismal confessions of the 'apostolic-catholic Church' through diverse traditions (e.g., Roman, Gallic, British, German, and Icelandic) up to and including the rise of Protestantism. Until the early twentieth century, it was widely assumed that the results of conscientious scholarly research in this area would confirm the narrative that the baptismal faith, in the form of an explicit declaratory creed, took a recognisable, if not final, shape in the early second century.

One can see the shift away from this consensus narrative by comparing two articles bearing the same title in the *Journal of Theological Studies* (*JTS*), the first from the journal's inaugural issue in 1899 and the other from its centenary in 1999. As the lead article in the inaugural issue, W. Sanday's 'Recent Research on the Origin of the Creed' supported a second-century date for the so-called Roman Creed first cited by Marcellus of Ancyra. Since Ussher in the seventeenth century, this had been recognised as the ancestor of the Apostles' Creed cited by Rufinus. Sanday's argument was that the Nicene and Apostolic Creeds were 'really varieties ... of the same fundamental creed', a derivation that holds even if, as Sanday believed, this creed took two forms, an Eastern and a Western, beginning in the early second century.[11] With its harmonious, organic narrative of creedal development, the piece uses the critical study of early Christianity to bolster rather than undermine orthodox commitment in the modern church. As Maurice Wiles noted in a piece for the centenary issue, in the early decades of *JTS*, 'There was a remarkable confidence that reason rightly used would always lead to the truth, and that that truth would not conflict with the catholic truth by which the church had always lived.'[12] Things had not always been thus. In 1711, William Whiston had famously argued that the original creed was the quasi-Eunomian confession found in the *Apostolic*

---

[9] E.g., Hort 1876: 76; Kattenbusch 1894: 228–45; Harnack 1896: 748–49; Burn 1899: 101–2; Lietzmann 1922: 24.
[10] Kelly 1972: 217–26, 310–31.   [11] Sanday 1899: 3.
[12] Maurice Wiles 1999: 501. Cf. the exchange between Harnack and Batiffol in Batiffol 1911, 5th French edn, 1909: viii–xvi.

Constitutions, which he dated to the year 64; therefore, for him, the original Christianity detected by scholarly study was Eunomianism. By the time of Sanday's essay, no one accepted this radical view. Yet the ease with which Sanday reconstructed the ancestor to the Apostles' Creed was also subject to scrutiny. In the *Journal*'s 1999 centenary issue, Wolfram Kinzig and Markus Vinzent reprised Sanday's theme, though with quite different results.[13] No longer are the Nicene and Apostles' Creeds seen as variations of a common ancestor. The genealogical questions that dominated research a century ago no longer occupy centre stage. Indeed, the authors claim that Marcellus was the author of what had been falsely dubbed the Roman Creed (R), the ancestor of the Apostles' (T). While Kinzig has since backed away from the claim that Marcellus authored R, he has not returned to the organic model of an ur-creed evolving over time into the Nicene and Apostles' Creeds.[14]

The recent publication of Kinzig's four-volume anthology *Faith in Formulae* provides a suitable occasion to revisit the question of how we ought to classify and organise creeds, and whether our conceptions match our late antique evidence. Kinzig's monumental work differs significantly from previous anthologies, and yet it exhibits a similar tension in its description of where the fourth-century creeds came from. On one hand, the editor insists that the 'declarative creed' is not an organic and primitive outgrowth of the second century, but rather a by-product of the 'Constantinian revolution' and in particular of the dogmatic controversies surrounding Arius – though interrogative creeds and rules of faith, as well as other non-creedal summaries, pre-existed the emergence of this type. The declarative form has roots in the earlier 'rules of faith', but Kinzig notes that the earliest extant exemplar of a declarative creed comes in Arius' letters. After mentioning bishop Alexander's own creed, Kinzig then cites the various Greek conciliar creeds beginning with Antioch in 324/25 CE and Nicaea in 325 CE as exemplifying the same type.[15] In Kinzig's words, 'The doctrinal controversies of the fourth century ... required that the "spirit" of the faith had to be written down as "letter".'[16] Thus, Kinzig treats the production of fourth-century creeds not as an epiphenomenon of organic development but as a response to concrete ecclesiastical and political moments. For Kinzig, from the earliest stage, creeds had one or both of two functions: either a catechetical and missionary

---

[13] Kinzig and Vinzent 1999: 535–59.
[14] Kinzig 2017: 1.12. On Marcellus, Kinzig follows Heil 2010. See also Kinzig, Markschies, and Vinzent 1999.
[15] Kinzig 2017: 1.8–9.   [16] Kinzig 2017: 1.12.

function or a doctrinal function.[17] Kinzig maintains that fourth-century declarative creeds as a subset served only the latter function of sorting orthodoxy from heterodoxy, and he notes in passing the prominence of anathemas in these creeds.

On the other hand, Kinzig wants to keep all of his documents together, and so he must merge the fourth-century Greek declarative creeds that are of a strictly doctrinal purpose with creeds that lack anathemas and serve primarily a catechetical purpose – the Apostles' Creed and others. The mechanism for combining these documents is to characterise the declarative creed as a 'literary genre'.[18] For Kinzig, this genre is defined not merely by a conventional set of titles – usually πίστις, ἔκθεσις τῆς πίστεως, or σύμβολον τῆς πίστεως – but most importantly by a common 'structure' and 'wording'.[19] Equating genre with form is crucial for the anthology, since 'creeds', taken in the most elastic application of the term, had no single *Sitz im Leben* and their intended functions varied. As with his anthologising predecessors, the part of the creedal text that matters for Kinzig is the creedal profession; eliminating any framing material, as well as the original anathemas and signatures, is crucial for the task of constructing the declarative creed as a genre including both conciliar and catechetical creeds. Kinzig makes clear his hermeneutical assumptions as he lays out his 'Criteria for the Choice of Texts': 'Thirdly, when dealing with explanations of the creed it was not always possible to extract the wording of the creed from its explanatory context. Again, in cases of doubt I have included the full texts of the expositions, and added suggestions as to how the underlying creeds might be reconstructed.'[20] The procedure, therefore, is to extract and to reconstruct 'underlying creeds', meaning professions of faith. For Kinzig, 'explanatory context' regrettably must in some cases be included, but solely because in some cases it is difficult to separate it from the creed proper. If the declarative creed was a genre that in its earliest exemplars came with framing material, anathemas, and signatures, and if it must stretch to include exemplars such as catechetical creeds that did not include such material, then necessarily such accompaniments must be construed as inessential to the form. Of course, it is of the nature of genres to be used in various ways, as new texts adapt old forms to suit their purposes. But one might question whether it is appropriate to begin by identifying a genre narrowly with a form, while excluding from the ideal type prominent parts of the original texts (the *praefationes*, the anathemas, the signatures, and so on) and ignoring the *Sitz im Leben* of the text.

---

[17] Kinzig 2017: 1.7–8.   [18] Kinzig 2017: 1.2, 4, 11, 29.
[19] Kinzig 2017: 1.2.   [20] Kinzig 2017: 1.29.

In the case of catechetical creeds, to be sure, we often have no idea when and by whom they were composed, but the same is not true of the declaratory creeds by individual clerics and by church councils.

The following offers a different story of the fourth-century Greek declarative creed, and in particular of the Nicene Creed. For clarity, I will use the following terminology for the elements of a creed:

- External frame: the text (e.g., a synodical letter or historical account) in which the creed has come down to us. There can be more than one external frame (e.g., a letter quoted in a history)
- Internal frame (usually just a *praefatio*; sometimes there is additional material at the end)
- Profession of faith (the 'We/I believe that' portion, typically taking a Trinitarian form)
- Anathemas
- Signatures.

In much modern usage, a creed has become synonymous with a profession of faith; many anthologies present *only* that portion, and the vast majority of modern commentary on creeds has to do with the contents of their professions. I will argue, based on an overview of select fourth- and fifth-century Greek evidence, that a different way of presenting and evaluating creeds – a different *ordering* of our knowledge – is necessary for synodal creeds than for others. In some cases, all the aforementioned elements, including a creed's external frame, are utterly necessary to understanding it; this is especially true for individually authored creeds pertaining to dogmatic issues. In all cases, we need to attend *at least* to the profession together with the appended anathema(s), since the anathemas often embodied a creed's decisive interventions into contemporary debate.

Over a century ago, C. H. Turner articulated the difference between Nicaea and what he thought to be its predecessors: 'the old creeds were creeds for catechumens, the new creed was a creed for bishops'.[21] Today one might dispute much of what Turner took for granted about the 'old creeds', and in particular the assumption that there were pre-Constantinian declarative creeds that derived from a common ancestor of more or less apostolic origin. Still, Turner is surely right about the new creed, that of Nicaea and its successors. The history of these creeds is inseparable from the changing institution of the episcopacy. As Turner likewise noted, the concrete literary element that the new creed – the bishops' creed – added was the

---

[21] Turner 1910: 24.

anathema. Nicaea's was the first creed to contain an anathema (unless we count the creed associated with Antioch in 324/25 CE), a fact directly tied to its origin and audience:

> Here for the first time, then, in the history of the Creeds we meet with anathemas: but for the first time also the Creed is being employed with the specific object of testing episcopal orthodoxy, and we cannot dissever the one phenomenon from the other. The anathemas are there because, and only because, the Creed is no longer the layman's confession of faith but the bishop's.[22]

We gain insights into how these bishops used anathemas by noting similarities between them and another product of fourth-century councils overlooked in much modern study of creeds: disciplinary canons. We know that many councils that produced a creed also produced a set of decrees on church law. Not every council that produced a creed also produced canons and not every council that produced canons also produced a creed. Of course, most canons are uninteresting for *Dogmengeschichte* so, insofar as creedal anthologies are driven by the latter, it is understandable that they exclude canons. Genres are pragmatic and the anthologies' ends of quick reference and easy comparison are not well served by maximal inclusion. Yet, there are overlooked but important similarities, identified in the next section, between the procedures whereby canons and anathemas were produced, published, and collected.

Councils, Canons, and Creeds: The Importance of Anathemas and Signatures

In the case of canons, there is a solid scholarly literature on (1) the procedures whereby they were decided, (2) the forms in which they were published, and (3) the process by which they were collected. Examining each point, however tentatively, will shed light on the processes whereby conciliar creeds were composed, distributed, and organised. Moreover, it will be clear that, at each stage, the participants, authors, and compilers viewed the anathemas and the signatures as the decisive elements in the creed.

Procedure

Athanasius' *De synodis* is not principally about the Council of Nicaea, but he does mention that council several times in order to draw a contrast with

---

[22] Turner 1910: 28.

more recent synods, especially the twin councils of Seleucia and Rimini. One of his criticisms is that the leading bishops – Ursacius, Valens, and Germinus – failed to give an appropriate 'pretext' (πρόφασις) for the synod to occur.[23] Their stated reason, evidently, was quite vague: 'they cite matters of faith' (σχηματισάμενοι περὶ πίστεως).[24] If there were a pressing need – some new heresy to condemn – Athanasius states precisely what they should have done: 'Let them in writing anathematise the heresies (one of which is the Arian heresy) prior to this synod, just as those at Nicaea did, so that these men might appear to have some convincing pretext for saying more novel things.'[25] A synod may have more than one goal – Athanasius maintains that Nicaea had a twin rationale of standardising the celebration of Pascha and anathematising the 'unnatural' heresy of Arius[26] – but it must have *at least one*. Moreover, the pretext, stated in writing in advance, must be precise. Athanasius implies that the document of summons to Nicaea must have contained an anathema.

Though we lack acts for the fourth-century councils, several scholars have maintained that, like the third-century North African councils we learn about through Cyprian's correspondence, they followed a broadly parliamentarian procedure akin to that of the Roman Senate.[27] The procedure in question would have contained the following elements:

As in the Senate, a *relatio* setting forth the matter to be discussed was read to the assembled bishops, followed by a roll-call in which each of them, again in imitation of the senators, stated his *sententia* … The resolution [the bishops] finally voted was, as in the Senate, written up in the form of a letter sent to interested parties.[28]

Interestingly, as Philip Amidon notes, in Cyprian, we see that the *relatio* stage could involve reading correspondence related to the matter at hand.[29]

---

[23] For the rhetorical background of this term, see Pearson 1952. My thanks to Michael Champion for the reference.
[24] Athanasius, *Syn.* 1 (Opitz 1935: 231.18–232.1; ET: 152).
[25] Athanasius, *Syn.* 6 (Opitz 1935: 234.16–18; ET: 156): γράφοντες τε ἀναθεματιζέτωσαν τὰς πρὸ τῆς συνόδου ταύτης αἱρέσεις, ἐν αἷς ἐστι καὶ ἡ ἀρειανή, ὥσπερ οἱ ἐν Νικαίᾳ πεποιήκασιν, ἵνα δόξωσι καὶ αὐτοὶ πιθανήν τινα πρόφασιν ἔχειν τοῦ καινότερα λέγειν.
[26] Athanasius, *Syn.* 5 (Opitz 1935: 234.4–5; ET: 155–56).
[27] See Amidon 1983: 329 (and the older studies by Batiffol and Baynes discussed in the article). See also Hess 2002: 24–27 (who cites precedents in the work of J. A. Fischer, H.-J. Sieben, Elisabeth Herrmann, and Jean Gaudemet); Stephens 2015: 176. An important qualification of the language of 'procedure' can be found in Van Nuffelen 2011: 245.
[28] Amidon 1983: 329. Amidon refuses the more sweeping conclusions that Hess draws from this resemblance, namely, that councils that employed senatorial procedure were thereby claiming no more than a *moral* authority, meaning that the canons were not viewed as legally binding (1983: 335). Stephens supports Hess's claim (2015: 176).
[29] Amidon 1983: 329.

If we apply this to Athanasius' account of Nicaea, then the *relatio* might have involved reading out the pre-circulated anathema and this would have been followed by the gathering of the bishops' opinions on the matter. We have two reports of the events from participants, and it is not impossible that at least one of these pertains to this stage in the council's deliberations.

I will examine the two accounts in order, bearing in mind that neither should be treated as one would treat official minutes or acts. The first comes from a fragment of a letter by Eustathius of Antioch preserved by Theodoret of Cyrrhus in his *Church History*. Eustathius begins with the curious fate of the creed – the 'doctrine of faith' (πίστεως διδασκαλίαν) – presented by one Eusebius (presumably the bishop of Nicomedia).[30] After presenting it to the council, the document was ripped to shreds (διαρραγέντος) – perhaps literally so.[31] We do not know the text's contexts. Ambrose of Milan gives the tantalising report that what Eusebius of Nicomedia presented to the council was a caution against calling the Son uncreated, as it might imply his consubstantiality.[32] If this has any historical value, it could relate to the *sententiae* stage of the council; in this case, Eusebius' 'doctrine of faith' (πίστεως διδασκαλίαν) would be not a creed, but a comment on the conciliar creed and anathema. It must have had physical form if it was literally ripped to shreds.[33] According to Eustathius, after Eusebius' text was destroyed, the bested though not condemned Eusebians – or, as he calls them, 'Ariomaniacs' – saw no alternative but to comply with the majority. Our narrator sees the compliance as a pure feint. What interests us is that the narrator encapsulates the act of compliance in two verbs: 'They leaped forth to *anathematise* the forbidden dogma *by subscribing* in their own hand to the approved document.'[34]

Perhaps Eusebius' presentation was not part of a gathering of *sententiae*; perhaps instead it was a defence against some allegation of heterodoxy. Such a proposal would make sense in light of his known associations with Arius, the *bête noire* of the conciliar majority. The internal evidence

---

[30] So Hanson 2005, 1st edn, 1988: 160–61. Theodoret preserves two letters by Eusebius, which surely correspond in some manner to his creed.

[31] See Eustathius of Antioch's letter cited in Theodoret, *Hist. eccl.* 1.8.1–5. (Parmentier and Scheidweiler 1954: 33–34). The same verb (διέρρηξαν) is used also in Theodoret's own narrative introduction to the letter: *Hist. eccl.* 1.7.15 (Parmentier and Scheidweiler 1954: 33).

[32] Ambrose, *De fide* 3.15.125.

[33] For document destruction in the Latin tradition, see Howley 2017 and Coogan 2018. I thank Jeremiah Coogan for these references.

[34] Eustathius of Antioch, in Theodoret, *Hist. eccl.* 1.8.3 (Parmentier and Scheidweiler 1954: 33): ἀναθεματίζουσι μὲν προπηδήσαντες τὸ ἀπηγορευμένον δόγμα, συμφώνοις γράμμασιν ὑπογράψαντες αὐτοχειρί.

does not enable a decision between these two interpretations of Eusebius of Nicomedia's motivation, and either could find supporting evidence in the account of the proceedings in Eusebius of Caesarea's *Life of Constantine*.[35] Eusebius presents the meeting, on the one hand, as an open and pacific airing of diverse viewpoints overseen by Constantine and, on the other hand, as rife with allegations and defences. Eustathius' picturesque account is all frame with no actual cited creed. What matters to him is the twofold act of compliance: signing and anathematising. Theodoret presents this capitulation as the council's final act and links the churches of his day with the events: 'Thus, when all in harmony had drawn up the faith that even up to the present is regnant in the churches and had confirmed it with subscriptions, they disbanded the council.'[36] We might find it curious that Eustathius omitted the actual creeds produced by Eusebius and the council, but he seems to have been following a deep tradition. We find numerous letters from gatherings of bishops cited in Eusebius of Caesarea's *Church History*. In each case, the information conveyed is simple: who attended, what they discussed, what they decided, and who signed.[37]

We can turn to Eusebius of Caesarea's *Letter to His Diocese*, which Athanasius appended to his *De decretis*. This document has been probed for the light it sheds on the origin of the Nicene profession – precisely as Athanasius intended it to be used. In the letter, Eusebius cites a creed that he presented at the council. Thus, for this creed we have a dual external frame (Eusebius' letter and Athanasius' text), and the narrative provided by these frames is essential to interpreting Eusebius' creed. In contrast to his Nicomedian namesake, whom he does not mention, Eusebius of Caesarea declares that his creed met with the approval of all, with special note of Constantine's support. It was, on his telling, used as the basis for the Nicene profession itself; only the *homoousion* was added at the emperor's insistence and after some investigation of its meaning. We cannot say why Eusebius' creed pleased everyone. It does include an anathema of 'every godless heresy'.[38] Many scholars have taken Eusebius'

---

[35] Eusebius of Caesarea, *Life of Constantine* 3.6–14, esp. 3.13.

[36] Theodoret, *Hist. eccl.* 1.7.16 (Parmentier and Scheidweiler 1954: 33): οὕτω δέ … συμφώνως ἅπαντες τὴν μέχρι καὶ νῦν ἐν ταῖς ἐκκλησίαις πολιτευομένην πίστιν ὑπαγορεύσαντες καὶ ταῖς ὑπογραφαῖς βεβαιώσαντες διέλυσαν τὸ συνέδριον.

[37] See the many examples of second- and third-century episcopal correspondence produced by Eusebius of Caesarea (e.g., *Hist. eccl.* 5.19, 25). The fullest study on the phenomenon of signing creeds, together with an account of the Roman legal and epistolary background, is Amidon 2002.

[38] Eusebius, *Letter to His Diocese*, in Athanasius, *De decretis* 33.5 (Opitz 1935: 29.23).

creed, extracted from its internal and external frames, to be in essence the Caesarean baptismal creed *and* the source of the Nicene; there are two equations here, both unsustainable.[39] Eusebius does indeed link his creed with the baptismal faith, as do many fourth-century creeds. We should, however, resist a simple equation between his text and the text Caesarean Christians learned as catechumens. First, Eusebius' creed includes a somewhat autobiographical and highly apologetic internal frame that is quite obviously of his own composition. He claims to be relating his baptismal faith, but it is not clear that he is citing a pre-existing text. If the general pattern that we see in other cases applies here, the council members who approved (signed?) Eusebius' creed did so on the basis principally, perhaps exclusively, of its anathema, which would have been composed by Eusebius himself. If so, the relevant part was unambiguously of Eusebius' own composition. There is a plausible background that might explain why he offered a creed. At a council in Antioch earlier the same year, Eusebius had been excommunicated. This could be his petition for re-admittance.[40] If so, the procedure of the council was not merely deliberative but also included trials of orthodoxy.

Something similar goes for the council of Jerusalem, mentioned as the first Arian synod by Athanasius. While this council did not produce a creed, its synodical letter states that the assembled bishops had reviewed Arius' creed and judged it orthodox. Such a procedure might also lie behind the creed of Theophronius of Tyana, produced at the Dedication Council of Antioch in 341 CE and cited by Athanasius, who mentions that it was signed by the other bishops.[41] In sum, we see in our rather meagre fourth-century evidence some indications that councils conducted themselves in ways akin to parliamentary procedures (the Senate, municipal assemblies, and the like) *and* to trials, and that this dual conception of procedure shaped their participants' collective and individual production of creeds, and especially of anathemas.

---

[39] For the decisive argument against viewing this creed as the source of the Nicene Creed, see Kelly 1972: 217–26.

[40] See Radde-Gallwitz 2016: 472–73, following Kelly 1972: 224.

[41] Note the difference between taking Theophronius' creed as apologetic (on which, see Kelly 1972: 110, 266–68; Radde-Gallwitz 2016: 474–75), and the anthological approach. In the anthological tradition, Theophronius' creed is of interest as a source for the reconstruction of the primitive, ante-Nicene Cappadocian creed. Kattenbusch noted similarities between it and two other creeds from roughly the same region: the creed of Asterius and the second creed of the Dedication Council in 341 CE. Sanday (1899: 19) pushed further, taking each as a variant of the ur-creed used in baptism in the region of Cappadocia. The two approaches are not strictly mutually exclusive, but they ask different questions of the source material.

Publication

The canonical decisions of a council were written up, signed, and distributed in a synodical letter. Hess has dubbed the form in which these were initially published the *dixit-placet*, which resembled minutes of the meeting. In such documents, in an almost dialogue setting, one bishop proposes a decree (N. *dixit*), which is then confirmed by the consent of all present (*placet*).[42] This form was replaced gradually by a simpler *placuit* form omitting the initial proposal. Hess notes the senatorial roots of this form and argues that a published canon list was meant to resemble a senatorial *liber sententiarum*: 'Series of canons ... are accompanied by a brief and usually introductory statement (the *praefatio*) that identifies the place and circumstances of the meeting, and also by a list of subscriptions'; Hess notes that both of these features 'were common to records of various kinds of meetings, including the senate, in government and in society'.[43]

The authority of the documents was rooted in 'the personal *auctoritas* of the participants and the breadth of *consensus* determined by their number'.[44] This information was conveyed to recipients of the framing letter in the *praefatio* and the list of signatures. Something similar can be said regarding creeds. In the fourth century, the Nicene Creed was almost always glossed with some such phrase as 'the faith put forth by the 318 fathers'. The creed's authority was rooted in the relatively large number of its signatories, even if the number varied in different reports; thus, the number had significance even apart from any mystical associations with the size of Abraham's army. Among the other creeds cited in Athanasius' *De synodis*, we see various exemplars with *praefationes* or (partial) signature lists lending authority to the document.[45] In one case, that of the so-called 'Dated Creed', Athanasius complains that the bishops have included the date of publication in the creed's preface, but in light of the parliamentary background, this would not have seemed so odd. Sometimes a creed's multiple signatures lent it authority; other times only one signature needed to be cited. We will discuss Basil's *Epistle* 125 below; for now, it is worth noting that the purpose of publishing this creed is to show that Eustathius signed the Nicene Creed, together with the anathema that Basil added to it.

I noted earlier the typical form that canons took (*dixit-placet* and *placuit*). There are two interesting exceptions to the pattern described by Hess. In the case of two councils, there is ambiguity between anathemas and canons.

---

[42] Hess 2002: 69–70.   [43] Hess 2002: 69, cf. 74.   [44] Hess 2002: 75.
[45] Athanasius, *Syn.* 8, 21. Signatures are mentioned various places, e.g., *Syn.* 24.

The twenty canons of the council of Gangra (*c.* 355 CE),[46] which address disciplinary rather than doctrinal matters, actually take the classical Pauline (Gal 1:8) form of anathemas: 'If someone says X, let him be anathema' (εἰ τις λέγει ... ἀνάθεμα ἔστω). The first canon of the council of Constantinople (381 CE) contains the council's doctrinal anathemas, whereas the other canons attend to disciplinary matters. It is not hard to imagine how anathemas and canons could be combined or confused in these ways; these were the two parts of the council's publications that showed in concrete terms the results of its authoritative consensus.

Collections

At first glance, it seems that the analogy between conciliar canons and creeds breaks down when we start to examine how these texts were collected. The fourth century witnessed the first known collections of canons from diverse sources, but creeds were not collected in the same way. Instead of omnibus collections, the only sort of thing we can call a 'collection' of creeds in fourth-century Greek is Athanasius' *De synodis*.[47] This epistolary history of the synods leading up to Seleucia and Rimini fits its documents into a narrative of heresy, duplicity, and opportunism on the part of Athanasius' episcopal opponents and their imperial patron Constantius II. By contrast, the canonical collections offer no narrative whatsoever.

Yet, a closer look reveals editorial hands at work in the canonical collections – not, of course, pursuing the same agenda as Athanasius, but nonetheless actively reshaping received material. I will mention four fourth-century examples.

(1) From letters of bishops and Eusebius' *Church History*, we know of disciplinary canons from the pre-Constantinian era. The first known attempt to collect disciplinary canons from councils of the fourth century included those written at the synods of Ancyra, Caesarea, Neocaesarea, Gangra, Antioch, and perhaps Laodicaea.[48] This edition was possibly made by Euzoius, Homoian bishop of Antioch from 361–76 CE.[49] His anti-Nicene agenda arguably explains the absence of Nicaea's canons from this corpus. (2) A revision of this collection was made, which survives only

---

[46] Barnes 1989: 121–24.

[47] I bracket the question of whether the same could be said for Latin sources, though I suspect a similar case could be made for such texts as Hilary's *De synodis* and the *Collectanea Antiariana Parisina* (ed. Feder, CSEL 65).

[48] See L'Huillier 1976; Stephens 2015.   [49] So Hess 2002: 53, following Schwartz.

in Latin and Syriac translations. In this expanded version, which Eduard Schwartz reasoned was made by the pro-Nicene bishop Meletius of Antioch, the canons of Nicaea are added at the head. At some still later point, the canons of Constantinople 381 and Chalcedon were added to Meletius' collection. As with Euzoius' work, the documentary and pastoral task of producing or revising this canonical collection was governed by its editor's assumptions about which councils counted as legitimate tradition. Crucially, in all cases the *ratio edendi* was cumulative: canons were added, in some order or another, to those already in the collection, which were not thereby replaced.[50] Similar points can be made about collections of canons produced by individual bishops for some colleague. Here we can mention (3) the 188 canons of Basil of Caesarea, contained in three letters to Amphilochius of Iconium, and (4) Gregory of Nyssa's *Canonical Letter to Letoius*.[51] Unlike the collections of conciliar canons, neither Basil nor Gregory attempts to document all relevant prior tradition. However, like those collections, the canonical letters of Basil and Gregory display a striking deference to tradition as well as a strong editorial hand. Gregory even arranges canons around the structuring principle of the Platonic tripartite soul, correlating sins treated in penance with the part of the soul whence they arise.

Individual bishops felt free to arrange their inherited material in whatever order suited their presentation. This liberty affected not only the order but also the content of their collections: Peter L'Huillier has noted that while Basil in another letter (*Ep.* 55) mentions one of Nicaea's canons, in the canonical letters he ignores them.[52] The freedom was not total and did not extend to the construction of new material: Gregory of Nyssa, while bitterly complaining of oversights in previous tradition, felt he could not add a canon for the sin of avarice where none existed already.[53] But surely *councils* did not feel so constrained, as they did precisely add new canonical decrees to old ones.

All of this forms a possible context for understanding how councils handled anathemas. Perhaps anathemas of previous councils could simply be tacked on to subsequent ones. Given the ambiguity we noted above between canons and anathemas, it is worth asking whether the same phenomenon of selective and adaptive collection of anathemas occurred.

---

[50] See Schwartz 1960, orig. pub. 1936: 196–203.
[51] Trans. Radde-Gallwitz in Muehlberger 2017: 143–67 (Basil) and 168–77 (Gregory).
[52] L'Huillier 1997: 125–26.
[53] Gregory of Nyssa, *Epistula canonica*, Canon 6 (Mühlenberg 2008: 9.18–11.14; for English trans. see Muehlberger 2017: 175–76).

Did each creed need to be transmitted inviolate or was it adaptable? To answer these questions, we need to spend some time with the history of the principal creed of our period, the Nicene, and in particular the fate of its anathema.

The Nicene Anathema and Its Legacy

It is a truism of modern scholarship that, following Eusebius of Caesarea's *Letter to His Diocese*, it was not until the 350s that the Nicene profession itself, and in particular the phrases 'from the Father's substance' and 'same-in-substance with the Father', became the subject of extended debate and commentary. Various explanations have been given for this gap.[54] There is a tendency in this literature to conflate the Nicene profession with the Nicene Creed *simpliciter*. Accordingly, neglect of the profession between 325 CE and the early 350s CE equates to neglect of Nicaea as such. Yet, if we look at the same period with an eye to the Creed's anathema, a different picture emerges. I suggest that this is because the anathema was what mattered, and that it entered into 'collections' of anathemas at subsequent councils in a way not altogether unlike what we have just observed in the case of disciplinary canon collections. Moreover, the pattern established by councils in these decades was followed by such later pro-Nicene luminaries as Basil of Caesarea and Cyril of Alexandria, as well as at the Council of Constantinople in 381 CE.

The following table aims to summarise the *Nachleben* of the Nicene anathema up to 351 CE.

Nicene Creed (325 CE)[55] Now as for those who say: There was when he did not exist, and before he was begotten, he did not exist, and that he came to be from nothing, or from a different subsistence or substance, claiming that the Son of God is either changeable or mutable, these people the catholic and apostolic church anathematises.	τοὺς δὲ λέγοντας· ἦν ποτε ὅτε οὐκ ἦν καὶ πρὶν γεννηθῆναι οὐκ ἦν καὶ ὅτι ἐξ οὐκ ὄντων ἐγένετο ἢ ἐξ ἑτέρας ὑποστάσεως ἢ οὐσίας φάσκοντας εἶναι ἢ τρεπτὸν ἢ ἀλλοιωτὸν τὸν υἱὸν τοῦ θεοῦ τούτους ἀναθεματίζει ἡ καθολικὴ καὶ ἀποστολικὴ ἐκκλησία.

---

[54] See Kelly 1972: 254–62; Ayres 2004a: 337–59; Stephens 2015: 114–18; Scott 2018: 12–16.
[55] Nicene Creed (Dossetti 1967: 226; ET, 115).

Dedication Council of Antioch (341 CE), Third Creed, sole anathema[56] Now as for those who say that the Son is from nothing or from another subsistence, rather than from God, and that there was a time when he did not exist: the catholic church recognises them as foreign.	τοὺς δὲ λέγοντας ἐξ οὐκ ὄντων τὸν υἱὸν ἢ ἐξ ἑτέρας ὑποστάσεως καὶ μὴ ἐκ τοῦ θεοῦ καὶ 'ἦν ποτε χρόνος ὅτε οὐκ ἦν' ἀλλοτρίους οἶδεν ἡ καθολικὴ ἐκκλησία.
Macrostich Creed (344 CE), first anathema[57] Now as for those who say that the Son is from nothing or from another subsistence, rather than from God, and that there was a time or an age when he did not exist: the catholic and holy church recognises them as foreign.	Τοὺς δὲ λέγοντας ἐξ οὐκ ὄντων τὸν υἱὸν ἢ ἐξ ἑτέρας ὑποστάσεως καὶ μὴ ἐκ τοῦ θεοῦ καὶ ὅτι ἦν χρόνος ποτὲ ἢ αἰών, ὅτε μὴ ἦν, ἀλλοτρίους οἶδεν ἡ καθολικὴ καὶ ἁγία ἐκκλησία.
Creed of the First Synod of Sirmium (351 CE), first anathema (with second and third for comparison; there are 27 total)[58] 1. Now as for those who say that the Son is from nothing or from another subsistence and not from God, and that there was a time or an age when he was not, the holy and catholic church recognises them as foreign. 2. Again we will say: if someone calls the Father and the Son two gods, let him be anathema. 3. And if anyone says ... let him be anathema.	1. Τοὺς δὲ λέγοντας ἐξ οὐκ ὄντων τὸν υἱὸν ἢ ἐξ ἑτέρας ὑποστάσεως καὶ μὴ ἐκ τοῦ θεοῦ καὶ ὅτι ἦν χρόνος ἢ αἰών, ὅτε οὐκ ἦν, ἀλλοτρίους οἶδεν ἡ ἁγία καὶ καθολικὴ ἐκκλησία. 2. Πάλιν οὖν ἐροῦμεν· εἴ τις τὸν πατέρα καὶ τὸν υἱὸν δύο λέγει θεούς, ἀνάθεμα ἔστω. 3. Καὶ εἴ τις λέγων ..., ἀνάθεμα ἔστω.

[56] Athanasius, *Syn.* 25 (Opitz 1935: 251.14–16; ET: 178, slightly adapted).
[57] Athanasius, *Syn.* 26.2 (Opitz 1935: 252.4–6; ET: 179, slightly adapted).
[58] Athanasius, *Syn.* 27 (Opitz 1935: 254.32–36; ET: 183, slightly adapted).

Our source for these later creeds is Athanasius' *De synodis*. Athanasius, of course, wants us to see these synods as motivated by hostility towards Nicaea.[59] If, however, we do not assume such hostility, we see a different pattern. In their anathemas, the synods of 341, 344, and 351 CE appear to affirm Nicaea's anathema; the attitude seems to be one of acceptance, even deference, as well as gradual clarification and expansion.

There are minor differences among the presentations of the anathema, but it seems substantially the same in all versions. The order is changed slightly beginning with the Antiochene Council's Third Creed, which was written to convey the council's decree to Constans, then the Western Augustus.[60] Beginning with that creed, the denial of *ex nihilo* is placed at the beginning of the anathema. One point – the notorious lacuna around temporality – is filled in, presumably to clarify the sense: Nicaea's 'there was when he did not exist' (ἦν ποτε ὅτε οὐκ ἦν) becomes 'there was *a time* when he did not exist' (ἦν ποτε χρόνος ὅτε οὐκ ἦν) and then, for good measure, 'that there was *a time or an age* when he did not exist' (ὅτι ἦν χρόνος ἢ αἰών, ὅτε οὐκ ἦν).[61] Beginning with Antioch's third creed, the Nicene 'from another hypostasis or substance' (ἐξ ἑτέρας ὑποστάσεως ἢ οὐσίας) is decisively revised to 'from another hypostasis and not from God' (ἐξ ἑτέρας ὑποστάσεως καὶ μὴ ἐκ τοῦ θεοῦ). The Nicene clauses 'before he was begotten he did not exist' (πρὶν γεννηθῆναι οὐκ ἦν) and 'changeable or mutable' (ἢ τρεπτὸν ἢ ἀλλοιωτὸν) drop out beginning with the same creed, though we will see below that the first of these clauses still echoes in the Dedication Council's more famous Second Creed. And the principal verb modifying the (holy, catholic, apostolic) church changes from 'anathematises' (ἀναθεματίζει) to 'recognises as foreign' (ἀλλοτρίους οἶδεν). These are benign clarifications offered in documents that clearly view Nicaea's

---

[59] Athanasius, *Syn.* 1; 7; 14; 32, a representation echoed in later sources: e.g., Socrates, *Hist. eccl.* 2.10.

[60] In addition to Athanasius, *Syn.* 25, see Socrates, *Hist. eccl.* 2.18.

[61] One might take such expansions as attempts at evasion. On this line, the intent of the seemingly innocuous additions would be to specify the prohibited position so narrowly that one's own vaguer commitments escape censure. Perhaps the authors would condemn positing a *time* or *age* when the Son was not, while still positing some temporal or quasi-temporal origin for the Son. According to this view, the strategy would be to undermine Nicaea's theology by reinterpreting it. Mark DelCogliano pressed this issue during the Rome Seminar. (The same line applies to the other changes detailed in the paragraph.) I remain sceptical as to the intent of the Council Fathers in 341 CE, and I see the issue as irrelevant for the current argument. DelCogliano's reading of their intention, if correct, would in fact add greater interest to my claim for Nicaea's authority in 341 CE, since it would show that *even those who disagreed* theologically with the anathema respected its authority. Otherwise, there would have been no need for such creative revision.

anathema as authoritative. So closely do the later documents follow it that they repeat its 'those who say' (τοὺς δὲ λέγοντας) form, which becomes quite noteworthy in Sirmium's creed, where the Pauline alternative form – 'if anyone says' (εἴ τις λέγει/λέγων), paired with 'let him be anathema' (ἀνάθεμα ἔστω) – predominates throughout the remaining twenty-six anathemas (cf. Gal 1:8; 1 Cor 16:22).

This alternative form is used in the Second Creed of the 341 CE Dedication Council. A close examination reveals similar content despite this difference in form:

Dedication Council of Antioch (341 CE), Second Creed[62]	
And so, since we have held this faith from the beginning and hold it to the end, in the presence of God and Christ we anathematise every heretical falsehood. And if anyone teaches something contrary to the sound faith of the scriptures, saying that a time, or a period, or an age exists or passed before the Son was born, let him be anathema. And if anyone says that the Son is a creature like one of the creatures, or something born like one of the things born, or something made like one of the things made, and not as the divine scriptures handed down each of the terms just mentioned; or if he teaches or proclaims anything else contrary to what we have received, let him be anathema.	ταυτήν οὖν ἔχοντες τὴν πίστιν καὶ ἐξ ἀρχῆς καὶ μέχρι τέλους ἔχοντες ἐνώπιον τοῦ θεοῦ καὶ τοῦ Χριστοῦ πᾶσαν αἱρετικὴν κακοδοξίαν ἀναθεματίζομεν. καὶ εἴ τις παρὰ τὴν ὑγιῆ τῶν γραφῶν [ὀρθὴν] πίστιν διδάσκει λέγων ἢ χρόνον ἢ καιρὸν ἢ αἰῶνα ἢ εἶναι ἢ γεγονέναι πρὸ τοῦ γεννηθῆναι τὸν υἱόν, ἀνάθεμα ἔστω. καὶ εἴ τις λέγει τὸν υἱὸν κτίσμα ὡς ἓν τῶν κτισμάτων ἢ γέννημα ὡς ἓν τῶν γεννημάτων ἢ ποίημα ὡς ἓν τῶν ποιημάτων καὶ μὴ ὡς αἱ θεῖαι γραφαὶ παραδέδωκαν τῶν προειρημένων ἕκαστον [ἀφ' ἑκάστου], ἢ εἴ τι ἄλλο διδάσκει ἢ εὐαγγελίζεται, παρ' ὃ παρελάβομεν, ἀνάθεμα ἔστω.

While more verbose than the others cited above, much of the terminology from the Nicene anathema is present here.[63] Of the anathemas we have cited, this one alone echoes the Nicene 'before he was begotten he did not exist' (πρὶν γεννηθῆναι οὐκ ἦν) with its 'saying that a time, or a

---

[62] Athanasius, *Syn.* 23 (Opitz 1935: 249.33–250.2; ET: 176).
[63] Noted by Ayres 2004b: 120.

period, or an age exists or passed before the Son was born' (λέγων ἢ χρόνον ἢ καιρὸν ἢ αἰῶνα ἢ εἶναι ἢ γεγονέναι πρὸ τοῦ γεννηθῆναι τὸν υἱόν). The creed's expansions that have no direct parallel in Nicaea either are generic condemnations of every heresy or are directed against slogans associated, however tendentiously, with Arius and his partisans.

In all of these documents, then, the Nicene anathema either is the only one or appears first in a list of anathemas. That the Nicene anathema is rewritten does not negate the point. The verbal echoes, together with the placement, demand explanation. Let me bracket the period from Nicaea until Antioch (341 CE); the only synod mentioned by Athanasius in that time frame is the Council of Jerusalem in 335 CE, which did not produce a creed. My conclusion is that in the decade from Antioch (341 CE) until Sirmium (351 CE), among Eastern bishops, the Nicene Creed, and in particular its anathema, was authoritative.

It was not that the wording of Nicaea's anathema was sacred; it was not that the anathema needed to be cited as Nicaea's; still, a recognisable version of the anathema was apparently expected to appear among a creed's anathemas. With that said, Nicaea's authoritative status did not preclude the promulgation of additional anathemas directed at new problems. It seems that, for these bishops, development happened by interpretative revision of the authoritative Nicene anathema and by the multiplication of new anathemas. There is a partial parallel between such accumulation of anathemas and early collections of canons, which followed a chronological order, as the earliest canons were placed at the head of the list and subsequent ones were tacked on. A great deal of effort has been expended explaining Nicaea's absence in the quarter century after the council, but I want to suggest that Nicaea, embodied in its first anathema, was there all along.

Had the 'Eusebians' not consented to Nicaea in their earlier creeds, the argument of Athanasius' *De synodis* would make no sense. This work was written in 359 CE, with a revision in 361 CE. By this time, important changes had occurred. In the late 350s CE, various Homoian councils, under the patronage of Constantius, had forbidden the use of the term *ousia* in creedal statements, a prohibition that would outlaw both the Nicene Creed and the Second Creed of the Dedication Council in Antioch.[64] Athanasius maintains that the instigators of these councils of the late 350s either had been present at Nicaea or had at some prior point anathematised the Arian heresy, which is equivalent in his mind with support

---

[64] See Ayres 2004b: 134–35.

for Nicaea. His claim is that they are revoking their previous opposition to Arius and therefore revoking their support for Nicaea. Clearly, not all of the anti-Nicene bishops active at the end of Constantius' reign had been present at the Council of Nicaea in 325 CE. Athanasius' point presumes, therefore, that the creeds to which these bishops and their allies subscribed from 341 to 351 CE included the Nicene anathema.

At the same time, in both *De synodis* and *De decretis*, Athanasius was busy expanding the authority of Nicaea to include the entire creed: its profession and anathemas.[65] Even so, in his comments on the profession, Athanasius discusses only the dogmatically significant phrases, 'from the substance of the Father' and 'same-in-substance', and thus he shows no interest in those elements of Nicaea that resemble the Apostles' Creed.

In 358 CE, a gathering of bishops known as Homoiousians, led by Basil of Ancyra, anathematised the Nicene profession of *homoousion* and omitted the Nicene anathema. Hence by the end of the 350s CE, support for Nicaea had become an all-or-nothing affair. That does not mean its supporters viewed its text as entirely fixed. Even if they treated the Creed's existing words as unalterable, some of them advocated for new amendments in the form of anathemas. The clearest example of this strategy appears in various letters of Basil of Caesarea from the 370s CE. We can mention two cases in which Basil recommends the strategy (*Ep.* 113 and 114, both addressed to clergy in Tarsus) and another (*Ep.* 125) in which he implements it. In *Epistle* 113, Basil proposes a method for handling cases of blasphemy against the Holy Spirit. He takes this to be such a widespread phenomenon that it cannot be eradicated from the church, though he maintains that a procedure is possible for distinguishing those blasphemers who may be held in communion (from which position they might be brought to the truth) from those who must be expelled: 'Let us then seek nothing more, but merely propose the Creed of Nicaea to the brethren who wish to join us; and if they agree to this, let us demand also that the Holy Spirit shall not be called a creature, and that those who do so call Him shall not be communicants with them. But beyond these things I think nothing should be insisted upon by us.'[66] *Epistle* 114 reiterates the point. In *Epistle* 125, we see Basil using this method for handling his one-time mentor and friend Eustathius of Sebasteia, whom he now treats as a Pneumatomachian. The letter includes an opening frame and then cites Nicaea verbatim, plus the added anathema, and, crucially, Eustathius' signature.

---

[65] See Ayres 2004a; Scott 2018: 19–24.
[66] Basil, *Ep.* 113 (Courtonne 2003: 17; ET Deferrari 1928: 225).

Epiphanius of Salamis seems to have held a comparable attitude to Nicaea. His *Ancoratus*, written in 374 CE, concludes with two chapters aimed at presenting the orthodox faith which his colleagues can transmit in catechesis. In the first of these chapters, chapter 118, a creed appears that is called that of the more than 310 bishops. In the present state of the text (which survives in only one Greek manuscript, as well as an earlier Ethiopic manuscript), the creed cited is the so-called Nicene-Constantinopolitan Creed of 381 with the Nicene anathema tacked on. Several factors, most notably the frame denoting the creed's authors, indicate that this creed has been interpolated by a later copyist. The original version of chapter 118 must have cited the Nicene rather than the Nicene-Constantinopolitan Creed – or, more likely, a local catechetical creed similar to the one cited by Cyril of Jerusalem but revised with phrases from the original Nicene Creed and thus capable of being denoted Nicene by Epiphanius.[67] More interesting for present purposes is chapter 119. Here, Epiphanius supplements the previous creed with 'an anti-Apollinarian, anti-Macedonian commentary', as well as non-Trinitarian additions to the third article.[68] The commentary is interlaced with the creed and includes both additional affirmations and negations. For instance, to Nicaea's confession that Christ 'became man', Epiphanius adds, 'that is, assumed a perfect man, soul and body and mind and all that is a man apart from sin; who not from the seed of man nor <having come to be> in a man, but in himself formed anew flesh into one holy unity, not just as he breathed and spoke and operated in the prophets, but perfectly became man'.[69] These are the sorts of expansions one tends to find in anathemas in other creeds. Epiphanius' Second Creed maintains the Nicene anathema and adds another directed at 'those who do not confess a resurrection of the dead and all the heresies which are not of this right faith'.[70] The faith in question, I presume, is the commented form presented in chapter 119, even as the author aims to portray these additions as merely making explicit Nicaea's implicit ideas. Thus, Epiphanius includes an anathema against anyone who disputes the various points in his commentary as well as against those who dispute the original text of Nicaea itself.

The framing of Epiphanius' Second Creed is interesting. Evidently, he did not share Athanasius' dislike for including information pertinent to the Creed's date in its *praefatio*. For Epiphanius, the dates specify the concrete point when there arose a need for a new statement of faith:

---

[67] Kelly 1972: 310–11. [68] Kelly 1972: 319–20.
[69] Epiphanius, *Anc.* 119.5–6 (Holl 1915: 148.13–18; ET: 224–25).
[70] Epiphanius, *Anc.* 119.12 (Holl 1915: 149.9–11; ET: 227).

Since in our generation some other successive heresies emerged, that is, in the time of Valentinian and Valens, the emperors in the tenth year of their reign and again in the sixth year of Gratian, that is, in the nineteenth year of Diocletian the tyrant – because of this, both you and we, and all the orthodox bishops, and in short the entire holy catholic church, against the heresies which have emerged subsequently, in accordance with the faith of those holy fathers which has been ordained earlier, thus speak, especially to those coming to holy baptism, in order that they may declare and speak thus.[71]

While the form of Epiphanius' proposed creed is different from Basil's, the idea of settling new disputes by placing the newly offensive ideas under the ban seems to be the same.[72] Epiphanius also, incidentally, stresses the catechetical use of his statement of faith. This emphasis is apparently unique among our surviving examples. It does not seem to invalidate Turner's distinction between bishops' and catechumens' creeds, since Epiphanius is only addressing catechumens indirectly via his immediate audience of bishops. His envisioned audience is closer to that of Gregory of Nyssa's *Catechetical Oration* (addressed to catechists) than to that of Cyril of Jerusalem's *Catecheses* (addressed to catechumens).

The wording of Constantinople 381's first canon, which as noted contains all of its anathemas, is worth quoting in connection with the original Nicene anathema:

The faith of the 318 fathers who met at Nicaea in Bithynia must not be set aside but must be maintained as binding, and every heresy must be anathematised, and in particular that of the Eunomians, or Anomoeans, and that of the Arians, or Eudoxians, and that of the Semi-Arians, or Pneumatomachians, and that of the Sabellians, and that of the Marcellians, and that of the Photinians, and that of the Apollinarians.[73]

The council fathers insist that Nicaea remains in effect, even as they add anathemas of various new groups, including Eunomians and Pneumatomachians.

The final example that I will mention occurs in Cyril of Alexandria's *Third Letter to Nestorius*. Like Cyril's *Second Letter to Nestorius*, the bulk of this document consists of commentary on the Nicene Creed: expansions, clarifications, and especially added negations. To this commentary, Cyril appends the famous Twelve Anathemas, which Nestorius must sign to give

---

[71] Epiphanius, *Anc.* 119.1–2 (Holl 1915: 147.24–148.3; ET: 224, altered slightly).
[72] See Scott 2018: 25–28.
[73] Canon 1, Council of Constantinople 381 (Greek: Mansi 1759: 3.557–58; ET: Kelly 1972: 306).

assurance of orthodoxy. Cyril gives no indication that he intends his anathemas to be added to the creed universally.[74] Their fraught reception is well known. The key point is his use of the familiar method of addressing new problems by adding to Nicaea's authoritative anathema.[75]

The examples I have cited from Basil, Epiphanius, and Cyril are creeds proposed as conditions for admission or readmission to communion. Nicaea also factors, though more obliquely, in a document intended to persuade its envisioned audience of the author's own Nicene *bona fides*: Gregory of Nyssa's *Epistle* 5. In the frame, Gregory explains that he has been accused of holding views contrary to Nicaea. His method of self-defence was to compose a creed. The key feature for us is the anathemas: 'But if someone proclaims two or three gods or three deities, let him be anathema. And if someone, following Arius' perversion, proclaims that the Son or the Holy Spirit came into being from nothing, let him be anathema.'[76] The first of these, I believe, is the matter behind the problem addressed in Gregory's *To Ablabius*.[77] The second is a reworking of Nicaea, expanding it to cover the Spirit in Basilian fashion. So, beginning with Basil, among pro-Nicenes, when creeds were being used as tests for a third party to sign, Nicaea's entire creed was proposed for signature, with an added anathema or anathemas; in the case when a creed was used as testimony to its author's orthodoxy, Nicaea's anathema appeared in an edited form and coupled to a different profession and another anathema. It seems that this anathema was inescapable for most of the century after its composition, forming the first building block in the adjudication of orthodoxy.[78]

Conclusion

In the fourth century, anathemas were arguably the principal point of reference for the bishops who wrote and used synodal creeds, both during and after the council proceedings. It follows that, if we want to avoid equivocation, we need to keep creeds containing anathemas distinct from the catechetical creeds we begin to see in the later fourth century, which lack anathemas. That they have not received due attention in modern study is perhaps one legacy of the organisation of knowledge embodied in creedal

---

[74] Cyril of Alexandria, *Third Letter to Nestorius* 12 (Schwartz 1927: 40–42; ET: in Crawford 2022).
[75] See Scott 2018: 54.   [76] Gregory of Nyssa, *Ep.* 5.8 (Maraval 1990: 162).
[77] Argued in Radde-Gallwitz 2018: 40–42.
[78] I borrow the 'building block' metaphor from Kinzig and Vinzent (1999: 555–59), who use it for professions of faith; cf. Kinzig 2017: 1.8.

anthologies. Over fifty years ago, Yves Congar remarked that Denzinger's collection 'has the great drawback of baldly presenting documents in isolation from the historical and theological culture that alone enables them to be correctly interpreted'.[79] I would add that attention to this 'historical and theological culture' reveals significant ruptures in the tradition of the declarative creed, particularly as it emigrated from the quasi-legal context we have examined here to its more familiar role in Western liturgies, where it acquired a new frame and severed its original link with the collective, ritual cursing of heresy. Throughout late antiquity, creeds with anathemas were the province of bishops, as they dealt, individually and collectively, with their fellow bishops and, at times, with imperial officials. In Byzantine tradition, as Andrew Louth has shown, it was only at the ceremony marking the Triumph of Orthodoxy in 843 CE that the laity were 'made complicit' in the act of anathematisation, as they repeated condemnations written for the occasion – an event ritually re-enacted each year.[80]

If we focus on anathemas, our understanding of doctrinal development changes considerably. Bishops of the fourth and early fifth century treated anathemas as the way to tackle new doctrinal problems as they arose. As a result, anathema lists emanating from councils resemble lists of canons collected in the fourth century. Even councils that have been treated as anti-Nicene because of their professions of faith can be seen as implicitly endorsing Nicaea by their inclusion of its anathema at the head of their list of anathemas. The principle of organisation here was cumulative, and it was promoted even by obvious supporters of Nicaea like Basil of Caesarea and Cyril of Alexandria. To appreciate its logic, we must distinguish what C. H. Turner called 'creeds for bishops' from 'creeds for catechumens'. In the hands of late antique bishops, Nicaea proved more adaptable than a documentary collection can easily convey.

---

[79] Congar 2004, French edn, 1963: 131–32.   [80] Louth 2007: 133.

14 The Arian Controversy and the Problem of Image(s)

REBECCA LYMAN

Introduction

As Lewis Ayres has insightfully suggested, the historical Arius was not the eponymous founder of a heretical movement, but rather a catalyst for continuing theological debates.[1] Polemical constructions eventually linked him to most, if not all, objections to Nicene orthodoxy, but the original teachings of Arius, as far as can be reconstructed from the mutilated fragments preserved by his opponents, were largely discarded.[2] This discontinuity provides the opportunity for exploring the social and religious context that shaped Arius' short-lived 'obstinate, consistent, and radical agnosticism'.[3] As Richard Vaggione notes, the doctrinal conflict became a mass movement almost overnight: 'more to the point, it provoked a polemical outburst whose immediacy and emotional content were out of all proportion to the alleged provocation'.[4] Clues about the shape of the original controversy in Alexandria and its theological volatility emerge by examining the extant evidence within the situational categories of lived religion, especially in relation to the events preceding it, i.e., the 'Great Persecution' and its ongoing political, literary, and spiritual aftermath.[5] While scholars are rightly cautious about ancient Christian rhetoric concerning violence and martyrdom, the imperial destruction of churches and Christians in the Eastern empire left the growing Melitian division in Egypt, framed the new theological constructions of Christian religion by Eusebius of Caesarea, and underlay both the rising cult around the victims and the expanding ascetic movement as their successors in performative holiness and destroyers of polytheism.[6] The main protagonists of the conflict, Arius and

---

[1] Ayres 2004b: 12 n. 3.
[2] Wiles 1996. On the construction of 'Athanasian Arianism', see Gwynn 2007a: 177–202.
[3] Williams 1987, rev. edn, 2001: 166.
[4] Vaggione 1989: 63–87. See Löhr 2006a, 2006b.
[5] Conant 2020: 38. Elizabeth DePalma Digeser (2018: 261–81) explores religious identity and Arius in this era. On reframing the controversy in this context of the Great Persecution, see also Lyman 2021.
[6] For a recent summary on definitions of 'martyr' and martyr accounts, see the editors' 'Introduction' in Maier and Waldner 2021: 1–13; cf. Barkman 2014; Bremmer 2021.

Alexander, began their clerical careers in the midst of persecution, perhaps as rivals in a sudden episcopal election after the execution of Achillas. In intertwined academic and martyr genealogies, Eusebius of Caesarea celebrated his teacher Pamphilus, and Eusebius of Nicomedia was imprisoned with Lucian of Antioch, the martyr whose reputation Arius invoked and Alexander denied.[7] After a religious vision of his own, Licinius fostered an inclusive henotheistic model of imperial religion that included contacts with Neoplatonists as well as with Eusebius, bishop of Nicomedia.[8] Licinius continued to require traditional religious sacrifice for members of his household and the army, which resulted in exile, apostasy, and martyrdom for a small number of Christians.[9] The measures he invoked to control disruptive Christian public behaviour may be linked to the public disorders in the early Alexandrian conflict.[10]

In his study of the cultural conflicts and economic exchanges between the Algonquin tribes and invading French traders in the seventeenth-century Great Lakes region, Richard White outlined a period of 'middle ground' in which self-interest and necessity stimulated new amalgams of language and behaviour to create and define a mutually comprehended world.[11] The decade between the 'Edict of Milan' in 313 CE and the outbreak of schism in Alexandria could be approached in a similar manner to chart Christian theological and religious adjustments to the novel reality of imperially sponsored tolerance. Recent studies of Eusebius of Caesarea have focused less on his theological errors than on his literary and theological creativity in this period of a 'process of Christian naturalization'.[12] Eusebius composed his massive 'literary experiment' of the *Praeparatio evangelica* and the companion volume, *Demonstratio evangelica*, to be an exposition of the 'new religion' of Christianity by subordinating the religious traditions and texts of Judaism and Greco-Roman culture to the fulfilment of true piety found only in Christian monotheism.[13] Correct piety was revealed only through the Word, while the Father remained invisible and nameless. As in earlier apologists, this defence of transcendent monotheism was in the end a 'Christophany'.[14]

---

[7] On Alexander and Arius, see Parvis 2006: 73. On Lucian of Antioch as martyr and his connection to Arius, see Brennecke 1993: 170–92; Löhr 2006a: 531–33; 2006b: 134–35.
[8] Barnes 1981: 68, 70–71.
[9] Barnes (1982: 180–91) summarises the evidence concerning 'some martyrdoms'.
[10] Barnes 1981: 71.   [11] White 1991.
[12] Johnson and Schott 2013: 13; Johnson 2014; Corke-Webster 2019. On the strategy of Eusebius in response to trauma, see Corke-Webster 2012: 51–77.
[13] Johnson 2006a; Morlet 2011: 119–50.   [14] Bucur 2018: 236–40.

In Eusebius, as also in Athanasius' early works *Contra gentes* and *De incarnatione*, the defeat of idolatry by the presence and teaching of the incarnate Word proves the decisive truth and visible transforming power of Christianity.[15] The changes were rung on this theme rhetorically not only in the contrast between inanimate religion and living wisdom in the incarnation, but as embodied in the spiritual power and practices of the Christian community: virtuous people of the new covenant – men and women, rich and poor, learned and unlearned – replaced lifeless idols of wood and stone.[16] Eusebius' narratives of martyrdom in the *Ecclesiastical History* and the *Martyrs of Palestine* showcased the moral fortitude of the confessors and martyrs; the keyword for his descriptions was *upomene*, in which the calm endurance of the tortured revealed their likeness to God.[17] Eusebius here illustrated a principle of 'iconoclash', that is, the replacement of false images by true ones rather than an iconoclastic destruction.[18] A living plant that enabled healing was more efficacious, if not more wonderful, than the memorial statue of Jesus (*andrianta eikona tou Iesou*) that pagans had erected in Caesarea Philippi.[19] In the fragments of the *Letter to Constantia* attributed to him, Eusebius opposed her conventional desire for an image of Christ, not only naming this as a practice of the Manichees and pagans, but asserting the impossibility of portraying either the 'true and unchangeable' image or the material image now transformed by the incarnation.[20]

The problem of monotheism and image in the texts of Arius and Alexander has been thoroughly mapped within the genealogy and development of later Trinitarian theology.[21] Christian theologies of the incarnate divine image of course have a long and complex history, especially after the fourth century.[22] The divisive effects of these competing theologies of generation in Alexandria, however, seem linked to broader religious issues surrounding religious competition and legacies of violent relationship to material cults as well as theological or philosophical principles. The centrality of *creatio ex nihilo*, at least in part in response to Manichaean teaching in Egypt, set this conflict about the nature of the Son apart from earlier Christian

---

[15] Kofsky 2002: 100–37; Anatolios 2011: 27–31. [16] Eusebius, *Dem. ev.* 1.6.21–22.
[17] Eusebius, *Hist. eccl.* 8.3–4; 8.45; 8.69, in Verdoner 2011: 114–17; Castelli 2004: 104–95.
[18] See discussion in Van Nuffelen 2013: 133–49; on 'iconoclash', see Koerner 2004: 12.
[19] Eusebius, *Hist. eccl.* 7.18.
[20] PG 20.1545–50. As better attributed to Eusebius of Nicomedia, see Parvis 2006: 41 n. 15; on recent arguments for Eusebius of Caesarea and his theology of images, see Van Nuffelen 2013: 144–45.
[21] DelCogliano 2006; Robertson 2007; Young 2011; Edwards 2013a.
[22] Gwynn 2007b; Francis 2020.

arguments as well as contemporary philosophy.[23] Winrich Löhr has most recently defended Arius' monotheism as reflecting traditional and devotional, if not anti-philosophical, Christian themes.[24] Other scholars have returned to the possible shape of Arius' christology, mapping the underlying shifts by Methodius and others in describing humans as created in the image of God in both body and soul as reflecting issues of materiality in models of incarnation and asceticism.[25]

The contemporary conflicts, then, were not only how the Son imaged the Father, but also how humans in body or soul imaged God. In this context, Alexander's polemic concerning changeability and the testimonies from the early debate concerning self-determination preserved by Athanasius may suggest not an adoptionist or exemplarist christology, but rather underlying conflicts concerning shifting anthropological definitions and the reception of the incarnate Son as divine image.[26] Methodius has often been cited in relation to Arius' refutation of eternal generation, but his central use of the power of divine will to recreate and perfect the human material image is also important in how disputes on the human image and spiritual practices shaped reflection on christology.[27] In his *Symposium*, Methodius linked the perfection of the incarnate Christ, the Second Adam, to virginity. Virgins were the perfect living and visible image of humanity, to be celebrated like the martyrs, and the answer to idolatry as a living image of God.[28] As a doubled image of body and soul, virgins portrayed the unchanged body and as well as the freely obedient soul illustrating the remodelling of humanity from corruption to incorruption.[29] Ancient Christian debates on incarnation were shaped not only by philosophical and theological legacies but, with regard to the body, by surrounding practices of visuality and material images; the 'living icons' of martyrs and ascetics were visible bridges to the hidden transcendent world, whose popularity as objects of devotion and divine power exploded in the decades after the Great Persecution.[30]

---

[23] Lyman 1989; Heil 2002.   [24] Löhr 2006b: 149; Anatolios 2011: 42–52.
[25] Bracht 1999; Anatolios 2011: 51; Cartwright 2015.
[26] On the description of changeability as purely orthodox polemic, against the proposals of Robert Gregg and Dennis Groh (1981) or as suffering by Richard Hanson, see Gwynn 2007a: 194–202.
[27] See discussion in Williams 1987, rev. edn, 2001: 169–70. Bracht comments that Methodius' use of divine will, unlike that of Arius, was focused on anthropology in opposition to dualism (Bracht 1999: 232).
[28] Methodius, *Symp.* 8.11; 6.2; 8.2; 10.2; cf. Bracht 1999: 131–35. On his performative christology, see Brown Hughes 2016: 51–76.
[29] Methodius, *Symp.* 2.6–7; 3.7–8.
[30] Francis 2003; Neis 2012; Neis 2015; Pongratz-Leisten and Sonik 2015; Brand 2020.

What have appeared to be ruptures in Christian theology by Arius, i.e., his defence of an apophatic deity, his central use of *creatio ex nihilo*, and the (un)changeable or self-determined nature of the Son, were in fact elements of contemporary anti-idolatry theology. These theological arguments may reflect a collection of values to be defended rather than an alternative theology, and resulted in a short-lived, if popular, oppositional theology to curb Alexander's alleged mistakes on materiality and visuality in a shifting world of imperial polytheistic patronage and tolerance.

Rethinking Theological Conflict and Lived Religion in Alexandria

Recent scholarship continues to make clear that not only do persisting heresiological categories shape our historical narratives, but so also do anachronistic assumptions about continuities of Christian spirituality, worship, or authority.[31] Before the era of the imperial councils, local Christian disputes often remained open-ended, with varied alliances authorising some practices or leading to divisions that continued to co-exist. The extant documents of the early debate in Alexandria thus preserve only brief public and performative epistolary exchanges among local clergy, which may suggest why genealogical traces of separate schools or exegetical arguments on either side have been so difficult to confirm.[32] Not only do we often lack significant evidence, but also these local conflicts often do not fit our assumptions about Christian identity or even the broader histories of late antique religion we use to frame them.[33] In the early Alexandrian controversy, historians have cross-referenced the polemical reports with the few extant sources to verify authenticity or, in some cases, to argue that these must be discarded almost entirely as orthodox inventions.[34] One danger with this practice can be rather narrow classifications of what and how we may think ancient Christian theologians might properly argue.[35] For example, the report that the Father is unseen or unknown by the Son would probably be considered merely polemical, if we did not have the relevant, and highly qualified, fragments from the *Thalia*. The descriptions of

---

[31] Elsner 2020b: 2–9; cf. Bradshaw 2002; King 2010: 66–84; Vinzent 2016.
[32] Poster 2001: 24–28.   [33] Mitchell 1991: 114.
[34] Gwynn helpfully contrasts the lists of charges used by Alexander and Athanasius with recent evidence and discussions (2007a: 189–220).
[35] For theological filters on reconstructing the history of Arius, see Wiles 1996.

mutability have also lingered as a problem not only for textual reasons but also for reasons of ancient theological probability.[36]

However, what appear from later norms to be puzzling statements can be important survivals of ancient religious practice and belief. The study of 'lived ancient religion' in late antiquity has been limited and obscured by disciplinary boundaries as well as by treating contemporary religious movements as living in distinct worlds.[37] The relation between ancient religious institutions and individual actions may be better explored through four key notions: appropriation, agency, situational meaning, and mediality.[38] The division in Alexandria was a significant public movement that included a number of clergy and laity whom Alexander claimed brought lawsuits against him, met in separate assemblies, and perhaps had differing worship.[39] To characterise Arius as a 'teacher' with philosophical interests obscures the central historical evidence of his agency as a presbyter amid a significant group of clergy and people challenging the orthodoxy of the local bishop.[40] Alexander as bishop claimed equal intellectual and spiritual teaching authority with his opponents, as well as more humility and continuity with tradition, but also admitted in his attempt to gain clerical support that the people were against him.[41]

To pay close attention to 'situational meaning' is to understand religious or theological definitions not as generated by coherent world-views, but rather by a complexity of interests, beliefs, and satisfactions.[42] The defence of monotheism in the collective clerical letter to Alexander not only emphasised traditional Christian formulas but also added several contemporary errors in Egypt including the spiritual dualism of the Manichees and a controversial ascetic, Hieracas.[43] According to Epiphanius, Hieracas based

---

[36] Gregg and Groh's (1981) attention to mutability was criticised as an uncritical reliance on orthodox polemics and a modernist filter; 'Western post-Augustinian' in Anatolios 2011: 48; Williams also suggests that 'Lyman, like Gregg and Groh, seems to move too rapidly to the distinctively modern assumption that what is of theological interest in all this must be a human biography' (Williams 1987, rev. edn, 2001: 258).

[37] Gasparini et al. 2020: 1; Vinzent 2016: 107–9.   [38] Gasparini et al. 2020: 2; Vinzent 2016: 102–6.

[39] *Ur.* 14.1–6. On Egyptian lawsuits as public displays of redressing grievances, see Bryen 2008. On Christian disputes, see Humfress 2007: 153–61.

[40] On the problem of Arius as 'teacher', see Lyman 2010: 241–42. On the interwoven world of Christian leadership, see Eshleman 2012; Vinzent 2016: 102.

[41] *Ur.* 14: vulgar speech; 14.44: uneducated mud; 14.9: arrogance: 14.49; if ministers unite, the people will follow: 14.60. Arius appeared to threaten Constantine after Nicaea that 'we have the masses' (*Ur.* 34).

[42] Gasparini et al. 2020: 2.

[43] *Ur.* 6.3. Alexander refers to other groups in his response, but not these two ascetic Christian competitors. Athanasius will later address both groups.

his theology on the *Ascension of Isaiah*, in which God was flanked by the Beloved and the Holy Spirit.[44] The *Ascension of Isaiah* is an apocalyptic text of Jewish and Christian origins concerning the revelation of God through the mystical ascension of the suffering; the deity is invisible except to the transformed righteous who ascend through intermediaries and levels of glory. The Beloved One is a transformable and visible divine being; he functioned so to speak as the visible presence of the invisible deity.[45] The Manichaean movement also celebrated martyrdom and used didactic images including icons, narratives, and diagrams to explore six theological themes as part of the original set, *The Book of Pictures*.[46] Composed in part against pagan cults, these 'forms of art as manifestations of the divine' trained the eye to discern glimpses of light: 'the one who hears can see'.[47] A reference in the clergy letter to their common opposition with Alexander to 'something pre-existing that turned into something else' might refer to 'Son' as an economic term, as in Lactantius, or Porphyry's possible jibe concerning the confusion of Son and Logos.[48] Theologians defended the reality of the struggles and obedience of Jesus against both Manichees and philosophical critics who questioned if a god could change.[49] Equally important, both Christian groups had distinctive teachings with regard to visuality, materiality, and human nature in line with their theologies of generation.[50]

Finally, the shape of communications inevitably involves concerns to do with surrounding material culture and embodiment, which has attracted increasing notice in ancient Christian studies.[51] In relation to public space and imperial patronage, Alexander expanded the church of St Theonas and used it as his episcopal residence; he may have also transformed a local temple of Kronos into a church dedicated to St Michael.[52] According to a later life of the bishop Peter, a dispute occurred immediately after his execution in 311 CE as to whether he should be buried near the church of Theonas or in Boukolon near the shrine of Mark.[53] While the place of Arius' parish remains obscure, if 'Baukalis' and Boukolon could be reconciled this would put him adjacent to the traditional, and perhaps competing, site of

---

[44] Epiphanius, *Pan.* 67.3–4.   [45] Knight 2012. On heavenly hierarchies, see Williams 1987/2001.
[46] Brand 2020; cf. *kephalion* 151 in Gulácsi 2015: 490–94.   [47] Gulácsi 2018: 217–20.
[48] Lactantius, *Inst.* 4.6.1–2; a report from Theophylactus is no. 214 (Harnack no. 86) in Berchman 2005: 220. For commentary see Edwards 2013b: 246 n. 33.
[49] Sandnes 2016; on Origen and Celsus, see pp. 65–70.   [50] Brakke 1995: 44–55.
[51] Nasrallah (2019: 18–39) gives a cogent overview of defining and using material culture for literary sources. Cf. Vinzent 2016.
[52] Hass 1997: 209–10, 269. On later uses of landscape, buildings, and religious identity, see Shepardson 2014.
[53] See Vivian 1988: 45–47.

the martyrium of St Mark.[54] The martyrium, the tombs, and the suburbs were popular places for early ascetics as well as religious devotions that could explain in part the broad support of Arius and his colleagues, and his association with ascetics.[55] The restoration of church property, including the restoration of property to the survivors of martyrs, and if not to them, to the local church, could also have provided significant sums as imperial patronage shifted in these early decades, and perhaps inspired the alleged lawsuits. Constantine resolved some conflicts by declaring in 324 CE that graves of martyrs belonged to the church.[56]

Alexander's definitions of one divine nature shared by the Father and the Son, including eternal image, also provoked accusations concerning different dimensions of materiality.[57] He used *aparallatokos* to describe the Son as image, and underscored the eternity and necessity of divine image.[58] His reference to the Son's likeness with reference to worship has a surprisingly defensive ring.[59] To his opponents, an implication may also have been that this exact likeness in divine nature could now be seen directly in the incarnation of the Son.[60] In his later metered hymn *Thalia*, Arius set out his theology as a narrow spiritual path, perhaps with direct reference to 'practical knowing' or *sapientia*, as teachings concerning Christian life and ways of seeking God.[61] Arius defended divine nature as inexpressible

---

[54] See Hass 1997: 213, 271–72. On other churches in Alexandria, see Williams 1987/2001: 42–43. On the evidence of Christian churches before 328 CE, see McKenzie 2007: 240–42. See the sceptical comment of McKenzie 2007: 242 and 407 n. 28. Perhaps Epiphanius misheard, since in Egyptian Greek there seems to have been a frequent interchange of *alpha* and *omicron* as part of the bilingual interference of Coptic vowels; see Gignac 1975: 288–89.

[55] Hass 1997: 271–72; on the question of ascetic women in Alexandria, see Burrus 1991: 229–48; Brakke 1995: 57–79; Elm 2004: 331f. Richard Vaggione (2000) notes that women of varied sorts were usually active in debates as well as targets of propaganda.

[56] This declaration of restoration appears several times in 313 CE (*Hist. eccl.* 10.5.1–14; 9.10.7–11) and 324 CE by Constantine (*Vit. Const.* 2.46).

[57] *Ur.* 1.2, 4–5. To Eusebius of Nicomedia Arius lists, if not ridicules, Alexander's assertions of co-existence and the Son as a part. Mark Edwards (2012; 2013a: 138–41) reviews reactions to Alexander. Origen expresses reservations on expressions of begotten of the Father's essence as implying the Father was divided, corporeal, and akin to pregnancy in *Comm. Jo.* 20.157–59.

[58] On Alexander's discussion of *eikon*, see *Ur.* 14. 38, 39, 47, 48, 52; see Parvis 2006: 53.

[59] *Ur.* 14.52: 'We will continue worshipping him as we have been, piously and respectfully referring to him with the terms "was" and "ever" and "before all ages". We do not reject his divinity but instead credit to him his perfect likeness to his Father in every way.'

Ur. 14.6: We drove them out of our church that worships the divine Christ. His opponents of course called the Son divine but did describe that 'he is over him as his God' in *Ur.* 6.5. On the variety of prayers through and to Christ, see Bradshaw 2012: 249–60.

[60] *Ur.* 14.39: Alexander quoted John 14.8–9 and described the Son as a mirror.

[61] On wisdom literature, see Elliot 2013; on hymns as possible evidence for religious experience, see Gordon 2020.

and invisible, even to the Son, so it was through the known limits of the Son as begotten that we are able to praise and worship the unbegotten God.[62] Addressing the problem of sight and knowledge specifically, Arius asserted that the invisible was seen according to the power by which God was able to see and according to individual measure; the Son endures (*upomene*) to see the Father, as determined.[63] This description parallels earlier descriptions of the goal of God's gracious self-revelation and spiritual transformation in Irenaeus and Origen.[64]

Within a larger context of late antique religion, these assertions about the means of revelation and image are arguments about visuality and divine nature. As Clifford Ando pointed out, if the modern research on image tends towards archetype and representation, the ancient issue was approaching and responding to the presence of the gods in material images.[65] Many studies have investigated the 'rising textual noise' in late antiquity concerning the definition of 'image' and the varied means of vision in encountering the divine, including 'epiphanic viewing'.[66] An essential part of the practices of religion within the highly visual culture of antiquity were the 'rules of engagement' as embodied in pilgrimage and temples in order to encounter the god.[67] As in formulating christology, a 'living' image or animated statue expressed the gap between mortals and divinity and a means of contrasting two entirely distinct modes of being.[68] As Jaś Elsner has recently commented, with the unusual exceptions of Judaism and Christianity, 'visual and material culture in many respects *constitute* religious experience and are much more than merely expressions or illustrations'.[69]

Christian ambivalence about the nature of the material images surrounding them is well known, but this did not preclude using them to think with.[70] Especially with reference to the visual encounter with the divine, biblical accounts of theophanies resulted in varied receptions in Judaism

---

[62] *Thalia* in Athanasius, *C. Ar.* 1.5.   [63] *Thalia* in Athanasius, *Decr.* 15.
[64] Origen, *Princ.* 1.1.8–9 on invisibility of God, though 'seen' by the pure of heart; cf. *Cels.* 7.39, 44: one may see through the eyes of the soul; 7.44: even uneducated Christians know to shut eyes to 'see'. Irenaeus, *Haer.* 4.20.5: 'for man does not see God by his own power, but when he pleases he is seen by men, by whom he wills and when'. Origen, *Comm. Jo.* 20.47: we will see the Father as the Son sees him, no longer through an image.
[65] Ando 2008: 21–42; cf. Francis 2009: 285–87; Arnhold, Maier, and Rüpke 2018; Markschies 2019.
[66] Elsner 2007, 2012; Platt 2011.   [67] Clarke 2012.
[68] Stewart 2003: 35–44. On the slippage of terminology with regard to divine and human images, see Stewart 2003: 22–28. Cf. Steiner 2003: 135–84.
[69] Elsner 2020b: 11. On problems of art and religion, see Elsner 2020b: 126–27. On problems of writing religious history with material culture, see Elsner 2020b: 78–80.
[70] Nasrallah 2010; Jensen 2013: 309–43; Kristensen 2013; Peppard 2015.

and Christianity.[71] Not surprisingly, in Christianity there were also diverse answers concerning the created image of God in humanity drawn from the multiple scriptural references, distinct cosmologies, and pieties of different communities.[72] As traced by Marguerite Harl, in Alexandria *agalma* was used by Philo as equivalent to *eikon* to understand humanity as created in the divine image by God.[73] Clement described humans as an animated statue (*agalma empsuchon*) with the mind as the image of God in the temple of the body.[74] By contrast Origen only rarely used this term and replied to Celsus that of course Christians did not have cult statues, but rather the *agalma* of virtue to be imitated.[75] Origen's defence of the image as the inward part of humanity was to guard against any sense of God as composite, and to focus on the journey of the soul towards God, who as invisible and incorporeal was known only through the revelation by the Logos.[76] Methodius described Christ as the 'second incarnation of the Word', both icon and exemplar, whose flesh and image was identical to Adam in order to restore and perfect human nature as the 'arch-virgin'; as a creation of God, matter is not a fault, but an expression of freedom as God created both form and matter.[77] This doubling of image to include the inner and exterior with analogy to statue was also seen in Eustathius of Antioch.[78] The proliferation of Christian living 'images', both faithful and immobile, in the ascetic movement and martyrdom accounts can be seen as a reflection as well as a replacement of ancient religious values: no longer inanimate wood or stone, but enfleshed human beings may reveal the divine power of God in Christ.[79] In the fourth century, Harl notes, the metaphor of *agalma* was inverted in order to emphasise the manifestation of the divine, so the *agalma* is no longer the inner mirror of divinity, but the outer revelation in christology; Eusebius replaced *soma* with *agalma* to underline the body of Jesus is a revelation and presence of the divine.[80] The body as *agalma* to manifest the invisible deity reflected the contemporary ambivalence concerning image and materiality to represent the divine. Marcellus of Ancyra asserted that *eikon* referred not to the Logos, but to the incarnate Image that could be seen.[81]

---

[71] On rabbinic exegesis of theophany, see Neis 2013: 43–81; Heath 2016: 220–36. On pre-Nicene theophanies, see Bucur 2019.
[72] Hall 2007.   [73] Harl 2009: esp. 64 and 51 n. 3 on *agalma*.
[74] On use by Plotinus, Porphyry, and Clement, see Harl 2009: 55–64. On gender and elite aspects of Clement's description, see Nasrallah 2010: 272–95.
[75] *Cels.* 8.17–18; Harl 2009: 64–65.   [76] 1 Cor 6:19: *Cels.* 6.63–65; Harl 2009: 64–65.
[77] Bracht 1999: 141–42, 213–16.   [78] Cartwright 2012; 2015: 158–63.
[79] Kristensen 2013: 68. On the formation of martyrs as sages and heroes, see Fialon 2018: 316–62.
[80] Harl 2009: 69.   [81] Cartwright 2012: 202.

While the patterns of language and exegesis link the Alexandrian clergy to earlier and contemporary Christian authors, the central oppositions concerning transcendence and materialism, image and visuality, and warnings of apostasy signal their awareness of surrounding religious rivals while asserting their own values concerning Christian belief and practice.[82] Rather than charting rebellion, submission, or failure in religious conflicts as a relation to an institution or belief structure, one can recover the moral or ethical frameworks that construct subjects whose piety may not fully be understood without paying closer attention to the multiple ways in which one may inhabit norms as well as material environments.[83] The conflicting values emerge in Alexandria in relation to several facets of lived religion. Whatever their ecclesiastical rank, they encounter each other as teachers in religious community through public discourse in an already divided church. Their commitments to understanding formulations of generation and soteriology are also shaped by other competing, if erroneous, Christian groups, with regard to issues which separate all Christians from Greco-Romans, i.e., divine nature, visuality, and anthropology even as they affirm suffering and transformation. Finally, if imperial patronage had increased Alexander's status and budget, the legacy of persecution remained in the correspondence and rhetoric of the communications, if not in the surrounding tombs.

The Problem of Image(s) and Mutability in Alexandria

In his polemic against his opponents as adoptionists, Alexander never underestimated the importance of spiritual progress to faithful Christian life, but rather he objected to this essential Christian definition of transformative human nature and image being applied to the divine Son: they filled their heads with texts of suffering and kenosis.[84] For Arius the origin of the Son from the Father must not compromise a definition of divinity whose transcendence and singularity may not be wholly seen nor known apart from deliberate self-discourse. If we think of this conflict as centred on constitutive problems of the christological union, the criticism of Eustathius of Antioch – who described Arius' theology as lacking

---

[82] On opponents as apostates: *Ur.* 4b.3, 17 (Eusebius to Alexander); *Ur.* 7.3: they take care lest they get arrested. *Ur.* 14.6: they ridiculed and instigated a persecution; *Ur.* 55: they are ready to die and be tortured; *Ur.* 59: they publicly mock Christianity.
[83] Mahmood 2005; Beekers and Kloss 2017.   [84] *Ur.* 14.37.

both true divinity and complete humanity, i.e., only a soulless body or statue – was apt.[85] If we oppose *mimesis* and *theosis*, as will an older Athanasius, then we may criticise a mere exemplary soteriology that has confused the traditional distinction between the divine image and the created image in humanity.[86] However, if we frame the early public argument in Alexandria as concerning visuality and material images in the context of religious practices of monotheism, martyrdom, and asceticism, the theological dispute reveals layers of the relation between discourses opposing idolatry, lived religion, and theological reflection. Narratives of *kenosis* were an *ekphrasis* not only of self-emptying or obedience, but of the revelation of transformative divine power in both christology and martyrdom.[87]

In his later polemical work *Contra arianos*, written to discredit the opponents of Nicaea by association with Arius, Athanasius included a list of questions that he alleged had been asked by Arius and his colleagues to 'boys and women in the streets of Alexandria'.[88] They echo charges from the correspondence of the earliest conflict, and perhaps are the 'uneducated theology' of Alexander's complaints, but should be read as a *testimonium* rather than a fragment.[89] Thus, Athanasius repeated and expanded various versions of the third group of the four questions as part of his polemic about mutability. In *Contra arianos* 1.35, Athanasius reported a series of questions asked in the streets:

Is he free willed (*autexousios*) or not? Is he good (*kalos*) from choosing (*prohairesis*) according to free will (*autexousios*), and can, if he chooses (*thelese*), change, being of a changeable nature (*treptos on phuseos*)? Or being like stone (*lithos*) or wood (*xulon*) has he not free choice (*prohairesis eleutheran*) to turn to this or that way?[90]

---

[85] Gwynn (2007a: 198–201) discussed problems with this model that Hanson and Lorenz (1979) drew upon. Cartwright (2015: 61), however, discusses the recent work of Karl-Heinz Uthemann, which supports the moral agency which Gregg and Groh (1981) and Lorenz (1979) discerned.

[86] Athanasius, *Decr.* 20.3; On the importance of *theosis*, see the summary of Gwynn 2007a: 198. Candida Moss (2010: 164) notes that, in contrast to later models, the earlier language of exaltation in martyrdom accounts may have indicated shared status.

[87] Stephanie Cobb (2016: 1–14) discusses the portrayal of divine power. Eusebius portrayed the submission of the Son and confrontation with the demons on the cross in *Dem. ev.* 10.8; *Theoph.* 3.44.

[88] *C. Ar.* 1.22; 1.35; 2.18. On *Contra arianos* in context of Athanasius' polemics, see Gwynn 2007a: 21–26.

[89] Timothy Barnes (1993: 55) speculated Athanasius relied on his memory and materials from Marcellus. Marcus Vinzent (1993: 250) accepts these as probably original. On the difference between a fragment and a *testimonium*, see Magny 2014: 23–26.

[90] These questions were set out more briefly in 1.22 and 2.18.

In 1.5, Athanasius reported this statement as a conclusion rather than a question as part of his quotations from the *Thalia* of Arius: 'And by nature as others, so the Word himself is alterable (*treptos*) and remains good by his own free will (*autexousios*).'[91]

In the first and longest testimony, traditional Christian autonomy is contrasted to inanimate physical nature (wood or stone) that is incapable of independent movement. This is a commonplace philosophical definition of the soul, but also had a long use in Christian apologetics against material images of divinity.[92] The predicate 'Word', unlike Arius' usual use of Son, in the third testimony, however, is a characteristic Athanasian intervention to shape a teaching into a nonsensical statement. Stead, however, accepted this as an authentic saying echoing Arius' usual constructions.[93] As a whole, these testimonies are not about advancement or adoption, but rather the Son as genuinely ethically capable and animate, i.e., that his changeability reflects not only a traditional Christian anthropology of *autexousios*, but in the context of idolatry, a living image as the appropriate revelation of God. The association of *autexousios* and *treptos* is not consistent, which may also reflect an Athanasian spin on the Son as created. Yet, this combination of the (un)changing being of the Son as directly created might also echo the direct creation of body and soul in Methodius. The Son is directly begotten or created as the Second Adam who reveals both the divine will and the human fulfilment of divine knowledge and life.

This argument has parallels with a fragment from Porphyry's *On Images*, which is engaged in contemporary works by Eusebius in *Preparatio evangelica* and by Athanasius in *Contra gentes*. In an excerpt on images (*agalma*) discussed by Eusebius, Porphyry argued that invisible gods could be grasped through visible forms, i.e., statues; only the unlearned saw them as 'wood or stone' just like only an illiterate would see knowledge from a book as simply 'papyrus'.[94] Eusebius ignored the obvious appeal to practices of spiritual seeing and replied in accordance with traditional arguments: 'lifeless materials cannot bear the divine image'. Since the human body had no likeness to the mind of God, worshipping or contemplating a human statue was only seeing 'a deaf and dumb image of living flesh in lifeless and dead matter'; only the soul is the image and likeness of God, being immortal, incorporeal, rational, and capable of virtue and wisdom. Material images were therefore especially false because they expressed not

---

[91] Athanasius, *C. Ar.* 1.5.   [92] Meijering 1984: 56–58.
[93] Stead 1983: 253. Cf. Löhr 2006b: 133. Vinzent (1993: 284) sees this as a mixture of Arius and Asterius.
[94] Eusebius, *Praep. ev.* 3.7–10; cf. Miles 2015; Smith 2000: 39.

the whole man, but the worst part of him, not showing a trace of soul and life. It would thus be impossible to find divine power through the images of lifeless matter and only the properties of a moral soul can be a true 'image' or statue of the transcendent God or the true alphabet of revelation.

In *Contra gentes*, an early work against both idolatry and dualism, including perhaps Manichees, Athanasius also engaged the fragment.[95] He first argued, like Eusebius, that the notion of God would be better understood through living beings, rational and irrational, and not looked at in lifeless and unmoving objects of wood and stone. He then affirmed the ultimate creative power of God and divine nature as incorporeal, incorruptible, and immortal.[96] The only true road to God is in each soul and mind, where God may be seen and apprehended.[97] The work ends with the definition of the Son as the only and exact image, *eikon aparallaktos*.[98]

Arius in some ways is closer to Athanasius' anti-idolatry and anti-dualist theology in *Contra gentes* than to Eusebius' mediating theology of image.[99] In the fragments of his letter preserved by Constantine, Arius continued to distinguish sharply between God and the Son. Divine nature may not be demoted nor circumscribed. Constantine wondered, how is a form or a figure or an image an outrage?[100] The Son is less an ontological mediator than a visual go-between, who as a living image points to God, as stated in the *Thalia*, as well as presenting the unchanged presence of a transformed humanity. The centrality of self-determination and the affirmations of divine power suggest a deeply anti-fatalist and anti-dualist vision of Christian theology and practice. As suggested above from our extant evidence of a local controversy, Arius may have been defending a traditional set of anti-idolatry religious values concerning divine power and human nature rather than a coherent theological system. Not surprisingly, after the early controversy in Alexandria, Athanasius explored the necessary values of *eikon*, vision, and materiality more thoroughly in the classic text of christology and *theosis*, *De incarnatione*. Athanasius' later example of *aparallaktos* with reference to the imperial *eikon*, paraphrasing the Johannine Christ, would perhaps be the fulfilment of Arius' worst expectation of Alexander's theology.[101]

---

[95] Meijering 1984.   [96] Athanasius, *C. Gent.* 19–21.   [97] Athanasius, *C. Gent.* 30.
[98] Athanasius, *C. Gent.* 46.
[99] Ayres 2004b: 58–59; Robertson 2007: 37–68; Johnson 2014: 125–32.   [100] *Ur.* 34.32.
[101] 'I and the Emperor are one; for I am in him and he in me'; cf. Peppard 2013: 400–405. Francis (2020: 303) discusses Athanasius use of the image of the emperor in *C. Ar.* 3.5 and the visual culture already 'baptised' by Athanasius and others.

Framed by the legacy of surrounding material practices and religious debates among Christians, the accusations of materiality and changeability in the Alexandrian debate on monotheism were deeply intertwined with contemporary questions of visuality and of material images of God. Elements of Arius' teaching against Alexander echoed traditional Christian refutations of visuality and materiality in polytheism and dualism: the one living creator of all must be revealed only through the Son as a living image, in contrast to inanimate 'wood or stone'.[102] In the decade after the Great Persecution, these assertions were not merely a cultural or traditional cliché in apologetic discourse, but deliberate signals concerning past trauma and heroism.[103] This phrase also linked the divine *kenosis* of the incarnate Son to the faithfulness of the martyrs and the ascetics as transformed human images of divine power and presence.[104] The apologetic phrase of 'wood and stone' eventually became a 'ritual speech' of monks included in their physical attacks on Greco-Roman images and temples.[105] Over the fourth century the portrayals of the deaths of martyrs became powerful texts of *ekphrasis*, constructed to explain the struggles of the martyrs as living models of Christian virtue and ultimate divine power.[106] Woven into these literary narratives and the continuing theological debates were the lived religious experiences of those whose own lives were shaped in diverse ways by their *ekphrasis* on the narratives and presence of the incarnate Son.

---

[102] Arnobius, *Contra* 1.42: The virtues of Jesus reveal his divinity. Lactantius, *Inst.* 2.2: A living God has a living image.
[103] Fournier 2020: 9–11.   [104] Brakke 2006: 23–47.
[105] Brakke 2008; Frankfurter 2008: 148–49.   [106] Moss 2010: 21, 46; Cobb 2016: 63–121.

15 Imagining Ephrem the Author

JEFFREY WICKES

Introduction

A set of fifteen Syriac hymns – *madrashe* – honour the ascetic Abraham Qidunaya, who died in 367 CE. They are attributed to the poet Ephrem (d. 373 CE) and most scholars think he wrote some of them, though probably not all.[1] The arguments for or against their authenticity are complex but relate, in part, to three lines that appear in the second hymn. The poet sings:

Little by little, the waves of your delightful story stole me away.
Into the waves I fell and thrashed about. Though I did not abandon your story,
I can repeat nothing from it.[2]

Edmund Beck (d. 1991), the critical editor of the majority of Ephrem's Syriac hymnody, edited these lines in 1972, by which time he had spent nearly twenty years working on what he took to be the authentic poems of Ephrem.[3] He knew these hymns on Abraham were early – their style was nearly identical to that of authentic Ephrem and they appear complete in a late sixth- or early seventh-century manuscript – but he thought the attribution dubious.[4] When he read these lines, they struck him as clearly Ephremic in tone and language, but radically un-Ephremic in referent. From Beck's perspective, authentic Ephrem could only apply such language of surpassing wonder to God.[5] To sing such words in reference to a saint – a

---

[1] For the critical edition and German translation of the *Madrashe on Abraham Qidunaya*, see Beck 1972a (CSCO 322–23). On the question of their authenticity, see Beck 1972a (CSCO 323): v–x. For a recent English translation and an updated discussion of their authenticity, see Hayes 2012: 14–21, 31–54, 214–23.

[2] Unless otherwise noted, all translations are my own. This translation is adapted from Hayes 2012: 358–59.

[3] For a list of Beck's editions, see Brock 2007a. Throughout this chapter, I use the term 'poem' as a generic term to refer to both the metered genres in which Ephrem wrote: *madrashe*, a stanzaic, metered song, with a melody and a sung refrain, and *memre*, a metered homily-like genre, which carries no melody or refrain, but which was probably intoned in a *recitativo* style.

[4] The hymns appear in BL Add. MS 14,592. On the manuscript, see Wright 1870–72: 2.684–90, fols. 57a–61b.

[5] Compare these lines from the *Madrashe on Virginity* 7.15, which Beck took as genuine: 'Who has buried my weak self beneath relentless waves? / As the waves of oil have lifted me up, they have

human being? In 1972, this struck the Benedictine Beck as 'ridiculous', and unbefitting of the literary and spiritual genius of the author Ephrem.[6]

These *madrashe* on Abraham form one piece of a tapestry of works that Beck edited and deemed close chronologically and stylistically to authentic Ephrem, but ultimately, at least in part, inauthentic. His determination of a work as authentic or inauthentic was wrapped up with his conception of Ephrem as author, saint, deacon, and hymnographer, a conception that he built almost entirely without recourse to Ephrem's biographical tradition. This chapter traces the way that Beck situated questions of authorship and authenticity at the centre of his organisation of the unwieldy body of Syriac poetry ascribed to Ephrem. Faced with an unreliable biographical tradition, and a poetic corpus in which the boundaries between the authentic and inauthentic blurred, Beck constructed a history, a chronology, and a notion of literary genius and consequent decline to map this corpus. I suggest that such a focus has often rested on questionable assumptions about the context of the poetry and has been pursued at the expense of other modes of organising this corpus. Within the context of this volume, which surveys the maps late antique Christians created to navigate their world, I use Edmund Beck and his editing of Ephrem's corpus to ask how our own histories of scholarship have shaped, and at times even determined, the patterns we see in the literature we study, and the models we build to organise the past.

In Search of Ephrem

Ephrem the Syrian appeared on the historical stage in two ways. Biographically, a narrative tradition began in Latin in 392 CE, developed in decisive ways over the course of the fourth and fifth centuries in Greek, and took canonical shape in the sixth century in Syriac.[7] Literarily, a body of mostly poetry but also some prose, written in Syriac but extant also (occasionally exclusively) in Armenian, was externally attested by the end of the fifth century and begins to appear in extant manuscripts in the early sixth century.[8] These two streams – the biographical and the literary – make no apparent

---

given me Christ's story. / Christ's waves have struck me, and given me the symbols of oil. / Look: waves crash against waves. I am stuck in the middle!' For the text, see Beck 1962 (CSCO 223).
[6] Beck 1972a (CSCO 323): vii.
[7] For a succinct account of the biographical tradition, as well as an edition and English translation of the Syriac texts, see Amar 2011 (CSCO 629–30).
[8] See Brock 2007a.

reference to one another.[9] The earliest biographical tradition appears unaware of any but the most general of details related to Ephrem's literary life. And the literary tradition preserves little to no detail that resonates with the budding biographical tradition. Added to this complexity is the vast literary corpus that would come to be attributed to Ephrem in, mostly, Greek, Syriac, and Armenian. Some of this pseudonymous tradition is late and obviously inauthentic.[10] But much of it appears also to have emerged between the fourth and sixth centuries, and without obvious markers of historical or linguistic anachronism.

The literature that has come to be seen as authentic also does not reveal much in the way of an author, if by 'author' we mean a historical person with a concrete biography – birth, death, places of residence, names of friends, colleagues, opponents, or students. Never does the poetry's 'I' identify with any proper noun, much less the name 'Ephrem' (though four *madrashe* signed themselves as acrostics on that name).[11] Scattered among thousands of lines of verse, we hear the names of four bishops, a few place names, some (mostly dead by the time Ephrem wrote) opponents, an apostate emperor, and a few historical events.[12] Yet even these concrete historical references are embedded in a poetic corpus prone to detach them from their mundane, chronological existence.[13] If by 'author', however, we mean a set of consistent ideological commitments or a consistent literary style, then we can at least make the case for an authorial presence lurking in the literature attributed to Ephrem – some unifying voice and vision that we can uncover and piece together, which links certain poems and excludes certain others. But the boundaries between the authentic and inauthentic grow porous when using these criteria of theological commitment and literary style. Just as the 'I' of the early Syriac poetry attributed to Ephrem never revealed a biographical self, neither did that 'I' explicate its theological, psychological, or literary commitments – it never drew for us the boundaries of its own authorial self.

---

[9] One exception here is the *Memra on Ephrem* by Jacob of Serugh. The latter, while not offering much biographical detail, at least does not contradict what has come to be seen as the authentic hymnody. See Amar 1995.

[10] See, for example, the *Memra on the End*, which, under the name of Ephrem, prophesies the advent of Islam. See Beck 1972b (CSCO 320–21).

[11] Acrostics appear in *Madrashe against Heresies* 40; *Madrashe on Faith* 49; *Madrashe on Nisibis* 2; and the solitary *Madrasha on the Church*.

[12] For the names of bishops, see *Madrashe on Nisibis*. The local Edessan martyrs, Shmona and Gurya, are also mentioned in the same collection. A few opponents are named in *Madrashe against Heresies*. Julian is named in *Madrashe against Julian*.

[13] See Hartung 2018: 315–17.

In spite of the problems surrounding Ephremic authorship, the reception in the West of the literature ascribed to Ephrem has tended to assume that a single author – a genuine Ephrem – stood at the head of that literary tradition, and that authorship was crucial for organising the corpus. The earliest printings of the Syriac sources began by printing the biographies of Ephrem, and only then turned to the literary works.[14] Even Anton Baumstark and Arthur Vööbus, who admitted that the Syriac biographical tradition was full of 'pious legends', began their treatments of Ephrem by trying to reconstruct reliable biographies.[15] Yet this search for Ephrem the author took a distinct turn in the editing work of Beck, undertaken between the 1950s and the 1970s. Ironically, though Beck mostly rejected the traditional biographical sources and positioned the literary works ascribed to Ephrem at the heart of his inquiry, he still assumed, and went in search of, a single author. But because these literary works were so reticent about the specifics of their authorship, Beck imaginatively constructed the notion of author, of which authenticity was predicated, as the privileged way of unifying materials that were obviously related to one another in some way, yet whose contents were diverse enough that their shared authorship could not be taken for granted.

Ephrem's Reception in Late Antiquity and Modernity

Though Beck's organising of Ephrem's corpus has shaped the modern study of Ephrem in a way that no other system has, his work did not arise from nowhere. Beck drew on a series of organisational models – both late antique and modern – that placed before him a corpus of Ephremic poetry and began the work of prioritising and vetting the authorship of that corpus. These sources provided Beck with a corpus that could feasibly be attributed to Ephrem and a series of loose criteria that, once refined, could be used to further winnow down that corpus. Surveying this material also helps us to see just how much smaller Beck's corpus of authentic materials was than that of any scholar that preceded him. At the same time, it helps us to see that Beck was unique not only in the extent and depth of his reflection on questions of authenticity, but also in the way he predicated his

---

[14] See Assemani 1732: 1.vff. While Lamy's later edition began by printing the hymns, not the biographical sources, he framed this with a long discussion of the biographical sources. See Lamy 1882: 1.xxii–xxxii.
[15] Baumstark 1922: 33–35. Vööbus 1958: 11–58.

notion of authenticity on ideas such as historical context, ascetic culture, psychological profile, theological development, and literary genius.

Excluding manuscripts, about which I will speak more below, the late antique source that most decisively shaped the contours of the Ephremic corpus that Beck inherited was a late fifth-century florilegium by Philoxenus that attributed 105 quotations to Ephrem.[16] Philoxenus did not address questions of biography, authorship, or authenticity in his discussion of these Ephremic quotations but simply organised passages from Ephrem and other fathers around theological points. This florilegium has been invaluable in the modern study of Ephrem in that it provides a glimpse of how works attributed to Ephrem were circulating just over a century after his death. Beck eventually deemed authentic a significantly smaller corpus of Ephremic works than did Philoxenus.[17]

The modern sources that stood in the background of Beck's discussion of Ephremic authorship include both a series of non-critical printings of texts ascribed to Ephrem from the seventeenth through twentieth centuries, and, more importantly for our purposes, a series of twentieth-century monographs and encyclopaedias.[18] It is these twentieth-century treatments – by Francis Burkitt, Anton Baumstark, and Arthur Vööbus – that offer the first attempts to assess the authenticity of the Syriac works attributed to Ephrem.

Francis Burkitt, in his 1901 study of Ephrem's gospel quotations, first articulated criteria to determine Ephrem's authentic corpus. Strictly speaking, Burkitt put forward only one criterion – that those works contained in pre-Islamic manuscripts transmitted an unmistakably authentic corpus.[19] Bound up with this criterion was a functional second. Burkitt argued that the New Testament Peshitta emerged only after Ephrem and that authentic Ephremic works would thus quote readings only from the Diatessaron and the Old Syriac. However, he used the first criterion – manuscript age – to limit the second – New Testament text. For whereas all works included in pre-Islamic manuscripts quoted older versions of the New Testament,

---

[16] This florilegium, contained as part four of Philoxenus' *Memra against Habbib*, appears in Graffin 1982. There is also a late fifth- or early sixth-century anonymous index that organised large swathes of Ephrem's hymnody according to melody (*qale*) that is very important for our determination of the early shape of Ephrem's corpus. See de Halleux 1972. However, this was not edited until 1972, and I have found no evidence that it shaped Beck's thinking on Ephremic authorship.

[17] On Ephrem's relationship to this florilegium, see Sebastian Brock 1997: 491–94. Also Van Rompay 2007.

[18] On the printings that preceded Beck's editions, see Brock 2007a.

[19] Burkitt articulates his conception of Ephremic authenticity in Burkitt 1901: 21–27.

not all works that quoted older versions of the New Testament were found in pre-Islamic manuscripts. This discrepancy notwithstanding, Burkitt felt manuscript age was the surest way – even if overly conservative – to establish authenticity.[20]

Twenty-one years after Burkitt's study, Anton Baumstark produced his magisterial *Geschichte der syrischen Literatur*, a survey of Syriac literature from its origins to roughly the fifteenth century.[21] Within this broader history, Baumstark devoted twenty-one pages to Ephrem.[22] Baumstark's treatment does not establish precise criteria for determining authenticity, nor does it lay out in any clear way precisely the corpus he took to be authentic. Nevertheless, as Baumstark's discussion developed, certain criteria did emerge. Like Burkitt, Baumstark privileged works that appeared in pre-Islamic manuscripts and drew on pre-Peshitta versions of the New Testament. Yet, he gave greater weight to the list of works contained in Philoxenus' florilegium, considering all of them authentic.[23] Baumstark also gave value not just to date, but to type of manuscript. He thought liturgical manuscripts – with their constant reuse, capacity for editing and corruption, and tendency to group multiple authors together – less reliable than manuscripts organised around authors (preferably single authors).[24] He generally thought whole *memre* were more likely to be inauthentic than whole *madrashe*.[25] At the same time, Baumstark was cognisant of a corruption characteristic of the transmission of *madrashe*. The manuscript tradition demonstrated the way that *madrasha* stanzas could be separated from their original compositions, and joined and rejoined into endlessly new, yet corrupt, compositions.[26]

The final, and arguably most important, chapter in the lead-up to Beck's editing of Ephrem's works, one that actually overlapped with the earliest

---

[20] For the list of works Burkitt considered genuine, see Burkitt 1901: 21–27.
[21] Baumstark 1922.   [22] Baumstark 1922: 31–52.   [23] Baumstark 1922: 35 and 43.
[24] Baumstark 1922: 44. On the corruption of Ephrem's corpus attested especially in the liturgical manuscripts, and an argument for a certain intentionality at work in that corruption, see Butts 2017.
[25] Baumstark 1922: 42. He does not explain his reasoning here, but it seems to be basically descriptive: there are simply more inauthentic *memre* than there are *madrashe*.
[26] Baumstark 1922: 35–36. Baumstark never gives a precise list of works he considered authentic, but he seems to assume the authenticity of the commentaries on Exodus and Genesis, the *Madrashe against Heresies, against Julian, on Azymes, on the Church, on the Crucifixion, on the Deceased*, portions of *on Epiphany, on Faith, on the Fast, on Nativity, on Nisibis, on Paradise, on Virginity*, and *Memre against Bardaisan, on Jonah, on Nicomedia, on Rogations, on our Lord*, the *Letter to Publius*, and the *Prose Refutations*.

phase of that editing, came in the work of Arthur Vööbus. Vööbus argued for the outlines of Ephrem's literary corpus in two primary places – initially in *Literary, Critical, and Historical Studies in Ephrem* (1958) and again in *History of Asceticism in the Syrian Orient*, Volume II (1960). Like Baumstark, Vööbus articulated a number of criteria to vet the authentic corpus of Ephrem – date of manuscript, style, biblical version. Anticipating Beck, however, Vööbus also attempted to garner a sense of the character of authentic Ephrem. He accepted the authenticity of many works that Beck would come to reject because of his sense of their similarity to an Ephremic religious 'psychology'. In this way, Vööbus mirrored Beck's construction of Ephrem as an author with a certain kind of psychological profile. Crucially, too, Vööbus' Ephrem was very much wrapped up with a history of asceticism – a history that took for granted the authenticity of many of the ascetic works Beck would reject. On the whole, Vööbus operated with a much more expansive sense of authentic Ephrem's corpus, including especially the ascetic works that Beck would increasingly distance from authentic Ephrem.

Edmund Beck's Ephrem

With the exception of Vööbus' articulation of Syriac ascetic culture, the criteria that these scholars articulated for determining an authentic Ephremic corpus concerned almost entirely date of manuscript, New Testament text, and modes of transmission. They did not grapple with what it meant to attach a piece of literature to an 'author' – what that attachment reveals and implies about the person to whom it is attached, as well as about the works that are and are not attached. Beyond a basic chronology and geography (that is, that Ephrem's life spanned the first three quarters of the fourth century and that he lived in Nisibis and Edessa), they did not assume anything about who Ephrem was or what he thought. This would change with the work of Edmund Beck.

Beck, more than any other scholar, has been rightfully recognised for establishing the textual foundation for the modern, critical study of Ephrem. It was Beck who drew a circle around the works we now think of as genuine and representative of the 'real' Ephrem. The corpus that emerged as genuine following his editing work was significantly different from that which was considered authentic when he began. Most generally, Beck rejected outright, or cast serious doubts upon, the authenticity of a series of poems and prose works that related to asceticism and the cult of the saints.[27] Beck's authentic corpus did not arise out of the discovery of previously unknown artefacts or texts. Rather, it emerged from Beck's construction of Ephrem as an author with a personality, theological commitments, a history, a style, a piety, and a psychology. Beck began to conceive Ephrem as a voice somehow distinct from, and logically prior to, the literary corpus he brought into being, yet at the same time as the primary form that held that corpus together.

Beck's construction of Ephrem as author was as important for the way it excluded texts as it was for the way it included them. And this exclusion depended more upon the subtle authorial persona for which he argued than it did upon the more concrete criteria to which previous scholars had pointed. Beck acknowledged the importance of these latter criteria – date, type of manuscripts, and biblical versions – and added two more – knowledge of other texts and linguistic developments. But he generally concluded that manuscript type and date could reveal only a limited amount about a work's authenticity. He deemed inauthentic works that appeared in early manuscripts, and authentic works that appeared late.[28] Similarly, he argued against the authenticity of certain works that cited early Syriac biblical versions.[29] Beck further made linguistic arguments to craft a sense of an authentic corpus of Ephrem. One of the most basic of these arguments involved the term for 'Holy Spirit'. As is generally well known, in the century after Ephrem, the Syriac term for the Holy Spirit would shift from the feminine *rûḥ qûdšâ* ('spirit of holiness') to the masculine *rûḥâ qûdšâ* ('Holy Spirit').[30] Beck could point to a particular usage in poetry ascribed to Ephrem to argue for or against a work's authenticity. Here, too, however, he pointed to the use of this phrase in the feminine most often where

---

[27] Most notably, the *Madrashe on Abraham Qidunaya, on Confessors, on Julian Saba, on the Maccabean Mother*, several eschatological and apocalyptic *memre*, two *Memre on Ihidaye*, the *Letter to the Mountaineers*, and the *Testament of Ephrem*. For a full list of Beck's final canon, see Melki 1983.

[28] On the limited use of manuscript date and type, see Beck 1958: 356 and Beck 1972b (CSCO 320): v. He accepts the third *Memra on Reproof* as authentic in spite of the thirteenth-century date of its manuscript (Beck 1970a (CSCO 305): vii.). While he ultimately will consider the *Memra on Magic and Magicians* as inauthentic, he does think it is very early, in spite of its late manuscript date (845 CE) (Beck 1972b (CSCO 320): vii).

[29] In fact, Beck referred to the evidence of biblical versions primarily in cases where he argued against a poem's authenticity in spite of the early versions of the biblical text it cited. See the first *Memra on Repentance* from Beck 1970a (CSCO 305): xix; *Memra on Palm Sunday* from Beck 1970b (CSCO 311): x; *Memra on Magic and Magicians* from Beck 1972b (CSCO 320–21): vii. In the few cases where a work that he edited cited a later biblical version, he would note this as an argument against its authenticity. See *Madrashe on Confessors* 9, which cites Exod 20:7 with a variant from the Peshitta of Matt 5:33.

[30] See Brock 1990 and Harvey 2004.

he argued *against* an early work's authenticity.[31] Beck also developed a sense of a closed Ephremic lexicon, and, on its basis, used the presence of hapax legomena to argue against a work's authenticity, or the presence of a particular Ephremic use of a word to argue for a work's authenticity.[32] Finally, in the case of certain poems, Beck argued that their dependence upon post-Ephremic texts demonstrated their inauthenticity.[33]

But these concrete criteria factored minimally as Beck continued to edit the corpus of poetry ascribed to Ephrem. This shift, from a sense that Ephremic authorship could be decided through attention to very specific textual criteria, to a dependence upon criteria far more subtle, developed over the course of Beck's work. The shift can be observed compellingly in his changing treatment of a *memra* 'On the Ihidaye and Desert Dwellers'.[34] Beck first discussed the authenticity of this *memra* in 1958. In this initial treatment, he assumed its authenticity on the basis of concrete criteria – its use of the feminine *rûḥ qûdšâ* ('spirit of holiness') and its use of a certain term, *drāšâ* ('debate'), in a particularly Ephremic way.[35] However, when he critically edited the work fifteen years later, his position had changed. At that time, in spite of the criteria that had suggested its earlier date, he leaned on criteria of a more subjective nature. He identified its style as overly simplistic, pointed to rhetorical techniques that he felt were idiosyncratic, and suggested that it articulated an eschatology out of character with authentic Ephrem.[36] Though the apparently concrete criteria suggested its early date, its style and theology suggested its misalignment with the real Ephrem.

It is in Beck's development of these subtler criteria that we see his notion of Ephrem the author come to life. As Beck's body of critical editions developed, so did a distinct author. His notion of authorship emerged especially when he discussed Ephremic literature whose authenticity he felt could not

---

[31] That is, he would cite the feminine form as an initial point in favour of a work's authenticity, but then cite other evidence to argue for its inauthenticity. See, for example, his discussion of the *Memra on the Word that the Ecclesiastes Spoke* in Beck 1970a (CSCO 305): viii.

[32] See the *Memra on Palm Sunday*, which uses two Greek loan words not otherwise attested in Ephrem (Beck 1970b (CSCO 311): ix–x); 'The Letter to the Mountaineers', which uses the *ṭurāyê*, which Beck argues does not appear in the authentic corpus (Beck 1973 (CSCO 334–35): ix). *Memra on the End and the Judgment*, which uses the word 'Trinity' (Beck 1972b (CSCO 320–21): viii).

[33] Beck argues that *Madrashe on Abraham Qidunaya* 7–15 display knowledge of the Syriac *Acta of Abraham*, which postdate Ephrem (Beck 1972a (CSCO 323): vi). See also the *Memre on Divine Begetting* and *On Holy Week*, both of which bear close similarities to poems by Jacob of Serugh of the same name. Beck 1975 (CSCO 364): vi–ix and Beck 1979 (CSCO 413): 12.

[34] Beck 1973 (CSCO 334–35). Commentary in Beck 1973 (CSCO 335): vi–viii.

[35] Beck 1958: 356–57.   [36] Beck 1973 (CSCO 335): vi–viii.

be taken for granted. The most basic of criteria that he developed – one that he would, however, never articulate outright – was his sense of a canon of indisputably authentic works – mostly *madrashe* – whose authenticity he never called into question or even discussed.[37] This is one of the basic facts of Beck's editing activity that has not been observed but is crucially important to the work he carries out: there are certain works that Beck uses to form the basis of his portrait of Ephrem the author – that demonstrate and distil Ephrem at his most essential – but whose authority in his overall project he never defends. Beck never outlines this internal canon, but we can think of it in two ways – as works that he edited but whose authenticity he never called into question (*Madrashe against Heresies, Madrashe on the Church, Madrashe on Faith, Madrashe on the Fast, Madrashe on the Nativity, Madrashe on Nisibis, Madrashe on Paradise, Madrashe on Virginity*, and *Memre on Faith*), and as a series of works to which he would routinely refer in his delineation of the authentic status of other works.[38] The latter canon is even smaller than the first, consisting especially in the *Commentary on Genesis, Madrashe on Paradise, Madrashe against Heresies, Madrashe on Faith, Madrashe on the Nativity, Madrashe on Nisibis, Madrashe on Virginity*, and *Memre on Faith*.[39] These works played a tremendously important role in Beck's construction of Ephrem the author, and in his discussion of works whose authenticity he felt could not be taken for granted. This internal canon allowed him to construct a basic picture of a single author, with singular commitments and agendas, consistent theological positions, and a consistent and fairly closed lexicon.

Beck's treatment of a *memra* 'On Reproof' provides an example of how this central canon shapes his idea of Ephremic authorship.[40] He admits from the outset that the authenticity of this *memra* is difficult to discern. Ultimately, he argues for its authenticity on the basis of a favourable comparison with passages from the *Madrashe against Heresies, Madrashe on*

---

[37] That is, in his editions of certain works, he would address authenticity before anything else. See, for example, the introduction to Beck 1970a (CSCO 306), which is entirely a discussion of the works' authenticity. However, in his editions of works such as the *Madrashe on Paradise*, he never addresses questions of authenticity at all but simply takes them for granted.

[38] He would also cite in this category the *Comm. Gen.* and *Prose Refutations*, which he did not edit, but whose authenticity he considered incontestable.

[39] These are the works to which he routinely returns when trying to discern the authenticity of a dubious work. Among this collection, the *Madrashe on Paradise*, which Beck refers to as an 'early work', seems to have occupied a special place. It is the work to which he refers more than any other and seems to have taken it to distil Ephrem's essence in a special way.

[40] Beck edits three *Memre on Reproof* in Beck 1970a (CSCO 305-6), all of which he thinks are genuine. I refer here to the second of the three.

Nisibis, and *Memre on Faith*. Compared with the latter, the *memra* 'On Reproof' can be seen to form a single textual unit with Ephrem's genuine canon – the product of a single mind possessed of immense psychological depth, capable of producing striking literary images (more on these latter qualities below). Yet it is essential to note that the corpus that forms the foundation of this comparison is composed of works whose authenticity and relationship to one another Beck never establishes per se. Taking their authenticity for granted, he then extends that authenticity to other works, to include them in, or exclude them from, the canon.

Beck's assumption of a secure, internal canon formed the basis for the other criteria he would use to build a corpus of authentic and inauthentic Ephremic literature. From this internal canon, he developed, first, a concept and a history of Syriac asceticism that would provide one of his most crucial criteria for vetting the works ascribed to Ephrem. Beck laid the foundation for this work in two articles, 'Ein Beitrag zur Terminologie des ältesten syrischen Mönchtums' in 1956 and 'Asketentum und Mönchtum bei Ephraem' in 1958.[41] The first article was concerned primarily with arguing for particular Ephremic meanings for certain ascetic terms. Central to this project was the Syriac term *ihidaya* (plural, *ihidaye*), which derives from the noun *ḥad*, 'one', and carries the basic meaning of 'alone' or 'single'. As Syriac monasticism developed in the fourth through sixth centuries, this term would take on the resonance of 'solitary', 'hermit', and simply 'monk'.[42] In fact, in one of Beck's first published works – a 1951 commentary on the *Madrashe on Paradise* – he translated *ihidaya* with the Latin *eremita*.[43] However, by 1956, his position had changed. In 'Ein Beitrag zur Terminologie des ältesten syrischen Mönchtums', Beck argued that in early Syriac literature – by which he meant Aphrahat's *Demonstrations* (c. 340s) and Ephrem's *madrashe* – *ihidaya* meant, quite simply, 'celibate'. His insistence upon this meaning was connected to his observation that, especially in Aphrahat, the *ihidaye* together formed a group called the 'children of the covenant' (*bnay/bnat qyama*). He took the latter to be a sacramentally integrated 'office' in the Syriac church, as integral to the sacramental community as priests, deacons, and readers.[44] By definition, then, the *ihidaye* could not, in Beck's mind, be hermits.[45]

---

[41] Beck 1956, 1958. [42] On this term, see more recently Griffith 1995. [43] Beck 1951: 70.
[44] Beck 1958: 343–44. Beck's primary source for this is actually not Ephrem, but Aphrahat. Ironically, the only Ephremic source he cites to link the *ihidaya* with baptism is the *Madrashe on Epiphany*, a collection whose authenticity he will otherwise doubt.
[45] Beck 1956 responds immediately to Adam 1953–54, which argued that *ihidaya* sits behind the Greek *monachos*.

In 'Asketentum und Mönchtum bei Ephraem', Beck expanded this primarily linguistic argument into a broader concept of the development of Syriac ascetic culture. As Beck articulated it, the early fourth century offered two distinct and mutually exclusive options: an Egyptian-style monasticism marked by total flight from society (Pachomian, cenobitic monasticism would arise later in response to this), and an early Syriac-style asceticism marked primarily by sexual continence, but which emerged in close physical proximity to the hierarchical, sacramental church.[46] Within the corpus ascribed to Ephrem, a clear chronological and geographical relationship existed between these two movements. Egyptian-style asceticism did not emerge in Ephremic literature until roughly the late 360s, when Ephrem encountered it in Edessa, while Syriac-style asceticism emerged earlier (certainly by the first half of the fourth century) and closer to Persia, and is reflected in the Ephremic literature most safely identified as authentic. This historical schema formed one of the most basic criteria for Beck's assessment of the poems ascribed to Ephrem: those poems that suggested an asceticism firmly connected to the ecclesiastical community were more likely early and more likely authentic, and those that indicated an ascetic flight from society were more likely late and more likely inauthentic. In Beck's view, almost none of the literature that could be safely ascribed to Ephrem registered flight from society as an ascetic virtue. Among the works whose authenticity can be assumed, it is only in the *Madrashe on Virginity* – a work Beck deemed late – that Ephrem even registered the existence of solitary monks.

From Beck's perspective, Ephrem's authorial persona thus developed over time in response to the ascetic cultures he encountered. In his early life, he knew only of a community-based asceticism, intimately connected to the sacraments and the hierarchy of the church. In his later life, having moved to Edessa, he encountered ascetics who had withdrawn from society, living on its outskirts as hermits. In Beck's mind, this development extended beyond Ephrem into pseudo-Ephremic literature that privileged ascetics who had, apparently, cut ties entirely with the gathered community.[47] Beck's chronology of asceticism maps onto, and beyond, the chronology of an author's life.

---

[46] Beck sees antecedents for this pre-monastic valuation of virginity in, for example, Origen and Methodius. However, Beck (1958: 343) sees Syriac Christianity as unique in situating these ascetics right in the middle of the sacramental life of the church.

[47] See his comments on the *Memra on the Ihidaye and the Mourners*, which present the bodies of the ascetics as 'temples of the spirit and their mind churches. / Their prayer is a pure censer

Beck's parsing of the relationship between Ephrem and the history of asceticism inevitably begs questions of authorial development. If Ephrem could have encountered solitary monks late in life, why could he not have come to praise them in the vociferous terms of the works Beck considers pseudonymous? Generally speaking, Beck allowed apparent contradictions and developments in the content of Ephremic poetry when he saw those contradictions as either superficial or emerging from biographical change. For example, he tolerated authentic poetry using rhetorical tropes in different, perhaps contradictory ways, but he could not countenance the idea that the same author would interpret the same biblical passage in different ways or would imagine the afterlife in apparently contradictory ways.[48] The latter sort of evidence suggests, for Beck, a certain degree of inauthenticity.

But Beck thought about Ephrem's development in relation to asceticism in a very specific way. He assumed that the world Ephrem beheld did develop and change, especially as the poet travelled from Nisibis to Edessa, and that that development registered in the content of what he wrote. But though Beck's Ephrem beheld radically new forms of ascetic life in Edessa, Ephrem himself did not change. Beck's Ephrem lived and died as a deacon and hymnographer whose commitments were to the institutional, sacramental, communal church. This assumption of personal stability became important for Beck's vetting of the corpus, especially as he edited works that praised 'late' forms of asceticism, but which appeared in every other

---

and their prayers sweet incense'. The poem goes on to say that the ascetic 'props up his cross and becomes a church' (Beck 1958: 360). This is the second *memra* that he edits in Beck 1973. As this passage makes clear, there is a sense of a normative, eucharistic ecclesiology embedded in Beck's chronological sequencing of asceticism. Alongside the development from an ascetic culture woven into the fabric of the physical, urban church to one that privileged physical seclusion is a connected ecclesiological development from one that privileged the communal, sacramental, hierarchically organised church, to one that saw the ascetic as a self-contained, solitary, sacramental body. At one point, Beck describes the latter ascetics as having been ripped from the sacramental life of the gathered community (1958: 359). Like ascetic hermits, Beck assumes that what he sees as an isolationist, spiritualised ecclesiology developed late, and that it misrepresents the ecclesiological sensibilities of the genuine Ephrem.

[48] See his comments on the third *Memra on Reproof*, which uses a metaphor of the wolf and the bear in a way that contradicts the use of the same metaphor in the second *Memra on Reproof*, which Beck thinks is also authentic. The contradiction troubles Beck, but because it does not concern an idea 'of a general and foundational sort' (*eine Bedenken allgemeiner und grundsätzlicher Art*) he allows both *memre* to stand as authentic (Beck 1970a (CSCO 306): x). However, he notes that in the *Memra on Palm Sunday*, Zion remains asleep when Jesus enters Jerusalem, whereas *Madrashe on Nativity* 6.23 emphasises the city's jubilation. In Beck's mind, both cannot be the product of a single author (Beck 1970b (CSCO 311): x). On eschatology, see below.

way Ephremic. Beck was willing to imagine a scenario in which Ephrem beheld and even praised these 'late' ascetic forms from the outside. But he deemed unquestionably inauthentic any literature in which the 'I' spoke as a hermit.[49]

On the one hand, Beck's argument for Ephrem's stability – his argument for why Ephrem could not have become, for example, a monastic disciple of Julian Saba – depends upon a certain kind of common sense: by the time Ephrem arrived in Edessa, he would have been too old to adopt such a new form of life.[50] On the other hand, Beck based his argument for the stability of Ephrem's life – as a non-monk, non-solitary – on an assumption of a radical division between early, communal and late, solitary forms of life. Commenting on an early Syriac work ascribed to Ephrem that Beck took to be inauthentic – 'The Letter to the Mountaineers', which exhorts monastics to flee the world and not look back – Beck asserts: 'Such words, in the world of Ephrem's Edessan period – the world of the teacher, the hymnographer, the chorus-leader, the advisor to bishops – are *impossible*.'[51]

Alongside Beck's notion of developing ascetic culture – or, rather, his parsing of a corpus that appeared to value contradictory ideals of the ascetic life – Beck developed two similar historiographical notions to organise the corpus ascribed to Ephrem. The first of these involved notions of eschatology and the second a theology and poetics of sanctity.

Like Beck's recounting of asceticism, he saw the eschatology that emerged in the corpus ascribed to Ephrem as manifesting both early authentic and late inauthentic forms. Also like his recounting of asceticism, Beck's charting of eschatological development depended upon his assumption of a core, closed canon of indisputably authentic works that distilled an eschatological vision that was both early and authentic. However, whereas Beck imagined the possibility for Ephrem to have encountered new ascetic styles, and for these styles to have registered in the content of his poetry, he can countenance no possibility for change in the way Ephrem spoke about the afterlife. He argues that genuine Ephremic eschatology manifested two central ideas with an unflinching consistency: first, that body and soul are separated at death, not to be rejoined until the day of judgement; second, that while saints could intercede on behalf of others on the day of judgement, they could not do so before then. This simple schema played a powerful role in Beck's editing decisions. He doubted, for example, the authenticity of a poem 'On the

---

[49] Beck 1958: 357–58.   [50] Beck 1958: 357–58.   [51] Beck 1958: 358. Emphasis mine.

Word which Qohelet Spoke' first on stylistic grounds, but then admitted the subjective character of this criterion. In order to provide objective heft, he pointed to the poem's eschatology, which depicted the soul at judgement immediately after death. In Beck's mind, such a contradiction signalled the obvious inauthenticity of the poem.[52] Another poem, 'On the fear of God and the end', insisted that there would be no intercession on behalf of others on the day of judgement, a position that Beck deems 'impossible' for authentic Ephrem to have articulated.[53] In Beck's mind, eschatology was simply not an area where a single author could contradict himself or change positions.

A final theological idea that Beck used to separate the authentic from the inauthentic involved a poetics of sanctity. As with each of the authentic Ephremic theologies that Beck articulated, this poetics of sanctity built initially from a core, internal canon – specifically, from the *Madrashe on Faith*. The latter consists in eighty-seven hymns that are thought to have arisen between the 350s and 370s in response to the controversies surrounding the divinity of Christ and the Holy Spirit. One of the primary theological characteristics of these hymns is their repeated insistence that God stands beyond human investigation. These hymns do not develop this point in a general way, but through a specific set of terms and formulaic phrases.[54] Given Beck's early work on these *madrashe*, which were one of the first collections he edited, he immediately noticed that in each of the early hagiographical hymn collections ascribed to Ephrem – the *Madrashe on Abraham Qidunaya*, *Madrashe on Julian Saba*, and *Madrashe on Confessors* – this same apophatic language was ascribed to the saints. The poet depicted Abraham Qidunaya's life as transcending the capacity of human speech. Using language identical to the theological language of the *Madrashe on Faith*, the *Madrashe on Confessors* presented the stories of the martyrs as like the sea in their immeasurability. And in the *Madrashe on Julian Saba*, the poet meditated on his own inability to describe Julian Saba, just as the poet of the *Madrashe on Faith* had decried his inability to describe the divine Christ. Witnessing this referential shift in apophatic

---

[52] Beck 1970a (CSCO 305): xi. In this case, he compares this poem with *Madrashe on Paradise* 2.3–5 and *Madrashe on Nisibis* 73.4, both of which suggest that Christ judges all souls and bodies together at the final judgement. Another poem ('On the Solitaries and the Desert Dwellers') presents the souls of solitaries going straight to heaven after death, which Beck cites as evidence for the work's inauthenticity (1973 (CSCO 334–35): viii). He makes the same argument for Memra II in Beck 1973 (CSCO 334–35): vii.
[53] This *memra* also suggests that all will be resurrected as fully developed human beings, against which Beck compares *Madrashe on Paradise* 7.8; 14.10; 14.13.
[54] See Wickes 2019: 24–42.

language from Christ to the saints, Beck could only condemn it as ill-suited to the authentic Ephrem. In the *Madrashe on Abraham Qidunaya*, Beck feels that Ephrem's language has been torn from its authentic context and applied 'in a sometimes even ridiculous manner to the saints and their worshippers'.[55] In his discussion of *Madrashe on Julian Saba*, he refers to it as a 'devaluation of Ephremic images'.[56] While Beck attributed many of the works he deemed inauthentic to the students of Ephrem, these 'ridiculous devaluations' of Ephremic theology he felt could be attributed only to authors who knew the works of Ephrem but had never encountered the poet himself.[57]

The historical frameworks that Beck constructed and placed Ephrem within all implied narratives of decline – from true, ecclesial asceticism to a solipsistic, anti-sacramental, anti-communal asceticism, or from a theological poetics that rightly understood God as the only object of a thoroughgoing apophaticism to one that rhetorically and theologically blurred the boundaries between God and humans. At the most basic level, these histories, by organising an authentic Ephremic corpus and building an inviolable wall around it, also constructed the author of whom this authentic corpus could be predicated. Not surprisingly, the corpus ascribed to Ephrem became wrapped up, in Beck's schema, in the same narrative of decline that marked the world within which it arose. The implication of Beck's vetting of Ephrem's corpus was that he was an original genius who wrote single, unified works of immense sophistication. As the works were transmitted, however, the authentic works became increasingly diffuse – broken down into fragments, which were then reassembled into new, inauthentic works. Or, new, second-rate poets – sometimes students, but sometimes mere imitators with no organic connection to the original genius – simply wrote mediocre poems to which they attached Ephrem's name.

Beck's notion of Ephrem as literary genius played a powerful role in his vetting of the authentic corpus. Quite simply, it meant that he would deem inauthentic any work he deemed to be of low quality, no matter how many concrete criteria of authenticity it met. A *memra* 'On Repentance', for example, consistently cited Old Syriac versions of the New Testament, but was, at the same time, overly simplistic. The latter quality trumped the biblical version, and so the work was deemed inauthentic and late, despite its use of an early biblical version.[58] A *memra* 'On Solitaries and

---

[55] Beck 1972a (CSCO 322–23): vii.
[56] Beck 1972a (CSCO 322–23): xv.
[57] Beck 1972a (CSCO 322–23): xv.
[58] Beck 1970a (CSCO 305–6), *memra* 7.

Mourners', despite its use of the antiquated feminine 'Holy Spirit', and a genuinely Ephremic reading of Gen 28:11, was vetted as inauthentic, and thus late, because Beck saw its style as too simplistic for genuine Ephrem.[59] Beck found the *memra* 'On the Word which Qohelet Spoke' full of 'empty repetitions, prosaic turns of phrase, empty executions of images',[60] and thus inauthentic. He wrestled with the authenticity of a *memra* 'On Admonition', because it betrayed an Ephremic eschatology and its first-person pleading sounded similar to that of the authentic hymns. In the end, however, he remained hesitant to accept its authenticity, because of the poem's 'piety', which he felt contradicted the 'real piety' of Ephrem.[61]

Just as literary mediocrity could damn a work to post-Ephremic inauthenticity, no matter how many indicators of its early date, literary genius could ensure a work's authenticity. Beck argued for the authenticity of a *memra* 'On Reproof' because of its 'psychological depth', as well as its striking imagery and sophisticated rhetorical technique.[62] He admitted that the 'rhetorical prolixity' (*Weitschweifigkeit*) of the *memra* 'On Jonah and the Ninevites' was unique within Ephrem's corpus but felt it such a masterpiece of Syriac rhetoric that its authenticity was likely.[63] Similarly, Beck observed that the text of the *memra* 'On the Sinful Woman' had been tampered with, a quality that usually suggested a work's lateness and inauthenticity. In this case, however, Beck was so taken with the rhetorical skill of certain parts, that he concluded that such parts must result from the hand of the authentic Ephrem.[64] In these cases, Beck's assumptions about literary genius – what it constituted, and also that 'Ephrem' was one – was the primary guiding criterion in his assessment of a work's authenticity

---

[59] Beck 1973 (CSCO 334–35): vii–viii. Beck is also suspicious of the un-Ephremic eschatology that this *memra* articulates.

[60] Beck 1970a (CSCO 305–6): x. He admits that the second part is more impressive stylistically and thus wonders whether the poem is a mixture of authentic and inauthentic.

[61] Beck 1970a (CSCO 305–6): xi–xvi. In distancing authentic Ephrem from the 'piety' of this *memra*, he seems to have in mind primarily what he feels is an overly self-condemnatory tone. The examples in which Beck discounts a work's style could be multiplied. See 'On the Word that Isaiah Spoke' (Beck 1970a (CSCO 305–6), *memra* 6), which Beck says is characterised by pointless repetitions and a generally prosaic style. Beck 1970a (CSCO 305–6), *memra* 7 ('On Repentance') and Beck 1973 (CSCO 334–35), *memra II* ('On the Ihidaye and the Desert-Dwellers') are both overly simplistic. Beck 1973 (CSCO 334–35), *memra I* is disjointed and unclear. In all of these cases, Beck feels this style is ill-suited to authentic Ephremic genius.

[62] Beck 1970a (CSCO 305–6): vii–viii.

[63] Beck says of this *memra*: 'That Ephrem plays here more than usual with these [rhetorical] elements is by no means surprising given his masterly command of the language' (Beck 1970b (CSCO 311): vi).

[64] Beck 1970b (CSCO 311): xi–xii.

and, inadvertently, its early or late date. Rhetorical genius was enough to admit a work into the canon of authenticity, rhetorical mediocrity enough to banish it.

Rerouting Ephrem's Authorship

For Beck, Syriac asceticism, eschatology, sanctity, and literary quality could be categorised according to early and late forms, and Ephrem's corpus thus dated similarly in terms of early and late, authentic, questionable, and inauthentic. Yet scholarship on late antique Christianity since Beck has challenged each of the historiographical foundations upon which he stood in organising Ephrem's corpus. Contrary to what Beck often assumed, for example, about the communal, ecclesial character of fourth-century Syriac Christianity, we can readily find examples of solitary ascetics even in Ephremic works that Beck deemed early and authentic.[65] We know further that eschatology and beliefs surrounding the intercession of the saints were notoriously unstable throughout the late antique and early Byzantine worlds, and that single authors, and certainly whole communities, rarely had systematic, consistent views of the afterlife.[66] The gushing piety that often accompanied the cult of the saints – piety that might seem from a modern perspective to confuse God and the saints – can no longer be dismissed as merely 'popular' or 'superstitious'.[67] We are also increasingly aware of the way that classical aesthetics have led us to denounce late antique literary aesthetics in hasty ways.[68] Finally, scholars have begun to argue against the primarily authorially focused character of patristics and early Christian studies, noting that it leads us to ignore works we deem inauthentic, when those works were often just as valued in late antique society as the works we deem authentic.[69] On each count, then, the context Beck built around Ephrem's authorship and authenticity has been challenged. We are deeply indebted to, and absolutely dependent upon, the work of careful, textual editing that he did. But are there ways to rethink his contextualisation of the texts he edited, especially his organising of them

---

[65] See *Madrasha on Nisibis* 15.9, in which the bishop Vologese is said to be 'holy (*qaddîšâ*) in his body and alone (*ihidaya*) in his house'.

[66] See Filoramo 2014 and Taft 1996.

[67] See Peter Brown's classic critique of our application of 'high' and 'low' to the cult of the saints in Brown 2015, 1st edn, 1981: 13–22.

[68] See Roberts 1989: 1–13. [69] See Muehlberger 2015.

first and foremost according to categories of authenticity and inauthenticity? I would like to suggest three such ways.

The first builds on Blake Hartung's recent suggestion that we organise our study of Ephrem's corpus around metres and melodies, rather than according to the large collections in which the tradition has transmitted them.[70] Pointing out that such collections appear only in the late fifth century and may well have been constructed without any oversight by Ephrem, Hartung makes the persuasive argument that the smaller 'sub-collections' embedded within these later collections likely reflect the earliest stratum of the *madrashe*'s written existence. While these sub-collections are still grouped, through scribal colophons, around the name Ephrem, they use metre and melody as a more fundamental organising principle. Hartung's suggestion thus depends as much upon form – the form of melody and metre – as an organising principle as it does upon authorship and authenticity. Hartung sees this renewed emphasis on sub-collections as providing a path back to the neighbourhood of the fourth-century poems that Ephrem wrote, and so questions of date and authenticity still linger in the background. Nevertheless, his emphasis on the forms of melodies and metres suggests a way out of such foci. The melodies and metres that were attached to the name 'Ephrem' migrated between the works Beck considered authentic and inauthentic, and even beyond the name 'Ephrem'. Intentionally or not, Hartung thus offers a way out of a strictly historicist approach to this poetry, one that can blur the boundaries between – from our perspective – authentic and inauthentic, and the historical boxes of the fourth, fifth, and sixth centuries.

A second approach would see the sometimes fragmentary character of the *madrashe* not as evidence of late decline, but as worthy of study in its own right. Though Hartung emphasises literary form over authorship – and certainly over biography – he still seems to assume a certain intrinsic, superior value to earlier materials. Indeed, one of the most enduring aspects of Beck's project was the way it embedded Ephremic materials in a narrative of decline that mapped onto authenticity and inauthenticity the further values of unity and multiplicity and of literary excellence and mediocrity. Sebastian Brock has characterised the gift of contemporary Ephremic scholarship as precisely its ability to work with the real Ephrem, now salvaged from the literary fragmentation that he experienced after death. Brock wrote: '[I]t is only now, in our own lifetimes, that we are in

---

[70] Hartung 2018. I should disclose here that I directed Hartung's dissertation but did not supervise the research that led to this article.

a position to encounter the real St Ephrem, who has hitherto had to hide behind the misleading medieval tradition where his genuine works had been sadly abbreviated and where many mediocre poems "in the meter of Ephrem" had misleadingly been attributed to him' (2007b: 20).

Brock has pointed especially to eighth- and ninth-century liturgical manuscripts as crucial evidence for the way Ephrem's corpus was corrupted.[71] But he has also shown that such a process can be attested as early as the sixth century and is thus concurrent with the editing of the manuscripts that provide our earliest sources for Ephrem's unified poetry.[72] Rather than reading this fragmentation as an aberration – a mediocre departure from the authentic, unified Ephrem – I would suggest that it poignantly reflects the aesthetic character of the *madrasha*, inclusive of the materials that have been deemed authentic and inauthentic. The *madrasha* is a stanzaic genre, and each stanza is interrupted by a refrain and forms a semantic unit within itself. Sometimes over the course of a whole *madrasha* – a collection of several stanzas – these stanzas seem to form a neat semantic whole, but sometimes not. This characteristic seems to link these poems to late antique culture broadly. Michael Roberts has argued that, unlike a classical aesthetic that privileged 'the unity of the whole, the proportion of the parts, and the careful articulation of an apparently seamless composition', late antique poetry not only let the seams show but blatantly advertised them.[73] This fragmentary character, if freed from the quest for authenticity and chronological development or denouement, can lead us further to recognise the *madrasha* as participating in a wide-ranging late antique poetic culture.

A third suggestion for rethinking our organisation of Ephrem's corpus would be to focus on the poetry – especially the *memre* – that is thematically linked with late antique Syriac poems ascribed to authors other than Ephrem. *Memre* 'On Repentance', for example, are ascribed to Ephrem, Isaac, Jacob, and doubtlessly others.[74] Beck edited two such *memre* ascribed to Ephrem, deemed both inauthentic, and then did not discuss them again. But if we sideline this concern with authenticity, we may well see a tapestry of poems related to one another in surprising ways – perhaps in terms of obvious influence and derivation, but perhaps also in terms of synchronous conversation, networking, and religious debate and dialogue.

---

[71] Brock 1997: 494–97; Brock 1999: 21–22; Brock 2004: 18–19.
[72] Brock 2004: 286.   [73] Roberts 1989: 3.
[74] For Ephrem's *memre* 'On Repentance', see *memre* 7 and 8 in Beck 1970a (CSCO 305–6). For Isaac's, see Bedjan 1903: 76–80, 259–71, 253–59, 127–34, 621–41. For Jacob's, see Bedjan, 1905: 1.646–68, 668–82.

We may also gain new insights into the way late antique poets and readers conceived authorship, as we try to understand why one *memra* 'On Repentance' would get ascribed to Ephrem, another to Isaac, and another to Jacob. Organising material according to form – the metered speech of the *memra* – and content, while it would likely frustrate attempts at periodisation according to centuries, would just as likely reveal modes of organisation that, in our focus on authenticity and chronology, elude us.

Conclusion

In this chapter, I have tried to conceptualise Beck's handling of authorship and authenticity in his editing of Ephrem's works. While Beck's textual editing stands as one of the great achievements of modern Syriac scholarship, his organisation of the corpus around questions of authenticity and authorship depended upon historiographical assumptions that have since been challenged. I have focused in this chapter on the way modern scholars have organised the corpus of Ephrem, rather than on Ephrem's own organising of the world. Yet, my sense is that by shifting our attention away from questions of authorship and authenticity – at least as we understand these ideas – we can begin to imagine other ways of organising late antique literature, ways that may in fact be more sensitive to that literature's own structuring of its world.

16 | Homilies as 'Modes of Knowing': An Exploration on the Basis of Greek Patristic Festal Sermons (*c.* 350–*c.* 450 CE)

JOHAN LEEMANS

Introduction

In Lent of (probably) the year 386 CE,[1] a priest named John, active in Antioch and later nicknamed Chrysostom, was delivering a series of sermons on the opening chapters of the book of Genesis.[2] In what is now extant as the fourth of these sermons, he indulges in a lengthy reflection on various forms of government. This apparently caused the attention of some members of the congregation to drift away, to the extent that John felt the need to reclaim it:

> Wake up there, and dispel indifference. Why do I say this? Because while we are discoursing to you on the scriptures, you instead are averting your eyes from us and fixing them on the lamps and the man lighting the lamps. What extreme indifference is this, to ignore us and attend to him! Here am I, lighting the fire that comes from the scriptures, and the light of its teaching is burning on our tongue. This light is brighter and better than that light; we are not kindling a wick saturated in oil, like him: souls bedewed with piety we set alight with the desire for listening.[3]

As this passage shows, homilies offer fascinating access to the intellectual world of Christian late antiquity. Here the homilist, equipped with *paideia*, rhetorically gifted, and a skilled and enthusiastic interpreter of the scriptures, had been drifting away a bit too far from the subject. Instead, some had directed their gaze and attention to the man lighting the lamps. However lofty the subject and the liturgical context, the homilist had to fight to retain his audience's attention. The homilist was playing the leading role in creation and communication of knowledge, but the audience was not a passive partner. Moreover, the detail of the man lighting the lamps is a salutary reminder that these homilists were not delivered in a void, but in the concrete, material context of a church setting.[4] Homilies were part of a

---
[1] For date and location of this sermon, see Brottier 1998: 11–12.
[2] In this chapter, the words 'sermon' and 'homily' are used as synonyms.
[3] Greek text: Brottier 1998: 238–41; ET: Hill 2004: 72–73.
[4] For this dynamic between church building and rituals, see the beautiful study of Yasin 2009.

concrete liturgical event, with a stable format and accompanying expectations. Here we likely have to do with a priest instructing catechumens on the creation narrative, one of the set topics for the introduction to the faith that catechumens received before their baptism.

In this chapter, I would like to explore the dynamics of the intellectual world into which sermons give us access. This exploration will draw on the corpus of Greek patristic sermons of 350–450 CE. Many sermons from this period still bear the traces of oral delivery and of preacher–audience communication. In later sermons, by contrast, these traces are less visible or have been effaced to disappear completely with the introduction and expansion of the desk sermon.[5] Thus, sermons by preachers such as the Cappadocian Fathers, John Chrysostom, Severian of Gabala, and Proclus of Constantinople offer a double – though dialectically interrelated – access to homiletical modes of knowing: how did the preacher create and order his knowledge and how did he try to get it across to his audience? Moreover, as liturgical texts and part of the liturgy, these sermons are not only theological texts but also a *theologia prima*: a liturgical praxis and theology that precedes the theological reflection in the more academic, content-related sense of the word.[6] In these sermons more happened than reading a text to an audience: the preacher (often speaking *ex tempore*) enveloped his audience into a shared world, as it were, and took them for the duration of the sermon to a spiritual world, detached from the concrete here and now. For the sake of coherence, I will mostly focus on the festal sermons of these preachers: sermons delivered on the main feast days of the church (Christmas, Ascension, Pentecost) and, locally at least as important, festal sermons delivered on the feast days of martyrs.

For my exploration of the intellectual world of these late antique Christian sermons, I will follow four avenues. First, I will highlight the importance of rhetoric and of the scriptures in the tissue of knowledge that these sermons constitute. Next, I will turn to how these sermons are not only part of the liturgy but in themselves liturgical events for which the frontiers between past, present, and future are suspended. Finally, some examples will show that the homilist had much freedom when delivering a sermon but that there were also boundaries to that freedom. Those four avenues offer a broad panorama of what late antique Christians were contributing to the intellectual world of late antiquity and how they achieved this.

---

[5] This gradual transition is well documented in Cunningham and Allen 1998.
[6] I borrow this term loosely from the discipline of liturgical theology as developed by David Fagerberg (e.g., 2004).

Rhetoric and Homilies

Sermons, in oral or written form, are a combination of form and content; both are inseparable, especially when trying to understand the modes of knowing operative within them. Greek Christian preachers of the fourth and fifth centuries CE were skilled and experienced orators, and an appreciation of this is essential to our purpose. Their sermons (and other writings!), however different in style, are deeply indebted to the rhetoric of the Second Sophistic, which they adopted and adapted to their own purposes. Their works can be seen as the result of 'the Christianisation of classical rhetoric': the dynamic interplay between Christian 'content' and classical 'form' that resulted in something new. The influence of the rhetorical handbooks may be observed at the level of the structure of their writings, meaning that they prescribed for many literary genres a list of *topoi* that would be successively addressed or touched upon. The hagio-biographical writings of the Cappadocians and John Chrysostom perhaps exhibit the clearest examples of this.[7] But it is especially the influence of rhetoric on the style of the sermons that is vital to grasp the specificity of the mode of knowing present in them. Indeed, the construction of the sentence, the building of the periods, the search for symmetry and rhythm gave these homilies a melodious sound, in some passages coming close to the hymnic.[8] The ubiquitous presence of these stylistic features and the rhetorical tricks in these sermons together substantially contributed to a theatrical, exuberant character and the love for the stylistic relief typical for the Second Sophistic. The frequent use of the hyperbole, comparisons, periphrastic turns, paratactic and antithetic parallelisms, fictitious monologues and dialogues, and *ekphrases* resulted in an elevated, rhythmic, sonorous language that in some instances must have come close to music. It was a liturgical language that to no small extent helped to get across the message that the homilist was offering as a *Totalerlebnis* to his audience; he was offering them access, through his sermon, to a spiritual world, a world of artistry through which and in which the Christian message of the sermon was evoked and communicated. The style underlined the content but also added to the environment within which the sermon functioned. In short, the rhetoric of the Second Sophistic made a sermon into a liturgical event. Certainly this melodious effect and elevated, exuberant style, replete with the aforementioned stylistic features, was not as strongly present in the different homilists. Asterius of Amaseia, for instance, was definitely less

---

[7] With regard to Gregory's writings, see the literature mentioned in Leemans 2005: nn. 4–7.
[8] For analysis of Gregory of Nyssa's homilies from this perspective, see Klock 1987.

strongly inclined to develop this aspect than Gregory of Nyssa. At the other end of the spectrum, we meet somebody like Proclus of Constantinople, whose poetic, artistic, almost baroque or rococo style announces a seemingly seamless transition to the *kontakia* of Romanos the Melodist.

The following example demonstrates how these stylistic features contributed to the content of the sermon and to the message that the preacher wanted to get across to his audience, as well as to the creation of a liturgical ambiance, to the sermon as liturgical event. The example is taken from the opening of Gregory of Nyssa's *First Homily on Stephen the Protomartyr*, delivered on the traditional feast day of the martyr, December 26th:

Ὡς καλὴ τῶν ἀγαθῶν ἡ ἀκολουθία,
ὡς γλυκεῖα ἡ τῆς εὐφροσύνης διαδοχή.
ἰδοὺ γὰρ ἑορτὴν ἐξ ἑορτῆς καὶ χάριν ἀντιλαμβάνομεν χάριτος.
χθὲς ἡμᾶς ὁ τοῦ παντὸς δεσπότης εἱστίασε,
σήμερον ὁ μιμητὴς τοῦ δεσπότου.
πῶς οὗτος ἢ πῶς ἐκεῖνος;
ἐκεῖνος τὸν ἄνθρωπον ὑπὲρ ἡμῶν ἐνδυόμενος,
οὗτος τὸν ἄνθρωπον ὑπὲρ ἐκείνου ἀποδυόμενος.
ἐκεῖνος τὸ τοῦ βίου σπήλαιον δι' ἡμᾶς ὑπερχόμενος,
οὗτος τοῦ σπηλαίου δι' ἐκεῖνον ὑπεξερχόμενος.
ἐκεῖνος ὑπὲρ ἡμῶν σπαργανούμενος,
οὗτος ὑπὲρ ἐκείνου καταλιθούμενος.
ἐκεῖνος ἀναιρῶν τὸν θάνατον,
οὗτος ἐπεμβαίνων τῷ θανάτῳ κειμένῳ.

How beautiful the succession of goodness,
how sweet the succession of joy!
For look how we receive feast for feast and grace for grace.
Yesterday the Master of Everything entertained us hospitably,
today the Master's imitator is doing the same.
How the former and how the latter?
The former by putting on humanity because of us,
the latter by putting off humanity because of Him;
the former by entering the cave of life because of us,
the latter by leaving the cave because of Him;
the former by being wrapped up in swaddling clothes because of us,
the latter by being lapidated because of Him;
the former by annihilating death,
the latter by trampling upon the allayed death.[9]

---

[9] Gregory of Nyssa, *In Stephanum I* (ed. Lendle, GNO X, 1/2: 75.6–13; ET: Leemans 2005: 121–24).

This passage foregrounds Christ and the Protomartyr using an antithetical construction. The opposition is developed in six couplets. Moreover, each clause of each couplet has at least one keyword in common, which creates an echoing effect. This elaborate symmetrical construction at the beginning of the panegyric is a rhetorical masterpiece, aimed at delighting the audience and satisfying its sense of linguistic beauty and rhetorical ability. Yet it is also more than that: it presents the Protomartyr, the main character of the homily, as an imitator of Christ and it is precisely in this feature that Stephen should be a source of inspiration and a model to follow. Moreover, the repetition of the him–us opposition stylistically underlines the soteriological theologoumenon that Christ's life and death were for our salvation, whereas Stephen's occurred in imitation of Christ's. In this way, this antithesis sets the tone of the homily and directs how Gregory wishes his audience to perceive Stephen: not as a biblical character, but as a laudable imitator of Christ. The elevated style and skilful use of antithesis also opens up space for the sermon to develop as a liturgical event. In the rest of the sermon, Stephen's story in Acts 6–7 will be retold and the audience will be enveloped in it.

Another stylistic feature that is easily detectable in sermons is the *ekphrasis*: a detailed description of an object, a person, a place, or a natural phenomenon that brings it in all precision before the mental eye of the listener, and makes it present in words as if it is really present.[10] Here, too, the preacher can give his rhetorical abilities free rein. But the *ekphrasis* is also used to play on the emotions or to serve other purposes. In his *First Homily on Love for the Poor*, Gregory of Nyssa wants to kindle in the hearts of his congregation feelings of empathy leading to practical support for a large group of refugees who had landed in Nyssa. He describes their fate as homeless beggars in a long, heart-breaking *ekphrasis*. Later in the same homily, he urges his audience to mirror God's *philanthropia* towards humanity in his act of the creation of the world in their own behaviour towards the poor. A long *ekphrasis* of the bounty, beauty, and generosity of creation and its benefit for us (food, clothes, spices) supports Gregory's point. Here again the beauty of his mellifluous, long, paratactic, flowing sentences adds to the greatness and importance of the topic and is instrumental in drawing the audience into the world the homilist is creating for them.[11]

---

[10] The best study on *ekphrasis* is Webb 2009.
[11] Gregory of Nyssa, *De pauperibus amandis I*, ed. van Heck in GNO IX: 96.17–97.9 (*ekphrasis* on the plight of the refugees) and GNO IX: 100.20–102.14 (*ekphrasis* on the bounty of creation).

Bible and Liturgy

A second fruitful avenue to make sense of patristic sermons is to take a closer look at their use of the scriptures. As the Bible is ubiquitous in these texts, the homiletical genre very flexible, and homilists extremely creative, we can only scratch the surface of showing how the scriptures contribute to the communicative power of homilies. The scriptures play an essential role at two levels. First, they constitute the main subject matter of many patristic homilies. Second, they provide a language, a world of images, a reservoir of borrowings that constituted a reference framework common to the preacher and his audience.

The first level is that of the scriptures providing the subject of the sermon. Indeed, many sermons present themselves as an elucidation, a commentary on a scriptural unit, be it an entire book, a chapter, or a single verse. Gregory of Nyssa has sets of homilies on Ecclesiastes, the Song of Songs, the Beatitudes, and the Lord's Prayer. Basil has a set on the Hexaemeron and Chrysostom's sets on the Pauline letters and on Genesis (short and long series) are well known. One should be careful not to jump to conclusions too quickly on the level of initial delivery: some of those sermons were probably delivered consecutively but others (e.g., Chrysostom's on the Pauline letters) were only later brought together in the *seriatim* collection we have today.[12]

Besides these series of homilies, there are a large number of '*in illud* sermons', sermons on one verse or pericope. Often these sermons offer a more or less verse-by-verse commentary on the pericope in question. The corpora of Amphilochius of Iconium and Asterius of Amaseia showcase good examples of this way of proceeding. Here scripture dictates the form of the homily.[13] In Asterius of Amaseia's case, his exegetical sermons so closely follow the scriptural text he is commenting on that in one instance it forms a good argument to postulate that a sermon is incomplete because it breaks off halfway through the pericope.[14] Content-wise, these exegetical sermons vary widely. Depending on the verse and/or the preacher, the content of the sermon may be exegetical, doctrinal, morally exhortatory, spiritual, or, often, a mixture of some of these. In many cases, we do not have a liturgical context for these exegetical sermons. We may surmise that they were tied to a liturgical season (e.g., *Hexaemeron* homilies were part of the catechumens' training during Lent) and that they were following some

---

[12] See Allen and Mayer 1994: 21–39; 1995: 270–89; Allen 1996: 397–421; 1997: 3–21.
[13] On Amphilochius, see also Chapter 17 by Cilliers Breytenbach, this volume.
[14] His *Homily on Lazarus and the Rich Man* (Luke 16:19–31); cf. Speyer 1986: 628.

sort of 'proto-lectionary', the footprints of which can be traced much more firmly in the Latin West through the sermons of Augustine than for the Greek East.[15]

This first level, that of the scriptures providing the subject of the sermon, is quite clear. As mentioned earlier, there also is a second level. The scriptures were an important common frame of reference and a reservoir of arguments, images, and comparisons for the homilist to draw upon whenever he deemed it necessary. Sometimes these biblical exempla or quotations fall out of the blue (at least for today's reader), sometimes there is an associative link, sometimes they are very predictable. It is impossible to do even minimal justice to the wealth and complexity of the contribution of the scriptures to the content of the sermon as a liturgical event. Fundamental here is the versatility of the scriptures and the variety and adaptability of their content. This is enhanced by the homilist's creative freedom to cut out a verse, part of a verse, an expression, or a much longer part of the scriptures, whatever he saw fit given his purpose. All parts of scripture reveal truth; hence, each word, expression, citation, or allusion shares in this hallowed character. Scriptural borrowings not only lend authority to a sermon but, more importantly and often more discretely, also add to it the patina of time-honoured wisdom and truth. Furthermore, the scriptures were part of the liturgy through the readings and, hence, at the forefront of the minds of the audience. Finally, the members of the audience will have had a (varying) degree of religious and biblical literacy, including knowledge of the main storylines and protagonists, key verses, fundamental biblical-theological concepts, and other recurring features and patterns. Against this background, we may now briefly discuss some recurrent ways in which scriptural borrowings are used by homilists.

Let us begin with biblical characters as exempla. Indeed, the use of the main biblical characters – the stories about them and what they stood for (or could be made to stand for!) as biblical exempla – is omnipresent in the sermons. A few passages suffice to illustrate how the Bible inspired a mimetic ethics. In the prologue to the *First Homily on the Martyrs of Sebaste*, Gregory of Nyssa asks his audience the following rhetorical question:

To which of the readings shall I turn my attention in order to find a fitting homily for those present here? Job is of great use in this regard because he teaches the virtue of courage through examples from his own life; the author of Proverbs because he does the same through riddles …[16]

---

[15] For Augustine, see Margoni-Kögler 2010. For Asia Minor, see Leemans and Tamas 2022.
[16] Gregory of Nyssa, *Mart Ia* (ed. O. Lendle, GNO X, 1/2: 137.17–138.2; ET: Leemans et al. 2003: 93).

And in the prologue to Basil's *Homily on Gordius*, we read:

I mean that the life of Joseph is an encouragement to chastity (cf. Gen 39:8), and the tales of Samson [are an encouragement] to bravery (cf. Judg 14:5–9).[17]

These are no singular instances. Job occurs regularly in Gregory's oeuvre as the exemplary personification of the virtue of courage[18] and the virtue of Joseph in resisting sexual temptation in the episode with Potiphar's wife is recounted *in extenso* in Gregory's sermon *The Person Who Commits Impurity Sins against His Own Body*.

A second feature is the connection between biblical pericopes and liturgical feasts. More generally, one may surmise that any local congregation was aware of the main lines of the stories about Jesus' birth, death, and resurrection as well as his deeds and words. Oft-quoted *loci classici* like the beginning of the Johannine prologue were well known and provided hearers with a framework of what to expect, enabling them to recognise major anchor points in the flow of the preacher's words. But especially scriptural key passages related to the main Christian feasts (Christmas, Easter, Pentecost), and their underlying theologoumena (the feast's *hypothesis*) will have been well-known. A fascinating example of a catechetical process that will have deepened the hearer's knowledge is offered in Gregory of Nyssa's *Homily on the Day of Lights* (Epiphany). In this sermon, the Lord's baptism in the Jordan was commemorated and celebrated, but it was also the day on which baptisands-*in-spe* could enrol for the formation period leading to their baptism during the Easter vigil. A substantial part of the sermon is devoted to a very long list – all in all, twenty-five – of scriptural passages from the Old Testament that constitute, in one way or another, a typology of baptism. Each passage is briefly presented and then interpreted to clarify the link with baptism. Moreover, they are ordered according to biblical book and thus offer a panoramic *tour d'horizon* of traditional (and less traditional) Old Testament prefigurations of baptism.[19]

Third, the Psalms contributed to making sermons into liturgical events. They had been sung during liturgy before the sermon and were a constitutive part of the church's liturgy. Their hymnic qualities added to the liturgy as event, and their inclusion in the sermon helped to turn it into a festal sermon. Thus, Gregory of Nyssa's sermons *On Ascension* and *On Pentecost*

---

[17] Basil of Caesarea, *In Gordium* 1 (PG 31: 491; ET: Leemans et al. 2003: 93).
[18] Leemans 2008: 227–44.
[19] Gregory of Nyssa, *In diem luminum* (ed. Gebhardt, GNO IX: 230.19–237.23). I briefly discuss the passage in Leemans 2016a; cf. Hupsch 2016.

have a verse of a psalm that is repeatedly quoted and hence functions as a sort of refrain. The following example from the prologue of Proclus' *Homily on the Incarnation and on the Lampstand of Zechariah* makes clear why the psalms were important for the liturgy of the church, but it also illustrates the role of rhetoric and clarifies how this helps to set a joyful stage for the rest of the sermon:[20]

1. The lyre of the psalms is beautiful; the harp of the Spirit is inspired by God
    (cf. 2 Tim 3:16). The prophetic song is both joyful and fearsome.
The singing of psalms is always salvific, melodiously lulling the passions to sleep.
What the pruning hook is to thorns, a psalm is to sadness.
A chanted psalm shears away despondency and cuts off sorrow at its root.
It sponges away the passions and silences lamentations.
It removes worldly cares,
comforts the suffering,
moves sinners to repentance,
awakens one to piety,
makes cities of the desert,
and chastens those in cities.
It unifies monasteries,
advocates virginity,
teaches gentleness,
lays down the law of love,
blesses love for the poor,
prepares for endurance,
raises to heaven,
fills the church with the faithful,
sanctifies priests,
repels demons,
prophesies things to come,
proclaims mysteries in advance,
and promulgates the Trinity, saying: 'The Lord said to my Lord: Sit at my right
    hand until I make thine enemies a footstool for thy feet' (Ps 109:1). The psalm
    proclaims that the Son sits on the throne of God, it does not denounce the one
    who shares the Father's essence as a ministering servant.
2. This is why the blessed David, while just now singing a hymn
to the inexhaustible nature,
to the omnipotent essence,
the insuperable will,
the grace which does not tarry,
the supreme Creator,

---

[20] Constas 2003: 164–67.

the sovereign Son,
the unconditionally free God,
the Lord subject to none, cried out and said: 'How great are thy works, O Lord! In wisdom thou hast created them all!' (Ps 103:24).
Let Arius and Eunomius, Macedonius and Nestorius be ashamed,
that four-horse chariot of the devil,
those surging summits of heresy,
those rocky reefs of blasphemy,
those shipwrecks of souls,
those hidden ledges of impiety,
those deceitful merchants who upset the balance of the Trinity.
They should listen to David when he says: 'How great are thy works, O Lord! In wisdom thou hast created them all!' (Ps 103:24). David magnifies creation, but those blasphemers diminish the Creator!
Nevertheless, all the works of our Lord Christ are wondrous beyond any expectation, for they are the awesome works of the Word of God, and as a sign of the Creator's power they readily conquer the swiftness of the tongue.

The beginning of the homily explains the many ways in which the singing of psalms may be wholesome for the Christian and therapeutic for the soul. Using Ps 109:1 as a hinge, the homilist then turns to the Psalms promulgating the Trinity. This passage demonstrates that Proclus is not afraid to include in a festal sermon quite intricate theological arguments regarding the Son's divinity, here using Ps 103:24 as a scriptural foundation. This is no exception at all. Proclus, like other homilists, puts forward scriptural arguments in defence of trinitarian and christological claims and did not eschew offering sophisticated theological arguments to a large audience on a big feast day.[21]

Living the Here and Now – Transcending the Here and Now

When delivering a festal sermon, our homilists continuously negotiated the space between the here and now of the present, on the one hand, and the past and the future, on the other. At the epistemological level, one can say, they continuously moved between the temporal and the eternal. The discursive, spiritual world in which they enveloped their audiences had its focal point in the here and now of this particular service in this particular church building in this particular year but, as a liturgical event, stretched

---

[21] For Gregory of Nyssa, I develop this point in Leemans 2009: 61–83.

out to become part of the divine plan of salvation. All aforementioned aspects are not equally strongly present in all festal sermons, but one often finds glimpses even if they are not fully articulated.

The Cappadocians' festal sermons on martyrs are an interesting case in point. First of all, they are firmly grounded in the here and now. The homilist welcomes the congregation in the church, they are praised for having come in large numbers, from near or far. The church building is mentioned and sometimes described in loving detail. The presence of the martyr's relics is highlighted and brief references to the concrete world of daily life strengthen the here-and-now aspect even more. Yet the ultimate purpose of the homilist was to present the martyr as a model of steadfast adherence to the Christian faith in difficult circumstances. To that end, the story of the martyr's life, suffering, and death had to be told in a manner that was generic enough. Omitting particular historical details and using many periphrastic turns to indicate the main characters, the martyr's story was basically reduced to a fight between good and bad, between God and the Devil (and their accomplices). Even the angels lend the martyr support and cheer for him. The story was told with gusto, using all the stylistic features available: hyperbole, fictitious monologues and dialogues, and biblical references. In this way, the audience became part of the story, identified with the hero, and was enveloped in the narrative. It was a story of the past that had become the present and meant to inspire its hearers for the future. With the latter in mind, the audience was reminded of all the good deeds or even miracles the martyr had done for them, and the hope was expressed he would continue to do so. The hearers were encouraged to take the martyr as example for their lives as Christians. Owing to its generic nature, contemporary pastoral challenges could be grafted onto the story of the martyr. Ultimately, even the border of the temporal and the eternal was abolished: the hearers received the promise that the martyr from his heavenly abode would intercede on behalf of the Christian community that was keeping and venerating his relics.[22] In festal sermons delivered on major feast days, we also see this continuous dynamic at work, between past, present, and future as well as between the here and now and the eternal divine salvific plan in which every Christian has a place. Sermons on Pentecost are fruitful material because here, too, we have an 'historical event' (the coming of the Spirit as described in Acts) which has links to the present and the

---

[22] Much of what is summarised here can be read *in extenso* in the general introduction to Leemans et al. 2003. For a survey of how, at the level of discourse, contemporary challenges could be grafted onto the martyr's story, see Leemans 2012.

future as well as being part of both the temporal and the eternal realm.[23] To illustrate this dynamic between past, present, and future, I offer a reading of Proclus of Constantinople's brief Pentecost sermon (CPG 5815).[24]

In this sermon, Proclus reflects on the story of Acts, the meaning of the coming of the Spirit, and the divinity of the Spirit. The sermon is powerful because Proclus skilfully exploits the tension between the biblical 'then' and the liturgical 'now'. A masterful use of style and rhetoric adds to the liturgical power of the sermon. In this way, the homilist not only gets a message across to his audience but envelops the audience in it, makes them part of the message, and exhorts them to embody this Spirit-filled presence in their lives outside the liturgy. *Lex orandi* and *lex credendi* ultimately became a *lex agendi*.

Proclus is an experienced festal homilist. His central theme is the coming of the Spirit with Pentecost and its place in the entire plan of salvation. In developing this theme, he draws on the continuity between the biblical past, the coming of the Spirit to the apostles with the first Pentecost, and the Spirit's continuous presence, 'today', in the liturgical celebration and in the lives of the members of his congregation. This suggests quite a straightforward narrative, but in fact the preacher's train of thought is associative. He is not developing an argument; his concern is to sketch a strongly biblically inspired panorama of the Spirit's role in the history of salvation – past, present, and future.

The opening sentences immediately dive into the main theme:

Today, beloved, the grace of the Holy Spirit has visited us
Having taken its beginning from this very day;
And while increasing in power and strength, is extolled up to this very day.

The opening word 'today' (*sèmeron*) is a common opening of a festal sermon. The reason of the feast is immediately announced: it is the coming of the Spirit that is commemorated and celebrated. The next two clauses develop the *double entendre* of the 'today', which refers both to the historical Pentecost and to the actual celebration: 'Having taken its beginning from this very day; and while increasing in power and strength, is extolled up to this very day.'

---

[23] I have worked this out for Gregory of Nyssa's Pentecost sermon in Leemans 2016a (section 4).

[24] Proclus, *Hom*. 16 (ET: Barkhuizen 2001: 205–9. The text in Migne (*PG* 65: 805–8) is still in use today (and is the basis for Barkhuizen's translation), even though it is a reprint of the 1630 edition by V. Riccardi, based on a single manuscript of the Vatican Library. Since then many new manuscripts have emerged.

There is a clear parallel structure and repetition (*apo tès sèmeron hèméras / mèchri tès sèmeron hèméras*). In this way, Proclus underlines the Spirit's continuous salvific presence. It began with the 'historical Pentecost' and lasts until the very Pentecost on which the sermon is held. This double meaning of the 'today' situates the audience within the sacred realm of a 'liturgical now', which embraces the entire period from the very first Pentecost to the present one. In the rest of the sermon, Proclus explores the topic by brushing a sketchy panorama with three main focal points: (1) a list of biblical exempla; (2) a stress on the divinity of the Spirit; and (3) the presence of the Spirit in the present liturgy and in the baptism that had just been administered. As a skilful liturgist, Proclus does not treat these topics in a discursive manner but rather weaves a tapestry in which the topics are intertwined. The divinity of the Spirit runs as a red thread through the sermon, which is reasonable as his divine nature is the *sine qua non* for the salvific nature of his presence.

With the three mentioned topics in mind, let us now follow more closely how Proclus develops his sermon. Proclus starts with the apostles' speaking in other tongues. He develops this theme extensively: The Spirit's grace emboldened the apostles to fluent speech, it encouraged Peter and the other apostles, and it 'rescues my poor and beggarly mind from timidity', he says. The example of Peter is discussed at length: before the coming of the Spirit, he renounced the Lord in the presence of a maidservant, but after the coming of the Spirit he confessed his faith with boldness. When the Jews judged the Spirit-filled eloquence of the apostles as a sign of drunkenness, the same Peter rebuked them, pointing out that it was only the third hour of the day (Acts 2:13–15).

The motif of 'the third hour' helps Proclus make, by association, a transition to the second main topic of the sermon: the divinity of the Spirit, which really is the core theme of the sermon and of many other Pentecost sermons.[25] The divinity of the Spirit is argued for on the basis of five scriptural arguments, all tied to the story told in Acts. First, the coming of the Spirit at the third hour of the afternoon, as we read in Acts, was not a coincidence but (almost) a decision of the Trinity. The cross had been planted on the third hour and therefore the Spirit also 'came to rest upon the disciples in the third hour'. Second, the Spirit came in the form of fire. This, too, is a sign of his divinity, as we read in Heb 12:29 that 'our

---

[25] This is the case in Pentecost sermons by Gregory of Nazianzus, Gregory of Nyssa, Severian of Gabala, John Chrysostom, Proclus of Constantinople, and Leontius of Constantinople (Leemans 2016b).

God is a consuming fire'. Third, a sound came from heaven, like the rush of a mighty wind (*pnoè*) (Acts 2:2). This happened, Proclus comments, 'in order that it might be revealed that the Spirit is God'. The fourth is a lengthy and quite intricate scriptural argumentation, introduced by the words 'be instructed (*didachthèti*) that the Spirit is God'. The argumentation is based on a condensed version of Isa 6:1–10. The quotation opens as follows: 'I saw the Lord sitting on a high and lofty throne. And the seraphs stood around him. And he said to me: "Who will go to this people and whom shall I send to them? For the heart of this people has grown dull and their ears are hard of hearing".' Proclus connects this quotation from Isaiah with Acts 28, where the following statement is put into Paul's mouth: 'The Holy Spirit was right in saying concerning you [the Jews in Rome] through Isaiah the prophet: you shall indeed hear but never understand.' Proclus identifies the Isaiah quotation referred to in Acts 28 with the one from Isaiah 6 quoted above. From this it follows that the 'I' and the 'me' in the Isaiah quotation can be identified with the Spirit who, hence, was also 'sitting on a high and lofty throne'. He is, in other words, on par with the Lord. The conclusion must be that the Spirit shares the divine nature, that he is 'both Lord and God'. A fifth and final argument in favour of the Spirit's divinity is that in many other scriptural passages the Spirit is often mentioned in one breath with the other persons of the Trinity, as in Ps 32:6: 'the heavens were established by the word of the Lord, and by the Spirit of his mouth all their might'.

Next Proclus transitions smoothly to his third main topic: the presence of the Spirit after Pentecost in general and in baptism in particular. For one of the archetypal scriptural passages in which the Trinity as a whole is present is, of course, Jesus' baptism in the Jordan. The Father's voice speaks from the heavens above, the Son is present, and so is the Spirit, in the form of a dove.

In the final section of the sermon, Proclus again mentions the fiery tongues of the Pentecost narrative of Acts. In line with many homilists before him, Proclus interprets these fiery tongues as a distribution of the charismata: 'This Spirit distributes the gifts of all blessings, apportioning to each one individually as he wills' (the latter half is a quote from 1 Cor 12:11). Proclus thus briefly mentions the role of the Spirit in the life and work of the apostle Paul, in inspiring the archangel Gabriel in the Lukan infancy narrative, and in the blinding of the magician Elimas (Acts 5:4). The examples are seemingly chosen at random yet illustrate the continuous work of the Spirit. Proclus then ends his sermon as follows:

And may he also now come upon us and bless us.
For he is blended with the water,
And melts away our sins like a fire,
And shines on the newly enlightened like a light,
And is merciful towards us as God,
Because glory and power beseem him forever more. Amen.

The sermon ends with a prayer for blessing. The focus is on baptism and on the Spirit's salvific presence in the water that will cleanse the newly baptised and melt away their sins. Yet Proclus' prayer extends beyond this baptism. He also prays that the Spirit may also come to rest upon 'us' (the congregation and its bishop) and that he may bless 'us'. As the Spirit is 'merciful as God', Proclus takes for granted that God's Spirit indeed is present to bless his congregation abundantly. In this way, at the end of the sermon, he has arrived at the today of his own day, of the very feast of Pentecost that is being celebrated at that very moment. God's Spirit, this divine salvific power that had been given to the disciples at Pentecost, has finally reached the Constantinopolitan church in which Proclus' congregation is listening to their preacher. Beginning from the 'then', he finally arrives in the 'now' of the present. The liturgical power of this sermon lies in the continuity Proclus establishes between the then and the now, a continuity that is not historical but theological and liturgical in nature. In this way, a mode of knowledge is shaped that goes far beyond the purely cognitive aspect. The hearer of this sermon is wrapped into the preacher's flow of words that opens up a panorama, a reality to become part of, that is ultimately no longer a human reality but a divine one in which humans are invited to participate. It is a participatory, experiential knowledge of humans partaking in the divine plan of salvation.

The Preacher's (Un)limited Command of Homiletic Modes of Knowing

From what has been said so far, it emerges that the preacher was the one who was ordering the knowledge and offered it through sermons to his audience in the way he wanted. By and large this is correct: in the dynamic between the preacher and his congregation, the homilist was the one pulling the strings. He had considerable liberty in choosing the topic of his sermon and the way he wanted to approach and structure it. There are even quite a few instances where the homilist did something rather unexpected when he wanted to. One can think here of Chrysostom, who made, when preaching on the creation narrative, an excursus on various forms of government (as in the passage at the beginning of this contribution). This suggests an almost unlimited power for the homilist. This seems to have been especially the case with sermons on martyr festivals when the congregation may have expected an encomium on the martyr of the day but found the homilist seizing upon the opportunity of having a large crowd to do something entirely different. Basil of Caesarea's *Homily on Psalm 114* is a good example. The introduction of this homily informs us that it was delivered on the occasion of a *panèguris* on which the presence of the Caesarean bishop was expected. The congregation was present in church at midnight, but Basil did not show up before noon of the following day. In his homily, he congratulates the people because of their patience during this long time of waiting and because they put the veneration of the martyrs above their sleep. The text mentions that while the congregation was waiting, they had been singing psalms.[26] When Basil finally arrived, the people were singing Psalm 114. Basil did not deliver a homily on the martyr or martyrs whose feast day was celebrated but discussed, after an apology for his late arrival, the psalm that the congregation had been singing when he entered the church. He promised to keep his homily rather short, as to allow people to go home and take some rest.[27] The Caesarean bishop's *Homily on Julitta* is similar. Basil keeps the first part of his homily, in which he treats the deeds and merits of Julitta, a female martyr from Caesarea, extremely short and then continues his sermon of the day before on the importance of performing acts of gratitude.[28] Asterius of Amaseia opens his *Homily on Avarice* with a reflection on the spiritual importance of *panègureis* but then moves quickly to the theme of avarice, the topic of the previous day to which also the lions' share of this homily is devoted.[29]

But the homilist was not always in full control of the sermon. Sometimes he was forced by the situation to improvise. A priori, this is not surprising

---

[26] Basil, *Homily on Psalm 114*, 1 (PG 29: 484 A9–B2; ET: Way 1963: 351): 'Having arrived so long in advance at these sacred precincts of the martyrs, you have persevered from midnight until this midday appeasing the God of the martyrs with hymns, while awaiting our arrival. The reward, therefore, is ready for you, who prefer honor for the martyrs and the worship of God to sleep and rest.'

[27] Basil, *Homily on Psalm 114*, 1 (PG 29: 484 B13–C4; ET: Way 1963: 351): 'In order that we may not be distressed at detaining you further, after discoursing briefly on that Psalm which we found you singing on our arrival, and feeding your souls with the word of consolation according to the power that is ours, we shall dismiss all of you for the care of your bodies.'

[28] The sermon is edited in PG 31: 237–62. The part about Julitta is PG 31: 237–41 (chs. 1 and 2).

[29] Datema 1970: 27–37. Only the *prooemium* (p. 27) touches upon the occasion of the *panèguris*.

at all: a bishop had to preach two to three times a week (at least), so it is logical that he could not always be well prepared. Moreover, his experience as a homilist, his theological and rhetorical training, had prepared him for this role. Furthermore, often there were stenographers who took notes of the sermon and thus allowed the homilist to revise it and have an 'authorised copy' circulated. Improvisation was thus part and parcel of patristic sermon delivery and it belonged to the homilist's skills to cope with it.[30]

In the extant patristic sermons, we find extraordinary cases of improvisation that may have been less exceptional than one might think. A first fascinating example of improvisation on the homilist's part is offered by Basil's *Homily on Mamas*. About this martyr nothing specific was known except that during his life he had been a shepherd. Moreover, it was one of the first times that Basil had to preach Mamas' *panèguris*.[31] He thus had no earlier exempla to hark back to. Basil solves the problem by keeping his homily short and expounding largely and in general on the gathering of the *panèguris*. In the ensuing parts, he treats some biblical shepherds, discussing their merits and shortcomings, and ends with the topics of Christ as the Good Shepherd and the heretics as bad and untrustworthy shepherds.[32] All in all, a not very original, even predictable approach. But there is more. To nurture his audience's ardent veneration of Mamas, Basil solves the problem of his lack of knowledge on Mamas by creating for the congregation the possibility of informing each other. In the beginning of his homily, he asks everybody to remember all that they know about the martyr and to join all these pieces of information in a kind of common oration in praise of Mamas.[33] He encouraged them to try to remember how often Mamas appeared to them in a dream, how much support they received from him, how many sick people he cured, travellers he protected, dead children he resurrected from the death: 'Share with each other: anybody who knows (should share) with somebody who doesn't and he who does not know must receive from he who does. In this way you must by putting together (your knowledge) feed each other and thus meet our weakness.'[34] This brainstorming *avant la lettre* provides fascinating insight into the concrete reality of a particular liturgical service.

We find an even more radical interruption in John Chrysostom's *On Eutropius*. When the powerful Eutropius, who had been one of Chrysostom's

---

[30] Olivar 1991: 589–641; Hammerstaedt and Terbuycken 1996: 1212–84.
[31] On the date of this homily, see Troiano 1987: 147–57.
[32] Cf. the edition of this homily in PG 31: 589–600.
[33] Basil, *On Mamas* 1 (PG 31: 589C–D5). [34] Basil, *On Mamas* 1 (PG 31: 589D1–5).

main enemies in Constantinople, had fallen out of imperial favour, he rushed into the church where Chrysostom was presiding at a liturgical service and preaching. John interrupts the flow of his sermon and turns it into a vehement plea for Eutropius' right of asylum in the church, even though he had tried earlier on to take away any legal foundation for it.[35]

A dramatic example of improvisation going awfully wrong is offered by Gregory Nazianzus's *Oration in Praise of Cyprian*. Gregory delivered this sermon when he was presiding over the small Neo-Nicene congregation of the Anastasia Church in a predominantly Arian city. He was not aware of the details of the liturgical calendar (or didn't pay enough attention to it), and hence he had almost forgotten about the feast of St Cyprian. Rushing back to the city (he had sought some peace and quiet outside it), he had not had time for a solid preparation. The result is surprising: the Cyprian whom Gregory presents to his audience is a Janus figure, half the famous bishop of Carthage, half a far less illustrious homonymous martyr of Antioch.[36] Gregory of Nyssa's *Christmas Homily* and, more clearly, his *Against Those Who Deal with Rebukes with Difficulty* are other examples of Cappadocian sermons with a great deal of improvisation at work.

Some passages go one step further and indicate that the homilist had his freedom reined in by the audience and had been forced to adjust the content or *ductus* of his sermon. A spectacular example can be found in Gregory of Nyssa's *First Homily on the Forty of Sebaste* (Ia). Gregory's Sebastene audience, by cheering and applauding, was making a lot of noise. In the text, one can follow how he tried to cope with the problem. At first, he asked his audience to be quieter, likening them to the noise of the sea that could not be overcome by his voice; but when this did not help, Gregory had no other choice than to end his homily almost before he had embarked on the subject.[37] The next day he resumed his sermon, referring back to what happened the day before and, this time, delivering the rest of the sermon according to plan.

Basil of Caesarea's homiletical oeuvre contains two beautiful illustrations of how interaction with his audience led to a change in the direction of the sermon. In his *Eighth Homily on the Hexaemeron* he reacts to non-verbal communication from his congregation. Apparently, some members of the congregation were able to follow Basil's train of thought in great detail and they caught him on something he had overlooked and forgot to comment

---

[35] John Chrysostom, *In Eutropium* (PG 51.2: 391–96).
[36] Gregory of Nazianzen, *In laudem S. Cypriani* (Mossay and Lafontaine 1981: 40–85, esp. 40–41); cf. Bernardi 1968: 161–62.
[37] In the GNO edition by Lendle (GNO X, 1/2), the passage runs from 141.27 to 142.16.

upon. They first looked at each other for confirmation that they had indeed understood him well; then they got his attention by signs of their hands and by moving their heads. Basil understood what these listeners wanted to convey to him. He interrupts his sermon and explains to his audience what had happened and why he stopped speaking. Then he gives his attentive interlocutors their due before continuing the sermon.[38] A more dramatic example is offered by Basil's sermon *On Detachment*, delivered (probably) in July 372 to a congregation in Armenian Satala. In the long first part of his sermon, he addresses especially the more well-to-do members of his audience, exhorting them to give alms to the poor and to be more sensitive in general to their fate and plight. When Basil is about to bring his sermon to a close and pronounce the doxology, his audience protests. The day before, a fire had destroyed part of the city, including houses of some Christians present in church who faced poverty as a consequence of the fire. Especially given the train of thought Basil had developed so far, it is understandable that the audience expected Basil to address the issue and to speak words of advice, support, and consolation. So Basil does exactly that; in dialogue with his audience he treats the theme that his audience had more or less imposed on him and he does so in dialogue with them.[39]

Finally, there is a hint that Gregory of Nyssa treated a pressing pastoral and theological problem at the end of his *First Sermon on the Forty of Sebaste (Mart Ib)* because he had been asked to do so by one of the members of his congregation.[40] The passage concerns Gen 3:24, a hotly debated verse,[41] in which we read that after Adam's expulsion from Eden, cherubim with revolving fiery swords were guarding the entrance to paradise. This raises the question: if the gates to paradise are guarded that well, how will the martyrs get access to it and, a fortiori, how will eventually, maybe, ordinary Christians? Will it be possible at all? The matter is even more complicated by Jesus' promise to the 'good murderer' that 'today you will be with me in Paradise' (Luke 23:43 NRSV). So apparently it *is* possible. But how? Gregory had dealt with Gen 3:24 a few days earlier in a sermon (*prôèn*) with insufficient detail or without coming to a satisfactory exposition. Apparently, aspects had been left unaddressed or open, and this urges him to come back to it on this later occasion. He does not explicitly

---

[38] Basil of Caesarea, *Homilia VIII in Hexaemeron* 2 (Giet 1968: 436–38).
[39] Basil of Caesarea, *Quod rebus mundanis adhaerendum non sit* (ed. PG 31: 540C–564B). The *caesura* between parts I and II is at ch. 9 (PG 31: 556C).
[40] Gregory of Nyssa, *Mart Ib* (ed. O. Lendle (GNO, X, 1/2, 155.20–156.20).
[41] A detailed survey of the history of interpretation from Philo onwards is offered by Alexandre 1986.

mention that he is acting on the request of members of his congregation, but this seems plausible for four reasons: (1) it is a very precise topic; (2) there is a pressing pastoral and theological problem behind it (access to salvation); (3) from other passages we know Gregory was in the thick of his parish members and receptive to their questions and concerns; (4) the passage reveals uneasiness in having to come back to this, a bit of a hesitant, difficult transition from the main topic of the sermon. It feels a bit like an afterthought, a tacked-on addendum. So, at the end of his sermon on the Forty, which he cuts short for this reason, Gregory addresses the question (*zètèma*) prompted by Gen 3:24 and, probably drawing on Basil's ideas,[42] he solves it. He acknowledges that Gen 3:24 raises serious problems and that the interpretation of those fearing for a more difficult access to salvation is legitimate. Yet, there is no danger: access to paradise for the Forty and for all good Christians is guaranteed because the cherubim are holding revolving swords, meaning that with some cleverness and carefulness these can be evaded. The saints will have access to paradise in this way and so will ordinary Christians, as Gregory shows by the final words of the sermon, before the doxology, in which he expresses the wish that, thanks to the prayer of the Forty, many may be granted access to paradise.

Conclusion

In this exploratory chapter, I have documented some modes of knowing in patristic sermons, mainly from the Cappadocian Fathers. In the process, I hope to have shown the dynamic character of sermons, the flexibility of the genre, and the endless possibilities that it offered to the preacher to spread the word of God and inspire his audience, drawing them into the liturgical and spiritual world that he created for them. In so doing, I have followed four avenues. First, I underlined how apt use of rhetoric structured the sermon and shaped it stylistically so that it had a sonorous effect that added to its melodious tone. Second, I showed how the role of the scriptures is pivotal in the process of creating the sermon, both by determining it with its subject and by providing images, comparisons, metaphors, and stock verses. In brief, the scriptures provide a common reference work for preacher and audience. Especially the Psalms were instrumental in making sermons into a liturgical experience for the hearers. Rhetoric and the scriptures were the two key elements to make sermons into something

---

[42] Basil of Caesarea, *Exhortatio ad baptismum* 2 (ed. PG 31: 428C1–10).

more than just a transfer of cognitive knowledge. This is supported by a theological and liturgical epistemology, in which the sermon transcends the concrete here and now to encompass the past, present, and future of God's plan of salvation for humanity. The last section has shown how the preacher was also not unlimited in being the master of the mode but was at times confronted with situations that put limitations on him in this role. The master of the mode of knowledge was not so much an absolute monarch but, at best, also a servant of the Word and of his congregation.

17 | Dissemination of Biblical Narratives, Motifs, and Figures through Early Christian Inscriptions and Homilies

CILLIERS BREYTENBACH

Introduction

How was Christian knowledge, including specific narratives and motifs from the Bible, used in early Christian inscriptions and in the homilies of Amphilochius, bishop of Iconium in the later fourth century? Early Christian knowledge circled around the Bible. Unlike, for example, the Elysian mysteries, where participation in the procession was the main event, early Christianity did not circle around ritual. It was a movement that filled a cognitive space, mediation of knowledge being a major aspect of their religion (1 Cor 15:1–2; Matt 28:19–20). Baptism and the Lord's Supper were integrated into the proclamation of Jesus' death, lordship, and *parousia*. This tradition of proclaiming, teaching, and instructing intensified with the development of the formal instruction during pre-baptismal catechesis in the third century.[1] Bishops and presbyters were required to know the narratives from the Greek translation of the Hebrew Bible and to teach what Jesus and the apostles taught. Biblical texts thus played a decisive role in this instruction, and bishops and presbyters and readers (or lectors) were vital to mediate this content. For the ability to read, Christians relied on Hellenistic education and some Christians were rhetorically trained. Such orators contributed decisively to the dissemination of knowledge of the Bible through sermons attended by large congregations, especially on festive occasions like Easter. The homilies of the late fourth-century bishop Amphilochius of Iconium serve as an example.[2]

I thank my student assistant Anamika Wehen for her tireless support in helping me to get access to literature in the Corona year and for editing and proofreading the final manuscript. I also thank the following persons and institutions for the cordial permission to reprint the following illustrations: Fig. 17.1: Charlotte Roueché; Fig. 17.2: Ephorate of Antiquities of Magnesia; Figs. 17.3–17.5: Verlag Dr Rudolf Habelt, Bonn; Fig. 17.6: Epigraphic Museum at Athens; Fig. 17.8: Christian Wallner; Plate 17.1: Prof Sheila Campbell, Pontifical Institute of Mediaeval Studies, Toronto.

[1] On Christian education generally, see Gemeinhardt 2016.
[2] On the role of bishops and presbyters in teaching, see Breytenbach and Zimmermann 2018: 589–94, 585–86, 602–3.

Iconium was at the centre of an area of ancient Asia Minor which left us with thousands of epitaphs marking the graves of Christians and several building inscriptions from early Christian churches.[3] The numerous scriptural allusions and citations in this epigraphic evidence vividly illustrate the knowledge and use of scripture in specific locations and among ordinary Christians. Taken together, the homilies of Amphilochius and the Christian inscriptions show that specific passages from the Bible formed the nodes of an interrelated network of scriptural knowledge that Guy Stroumsa aptly described as ancient Christianity's 'scriptural universe'.[4]

Dissemination of Knowledge of the Scriptures in Inscriptions

Following ancient practice, early Christians inscribed tombstones with funerary epitaphs, added inscriptions mentioning the donors to new or renovated buildings (sometimes as part of larger mosaics), and set up stones inscribed with invocations and prayers. These inscriptions were meant to be read – by those passing by the graveyard next to the road leading out of the city, by those entering the church passing under the inscribed lintel, by those setting foot on its mosaic floor, by those standing around the inscribed baptismal font or coming to receive the Eucharist. Sepulchral epitaphs, building inscriptions, and votive inscriptions mention the names of the deceased, the bereft, the donors, or the dedicators.

This chapter focuses on Christian inscriptions, specifically on explanatory inscriptions referring to biblical narratives or on inscriptions citing or alluding to the Bible. Although few and far between, there are also Jewish inscriptions citing the Bible.[5] So when is an inscription Christian? Crosses are, of course, one of the major indicators that a monument is Christian.[6] Other indicators are the occurrence of terms like bishop, presbyter, or deacon[7], a *nomen sacrum*,[8] Christ monograms (⳩), staurograms (⳨),[9] an alpha and omega, or various combinations of these signs, as, for example, the inscriptions from Néa Anchiálos close to Thebes in Thessaly.[10] It is

---

[3] On citations from the LXX in Christian inscriptions from Asia Minor, see Breytenbach 2012. Christian inscriptions are referred to by their *Inscriptiones Christianae Graecae* (= ICG) numbers. The 2019 repository of ICG can be consulted at: http://repository.edition-topoi.org/collection/ICG. The fuller current database can be consulted under https://icg.uni-kiel.de.
[4] Stroumsa 2016. [5] See van der Horst 2014. [6] ICG 3821, 3836.
[7] ICG 3828, 3822, 3829. [8] ICG 3823. [9] ICG 3824.
[10] ICG 3814: Μη⟨μ⟩- Α ⳨ Ω -⟨ό⟩ριον | Δομνίνου. The staurogram is part of a cross.

not necessary to rehearse the criteria for identifying Christian inscriptions here, since they have been treated elsewhere.[11]

What distinguishes Christian inscriptions from many non-Christian epitaphs is that, rather than drawing on Homer and Hesiod, they often show the influence of the Bible on names and the form of invocations and allude both to biblical narratives and to figures in those narratives and other motifs from biblical texts. A mode of scriptural knowledge is reflected in many inscriptions. Several deceased or bereft in funerary epitaphs and several donors mentioned in building inscriptions had biblical names. As such, naming was an important mode of transferring biblical content in ancient Christianity. Their naming practice kept alive the memory of Mary, Paul, Peter, John, Andrew, Stephen, Susanna, and Thomas and of the narratives in which they were embedded. We shall, however, not explore this further here[12] but, rather, turn to the influence of biblical phrases and narratives on the texts of Christian inscriptions.

That the Greek translations of the Hebrew Scriptures played a major role in early Christianity is well known. When 'Paul' instructs 'Timothy' 'to give attention to reading, to exhorting, and to teaching', in 1 Tim 4:13, 'reading' (ἀνάγνωσις) most probably refers to public reading from scripture. Paul's letters and the Apocalypse were meant to be read in Christian assemblies. Through reading in Christian assemblies, the Pauline letters and an early narrative on Jesus' passion and crucifixion leading the way, those texts that were to become the New Testament also gained influence.[13] 'From the first to the fourth century CE, the material support of the book underwent a dramatic change, in the passage from *volumen*, or roll, to *codex*.'[14] Papyrus codices of the Pauline corpus are attested since the second century and of the gospels since the third.[15] There is even iconographic evidence for the importance of a holy book in early Christianity. On the Lycaonian-Isaurian border, codices were depicted on Christian gravestones as early as in the third century,[16] and in Messene on the southwestern Peloponnese the lector Paramonos donated a mosaic floor for a room where books were kept.[17] Christianity became a religion of the

---

[11] See Breytenbach and Zimmermann 2018: 8–13.
[12] See Breytenbach and Zimmermann 2018: 399–418.
[13] See $\mathfrak{P}^{46}$ and $\mathfrak{P}^{75}$. On the emergence of the Christian canon, see Schmid and Schröter 2019: 338–56.
[14] Stroumsa 2016: 12; cf. 14–15. But see also recent arguments for somewhat later dating of each of these examples, e.g. in Nongbri 2018.
[15] See $\mathfrak{P}^{46}$, $\mathfrak{P}^{45}$, and $\mathfrak{P}^{75}$.
[16] ICG 811 (Aydoğmuş), 984 (Alisa). See Breytenbach and Zimmermann 2018: 199–200, 203.
[17] ICG 3482.

book, a textual community.[18] For early Christianity, the Bible was primarily a liturgical book, lections from it were read, phrases from it used in prayer, and biblical passages interpreted in liturgical settings. On the other hand, '[T]he Bible was considered as the foundation of Christian liturgy, and deeply influenced its development'.[19]

The recourse to scripture guides and authorises the liturgical action. From Greece to eastern Asia Minor, inscriptions kept the words from the Psalms present to literate Christian clergy who could read them out loud during assemblies of the Christian communities.[20] Scripture was not used in isolation. Its use in inscriptions reveals that the citation of or allusion to scripture or the use of scriptural phrases were intertwined with other aspects of Christian teaching and piety. Scripture was used, for example, to praise God or in invocations for help. In a broad sense, one can say that in such cases it was used in the context of prayer, 'praying by the scriptures and with the scriptures'.[21] Several fifth- or sixth-century inscriptions quote lines from the Greek translation of the Hebrew Bible. A few examples should suffice. The benediction εὐλογητὸς ὁ θεός occurs on an arch found in Anazarbus in Cilicia.[22] It also introduces the epitaph on the gravestone of a lector from Athens with the biblical name 'John'.[23] Using a phrase from the Psalms,[24] Heraclius from Savatra in Lycaonia invokes God in his sorrow for the loss of his beloved brother named after the apostle Paul: θε(ὸς) βοήθι.[25] Such benedictions and invocations for help document the influence of the Bible on the prayers of early Christians.[26]

Psalms are used in other contexts too. Ps^{LXX} 117:20 ('This is the gate of the Lord; righteous ones shall enter in it'[27]) is quoted on lintels above the entrance doors of many early Christian churches: from Corfu (Κέρκυρα) in the west, from Athens, and as far as Thebasa on the eastern edges of Lycaonia, some from the fifth century.[28] By the end of the fourth or sometime in the fifth century, Ps^{LXX} 42:4 ('And I will go in to the altar of God, to God

---

[18] See Stroumsa 2016: esp. ch. 4, 'Scripture and Culture'.
[19] Rouwhorst 2013: 824; cf. 840–42.
[20] If one would regard the Eucharist and baptism as cult, G. Stroumsa's catchy 'book as cult' would apply here. See Stroumsa 2016: 15: 'In the religious culture of late antiquity, books had important performative aspects, such as their role in public ritual, both in the synagogue and in the church.'
[21] Stroumsa 2016: 85.   [22] See Breytenbach 2012: 278.   [23] ICG 2193.
[24] Ps^{LXX} 53:6; 69:6; 78:9; 93:18; 108:26; 118:86, 117.
[25] ICG 537 with comment in Breytenbach and Zimmermann 2018: 232–33.
[26] For more examples, see Breytenbach 2012: 283–85, 287–90.
[27] Ps^{LXX} 117:20: αὕτη ἡ πύλη τοῦ κυρίου, δίκαιοι εἰσελεύσονται ἐν αὐτῇ (NETS).
[28] See ICG 4154, 1879, and 733. More examples east of the Amanus in Breytenbach 2012: 285–86.

who gladdens my youth') is quoted in two mosaics on the floor of a basilica in Pisidian Antioch.[29] From the fourth century on, Ps^{LXX} 28:3 ('The voice of the Lord is upon the waters') is quoted on stoups or baptismal fonts over a wide area,[30] indicating that the baptismal water has a life-saving effect, since the voice of the Lord is upon the water. The water goes along with his word.[31] From these examples it becomes clear that over a wide area, entrance into the church, approach to the altar, or gathering around the baptismal font were all placed 'under' phrases from the Psalms.

The majority of our examples are from the fifth century, when more Christian church buildings rose. The practice of disseminating biblical language in prayers praising God and invoking his help, however, reaches back to the apostolic age.[32] The use of the Psalms from the LXX to define ecclesiastical space sets in with the earliest extant churches. The context, in which they were mediated, seems to be 'liturgical'. This use was not confined to Attica and Asia Minor but was an ecumenical phenomenon.[33] Next to the Psalms, the book of Isaiah was also integrated in liturgical practice. This can be briefly illustrated further by examples from Phrygia.

Citations from Isaiah and the Psalms in Inscriptions from Liturgical Contexts in Southeast Phrygia[34]

An inscription from a church in Afyonkarahisar in southeast Phrygia that quotes Isa^{LXX} 1:16–18 might be from the fifth century.[35] Isa^{LXX} 1:16–18 is not quoted in the NT, but it became important in Christian writings from the end of the first until the later part of the fourth century.[36] Because of the initial phrase λούσασθε καθαροὶ γένεσθε ('Wash yourselves, become clean!') in Isa 1:16, it was quoted explicitly in connection

---

[29] ICG 1334A: καὶ εἰσελεύ|σομαι πρὸς | τὸ θυσιαστή|ριον τοῦ θεοῦ· B. πρὸς τὸν θε[ὸν] | τὸν εὐφ[ραί]| νοντα τ[ὴν]| νεότητ[ά μου]. See also ICG 4160. For the quotation of Ps^{LXX} 5:8 within the mosaic floor of a Byzantine church in Arycanda in Lycia, see Breytenbach 2015.

[30] E.g., ICG 1093 (Prymnessos in Phrygia): ✝ φωνὶ Κυρίου ἐπὶ τῶν ὑδάτων. ✝. See also ICG 3691 (Thessalonica) 1322 (sixth-century Psidian Antioch = Yalvaç), 3366 (Laconia).

[31] See Breytenbach 2012: 766–68.

[32] Εὐλογητὸς ὁ θεὸς καὶ πατὴρ τοῦ κυρίου ἡμῶν Ἰησοῦ Χριστοῦ (2 Cor 1:3; cf. Eph 1:3; 1 Pet 1:3); κύριος ἐμοὶ βοηθός, [καὶ] οὐ φοβηθήσομαι … (Heb 13:6).

[33] The use of the Bible in inscriptions is very widespread; see Felle 2006.

[34] This is a summary of previously published research. See Breytenbach 2014: 759–74.

[35] ICG 1009: For a comparison between the inscription and LXX manuscripts, see Breytenbach 2014: 762–63.

[36] Quoted by Athanasius, *Ep. Marcell.* 9 (PG 27: 17–20); Gregory of Nazianzus, *Or.* 11.4 (SC 405: 336–38).

Figure 17.1 ICG 1008 (Photo MAMA vi 385)

with baptism.[37] 'On the inscription in the church at Afyonkarahisar the Isaiah text reflects part of the liturgy and it is likely that the phrases "wash yourself, become clean, remove your evil deeds ... cease from your evil deeds" are to be interpreted in the context of baptism.'[38] Within the liturgical context, the last lines in 1:18 'even though your sins are like crimson, I will make them white like snow; and though they are like scarlet, I will make them white like wool' were taken to refer to absolution.

A catena of texts from the Psalms (Ps^{LXX} 31:1; 33:9, 6; 26:1; 96:11) quoted on a lintel from the same building (Fig. 17.1)[39] serves to express the forgiveness or covering of sins and the blessings that come from it. The use of these texts from the Psalms by early Christian writers suggests that the catena reflects the practice of absolution after penitence leading up to the baptism or Eucharist.[40]

A citation conflating Isa^{LXX} 61:1a, 10b–c, and 25:6–7a possibly stems from the same church and was probably used in a baptismal context.[41]

Biblical Motifs and Narratives in Inscriptions from Thessaly

Recourse to the LXX goes beyond citations from the Psalms and Isaiah. Narratives from the Bible, like those of Daniel in the lions' den or the good shepherd, were used as motifs in frescos within early Christian tombs or

---

[37] 1 Clem. 8:4; Justin, 1 Apol. 44.3; 61.7 (Marcovich); Dial. 18.2; 44.4 (Marcovich); Clement of Alexandria, Quis div. 39.4–5 (GCS 17: 185–86); Cyprian, Test. 1.24 (CSEL 3/1: 59); Basil of Caesarea, Regula brevis tractatae 13 (PG 31: 1089–92); Ambrose, Myst. 7.34 (CSEL 73: 102–3); Gregory of Nazianzus, Or. 14.37 (PG 35: 908); Gregory of Nyssa, In diem luminum 235 (Gebhardt); Oratio catechetica 103 (Mühlenberg).

[38] Breytenbach 2014: 763.

[39] ICG 1008. For a comparison between the inscription and LXX manuscripts, see Breytenbach 2014: 763–64.

[40] See the references to works of Cyril of Jerusalem, Ambrose, and Gregory of Nyssa in Breytenbach 2014: 764.

[41] ICG 2010. See Breytenbach 2014: 764–65.

to decorate the sarcophagi of affluent Christian families in Macedonia and Rome.[42] Early Christian mosaics also depict motifs from biblical narratives from Rome to Palestine. Expanding on previously published research,[43] I add new examples from Thessaly.

Before we proceed, we must clarify one important prerequisite for the dissemination of biblical knowledge into liturgical and sepulchral space. Lectors, deacons, and presbyters, who ought to be literate, and of course bishops, were seminal in keeping biblical tradition alive through public reading and homilies. There were of course also readers in other regions.[44] Thessaly, which left a notable number of epitaphs attesting to a tradition of lectors reading scripture to others, can serve as an example.

A sixth-century teacher (διδάσκαλος) from Néa Anchiálos in Thessalian Thebes bore the ethnonym *Germanus*,[45] but as his wife Alexandria, the majority of readers from there had Greek names that were popular among Christians (Ἐ[λπίδ]ιος in ICG 3810; Ὀνήσιμος in 3855 and 3873), or names confined to Christians in Thebes (Κυριδίων in 3837, see 3819), or originally Christian names like Πέτρος. On his memorial, Peter is first remembered as a lector, and then it is stated that he made a living as a greengrocer (κραμβιτᾶς).[46]

Quotations from and Allusions to the New Testament

Sometimes phrases from the New Testament became part of the liturgy of the early church and are thus quoted on monuments. The epitaph on the gravestone of Antoninus in Thebes ends citing the prayer from the earliest Christian Eucharist liturgy in 1 Cor 16:22: μαράνα θά ('Our Lord, come!').[47] A stamp for Eucharistic bread from Antikyra in Thebes, for example, takes up the formula from the Psalms: Εὐλογί[α Κυρίου ἐφ᾽ ὑ]μ(ᾶ)ς.[48]

---

[42] ICG 3144; Breytenbach 2007: 155, 158, 170–71; Dresken-Weiland 2010.
[43] See Breytenbach 2015.
[44] For the strong tradition of readers in Attica, see Breytenbach and Tzavella (2023) (= ECG 1). The role of the Christian harper (ψάλτης) Andreas in Thebes remains unclear (ICG 4005). For readers in Lycaonia, see Breytenbach and Zimmermann 2018: 663–65.
[45] ICG 3859.
[46] ICG 3815: † | † Ἔνθα κατά|κιτε ὁ τῆς εὐλαβοῦς | μνήμης Πέτρος ἀν|αγνόστης καὶ ἡ σύν|βιος αὐτοῦ Ἡρίνη, ἔχον | τὴν μέθωδον κραν|βιτᾶς. | ☙ † ☙.
[47] ICG 3878. + Ἀντω|νίνο[υ] | Μαρα[ναθά (?)]. See earlier examples from Athens (ICG 2096) and Argolis (3358).
[48] ICG 4083. The text encircles a ⚚ combined with an encircled cross ⊕ (as in the sixth-century ICG 3850) with Α Ω. For the text, see Ps^{LXX} 3:9; 128:8 (... εὐλογία κυρίου ἐφ᾽ ὑμᾶς ...); Prov 10:6, 11.

A Eucharistic seal from Labadeia has a bird in the centre of the medallion. The text around it resounds the *Sanctus* introduced in the eucharistic liturgy by the fourth century.[49] It cites Ps^{LXX}117:26, which the gospels, following Mark 11:9, place on the lips of the crowd hailing Jesus when he enters Jerusalem: 'Blessed is he who comes in the name of the Lord.'[50]

Symbols Referring to Biblical Narratives, Sayings, or Motifs

Sometimes the relation to the text of a biblical passage is merely indicated by the iconography. It is assumed an onlooker would recognise, e.g., the cross or staurogram above, in, or below the inscription, knowing that it refers to the crucifixion of Jesus Christ as told in the passion narratives in the gospels. The depiction of doves also falls into this category. Following the narrative of Jesus' baptism where the Spirit is visualised descending as a dove (ὡς περιστεράν in Mark 1:10) unto Jesus, the dove signified first and foremost the Holy Spirit. The dove underneath the epitaph on the gravestone of a fifth-century family from Néa Anchiálos in Thebes in Thessaly may serve as an example.[51]

In Matthew's Gospel (10:16), Jesus commanded his disciples to be pure (ἀκέραιος) like doves. In early Christian iconography, doves and peacocks are the most common birds.[52] The bird in the centre of the beautiful mosaic medallion in the central panel of the mosaic floor in the narthex of the church of Olosson cannot be identified with certainty. It is encircled by an inscription in which the donor, Mary, invokes St Andrew to remember her.[53] An olive branch surrounds the bird, which makes it likely that it is a dove. A dove could symbolise attributes of Mary, like her purity caused by the Holy Spirit.

The dove can also represent the person. Two doves drink from a chalice under the inscription marking the 'sleeping place' of Symeonios and his wife Olympia in sixth-century Néa Anchiálos, symbolising their participation in the Eucharist (see Fig. 17.2).[54] 'In Early Christian art, the popular presentation of a dove drinking from a fountain or pecking at bread signified the spiritual nourishment of baptism and the Eucharist.'[55]

---

[49] See *Apos. Con.* 8.13 and Hayward and Louth 1999.
[50] ICG 4098: + Εὐλογημένος ὁ ἐρχόμε(νος). Ps^{LXX} 117:26: εὐλογημένος ὁ ἐρχόμενος ἐν ὀνόματι κυρίου.
[51] ICG 3818. Doves on monuments from Attica in ICG 1848, 2106, 2173. See also Poeschke 1968.
[52] For doves, see below; for peacocks, see ICG 4026, 4031, and several examples from Thessalonica in Breytenbach 2007: 61 and 146, 62 and 149, 68 and 155.
[53] ICG 3961: Ἅγιε Ἀνδρέα, μνήσθητι τῆς δούλης σου Μαρίας. For the image, see Larisa Culture Index, accessed on 3 April 2020.
[54] ICG 3835. A similar depiction occurs above the epitaph on the koimeterion of Synodios, a subdeacon from Brauron in the Mesogeia (ICG 2106).
[55] Apostolos-Cappadona 2008: 177.

Figure 17.2 An *ekphrasis* from the Damokratia Basilica, Demetrias, Thessaly (ICG 3835) (Photo, Papanikola-Bakirtzi 2002)[56]

[56] Papanikola-Bakirtzi 2002: 100, no. 86.

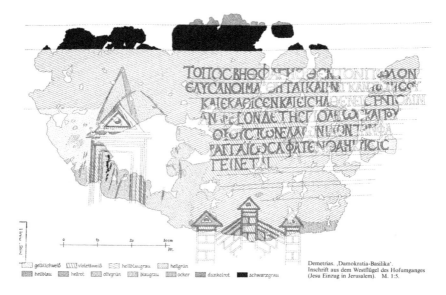

Figure 17.3 An *ekphrasis* of biblical narrative, Damokratia Basilica in Demetrias in Thessaly (ICG 3959) (Drawing, Habicht 1987: Tafel 55)

Ekphrases to Depicted Biblical Narratives from the Damokratia Basilica in Demetrias in Thessaly

In a few isolated instances, the iconography on monuments alludes to a biblical narrative. This is sometimes indicated by reference to the biblical text in an accompanying inscription. We focus on those instances where the citation of or allusion to a biblical pretext refers to a drawing on the monument itself. In such cases it is better to speak of *ekphrasis*.[57] Selecting important traits of the biblical pretext, the inscription mediates between the iconic representation and the commonly known narrative it refers to.

Paraphrasing Mark 11:1–11 and parallels, a *dipinto* inscription from the end of the fifth century identifies the depiction on the wall of the western side of the courtyard near the door to the narthex of the Damokratia Basilica in Demetrias in Thessaly as τόπος Βηθφαγη. The text runs: 'Place Bethphage, where the disciples unbound the colt and brought it to Jesus, and he sat (upon it) and entered the city. In the midst of the city and of the Mount of Olives they saw the gorge of Josaphat, where the judgement will take place' (see Fig. 17.3).[58] The text has an ekphrastic function and identifies the

---

[57] On *ekphrasis* see Webb 2009; Leatherbury 2020.
[58] ICG 3959: *vacat* | Τόπος Βηθφαγη, ὅθεν τ[ὸν π]ῶλον | ἔλυσαν οἱ μαθηταὶ καὶ ἤνε[γκαν] τῷ Ἰησοῦ | καὶ ἐκάθισεν καὶ εἰσῆλ[θεν εἰ]ς τὴν πό[λιν] | ἀνάμεσον δὲ τῆς πόλεως καὶ τοῦ || ὄρους τῶν ἐλαῶν ἴδον τὴν [φά]|ραγγα Ἰωσαφατ, ἔνθα ἡ κρίσις | γείνεται. *vacat* | *vacat*. (trans. ICG). Text: Habicht 1987: 269–306, 301.

images on the wall. It is presumed that the onlooker will know the narrative, since Jesus' entry into Jerusalem was commemorated annually on Palm Sunday. Drawing on the biblical narrative, the inscription and the depiction mediate the site from the holy land into the church and keep the story alive.[59] The gorge of Josaphat refers to the place where, according to Joel 4:2, 11–12, 14, the Lord will judge the nations. Just like Eusebius had done, the inscription identifies the gorge of Josaphat with the Kidron Valley, which separates the Temple Mount from the Mount of Olives.[60] The *dipinto* not only commemorates Jesus' entry into Jerusalem but also reminds the viewer that Jesus will also return to Jerusalem for the final judgement.

Fragments from the northern wall of the courtyard paraphrase the text of Gen^{LXX} 28:12 but relocate the topos of Jacob's dream from Beer-sheba (בְּאֵר שֶׁבַע), which is correctly translated in the LXX with Φρέαρ ὁρκισμοῦ 'well of the oath' (Gen 21:31) to Bethlehem: 'The city of Bethlehem, where Jacob saw the dream inspired by God: the stairway set up into heaven and the angels of God going up and coming down' (see Figs. 17.4 and 17.5).[61] Bethlehem features here in the basilica because this reception of Gen 28:12 presupposes its use in the New Testament. Narratives from the (in Christian terms) 'Old' Testament were interpreted within the Christian hermeneutic as referring to Christ. It is this *interpretatio Christiana* that made it possible to apply the passages within liturgical contexts in Christian churches. In our example from Demetrias in Thessaly, this is the case. The Johannine Jesus alludes to Gen 28:12 in John 1:51, when in answering Nathanael he describes himself: 'Very truly, I tell you, you will see heaven opened and the angels of God ascending and descending upon the Son of Man' (NRSV). In John 3:13, he repeats: 'No one has ascended into heaven but he who descended from heaven, the Son of Man.' Jesus as the Son of Man connecting heaven and earth is described in terms of Jacob's dream of the ladder; therefore, the ladder must be at Bethlehem where, according to Matthew and Luke, Jesus was born. In several homilies from the third century, the connection between the Son of Man and the ladder of Jacob is presupposed.[62]

---

[59] See Leatherbury 2020: 203–5.
[60] Habicht 1987: 302, with reference to Eusebius, *Onomasticon* (Klostermann 1904: 118.18).
[61] ICG 3954: [Πόλι]ς Βηθλεεμ, ὅπου Ἰακω[β εἶδεν] | [θεῖον] ἐνύπνιον, τὴν κλίμακα ἐσ[τη]][ριγμένην] εἰς τ[ὸ]ν οὐρανὸν καὶ τοὺς | [ἀγγέλους το]ῦ θεοῦ ἀναβένοντα[ς] || [καὶ καταβένο]ντας. *vacat.* Gen^{LXX} 28:12: καὶ ἐνυπνιάσθη καὶ ἰδοὺ κλίμαξ ἐστηριγμένη ἐν τῇ γῇ ἧς ἡ κεφαλὴ ἀφικνεῖτο εἰς τὸν οὐρανόν καὶ οἱ ἄγγελοι τοῦ θεοῦ ἀνέβαινον καὶ κατέβαινον ἐπ' αὐτῆς. See the drawing in Habicht 1987: Tafel 53.
[62] See Gregorius Thaumaturgus, *Sermo in omnes sanctus* 1201.28–40 (PG 10); Didymus Caecus, *Fragmenta in Joanneum* 1 (on John 3:13, see Reuss 1966: 177). For Severianus, *In dictum apostoli: Non quod volo facio* 669 (PG 4203), the ladder is εἰκὼν τοῦ σταυροῦ.

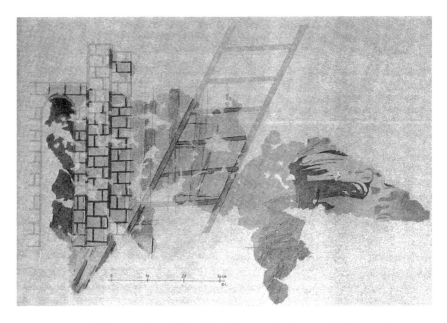

Figure 17.4 Bethlehem and Jacob's ladder (Photo, Habicht 1987: Tafel xxviii)

Figure 17.5 ICG 3954 (Photo, Habicht 1987: Tafel xxviii)

The interaction between biblical texts from the LXX, Christian interpretation, and liturgical context becomes even clearer in the next example from the Damokratia Basilica. Three of the nine *dipinto* fragments from the western wall of the courtyard could be restored.[63] Joined together, fragments 2 and 5 allude to Josh 9:2e and 2d: 'blessings ... curses ... Gerizim ... and Mount ... Gaibal'.[64] Fragments 2 and 4 paraphrase Josh 5:9, the final verse of the narrative about the second circumcision of the sons of Israel by Joshua in Josh 5:2–9: 'Place Galgala, where Joshua circumcised the sons of Israel, where they also were released from the reproach of Egypt'.[65] The setting of the story about the crossing of the river Jordan at Gilgal in Josh^{LXX} 4:22–23 and 5:1 draws on the narrative of Exod 14:21–31 when the Lord divided the sea 'and the children of Israel went into the midst of the sea on dry land' (Exod 14:22, 29). The riders, chariots, and horses of Pharaoh were destroyed. On that day, God delivered Israel from the hand of the Egyptians (Exod 14:30). Joshua piled twelve stones from the river as a token in Galgalas (Gilgal), that the Lord God had dried up the water of the Jordan before Israel as he did to the waters of the Red Sea (ἡ ἐρυθρὰ θάλασσα, Josh 4:23). In 1 Cor 10:1–5, Paul alludes to the events in the Exodus narrative as τύποι (1 Cor 10:6) for the Christians, inaugurating a tradition of exposition in which the passage through the Red Sea foreshadows Christian baptism.[66] In the section below on Amphilochius of Iconium's homily on baptism, we shall return to a similar use of Exod 14 and 15.

The fact that Josh 4 and 5 also draws on Exod 14 and because the name Jehoshua (יְהוֹשֻׁעַ) and its shorter form Jeshua יֵשׁוּעַ), the name of Jesus, were both rendered in Greek with Ἰησοῦς, also explains why this passage was associated with baptism in early Christianity. However, the story in Josh 5 is about a second circumcision. In the light of the Pauline notion that faith is the (second) circumcision of the heart (Rom 2:29; 3:30; 15:8) and that baptism superseded circumcision (Col 2:11–12), the text of Josh 5 allowed further Christian exposition of the meaning of baptism in early Christianity.[67]

---

[63] See the drawing in Habicht 1987: Tafel 54.
[64] ICG 3958b frag. 3: vacat | ΕΙCΙΝΤΑΔΥΩ *vac* | Υ εὐλογίας vac | - - κα]τάρας *vac* | - - Γαρι]ζιν *vacat* | *vacat*. – frag. 5: *vacat* | vacat καὶ ὄρος vacat | vacat <Γ>αιβαλ vacat | vacat.
[65] ICG 3958a: *vacat* vacat | [τόπος Γαλ]γαλα, ἔνθα περ[ιέτε]μεν Ἰησ[οῦς] | [τοὺς υἱοὺς Ἰσρα]ηλ, ἔνθα καὶ [ἐλύθησ]αν *vacat* | [ἀπὸ τοῦ ὀνειδισμοῦ] Ἐγύπτου. *vacat*. (trans. ICG) Josh^{LXX} 5:9: καὶ εἶπεν κύριος τῷ Ἰησοῖ υἱῷ Ναυη ἐν τῇ σήμερον ἡμέρᾳ ἀφεῖλον τὸν ὀνειδισμὸν Αἰγύπτου ἀφ' ὑμῶν καὶ ἐκάλεσεν τὸ ὄνομα τοῦ τόπου ἐκείνου Γαλγαλα.
[66] On this, see Breytenbach 2015: 481–82.
[67] On the replacement of circumcision as a ritual of initiation by baptism, see the differentiating discussion by Rouwhorst 2019.

This interpretative model is not confined to Thessaly. For Pseudo-Athanasius in Alexandria, circumcision in Galgala served as typology for the baptism through Christ.[68] The circumcision, literally the circular cutting off of a part of the whole (from περιτέμνω 'to cut off around'), is a shadow (σκιά) of the things to come. Commenting on Josh 5:9,[69] Pseudo-Athanasius argues that when the circumcision is a removal (ἀφαίρεσις) of part from the generation in Egypt, it means that uncircumcision (ἀκροβυστία) is a token of Egyptian nature and origin (αἰγυπτιακῆς σχέσεως καὶ γενέσεως). According to him, circumcision generally appears to be given in order that death as the reproach of the trespass (ὁ ὀνειδισμὸς τοῦ παραπτώματος) of Adam is taken away from the mortal descendants of Abraham so that they would no longer be subjected to Gen 3:19: 'earth are you and to earth you shall go'. For Pseudo-Athanasius, the reproach for the trespass in Eden was removed at Gilgal as 'typos' of the baptism through Christ (Τοῦτο δὲ ἐγένετο τότε εἰς τύπον τοῦ διὰ Χριστοῦ βαπτίσματος). Reflecting on Rom 6:6; Col 3:9; Titus 3:5; and 1 Pet 1:23, he continues:

Then it happened in part, as in shadow, but now, as the apostle said, 'We stripped off the entire earthly origin through the bath, we are new begotten, so that we do not die according to the previous origin, but according to the circumcision of putting off the body, which we stripped off through baptism, we shall live.' As the Lord said to Joshua 'I removed the reproach of Egypt on this day from them', so much more would he say to every one of those being baptised now 'On this day I removed the reproach of the earthly origin and the reproach of the destruction of the death from you, on this day.'[70]

Such interpretative models were treasured for a long time. In his third *Question on Joshua*, Theodoret of Cyrus (d. c. 466) also comments on Josh 5:2 that the second circumcision of the children of Israel foreshadows reality in an important way. Drawing on Acts 2:38; Col 2:11; and Rom 2:29, he argues that those Jews 'who believed in the Savior, though already possessing

---

[68] See Pseudo-Athanasius, *De sabbatis et circumcisione* 23–53 (PG 28.141). The text might be spurious.

[69] Josh 5:9: ἐν τῇ σήμερον ἡμέρᾳ ἀφεῖλον τὸν ὀνειδισμὸν Αἰγύπτου ἀφ' ὑμῶν ('On this day I removed the reproach of Egypt from you').

[70] Athanasius, *De sabbatis et circumcisione* 39–53: Τότε γὰρ ἐκ μέρους ἐγένετο, ὡς ἐν σκιᾷ, νῦν δέ, ὥσπερ εἶπεν ὁ Ἀπόστολος, ὅλην τὴν γηΐνην γένεσιν ἀπεκδιδυσκόμεθα, διὰ τοῦ λουτροῦ ἀναγεννώμενοι, ἵνα μηκέτι κατὰ τὴν πρώτην γένεσιν ἀποθνήσκωμεν, ἀλλὰ κατὰ τὴν περιτομὴν τῆς ἀπεκδύσεως τοῦ σώματος, ἣν διὰ τοῦ λουτροῦ ἀπεκδιδυσκόμεθα, ζήσωμεν. Ὥσπερ δὲ εἶπεν ὁ Κύριος τῷ Ἰησοῦ· Ἀφεῖλον τὸν ὀνειδισμὸν Αἰγύπτου ἐν τῇ σήμερον ἡμέρᾳ ἀφ' ὑμῶν· οὕτως πολλῷ πλέον λεχθείη ἂν ἑκάστῳ τῶν νῦν βαπτιζομένων· Ἐν τῇ ἡμέρᾳ ταύτῃ ἀφεῖλον τὸν ὀνειδισμὸν τῆς γηΐνης γενέσεως, καὶ τὸν ὀνειδισμὸν τῆς τοῦ θανάτου φθορᾶς ἀπὸ σοῦ, ἐν τῇ σήμερον ἡμέρᾳ.

the Mosaic circumcision, received as well the spiritual. The phrase "a second time," therefore, prefigures the reality, as it is impossible for the flesh to be circumcised twice.'[71] The name of the place was Galgala (Gilgal), which he interprets in *Question* 4 as 'freedom'. This signifies the deliverance from bondage and idolisation in Egyptian slavery and the entrance into the promised land. 'As for us, we learn that whoever is accorded most holy baptism and receives the spiritual circumcision lays aside the disgrace of sin.'[72]

Not only is the ekphrastic relation between the inscriptions alluding to Genesis and Joshua and the drawings remarkable but so also is the intertextual web in which the biblical texts are placed through its use in the narthex of a Christian church. The text from Joshua already refers to Exod 14, and the Red Sea and this connection facilitated its use in a baptismal context. All the LXX stories alluded to must be understood in the light of their Christian reception in John 1:51 and in light of Paul's view on the circumcision of the heart in Rom 2:29 and on how baptism supersedes circumcision in Col 2:11. Knowledge of scripture is transmitted through a web of intertextual relations woven since the earliest Christian writings. The *dipinti* in Demetrias are not merely the work of an artisan; they refer to an emerging 'scriptural universe'.[73] The examples in the next section show that this way of mediating scripture was not confined to Phrygia or Thessaly, but that it was a widespread phenomenon throughout the Christian world of late antiquity.

The Trisagion from Isaiah 6:3 and the Lamb from Revelation 5:8

On a fourth- or fifth-century marble plate from Athens, a lamb is depicted with its head against the background of a large cross. The edges of the cross have peculiar circles; below the crossbar the upright is flanked by an alpha and an omega. The lamb depicts the slain ἀρνίον of Rev 5:6: 'Then I saw between the throne and the four living creatures and among the

---

[71] Theodoret, *Quaestiones in Octateuchum* 274.18–21 (Marcos and Sáenz-Badillos): οἱ τοίνυν ἐξ Ἰουδαίων τῷ σωτῆρι πεπιστευκότες, τὴν μωσαϊκὴν περιτομὴν ἔχοντες, προσέλαβον τὴν πνευματικήν. τὸ τοίνυν 'ἐκδευτέρου' τὴν ἀλήθειαν προτυποῖ· τὴν γὰρ σάρκα δὶς περιτμηθῆναι τῶν ἀδυνάτων. Trans. Petruccione 2007: 273.

[72] Theodoret, *Quaestiones in Octateuchum* 276.8–10 (Marcos and Sáenz-Badillos): καὶ ἡμεῖς δὲ μανθάνομεν, ὡς ὁ τοῦ παναγίου βαπτίσματος ἀξιούμενος, καὶ τὴν πνευματικὴν περιτομὴν δεχόμενος, τὸ τῆς ἁμαρτίας ὄνειδος ἀποτίθεται. Trans. Petruccione 2007: 277.

[73] Stroumsa 2016.

Figure 17.6 ICG 1881 (Photo IG II/III² v 13303)

elders a Lamb standing as if it had been slaughtered, having seven horns and seven eyes' (NRSV). The lamb is the Christ, who is the Alpha and the Omega, the first and the last (Rev 22:13). The cross behind its head simultaneously serves to express that the lamb is slain and the circles on the edges serve to indicate eyes, the seventh eye being in the head. In the Apocalypse, the four beasts were reciting the trisagion from Isa^{LXX} 6:3.[74] Only part of the inscription in the circle is extant: ΑΓΙΟΣΑ. Since Isa 6:3 is widely used in early Christian inscriptions,[75] it is better in light of the image of the seven-eyed lamb to draw on its reception in Rev 4:8 for the reconstruction of the text following the ἅγιος ἅ- … in an inscription from Athens (see Fig. 17.6).[76]

---

[74] See Rev 4:8 (καὶ ἀνάπαυσιν οὐκ ἔχουσιν [sc. the four beasts] ἡμέρας καὶ νυκτὸς λέγοντες· ἅγιος ἅγιος ἅγιος κύριος ὁ θεὸς ὁ παντοκράτωρ, ὁ ἦν καὶ ὁ ὢν καὶ ὁ ἐρχόμενος) and Isa^{LXX} 6:3 (ἅγιος ἅγιος ἅγιος κύριος σαβαωθ πλήρης πᾶσα ἡ γῆ τῆς δόξης αὐτοῦ).

[75] On the trisagion in Christian inscriptions from Asia Minor, see Breytenbach 2014: 768–69.

[76] ICG 1881: Α – Ω | [ἅγιος] ἅγιος ἅγ[ιος κύριος ὁ θεὸς ὁ παντοκράτωρ].

Epigraphic Examples from Other Regions

Paradisiac Peace from Isaiah 11:6

The book of Isaiah expects that animals that are natural enemies will live peacefully together.[77] Mosaic builders used this paradisal motif of the leopard and the lamb from Isa 11:6 to express the role of Christ as inaugurator of the kingdom of peace. A figured floor panel in the eastern end of the nave of a fifth-century church at Anemurium on the Mediterranean coast of Rough Cilicia may serve as an example.[78] A leopard and a goat stand on either side of a palm tree, the trunk of which is entwined by a serpent.[79] The badly damaged *ekphrasis* cites parts of Isa^{LXX} 11:6 in inverted order.[80] The mosaic illustrates the reception of the paradise motif of the peaceful kingdom taken from Isa 11 in the design of the interior of the basilica. The future fulfilment that is connected with Christ's advent is illustrated in several other Christian churches in colourful mosaics.[81] In the mosaics on the floors of the churches, Isaiah's expectation is transferred into images. The peace between predator and prey signifies the meaning of the birth of Christ. The location of the mosaic depicting the peaceful kingdom in front of the altar in the apse illustrates that the messianic age has been inaugurated with the little child, and that the full realisation of paradisiacal peace is expected with his return (see Plate 17.1).[82] This motif from Isa 11:6 was used in Christian literary texts in a comparable manner.[83]

Jonah and the Son of Man of Matt 12:39

At Çukurkavak on the northern slopes of the Taurus Mountains south of Konya (Iconium), an important find was made, the so-called Jonah

---

[77] Isa 11:6–9 (NETS): 'And the wolf shall graze with the lamb, and the leopard shall rest with the kid, and the calf and the bull and the lion shall graze together, and a little child shall lead them. And the ox and the bear shall graze together, and their young shall be together, and together shall the lion and the ox eat husks.'

[78] Russell 1987: no. 14 (cf. Russell 1980: 270).   [79] See Campbell 1998: pls. 206–8, esp. 208.

[80] *SEG* 37.1278 and 1311 (cf. MAMA II 106–107): καὶ παιδίον] μικρὸν ἄξι αὐτούς καὶ πάρδ[α]λι[ς] συν[αναπ]αύ|σετ[αι ἐρίφῳ]. Cf. Isa^{LXX} 11:6b: καὶ πάρδαλις συναναπαύσεται ἐρίφῳ ... καὶ παιδίον μικρὸν ἄξει αὐτούς ('And the leopard shall rest with the kid ... and a little child shall lead them', NETS). For more detail, see Breytenbach 2015.

[81] For treatment of and references to similar mosaics in a cathedral in Corycus or in a church at Elaiussa/Sebaste, both on the Cilician coast, in a basilica in Karlık near Adana in Cilicia Campestris, and several in Syrio-Palestine, see Breytenbach 2015.

[82] For alternative models of interpretation, see Campbell 1995.

[83] Tertullian, *Herm.* 11; Origen, *Princ.* 4.2.1; Eusebius, *Comm. Isa.* 62 on Isa 11:6, 8–9.

Figure 17.7 ICG 829 (Photo C. Breytenbach)

inscription.[84] A person named [Ta]ta erected a huge marble block for Mithius and Paulus, his uncles, for memory's sake. Below the decoration is engraved: 'Huge fish and Jonah' (see Fig. 17.7).[85] The widely used narrative of Jonah and the huge fish forms the iconographic backdrop against which the inscription and the monument must be understood. In early Judaism, the narrative of Jonah rescued by the fish is, in line with Daniel surviving the lion's den and the three men rescued from the fire, an example illustrating God's ability to save from a perilous situation.[86] The author of the text of the inscription, however, most probably obtained the motif via Matt 12:39–40. The first evangelist compares Jonah in the belly of the big fish to the Son of Man who will be in the heart of the earth for three days, applying the motif to the burial of the Son of Man. The early Christian kerygma of his resurrection after three days (1 Cor 15:3–4) is clearly presupposed in this context. This is quite distinct from Luke 11:29b–30, where Jonah's sign is addressed to the men of Nineveh. Matthew's appropriation of the Q-text vibrates through the works of the early Christian authors,[87] expressing the belief that, as in the case of Jonah, whose body was not digested by the sea monster, the believer[88] will by the power of God come out of the grave unscathed.[89] When the fish or the sea monster swallowed Jonah, he was

---

[84] For a fuller treatment, see Breytenbach and Zimmermann 2018: 183–87.
[85] ICG 829: […] [- -]τα ἀνέστησεν Μιθιον κὲ Παῦλον τοὺς θείους αὐτοῦ | μνή{σ}μης χάριν. [decoration] κέτος κὲ Ἰώνας.
[86] 3 Macc 6:8; Josephus, *Ant.* 9.213.
[87] Cf. Justin, *Dial.* 107; Irenaeus, *Haer.* 5.5.2; 5.31.1; Methodius of Olympus, *Res.* 2.25.8–9; Gregory of Nyssa, *In Christi resurrectionem oratio I*, PG 46: 604B; *Apos. Con.* 5.7.12; Cyril of Jerusalem, *Catechesis* 14.18.
[88] Tertullian, *Res.* 58.8–10.   [89] Tertullian, *Res.* 32.

not only rescued from drowning, but he also entered into an intermediate state like Jesus and had an exemplary role. The iconographic evidence on the popularity of the Jonah motif goes beyond our monument, and even beyond Roman sarcophagi and catacombs.[90] The use of the Jonah cycle on the gravestone from Çukurkavak shows us that Mithius and Paul, the deceased, are like the interred Son of Man, the earth in which they were buried being compared to the belly of the big fish. They are in a transitory state, waiting on the crucified who will return, resurrecting the buried. God shall resurrect those that have believed in Christ Jesus, just as Christ himself was resurrected.[91]

Amphilochius of Iconium and Scripture

Amphilochius was a good choice to be made bishop of Iconium in AD 373.[92] His rhetorical training benefited his preaching, and his sermons displayed deep knowledge of the Old and the New Testaments in Greek. For him, scripture was divine and the Bible was the basis and norm for Christian education. Karl Holl correctly branded Amphilochius as a 'biblischer Theologe'.[93] Citing 2 Tim 3:16 in *Iambi ad Seleucum* (186, 319, and 262–63), he regards both testaments as γραφαὶ/βίβλοι θεόπνευστοι.[94]

In his homilies, the bishop of Iconium exposed his audiences to several of these books that were according to the canon θεόπνευστος, 'God inspired'. Amphilochius did not allude to, quote, or comment upon the whole canon. His sermons are generally based on a central passage from scripture, but in his argument, he alludes to several other passages too.[95] We may assume that they were addressed to audiences in Iconium.[96] They thus give us an impression of the use and dissemination of scripture

---

[90] As Dresken-Weiland (2010: 98–115) illustrated, from the third century onwards the Jonah cycle decorated Christian graves from Constantinople over Konya to the east of the Roman empire and south to Alexandria. This iconographic evidence on the popularity of the Jonah motif is not confined to Roman sarcophagi and catacombs. See also Dresken-Weiland 2010: 116–18. Harl (2014) argued that these narratives shaped the formation of the Christian liturgical collections of odes or canticles.

[91] For the interpretation of the figure-like cross, see Breytenbach and Zimmermann 2018: 186–87.

[92] On Amphilochius' role as bishop, see Breytenbach and Zimmermann 2018: 589–94.

[93] Holl 1904: 114.

[94] Cf. Amphilochius' list of the θεόπνευστοι βίβλοι of the Old and New Testament, *Seleuc.* 261–319.

[95] Cf. the general remarks of Holl 1904: 64–79.   [96] See also Holl 1904: 111.

in central Asia Minor at the end of the fourth century. For the purpose of this paper, we focus on Amphilochius' sermon on baptism.[97]

Amphilochius' De recens baptizatis

The homily celebrates the newly baptised at Easter. In his introduction, Amphilochius quotes several psalms[98] in praise of purity and maidenhood and in commendation of charity and almsgiving to the poor. To illustrate how baptism changes life, bringing hope, he quotes Ps^{LXX} 32:3: 'Sing him a new song!' 'Now the grief of the dead is expelled, for the splendour of the resurrection arrived.'[99] In describing the meaning of baptism, Amphilochius combines several aspects of Paul's letters. Amphilochius says the old sin has disappeared, Adam is renewed, Eve restored into heaven; he introduces a quotation from 2 Cor 5:17: ἰδοὺ γέγονεν πάντα καινά. In 1 Corinthians, Paul described the exodus through the Red Sea in terms of Christian baptism.[100] Aware of this line of interpretation,[101] Amphilochius requested his audience to rise with him and the choir to sing the song of Mary, the sister of Moses from Exod^{LXX} 15:21. 'Let us sing to the Lord, for gloriously he has glorified himself. What had he done? Horse and rider he threw into the sea.'[102] He then comments that the Lord plunged the horse, the sin of being besotted with women, and the rider, the daemon crouching on this sin, in the baptism of the water bath.[103] He repeats the first stich from Exod 15:21 ('Let us sing to the Lord, for gloriously he has glorified himself'), adds Exod 15:4 ('he cast Pharaoh and his power into the sea'), and interprets: 'This

---

[97] On Amphilochius, *Contra Haereticus* (Datema 1978: 185–214), cf. Breytenbach and Zimmermann 2018: 5.5.8. On the speech against the heretics (*Pater si possible est*, Datema 1978, 139–52) given on the day of St Stephen (December 26), cf. Breytenbach and Zimmermann 2018: 5.6.2; Holl 1904: 84–104.

[98] Ps^{LXX} 140:2; 51:10; 91:13; 32:3.

[99] Amphilochius, *De recens baptizatis* 45–46 (Datema 1978: 156): νῦν τὸ πένθος τῶν νεκρῶν ἐδραπετεύθη, τὸ γὰρ φέγγος τῆς ἀναστάσεως ἐλήλυθεν.

[100] 1 Cor 10:1–2.

[101] See also Tertullian, *Bapt.* 9.1. In Ali Demirici in the Çayıralan district about 350 km east of Ankara, an originally Jewish architrave depicting the scene from Exod 14:27–28 was found. Christians reused it, probably as lintel of the doorway of a baptistery; cf. Breytenbach 2015: 480–82.

[102] Amphilochius, *De recens baptizatis* 56–57 (Datema 1978: 157): Ἄσωμεν τῷ κυρίῳ, ἐνδόξως γὰρ δεδόξασται. Τί γὰρ πεποίηκεν; Ἵππον καὶ ἀναβάτην ἔρριψεν εἰς θάλασσαν. The quotation follows Codex Vaticanus (B).

[103] Amphilochius, *De recens baptizatis* 57–59 (Datema 1978: 157): Ἵππον μὲν τὴν θηλυμανῆ ἁμαρτίαν, ἀναβάτην δὲ τὸν ἐπὶ τῇ ἁμαρτίᾳ καθήμενον δαίμονα ἐν τῷ βαπτίσματι τοῦ λουτροῦ κατεπόντισεν (sc. Κύριος).

Figure 17.8 *Ekphrasis* of Exod 15:8, ICG 2306 (Photo, Wallner, *Inschriften*, 110–12, no. V.1)

is the devil and the dark and polluted army of his daemons he (the Lord) surrounded with sea.'[104]

It might be possible to interpret a find from Cappadocia, now in the Yozgat Museum, in this light. The frieze on this white marble stone shows the moment before the chariots of Pharaoh will be covered by the water as depicted in Exod 15:8 (see Fig. 17.8).[105] '[T]he waters were congealed like a wall; the waves were congealed in the midst of the sea' (NETS). It shows to the left the chariot of Pharaoh, to the right a wave of the Red Sea, Moses, the people and the pillars of cloud and fire.

Baptism is more, however, than the drowning of evil forces. On the same line as Athanasius,[106] Amphilochius no longer fears hearing Gen 3:19, 'earth you are and to earth you will depart'. Combining key quotations from the letters of Paul, he says: 'In baptism I lay off earth and put on heaven and I hear, "heaven you are and to heaven you shall return," "for as many of you as were baptised into Christ have clothed yourselves with Christ." And "as was the man made of earth, so are those who are of the earth; and as is the heavenly man, so also are those who are of heaven."'[107] To prove that he and his audience are bound to ascend with the clouds and to return into heaven, Amphilochius quotes the 'testimony' of Paul: 'we will be caught up in the clouds to meet the Lord in the air; and so we will be

---

[104] Amphilochius, *De recens baptizatis* 60–63 (Datema 1978: 157): ... τουτέστιν τὸν διάβολον καὶ τὸ σκοτεινὸν καὶ ἐναγὲς τῶν δαιμόνων αὐτοῦ στρατόπεδον ἐν τῷ λουτρῷ τοῦ βαπτίσματος ἐθαλάσσωσεν (sc. Κύριος).

[105] ICG 2306. Full text, translation, and illustration in Wallner 2011.   [106] See p. 316 above.

[107] Amphilochius, *De recens baptizatis* 63–68 (Datema 1978: 157): Οὐκέτι φοβοῦμαι ἀκούειν· Γῆ εἶ καὶ εἰς γῆν ἀπελεύσῃ· ἐν γὰρ τῷ βαπτίσματι τὴν γῆν ἀπεθέμην καὶ οὐρανὸν ἐνεδυσάμην καὶ ἀκούω· οὐρανὸς εἶ καὶ εἰς οὐρανοὺς ἀπελεύσῃ· ὅσοι γὰρ εἰς Χριστὸν ἐβαπτίσθητε Χριστὸν ἐνεδύσασθε (Gal 3:27), καί· οἷος ὁ χοϊκός, τοιοῦτοι καὶ οἱ χοϊκοί, καὶ οἷος ὁ ἐπουράνιος, τοιοῦτοι καὶ οἱ ἐπουράνιοι (1 Cor 15:48). The quotations match Codex Vaticanus (B).

with the Lord forever'.[108] From the text of these quotations, it is clear that Amphilochius had access to a text almost identical to that of Codex Vaticanus. The quotations he selects from Paul's letters and the way he strings them together illustrate a good knowledge of the letters and take up key elements of Paul's preaching.

Returning to the occasion of the newly baptised, Amphilochius quotes Ps^{LXX} 117:24, a central reference text since the beginnings of Christianity:[109] 'This is the day that the Lord made; let us rejoice and be glad in it.'[110] The reason for the joy is the experience of the love of God and the hope of eternal life. From what follows, it is clear that the Eucharist followed the baptism. The heavenly bread (ὁ οὐράνιος ἄρτος) is the provision for eternal life (ζωῆς αἰωνίου ἐφόδιον) and those receiving should do so with pure hands made bright by good deeds (καθαραῖς παλάμαις ὑποδεξάμενοι … εὐποιΐαις λαμπρυνομέναις).[111] Amphilochius tells his audience: 'The divine and heavenly mixed wine (κρᾶμα) we should sip with rose red lips … purpled by the blood of Jesus Christ.'[112] True to the Pauline paradox of the death of Christ, Amphilochius exclaims: 'Oh death of Christ, death's death which gushes forth sweet life in bitterest death'.[113] It is the cross that is saving the world through Jesus Christ the Lord.[114] He understands the crucifixion in the light of the orthodox christology of Nicaea: καὶ ὁ υἱὸς τοῦ θεοῦ ἐπὶ σταυροῦ ἀνεφέρετο καὶ τῇ σαρκὶ ὑπὲρ ἡμῶν ἐσταυροῦτο καὶ πάσχουσα ἡ σὰρξ ἡ θεότης οὐκ ἔπασχεν.[115] In conclusion he mentions several names of Christ: the 'way, door, shepherd, and light' come from the Gospel according to John,[116] 'cornerstone' comes from Isa 28:16 via Eph 2:20, 'mustard seed'

---

[108] Amphilochius, *De recens baptizatis* 68–71 (Datema 1978: 157): Δεῖ ἡμᾶς νεφέλαις ἐπιβῆναι καὶ εἰς οὐρανοὺς ἀναδραμεῖν· οὐκ ἀμάρτυρος ὁ λόγος, ἄκουε τοῦ Παύλου λέγοντος· Ἁρπαγησόμεθα ἐν νεφέλαις εἰς ἀπάντησιν τοῦ κυρίου εἰς ἀέρα·καὶ οὕτως πάντοτε σὺν κυρίῳ ἐσόμεθα (1 Thess 4:17). The quotation matches Codex Vaticanus (B).

[109] Paul alludes to this Psalm (e.g., Rom 8:31 and 2 Cor 6:9), which was quoted by the gospels (cf. Mark 11:9–10; Matt 21:9, 42; 23:39; Luke 13:35; 19:38; 20:17; John 12:13), Heb 13:6, and 1 Pet 2:4, 7, its twentieth verse appearing on the lintels above the entrance to various churches contemporary with Amphilochius (see Breytenbach and Zimmermann 2018: 5.6.3).

[110] Ps^{LXX} 117:24: αὕτη ἡ ἡμέρα, ἣν ἐποίησεν ὁ κύριος, ἀγαλλιασώμεθα καὶ εὐφρανθῶμεν ἐν αὐτῇ.

[111] Amphilochius, *De recens baptizatis* 78–81 (Datema 1978: 158).

[112] Amphilochius, *De recens baptizatis* 82–84 (Datema 1978: 157): Καὶ τὸ θεῖον καὶ οὐράνιον κρᾶμα ῥοδοειδέσι χείλεσιν ἀρυσώμεθα (οὐ φοινίκί τινι ἐρυθαίνοντες, ἀλλὰ) τῷ αἵματι Ἰησοῦ Χριστοῦ πορφυρίζοντες.

[113] Amphilochius, *De recens baptizatis* 91–93 (Datema 1978: 158).

[114] Amphilochius, *In occursum Domini* 257–58 (Datema 1978: 71–72).

[115] Amphilochius, *De recens baptizatis* 95–97 (Datema 1978: 158).

[116] Cf. the allusions to John 14:6; 10:7; 10:11; and 1:9 in Amphilochius, *De recens baptizatis* 160, 127, 130, 142, 150–51.

from Matt 13:31, 'sheep' from Isa 53:7, 'sun of justice' from Mal 3:20 and 'worm' (σκώληξ) from Ps^{LXX} 21:7.

In Amphilochius' use of scripture, two aspects are notable: on the one hand, focusing on the text, each of Amphilochius' sermons illustrate that the bishop himself drew on a wide range of passages from various books of the Bible. On the other hand, the manner in which Amphilochius used scripture in his sermons illustrates that he could presuppose that his audience knew several stories from the scriptures by heart. Taken together, these two aspects illustrate the wide dissemination of the Greek Bible by the end of the fourth century.[117]

By the end of the fourth century, the homilies given during the church services on Sundays and on the occasion of the great feasts played a major role in disseminating knowledge of the Bible in the bishopric. The weekly reading of the Bible, the homilies, and the catechesis, and the use of biblical phrases in the liturgy all sustained and expanded knowledge of the Bible among the faithful, as can be seen from the allusions to and quotations of the Bible in the texts of inscriptions over a wide area.

Conclusion

Epigraphy nuances our knowledge of the dissemination of biblical content in late antique Christianity. One of the most obvious ways in which biblical knowledge was kept alive was through naming. By giving their children the names of biblical figures, especially of the apostles, their memory was kept alive. Biblical phrases influenced the way in which early Christians prayed. Benedictions and invocations for help inscribed on stone reflect the language of the Psalms. Like the widely used trisagion from Isa 6:3, they show the influence of the LXX on the language of early Christianity. On the other hand, the use of these phrases reinforced the role of the Bible in the liturgy. Texts like Ps^{LXX} 117:20 ('This is the gate of the Lord; righteous ones shall enter in it'), Ps^{LXX} 28:3 ('The voice of the Lord is upon the waters'), Isa^{LXX} 1:18 ('even though your sins are like crimson, I will make them white like snow; and though they are like scarlet, I will make them white like wool'), and Ps^{LXX} 42:4 ('And I will go in to the altar of God, to God who gladdens

---

[117] It is particularly interesting that the text form used consequently reflects that of Codex Vaticanus. See Breytenbach 2012.

my youth') accompanied entrance into the church, receiving baptism, absolution, and the Eucharist.

Since Paul, leading figures instructed Christians[118] using narratives about Adam, Abraham, Moses, Joshua, and Jonah as τύποι for Christ or baptism.[119] The teaching of bishops and presbyters was based on these texts and lectors read such texts to Christian communities, ensuring that narratives from the Bible were present among Christians. Interpreted in the light of the Christ event, the meaning of these narratives was reinforced through homilies, as one can see from the fourth-century sermons of Amphilochius of Iconium. From the fifth century onward, ekphrastic inscriptions in churches captioned mosaics and *dipinti* that illustrated various stages in Jesus' life: his birth as the advent of the paradisiac peace (Isa 11:6), his triumphal entry into Jerusalem (Mark 11:1–11 and parallels), and his resurrection after three days like Jonah who was spat out by the big fish (Matt 12:38–40). Other depictions include the slaughtered lamb (Rev 5:8), as well as the liberation from the Egyptians through the Red Sea (Exod 14–15) and the circumcision of the Israelites at Gilgal (Josh 5:9) as foreshadowing Christian baptism. The similar reception of these motifs from the Bible in the literary works of Christian writers shows that the inscriptions and depictions were part of a larger network of texts, woven with threads from the LXX and the emerging New Testament, that sustained central aspects of early Christian liturgy, which to a large extent commemorated past events. The Eucharist was about remembering the meaning of the death of the Lord. Annual Christian feasts were embedded in the narratives about the birth, passion, death, and resurrection of Jesus Christ. The Exodus and circumcision were understood as a prefiguration of baptism. Liturgical actions, even ones as simple as addressing God as Creator, presupposed narratives such as those about the creation, the Exodus, the passion of Christ, and the victory of the Lord over death. As non-literary evidence, inscriptions contribute substantially to understanding the practice of early Christian dissemination and transmission of biblical narratives and motifs underpinning their faith. The studying, teaching, preaching, and liturgical use of narratives and motifs from the Bible by bishops, presbyters, and readers[120] functioned as ways to involve ordinary people who came to

---

[118] See 1 Cor 15:2; Rom 6:17.

[119] See Rom 5:14; 4:1, 23–24; 1 Cor 10:6; Heb 8:5; Josh 5:9; Matt 12:39, 41.

[120] On the requirement that clergy should be able to read, see note 2. On the teaching of bishops and presbyters, see Gemeinhardt 2016: 40–43.

the churches in the actions of listening to, looking at depictions of, and partaking in worship moulded by these narratives and motifs. For the first time in history, people of various regions and social classes were instructed from the same books. The readers, presbyters, and bishops who had command of letters thereby mediated knowledge of the scriptures to those who listened to the teaching, participated in liturgy, and looked at mosaics and *dipinti* in church buildings.

18 | How to Make Use of Pagan Knowledge without Separating Oneself from the Church's Milk: The Function of Otherness in Gregory of Nyssa's Theory of Self-Perfection

JAN R. STENGER

Introduction

Is there a Christian *paideia*, a characteristically Christian way of acquiring, ordering, and using knowledge? This question occupied the minds of the three Cappadocians ever since Basil and Gregory of Nazianzus travelled to Athens in order to study rhetoric while Gregory of Nyssa received at home a thorough training in literature and philosophy.[1] Their study of the Greek classical writers and thinkers left conspicuous marks on their works and their theology later in life, but was never unproblematic, as documented by Basil's *Address to the Young* and Nazianzen's invective against the emperor Julian (*Or.* 4). Gregory of Nyssa (*c.* 335–394) turned to the question of the proper engagement with classical *paideia* over and over again, in particular when he paid literary tribute to his siblings Macrina and Basil and to Gregory Thaumaturgus, about whom he knew through his grandmother.[2]

Education and learning also play a central role in the *Life of Moses*, which combines a historical account, based on Exodus and Numbers, of Moses' biography with an allegorical interpretation. Composed probably around 390 at the request of a certain Caesarius, the biography prominently features Moses' upbringing at the Pharaoh's court and his instruction in the disciplines.[3] As the introduction makes clear, the *Life* pursues a pedagogical

---

[1] On modes of knowing in the Cappadocians' homilies, see also Chapter 16 by Johan Leemans, this volume.

[2] See the *Life of Macrina* (SC 178), *On the Soul and Resurrection* (GNO 3.3), the eulogy for his brother Basil (GNO 10.1), and the *Life of Gregory Thaumaturgus* (GNO 10.1). For Gregory's depiction of Macrina as a philosopher, see Stenger 2022: 119–28 and Chapter 19 by Dawn LaValle Norman, this volume.

[3] Caesarius is addressed in Gregory of Nyssa, *Mos.* 2.319 (SC 1.324; the address, not transmitted in some of the manuscripts, is not put in the text of GNO 7.1.143; see the apparatus). Nothing further is known about him. For the probable date of the *Life*, see Daniélou (1968: 15) and Jaeger (1954: 132–42), who discuss its close relationship to *De instituto Christiano*.

goal: it intends to give counsel concerning the perfect life and to encourage the addressee, as well as any reader, to seek the path of virtue.[4] Gregory is known for his reflective approach to literary composition, and the *Life of Moses* is no exception.[5] Before he recounts the events recorded in the Pentateuch, he reflects on the possibility of human perfection and, in addition, on the challenge of representing and communicating the perfect life. Even though it has to be acknowledged that perfection cannot be adequately described, let alone attained by human beings, Gregory wants to provide to his readers the Old Testament figure of Moses as a model to emulate so that by imitating his example they may conduct their lives in a virtuous manner.[6] Yet, while ancient preachers often exhorted believers to imitate saintly exemplars without addressing the methodological problems involved in this task, Gregory raises a fundamental question that points to the rationale of the *Life*. Anticipating the reader's response to his text, he asks,

> 'What then?', someone will say, '[How shall I imitate them,] since I am not a Chaldaean as Abraham is remembered to have been, nor was I nourished by the daughter of the Egyptian as the report about Moses prevails, and in general I do not have in these matters anything in my life corresponding to anyone of the ancients? How shall I place myself in the same rank with one of them, when I do not know how to imitate anyone so far removed from me by the circumstances of his life?'[7]

The imagined reader here draws our attention to the central problem of pedagogical mimesis and, more generally, to the challenge of hermeneutics. How can the wide gap between the reader in the present and the role model situated in the remote past be bridged? How is imitation possible if its object is so different that the subject cannot find any point to relate to? With these metatextual comments, Gregory suggests that the encounter with an exemplary figure for the sake of self-perfection necessarily involves an element of otherness. Moulding the self in the quest for the perfect life requires the subject to assimilate him- or herself to an object, but on the other hand, the object must not be so different and alien as to preclude imitation. By couching the hermeneutical challenge in ethnic and geographic terms ('Chaldaean', 'Egyptian'), the *Life* highlights the enormous distance that has to be negotiated in the pedagogical process. As a solution to the

---

[4] Gregory of Nyssa, *Mos.* 1.2–3 (GNO 7.1.2–3; SC 1.46).   [5] See Jaeger 1961: 84.
[6] Gregory of Nyssa, *Mos.* 1.15 (GNO 7.1.6–7; SC 1.54).
[7] Gregory of Nyssa, *Mos.* 1.14 (GNO 7.1.6; SC 1.54): Τί οὖν, ἐρεῖ τις, εἰ μήτε Χαλδαῖος ἐγώ, ὥσπερ ὁ Ἀβραὰμ μνημονεύεται, μήτε τῆς θυγατρὸς τοῦ Αἰγυπτίου τρόφιμος, ὡς περὶ τοῦ Μωϋσέως ὁ λόγος κατέχει, μηδ' ὅλως ἐν τοῖς τοιούτοις πρός τινα τῶν ἀρχαίων ἔχω τι κατὰ τὸν βίον κατάλληλον, πῶς εἰς τὴν αὐτὴν τάξιν ἑνὶ τούτων ἐμαυτὸν καταστήσω, μὴ ἔχων ὅπως τὸν τοσοῦτον ἀφεστῶτα διὰ τῶν ἐπιτηδευμάτων μιμήσομαι. Translations are adapted from Malherbe and Ferguson 1978.

problem, Gregory proposes an allegorical reading of Moses' biography, an interpretation that brings out the general idea, the *dianoia*, by stripping it of contingent historical accretions.[8] Allegory is intended to make the other more familiar in order to facilitate understanding and imitation. This interpretative manoeuvre will allow readers to recognise the points of contact, the kinship as it were, that enable them to apply the model to their own lives.

The aim of this chapter is to show that Gregory's *Life of Moses* introduces the negotiation of otherness as a key mechanism in the process of what, with Wilhelm von Humboldt, we might call *Bildung*, the endeavour of both intellectual and ethical formation.[9] It addresses the question of how Gregory solves the hermeneutical challenge underlying the acquisition of knowledge that is necessary for self-perfection. I will argue that, instead of closing the gap completely, he makes the gulf of otherness productive and uses it for establishing a Christian mode of digesting knowledge.[10] It will become clear that otherness in the process of formation operates on different levels. Taking the category of distance (τὸν τοσοῦτον ἀφεστῶτα) as a key to Nyssen's conception of Christian *paideia*, I hope to make two contributions to research on this topic. First, my argument builds on Werner Jaeger's observation that the idea of *morphosis*, meaning the creative and sculptural activity of the educational process, is at the heart of Gregory's view of human progress.[11] Regarding this idea Jaeger states:

> One essential feature of Greek paideia that made it unique among all the different conceptions of human education in other nations is that it not only contemplated the process of development in the human subject but also took into account the influence of the object of learning.[12]

---

[8] Gregory of Nyssa, *Mos.* 1.14–15; 2.45; 2.105; 2.221–23; 2.251; etc.

[9] Man's purpose, as prescribed by reason, Humboldt says, is 'the highest and most harmonious formation of his capabilities into a unified whole' (*Ideen zu einem Versuch, die Gränzen der Wirksamkeit des Staates zu bestimmen*) (1903, 1st edn, 1792: 106). The two conditions for a successful process of formation are freedom and a variety of situations. Humboldt recognises that, in order to bring his human nature to fulfilment, the individual needs an object on which he can exercise his powers; to put it differently, for this purpose man needs a world outside himself (*Theorie der Bildung des Menschen* (Humboldt 1903, 1st edn, 1793: 282–83)). The term *Bildung* seems particularly apt in our context because, in its Humboldtian sense, it not only expresses the broad scope of formative processes pertaining to intellect and character but also rests on the idea that in order to develop the notion of humanity in ourselves to its full meaning, we need to connect our 'I' with an object that is not what we are. See Wulf 2003 and Gjesdal 2015. I have discussed Humboldt's idea of *Bildung* in relation to late antique conceptions of education in Stenger 2022: 189–94.

[10] See also Stenger 2022: 212–23. [11] Jaeger 1961: 86–100.

[12] Jaeger 1961: 91. This is one of the main threads of Jaeger's magnum opus, *Paideia: The Ideals of Greek Culture* (German orig. in 3 vols., 1933–44).

Whether this approach to education was unique or not, my analysis shall explicate in more detail than Jaeger's the relationship between likeness and otherness that is the backbone of Gregory's educational thinking. Second, existing research has foregrounded the provocation that pagan *paideia* posed to fourth-century churchmen because of its alleged foreignness. It has, for instance, been argued that Gregory's thinking is characterised by an antagonism between anthropocentric Hellenic *paideia* and God-oriented Christian formation.[13] The following discussion shall demonstrate that this image of cultural polarity is too simplistic and that, by contrast, the *Life* makes the case for a positive effect of the tension of foreignness and kinship.

Gregory of Nyssa's Theory of Human Perfection

First a rough outline of Gregory's educational thinking is in order, as the context in which he situates Moses' engagement with various types of knowledge. The elements of his thought on human formation and progress are all included in the *Life* itself and receive detailed treatment also in other writings, above all in the treatises *De instituto Christiano* and *De perfectione*.[14] Gregory's premise is that the human being is by nature an educable being, capable of giving shape to him- or herself according to a chosen goal (*Mos.* 2.3). To make clear how he conceives of this activity, Gregory draws an analogy to the fine arts, suggesting that humans have the ability, and the task, to shape themselves as the sculptors of their own lives, as if life were a pliable substance that could gradually be assimilated to a preconceived idea (2.313). The belief that self-formation resembles the creative activity of an artist is also the reason why, as Jaeger notes, Gregory frequently has recourse to the term *morphosis* and related expressions when discussing the process of perfection.[15] In addition to the idea of creatively shaping human life, another implication of the metaphor is that the sculptor, that is, every human being, has to have a plan, an idea of the final artwork, according to which the material is formed. In Gregory's theological anthropology, the ultimate goal of every formative endeavour is perfection, namely the

---

[13] Van Lengerich 1994: 20–24, 295. For Gregory's encounter with, and assimilation of, classical philosophy, see Pelikan 1993.

[14] Both treatises are edited in GNO 8.1. For their theology see Jaeger 1954 and van Lengerich 1994. See also Leuenberger-Wenger 2008 on Gregory's idea of human perfection in the context of his ethics.

[15] Jaeger 1961: 87. See also the relevant entries in the Brill *Lexicon Gregorianum: Wörterbuch zu den Schriften Gregors von Nyssa* (10 vols.).

contemplation of God, as illustrated in Moses' encounter with God.[16] This goal can be pursued only through the life of virtue, seen in truly Platonic fashion as the ascent from the material world to the divine.

From the perspective of salvation history, human self-perfection may also be viewed as a restorative process, because what the human being, by following the path of virtue, seeks to accomplish is to regain likeness to God.[17] Since in Adam's fall, man has violated his natural goodness as *imago Dei*, he is now commanded to eradicate any evil from his life and to beautify himself with what is incorruptible and unchangeable until he becomes like God.[18] Gregory's conceptualisation of this process is evidently indebted to Plato's notion of the assimilation to God to the highest possible degree (ὁμοίωσις θεῷ).[19] For Gregory, the idea that man seeks to overcome alienation and become like God entails two important qualifications. For one thing, it is impossible to complete the formative path without God's help. Only if divine grace assists humans in their quest for the good can they hope to cleanse their lives from passions and vices in order to free themselves from the world of materiality. Man's dependence is thus a core element of Gregory's educational thinking.[20] This also becomes apparent when we look at how humans are to work towards the goal of virtue. In order to cleanse his life from corruption and defilement, man needs an exemplar, an embodiment of perfection. To take up Gregory's analogy of the sculptor, we could say that, for human life to take a particular shape, there must be a suitable model. In the case of the Christian life, this means that Christ himself has been provided as the archetype to which humans ought to conform their lives.[21] As Gregory states in *De perfectione*, 'the one road to the pure and divine life for lovers of virtue is knowing what the name of Christ means, in conformity with which we must shape our lives'.[22]

---

[16] Cf. Gregory of Nyssa, *Mos.* 2.157–58 (GNO 7.1.84–85; SC 1.206).

[17] Cf. Gregory of Nyssa, *Or. cat.* 8 and 15 (GNO 3.4.31, 43–44).

[18] The idea of man as *imago Dei* occurs in the *Life of Moses* only at the end, in 2.318 (GNO 7.1.143; SC 1.322–24). However, it has a central place in Gregory's Christian anthropology. See *Perf.* 269–72 M. (GNO 8.1.194–95), *Prof.* 244–45 M. (GNO 8.1.135–38). See Jaeger 1954: 73–76; Boersma 2013: 104.

[19] Plato, *Theaet.* 176a–b, *Resp.* 6.500c, 10.613a. See Merki 1952.

[20] Gregory of Nyssa, *Mos.* 2.44 (GNO 7.1.45; SC 1.130). For Gregory's doctrine of synergy, see Jaeger 1954: 85–107 and Boersma 2013: 217–20.

[21] See, e.g., Gregory of Nyssa, *Prof.* 244 M. (GNO 8.1.135–36), further *Mos.* 2.318 (GNO 7.1.143; SC 1.322–24).

[22] Gregory of Nyssa, *Perf.* 256 and 260 M. (GNO 8.1.178, 181): μία πρὸς τὴν καθαράν τε καὶ θείαν ζωήν ἐστι τοῖς φιλαρέτοις ὁδὸς τὸ γνῶναι τί σημαίνει τὸ τοῦ Χριστοῦ ὄνομα, ᾧ χρὴ καὶ τὸν ἡμέτερον συμμορφωθῆναι βίον, διὰ τῆς τῶν λοιπῶν ὀνομάτων ἐμφάσεως εἰς ἀρετὴν ῥυθμιζόμενον.

The second modification is that the goal of perfection is never attainable. In the introduction to the *Life of Moses*, Gregory expounds that, as the apostle has taught, perfection has no limit and that the good is limited only by the presence of its opposite.[23] What is more, God, as the essence of goodness, does not admit of an opposite, so that his nature is unlimited and infinite. As a consequence, the person pursuing the life of virtue, i.e., participating in God being absolute virtue, has a desire that never reaches fulfilment. Thus, 'the perfection of human nature consists in its very growth in goodness' and is by necessity an unlimited progression (ἐπέκτασις).[24] The tension of fundamental difference or otherness is inscribed in Gregory's theory of self-formation from the outset, as the ontological gap between humans and their ideal goal.

Moses as Paradigm of the Educated Christian

In Gregory's allegorical interpretation, Moses' entire life perfectly illustrates these principles. His biography is presented as a continuous ascent, completed through several stages, which culminates in the contemplation of God. From childhood on, his actions and conduct evince the desire for goodness and perfection, until he has liberated his soul from the world of materiality and climbed to the top of Mount Sinai, where he attained ever deeper knowledge of God. It is therefore appropriate to call Moses 'a good sculptor who has fashioned well the statue of his whole life' and to consider him a true servant of God, an accolade to which Gregory encourages his readers to aspire.[25] Although the Old Testament lawgiver certainly attained to a degree of perfection that for ordinary Christians is beyond reach, Gregory's pedagogy is optimistic that his biography can serve as a blueprint for the true Christian life also under the very different conditions of the late Roman empire.

In the same way as Philo of Alexandria, in his allegorical reading, had interpreted Moses' life as an illustration of the highest form of human

---

[23] Gregory of Nyssa, *Mos.* 1.5–8 (GNO 7.1.3–4; SC 1.48–50), quoting Phil 3:13, which has been called by Daniélou 1968: 49 n. 1 'le leit-motiv de tout le traité'. For the idea of divine infinity in the *Life*, see Böhm 1996: 54–57; Geljon 2005: 162–63; Boersma 2013: 232–34. It is particularly prominent in Gregory's treatise *Against Eunomius*.

[24] Gregory of Nyssa, *Mos.* 1.10 (GNO 7.1.5; SC 1.50): τάχα γὰρ τὸ οὕτως ἔχειν, ὡς ἀεὶ ἐθέλειν ἐν τῷ καλῷ τὸ πλέον ἔχειν, ἡ τῆς ἀνθρωπίνης φύσεως τελειότης ἐστί. For the idea of perpetual progress see *Cant.* 8 (GNO 6.245–46); *Mos.* 2.225 (GNO 7.1.112; SC 1.262); *Perf.* 285 M. (GNO 8.1.212–14). See Alexopoulos 2006; Mateo-Seco 2010; Boersma 2013: 232–34, 243–45.

[25] Gregory of Nyssa, *Mos.* 2.313–15 (GNO 7.1.140–41; SC 1.318–20).

existence, so Gregory, who was clearly influenced by Philo, wanted his contemporaries to emulate Moses and translate the general idea of his biography to their own lives.[26] Significantly, Nyssen evoked the lawgiver as a paradigmatic figure also when he commemorated Gregory Thaumaturgus and his own older brother, Basil. And he did so under one particular aspect. In both the *Life of Gregory Thaumaturgus* and the funeral oration for Basil, Moses is mentioned as an analogy for the attitude to studies and learning. Just as Moses had, as Acts 7:22 reported, imbibed Egyptian wisdom, so the Wonderworker and Basil did not confine their intellectual interests to Christian teachings and the scriptures, but also deemed it apt to have training in 'outside' or 'foreign' learning, that is, to study pagan Greek literature and philosophy.[27] The repeated reference to Moses' intellectual formation shows that Gregory had in mind the experience of many a late antique Christian: he wanted to advise them on how to deal with Hellenic *paideia* as nurtured by the established schools.

Moses' early education is given a prominent place also in the *Life*. Right at the beginning of the historical part, after he has related the circumstances of Moses' birth, Gregory gives some information on the learning with which the adolescent was made familiar in the household of the Pharaoh's daughter.

After he had left childhood and had been educated in foreign studies during his royal upbringing, he did not choose the things considered glorious by the foreigners nor did he agree any longer to acknowledge as his mother that woman by whom he had been adopted, but who was not his real mother; instead he returned to his natural mother and attached himself to his own kinsmen.[28]

It is remarkable that Gregory inserts here into the narrative an element that is not included in Exodus, but found only in Acts, Philo's *Life of Moses*, and later Christian literature.[29] Apparently, the glimpse of Moses' intellectual

---

[26] For Philo's influence on Gregory, see Geljon 2002.
[27] Gregory of Nyssa, *Thaum.* 901 M. (GNO 10.1.10); *Laud. Bas.* 789, 808–9 M. (GNO 10.1.110, 126). In Gregory's eulogy of Basil, Moses is seen as the model for Basil's entire life. See Damgaard 2013: 183–201.
[28] Gregory of Nyssa, *Mos.* 1.18 (GNO 7.1.7–8; SC 1.58): Ἐκβὰς δὲ ἤδη τὴν ἡλικίαν τῶν παίδων, ἐν βασιλικῇ τῇ τροφῇ καὶ παιδευθεὶς τὴν ἔξωθεν παίδευσιν, ἃ δόξης ἐνομίζετο παρὰ τοῖς ἔξωθεν οὐχ ἑλέσθαι οὐδ᾽ ἔτι καταδέξασθαι τὴν σεσοφισμένην ἐκείνην ὁμολογεῖν μητέρα ᾕπερ εἰς υἱοῦ τάξιν εἰσεποιήθη, ἀλλ᾽ ἐπὶ τὴν κατὰ φύσιν ἐπανελθεῖν πάλιν καὶ τοῖς ὁμοφύλοις ἐγκαταμιχθῆναι· Malherbe and Ferguson's translation 'that wise woman' is a misunderstanding of the Greek; the participle σεσοφισμένην means 'craftily devised', underlining that the princess was not Moses' true mother. See also *Laud. Bas.* 809 M. (GNO 10.1.126): ἠρνήσατο μετὰ ταῦτα ὁ Μωϋσῆς τῆς ψευδωνύμου μητρὸς τὴν σεσοφισμένην συγγένειαν.
[29] Acts 7:22; Philo, *Mos.* 1.5, 20–24; Clement of Alexandria, *Strom.* 1.23.153 (after Philo).

upbringing was, in his view, so relevant to the way in which Christians of late antiquity were to conduct their lives that he added it to the paraphrase that otherwise followed closely the Old Testament. When immediately before this passage Gregory relates how the princess encounters the ark carrying the baby over the Nile's waves, he highlights that the infant instinctively refused the stranger's nourishment and was nursed at his mother's breast. This is then reiterated, in slightly more elaborate fashion, in the quote, in which it is again stressed that the princess was merely Moses' 'feigned' mother, who had adopted him, whereas the child returned to his biological mother and kinsmen. With the contrast of ἔξωθεν and τοῖς ὁμοφύλοις, the *Life* introduces the leitmotif that pervades the narrative and its allegorical exegesis: over and over again we are reminded of the opposition of 'foreign' and 'kin', often referred to by the ethnic names 'Egyptian' and 'Hebrew'. This antagonism is graphically conjured in the passage immediately following the quote. There Gregory mentions that, in a fight between a Hebrew and an Egyptian, Moses sided with his countryman and killed the foreigner, whereas on another occasion, when two Hebrews were fighting with each other, he reconciled them as 'brothers' bound together by nature.[30]

Thus, Moses' education is bookended by two references to the polarity of otherness and sameness. To add to this sense of dichotomy, the passage quoted above twice underscores the alien nature of the knowledge to which the boy was exposed. Not only was he 'educated in foreign education' (παιδευθεὶς τὴν ἔξωθεν παίδευσιν), but this type of education was also held in high esteem by the 'outsiders', the non-Jews. In a very conspicuous manner, the *Life* presents the *paideusis* which seems to be Moses' exclusive intellectual formation as inherently alien, as something not really belonging to the people of Israel. By virtue of its association with his royal stepmother, the Egyptian knowledge appears even as false and unnatural. Intriguingly, however, the presentation of the sentence intimates that it was precisely the training in feigned foreign learning that both chronologically and logically preceded Moses' return to his biological mother and true origins. We will return to that point later. For the moment it suffices to state that the first paragraphs of the historical account suggest that learning and self-formation somehow perforce involve an engagement with otherness, in a kind of dialectical process. The alien element had to be counterbalanced by what was truly one's own. Gregory's reader was to learn the lesson that just as the future lawgiver had been trained in Egyptian wisdom, so fourth-century Christian education included an element of 'external' *paideusis*.

---

[30] Gregory of Nyssa, *Mos.* 1.18 (GNO 7.1.8; SC 1.58). See Exod 2:11–13.

Gregory's introduction of the Egyptian learning into the Exodus narrative indicates, first, that otherness in the process of formation is operative not only in imitating exemplars such as Moses, but also in dealing with existing knowledge; and second, that the Christian life of virtue in some sense necessitates a critical engagement with classical *paideia*. With the latter point, which also comes to the fore in the *Life of Gregory Thaumaturgus*, Gregory takes up a topic that resonated with most well-educated Christians of this period. After having touched upon this controversial issue in the historical narrative only briefly, he returns to it in more detail in the allegorical explanation:

The ark, constructed out of various boards, would be the education put together from various disciplines, which holds the one whom it carries above the waves of life. Although he is borne along by the rushing of the waves, he will not be carried far by the tossing of the waters as long as there is this education. Instead being washed to the firm bank, that is to say, outside the turmoil of life, he will be naturally thrust by the motion of the waters onto the firm bank.[31]

While Gregory's allegorical interpretation in general owes much to Philo's precedent, he departs from his model in this particular case. That the ark of the Exodus narrative stands for an education comprising a variety of disciplines is a reading without exact parallel in the Jewish-Christian tradition.[32] Apparently, Gregory here wants to intimate a close resemblance between Moses and well-educated late antique elites, who had, on top of their rhetorical schooling, acquired knowledge in the liberal disciplines. Later, when the Israelites' departure from Egypt is discussed, this relationship becomes more explicit. There the *Life* adds that a thorough training in foreign *paideia* includes not only moral and natural philosophy, but also geometry, astronomy, dialectic, and whatever learning was available outside the church.[33] If, at first glance, the parallel between the ark constructed from various boards and the liberal arts curriculum seems a bit forced, the underlying intention then becomes clear in the following lines: in the same way as the basket of the historical account saves the baby's life from the

---

[31] Gregory of Nyssa, *Mos.* 2.7–8 (GNO 7.1.35; SC 1.110): Κιβωτὸς δ' ἂν εἴη ἐκ διαφόρων σανίδων συμπεπηγυῖα ἡ ἐκ ποικίλων μαθημάτων συμπηγνυμένη παίδευσις, ἡ ἄνω τῶν κυμάτων τὸν δι' αὐτῆς ἐπιφερόμενον τοῦ βίου ἀνέχουσα, ἧς ὑπαρχούσης, οὐδὲ ἐπὶ πολὺ τῷ σάλῳ τῶν ὑδάτων ἐμπλανηθήσεται ταῖς τῶν κυμάτων ὁρμαῖς συμπεριφερόμενος, ἀλλ' ἐπὶ τοῦ σταθεροῦ τῆς ὄχθης, τουτέστιν ἔξω τοῦ βιωτικοῦ σάλου γενόμενος, αὐτομάτως ὑπὸ τῆς φορᾶς τῶν ὑδάτων πρὸς τὸ σταθερὸν ἀπωσθήσεται.

[32] See Geljon 2002: 85–86. For the idea of taking various elements of learning from diverse sources and weaving them together, see Philo, *Somn.* 1.205 (on Bezaleel, cf. Exod 31:2–5).

[33] Gregory of Nyssa, *Mos.* 2.115 (GNO 7.1.68; SC 1.174).

dangerous waters, good knowledge of the classical disciplines protects against the turmoil of life. As it is the aim of the life of virtue to escape from the world of materiality and complete the ascent to the divine, the encyclopaedic Hellenic *paideia* appears to make a significant contribution to the path of perfection. Although it is not fully explained how, a structured and methodical instruction, as it was offered by the established schools, is seen by Gregory to disentangle Christians from the chaos of human affairs and carry them above the confusion to what is firm and stable, that is, virtue.

How Hellenic knowledge, which we have seen is conspicuously 'alien', contributes to Christian self-formation is further elucidated in the passage on the exodus from Egypt. Following an interpretation already proposed by Origen, Gregory understands the Old Testament narrative in the sense that those who follow their leader, embodied by Moses, to the goal of virtue should take with them, as a viaticum as it were, the treasures of the enemies.[34] The higher meaning of the biblical passage, the *Life* explains, 'commands those participating through virtue in the free life also to equip themselves with the foreign wealth of learning by which foreigners to the faith beautify themselves'.[35] Once again, Gregory underscores the foreign nature of the pagan disciplines but insists that they can serve as equipment on the Christian road to perfection. While other Christian readings of the Exodus' spoliation episode emphasise the selectiveness of the Christian's use of pagan learning, advising that only useful teachings should be adopted, Gregory indicates the way in which classical education, epitomised in the disciplines mentioned above, could be utilised. 'Many', he says, 'bring to the church of God their profane learning as a kind of gift: Such a man was the great Basil, who acquired the Egyptian wealth in every respect during his youth and dedicated this wealth to God for the adornment of the church, the true tabernacle.'[36] The things learned in the schools according to the traditional curriculum will be of great use at a time

---

[34] Gregory of Nyssa, *Mos.* 2.112–16 (GNO 7.1.67–69; SC 1.172–74). Cf. Exod 3:21–22; 12:35–36. Origen, *Ep. Greg.* 1–3. As to the Christian appropriation of pagan learning, it is Augustine's allegorical reading of the spoliation that has gained particular prominence (Augustine, *Doctr. chr.* 2.40.60–42.63). See also Philo, *Mos.* 1.140–42. Chin (2008: 88–93) discusses Augustine's interpretation. See also Allen 2008 and Stenger (forthcoming).

[35] Gregory of Nyssa, *Mos.* 2.115 (GNO 7.1.68; SC 1.174): ὁ κελεύων τοὺς τὸν ἐλεύθερον βίον μετιόντας δι' ἀρετῆς καὶ τὸν ἔξωθεν τῆς παιδεύσεως πλοῦτον παρασκευάσασθαι, ᾧ οἱ κατὰ τὴν πίστιν ἀλλόφυλοι καλλωπίζονται.

[36] Gregory of Nyssa, *Mos.* 2.116 (GNO 7.1.68–69; SC 1.174–76): Πολλοὶ τὴν ἔξω παίδευσιν τῇ τοῦ Θεοῦ Ἐκκλησίᾳ καθάπερ τι δῶρον προσάγουσιν, οἷος ἦν ὁ μέγας Βασίλειος, ὁ καλῶς τὸν Αἰγύπτιον πλοῦτον ἐμπορευσάμενος κατὰ τὸν τῆς νεότητος χρόνον καὶ ἀναθεὶς τῷ Θεῷ καὶ τῷ τοιούτῳ πλούτῳ τὴν ἀληθινὴν κατακοσμήσας τῆς Ἐκκλησίας σκηνήν.

when the divine sanctuary of mystery is equipped with the riches of reason. What an exemplary Christian intellectual such as Basil demonstrates is the significant role of rationality made available by philosophy, dialectic, and the other arts to Christian doctrine. Taken together with the earlier passage on Moses' ark, this intimates that the exercise of reason, the theoretical and contemplative element so prominent in pagan studies, becomes an important aid when the Christian is proceeding on the path from the ever-changeable material realm to the heights of the divine. However, as the metaphors of beautification and embellishment imply, foreign *paideia* is assigned an unequivocally subservient role. It remains on the outside and is purely instrumental, like the items carried off by the Israelites.

Objectifying Classical *Paideia*

By interpreting the spoliation narrative in this way and holding up his brother as an example, Gregory seems to advocate a rather liberal use of the traditional education system and its curriculum. With the reference to philosophy and other branches of knowledge, he suggests that the methods and contents taught by formal education can add to Christian faith and truth in such a way that Christianity becomes more rational and intellectual, if we may put it in these terms. While a number of fourth-century Christians, especially those with inclinations to asceticism, were sceptical, if not outright opposed to the use of Hellenic *paideia*, Gregory makes a plea for its integration into Christianity and even into the life of perfection. Yet the Christian engagement with Greek *paideusis* is not as straightforward as it seems. It is no coincidence that, for his reading of the departure from Egypt, Gregory had recourse to Origen's exegesis, which had recommended the episode as a template for the right way of using pagan teachings. For it was in the act of spoiling and leaving Egypt that Gregory found an image congenial to his view of a Christian *paideia*. The story of how Moses and his people stripped the foreigners of their possessions and took the valuable things with them to the promised land perfectly encapsulated the duality of otherness and appropriation that structures Gregory's educational thinking. Accordingly, the allegorical interpretation does not allow the notion of foreignness to recede into the background. Conversely, the alien nature and difference of Greek learning is once again thrown into high relief. The repeated references to the Egyptians or 'foreigners' and to the spatial movement by which the 'riches' are brought into the church heighten our awareness that *paideusis* remains alien and different, almost displaced.

This quality raises the fundamental question of whether an integration is possible in the first place. When we return to Moses' beginnings, we notice that the *Life* has already drawn attention to the provocation posed by 'outside' learning. We mentioned above that the passage on Moses' education in the royal household of the pharaoh is immediately followed by his intervention in the fight between a Hebrew and an Egyptian. Returning to this event in the allegorical section, Gregory ties it even closer to the theme of knowledge:

> It is true that he who looks to the foreign doctrines and to the doctrines of the fathers will find himself between two antagonists. For the foreigner in worship is opposed to the Hebrew teaching, and contentiously strives to appear stronger than the Israelite. And so he seems to be to many of the more superficial who abandoned the faith of their fathers and fought on the side of the enemy, becoming transgressors of the fathers' teaching. On the other hand, he who is great and noble in soul like Moses slays with his own hand the one who rises in opposition to true piety.[37]

This passage not only employs ethnic categories to emphasise the difference between pagan teachings and Christian truth but even presents the Christian encounter with Greco-Roman culture as a veritable battle. While, from the times of the Apostle Paul on, Christians were used to seeing their relationship with non-Christians and the surrounding culture in terms of ethnicity, the *Life of Moses* here goes a step further by combining ethnic difference with the concept of fight.[38] There is an enmity that defies any attempt at reconciliation. It is, to put it differently, a question of either/or, of victory or defeat, which admits of no mean. To add to the sense of incompatibility, Gregory joins the motif of fight with the polarity of paternal heritage, or tradition, versus apostasy, suggesting that those who embrace outside learning too eagerly defect from the true and pure faith, thus betraying their own origins. But Gregory takes his reading here still to another level. First, he insists that foreign philosophy utterly fails to

---

[37] Gregory of Nyssa, *Mos.* 2.13 (GNO 7.1.37; SC 1.112–14): Ἀληθὴς δὲ ὁ λόγος ὅτι δύο πολεμίων μέσος γενήσεται ὁ πρὸς τὰ ἔξωθεν δόγματα καὶ τὰ πάτρια βλέπων. Ἀνθίσταται γὰρ ὁ κατὰ τὴν θρησκείαν ἀλλόφυλος τῷ Ἑβραίῳ λόγῳ, ἰσχυρότερος φανῆναι τοῦ Ἰσραηλιτικοῦ φιλονεικῶν. Καὶ πολλοῖς γε τῶν ἐπιπολαιοτέρων τοιοῦτος ἔδοξεν, οἳ καταλιπόντες τὴν πατρῴαν πίστιν τῷ ἐχθρῷ συνεμάχησαν, παραβάται τῆς πατρίου διδασκαλίας γενόμενοι. Ὁ μέντοι κατὰ τὸν Μωϋσέα μέγας τε καὶ γενναῖος τὴν ψυχὴν νεκρὸν ἀποδείκνυσι τῇ παρ' ἑαυτοῦ πληγῇ τὸν τῷ λόγῳ τῆς εὐσεβείας ἀντεγειρόμενον.

[38] Krolikowski (2010: 572–74) unconvincingly attributes the negative attitude towards Greek *paideia* expressed in this passage to Gregory's 'trauma' triggered by the emperor Julian's edict on teaching. His highly psychologising reading fails to take into consideration the fundamental ambivalence about classical culture evinced by the Cappadocians and other ecclesiastical writers.

attain true knowledge of God, as reflected by the princess's barrenness. It is, though, not only insufficiency that distinguishes Greek philosophy from Christian wisdom. What is more, pagan learning is opposed to Christianity with regard to religion and theology, as the allegorical interpretation of Moses' upbringing among the Egyptians makes clear:

> Now after living with the princess of the Egyptians for such a long time that he seemed to share in what was held in respect by them, he must return to his natural mother. Indeed, he was not separated from her while he was being brought up by the princess but was nursed by his mother's milk, as the history states. This teaches, it seems to me, that if we should be involved with foreign teachings during our education, we should not separate ourselves from the nourishment of the church's milk, which would be her laws and customs. By these the soul is nourished and matured, thus being given the means of ascending the height.[39]

The study of foreign *logoi*, Gregory insists, must not get such a strong grip on the Christian student that he is alienated from his religious affiliation and tempted to abandon the laws of the church. The fight of the Egyptian against the Hebrew, he elaborates further, is 'like the fight of idolatry against true religion, of licentiousness against self-control, of injustice against righteousness', and he reiterates that the victory of true religion is the death of idolatry.[40] In Gregory's view, we would miss the significance of the antagonism if we understood it simply in terms of intellectual superiority and inferiority, respectively. Rather, it has to be seen as a religious conflict, as Christianity's triumph over paganism, because Greek philosophy is intertwined with the cult of the pagan gods. Like Tertullian and the *Life of Antony*, Gregory emphasises the opposition of Greco-Roman culture and Christian faith; he seeks to draw a line as sharply as possible between the followers of Jesus and the pagan world surrounding them.[41]

---

[39] Gregory of Nyssa, *Mos.* 2.12 (GNO 7.1.36–37; SC 1.112): Οὐκοῦν τοσοῦτόν τις τῇ τῶν Αἰγυπτίων βασιλίδι συζήσας, ὅσον μὴ δοκεῖν ἄμοιρος εἶναι τῶν παρ' ἐκείνοις σεμνῶν, ἀναδραμείτω πρὸς τὴν κατὰ φύσιν μητέρα, ἧς οὐδὲ παρὰ τῇ βασιλίδι τρεφόμενος ἀπεσχίσθη, τῷ μητρῴῳ γάλακτι, καθὼς ἡ ἱστορία φησί, τιθηνούμενος, ὅπερ μοι δοκεῖ διδάσκειν, εἰ τοῖς ἔξωθεν λόγοις καθομιλοίημεν ἐν τῷ καιρῷ τῆς παιδεύσεως, μὴ χωρίζεσθαι τοῦ ὑποτρέφοντος ἡμᾶς τῆς Ἐκκλησίας γάλακτος. Τοῦτο δ' ἂν εἴη τὰ νόμιμά τε καὶ τὰ ἔθη τῆς Ἐκκλησίας, οἷς τρέφεται ἡ ψυχὴ καὶ ἁδρύνεται, ἐντεῦθεν τῆς εἰς ὕψος ἀναδρομῆς τὰς ἀφορμὰς ποιουμένη. See also *Laud. Bas.* 808–9 M. (GNO 10.1.125–26).

[40] Gregory of Nyssa, *Mos.* 2.14 (GNO 7.1.37; SC 1.114): Μέσος γὰρ ὁ ἄνθρωπος οἷόν τι ἔπαθλον ἀγῶνος τοῖς ἐκ τοῦ ἐναντίου μεταποιουμένοις πρόκειται· καὶ ᾧπερ ἂν προστεθῇ, τοῦτον νικητὴν τοῦ ἐναντίου ποιεῖ· οἷον εἰδωλολατρεία καὶ θεοσέβεια, ἀκολασία καὶ σωφροσύνη, δικαιοσύνη καὶ ἀδικία, τύφος καὶ μετριότης, καὶ πάντα τὰ ἐξ ἀντιθέτου νοούμενα Αἰγυπτίου τινὸς ἀντικρύς ἐστι πρὸς Ἑβραῖον μάχη.

[41] See, for example, Tertullian, *Praescr.* 7.9; Athanasius, *Vit. Ant.* 72–80. See Stenger (forthcoming) for an overview and further literature.

Even though he acknowledges the positive contribution made by the classical education system, he does his best to paint it in dark colours. Greek philosophy is associated with miscarriage, falsehood, and vice, so that Moses feels shame (αἰσχύνη) to be called the son of such a mother. Significantly, Gregory reaffirms his alleged aversion to Greek *paideia* by repeating these strong verdicts in the eulogistic oration for Basil, when he summarises the lawgiver's attitude to pagan learning.[42] In contrast to the hermeneutical otherness mentioned earlier, this type of alienness is seen in a predominantly negative light, as a menace.

It is the well-known rhetoric of difference that Gregory employs here to throw the problematic nature of classical *paideusis* into high relief.[43] Yet, he deepens the trench between Christian religion and philosophy by projecting onto it the ethnic distinction between Hebrews and Egyptians, and further, the dichotomy of nature and artifice. When we notice the prominence of the notion of difference in the *Life*, this raises the question as to whether Gregory had recourse to this trope simply because he wanted to demarcate Christian identity in the sharpest possible way. Arthur Urbano has argued that Gregory, though he was open to the usefulness of *paideia*, still fell back into the habit of casting it as essentially foreign:

> While Gregory may have 'recognized' the broader contours of the competition with the Greeks, he still 'misrecognized' the extent to which Christian intellectual culture had a kinship to Greek paideia. This misrecognition results in an objectification of Greek wisdom as something completely identifiable and separable from Christianity.[44]

Urbano is right to point out that the *Life of Moses* objectifies Greek erudition, as Gregory postulated a clear dividing line where in fact there was kinship. Nyssen objectifies classical culture so as to advocate Christianity as the superior alternative. It is, however, misleading to term this a misrecognition, as if he had been unaware of how much Christianity was part of Greco-Roman civilisation. After Clement of Alexandria and others had discerned traces of Jewish-Christian wisdom in pagan philosophers, and at a time when Basil in his *Address to the Young* saw some pagan teachings as 'related to us' and 'akin' to Christian truth, Gregory was certainly alive to the ground shared by Christian intellectual culture and Greek *paideia*.[45] Thus, it was a purposeful mental operation that assigned to Hellenic *paideia* a

---

[42] Gregory of Nyssa, *Laud. Bas.* 809 M. (GNO 10.1.126).   [43] See Cameron 1991.
[44] Urbano 2013: 119.
[45] Clement of Alexandria, *Strom.* 1.25.165; Basil, *Leg. lib.* 7.6–13. For the so-called dependency theme in Christian writers, see Ridings 1995 and Boys-Stones 2001: 176–202.

precisely defined and circumscribed place and function within his conception of the life of perfection.

That this objectification was a key part of Gregory's mapping of the educational field becomes apparent when we take a closer look at the method proposed for dealing with the foreign element. We have already seen that the *Life* follows Origen in reading the spoliation of the Egyptians as an image of how Christians should 'borrow' from Greek culture what is useful and put it in the service of Christian truth. Significantly, Gregory emphasises twice that this is a 'command' to those who participate through virtue in the free life, implying that the appropriation of pagan doctrines is a matter of necessity.[46] Further, Gregory's reading hints that the use of Greek *paideia* is justified only if it is done within and for the church; the pagan disciplines do not have a value in themselves and are not to be pursued independently from faith. Thus, pagan intellectual culture is confined to an instrumental and subservient role, and it remains identifiable as something of foreign origin, which means that it has to be translocated. As the notion of borrowing suggests, the use that Christians are to make of the traditional curriculum is a subservient one.[47] That it is an intermediary stage on the road to virtue, but not the final destination has also been pointed out before, in the interpretation of Moses' marriage with the foreign woman Zipporah.[48] In Gregory's view, the union with the Midianite wife illustrates the way in which the Christian ought to deal with a cultural tradition outside Christianity. The lesson that this episode teaches is that some foreign teachings are not to be rejected when we strive for virtue. 'Indeed', Gregory says, 'moral and natural philosophy may become at certain times a comrade, friend, and companion of life to the higher way, provided that the offspring of this union introduce nothing of a foreign defilement'.[49] It is essential that the Christian utilises pagan *paideia* as propaedeutic, because it eases the departure from the material world and prepares the acquisition of virtue, but only for a limited period, until he, like Moses, returns to his true mother, the church.

---

[46] Gregory of Nyssa, *Mos.* 2.115 (GNO 7.1.68; SC 1.174): κελεύων and κελεύει.

[47] Pace Urbano 2013: 124, Gregory, in his reading of the spoliation, does not develop a Christian curriculum outside of and independent from Greek schools. Rather, he shows how elements of the traditional curriculum can be made profitable for Christian formation.

[48] Gregory has briefly mentioned Moses' 'foreign wife' (without name) and their children in 1.19 and 22. In both passages, he stresses her foreignness.

[49] Gregory of Nyssa, *Mos.* 2.37 (GNO 7.1.43; SC 1.126–28): Καὶ γὰρ ἡ ἠθική τε καὶ φυσικὴ φιλοσοφία γένοιτο ἄν ποτε τῷ ὑψηλοτέρῳ βίῳ σύζυγός τε καὶ φίλη καὶ κοινωνὸς τῆς ζωῆς, μόνον εἰ τὰ ἐκ ταύτης κυήματα μηδὲν ἐπάγοιτο τοῦ ἀλλοφύλου μιάσματος. While here Gregory mentions only two branches of philosophy, he adds the third, logic, in 2.115. For Moses' marriage with the daughter of the priest Jethro, see Exod 2:16–22 and 4:19–27.

Apart from being temporary, the exploitation of foreign learning is legitimate. To his recommendation that we associate with foreign wisdom Gregory adds the exhortation to scatter the wicked shepherds from their unjust use of the wells, meaning the wicked pagan teachers who have made illegitimate use of instruction.[50] It is thus not only an act of cultural borrowing, but also one of returning non-Christian teachings to their proper use – a view advocated also, if more elaborately, by Augustine in his reading of the spoliation episode.[51] For Hellenic doctrines to be used properly, Christians first need to purge them. Since philosophy contains false teachings alongside true knowledge, it is vital to strip it of erroneous doctrines and exercise careful discrimination. Like Basil in his recommendations on Greek literature, his brother advises readers to separate wicked and harmful teachings from those which are in agreement with and related to Christian truth. Expressed in allegorical terms this means: 'There is something fleshly and uncircumcised in what is taught by philosophy's generative faculty; when that has been completely removed, there remains the pure Israelite race.'[52] The good doctrines, Gregory explains, are contaminated by what pagan philosophy absurdly has added. He conceptualises the engagement with Greek *paideia* as a kind of subtraction: as the pagans have obscured and defiled the true teachings, it is necessary to remove the foreign elements so that the pure core can be seen again. Knowledge is stripped of its negative and threatening otherness. On the other hand, it seems to be precisely this operation of discrimination that enables the Christian to recognise fully what genuinely belongs to him.

Projecting the Jewish practice of circumcision onto the Christian dealing with philosophy, the *Life* intimates that the appropriation of foreign doctrines is virtually a religious rite, one that puts a Jewish, viz. Christian, mark on them, as a visible sign of their translocation and the now 'right' use. What is more, with the mention of Basil and others who have already emulated the Israelites in borrowing the Egyptian riches, Gregory insists that the reappropriation is not a process that has been completed once and for all, but a continuing activity. He makes clear that every Christian on the journey to virtue ought to reperform, like Basil, the 'exodus script', to wrestle from the foreigners their knowledge and transfer it to the church. I would like to argue that Gregory wanted his readers to see this process of infinite recuperation as their emancipation. In the introduction, when

---

[50] Gregory of Nyssa, *Mos.* 2.17 (GNO 7.1.38; SC 1.116).
[51] See Augustine, *Doctr. chr.* 2.40.60. For the Christian idea of the 'right' use, see Gnilka 1984.
[52] Gregory of Nyssa, *Mos.* 2.39 (GNO 7.1.44; SC 1.128): Ἔστι γάρ τι τῆς φιλοσόφου γονῆς ἐν μαθήμασι σαρκῶδές τε καὶ ἀκρόβυστον, οὗ περιαιρεθέντος τῆς Ἰσραηλιτικῆς εὐγενείας ἐστὶ τὸ λειπόμενον.

he brings up the hermeneutical challenge mentioned in the beginning of this article, he expounds to the imagined interlocutor, 'no one is banished from the life of virtue by living in Egypt or spending his life in Babylon'. The intention of the *Life* is to show 'how, by removing ourselves from such Chaldeans and Egyptians and by escaping from such a Babylonian captivity, we shall embark on the blessed life'.[53]

This metatextual comment suggests that every engagement with Greek learning and, more generally, every step in the process of self-formation means departing from something foreign and returning to one's natural home, where perfection can be found. It seems that the encounter with an alien object, the negotiation of otherness, is an indispensable ingredient in the acquisition of the knowledge leading to virtue. This is also what Moses' relationship with his Egyptian stepmother teaches: in the historical narrative, his education in 'outside' *paideusis* is bound up with his rejection of the woman who had adopted him and the return to his biological mother. The allegorical interpretation resumes this theme but gives it a significant twist by adding that, according to scripture, Moses should not reject the stepmother until he recognises his immaturity.[54] The hidden meaning is that in the involvement with pagan knowledge we must not be separated from the church, represented by the biological mother. As the metaphors of the milk and nourishment indicate, Christian self-formation is conceptualised as transformative feeding of infants.[55] The nourishment provided by faith is an element that maintains a natural bond between the believer and the mother church; the milk, in analogy to human breastfeeding, helps to realise one's innate potentials and develop one's true identity. Greek learning, by contrast, is seen as a secondary and external addition, something which is acquired but does not belong to one's true being.[56] Nonetheless, it can serve as a cognitive device that assists self-understanding.

When Gregory's readers harness the education they have acquired in the schools, they must tread a fine line between estrangement and total

---

[53] Gregory of Nyssa, *Mos.* 1.14 (GNO 7.1.6; SC 1.54): οὔτε τῇ ἐν Αἰγύπτῳ ζωῇ οὔτε τῇ ἐν Βαβυλῶνι διατριβῇ τοῦ βίου τις τοῦ κατ' ἀρετὴν ἐξοικίζεται ... ὡς διιδεῖν ἐκ τῆς ἱστορίας ποίων Χαλδαίων ἢ Αἰγυπτίων πόρρω γενόμενοι καὶ ποίας Βαβυλωνίων αἰχμαλωσίας ἀπολυθέντες τοῦ μακαρίου βίου ἐπιβησόμεθα.

[54] Gregory of Nyssa, *Mos.* 2.10 (GNO 7.1.36; SC 1.110–12).

[55] See Gregory of Nyssa, *Laud. Bas.* 808–9 (GNO 10.1.125–26), with a comparison between Basil and Moses.

[56] For the connection between nourishment and the formation of the soul in Christian thought, see 1 Cor 3:1–3. The trope of nourishment in Gregory's understanding of the formation of the human person is discussed by Penniman 2015b (especially 507–12 on the *Life of Moses*), again in Penniman 2017: 138–64.

rejection. On the one hand, they have to draw on the resources of *paideia* for the benefit of their self-perfection. On the other, they must avoid losing themselves to the foreign and dangerous object in order not to abandon true religion. On the basis of the lawgiver's biography, the *Life* advocates a delicate negotiation of otherness and kinship in which the foreign object serves as a foil. In the same way as Moses, through his education in Egyptian knowledge, matures and comes to know his true identity, the late-antique Christian will become aware of his religious affiliation through critical engagement with a *paideia* which must remain alien: there is a necessary distance in Christian education. In the same vein, Gregory Thaumaturgus, notably in parallel to Moses, by being confronted with the deficient doctrines of the Greek philosophers, comes to understand Christianity and embrace true faith. He, too, goes through an encounter with foreign wisdom before he fully realises what his true destiny is.[57]

Conclusion

It is characteristic of the late fourth and early fifth centuries that ecclesiastical writers were ruminating about the right method for the acquisition and use of knowledge. With Christianity increasingly spreading across all segments of the society, it seemed urgent to devise new ways in which Christians could engage with elementary and higher learning without betraying their religious affiliation. Among others, Basil the Great, John Chrysostom, Jerome, Augustine, and John Cassian, rather than setting up a fully fledged curriculum for Christian education, tried to establish methodologies and theoretical approaches for the acquisition of spiritual knowledge and engagement with worldly or pagan learning. With the *Life of Moses*, Gregory of Nyssa made another contribution to this discussion, proposing the Jewish lawgiver's biography as a blueprint for late antique Christians to engage with pagan *paideia* and, more generally, give shape to their lives. Interpreted in allegorical manner, the spoliation narrative of Exodus provided the script for how Christian members of the upper echelons of society were to deal with the disciplines of the classical education system. Gregory expected from them a re-performance of the Israelites' appropriation of the Egyptian riches and the departure from the foreign land. In this way, Christians could legitimately take part in the erudite culture of Greco-Roman

---

[57] Gregory of Nyssa, *Thaum.* 900–1 M. (GNO 10.1.9–10), drawing a parallel to Moses' schooling in Egyptian wisdom.

antiquity and make use of it for their own ends. The two conditions were, first, that this exploitation was uncompromisingly oriented towards the perfect Christian life and, second, that it was subordinated to Christian faith. In the *Life of Gregory Thaumaturgus*, Nyssen found a felicitous image for this, saying that Abraham used 'outside' wisdom like a stepping stone or rung in order to become more lofty through it, to rise to the imperceptible things.[58] In similar vein, Moses in his self-perfection set foot on the ladder which God set up and continually climbed to the step above.[59]

At the same time, Gregory re-evaluated the role of otherness. What the *Life* suggests is a constant negotiation of foreignness and kinship that makes this tension productive for the process of self-perfection. This is greatly facilitated by allegory as the literary method for unearthing from otherness the treasures to be exploited for perfecting one's life. Although pagan philosophy posed a dangerous threat to Christian religion, Gregory's allegorical reading insisted on the need for critical engagement with it. On the one hand, classical learning was harmful, because it was associated with idolatry and contained false teachings; thus, it threatened to alienate the student from true religion. But on the other, it paved the way to virtue and the separation from the material world. What is more, the examples of Moses and Gregory Thaumaturgus demonstrated that, in order to become aware of one's true nature and origin, it was essential to encounter something foreign, a distant object, ambivalent though it was. It is through the feigned Egyptian mother that Moses matures and recognises his kin, while the Wonderworker needs pagan education as a catalyst to arrive at an understanding of Christianity. In Gregory of Nyssa's constructivist picture, the otherness of pagan *paideia* was not a danger *tout court* but had a positive role to play in personal progress. He assigned to it a dual value: one benefit was material, that is, the contribution made by classical education through formal knowledge to the life of virtue. The other benefit was formative, namely developing in Christians a sense of their religious identity and belonging.

---

[58] Gregory of Nyssa, *Thaum.* 901 M. (GNO 10.1.9): ὑποβάθρᾳ χρήσασθαι τῇ περὶ ταῦτα γνώσει πρὸς τὴν τοῦ ὑπερκειμένου ἀγαθοῦ θεωρίαν, λογισάμενον, ὡς εἰ τὰ τῇ αἰσθήσει ληπτὰ τοιαῦτα, τί ἂν εἴη τὰ ὑπὲρ αἴσθησιν; καὶ οὕτως τοῦ ζητουμένου τυχεῖν, οἷον ἐπιβάντα τῆς ἔξω σοφίας, καὶ γενόμενον δι' αὐτῆς ὑψηλότερον, ὥστε προσεγγίσαι τρόπον τινὰ δι' αὐτῆς τοῖς ἀλήπτοις. This is seen as a parallel to Gregory Thaumaturgus' intellectual formation.

[59] Gregory of Nyssa, *Mos.* 2.227 (GNO 7.1.113; SC 1.262–64), with reference to Jacob's ladder (Gen 28:12).

19 | Female Characters as Modes of Knowing in Late Imperial Dialogues: The Body, Desire, and the Intellectual Life

DAWN LAVALLE NORMAN

Introduction

In one of Augustine's earliest-surviving works, a character mutinies. His mother Monica objects to the role that her son has written for her in the philosophical dialogue, the *De ordine*:

And meanwhile my mother came in and asked us how far we had gotten, for the topic under investigation was known to her, too. When I had commanded that her entrance and her question be written down, as was our custom, she said, 'What are you doing? For have I ever heard of women introduced in this type of discussion in those books which you all read?'

atque interea mater ingressa est quaesiuitque a nobis, quid promovissemus; nam et ei quaestio nota erat. Cuius et ingressum et rogationem cum scribi nostro more iussissem. 'quid agitis?' inquit; 'numquidnam in illis quos legitis libris etiam feminas umquam audiui in hoc genus disputationis inductas?' (Augustine, *Ord*. 1.11.31)

Monica has just entered from offstage and assumes that her role will be a non-speaking part. Like so many others that inhabited the real ancient world, she takes for granted that she will be invisible in the literary ancient world, and that any comment that she might make will not be immortalised for posterity. After all, that is the way that it has always been in philosophical dialogues, a fact that Monica knows even though she claims never to have read one herself. According to Augustine's record of Monica's views, the dialogue is an imaginary world where the characters are men, and in this assessment, Monica is almost entirely correct. Augustine advertises his innovation in the genre by scripting her shock and following it with his own lengthy justification for keeping her words on the official record.[1]

---

[1] Augustine claims throughout his dialogues to be using official note-takers (*notarii*) to record his conversations with his students, friends, and family. This unusual choice has caused an even greater focus on the question of historicity for Augustine's dialogues than for other dialogues, and has left a long bibliography (for which, see recently Kenyon 2018: 3–4). More interesting to

Clearly, for Augustine, writing a woman into his dialogues was something that needed to be talked about.

In this chapter I will examine how Christians came to use women's voices in philosophical dialogues, an obvious innovation in the genre, in order to express new values. Female characters were brought into philosophical discussions because of the traditional link between women and the life of the body. Writers used women to explore the changing values assigned to embodiment in a philosophical milieu predominantly inspired by Platonism. I will look in particular at two Greek authors, Methodius of Olympus and Gregory of Nyssa, who precede Augustine's inclusion of his mother in his dialogue. These two thinkers wrote dialogues that strikingly use the female voice in ways that I will argue work explicitly towards rearranging the hierarchy of value between the intellect and the body within the Platonic world.

Because philosophy was primarily a man's activity in the ancient world, philosophical dialogues rarely included women at all.[2] Before Monica, in fact, we have no evidence that a woman took part in any previously written Latin philosophical dialogue. On the Greek side, the situation is less stark, and there was a small but important tradition of putting certain types of women's voices to use in the Greek dialogic tradition. But even those Greek dialogues that included women's voices avoided putting women what I will call 'onstage', that is, speaking *in propria persona* within the drama of the dialogue. Sometimes (but even then, only rarely) conversations men had with women were *related* in Greek dialogues, happening, as I call it, 'offstage'.

---

me is the literary use to which Augustine puts his insistence that the dialogues are stenographic notes of actual conversations. Monica's exclamation quoted here comes immediately after Augustine's two young students, Licentius and Trygentius, have also unsuccessfully asked Augustine to strike their mistakes from the written record of the conversation (*Ord.* 1.11.30). Even though Monica did not 'hear' their request, all three of these interlocutors who ask Augustine that their words not be taken philosophically are rejected by Augustine's insistence on 'accuracy' for educational purposes. Conybeare treats the play between written and real for Augustine's literary purposes (2006: 27–35). The most extensive discussion of Augustine's use of *notarii* in his Cassiciacum dialogues is still Meulenbroek (1947).

[2] As Madeleine Henry has said in her study of the figure of Aspasia, 'philosophical discourse almost exclusively represents male discussants engaged in an examination of the good life as lived in a community dominated by men' (1995: 29). Pythagoreanism seemed importantly different in this regard, and early on there were female members of the philosophical community, according to Iamblichus' *Life of Pythagoras*, which ends with a list of female Pythagoreans (36.267). From the later period of non-Christian philosophy in the Platonic tradition, there are notable women such as Sosipatra, the non-Christian philosopher from the early fourth century CE whose biography is told by Eunapius, *Vit. Phil.* 466–71, and the fifth-century CE mathematician Hypatia of Alexandria, the most fulsome account of whom can be found in Socrates Scholasticus, *Hist. eccl.* 7.15. For overviews of the evidence of ancient female philosophers, see Waithe 1987; Taylor 2006: 173–226 (chapter 8: 'Paradigms of "Women" in Discourses on Philosophia'), and for the Pythagorean women philosophers, see Dutsch 2020 and Pellò 2022.

But the only sustained examples of women speaking directly in their own voices in philosophical dialogues come in the third and fourth centuries CE, when there was a burst of inclusion across Greek and Latin Christian writers. For this chapter, I will not focus on the historical lives of the women behind the characters or what their inclusion in the story might add to narratives of social history, however interesting that may be, but rather on their literary portrayal.[3] I will also limit myself to philosophical dialogues to the exclusion of other genres, such as biography or drama, where women's voices were used differently.[4] Men began to find a new use for women's voices in this time: they started to use them as philosophical authorities who were granted direct speech.[5]

Throughout this whole timeline, from the Socratics to Augustine, men used women's voices in philosophical dialogues to speak as experts on the body, especially in three aspects: birth, the physical details of death, and erotic desire. These connections were inaugurated by Plato and Xenophon. However, a changing anthropology, and especially the belief that the body persisted after death, led certain Christian authors to increase the role given to female characters. When the body was revalued and brought into the centre of philosophical focus, women's voices moved from reported speech into direct speech. Simultaneously, late ancient Christian authors reflected on the inherent connection between erotic desire and the genre of the dialogue itself, matching their subject to their form. Using female characters in their dialogues helped male authors come to know certain things that using male voices could not do as well, by thinking through specific topics 'like a woman'; the female, with her culturally embodied nature, became a model of an ideal life which insisted on the persistence of the body, even in the afterlife.

In the first part of this chapter, I will briefly sketch the role that women played in Greek philosophical dialogues *before* late antiquity, looking particularly at the Socratics. Once this background has been established, I will turn to the two primary examples from the Greek-speaking world

---

[3] For some thoughts on the inherently literary nature of most of our evidence for women (and here, especially of early Christian women), and the difficulty of getting from these male depictions to the actual women behind them, see Kraemer 2010: 6–12 and, most influentially, Clark 1998. For an investigation into the role women played in persuading powerful men during the period of Gregory the Great, see Chapter 36 by Bronwen Neil, this volume.

[4] For more on the genre of the dialogue, see Neil's comments on Gregory the Great's *Dialogues* in Chapter 36, this volume.

[5] As such, this is one of a number of larger changes to the genre that were happening in the imperial period. The genre of the dialogue and the changes it underwent during its long history have been the subject of recent investigations in Föllinger and Müller 2013; Cameron 2014.

of female philosophers who take up roles in dialogues in late antiquity: Methodius of Olympus' third-century *Symposium* and Gregory of Nyssa's fourth-century *On the Soul and Resurrection* (*De anima*). Although they differ from each other in many particulars, both dialogues feature women as primary speakers, and both also take the opportunity to deal with issues of the body, its desires, and death explicitly. Even more strikingly, both of these dialogues first contain the opinion that all emotions should be avoided, subsequently overcome that position in the course of conversation, and end with the idea that desire should not be avoided, but rather correctly used and directed, leading humans to their eschatological destiny, a destiny that necessarily includes a purified body. The link between a dialectic that moves towards an end that includes some type of embodiment and the inclusion of women is not accidental, but rather culminates a long history of connecting these ideas.

Women in Classical Philosophical Dialogues

Despite their shadowy presence, the women of the Socratic dialogues had a substantial influence on the development of the discourse around philosophically verbal women. Plato includes the speeches of two women in his dialogues: the priestess Diotima in the *Symposium* and Pericles' mistress Aspasia in the *Menexenus*. Both are styled 'teachers',[6] but neither are allowed to do their teaching onstage. Rather, the teaching takes place before the dramatic moment of the dialogue. In the *Symposium*, when it comes to Socrates' turn to eulogise Eros, he chooses to 'relate' what he learned from a priestess named Diotima, recreating her teaching as an inset dialogue and ventriloquising her side of the discussion. The intrusion of Diotima's voice, even though ventriloquised through Socrates, into the all-male *Symposium* is the most striking and influential of the Socratic women. As David Halperin has claimed, Diotima's femininity is useful to Plato because it allows him to focus on two aspects of love that were specifically coded feminine in the ancient world, but which Plato wanted to include in his ideal construction: (1) the mutuality of desire (reflected in the method of the dialogue form itself) and (2) a procreative rather than possessive goal for love. Diotima's espousal of the ladder of love in the *Symposium*, and the systematisation and channelling of desire for ascent, is, in this reading,

---

[6] Diotima: ἣ δὴ καὶ ἐμὲ τὰ ἐρωτικὰ ἐδίδαξεν, Plato, *Symp.* 201d; Aspasia: ᾧ τυγχάνει διδάσκαλος οὖσα οὐ πάνυ φαύλη περὶ ῥητορικῆς, Plato, *Menex.* 235e.

bound up with her 'feminine' range of experience. Even if Elizabeth Pender is correct to assert that Diotima's description of birth sounds suspiciously like male ejaculation,[7] nevertheless Plato's choice to depict a woman as the expert in love would echo down the ages. However, the use of the female to focus on issues of birth here (Halperin's second point) serves the explicit goal of advancing from a focus on physical birth to spiritual birth. Eros for other bodies is very low on the ladder, and as the soul ascends, it purifies its desires of all earthly beauty, leaving the body and its lower desires behind. The analogy of birth, with all of its connections to the mess of bodily fluids and pain, is superseded. Plato's *Symposium* appropriates the feminine, bodily type of birth into a masculine, spiritual type of birth. The woman and her concomitant physicality do not persist during the process of ascent.

Although Diotima is the most well-known today, the more important woman for the ancient dialogue as a genre was Aspasia.[8] At least three other writers of Socratic dialogues besides Plato featured Aspasia in their works: Antisthenes, Aeschines, and Xenophon.[9] Unlike the shadowy Diotima, who may or may not have been invented by Plato, Aspasia was a well-known historical figure, the mistress of Pericles, a foreigner of dubious sexual status. In Plato's *Menexenus*, Aspasia is said to have taught Socrates the art of *rhetoric*, but in other versions of the story, she taught Socrates the art of *erotics*.[10] Barbara Ehlers argues that the tradition that made Aspasia a teacher of the erotic arts stems from the lost *Aspasia* dialogue of Aeschines. In her reconstruction of the dialogue, she argues that Socrates recommends Aspasia as the best teacher of virtue to the youth on the basis that she knows how to use *eros* to direct men to achieve *arete* (Ehlers 1966). Aspasia's role in Antisthenes' dialogue bearing her name

---

[7] Pender 1992, which influences the modified and expanded treatment of the theme in Leitao 2012: 182–226.
[8] The prominence of Aspasia has actually led some scholars to say that both Socratic women, Diotima and Theodote (discussed below), are fictional stand-ins for the historical Aspasia (see the dissenting views of Henry 1995: 48 and Halperin 1990: 122–24).
[9] For the Aspasia of Antisthenes, see Prince 2015: 146–47, 414–21 and, most recently, Kennedy 2017. For Aeschines' *Aspasia* see Ehlers 1966, and for both Antisthenes and Aeschines among the Socratic fragments, see Giannantoni 1991. As Plutarch says litotically in his *Life of Pericles*, 'not slight nor small is the talk about her among philosophers' (καὶ τοῖς φιλοσόφοις οὐ φαῦλον οὐδ' ὀλίγον ὑπὲρ αὐτῆς παρέσχε λόγον. Plutarch, *Per.* 24.2–3).
[10] Maximus says that Aspasia and Diotima were Socrates' teachers in the erotic arts (ἀλλὰ καὶ διδασκάλους ἐπιγέγραπται τῆς τέχνης, Ἀσπασίαν τὴν Μιλησίαν καὶ Διοτίμαν τὴν Μαντινικήν), and that his students were Alcibiades, Critoboulus, Agathon, Phaedrus, Lysis, and Charmides (Maximus of Tyre, *Diss.* 18.4). Synesius says that Socrates used to frequent Aspasia to learn erotica (προσένεμε γὰρ Ἀσπασίᾳ τὴν δύναμιν ταύτην, ᾗ προσεφοίτα **κατὰ χάριντοῦ τὰ ἐρωτικὰ παιδευθῆναι**, Synesius, *Dio.* 15.2).

is more opaque, mostly because our surviving fragments do not seem to focus on Aspasia at all, but rather on the men who surrounded her. Although their fragmentary nature makes final conclusions difficult, it seems that in both dialogues of Aeschines and Antisthenes, as in Plato, Aspasia was not permitted to speak onstage with her own voice. The same is true for the use of her character by Xenophon, where Socrates mentions Aspasia's wise words to him on the topic of proper matchmaking (Xenophon, *Mem.* 2.6.36) and recommends her as a teacher of spousal harmony (Xenophon, *Oec.* 3.14). Her role in Plato's *Menexenus* is not connected with desire like Diotima's role in the *Symposium* or the use of Aspasia in Aeschines' *Aspasia*. Rather, she is reported to have taught Socrates how to give funeral speeches.

In Plato's *Menexenus*, Aspasia comes to represent the physical side of death, the other end of birth. The model speech she performs focuses on the earth as the mother of all the Athenians (Plato, *Menex.* 237b–39a).[11] The mother earth does three things: she bears, nurtures, and receives her children into their natural home again when they die (καὶ νῦν κεῖσθαι τελευτήσαντας ἐν οἰκείοις τόποις τῆς τεκούσης καὶ θρεψάσης καὶ ὑποδεξαμένης, Plato, *Menex.* 237c). Plato's Aspasia turns to the female body as birthing mother and burying mother, emphasising the connection between maternity, materiality, and death widespread in ancient Greek thought.[12] But the *Menexenus* is not the *Phaedo*: it is not focused on the immortality of the soul, but rather on the memory that persists of the war dead in civic life. That is cold comfort to Platonists, and Aspasia's feminine connection with death is in the limited, earthly notion of cessation of civic existence rather than in freedom from the bodily bondage emphasised in the *Phaedo*. Only under the influence of Christian notions of death would women be invited into the *philosophical* understanding of death, coupled with the belief in the persistence of the body in death.

Despite the fame of Diotima in the later tradition and in modern scholarship and the prevalence of Aspasia among a variety of early Socratic writers, it is a less well-known character who is the *only certain pre-Christian* example of a woman talking onstage in any Greek philosophical dialogue. In *Memorabilia* 3.11, Xenophon relates a short and sassy story about how

---

[11] Plato claims that Aspasia said in her speech: 'It is most just to honour the mother herself first' (δικαιότατον δὴ κοσμῆσαι πρῶτον τὴν μητέρα αὐτήν· Plato, *Menex.* 237c).

[12] Through linking the female earthly body with rhetoric, he also emphasises rhetoric's connection with death rather than with the life-giving erotics of philosophy that the female provides in the *Symposium*. For an influential chapter on the link between earth and the female body, see DuBois 1988: 39–64 (Chapter II.3, 'Metaphors of the Female Body: Field').

Socrates visited a beautiful *hetaera* named Theodote while she reclined modelling for a painter.[13] Their conversation revolves around the erotic art of attraction. While Theodote is at first described as the one whose livelihood depends upon being persuaded (to give her sexual favours), in the end she is left begging *Socrates* to be persuaded by her (to visit her more often and teach her the erotic art). Socrates playfully turns the tables and transforms the desire expected of *him* into Theodote's desire to learn from Socrates, switching the expectations of who will be the erotic instructor. The beautiful woman's presence allows Xenophon to address the issue of the use and direction of desire, just as Plato had used Diotima's femininity for similar purposes.

In sum, in most surviving ancient philosophical dialogues, women play absolutely no role at all. When they do appear, which is rarely, it is almost always in reported conversation of men. The only exception to this is the brief onstage dialogue between Socrates and Theodote in Xenophon's *Memorabilia*. Cutting across all of these uses, there is a persistent insistence that their realm of expertise lies in the bodily processes of birth, death, and physical desire. In the following Christian examples, however, the women move up a level of representation. They are no longer ventriloquised by men within the story, but the male authors of the dialogues allow them to speak 'in their own voices' within the fiction of the dialogue. The emergence of the female voice occurs at the same time as a new valuation of the body and a belief in its continuance beyond death. The body is no longer only a necessary stepping-stone but will itself be transformed in order to be included in the final goal of ascent. Male authors used female voices to speak new conclusions concerning the persistence of the body and its desires in the afterlife. To do so, they took advantage of the traditional cluster of ideas that we have investigated up to this point.

Women in Late Imperial Dialogues

Against such a background of woman's nearly complete silence onstage in philosophical dialogues, there stand out in contrast two substantial dialogues written in the third and fourth centuries CE in Asia Minor, both of which feature women as their main philosophical protagonists. The authors of both works were Christian men who lived in related literary

---

[13] Goldhill 2010 is an illuminating article on the playful switching of erotic education in this passage.

and philosophical milieus.[14] Methodius of Olympus' *Symposium*, written in the late third century in Lycia, is the most extreme, featuring an entirely female cast. His dialogue stars ten women who have been brought together by their hostess Virtue, daughter of Philosophy, for a party, after which Virtue asks each guest to make a speech on the topic of chastity. Most of the women are otherwise unknown, with the exception of Thecla, who had been made famous by her second-century *Acts* as a companion of St Paul and an important (and controversial) Christian teacher.[15] After the competition, a description of which forms the main body of the dialogue, Thecla is chosen by Virtue as the winner of the speech competition and leads the other virgins in a hymn, before the dialogue fades out to the framing narrators, who are also women, as they begin a new discussion on the topic of desire.

The second dialogue, *On the Soul and the Resurrection*, was written by Gregory of Nyssa in about 380 CE, almost one hundred years after Methodius. Gregory writes a dialogue between himself and his sister Macrina, whose dramatic date is the days immediately preceding his sister's death. Gregory takes the inferior position in the conversation, and the dialogue presents Macrina as Gregory's teacher,[16] as she re-convinces Gregory of the immortality of the soul in the wake of their brother Basil's death.

In both cases, the women involved have embraced a life of celibacy and encourage asceticism in the dialogue. And despite the fact that they present different types of female body (Methodius' virgins are young and beautiful, while Macrina is old, sick, and dying), they both manage to stoke the desire of those who look at them – either by their virginal beauty or by the familial closeness of sisterhood. This ability to stir desire causes the conversations to take a particular turn in both cases, and the role of the emotions in the holy life is addressed directly. In both dialogues, the main interlocutor first presents a vision of the holy life that avoids all involvement in emotions, before this view is dialectically overcome in the course of conversation. Unlike Plato's *Symposium*, these two Christian authors display the removal

---

[14] It has been argued that Gregory knew Methodius' *Symposium*, and so knowingly follows Methodius' trail-blazing footsteps of including women in philosophical dialogues, for which see Silvas 2008: 20 and 157 (although the authorship of the work which used to be thought to contain Gregory's direct reference to Methodius' *Symposium* has been reassigned to Anastasius of Sinai; see the edition of Uthemann 1985). Both dialogues have Thecla somewhere in the background: in Methodius, she is one of the main characters, and in the second, Macrina's secret family name is Thecla, according to Gregory of Nyssa's biography of his sister (Gregory of Nyssa, *Life of Macrina* 3.2; Silvas 2008: 112 and LaValle Norman 2022: 25–28).

[15] For the cult of Thecla, see Davis 2001; Johnson 2006.

[16] He repeatedly calls her ἡ διδάσκαλος; e.g., 1.6 (12M); 2.1 (12M); 4.1 (16M); 5.8 (17M). For citations of the *De anima*, I use the page and line numbers of the critical edition of Spira 2014, followed by the Migne page.

of resistance to desire within the drama of the dialogue, which draws new attention to the topic. Both of these Christian dialogues likewise embrace an anthropology that believes in the persistence of the body after death, which goes hand in hand with a new verbosity of philosophical women, even *with* their traditional connection with the body.

Methodius of Olympus' *Symposium*

I will turn first to the all-female dialogue of Methodius, which is the earlier dialogue of the two. There are two moments in Methodius' dialogue that are particularly germane to the nexus of desire, the body, and gender:[17] the speech delivered by Thecla and the concluding discussion by the external narrators. The more explicit of the two is the latter. Through the lens of this final debate, it comes into retrospective focus that similar concerns were addressed throughout the earlier parts of the dialogue as well, including certain sections of Thecla's speech to which we will turn next.

After she has heard the report of the party, Eubulion, who had been a passive listener up to this point, asks Gregorion her opinion on which is better: to be completely unaffected by desire or to experience desire but have control over it. Gregorion begins with the view that it would be better to avoid desire entirely and to remain sealed shut and preserved from external-induced imagination.

GREGORION: Because first of all, they hold their soul pure and the Holy Spirit always dwells in it, not dragged about and roiling with *phantasiai* and thoughts of self-indulgence, with the result that they are polluted through thinking about them. But they are wholly unreceptive both in their flesh and in their heart, having tranquillity from the desire of their passions (τῆς ἐπιθυμίας … τῶν παθημάτων). On the other hand, others are enticed through external sight with *phantasiai* and receive desire (τὴν ἐπιθυμίαν) flowing in upon them like a river into their hearts. Even if they think that they are striving and fighting against pleasures, nevertheless they are often contaminated, having been defeated in their thoughts.

ΓΡΗΓ. Ὅτι πρωτον μὲν καθαρὰν ἔχουσιν αυτην τὴν ψυχὴν καὶ ἀεὶ τὸ πνευμα τὸ ἅγιον ἐν αυτη κατοικει μὴ περιελκομενης αυτης καὶ ἐπιθολουμενης φαντασιαις καὶ λογισμοις ἀκρασιας, ὥστε καὶ διὰ της ἐνθυμησεως ἐπιλωβηθηναι ποτε· ἀλλ' εἰσὶν ἀνεπιδεκτοι παντη καὶ κατὰ τὴν σαρκα καὶ κατὰ τὴν καρδιαν οὗτοι της ἐπιθυμιας γαληνην ἄγοντες των αθηματων. Οἱ δὲ διὰ της ὄψεως ἔξωθεν

---

[17] An expanded version of the following argument about the role of *phantasiai* in Methodius' *Symposium* can be found in LaValle Norman 2019: 81–89.

> δελεαζομενοι ταις φαντασιαις καὶ ἐπεισρεουσαν δεχομενοι τὴν ἐπιθυμιαν δικην ῥευματος εἰς τὴν καρδιαν ουδὲν ἧσσον μολυνονται πολλακις, κἂν νομιζωσιν ἀντιφιλονεικειν καὶ μαχεσθαι πρὸς τὰς ἡδονὰς ἡσσωμενοι τὸν λογισμον. (*Symp.* Epilogue 295–96)

Gregorion here seems to be saying that *all* desire (τὴν ἐπιθυμίαν) is negative, caused by sense perception (διὰ τῆς ὄψεως ἔξωθεν) creating internal mental images (ταῖς φαντασίαις). At first, she specifies 'desire of the passions' (τῆς ἐπιθυμίας … τῶν παθημάτων), which might allow for the bifurcated understanding of desire put forward in Thecla's eighth speech, where Thecla differentiates the desire of the flesh (ἐπιθυμία … σαρκὸς) and the desire of the soul (ἐπιθυμία … ψυχῆς) (*Symp.* 8.17.230).[18] However, by the end of her description, Gregorion has left off any limiting genitive and speaks pejoratively of desire itself, which acts as a polluting river rolling through the heart caused by mental images entering the senses from without.

However, this preliminary argument is demolished by Eubulion's spirited response. She replies that the chaste virgin *should* allow input into her senses, which had been called by another virgin symposiast the 'gates of wisdom' and 'the five pathways of virtue' (σοφίας … πύλας; τῶν πέντε διόδων τῆς ἀρετῆς; *Symp.* 6.3.139). By using the senses correctly, Eubulion claims, fortitude is increased, which is 'the *dynamis* of virtue' (δύναμις ἀρετῆς ἐστιν ἡ ὑπομονή, *Symp.* Epilogue 301). Virtue is not found in a closing off, but in allowing in and controlling impressions from without.[19] Methodius' staging of this concluding debate implies resistance to the use of desire (ἐπιθυμία) from within the Christian community, represented by Gregorion. Plato emphasised the need to use the lower desires to ascend to a more purified form of desire for the good in and of itself. Therefore, Methodius here responds to an internal Christian resistance towards desire with a more Platonic concept of harnessing desire for progress.

From this point, looking back over the dialogue as a whole, it is clear that the speeches of the virgins support Eubulion's incorporation of the imagination-caused desire into the holy life. Through imagination, desire

---

[18] 'For two impulses exist in us: there exists desire of the flesh and desire of the spirit. It is from these that the two things take their names: for the one has the name of virtue and the other of vice.' Δύο γὰρ κινήσεε ἐν ἡμῖν ἔστον· ἐπιθυμία πεφυκότε σαρκὸς καὶ ψυχῆς, διαφέρετον ἀλλήλοιν. Ὅθεν καὶ δύο ἐλαβέτην ὀνόματε· ἡ μὲν γὰρ ἀρετῆς, ἡ δὲ κακίας (*Symp.* 8.17.230).

[19] This passage has been misunderstood by Simon Goldhill: 'Methodius' Gregorion and Euboulion end by agreeing ("Aye, by *Sophrosune*!") that it is "better to maintain virginity without experiencing desire than to be able to control one's desire" (*Epilogue* 293)' (Goldhill 1995: 4). Goldhill's comment could have found better support in the final speech by Virtue, which encourages the women to be like well-caulked ships, not allowing the moisture of sin to get in and sink the boat (*Symp.* 11.283).

for the eschaton is fuelled. First of all, Gregorion has failed to realise that she has herself been involved in a monumental task of the imagination through vividly relating the contents of the party to Eubulion in the first place. Immediately after Thecla's speech has been recounted, the two of them comment upon her contribution, and upon her impact as a speaker.

EUBULION: How truly magnificent and in the spirit of a contest was Thecla's discourse, Gregorion!

GREGORION: What then if you had heard that woman, dialoguing with a flowing and well-turned tongue, with great grace and pleasure; so that someone applying themselves would be amazed at her beauty, blossoming with words. How unaffectedly and truly having been brought to one's mind's-eye (ὡς ἐνδιαθέτως καὶ τῷ ὄντι φανταζομένη), she completed those things about which she was speaking, as her face blushed with modesty. She is wholly fair in body and soul.

ΕΥΒΟΥΛ. Ὡς λίαν ἀγωνιστικῶς ἡ Θέκλα καὶ ἐνδόξως, ὦ Γρηγόριον.
ΓΡΗΓΟΡ. Τι ουν, ει αυτης εκεινης ηκηκοεις ρυδην και ευτροχῳ τῃ γλωσσῃ μετὰ πολλης χαριτος και ἡδονης διαλεγομενης; ὥστε αγασθηναι τινα προσεχοντα και της μορφης επανθουσης τοις λογοις, ὡς ενδιαθετως και τῳ ὄντι φανταζομενη περὶ ὧν ἀφηγειτο διετελει ὑπερυθραινομενης αυτη της ὄψεως αἰδοι· ὅλη γὰρ εἶναι πεφυκε λευκὴ καὶ σωμα καὶ ψυχην. (*Symp.* 8.231)

As Gregorion describes what it was like to be there in person, the image is instantly created in the reader's own imagination, down to the details of Thecla's lovely (though modest) body. Gregorion tries to make present in Eubulion's mind what she has missed, and in so doing, makes it simultaneously present in each reader's mind as well. Gregorion stirs Eubulion's desire for the famous Thecla, not only to hear her words, but even to see her attractive presentation. We are reminded of how Socrates used the sight of the beautiful body of Theodote to begin a discussion about desire in Xenophon's *Memorabilia*. The female body on show has moved from that of a prostitute to a chaste virgin, and the internal audience has likewise shifted genders from all-male to all-female. Yet the ability of beautiful women to cause desire is once again emphasised, and that potentially dangerous power is presented as an opportunity. However, unlike the abandonment of the body in Diotima's ascent to contemplation of the beautiful, here Gregorion calls upon us to admire Thecla's beauty *in both body and soul* (καὶ σῶμα καὶ ψυχήν). In Methodius' world, the material is not left behind in the presentation of the ideal life but is incorporated.[20]

---

[20] An explicit place where this dynamic occurs is between the first three speakers of the event narrated in the *Symposium*. The first speaker, Marcella, states that with the coming of Christ,

Methodius' defence of desire is an extension of the Platonic teaching in the *Symposium*. However, the goal of that desired good life has changed in a central way. The 'lower' type of desire, the one involved in embodiment, is now included as well. The persistence of the body is such a central belief to Methodius that he devoted an entire dialogue to it, the *De resurrectione*, where he argued that the material elements of the body, and not only its form, will be rejoined at the resurrection. Tied to his embrace of the physical in the process of ascent comes the emergence of his female voices from ventriloquism to direct speech.

Gregory of Nyssa's *On the Soul and the Resurrection*

The next author, like Methodius, also takes his model from among the works of Plato, crafting a *Phaedo*-esque deathbed conversation about the immortality of the soul rather than the bustling party atmosphere of the *Symposium*. And while the most striking prototype for Gregory of Nyssa's sister Macrina in his dialogue *On the Soul and the Resurrection* is Socrates waiting for his death in the *Phaedo*, scholars have also repeatedly suggested *Symposium*'s Diotima as Gregory's model as a Platonic female teacher.[21] I argue that narratives such as these forget Theodote and the already existing Christian tradition of putting women onstage as teachers in philosophical dialogues that we saw in Methodius. Instead of seeing Macrina as unique because of her biography and personal connection to the author, I will look at her role in line with the lengthy tradition of using women's voices to focus on questions of desire in philosophical dialogues. Women are a mode of knowing, and authors come to different conclusions by using this mode in new ways.

Methodius built on the connection between women and desire that Plato already made in the *Symposium*, respecting the segregation of genders.[22] Gregory of Nyssa does something quite different, both because he mixes the genders of the onstage speakers and because he imitates a different

---

the period of marriage is over, and the perfect life is now to be found in virginity. The second speaker, Theophila, disagrees and argues that procreation is meant to continue. She matches her argument to her case by using physiological knowledge to support her claims. The third speaker, Thalia, presents a synthesis of the disagreeing first two speakers. She argues for the continuation of procreation, but also the primacy of the spiritual interpretation of procreation.

[21] Burrus 2005: 252, 255; Ludlow 2009: 469; Roth 1992: 20–21.

[22] The one other place where Methodius relates a woman speaking, in his dialogue the *De lepra*, the main interlocutors are both men, and the woman's voice is reported indirectly, as in Plato. She is not onstage and does not even have her name mentioned, being referred to only as a 'woman from Lycia'.

Platonic dialogue which uses women in a very different way from the *Symposium*. To understand this, we need to look back to Plato's *Phaedo*. Socrates' wife, Xanthippe, plays a very minor role in the Socratic works that have survived. She is mentioned twice by Xenophon (*Mem.* 2.2.7–9; *Symp.* 2.10), but it is only in Plato's *Phaedo* where we get to catch a glimpse of her.

We found Socrates recently released from his chains, and Xanthippe – you know her – sitting by him, holding their baby. When she saw us, she cried out and said the sort of thing that women usually say: 'Socrates, this is the last time your friends will talk to you and you to them.' Socrates looked at Crito. 'Crito,' he said, 'let someone take her home.' And some of Crito's people led her away lamenting and beating her breast.

κατελαμβάνομεν τὸν μὲν Σωκράτη ἄρτι λελυμένον, τὴν δὲ Ξανθίππην – γιγνώσκεις γάρ – ἔχουσάν τε τὸ παιδίον αὐτοῦ καὶ παρακαθημένην. ὡς οὖν εἶδεν ἡμᾶς ἡ Ξανθίππη, ἀνηυφήμησέ τε καὶ τοιαῦτ' ἄττα εἶπεν, οἷα δὴ εἰώθασιν αἱ γυναῖκες, ὅτι 'Ὦ Σώκρατες, ὕστατον δή σε προσεροῦσι νῦν οἱ ἐπιτήδειοι καὶ σὺ τούτους.' καὶ ὁ Σωκράτης βλέψας εἰς τὸν Κρίτωνα, 'Ὦ Κρίτων', ἔφη, 'ἀπαγέτω τις αὐτὴν οἴκαδε'. Καὶ ἐκείνην μὲν ἀπῆγόν τινες τῶν τοῦ Κρίτωνος βοῶσάν τε καὶ κοπτομένην· (Plato, *Phaed.* 60a, trans. Grube)

Only once Xanthippe and the baby are removed can the philosophical dialogue begin. Her removal from the scene is simultaneous to the removal of the chains from Socrates' ankles. The pleasure he feels from the release from his bounds implicates Xanthippe too as an irksome bond that ties him down. He gets rid of both chains at the same time. But perhaps the parallel in the initial μὲν ... δὲ clause speaks more to the restrictions experienced *by* Xanthippe rather than Xanthippe as a restriction. While Socrates gets rid of his chains, Xanthippe is holding a little child (ἔχουσάν τε τὸ παιδίον). She either cannot or chooses not to remove the chain of the physical obligations of motherhood in order to move to the disembodied afterlife that Socrates embraces. Xanthippe cannot participate in the following conversation. The woman gets in the way of philosophy with her emotional response to death and loss, performing the typical female role of lamentation (βοῶσάν τε καὶ κοπτομένην). Socrates makes this gendered link explicit at the end of the dialogue when he chastens the men for crying:

'What is this,' he said, 'you strange fellows. It is mainly for this reason that I sent the women away, to avoid such unseemliness, for I am told one should die in good omened silence. So keep quiet and control yourselves.'

Ἐκεῖνος δέ, Οἷα, ἔφη, ποιεῖτε, ὦ θαυμάσιοι. ἐγὼ μέντοι οὐχ ἥκιστα τούτου ἕνεκα τὰς γυναῖκας ἀπέπεμψα, ἵνα μὴ τοιαῦτα πλημμελοῖεν· καὶ γὰρ ἀκήκοα ὅτι ἐν εὐφημίᾳ χρὴ τελευτᾶν. ἀλλ' ἡσυχίαν τε ἄγετε καὶ καρτερεῖτε. (Plato, *Phaed.* 117d–e, trans. Grube)

The men are able to do as they are asked and stop crying. Apparently, their maleness allows them to control their emotions (καρτερεῖτε) in a way that would be impossible for someone whose feminine gender made such control impossible, like Xanthippe.[23]

Gregory's choice to base his dialogue with his sister on the *Phaedo* rather than on Plato's *Symposium*, Plato's *Menexenus*, or Xenophon's *Memorabilia* brings with it different connotations of women in the philosophical tradition. Xanthippe's character in the *Phaedo* reminded us of the bondage that women's bodies in particular feel to the physical world, and its cycles of birthing and dying. When Gregory chooses to cast his sister in the dying role of Socrates, he casts himself in the role of Socrates' weeping male disciples (Plato, *Phaed.* 117c–e) and not that of his weeping wife. He is a man who can be chastened into controlling his emotions.[24]

Like the earlier tradition, Gregory plays with women's association with *desire*. However, instead of attractive, athletic female bodies, Macrina presents a different side of the spectrum – a withered, sick old woman who cannot move and is attended by medical assistance. Yet, she too is able to create desire in her male viewer. Her brother Gregory is caused increased grief upon seeing her, because he desires her physical presence to remain and is overcome with sorrow imagining its imminent departure. Like Phaedo says of himself in the eponymous Platonic dialogue, 'I was weeping for myself, not for him' (Plato, *Phaed.* 117c). But through her dialectic, Macrina reorients Gregory's original inappropriate desire and replaces it with the desire for the life to come.

Scholars have struggled to understand the precise role of desire in this dialogue, often by combining it with the companion narrative in the *Life of Macrina*.[25] However, in this chapter I set aside the *Life of Macrina* in order to develop a genealogy of the moves made specifically in the dialogic form. Disaggregating *On the Soul and Resurrection* from the

---

[23] There is one more brief section where women intrude in the *Phaedo*. In the last moments, Socrates' three sons and the women of his family come and get instruction from him (Plato, *Phaed.* 116b), only to be sent away again so that Socrates can rejoin his male friends to drink the poison and finish their philosophical conversation.

[24] In this, I think that Sarah Coakley's analysis of this scene needs to be expanded. She only mentions Gregory's connection to the feminine passions in this opening (Coakley 2000: 165). However, looking at the parallels in the *Phaedo*, it seems clear that Gregory is behaving like a male who has forgotten his manliness rather than as a woman at a family deathbed. Like Socrates' followers, and unlike Xanthippe, Gregory is able to get a hold of himself. This could play nicely into Coakley's overall argument in her article about the fluidity of gender in Gregory of Nyssa.

[25] Important articles on related questions in the *Life of Macrina*, which will not be treated here, are Frank 2000a; Krueger 2000; Smith 2004a; and parts of Champion 2014.

Life of Macrina helps to focus on the unique uses of women's voices in dialogues, which has a very different history from the use of women's voices in biography, a genre which never shared the same resistance to reporting women's direct speech.

In the opening setting of the dialogue, we learn that the most famous brother of Gregory and Macrina, Basil of Caesarea, has recently died, and the reason for Gregory's visit to his sister is to find consolation in mutual grief. But when Gregory arrives at their old family estate, now turned into a monastic establishment headed by Macrina, he finds to his surprise that his sister too is close to death. Words of emotion stuff the opening, narrative scene-setting paragraph. Gregory comes with his soul *full* of grief for his brother's death (περιώδυνος ἦν ἡ ψυχὴ, *De an.*, ed. Spira 1.8 [12M]), grieving *exceedingly* (ὑπεραλγοῦσα, *De an.*, ed. Spira 1.9 [12M]). These are not just normal emotions but require intensifying prefixes. Then a fresh grief attacks him through his eyes (said twice: *De an.*, ed. Spira 1.10 [12M] and 2.10-12 [12-13M]) when he sees the state of Macrina, lying prone, attended by a doctor.

Macrina, instead of mourning together with her brother as he had hoped, responds with a rejection of grief from the Christian scriptures.

But she, in the style of those skilled in horsemanship allowing me to be carried away for a little while by the impulse of my passion (τῇ ῥύμῃ τοῦ πάθους), tried afterwards to rein it in, just like straightening the rebellious part of the soul with the bit of private reasoning. And she cited the apostolic text, namely that it was necessary not to grieve for those who had fallen asleep (1 Thess 4:13). For this passion (τὸ πάθος) only belongs to those who have no hope.

Ἡ δὲ κατὰ τοὺς τῆς ἱππικῆς ἐπιστήμονας ἐνδοῦσά μοι πρὸς ὀλίγον παρενεχθῆναι τῇ ῥύμῃ τοῦ πάθους, ἀναστομοῦν ἐπεχείρει μετὰ ταῦτα τῷ λόγῳ, καθάπερ χαλινῷ τινι τῷ ἰδίῳ λογισμῷ τὸ ἀτακτοῦν τῆς ψυχῆς ἀπευθύνουσα, καὶ ἦν αὐτῇ τὸ ἀποστολικὸν λόγιον προφερόμενον, τὸ μὴ δεῖν ἐπὶ τῶν κεκοιμημένων λυπεῖσθαι· μόνων γὰρ τοῦτο τῶν οὐκ ἐχόντων ἐλπίδα τὸ πάθος εἶναι. (*De an.*, ed. Spira 2.3-8 [12M-13M])

The author scripts Macrina as combining the Platonic control of the unruly horse of passion with the passage from the letters of Paul to counter the emotions that Gregory is inappropriately displaying. But before she controls it, the readers are invited to join Gregory in his grief. Among his many works, this is the only one which Gregory chooses to put in the genre of a dialogue and thereby to invite his readers into the experience of such intense emotion. Why would the author Gregory start with depicting his own deep emotion, desire, and loss only to have those emotions refuted in the second paragraph by his main interlocutor? What role can emotions play, and why, if Gregory knows that seeing grief stirs up grief in others, does he present this sad scene to his readers and risk their complicit involvement?

Gregory of Nyssa's *On the Soul and Resurrection* takes the theme of desire, emotions, and their role in the Christian life head-on, so much so that Burrus has called this a 'dialogue on desire'.[26] The dialogue accomplishes this in two ways. The first is through Macrina's use of Gregory's disordered emotions as an impulse to philosophise in the first place, and the second is in the modification of Macrina's initially harsh anthropology through her dialectic with Gregory into an anthropology that admits the vital role of the emotions in the holy life. Like the closing of Methodius' *Symposium*, Gregory of Nyssa's *On the Soul and Resurrection* stages resistance to desire only to overcome that resistance dialectically.

Although Macrina at first rebukes Gregory for his disordered emotions, a few paragraphs later Macrina decides to use Gregory's disordered emotional state to help fuel their discussion.

'Therefore', my teacher said, 'it is necessary to seek whence the speech takes its proper beginning about these things. If it seems good to you, you can be the fellow-fighter of the opposing opinions (τῶν ἐναντίων δογμάτων ἡ συμμαχία). For I see that your reasoning has been all riled up (ὑποκεκίνηται) towards such an attack. Perhaps thus the reasoning of truth will be discovered after the antithesis.'

Οὐκοῦν ζητῆσαι χρή, φησὶν ἡ διδάσκαλος, ὅθεν ἂν ἡμῖν τὴν δέουσαν περὶ τούτων ἀρχὴν ὁ λόγος λάβῃ. Καὶ εἰ δοκεῖ, παρὰ σοῦ γενέσθω τῶν ἐναντίων δογμάτων ἡ συμμαχία· ὁρῶ γὰρ ὅτι σοι καὶ ὑποκεκίνηται πρὸς τοιαύτην καταφορὰν ἡ διάνοια. Εἶθ' οὕτως ὁ τῆς ἀληθείας μετὰ τὴν ἀντίθεσιν ἀναζητηθήσεται λόγος. (*De an.*, ed. Spira 7.3–7 [20M])

Macrina decides not to ignore Gregory's emotional state, but to use it to her advantage, allowing it to spur on the conversation. She *shows* us how emotions can be channelled and guided.[27] As Rowan Williams has said, 'Macrina thus brings the pain of human loss within the pedagogy of the spirit.'[28] In the course of their conversation, Gregory is freed from his disordered grief through the growth of his intellect's control over it, until he admits that in the beginning he was subordinating his logical faculty to his

---

[26] Burrus 2005: 252.
[27] Gregory playing devil's advocate echoes the role he must play as a composer of philosophical dialogues more generally. The assigning of the devil's advocate role explicitly at the beginning of the dialogue was also something that Methodius utilised in his dialogue *On the Resurrection*, which may have influenced Gregory here.
[28] Williams 1993: 231.

passions.[29] Readers watch the process of control over desire for what has gone and reorientation of that desire towards God. That process is inherently dialectical: Gregory has elegantly matched his genre to his argument. He allows his readers to go through the same process that he depicted himself going through in the narrative.

After such an emotional scene-setting, the role of emotions becomes an explicit topic of conversation between the brother and sister, and Macrina's view of the emotions changes over the course of the dialogue.[30] Macrina first defines the soul as an *intellectual* power that gives sense perceptions their comprehensibility. The soul sorts out the information handed to it by sense perception, interpreting it through the power of intelligence. But is the soul only the seat of the intellect, Gregory asks, or is it also the seat of emotions, the means of desire and fear? Macrina in her first answer explicitly rejects the Platonic image of the soul as a chariot with two horses and one charioteer.[31] She does not allow desire (one of Plato's pulling horses) to be an inherent part of the soul, because desire cannot coexist with satiety, and Christianity does not believe in continual cycles of existence, as she will argue in detail later. She says instead that emotions are accretions around the soul and not the soul itself – like warts.[32] She thereby narrows down Plato's definition of the soul: what is essential to the soul is the charioteer alone rather than the entire chariot complex. The disobedient horse can be unhitched from the chariot. But Macrina is immediately corrected from her initial anti-emotion view by Gregory's retort of a raft of biblical citations pointing to the positive use of emotions. Through dialectic it becomes clear that the emotions are *not* bad in and of themselves, and in fact form a non-moral tool that the soul must use correctly in order to advance.

That such a discussion of the role of emotions in the holy Christian life takes place using a female character is no accident, but rather shows Gregory's creative reuse of the traditional link between women and emotions. Other scholars tend to take Macrina's 'masculine' role as Gregory's teacher as an example of Gregory of Nyssa's belief that gender is non-essential to personhood and does not persist in the afterlife.[33] But in my analysis, I have focused not on an overcoming of gender roles, but rather on Gregory's continued use of topics traditionally coded feminine. Although, at first, we

---

[29] Ἐγὼ δὲ (καὶ γὰρ οὔπω τοῦ πάθους τὸν λογισμὸν ἀνεδεξάμην) θρασύτερόν πως ἀπεκρινάμην, οὐ πάνυ περισκεψάμενος τὸ λεγόμενον.
[30] This is the argument of Chapter 3, 'The Nature of the Passions', of J. Warren Smith's work (2004b: 75–103).
[31] *De an.*, ed. Spira 33.13–17 (51–52M). [32] *De an.*, ed. Spira 38.10–14 (56M).
[33] Ludlow 2013: 219; Harrison 1990.

might think of Gregory as feminised and Macrina as masculinised, I am arguing that Macrina's female gender is what allows certain topics to be the focus on the dialogue in the first place.

But perhaps even more germane to the change in the gender of the characters from the *Phaedo* is Gregory and Macrina's belief in the resurrection of the body. I am not specifically interested here in the vexed question of the persistence of gender in the afterlife for Gregory.[34] Instead, I am interested in the connection between a concern for the body and using women's voices in philosophical dialogues. Macrina fits perfectly into the trend that links women's voices with expertise about the body. Macrina's knowledge of physics, both cosmological and anthropological, is impressive.[35] Xanthippe, with her baby on her knee, could not be brought into Socrates' discussion of the soul's journey beyond the body. But Macrina, old, sick, and dying, can be brought into the discussion (and even lead it!) on the discussion of the soul's regathering of all of its particular molecules in a grand resurrection of the physical body. The acceptance of the body in the afterlife, no matter how much it changes in the transition, permits women with their physical expertise to take on a more central role in philosophical dialogues.

Conclusion

The two Greek Christian dialogues of the third and fourth century CE that feature female philosophers as primary interlocutors, Methodius' *Symposium* and Gregory of Nyssa's *On the Soul and Resurrection*, both deal with embodiment and desire in the pursuit of and enjoyment of the afterlife. In particular, they create a nexus of three important concepts: women, desire, and embodiment. We first saw these links exploited in the Socratic dialogues of Plato's *Symposium* and Xenophon's *Memorabilia*. Christian authors take up these traditional links, but in distinction to the female characters in the preceding Greek tradition, who are not allowed to speak directly as philosophers, but (if they were *lucky*) only had their words reported by men to other men, these female characters directly present their philosophical arguments to the readers. Hand in hand with inviting their female characters onstage, both Methodius and Gregory argue that

[34] For this, see especially Harrison and Ludlow (Harrison 1990; Ludlow 2013: 166–81).
[35] Ludlow's work on the scientific analogies in the dialogue shows that Macrina's use of examples from science back up the dialogue's broader dialectic from material, to rejection of material, to synthesis of material and immaterial, supporting this chapter's thesis (2009).

the body, along with its emotions, can be harnessed and used for progress. It is better to involve them than to deny them entirely. Finally, even once the goal is achieved, the body does not disappear, as it does for Plato. The body will be reconstituted in the eschaton, which means that women, with their traditional expertise in the body, have greater philosophical importance when talking about the final end of humanity.

Richard Hawley, in his study of women in ancient philosophy, has suggested that it was 'ironic' that early Christians preserved evidence of ancient female philosophers, based on his assumption that ancient Christians would rather have actively tried to destroy evidence of ancient female philosophers.[36] I have argued in this chapter that early Christians did not preserve the memory of philosophical women *despite* their Christianity, but rather precisely because of the commitments of their new faith. And they not only preserved evidence of *ancient* philosophical women but created and promoted new ones. Because of their focus on the value of the body and its emotions (as long as used correctly), what had been a Platonic overstepping of the feminine became an embrace of the embodied and desiring character of 'women'. Women were given a new amount of power in the imaginary world of dialogues partly because men had changed what they cared about. Writers such as Methodius and Gregory decided it was worthwhile to occupy a woman's mind imaginatively in order to explore new connections, such as the persistence of the physical body in the afterlife. The creation of characters such as Macrina, Thecla, and the other virgins at Methodius' party, completely apart from the question of their existence as real women, permitted these male writers to think through issues differently, using female voices to speak new conclusions about the utility of the body and its desires.

---

[36] Hawley 1994: 83.

20 | The Christianity of Latin Christian Poetry

MARK EDWARDS

Introduction

Before fiction became for most readers the dominant form of literature, books were perceived (or at least were advertised) chiefly as means to the propagation of knowledge. In the ancient Mediterranean world, even poetry was assumed to owe its value, if it had any, to its power to improve the soul or enrich the memory; history, however tendentious, was always in principle held to the test of veracity,[1] while philosophy and rhetoric were sometimes rivals but more often allies in the education of the political class. Travel being slow and perilous even for the few who could afford it, there was much that could be learned only through the medium of writing; the consequence was that the number of books that one had read (or sometimes only the number that one possessed) became the measure of education. To put this in more modern terms, the consumption and production of books not only enlarged one's pecuniary capital but amplified one's intellectual, cultural, and social capital.[2] Not to have read Aratus, for example, was to be ignorant; on the other hand, an astrologer who knew more of his science than Aratus but had not read Aratus himself would be deemed unlettered and therefore unlearned.[3] In the present chapter, I suggest that we should consider the beginning of Christian poetry as a double endeavour, on the one hand to promote what I shall call a first-order knowledge of truths that had hitherto been neglected in polite circles, and on the other to enhance the second order of knowledge by adding to the canon of works that an educated person ought to have read.

With this end in view, I have little to say on the questions which have inspired the majority of recent monographs on the first Latin poets of Christendom. These have generally been produced by scholars whose chief

---

I am grateful to Michael Champion, Jeremiah Coogan, Matthew Crawford, Michael Hanaghan, and Dawn LaValle Norman for their comments on previous versions of this chapter.

[1] In Lucian, *How to Write History*, and also by implication in Cicero's letter to Lucceius (*Fam.* 5.12), where he is asking for a delinquency in his favour. The rule is clear, and if it was almost always broken, so it is today.

[2] For this nomenclature, see, e.g., Bourdieu 1993.   [3] See further Gee 2013.

objective is to illustrate the survival, by a fusion of metamorphosis with mimicry, of the Latin verse tradition.[4] Delicate, nuanced, and erudite as they have been, their discussions have opened to us an unsuspected world of experimentation in which all is new, although nothing is intractably unfamiliar: they have exploded once and for all the assumption that late antique writers are merely derivative where they evoke their classic predecessors and always poetasters where they do not. There is, by contrast, little consideration of the aims which these authors may have entertained as Christians, profiting by and making their own contribution to the gradual eclipse of paganism by the cultural and political ascendancy of the church.[5] This is the subject that I wish to broach, with no pretence or hope of coming to any definitive results, as I pass in this chapter from Juvencus, whose ostensible aim is to bring a new hero to the attention of patrons of Latin epic, through the efforts of Prudentius to create a whole library of Christian classics, to the wily indirection of Ausonius, who can write, two generations after Juvencus, as though the gospel were already so well known that it need no longer be proclaimed.

Juvencus

The first complete digest of the gospels in Latin (150 years after Tatian's Greek or Syriac *Diatessaron*), is the *Libri Evangeliorum Quattuor*, a hexameter epic in four books attributed to one Juvencus and dated to 329 by Jerome.[6] It is clearly a product of the reign of Constantine, whom it acclaims at 4.808, and, as Roger Green says[7], there is consequently no reason to doubt Jerome's date. Juvencus therefore wrote at a time when Christians had almost lost their fear of persecution but had not yet persuaded the world, or even themselves, that the scriptures had any claim, apart from their antiquity and veracity, on a cultivated audience.[8] To make poetry rather than prose his vehicle was a bold choice for Juvencus, the motives of which we shall be in a better position to canvass after a brief reconnaissance of his text.

It was common for a book of Latin poems, or some programmatic portion of it, to commence with the device known as *recusatio*, in which the author declares that certain subjects have already been worked to exhaustion

---

[4] See the seminal work of Roberts 1989 and, most recently, Hardie 2019. On the permutation of classical tropes in Prudentius and Ausonius, and on their attempts to place themselves in a narrative that encompasses both scriptural and classical antiquity, see Pelttari 2014.
[5] See here the remarks of Jauss 1982: 18.
[6] Jerome, *Vir. ill.* 84. For Juvencus, see the edition of Marold 1886.
[7] Green 2006: 3–6.   [8] Gao 2002: 39–45.

by his predecessors, or else that they lie outside his present capacities or interest. In the third book of his *Georgics*, Virgil declines to treat a number of heroic or pathetic themes which he deems to be hackneyed, undertaking instead to erect a temple celebrating the feats of Augustus. In fact, he devotes no more of Book 3 to this edifice than the proem in which he imagines its adornments; on the other hand, the lines in which he passes over Eurystheus, Busiris, and Hylas (*Georg.* 3.4–6) afford our only evidence that these figures had ever been treated in Latin verse. This playfulness suggests that the *recusatio* was already an established trope. Propertius introduces a new variation in the third book of his elegies, presenting himself as the first to drink water from the pure spring of Callimachus, who was best known for the fastidious diction of his elegiacs; while this claim sits oddly on one who is writing a generation after Catullus, it allows him to take the narrow path of amatory verse in contrast to the highway which is thronged by eulogists of Rome's martial glories. Virgil in his sixth *Eclogue* had already been warned by Apollo to leave the recital of 'kings and battles' to those who had the epic calling; this prorogation of the *Aeneid* entailed no change of metre, but when Ovid learned that he must serve his apprenticeship as a poet of love, he was also obliged to exchange hexameters for elegiacs.[9]

Whereas all these poets make some pretence of divine instruction, Persius scoffs in the prologue to his satires that his tongue is moved by hunger rather than Helicon, thus disavowing the trite hypocrisy of disavowal. Juvencus was as resolved as any pagan writer of epic to excel his predecessors; but was not the *recusatio*, like the epic itself, a form wrung dry by every possible experiment? At the outset we might think that he has added nothing to the familiar practice of eschewing the subjects which have brought renown to the older poets:[10]

Sed tamen innumeros homines sublimia facta
Et virtutis honos in tempora longa frequentant,
Accumulant quorum famam laudemque poetae.
Hos celsi cantus, Smyrnae de fonte fluentes,
Illos Minciadae celebrat dulcedo Maronis.

Countless nonetheless are those whose outstanding feats and honoured virtue surround them through the ages, as poets heap up their fame and praise. Some are commemorated by noble songs which flow from the fount of Smyrna, others by the sweet diction of Maro. (Juvencus, Preface 6–10)

---

[9] Propertius, *Elegies* 3.1.1–12; Virgil, *Ecl.* 6.1–5; Ovid, *Am.* 1.1.1–16.
[10] Preface 6–10 (Marold 1886: 2). The poets to whom Juvencus alludes are Homer and Virgil.

But whereas the convention in the ancient world was to seek an alternative path to fame by raising some new subject to the dignity of epic or elegiac verse, Juvencus protests that Christians have no use for such vicarious longevity. It is not by their own artifice but by Christ that they live, and not in the fickle memory but forever and in the flesh:

Quod si tam longam meruerunt carmina famam.
Quae veterum gestis hominum mendacia nectunt,
Nobis certa fides aeternae in saecula laudis
Immortale decus tribuet, meritumque rependet.
Nam mihi carmen erit Christi vitalia gesta,
Divinum populis falsi sine crimine donum.

But if songs which mingle lies with the deeds of the ancients have deserved such lasting praise, my confident assurance of eternal praise through all the ages will certainly confer immortal glory on me and repay my merit; for my song will be the lifegiving deeds of Christ, a divine gift to the nations[11] that incurs no charge of falsehood. (Juvencus, Preface 15–20)

Pagan poets mingle truth with falsehood, as they confess,[12] whereas the record of Christ's ministry is handed down by four unimpeachable witnesses[13] and is therefore the only proper subject for an eternal song. And so, by a rapid tergiversation, the poet should have no ambition for his own work but for the genuine immortality which accrues to us by *fides* or faith in Christ. Whereas Ovid (for instance) boasted that his *Metamorphoses* would be proof against both fire and the wrath of Jove,[14] Juvencus anticipates not lasting honour in this world but an exemption from the flames that on the last day will consume the pagan bards with all their works:

Nec metus, ut mundi rapiant incendia secum
Hoc opus; hoc etenim forsan me subtrahet igni
Tunc, cum flammivola descendent nube coruscans,
Iudex, altithroni genitoris gloria, Christus.

Nor do I fear that this work will be snatched away in the combustion of the world; indeed, this will perhaps exempt me from the fire when from the heaven-borne cloud of flame the judge descends, Christ the glory of his Father enthroned on high. (Preface 21–24)

---

[11] Cf. Luke 2:32 and Juvencus 1.210.
[12] Hesiod, *Theog.* 27–28. The Latin precursor to Juvencus is Lucretius, who urges at *Rer. nat.* 5.1ff. that Epicurus has rendered greater services to humankind than Hercules.
[13] See Marold 1886: 1.   [14] Ovid, *Metam.* 15.871–79; cf. Horace, *Carm.* 3.30.

The conflagration that Ovid pretends to foresee without fear is no conceit after all; Juvencus, however, hopes that it will spare not only his work but himself in acknowledgement of that work. Perhaps he recalls Paul's promise at 1 Corinthians 3:15 that those who build on Christ will invariably be saved, though some must stand the test of fire; in any case, he turns the classical trope on its head by aspiring to outlive his poem rather than to procure survival through it. Of course, we may doubt whether any poet can be sincerely indifferent to the fortunes of his work in the present world while it endures, but we must also grant to Juvencus that the product is consistent with his professions. Although it is not a cento,[15] either of Virgilian tags or of biblical verses, it also offers little pretence of originality, either in style or in content. There is no innovation upon the gospel narratives, no doubt because he is wary of misinforming a pagan reader; there is no departure from classical diction except where the subject matter requires the adoption, or occasional creation, of a term for which the poets who served him as models had no use.

Virgil is saluted in the proem as Juvencus' master in style, the appellation Maro Minciades being formed by the coupling of his cognomen with a patronymic derived from the river near which he was born – a novel calque on 'Maeonides', the long-established epithet for Homer. Often the Virgilian echoes bring out the disparity between the new work and its model, for as Roger Green observes, 'there is not much Aeneas in Juvencus' Christ'. On the contrary, the deliverance of Christ to Pilate (*post terga revinctum ... magno clamore trahebant* at 4.588–89) echoes the discovery of Sinon at *Aeneid* 2.57–58. Yet Sinon was a liar, mistaken for a true informant, whereas Christ is the saviour mistaken for a villain. Again, Juvencus' storm scene at 2.25–38 has many Virgilian reminiscences, but there is no human in any pagan epic who can still a storm as Christ does at 2.35.[16] Coalescence with classical models is, however, observable, e.g. at 1.679–89, where the paraphrase of Matt 7:13–14 on the broad and narrow gates is eked out by reminiscences of the 'two paths' motif in Prodicus' 'Choice of Heracles' and the 'Pythagorean' *Tabula Cebetis*. Green notes that Juvencus' description of the place of the lost at 4.284–87 combines Matt 25:41 (on outer darkness) with features of Virgil's Tartarus, perhaps with further evocations of Statius and Valerius Flaccus.[17] While we cannot

---

[15] On the cento of Proba (not wholly bereft of original composition), see Dijkstra 2016: 103–6 with McGill 2016: 3–32, 145, etc.

[16] Cf. Mark 4:39 and Green 2006: 62–63.

[17] Green 2006: 95, quoting Statius, *Thebaid* 1.85 and Valerius, *Argonautica* 2.192, with a hint that classical precedents may have led Juvencus to expand the Matthaean text with allusions to the mental pains of the damned.

be sure that Juvencus knew them,[18] these poets furnished a precedent for narrating events in their chronological order, rather than plunging *in medias res*, as Horace prescribes and as Virgil had chosen to do in the manner of Homer.

Hence it was as much the poet's design to differ from Virgil as to imitate him[19] – a natural ambition, we might say, when his aim is to win for himself the renown that has already accrued to the object of his emulation. In contrast, however, to Horace who covets a reputation that will outlive the pyramids, in contrast to Ovid who summons fate and the Muse to verify his immortality, in contrast even to Virgil who seems to play on his own name when he records that he wrote the *Georgics* in Parthenope[20] – in contrast, we may say, to the very rationale of literary production in the ancient world, Juvencus not only omits to name himself but yields his closing lines to another, who is at most his dedicatee, not his patron or the ostensible subject of his praise:

Haec mihi pax tribuit, pax haec mihi saecli
Quam fovet indulgens terrae regnator apertae
Constantinus, adest cui gratia digna merenti,
Qui solus regum sacri sibi nominis horret
Inponi pondus, quo iustis dignior actis
Aeternam capiat divina in saecula vitam
Per dominum lucis Christum, qui in saecula regnat.

The peace of Christ has made this possible for me, and also the peace of the world, which is benignly sustained by Constantine, the ruler of the earth's whole expanse, to whom grace is given according to his desert. He alone among monarchs feels the awful weight of the sacred name on his shoulders, so that he may be more worthy by his righteous deeds to receive eternal life for godlike ages, through Christ the lord of light, who reigns from age to age. (Juvencus, 4.805–11)

The Motives of Juvencus

This harmony of the gospels is, in fact, one of three didactic works in Latin which pay court to Constantine.[21] The earliest, though of very uncertain

---

[18] Green 2006: 12. [19] See McGill 2016: 31 on 'Kontrastimitation'. [20] *Georgics* 4.563–66.
[21] Or four, if to Lactantius, Firmicus, and Juvencus himself we add some parts of Optatianus Porfirius, on whom see now Squire 2016.

date, is the *Divine Institutes* of Lactantius,[22] which purports to be not merely a new apology but a manual of Christian thought and practice; the appeals to Constantine may not belong to the earliest conception of the work, but the emperor's *Oration to the Saints* provides strong evidence that he had read at least one edition with approval. Much later, and punctuated by strong echoes of Lactantius, is the *Mathesis*, or primer of astronomy, in which Firmicus Maternus defends this science against the false charges which have led Constantine to enact a new law against it. Professing a monotheism consistent with action through lesser deities, Firmicus does not say whether he thinks himself a Christian or takes Constantine to be one. Juvencus makes no secret of his convictions and could not doubt that they were shared by his addressee, who had recently commissioned the preparation of some fifty copies of the New Testament in a single city.[23] This concern for the integrity of the sacred corpus, however, hardly proves by itself that he would have welcomed the translation of the four gospels into a smooth tale that would necessitate the extrusion of certain elements, or into a metrical form that could not but obscure the simplicity of the original. It is only the *Oration to the Saints*, with its citations from the fourth *Eclogue* to complement its indiscriminate culling of episodes from all four of the gospels, that appears to condone the use of classical precedents in the glorification of Christ.

Constantine's New Testaments, we are told, were designed for a host of new believers whose thirst for instruction had been quickened or enhanced by his victories in the east.[24] We need not doubt that the simultaneous publication, here and in other centres, of so many copies from the same archetype contributed to the fixing of the Greek canon. We hear of no such direction being given in the West, and we possess no full Latin copy of the New Testament from the fourth century.[25] We cannot, therefore, say how many readers of Juvencus would have been able to consult a literal rendering of the gospels, and there may have been many whose only source of knowledge was his poem. Among these we may include not only Christians but pagans who either lacked the opportunity to acquaint themselves with the gospels or were indisposed to read a text which they knew to be slender

---

[22] See Barnes 1973; Edwards 2015b: 73–76.

[23] Eusebius, *Vit. Const.* 4.36. On the question as to whether these were pandect Bibles or New Testament codices, see Grafton and Williams 2006: 216–21.

[24] Eusebius, *Vit. Const.* 4.36. The role of Constantine in forming the canon has been variously estimated; the longest discussion is that of Dungan 2006.

[25] For an edition of a partial text antedating the Vulgate, see Gasquet 1914. Jeremiah Coogan points out to me that Latin codices from the fourth century containing at least the remnants of multiple gospels include the codices Bobiensis and Vercellensis, and that a fragment from another fourth-century gospel book is preserved in the endpapers of MS Stutt. HB VII 64.

in literary merit, as such merit was judged in the forum or the schools. The majority of Victorians would have found the hagiography of the Buddha jejune and puerile if they had come upon a translation of some original text, but Sir Edwin Arnold's life of him in blank verse, *The Light of Asia*, outsold its companion-piece on Christ, *The Light of the World*, in part no doubt because it was not competing with any canonical narrative.[26]

Nor should we assume that only a learned audience would prefer hexameters to prose. As the studies of Agosti and others remind us,[27] hexameters are frequent in both Greek and Latin inscriptions which would surely have missed their purpose if they were legible only to the well-to-do.[28] Those with less leisure would certainly have no reason to charge Juvencus with verbosity; the median length of each of his four books is about 800 lines, a little less than the median for the *Aeneid*. It cannot therefore be said that an attempt to be more comprehensive would have swollen the book to unmanageable dimensions: mechanical factors cannot explain the absence of the conversation with Mary and John from the cross which is recounted in the Fourth Gospel or the failure of Juvencus to begin, as the *Diatessaron* does, with the prologue to the same text which declares Christ to be the Logos who was 'with God in the beginning' (cf. John 1:2). His reticence does not seem to betoken any doubt of Christ's divinity, which is attested elsewhere in the poem; it may be that he simply found it difficult to accommodate such a passage in an imitation of heroic narrative or to cast its novel teachings into the idiom of Virgil. It may also be, however, that he was observing Paul's injunction not to draw those who are weak in faith into doubtful disputations (Rom 14:1). Why set oneself at the outset the conundrum of deciding whether *logos* was best rendered as *ratio*, *sermo*, or *verbum*, as 'reason', 'speech', or 'word'?[29]

Attempts to divine an author's aims from the mere inspection of his works, without knowledge of his audience or the ambient circumstances, will always be questionable, even when they are not carried to the extremes that characterise New Testament scholarship. We may feel that artistic motives may be ascribed with greater confidence to a Latin poet than to an evangelist, and conversely that the poet would not consciously adopt a distinctive position on matters of faith. On the other hand, just as no one writes without artifice, so no aesthetic decision can be wholly severed from other beliefs to which the author subscribes. Let us take as an example the

---

[26] Arnold 1879, 1893. [27] See e.g. Agosti 2016.
[28] On the use of Homer in elementary education, see Morgan 1998: 59, 93, 144, and especially 308.
[29] Cf. Tertullian, *Prax.* 5.

raising of Lazarus, an episode which, as Scott McGill points out, has been inserted into a narrative of the passion drawn largely from Matthew.[30] It is followed immediately in the poem by Matthew's version of the plot preceding the arrest of Jesus in Holy Week; a conspiracy against Jesus, however, is also the immediate sequel of the Lazarus episode in the Fourth Gospel. By returning to Matthew when he might have continued with John, is Juvencus ascribing a certain primacy to Matthew, who is named first in the prologue attached to his poem, and probably held the first place, then as now, in Latin codices of the gospels? Or is the conjunction of two sources where he might have followed one alone designed to illustrate the harmony of the New Testament? Should we argue, rather, that he postponed this miracle to the week of the passion not because he preferred the chronology of one gospel to that of the other, but because the architecture of his poem required that the most portentous of the Saviour's works should be his last?

It is safest to assume that he had no intention of honouring one evangelist more than another, any more than he wished to take a side in any current ecclesiastical controversy. We may also surmise that he had no quarrel with the stylistic or architectonic conventions of pagan literature; the displaced echoes of Virgil which we noted above would be lost on future readers if his poem were to drive Virgil into the obscurity into which the latter had already driven Naevius. Juvencus writes in the spirit of Lactantius, who represents Christianity as the consummation of all that is best in Latin culture; Constantine, so far as we can judge, was of the same mind, and it was not a Christian sovereign, but Julian the Apostate, who enacted a law forbidding the 'Galileans' to study writings which might sully the purity of their ancestral faith.

Prudentius[31]

Julian's interdict on the Christian teaching of pagan literature is recorded by Ammianus Marcellinus with the comment that this was the most unjust of his measures against the Christians.[32] It seems indeed to have been the principal cause of posthumous obloquy, for exclusion from the schools which taught the classics was exclusion from any powerful or remunerative

---

[30] McGill 2016: 21–22.

[31] Prudentius may be read most conveniently in the Loeb Classical Library edition of Thomson 1949–54. The fullest commentary is that of Lavarenne 2002.

[32] Ammianus, *Histories* 20.10.7; 25.4.20; cf. *Theodosian Code* 13.3.5 and Hardy 1968. Against the view that it was purposely coercive, see McLynn 2014.

office, and hence a betrayal of ancestral dignity for those families which traditionally held such offices. At the same time, it was also the logical complement to the Christian rejection of the gods in whose honour the texts had been composed. While pagans were indignant to see their enemies frequenting the schools of rhetoric and philosophy in ever-increasing numbers, educated Christians must have wondered why these schools enjoined the perusal of the same authors who were subject to weekly invective from the pulpit. Basil commends a discriminating use of pagan literature in his advice to the young,[33] but Apollinarius adopted a surgical rather than a palliative remedy when he versified the Septuagint in the metres of Homer and Pindar while creating a substitute for the Platonic dialogue in his paraphrases of the New Testament.[34]

Latin continued to show more originality than Greek, in Christian as in pagan verse of the later empire. The small library which Prudentius adds to the fruits of his native tongue includes the *Psychomachia*, a small epic in which the combatants are personified vices and virtues;[35] *Apotheosis* and the *Hamartigenia* (brief epics on the nativity of Christ and the birth of sin); a suite of daily hymns, the *Cathemerinon*; and a series of panegyrics, the *Peristephanon*, to which we owe some of the most memorable details in our legends of the saints. In these, as in his great diatribe against the restoration of the Altar of Victory (*Contra Symmachum*), passages which appear to be wholly new stand side by side with variations on Horace, Virgil, and other authors, which have been ably discussed in recent scholarship.[36] Such adaptation, however, was the sinew of creativity in the golden and silver ages of Latin literature, and no work by Prudentius is bare pastiche,[37] any more than this could be said of Lucretian or Catullan reminiscences in Virgil. He may not have had the arrogance to imagine that his verse would outlive its precursors, but he can be read more independently of them than Juvencus. On the other hand, while his diction teems with allusions to the scriptures, Prudentius never engages in paraphrase: his poetry is not a propaedeutic for new believers but the ensign of an ever-advancing church.

---

[33] See Wilson 1975.
[34] On Christian poetry of the fourth century as a response to Julian, see Ludlow and Lunn-Rockliffe 2019: 634, esp. n. 25.
[35] I shall not attempt here to add anything to Pelttari 2019. [36] See Pucci 1991.
[37] On the 'aesthetic' and 'logical' principles of the collection, see Rand 1920: esp. 72 and 80, where he observes that Prudentius is 'filling the framework of Pindaric and Horatian hymns with Christian feeling and belief and Christian story'.

It will not be necessary to repeat here the perspicacious observations of other scholars on Prudentius' evocations of earlier Latin poets.[38] It may, however, be useful to draw attention to his fondness for pervasive images which have both a scriptural and a pagan ancestry. Thus, the snake is notoriously a frequent intruder in Virgil, whose unseen snake in the grass at *Eclogues* 3.93 becomes a vivid metaphor at *Aeneid* 2.380, where the Greeks shrink from false allies whom they have just perceived to be Trojans as a man shrinks from a snake whom he has startled in a bush. Laocoön and his sons are crushed by the coils of two stupendous serpents sent from the deep by Poseidon; the words in which they are described echo *Georg.* 1.53, where Italy is said to be free of such vermin. This assurance is belied by the catalogue of snakes at *Georg.* 3.314–19; the serpent which is cast into the bosom of Amata by a Fury is invisible, but all the more pernicious in its effects.[39] In Book 2 of the *Aeneid*, Pyrrhus is compared to an arched and glittering *coluber* as he dispatches Priam, while Helen, *Vestae limina servantem*, has the attributes of Eurydice's subtle assassin at *Georg.* 4.459.[40] A Gorgon surrounded by hissing serpents adorns the shield of Aeneas; a snake expiring after a blow provides a simile for a ship foundering on the rocks; the snake which is seen as an omen at the tomb of Anchises may represent his soul.[41] The serpent is thus on most occasions a symbol of guile, swift death, and unreasoning malignity – in each guise, therefore, a synecdoche for natural evil, not a metaphysical antitype to the good or the divine.

By contrast, in Prudentius, it is neither a natural beast nor a figure of speech, but the form in which the devil preys ubiquitously upon a world which serves him most when it knows him least. At *Cathemerinon* 3.101–2, the treacherous serpent beguiles the simple Eve, only to hear at 3.126–27 that she will be avenged when his three-tongued head is trodden by her heel. This allusion to the *titulus* in Latin, Greek, and Hebrew, which was set above the head of the crucified Saviour, is offset at 6.140–45 by the banishment of the twisting serpent who disturbs peaceable hearts with his multitudinous coils. No wonder that, in contemplating the death of Jesus, the serpent feels a terrible wound which breaks his sibilant neck and causes his venomous gall to desert him (9.88–90). Hence, it is now permitted to enter the garden of which the serpent robbed humanity (10.163–64), even while those without continue to rage as though they have poison in their veins or were stung by furies (11.91–92). The reptile in the *Cathemerinon* is always Satan, and the sequence of allusions leads us from his first victory to his

---

[38] See, e.g., Palmer 1989. [39] *Aeneid* 2.205–31; 7.346. [40] *Aeneid* 2.471–75; 576.
[41] *Aeneid* 8.435–38; 5.273–75; 5.80–84.

exorcism. Prudentius' implicit revision or critique of Virgil[42] is best understood if we compare the prose tract in which Firmicus Maternus, now an undisguised believer, had exhorted the sons of Constantine to suppress the 'errors of profane religion'. The itinerary of false cults circles the regions of the known world, culminating in the discovery of the serpent as the idol of superstition in Rome itself. In his subsequent exposition of the true doctrine, Firmicus reminds his Christian sovereigns that the serpent is the deceiver of our first parents, the instigator of idolatry, and hence the chief destroyer of human souls.[43] Rome's fathers, who revered him as a god, were therefore ignorant or depraved; the judgement on Virgil implied by the recurrent apparition of the serpent in Prudentius may not have been so condemnatory. It is possible that, like Lactantius and Constantine,[44] he regards him as a prophet who was not fully cognisant of all the truths that are adumbrated in his songs.

A survey of Prudentius' uses of *faenus* ('interest') would reveal a similar leavening of its classical by its biblical, or more precisely by its parabolic associations. While many Romans drew a handsome revenue from lending, it is always assumed in poetry that such profits are base, not only when paupers envy them (as in Juvenal's ninth *Satire*) but when they are enjoyed yet hypocritically disowned, as in the praise of the simple life by the usurer Allius in the second *Epode* of Horace. Historians knew that those oppressed by debt were apt to seek relief in brigandage or rebellion, and that statesmen had from time to time secured both popularity and peace by releasing them from their obligations. Usury is forbidden in the Old Testament, and the tax-collectors who fleeced the poor on Rome's behalf were among the most despised of the Jewish contemporaries of Jesus. Nevertheless, in his parable of the talents (Matt 25:14–30), Jesus presents himself as a master who punishes servants when they fail to augment the deposits entrusted to them, and his images from agriculture are sometimes accompanied by a figure for increase ('thirtyfold, sixtyfold, a hundredfold'), which would be conceivable only in financial husbandry (Matt 13:8). In the second hymn of Prudentius, *faenus* is mere lucre, the talisman of Roman avarice (*Cathemerinon* 2.25); in the seventh, however, he promises that the man whose right hand is greedy for praise and prodigal of wealth will reap a hundredfold in interest (7.220). In the *Apotheosis*, or *Nativity of Christ*, *faenus* in its other sense of 'grass' still signifies interest, but in a spiritual sense, when

---

[42] On Prudentius as a skilled interpreter of Virgil, see Hardie 2017.
[43] See Firmicus, *Err. prof. rel.* 21 and 26.
[44] Lactantius, *Inst.* 7.24; Constantine, *Coet. sanct.* 19–21.

it provides a seat for the crowd on whose behalf Christ multiplies a handful of loaves and fishes (712). In the *Psychomachia*, an essay in extended personification which spawned half the poetry of the Latin Middle Ages, it is Virtue who, by emptying her purse, lays up the interest on eternal wealth while dealing a fatal blow to Avarice (583). By eschewing the filthy coin of earth, she lays up an incorruptible treasure in heaven: the transition from the carnal to the spiritual sense of *faenus* prefigures the extinction of worldly opulence by the kingdom of those who beg.

Another striking instance of the interpenetration of pagan and Christian symbolism has been pointed out by Mark Tomlinson in a hitherto unpublished thesis on 'The Influence of Pagan Sacrificial Thought on Christian Martyr-Soteriology'.[45] Truly or idly, Ovid relates that the Lemuria, a festival for the expulsion of evil spirits, was initially named the Remuria, and dedicated to Remus, the brother of Romulus, who was struck down after jumping in derision over the walls which were being erected by his brother (*Fast.* 5.451–80). Historians have observed that the shedding of blood to cement the walls of a nascent city is a well-attested rite.[46] In his eulogy of the martyr Lawrence, Prudentius acclaims him as the true protector of the capital, contrasting him with a number of ancient leaders who had rescued it from siege or occupation (*Peristephanon* 2.9–16). The foes repelled by Lawrence are supernatural, as the founders of the Lemuria understood, without perceiving that the gods whom they continued to worship were more to be feared than those whom they had banished. Lawrence is put to death because, when an avaricious prefect demands a public show of the church's hidden riches, he assembles the poor, the widows, the disabled, and the fatherless in order to point a characteristically Prudentian moral (*Peristephanon* 2.45–167). Romulus and Remus, as he reminds his interlocutor at *Against Symmachus* 2.299, had only *faenus* or hay as a coverlet for their royal couches. The gathering of this spiritual bounty requires Lawrence to make a full circuit of the city, another act which often formed part of a pagan ritual of consecration (*Peristephanon* 2.142). Thus, the assimilation of the legend to pagan customs is in no way a validation of these customs but a judgement on those who perform them in ignorance of that coming world in which the wages of the oppressor will no longer be paid in gold.[47]

The revaluation of the literary symbol in Prudentius marks the transition from a pagan to a Christian epistemology. The poets for whom the

---

[45] Tomlinson 2010.
[46] For references (esp. Ennius, frag. 1.74 Skutsch) and recent bibliography, see Serrati 2015: 11.
[47] On other subversive elements in *Peristephanon* 2, see Conybeare 2002.

snake was a ubiquitous synecdoche for danger were not yet conscious of the spiritual poison which has lurked in our hearts since Eden; the great of this world who have lived by *faenus* or usury will soon learn that the revenues of heaven are reserved for those whose *faenus* in this world is a dinner of herbs. The blood of Remus could not preserve Rome from the Gauls, but she has unwittingly made a talisman of the murdered Lawrence, brother to the weak, the poor, and the naked of this world, who will not be the weak, the poor, and the naked of the next.

Ausonius of Bordeaux

The teacher and poet Ausonius,[48] who had the future emperor Gratian as his pupil and was rewarded with a consulship, would have prospered less had he not embraced the religion of his patron.[49] In his most openly Christian composition, the *Paschal Verses*, he celebrates the divine majesty of the emperor and his coregents, who share a single realm without division, in language redolent of current teaching on the trinity.[50] The *Gryphus Ternarii Numeri* is a catalogue of significant and symbolic triads, the tacit application of which was unlikely to be lost on Christian readers.[51] For the most part, however, his poems declare no allegiance to the church, and his occasional professions of faith are assumed to be lukewarm, late, or insincere. Such judgements presuppose that a Christian author should never fail to advertise his Christianity, and it is indeed true that, unless an exception ought to be made for Firmicus Maternus,[52] we know of no private person before Ausonius who failed to observe this rule from the time of his entry into the church. An emperor will at times be bound to speak for all his subjects, and a neophyte such as Marius Victorinus could not obliterate or emend all that he wrote before his conversion, but could a poet reckon himself a Christian yet take the imitation of his classical models so far as to make believe that their gods were still his?

It is clear that we can return an affirmative answer to this question in later epochs, unless we are to conclude that almost every Elizabethan

---

[48] For his works see Green 1991, 1999.   [49] Green 1993.   [50] Green 1991: 15–16.

[51] Green 1991: 111–16. Hardie 2019: 186–87 cites the *Gryphus* to reinforce his suggestion that *ex tribus est unus* in Epigram 82 is a ludic allusion to the doctrine of the trinity, and is even willing to find a reminiscence of christological or eucharistic formulae in Epigram 83, where vinegar 'becomes what it was not' by transformation into wine (he also compares the miracle at Cana from John 2:1–12).

[52] See Edwards 2015b: 75. Julius Africanus is an enigma that I cannot address in this chapter.

was a pagan. Even where false gods are not expressly invoked, such unimpeachable Protestants as Milton and Marvell may compose verses which are simply erotic, salutatory, or descriptive, giving no expression to the religious sentiments which inform their other writings. Just as we do not assign 'Gratiana singing and dancing' to Marvell's pagan youth, so we do not attempt to conjure it into an allegory. In other poems, we find intersecting languages which enable us to say that only a Christian could have written (say) 'The Nymphs Complaining for the Death of her Faun', but not that its overall tenor is Christian, or religious rather than pastoral.[53] As a victim of 'wanton troopers', the faun might represent Christ as the principal casualty of a war that was prosecuted by both sides in the name of religion; his identity, we may think, cannot be mistaken when the nymph exclaims, 'There is not such another in / The world to offer for their sin'. But who, if the faun is Christ, is the faithless Silvio, who presented him as a gift to the nymph before he abandoned her and 'left his deere, but took my hart'? The bad pun is redeemed by the final conceit, in which the faun feeds, like the bridegroom of the Song of Songs, in a garden of roses and lilies so that he might, had he lived, have become as red within as the one and as white without as the other. It would nonetheless be peremptory to deduce that he 'is Christ' after all; on the other hand, it would be absurd to question Marvell's faith because of his ludic use of sacred imagery.

The Crucifixion of Cupid (*Cupido Cruciatus*)

I dwell on this example because it may furnish an analogue for one of the most celebrated works of Ausonius, the *Cupid Crucified*.[54] It opens in the underworld, with explicit allusions to the topography of this realm in the sixth book of the Aeneid. It ends with the flight of Love through the gates of ivory, the same gate through which Aeneas quits the underworld, although it is the portal of 'false dreams'. The intervening plot, however, is more reminiscent of the death of Orpheus in Ovid than of any scene in Virgil.[55] The *dramatis personae* are women who have died for love and each of them, forgetting her own infirmities, ascribes her ruin

---

[53] For text see Smith 2003: 69–71. On p. 68, Smith remarks: 'While some have acknowledged literary presences within the poem that were conventionally understood to be allegorical (such as the Song of Songs), they have nonetheless denied that the poem is referring to anything in particular.'
[54] Green 1991: 139–43.   [55] Ovid, *Metam.* 11.1–43.

to supernatural agency. When Love himself attempts to make a secret journey through the nether region, his sharp-eyed victims fall upon him without mercy. Hanging him on a myrtle, they rain punitive blows upon him, and their violence is redoubled when his mother Venus joins them, hoping to expiate her own shame. Indeed, she is so intemperate in her blows that the other women repent and intervene to restrain her, permitting Love to make his escape.

Despite its central theme, the poem has rarely been interpreted in modern times with reference to Christ, although it may have been so construed by its seventeenth-century translator, the devoutly Christian poet Henry Vaughan.[56] The setting in the underworld is no impediment to such a reading, for Christ's descent to Hades to vanquish Satan and thereby liberate the just dead was already the subject of a number of elaborate narratives in the fourth century.[57] Nor can it be maintained that, in taking Orpheus as his pattern, the poet excludes the identification of Love with Christ, for other illustrations of the coalescence of Orpheus with Christ in art and literature are not far to seek in the early Christian centuries. In a recent monograph,[58] Miguel Herrero de Jáuregui has described one extant picture in which the two figures are conflated: interpretation is therefore not foreclosed by the preface in which Ausonius traces his inspiration to a painting, whether or not we are disposed, with Roger Green,[59] to take the vivacity of the poem as evidence that his claim is true. It hardly needs to be said that Christ was the most notorious victim of crucifixion even for a pagan reader of this period; a Christian might also have been aware of the aphorism 'my love is crucified', which had lately acquired new currency in the long recension of the letters attributed to Ignatius of Antioch. Quoting from an earlier (and all but identical) redaction of Ignatius' *Letter to the Romans*, Origen had taken Love as a sobriquet for Christ in his *Commentary on the Song of Songs*.

With the caveat that I no more wish to affirm that Love in Ausonius means Christ than that the faun in Marvell is Christ, I wish to argue that a readiness to hear echoes of scripture and Christian tradition will enrich our appreciation of certain passages in *Cupid Crucified*. I shall make no claims regarding the intention of the author, except to promise that I shall not cite any text which he is unlikely to have read.

---

[56] Davis 2008: 65–74.
[57] See yet again Firmicus, *Err. prof. rel.* 24.2. For the origins of the tradition, see Eph 4.17–20; 1 Pet 3:18–19, Rev 1:8, etc.; Pol. *Phil.* 1.2; Irenaeus, *Haer.* 4.27.2; Origen, *Cels.* 2.43.
[58] Herrero de Jáuregui 2010: 118–25.   [59] Green 1991. Contrast Laird 1996: 100 and notes.

I begin with the scene in which the women catch sight of Cupid:

Agnovere omnes puerum ...
Agnoscunt tamen et vanum vibrare vigorem
Occipiunt, hostemque unum loca non sua nactum
Cum pigros ageret densa sub nocte volatus
Facta nube premunt.

All recognised the boy ... They recognise him nonetheless, and begin to flex their phantom sinews. Forming a cloud, they envelop their single enemy, as he winged his toilsome way through the dense night, occupying a place not his own. (Cupid Crucified 47, 51–54)

Puer, representing *pais* in Greek (which may mean 'child' or 'servant') is the designation of Christ at Acts 5:27, and he had already been identified, as we have seen, with the *puer* of Virgil's fourth *Eclogue*. Both Homer and Virgil represent shades as intangible, hence incapable of exercising more than *vanus vigor*; but mortals as a race are *vani* at Ps 61[62]:10 and Wisd 13:1. Cupid fails to imitate the secrecy of Christ's coming to earth[60] and suffers in 'a place not his own' the opposite misfortune to that of Christ, who 'came to his own and his own knew him not' (John 1:11).[61]

The crucifixion follows in short order (59–64):

huius in excelso suspensum stipite Amorem
devinctum post terga manus substrictaque plantis
vincula maerentem nullo moderamine poenae
afficiunt. reus est sine crimine, iudice nullo
accusatur Amor. se quisque absolvere gestit,
transferat ut proprias aliena in crimina culpas.

On a high branch of this [myrtle tree] they hanged Love. Binding his hands behind his back, and fettering his feet with painful chains, they heaped punishments upon him with no remission. Love is on trial for no offence, he is accused without a judge. Each one strives to prove her innocence so that she may lay her own guilt to another's charge.

The myrtle is not significant in Christian iconography. It is said by Ausonius to be the tree on which Proserpina crucified Adonis because he spurned her love for that of Venus. Although he is said by Ovid to have been the child of Myrrha (*Metam.* 10.503–4), the crucifixion is not an attested detail. Lipsius conjectures that it formed the end of the story in

---

[60] Cf. Phil 2:6; 1 Cor 2:8; Ign. *Magn.* 8.2.
[61] In the Vulgate, this reads *in propria venit et sui non receperunt*.

which Proserpine/Persephone falls in love with Adonis after his death and so becomes the rival of Venus. Jupiter is said to have allotted him to each goddess at a different time of the year, but Ausonius implies that Adonis refused to accept the alternation. This may be his own invention, just as Firmicus in his account of the rites of Attis is the first to record that the adepts were consoled by a promise of the god's resurrection.[62]

The locution *Reus sine crimine* seems to be unattested before Ausonius but is patently a more apposite description of Christ in the gospels than of Love in the present poem. It is not true, of course, that Christ was sent to the cross *iudice nullo*, but a mob comes near to throwing him from a rock at Luke 4:29–30, while he is in danger of being stoned at John 10:32. The locution *aliena crimina* seems to be first attested here; it occurs again in Augustine, *On the One Baptism* 14.23–24, where it signifies sins committed by others which cannot render the sacraments of the catholic church invalid for those who receive them in faith. It is standard Christian doctrine, of course, that all the sins for which Christ died are foreign to his own nature.[63]

The intervention of the mother (80–85) is a surprising detail, though it might have been foreseen by an astute reader of the Fourth Gospel:

alma Venus tantos penetrat secura tumultus.
nec circumvento properans suffragia nato
terrorem ingeminat stimulisque accendit Amaris
ancipites furias natique in crimina confert
dedecus ipsa suum, quod vincula caeca mariti
deprenso Mavorte tulit.

Benign Venus makes her way through these violent tumults with impunity, but makes no haste to succour her beleaguered child. She redoubles his fearful suffering, goading them with harsh words to inflame their furious onset from both sides. She lays to her son's charge her own dishonour when she blindly donned the chains in which her consort took Mars captive.

Christ's mother is a spectator of his execution at John 19:25. The evangelists, who call her Mary, tell us that she was a virgin, but Jews and pagans were happy to spread abroad the name of the soldier who had sired her miraculous child.[64]

---

[62] Firmicus, *Err. prof. rel.* 22.1.
[63] While Ausonius cannot have read Augustine, he may have been familiar with Cyprian's distinction between *propria* and *aliena peccata* at *Ep.* 64.5.
[64] Origen, *Cels.* 1.28; 1.32.

As Venus is the antitype of Mary, so Cupid escapes the fate of Christ (79–98):

Tum pia mater grates agit cessisse dolentes
Et condonatas puero dimittere culpas.

Then (to their delight) the pious mother urges them to desist from grieving, to forgive the boy's offences, his debt being paid.

Condonare initially means to sacrifice, or to pay a debt. *Dimittere* can have a similar meaning, and both occur together in this sense at Caesar, *Civil War* 3.69. Christians, however, would be familiar with *demittere* as 'remit' from the Lord's prayer (*demitte debita nostra*), as also with the *nunc dimittis* intoned by Simeon at Luke 2:29. On the other hand, neither the poet's theology nor the argument of his poem requires that the sacrificial sense of *condonare* should be ignored.

Thus Cupid in this poem is not Christ, but the subliminal awareness of the gospel narrative creates a fleeting resemblance at a number of points, which is offset at once by an equally striking incongruity. This jarring intersection of amatory and religious imagery was to be a recurrent feature of European poetry in the Middle Ages, in which a knight could pay his devoirs to another man's wife as though she were the Virgin, while Mary herself was addressed with all the unction that would grace a petition to an earthly queen.[65]

Ausonius may strike us as the most modern of the poets considered here, and he can be read most sympathetically if we reflect that the waning influence of the church in the last few centuries has been accompanied by a waning need for its influence. Few know the way to Calvary, but the footfall of Christ is heard in every political manifesto, and the precepts of the Sermon on the Mount are more widely practised now than in the days when everyone professed them. This universalisation of the Christian sensibility – this secular gospel, as some would style it – first becomes apparent in the literature of England's Augustan age, the eighteenth century. Whereas the first Augustans could congratulate the poor on their obscurity while lamenting the great who had died without a Homer to remember them,[66] Gray's 'Elegy in a Country Churchyard' raises the humble to parity with the heroic, in life as in death:

Some village Hampden that with dauntless breast
The little tyrant of his fields withstood;

---

[65] Schubart 1952: 124–26.   [66] Virgil, *Georg.* 2.458; Horace, *Carm.* 4.9.25.

Some mute inglorious Milton laid to rest
Some Cromwell guiltless of his country's blood.

It has been observed that Ausonius was among the poets that Thomas Gray read in youth,[67] before Gibbon had affirmed that his poetical fame condemns the taste of his age.[68] That fame rests above all on his exhaustive catalogue of the finny tribes which populate the river Moselle. When he comes at last to its human denizens, however, he strikes the chord that we hear again from the churchyard of Stoke Poges:[69]

Nec sola antiquos ostentat Roma Catones
Aut unus tantum iusti spectator et aequi
Pollet Aristides veteresque illustrat Athenas.

It is not only Rome who boasts her illustrious Catos, and that one man Aristides, ornament of ancient Athens, is not the sole scrutineer of the just and right.

If Gibbon could not applaud this liberation of the ethos from the dogmas of Christianity, the reason was that he stood at the end of a cycle of which Ausonius marks the beginning. For Ausonius, Christianity was new but incontrovertible, while paganism was as obsolescent as Christianity is now often held to be. In both his ludic and his elegiac moods (which are not always distinguishable), Ausonius is consciously epigonal, the restorer of pagan arts in a Christian world which is all the more ready to tolerate them because their temples are in decay. Nevertheless, for him and for his contemporaries it may have been as hard to plant both feet firmly in the church as it was hard to take both feet out of it in the century of Aldous Huxley, Benjamin Britten, W. H. Auden, and Geoffrey Hill.

Concluding Review

Let us assume that Juvencus achieved the least that he must have hoped for – to have his own epic placed on library shelves next to those of Virgil, Lucian, and Ovid, to be ordered from time to time, or in the best case even copied for personal use, by members of the pagan elite who were either ignorant of the New Testament or thought it beneath their notice. In what

---

[67] Mack 2000: 127.
[68] Gibbon 1914–1919, original edition 1776–1779: chapter 27 n. 1. As an aesthetic judgement this is rebutted (for example) in Nugent 1990.
[69] *Moselle* 387–89, at Green 1991: 127.

ways could it be said to increase the knowledge of such readers? Firstly, and for them, at least, most importantly by acquainting them with historical facts that were not only worthy of memory but conducive to the healing and deliverance of the soul. Such knowledge, for those who embraced not only the facts but the Christian reading of them, would put an end to prejudicial views of the church and to chimerical desires for a pagan successor to Constantine. At the same time, once the merits of the poem were understood, it would not only add a new classic to the repertory of second-order knowledge – the knowledge that consists in being well-informed about books – but expose the insufficiency of much that had been hitherto taken for knowledge of both the first and the second order. By the device that Scott McGill styles *Kontrastimitation*,[70] it would teach the pagans not only that Christ is superior to any pagan hero and his Father more potent than any graven image, but that poetry can be as free from deceit as Plato himself could have wished (cf. *Republic* 595), without forfeiting its power to entertain. As McGill also says, it is a hybrid,[71] attiring in stately hexameters a subject which has nothing to do, in the common sense, with kings and battles, the proper stuff of epic. And this is more than a new variation of literary timbre: it is also a refutation of a venerable dichotomy between the universal truth of poetry and the mere contingency of narrative.

Juvencus, as we have seen, could hope to add to both the first-order and the second-order knowledge of his readers by composing a metrical paraphrase of the gospels. For Prudentius this was no longer true, since those who had not yet come into the church in his day were obstinate recusants who would not waste their leisure on Christian literature of any kind. He might, as the better poet, have aspired to displace Juvencus in the second order of knowledge; instead, he chose to versify the lives of saints, of whom only a few would have been familiar to any one believer, and the narrative of the fall, which not only lent itself to much poetry embellishment but demanded a theological explanation. That other, and more profitable, branch of learning that teaches us how to glorify the Creator in our lives is addressed in the hymns and the *Psychomachia*, in writing by which Prudentius augments the canon of Latin verse not only with new stanzaic forms but with a new conceit, the personification of virtue and vice, which proved more seminal in the Middle Ages than the innovations of all other Christian poets rolled into one. Even if the remaining pagans were unredeemable, there were now Christians, in greater numbers than ever, whose tastes had yet to be weaned from pagan literature, with all its temptations

---

[70] McGill 2016: 31. [71] McGill 2016: 1, 12, 26.

to licence and idolatry. In his castigation of Symmachus, Prudentius leaves no doubt that true religion cannot co-exist with any relic of Satan's empire; that is a work for emperors, but his task as a poet was to find his own way of converting every pagan temple into a Christian shrine.

It is fair to say that no first-order knowledge of Christianity can be gleaned from the works of Ausonius; it is probably fair to say that there is no other Christian poet of late antiquity in whom the aspiration to join the literary canon has so completely ousted any didactic aim. The Oxford Classical Text of his works, unrivalled by either Juvencus or Prudentius, affords more proof than we could ever have needed that no sea change had been effected in the tastes of the Roman elite. At the same time, the measure of this failure, if provisionally we may call it so, is that even such a poem as the *Crucifixion of Cupid* cannot be fully appreciated unless we are conscious of its Christian milieu. From this it follows that Ausonius was a professing Christian and expected his readers to be so, notwithstanding his reluctance to issue even one unambiguous proclamation of his faith. Yet it may be that we see here not so much a failure of Christianisation as a different contribution to its success: the *Crucifixion of Cupid* does not perpetuate any existing pagan myth but seems to hint instead that myth will die with the old religion unless it is covertly inoculated with Christian motifs. Where Christianity publicly undertook to succeed its forerunners, it could be publicly opposed, as its theology was opposed by the Neoplatonists and its monasteries by Eunapius and Rutilius Namatianus.[72] By contrast, a surreptitious Christian undertone in literature that was superficially classical in content and form accelerated the weakening of a culture that was already losing its hold on the elite. Prudentius and Ausonius exemplify that combination of forces which, according to Arnold Toynbee,[73] is required to bring about the end of any great civilisation – duress from without and schism in the soul.

---

[72] For doubts regarding the paganism of both Rutilius and Claudian, see Cameron 2010: 207–9.
[73] Toynbee 1979.

21 | Ambrose's Hymns as Modes of Knowing the 'Real'

BRIAN DUNKLE, SJ

Introduction

As the inscription for *A Grammar of Assent*, John Henry Newman chose the famous line from Ambrose of Milan's *On the Faith*: *Non in dialectica conplacuit deo saluum facere populum suum*: 'It did not please God to save his people through dialectic.'[1] The quotation captures an essential feature of Newman's epistemology, which challenged the dominance of empiricism by distinguishing the merely 'notional assent' that is given to deductive propositions from the 'real assent' that is characteristic of authentic human knowing; real assent, often identified with belief, does not rely on dialectical inference, but rather on direct apprehension, which leads the knower to action.[2] According to Newman, the epistemology of 'real assent' should inform theological rhetoric. By imitating God's chosen mode of salvation – that is, through embodied involvement rather than through dialectic – the most effective apologies do not employ abstract arguments, but rather vivid imagery which elicits belief.

Newman's choice of Ambrose as muse raises the question of the bishop's own views on the place of argument in catechesis and pastoral care.[3] Of course, Ambrose's hostility towards philosophical sophistication and, more specifically, dialectic, is a commonplace among apologists, both pagan and Christian.[4] Yet Newman seems to have spotted a genuine concern in the bishop's epistemology.[5] Ambrose's distrust of dialectic extends beyond a mere rhetorical trope; it is a theme that he rehearses throughout his career

---

[1] Newman 1979, citing *Fid. Grat.* 1.5.42 (CSEL 78.18). All translations are my own.
[2] For background, see the introduction by Nicholas Lash in Newman 1979: 1–22.
[3] Newman was hardly the first to be struck by Ambrose's language. His Homoian rival, Palladius of Ratiaria, cited the same passage (among others) in his refutation of *De fide*, which survives in the *Scholia* on the Council of Aquileia; frag. 54 on fol. 336r (CCSL 87.172).
[4] Among philosophers, see Cicero, *De or.* 2.157–58; Seneca, *Lucil.* 45.5; among theologians, Paul, of course, is the pre-eminent source (e.g., 1 Cor 3:18–23), but see also Athanasius, *Ep. Aeg. Lib.* 1; *C. Ar.* 1.1; Hilary of Poitiers, *Trin.* 1.13; for a review of this issue, see de Ghellinck 1948: 245–310.
[5] Newman knew Ambrose's work well; see his essay, 'What Does St. Ambrose Say about It?', originally published in the *British Magazine* and subsequently included in the volume *Primitive Christianity*, which he republished in *Historical Sketches*, vol. I (1872): 339–74.

from the early *On the Faith* to the late *Explanation of the Psalms*.[6] Indeed, Goulven Madec, in his influential study of Ambrose and philosophy, notes the 'excess' of his animus.[7]

To be sure, scholars have both qualified Ambrose's blanket denunciations of dialectic and demonstrated his extensive engagement with classical thought;[8] nevertheless, all agree that the bishop had less interest than many of his contemporaries in extended technical disputation. His doctrinal treatises, especially *On the Faith, On the Holy Spirit*, and *On the Sacrament of the Lord's Incarnation*, make few theoretical contributions to the christological and trinitarian debates of late fourth-century Milan.[9] Even as the bishop is now recognised as less 'derivative' than once maintained,[10] his originality is located more in the mode than in the content of his compositions.[11]

But that mode of composition gave rise to his most enduring contribution to the history of theology: his hymns. To borrow from Newman's categories, I suggest that Ambrose's hymns prioritise a mode of knowing that is both 'non-dialectical' and 'real'. As I argue in this chapter, Ambrose's approach is especially evident when his hymns are read in light of his popular sermons; both genres aim less to critique through analysis than to 'build up' (*adstruere*) through compelling imagery and a programme of sensitisation.[12] Ambrose regularly renders abstract, narrative, and conceptual claims by means of personal, concrete, and actualising images that present his congregation with real objects of assent.

To illustrate this approach, I compare Ambrose's treatment of the miracles associated with the early life of Christ in his *Expositio on Luke* and in his hymn for the Epiphany, 'Illuminans Altissimus'. The bishop's 'real', embodied rhetoric is evident in the sermon and heightened further in the corresponding hymn.[13] In the final section, I argue that such an approach distinguishes Ambrose's hymns from the verse compositions of his Latin contemporaries Hilary of Poitiers and Augustine of Hippo. By crafting his

---

[6] Ambrose, *Enarrat. Ps.* 36.28. [7] Madec 1974: 49.
[8] For a review of the recent scholarship, see Harmon 2017: 201–2; classic studies include Courcelle 1950: 29–56; Hadot 1956: 202–20; Savon 1977; Lenox-Conyngham 1993: 112–28.
[9] Given that Ambrose's 'technical' treatises contain sermonic material, the distinction among genres is not hard and fast; on the challenges of identifying the sermons in the surviving works of Ambrose, see Savon 1999: 33–35 and Gerzaguet 2018: 162–63. For a brief review of Ambrose's theological merits, see Markschies 1995b: 63–66.
[10] For the standard dismissals, see Jerome's preface to his translation of Didymus's *De Spiritu Sancto*; and Hagendahl 1958: 372.
[11] See especially Markschies 1995b and Selby 2020.
[12] I have explored these issues in Dunkle 2016: 93–99.
[13] Text from Charlet in Fontaine 2008, 1st edn, 1992: 345–47. Note that editions vary in the spelling of the hymn's title; even Fontaine prints 'Illuminans' in the heading but 'Inluminans' for the hymn.

hymns in the model of his catechetical preaching rather than of his apologetical works, Ambrose created a hymn corpus that could nurture in his congregation spiritual modes of knowing.[14]

Ambrose's Preaching and Hymns as 'Building Up Faith'

The parallels between Ambrose's preaching and his hymns are well known.[15] Of the thirteen hymns regularly attributed to the bishop, at least six treat themes and figures that appear in his sermons: 'Aeterne rerum conditor', his hymn for the cockcrow, overlaps with sections of his *Hexameron*; 'Iam surgit hora tertia', for terce, corresponds with his *Expositio on Luke*, as does the hymn for Epiphany, 'Illuminans Altissimus', which I treat below; his hymn to Agnes has extended parallels with a passage from *De uirginibus*; his hymn to Victor, Nabor, and Felix contains sections from his preaching on Luke; and his hymn to Lawrence resembles his treatment of the saint in *De officiis*.[16] Ambrose, it seems, was drawn to present the same material in both genres.

The links have long intrigued scholars. Textual critics generally focus on the lexical correspondence to address issues of attribution, which are especially vexing in the study of the hymns.[17] Any repetitions may support Ambrosian authorship, although the arguments for dependency are complicated: verbal reminiscences do not establish priority between the two texts and they could also be attributed to learned imitation by one of Ambrose's successors or collaborators.[18]

At the same time, the many parallels point to the specific pastoral aim that characterises many of Ambrose's works, namely, 'building up [the] faith' (*adstruere fidem*).[19] According to Thomas Graumann, the phrase functions as a virtual 'Auslegungsmotto' for much of Ambrose's biblical

---

[14] On the Bible in Cyprian's catechesis, see Chapter 9 by Edwina Murphy, this volume.

[15] On parallels with his mystagogical preaching, see Dunkle 2016: 85–115; Fontaine 2008, 1st edn, 1992: 74; on the interaction of genres in the Theodosian period, see Fontaine 1976: 124–70. A valuable study on correspondences in his hymns for saints, see Lanéry 2008: 217–75.

[16] For the pertinent references, see the apparatus to the hymns in Fontaine 2008, 1st edn, 1992. Note also that the hymn, 'Grates tibi, Iesu, nouas', which treats the *inuentio* of the martyrs Protasius and Gervasius, has close parallels with *Ep.* 10.77, a letter to his sister Marcellina; on dating Ambrose's works, see Visonà 2004: 58–145.

[17] For an overview of the issues of priority for 'Illuminans Altissimus', see Charlet in Fontaine 2008, 1st edn, 1992: 340–43, who rejects the attribution of the hymn to Ambrose and therefore dates the sermon before the hymn; for a review of the debate and a robust defence of Ambrose's authorship, see Zerfass 2008: 40–61; for a defence on stylistic grounds, see Springer 1995: 228–37.

[18] See Charlet in Fontaine 2008, 1st edn, 1992: 343; Zerfass 2008: 54–58.

[19] On the objective and subjective sense of *fides* in Ambrose's hymns, see Dunkle 2016: 103.

interpretation.[20] Indeed, in the section of *De fide* from which Newman borrows his epigraph, the bishop uses such language to critique the dialectic of his opponents: 'in the opinion of the philosophers, dialectical disputation does not have the power to build up [*uim adstruendi*], but only the goal of destroying [*studium destruendi*]'.[21] In contrast to his opponents, Ambrose maintains that his own position is constructed entirely on the basis of the wisdom of the *piscatores*, that is, the concrete evidence of fishermen evangelists.[22]

Ambrose often links the language of building up [the] faith with his understanding and use of *exempla*, which impress the audience by the strength and vivacity of the sensory image.[23] In his *Expositio on Luke*, for example, Ambrose argues that the miraculous events related to the birth of Jesus – including the cure of Zachariah, the birth of John the Baptist, the virgin birth, and the adoration of the Magi – serve by their vividness to bolster the belief of readers.[24] Likewise, in his treatment of the angels' appearance to the shepherds (Luke 2:8–20), Ambrose stresses the affective force of the repeated announcements by the angel: 'Observe how divine concern builds up faith [*fidem adstruat*]. The angel instructs Mary, the angel instructs Joseph, the angel instructs the shepherds. It was not enough that there be a single sending: for God establishes every word on two and three witnesses' (cf. Deut 19:15 and Matt 18:16).[25] Divine pedagogy repeats miracles for at least two reasons: on the one hand, as scripture maintains, only multiple witnesses are reliable; on the other, the repetition of the message itself effectively imprints on observers the miraculous nature of the event. Mary, Joseph, and the shepherds can both rely on and be formed by the many proofs of the same miraculous birth.

---

[20] Graumann 1994: 157.
[21] Ambrose, *Fid. Grat.* 1.5.42 (CSEL 78.17): *Omnem enim uim uenenorum suorum in dialectica disputatione constituunt, quae philosophorum sententia definitur non adstruendi uim habere, sed studium destruendi*. The *philosophorum sententia* refers most likely to Cicero; see *Fin.* 2.6.17 and *Acad. pr.* 2.91. The specific charge that dialectic is a technology for 'tearing down' is suggested earlier by Tertullian, who, however, claims that it 'composes' (*struendi*) as well: *Praescr.* 7.6 (CC 1.193): *Miserum Aristotelem! qui illis dialecticam instituit, artificem struendi et destruendi*; see Madec 1974: 48 n. 141.
[22] See *Fid. Grat.* 1.8 and 1.13; cf. *Incarn.* 9.89. On Ambrose's frequent reference to the ideal of the *piscatores*, see Madec 1974: 214–24.
[23] See Lanéry 2008: 45–47; Harmon 2017: 204; on exemplarism in John Chrysostom, see most recently Dupont and Finn 2019: 190–217. On sermons as 'goads' (*stimuli*), see Ambrose's *Ep.* 7.36.5–7, a letter that Camille Gerzaguet calls 'Ambrose's *De doctrina christiana*'; Gerzaguet 2018: 160.
[24] For parallels in Augustine, see Chapter 25 by Robin Jensen, this volume.
[25] Ambrose, *Exp. Luc.* 2.51 (CCSL 14.53): *uidete quemadmodum diuina cura fidem adstruat. angelus Mariam, angelus Ioseph, angelus pastores edocet. non satis est semel missum; duobus enim et tribus testibus stat omne uerbum.*

Modelling his pedagogy on God's own, Ambrose not only refers to the scriptural methods of building up faith but also uses exemplarity and reinforcement to do so himself. Thus, in *De mysteriis*, he revisits the rite of initiation that the neophytes have undergone by recounting the miraculous transformation of the baptismal waters. He first explains the plausibility of the sacramental consecration deductively, reminding his audience that Christ is the transcendent creator. He then qualifies that explanation, stating that he prefers *exempla* to arguments: 'But why do we employ arguments? Let us employ his *exempla* and build up [*adstruamus*] the truth of the mystery by mysteries of the incarnation.'[26] Rather than abstract christological concepts, the image of the virgin birth itself is most effective in showing that Christ has power over nature.[27] Ambrose adopts the approach in much of his preaching: as Marcia Colish and Warren Smith have shown, Ambrose's sermons on patriarchs build up faith through an exemplaristic ethics that is adapted to a broad and mixed congregation.[28]

Both external and internal evidence suggests that a similar rhetoric of building up faith by means of *exempla* and reinforcement characterises his hymns.[29] Augustine's account of their origins, recorded in Book 9 of *Confessions*, provides the classic origin story for Ambrose's hymns during the 'basilica crisis' of 386: 'Then was established the singing of hymns and psalms according to the manner of the eastern regions, so that the people not grow weary on account of the tedium of their sadness.'[30] For Augustine, the central aim of the hymns was not the communication of doctrinal precision, but rather the moral encouragement of Ambrose's people as they resisted the empress Justina's Arian forces, who were attempting to claim the Basilica Portiana for their worship. Ambrose himself identifies his hymns as 'spells' (*carmina*), most likely on account of their distinctive emotional, even visceral, impact on singers and listeners.[31]

Recent scholars have noted the affective force of the stylistic features of Ambrose's hymns. His use of iambic dimeter and a strict, eight-stanza form, which are otherwise rare in Latin verse, indicates his desire to render the hymns accessible to a wide audience through the aural effects of a

---

[26] Ambrose, *Myst.* 9.53 (CSEL 73.112): *sed quid argumentis utimur? suis utamur exemplis incarnationisque mysteriis* **adstruamus** *mysterii* **ueritatem**.

[27] On his methods of mystagogy, see Satterlee 2000; Vopřada 2016: 25–146.

[28] For analysis, see Colish 2005 and Smith 2011.

[29] Fontaine 2008, 1st edn, 1992: 11–123, provides the necessary background.

[30] Augustine, *Conf.* 9.7 (CCSL 27.142): *tunc hymni et psalmi ut canerentur secundum morem orientalium partium, ne populus maeroris taedio contabesceret, institutum est.*

[31] Ambrose, *Ep.* 75a.34; see also Paulinus of Milan, *Vita Ambrosii* 13.3 and Ambrose, *Ep.* 75a.34, who presents his hymns as casting a 'spell' (*carmen*); see Harrison 2019a: 12.

relatively simple accentual scheme.³² He favours vivid, sensual vocabulary as well as abundant *exempla* rather than technical exposition. Moreover, he regularly repeats key terms to heighten their impact and to imprint them on the singers' imaginary.³³ Ambrose's hymns employ indexical terms, which call the singers' attention to the present moment, and pithy, memorable phrases, which would function to arouse the imaginations of his congregation and to rally them to his pro-Nicene cause.³⁴ All of these features, I suggest, relate to Ambrose's preference for the real over the notional.³⁵

Ambrose's *Expositio on Luke* and 'Illuminans Altissimus'

For the sake of illustration, I consider the most extensive overlap between sermon and hymn, which appears when Ambrose treats select miracles of Christ both in his *Expositio* on Luke and in his hymn for the Epiphany 'Illuminans Altissimus'.³⁶ Comparison of the respective treatments illustrates the distinctive compositional methods that I have discussed.

The Baptism of the Lord

In Books 1 and 2 of the *Expositio*, Ambrose refers only briefly to the baptism of the Lord, the central event celebrated on the Epiphany in fourth-century Milan.³⁷ His most direct reference to the baptism occurs in Book 2, when he specifies its motive: 'The Lord was baptised, desiring not to be purified himself, but to purify the waters, so that, washed clean by the flesh of Christ, which did not know sin, the waters might have the power to baptise.'³⁸ Ambrose summarises the standard patristic understanding of

---

[32] Springer 1991: 76–78.   [33] Dunkle 2016: 93–100.

[34] In general, den Boeft 2008; see Charlet 1988 and Springer 2014 on 'Aeterne Rerum Conditor'; den Boeft 2003: 27–40; for Ambrose's hymns as acclamations in the Roman style, see Williams 2013: 108–34. On repetition in the hymns, see Springer 2014: 155–77.

[35] For some parallels in Byzantine poetry and preaching, see Chapter 29 by Sarah Gador-Whyte, this volume.

[36] Both dated to the late 380s; see Visonà 2004: 96–97 and 114–16. On the parallels between Ambrose on Luke (SC 45 and 52) and Origen, see SC 87: 563–64; Blackburn Griffith 2016: 199–225. For exegesis of the multiplication of loaves in this passage, see Graumann 1994: 222–24.

[37] On background to the baptism of the Lord and the Epiphany at Milan in relation to the hymn, see Frank 1971: 115–32.

[38] Ambrose, *Exp. Luc.* 2.83 (CCSL 14.67): *baptizatus ergo est dominus non mundari uolens, sed mundare aquas, ut ablutae per carnem christi, quae peccatum non cognouit, baptismatis ius haberent.*

the Lord's baptism as a moment when the waters, rather than Jesus himself, were endowed with sanctifying power.[39]

While the interpretation is familiar, Ambrose's mode of presentation is distinctive, elevating the concrete over the abstract. Ambrose makes the waters (*aquae*) and the flesh (*carnem*) of Christ the active subjects of the transformation: the waters obtain a power by means of the agency of Christ's flesh; Christ's flesh is itself sinless. The move to the embodied agency of the physical reflects Ambrose's preference for the sensual over the abstract, the real over the notional.

'Illuminans' exhibits a similar preference. As in the sermon, the treatment of the baptism is notably brief, especially for a hymn on the Epiphany.[40] The first stanza invokes Christ in language appropriate for the feast, as the 'illuminating Most High', alluding to ancient titles for the sacrament as itself 'illumination'.[41] The second stanza specifies the meaning of the day that is celebrated: as when three times in the past the waters of the Jordan turned back, so now Christ transforms the waters of baptism.

While the narrative is minimal, Ambrose renders it concretely. He actualises the baptism by referring it to the 'present day' (*praesenti die*). He personalises the narration by addressing Christ in the second person. The effect, at the invocation of the hymn, is to bring the biblical account to vivid display before the singers' imaginations.[42]

The Adoration of the Magi

The concrete and the real also figure in Ambrose's treatment of the adoration of the Magi. In Book 2 of the *Expositio*, Ambrose turns from the text of Luke to the Gospel of Matthew to treat the episode.[43] Ambrose's account of the adoration focuses on the agency of the star, who is Christ himself guiding the visitors.[44] Christ, Ambrose explains, 'comes forth from the womb, but he also flashes forth from the sky [*e caelo*]'.[45] Ambrose then makes the link explicit:

---

[39] See, e.g., Basil, *Bapt.* 2.1.
[40] On *breuitas* in the hymns, see Fontaine 2008, 1st edn, 1992: 78.
[41] Zerfass 2008: 160–61.
[42] For parallel techniques for actualisation in Romanos, see Chapter 29 by Gador-Whyte, this volume.
[43] Ambrose, *Exp. Luc.* 2.49 (CCSL 14.52–53): *Haec de Matthaeo pauca libauimus, ut clareret infantiae tempora a diuinitatis operibus minime uacasse.*
[44] Ephrem the Syrian also interprets the star as possessing the agency of the Word; see Crawford 2015a: 75, 92–93.
[45] Ambrose, *Exp. Luc.* 2.43 (CCSL 14.50): *Ex utero funditur, sed coruscat e caelo.*

Therefore, since this star is the way, the way is Christ, because according to the mystery of the incarnation, 'Christ is the star'; for 'A star will rise from Jacob and a man will spring up from Israel' [Num 24:17]. Hence where Christ is, so too is the star; for he himself is the bright morning star [Rev 22:16]. Thus he is the one who indicates himself by his own light.[46]

Just as Ambrose had presented the waters and Christ's flesh as agents in the baptism, Ambrose personalises the star as Christ, who indicates himself (*se signat*) to the shepherds; again, he attributes to the natural world a vivid role in salvation history. The bishop's congregation, then, is led to know divine agency at the Epiphany not through reflection on abstract concepts, such as causality or participation, but through the concrete activities of nature. Ambrose's method draws on scriptural identifications – Christ *just is* the 'star from Jacob' and the 'bright morning star' – to offer to the congregation biblical exegesis that is both concrete and personal.

'Illuminans' develops this approach in song. The corresponding stanza of the hymn closely resembles the prose presentation. The congregation sings:

Or when, as a star sparkling in the sky,
you indicated the virgin birth
and on this day you led the magi
to adoration at the manger.[47]

Key terms – *caelo, signaueris, duxeris, adoratum* – have direct parallels in the prose account.[48] As in the sermon, Ambrose identifies the star shining in the sky with Christ himself. The basic narrative and central themes of the sermon are present in the hymn.

Yet the hymn further actualises the prose account. By employing the second person, in reference to Christ who 'signalled' the virgin birth and who 'guided' Magi to the adoration at the manger on 'this day', Ambrose stresses Christ's presence and agency on the feast. Indexical terms (*hoc die*) prompt the congregation to envision the present moment in light of sacred history.[49] The hymn adds a measure of vivacity to the prose account.

---

[46] Ambrose, *Exp. Luc.* 2.45 (CCSL 14.51): *Ergo stella haec uia est et uia Christus, quia secundum incarnationis mysterium Christus est stella; ipse enim est stella splendida et matutina. sua igitur ipse luce se signat.*

[47] Charlet in Fontaine 2008, 1st edn, 1992: 345: *Seu stella partum uirginis / caelo micans signaueris / et hoc adoratum die / praesepe magos duxeris.*

[48] Cf. Ambrose, *Exp. Luc.* 2.45 (CCSL 14.51): *duae quippe sunt uiae, una quae ducit ad interitum, alia quae ducit ad regnum.*

[49] See Dunkle 2016: 92–93; for parallels in Romanos, see Chapter 29 by Gador-Whyte, this volume.

The Multiplication of the Loaves and the Wedding at Cana

A similar stress on the personal, concrete elements appears in Ambrose's treatment of the two central miracles of the hymn – the multiplication of the loaves and the transformation of the water to wine at Cana – which he also presents in close proximity in the *Expositio* treatment of Luke 9:10–17.

As Ambrose explains the multiplication in the *Expositio on Luke*, he introduces the miracle at Cana, recorded in John, as a comparable version of the sort of changes that God brings about.[50] The highlighted terms appear in both the sermon and the hymn:[51]

Exp. Luc. 6.85 uideres inconprehensibili quodam **rigatu inter** diuidentium **manus** quas non fregerint fructificare particulas et **intacta frangentium** digitis sponte sua **fragmenta subrepere**.[52] qui **haec** legit quemadmodum **iuges aquarum miretur meatus** et liquidis **fontibus stupeat** continuos **fluere** successus, quando etiam **panis** exundat et naturae solidioris **rigatus** exuberat? …	uel **hydriis** plenis **aquae uini saporem infuderis**; **hausit minister** conscius quod ipse non **impleuerat**, **aquas colorari uidens**, **inebriare** flumina; **mutata elementa stupent** transire in **usus** alteros.
6.87 nec dubites uel quod **in manibus ministrantium** uel in ore **edentium cibus crescat**, quando ubique nostri operis testimonium ad firmamentum credulitatis adsciscitur. sic in nuptiis ex **fontibus uina ministris** operantibus **colorantur** et ipsi qui **inpleuerant hydrias aqua uinum** quod non detulerant **hauriebant**. conprehende, si potes, tanta rerum miracula. hic **edentibus** populis **crescunt** suis **fragmenta dispendiis** et de **quinque panibus** maiores reliquiae quam summa est colliguntur, illic in **alienam speciem** uertuntur **elementa** nec suos patitur natura defectus nec suos agnoscit ortus, **usus** tamen proprios recognoscit. quin etiam melior est **mutati uini** natura quam nati, quia in arbitrio creatoris est et quos **usus** uelit adsignare naturis et quas naturas inpertire gignendis. **uide** quantis operibus opus adstruat dum **aquam minister infundit**, odor transfusus **inebriat, color mutatus** informat, fidem quoque **sapor haustus** adcumulat.	Sic **quinque milibus** uirum dum **quinque panes** diuidit, **edentium** sub dentibus in **ore crescebat cibus**, multiplicabatur magis **dispendio panis** suo. Quis haec **uidens mirabitur iuges meatus fontium**? **Inter manus frangentium panis rigatur** profluus, **intacta** quae non **fregerant fragmenta subrepunt** uiris.

---

[50] Ambrose, *Exp. Luc.* 6.87.

[51] Texts from CCSL 14.205–206 and Charlet in Fontaine 2008, 1st edn, 1992: 345–47. For a similar comparison of the two texts, see Zerfass 2008: 49–50.

[52] On this reading over *subripere*, see Zerfass 2008: 49 n. 222; I discuss the significance below.

6.85 You would have observed the particles multiply by a certain incomprehensible streaming among the hands of those who share them without breaking them, and the fragments winding their way on their own, untouched, in the fingers of those who do break them. How would anyone who reads this event marvel at the ceaseless flow of the waters and wonder at the endless issue from the liquid sources, when even the bread abounds and the stream of a firmer nature overflows? …	Or when you infused the flavour of wine into vessels filled with water; the minister drank what he knew he himself had not poured in, As he saw the waters change colour, and their streams intoxicate; the elements, once changed, marvelled that they had passed over to new purposes.
6.87. Do not doubt that the food increases, whether in the hands of the minister or in the mouths of those who eat, whenever the testimony of our work is established as the foundation for credibility. For in the same way, at the wedding, the wine that came from founts of water changed colour as the ministers were at work, and those who had filled up the jars with water drank wine that they did not pour out. If you can, understand such marvellous works. In the scene from Luke, even as the fragments are being distributed, they increase while the people are eating, and there are more remains gathered from the five loaves than there was total [to begin with]; in the miracle at Cana, the elements are turned into another form and the nature [of the water] neither suffers its own loss nor understands the source, but yet it does recognise its proper ends. For indeed the essence of the wine that has been transformed is better than that which was produced naturally, because it is in the judgement of the Creator both to assign to natures whatever ends he wishes and to impart whatever natures he wishes to what is born. See by what great works he accomplishes his miracle. While the minister pours out the water, the aroma that is poured out now intoxicates, the colour that is transformed instructs, and the flavour when imbibed increases faith.	So too when he divided five loaves of bread among five thousand men, the food increased in their mouths beneath the teeth of them as they chewed, The bread multiplied the more it was shared. Seeing this miracle who would wonder at the ceaseless flow of the founts [of wine]? The overflowing bread flowed among the hands of those who broke it, the untouched fragments, which they had not broken, winded its way among the men.

In the prose account, Ambrose presents the shows of power in vivid, sensory terms, which emphasise the crowds' physical engagement with the miracle: the bread multiplies in their hands and their mouths, while the aroma, the colour, and the flavour of the wine are transformed. In his *ekphrasis* of the biblical scenes, Ambrose maintains that the sensual detail of the conversion of the water 'piles up on' (*adcumulat*) the faithfulness of the miracle by rendering the change real and sensible.[53] The imperatives (*comprehende, uide*), the present tense, and the emphasis on paradox heighten the emotional effect. Ambrose accentuates the sensory wonder of his congregation.[54]

Ambrose's stress on the sensory acquires further impact in light of his own link between exegesis of the two miracles in the *Expositio* and the celebration of the Eucharist: 'In the ministry of the apostles [in distributing the bread], the coming division of the Body and Blood of the Lord is anticipated.'[55] As in his mystagogies, Ambrose encourages the congregation to know the 'reality' of the elements of the bread and wine not by arguments, but by a deep encounter with the scripture and the liturgy.[56] Authentic knowledge of both scripture and rite is available only through a transformed sensory experience of the text and the sacrament.

The Miracles in 'Illuminans'

Approximately two-thirds of the terms in corresponding stanzas of the hymn, and almost all of the noteworthy language, appear in the *Expositio*.[57] The sensory terms are especially prominent: the savour (*saporem*) of the wine and the transformation of the colour (*colorari*) of the waters both parallel the sermon's description of the miracle. The impact is heightened by the reference to the gaze of the minister (*uidens*) upon the altered water; indeed, even the explanation of the motive corresponds closely to the sermon: 'Seeing this miracle who would wonder / at the ceaseless flow of the founts [of wine]?' Like the sermon, the hymn aims to render the miracle at Cana present to the senses of the congregation.

At the same time, the hymn heightens the concrete and embodied features of the sermon. The fragments of bread 'crawl' (*subrepunt*) – a term

---

[53] On *ekphrasis* in classical rhetoric, see especially Webb 2009.
[54] Note that the entire passage is probably an Ambrosian innovation. While much of the *Expositio* is borrowed directly from Origen's *Homilies on Luke*, Origen has no surviving treatment that links the multiplication of loaves with the miracle of Cana. We thus have some indication that Ambrose is here offering his own distinctive interpretation of the episodes. On the textual parallels, see Blackburn Griffith 2016: 199–225.
[55] Ambrose, *Exp. Luc.* 6.84 (CCSL 14.204): *in apostolorum ministerio futura diuisio dominici corporis sanguinisque praemittitur*; Zerfass 2008: 188–92.
[56] On ritual and the 'eyes of faith', see Frank 2001: 619–43.
[57] For extended analysis, see Zerfass 2008: 157–209.

characteristic of animate agents – among the crowds; Ambrose uses the same term in the *Expositio*, but there he includes the expository *sua sponte*, thereby calling attention notionally to the 'mechanics' of the bread's diffusion.[58] While the sermon mentions only the food in their 'mouths', the hymn specifies their 'teeth' (*sub dentibus*) as well; the sensual impact, already present in the sermon, is further articulated in visceral terms. As in treatment of the baptism, the hymn transfers agency to the inanimate: the waters of the vessels are themselves awed (*stupent*) to be transferred into other uses.[59]

Furthermore, certain didactic and abstract features of the sermon's account are absent from the hymn. Both in the passage quoted above and in the intervening paragraphs, the prose account includes references to the 'rationale' behind the miracles: God's mode of instruction by miracles 'builds up' (*adstruat*) by means of many shows of power (*operibus*). 'Illuminans', by contrast, includes no explanations. Furthermore, unlike the hymn, the prose account relies on the abstract language of *natura* to explain the changes. In 'Illuminans', Ambrose shows no concern to analyse the event, but only to render it sensible and thereby to bring it to life.

As the hymn forgoes exposition, it also heightens the prose account's emphasis on the transcendent and the wondrous. Both the fourth (central) and the eighth (final) stanzas stress human limitations: the minister at Cana knows that he was not the one who poured the wine that all are tasting; likewise, the five thousand did not break (*non fregerant*) the fragments, which were untouched (*intacta*). In both cases, the congregation's 'incapacity' is expressed through a relative clause in the pluperfect, denying what is contrary to fact. In both cases, divine action alone accounts for the miracle. Whereas the *Expositio* specifies the agency of the divine Creator, the hymn presents the miraculous by means of passive expressions, a subtle but vivid indication of the transcendent at work:[60] the streams of the Jordan are 'turned back' (*conuersa*); the water is 'transformed' (*mutata*) and the bread 'multiplied' (*multiplicabatur*); the abundant bread is 'conveyed' (*rigatur*) through the hands of those who break it. The miracles are accomplished not by the agents in the narrative but mysteriously, by God alone.

The rhetorical approach that I have outlined in 'Illuminans' appears throughout Ambrose's hymns and is especially evident in those hymns that correspond to sermonic material. The treatment of Lawrence in the

---

[58] See Charlet in Fontaine 2008, 1st edn, 1992: 359.
[59] The strangeness of the image – the water itself marvelling at its own transformation – has led many editors to emend the number of the verb so that the minister instead of the elements does the marvelling. See Zerfass 2008: 151.
[60] Charlet in Fontaine 2008, 1st edn, 1992: 359.

hymn 'Apostolorum supparem' follows the presentation in *De officiis* in its common concern for a graphic, sensory depiction of the martyr's death on a grill; but the hymn condenses the famous exchange between Lawrence and his executioner to bring it more forcefully to the congregation's senses, while eliminating the didactic portions of the prose version.[61] Ambrose's hymn for Agnes, 'Agnes beatae uirginis', shows a similar link to his prose treatment of the saint in *De uirginibus*.[62] Ambrose's three surviving hymns in celebration of the Lord's feasts – Christmas, Epiphany, and Easter – employ the vocabulary of awe and wonder to inspire the congregation.[63] In the words of Newman, these hymns do not demonstrate proofs but rather 'excite images'.[64]

Alternatives in Hilary and Augustine

The rhetoric of Newman's 'real' in Ambrosian hymns may seem merely an obvious aesthetic choice or even a feature proper to verse compositions according to their genre; we expect poetry to be imagistic. But the singularity of Ambrose's approach comes into sharp focus when we compare his hymns with the verse of his Latin contemporaries. The surviving songs from Hilary of Poitiers and Augustine offer a different mode of communication, which is both more abstract and didactic and less sensual and 'real' than that employed by Ambrose's hymns. Given the limits of space, my comparison must be brief.

Hilary of Poitiers

Hilary's hymn-writing project, attested by Jerome and early councils, survives in the form of extended fragments from three different hymns.[65] By contrast with Ambrose, who adopted a relatively popular metrical form, Hilary's hymns are composed according to learned, classical models.[66] The first, 'Ante saecula qui manes', is an abecedarian – an acrostic with stanzas arranged alphabetically, which aids memorisation – and presents a detailed, creedal exposition of the divinity of Christ and the mechanics

---

[61] For extended analysis, see Nauroy 1989: 559–615.   [62] Treated in Lanéry 2008: 241–42.
[63] Dunkle 2016: 141–42; cf. Newman 1979: 113.   [64] Newman 1979: 113.
[65] Dunkle 2016: 32–36; see *Gesta Concilii Toletani* 4.13; Jerome, *Comm. Gal.* 2.3.
[66] For some comparison, see Fontaine 1981: 81–94 and Moorhead 2010: 81–82.

of the incarnation. Distinctive Nicene language abounds; in the 'L' stanza, as a representative instance, Hilary describes Christ in terms drawn almost directly from the Creed itself:

Light gleams from light
and True God subsists out of True
God, born unbegotten, having nothing other
than has his Father, who cannot be born.[67]

The second hymn, also an abecedarian, narrates the crucifixion. While there are a few parallels to Ambrose's sensual language, Hilary generally favours mythological references (*Stygis, Flegethon, Tartari*), aiming for a learned poetic effect.[68] The third hymn, which survives only as a few stanzas, recounts the attacks of Satan before his overthrow through the incarnation.

Although the evidence is limited, all three fragments suggest that Hilary's approach is both didactic and narrative. In comparison with Ambrose's hymns, Hilary's lack any especially embodied and actualising language: we find few indexicals, for instance, or sensory terms. The features that render the hymns effective for memorisation, such as an alphabetic sequence and classicising metre, do not necessarily 'excite' imaginations. While both bishop-hymnists aim to 'impress' a congregation with their theology, Hilary relies especially on memorable forms for expressing that theology, while Ambrose prioritises the 'reality' of the content.

Augustine's *Psalmus contra partem Donati*

A related contrast appears when we look at the lone extended hymnodic effort of Augustine. In response to the Donatist hymns that were circulating in Carthage and gaining popularity in the early 390s, Augustine, still a priest, composed his *Psalmus contra partem Donati*, a lengthy abecedarian jingle with an innovative metrical form based on natural stress accents rather than metrical quantities.[69] By his own account, Augustine hoped that the form would be easily memorised (*inhaerere memoriae*) and help educate his people on the issues at stake.[70]

---

[67] Hymn 1 (CSEL 65.211): *Lumen fulsit a lumine / deusque uerus subsistit ex deo / uero, non aliud habens / ortus unigena, quam innascibilis pater.*
[68] Hymn 2 (CSEL 65.213).
[69] On Augustine and music, see the recent work of Carol Harrison, especially Harrison 2019b.
[70] Augustine, *Retract.* 1.20.

The text of the *Psalmus* is almost entirely didactic. It narrates the history of the Donatist schism in polemical detail.[71] With obvious apologetic intent, the *Psalmus* proposes rhetorical questions, cites biblical references to the evils of division, and repeats a refrain that would rally the congregation to oppose their Donatist rivals: 'All you who enjoy peace, judge now what is true.'[72] Biblical images are explained at length: 'Our Lord wanted to warn us by comparing the kingdom of heaven to the net cast into the sea.'[73] While Augustine's metrical schema is intentionally popularising, his vocabulary is often notional, technical, and abstract, employing terms that are specific to the controversy itself. The *Psalmus*, for instance, prays for release from the 'pseudoprophets' (*pseudoprophetis*) and critiques the opponents' practice of 'rebaptism' (*rebaptizare*); the prominent names and titles that are mentioned, including *macharius* and *circumcellio*, would be familiar only to those already involved in the struggles. Again, the sensual language and the actualising terms, so characteristic of Ambrose's hymns, are virtually absent from Augustine's apologetic verse.[74]

The didactic approach of Hilary and Augustine may help explain the relative obscurity of their projects. Jerome hints that Hilary's hymnodic efforts, which survive as three fragments in a single manuscript, failed to appeal to the Goths in southern Gaul.[75] And Augustine's reference in his *Retractationes* to his *Psalmus contra partem Donati*, leaves the impression that the text was for him an experiment rather than an effective strategy. Despite their prominent profiles and theological gifts, neither approached Ambrose's genius for popularising their songs.[76]

Conclusion

The unique success of Ambrose's hymns must arise partly from his commitment to modes of knowing that were attuned to the real and the embodied. Appealing to the spiritual senses and the imaginations of his congregation,

---

[71] Cf. vv. 47–48 (BA 28.156): *dixerunt maiores nostri et libros fecerunt inde qui tunc causam cognouerunt quod recens possent probare.*
[72] V. 1 (BA 28.150): *omnes [uos] qui gaudetis de pace, modo uerum iudicate.*
[73] Vv. 8–9 (BA 28.150): *propter hoc dominus noster uoluit nos praemonere / comparans regnum caelorum reticulo misso in mare.*
[74] To be sure, Augustine was himself quite capable of adopting an imagistic approach similar to Ambrose's in his sermons, as Robin Jensen demonstrates in Chapter 25, this volume.
[75] Jerome, *Comm. Gal.* 2.3.
[76] There has been a recent surge of interest in Augustine's approach. See Nodes 2009; Hunink 2011; Van Reyn 2015.

Ambrose employed visceral and dense vocabulary that promoted a certain imaginative engagement with the events and *exempla* that were sung. Even apart from the musical features of the hymns, which are lost to us, the lyrics themselves are sufficient to inform and delight an audience, and to introduce them to a new epistemology.[77]

Cardinal Newman most likely recognised that these 'real' traits pertained to the success of Ambrosian hymnody. At least, he imitated them in his own career. Newman himself was committed to non-discursive genres, especially in his sermons, as the most effective in communicating a thick account of the Christian faith. He was likewise a hymn-writer, who himself rendered Ambrose's hymns into English compositions that are still used liturgically today.[78]

---

[77] Scholars remain agnostic on the hymns' melodies, but on the musical features and attempts at a reconstruction, see the arguments of Migliavacca in Banterle et al. 1994: 181–215. On the ways in which sound and music might convey knowledge in early Christianity, see Harrison 2019b: 1–4.

[78] See Newman's 'Framer of the Earth and Sky', a rendering of 'Aeterne Rerum Conditor'. For a list of his compositions, including his translations of Ambrose's hymns, see www.Hymnary.org, John Henry Newman.

22 | Confused Voices: Sound and Sense in the Later Augustine

CAROL HARRISON

Introduction

My basic question is: do we need words to make sense or will sound do? From antiquity through to the present day, words have traditionally been prioritised over other modes of knowing as a rational, discursive, deliberated, and verifiable form of human reflection and communication. In contrast, non-verbal sounds, music, and the non-literary or non-verbal arts, such as sculpture, painting, and dance, have been mistrusted as irrational, intuitive, spontaneous, and subjective. Words, which spring from the intellect and inform the intellect, have been preferred to sounds which originate in the affections and form the affections.

In classical grammatical theory, this contrast was commonly expressed in terms of a distinction between what was called the confused voice and the articulate voice, the *vox confusa* and the *vox articulata*. This distinction was a commonplace for the fourth- to fifth-century Christian bishop of Hippo, Augustine, who will be the subject of this chapter. His contemporary, the grammarian Donatus, describes it thus: 'Sound (*vox*) is air that is struck which is perceptible to the ear, in and by itself. Every sound is either articulate or confused. Articulate sound can be captured in letters, confused sound cannot be written.'[1] In order to illustrate the *vox confusa*, classical authors tended to give the example of the (frequently onomatopoeic) sounds made by animals: the whinnying of a horse (*hinnitus*), the bellowing of a bull (*mugitus*), the roaring of wild beasts (*rugitus*), the hiss of snakes (*sibilus*), and the croak of frogs (*coax*).[2] I suppose we might add the *oink* of a pig or the *baah* of a sheep. For classical writers, these are all formless

---

The project is funded by the Polish Minister of Science and Higher Education within the programme under the name 'Regional Initiative of Excellence' in 2019–2022, project number: 028/RID/2018/19.

[1] Aelius Donatus (*c.* 350), *Ars Maior* 1.1 (ed. Copeland and Sluiter 2009: 87): *vox est aer ictus, sensibilis auditu, quantum in ipso est. Omnis vox aut articulata est aut confusa. Articulata est quae litteris comprehendi potest; confusa quae scribi non potest.*

[2] See Butler 2015: 113–15. Michael Hanaghan has drawn my attention to the fact that the Latin word for ghost (*boö*) is related to their supposed sound.

voices which, even though they can on occasion be written down, do not signify anything beyond the raw sound they make; they are non-verbal, mute, irrational noises, without sense. But there are other voices, which are similarly non-verbal, which I think we would all agree *do* convey a degree of meaning. The tone or timbre of someone's voice, their accent or rhythm of speech, a certain inflection or melodic lilt, an emotion-filled cry might well be non-verbal but are still powerfully communicative. Similarly, a person's singing voice or the sound of a particular composer's work can be instantly recognisable without any words being spoken.

When it comes to the sound of the voice, then, words and writing are clearly not the only way of conveying meaning. Even animal voices, we might argue, can convey excitement, hunger, aggression, fear … and we have only to think of the human sounds of laughter, of sighing and groaning, or the cooing and babbling of an infant, which all strictly belong to that category of voices which, according to Donatus' definition, are confused, to realise that the definition needs some qualification. These voices, may, indeed, often be spontaneous, involuntary, seemingly irrational explosions of sound, but I argue that they are nevertheless sounds which are not without sense. Donatus himself recognises this when he discusses the affective force of the part of speech known as *interiectio* or interjection. He writes: 'The interjection is the part of speech inserted into other parts of speech to express the disposition of the soul: either fearful, as *ei*; or desiring, as *o*; or sorrowful, as *heu*; or joyful, as *euax*.'[3] Indeed, as Mark Amsler observes, Donatus and other Latin grammarians acknowledged that such expressions could effectively undermine grammatical form in order to comprehend and communicate the strong emotions that gave rise to them. He observes, 'For Donatus, Servius, Diomedes, and other Latin grammarians, the speaker's emotional or mental state ("affectus mentis") can make phonological, syntactic, or semantic features of an utterance irregular, but the utterance can still be communicative even though it violates the principle that meaningful speech is rational, rule-ordered, and conventional.'[4]

---

[3] Donatus, *Ars Maior* 652.5–6 (cited by Amsler 2019: 27).

[4] Amsler 2019: 28. Similarly, in *The Edge of Words: God and the Habits of Language* (2014), Rowan Williams examines the ways in which our experience of our environment, of ourselves, of other human beings, and ultimately of God pushes us to the very edge where language falters, cracks, and explodes under the pressure of a reality which exceeds it and which it cannot readily grasp. Pressed to breaking point by an ultimately unknowable, irreducible, inexhaustible other, which generates an endless multiplicity of different representations, language, he argues becomes 'a wilder and odder thing than we usually notice' (xiii). In exploring these oddnesses, Williams cogently argues for an appreciation of what we have so far identified as the *vox confusa*. He writes, '"Extremity" in language works by pushing habitual or conventional speech

The late fifth- or early sixth-century grammarian Priscian is another example. Following Donatus, he acknowledges that interjections are a particular class of word which sometimes do not conform to proper accentuation or which imitate non-verbal sounds, such as giggles or expressions of disgust, in order to express the speaker's emotions.[5] Priscian also significantly nuances Donatus' account of the *vox confusa* and the *vox articulata* by introducing a fourfold definition of voice (*vox*): he writes that 'There are four different kinds of sound: "articulate", "inarticulate", "literate", "illiterate".'[6] Articulate and inarticulate sound are defined by whether they originate in the mind of the speaker: '"articulate" sound … is expressed in combination with a mental meaning of the speaker. Inarticulate … does not originate in any mental affection' (1.1). One, we might say, is rational; the other is irrational. Priscian's literate and illiterate sound (*vox*) are like Donatus' articulate and confused voices: '"Literate" sound can be written, "illiterate" sound cannot' (1.1). Priscian's fourfold distinction can therefore comprehend the sort of non-verbal (most often, unwritten) voices which we have identified as nevertheless significant, which convey meaning. In his definition we can have 'articulate' sounds, which originate in the mind of the speaker, which are also 'illiterate' because they cannot be written down. So, he comments, 'when human beings hiss or groan … these sounds indicate some intention of the person who delivers them but cannot be written' (1.1). Likewise, we can have inarticulate literate sounds, like *coax* – the croaking of a frog – which do not signify anything but can be written down; or inarticulate illiterate sounds, like creaking or lowing, which neither signify anything nor can be written or understood.

In this chapter, I focus on the theological significance of what, in Donatus' terms, are 'confused voices', but which might more accurately be described in Priscian's terms as articulate illiterate voices; or, in the work of both these grammarians, the voice of affective interjections: voices which signify something but which cannot (usually or easily) be written down because they are non-verbal. As the Slovenian philosopher, Mladen Dolar, writes of what he calls the 'semiotics of coughing': 'one coughs while preparing to speak … one can use coughing as bidding for time for reflection, or as an ironic commentary which jeopardises the sense of the utterance;

---

out of shape – by insisting on developing certain sorts of pattern (rhyme, assonance, metre), by coupling what is not normally coupled (metaphor, paradox), by undermining surface meanings (irony) or by forcing us to relearn speaking or perceiving (fractured and chaotic language, alienating or puzzling description)' (150).

[5] Priscian, *Institutiones grammaticae* 20:20.4; 3:91.3–4 (ed. Amsler 2019: 29).

[6] Priscian, *Institutiones grammaticae* 1.1 (ed. Copeland and Sluiter 2009: 172–73).

as a notification of one's presence; as an interruption of a difficult silence; as part of the pragmatics of telephone communication'.[7] So, clearing my throat with a deliberate and meaningful cough, I would like to explore what the theological significance of these non-verbal voices might be for Augustine of Hippo, that early Christian bishop who has had such an influence on Western thought – and Western semiotics.

Augustine clearly had an ambivalent relationship with language: ideally, he thinks that we would communicate in a much more direct and intuitive way, simply apprehending the mind of another person in the same way as we understand something in our own minds. We would not have to resort to words at all, which really amount to no more than a very crude and rude vehicle for carrying our wordless thoughts from mind to mind. This is evident in what he says in the *Confessions* about the ways in which he first learned to speak: by observing and imitating the sounds, gestures, facial expressions, and tone of voice (*sonitu vocis*) of those who spoke, which he calls 'natural words common to all races' (*verbis naturalibus omnium gentium*).[8]

I would like to hold on to that 'tone of voice' and those 'natural words' as we begin to trace a path which will hopefully lead us through Augustine's cautious, early middle-aged lack of interest in mere sound without words, to his later, wilder, bolder willingness to abandon words in favour of the pure – often mellifluous and joyous, sometimes rude and startling – sound of the *vox confusa*.

Let us begin with *De doctrina christiana*, the first three books of which are very much the project of Augustine's early middle age (Books 1–3 were written in 396 CE). In it, the sound of the voice lies close beneath the surface of Augustine's even, systematic prose, threatening rudely to interrupt at every turn; but each time it politely clears its throat, Augustine is quick to silence it. His focus in this work is on words, and especially the words of scripture, and he will not allow any extraneous sounds to distract him from that focus. In his careful account of different

---

[7] Dolar 2006: 24. Dolar's comments are, of course, just as relevant to bodily gestures and facial expressions, which similarly communicate a good deal in a non-verbal manner. Classical and early Christian writers were especially conscious of this when they turned to reflect on the ways in which the rhetor should use bodily gestures and facial expressions in order to move and persuade their audience. These reflections usually appear in the section of rhetorical treatises devoted to *pronunciatio*.

[8] *Conf.* 1.8.13; 1.13.20–14.23. As Amsler (2019: 28) observes, there was some discussion as to whether interjections were not proper to particular languages and whether they could be translated (e.g., Isidore of Seville, *Etymologiae sive origines* 1.14).

categories of signs in Book 2, Augustine does acknowledge the many non-verbal signs – including animal noises and the sound of trumpet, flute, and harp – which can, in some circumstances, signify something, but he swiftly makes clear that they are inferior to words and that they will not detain him further.[9]

These non-verbal sounds are not, however, so easily silenced: whether it is a resounding belch brought forth by the beloved disciple in writing the prologue of his gospel, signifying the unknowable and unutterable divinity of the eternally begotten Word,[10] or a jubilant, wordless shout of uncontainable joy which bursts out of the singing of a psalm in order to express praise of an ineffable God ('the heart's cry of joy is its understanding'[11]) these sounds resound with theological significance and give the lie to Augustine's peremptory dismissal of them in the *De doctrina christiana*.[12]

Voice and Word: John the Baptist and Christ

In a series of sermons on John the Baptist, preached annually on his feast day, which date from 401–13 CE (so slightly later middle age), we find Augustine giving rather more attention to the voice than he was inclined to do in *De doctrina*. In these sermons, John the Baptist and Christ are described in terms of the voice (*vox*) and the word (*verbum*) respectively. Deploying Donatus' distinction between the *vox confusa* and the *vox articulata*, Augustine makes it clear that a voice is not necessarily a significant sound; it can simply be a meaningless noise, like someone yelling, groaning, or wailing. 'Voice', as he puts it, is a 'formless sound (*informis ... sonus*), bearing or carrying a noise to the ears, without any meaning (*ratione*) to the intelligence. A word, however, unless it signifies something, unless it carries something to the ears and something else further to the mind, is not called a word' (288.3). His point appears to be that a voice is worthless unless it takes verbal form, and we might therefore well read him as simply once again dismissing the *vox confusa* and the ability of wordless sound to signify anything significant at all.[13]

But in drawing the contrast, or rather the relation, between John and Christ, the forerunner and the incarnate Word, Augustine goes a long way to demonstrating the importance of the sound of the voice. For without

---

[9] *Doctr. chr.* 2.1.2–2.3.4.   [10] *Serm.* 341.5 (Dolbeau 22); *Enarrat. Ps.* 44.   [11] *Enarrat. Ps.* 99.3.
[12] Barthes 2002: 6–7; 150 on the *jubilus*.   [13] *Serm.* 288.2.

John's *voice*, Christ, the Word of God, could not be heard or apprehended. Of course, John must decrease so that Christ can increase; the voice must give way to the Word: 'the voice is sent ahead, so that the Word later on may be understood (*intelligatur*)'.[14] Augustine uses one of his favourite analogies to explain this to his congregation: when we apprehend something in our mind or heart, we conceive a word which, he tells them, is 'held by the memory, got ready by the will, kept alive by the intelligence (*tenetur memoria, paratur voluntate, vivit intellectu*)'.[15] But we should also note the important fact that this word (*verbum*) – the inward conception which takes place in the mind or heart – is, in fact, non-verbal: 'it is neither in Greek, or Latin, or Punic, or Hebrew, or any other tongue',[16] he comments. In order to communicate this non-verbal 'word' to the mind of another, however, we must find a way of bringing it forth, selecting an appropriate language so that it can be heard and thereby transferred to the mind of our hearer.[17] Thus, a non-verbal word, conceived in the heart, which precedes voice and linguistic formulation, is conveyed by the physical voice when it is sounded and spoken, and thereby reaches the mind of another, where it once again becomes a non-linguistic word in the heart of the hearer.

That Augustine uses the same word, *verbum*, for the inward, intuitive, non-verbal conception in the mind or heart *and* for its outward expression can trip us up – indeed, we will see that it trips *him* up. *Verbum* is used, at one and the same time, of both inward signification and external sign, of what is understood and what is spoken and heard. The voice, however, has a crucial role to play in mediating between these two senses of *verbum*, for without voice, the inner, non-linguistic conception cannot be articulated, conveyed, or understood. The silent word, then, held in the memory, made ready by the will and kept alive by the intelligence, is like the inward joy welling up within, which bursts forth in the *jubilus*; or like the child gestating in the womb of a pregnant woman which must inexorably come forth;[18] or (with some important qualifications which we will note below in relation to *De trinitate*) like the eternally begotten Word of the Father, belched forth by John the beloved disciple; or even like the eternal Word of God made flesh for our salvation. In all these cases an inner, non-linguistic 'word' is given physical form, voice, and sound in order to articulate and convey what cannot otherwise be heard and understood by another. Similarly, John the Baptist, like all prophets and preachers,[19] is the voice which

---

[14] *Serm.* 288.2. [15] *Serm.* 288.3. [16] *Serm.* 288.3. [17] *Serm.* 288.3. [18] *Serm.* 293A.7.
[19] *Serm.* 293A.4.

communicates, or at least gestures towards, the unknowable and ineffable mystery of the eternally begotten Word made flesh. Hearing John, we can then believe the Word, apprehending Him in our minds and hearts, beyond all sound or spoken words.

The question we are left with amidst all these words and voices, then, is: does the voice have to be verbal in order to signify? Does it have to be a *vox articulata* in Donatus' terms, an articulate literate voice in Priscian's? The fact that John is described as a voice in contrast to the Word; that it is his *voice*, not his words or the content of his teaching, that is identified as enabling us to apprehend Christ, the eternal and incarnate Word; that what his voice or cry conveys is ultimately a non-verbal, inner conception, which is not in the words of any particular language, suggests that the voice and the sound of the voice are just as important as any verbal form they might take; that it is sound itself, just as much as words, which conveys meaning. Indeed, in these sermons on John the Baptist, Augustine appears to take the radical step of stating quite clearly that what defines a 'word' is not its verbal or non-verbal form, but the fact that it conveys belief and understanding. Just as in *Enarrat. Ps.* (99.4) he comments that 'the cry of the heart is its understanding', so in these sermons he observes in relation to John: 'what is a voice that can be called a word? Where something is understood, a voice that means something is a word' (*quae est autem vox quae dicitur verbum? Ubi intelligitur aliquid, vox significans verbum est, Serm.* 289.3). 'Let us hold on to the Word, let us not lose the Word conceived in the very marrow of our minds (*verbum medullitus conceptum*). Do you want to see the voice disappearing, and the divinity of the Word remaining? ... We all believe in Christ; we all hope for salvation in Christ; that's the word the sound of the voice conveyed' (*Serm.* 293.3).[20]

I think that what we are witnessing here is Augustine being forced, at every turn, to reconsider and revise the very words in which he reflects on words. He uses words such as *verbum* or *vox* only to qualify, redefine,

---

[20] Aristotle might help us here: as Augustine states that what defines a 'word' is not its verbal or non-verbal form, but the fact that it conveys meaning, so Aristotle states that what defines a 'voice' (*phônê*) is not just that it sounds but that it conveys meaning. Both, therefore, cut through the customary distinction between the *vox confusa* and *vox articulata* to arrive at a 'voice' or 'word' which can be non-verbal, unwritten, but which is defined by its power to signify. In addition, for Aristotle, the voice, created by breath striking the windpipe, conveys meaning only when it is made by a creature which possesses a soul, and who retains a mental representation of what is sounded: 'it is necessary for what does the striking to be ensouled and to proceed with a definite imagination (*meta tinos phantasies*), since it is certainly the case that voice is a definite significant sound, and not merely that of inhaled air' (*De an.* 420b32–35, trans. Shields 2016: 40–41).

and turn them upside down. True words – the eternally begotten Word and the inward word in our mind and heart – are, in fact, silent and non-verbal; and voice is not the articulate literate voices of verbal expression but the articulate illiterate voices of non-verbal calls, cries (and even belches). There is no language to express what Augustine is using the language of word and voice to try to express. Rather, he is simultaneously using words to efface words, rendering himself speechless – or at least wordless. What remains is either the silence of God's presence or the cry of the human voice gesturing towards God.

This is made clear, I think, in the full text of *Sermon* 293 on John the Baptist, which came to light only in the 1990s and is now known as *Sermon* 293A or Dolbeau 3 (which Dolbeau dates to 407 CE).[21] Paragraphs 5–11 were omitted in medieval manuscripts, but they are invaluable in reconciling some of the difficulties and confusions in Augustine's consideration of Christ and John the Baptist, the Word and the voice. In this sermon, the contrast between word and voice is drawn much more sharply: 'word (*verbum*)' is used only of Christ, the eternal Word, and of the inner, non-linguistic conception which we have in our minds. 'Voice (*vox*)' is used only of the transitory sounds by which we attempt to express this inner conception, and which then pass away (293A.5). So, as well as making the point that the inner word, conceived in the mind, is not in any language, Augustine also makes clear that in order to express this inward word we need to find a specific language, appropriate for our hearer: Latin for a Latin speaker, Punic for a Punic speaker. But we should note that, in doing so, he does not describe these languages as *words* (that is reserved only for the inner conception), but, in accordance with his strict division between inner word and outer voice, Latin, Punic, Greek, and Hebrew are described simply as *voices* (293A.7). Thus, when he gives the example of 'God', who is conceived inwardly, in no language, but who, in order to be expressed, is voiced in different verbal sounds, depending on the hearer, he observes:

When I wanted to bring forth, to proffer what I had conceived in my mind about God, if I found a Punic speaker, I said *Ylim*; if I found a Latin speaker, I said *Deus*; if I found a Greek, I said *Theos*; before I found any of them, what was in my mind was neither Greek nor Punic nor Latin. So what I conceived to be brought forth was a word; what I provided it with to bring it forth was a voice. (*Serm*. 293A.8)

This lays the ground for a much clearer and more cogent account of Christ the Word and John the voice. For the one who speaks, the word or inward

---

[21] Denecker and Partoens 2014.

conception comes first; the voice follows. For the one who listens, the voice comes first; the word follows. 'Thus, that the Word [Christ] might come to us', Augustine comments, 'the voice preceded it' ... 'the voice makes a sound and passes away, the Word abides' (293A.10). In the contrast between John and Christ, therefore, all language, all verbal expression, is in reality no more, and no less, than a sound or voice which gestures and points to the true Word.

Voice and Word: Formless Matter and Creation

Voice and word appear again slightly later, in the works of Augustine's late middle age, in the rather different and difficult context of his reflections on the creation of the world from formless matter.

Against the Manichees and philosophers, Augustine wishes to argue that, in the act of creation, God was not constrained by time or by any sort of pre-existent matter. His account of creation is a distinctive one: he describes it as a simultaneous moment of creation, conversion, and formation (*creatio – conversio – formatio*) – what he calls 'concreation' – which comes about when God speaks through his Word, calls creation into existence from nothing, and gives formless matter form.[22] In this context, human beings, who possess reason and will, are created and formed by responding to God's call in turning towards Him. It comes as no surprise to find Augustine expressing these ideas in a number of texts in terms of voices and words; sound and song; the *vox confusa* and the *vox articulata*. In *Contra adversarium legis et prophetarum* (written in 419/20 against the Manichees), for example, Augustine writes:

Therefore God made matter. Neither is it to be considered evil because it is unformed, but it is to be understood as a good, because being formable is the capacity. For if form is something of the good, being capable of the good is something of the good. Just as a confused voice is a clamour without words, an articulated voice comes about when it is formed into words (*sicut vox confusa est clamor sine verbis, vox vero articulata sit cum formatur in verba*). Therefore, the former is formable and the latter is formed. The former receives form and the latter has form. It is clear which of these is that from which something comes about. No one says that the sound of the voice comes from words (*de verbis fieri sonum vocis*), but who does not understand that spoken words come about from the voice? Neither is it to be thought that God first made unformed matter and then after an interval

[22] On this, see Vannier 2016.

of time formed that which he had made unformed. But as sounding words come about from the speaker (*sicut a loquente fiunt verba sonantia*), when the originally unformed voice does not later receive form but is produced formed (*non prius vox informis post accipit formam, sed formata profertur*), so God should be understood to have made the world from formless matter, so as to have concreated (*concreasse*) it with the world.[23]

Here we must pause, for in this text Augustine appears to be denying the very existence of the voice, save as the raw, formable sound which comes into existence and receives form only by being simultaneously formed into words. Are we therefore to read him as maintaining that there is no voice other than words?

Contra adversarium is not an isolated example. Augustine draws the same analogy between formless matter and creation; sound (*sonus*) and words in his *Confessions*, written almost twenty years earlier. Here he again observes that, just as there is no gap between sound (*sonus*) and song (*cantus*), so there is no gap between formless matter and form. Rather, matter and form, like sound and song, are created simultaneously.[24]

Can these texts be reconciled with the ones we have already encountered, where confused voices are given a significant role in communicating the Divine Word, or are they simply an example of Augustine using the analogy of voice and word in an entirely different way, in a different context, motivated by different aims?

In reflecting on this question, we need to bear in mind a number of issues: first, it is clear that, for whatever reason, in reflecting on creation, Augustine wishes to separate out theoretically formless matter and form (voice and words). This is not a temporal or spatial separation, but a distinction between what is inchoate but formable and what has form. The difficulty in making this distinction is one we have already encountered: how can what is inchoate and formless be described? Augustine clearly found it tempting to use the analogy of the *vox confusa* – that raw, inchoate, formless voice which, in taking the form of words, becomes a *vox articulata* – and this is precisely what he does in these two works.

It is interesting to find modern philosophers of voice giving much the same centrality to words, even while they acknowledge the signifying power of the comparatively formless, non-verbal voice. In attempting to categorise the ways in which voice is manifest, Mladen Dolar helpfully, I think, distinguishes between the pre-linguistic voice, the voice in speech, and the post-linguistic

---

[23] *Leg.* 1.8.11–9.12.   [24] *Conf.* 12.29.40.

voice; what in classical terms might be categorised as Donatus' *vox confusa* (pre-linguistic), the *vox articulata* (linguistic), and Priscian's articulate illiterate voice (post-linguistic). The pre-linguistic voice, Dolar suggests, is heard in purely physiological sounds, such as involuntary coughing and hiccups, or in the pre-symbolic voice of the infant who has not yet learned to speak, but who can make sounds – which, borrowing from Jakobsen, he calls 'sound gestures' – such as cooing and babbling. The 'post-linguistic' voice, on the other hand, is one that lies beyond language and is found in sounds such as laughter (as we have seen classical grammarians observe of interjections) – a sound which, Dolar notes, is often involuntary and 'looks like a regression to animality', but is, in fact, 'a highly cultural product' which exceeds language.[25] It is revealing that all of Dolar's categories for defining the voice use language as a paradigm. Although he is perfectly happy to allow that pre-linguistic and post-linguistic voices, such as coughing, babbling, and laughing, can indeed signify, he, like Augustine, is reluctant to lose sight of the paradigm of words. Dolar's pre- and post-linguistic voices, like Augustine's, can only be understood in relation to words; they signify as the absence of words. He comments, 'the pre-symbolic acquires its value only through opposition to the symbolic, and is thus itself laden with signification precisely by virtue of being non-signifying'.[26] Alternatively, it can signify in the same way as words, as in the sound gestures of the infant addressing another and eliciting a response.[27] Similarly, the post-linguistic voice can signify in tension with words: singing, for example, is 'expression beyond meaning, expression which is more than meaning, yet expression which functions only in tension with meaning – it needs a signifier as the limit to transcend and to reveal its beyond … expression beyond language is another highly sophisticated language'.[28] Non-verbal voices – or what Dolar calls the 'non-voice' – are therefore no more and no less than the raw matter which precedes, gives form to, and exceeds language; although they are non-verbal, they are defined and have no function except in relation to words. Dolar therefore concludes, 'So the paradoxical facit [sic] would be that there may be no linguistics of the voice, yet the non-voice which represents the voice untamed by structure is not external to linguistics' (32). In short, voices signify.

We find a similar approach to the non-verbal voice in Adriana Cavarero's *For More Than One Voice*. She, too, does not resist the temptation to speak of the raw, inchoate, formless matter which precedes, gives form to, and sometimes exceeds language, in terms of the voice. Prompted by

---

[25] Dolar 2006: 23–32. [26] Dolar 2006: 24. [27] Dolar 2006: 26–29. [28] Dolar 2006: 30–32.

Julia Kristeva, she develops this understanding of voice in relation to the notion of the 'semiotic chora', which Plato describes in the *Timaeus*.[29] For Plato, the 'chora' is the matter which is used in creating the physical world according to the eternal and immaterial forms or ideas. Of course, the *chora* itself is almost impossible to pin down, since it is by definition inchoate, formless, and therefore cannot strictly be articulated in conceptual terms. As Cavarero puts it, 'it is the amorphous receptacle, the space of materialisation, the wet nurse. Plato speaks of the *chora*, but in all rigor, he admits that it has no name and that one can only give a bastardised discourse about it.'[30] Like Augustine, and like Dolar, Cavarero therefore resorts to the analogy of the voice and mentions especially the tones, repetitions, and rhythms which structure and pervade the voice, before language, in language, and after language. She writes of the sounds that exceed language in a manner very similar to Dolar's description of post-linguistic voices such as laughter or singing and Augustine's description of the *jubilus* or belch: 'there are texts that are pervaded by a musical rhythm, in which vocality explodes through the linguistic signifier, comes to the surface, and commands the meaning. Poetry, understood as "poetic text" is the most efficacious example of this'[31] ... 'Both generating and destabilizing, the semiotic vocalic is therefore – at the same time – the precondition of the semantic function and its uncontrollable excess ... Thus, the poet simply indulges an ancient pleasure and resurrects the rhythmic waves whose undulation makes language move' (138).

Cavarero's admission that the *chora* is, in reality, a metaphor for what cannot be named or described, is worth noting, and I think that when we find Augustine using the analogy of the *vox confusa* and *vox articulata* to describe the way in which formless matter is simultaneously given form in creation, we should be prepared to make the same admission: that the *vox confusa* is here no more than a metaphor for what cannot, in reality, be described in words, not least because it precedes and exceeds language, as well as being the substance of language. In other words, we can apprehend and identify the *vox confusa*, but we cannot express it, except in words.

This gives us a clue as to why, as well as theoretically separating out formless matter and form, Augustine also wishes to argue that, in practice, when formless matter is brought into existence from nothingness, it is *simultaneously* given form by God. He is insistent that for something to exist it must possess form; that what is formless and inchoate, by definition, does not

---

[29] *Tim.* 48e4. [30] Cavarero 2005: 135. [31] Cavarero 2005: 136.

exist in any discernible form and therefore cannot be described until the moment when it is concreated – or simultaneously given form – by turning or converting towards the Creator. *All* voices, then – the non-verbal and the verbal; the confused and the articulate; the pre-linguistic, linguistic, and post-linguistic – are, by definition, *formed* sound; otherwise, they would not exist, and we would not be able to conceive of, or, indeed, hear them. Most importantly, they receive this form by converting or turning towards their Creator.

So, to return to our question: is there a contradiction in Augustine's different uses of the analogy of the *vox confusa* and the *vox articulata*? Is it the case that, in a context such as *Sermon* 293A, the *vox confusa* comprehends all human voices – verbal and non-verbal – in contrast to the eternal Word of God, whilst in the context of explaining the simultaneous creation, conversion, and formation of matter, the non-verbal voice/formless matter is only evident insofar as it is inseparable from and indistinguishable from words?

I argue that the contrast is perhaps not as stark as it might at first appear. Augustine's basic point both in the sermon and in his reflections on creation is that something exists only when it receives form and that for human beings this happens only when we turn towards our Creator. The voice, then – whether confused or articulate – whether it is John the Evangelist's belch, the *jubilus* of the Psalmist, the cry of John the Baptist, or an articulate human word – is an inchoate cry until it responds to and converts towards the creating and redeeming Word of God. The key to resolving the apparent contradictions in Augustine's treatment of voice and word, then, is, I would like to suggest, christology.

Voice and Word: A Christological Interpretation

This is made clear, I think, in the first book of *De Genesi ad Litteram* (401/415 CE) where we find the three basic concerns we have identified above – the theoretical separation of matter and form; the inseparability of matter and form in practice; and the conversion or turning which unites matter and form in a moment of concreation – being brought together in Augustine's reflections on the beginning of Genesis. In this commentary, he continues to use the analogy of voice and word in relation to creation, but, as in *Sermon* 293A, 'voice' is once again used only of human voices (verbal and non-verbal); 'word' is used only of the Divine Word.

When God is said to 'speak' in Genesis, in the beginning, and to say 'Let it be made', Augustine insists in Book 1 of *De Genesi ad litteram* that he is not speaking in any human way; he is not speaking with an outward, corporeal, temporal sound or voice; nor with imperfect words that tend towards nothing – not, as he puts it, 'with the sound of a voice nor with thoughts running through the time which sounds take'.[32] Rather, when God is said to 'speak' in the beginning, and to say, 'Let it be made', he is 'speaking' inwardly, incorporeally, and non-verbally; he is speaking within Himself, in the Word which is eternally begotten of the Father: 'it is by the Word, always adhering to the Father, that God eternally says everything ... with the light, co-eternal with himself, of the Wisdom he has begotten'.[33] It is this Word who, as the 'beginning', brings inchoate creation into existence, and who, in saying 'Let it be made', simultaneously calls it from its formlessness and imperfection to receive form and perfection. Augustine comments, 'Accordingly, where scripture states, *God said, Let it be made*, we should understand an incorporeal utterance of God in the substance of his co-eternal Word, calling back to himself the imperfection of the creation, so that it should not be formless, but should be formed, each element on the particular lines which follow in due order.'[34] He adds that, when creation is thus turned towards its Creator, to the unchangeable light of the Wisdom and Word of God, it 'imitates the form of the Word which always unchangingly adheres to the Father, and receives its own form, and becomes a perfect, complete creature'.[35]

It is in this respect that the turning of the creature towards God is the key to its formation. As Augustine puts it:

Eternal Wisdom, of course, is the origin or beginning of the intelligent creation; this beginning, while abiding unchangeably in itself, would certainly never cease to speak to the creature for which it is the beginning and summon it by some hidden

---

[32] *Gen. litt.* 1.4.9: *neque sono vocis neque cogitatione tempora sonorum volvente*.

[33] *Gen. litt.* 1.4.9.

[34] *Gen. litt.* 1.4.9: *ut in eo quod Scriptura narrat, Dixit Deus, Fiat, intelligamus Dei dictum incorporeum in natura Verbi ejus coaeterni revocantis ad se imperfectionem creaturae, ut non sit informis, sed formetur secundum singula, quae per ordinem exsequitur*.

[35] *Gen. litt.* 1.5.10. As we see him observe in *De trinitate* 15, in reference to divine simplicity, Augustine adds here (1.5.10) that the creature is entirely *unlike* the Word of God. For the Word, he observes, 'not only is it the same thing to be as to live, but to live is for him the same as to live wisely and blessedly' (*cui non solum hoc est esse quod vivere, sed etiam hoc est vivere, quod est sapienter ac beate vivere*). For the creature, on the other hand, called into being from nothing, to be is not the same as to live, and to live is not necessarily to live wisely or blessedly; there is a time when the creature was not, and it can turn away and become foolish and miserable.

inspiration to turn to that from which it derived its being, because in no other way could it possibly be formed and perfected.[36]

This is confirmed, I think, by Augustine's later christological reflections in Book 13 of *De trinitate*, this time in relation to the incarnate Word. Reflecting on scripture, and especially on the Prologue of John's Gospel, Augustine distinguishes the knowledge which is based on sense perception and conscious reasoning (*scientia*) from the knowledge which is based on eternal wisdom and contemplation (*sapientia*). This distinction is based on his observation that the first few lines of the Prologue, which refer to the eternally begotten Word, relate to Wisdom while those which describe the sending of John the Baptist to bear witness to Him, relate to sense perception and conscious reasoning.

Augustine illustrates these distinctions, as he so often does, with a linguistic analogy: the relation of sound, words, and meaning. First of all, he suggests that we apprehend sound through the senses, impressed upon and retained by the memory, and that we apprehend meaning when we recollect these mental images by conscious reflection (*animi ratione*) (13.1–4). But he is aware that not all meaning can be readily apprehended in this way. 'Faith', for example, is 'a thing of the heart … deep inside us (*cordis est res ipsa … in intimis nobis*)' (13.5); it is not a matter of sense perception or conscious reflection, but rather a matter of absolute certitude (*certissima scientia*) that, as Augustine puts it, 'the whole man, who consists of soul and body … is going to be immortal, and therefore truly happy' (13.12).[37] How this inner certitude comes about, how we fallen human beings come to believe, is, Augustine urges, on the strength of divine authority (*non argumentatio humana, sed diuina auctoritate*) (13.12), revealed to us in the incarnation.[38] Augustine's point appears to be that the sound and words in which faith is articulated and communicated remain meaningless unless they are a matter of faith in and love of Christ, the incarnate Son of God. To demonstrate this, he distinguishes between an outer trinity of sound or words and an inner Trinity of belief and love. What use, he asks, are mere sounds and

---

[36] *Gen. litt.* 1.5.10.

[37] See also Chapter 21 by Brian Dunkle, this volume, which similarly contrasts 'notional' with 'real' assent as a way of understanding Ambrose's hymns.

[38] He observes, 'But in case this feebleness that is man, which we see and carry about with us, should despair of attaining such eminence [becoming immortal], it went on to say, "And the word became flesh and dwelt among us" (John 1:14), in order to convince us of what might seem impossible by showing us the opposite. For surely if the Son of God by nature became Son of man by mercy for the sake of the sons of men … How much easier it is to believe that the sons of men by nature can become sons of God by grace and dwell in God; for it is in him alone and thanks to him alone that they can be happy, by sharing in his immortality; it was to persuade us of this that the Son of God came to share in our mortality' (13.12).

words – heard, impressed, stored, and recollected – if we do not know what they signify? If, for example, someone who does not know Greek hears a Greek word, it is nothing but a senseless sound of words (*verborum soni*); it is merely an outer trinity.[39] But when we not only hear but also believe it to be true, and love it, then we apprehend the meaning and live 'according to the trinity of the inner man (*cum autem vera esse creduntur, et quae ibi diligenda sunt diliguntur, jam secundum trinitatem interioris hominis vivitur*)' (13.26). Thus, it is not only through memory and reasoning, but also through faith and love – and most especially faith in, and love of, the Word made flesh, that we are able to move from an outer to an inner trinity; from knowledge to wisdom; from sound to meaning; from human voices (both non-verbal and verbal) to the Word.

The relation between the silent, eternally begotten Word of the Father, who takes flesh in order to reveal Himself to us, on the one hand, and the *verbum mentis* or inner word, which we conceive within, and which our noisy, temporal words seek to convey to the mind of another, is one that Augustine often observes,[40] but it is articulated most clearly, perhaps, in the final book of *De trinitate*. Here he enumerates the ways in which we know something: the first is through an innate consciousness (e.g., 'I want to be happy'; 'I know that I am alive'); the second is through sense perception; the third is through the testimony of others (*quae per se ipsum, et quae per sensus sui corporis, et quae testimoniis aliorum percerpta scit animus humanus*). It is from these, stored within what he calls the treasury of the memory (*thesauro memoriae*), that we can bring forth a true word (*verbum verum*), by which we can be said to know them:

From them is begotten a true word when we utter what we know, but a word before any sound, before any thought of sound. For it is then that the word is most like the thing known (*rei notae*), and most its image, because the seeing which is thought (*visio cogitationis*) springs direct from the seeing which is knowledge (*visio scientiae*), and it is a word of no language, a true word from a true thing (*verbum verum de re vera*), having nothing from itself, but everything from that knowledge from which it is born. (*Trin.* 15.22)

---

[39] 'He is certainly not acting according to a trinity of the inner man but rather one of the outer man, because all that he remembers and looks at when he wishes and as he wishes is something belonging to the sense of the body which we call hearing, nor by such thinking is he dealing with anything but the images of bodily things, namely of sounds' (13.26). *Nullo modo tamen dixerimus istum, cum hoc agit, secundum trinitatem interioris hominis agere, sed potius exterioris: quia id solum meminit, et quando uult, quantum uult intuetur, quod ad sensum corporis pertinent, qui vocatur auditus, nec aliud quam corporalium rerum, id est sonorum, tali cogitatione imagines versat.*

[40] Cf. *Conf.* 12; *Tract. ev. Jo.* 1.

Whilst there is an obvious and intended similarity with the eternal trinity, and especially the eternally begotten Word, Augustine is quick to point out that there is also a vast difference between the way in which we know and the manner in which the Godhead knows; between our words and the eternally begotten Word (15.22). This is because for the Father and his eternally begotten Word, existence, knowledge (*scientia*), and wisdom (*sapientia*) are one: 'in the wonderful simplicity of that nature it is not one thing to be wise, another to exist, but being wise is the same as being (*quod est sapere, hoc est et esse*)' (15.22). For us, created, mutable beings, it is of course very different: 'for us to be is not the same thing as to know or to be wise' (15.22); we can be ignorant, or unaware, or simply forget and still continue to be (15.22; 24). Our inward knowing is not co-eternal with our being, rather it must be preceded by thought, which brings it to consciousness (15.25).[41] So, although our bringing forth of an inner word is *like* the begetting of the Word, since it is born of knowledge, as the Word is born of God, Augustine stresses that it is also very *unlike* the Word of God. Whereas in begetting the Word God utters Himself, in bringing forth an inner word we utter something that was once unformed and did not yet exist, which is given form by our thinking (and which, Augustine has demonstrated, is in turn dependent not only on an inward intuition but on sense perception and the testimony of others). Our 'inner word' is not part of our substance but is simply created and brought into existence by our thought. Although Augustine does not here draw out the unlikeness between the incarnate Word of God and human words, in reference to our outward, sounded words, as well as our inner words – his subject here is the eternally begotten Word, not the incarnate Word – it is of course also the case that our spoken words are utterly unlike the incarnate Word. There is, again, no substantial identity between what we think and know and what we say or do; indeed, our words more often than not serve to lie, to veil our thoughts, to mislead, and to be misunderstood. Our spoken words are no more, and no less, than an indication of our fallen inability to convey what is in our minds, or know the truth in another's mind, directly; of our

---

[41] 'if there can be some everlasting knowledge (*scientia sempiterna*) in the mind, while there cannot be everlasting thought about this knowledge, and if our true and innermost word is only uttered by our thinking (*cogitatione*), only God can be understood to have an everlasting Word co-eternal with himself'. Likewise, Augustine argues that the eternally begotten Word's everlasting existence is not the same as our permanently having a formless idea always within ourselves which is formable and which simply needs to be thought in order to be given form. Rather, the eternally begotten Word is always in the form of God and is never formless or formable.

fallen need for sounded words, which are far removed from the inward, true word which we conceive within. In this context, the subversive sound of non-verbal voices, the cacophony of joyful cries, mournful wails, longing sighs, and sinful groans, are no doubt a more accurate articulation of the gap which lies between our inward word and our voiced expression of it, than words can ever be. I therefore argue that in this context, the *vox confusa* is, in fact, a clearer expression of our createdness and fallenness, on the one hand, and of our inability to articulate fully our praise for our transcendent Creator, and our joy and thanksgiving for our redemption, on the other. In both cases, confessing sin and confessing praise, the *vox confusa*, ironically, proves to be more articulate, and to make more sense, than the *vox articulata* of spoken and written words.

The Voice in Song

And what of the later works? I do not think that the wild Augustine, happy to exploit the voice of non-verbal sound, disappears, even if it is sometimes difficult to glimpse him in the midst of the rather joyless later works against Julian – though even here, as we will see, it is not entirely suppressed. The sound of the voice erupts at significant points, and it is a sound which is not just sensuous, but which makes sense. Not surprisingly, as in the case of the *Enarrationes*, it is often reflection on the nature and power of music – that non-verbal sound par excellence – that prompts Augustine to do this.

To conclude this chapter, there are two late texts which I would like to mention briefly in this respect. The first is, in more ways than one, a rather extraordinary section of *De civitate Dei*, Book 22 (413/427 CE). In chapter 8, we find Augustine setting out a forceful apology for miracles to counter those who are wondering why they no longer happen, and who are therefore undermining the one great miracle of Christ's bodily resurrection. Giving an account of some less well known, post-biblical miracles, done in Christ's name and power, which he has either heard of or witnessed for himself, it is a chapter of high drama and extreme emotions, expressed in a cacophony of confused voices which, in their turn, defy any attempt at articulate verbal description. Referring to the agonised prayers of someone who has had one operation and is about to undergo further, complicated, surgery, Augustine writes: 'he … hurled himself forward, as if someone had pushed him flat on his face; and he began to pray. It is beyond the power of words to express the manner of his prayer, his passion, his agitation, his flood of tears, his groans and sobs which shook his whole frame and almost stifled his breath.' The reaction which follows the news that a miraculous healing has made the operation unnecessary is just as indescribable: 'the rejoicing that followed, the thanksgiving to God, the merciful and almighty, which poured from every mouth with tears of happiness – all this I have not words to express'.[42] Where words fail, it appears that tears, facial expressions, bodily gestures, and the *vox confusa* take over.

In Augustine's account of the miracle of the healing of a demon-possessed youth, who is lying like a corpse on the point of death, confused voices sing, roar, shriek, and declaim as the miracle is effected – not, we should note, by words, but by the voices of a group of devout faithful singing a hymn: 'When he lay there ... the lady of the house came in with her maidservants, accompanied by some other devout souls, for the customary evening hymns and prayers (*hymnos et orationes*); and they began to sing a hymn (*hymnos cantare*). The youth was shaken out of his coma by their voices (*voce ille*), as if by a sudden shock; and with a terrifying roar (*fremitu*), he seized hold of the altar ... then with a mighty shriek (*grandi ejulatu*) the demon begged for mercy ... and withdrew from the man' (22.8). Passing over other miracles accompanied by 'tumultuous groans (*ingenti gemitu*), and resounding with lamentations (*ejulatibus personantem*)', we reach the end of this chapter of miracles, where, describing the uproar of shouts; the cries of joy and thanksgiving, which arose from his congregation following a double healing in the basilica at Hippo, Augustine writes: 'Then indeed there arose such a clamour of wonder, such a continuous shouting, mingled with tears, that it seemed impossible that it should ever end ... they rejoiced in the praises of God with wordless cries (*voce sine verbis*), with such a noise (*tanto sonitu*) that my ears could scarcely endure it' (22.8). These deafening, raucous, wordless cries are most definitely not meaningless, confused voices; they articulate the otherwise inexpressible faith, joy and thanksgiving welling up in the hearts of the exultant congregation: 'Now was there anything in their hearts as they rejoiced except the same faith in Christ for which Stephen shed his blood?', Augustine concludes (22.8).

The sensuous sound of music, which transforms, heals, and inspires faith, reappears in *Contra Julianum* (421/22 CE).[43] Julian had argued that

---

[42] *Civ.* 22.8.

[43] This is not the first time Julian was associated in Augustine's mind with music. He was the son of Memorius, to whom Augustine had sent Book 6 of his *De musica* in 408/409. In a covering letter (*Ep.* 101.4), Augustine mentions Memorius' son Julian with great affection.

if Augustine does not allow for the pleasure of the senses (*sensuum voluptatem*) before the fall, including, of course, the pleasure which accompanies sexual intercourse (*voluptas genitalium*), then he must hold that the senses were given by the devil, not by God.[44] This prompts Augustine to distinguish between the pleasure of the senses, which is necessary for health, piety, and virtue, and the pleasure which is unnecessary and which can become carnal concupiscence (*concupiscentia carnalis*).[45] He gives an example from hearing: a song can stir to love of piety, but it can also be a matter of mere sensual delight in the sound of silly, shameful words: 'The mind is surely stirred to a love of piety (*pietatis affectum*) when it hears a song to God (*diuino cantico*), but even in this case it is blamed if the desire to hear wants the sound (*sonum*) instead of the meaning (*sensum*). How much more it is blamed if it takes delight in silly or even shameful lyrics.'[46] That Augustine expresses the distinction between bad and good singing in terms of sound and sense (*sonum* and *sensum*) should not mislead us: he is not thereby rejecting the sound but – as in the more well-known passage on the ambivalent power of music in *Confessions* 10 – only sound which leads to carnal concupiscence, rather than moving the hearer to devotion. It is worth noting that he uses the same term in both texts to describe the positive effect of listening to music: it inspires feelings of devotion.

He clarifies the distinction between the good and bad pleasure of the senses – as he so often does – by contrasting what happened in paradise, before the fall, with what is now the case for fallen human beings. Hearing, like all the senses, would have been a matter of will, not of carnal concupiscence (*carnalis concupiscentia; motus libidinis*); the pleasure which it naturally afforded would have been subject to the will and directed towards good ends.[47] And so he comments that

> [i]t is one thing to consider even bodily beauty, whether visible beauty as in colours and shapes or audible beauty as in songs and melodies (*cantis atque modulis*). Only a rational animal can engage in such a consideration. The arousal of desire (*commotio libidinis*) is something else, and it must be reined in by reason (*ratione*).[48]

But again, this should not mislead us. The contrast between reason and lustful desire is not one that excludes delight in bodily beauty or the beauty of songs and melodies. Rather (as in the distinction between sound and sense), what Augustine is making clear is that the feeling of devotion (*affectus pietatis*) which the beauty of songs and melodies can prompt is not to

---

[44] C. Jul. 4.65.   [45] C. Jul. 4.65.   [46] C. Jul. 4.66.   [47] C. Jul. 4.69.   [48] C. Jul. 4.73.

be equated with carnal concupiscence (*carnalis concupiscentia*). There can be a good pleasure of the senses, which leads to loving devotion; one in which reason and will not only rationally judge but also affectively delight in God. In other words, there can be an appreciation of beauty – including the beauty of songs and melodies – which does not consist in sensual desire or carnal concupiscence, but rather in loving devotion; the will and reason operating both at the level of intellect, and at the level of faith and love. It can be rational, then, to believe, to delight, to jubilate, to praise, to love; reason cannot be separated from will and love.

In arguing that the concupiscence suffered by the genital organs is no different from the sort of concupiscence or pleasure suffered by other bodily senses, Julian had cited the well-known story, recounted by Cicero, of the inebriated youths, who, aroused by a flute player, broke down the doors of a chaste woman, and of Pythagoras' suggestion that the flautist play a slower and graver melody in order to calm them down.[49] In this instance, as in the case of all concupiscence, Julian had observed that the drunken youths had consented to concupiscence, rather than commanded it; their actions were not subject to their will but were aroused by other stimuli (presumably drink) and later quieted by melody. Augustine agrees with him: the actions of the drunken youths were governed, not by the will or by good desire, but by wrongful, carnal concupiscence.

But in doing so, Augustine appears to be acknowledging two things: first, the fact that the senses do also suffer concupiscence, like that of the genital organs, which is not willed but which rather subjects them; second, that the senses can take pleasure in bodily beauty or the beauty of songs and melody, which is subject to the will. The fact that it can do so is not reason to think that carnal concupiscence is therefore good, as Julian wants to argue. Rather – significantly – what Augustine appears to be doing here is putting music on a par with the will in subjecting sensual concupiscence and wrongful desire. It moves us towards feelings of devotion. This is, I think, endorsed by his reference to David's playing for Saul as an alternative Christian analogy of the effect of the flautist on the drunken youths: 'As a man of the church, you ought, of course, to have learned from the music of the church rather than from that of Pythagoras of the effect that David's harp had upon Saul when he was troubled by an evil spirit and recovered from that malady when the holy David played the harp.'[50]

---

[49] *Counsels* (now lost). For various versions of this story, see Sorabji 2002: 91 n. 59. The player changed from the Phrygian to the Doric mode.
[50] *C. Jul.* 5.23.

What can we conclude? I would like to suggest that in his readiness to rethink what the word, 'word' actually signifies; to embrace non-verbal thought and non-verbal sound; to identify meaning with faith and love; to emphasise the role of the voice of John the Baptist and the prophets; to deploy a resounding belch to communicate the ineffability of the eternally begotten Word; to simply sing in spontaneous, involuntary cries of wordless joy; and to acknowledge the miraculous, revivifying, inspiring power of music – we discover another, wilder Augustine: one who is prepared to relinquish words in order to embrace – in faith and love – what words cannot fully comprehend.

23 | Precision and the Limits of Autopsy in Augustine's Critique of Pagan Divination

MICHAEL HANAGHAN

Introduction

In *De doctrina Christiana*, Augustine blends his criticism of astrology into his refutation of omens and the danger that daemons pose (*Doctr. chr.* 2.23.36):[1]

Omnes igitur artes huiusmodi vel nugatoriae vel noxiae superstitionis, ex quadam pestifera societate hominum et daemonum ... in omnibus ergo istis doctrinis societas daemonum formidanda atque vitanda est ... quae omnia tantum valent quantum ... cum daemonibus foederata sunt.[2]

All arts of this kind are either useless or guilty of superstition, arising from the destructive union of man and daemons ... Accordingly, in regard to all these branches of knowledge we must fear and shun the fellowship of daemons ... and all these omens only are in force in so far as ... they have been arranged with daemons.

Augustine considered pagan ways of divining the future as a broad category (*omnes artes*) with multiple subcategories.[3] Astrology was one of the *ars nugatoria*, and so he accordingly denies its efficacy, while daemonic

---

[1] O'Loughlin (1999: 90–92) and De Vicente García (2001: 190–91) highlight Augustine's linking of astrological and daemonic divination. Hegedus (2007: 125–38) surveys where this claim occurs in early Christian authors, but Augustine's source for categorising divination as stemming from daemons may well be Apuleius, *De deo Socr.* 6.3: *per hos ... omnes praedagiorum species reguntur*, 'They rule over all forms of predicting the future.' Apuleius explicitly draws on Plato, *Symp.* 202e, for these remarks: διὰ τούτου [τοῦ δαιμονίου] καὶ ἡ μαντικὴ πᾶσα χωρεῖ καὶ ἡ τῶν ἱερέων τέχνη τῶν τε περὶ τὰς θυσίας καὶ τελετὰς καὶ τὰς ἐπῳδὰς καὶ τὴν μαντείαν πᾶσαν καὶ γοητείαν, 'Through it [τὸ δαιμόνιον] are conveyed all divination and priestcraft concerning sacrifice and ritual and incantations, and all soothsaying and sorcery' (LCL 166: 178).

[2] PL 34: 53.

[3] Cf. Augustine *Tract. Jo.* 7.12.2. where Augustine thinks that pagan magical and ritual practices work but are not preferable; and Augustine, *Ep.* 55.20, which indicates that bibliomancy with the Gospels is preferable to consulting daemons. Augustine, *Conf.* 4.3.4 offers the fact that astrologers do not consult spirits as a reason why Augustine once visited them. For the importance of divination to early Christian thinkers see Peter Struck's chapter in this volume (Chapter 8).

divination falls into the latter category, *ars noxia supersitionis*, as it was potent, dangerous, and should not be practised.[4]

This chapter argues that the limits of human autopsy offer an epistemological link between Augustine's criticisms of astrological and daemonic divination. The minute calculations that astrology requires are beyond human sense perception and so are the tricks used by daemons, which Augustine equates to abilities specific to animals, such as the olfactory skill of dogs.[5] I begin by examining how criticisms of astrology prior to Augustine focused on the exactitude required for successful predictions and used hypothetical birth scenes to attack the impropriety and impracticality of making natal observations with such precision. I then show how these earlier criticisms by classical and Christian authors influenced Augustine's criticism of astrology. Lastly, I link the limits of human autopsy, which fundamentally prohibit the practice of astrology, to Augustine's critique of daemonic divination, and detail how Augustine used Apuleius prior to his extensive rebuttal of Apuleian thought in *De civitate Dei*.[6]

Modern criticism has largely ignored Augustine's daemonology and cast doubt on the rhetorical strength of his argument against astrology.[7] Pingree, for example, claimed that 'Augustine's great attack on astrology ... [is based on] the problems of twins and of free will, and on assertion of demonic involvement, not on a detailed knowledge of the practices of astrologers.'[8] This approach has three fundamental problems. Firstly, it denies a unified thesis to Augustine's criticism of pagan ways of divining the future, and so looks to separate his criticism of astrology from daemons, when (as argued here) both arguments rely on the limits of human autopsy. Secondly, it belittles the prominence of daemons in Augustine's thought and their significance

---

[4] Cf. Augustine, *Ep.* 102.18, where Augustine refers to the worship of daemons as *noxia superstitio*. Augustine elsewhere admits that daemons sometimes predict the future correctly, see *Gen. litt.* 12.13.38. O'Neill 2011: 20–21 is correct in his critique of Evans' (1990: 106–7) claim that Augustine limits daemonic power to the mere appearance of power, which would make it an *ars nugatoria*, not an *ars noxia*. Augustine, *Agon.* 3.3 denies that daemons live among the sun, moon, and stars, but this falls short of invalidating the link between daemons and astrology.

[5] Augustine, *Div.* 3.7, analysed below.

[6] Schlapbach (2013: 133) notes a general similarity between Augustine's characterisation of daemons in *Div.* and the Platonists, including Porphyry and Apuleius, with the exception of daemonic divinity, which Schlapbach mentions. Pépin (1999: 74) notes the primary influence of Apuleius on Augustine's daemonology in *Div.* but does not examine this in any detail.

[7] For the scholarly trend of avoiding Augustine's daemonology, see O'Neill 2011: 9, notwithstanding significant contributions by Köckert 2016: 235–62 and Limonata 2017: 3–14, which have gone some way towards correcting this deficit.

[8] Pingree 1986–1994: 486, discussed in Hegedus 2007: 60–61. For an opposing view, see O'Loughlin 1999: 83–103.

to Augustine as a key source of pagan divination. Lastly Pingree explicitly assumes that Augustine does not characterise astrology correctly owing to his ignorance of its practice. This assumption warrants careful reconsideration.

Augustine was highly effective in his rhetorical attacks and was notorious for (mis)characterising the views of others, or even inventing them, as he did in the Donatist controversy, when the persistent silence of his opponents left a void that Augustine filled as their self-appointed proxy, sketching weak arguments that he could then deconstruct in detail.[9] This misrepresentation is not evidence that Augustine had failed to grasp what Donatists stood for but, rather, indicates that Augustine chose to represent the schism and its supporters in a way that highlighted the weakness of their ideas. The same rhetorical pragmatism is evident in Augustine's apparent and occasional mischaracterisation of astrology, which was a particularly dangerous topic for Christian thinkers given the taboos associated with its practice. At the end of his criticism of astrology in his *Hexaemeron*, for example, Ambrose pauses to make sure that no one thinks that he knows more about astrology than he ought.[10] Ambrose ends his discussion of astrology by claiming that concerns for his reputation forced him to curtail his treatment.[11] In speaking of astrology, Augustine similarly risked coming across as a secret admirer.[12] He therefore needed to keep his focus on refuting rather than summarising astrology. Any flaws in his summary probably reflect Augustine's rhetorical mischaracterisation of the opposing argument, or the careful posturing of Augustine's persona, rather than a genuine indication of his level of knowledge regarding astrology.

Exactitude in the Critique of Astrology: Ptolemy, Cicero, Basil of Caesarea, Ambrose

In the second century CE the polymath Claudius Ptolemy composed, in four books, the great treatise on astrology of antiquity, his so-called

---

[9] Miles 2008: 135–48.
[10] Ambrose, *Hex.* 4.5.20: *Multa diximus, plura nolumus; ne quis ea quae a nobis de illorum assertionibus usurpantur ad refellendum, ad recognoscendum assumpta arbitretur.* 'I have said a lot about this, I don't want to say anymore, lest anyone might think that what was adopted by me from the assertions of astrologers for the purpose of refutation, was actually taken up to affirm it.'
[11] Ambrose claimed that his engagement with astrology enabled him to confront astrologers directly. This justification also prefaced the criticism of astrology in Pseudo-Clementine *Recognitiones* 10.9.
[12] Augustine, *Conf.* 4.3.4–6 merely shows that Augustine once consulted astrologers. For a detailed discussion of his early interest in astrology, see O'Loughlin 1992: 101–25; 1999: 84–87; Hegedus 2007: 45–47.

Tetrabiblos.[13] Ptolemy stressed a crucial weakness of astrology: it needed to be incredibly precise, especially when determining the point in time of a person's entrance into the world.[14] This had to be calculated with supreme exactitude (Ptolemy, *Tetrabiblos* 3.2):

Ἐπειδὴ περὶ τοῦ πρώτου καὶ κυριωτάτου, τουτέστι τοῦ μορίου τῆς κατὰ τὴν ἐκτροπὴν ὥρας, ἀπορία γίνεται πολλάκις, μόνης μὲν ὡς ἐπὶ πᾶν τῆς δι' ἀστρολάβων ὡροσκοπίων κατ' αὐτὴν τὴν ἔκτεξιν διοπτεύσεως τοῖς ἐπιστημονικῶς παρατηροῦσι τὸ λεπτὸν τῆς ὥρας ὑποβάλλειν δυναμένης, τῶν δ' ἄλλων σχεδὸν ἁπάντων ὡροσκοπίων, οἷς οἱ πλεῖστοι τῶν ἐπιμελεστέρων προσέχουσι, πολλαχῇ διαψεύδεσθαι τῆς ἀληθείας δυναμένων ...[15]

Difficulty often arises with regard to the first and most important fact, that is, the fraction of the hour of the birth; for in general only observation by means of horoscopic astrolabes at the same time as the birth can for scientific observers give the minute of the hour, while practically all other horoscopic instruments, on which the majority of the more careful practitioners rely, are frequently capable of error ...

According to Ptolemy, the exact moment of birth was difficult to ascertain without the use of an astrolabe, a small mechanical device that allowed the user to mark the position of planets relative to one another.[16] He distinguished two types of astrology: as practised with an astrolabe and as practised by most, who mean well but fail to achieve reliable precision without the correct equipment.[17]

The exactitude that astrology demanded was part of its claim to be an authoritative and highly skilled practice with the potential to provide important knowledge, but this precision came to be seen by others as a potential weakness. For example, Cicero, in his treatise *De divinatione*, used the persona of Marcus to express disappointment that astrologers do not rely on mathematics to calculate planetary positions but instead hope to ascertain the exact position of the stars at the pivotal moment of birth by observation alone: '[Chaldeans] make their judgements relying on the highly deceptive perception of their eyes, when they ought to view (*videre*) these matters using reason (*ratione*) and thought (*animo*)'.[18] Autopsy is

---

[13] Hankinson (2003: 293) briefly summarises Ptolemy's arguments. For more detail, see Tester 1987: 83–88.

[14] Ptolemy highlights this difficulty towards the beginning of the work, at *Tetrabiblos* 1.3. The demand for precision features in Manilius, *Astronomica* 1.57.

[15] LCL 435: 228.   [16] Ptolemy, *Tetrabiblos* 3.3.   [17] Ptolemy, *Tetrabiblos* 3.3.

[18] Cicero, *Div.* 2.91 [*Chaldaei*] *oculorum fallacissimo sensu iudicant ea quae ratione atque animo videre debebant*. Beard (1986: 34) and Schofield (1986: 55–56) caution against conflating the persona that Cicero adopts in *De divinatione* with Cicero's actual views.

fundamentally unable to provide the kind of accuracy and precision that astrology requires. Eyes can be tricked, and so a judgement that relies on them cannot be trusted.[19] Cicero denies the astrologers the ability to see clearly by using *videre* with *ratio* and *animus*, thereby contrasting correct modes of knowing with the false judgements of astrologers. In Marcus' reasoning, knowledge obtained by sense perception is necessarily imperfect, even when accurate, and so must always be inferior to mathematical or higher-order reasoning. Precision is therefore only possible through reason, not observation.[20]

Two hundred years or so after Ptolemy's treatise, Basil of Caesarea composed and circulated his homilies on creation, his *Hexaemeron*. Basil prefaced his discussion of astrology by noting that his attack was firmly grounded in previous criticisms (*Hex*. 6.5): Ἐρῶ δὲ οὐδὲν ἐμαυτοῦ ἴδιον ('I won't say anything that is mine').[21] This claim operates as an Alexandrian footnote, signalling Basil's use of previous criticisms of astrology and of what astrologers and their proponents say about their own practice, and so subtly disclaims that Basil has any direct knowledge of astrology.[22] Like Ptolemy, he seized on the precision demanded by astrology, not to promote astrolabes but rather as a way of debunking its entire practice (Basil, *Hex*. 6.5):

Οἱ τῆς γενεθλιαλογίας ταύτης εὑρεταὶ ... εἰς στενὸν παντελῶς ἀπέκλεισαν τοῦ χρόνου τὰ μέτρα· ὡς καὶ παρὰ τὸ μικρότατον καὶ ἀκαριαῖον, οἷόν φησιν ὁ ἀπόστολος, τὸ ἐν ἀτόμῳ, καὶ τὸ ἐν ῥιπῇ ὀφθαλμοῦ, μεγίστης οὔσης διαφορᾶς γενέσει πρὸς γένεσιν.[23]

The inventors of astrology .... completely separated passages of time into narrow divisions, as if in the least and shortest interval, 'in a moment, in a twinkling of an eye' [1 Cor 15:52] to speak with the words of the Apostle, with their being the greatest difference between one birth and another.

Basil claims that a split second must be distinguished for astrology to work. The allusion to 1 Cor 15 points the reader in the direction of Paul's separation of celestial and terrestrial bodies at 1 Cor 15:40, and so undermines the claim that events on earth are linked to celestial signs. To make his

---

[19] Cf. Augustine, *Mag*. 11.38; Vergil, *Ecl*. 2.25-37; Lucretius, *De rerum natura* 4.379, for which see Nuzzo 2006: 147.
[20] A similar critique occurs in Sextus Empiricus, *Math*. 6.52-54.
[21] For a summary of Basil's arguments against astrology, see Riedinger 1956: 47-48.
[22] For the function of this kind of allusion and use of the term 'Alexandrian footnote', see Hinds 1998: 2, and more recently Nethercut 2018: 78 n. 8. For Basil's use of Origen at *Hex*. 6.5-7, see Robbins 1912: 41 and, in greater detail, Rasmussen 2014: 471-85; for this remark in particular, see Rasmussen 2014: 478.
[23] PG 29: 128-29.

argument more vivid and to stress the exactitude required, Basil includes a detailed hypothetical birth (*Hex.* 6.5):

Τιθέντες τοίνυν τὰς γενέσεις τῶν τικτομένων, ἴδωμεν εἰ τὴν ἀκρίβειαν ταύτην τῆς τοῦ χρόνου διαιρέσεως ἀποσῶσαι δυνήσονται. Ὁμοῦ τε γὰρ ἐτέχθη τὸ παιδίον, καὶ ἡ μαῖα κατασκοπεῖ τὸ γεννηθὲν ἄρρεν ἢ θῆλυ· εἶτα ἀναμένει τὸν κλαυθμόν, ὅπερ σημεῖόν ἐστι τῆς ζωῆς τοῦ τεχθέντος. Πόσα βούλει ἐν τούτῳ τῷ χρόνῳ παραδραμεῖν ἑξηκοστά; Εἶπε τῷ Χαλδαίῳ τὸ γεννηθέν. Διὰ πόσων, βούλει, θῶμεν τῶν λεπτοτάτων τῆς μαίας τὴν φωνὴν παρελθεῖν· ἄλλως τε καὶ εἰ τύχοι ἔξω τῆς γυναικωνίτιδος ἑστὼς ὁ τὴν ὥραν ἀποτιθέμενος; Δεῖ γὰρ τὸν τὰ ὡροσκοπεῖα καταμαθεῖν μέλλοντα, πρὸς ἀκρίβειαν τὴν ὥραν ἀπογράφεσθαι, εἴτε ἡμερινὰ ταῦτα, εἴτε νυκτερινὰ τυγχάνοι. Πόσων ἑξηκοστῶν σμῆνος ἐν τούτῳ πάλιν παρατρέχει τῷ χρόνῳ;

Let us see then, in determining the birth of infants, if they can preserve this precise division of time. At the same place the child is born, and the midwife ascertains the sex; then she awaits the wail which is a sign of its life. Until then how many seconds have passed do you think? The midwife announces the birth of the child to the Chaldaean: how many minuscule moments shall we count until she opens her mouth, especially if he who records the hour is outside the women's apartments? And we know that he who consults the dials, ought, whether by day or by night, to mark the hour with precise exactitude. What a swarm of seconds passes back and forth during this time![24]

Basil imagines a scene where a child is born, but the astrologer has trouble gaining access and recording accurately what happens. The precision involved is stressed through the repetition of ἀκρίβεια. Several moments pass before the astrologer is informed of the infant's birth, a time during which the newborn's sex and vitality are checked. By the time the astrologer is told of the infant's birth, it is too late; the astrologer cannot take their measurements with the meticulous precision needed.

Basil's hypothetical birth scene shows the impracticality of precise astrological measurements.[25] A few decades later, Ambrose of Milan composed his own homilies on creation, largely paraphrased from Basil's. Like Basil, Ambrose attacked genethlialogy by using a hypothetical birth scene (*Hex.* 4.4.14):

Constitue partum feminae; obstetrix utique eum primo cognoscit explorat vagitum, quo nati vita colligitur, attendit, utrum masculus sit an femina. Quot vis inter

---

[24] Rasmussen (2014: 481–82) notes Basil's extensive use of Origen for this passage with the exception (which he notes) of the final rhetorical flourish.
[25] Cf. Origen, *Philoc.* 23.6 on the inability of mankind to observe the movement of stars; *Philoc.* 23.17 for the precision astrologers claim that they need; and Eusebius' inclusion of Origen's criticisms of astrology at *Praep. ev.* 6.11. Rasmussen (2014) focuses on the latter in his analysis of Basil's use of this text.

has moras praeterire momenta? Pone mathematicum praeparatum. Numquid potest vir interesse puerperio? Dum mandat obstetrix, audit Chaldaeus, ponit horoscopium, in alterius sortem iam nati fata migrarunt, de altero quaeritur et alterius genitura proponitur. Pone veram esse eorum opinionem de nativitatum necessitatibus, non potest vera esse collectio.[26]

Imagine a woman is giving birth; the midwife is certainly the first to observe it, she looks out for the cry, which confirms the child's life, and notes whether the child is male or female. How many moments are you willing to allocate to these delays? Suppose an astrologer is ready. Can a man even be present at a birth? While the midwife is providing the information, the Chaldaean listens, sets up the horoscope, the fates of the child have already moved into another person's destiny. As an inquiry happens into one person, the birth of another is already being established. Allow that their view concerning the importance of birth is true; the gathering of this information cannot be true.

The same practical difficulties feature in both accounts; the nurse is delayed while postnatal checks are done on the infant.[27] Ambrose extends his account by raising the impropriety of an astrologer being present at the birth and adding the calibration of the horoscope as a further delay. Both hypothetical birth scenes illustrate their main argument: natal data, as recorded by an astrologer, are corrupted. Even if astrology were theoretically possible, pragmatic considerations inhibit its practice.

Prior to Augustine, critics had identified major weaknesses of astrology. Cicero had highlighted astrologers' misplaced reliance on their own autopsy to make detailed scientific measurements; Ptolemy had stressed the exactitude required. Neither of these necessarily precludes the possibility of astrology taking place. In Cicero's thinking, the precision that astrological calculations require must be mathematical, not observational, while Ptolemy allows that detailed precision is achievable with the right equipment. Basil and Ambrose exploit these concerns for astrological precision by using a hypothetical scene to stress the impossibility and impropriety of astrologers achieving this precision.

Augustine's Critique of Astrological Divination

According to Augustine, the defining moment in his thinking on astrology came during a conversation he had with his dear friend Firminus, related

---

[26] *Bibliotheca Patrum ecclesiasticorum Latinorum* 9.2, 87.
[27] Hegedus (2007: 31) notes how Ambrose's account closely parallels Basil's.

in his *Confessiones*.[28] In the dialogue, Firminus tells an exciting if improbable story.[29] His father shared an interest in astrology with a friend who owned a slave girl. Both the slave girl and Firminus' mother became pregnant at the same time, went into labour at the same time, and gave birth at the exact same time. Firminus states that this was discovered when messengers were sent from each house to report the respective births and met at the exact halfway point. Even though Firminus and the slave girl's son were supposedly born at the exact same time, they went on to live dramatically different lives, one as the heir to a wealthy estate, the other born into slavery. The narrative stresses that the two pregnancies progressed at the same time, culminating in the simultaneous births and that both interested parties, Firminus' father and the master of the slave girl, watched over the pregnancies with intense and detailed supervision.[30] The problem of simultaneous birth prompts Augustine to reflect on the claims astrologers make (*Conf.* 7.6.10):

hinc autem accepto aditu, ipse mecum talia ruminando, ne quis eorundem delirorum qui talem quaestum sequerentur, quos iam iamque invadere atque inrisos refellere cupiebam, mihi ita resisteret, quasi aut Firminus mihi aut illi pater falsa narraverit, intendi considerationem in eos qui gemini nascuntur, quorum plerique ita post invicem funduntur ex utero ut parvum ipsum temporis intervallum, quantamlibet vim in rerum natura habere contendant, conligi tamen humana observatione non possit litterisque signari omnino non valeat quas mathematicus inspecturus est ut vera pronuntiet. et non erunt vera, quia easdem litteras inspiciens eadem debuit dicere de Esau et de Iacob, sed non eadem utrique acciderunt. falsa ergo diceret aut, si vera diceret, non eadem diceret: at eadem inspiceret. non ergo arte sed sorte vera diceret.[31]

An opening thus made, ruminating with myself on such matters, so that none of those delinquents (who seek to profit from such a trade, and whom I longed to attack, and with derision to confute) might confront me with the claim that Firminus had lied to me or his father to him; I turned my thoughts to those that are born twins, who for the most part come out of the womb so near to one another, that this small interval (such is the power that they claim it has over the nature of things) cannot be noted by human observation, or be at all expressed in those signs which the astrologer is to inspect to make true predictions. They cannot, of course, be true: for looking into the same signs, [an astrologer] would have predicted the

---

[28] Augustine, *Conf.* 7.6.8–10. Stock (1996: 50–51) links Augustine's change in attitude to his discussion with Vindicianus, described at Augustine, *Conf.* 4.3.
[29] Augustine, *Conf.* 7.6.8.
[30] Augustine, *Conf.* 7.6.8: *examinatissima diligentia; cautissima observatione*.
[31] LCL 26: 314–16.

same fate for Esau and Jacob, but their fates were different. So either he would have spoken falsely, or if he actually spoke the truth, then he would not have said that their fates were the same, even as he looked at the same measurements. So he would have spoken the truth not by skill but by chance.

The scriptural example of Esau and Jacob is apt for two reasons: Jacob supposedly entered the world holding Esau's heel, so any distinction in the times of their births must be arbitrary; and Jacob ultimately acquired Esau's position as firstborn son, something which even a simple attempt at forecasting the future would have struggled to predict.[32] Augustine repeats this argument, unprefaced by Firminus' story, in both *De doctrina Christiana* and *De civitate Dei*, repeatedly drawing attention to astrologers' inability to perceive and apply any meaningful temporal difference in the birth of twins. At *Doctr. chr.* 2.23.33, Augustine notes, 'but it can be that some twins are born so closely to one another that no difference in time between them can be determined and marked down in the numbers of their constellations' (*fieri autem potest ut aliqui gemini tam sequaciter fundantur ex utero, ut intervallum temporis inter eos nullum possit apprehendi et constellationum numeris annotari*).[33] This means, in effect, that some twins end up having 'the same constellations' (*easdem constellationes, Doctr. chr.* 2.23.33), as there is no observable difference in the time of their births. Consequently, astrologers cannot achieve the precision that they claim their science demands (*Doctr. chr.* 2.23.34): 'For even if I were to concede that this [the smallest interval of time] was really important, it still cannot be uncovered in the constellations by an astrologer; once he inspects these claims he may pronounce their fates' (*etsi enim concedam ut plurimum valeat, tamen in constellationibus a mathematico inveniri non potest, quibus inspectis se fata dicere profitetur*).[34] In *Civ.* 5.2.4, Augustine claims that astrologers try to force their claims 'from the smallest difference in time' (*de interuallo exiguo temporis*), which in the case of twins born in close proximity to one another cannot account for the similarity in their upbringing, raised in the same house, with the same means and parents, and the dissimilarity in their behaviour, actions, and lives.[35] In similar language to *De doctrina Christiana*, Augustine again asserts that the difference in twins' 'constellations cannot be comprehended' (*[geminorum] constellationibus comprehendi non potest, Civ.* 5.2).[36] Augustine clearly shows how the inability of astrologers to distinguish the natal moment of twins, who

---

[32] Augustine, *Gen. litt.* 25.26–34. [33] Green 1996: 94–96. [34] Green 1996: 96.
[35] Walsh 2009: 24. [36] Walsh 2009: 24.

live different lives, invalidates the practice of astrology, as the same data set must produce two different results. In effect, twins end up being born under the same stars. Astrologers either guess correctly or are wrong: there is no skill involved.[37]

Scholars have wondered whether Augustine follows Cicero in using a specific example of twins to reinforce his criticism of astrology.[38] This doubt has been fuelled by Augustine's combative and dismissive attitude towards Cicero's treatment of divination.[39] Just after the twins problem in *De doctrina Christiana*, there is an allusion to Cicero's *De divinatione* (Augustine, *Doctr. chr.* 2.23.36):

sic etiam de quibusque nascentibus … multi multa humanis suspicionibus quasi regulariter coniectata litteris mandaverunt, si forte insolite acciderint, tamquam si mula pariat aut fulmine aliquid percutiatur.[40]

so also from things that are born … many have drawn many conjectures of their own, and have committed them to writing, as if they were rules, if there happened to be something unusual in the occurrence, such as when a mule brings forth young or an object is struck by lightning.

Lightning flashes are typical omens and so would hardly be enough to sustain an intertextual connection, but mules rarely give birth.[41] Augustine explicitly identifies that he has read about these claims (*litteris mandaverunt*). Both lightning and a mule giving birth are mentioned by Cicero in book two of *De divinatione*, the same book that includes his articulation of the 'twins problem': 'But since entrails and lightning have been sufficiently discussed, portents still need to be discussed for a complete treatment of

---

[37] Augustine, *Civ.* 5.2–4; *Doctr. chr.* 2.22.33; cf. *Conf.* 7.6.9–10.
[38] Cicero, *Div.* 2.90 uses the Spartan kings and twin brothers Procles and Eurysthenes as examples. At this point in *Div.*, Cicero is paraphrasing Diogenes' criticism of astrology, so the possibility remains that Cicero is simply repeating Diogenes' examples. Ferrari (1977: 249) notes the similarity in Augustine's and Cicero's arguments but puts this down to coincidence. De Vicente García (2001: 190) sees Cicero as Augustine's model for these remarks. Origen briefly mentions twins at *Philoc.* 23.17, but it remains conjectural whether Augustine had access to this text at this point, for which see Ramelli 2013: 293.
[39] Barton (2002: 191 n. 39) supposes that Augustine may have read a lost work of Cicero's, owing to his criticism of Cicero at *Civ.* 5.2 and 5.5, but Augustine may simply not have considered Cicero's *Div.* as a treatise opposed to the practice of divination, as the first book's support of astrology is not wholly undermined by the criticisms in the second, especially at its end, where divination is allowed under certain circumstances. For the methodological difficulty in reading the arguments in *Div.* as Cicero's own, see Beard 1986: 34–35 and Schofield 1986: 55–56.
[40] Walsh 2009: 24.
[41] Adams (1993: 44 n. 19) notes that a mule giving birth is considered a prodigy owing to the animal's sterility.

soothsaying. A mule giving birth was mentioned earlier by you.'[42] Cicero also mentions a mule giving birth at *Div.* 2.28.61. These two references represent half of the total number of references to mules giving birth in extant Latin literature prior to Augustine.[43] This intertextual connection suggests that Augustine knew Cicero's treatise on divination in some detail as early as 397 CE, when he wrote the first three books of *De doctrina Christiana*, around the same time that he was writing *Confessiones*, and so when he looked to exploit the rhetorical potential of twins to undermine astrology in *Confessiones*, it is feasible that he followed Cicero's rhetorical structure in *De divinatione*, which he illustrated with a scriptural rather than historical example.

Augustine's Critique of Daemonic Divination

Augustine's first descriptions of aerial beings in the Cassiciacum dialogues laid the groundwork for his subsequent claims: daemons are not divine but are celestial animals, and the divine is superior to what humans cannot see. Rather than try to prove that daemonic divination does not work, as he does with the *ars nugatoria* of astrology,[44] Augustine engages in a moralistic condemnation *ad homines* against those who consult daemons.[45] This leads to a sustained effort to diminish daemonic powers by comparing the limits of human autopsy to daemons' visual prowess.[46] This claim first appears in *Ep.* 9.2, written in response to Nebridius' request for information regarding what Augustine terms *superiores potestates vel daemones* and probably composed in 387 or 388 CE.[47] In that letter, Augustine describes human senses as *hebetes* and *tardos*, 'blunt' and 'slow'.[48] An explicit comparison between the sensory perception of humans and aerial or ethereal beings follows '[aerial

---

[42] Cicero, *Div.* 2.22: *Sed quoniam de extis et de fulgoribus satis est disputatum, ostenta restant, ut tota haruspicina sit pertractata. Mulae partus prolatus est a te.* LCL 154: 426.

[43] Otto 1890: 232 also cites Suetonius, *Galb.* 4 and Juvenal, *Sat.* 13.64.

[44] Augustine, *Doctr. chr.* 2.23.36, discussed above.

[45] Augustine, *Div.* 3.7, blames *curiositas* as the main reason why men consult daemons, a theme that he expounds upon at *Serm.* 112A.3. Walsh (1988: 74–85) connects Augustine's use of *curiositas* to Apuleius', noting '[Augustine's] repeated use of *curiositas* to describe the perverted pursuit of other religious enthusiasms is a legacy from Apuleius' (82). Augustine does not cite scripture to support his attack on those who consult daemons in *Div.*, but he does elsewhere, as in *Serm.* 198.3.

[46] Bouton-Touboulic 2007: 21–24.   [47] PL 33: 72. For the dating, see Köckert 2016: 260.

[48] Augustine *Ep.* 9.3 (PL 33: 72). For discussion of this passage, see Smith 2017: 12–13.

or ethereal beings'] sensory perception is incredibly sharp – so much so that, in comparison, ours are not even worthy of consideration as sensory perception'.[49] The predictions that daemons generate by using these senses may well turn out to be accurate, but this falls short of being real knowledge of the future, as their superior senses and celestial bodies enable them to manipulate events and individuals and to misrepresent their observations as predictions.

In *De divinatione daemonum*, Augustine uses the limits of human autopsy to compare daemonic divination to the perceptual capacities of animals, even as he acknowledges that it is superior to these senses. This depiction of daemons responds to Augustine's characterisation of humans, who are easily impressed by daemons' ability to see the future because their own sight is so limited. Scholarly attention has largely focused on Augustine's refutation of Apuleius' daemonology in *De civitate Dei*, to the exclusion of Augustine's earlier works.[50] In this section, I read Augustine's daemonology in *De divinatione daemonum* alongside Apuleius' *De deo Socratis*, to show that Augustine's thinking and rhetoric regarding daemons were shaped by Apuleius' arguments well before he delivered his sustained criticisms of that second-century author in *De civitate Dei*.

De divinatione daemonum begins as a dialogue between clergy, which concludes with a question regarding daemons.[51] Augustine then promises to return to the questions in a written treatise, which constitutes the remainder of the text.[52] This programmatic insertion presents the treatise in a didactic context, with Augustine cast in the role of learned preacher. The insertion of narrative time allows a smooth transition from the text of the dialogue to the expression of the treatise, but this is quite disarming, since Augustine proceeds to offer a detailed and considered daemonology, informed by his reading and understanding of Platonists such as Apuleius and Porphyry.[53]

---

[49] Augustine, *Ep.* 9.3: [*aeriorum aethereorumve animalium*] *est sensus acerrimus, et in cuius comparatione noster ne sensus quidem putandus est*. PL 33: 72.
[50] For recent efforts, see O'Neill 2017: 39–58 and Smith 2017: 7–32, both of whom analyse Augustine's partial refutation of Apuleius' daemonology in *Civ.* but do not track Apuleius' influence on Augustine's earlier thought. See also O'Neill 2011: 14.
[51] Augustine, *Div.* 1.1–2.6. Kühn (2004: 326) compares the beginning of the text to the dialogue at Cicero, *Div.* 2.19–21.
[52] Augustine, *Div.* 2.6. This opening may well be a conceit, given that Augustine envisaged an entire treatise on daemonic powers in *Ep.* 9.2.
[53] For a succinct summary of Augustine's arguments, see Kahlos 2016: 176–77; for its context, Fiedrowicz 2005: 197–202, and for its structure Bouton-Touboulic 2007: 17–19 and Kühn 2004: 308.

The title *De divinatione daemonum* issues a paratextual challenge and correction to Cicero's great treatise *De divinatione* since, in Augustine's thought, all divination (excluding astrology as an *ars nugatoria*) is ultimately about daemons.[54] At the same time, it also responds to Apuleius' *De deo Socratis*, or, at least, what Augustine claimed Apuleius' work should have been called (Augustine, *Civ.* 8.14):

non est Socrati amicitia daemonis gratulanda, de qua usque adeo et ipse Apuleius erubuit, ut de deo Socratis praenotaret librum, quem secundum suam disputationem, qua deos a daemonibus tam diligenter copioseque discernit, non appellare de deo sed de daemone Socratis debuit.[55]

Socrates should not be congratulated on the friendship of the daemon, of which Apuleius was so ashamed that he entitled his book *On the God of Socrates*, when in keeping with his own argument, in which he so diligently and at such length distinguishes gods from daemons, he should have entitled *On the Daemon of Socrates*, not *On the God*.

The title of Apuleius' work fails to account for the distinction between daemons and gods, and so – according to Augustine – it mistakenly claims that Socrates had a relationship with a divine being. This is fundamental to Augustine's refutation of Apuleius' daemonology. So, while Apuleius may maintain that daemons are 'divine beings'[56] which 'are not readily visible to anyone, unless by their divine favour they permit themselves to be seen' (*nemini hominum temere visibilia, nisi divinitus speciem sui offerant*, *De deo Soc.* 11.2–4),[57] Augustine fundamentally rejects the divine status of daemons. This rejection does not entail a complete rejection of Apuleius' claims; in fact, many of the arguments that Augustine makes are either drawn selectively from Apuleius' treatise or represent an extrapolation and combination of Apuleian premises.

Apuleius defined daemons using five characteristics: 'animals by classification, rational in mind, emotional in spirit, aerial in body, eternal in time' (*genere animalia, ingenio rationabilia, animo passiva, corpore aeria, tempore aeterna*, *De deo Soc.* 13.3).[58] Augustine selectively focuses on three characteristics: their aerial bodies, age and experience, and animal

---

[54] The title is authentic. Cf. Augustine, *Retract.* 2.30: *ex quadam disputatione necessitas ut De divinatione daemonum libellum scriberem, cuius titulus iste ipse est* ('after a discussion it became necessary for me to write a treatise *On the Divination of Daemons*; this was its actual title'). See Pépin 1977: 54–55.
[55] LCL 413: 66.   [56] Apuleius, *De deo Soc.* 6.2–3: *divinae potestates*.   [57] LCL 534: 368.
[58] LCL 534: 372.

classification.[59] The first two are used to explain how daemons seem to be able to predict the future; they can see a long way, travel great distances at speed, and anticipate many things based on their vast experience.[60] Augustine uses their animal status to deny their divinity and to draw comparisons between the power of daemons to see the future and the senses of other animals. He lists four animals and their respective abilities which are superior to humans' and similar in a way to daemonic divination, but not as powerful. These are clearly not the acts of divine beings: a dog can sniff out prey, a vulture can find carrion from a long distance away, an eagle can see far into the distance, and herbivores know not to eat poisonous plants (since they divine that the plants will make them sick).[61] Daemons, like these other animals 'do not use a wiser intellect, but a sharper physical sense'.[62] Like other Platonists,[63] Apuleius offers a comparative analysis of the sensory abilities of humans and other animals, but specific elements unique to Apuleius are later found in Augustine: daemons are explicitly

---

[59] Augustine mentions Apuleius' characteristic of daemons at *Civ.* 8.16, where he notes that daemons are only unique in possessing celestial bodies, for which see O'Neill 2011: 14–15. These Apuleian characteristics are also found in Augustine's *Div.* As Wiebe (2014: 4–5) shows, Augustine subsequently distanced himself somewhat from the view that daemons possessed physical bodies. Cf. Origen, *Cels.* 4.92, which credits δαίμονές τινες φαῦλοι ('some evil daemons') with having insight into the future as they are γυμνοὶ τῶν γηΐνων σωμάτων ('devoid of earthly bodies'). It is unclear whether Augustine knew the specific arguments of Origen at this point, but according to *Conf.* 8.6.14–15, he was familiar with a version of Athanasius' *Life of Antony* in which daemons occupy the air and seemingly possess some aerial form which allows them to pass through doors; see Athanasius, *Vit. Ant.* 21, 28, 65.

[60] Apuleius, *De deo Soc.* 12: *aeterna aequibilitate*. [61] Smith 2017: 15.

[62] Augustine, *Div.* 3.7: *non utique prudentiore intellectu animi, sed acutioris corporis sensu*.

[63] Porphyry, *Abst.* 3.23: Ὥσπερ ὄψεώς ἐστιν πρὸς ὄψιν διαφορά ... Καὶ γὰρ ἐκείνων πολλὰ τοῦτο μὲν μεγέθει καὶ ποδωκείᾳ, τοῦτο δὲ ὄψεως ῥώμῃ καὶ ἀκοῆς ἀκριβείᾳ πάντας ἀνθρώπους ἀπολέλοιπεν ('The sight of one animal differs from that of another ... For many brutes surpass all men in magnitude of body, and celerity of foot, and likewise in strength of sight, and accuracy of hearing'); Nauck (1860: 148) argues that Porphyry was influenced by Plutarch, *Soll. an.* 962C–D, which he quotes directly. See Mossmann 2005: 147–54 for discussion of Plutarch's rhetorical strategies and especially the comparative framework that he uses. Augustine acknowledges in *Conf.* 7.9.13 that he had read *quosdam Platonicorum libros ex graeca lingua in latinam versos* ('some Platonists' books translated from Greek into Latin') LCL 26: 320, but does not specify what these were; for discussion, see King 2005: 213–16. Pépin (1977: 56–57) noted connections between Augustine's thought and Porphyry's. The specific connection made here is supported by Gilson's (1946: 43–52) argument that Augustine, *Conf.* 7.9.15 drew on Porphyry *Abst.* 3.16. O'Neill (2011: 18) traces Augustine's argument but does not link it to Porphyry (and through Porphyry, Plutarch). Augustine names Porphyry among the Platonist philosophers at *Civ.* 8.12 but reserves his highest praise for Apuleius: *Apuleius Afer extitit Platonicus nobilis* ('Apuleius Afer stands out as a celebrated Platonist'); LCL 413: 58, on which see Hagendahl 1967: 682.

named in the comparison of animal sensory abilities and human abilities are limited by their poor eyesight (4.7, *obtutus hebes*).[64] Ultimately Augustine allows that the only way that humans can predict the future is by experience. When specific circumstances occur, someone with experience may recognise the similarity between those circumstances and their previous experience, and so predict the same outcome as happened when those circumstances last arose. For Augustine, this is no different from how daemons sometimes appear to predict the future, which they are better at doing, as being older, they have more experience – but experience is not a divine characteristic.[65]

Augustine reduced daemonic divination (in part) to a unique form of eyesight, particularly impressive to humans because of our very limited ability to see things, including the future. The influence of Apuleius' arguments appears in Augustine's characterisation of daemonic vision, even as he rejects Apuleius' consideration of daemons as divine beings. This influence may be detected early in Augustine's thought and is a critical component of his *De divinatione daemonum*, some twenty years before Augustine offered a detailed rebuttal of Apuleius in *De civitate Dei*.

Conclusion

Augustine distinguished between the *ars nugatoria* of astrology and the *ars noxia* of daemonic divination, but this distinction existed within a broader recognition that both pagan modes of predicting the future relied on deceit and trickery, whether astrologers claiming to see differences that are unobservable or daemons predicting outcomes using an array of abilities, including their highly attuned sensory perception. This critique relied on the limits of human perception in two ways. As the actors who

---

[64] Apuleius, *De deo Socr.* 3.8: [*homines*] *efferarint, ut possit videri nullum animal in terris homine postremius* ('humans have grown so bestial that it could be thought that no animal on earth is lower than a human'); LCL 534: 342. Augustine uses the same adjective *hebes* to describe human sensory perception in *Ep.* 9.3: *sensus, tam hebetes.* TLL s.v. 3b lists eight examples of *hebes* used to describe human vision: Cicero, *Fin.* 4.65; Seneca, *Nat.* 1.3.7; *Herc.* frag. 653; *Ep.* 90.28; Suetonius, *Dom.* 18.1; *Ner.* 51; Livy 5.18.4; and Columella, *De re rustica* 6.6.1, in addition to Apuleius. On divergent ancient valuations of vision as a mode of perception see Chapter 25 by Robin M. Jensen, this volume.

[65] Augustine, *Div.* 5.9: *enim quia praevidet medicus quod non praevidet eius artis ignarus, ideo iam divinus habendus est?* ('For a doctor sees a future which someone ignorant of his skill does not see, and so should he be thought of as divine too?') (CSEL 41: 607). This argument is discussed by Bouton-Touboulic 2007: 27. See also Augustine, *Div.* 4.7; 6.10.

made predictions, astrologers simply did not have the observational power to note minute differences in birth. This meant that astrologers could not have the accurate data which underpinned their claims of intellectual authority. In the case of daemonic divination, the limits of human observation created a yardstick of sorts, which daemons could surpass and so make the impression that they had perceived the future, when in fact their perception of the present, combined with their other non-human features, enabled them to anticipate outcomes. In *De doctrina Christiana*, Augustine connects astrology to daemonic divination on the basis of his moral disdain for both practices (2.22.34): 'Accordingly these opinions developed from indications of events based on human presumption, should be classified to the same categories as if they were determined and agreed upon with daemons' (*quare istae quoque opiniones quibusdam rerum signis humana praesumptione institutis ad eadem illa quasi quaedam cum daemonibus pacta et conventa referendae sunt*).[66] The noun *praesumptio* underscores that actual human observation or perception does not take place; instead, divination relies on an arrogant confidence trick that misrepresents its claims as truth. Other forms of divination which Augustine describes, of a kind presumably so petty as not to need daemonic involvement, rely equally on human observation. In that case, however, the issue is not whether, for example, someone was actually observed sneezing while putting on slippers, but the total pointlessness of making and interpreting such observations as having any real bearing on the future.[67]

Augustine's argument builds on classical and Christian criticisms of astrology in ways that show Augustine thinking alongside his intellectual forebears, even as there are clear differences in emphasis and argument. Cicero's *De divinatione* offers an example of twins to support a preference for reason over perception; Augustine also uses the example of twins, selecting the biblical example of Jacob and Esau: twins who were still touching when they were born, and thus born simultaneously, but also twins who suffered a reversal in fraternal fates, as the younger brother came to usurp the position of the eldest. This enables Augustine to expand Cicero's critique, beyond a preference for reason over perception, to claim that astrology is incapable of accurate prediction. In a similar way, Augustine capitalises on Apuleius' daemonology, altering his claims so as to undermine the divine status of daemons, while drawing on the physical traits that Apuleius uses to explain daemonic sensory perception as the source of their superhuman

---

[66] Green 1996: 96.
[67] Augustine, *Doctr. chr.* 2.20.31: 'most pointless observations' (*inanissimarum observationum*).

observational powers. These arguments are enhanced by Augustine's use of Ambrose's and Basil's criticisms of the immorality and impracticality of making detailed astrological observations at a live birth. The limits of the human condition provide Augustine with an ordering principle that structures and unites these different modes of knowing the future as practices directly opposed to a Christian life.

24 | The Duplex Via: Authority and Reason at Cassiciacum

GERALD P. BOERSMA

Introduction

Augustine's three earliest writings, *Contra academicos*, *De beata vita*, and *De ordine* form a literary unit. The three Cassiciacum dialogues share a literary genre, characters, and setting. Further, each of the dialogues makes internal reference to the other two.[1] The setting of the dialogues is the fall of 386 at the bucolic villa of Augustine's friend, Verecundus, in an airy, mountainous region just outside of Milan.[2] The dialogues feature Augustine in the role of a teacher engaged in philosophical discourse with close friends and family. The only further attestation we have to this time at Cassiciacum is from the *Confessions* and the *Retractationes*. Augustine tells us that after his conversion he retreated to Cassiciacum for a time of contemplative leisure. Upon his return to Milan, before his baptism during Easter of 387, Augustine composed the dialogues.

Since one of the common variables to the dialogues is the continuity of the Christian faith with classical philosophy, I want to pursue the following question: How does Augustine understand the relation between faith and reason or, more precisely, the relation between the *auctoritas* (of Christ and of the Catholic Church) and reason?[3] Many commenters, including John O'Meara, Robert O'Connell, Olivier du Roy, and, more recently, Brian Dobell contend that in the dialogues Augustine presents authority

---

[1] In the preface to the recently published critical edition of the Cassiciacum dialogues, Therese Fuhrer and Simone Adam describe these three texts as an 'independent trilogy' (Fuhrer and Adam 2017: vii). I have followed the translations of the three dialogues in FC 1 (1948).
[2] The *Soliloquia* are often included in the Cassiciacum dialogues because Augustine penned this work at the same time in Milan. However, the *Soliloquia* are an *interior* dialogue between Augustine and his reason. Further, the common subject matter, *mise-en-scène*, and characters of the Cassiciacum dialogues are not shared with the *Soliloquia*. Brian Stock (2010) offers an excellent analysis of the significance of the distinction between the external and internal dialogue for Augustine.
[3] For the significance of the terms 'authority' and 'reason' in Augustine's theology, and especially for the role they play in his early thought, see Lütcke 1986–1994: 498–510; Catapano 1986–: 1069–84.

and reason as two distinct paths of ascent to God. The path of authority is the safe and secure road now made available to all through Christian revelation. This path teaches moral excellence and promises happiness and wisdom in the life to come. The path of reason is a more treacherous (but rewarding) road accessible only to the few. This path promises happiness and wisdom already in this life through the study of the liberal arts and philosophy. I disagree with this reading. My contention is that in the dialogues, Augustine does not conceive of authority and reason as two diverse paths of ascent, but as distinct elements that constitute one integrated path of ascent. Authority and reason are coordinate means of ascent to wisdom and happiness (*Ord.* 2.5.16; 2.9.26).[4] I will first analyse how Augustine defines these two terms at Cassiciacum. I will then consider the two main reasons why many commentators hold that authority and reason represent two distinct paths of ascent. Third, I will argue that authority and reason operate dialectically, that is, while they can be characterised as opposing forces, authority and reason ultimately operate in tandem to purify and enlighten the soul for the ascent to God. Finally, I will argue that the integrated, dialectical relation of authority and reason comes to the fore most clearly when we consider the responsibility of reason to offer an *intellectus fidei*, an intellectual account of the mysteries delivered by authority.

The focus of this volume – Christian epistemology – is a mainstay of Augustine's long literary career. Faith's 'ways of knowing' occupy much of Augustine's intellectual landscape. 'Ordering knowledge' from distinct sources – philosophy and revelation, reason and authority – constantly exercise Augustine's thought. In part, this fascination is born out of Augustine's own intellectual experience: his long dalliance with the Manicheans and the decisive intellectual breakthrough occasioned by his encounter with Platonic literature. Here I engage Augustine's earliest writings, which already evince his conviction that faith is a type of knowing, that reason necessarily avails itself of faith, and that believing involves thinking. Augustine is a significant *theological* voice in the conversation devoted to Christian epistemology in late antiquity. His decisive contributions reverberate through the Christian tradition, reaching a certain apogee in the diverse scholastic articulations of the Augustinian principle, *crede ut intellegas*. The tension between the Christian theological imperative that truth is (at least in theory) accessible to all and the consensus that dominated the

---

[4] My reading of the dialogues is more proximate to those who recognise a convergence between authority and reason already at Cassiciacum: Holte 1962: 303–28; Mandouze 1968: 266–71; van Fleteren 1973; Harrison 2006: 67–73.

refined 'epistemic schemes' of the late antique intellectual world, namely, that eternal truth and philosophical wisdom are the preserve of an intellectual elite, is a central focus of this volume. Augustine's transposition of the Platonic distinction between the few and the many into a Christian key (a central theme in this chapter) is one striking example of Christian epistemology grappling with its diverse intellectual inheritances.

Authority and Reason Defined

The dialogues present authority as a person in whom one can invest trust for life's moral and intellectual direction.[5] Authority opens the door to hidden truth (*Ord.* 2.9.27) and lays the ground for reason. In a certain respect, then, ascent to wisdom and happiness is a movement from the cradle of authority (*auctoritatis cunabula*) to a grasp of reason itself (*ipsa ratio*) (*Ord.* 2.9.26). Nevertheless, as we will see, from stem to stern, authority and reason are complementary features of the ascent to God. A fundamental demarcation obtains between divine and human authority (*Ord.* 2.9.27). While the 'authority of upright men' is generally a good guide for the uneducated (*Ord.* 2.9.26), it remains fallible and not always or altogether trustworthy (*Ord.* 2.9.27). The only human *auctoritates* mentioned in the dialogues are philosophers; they epitomise 'the authority of our ancestors' (*Acad.* 1.3.7). Augustine references 'Plato, Socrates and all the other ancients' (*Acad.* 2.6.14; 3.18.41). Cicero also appears frequently as a 'yoke' and 'weight' of authority (*Acad.* 1.3.9; 1.9.24; 2.10.24; 3.7.14). Alypius piously bows his head to the authority of the eminent Sceptic philosophers (*Acad.* 2.13.29). But transcending all human authority is the divine *intellectus*, sent to assume a human body and now made present in the sacraments (*Acad.* 3.19.42; *Ord.* 2.9.27). No authority is more powerful than that of Christ (*Acad.* 3.20.43). In *De beata vita*, Augustine contrasts 'the authority of those who have given us the tradition of the divine mysteries' with the human authority that shines in the books of the Platonists (*Beat.* 1.4). Divine authority unambiguously attests that the Son of God is eternal wisdom, who is also truly God (*profecto deus*) (*Beat.* 4.34).

Three distinct uses of 'reason' are in play at Cassiciacum. First, the cosmic order displays reason – it is 'reasonable' (*rationabile*) (*Acad.* 1.1.1; *Ord.*

---

[5] Augustine is heir to a Latin philosophical tradition that considers the relation between reason and authority. Karl-Heinrich Lütcke has pointed to this theme in both Cicero and Seneca (Lütcke 1968: 45–46).

1.1.2; 2.11.31). Second, reason distinguishes the human person from the beasts; man is 'rational' (*rationalis*) (*Acad.* 1.7.20; *Ord.* 2.19.49). Finally, eternal reason (*ratio*) orders and guides all things. Augustine proposes a distinction between *rationalis* (referring to creatures possessing the faculty of reasoning) and *rationabile*, that which is done 'according to reason':[6]

> We could call these baths or our discourse *reasonable* (*rationabiles*); but him who constructs the baths, or ourselves who are now discoursing, we could term *rational* (*rationales*). Reason, then, proceeds from a rational soul (*anima rationali*) into reasonable things (*rationabilia*) which are done or spoken. (*Ord.* 2.11.31)

The three senses of the term 'reason' are construed hierarchically. It is by attending to the order and reason in the cosmos (*rationabile*) that the rational creature (*rationalis*) can ascend to eternal *ratio*. Rational creatures (*rationales*) are able to perceive cosmic reason and can delight in this order. Beyond what the senses perceive, they can apprehend 'beauteous reason (*pulchritudo rationis*) signalling something' (*Ord.* 1.8.25). Rational creatures (*rationales*) are capable of apprehending 'another Reason (*alia ratione*) that rules over all things from on high' (*Ord.* 1.8.25). Few, however, perceive this divine and deeply hidden reason (*occultissima ratio*) (*Ord.* 2.7.24).

Augustine's definition of reason is revealing: 'Reason is a movement of mind (*mentis motio*) capable of distinguishing and connecting the things that are learned' (*Ord.* 2.11.30). Reason is a dynamic, teleologically ordered movement (*motio*) that proceeds upwards, by way of distinctions and connections – rung by rung – to discern the intelligibility of the cosmos.[7] It proceeds from discerning order in the material cosmos to an understanding of the immaterial reason that orders all things. Reason's proper activity is to offer intellectual demonstrations about truth (*ratio demonstrauit*) (*Beat.* 2.14; 3.17; 3.21; 4.23; 4.29; 4.33; *Ord.* 7.22). The itinerary of the mind's motion (the cognitive content of which is filled in by the liberal arts) promises to disclose, at its culmination, the immaterial reason that animates the material cosmos while itself wholly transcending all things. But this is a rare achievement: 'To this knowledge, few are able to arrive in this life; even after this life, no one can exceed it' (*Ord.* 2.9.26). Reason's

---

[6] *Ord.* 2.11.31: *nam rationale esse dixerunt, quod ratione uteretur uel uti posset, rationabile autem, quod ratione factum esset aut dictum.*

[7] John O'Meara captures the dynamic character of *ratio* operative in the dialogues: '*Ratio* in Augustine's early *Dialogues* stands for the discursive function of the *mens* (i.e., *ratio* in the strictest sense), or for the completed act of that function (i.e., *intellectus*) or, by a natural transference for the truths attained or attainable by such function. That is to say, *ratio* is the process of the fullest human intellectual perception as Augustine conceived it, and is sometimes used also for the truths perceived' (O'Meara 1951: 344). See also du Roy 1966: 130–42.

full mental motion is seldom realised. Among the few who have leisure and talent, reason is often squandered and used to obtain only more of what is fleeting and effervescent, that is to say, reason is used for a life *least* according to reason. Few people desire to penetrate the nature and quality of reason itself (*Ord.* 2.11.30).

Rationality and mortality are the two elements punctuating the classical definition of the human person.[8] These two elements are construed hierarchically. That which is rational aspires 'up' to the transcendent and the eternal, to the stability of being itself, while that which is mortal inclines 'down' to the effervescent and transient, to the world of becoming. Further, moral hues colour the predicates 'rational' and 'mortal' – they become epithets for the character of one's life. By living 'according to reason', man follows that in him which is immortal and furnishes a way of escape from the mortal nature into which he has fallen.[9] As such, reason, the highest part of the soul, should direct and govern the body (*Acad.* 1.2.5). Augustine writes,

Just as the soul's upward movement (*progressus animae*) has fallen down (*lapsus*) to the things that are mortal, so ought its return be to reason. By the one term, *rational*, man is distinguished from the brute animals; by the other term, *mortal*, he is distinguished from God. Therefore, unless it holds fast to the rational element, it will be a beast; unless it turns aside from the mortal element, it will not be divine. (*Ord.* 2.11.31; trans. altered)

At Cassiciacum, Augustine and his entourage aspire to live a life *secundum rationem* – a phrase used four times (*Acad.* 1.3.9; 1.4.1; 1.4.12; 1.9.24). Reason is what is highest in the human person, and to live according to reason is to set oneself on a path towards union with eternal Reason. Augustine exclaims with enthusiasm, 'This is the life we are living!' (*vitam nos vivamus*) (*Ord.* 1.2.4). Licentius offers an enticing description of this philosophical life:

He is happy, because, to the utmost of his power, he is extricating himself from the entanglements of the body and devoting himself to sheer introspection; because he is not allowing himself to be torn asunder by inordinate desires, but always tranquilly directing his mind towards itself and towards God; and because he is doing all this in order to make a thoroughly good use of reason (*ratione perfruatur*) at the present time ... so that on the last day of his life he may be found prepared for what he has been longing to obtain. (*Acad.* 1.8.23)

---

[8] *Homo est animal rationale mortale* (*Ord.* 2.11.31). See Aristotle, *Top.* 132b2; Sextus Empiricus, *Pyr.* 2, 25; Cicero, *Luc.* 7, 21.
[9] I am agnostic about the fraught question of whether the 'fall of the soul' into a mortal nature should be understood in Plotinian terms or within the African theological tradition of original sin.

Living the philosophical life – a life directed by reason (*Ord.* 5.16) – is a happy mortal life that prepares one for immortal happiness. Reason promises a rich harvest (*Ord.* 1.24) to those who follow the course she charts (*ratione institutus cursus*) (*Beat.* 1.1.1).

Authority and Reason: Two Paths?

Many scholars, including John O'Meara, Robert O'Connell, and Olivier du Roy, maintain that the distinction between authority and reason marks a foundational structural demarcation in Augustine's early thought, a hermeneutical fault line for thinking through all major theological and philosophical questions. These commentators argue that, in the dialogues, Augustine proposes two distinct and independent paths of salvation: the path of authority safely travelled by the many and the path of reason arduously traversed by the few. Only after Augustine's return to Africa would he come to have less confidence in the ability of reason to ascend to God. His increasing exposure to the theological tradition, his deliberate reading of scripture, and the universality of his pastoral mandate would have led Augustine to abandon the *duplex via* and, instead, to prioritise the starting point of faith, later expressed in the dictum *crede ut intelligas*.[10]

Two arguments seem to give credence to the position that reason and authority represent two distinct paths of ascent in the dialogues. First, Augustine seems to adopt the Platonic distinction between the 'few' and the 'many' without emendation. For Plato, only the few are capable of living the philosophical life, of coming to know truth, and thereby achieving a degree of happiness and wisdom. The many are consigned to run after shadows, living only for what is effervescent.[11] Augustine's Platonic inheritance is quite content to consign the many to a life that is less than fully human. The two most well-known images of the *Republic* – the analogy of the cave and of the divided line – suggest that the distinction between the few and the many is a distinction predicated on the ability to distinguish between the intelligible and the sensible and to live according to that

---

[10] Cf. O'Meara 1951: 344–46; O'Connell 1968: 236–57; du Roy 1966: 126–30. More recently, Brian Dobell also followed this scholarly consensus. In fact, he structures his entire book into two parts corresponding to what he understands to be the two distinct paths of salvation outlined in Augustine's early writings, namely, the way of authority for the many and the way of reason for the few. He claims, 'Neither way is necessary, and both ways are individually sufficient, for salvation' (Dobell 2009: 27).

[11] Cf. *Resp.* 493e–494a; *Apol.* 25b.

knowledge.[12] The many do not live according to what is highest in them but contend about shadows projected on a cave wall.

What Augustine terms the *duplex via* can seem to map neatly onto the Platonic distinction between the 'few' and the 'many'. A number of texts in the dialogues might lead one to the conclusion that Augustine adopts this Platonic distinction *tout court*:

> When the obscurity of things perplexes us, we follow a twofold path (*duplex via*): reason (*rationem*), or at least, authority (*auctoritatem*). Philosophy sends forth reason, and it frees scarcely a few. (*Ord.* 2.5.16)
>
> The authority of upright men seems to be the safer guide for the uninstructed multitude, reason is better adapted for the educated. (*Ord.* 2.9.26)

Moreover, in the hortatory protreptic at the outset of each dialogue, Augustine makes clear that only the few are able to follow the path of philosophy that leads to wisdom, happiness, and eternity. After all, such a life requires leisure (*otium*) and intellectual talent (*ingenium*), both of which are not only in short supply, but wholly serendipitous – they are *fortuna*'s favour.[13] Many do not have the opportunity or talent for formal instruction in the liberal arts. They will have to be 'content to follow authority alone' (*sola auctoritate contenti*) (*Ord.* 2.9.26). Their vocation is to live a morally upright life that will have its reward after death when they 'will be liberated with greater facility ... as they have lived the more virtuously' (*Ord.* 2.9.26). Augustine does (perhaps grudgingly) acknowledge that those, like his mother, who do not aspire to master the liberal arts but faithfully trust divine authority have what is sufficient to achieve happiness. Nevertheless, speaking for himself, he remarks, 'I know not how I could call them happy as long they live among men' (*Ord.* 2.9.26).[14]

---

[12] *Resp.* 509d–520e.

[13] Augustine makes a lot of Lady Fortune (*fortuna*) in the Cassiciacum dialogues. Her ministrations lead some to the tranquil life of philosophy, while most others thrash about in a turbid life of ignorance, vice, and indulgence. For classical thought, *fortuna* can denote either prosperity or misfortune, but the decisive point is that her designs lie beyond human agency. Augustine makes mention of *fortuna* forty times in the dialogues. Outside of the dialogues, however, *fortuna* receives little attention in Augustine's corpus.

[14] Cf. *Retract.* 1.3.2. Carol Harrison considers this line 'to be more a statement of personal opinion than anything else' (2006: 45). Augustine's *own* mind, so eager to comprehend and grasp the contents of the faith, could not stomach the idea of resting content with faith, but he recognised that the faith itself sanctioned the legitimacy of this posture. Harrison writes, 'How can anyone be content simply to believe, to accept authority, and not desire to know and grasp the truth which they have been taught and which they worship? Augustine the intellectual, and Augustine the former Manichee, would find this incomprehensible. But Augustine the Christian is also bound to acknowledge the pre-eminent authority of the Christian faith' (2006: 46).

Robert O'Connell's treatment of the distinction between the few and the many is representative:

> Augustine's whole discussion of faith and reason pivots on a distinction between the 'many' and the 'few'. Not all are capable of pursuing the arduous upward way through the study of the liberal disciplines. Not all, in other words, are candidates for the way of 'reason' … The way of 'authority', then, is the indispensable way for the 'many', the 'unlearned', for those both 'uninstructed' and, indeed, incapable of the instruction demanded by the way of reason.[15]

O'Connell chafes at the 'intellectualism of [the] Plotinian way of salvation' exhibited in these early works, which seems to consign the many to plodding obediently after authority, reserving the intellectual life and the pursuit of truth to the few.[16] What is missing in this analysis, however, is the recognition that Augustine radically reconfigures this Platonic division. There are no longer two classes of people: the few who achieve wisdom and happiness and the many who flit about, getting and spending, carousing and copulating. Instead, all are called to transcend the cave; all are able to possess wisdom and happiness.[17] The division between the few and the many is no longer a distinction of natures, demarcating two types of people.

Admittedly, Augustine shares with the broader ethos of Platonic thought a steely realism, convinced that most are simply intellectually unfit for the curriculum of the liberal arts that lead to the philosophical life. Indulgence (*piger*), a life of business (*negotium*) that affords no time for leisure, or simply a lack of intellectual aptitude for the rigours of study (*durum ad discendum*) entail that most are not cut out for reason's rigorous regime as Augustine outlines it in *De ordine* (*Ord.* 2.5.15). But Augustine does not gainsay the path of faith. Faith is not, as it is in the Platonic lexicon, second-rate knowledge or opinion (*doxa*) but is divine and authoritative. To trust divine authority (ecclesially mediated) for what one cannot himself demonstrate is not a cause of ignominy:

> Let them provide for themselves a stronghold of faith (*fidei praesidia*), so that He, who suffers no one that rightly believes in Him through the mysteries (*per mysteria*

---

[15] O'Connell 1968: 248–49.   [16] O'Connell 1968: 227.

[17] Little has been written on Augustine's adoption and transposition of the Platonic distinction between the few and the many. Pierre Manent is an important exception: 'Christianity's point of impact is the separation between the few and the many. What Christianity attacks is not social or political inequality but the pertinence of the distinction between the few and the many, the philosopher and the nonphilosopher, with regard to the capacity to attain or receive the truth' (2013: 272). See also Harmon 2019.

bene credentem) to perish, may by this bond (*vinculo*) draw them to Himself and free them from those dreadful, entangling evils. (*Ord.* 2.5.15)

It remains the case that few intentionally and wholly devote their lives to contemplative speculation about divine realities, and most are content to follow authority. Nevertheless, Augustine's treatment of authority and reason does not map seamlessly onto the distinction between the few and the many. As I will argue shortly, this schema fails to do justice to the interrelated character of authority and reason in the dialogues. For Augustine, authority is reasonable and subject to rational interrogation. And, on the other side of the coin, the object of reason's investigation is dependent on authority, an authority that never becomes supererogatory. One never graduates beyond authority into a type of autonomous reason.

The second argument often advanced in defence of the claim that reason and authority represent two distinct paths of ascent at Cassiciacum is that Augustine seems to maintain the intrinsic superiority of reason over authority. Only reason can achieve, *already in this life*, wisdom and happiness, whereas authority promises its inductees wisdom and happiness in the life to come.[18] Again, Robert O'Connell is representative:

Augustine's dialogues at Cassiciacum show him seriously entertaining the possibility that this end is attainable even during 'this life', even while the soul 'bore the body': attainable, not only for a moment here and there, but in a semipermanent way. Even while 'in' the body, the soul could become so purified of bodily desires, so liberated from bodily preoccupations, that it could enter this circle of lasting joy, the 'happy life'.[19]

The man whose mind has been sharpened, his inner eye strengthened, 'comprehends' at length the triadic divinity of Reason, Intellect, and even 'what, beyond all things, is the Source of all things' ... Heaven can be dwelt in even now; even in the body, the soul can achieve effective disincarnation, unabating contemplation, unbroken happiness.[20]

That, at Cassiciacum, Augustine believed the life of reason can yield happiness and wisdom seems incontestable. Those who outgrow the 'cradle of authority' (*auctoritatis cunabula*) and lay hold of 'reason itself' (*ipsa*

---

[18] The majority of Augustine scholars take it as axiomatic that, at Cassiciacum, Augustine held the possibility of beatitude to be a distinct possibility *in via*. Van Fleteren writes, 'In the Cassiciacum dialogues, the texts are numerous and the evidence indisputable that Augustine thought that man could reach such a vision in this life' (van Fleteren 1977: 9). See also Teske 1994: 289–90; Dobell 2009: 65, 121, 198, 223. An important exception in this respect is Harrison 2006: 63–66.
[19] O'Connell 1968: 236.   [20] O'Connell 1968: 253.

ratio) achieve something intrinsically more noble than what authority can deliver in this life. Reason discloses a personal intellectual apprehension of the highest reality; the few can see for themselves that which the many are consigned to believe in faith. The concluding paragraph of *De beata vita* holds out the transcendent goal at which reason aims: 'This, then, is the full satisfaction of souls (*satietas animorum*), this is the happy life (*beata vita*): to recognise piously and completely the One through whom you are led into the truth, that nature of the truth you enjoy, and the bond that connects you with the supreme measure' (*Beat.* 35).[21] Nevertheless, the dialogue concludes with the aspirants 'not yet wise and happy' (*Beat.* 35). Reason's grasp of divine truth should not be equated with beatitude. Despite the soaring rhetoric about the philosophical life, the role of reason remains *preparatory* for beatitude. Augustine's early optimism regarding the ability of the liberal arts and philosophy to lay hold of an intellectual vision of the truth should not be confused with the stability and eternity of the *visio dei*.[22]

In *De ordine*, Augustine encourages Licentius to study the *disciplinae* precisely because they equip the soul to embrace truth and live the happy life (*beata vita*) (*Ord.* 1.8.24). But this happy, philosophical life is distinct from eternal life, which the dialogues make clear is realised only when the soul has escaped the body. The goal of the philosophical life – to 'see God' (*Deum videre*) (*Ord.* 2.19.51) – can be realised only after death. Drawing on the cadence of the *Symposium* and *Enn.* 1.6, Augustine exclaims

What kind of eyes those shall be! How pure! How beautiful! How powerful! How constant! How serene! How blessed! And what is that which they can see! What is it? I ask. What should we surmise? ... I shall say no more, except that to us is promised a vision of beauty – the beauty through whose imitation all other things are beautiful, and by comparison with which all other things are unsightly. (*Ord.* 2.19.51)

The vision of beauty is an eschatological hope for which the exercise of reason is preparatory. Although some passages in Augustine's early corpus could be read to argue that the vision of God can be possessed even

---

[21] There is almost certainly a trinitarian referent entailed in the description of the truth, the bond, and the supreme measure. See du Roy 1966: 154–65.

[22] If Augustine held that the stability and eternity of the *visio dei* obtains for some in this life, one would expect more vigorous censure of this position in *Retract*. In fact, Augustine only remarks that he is displeased to have said that happiness is found in the mind alone and that the happy life consists, rather, in an immortal body subject to the spirit (*Retract.* 1.2.1). The principle reprimand of *De ordine* in *Retract.* is of the undue value afforded the liberal arts (*Retract.* 1.3.2–3).

in via (*Beat.* 35; *Ord.* 1.8.24; *Solil.* 1.6.12), this does not comport with the overall sense of his early theology that beatitude – eternal life – is possible only after death. Admittedly, reason has an objective pre-eminence over authority because of its capacity to discern *already in this life* the order and providence of God that faith can only believe. But this does not entail that reason affords a direct, unmediated, and unchanging simple vision of God *in via*. If at Cassiciacum (and perhaps for a period thereafter) Augustine seems to hold that happiness – the intellectual vision of God – lies within the reach of the few, it is an intellectual perception in the order of an *intellectus fidei*, an intellectual grasp of divine realities that most are required to accept on authority.

The neat partition between the few who follow reason and the many consigned to trust authority is, in fact, more complicated. It does not neatly map onto the Platonic distinction between the few and the many. Nor does Augustine imagine that unaided reason can ascend to the beatific vision in this life.

Purification and Paedagogy

Authority and reason are, in fact, already thoroughly integrated at Cassiciacum, and the principle *crede ut intelligas* is already operative to a much greater extent than many commentators admit. In the dialogues, authority and reason intersect and overlap. If reason has an objective priority to authority in that it enables its inductee, already in this life, to obtain happiness and wisdom in knowing divine truth, authority has a relative priority in the temporal process of coming to learn. Diligent students who aspire to the philosophical life, Augustine explains, are 'of necessity led in a twofold manner: by authority and by reason. In point of time, authority is first; in order of reality, reason is prior (*tempore auctoritas, re autem ratio prior est*). What takes precedence in operation is one thing; what is more highly prized as an object of desire is something else' (*Ord.* 2.9.26). The path of reason begins with education, which inescapably requires an initial disposition of trust in authority. Augustine's long foray against the Sceptics in *Contra academicos* makes clear that methodological scepticism is an impossible starting point on the path of reason. Without the quickening of faith extended by trust in authority, the soul finds itself in a rut, the tyres are spinning, reason is unable to gain any traction to ascend. The life of reason requires the student first to be docile (*docilis*) to instruction: 'For those who seek to learn great and hidden truths authority alone opens the door' (*Ord.* 2.9.26). Thus, while reason has an objective priority (*re ... prior est*), authority takes temporal precedent.

Nevertheless, the chronological priority of authority is not absolute. Augustine admits that authority entails an initial judgement both in the determination that such belief is reasonable and in the determination of *which* authority to trust.[23] (There are good teachers, authorities worthy of trust; as well as bad teachers, sophists, and blowhards. The conundrum is that reason – even before it is fully formed – must judge who is a trustworthy authority (*Ord.* 2.9.26).)[24] In this respect, reason and authority are always coextensive: If I extend trust in an authority, I believe that to be reasonable, and when I reason, an appeal to authority is necessarily present. Some hold that reason and authority mark successive stages in the soul's ascent, such that a person graduates from the 'cradle of authority' to 'reason itself' (*Ord.* 2.9.26).[25] More accurate, I believe, is the contention that authority and reason dialectically constitute each other in a type of circular logic, each intersecting and overlapping with the other. We are dealing with a chicken and egg problem. Van Fleteren is closer to the mark when he describes the *duplex via* as 'one bipartite way'.[26] Authority and reason are not two distinct, parallel paths of ascent, but two lanes of the same road. While they can be distinguished, they function inseparably.

The ascent of the soul – the grand motif that fuels Augustine's early writings – palpably demonstrates the dialectical character of authority and reason, that is to say, these two seemingly antinomous realities function synchronically. They operate jointly in effecting moral purification and pedagogical instruction, thereby equipping the soul with the requisite volitional and intellectual aptitude for the ascent.

---

[23] Much later Augustine will articulate the omnipresence of reason in faith's assent: 'Who does not see that thinking comes before believing? No one, of course, believes anything unless he first thought that it should be believed ... In fact, the very act of believing is nothing other than to think with assent. Not everyone, after all, who thinks believes, for many think in order not to believe. But everyone who believes thinks, and a believer thinks when believing and, in thinking, believes' (Augustine, *Praed.* 2.5, trans. Teske, WSA 1/26: 151).

[24] This is a species of 'Meno's Paradox' (*Meno* 80d–e), in which Plato questions whether it is possible to learn anything new: '[A] man cannot search either for what he knows or for what he does not know[.] He cannot search for what he knows – since he knows it, there is no need to search – nor for what he does not know, for he does not know what to look for' (Plato, *Meno* 80e, trans. Grube).

[25] Dobell and Lütcke maintain that authority and reason represent distinct stages in the soul's ascent. See Dobell 2009: 49; Lütcke 1968: 64–65.

[26] Van Fleteren 1973: 48.

Moral Purification

The philosophical life at which the community at Cassiciacum is aiming is one of both intellectual and moral formation. This is a repeated emphasis: 'This science (*disciplina*) imposes a twofold order (*geminum ordinem*) of procedure on those who desire to know it, of which one part pertains to the regulating of life, and the other pertains to the directing of studies (*una pars vitae, altera eruditionis*)' (*Ord.* 2.8.25). Throughout the dialogues, but especially in the protreptic – the direct address at their outset – Augustine urges his reader to a moral conversion towards the philosophical life.[27] Such hortatory enjoinders (*exhortatio*) stand firmly in the rhetorical tradition of Cicero's *Hortensius* and Aristotle's *Protrepticus*.[28] Moral purification is an essential feature of the exercise of reason; the sublime heights of reason are accessible only to him who 'lives well, prays well, studies well' (*Ord.* 2.19.51). As Carol Harrison remarks, for Augustine and the broader classical philosophical tradition, the practice of reason is never simply an intellectual exercise:

> We must not forget that this ascent is not just a rational purification, but also, as in Neoplatonism, a moral one. The two are inextricable: the soul can be in a position to contemplate the truth only if it is pure and virtuous. Progress in the truth is at the same time a purgation of the soul, a training in virtue, away from involvement in temporal, mutable things and towards eternal, immutable truth ... Like the classical sage, the Christian must observe the truth in a particular mode of life in order to seek it by reason.[29]

The submission of the intellect to the order of the cosmos through study concomitantly effects moral order in the soul. The law of God, recognised in the created order, is 'transcribed' onto the souls of the wise:

> It is not by faith alone, but by trustworthy reason, that the soul leads itself little by little to most virtuous habits and the perfect life. For to the soul that diligently considers the nature and the power of numbers, it will appear manifestly unfitting and most deplorable that it should write a rhythmic line and play the harp by virtue of this knowledge and that its life and very self – which is the soul – should nevertheless follow a crooked path and, under the domination of lust, be out of tune by the clangor of shameful vices. (*Ord.* 2.19.51)

The increased recognition of external order in the cosmos should inculcate attention to the order of one's soul. The *disciplina* of contemplating the divine order serves not only to advance understanding but also to ennoble one's manner of life (*ut tanto se sciant vivere melius tantoque sublimius*, *Ord.* 2.8.25).

---

[27] Doignon 1986: 21–37.   [28] See Schlapbach 2003: 7.   [29] Harrison 2006: 44.

From his earliest writings, however, Augustine is attentive to both the inability of reason to fully purify its devotees (much less the many) and the attendant pride that lurks behind this aspiration. Divine authority complements and extends the moral purification effected by reason. The incarnation and its extension in the sacramental economy extends moral purification to all. The breadth of its purifying power to 'liberate' (*liberant*) the many completes and broadens what reason does for the few (*Ord.* 2.5.16). The contrast between the *ascent* of reason and the *descent* of divine authority is equally a contrast between pride and humility. This antinomy, first presented in the dialogues, subsequently becomes a mainstay of Augustine's writings (e.g., *Conf.* 7; *Civ.* 10). The universal moral purification made possible by the declension of the divine *intellectus* into a human body is the supreme example of divine humility (*clementia*).[30] Already in the dialogues, Augustine criticises the pride of autonomous reason that would seek to ascend independent from the descent of divine authority. Augustine writes,

> Great, indeed, though it be that so great a God has for our sake (*propter nos*) deigned to assume and activate (*assumere atque agere*) a body of our own kind (*nostri generis corpus*), yet the more lowly it appears, so much the more is it replete with clemency (*clementia*) and the farther and wider remote from a certain characteristic pride of ingenious men. (*Ord.* 2.5.16, trans. altered)
>
> By deeds (*factis*) [divine authority] shows its power; by humility, its clemency (*clementia*); by commandment (*praeceptione*), its nature. And all this is being delivered (*traduntur*) to us so distinctly and steadily by the sacred rites (*sacris*) into which we are being initiated: therein the life of good men is most easily purified, not indeed by the circumlocution of disputation, but by the authority of the mysteries (*mysteriorum auctoritate purgatur*). (*Ord.* 2.9.27, trans. altered)

Few are able to live the contemplative life, and it is not at all clear that such a life can be lived stably nor that it is equivalent to eternal life. As such, the mysteries communicate divine authority to *all*, purifying through effective words (*factis*) and deeds (*praeceptione*). Divine authority purifies its followers through sacramental rites with a power and efficacy absent from the purification philosophy promises.[31] Already in the dialogues there is a subtle censure of the pride that lurks in the corridors of philosophy that would reject the descent of divine *clementia* to the many and the possibility

---

[30] Divine *clementia* is the *ratio* for the incarnation in each of three passages that explicitly treat the incarnation at Cassiciacum (*Ord.* 2.5.16; 2.9.27; *Acad.* 3.19.42).

[31] The criticism of philosophy's inability to purify its inductees perhaps gives weight to the contention that Augustine's early works already exhibit an anti-Porphyrian polemic. See Theiler 1933; Hadot 1960; O'Meara 1969.

of universal purification. The descent of divine authority completes and extends the moral purification that constitutes an inextricable part of classical philosophical life.

Intellectual Pedagogy

The retreat at Cassiciacum is described as *schola nostra*, and Augustine serves as the *magister* of the gathered philosophical colloquy.[32] *De ordine* offers Augustine's most detailed précis of the ideal liberal arts curriculum. The goal of this sequence of study is to familiarise the soul with immaterial and eternal realities; it is to train the mind in the power of abstraction.[33] The curriculum should aid the inductee in his ascent from corporeal realities to incorporeal. Carol Harrison explains that, in *De ordine*, the liberal arts effect an 'inward turn and ascent, as they facilitate the movement from multiplicity to unity, from temporal fragmentation to eternal simplicity and truth'.[34] The structure of learning corresponds to the structure of the universe. Attending to the order of study is vital if one is to apprehend the order of the universe.[35] Beginning with the temporal, particular, and material, one ascends to the eternal, universal, and immaterial. As Augustine explains, 'Now in music, in geometry, in the movements of the stars, in the fixed ratios of numbers, order reigns (*ordo dominatur*) in such a manner that if one desires to see its source (*fontem*) and its very shrine (*penetrale*), so to speak, he either finds in these, or he is unerringly led to it through them' (*Ord.* 2.5.14).[36] The liberal disciplines disclose *rationes* that

---

[32] As Philip Cary writes, 'The Cassiciacum Dialogues are paedagogical in focus. Like Plato's Socratic dialogues (and interestingly, unlike Cicero's philosophical dialogues), the nature of teaching and learning is near the center of attention here, not only as a topic of conversation but as a matter for drama. The Cassiciacum Dialogues do not just talk about the search for wisdom and truth; they dramatize it' (1998: 142).

[33] There is much written on the classical tradition of the liberal arts and Augustine's place in that tradition. The best entry remains Marrou 1938: 187–327.

[34] *Retract.* 1.3. Cf. Harrison 2006: 43.

[35] Harrison underscores that the disciplines are not arbitrary, 'but a means of expressing and attaining the truth from which they derive: God is unity, order, harmony, simplicity, the archetype and source of the truth which informs the disciplines, and to which they lead. Since God is eternal truth, the exercise of reason, the highest part of the soul, is less a matter of rational exercise and argument as a religious and mystical quest for self-knowledge and knowledge of God' (2006: 43).

[36] Lewis Ayres notes the Platonising orchestration of the liberal arts: 'In clearly Platonist fashion, the Augustine of the *De ordine* insists that the *artes* find their unity in reason's uncovering of the harmonic and numerical form of all that enables an ascent towards contemplation, and that dialectic is a skill which attends to the order and structure of reality itself' (2010: 126). On

govern all things and lead the student up to the eternal *ratio* itself in which all finite *rationes* participate.[37]

The formal character of the liberal disciplines is the perception of the order and reason inscribed in the material universe. Augustine identifies this intelligible order with number (*numerus*) that pervades all things. The purpose of these studies is to ascend from that order to the eternal reason that governs all things:

> In all these branches of study (*disciplinis*), therefore, all things (*omnia*) were being presented to reason as numerically proportioned (*numerosa*). And they were all the more clearly visible in those dimensions which reason, by reflection and contemplation, beheld as most true; but it used to recall rather the shadows and vestiges of those dimensions in the things that are perceived by the senses. (*Ord.* 2.15.43)

The ascent through the liberal arts trains reason to apprehend the immaterial order (*numerus*) that animates perceptible reality. Through the *liberales disciplinae*, reason learns to judge the sensible and material according to an immaterial standard (*numeri*), which it recognises as governing the 'shadows and vestiges' of the physical order. The liberal arts are propaedeutic to a (Platonic) philosophical conception of the 'simple, true and certain unity of all things' (*Ord.* 2.16.44). The inductee transcends simple faith, now apprehending divine realties 'not merely as truths to be believed, but also as matters to be contemplated, understood and retained' (*Ord.* 2.16.44).

Study of the *disciplinae* remains the preserve of the few, those of 'good talent and leisure', who have given themselves fully to study.[38] Augustine soberly reminds that reason's path 'is very difficult except for some very gifted person who even from boyhood has earnestly and constantly applied himself' (*Ord.* 2.16.44). Moreover, even the few who ascend to a contemplative vision of simple unity frequently lapse from the heights of philosophical contemplation back to this sullied flesh. Here, where reason proves weak or faltering, divine authority intercedes and shores up reason's wings. The divine *intellectus* comes in a fleshly mode to the fleshly minded; he willingly debases (*depresserit*) himself to become an object of sense precisely so that all can learn to

---

the development of the liberal arts in the later Latin tradition, see Chapter 35 by John Magee (this volume) on Boethius and Cassiodorus; for an earlier Christian attempt to order the various disciplines, see Chapter 5 by Matyáš Havrda (this volume) on Clement of Alexandria.

[37] Ryan Topping remarks, 'Through these arts we are able to grasp the rationality immanent within the world ... In Augustine's hand the liberal curriculum has become a microcosm of the order and rationality present within creation' (2012: 132–33).

[38] *Ord.* 2.7.24; 2.9.26; 2.16.44; *Mus.* 6.1.1.

detach themselves from things of sense and ascend to immaterial and eternal truth. Augustine writes,

> We must therefore, accept as divine that authority which not only exceeds human power in its outward manifestations (*sensibilibus signis*), but also, in the very act of leading a man onward (*ipsum hominem agens*), shows him to what extent it has debased (*depresserit*) itself for his sake and bids him not to be confined to the senses, to which indeed those things seem wondrous, but to soar upward to the intellect (*ad intellectum evolare*). At the same time it shows him what great things it is able to do, and why it does them, and how little importance it attaches to them. (*Ord.* 2.9.27, trans. altered)

In this text and in the passages quoted above (*Ord.* 2.5.16; 2.9.27), we have a clear expression of the pedagogical christology that marks Augustine's early theology of the incarnation. The material and sensible signs of the Incarnate Christ become for the many a *via* of ascent to immaterial truth.[39] In its most epigrammatic form, the purpose of the incarnation is to 'rise through what is human to what is divine'.[40] Divine pedagogy finds its fullest expression in the incarnation, in which divine authority expresses itself in sensible signs (*sensibilibus signis*) consisting of words (*praeceptione*) and deeds (*factis*). These signs are a divine accommodation (*clementia*) to meet the many in their intellectual weakness and spiritual immaturity. However, one ought not to rest in amazement at the 'outward manifestation' of the incarnation. This divine sign (like all signs) is penultimate; the sensible is to be used only to ascend to the intelligible.[41] The sacramental mysteries attest to this same principle, or, more accurately, the sensible order of the incarnation is extended (*traduntur*) into the sacramental economy. Like the incarnation, the sacraments consist of sensible signs – deeds (*factis*) and words (*praeceptione*) – that lead beyond themselves to the eternal and intelligible.

The pedagogical christology of the dialogues serves what Tarcisius van Bavel and others have recognised as an 'Antiochian' bent in Augustine's

---

[39] This pedagogical christology is especially evident in *De magistro* and *De vera religione* in which Christ is, above all, an exemplar of the moral life.
[40] *Mor.* 1.17.30 (trans. Teske, WSA I/19, 45): *per humana in diuina consurgant*.
[41] Van Fleteren highlights the signatory valence of Augustine's early theology of the incarnation: 'Signs which transcend human power are not alone sufficient to testify to divine authority. Rather, the incarnation, described against the background of a Neo-platonist metaphysic, is a sign of this authority. The teaching of this incarnate authority, that man must not be held by the sensibles, but must flee to the intellect is characteristically Neoplatonic, perhaps Porphyrian. The miraculous events are done for this purpose and are of low estimation in themselves' (1973: 53).

early christology, in which Augustine readily avails himself of *homo susceptus* language. The divine *intellectus* proceeds from the ingenerate First Principle (*principium sine principio*) for our salvation (*nostram salutem*), without thereby being in anyway diminished (*sine degeneratione*) (*Ord.* 2.5.16). The divine *intellectus* bends down (*declinaret*), submitting (*submitteret*) himself to a human body (*Acad.* 3.19.42). The operative verb in this paradigm is *assumere*: 'So great a God has for our sake (*propter nos*) deigned to assume and activate (*assumere atque agere*) a body of our own kind (*nostri generis corpus*)' (*Ord.* 2.5.16, trans. mine).[42] The pedagogy of the divine *intellectus* secures and extends reason's intellectual ascent through the liberal arts and philosophy.

Reason and divine authority operate in tandem to effect moral purification and intellectual enlightenment. These two functions come together in Augustine's most extensive and explicit discussion of the incarnation, at the conclusion to *Contra academicos*. Augustine offers an abbreviated history of philosophy, recapitulating how, among the amalgam of ancient philosophical schools, the Platonists and the Aristotelians stood out from the Hellenic medley in offering a serious account of erudition, doctrine, and morals. A sublime synthesis of these two schools resulted, by which we can safely assume Augustine means Neoplatonism.[43] Augustine writes,

> For, it is not the philosophy of this world – the philosophy which our sacred mysteries rightly detest. It is of the other world, the intelligible world – a world to which even the most acute reasoning would never lead souls blinded by the multiform darkness of error and smeared with so much grime from the bodies. That most subtle Reason (*ista ratio subtilissima*) would never call back souls to that intelligible world if the most high God had not vouchsafed – through clemency (*clementia*) towards the whole human race (*populari*) – to send the authority of the divine intellect (*divini intellectus auctoritatem*) down even to a human body, and caused it to dwell therein, so that souls would be aroused not only by divine precepts (*praeceptis*) but also by divine acts (*factis*), and return to their very selves and gaze up upon their fatherland without any disputatious wranglings. (*Acad.* 3.19.42, trans. altered)

The path of reason shines brightest among the Neoplatonists; this philosophy is true in an unqualified sense (*una verissimae philosophiae*

---

[42] In this regard, the phrase *ipsum hominem agens* (*Ord.* 2.9.27) (translated above by Russell as 'leading a man onward') could be translated as 'activating a man' to better capture Augustine's 'Antiochian' proclivities. See O'Connell 1968: 265.

[43] These (Neoplatonic) philosophers taught that 'Aristotle and Plato blend and chord in such a manner that to the inattentive and unskilled they seem to be out of harmony' (*Acad.* 3.19.42). While many assume Plato and Aristotle offer rival accounts of the world, these men of extreme acumen and brilliance (*acutissimi et solertissimi viri*) recognise the common truth they taught.

disciplina).[44] Here reason at its most profound (*ratio subtilissima*) gives clear direction to the intelligible world. But, apart from divine authority, reason cannot extend sufficient moral purification or intellectual illumination to lead its devotees to a successful consummation of the ascent to the intelligible world. *Contra academicos*, more forcefully than *De ordine*, underscores the limitations of autonomous reason. Embodied creatures, mired in things of sense, have no hope of independently achieving the end to which reason points. God's mercy (*clementia*) intervenes. In contrast to philosophy, the humility of Christ is manifest in the universal scope of his saving intent. Divine authority revealed in the incarnation is capable of purifying all people (*populi*) through the mysteries, teaches through signs of word and deed, and thereby aids reason in achieving its anagogical end. In contrast to the 'disputatious wranglings' of the philosophers, the divine *intellectus* teaches with authority through sensible but effective signs – in words (*praeceptis*) and deeds (*factis*). The effect is dramatic: All are enabled to ascend, to turn within, and gaze *ad patriam*.

The Integration of Authority and Reason

The integrated, dialectical relation of authority and reason is perhaps most evident when we consider the principal task the dialogues assign to reason. Reason is charged with offering an *intellectus fidei*, an intellectual account of the mysteries delivered by authority. Augustine's description of a 'twofold path' of reason and authority (*Ord.* 2.5.16) might tempt us to imagine two opposing paths, one designated for the 'elite' and the other for the 'common man', but this would be a mistake. The context of Augustine's reference to a 'twofold path' makes clear that while the roles of authority and reason are distinguished, they operate in tandem:

When the obscurity of things perplexes us, we follow a twofold path (*duplex via*): reason (*rationem*), or at least, authority (*auctoritatem*). Philosophy sends forth reason, and it frees scarcely a few. By itself it compels these not only not to spurn those mysteries, but to understand them insofar as they can be understood (*non contemnere illa mysteria, sed sola intellegere, ut intellegenda sunt, cogit*). (*Ord.* 2.5.16)

---

[44] There is some ambiguity as to whether *una verissimae philosophiae disciplina* refers to Neoplatonism or to the Christian faith. I follow the majority who hold this to be a reference to Plotinus. In this regard, see du Roy 1966: 114–18. Ragner Holte contends that *verissimae philosophiae* is a sobriquet for Christianity (Holte 1962: 107–9).

The verbs describing the activity of reason contain important connotations. Reason seeks to understand (*intellegere*), to peer into the mystery. Having attained a degree of perception and comprehension, reason aims to hold the mysteries together as a whole before the mind's eye (*cogere*), that is, to perceive the integral harmony and sapiential unity of the faith. Reason is warned not to spurn the mysteries (*contemnere mysteria*), but to understand them as they ought to be understood. Reason's task is to penetrate the intelligibility of the mysteries. As such, despite Augustine's claim that reason has objective priority (*re ... prior est*) to authority (*Ord.* 2.9.26), there is also a sense in which authority claims objective priority. Authority provides the content of revelation that reason subsequently engages. Ryan Topping perceptively notes, 'The twofold method is what those who *already* accept Christian revelation may walk upon: these are not alternates open to Platonists, but only to those who have submitted themselves to the efficacy of the mysteries.'[45] Taken as a whole, the dialogues suggest both that the chronological priority of authority is relativised and that the intrinsic priority of reason is relativised. They are coextensive. Reason supervenes upon the contents of the faith, 'working over', so to speak, that which faith holds on divine authority. The quotation continues,

> The philosophy that is true (*vera*) – the genuine (*germana*) philosophy, so to speak – has no other function than to teach (*doceat*) what is the First Principle of all things – Itself without beginning (*principium sine principio*), – and how great an intellect (*intellectus*) dwells therein, and what has proceeded therefrom for our welfare (*nostram salutem*), but without deterioration of any kind. Now, the venerated mysteries (*mysteria*), which liberate persons of sincere and firm faith – not indiscriminately, as some say; and not harmfully, as many assert – these mysteries teach that this First Principle is one God omnipotent (*unum Deum omnipotentem*), and that He is tripotent (*tripotentem*), Father and Son and Holy Spirit. (*Ord.* 2.5.16)

Here we have an arresting example of how Augustine understands reason to penetrate the content of what authority delivers. The central mysteries of the faith – the doctrines of the incarnation and the Trinity – are considered within the metaphysical structures of the philosophy described as *vera* and *germana* (presumably that of Plotinus). By perceiving the intelligibility (*rationabile*) of creation, reason is led (*doceat*) to acknowledge a transcendent and eternal cause that is itself uncaused: *principium sine principio*. The mysteries deliver trinitarian specificity to Plotinian metaphysics. The Nicene confession of the Trinity and the incarnation received

---

[45] Topping 2012: 170.

through the mysteries of the Church completes and make spiritually effective the truths that Platonism points towards in an obscure manner.[46]

Conclusion

The widely held contention that at Cassiciacum authority and reason represent two distinct paths of salvation might prima facie seem plausible. After all, the distinction between the few and the many is a salient feature of Augustine's Platonic inheritance. This distinction, then, maps neatly onto the dialogues: while the many must rest content trusting divine authority to deliver salvation in the life to come, the few are permitted already in this mortal coil to ascend on the path of reason to beatitude. The exalted role that the liberal arts and philosophy play at Cassiciacum (a status that is nonpareil in patristic literature) in the ascent of the soul gives further support to this thesis. Despite the air of plausibility and the seeming textual warrant for these arguments, they do not stand up under scrutiny. Rather, the dialogues present authority and reason as dialectically constituted. Although they operate according to distinct modalities, they are woven into one integrated path of ascent. Reason supervenes on authority; it aims at an intellectual reckoning of what faith believes. In this sense, authority has chronological priority because the practice of reason requires a prior trust in what authority delivers. But this priority is not absolute. I can only trust what I already hold to be reasonable. Reason and authority mutually impinge on one another.

It is especially in the omnipresent theme of ascent that we can see how Augustine envisions the dialectical relation between reason and authority. For the philosophical schools of antiquity, a disciple's induction into the practice of reason was far from an exclusively cerebral affair. Ascent through the liberal arts, culminating in philosophy, promises an intellectual

---

[46] It is striking that here Augustine appeals in an explicit fashion to Nicaea. There is the creedal affirmation of *unum Deum omnipotentem*, and the *tripotentem* Godhead is named. It is exceptionally rare to find the term *tripotentem* used in Latin theology (this is its only occurrence in Augustine); however, it is used twice by Victorinus (*Adv. Ar.* I.50; I.56). On these grounds, Nello Cipriani speculates that Augustine was familiar with the *Adversus Arium* (Cipriani 1994: 264–65). Building on Cipriani, Lewis Ayres argues that since Augustine adopts Victorinus's '*tripotentem*' but not his '*tres potentiae*' (because the latter seems to run afoul of the unity of operations taught at Nicaea), we can see Augustine's early familiarity with Nicene debates. At the time of the composition of the Cassiciacum Dialogues, it seems Augustine was quite familiar with the terrain of Latin Nicene theology. Ayres concludes, 'We have strong evidence for an initial literary engagement with Latin Nicenes towards the end of 386' (2010: 29).

apprehension of the order and unity of all things. But like can only be seen by like: cosmic order and unity can be perceived only by a soul that is itself ordered and unified. Reason's ascent (*mentis motio*) from the distraction of mutable and temporal realities to the attention to immutable and eternal truth requires moral purification. The challenge, of course, is that such equanimity of soul – the life of unruffled stability proper to *theoria* – cannot be sustained while living in the body, nor can it contend with mortality. In short, reason cannot deliver the moral purification or intellectual illumination it promises. And, worse, Augustine diagnoses a pervasive pride in reason's autonomous attempt at purification, illumination, and ascent. Divine authority is itself eternal reason (*intellectus*) but now extends itself in humility (*clementia*) to all. The declension of the divine *intellectus* into a human body purifies and teaches the many through sensible signs – words and deeds – with the purpose of leading all beyond such sensible signs. The ecclesial mysteries are the sacramental extension of this incarnational principle that allows all to achieve what philosophy claims as the exclusive preserve of the few, namely, to 'return' to themselves and to 'gaze upon the fatherland' (*Acad.* 3.19.42).

Augustine's commitment to the doctrine of the incarnation at Cassiciacum requires that he radically reconfigure the Platonic distinction between the few and the many. There are no longer two classes of people with *insuperably* divided natures. Instead, *all* are called to the happiness and wisdom that is the vision of God, *all* require the aid of divine authority to realise this gift, and *none* obtains the stability and simplicity of such a vision in this life. Admittedly, some more than others are dispositionally suited to reason from the cosmic order to divine realities. Augustine's own experience is representative in this regard. Although he readily admits that the descent of divine *intellectus* now extends the promise of the happy life even to those with no familiarity in the liberal arts or time and talent for philosophy, his *own* disposition is one that cannot rest content on authority:

We are impelled towards knowledge by a twofold force: the force of authority and the force of reason. And I am resolved never to deviate in the least from the authority of Christ, for I find none more powerful. But, as for what is attainable by acute and accurate reasoning (*subtilissima ratione*), such is my state of mind that I am impatient to grasp what truth is – to grasp it not only by belief, but also by comprehension (*non credendo solum, sed etiam intellegendo apprehendere*). (*Acad.* 3.20.43)

Augustine's own creative use of Plotinus to articulate the metaphysical ligaments of the doctrine of the Trinity, the incarnation, and the drama of creation and redemption is perhaps the most compelling illustration of how he envisions the dialectical nature of authority and reason. Reason attempts an *intellectus fidei*, a rational account of what authority delivers. Reason seeks to penetrate the mysteries confessed on divine authority. As such, the dialogues overcome the antinomy Augustine identifies in classical philosophy between the few and the many, between reason and authority, and between philosophy and faith. And the dialogues, therefore, already anticipate Augustine's aphoristic remarks a few years later in *De vera religione*: 'We must repudiate all those who neither philosophise about sacred matters, nor attach sacred rites to philosophy.'[47]

---

[47] *Ver. rel.* 7.12.

25 | The Object of Our Gaze: Visual Perception as a Mode of Knowing

ROBIN M. JENSEN

Introduction

> The eye is the lamp of the body. So, if your eye is sound, your whole body will be full of light; but if your eye is not sound, your whole body will be full of darkness
>
> Matt 6:22–23

The Christian tradition has often judged words heard or read to be superior to things seen. From earliest times, theologians have presumed that faith was more reliably and effectively articulated and transmitted in words than by images. Thus, faith is best received, as Saint Paul asserted, 'from what is heard, and what is heard is through the word of Christ' (Rom 10:17). From this, one might assume that knowledge of holy scripture (the word of Christ) is best conveyed through such verbal forms as homilies, catecheses, exegetical treatises, and theological expositions, rather than by visual perception of things in the world or imagined in the mind.

This conviction has long and firmly established precedents. Ancient philosophers and theologians often deemed images to be at best imitative and at worst deceptive or fraudulent. Among them is Plato, who disparaged sensory experience – particularly sight – as untrustworthy and liable to error. Yet, despite the enduring influence of philosophers' distrust of the senses, early Christian theologians did not universally regard the faculty of sight or the act of seeing as inherently untrustworthy. In fact, early Christian teaching developed a nuanced theory of how vision initiates and sustains awareness of spiritual matters, including an imperfect or fleeting comprehension of the invisible, transcendent, and ineffable Divine. To this end, they granted equivalent powers to both eyes and ears as organs of perception and conduits of sacred knowledge.

The Incarnate Word and the Visible Image

Although it had precedents in pre-Socratic thought, the concept of Divine Word – the Logos – as the source of all things is pre-eminent in Christian theology, most notably in the prologue to the Fourth Gospel (John 1:1–3). Pre-Christian philosophers also regarded the Logos as the principle of reason, the ordering of intellectual thought, and the basis for human speech. An equally important scriptural passage, however, was the declaration that humans are created in God's image and after God's likeness (Gen 1:26). While Christian interpreters usually understood this assertion to refer to human rationality, memory, or intellect rather than any external or physical resemblance to the Divine One, it also justified identifying the Second Person of the Trinity as Image (*eikon*) as well as Word (*logos*). This identification is, in fact, asserted in the New Testament, when Christ is professed to be the 'image of the invisible God, the firstborn of all creation' (Col 1:15). Thus, even though God is declared to be beyond sight (cf. 1 Tim 6:16), this passage grants the Pre-Incarnate Christ a title that is defined visually as well as linguistically. Moreover, the epistle to the Hebrews reiterates the idea of the Son as God's image: 'He is the reflection of God's glory and the exact imprint of God's very being' (Heb 1:3).

These texts notwithstanding, Christians inherited from both Jewish teaching and Greco-Roman philosophy the belief that God is utterly invisible and transcends any imagined physical appearance.[1] For example, in the early third-century dialogue written by Marcus Minucius Felix, the protagonist explains to his pagan companion that the lack of any visual representations of the Christian God was a compelling reason to believe in him. Following Paul's declaration to the Romans that what can be known about God is evident in creation (Rom 1:18–19), he insisted that Christians neither see God in God's being nor conceive of that Being in their minds (*Oct.* 32.4).

Yet, Christian teaching clearly affirms that the invisible divine Being became visibly manifest – in a unique way – in Christ. Jesus' incarnation – his corporeal and visible appearance in human form – required early Christians to re-evaluate and nuance proclamations about God's absolute invisibility. Christ was revealed in discernible flesh and accessible to his followers' ears and eyes, teaching them by both his words and his actions. Thus, during Jesus' earthly life, the Divine Son was comprehended both

---

[1] For a general discussion of this, see Jensen 2005 (esp. chapter 3, 'The Invisible God and the Visible Image', 69–100); Finney 1994.

intelligibly *and* sensibly, while the New Testament attested that Divine Father was only occasionally audible as a voice from heaven (cf. Matt 3:17, 17:5 and parallels).[2]

Having seen Christ in his earthly life was the mark of a reliable witness. The Gospel according to Luke opens with the author proclaiming his authority as an eyewitness to the things he will recount (Luke 1:1–2). Luke's proclamation is echoed in the First Epistle of John, where the author confirms the significance of having heard, seen, and touched the Eternal Son in order to testify to his manifestation (1 John 1:1–3). Perhaps most tellingly, a famous passage from John's Gospel has Jesus simply claiming: 'Whoever has seen me, has seen the Father' (John 14:9). Paul himself claims the authority of an eyewitness when he emphasises the importance of Jesus' appearance to him on the way to Damascus – an event that grants him apostolic status (1 Cor 9:1; 15:8).[3]

Further challenging the idea that written texts and spoken words are the primary and perhaps only trustworthy mode for imparting knowledge of God is the fact that scripture frequently refers to the human yearning to see God and suggests that one day such vision may be granted. Whereas the psalmist pleads, 'Do not hide your face from me' (Ps 27:9), and asks 'When shall I come and behold the face of God?' (Ps 41:2), in his first epistle to the Corinthians, Paul affirms that such a wish will be granted to the righteous: 'For now we see as in a mirror, dimly, but then we will see face to face' (1 Cor 13:12). Paul reiterates this in his second letter to the Corinthians, where he declares that seeing the glory of the Lord will transform the faithful from one degree of glory into another (2 Cor 3:18). Similarly, the First Epistle of John maintains: 'When he is revealed we will be like him, for we will see him as he is' (1 John 3:2). Finally, Jesus' words in the Sermon on the Mount also appear to affirm an unmediated vision: 'Blessed are the pure in heart, for they will see God' (Matt 5:8).

Ancient Critiques of Sensory – Especially Visual – Perception

Despite this biblical allowance for visual perception as an effective means of encountering and knowing God, the influence of ancient thinkers who judged the sense of vision to be unreliable persisted. Even while allowing

---

[2] On the early development of the Christian notion of the spiritual senses, see Chapter 2 by Jane Heath, this volume.

[3] On these New Testament texts in particular, see Heath 2016. Note that Acts 9:3 does not precisely describe a christophany, but only that Paul saw lights and heard a voice speaking to him.

that knowledge was initially stimulated by information gained through sensory experience, they still distrusted what eyes observed on their own. Optical illusions, lack of light, and failing eyesight were among physiological reasons for this, but philosophers also regarded external images as essentially deceptive for other, more complex, reasons.

The most famous formulation of such disregard comes from Plato, whose general distrust of sensory experience included the physical act of seeing. While Plato admitted that mental images arise from sensory apprehension of external objects (the realm of appearances), he judged them as prone to being defective to the extent that they were based on secondarily derived comprehension rather than on cognition arising within the soul or mind. He argued that images are essentially unlike their models for, if they were truly identical, they would not be images. In Plato's view, mental concepts or ideas were more dependable, since they were unlikely to be based on partial, illusory, or false visual observations (*Resp.* 10.601c).

Plato's misgivings about the 'realm of appearances' are evident in his critique of visual art. For him, images made by artists were mere copies of copies (objects whose recognition was derived from their likeness to an ideal, abstract form). This made them exceptionally prone to be misrepresentations, insofar as they were distant from the reality of the model or prototype – or the truth (*Resp.* 2.377c–383c; 595a–608b). Nevertheless, Plato also allows that images serve a useful function to the extent that they participate – albeit in a very limited sense through external appearance – in the reality of that ideal form or model they represent. Images thereby permit the beholder to have an intimation of the reality and, perceiving their provisional nature, the viewers may realise the need to transcend mere external appearances to progress towards truth and value the importance of exchanging the palpable physical realm for the invisible spiritual one. Thus, Plato grants that the experience of beautiful things in the world engenders comprehension of the abstract idea of Beauty as such (*Symp.* 211c).

Early Christian philosophers, like Plato, granted bodily sight a useful – albeit initial – role in the work of discerning truth. For example, Tertullian cites Plato's disparagement of sensory experiences when he refers to the famous example of an oar that looks bent when immersed in water (*An.* 17, citing *Tim.* 44d–47e). Tertullian recognises the fundamental distinction between corporeal things, manifest to bodily sight, and spiritual things, accessible only to the human rational faculty. Yet he acknowledges that spiritual truths are often initiated by sensible experience of the external, physical realm and that, therefore, the intellect could not effectively operate apart from the bodily senses (*An.* 18). Significantly, Tertullian cites Paul's

Epistle to the Romans, where the apostle asserts that while eternal power and divine nature are essentially invisible, they have and can be understood and seen through the things God has made (Rom 1:20).

As noted above, belief in the incarnation obliged Christians to modify the belief that God is utterly invisible in order to make an exception for the Divine Son, who was visible in life and appeared even after death to the Apostle Paul and the protomartyr Stephen (Acts 7:55). Christ's human, corporeal appearance not only allowed physical and visible apprehension of God, but some fourth-century theologians, like Athanasius of Alexandria, regarded it as an essential part of Christ's saving mission. In his treatise *On the Incarnation*, Athanasius describes the fallen children of Adam and Eve as blinded by sin, deceived by demons, and utterly unaware of their potential for redemption. As such, they desperately needed God's coming in the person of Christ to be redirected and restored (*Inc.* 14.4–6). Because signs of God in the created world were available to humans from the beginning, Athanasius reasons that humans were not alert to or aware of them, but kept their eyes downcast. Hence, God condescended to humanity's need to see the divine in a corporeal body like theirs, so that they might know God through that body.

More than merely seeing Christ as a human body, however, Athanasius emphasises the significance of witnessing Christ's human actions in the world (*Inc.* 14.8). He insists that Christ did not come merely to be a sacrifice – to die on a cross and then be raised from the dead – for by this means he would have rendered himself invisible and inaccessible to human sense perception. Rather, he says that Christ came expressly to perform works that would reveal him as God and not only as a human man (*Inc.* 16.3–5). For Athanasius, visual observation (with bodily eyes) was critical for humans to accept Christ as the Divine Word: the invisible one made visible. But what humans needed to observe was more than his external, bodily appearance. They also needed to see him in action in order to be filled with the knowledge of God (Eph 3:19).

In his treatise, Athanasius also stresses that, in recognising Christ as the Divine Word, humans realise their own divine potential. Athanasius describes the Divine Logos as a painter or art restorer, who came to restore the human soul – created in the image of God but blemished, obscured, and defaced through the continued accumulation of sin (*Inc.* 14.1–2). The divine artist did not discard the damaged portrait but instead brought the model back to the studio to repair the work. Once the image is cleaned and renewed, the likeness returns to its original state, and the soul beholds as if in a mirror the very likeness of the Word that in turn shows forth the image of the Father (*C. Gent.* 2.34). Salvation is assured through the grace of divine self-revelation and the human act of visual perception.

Plotinus and Neoplatonism: Theories of Participation

As a contemporary to many early Christian writers, the works of Plotinus are particularly relevant to how philosophers regarded the faculty of sight and its role in generating knowledge. Plotinus followed Plato in his caution about the trustworthiness of the senses and judgement that physical matter is inferior to soul or mind. He also allowed that images (as well as works of art) were useful guides or signs, able to assist the viewer's comprehension of higher realities. Yet, he granted visual images a more positive value, rather than understanding them simply as imitations of that reality and likely to be flawed or misleading. In Plotinus' view, the order and structure that are visually perceptible in the natural world imitate the transcendent world of ideas. Attentive observation of the external, visible world pointed beholders towards the invisible and transcendent, allowing them to discern the foundational structure and beauty contained in the realm of forms that was, above all, the basis for all sensory knowledge. In other words, the act of seeing best aimed at perceiving how everything fitted together and participated in the sublime truth that endowed it with its comprehensible form. Contemplation of a beautiful object – of art or in nature – leads to understanding of beauty itself, realised only in the spiritual realm (*Enn.* 5.8.9; cf. *Enn.* 5.5.12).

Plotinus' argument grants potential value not only to objects seen in nature, but also to works of art. According to Plotinus, artists begin by studying the natural world. Although the works they produce are basically derivative, they are also more than that because they are conceived in the artist's mind before being rendered visible in the finished object. For this reason, Plotinus believes that ideas can be expressed in material form. For example, a carved block of stone is not merely an imitation of a model; it expresses an idea. It draws upon nature, but by apprehending the transcendent form that lies beyond it, the artist's product is more perfect than the thing itself. In this way, artists incorporate their vision of the ideal and project that vision into their works, making them superior to their models, if one even exists. For example, Plotinus says, the great Phidias sculpted an image of Zeus only by imagining the form Zeus would take if he deigned to become visible (*Enn.* 5.8.1).[4]

---

[4] For a helpful summary of Plotinus' views on sense perception, see Emilsson 1988.

In *Ennead* 5.3, Plotinus elaborates his belief that observation of the beauty and structure of the natural world could lead viewers to rise above the material things they saw to appreciate that such material things were reflections or images of invisible realities beyond bodily sight. For Plotinus, therefore, knowledge initially relies upon the sense of sight, but he argues that the observer must transcend the visible and externally attractive in order to grasp internal and intelligible truths. Conscious and sustained attention, leads, step by step, in a kind of ladder of ascent towards the eventual comprehension of the divine One. Yet, all this begins with bodily eyes observing earthly beauty. Thus, matter has a positive function as the first stage of a spectator's ascent from external and visible things to internal and intelligible cognition.[5]

To explain this process, Plotinus emphasises the resemblance or principle of congruity between an object seen by the bodily eye and a Form perceived by the mind or soul. Thus, those who gaze upon images, whether pictures or statues, are prompted to recognise the unseen realities that they reveal. The raw physical material itself is a medium and the artist is the one who gives it form. When discerning viewers see an object, they perceive its pre-material form and model and are drawn towards that reality. Consequently, for Plotinus, the act of viewing initiates and aids the process of comprehension, prompting the spectator's gaze to evolve from appreciation of external beauty to awareness of intelligible beauty (cf. *Enn*. 4.3.1). Thus, an image is different from its model, but the fact of its likeness guides viewers to more perfect understanding.

For Neoplatonists of the fourth century, then, the devotee is aided and directed by visible things (e.g., images, names, buildings) towards the invisible ones, from the comprehensible to a gradually developing consciousness of the incomprehensible. If one had nothing to see, comprehension would be inhibited. Both the principles of participation and congruity begin to overcome any potential dualism between the spiritual and material realm.

This positive valuation of the external and visual realm has a parallel in Christian teaching around the same time, largely due to the belief that God is especially shown forth in the bodily incarnation and resurrection of Christ. Theologians like Origen, who resolutely believed God to be incorporeal and incomprehensible and who regarded the bodily senses as a consequence of the fallen state, also granted that by his coming in an actual human body, Christ revealed an otherwise unbearable glory, to which humans could gradually become accustomed. This he believed to be a

---

[5] See Plotinus, *Enn*. 5.8, 'On the Intelligible Beauty'.

divine accommodation to limited human faculties. By way of explanation, Origen gives an example of a statue of such enormous size that it filled the whole world and thus could not be perceptible as such. However, another statue, made in every way identical but not of immense size, allowed viewers to distinguish it and grasp the incomprehensible majesty and infinite brightness of the original (*Princ.* 1.2.8).

Similarly, the fourth-century Cappadocian Basil of Caesarea insists on the ineffability of the Divine Being yet maintains that by gazing at the beauty of an image one may distinguish the archetype. This, he says, accounts for the relationship of the Divine Word and God as that of image and prototype. Hence, the one who has a mental apprehension of the form of the Son can actually distinguish the image of the Father, beholding the unbegotten beauty through envisioning the Begotten. Basil sees the visioning process as initiated in the external realm and progressing to spiritual understanding and affirms that, while the physical and spiritual realms were not equivalent, they were inseparable from one another (*Ep.* 38.8).

In his treatise *On the Making of Man*, Gregory of Nyssa considers the ways in which humans bear the divine likeness, contending that it has nothing to do with shape, form, or colour but, rather, is based on an excellent character. He offers an analogy of God's creation of humans, somewhat like Athanasius', to the work of the artist, who paints with precisely selected and blended colours to transfer the beauty of the original to the copy. So, Gregory says, God also paints a portrait to resemble his own beauty, but for Gregory the hues are not colours but rather virtues (e.g., purity, alienation from evil, and mutual love). He concludes that humans have been given the ability to apprehend this by the faculties of sight and hearing, but most of all by the impetus to search them out and the discernment to appreciate how they are truly stamped with the divine likeness (*De hom. opif.* 5.1–2).

Augustine on Visualising and the Visible

Among Christian writers of the late fourth and early fifth centuries, the most expansive discussion of both the problems and the potential of visual experience in the quest for spiritual knowledge comes from Augustine. Augustine was inclined to distrust the visual arts as distracting, even while he conceded that beautiful creations of human hands could be regarded as divinely inspired or as having their ultimate source in the Divine Being. He expounds on this subject most fulsomely in the *Confessions*, where he describes the process of art-making as the imposition of an inward concept upon external material. Images, he insists, are not seen independently and then stored in the mind, but rather are recognised as inherent memories that are essentially recollected and recreated (*Conf.* 10.17–11.18). His thinking in many respects echoes Plato's, believing that artists drew upon eternal and intangible forms known in the mind to impress tangible forms on base materials rather than drawing solely from observation of things in the world to make copies of them in paint or stone.

> We do not draw images through our senses, but discern them inwardly not through images but as they really are, and through the concepts themselves we find that the process of learning is simply this: by thinking we, as it were, gather together ideas which the memory contains in a dispersed and disordered way, and by concentrating our attention we arrange them in order as if ready to hand, stored in the very memory where previously they lay hidden, scattered, and neglected.[6] (*Conf.* 10.11.18)

In this statement, Augustine makes an important point about the psychology of attention – that, when deployed, it provides, as it were, a way in and upward. One does not briefly glance and then move along to the next attractive object but, rather, focuses and then orders or categorises the experience in the mind.

In an earlier discussion of his 'vast hall' of memory, Augustine acknowledges that those sights held in the memory entered and penetrated by the use of the bodily organs: ears, nostrils, mouth, and eyes (*Conf.* 10.8.13). Recollection thereby depends on sensory experience. One sees objects. The objects, existing as they do in the external world, do not themselves penetrate the mind, nor are they stored in the memory as concrete or physical realities, but they nevertheless are essential to comprehension.

Despite this affirmation of the role of these bodily faculties, for Augustine sense perception, necessary as it is to attaining knowledge, is vastly inferior to inward reflection. He speaks about the 'rays of his eyes' as messengers, sent forth from the body to gain information about the external world. What they report to the mind, the mind then assesses and judges in order to understand. Citing Rom 1, Augustine allows that the invisible things of God are discerned in the created world. However, he argues that one must be careful not to mistake them for the reality to which they point – a reality that can only be grasped with the soul. Without judgement – without the action of the rational faculty – the act of seeing is meaningless and does not

---

[6] Trans. Chadwick 1991: 189.

foster insight. The senses have their proper place and function, but the mind is the guide towards truth (*Conf.* 10.6.10–10.7.11).

In his treatise on the Trinity, Augustine invites the reader to look around herself to see the beauty in the world – a man's well-proportioned face, cheerful expression, and good complexion, for example. Because one loves what is good, Augustine urges his readers to see good itself, for that way they will see God not as a good with some other good, but as the good of every good (*Trin.* 8.4). In other words, if one encounters something good with the bodily senses, one can come to appreciate and love the good itself – in that way perceiving God. Later in his treatise, Augustine refers to the faculty of sight as the most excellent of the bodily senses, and one with the most affinity to mental vision (*Trin.* 11.1). Augustine, however, had little appreciation or use for objects of art. Much like Plotinus, he believed that artists externalised images they had in their minds and so creations of this sort could be used to demonstrate how ideas already in the mind impressed form upon the material world. This was like God's creation of the world, although God was the ultimate source of both the material, the sensory powers, and the ability to use them (*Conf.* 11.5.7). The idea that artists started from an intellectual concept and then proceeded to fashion the image or object, rather than starting from observation of the object to reproduce it in some material, has implications for the mechanics of seeing itself. In this theory of optics, the object was not the source of the image, but rather a passive participant in the activity of gazing, reflection, and reproduction.

Augustine and Ancient Theories of Seeing

Augustine's theory of the mechanics of seeing, the idea that the mind emitted a ray that actively grasped the object in view, was not original to him. In fact, the above-quoted text of Matt 6:22 and its parallel in Luke 11:34 describing the eye as the lamp of the body – that, if healthy, will fill the whole body with light and, if unhealthy, will fill the body with darkness – may have roots in much older theories of vision.[7]

Expounding the physiology of sight was also a project of great interest to ancient philosophers, perhaps starting with Empedocles (495–444 BCE), who described perception as a twofold movement. One trajectory of effluences goes out from the object, while the other is transmitted by the

---

[7] On this passage and a summary of ancient vision theory, see Betz 1979; Allison 1987.

eye. He describes the eye as a lantern that holds a fire within it, and just as the lantern has a linen shield that the light penetrates, so the light moves from behind the pupil through the eye's covering membrane (B84). Plato contended that the eye emits a beam of fiery light that extends to the object in view and becomes one substance with the light of day (*Tim.* 45b–46a; *Resp.* 6 and 7). Aristotle believed the opposite, that sight was the passive response to a stimulus of some sort (e.g., light) that an object emanated through space and then projected replicas of itself into the receiver's mind (cf. *De an.* 2.7 and *Sens.* 2). Plotinus expounded and expanded Plato's idea, comparing the activity of the eye to the sense of touch – the finger reaching out to physically examine an object (*Enn.* 4.5.7.24; 5.5.7.24). This theory of 'extramission' proposes that when viewers turn their eyes towards an object, the eye extends an invisible beam that grasps hold of it. Seeing is, then, a kind of touching.[8]

Augustine elaborated this idea in several places, including in a sermon he preached on the Feast of Saint Vincent, probably around the year 413. Discussing the corporeal nature of the resurrected body, Augustine employs the act of seeing as evidence that the body, when unburdened by the sluggishness of its former fleshliness, could move about with great speed. He compares this to the way that sight works almost instantaneously:

In this very body which we carry around with us, I can find something whose inexpressible swiftness astonishes me: the ray from our eye, with which we touch whatever we behold. ... How big is the distance between you and the sun? Who could ever measure such distances as that? ... As soon as you wanted to see it, you reached it by seeing it. You didn't look around for machines to attempt it with, not with ladders to climb up to it, not for ropes to lift yourself up to it, not for wings to fly to it. Just opening your eyes constitutes reaching it.[9] (*Serm.* 277.10)

Returning to his treatise *On the Trinity*, Augustine proposes a more sophisticated explanation of the act of seeing. Here he distinguishes three elements of the process. First is the thing seen, which has a prior existence. Second is the act of seeing, which does not have a prior existence. Third is the conscious intention on the part of the observer to instigate and sustain the gaze. In this, one can see Augustine making a considered shift in his thinking about agent and recipient. He allows that while sight is inaugurated by the viewer and not by the object, and proceeds from the eye like a blind man's cane, it is, most importantly, the attention that the viewer pays the object that influences the observer's experience and response. One

---

[8] On this topic see Nightingale 2016.   [9] Trans. Hill 1994: 38–39.

can pass something and not actually see it, or only look at it without really noticing. The result of seeing is the perception, shaped and formed by the quality of the gaze itself. However, interestingly, Augustine also seems to give some agency to the object, which, he says emanates a likeness of itself to the seer (*Trin.* 11.2–6).

In his theory of vision, Augustine posits a reciprocal process by which some external object is sought by the eye, impressed upon the mind, retained in the memory, and – finally – impacts the viewer's soul. As they are impressed upon the soul, seen images are powerfully formative of spectators' character and actions, even against their own will or intention, and can work for good or ill. Augustine compares this power of images to shape individual dispositions to the long-standing belief that what a pregnant woman looks at will affect the appearance or temperament of her unborn child (cf. *C. Iul.* 5.14.51). As evidence, he cites the biblical story of Jacob, who wished to create a flock of speckled sheep by having the ewes impregnated while they looked upon spotted rods set into their water troughs (Gen 30:37–41; *Trin.* 11.15). The act of viewing can have permanent consequences.

Thus, echoing the two biblical passages from Matthew and Luke that ascribe a moral aspect to viewing and link physical sight with ethical formation, Augustine insists on the power of the image and its potential for positive or negative effects upon the soul – and even upon one's physical body. In his *Confessions*, Augustine presents the case of his friend Alypius, who had developed an addiction to gladiatorial games, and he describes the impact of his friend's attending the spectacles:

> He was struck in the soul by a wound graver than the gladiator in his body, whose fall had forced open his eyes … As soon as he saw the blood, he at once drank in savagery and did not turn away. His eyes were riveted. He imbibed madness. Without any awareness of what was happening to him, he found delight in the murderous contest and was inebriated by bloodthirsty pleasure.[10] (*Conf.* 6.8.13)

This, what he calls a 'lust of the eyes' (*concupiscentia oculorum*), Augustine describes as a kind of restlessness for information or experience for its own sake. He regards this need as a vain appetite for knowledge, driven by morbid curiosity, constant craving for more excitement, or just adventures for their own sake. These things become idols in that they are ends rather than means and, as such, do not lead beyond themselves. Sought and prized for themselves, they are no longer instrumental but claim an intrinsic but baseless value (*Conf.* 10.35.54).

---

[10] Trans. Chadwick 1991: 100–1.

In another of his works, *The Literal Commentary of Genesis*, Augustine discusses three distinct and hierarchically ordered kinds of vision. He uses the commandment 'you shall love your neighbour as yourself' to help make his argument. He begins with the first type of vision, which is seeing things in the external world that meet the bodily eye. This, he labels 'corporeal vision'. For example, one may read the words of the commandment or even see the neighbour in person. The second type of vision is the memory we have of objects that are no longer present to our gaze, or the imagination of things or beings that we have never actually seen. This he labels 'spiritual vision', and it corresponds to the neighbour who may be absent. The third and highest kind is the vision of things that have no precise likenesses and exist only in the mind, but which give the whole process of vision its ultimate meaning. Augustine here offers the example of 'love' and labels this vision 'intellectual'.[11] As he works out his theory, Augustine elaborates that the three types of vision are progressive; one leads to the next:

And so, after the eyes have taken their object in and announced it to the spirit, in order that an image of it may be produced there, then, if it is symbolic of something, its meaning is either immediately understood by the intellect or sought out; for there can be neither understanding nor searching except by the functioning of the mind.[12] (*Gen. litt.* 12.11.22)

Thus, while Augustine analysed the mechanics of seeing itself, he also distinguished different types of viewing evident in those who are materially minded versus those who are spiritually minded. The viewer's intention determined whether the sight was edifying and even elevating or, instead, degrading and harmful. In this way, the process of seeing is not simply a bodily activity but one directed by the will and informed by practised intentions. Faithful Christians will practise the kind of selective seeing and full active knowledge that makes them compassionate rather than cruel, loving rather than lustful, and pious rather than prurient (*Serm.* 51.1–2).

Augustine also allows that, of all the senses, sight is not only the most excellent (*Trin.* 11.1), but also the most active and becomes a way of speaking about all of the others. For example, he notices that we use the verb 'see' when we mean 'understand' or 'comprehend' (*Conf.* 10.35.54). For example, one says 'I see' or 'I observe' when they speak about rational perception, even if they don't actually refer to anything seen in the outer world.

---

[11] Augustine, *Gen. litt.* 12.6.15–16.   [12] Trans. Taylor 1982: 191–92.

Thus, sight is the human faculty most commonly linked with a purely mental process of discernment, and external visual experiences often provide the basic elements for interior cogitation: ideas, imaginative inventions, memories, judgement, etc. In the same way, the Greek word θεωρέω technically means 'behold' and the Latin *contemplatio* implies gazing as well as mentally meditating. In English, we say, 'in my view' to mean 'this is what I think'. Each of these verbal expressions indicates the role of seeing in human cognition.

Augustine and Spiritual Seeing

Augustine regarded physical objects and bodily sight as essential first steps in the visioning process, but he also believed that, for the viewer to grasp the true meaning of an image, it must be interpreted by the mind and retained in the memory. For him, conscious and intentional contemplation of an object changes its character, as it ceases to exist only in the external realm and enters the intelligible one. This, then, changes the meaning of 'seeing' altogether, insofar as it is no longer simply a means of acquiring knowledge of sensible things but can lead to knowing what is transcendent and invisible.[13] The complex act of seeing is an important bridge between body and soul and, as discussed above, is profoundly affective.

Like Plotinus, Augustine explains the process of visual ascent, proceeding upwards from appreciating the beauty of bodies both terrestrial and celestial, step by step to the soul informed by the body and from there to reason and judgement of that sensory knowledge (*Conf.* 7.17.23). He admits that such comprehension can be fleeting. He describes his first coming to faith as 'a flash of a trembling glance' in which he perceived the invisible divine nature but did not succeed in maintaining the vision. He lacked the strength to keep his inner eye fixed on the revelation. Despite his inability to hang on to the moment, Augustine retained the memory of the experience and the desire that he might have it again (*Conf.* 7.17.24).

In his *City of God*, Augustine elaborates his idea of spiritual sight. Developing the apostle Paul's description of the beatific vision (e.g., 1 Cor 13:12; 2 Cor 3:18), he explains that while the resurrected faithful will see with corporeal eyes, they will look upon only spiritual things. These blessed ones even behold God, either because the eyes possess an ability akin to that of the mind, or because they will see only by the spirit. However, in a manner

---

[13] See also Augustine, *Conf.* 10.8.13; 10.17–11.18.

distinctly different from Plotinus, Augustine believes that when the faithful attain this beatific vision, they nevertheless will see by means of their bodily eyes (*Civ.* 22.29). Augustine further held that in the resurrection the body and soul would be so perfectly aligned that humans would be able to know each other's thoughts, because thoughts themselves would be visible. In another place, Augustine explains that this vision is not ordinary bodily sight (although with resurrected corporeal eyes), but the keenness of a mind that had turned aside from all carnal sensory experiences and has come to 'see invisibly' (*Ep.* 147). In the world to come, the resurrected flesh of the saints will become spiritual, and so the physical faculty of sight likewise will be changed into pure spiritual sight, now in the mind's eyes. This, for Augustine, is the goal of the Christian life: the attainment of a particular and exceedingly sacred kind of transcendent vision. Corporeality itself is transformed and perfected. And as it is perfected, the act of beholding the Divine One is the fulfilment of the believer's deepest desire.

Nevertheless, for Augustine, observation does not inevitably lead to comprehension, much less belief. People often fail to notice the significant or beautiful things that lie directly before their eyes. As Augustine points out in his *Response to Simplician*, many people witnessed Christ performing miracles or raising the dead, but they did not come to faith, unlike the thief on the cross, who recognised the one next to him (*Div. quaest. Simpl.* 1.Q.2.14). In this respect, Augustine echoes Athanasius' emphasis on seeing Christ's works but extends the argument to account for differing human dispositions. While one person may glance at something, but be inattentive and unmoved, another observer will be powerfully affected by the same scene and even be transformed by the sight. Moreover, observation is not simply taking in a simple object but seeing it as part of a larger context. Ideas are perceived in actions, and memories are made up of sensible experiences. In this sense, outward actions are truly a form of language. Mercy, for example, is not simply an idea: it is understood by seeing, doing, and recalling deeds of mercy.

For this reason, Augustine also believed that the living Christian community would be inspired by imaginatively creating mental images of Christ's miracles and Passion, along with the images of the martyrs undergoing their trials (*Serm.* 51.1–20). Like Athanasius, Augustine insisted that visible events, like the miracles of Christ, were God's way of calling people to pay attention and of reawakening them to better understanding of God's purposes (*Tract. ev. Jo.* 24.1). While Augustine probably neither knew nor condoned complex narrative depictions in actual pictorial art, he certainly encouraged people to imagine them. Yet in Christ's earthly life displaying these wonders to the eyes of otherwise dulled or distracted witnesses prompted the faithful to marvel at the invisible God through his visible acts and thereby to be brought to faith. Jesus teaches by showing, with actions as much as with words. Augustine adds that this could lead to a longing to see, in an invisible manner, the One who was the source of these visible things. He goes on, then, to assert that these experiences of seeing have their own kind of language, because Christ is the Word of God and so his deeds are, in a real sense, actually words. Just like letters on a page that one needs to know how to read in order to understand, Christ's signs and wonders are signs that one must understand to appreciate (*Tract. ev. Jo.* 24.2).

Nevertheless, Augustine made a distinction between seeing external objects and seeing God. He says that God gave humans bodily eyes to see things, but a mind for comprehending God. So, while some might see the miracles of Christ with their eyes, they had to appreciate the transcendent reality to which those miracles point with their rational minds. The vision of God, such as it is, is finally spiritual and not corporeal. This, of course, does not mean that Augustine thought Jesus was invisible, but only that his appearance does not manifest the nature of God in anything like its entirety. Furthermore, to assert that one person of the Holy Trinity is visible while the others are, in their essence, invisible is to undermine the co-equality of the three. To the extent that any of them appear, they do so by their will and not according to their nature. The Trinity is invisible and immutable, and to the extent that One Person becomes visible, it is because God appears in the form God wills entirely by God's initiative so that his essential incomprehensibility remains unchanged (*Ep.* 147).

Conclusion

Although Augustine rarely refers to actual works of art, his emphasis on perceiving Christ's divine actions (and not only his countenance or physical body), as well as on mentally envisioning the courage and suffering of martyrs, accords almost perfectly with early Christian iconography, which is almost entirely narrative in its content. Despite the claims of those historians who judge that commandment-conscious early Christians would have eschewed pictorial art as idolatrous, the surviving evidence demonstrates that they initially avoided only cult images of the pagan gods. In addition, perhaps because they resembled these 'pagan idols', to a large extent they also avoided free-standing or uncontextualised portraits of

Figure 25.1 Front of a frieze sarcophagus, showing image of Christ healing and working wonders, c. 300–25. Vatican Museo Pio Cristiano. Photo credit: Vanni Archive/Art Resource, NY

Figure 25.2 Front panel of a child's sarcophagus, with images of Christ healing and working wonders, c. 325–30. Vatican Museo Pio Cristiano. Photo credit: Vanni Archive/Art Resource, NY

Christ, biblical characters, or the saints. Instead, the compositions found among Christian catacomb paintings, sarcophagus reliefs, and church pavements and murals reveal that the images the faithful chose for their tombs, domestic décor, or places of worship concentrated on presenting exemplary stories from the Old Testament alongside the deeds and actions of Jesus as healer and wonder-worker, the adoration of the magi, and the martyrdoms of Peter and Paul (Figs. 25.1, 25.2). Anonymous bystanders often appear in the scenes, perhaps attesting to the importance of witnessing these events and of prompting the viewer to imagine themselves in their place. The seer could thus comply with Augustine's recommendation that they reconstruct the episode and see it for themselves, possibly linking the image with the story, reinforcing and amplifying a mental construct with a visual experience.

As noted above, Augustine rarely refers to specific examples of pictorial art. In one sermon, however, he refers in positive terms to a lovely painting (*dulcissima pictura*) of the stoning of Stephen. Using it as a kind of visual aid for his homily, he indicates that Paul can be seen, standing at the back of the crowd, holding the cloaks of the persecutors (*Serm.* 316.5). The pedagogical value of pictorial compositions of this kind was also justified by Paulinus of Nola, who in one of his poems refers to the painted scenes in the portico of his church. To anyone who would ask why he chose to do this, Paulinus responded that the pictures would inspire those who entered to be more like the virtuous and saintly figures they beheld (*Carm.* 27.542). Teaching by pictures is, as almost any pedagogue knows, sometimes the most effective way of transmitting and retaining knowledge.

Early Christian theologians thus positively incorporated the process of seeing, perception, recognition, and memory retention into their theology of divine revelation. They continued to explore the connections between physical sight and spiritual cognition through the next centuries, notably in the works of figures like Pseudo-Dionysius, John of Damascus, and Theodore the Studite. From Paul onwards, Christians respected the special place of the physical senses, and especially sight, for mediating non-verbal understanding of transcendent and immaterial realities. Human cognition did not need words or texts alone to become enlightened, nor did the eye or its action need to be regarded as fundamentally untrustworthy. Rather, seeing was understood as a dynamic and effective means of obtaining knowledge and as an aid to lifting the visionary to a new level of comprehension.

26 | Reconsidering the *Tholos* Image in the Eusebian Canon Tables: Symbols, Space, and Books in the Late Antique Christian Imagination

MATTHEW R. CRAWFORD

Introduction

In the early fourth century, the polymath bishop and scholar Eusebius of Caesarea achieved a milestone in the history of the book by producing a paratextual apparatus for the fourfold gospel that was the most complex system of textual segmentation, classification, and navigation that had thus far been invented for any literary corpus. The so-called Canon Tables proved to be as successful in terms of their wide transmission throughout late antiquity and the Middle Ages as they were innovative in Eusebius' own Alexandrian-influenced Caesarea of the early fourth century. The innovation of Eusebius' creation in terms of its function as a tool for interacting with a set of texts stands out sharply when viewed against the backdrop of the history of information technology in antiquity, as proposed elsewhere in this volume by Andrew Riggsby, and as I have argued at greater length in a recent monograph.[1] For the present chapter, I advance a parallel argument with respect to the visual aspects of the Canon Tables, namely that they are also remarkably innovative in the way they employ artistic imagery within a book to direct a viewer's imagination to the manifold contexts within which the gospels were significant.[2]

I would like to thank the participants in the 2017 ACU sponsored seminar in Rome who provided stimulating feedback on the initial draft of this chapter, especially Robin Jensen, as well as Jeremiah Coogan, Jaś Elsner, and Jacopo Gnisci who read and offered comments on subsequent versions.

[1] See Crawford 2019: chs. 1–2.
[2] The present chapter builds upon the recent argument of Jaś Elsner, who highlights the 'spectacular level of complexity and scholarly depth' in the 'architectural prefatory pattern' of the Canon Tables' decorative scheme and the 'high levels of artistry in the early Christian gospel book' in terms of 'the use of images and paratexts to structure a text and help its readership' (2020a: 108).

This function was possible because the gospel-book – a codex containing the four gospels – served as a nodal point in the late antique Christian episteme, containing a rich surplus of meaning exceeding the mere text or images on its pages. This can be seen in the central role it played in religious rites like catechesis, liturgical processions, and church councils. Yet even taking into account this wider penumbra of symbolic import, it would be a mistake to view the gospel-book as merely the repository of a static and clearly defined body of information. For late antique Christians it was, rather, something like what medievalist Mary Carruthers has called a 'cognitive machine', a term she employs to describe certain medieval images used as generative devices for organising and stimulating thought.[3]

Viewing the gospel-book as a 'cognitive machine' directs our attention beyond the obvious fact that the codex contains encoded information – whether in writing that can be decoded by a literate person or in pictures that a knowledgeable viewer could recognise and identify. It presses us instead towards questions about how readers and viewers found it to be a sacred object useful for thinking *with*, for provoking imagination and creativity, in short, as an instrument to be used for exploring and mapping knowledge in a much broader sense.[4] When viewed from this perspective, the gospel-book equipped with an exquisitely adorned set of Canon Tables illuminates an important late antique mode of knowing, marked above all by the assumption that material objects like churches and manuscripts could be carriers of abstract intelligible truths rooted in concrete historical events and places, which could be accessed and activated through the combined efficacy of image, text, and ritual operating in a complex yet unified whole.

Sets of Canon Tables surviving from late antique and early medieval manuscripts almost always contain a sophisticated decorative scheme consisting of architectural frames and a variety of flora and fauna. I take as my focus here one specific motif that often appears: the image of a round building commonly known as a *tholos* or *tempietto* which, when present, usually concludes the series of pages containing the prefatory Canon Tables. The chapter proceeds in four stages. First, I will provide an up-to-date catalogue of the surviving examples of this image and will argue that, while we cannot be certain whether Eusebius was its maker, similarities with surviving mosaics suggest that it originated in the fourth or fifth century. I will next examine the iconography of the image, surveying attempts

---

[3] Carruthers 1998: 198–220.
[4] For Eusebius' Gospel apparatus as a textual map, see Coogan 2017.

over the past eighty years to isolate its intended referent and will argue that such attempts are misguided, since the image is underdetermined and hence polyvalent, inviting the viewer to imaginatively engage in the process of meaning-making. Third, I will buttress this claim by highlighting the approach to sacred architecture evident in Eusebius' corpus, specifically a brief passage on the Church of the Holy Sepulchre and a fuller elaboration of his method in his oration delivered for the dedication of Paulinus' basilica at Tyre in 315. Finally, I conclude by considering what is distinctly late antique and distinctly Christian about the mode of knowing represented by the *tholos* image and the wider decorative scheme adorning the Canon Tables.

The Origins of the *Tholos* Image

The Surviving Examples

The surviving examples of the *tholos* image appear in a surprisingly diverse range of linguistic traditions across nearly a millennium, from the sixth century to at least the fifteenth. I group these images together, first, on the basis of a close iconographic similarity, in that they all depict a circular building with a domed roof supported by multiple columns. The second justification for considering these images as a group is that, with but one exception,[5] they are all connected to a set of Canon Tables (or once were), most commonly serving as the conclusion to the series of prefatory pages containing Eusebius' numeric matrices. Table 26.1 contains a list of the surviving examples of the image that have been identified, arranged roughly chronologically.[6]

---

[5] Among those examples listed here, the sole exception to this pattern is the version that appears in the Godescalc Gospel Lectionary (no. 3 in Table 26.1), which, as its name implies, is a gospel lectionary rather than a four-gospel codex. The Eusebian paratext was designed to function for a four-gospel codex, not a lectionary, so the absence of Canon Tables from this manuscript is not surprising, though the similarity of content between the two types of manuscripts perhaps explains why an artist thought it appropriate to include the *tholos*.

[6] According to The Index of Medieval Art (no. 58908), a *tempietto* also appears on fol. 355v of a gospel-book held at Hiera Monē tou Megalou Spēlaiou in Greece, but I have been unable to find any photographs of it or any scholarship discussing it. The *tholos*-style building occasionally appears in other kinds of manuscripts as well. As noted in Gnisci (2020: 76), a *tholos* is used as an opening page for a collection of Gregory of Nyssa's homilies in Stauronikita ms. 13, fol. 2r (see Weitzmann 1935: fig. 125). The structure is similarly used to frame the incipit of the *vita* of Gregory of Nazianzus in Iviron Monastery, ms. 27, fol. 413v (cf. Pelekanidis et al. 1975: 304 and fig. 45).

Table 26.1 Surviving examples of the *tholos* image

1	Rabbula Gospels: Florence, Laurentian Library, Plut. I.56, fol. 2r[1]	6th century	Syriac
2	Abba Garima I: Abba Garima Monastery, Ethiopia, AG II, fol. 258v[2] (see Plate 26.1)	6th–7th century	Geʿez
3	Godescalc Gospel Lectionary: Paris, Bibl. Nat., n.a. lat. 1203, fol. 3v[3]	c. 782	Latin
4	Gospels of Saint-Médard de Soissons: Paris, Bibl. Nat., lat. 8850, fol. 6v[4] (see Plate 26.2)	ante 827	Latin
5	Venice, Biblioteca Nazionale Marciana, MS gr. I. 8, fol. 3r[5] (see Plate 26.3)	9th century	Greek
6	Adishi Gospels: Mestia, Svaneti Museum, Georgian National Museum, MS 22, fol. 5v[6]	897	Georgian
7	Vatican, gr. 354, fol. 13v[7]	10th century	Greek
8	Erevan, Matenadaran, MS 9430, fol. 1r[8]	10th century	Armenian
9	Gospels of Mekhitarist Library, MS 697, fol. 6r[9]	10th century	Armenian
10	Etchmiadzin Gospels: Erevan, Matenadaran, MS 2374, fol. 5v[10] (see Plate 26.4)	989	Armenian
11	Second Etchmiadzin Gospels: Armenian Patriarchate, MS 2555, fol. 7r[11]	10th or early 11th century	Armenian
12	Gospels of the Armenian Patriarchate, MS 2562, fol. 3r[12]	10th–11th century	Armenian
13	Akkälä Guzay, Däbrä Libanos, fol. 7r[13]	12th–13th century	Geʿez
14	Ḥayq, Däbrä Ḥayq Ǝsṭifanos, fol. 12r[14]	1280–81	Geʿez
15	Addis Ababa, National Library, MS 28, fol. 14r[15]	c. 1300–39/40	Geʿez
16	Addis Ababa, The Institute of Ethiopian Studies, 3475a–b[16]	second half of 14th century	Geʿez
17	Säraye, Däbrä Maryam Qwäḥayn[17]	1360–61	Geʿez
18	Amba Därä, Maryam Mägdälawit, fol. 18r[18]	1362–63 or 1438–39	Geʿez
19	Paris, Bib. Nat., ms. ethiop. 32, fol.7r[19]	mid 14th to early 15th century?	Geʿez
20	Gospels of the Church of Abuna Gabra Masqal, Däbrä Mäʿar, fol. 10r[20]	1340–41	Geʿez
21	Zir Ganela Gospels: New York, Pierpoint Morgan Library, MS M.828, fol. 6r[21]	1400–1	Geʿez
22	New York, Metropolitan Museum of Art, accession no. 2006.100[22]	mid to late 14th century?	Geʿez
23	Walters Art Museum, MS W.836, fol. 6r[23]	mid to late 14th century	Geʿez
24	Gospels of the Church of Ura Masqal[24]	mid 14th to early 15th century	Geʿez
25	Lake Ṭana, Däq, Arsima Sämaʿǝtat[25]	mid 14th to early 15th century?	Geʿez
26	Täkwǝlädäre, Boru Meda Abärra Śǝllase, fol. 8r[26]	mid 14th to early 15th century?	Geʿez
27	Gospels of Däbrä Särabi, fol. 10r[27]	second half of 14th century?	Geʿez
28	Gospels of the Church of Kebran Gabriel[28]	c. 1344–1412	Geʿez
29	Däqqi Dašǝm, Qǝddus Mikaʾel, fol. 4r[29]	early 15th century?	Geʿez
30	New York, The Metropolitan Museum of Art, acc. no. 1998.66, fol. 16r[30]	early 15th century?	Geʿez
31	Private Collection, fol. 8r[31]	c. 1400	Geʿez

Table 26.1 (cont.)

32	Ğähğäh Giyorgis Gospel Book, Jäger II, miniature 10[32]	15th century	Geʿez
33	Golden Gospels of Dabra Sahel[33]	?	Geʿez
34	Yerevan, Matenadaran, MS 6342, fol. 8v[34]	1443	Armenian

[1] See Crawford 2019: 88, fig. 19; McKenzie and Watson 2016: 154, fig. 219; Underwood 1950: fig. 56. On the images in this manuscript, see especially Bernabò 2008, 2014.

[2] See Gnisci 2020: 74, fig. 4; Crawford 2019: 238, fig. 37; McKenzie and Watson 2016: pl. 42.

[3] See McKenzie and Watson 2016: 135, fig. 197; Underwood 1950: fig. 25; Nordenfalk 1938: Taf. 39a.

[4] See Crawford 2019: 238, fig. 38; McKenzie and Watson 2016: 137–38, figs. 198–99; Underwood 1950: fig. 26; Nordenfalk 1938: Taf. 39b.

[5] See Crawford 2019: 239, fig. 39; McKenzie and Watson 2016: 139, fig. 200; Underwood 1950: fig. 55; Nordenfalk 1938: 104, fig. 2.

[6] See Crawford 2019: 239, fig. 40; McKenzie and Watson 2016: 134, fig. 195; Grigoryan 2014: 15, fig. 6; Underwood 1950: fig. 44; Nordenfalk 1938: 115, fig. 5.

[7] A digitised version of the manuscript can be found at https://digi.vatlib.it/view/MSS_Vat.gr.354 (accessed 29 January 2021).

[8] See McKenzie and Watson 2016: 132, fig. 190; Grigoryan 2014: 14, fig. 4.

[9] See Grigoryan 2014: 13, fig. 3; Underwood 1950: fig. 37; Nordenfalk 1938: Taf. 33a.

[10] See McKenzie and Watson 2016: 133, fig. 193; Grigoryan 2014: 12, fig. 1; Underwood 1950: fig. 35; Nordenfalk 1938: Taf. 24.

[11] See McKenzie and Watson 2016: 133, fig. 194; Grigoryan 2014: 12, fig. 2; Underwood 1950: fig. 36; Nordenfalk 1938: Taf. 33b.

[12] See Grigoryan 2014: 14, fig. 5; Underwood 1950: fig. 34.

[13] See Gnisci 2020: 75, fig. 5.

[14] See Gnisci 2020: 76, fig. 6.

[15] See Gnisci 2020: 77, fig. 7.

[16] See Heldman, Munro-Hay, and Grierson 1993: 122.

[17] See Leroy 1962: 188, fig. 12.

[18] See Gnisci 2020: 82, fig. 10.

[19] See Underwood 1950: fig. 53.

[20] See Gnisci 2020: 69, fig. 2; McKenzie and Watson 2016: 142, fig. 203.

[21] See McKenzie and Watson 2016: 141, fig. 202; Underwood 1950: fig. 54.

[22] See Gnisci 2020: 68, fig. 1; McKenzie and Watson 2016: 142, fig. 204.

[23] See Gnisci 2020: 78, fig. 8; McKenzie and Watson 2016: 142, fig. 205.

[24] See McKenzie and Watson 2016: 143, fig. 206.

[25] See Leroy 1962: 189, fig. 13.

[26] See Gnisci 2020: 72.

[27] See Gnisci 2020: 80, fig. 9; McKenzie and Watson 2016: 143, fig. 207.

[28] See McKenzie and Watson 2016: 143, fig. 208.

[29] See Gnisci 2020: 72.

[30] See Lepage and Mercier 2012: 103, fig. 4.

[31] See Mercier 2000: 54.

[32] See Wright, Jäger, and Leroy 1961: pl. XXVIII.

[33] See McKenzie and Watson 2016: 143, fig. 209.

[34] See Grigoryan 2014: 17, fig. 7.

The distribution of these images is striking for a number of reasons. First is the breadth of the distribution in both geography and chronology. Yet despite this breadth, the surviving examples for the most part neatly form a handful of clusters. The image in the Rabbula Gospels (no. 1) is idiosyncratic, for reasons shortly to be discussed, and the Garima image (no. 2) from the sixth or seventh century, the earliest example of the most frequent model with flora and fauna, is an outlier in terms of its early date.[7] Two Latin manuscripts with the image then appear (nos. 3, 4), with no precursor in the Latin world nor any descendants. Perhaps these were copied from Eastern models imported during the Carolingian renaissance.[8] Similarly only two Greek examples survive (nos. 5, 7), which might be due simply to the accidents of survival, since few sets of Canon Tables in Greek from the early Byzantine period are extant. The earliest dated Georgian gospels, the Adishi Gospels from 897, have a version of the image (no. 6), and it appears shortly thereafter in several of our earliest surviving Armenian gospel-books dated to the tenth and eleventh centuries (nos. 8–12). The *tholos* page next turns up in Geʿez gospel-books in the twelfth or thirteenth century, being found in a stunning twenty-one manuscripts from Ethiopia over the next two centuries (nos. 13–33). The fact that it also appears in the Ethiopian Garima Gospels from the sixth or seventh century suggests that these later Ethiopian examples are probably not the result of an influx of foreign influences in the medieval period but are subsequent stages of an artistic tradition stretching back at least eight centuries whose earliest artefacts have almost entirely perished, in keeping with the paucity of extant manuscripts from Ethiopia dated earlier than the twelfth century. The final Armenian example (no. 34) is again an outlier, both in date and with respect to the iconography of the image, which has departed from the realistic architecture of the earliest examples in favour of a much more abstract style.

Despite some variation, the examples listed here show a surprising degree of iconographic stability, an observation that led scholars like Carl Nordenfalk and Paul Underwood to search for a common archetype behind them all.[9] Isolating and reconstructing a single archetype is complicated by the fact that there must have been a number of intermediary models that have perished, since common features appear in manuscripts

---

[7] Assuming, that is, that one follows the carbon-14 dating of the manuscript, as most scholars do (see McKenzie and Watson 2016: 31–41). For a dissenting voice, see Elsner 2020a: 109–11.
[8] As suggested by McKenzie and Watson 2016: 136.
[9] McKenzie and Watson (2016: 139–40) raise the possibility of multiple prototypes behind the various versions that have survived.

separated by centuries and by linguistic barriers. This difficulty, however, is no hindrance to the present argument, since my focus is on the manifold meanings later artists and viewers may have found in the image rather than the hypothetical single archetype lying behind all subsequent versions. Here it suffices to draw attention to some of the common features in these images and the interpretative possibilities they present.

The most basic model survives in a ninth-century Greek manuscript (no. 5). It shows a relatively simple structure with four pillars supporting a domed roof surmounted by a cross and including a small lamp hanging within. In contrast to most other surviving examples, the building in this manuscript is comparatively unadorned. Perhaps this minimalism is related to the fact that a short text serving as an introduction to the Canon Tables (known as the 'hypothesis inscription') is written between the columns, a feature that also appears in a less skilled version in a later Greek manuscript (no. 7)[10] and in several much later Ethiopian gospel-books (e.g., no. 19).[11] In these examples, one of the clear purposes of the *tholos* image is to frame this text and thereby serve as a visual and textual summary of the entire Canon Tables apparatus.[12] In keeping with its function as a symbolic summary of the entire Eusebian paratext, the *tholos* page in no. 5 occurs at the front of the series of Canon Tables and thus marks the reader's first encounter with the apparatus. The Gospels of Saint-Médard de Soissons (no. 4) similarly place the *tholos* at the front of the series, as do the Rabbula Gospels (no. 1), though in most of the surviving examples the image appears instead at the end of the sequence of prefatory pages containing Eusebius' paratext. In the Rabbula Gospels, the building frames standing portraits of Ammonius and Eusebius, as a way of drawing the reader's attention to the two people whose work went into the creation of the Canon Tables.[13] Thus, similarly to the version in no. 5, the *tholos* in the Rabbula Gospels is used to highlight material relevant to the entire Eusebian apparatus and so functions in a summative fashion.

---

[10] Cf. Underwood 1950: 108; Wallraff 2013: 9–10.

[11] This hypothesis inscription appears in some other manuscripts, like the Rossano Gospels, fol. 5r where it is inscribed within a wreath that serves as a frontispiece to the sequence of Canon Tables. Cf. Underwood 1950: 109; McKenzie and Watson 2016: 139. The version of the *tholos* in no. 19 also shows similarities to no. 5 in terms of the specific shape and proportions of the structure. Both images divide the space immediately above the columns into three differently coloured sections. These features suggest a common origin for these two versions, separated though they are by four centuries and a linguistic barrier.

[12] On frames in late antiquity, see Platt and Squire 2017, especially part V, 'Framing Texts'.

[13] On the Ammonius-Eusebius image in the Rabbula Gospels, see Underwood 1950: 110–11, who regarded it as an adaptation of the more standard *tholos* image.

In contrast to the use of the *tholos* to frame the hypothesis inscription in a handful of cases and to house the portraits of Ammonius and Eusebius in the Rabbula Gospels, the elements that frequently appear inside the building in the other surviving examples are curtains, usually knotted and sometimes tied to the columns (e.g. nos. 6, 7, 8, 9, 10, 11, 12, 19, 20, 21, 22, 23, 24, 27, 28, 33), as well as hanging lamps, sometimes so small that they are easily overlooked (e.g. nos. 8, 9, 10, 32). The significance of these elements is not as unambiguous as the hypothesis inscription or the dual authorial portrait of the Rabbula manuscript, but they open up a range of possible associations: the unveiling of scripture in the light of the gospel; the physical veiling or unveiling of parts of a church; Christ as the light of the world; the church as a lamp; and so on. Furthermore, unlike the minimalism of no. 5, almost all the surviving examples present a variety of flora and fauna surrounding the *tholos*, with nos. 2 and 8 as representative examples. Evergreen trees grow on either side of the building and birds scurry about on the grass-covered roof. In most later Ethiopian manuscripts, stags or antelope appear on either side of the building as well. These much later Ethiopian versions of the image must be somehow related to the two surviving Carolingian manuscripts (nos. 3, 4), since they, too, include deer and a multitude of birds. The two Carolingian models have eight columns in place of the usual four and both have a low wall around the interior of the columns, motifs that also appear in several of the Ethiopian manuscripts such as nos. 19, 20, 21, 22, 23, 24, 27, and 33. The Gospels of Saint-Médard de Soissons (no. 4) take this theme a step further by using a different perspective, allowing the viewer to see that the *tholos* is filled with water and has a small fountain in the centre of the pool.[14] Paul Underwood has, with justification, called this version the 'fountain of life' and argued that it symbolises baptism, an association that is also apt for the image in the Godescalc Gospel Lectionary (no. 3), which was commissioned in part to commemorate the baptism of Charlemagne's son Pippin by Pope Hadrian in 781.[15]

Such is the artistic imagery that frequently accompanies the *tholos* in its surviving examples. As implied in the preceding brief overview, we should not assume that the image in these various manuscripts had a single stable

---

[14] The manuscript repeats this motif by including a miniature version of the water-filled *tholos* in the tympanum under the arch housing canons 6–8 on fol. 11r (see Underwood 1950: fig. 29). Similarly, a miniature square *tempietto* supported by four columns and housing a fountain appears atop one of the architectural frames housing the Canon Tables in the Greek gospel-book Biblioteca Palatina, gr. 5, fol. 8r (see Eleuteri 1993: pl. i), as well as on fols. 3r and 5r (The Index of Medieval Art, nos. 130567, 130812). This same manuscript has a domed four-pillared canopy between portraits of Eusebius and Carpianus on fol. 12v (see Crawford 2019: 89, fig. 20).

[15] See Underwood 1950: 64–67.

meaning for those who viewed it over such a long span of time. Some versions add elements to bring out different associations. Moreover, even when the same imagery is used in different locales (e.g., the Carolingian empire versus medieval Ethiopia), it may have carried different meanings. What remains the same is the summative role of the *tholos* page with respect to the entire Canon Tables apparatus and its richly symbolic but abstract quality. In what follows, I turn to late antique material and textual evidence to consider how such a symbolic and abstract summation might have been used by its viewers in their cognitive projects.

Late Antique *Comparanda* for the *Tholos* Image

Since Carl Nordenfalk's influential 1938 monograph, it has been customary to assume that the *tholos* image goes back to Eusebius' archetype of the Canon Tables from which all later copies descend.[16] Three main lines of argument have been adduced to support this claim. First, the *tholos* image appears contemporaneously with our earliest complete sets of Canon Tables and was transmitted across nearly all the linguistic traditions into which the Eusebian apparatus was translated, suggesting that this motif entered the tradition early.[17] The second line of argument focuses upon the harmony of the *tholos* page with the rest of the decorative scheme found throughout the Canon Tables, specifically two design elements. First, the *tholos* displays notable iconographic consistency with the architectural frames used to house Eusebius' ten numeric matrices, which similarly consist of columns supporting arches. If, as Nordenfalk argued, the architectural frames were a component of Eusebius' archetype, then presumably the *tholos* page would have been as well.[18] Secondly, in Nordenfalk's meticulous reconstruction of the layout of Eusebius' archetype, the *Letter to Carpianus* occupied the first two pages, followed by the ten matrices spread out across the next seven pages. The addition of the *tholos* image as a concluding page would bring the total sequence to ten pages, making full use of the first five folios of a manuscript and conforming to Eusebius' preference for having precisely ten numeric matrices in his paratextual apparatus.[19]

The final argument that the *tholos* page derives from Eusebius himself stems from Nordenfalk's contention that it is intended to be a representation of the aedicula that Constantine built over the Holy Sepulchre in

---

[16] For recent analysis of the scholarly debate about Eusebius' view of sacred images, see Caillet 2014, who concludes that although Eusebius rejected depictions of the divine, he was open to figural or symbolic images.

[17] Nordenfalk 1938: 103–4.   [18] Nordenfalk 1938: 103.   [19] Nordenfalk 1938: 102–3.

Jerusalem (assuming of course that the aedicula was built by Constantine, which is itself debated).[20] The significance that this site held in Eusebius' imagination is evident from the fact that he delivered an oration in the emperor's presence on the symbolism of the Basilica of the Holy Sepulchre and preached the dedication sermon for it in 336 CE (more on this below). Furthermore, we know that Constantine sent Eusebius a request to have the Caesarean scriptorium produce copies of the 'inspired oracles' including 'magnificent adornment' (μεγαλοπρεπεῖ κατασκευῇ) for use in the churches of Constantinople.[21] Similarly, the eleventh-century Byzantine historian George Cedrenus noted in passing that Constantine, 'having made golden books of the gospels [covered] with pearls and [precious] stones, presented them to the great church, a remarkable wonder'.[22] Neither Eusebius nor Cedrenus explicitly describes decoration *within* manuscripts, but we can at least say that Constantine showed an interest in the production of richly adorned copies of sacred texts. An image such as the *tholos* page would theoretically have been suitable to such a programme, inasmuch as it would, on Nordenfalk's view, depict the emperor's own construction at Christianity's holiest site and was produced by the bishop who had taken a special interest in it.[23]

Nordenfalk's contention that this image goes back to Eusebius has been widely accepted, but it is far from conclusive. The first two lines of argument merely suggest that it appeared early in the Canon Tables tradition but do not rule out the possibility that it was a post-Eusebian innovation. Moreover, the third argument loses much of its force if one weakens the

---

[20] Nordenfalk 1938: 107–8. On the debate over what Constantine built at the site, see Biddle 1999: 68–69. For a reconstruction of the layout of Constantine's aedicula, see Biddle 1999: 117, and for the surviving images of the aedicula from the first millennium, see pp. 21–28. Diagrams of the layout of the overall complex can be found at Krautheimer 1975: 63–65. A short summary description of the aedicula is also available in Murphy-O'Connor 2012: 208–9.

[21] Eusebius, *Vit. Const.* 3.1. This passage of Eusebius and the following one from George Cedrenus were highlighted in Nordenfalk 1951: 16. Eusebius' passage containing Constantine's request is notoriously difficult to interpret. For a recent discussion, see Parker 2010: 19–22.

[22] George Cedrenus, *Compendium historiarum* 314 (I. Bekker, *Georgius Cedrenus Ioannis Scylitzae opera*, 2 vols. [Corpus scriptorum historiae Byzantinae; Bonn: Weber, 1838–39], 1.517). ἀλλὰ καὶ πτύχας εὐαγγελίων χρυσᾶς διὰ μαργάρων καὶ λίθων κατασκευάσας ἐν τῇ μεγάλῃ ἐκκλησίᾳ προσήγαγε, θαύματος ἀξίας. I am grateful to Roger Scott for sharing with me the unpublished translation of this passage produced by himself, John Burke, and Paul Tuffin, which I here follow.

[23] See De Vegvar 2006: 248: 'one can scarcely envision a reference that would have been closer to the concerns of both Eusebius himself and his imperial patron'. For an argument against the common view of Eusebius as Constantine's court theologian, which is often assumed in arguments that link the *tholos* to the aedicula at the Church of the Holy Sepulchre, see Johnson 2006b: 153–97.

connection between the image and the aedicula at the Holy Sepulchre, as I will do in the next section of this chapter. Nevertheless, even if we cannot be certain whether the *tholos* page was created by Eusebius himself, the image is undoubtedly at home in the world of late antique Christian art. In itself, the *tholos*-style building is neither uniquely late antique nor distinctly Christian, as can be seen in the *comparanda* from Petra and Pompeii originally adduced by Nordenfalk and recently reiterated by Judith McKenzie.[24] Nevertheless, material remains demonstrate that, by the fifth century, this style of building had taken on distinctly Christian associations.[25] The most famous examples are pilgrims' flasks, or *ampullae*, that were carried back to Europe by visitors to the Holy Sepulchre.[26] These depict the aedicula over Christ's tomb, consisting of a canopy supported by columns and surmounted by a cross, which is undeniably similar in structure to the building in our manuscripts.

Moreover, the *tholos* can be found in church mosaics from this same period. A floor mosaic from the Church of the Holy Martyrs at Taybat al-Imam near Hama, Syria, dated to 441 CE, depicts a *tholos* structure between buildings labelled Bethlehem and Jerusalem, with peacocks and fruit trees on either side (see Plate 26.5).[27] Within the *tholos*, beneath drawn curtains and a hanging lamp, is a lamb, and in the lower register of the mosaic an eagle sits at the source of the four rivers of paradise, from which stags drink and trees grow forth. A damaged fifth-century floor mosaic from Iunca/Younga (Mahares) in Tunisia similarly has a *tholos* in its centre, situated between unmarked buildings that presumably again represent Jerusalem and Bethlehem, and beneath the *tholos* once more stand deer drinking from the four rivers of paradise.[28] A similar image also appears in a mosaic from the fifth-century Church of Temanaa in Syria, where a *tholos* stands with a stag and a tree on either side and has birds on its roof and a lamp hanging inside.[29] Many of these features, of course, also appear in the *tholos* images associated with Canon Tables, such as the curtains and lamp,

---

[24] Nordenfalk 1938: 107; McKenzie and Watson 2016: 130. Cf. Klauser 1961: 195; McKenzie 2007: 97–98.

[25] For a survey of the architectural use and theological significance of canopies in Byzantium, see Bogdanović 2017.

[26] Nordenfalk 1938: 107–8. Cf. Underwood 1950: figs. 42–43, 49–52; McKenzie and Watson 2016: 134, fig. 196.

[27] See McKenzie and Watson 2016: 126, fig. 179; Broilo 2016: 316; Zaqzuq and Piccirillo 1999. The peacocks may symbolise immortality and eternal life, associations they had in non-Christian sources as well. See Maguire 1987: 39–40.

[28] See Underwood 1950: 115; McKenzie and Watson 2016: 126, fig. 180.

[29] See Jouéjati 2012; Gnisci 2020: 89, fig.12.

as well as garden and paradise motifs, including peacocks, trees, and stags, so a relation between the codex version of the image and the mosaics is compelling, as recognised over half a century ago by Underwood. The fact that the four rivers of paradise were often taken as an analogy for the fourfold gospel further strengthens the associative links between these church mosaics and the *tholos* page that appears alongside Canon Tables in gospel manuscripts.[30]

A final mosaic can be added to this short list which helpfully complicates the evidence by showing that the *tholos*-style building could also be put to other uses in Christian contexts during this period. The monumental Rotunda in Thessaloniki was originally a palace of the emperor Galerius, but by the late fourth or early fifth century it had been converted into a Christian church, at which point its dome was decorated with an elaborate scheme of mosaics depicting scenes of heavenly worship.[31] The best-preserved band of mosaics encircling the dome presents a two-storey complex of buildings that includes several round structures supported by four columns, similar to the *tholos* image (see Plate 26.6),[32] and within the building complex are other familiar motifs like hanging lamps, candles, knotted curtains, fountains, and various birds, including peacocks, along with worshipping figures standing in the orant position. Moreover, two panels feature as their central element domed pavilions supported by six columns, beneath which lie gem-studded books resting upon a pedestal in front of a green curtain.[33] There is no indication of what books are intended, but a four-gospel codex is surely the most likely candidate given its prominence in Christian worship. The most compelling interpretation of the mosaics views them in the context of the liturgical rituals that would have taken place in this sacred space: 'Early Christians using the Rotunda would have looked up to see patterns of their own worship, in idealized form surrounding them above.'[34] In other words, the mosaics were designed to

---

[30] On this and other such analogies for the fourfold gospel, see especially Coogan 2023.

[31] On the rotunda and its mosaics, see Nasrallah 2005; Bakirtzis, Kourkoutidou-Nikolaidou, and Mauropoulou-Tsioumi 2012: 48–127; Kiilerich and Torp 2017. Although most date the mosaics to the reign of Theodosius I, Charalambos Bakirtzis has proposed that they were completed under Constantine I (Bakirtzis, Kourkoutidou-Nikolaidou, and Mauropoulou-Tsioumi 2012: 115–16). I am grateful to Warren Woodfin for drawing these mosaics to my attention during our delightful stay at Dumbarton Oaks in autumn 2019.

[32] The second and sixth panels each include on their second storey two four-pillared *tholoi* with lamps hanging within them. See Bakirtzis, Kourkoutidou-Nikolaidou, and Mauropoulou-Tsioumi 2012: 64–65.

[33] For images and discussion, see Bakirtzis, Kourkoutidou-Nikolaidou, and Mauropoulou-Tsioumi 2012: 100–9. Cf. Nasrallah 2005: 491–92.

[34] Nasrallah 2005: 495.

remind participants that the church on earth was united in worship with the church in heaven, and that the events playing out before their eyes had a counterpart in a higher immaterial realm.

None of these mosaics replicates precisely the same image that we find associated with the Eusebian Canon Tables, but they do present numerous overlapping elements and thus, at a minimum, demonstrate that, even though the majority of surviving examples surveyed above date to the medieval period, the *tholos* image is at home in the context of late antique Christian art as early as the late fourth or fifth century. Before considering further the light these mosaics might shed upon the interpretation of the *tholos* image, we need first to survey briefly the various proposals that have been offered over the last century for its meaning.

The Iconography of the *Tholos* Image

Nordenfalk's argument that the *tholos* image was a depiction of the aedicula built by Constantine over the Holy Sepulchre rested upon its similarity to representations of the structure that can be found on *ampullae*. The connection to the Holy Sepulchre is especially clear in the version of the image in the ninth-century Adishi Gospels (no. 6), which, unique among all surviving examples, adds tall grills between the columns on either side, a feature that is also evident on the pilgrim *ampullae*. Moreover, within and around the *tholos* in the Adishi Gospels are several inscriptions in Georgian, the earliest of which, possibly contemporary with the manuscript, reads 'Holy resurrection on Sunday'.[35] Although Nordenfalk's identification of the *tholos* as Constantine's aedicula is widely accepted,[36] other proposals have been advanced. As already mentioned, Paul Underwood, in an influential study, conceded that the versions in the later Eastern manuscripts allude to the Holy Sepulchre but argued for the primacy of the two Carolingian images which he took to be symbolic representations of baptism as the 'fountain of life'.[37] Theodore Klauser, assuming that Eusebius included the image in the copies of the scriptures he prepared for Constantine in 331 CE and that the aedicula was not completed until several years later, concluded that the *tholos* could not depict the aedicula but rather represented the ciborium of Eusebius' own cathedral in Caesarea. Klauser also highlighted the oddity of the fact that the *tholos*, in most versions, is empty

---

[35] Cf. Underwood 1950: 93; McKenzie and Watson 2016: 134.
[36] Cf. Klemm 1972; de Vegvar 2006; Amirkhanian 2008–9. [37] Underwood 1950: 117–18.

and proposed that the vacant structure was an allusion to the fourfold gospel itself.[38] Several years later, Günter Bandmann proposed that the image is 'ein ideales architektonisches Ensemble' that refers simultaneously to the Holy Sepulchre, the fountain of life, and the altar in a church,[39] while Klaus Wessel highlighted several ways in which the *tholos* differs from the aedicula depicted on the *ampullae* and argued that it instead represented the ciborium at the sanctuary at Bethlehem.[40] More recently, Gohar Grigoryan, once again pointing out the chronological problem highlighted by Klauser, claimed that the *tholos* in the Armenian manuscripts is meant to 'represent a symbolic temple of God'.[41]

Such are the proposals for the meaning of the *tholos* image. In concluding the first half of this chapter, four observations upon the preceding overview are necessary to set the stage for the next phase of my argument. First, much scholarship on the *tholos* had the tacit or explicit goal of identifying what the image's creator, whether Eusebius or someone else, intended the building to represent. However, the attempt to isolate an original meaning risks obscuring the richness and variety in the surviving examples. I therefore take as my aim here to consider the manifold possibilities of interpretation the image presented to late antique viewers rather than to narrow its meaning to a single, original referent.

Second, while some late antique viewers would have viewed the *tholos* as a depiction of the aedicula built atop the Holy Sepulchre, we should not overlook the fact that, in most of the surviving examples, the image is rather oddly generic. As Elisabeth Klemm observed, various interpretations have arisen precisely because it is not obviously marked as a tomb.[42] The pilgrim flasks usually include additional details to make clear that they are specifically recalling the Holy Sepulchre, including grills between the two innermost columns and, between the grills, the opening of the tomb itself, or even the women at the tomb on Easter morning. The absence of these features in the *tholos* image renders it underdetermined and more polyvalent than the *ampullae* so often used as *comparanda*. The force of this observation is strengthened by the fact that the artist responsible for

---

[38] Klauser 1961. [39] Bandmann 1966: 28. [40] Wessel 1978: 962–67.
[41] Grigoryan 2014: 16. Grigoryan's argument is bolstered by the fact that Abba Garima I, which contains the earliest example of the most common version of the *tholos* image, has a companion codex of slightly earlier date (Abba Garima III) that includes a full-page depiction of a temple as the final page in the sequence of Canon Tables, seemingly in place of the *tholos* page, which might imply that the temple and *tholos* are thematically related (see McKenzie and Watson 2016: 121–28 and plate 14). On the temple image in Abba Garima III, see Watson 2021.
[42] Klemm 1972: 88.

the Adishi Gospels was apparently unsatisfied by the indeterminacy of the more common version of the *tholos* image, and so added additional features to clarify its intended referent. This generic quality is also evident in the striking fact that, as Klauser observed, the *tholos* is most often empty aside from lamps, which are usually comparatively small and scarcely take up the full interior space, or drawn curtains, which imply the presence of something within the building that would otherwise be veiled. Yet in most versions, the pulling back of the curtains has unveiled a surprising absence rather than any definite object.

Third, rather than viewing this indeterminacy as a problem, I suggest it is precisely what gives the image its potency, since it invites viewers to ponder for themselves what the picture before them represents or even imaginatively to supply the missing sacred object in the empty space within the *tholos*. This proposal becomes more plausible when the *tholos* page is viewed in the context of the overall decorative scheme found throughout the rest of the Canon Tables apparatus. What is invariably true in terms of the placement of the image is that it appears either at the beginning or, in most cases, at the end of the series of pages containing Eusebius' prefatory paratext, performing a summative or concluding function.[43] Moreover, we should recall that the dominant element in the decorative scheme on the preceding pages are the architectural frames housing Eusebius' *Letter to Carpianus* and his ten numeric matrices, which create a sort of artificial built environment within the book. As Bruno Reudenbach has emphasised, this symbolic setting exploits the real physical space created by reading a codex in contrast to a scroll. Whereas the scroll only moves left and right or up and down in a flat plane before the reader's gaze, the codex is broken into discrete pages that move through three dimensions of space as they are turned, creating depth and 'space' that is absent in the experience of reading a scroll.[44] The decorative architecture of the Canon Tables seems designed to intensify or render more explicit this spatial aspect of the codex by inviting readers to place themselves in the imagined world depicted on the pages of the book, moving through space as they turn the pages.[45]

---

[43] Nordenfalk likewise viewed the *tholos* as the logical conclusion to the preceding pages: 'Als Schlußseite der Kanones, die eine Zusammenfassung der Berichte der Evangelien von dem Leben und der Lehre Christi darstellen, würde jedenfalls eine Erinnerung an das Endziel des Erdenlebens Christi und den Inbegriff der christlichen Erlösungshoffnung als durchaus sinnvoll erscheinen' (1938: 108).

[44] Reudenbach 2009: 60–61.

[45] Reudenbach 2009: 65. Cf. de Vegvar 2006; Amirkhanian 2008–9. In a parallel fashion, Elsner (2020a: 108) comments: 'The architectural image [used as a prefatory illustration] in particular

Plate 2.1 Baptism. Fresco. Catacomb of Saints Marcellinus and Peter. Rome, Italy. 3rd century (Archivah / Alamy Stock Photo)

Plate 17.1 Apse mosaic, Anemurium (Photo: Campbell 1998: plate xv)

Plate 26.1 *Tholos* image in Abba Garima I (6th–7th century). Ethiopia, Abba Garima Monastery, AG II, fol. 258v (Photo © Michael Gervers, 2004)

Plate 26.2 Fountain of life image in the Gospels of St Médard de Soissons (before 827 CE). Paris, Bibliothèque nationale de France, MS lat. 8850, fol. 6v.

Plate 26.3 *Tholos* with a *hypothesis* inscription, serving as the frontispiece for the sequence of Canon Tables that follow in a Greek gospel-book (9th century). Venice, Biblioteca Nazionale Marciana, MS gr. I 8, fol. 3r.

Plate 26.4 *Tholos* image in Etchmiadzin Gospels (989). Erevan, Matenadaran, MS 2374, fol. 5v.

Plate 26.5 Taybat al-Imam near Hama, Syria, Church of the Holy Martyrs, floor mosaic (441 CE) (Photo © Judith McKenzie)

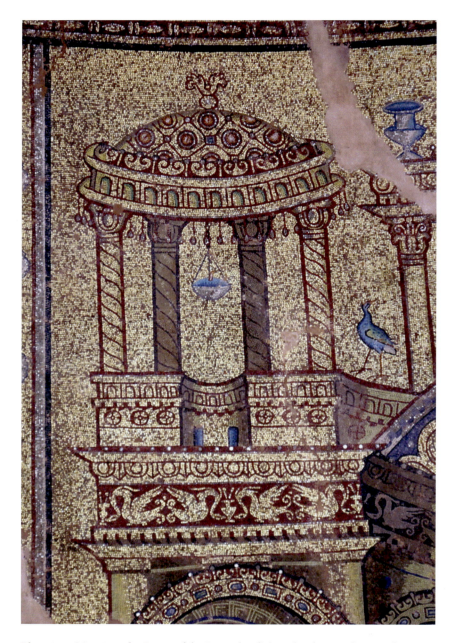

Plate 26.6 Mosaic in the Dome of the Rotunda of Thessaloniki. © Ephorate of Antiquities of Thessaloniki, Hellenic Ministry of Culture & Sports – Archaeological Resources Fund

The important point for my purposes is to observe that, on this interpretation, the framing columns and arches are designed to engage the viewer's imagination and active participation.[46] This, I suggest, might explain the generic quality of the *tholos* image, since this indeterminacy similarly draws the viewer into the process of meaning-making. In short, the overall decorative scheme puts the viewer in the position of being on an imagined journey, walking through or alongside each of the archways to reach the next stop along the way, achieving a climax with the *tholos* image that invites an imaginative response.[47]

Finally, the relevance of the aforementioned church mosaics for interpreting the *tholos* page has not been sufficiently recognised, when in fact they provide the closest analogues to it in light of their numerous overlapping motifs mentioned above. In fact, when viewed in conjunction with them, the *tholos* page could be viewed as a *pars pro toto* summary of any of these larger complex pictures, whether the garden paradise imagery of the mosaics from Syria and Tunisia or the heavenly worship scene depicted in the rotunda in Thessaloniki. None of these mosaics are mere representations of the physical world. It is true that two of them include buildings denoting Jerusalem and Bethlehem, but these structures are placed alongside a rich array of symbolic images, calling the viewer into a realm that includes but also transcends the world of everyday experience. So it is, I suggest, for the *tholos* page. It too, in most of its versions, does not refer unambiguously to a single physical structure but is instead open to a variety of identifications including actual physical church buildings, as well as the heavenly Jerusalem, along with the associations and rituals attached to these sites such as the death and resurrection of Christ, baptism, the Eucharist, and, not least, the four gospels which preserve the sacred record of these realities. The fact that the *tholos* can serve as a suitable summary of both sets of mosaics, and no doubt of still others as well, once more highlights its polyvalence. Viewers could fill out the image and situate it in symbolic settings familiar from other textual and visual sources.

---

focalises the *artefactual* nature of the book as something *constructed* of parchment or papyrus, carefully treated, rolled or stitched, inscribed and painted on.' On this aspect of the codex, see especially Boudalis 2018.

[46] A similar point has been made by Timothy O'Sullivan with respect to the use of porticoes to frame the famous series of paintings depicting scenes from the Odyssey from the first century BCE: 'This is the point of the portico frame: the metaphor of ambulatory philosophical contemplation that it imposes allows for individual reactions and personal interpretations and is thus meant to spur discussion among the strolling viewers' (O'Sullivan 2007: 525).

[47] The idea of a movement through imagined space culminating in the *tholos* page is also argued by Strøm-Olsen 2018: esp. 429.

Learning from Eusebius How to Think with Symbols and Space

The approach to the *tholos* image I have proposed gains additional support when considered in light of late antique textual sources that discuss built church structures. The author whose writings most clearly elucidate this point is Eusebius himself. I bring Eusebius' writings into the argument at this stage not because I hold that he himself was necessarily responsible for creating the *tholos* page for his original archetype of the Canon Tables, as if the passages that follow reveal his creative intent. As suggested above, the arguments that the image originated with Eusebius are ultimately inconclusive and the image is polyvalent. Nevertheless, Eusebius' writings are the earliest textual sources commenting directly on church buildings and it is unlikely that he was completely idiosyncratic in his treatment of them. I suggest that we can, therefore, take his writings as a plausible indication of what a late antique viewer of the *tholos* page might have thought when viewing it and how they might have been inclined to put it to use. Eusebius commented directly on two churches, the Church of the Holy Sepulchre and Church of Tyre, and in what follows I consider his treatment of each in turn.

Eusebius on the Church of the Holy Sepulchre

Eusebius is thought to have written at least four treatments of the structure Constantine erected over the Holy Sepulchre.[48] The first occurs in his extended narrative of Constantine's building projects on Christianity's three most sacred sites; it consists of a descriptive account that narrates the excavation of the site, the discovery of the tomb, and the building of a shrine on the location.[49] A second text is the oration appended to the end of the *Vita Constantini* as the *De laudibus Constantini* 11–18, which provides little description of the structure and focuses instead on Constantine and his role in redemptive history. In another passage of the *Vita Constantini*, Eusebius alludes to a third treatment of the Holy Sepulchre that he delivered in the emperor's presence in Constantinople in 335 CE, which is now assumed to have been lost.[50]

---

[48] For what follows, see Smith 1989: 239–40. For a more recent survey of Eusebius' comments on the Holy Sepulchre, see Spieser 2014.

[49] Eusebius, *Vit. Const.* 3.29–40.

[50] Eusebius, *Vit. Const.* 4.46. Eusebius stated that he planned to publish this oration to the emperor together with his tricennial oration, in other words in the same position as the text just mentioned as *Laud. Const.* 11–18, but because the description does not fit this oration, scholars have concluded that it must have been a separate work. Cf. Cameron and Hall 1999: 331.

The fourth text is similarly lost, but Eusebius' brief description of its contents is intriguing and suggestive. In his account of the Council of Tyre in 335, he reported that Constantine ordered the assembled bishops to travel to Jerusalem for the dedication of the new church there. This was a celebratory event, with a variety of speeches delivered, including one by Eusebius himself:

> This was the occasion when we also, being honoured with favours beyond us, graced the feast with a diverse array of speeches to those assembled, at one time interpreting in a written work the elaborate descriptions of the emperor's philosophical ideas, at another making prophetic visions apply to the symbols presently in hand.

> ἔνθα δὴ καὶ ἡμεῖς τῶν ὑπὲρ ἡμᾶς ἀγαθῶν ἠξιωμένοι ποικίλαις ταῖς εἰς τὸ κοινὸν διαλέξεσι τὴν ἑορτὴν ἐτιμῶμεν, τοτὲ μὲν {διὰ γράμματος} τῶν βασιλεῖ πεφιλοσοφημένων τὰς ἐκφράσεις {ἑρμηνεύοντες} <ποιούμενοι>, τοτὲ δὲ καιρίους καὶ τοῖς προκειμένοις συμβόλοις τὰς προφητικὰς {ποιούμενοι} <ἑρμηνεύοντες> θεωρίας.[51]

As suggested by the various brackets in the Greek text, editors suspect textual corruption in this passage, but the general import is clear enough. Three points are relevant for the present inquiry. First, Eusebius holds that the buildings constructed by Constantine encoded the emperor's 'philosophical ideas' (τῶν ... πεφιλοσοφημένων), which can be unfolded through the process of ἔκφρασις. The word ἔκφρασις was, of course, a standard rhetorical term for a vivid description of something, whether of a battle scene, a work of art, or, as in this case, a building.[52] Second, Eusebius highlights the σύμβολα that existed in the sacred space. Cameron and Hall have translated this term as 'rites', which is one possible meaning and could be what Eusebius has in mind here.[53] However, as early as Pythagoras, the word was laden with significant philosophical connotations and continued to have currency among Platonists well into late antiquity.[54] Eusebius' contemporary Porphyry, for example, used the word to refer to 'either a material entity standing in for a divine one (like a wax statue for Hecate), or a divine thing standing for a natural entity (like Hera for the air)'.[55] In discussing Homer's cave of the nymphs, he based

---

[51] Eusebius, *Vit. Const.* 4.45. Text: Winkelmann 1975: 139. Trans. Cameron and Hall 1999: 171, modified.

[52] *Ekphrasis* was one of the standard topics covered in the rhetorical manuals known as progymnasmata. See Aelius Theon, *Prog.* 7; Ps-Hermogenes, *Prog.* 10; Aphthonius, *Prog.* 12; Nicolaus, *Prog.* 11, all of which can be found in Kennedy 2003. The literature on *ekphrasis* is immense. Helpful places to begin are Webb 2016b and Squire 2015.

[53] See Grigg 1977: 4–5. [54] On σύμβολα among Pythagoreans, see Struck 2004: 97–107.

[55] Struck 2004: 217–18, referring to Porphyry's *On Philosophy from Oracles* and *On Images*.

his figural interpretation of the poet on the assumption that 'shrines' set up by ancient peoples contain 'mystical symbols' (συμβόλων μυστικῶν), which legitimated his interpretation of it as a 'symbol of the generated and perceptible cosmos' (κόσμου σύμβολον ἤτοι γενητοῦ αἰσθητοῦ).[56] Eusebius' usage arguably taps into these philosophical associations and presents the decoration of the church and its furnishings as material realities making known abstract or immaterial concepts. Finally, Eusebius ties these 'symbols', which express Constantine's 'philosophical ideas', to sacred scripture, specifically the 'visions' drawn from the Hebrew prophets. These, it would seem, unlock the meaning hidden within the symbols.

Although Eusebius' dedicatory oration at the Church of the Holy Sepulchre is lost, this short summary makes clear that he regarded the emperor's architectural achievements as expressive of philosophical ideas and, consequently, as amenable to a biblically inspired figural interpretation, probably in a manner akin to Porphyry's understanding of a σύμβολον as a nodal point in the web of meaning embedded in the universe that could be activated with the correct interpretation. It might be supposed that such an approach was restricted to uniquely holy sites like Christ's tomb. In what follows, however, we will see that Eusebius could apply this same method to other holy buildings. If this is how he wanted his hearers and readers to understand actual physical church structures at various locations, it is plausible that they would have extended this method to artistic representations of sacred architecture as well, regardless of whether the image at hand was a depiction of Constantine's aedicula or some other structure. Hence, in the following section I apply such a method to the *tholos* image, using another of Eusebius' texts as a model.[57]

Eusebius on the Church at Tyre

The passage above describing Eusebius' oration in Jerusalem is tantalisingly brief and leaves one wishing we could know more details about what

---

[56] Porphyry, *Antr. nymph.* 4, 7. Trans. Lamberton 1983: 24–25.
[57] Subsequent to the first drafting of the present chapter in 2017, the fruitfulness of bringing Eusebius' oration at Tyre to bear upon the Canon Tables decorative scheme was also highlighted by Strøm-Olsen 2018: 419–22, who justified the suitability of this exercise by commenting, 'It is reasonable to think that the elaboration of a visual protocol for the canon tables during this period would share this interest [in the link between physical architecture and spiritual symbolism] and that the design was intended to make specific allusion to a Christian space characteristic to those communities from within which they were produced' (p. 424). The following analysis is parallel to Strøm-Olsen's approach and we reach conclusions that are mutually reinforcing, though not identical.

he said on the occasion. Although the speech is lost, we can fill out our picture of what he was proposing by attending to another text in his corpus. Two decades prior to the dedication of Constantine's building in Jerusalem, Eusebius delivered a panegyrical oration at the dedication of another church, the basilica built in Tyre by bishop Paulinus.[58] This was 'likely one of [Eusebius'] first major public performances'[59] and its timing only shortly after the cessation of persecution made the re-establishment of the church a momentous occasion. Eusebius' oration at Tyre is the earliest literary description of a church that has survived, and as such it stands at the head of a long Byzantine tradition of *ekphraseis* of church buildings.[60] Reconstructing the features of this specific church is largely irrelevant to my argument. More important are the two contexts within which he situates his understanding of sacred architecture, one historical and one theological.[61] The historical context is the drastic change of fortunes the Christian church had recently experienced. A new church in Tyre was required because the earlier one had been destroyed in the Great Persecution. If, as is usually thought, Eusebius' oration was delivered around 315 CE,[62] these events would have been fresh on everyone's minds, and Eusebius used this background to good rhetorical effect, repeatedly mentioning the imperial efforts to destroy churches and burn the scriptures[63] and presenting the subsequent rededications of the rebuilt churches as 'clear proofs of the rule of our Savior' (τῆς τοῦ σωτῆρος ἡμῶν βασιλείας ἐναργῆ δείγματα).[64]

Eager to present the rebuilding of Paulinus' basilica as the fulfilment of prophecy, Eusebius invoked the text of Isa 35:1-7: 'Rejoice, O thirsty

---

[58] Scholars have rightly emphasised that Eusebius casts Constantine's Church of the Holy Sepulchre as the 'celestial Jerusalem' present on earth in material form (Wilken 1992: 82–100; Amirkhanian 2008-9: 209–10) and as the 'new temple' to replace the one built by Solomon (Ousterhout 1990), but the connection between a physical church space and the heavenly Jerusalem is already in place twenty years earlier, in relation to a church in an entirely different locale (cf. Ousterhout 2010: 233–34). Paulinus stands in the line of those great builders of the Bible – Bezalel, Solomon, and Zerubbabel (Eusebius, *Hist. eccl.* 10.4.3) – and the heavenly 'patterns' (παραδείγματα) that he follows in constructing the church derive from 'the so-called Jerusalem above' (τήν τε ἄνω λεγομένην Ἱερουσαλήμ, *Hist. eccl.* 10.4.70). Of course, the earthly Jerusalem would assume greater significance for Eusebius after Constantine's building efforts, but the ecclesiology presupposed in his interpretation of Paulinus' building implies that any church structure instantiates the 'archetypal patterns' in material form and so participates in the Jerusalem above as a 'new temple'.

[59] Schott 2011: 178.

[60] Webb 1999: 60, 66. On Byzantine *ekphrasis* in particular, see James and Webb 1991; Maguire 2008: 721–24.

[61] For an analysis of Eusebius' rhetoric in the oration, see especially Smith 1989.

[62] Barnes 1981: 162–63.   [63] Eusebius, *Hist. eccl.* 10.4.14–16; 10.4.28–32; 10.4.46–55.

[64] Eusebius, *Hist. eccl.* 10.4.20.

wilderness! Let the wilderness be glad, and let it blossom like a lily! And the desert places shall blossom and be glad ... because water has broken forth in the wilderness and a gully in a thirsty land; the dry place shall turn into marshlands, and in the thirsty land there shall be a spring of water' (NETS).[65] After citing this passage, he spent the next paragraph applying it to the church's recent reversal of circumstances, comparing the church to the 'lily' that has blossomed anew and spread sweet fragrance upon humanity. The water mentioned in the prophetic text represents the 'streams of divine regeneration bestowed by the washing of salvation' (τὸ νᾶμα τῆς θείας τοῦ σωτηρίου λουτροῦ παλιγγενεσίας). The desert brought about by the persecution has been transformed into 'marsh-meadows', while the dry ground has yielded 'a fountain of living water' (πηγὴ ὕδατος ζῶντος).[66] Here we begin to see what Eusebius probably had in mind when, in discussing the Holy Sepulchre, he 'made prophetic visions apply to the symbols' present in it. The sacred scriptures provided him with a stock of evocative imagery that could be used in *ekphrasis* to describe the recent events he and his contemporaries had experienced which were instantiated in the physical church structure before them.

The biblical passage Eusebius has focused upon is also suitable for the *tholos* image, which in almost all surviving examples includes garden and paradise motifs, as do the similar mosaics from Syria and Tunisia. I do not mean to suggest that the artists responsible for these productions were aiming at a straightforward depiction of this passage, but rather that the passage provides an intertext that is productive for stimulating the imagination of the viewer pondering their meaning.[67] A late antique viewer of the image who had read or heard Eusebius' oration would have been prompted to interpret the abundant plants and bird life surrounding the *tholos* as representing the rebuilding of the church at Tyre following its destruction in the Great Persecution. Although he does not cite it, the biblical passage from which Eusebius took his citation also speaks of the lame 'leap[ing] like a deer' and says that 'the joy of birds' will be present amidst the watery marshlands (Isa 35:6, 7), which reminds one of the animal life that typically accompanies the *tholos*. Moreover, Eusebius' mention of the 'streams of divine regeneration' brings to mind the Carolingian versions of the *tholos* page in which the four-columned structure has been

---

[65] Eusebius, *Hist. eccl.* 10.4.32. Eusebius quotes more of the passage than I have cited here.
[66] Eusebius, *Hist. eccl.* 10.4.34.
[67] As a methodological parallel to this exercise, see Nasrallah (2005: 496), who argues that the Pauline letter of 1 Thessalonians was a likely intertext for the mosaics adorning the dome of the rotunda in Thessaloniki.

turned into a fountain of life. There is no reason why such imagery would be suitable only for Paulinus' church at Tyre. Eusebius later used similar language for the Holy Sepulchre, saying that in Palestine, 'like a fountain, the life-giving stream gushed forth to all' (τοῦ ζωοποιοῦ νάματος πηγῆς δίκην ἀνομβρήσαντος εἰς πάντας).[68] The *tholos* image, therefore, is both rich enough in symbolic imagery but also ambiguous enough in its identification that when combined with this biblical passage it could be regarded as a depiction of the church at Tyre, the Church of the Holy Sepulchre, or indeed any church whatsoever that had been subjected to Eusebius' biblically inspired *ekphrasis*.[69]

According to Eusebius, the theological context for the rebuilding of the church at Tyre comes from the metaphor of the people assembled together as a 'building' analogous to the physical building erected under Paulinus' direction. In fact, to call it a 'metaphor' risks obscuring the ecclesiological reality Eusebius intends, if the term is understood in a merely rhetorical or ornamental sense. Eusebius in fact asserts that the physical building is modelled on the heavenly reality of the people redeemed by Christ and is caught up in the process of their salvation, not just by virtue of the rites that take place within it, but also because it encodes within its structure a map that reveals their journey. Just as the Son looks to his Father and does what he sees the Father doing (cf. John 5.19), so too Paulinus looks to Christ to find the 'archetypal patterns' (ἀρχετύποις ... παραδείγμασιν) and then forms in the church 'images of them in the closest likeness possible' (τὰς εἰκόνας, ὡς ἔνι μάλιστα δυνατόν, εἰς τὸ ὁμοιότατον). This modus operandi Eusebius finds prefigured in Bezalel who formed Israel's tabernacle in the wilderness, accomplishing 'the construction of heavenly types through the temple's symbols' (τῆς τῶν οὐρανίων τύπων διὰ συμβόλων ναοῦ κατασκευῆς).[70] Eusebius' usage of σύμβολον in this passage should not be overlooked in light of the passage I highlighted above describing his lost oration on the Church of the Holy Sepulchre. Strictly speaking, the reference here is to Bezalel, but

---

[68] Eusebius, *Laud. Const.* 9.15. This passage undermines the reconstructed historical development of the meaning of the *tholos* image posited by Underwood 1950: 117, who claimed that, prior to the end of the sixth century or beginning of the seventh, the Holy Sepulchre was not identified with the fountain of life in either textual references or material culture. On the contrary, Eusebius' passing comment indicates that this theological concept was already associated with the site from the outset of its discovery.

[69] Similarly, Ousterhout (2010: 251) concluded, 'What is perhaps more important is that the same [biblical] verses could have been used in the dedication of *any* Byzantine church. That is, although the allusions to the Temple have a powerful resonance at Hagia Sophia and the Holy Sepulchre, the association was neither exclusive nor all-encompassing.'

[70] Eusebius, *Hist. eccl.* 10.4.25.

Eusebius' comparison implies that Paulinus has constructed the basilica in Tyre by similarly incorporating 'symbols' to convey heavenly realities.

Assuming this ecclesiological scheme whereby the physical church has a 'nature that resembles the pattern of better things' (τῷ τοῦ κρείττονος παραδείγματι … τὴν φύσιν ἐμφερῆ),[71] Eusebius provides a twofold account of the basilica at Tyre.[72] The first is a brief and straightforward description of the various parts of the church that follows the *periegesis*[73] format, tracing the steps of a viewer as she works her way through the building complex, beginning at the outer enclosure, going through the forecourt, processing into the church itself up to the altar, and finally passing back outside to see the adjacent buildings.[74] In the second half of the account, Eusebius overlays another meaning upon the physical structure. Paulinus' building programme is seen as mirroring the 'renewal of the rational and God-given edifice in our souls' (τὰ τῆς ἐνθέου φημὶ καὶ λογικῆς ἐν ψυχαῖς οἰκοδομῆς ἀνανεώματα),[75] and various groups of persons within the church correspond to the components of the physical structure. So, for example, the 'outer enclosure' represents the majority of Christians who have an 'unerring faith' but cannot 'support a greater structure', the 'entrances' to the church are those who 'guide' the people who are in the process of entering the church, and so on right up to the altar, where Christ stands offering up the sacrifices and praises of all to the Father.[76] In this way Eusebius treats the layout of the church as following the progression of a Christian's spiritual life: the more interior a space or feature is, the more advanced a stage of attainment it represents.

In this section of the oration, we once more find a fruitful intertext for interpreting the *tholos* page, specifically in Eusebius' description of the forecourt or atrium[77] situated between the outer entrances into the

---

[71] Eusebius, *Hist. eccl.* 10.4.26.

[72] On Eusebius' twofold description, see Schott 2011: 193–96, who argues for its indebtedness to Philo and the Platonic tradition. Eusebius' debt to Philo was also recognised by Smith 1989: 234–38.

[73] On *periegesis*, see Webb 1999: 66–68. Christine Smith calls it a 'kinesthetic description' (1989: 230).

[74] Eusebius, *Hist. eccl.* 10.4.38–45. For brief architectural analyses of Eusebius' description, see Krautheimer 1975: 45–46; White 1990: 1.136.

[75] Eusebius, *Hist. eccl.* 10.4.55. Similarly, Vasiliki Limberis says about the *ekphrasis* of the martyrium of St Theodore by Gregory of Nyssa, 'Because the Christian theology of the *panegyris* has intervened, the *logos periegematikos* goes beyond its verbal realm of memory and imagination and ushers in the experience of the eternal' (2011: 59). The central argument of James and Webb (1991: 12) is that this was the primary purpose of *ekphrasis* in Byzantium: it 'made present not the actual picture, which could be seen, but the spiritual reality behind it'.

[76] Eusebius, *Hist. eccl.* 10.4.63–68.

[77] My usage of the terms 'forecourt' and 'atrium' for this space follows Krautheimer 1975: 45–46.

building complex and the entrance into the church building itself. This is true for both phases of his description of this space. In his first pass through it giving a straightforward description, Paulinus is said to have

> marked off an exceedingly large space between the temple and the first entrances, and adorned it all around with four transverse colonnades, fencing the place into a kind of quadrangular figure by the columns raised on every side, in between which are wooden barriers of lattice-work that enclose the space up to a suitable height. And in the midst of it he has left an open space so that people can see the sky, thus providing it with bright air that is open to the rays of light. And here he placed symbols of sacred purifications, by erecting fountains opposite the temple, whose copious streams of flowing water supply cleansing to those who are advancing from the sacred enclosures to the inner area. And this is the first stopping-place for those that enter, supplying at once adornment and splendour to the whole, and a way station corresponding to those people who are still in need of the initial instructions.[78]

A number of aspects of this passage are noteworthy. First, Eusebius emphasises the colonnades that surround this space, which are reminiscent of the columns that frame the numeric matrices of his Canon Tables. Second, Eusebius describes the fountains in this open courtyard as 'symbols' of purification, once more using the potent word σύμβολον. This specific symbol also recalls his earlier citation of the Isaianic passage about a 'fountain of living water' bursting forth in the desert and reminds one of the fountains that appear in some versions of the *tholos* image. Presumably Eusebius is referring to fountains used for ablutions prior to entering into the church building, rather than the baptismal font itself,[79] but, whatever the case, he clearly regards the fountains in this space as no mere source of everyday water but rather as offering water

---

[78] Eusebius, *Hist. eccl.* 10.4.39–40: διαλαβὼν δὲ πλεῖστον ὅσον τὸ μεταξὺ τοῦ τε νεὼ καὶ τῶν πρώτων εἰσόδων, τέτταρσι μὲν πέριξ ἐγκαρσίοις κατεκόσμησεν στοαῖς, εἰς τετράγωνόν τι σχῆμα περιφράξας τὸν τόπον, κίοσι πανταχόθεν ἐπαιρομέναις· ὧν τὰ μέσα διαφράγμασι τοῖς ἀπὸ ξύλου δικτυωτοῖς ἐς τὸ σύμμετρον ἥκουσι μήκους περικλείσας, μέσον αἴθριον ἡφίει εἰς τὴν τοῦ οὐρανοῦ κάτοψιν, λαμπρὸν καὶ ταῖς τοῦ φωτὸς ἀκτῖσιν ἀνειμένον ἀέρα παρέχων. ἱερῶν δ' ἐνταῦθα καθαρσίων ἐτίθει σύμβολα, κρήνας ἄντικρυς εἰς πρόσωπον ἐπισκευάζων τοῦ νεὼ πολλῷ τῷ χεύματι τοῦ νάματος τοῖς καθαρσίων ἐτίθει σύμβολα, κρήνας ἄντικρυς εἰς πρόσωπον ἐπισκευάζων τοῦ νεὼ πολλῷ τῷ χεύματι τοῦ νάματος τοῖς περιβόλων ἱερῶν ἐπὶ τὰ ἔσω προϊοῦσιν τὴν ἀπόρυψιν παρεχομένας. καὶ πρώτη μὲν εἰσιόντων αὕτη διατριβή, κόσμον ὁμοῦ καὶ ἀγλαΐαν τῷ παντὶ τοῖς τε τῶν πρώτων εἰσαγωγῶν ἔτι δεομένοις κατάλληλον τὴν μονὴν παρεχομένη.

[79] In his survey of the church, Eusebius nowhere else mentions the font unless the oblique reference about the side chambers at *Hist. eccl.* 10.4.45 refers to it. Krautheimer comments, 'A baptistery may have stood somewhere inside the vast precinct wall which enclosed the entire structure, including its forecourt' (1975: 45).

that plays a central role in the drama of redemption. Finally, even though this is Eusebius' straightforward *ekphrasis* of the physical church building, he is already slipping into the meaning of this space that he will give in his second pass through the church. The term he uses for this forecourt (διατριβή) works as a simple description of a place where an observer walking through the church might pause ('stopping place') but is also laden with philosophical connotations. Numenius, for example, in a passage Eusebius himself cited, used the word to refer to the 'school of Epicurus' which was 'like a true republic' (ἔοικέ τε ἡ Ἐπικούρου διατριβή πολιτείᾳ τινὶ ἀληθεῖ).[80] By referring to this space as a διατριβή where one receives 'initial instructions', Eusebius was probably deliberately playing on the polyvalence of the term and implying that the church itself is a sort of philosophical school.

The latter emphasis becomes explicit when Eusebius returns to this part of the basilica as he retraces his steps in his heavenly explanation of the architectural features. This time he says

Other people [the Logos] supported with the first outer columns that are around the quadrangular courtyard, guiding them to their first acquaintance with the letter of the four gospels.[81]

This forecourt comes after the outer enclosure of the entire complex, which represent those who simply have 'faith', and prior to those who have experienced 'divine washing', so it seemingly refers to catechumens receiving their 'initial instruction' in the scriptures. Strikingly, the specific part of the canon that Eusebius highlights is the fourfold gospel;[82] his mention of the 'letter' of the gospels is his way of referring to the bare literal sense of the text. Further on, he explains that those who have had the 'divine washing' go on to learn 'the innermost mystical teachings of scripture' (τῶν ἐνδοτάτω μυστικῶν τῆς γραφῆς δογμάτων).[83] In other words, progression in the Christian life is marked by a movement from the literal sense of the text available to catechumens to a deeper understanding of the 'mystical teachings' contained therein that is available only to the baptised.

---

[80] Numenius, frag. 24, *apud* Eusebius, *Praep. ev.* 14.5.3.
[81] Eusebius, *Hist. eccl.* 10.4.63: ἄλλους δὲ πρώτοις τοῖς ἔξωθεν ἀμφὶ τὴν αὐλὴν ἐκ τετραγώνου κίοσιν ὑπεστήριξεν, ταῖς πρώταις τῶν τεττάρων εὐαγγελίων τοῦ γράμματος προσβολαῖς ἐμβιβάζων·
[82] For a brief discussion of what Eusebius' comments here imply about the stages of catechesis in Palestine in the early fourth century, see Dujarier 1979: 70–71.
[83] Eusebius, *Hist. eccl.* 10.4.64.

To summarise, what Eusebius sees in the forecourt of Paulinus' church is a courtyard surrounded by colonnades on four sides, with a fountain in the middle. These columns 'correspond to' catechumens receiving their first instruction in the four gospels, who are expected to progress on from this point to a deeper understanding of scripture as they approach baptism which is represented by the fountain residing in the middle of the courtyard. Eusebius' treatment of the space presents a variety of possible associations with the architectural décor of the Canon Tables, including the *tholos* image. In fact, the *tholos* itself could be seen as the sort of 'symbol' that could be activated by a biblically inspired ekphrastic interpretation and used to theorise the philosophical truths hidden within the world of sensible experience.

On the one hand, the decorative scheme of the Canon Tables might refer to a physical church itself. A series of pages depicting archways could together constitute the colonnades that mark off the forecourt or the archways through which one walks to reach the forecourt. Perhaps the numeric matrices that fill the archways on the page could even be seen as the wooden latticework that stands between the columns. The paradisal imagery that surrounds the Canon Table archways recalls the presentation of Paulinus' church as a desert bursting with life, symbolised by the fountain in the middle of the courtyard. The *tholos* itself, as the conclusion to the sequence of Canon Table pages, might also refer to such a fountain (as it clearly does in the Carolingian examples) or might symbolise the church into which one enters after crossing the forecourt.

On the other hand, the decorative scheme of the Canon Tables can also evoke the theological, ritual, and hermeneutical themes that Eusebius associates with this part of the church. If the forecourt represents catechumens who are receiving their initial lessons from the gospels, this would be a particularly apt association for the Canon Tables that stand at the front of a four-gospel codex. Seen in this light, the viewer's imaginative movement through the pages re-enacts their literal entrance into the church building as well as their incorporation into the heavenly people of God via baptism, with the *tholos* serving as a potent symbol for their destination in both senses. One could overlay onto this progression through the pages of the codex the hermeneutical transition that Eusebius describes, with catechumens beginning at the literal sense of scripture and advancing, after their baptism, to its mystical meanings. On this interpretation, the final *tholos* page might refer to the mystical meaning of scripture that both constitutes and is made known in the church. Alternatively, the *tholos* could represent the intermediate stage of baptism through which one passes to reach the text of the gospels that follows the Eusebian paratext in a manuscript, now illumined to reveal its mystical meaning.[84]

What I have proposed in the last several paragraphs is intended to be suggestive rather than prescriptive in terms of its details.[85] It would press the analogy too far if one viewed the pages containing the Canon Tables as listing passages in the gospels with a literal meaning which one must consider first in order to understand the mystical meaning of the gospels represented by the *tholos*. On the contrary, the cross-referencing function of the Canon Tables does not so directly align with the approach to the decorative scheme I am here proposing since the parallels included in Eusebius' ten tables present a wide range of varying kinds and degrees of similarity.[86] Nor should one think that a church presenting a different architectural layout from Paulinus' basilica was unable to conform to the heavenly realities or to offer similarly fruitful imaginative possibilities when juxtaposed with the ornamentation of the Canon Tables, as if the specific analogies Eusebius draws between the physical and theological realms were the only interpretative options. Rather, what is important is the process or method that Eusebius is modelling for his hearers and readers, a way of using built space as a 'cognitive machine' for stimulating and organising thought by unlocking philosophically laden symbols through a biblically inspired *ekphrasis*. The same would plausibly hold true for artistic portrayals of sacred space such as the arches and concluding *tholos* of the Canon Tables.

---

[84] Strøm-Olsen (2018: 405) reaches a similar conclusion: 'I argue that the architectonic motif served as the basis for a decorative program that could adequately reflect the value of the tables themselves to the Gospels, and that the table design denoted specifically the idea of a passage through the space of a Christian temple, emphasizing the idea of an inner sanctuary where the mystery of the Word fused with the divine Logos as the focal point of salvation for the true Christian believer. Thus, the architectural setting of the canon tables can be read as a form of allegory, a figurative propyleum through which a Christian soteriology is accessed.'

[85] My point here aligns with Smith's conclusion that for Eusebius 'there is no *direct* relationships posited between mentions of buildings in the Bible, and the church at Tyre. Rather, the connection is one of identity of significance; identity of meaning on the spiritual level. The same idea may be materialized in different ways and with different images; this is why metaphor is evocative rather than definitive' (Smith 1989: 236). Ousterhout likewise remarks, 'Thus, architecture may comment on or interact with the rituals it houses, but I think it is a mistake to expect a direct symbolic correspondence. In the architectural setting, there was perhaps by necessity only a general association of form and meaning. It was the function – the liturgy – that added texture, nuance, and specificity' (1990: 52). Ousterhout is reacting against the association of form and meaning suggested by Krautheimer 1969, particularly with respect to how other church buildings are understood in relation to the Church of the Holy Sepulchre.

[86] On the hermeneutical implications of the Canon Tables, see Crawford 2019: ch. 3, which includes analysis of several of Eusebius' parallels. Later Irish scholars devoted themselves to classifying the kinds of parallels included in the tables. See Crawford 2019: ch. 6. The Canon Tables are also central to the theological reading of the gospels offered in Watson 2016.

These images too were amenable to being used as a cognitive machine by their late antique creators and viewers, and the ambiguity or polyvalence of the *tholos* is particularly well suited to such an undertaking.

Text and Image, Space and Ritual

To conclude, I want to return to late antique Christian modes of knowing and make two points, one more general and one specifically about the *tholos* image. First, we are so accustomed to illuminated manuscripts from the Middle Ages that we need to be reminded that books in antiquity were starkly different. Under the influence of Kurt Weitzmann, the common view in an earlier generation of scholarship was that there existed in antiquity an extensive and complex tradition of book 'illustrations' that could be recovered and reconstructed by attending to the influence of this tradition on a variety of other media.[87] Art historians have moved away from Weitzmann's thesis, pointing out the rarity of any kind of illustration in the papyri that have been preserved by the sands of Egypt[88] and rejecting the philological methodology he employed to develop his theory.[89] In the words of Michael Squire, 'scholarship on surviving codices has come to realize that the placing of images beside narrative texts in manuscripts was a specific invention of the (very) late antique world'.[90] Setting aside mathematical and technical manuals,[91] the earliest-surviving books containing extensive and planned images alongside narrative texts date to the fourth century CE, precisely the period from which also come Eusebius'

---

[87] See Weitzmann 1959, 1970.

[88] For a survey of the material and literary evidence for illustrated texts from antiquity, see Small 2003: 118–54, who concludes that '[i]llustrated rolls with pictures integrated with text begin in the second half of the first century BC, are rare in the first century AD, and increase slowly in popularity thereafter' (140–41). According to Elsner (2020a: 103 n. 34), however, 'The major collection of [illustrated] material from Oxyrhynchus remains unpublished.' Until it appears, claims about the rarity or abundance of illustrations in papyri must be treated as provisional, though it seems unlikely that we will uncover sufficient evidence to overturn the basic claim that complex schemes of pictures alongside narrative texts were uncommon before late antiquity. On two-dimensional representations in the Roman world, see Riggsby 2019: 154–201, especially the section 'Textual Illustrations' on pp. 157–64.

[89] For a critique of the method Weitzmann adapted for the study of images, see Brubaker 2008: 61–62. For a critique of Weitzmann's understanding of images as mere 'illustrations' of an accompanying text, see Squire 2009: 122–31.

[90] Squire 2011: 139.

[91] This is not to suggest that the late antique gospel-book had nothing in common with such 'practical texts'; for an exploration of similarities in possible modes of reading such books, see Coogan 2021.

Canon Tables.[92] This was not a development unique to Christian texts, since we also have a few roughly contemporaneous illuminated manuscripts of classical texts like the Vatican Vergil.[93] The inclusion of images alongside narrative texts should thus be seen as one of the innovative new modes of knowing that emerged in the period covered by this volume, one that brought with it a host of cognitive possibilities that were being creatively explored by authors, scribes, and artists.[94] The Canon Tables are thus merely one of the most creative and successful productions to arise from this wider milieu.

In a more precise sense, I suggest that the use of architectural imagery as an ornamentation scheme for the Eusebian Canon Tables, when viewed in light of the understanding of built architecture evident in Eusebius' corpus, represents a distinct mode of knowing that combines space, text, and ritual in a dense web of meaning. Jeremy Schott has argued that in his panegyric at Tyre, Eusebius turned the church into 'a textualized, exegetical space'[95] with his Philonic and Neoplatonic application of scriptural texts to Paulinus' church. In an analogous manner, Georgia Frank claimed that intrinsic to the development of pilgrimage in the fourth century was the cultivation of the pilgrim's 'eye of faith' by which one saw the events of scripture overlaid onto the holy places of Palestine.[96] This practice owed a great deal to Eusebius, given that he 'directed attention, for the first time in Christian history, to the religious and theological significance of space', specifically the *loca sancta* of Palestine.[97] Although it is tempting to extend this argument slightly further and argue that it was this interest in space that inspired Eusebius himself to create both the architectural frames that house his numeric matrices and the concluding symbolic *tholos* page, the evidence for attributing the *tholos* to him is ultimately inconclusive. Eusebius may have been responsible for these elements, but we cannot exclude the possibility that they mark a later development in the transmission of the paratext.

---

[92] For a survey of late antique prefatory *comparanda* relevant to the Canon Tables, see Elsner 2020a.

[93] For a survey of the earliest-surviving illustrated biblical manuscripts, see Lowden 1999. Squire (2011: 139) comments, 'The small handful of fifth-century codices featuring figurative images [alongside classical texts] are best understood as reflections of this early Byzantine development, bound up with the intellectual history of Christian theology at large.'

[94] We should not assume that images are reducible to the texts they accompany, nor that they are mere adornment that serves only an aesthetic purpose. On the contrary, as Jaś Elsner has put it, there is 'a continuous and revolving dialogue of image and text' (2020a: 108). Cf. James 2007; Squire 2009.

[95] Schott 2011: 189.   [96] Frank 2000b: 102–33.   [97] Wilken 1992: 88.

Yet imagining how these features might have functioned as a late-antique mode of knowing does not require determining their precise origin. If my interpretation of the Canon Table decorative scheme is persuasive, it suggests the inverse of the sort of scriptural overlay argued by Schott and Frank is also true. Christians in late antiquity brought sacred architecture into the book containing the sacred text and used this architectural imagery to emphasise the role that text played in the rituals carried out in those same physical spaces, as well as to the hermeneutical progression one experienced by undergoing those rituals. The influence between space and text was thus bidirectional. Like two mirrors turned to face one another, the sacred book depicted in artistic form the ritual practices and spaces in which the book itself was central.

Although put to creative use by Christians like Eusebius, this clearly was not a uniquely Christian mode of knowing; rather, it presents a range of similarities with Eusebius' Neoplatonic contemporaries. I have already mentioned Porphyry's interpretation of the cave of the nymphs as a 'symbol' filled with a multitude of other 'symbols' that together speak of the entrance of souls into the material realm and their exit from it, which is broadly comparable to the way in which Eusebius sees Paulinus' church as filled with 'symbols' based on 'archetypal patterns' that reveal the Logos' divine plan to gather the redeemed into a new ἔθνος. Moreover, Porphyry composed an entire treatise *On Images* in which he aimed to teach philosophy students how properly to view religious images, more specifically, how to discern the deeper Platonic reality behind the visible appearances of the gods.[98] Although Porphyry focused on generalised features in the way certain gods were commonly depicted rather than remarking upon any particular sculpture or painting that a religious devotee might encounter at a specific sacred site, his approach to visual imagery seems broadly parallel to the way Eusebius treated the symbols in the churches in Tyre and Jerusalem, insofar as both exercises are attempts to penetrate beneath the visible surface and discern hidden truths.[99] At least one further Neoplatonic parallel is relevant to the argument I have advanced. The sixth-century Neoplatonic commentator Olympiodorus asserted that Plato's *Alcibiades*

---

[98] The fragments of Porphyry's *On Statues* are collected in Smith 1993: frags. 351–60. For discussion of the treatise, see especially Johnson 2013: 165–71, who follows Krulak 2011 in viewing the text as a philosophical εἰσαγωγή. Most of the surviving fragments were preserved by Eusebius himself in Book 3 of his *Preparatio Evangelica*.

[99] On the conceptual frames that informed ancient viewing of art, see Elsner 1995: 88, who argues that late antiquity witnessed 'a transformation in viewing away from naturalist expectations towards the symbolism inherent in mystic contemplation'.

was the 'fore-gates' (προπυλαίοις) of the Platonic corpus, leading on to the *Parmenides* which was the 'holy of holies' (ἀδύτοις).[100] This comment highlights the crucial importance that the Neoplatonists placed on reading Plato's dialogues in a certain sequence. The order represented by Olympiodorus, as well as the temple metaphor that he employs, go back to Eusebius' contemporary Iamblichus who put the *Alcibiades* first in the sequence and the *Parmenides* last as the most advanced text.[101] Both Iamblichus and Eusebius, therefore, regarded the progression through a body of literature as akin to movement through a sacred space, leading to an ever deeper understanding of the subject matter at hand.

In light of such parallels, what was distinctive about the approach to Christian imagery examined in this chapter? Simply the obvious but important fact that we are dealing here with images in books. What is unique about the decorative scheme for the Canon Tables is that it takes the metaphor of a literary corpus as religious space and represents it in the sacred book itself, incorporating images amenable to the same kind of symbolic exegesis that one might apply to similar representations in other media. So far as we know, the Neoplatonists never did anything comparable. No surviving copies of Porphyry's *On the Cave of the Nymphs* include an image of the cave in question, nor do we know of any late antique collections of Platonic dialogues that employed sacred architecture as a framing device. Although, in the preface to his *On Images*, Porphyry drew an analogy between reading letters in a book and interpreting statues of the gods, nothing suggests he had in mind symbolic depictions of the gods in books that should be interpreted philosophically.[102] I do not mean to suggest that a Neoplatonic scribe or artist could not have produced such a book, merely that there is no evidence that any ever did, perhaps simply because the inclusion of images alongside non-technical literature was still relatively novel in the fourth century. In fact, Iamblichus and Porphyry

---

[100] Olympiodorus, *In Platonis Alcibiadem commentarii* 11. Text from Westerink 1956, trans. Griffin 2015: 83.

[101] Cf. Griffin 2015: 18–19. On the order of Plato's dialogues in the Neoplatonic curriculum, see Westerink 1962: XXXVII–XL; Festugière 1969; O'Meara 2003: 61–68.

[102] Porphyry, *De simulac.* frag. 351 Smith (*apud* Eusebius, *Praep. ev.* 3.7.1). The fragment reads Φθέγξομαι οἷς θέμις ἐστί, θύρας δ᾽ ἐπίθεσθε βέβηλοι, σοφίας θεολόγου νοήματα δεικνύς, οἷς τὸν θεὸν καὶ τοῦ θεοῦ τὰς δυνάμεις διὰ εἰκόνων συμφύλων αἰσθήσει ἐμήνυσαν ἄνδρες, τὰ ἀφανῆ φανεροῖς ἀποτυπώσαντες πλάσμασιν, τοῖς καθάπερ ἐκ βίβλων τῶν ἀγαλμάτων ἀναλέγειν τὰ περὶ θεῶν μεμαθηκόσι γράμματα. θαυμαστὸν δὲ οὐδὲν ξύλα καὶ λίθους ἡγεῖσθαι τὰ ξόανα τοὺς ἀμαθεστάτους, καθὰ δὴ καὶ τῶν γραμμάτων οἱ ἀνόητοι λίθους μὲν ὁρῶσι τὰς στήλας, ξύλα δὲ τὰς δέλτους, ἐξυφασμένην δὲ πάπυρον τὰς βίβλους. For a translation, see Krulak 2011: 353; Johnson 2013: 165.

may have still been reading Plato's dialogues on separate scrolls rather than in the form of a single codex, as Eusebius had for the gospels; it was the shift to the parchment codex, perhaps more than anything else, that facilitated elaborate schemes of images presented alongside text. Eusebius' decorated Canon Tables are, therefore, both indicative of the broader intellectual milieu in which he worked and emblematic of a distinct mode of knowing that emerged within Christian intellectual culture of the early fourth century and would lead to the rich medieval tradition of illuminated manuscripts.

27 | Condemning the Glutton of the Monastery: Rhetorical Strategies and the Epistemology of Philoxenos of Mabbug

JEANNE-NICOLE MELLON SAINT-LAURENT

Introduction

The Syrian metropolitan Philoxenos of Mabbug (440?–523 CE) spent his life fighting for the cause of the Miaphysites in the tumultuous decades following the Council of Chalcedon.[1] It is unlikely that simple Christians who found themselves on the side of the Chalcedonians or Miaphysites always understood the intricacies of christology that divided them.[2] The articulation of Christ's humanity and divinity presented a theological puzzle, but not everyone agreed that it was a Christian's job to solve it. Indeed, as Philoxenos claimed, speculative theology that pried into the hiddenness of Christ was a flawed approach to divine mystery. The competition to articulate a perfect christology, for Philoxenos, had led to heresy.

Philoxenos posits another response to the mystery of the incarnation, grounded in asceticism, reading scripture, shepherding religious communities, contemplation, and participation in the sacraments, as David Michelson has shown.[3] These practices lead to the attainment of the knowledge of God and to protect proper access to that knowledge.[4] This theme runs throughout Philoxenos' corpus.

I am grateful for the helpful feedback from the volume's editors and the response to my work from Professor Paul Blowers at the Modes of Knowing Conference in Rome, Italy (May 2019). I dedicate this article to a dear friend and colleague, Professor David Michelson, who taught me much about the importance of Philoxenos in Christian ascetic tradition. All mistakes remaining are my own.

[1] See Michelson 2014; Michelson 2011a: 1–8. A basic source for the study of Philoxenos is de Halleux 1963.
[2] See Tannous 2018: 11–110.
[3] This point is a vital contribution of David Michelson's (2014: 22, 61) scholarship on Philoxenos of Mabbug.
[4] In its most basic sense, we can understand asceticism as 'any act of self-denial undertaken as a strategy of empowerment or gratification' (Harpham 1987: xiii). Teresa Shaw (1998: 5) also adopts this definition in her book on fasting and sexuality in early Christianity.

Philoxenos addresses the monks under his care in his extended discourses or *memre* on the ascetic life.[5] Ascetic practice, as the works of Evagrius of Pontus had taught Philoxenos, was a struggle against demons, and the first of these to attack the monk was gluttony.[6] In *Memra* 10, against the lust of the belly or *On Gluttony*,[7] Philoxenos teaches that gluttony turns people into animals.[8] The weight of food covers the mind and deprives a person of the faculties of knowledge.[9] Philoxenos shows that a glutton's behaviour and attitude towards food and drink are rooted in false epistemologies of the self and God, and thus that gluttony leads to heresy and death.

To teach his monks about the dangers of gluttony, Philoxenos tells the story of a fallen monk who never knew God, because the temptations of his tummy distracted him so much. Philoxenos employs the rhetorical technique of teaching ascetic virtue using story and anti-exemplum. This discourse demonstrates that homiletic narrative was a mode of teaching in the late ancient church that was as useful as theological discourse or exegesis. Philoxenos vividly describes the glutton and creates a conversation with the gluttonous monk. By studying this embedded dialogue with an imagined gluttonous monk, we can uncover how Philoxenos advances his thesis about the danger of gluttony: it distorts the human person and prevents the knowledge of God.

This chapter proceeds in two main parts. In the first section, we will discuss gluttony and its danger to divine knowledge in Philoxenos' presentation. In the second section, we analyse Philoxenos' vivid description of the monastic glutton as an inverted hagiographic narrative. The chapter concludes with a note of Philoxenos' suggestions to remedy gluttony, which he grounds in the Eucharist. This chapter, therefore, connects with several others in this volume. It examines ascetic theology as a principal for structuring the self, and thus links with Paul Saieg's chapter on Irenaeus of Lyons. It is also concerned with Christian genres and modes of expression, and thus it links with Johan Leemans' chapter on patristic homilies and Brian Dunkle's on Ambrose's hymns.

---

[5] Philoxenos' discourse on gluttony is one of thirteen treatises on ascetical topics that he wrote to Syrian Miaphysite monks. See Kitchen 2013: 12–85.

[6] Evagrius calls gluttony 'first of the passions' (Evagrius, 'On the Eight Thoughts', 73).

[7] In this chapter, I follow Kitchen's translation and cite his page numbers for the English translation of Philoxenos' *Discourses*. For the *Discourse on Gluttony*, see Philoxenos, 'Gluttony', 370–425. The Syriac text of the *Ascetic Discourses* to which I refer throughout this article is contained in Budge 1893, vol. I. I cite the page number to the Syriac of Budge's edition. For a summary of some of the themes of the ascetical discourses of Philoxenos, see Kitchen 2010 and 2013.

[8] 'ܚܒܘܫܐ ܕܟܪܣܐ': Philoxenos, 'Gluttony', 276 (ET), 353 (Syr.).

[9] 'ܚܫܘܟܐ ܕܗܘܢܐ': Philoxenos, 'Gluttony', 276 (ET), 353 (Syr.).

Philoxenos' Anxiety about Gluttony in the Syrian Monastery: Context, Sources, and Characterisations

Philoxenos came from Beth Garma in present-day Iraq.[10] He was bilingual and moved between the Syriac- and Greek-speaking areas of the Eastern church. Philoxenos opposed the christology of Chalcedon because he believed that Chalcedon's wording obscured the full reality of the incarnation.[11] He was a bishop on the move, working to sustain communities and monasteries who dissented from Chalcedon.[12] His discourses reveal that men had become monks '[to escape] from servitude or debt, or as a result of the constraint of parents, or from the vexation of woman, along with all the other unhealthy reasons by which many are forcibly driven to come to be disciples of Christ'.[13] Monks could be indifferent to doctrine and practice and needed catechesis.[14] Sometime after 485 CE, Philoxenos wrote *On Gluttony*, a part of his ascetic *Discourses*, for the monks under his care.[15]

Gluttony, *regath karso* or 'desire of the stomach' in Syriac, turns the mind inwards to the belly's desires, replacing the love of God, neighbour, and self with a preoccupation with food, drink, and envy of another person's meal. Gluttony led to humanity's estrangement from God when Eve ate from the fruit of the tree of the knowledge of good and evil,[16] so theologians prescribed fasting as a remedy to guide Christians back to a paradisiacal state.[17] Early Christian thinkers identified gluttony as a 'vice of the soul with physical causes and effects, a psychological enemy that [could] be battled in part by physical methods'.[18] If eating led to sin, then some sort of un-eating, fasting, was necessary for redemption.[19] Late ancient Christians incorporated the medical insights of thinkers like Galen (who wrote about regimens for training gladiators),[20] and they presumed the interconnection

---

[10] Michelson 2011a. [11] Brock 1987: 102. [12] See Frend 1972; van Rompay 2005: 239–66.
[13] Philoxenos, 'Faith', 53 (ET), 70 (Syr.).
[14] See Philoxenos, *Letter to the Monks of Senun*, 89–90, as cited in Michelson 2014: 1.
[15] de Halleux 1963: 288; Kitchen 2013: xxxv.
[16] Gen 3:6. Many early Christian exegetes identified the transgression of Adam and Eve with eating. If gluttony was not the *sin* of Eden, it certainly was linked to man's estrangement from God. Evagrius notes: 'Desire for food gave birth to disobedience and a sweet taste expelled from paradise (Gen. 3: 6, 23)' ('On the Eight Thoughts', 74).
[17] Shaw 1998: 8–9. [18] Shaw 1998: 129.
[19] There is a robust literature on fasting in the early church, both the theology of fasting and the practical and social aspects. In addition to Shaw's *Burden of the Flesh*, see Beatrice 1998: 211–28; Grimm 2010; cf. Basil of Caesarea, *On Fasting and Feast* (trans. Holman and DelCogliano 2013).
[20] Galen warns that gladiators who eat too many lentils become flatulent. See Galen, *Alim. Fac.* 1.19 (6.529–30 Kühn). I am grateful for this reference that I found in Scarborough 1971: 103.

of diet, physiology, and care of the soul as they prescribed remedies to tame gluttony.[21] Christian monastic circles transmitted gnomologies and collections of sayings of Pythagoras that showed the interaction between Christian and Neo-Pythagorean ascetic traditions.[22] We find several sayings about the dangers of gluttony in the *Sentences of Sextus*: 'As you govern your stomach, you will also govern your sexual desire' (*Sext.* 240).[23]

For Christian authors, gluttony included not just overindulgence but eating foods too tasty, delicious, or decadent.[24] John Cassian (360–435 CE) identifies three types of gluttony: wanting a more delicate diet, consuming large amounts of food, and even wanting to eat before mealtimes.[25] Philoxenos draws upon the Greek and Syriac traditions to fashion his argument against the dangers of gluttony,[26] 'mother and nurturer' of all the passions.[27] Philoxenos is most dependent on Evagrius, however, for his articulation of the vice of gluttony.

Philoxenos read Evagrius in Syriac translation and integrated Evagrian theory of practice (in a modified form) into his theological framework,[28] transmitting Evagrian theology to the Syriac world. Syriac translators of Evagrius reworked his 'vision of spiritual progress into a two-step path to divine knowledge compatible with Nicene theology'.[29] Evagrius had classified the vices as demons that a monk needed to attack. Gluttony – together with fornication, love of money, sadness, anger, listlessness, vainglory, and pride – was one of the primary demons that assaulted monks.[30]

For Evagrius, gluttony tempted the monk to over-indulge in food and drink, and that led to fornication. Evagrius also made a direct link between the demon of gluttony and the knowledge of God: 'A soiled mirror does not produce a clear image of the form that falls upon it; when the intellect is blunted by satiety, it does not receive the knowledge of God.'[31] In the

---

[21] Shaw 1998: 23–24, 129.   [22] Pevarello 2018: 256–77.
[23] Wilson 2012: 241, as cited in Pevarello 2018: 272.   [24] Shaw 1998: 129–30.
[25] Cassian's discussion of gluttony or voraciousness of the belly is found in the Fifth of his 'Conferences'. The Fifth Conference came from his conversation with Abba Serapion, who distinguishes different types of gluttony. Cassian, *Conf.* 5.11: 199.
[26] Philoxenos' discourse fuses Greek and Syriac ascetic theology. See Brock 1987: 103.
[27] 'ܐܡܐ ܘܡܪܒܝܢܝܬܐ': Philoxenos, 'On Gluttony', 283 (ET), 363 (Syr.).
[28] Michelson 2014: 64.
[29] It is important to note that the Evagrian theology that Philoxenos received was in fact a redacted Evagrius. Syriac translators of Evagrius privileged practical elements of Evagrian ascetic theology but 'purged' Evagrius' work of tendencies towards speculative contemplation or his distinction of the human Christ and divine Logos, which did not harmonise with Miaphysite Christology (Michelson 2014: 84–85).
[30] Brakke 2009: 4.   [31] Evagrius, 'On the Eight Thoughts', 66–90.

Antirrhêtikos or *Talking Back*, his book about combatting demons, Evagrius classifies several thoughts (or *logismoi*) from the demon of gluttony. He compiles a list of biblical citations for the monk to speak out in his fight against gluttony. The demon tempts the monk to eat because he thinks he is ill,[32] and causes a monk to forget his duties to God and to demonstrate a lack of trust in divine providence.[33] He tempts the monk away from proper fasting,[34] makes the monk ungrateful for simple foods,[35] makes him recall the tasty foods and wines from the world,[36] and persuades the monk not to share with the poor.[37]

Philoxenian reception and transmission of Evagrius shaped Syriac asceticism henceforth.[38] Philoxenos grounded his epistemology in proper ascetic practice from his interpretation of Evagrian asceticism.[39] Ascent to divine knowledge began with a descent to the belly and a taming of its desires. Philoxenos does not express anxiety about food defiling the body (Matt 15:11), nor does he identify gluttony as a demon. Nevertheless, gluttony is the gateway sin that leads to other vices.[40]

Philoxenos identifies gluttony as irrational anxiety about food and an obsession with what meal lies ahead.[41] Gluttony misorients body and mind. The body becomes a vehicle that leads the monk astray. Gluttony, as an incorrect response to the gifts of creation, comes from disordered understandings of our human nature. In short, what we consume, how we consume it, and how much – these are indeed framed as epistemological questions in late antiquity because these choices directly affect our capacity to understand ourselves and hinder our approach to the knowledge of God. Food weighs down the mind. Philoxenos notes, too, that the sharpest parents who care about their children's education know not to overfeed their children, since a heavy body would weigh down the mind.[42] Gluttony turns a monk into a disgusting animal, turned downwards towards death.

Modern minds identify gluttony as a vice that leads to obesity and premature death. Philoxenos links gluttony and death explicitly. Death herself is a glutton. The glutton's behaviour mirrors Sheol, a hungry region that consumes the dead. Several passages in the Hebrew Bible had imagined

---

[32] Evagrius, *Talking Back*, 54.   [33] Evagrius, *Talking Back*, 54–55.
[34] Evagrius, *Talking Back*, 57.   [35] Evagrius, *Talking Back*, 58.   [36] Evagrius, *Talking Back*, 61.
[37] Evagrius, *Talking Back*, 63.   [38] Amar 1990: 66–89. Cf. Young 2011: 157–75.
[39] Michelson 2014: 83.   [40] Philoxenos, 'On Gluttony', 276 (ET), 353 (Syr.).
[41] Philoxenos, 'On Gluttony', 281–82 (ET), 361–62 (Syr.).
[42] Philoxenos, 'On Gluttony', 277 (ET), 356 (Syr.). Evagrius notes, too, that the prayers of a weighty God are too heavy to reach God. Evagrius, 'On the Eight Thoughts', 74.

that Sheol/ܫܝܘܠ, the underworld or place of the dead, was a hungry glutton with an insatiable appetite.[43]

The Syriac poets and homilists expanded upon this tradition, as we see, for instance, in the poetry of Ephrem the Syrian. Christ emptied the belly of Sheol, the dwelling place of the dead: 'This is the skilful Son of the carpenter, Who constructed his Cross over Sheol that devours all, and brought over humankind into the place of life.'[44] The Word had to take on a body to be swallowed up by Sheol. Christ's body tricked Sheol – death swallowed Christ and then Christ set free those who were in her womb. Thus, in the Syriac imagination, Sheol herself is a glutton, and an insatiable glutton is an image of death. Like Sheol, no matter how much the glutton has, he always wants more.[45] Elsewhere, Philoxenos condemns the glutton for making himself a tomb for food (ܩܒܪܐ ܠܗ ܠܡܐܟܠܬܐ), a perverted response to Christ who became food, died, and was buried so that the glutton might live.[46] Thus gluttony matters for Philoxenos because it brings a monk to his death. It transforms a monk into an image of death and turns him from the knowledge of God.

Imagining the Glutton of the Monastery: *Anti-exemplum* in Homiletic Discourse

Philoxenos' discourse *On Gluttony* is the inversion of a hagiography. It is replete with literary elements of hagiography, but instead of a hero for the emergent Syrian orthodox church, Philoxenos portrays an *anti-exemplum*, a glutton in the monastery, and presents his words and deeds. Philoxenos uses *prosopopoeia* (vivid description and impersonation of a person and his or her speech in character) to present a monk whose mind is enclouded by gluttony.[47] Prosopopoeia is a rhetorical strategy in which a narrator invents a voice for a historical or mythological speaker. Philoxenos constructs a glutton to question and condemn him. The monastic glutton is an idolater enslaved to his belly's desires. He is a sick, depressed man, a poison

---

[43] Proverbs speaks of the hungry womb of Sheol: 'Three things are never satisfied, four never say "enough"; Sheol, the barren womb, the land never satisfied with water, and the fire that never says, "enough"' (Prov 30:15). Habakkuk likewise imagines voracious death (Hab 2:4–5).
[44] Ephraem Syrus, *Sermo de Domino nostro* 4.4.
[45] 'Like Sheol, it receives what is fuel, but is never filled' (Philoxenos, 'On Gluttony', 282 [ET], 362 [Syr.]).
[46] Philoxenos of Mabbug, 'On Gluttony,' section 29; Budge, *Discourses*, 383.
[47] For *prosopopoeia*, see Mayoral and Ballesteros 2001 (www.oxfordreference.com/view/10.1093/acref/9780195125955.001.0001/acref-9780195125955-e-206); Enterline 2015.

to the monastic community, whose words and deeds lead others to heresy through his behaviour. Philoxenos' glutton exchanges knowledge of God for the pleasures of his body.[48]

The glutton of Philoxenos' story has no name. Instead, Philoxenos identifies him as the antithesis of a disciple, and then he narrates how the glutton's habits are opposed to those of a saint or a Christian ascetic. If the way to the knowledge of God is paved with ascetic practices that lighten the body, then the habits of the glutton weigh him down and lead him to Sheol until the glutton becomes an image of what consumes him.[49] Philoxenos constructs a 'gluttonous monk' to elicit visceral responses of disgust.[50]

To show the glutton's idolatry, Philoxenos guides his reader through the glutton's daily routine. The glutton's preoccupation with his belly's desires upsets and perverts the monk's ascetic practices. The love of food replaces his desire to pray or meditate on scripture and makes the glutton an idolater: 'Two eggs are dearer to him than the New and Old [Testaments]. Hearing about a vigil terrifies him. Prolonged prayer is a torture for him. … prayer is short, but the time of his eating is long.'[51] Philoxenos' glutton pays homage to the stomach with rituals and practices focused on meals and foods rather than God: a cult of the belly. The glutton's worship of the stomach prevents his mind from understanding God, as gluttony 'darkens the intellect from reflection on God and clouds the mind from the remembrance of Christ'.[52] He cannot think because all he is thinking about is food.

Gluttony disrupts the monk's sense of time, and it reveals that the glutton is not free. The gluttonous monk orders his day around food, losing his freedom to worship God. He is an addict, enslaved to the desires of the belly. Philoxenos denounces the glutton and how he wasted the gift of his free will: 'You are the master of creation by the will of your Maker. Why have you voluntarily [*lit.* by the desire of your freewill: ܒܨܒܝܢܐ] been made the servant of your belly?'[53] The soul should be the mistress who leads a subservient body, but in the case of the glutton, this hierarchy

---

[48] Philoxenos, 'Gluttony', 288–89, 318–19 (ET), 369–72, 409–10 (Syr.).
[49] Philoxenos, 'On Gluttony', 276 (ET), 354 (Syr.).
[50] 'Disgust is a powerful, visceral emotion … theorists have hesitated even to classify it as an emotion in the fullest sense, considering it more akin to involuntary reactions such as nausea, retching and the startle recoil. … [D]isgust is also an emotion that is at work in creating and sustaining our social and cultural reality' (Korsmeyer and Smith 2004: 6).
[51] Philoxenos, 'On Gluttony', 303 (ET, mod.), 389 (Syr.).
[52] Philoxenos, 'On Gluttony', 283 (ET), 364 (Syr.).
[53] Philoxenos, 'On Gluttony', 297 (ET), 382 (Syr.).

is perverted: 'the soul cannot lead the body freely [lit. as a free woman] but carries its weight like a slave'.[54] The uncomely body of the glutton is unhealthy and incapable of performing righteous deeds.[55]

Philoxenos constructs gluttony as an illness that enters the body and enervates it. The gluttonous monk's body can no longer be a vessel for a reformed Christian body; it stinks, just like death: 'It is equally an illness of both the soul and the body, a vessel of decay, a stinking smell, the source of the excrement of the body, a friend of darkness, a relative of gloom.'[56] The disordering of the body's desires blocks the glutton's ability to know he is sick. The glutton is grotesque because he 'tinkers/ ܡܬܦܪܣ' with his health. Rather than try 'to block the source of his illnesses' and 'suppress his gluttony a little',[57] he prefers illness to changing his gluttonous habits.

Philoxenos portrays the glutton as a pervert: instead of anticipating the glorified resurrected life or body, the glutton orients himself to his belly's desires. He directs himself towards mortality, corruptibility, and death. Unlike the modern psychologist, who might see gluttony as a result of depression, Philoxenos (as other ancient and medieval expounders on this topic) believed that gluttony was the cause of grief (ܥܩܬܐ) and sadness (ܟܪܝܘܬܐ).[58] This sadness makes the glutton turn inward, nourishing not charity but 'dullness of the heart'.[59] Incorporating an image from Prov 26:11,[60] Philoxenos calls gluttony 'the yoke-fellow of an avaricious dog returning to its vomit'.[61] The glutton's obsession with food dehumanises him and makes knowledge impossible, as gluttony is the 'defiler of the conscience, the destroyer of learning, annihilator of knowledge'.[62]

Philoxenos is especially concerned about the effects of gluttony on communal life. Unlike the 'holy fool' who feigns stupidity for the sake of the Lord,[63] the glutton is a real fool disgracing the monastic habit, drawing others down by his example as he places his hope in food rather than

---

[54] Philoxenos, 'On Gluttony', 279 (ET), 359 (Syr.).
[55] Philoxenos, 'On Gluttony', 277 (ET), 355 (Syr.).
[56] Philoxenos, 'On Gluttony', 285 (ET), 366 (Syr.).
[57] Philoxenos, 'On Gluttony', 303 (ET), 390 (Syr.).
[58] Philoxenos, 'On Gluttony', 285 (ET), 366 (Syr.). On monastic conceptions of grief and sadness, see also Chapter 28 by Jonathan Zecher, this volume.
[59] ܥܡܛܘܬ ܠܒܐ : Philoxenos, 'On Gluttony', 285 (ET), 366 (Syr.).
[60] 'As a dog returns to its vomit, so a fool repeats his folly.' This same proverb is found in 2 Pet 2:22.
[61] ܒܪ ܢܝܪܐ ܕܟܠܒܐ ܥܠܘܒܐ: Philoxenos, 'On Gluttony', 285 (ET), 366 (Syr.).
[62] Philoxenos, 'On Gluttony', 284 (ET), 365 (Syr.).
[63] The holy fool was a type of saint that became popular in the Byzantine and Syriac traditions. See Krueger 1996.

God. Gluttony that kills the body of the individual monk is contagious. It spreads in the community, infecting others and perverting the mealtimes of the monks: 'It eats by itself, the enemy of those who do not give it anything, an abominable image (ܕܠܐ ܚܙܘ), a vile resemblance that is not describable.'[64] Philoxenos constructs a glutton who also is *unaware* of the effects that his sinful habits have on those living around him. The vice of gluttony can be 'put on' like clothing.[65] When one monk puts on a form of 'dissoluteness', then others follow suit:

> The glutton, seeing his companion, adds more unto his own dissoluteness. The dissolute person looks at him and puts on (ܠܒܫ) his dissoluteness again like one coat over [another] coat. Whoever is grasped by the desire of his belly sees him and remains even more with his love. However, the valiant and ascetics suffer loss because they are scandalised by him, and his story draws them into a conversation they do not like. From all sides he stirs up war against them, whether [it be] not to lower themselves at the sight of his dissoluteness, or not to become prideful by their tenacity comparing their virtuous life with his dissoluteness. … Their life in the world is found to be in all ways a cause of harm for [other] people.[66]

Gluttony is a contagion that instils laziness and 'induces laxity (ܪܦܝܘܬܐ) in all who see it'.[67] The glutton is an icon inspiring a life of idolatrous worship of the belly, rather than of God.

Thus, the imposter of the monastery, the glutton, infiltrates and poisons the community. A terrible friend, his gluttony leads to another vice – envy – and he desires others' things.[68] He corrupts friendships by introducing food as bribery: 'He doesn't know how to acquire a friend without the belly … if there is murmuring against him, he thinks he can appease it with a gift of the stomach (ܡܘܗܒܬܐ ܕܟܪܣܐ).'[69] He manipulates food and hunger to make up for his mistakes. Too much food perverts the monk into a jealous fool: 'If he has angered someone by his foolishness (ܣܟܠܘܬܐ) and his jealousy, he runs with a gift of food to reconcile him. His hope is based on [food], and through it he thinks the bonds of his deeds can be released.'[70]

Through attributing speech to the imagined glutton (*prosopopoeia*), Philoxenos underscores the link between gluttony, epistemology, and the

---

[64] Philoxenos, 'On Gluttony', 285 (ET), 366 (Syr.).
[65] For clothing imagery in Syriac theology, see Brock 1982: 11–40.
[66] Philoxenos, 'On Gluttony', 299 (ET), 384 (Syr.).
[67] Philoxenos, 'On Gluttony', 285 (ET), 366 (Syr.).
[68] Philoxenos, 'On Gluttony', 282 (ET), 362 (Syr.). The glutton looks on the food of others with an envious eye, ܥܝܢܐ ܕܚܣܡܐ.
[69] Philoxenos, 'On Gluttony', 301 (ET), 387 (Syr.).
[70] Philoxenos, 'On Gluttony', 301–2 (ET), 387–88 (Syr.).

road to heresy. Philoxenos imagines the foolish words and narratives that the glutton speaks, and then he condemns them.[71] Philoxenos imagines that the glutton ridicules others practising asceticism, taunting his fellow monks who do their sacred reading, 'Have you nothing [better] to do?'[72] Gluttons call those zealous for the orthodox faith (as Philoxenos himself was) 'troublemakers'.[73] Instead of defending orthodoxy, the glutton is content to eat and says, 'Let us eat something that God has provided for us and be quiet.'[74] Such statements, for Philoxenos, demonstrate the glutton's complacency and mean 'Let us serve our belly and get rid of faith.'[75]

The speech of the glutton betrays his sympathy with heretics. Philoxenos characterises the glutton in the same way that he portrays theologians who investigate God, rather than approaching God in wonder: '[The glutton] labels the search for truth (ܒܥܬܐ ܕܫܪܪܐ) a disputation (ܕܪܫܐ), and he calls conversation about faith an investigation (ܥܘܩܒܐ).'[76] The glutton will not identify the knowledge of God because he is unworthy to recognise it: 'he reproaches divine teaching along with its teachers' and 'denounces the wisdom of Christ along with those who seek it'.[77] We can join these thoughts to Philoxenos' lament elsewhere in his corpus that monks would change their christological position because of failure in the knowledge of God: 'Indeed, they did not know it because they were not worthy to know it.'[78] Disordered thoughts and priorities about the body and its needs lead to incorrect beliefs about God.

The monastic fraud, the glutton, shuts his ears from the monastery's stories and twists sacred stories into plots that concern his belly. The glutton 'ignores all [other] stories and makes his own the center of attention. If a story should be told, whether of a work of labor or of a divine teaching, he craftily twists and disposes of it in order to bring about a tale of the stomach (ܬܫܥܝܬܐ ܕܟܪܣܐ) into the middle.'[79] The pious monk's stories praise Christian virtues, but those of the glutton make an idol of the belly.

The glutton channels his energy in the pursuit of food, just like a dog or a hog.[80] He devalues his own humanity and loses the capacity to speak about

---

[71] For imagined speech as a rhetorical tool, see Harvey 2005: 63–86.
[72] Philoxenos, 'On Gluttony', 287 (ET), 368 (Syr.).
[73] Philoxenos, 'On Gluttony', 288 (ET), 369 (Syr.).
[74] Philoxenos, 'On Gluttony', 288 (ET), 370 (Syr.).
[75] Philoxenos, 'On Gluttony', 288 (ET), 370 (Syr.).
[76] Philoxenos, 'On Gluttony', 287 (ET), 368 (Syr.).
[77] Philoxenos, 'On Gluttony', 287 (ET), 369 (Syr.).
[78] Philoxenos, *Letter to the Monks of Senun* 89–90. As cited in Michelson 2014: 4.
[79] Philoxenos, 'On Gluttony', 302 (ET), 388 (Syr.).
[80] Philoxenos, 'On Gluttony', 297 (ET), 382 (Syr.). Cf. Philoxenos, 'On Gluttony', 300 (ET), 385 (Syr).

wisdom. This exchange symbolises his rejection of knowledge. Philoxenos' appeal to animals is necessary to dehumanise the glutton and to construct an image of disgust. Like a dog, the glutton dashes to the table, but he cannot speak 'since like an animal he is deprived of all conversations of wisdom'.[81] Throughout his treatise, Philoxenos compares this monk's behaviour as being, in fact, 'worse' than that of an animal: at least, in Philoxenos' mind, an animal stops eating when it is full. Philoxenos compares the glutton to an animal to shame (ܒܗܬ) the glutton about his desires.[82]

The glutton is a monastic failure who does not understand that God created him to glorify God. Because he values his body's desires over the promise of divine knowledge, he has thwarted his commitment to askesis. His attention to eating brings his life's focus on his mortality rather than the possibility of sharing in Christ's resurrection and glory. Philoxenos rebukes the glutton: 'He has created everything for your glory, but you are exchanging his glory for your belly? God calls you to conversation with him, but is your thought tied down to the table?'[83] The glutton has forgotten the reason he became a monk in the first place. Gluttony destroys the memory of God (ܥܘܗܕܢܐ ܕܐܠܗܐ),[84] and that disorders all his practices. By turning his attention solely to the belly (which leads to other passions), the glutton offends God by staining God's beautiful work.

Philoxenos laments the gluttonous monk as a sickened image of God, who cannot know God because he has never identified himself as a work of God. Food prevents the glutton from properly using his senses, as desire plugs his ear from hearing the theological teaching that would lead him to God:[85] 'Who will not weep over this seeing that he damages a beautiful work of God (ܥܒܕܐ ܫܦܝܪܐ ܕܐܠܗܐ) by his laxity? That is, he is justly worthy of punishment, not only because he serves his lusts and enrages God by his desire, but also because he damages by his gluttony healthy members that were beautifully fashioned by the Maker?'[86] Philoxenos gives his audience a way to know and understand themselves. Understanding his physical constitution is the first step to knowing God and healing his relationship to his Creator: 'See, therefore, the cause of your [broken-down] constitution, O glutton (ܐܘ ܝܥܢܐ), and tremble before God, and do not damage yourself.'[87]

---

[81] Philoxenos, 'On Gluttony', 300 (ET), 385 (Syr.).
[82] Philoxenos, 'On Gluttony', 300 (ET), 386 (Syr.).
[83] Philoxenos, 'On Gluttony', 297 (ET), 382 (Syr.).
[84] Philoxenos, 'On Gluttony', 283 (ET), 364 (Syr.).
[85] Philoxenos, 'On Gluttony', 295–96 (ET), 380 (Syr.).
[86] Philoxenos, 'On Gluttony', 296 (ET), 380 (Syr.).
[87] Philoxenos, 'On Gluttony', 296 (ET), 381 (Syr.).

Freeing the Body from Gluttony and the Medicine of the Eucharist

Like many theologians of asceticism in late antiquity, the starting point for Philoxenos' construction of the glutton is the goodness of the human body. While Philoxenos depicts the glutton as a slave to his belly, the belly is not necessarily the monk's adversary. Indeed, affirming the body's goodness, Philoxenos reminds his reader that the body helps the ascetic limit food intake: 'For the Maker, in order to restrain the lust of the gluttons – has made the stomach of a limited capacity, so that by necessity, even though they do not wish, they will be inhibited from their lust.'[88]

Philoxenos urges his audience to consider a limited diet for a healthier body and soul: 'Besides the word of doctors, we should understand from experience as wise people that the cause of all evils, diseases, and ailments of the body is from too much food.'[89] Along with a smaller diet, labour is also vital for one's health. He who is healthy will never need a doctor or foolish remedies like purgatives, bloodletting, and drugs.

Throughout this text, Philoxenos emphasises that a rigorous programme that counters gluttony also trains one to understand the heavenly realm's reality more clearly. He presents Christ's table in heaven to the glutton as a more fitting counterpart to the offerings of this world: 'Christ has a table that has been promised to his friends – why do you suspend your attention to look at the time for table? There is another world with its heavenly blessings – why have you confined your life's confidence in the visible world?'[90] By addressing this imagined glutton, Philoxenos calls his readers to reform how they see themselves. The body must be reoriented towards God to know God and recognise God's presence. Furthermore, overeating misdirects our proper orientation and understanding of the Eucharist: 'The Lord has loved you to such an extent that he should become food for you.'[91] Through the eucharistic feast, the monk's eating is redeemed and reordered.

Conclusions

The church's intellectuals drew stricter lines of right belief and heresy in the fifth and sixth centuries and worked on rectifying the individual Christian

---

[88] Philoxenos, 'On Gluttony', 281 (ET), 360 (Syr.).
[89] Philoxenos, 'On Gluttony', 294 (ET), 377 (Syr.).
[90] Philoxenos, 'On Gluttony', 297 (ET), 381 (Syr.).
[91] Philoxenos, 'On Gluttony', 298 (ET), 382 (Syr.).

body. Christian asceticism offered a way to know God through a reformed body that symbolised the intersection of the human and divine. As debates about orthodox christology divided the church from the fourth century onwards, both Chalcedonians and Non-Chalcedonians prized ascetic bodies as symbols of holiness among their ranks. The identification and condemnation of vices was, therefore, an essential step in the emergent Christian epistemology.

Christian ascetics exchanged pain of the body for the hope of the knowledge of God.[92] Through committing themselves singleheartedly to a proper ordering of their body, Philoxenos wanted his monks to manifest orthodox christology and divine power. A stronger community of ascetics meant a more definite hierarchy of Christian heroes for the Miaphysite cause. So Philoxenos' anxiety that his monks govern their bellies was also, therefore, a plea for them to retain the authority that ascetics earned. The glutton is poison for the monastery because he tempts others to exchange a life oriented towards the divine for one that looks at the belly, gazing downwards towards death. One can only know God in a body that asceticism has trained. For Philoxenos, the glutton is a foolish idolater – an anti-monk, worshipping his belly instead of God.

To turn his readers' minds against gluttony's dangers, Philoxenos instilled images in their minds intended to disgust them. He composed a narrative of the deviant monk. Philoxenos' glutton is a monastic flop, an icon of Sheol. He creates a portrait of this idolatrous belly worshipper, a dog, a foul creature, whose choice to order his day according to food and his belly overturns the hierarchy of ascetic virtues. His gluttony leads to foolishness and heterodoxy. While we note the rhetorical strategies at play, it is also true that Philoxenos would not have been a persuasive teacher if the ideas that he suggested to his monks were far-fetched. While it may be a stretch to say that all monks were lazy or indulgent, many among his audience needed training in the ascetic discipline and a divine purpose for it. Philoxenos gives this to them in his discourse.

Philoxenos uses his discourse on gluttony to lament against broader disordered epistemologies about the body, mind, and knowledge of God. Philoxenos constructs the glutton as a metonymic figure, standing in for any Christian whose lax habits of the body inevitably lead to a flawed way of knowing God and ultimately to heresy. Disputations and argumentations

---

[92] Harpham notes that the distinctions between the exchange for pain and knowledge and the exchange of pain for power are perhaps mistaken (Harpham 2008: 485).

about faith and God's nature had led to divisions of the church. Philoxenos corrects idolatrous bodily habits to prevent heterodox understandings of God. By reforming the monks, Philoxenos orients the Miaphysite church towards theological knowledge built on wonder, ascetic practice, and the life of prayer and study.

While only a few could articulate Miaphysite theology, the story of the gluttonous monk was concrete.[93] Homiletic discourse and prosopopoeia were useful modes of instructing ascetics living in an era torn by theological controversies and anxiety over orthodoxy. Fighting gluttony, the gateway sin, was the first step in reordering the human person towards the knowledge of God.

---

[93] Brian Dunkle (Chapter 21, this volume) similarly argues that Ambrose's hymns relied on concrete exempla rather than abstract conceptual claims. For an alternate approach to distilling the Chalcedonian-Miaphysite debates into a more accessible form for non-experts, see Chapter 33 by Dirk Krausmüller, this volume.

28 | Evagrius of Pontus on Λύπη: Distress and Cognition between Philosophy, Medicine, and Monasticism

JONATHAN L. ZECHER

Introduction

> Distress is a worm in the heart, and devours the mother that births it.
> Evagrius of Pontus (c. 345–99)[1]

> Mourning is a golden nail in the heart, stripped of every transfixion and attachment, transfixed to the heart's watchtower by holy grief.
> John Climacus (c. 579–649)[2]

These two definitions seem, especially in English, to refer to quite different phenomena: distress (λύπη) and mourning (πένθος). Yet both describe a gnawing pain in the breast. Evagrius' 'distress' destroys the heart and, with it, the one who suffers it. John's 'mourning' is mobilised by 'holy grief' – also λύπη – to bring its sufferer to repentance. Clearly, λύπη is operating differently in the Evagrian passage than in the Climacian one, despite the similarity of sensation. In other passages, Evagrius speaks well of πένθος, and John worries over λύπη; the distinction is not one of authorial preference. Read together, these two definitions raise an important question: how could Christian ascetic writers like Evagrius and John define an apparently singular emotional experience in two such opposite ways?

The bifurcation of 'grief' into vice and virtue is a feature of Christian ascetic spirituality often discussed but poorly understood.[3] Certainly,

---

[1] *Oct. spir. mal.* 5.1 (PG 79: 1156B).
[2] *Scal.* 7.1 (PG 88: 801A): Πένθος ἐστὶ κέντρον χρύσεον ψυχῆς πάσης προσηλώσεως καὶ σχέσεως γυμνωθέν· καὶ ἐν ἐπισκοπῇ καρδίας ὑπὸ τῆς ὁσίας λύπης καταπηχθέν.
[3] One notable exception: Crislip 2023. Andrew Crislip, drawing on Ute Frevert's work in the history of emotions, rightly argues that Evagrius shows us emotions in transition – the sociocultural context of anchorite and coenobitic monasticism generated conditions that in turn generated, constrained, and even upended trains of thought, affective response, and cognitive function. One might point to the reconfiguration of agonistic relationships in monastic condemnation of anger, as well as to the bifurcation of λύπη that I explore here.

both λύπη and πένθος are familiar to readers of desert and other monastic literature. Λύπη is the fourth (sometimes fifth) of Evagrius' famous 'Eight Wicked Thoughts'. Though Evagrius does not dwell on it, for some ascetics, like Abba Poemen (fourth century) or the Byzantine monk Symeon the New Theologian (969–1025 CE), πένθος comprises the core practice of the Christian life. Scholarship on ascetic spirituality has assumed that the semantic difference is coterminous with a conceptual one, yielding studies of either the 'vice of sadness'[4] or the 'virtue of mourning'.[5] However, as this chapter will show, close study of Evagrius' account of λύπη demonstrates that the semantic distinction is much less important than a subtler psychological one, fashioned among the possible causes of a constellation of emotional sensations and practices within λύπη. Evagrius countenances an equivocality in the phenomenology of λύπη that is absent or rejected in the philosophical and medical accounts that inform him. Evagrius transforms the *meanings* rather than the *sensations* of λύπη, with implications for the human being both as a knowing subject and as a known object.

In what follows, I will not translate λύπη or πένθος. First, because no one English term covers the connotative range of these terms in philosophical, medical, and monastic literature. Second, because I want to trouble the comfortable but false distinction between 'grief' and 'mourning' that has haunted scholars thus far. I will first show how λύπη was organised, analysed, and articulated in Hellenistic lists of emotions, which elaborate the 'primary passions' or 'passions' found in Plato, Aristotle, and the Stoics. While 'primary passions' were accepted as features as well as modifiers of cognition, philosophical treatises mediated their experience and expression in culturally specific ways. Passion-lists, for example, negotiate the distance between these through two complementary functions: they constitute *affective lexica* for naming and communicating bodily states and intentional objects of emotional experience; and they generate *behavioural scripts* which in turn shape the practice of emotions. It becomes clear from these that, without exception, λύπη damages cognition and relationships, and that even public acts of mourning, while culturally acceptable, can catalyse its most deleterious effects. In the second part, I turn to Evagrius of Pontus to show how his commitments both to classical learning and to scriptural exegesis demand a new organisation of

---

[4] Barring Crislip's article, there is no study of λύπη in monastic literature as such. Rather, there are studies of 'sadness' or 'grief' in Evagrian thought: Stewart 2005; Burton-Christie 2009.
[5] The most important studies are Hausherr 1944; Müller 2000; Hunt 2004.

emotion that distinguishes between λύπη as a passion and λύπη as a virtue. Evagrius articulates a new understanding of the human as a *knowing subject*. I will conclude with a brief discussion of the emerging 'hermeneutic' of λύπη that this phenomenology necessitates, in which the human as a *known object* is reorganised and conceived.

Passion for Lists, Lists for Passions

There were in antiquity a few possible lists of primary passions, but it seems that generally the Stoic four were accepted. Stobaeus gives the canonical account. The Stoics, he says, define four passions (πάθη) as 'primary with respect to the genus [πρῶτα δ' εἶναι τῷ γένει]', and these are 'desire, fear, λύπη, and pleasure'.[6] The list is subtle and was probably not intended to exhaust the range of emotional experience. Rather, Stobaeus' list may be thought of as mapping a plane along which emotions arise and within which they can be named, organised, and managed. The plane is defined by two axes: voluntary motion (ὁρμή/ἀφορμή, impulsion/aversion) and temporality, or degrees of uncertainty (παρόν/μελλόν, present/future or perhaps present/non-present). The possibilities for emotional experience have, then, four corners: present-impulsion (ἡδονή, pleasure), present-aversion (λύπη, distress), future-impulsion (ἐπιθυμία, desire), and future-aversion (φόβος, fear). Between these four corners, the variety of experiences, expressions, and practices of emotion are, at least in principle, numerous. The four primary emotions imprint logically primary properties of human experience. Phenomenologically, however, experiences and practices of emotion take on myriad culture-bound forms.

Philosophers employed a second kind of list to negotiate the distance between universal, 'primary' passions, and their experiential and performative phenomenology. These lists are found in fragmentary texts, in doxographies, and in moral treatises. They are arranged taxonomically around the opposition of passions (πάθη) and virtues (ἀρεταί), which suggests mnemonic use and possibly a schoolroom context. The primary passions are genera (γένη), and their manifestations are species (εἴδη) of each. Under λύπη, lists include anywhere from four to twenty-five forms, the terms and definitions of which create affective lexica and engage behavioural scripts.

---

[6] Stobaeus, *Flor.* 2.7.10 (Wachsmuth 1884: 2.88.14–15).

Evagrius of Pontus on Λύπη 533

I discern two kinds of definition: one referring to a bodily movement or sensation, the other to an intentional object. Thus, Pseudo-Andronicus gives the following:

12. Ὄχλησις is λύπη that constricts, and offers no release.
13. Ὀδύνη is λύπη that comes swift and sharp.
22. Βαρυθυμία is λύπη that weighs down and does not allow one to stand.[7]

In his version, Diogenes Laertius modifies a couple of definitions to heighten their vividness. Thus, ἐνόχλησις is 'λύπη that constricts and makes spaces too small', and ὀδύνη 'toilsome λύπη'.[8] Each such definition highlights a physical experience – speechlessness, weight, constraint, suffocation – all of which are *painful* and so, by referring those experiences to an emotion (or affect) that is both named and, taxonomically, at least, understood, the list begins to craft a language for pain.

Other definitions refer readers to λύπη's intentional objects, which seem generally to be social circumstances:

1. Ἔλεος is λύπη at another's sufferings which that person suffers undeservedly [λύπη ἐπ' ἀλλοτρίοις κακοῖς ἀναξίως πάσχοντος ἐκείνου].
6. Συμφορά is λύπη at close-packed evils [λύπη ἐπὶ συμπεφραγμένοις κακοῖς].
10. Πένθος is λύπη at untimely death [λύπη ἐπὶ ἀώρῳ τελευτῇ].
15. Μεταμέλεια is λύπη at mistakes made, because they are one's own fault [λύπη ἐπὶ ἁμαρτήμασι πεπραγμένοις ὡς δι' αὐτοῦ γεγονόσιν].
25. Οἶκτος is λύπη at another's sufferings [λύπη ἐπ' ἀλλοτρίοις κακοῖς].[9]

In these definitions, perception predominates – how are one's own actions or the experiences of another interpreted? A Stoic might read the list quite differently from a Platonist: for the Stoic, the perception is a judgement which *causes* the emotion; for the Platonist, the emotion might cause the perception. For both, though, the list highlights the social reality of λύπη, that it is tied to relationships, to self-perception, to status, to norms and practices which are the background against which emotional arousal becomes visible.

More importantly, these definitions highlight the ways in which λύπη impairs human knowing. Examined with respect to its occasions, λύπη binds its sufferer to past and present miseries.[10] Of course, it is not that another's good fortune or one's misfortune *must* cause λύπη – such, at least, is the

---

[7] Pseudo-Andronicus, *De passionibus* 1.2 (Wachsmuth 1884: 14.8–10).
[8] *Lives* 7.112 (Hicks 1925: 216).
[9] Pseudo-Andronicus, *De passionibus* 1.2 (Wachsmuth 1884: 12.12–13, 14.2, 14.11–12, 15.9).
[10] In those analyses of λύπη that align it most closely with φόβος, one might include contingent futures as well. Perhaps what we find is that grief characterises a certain way of perceiving, among other things, temporal contingency.

claim of philosophical protreptics from Stoics, Peripatetics, and Platonists alike. For some, no occasion should be the cause of λύπη, and for all λύπη is inherently problematic. Nevertheless, λύπη's appearance makes its cause seem necessary, because its cognitive effects perpetuate and exacerbate the affective response to perceived frustrations. Thus, Pseudo-Andronicus has '24. Φροντίς is a distressed train of thought [λογισμὸς λυπουμένου]'. Λύπη colours how one thinks and, for that reason, it alters judgements, and distorts perception. Pseudo-Andronicus defines '16. Σύγχυσις' as 'λύπη that hinders one from seeing what will be [κωλύουσα διορᾶν τὸ μέλλον]',[11] while Diogenes Laertius amplifies this passion's effects, saying that it 'is an irrational λύπη that wears one down and hinders from seeing how things are [λύπην ἄλογον, ἀποκναίουσαν καὶ κωλύουσαν τὰ παρόντα συνορᾶν]'.[12] In both cases, λύπη so restricts cognitive capacities that it blinds its sufferer to the realities of their world. Left unchecked, it results in the more serious mental derangements of φρενῖτις, μανία, and μελαγχολία.[13] So understood, λύπη is the cause and initial stage of severe cognitive dysfunction and mental illness.[14]

In medical literature too, and especially in Galen's nosology, λύπη plays a role in mental illness, but it means something closer to 'anxiety' than 'grief'. Galen deploys various passion-lists. Usually resembling Stoic ones, his are governed by an interest in the pathological hazards of psychical passions. Moreover, 'bodily' and 'psychic' causes intermingle in his nosology.[15] Galen thus develops his own medical passion-lists,[16] in which λύπη features prominently, not, according to Susan Mattern, as 'a passive emotion, but a desperate, agitating force that drives its victims to extremes'.[17] In Galen's case studies, moreover, λύπη's meaning tends to shade into 'anxiety' – Mattern even compares Galenic λύπη with 'generalized anxiety disorder'.[18] In Galen's famous story of Justus' wife, who fell in love with a circus performer, it is not the *loss* of love that leads to her λύπη, but her worry over being discovered.[19] Her λύπη is concerned with possible futures.[20] Whether or not the modern psychiatric category is applicable, the general point holds true: For Galen, λύπη refers more usually to an emotional experience borne of cognitive uncertainty, and, while that

---

[11] *De passionibus* 1.2.1 (Wachsmuth 1884: 14.13). [12] *Lives* 7.112 (Hicks 1925: 185.216).
[13] Pigeaud 2006: 70–138.
[14] See, e.g., Holmes 2013a; Singer 2018; and the other essays in those volumes.
[15] Mattern 2016.
[16] See, e.g., *Ars Med.* 24; *Temp.* 2.6; *San. Tu.*1.5; 1.8; *MM* 8.2; 10.2; 10.4; 10.6; etc. On these, see Boudon-Millot 2013: 140.
[17] Mattern 2016: 208. [18] Mattern 2016: 203–23. [19] Galen, *Praen.* 6 (Nutton 1979: 100–2).
[20] Mattern 2016: 211–12.

uncertainty may often have an object, very often the experience is disproportionate or disconnected from the object.

What of πένθος, that great virtue of monks? Both passion-lists and lexicographical evidence demonstrate that, from antiquity through the Byzantine period, πένθος is tied to λύπη. Pseudo-Andronicus and Arius Didymus, as we have seen, classify πένθος as 'λύπη at untimely death' – whether another's or one's own is left ambiguous. Lexicographical entries demonstrate that the tie between πένθος and λύπη is maintained all the way through the Byzantine era. Hesychius (fifth century) defines πένθος as 'misfortune, wailing, λύπη [συμφορά. Θρῆνος, λύπη]'.[21] The entry for πένθος in the *Lexicon* of Pseudo-Zonaras (thirteenth century) summarises mourning's relationship to λύπη:

Mourning. A gloomy disposition of soul [διάθεσις ψυχῆς σκυθρωπή] arising from the deprivation of something much desired. It has no place in those who live in contentment. Or, a painful sensation [αἴσθησις ἀλγεινή] of the deprivation of one's delights. The word [πένθος] comes from 'depth' [τὸ βάθος] ... properly it pertains to the dying, because their λύπη is in their deepest parts.[22]

This definition recalls the language of passion-lists in its interest in cause ('deprivations') as well as cognitive-affective (the 'gloomy disposition of soul') and physiological ('painful sensation') analyses of the psychic experience that accompanies the action of mourning.

The passage in Hesychius accords with, and perhaps draws on, consolatory descriptions of mourning, which set culturally recognisable forms within moral psychology. Plutarch, for example, urges moderation rather than extirpation of passion but tells his exiled friend 'grieving and humiliating oneself is always useless and vain'.[23] Galen would disagree sharply with Chrysippus about the operation of passions but agree that distress constitutes a particularly nasty one.[24] Nemesius of Emesa (4th–5th century) might take the Stoics to task for their fatalism and materialism but nevertheless conclude his (Christian) passion-list by quoting Chrysippus: 'All λύπη is evil by its very nature [πᾶσα δὲ λύπη κακὸν τῇ ἑαυτῆς φύσει].'[25] Across philosophical schools,

---

[21] Hesychius, *Lexicon*, Π.1399; see also Julius Pollux, *Onom.* 3.99.2–5.
[22] Pseudo-Zonaras, *Lexicon*, Π (Tittmann 1967: 2.1536.1–10).
[23] Plutarch, *Exil.* 1, 599B–C: 'τὸ λυπεῖσθαι καὶ τὸ ταπεινοῦν ἑαυτὸν ἐπὶ παντὶ μὲν ἄχρηστον ἐστι καὶ γενόμενον κενῶς.' Cf. Iamblichus, *De vita pythagorica* 15.65: 'περιῆγε τὰ τῆς ψυχῆς πάθη νέον ἐν αὐτοῖς ἀλόγως συνιστάμενα καὶ ὑποφυόμενα, λύπας καὶ ὀργὰς καὶ ἐλέους καὶ ζήλους ἀτόπους καὶ φόβους, ἐπιθυμίας τε παντοίας καὶ θυμοὺς καὶ ὀρέξεις καὶ χαυνώσεις καὶ ὑπτιότητας καὶ σφοδρότητας'.
[24] Galen, *Aff. Pecc. Dig.* 1.7.2 (de Boer 1937: 24.14–16).
[25] Nemesius, *De natura hominis* 19 (Morani 1987: 80.15–16).

regardless of their psychology or ethical ideals, λύπη was understood to be, in itself and of itself, a problem for knowing, to say nothing of happiness.

The Fate of Lists

Christian writers inherited the philosophical apprehension over λύπη, not merely in a general sense that λύπη is detrimental to knowing and happiness, but in the more nuanced articulation of its experience which emerges from passion-lists. Christians made their own passion-lists that depended on Stoic and Galenic ones. We have already encountered lists in Byzantine lexica, and Nemesius of Emesa's version of Diogenes Laertius' list is picked up by Maximus the Confessor, John of Damascus, and others. The list has a long life in Christian literature because it is an important site of philosophical, medical, and theological reflection on the causes, sensations, and practices of emotion. As I turn to Evagrius, I would highlight three ways in which lists colour monastic accounts of λύπη and πένθος. First, lists provide psychological schemata: we shall see that Evagrius takes up the list-based approach to organising the production, experience, and practices of λύπη. Second, as we have seen, passion-lists are concerned with creating *affective lexica*, useful for articulating and narrativising experience. Third, lists' causal analyses of passion highlight interest in the cognitive process and worries over the debilitating effects of λύπη on cognition.[26] As we have seen, in these lists and in the literature more broadly, there was common consensus that all passions, but especially λύπη, impede human knowing. In the same literature, πένθος is inseparable from λύπη. It is a practice of grief, and so dangerous because, while culturally sanctioned, it catalyses λύπη's most deleterious effects. In this literature, emotional experience becomes a dimension of the knowing subject and its organisation an object of knowledge. Monastic authors like Evagrius would transform both subject and object of knowledge in their differentiation between godly and demonic λύπη, as well as between λύπη and πένθος.

The Christian Transformation of λύπη

Evagrius created what would become the most conspicuous and influential Christian passion-list: the 'eight wicked thoughts' (or 'spirits') which

[26] For a schematic and synthetic overview of λύπη's causes and effects in Christian literature, with copious references, see Larchet 2000: 195–205.

initiate corresponding passions. These are γαστριμαργία, πορνεία, φιλαργυρία, θυμός/ὀργή, λύπη, ἀκηδία, κενοδοξία, and ὑπερηφανία. The eight thoughts update and expand the 'four primary passions' within a Christian ascetic tradition. While the exact sources are not clear, it is certain that Evagrius' eight are, like the Stoic four, both *generic* and *generative* of a wide variety of emotional, cognitive, and ethical malfunctions.[27] Moreover, like the Hellenistic passion-lists, Evagrius' is fluid,[28] though generally keyed to divisions of the Platonic soul,[29] and is meant to reflect the order in which temptations are thought to attack monks.[30] Evagrius consistently maintains the venerable connection between λύπη and θύμος (or ὀργή) as twinned movements of the θυμικόν, both of which 'stir up the soul'.[31] However, he tightens this connection by making each a possible cause of the other. This flexibility as regards both the number and the order of 'thoughts' suggests that Evagrius, like his Hellenistic predecessors, views the list as a sketchpad rather than a procrustean bed. An examination of those texts in which Evagrius presents the eight thoughts shows not only his inheritance from Hellenistic philosophy, but also the ways in which his exegetical commitments and experience of monastic life demand its transformation. This chapter focuses on three points of novelty: first, the intentional objects and cognitive effects of λύπη, among which Evagrius includes beneficial and reasonable ones as well as irrational and deleterious; second, the use of metaphorical language to craft a new affective lexicon; and third, the new behavioural scripts required by his novel analysis.

Λύπη *in Two Tenses*

Evagrius' combination of technical precision with pedagogical flexibility makes it unwise to abstract a system from his writings, although many have attempted exactly that. Within any given text, Evagrius is semantically consistent and conceptually precise – but not so much between texts. Thus, in his extended discussions in *To Eulogius* and *On the Eight Wicked Spirits*, Evagrius analyses λύπη causally, as the result of frustrated desire, whether for pleasure[32] or revenge,[33] and, therefore, the antecedent cause

---

[27] Corrigan 2009: 76.
[28] Evagrius does not even tie himself to 'eight' thoughts. Sometimes he adds φθόνος or ἀναισθησία or καταλαλιά. See Zecher 2018; Stewart 2005: 30–31.
[29] *Mal. cog.* 17, 25; *Cap. prac.* 22; on which see Gibbons 2015: 310–11; so too Stewart 2005: 17.
[30] *Mal. cog.* 1.
[31] *Cap. prac.* 22 (SC 171: 552); note again the definition of λύπη with which this paper began – it is a worm in the *heart*.
[32] *Eulog.* 6.23–24 (SC 591: 296): Ἐπιθυμίαι ἀποτυχοῦσαι φυτεύουσι λύπας.
[33] *Oct. spir. mal.* 5.1 (PG 79: 1156B).

or an effect of anger.[34] Its operation (ἐργασία) is experienced as regret or even nostalgia. Evagrius describes in the *Praktikos* the potency of λύπη:

> Λύπη that follows the frustration of desires comes upon the monk thus: Some lingering thoughts bring the soul to remember house, parents, and its former way of life. And when they [i.e., the demons] see that the soul does not resist but, rather follows and pours itself into these imagined pleasures, then they seize it and baptise it in λύπη, since the old days are gone and, thanks to the monastic life, will not come again.[35]

In this passage, as elsewhere, λύπη is parasitic on other passions. That is, it is the *attachment* to an old life, as well as the judgement that it is *pleasurable*, that gives λύπη purchase in the soul.[36] In *To Eulogius*, Evagrius says λύπη follows on the experience of a baseless demonic joy in the heart (the organ of the θυμικόν, after all), because the 'spirit of λύπη' has made the heart 'captive' to falsity. Joy without cause – an imagined delight with no basis in reality.[37] A similar phenomenology holds for λύπη that follows frustrated anger: the *esprit d'escalier*, the dream of revenge and the feeling of impotence at being unable to realise it. In both cases, the mental pleasure of recollection and imagination leads to λύπη, which may itself be described as λύπη at an imagined but impossible *present*: family lost, rivals promoted, and one's failure in the midst of it all.

By contrast, in the *Antirrhetikos* and *De malignis cogitationibus* (*On Thoughts*), Evagrius draws on a valence of λύπη much more common in medical literature: λύπη as the psycho-physical distress attending an imagined and possible *future*. In his studies of dreams and demonic night-terrors, Evagrius' account is close to Galen's. In *On Thoughts*, Evagrius describes λύπη's action as follows:

> Often [dreams] cast anchorites into inconsolable sadness, showing them some of their own [relatives? brethren?] who are ill, or who are in danger on land or sea.

---

[34] *Eulog.* 9.12–16 (SC 591: 308), *Oct. spir. mal.* 5.1 (PG 79: 1156B), which quotes Chrysippus (frags. 395, 396, 397; Diogenes Laertius, *Lives* 7.113). While the precise wording is Chrysippus', the position goes back to Aristotle, *De an.* 1.1.403a30. So too *Cap. prac.* 10, 11, 23; *Vit. prol.*24–25; 4.1–6 (SC 591: 412, 420).

[35] *Cap. prac.* 10.2–10 (SC 171: 514): Κατὰ στέρησιν δὲ τῶν ἐπιθυμιῶν οὕτως ἐπισυμβαίνει· λογισμοί τινες προλαβόντες εἰς μνήμην ἄγουσι τὴν ψυχὴν οἴκου τε καὶ γονέων καὶ τῆς προτέρας διαγωγῆς. Καὶ ὅταν αὐτὴν μὴ ἀνθισταμένην ἀλλ' ἐπακολουθοῦσαν θεάσωνται καὶ διαχεομένην ἐν ταῖς κατὰ διάνοιαν ἡδοναῖς, τότε λαμβάνοντες αὐτὴν ἐν τῇ λύπῃ βαπτίζουσιν ὡς οὐχ ὑπαρχόντων τῶν προτέρων πραγμάτων οὐδὲ δυναμένων λοιπὸν διὰ τὸν παρόντα βίον ὑπάρξαι. For shades of 'regret', see *cap. prac.* 25: 'Πρόσεχε σεαυτῷ μήποτε φυγαδεύσῃς τινὰ τῶν ἀδελφῶν παροργίσας, καὶ οὐκ ἐκφεύξῃ ἐν τῇ ζωῇ σου τὸν τῆς λύπης δαίμονα.'

[36] So *Oct. spir. mal.* 5.9–11; 5.15–18 (PG 79: 1156C–D; 1157A–B).

[37] *Eulog.* 6.5–9 (SC 591: 294): 'Ἐφίσταται γὰρ χαρὰ πνευματικὴ καρδίᾳ οὐδενὸς προκειμένου, ὅτι τὸν ἡγεμόνα τῆς κατὰ Θεὸν λύπης μετέωρον εὑρίσκει· ἔπειτα δὲ καὶ τῷ πνεύματι τῆς λύπης τὴν ψυχὴν παραδιδοῖ, ὅτι τῆς πνευματικῆς αὐτῆς χαρᾶς αἰχμάλωτον ἐποίησεν.'

Sometimes the shipwrecks of the monastic life are predicted to these same brothers through dreams: They cast the brothers down from high ladders they had ascended, or blind them, so they must grope their way along the walls. They tell a thousand other terrors too ...[38]

In such dreams, it is not so much nostalgia as terror that constitutes 'inconsolable sadness'. Such dreams depict no lost pleasure, but only the possibility of misery. As for the *Antirrhetikos*, of the seventy-six thoughts and demons, twenty-two describe worries and curiosities about combat with demons, as well as the authority and fate of demons.[39] Another thirty-four describe various distracting or frightening visions, and the pretended violence of demons.[40] Three describe *actual* physical violence from demons.[41] Another eight describe experiences of worry or uncertainty for one's own or one's relatives' futures.[42] Two are too vague to define, and another two refer in very general fashion to 'fear' and 'trepidation' alongside sadness.[43] Only five refer to imagined sufferings in the monastic life – both physical, social, and spiritual – and even these may be future-oriented, while two refer to the humiliation one suffers from family members or worldlings.[44] The overwhelming majority of Evagrius' chapters on the topic refer to fear and anxiety centring on spiritual combat and the rigour of monastic life (64 or 69 of 76), while nostalgia and regret are almost entirely absent. The imagined future, although unreal, creates uncertainties that colour the monk's experience of the real present. The distress of anxiety refers, therefore, to an imagined, but as yet unreal present.

While anxiety and nostalgia seem quite different, these two causalities and phenomenologies of λύπη share key points, which together suggest that it is an emotion aroused by the fragility of human life and the precariousness

---

[38] *Mal. cog.* 28.15-22 (SC 438: 252-54): Πολλάκις δὲ εἰς λύπην ἀπαρηγόρητον τοὺς ἀναχωροῦντας ἐμβάλλουσι, δεικνύντες αὐτοῖς τινας τῶν ἰδίων νοσοῦντας καὶ κατὰ γῆν ἢ κατὰ θάλασσαν κινδυνεύοντας. Ἔστι δὲ ὅτε καὶ αὐτοῖς τοῖς ἀδελφοῖς προμαντεύονται δι' ἐνυπνίων τοῦ μοναδικοῦ βίου ναυάγια, ἀπὸ ὑψηλῶν κλιμάκων ἀναβάντας αὐτοὺς καταστρέφοντες καὶ τυφλοὺς πάλιν ποιοῦντες ψηλαφῶντας τοὺς τοίχους. Καὶ ἄλλα μυρία τινὰ τερατεύονται ...

[39] *Antirr.* 4.1-7, 12, 27-28, 30, 46, 50, 51-52, 57, 59, 66, 68-69, 71, 75.

[40] *Antirr.* 4.8-11, 13-21, 23, 26, 32-34, 38-39, 45, 47-49, 53-54, 56, 58, 62-65, 72; 29 and 31 are directed to God, but in context of night-terrors. It is worth considering how many of these chapters are explicitly nocturnal.

[41] *Antirr.* 4.35-36, 41.

[42] Oneself: *Antirr.* 4.25, 37, 43, 64, 68-69, 74, 76; relatives: *Antirr.* 4.42.

[43] *Antirr.* 4.40, 44 are vague; 61, 67 are vague but refer to fear. Many other chapters also refer to 'fear', 'terror', 'trembling', and 'trepidation'.

[44] Sufferings of the monastic life: *Antirr.* 4.50, 68-69, 74, 76; humiliation from others: *Antirr.* 4.60, 68. Two chapters discuss sadness over past sins (*Antirr.* 4.55, 73), a point to which we will return shortly.

of the monastic life especially. As the demands are greater in renunciation, the stakes are higher for failure. The monk is caught between a lost past and an uncertain future, in a present tinged with impossible or unreal fantasies. We might say that, for Evagrius, λύπη's cognitive dimension measures the disjunction between what could be the case and what actually *is* the case. Its affective dimension measures the pain of oscillating between fantasy and its frustration or persistent uncertainty. Put otherwise, λύπη is the pain of living in cognitive dissonance.[45]

'A Disease of Soul and Flesh'

What sort of pain is λύπη? Evagrius consistently maintains that λύπη has a physiological dimension which cannot be ignored. In the *Praktikos*, Evagrius concludes: 'The wretched soul – as much as it is poured into its imagined pleasures, so much is it contracted as it is humiliated at the realisation of their impossibility.'[46] 'Contraction' is, in Stoic psychology, the physical experience of the soul shrinking back[47] from what hurts it or what may hurt it in future. Evagrius might opt for the Platonising interpretation, that the heart, being the organ on which the θυμικόν supervenes or through which it operates, contracts. Either way, the experience of λύπη is both sensed and indicative of bodily movement. Evagrius amplifies this aspect of emotional experience when he refers to the result of distress. In *To Eulogius*, λύπη culminates, via a pathology of 'resentment' (μῆνις), in 'destructive *phrenitis* [φρενίτις λοιδορία]'.[48] Evagrius may have in mind Galenic medical claims that anxiety unchecked culminates

---

[45] Alongside the causes described, Evagrius imagines a third kind of cause for λύπη:

> Evil griefs are twofold, distinguishable in each operation: one comes upon the heart without a distressing cause being seen, and the other is violently born of all sorts of causes [Διτταὶ τῆς κακίας αἱ λύπαι τυγχάνουσιν ἐν ἑκάστῃ ἐργασίᾳ ἀπεζευγμέναι· καὶ ἡ μὲν ἐφίσταται καρδίᾳ λυπηρᾶς αἰτίας οὐ βλεπομένης· ἡ δὲ τίκτεται ἐξ ἀλλοκότων αἰτιῶν ὠθουμένη].
> (*Eulog.* 6.16–19)

Here frustration, regret, and anxiety all fall under the *second* category of 'all sorts of causes'. The first is more nebulous, and the lack of a 'visible' cause suggests that, contrary to Stoic thought, not all λύπη has intentional objects. Were it not unduly speculative to psychoanalyse the dead, it would be tempting (though perilous) to think that Evagrius is describing something like modern clinical accounts of depression, in which patients frequently cannot point to a cause for their experience, but only to the experience itself.

[46] *Cap. prac.* 10.10–12 (SC 171: 514): Καὶ ἡ ταλαίπωρος ψυχή, ὅσον διεχύθη ἐπὶ τοῖς προτέροις λογισμοῖς, τοσοῦτον ἐπὶ τοῖς δευτέροις συνεστάλη ταπεινωθεῖσα. I grant that mine is a very free translation, but it is clear from context that 'τοῖς προτέροις λογισμοῖς' refer to the 'ταῖς κατὰ διάνοιαν ἡδοναῖς' (line 7) and 'τοῖς δευτέροις' to the fact that these are gone and cannot return (lines 8–10).

[47] Or, in a Platonist account, of the organ in which the θυμικόν resides or operates.

[48] *Eulog.* 6.30–31 (SC 591: 296); so too *Mal. cog.* 12.9–14.

in a mental illness localised in the brain, which destroys both reasoning faculty and bodily function.[49] He certainly agrees with the Aristotelian dictum that 'pleasure and pain are common to soul and body'.[50] But it is interesting that he also draws on more specific medical discourses to craft a pathology according to which physical and cognitive damage are intertwined. Φρενῖτις, for example, is a brain disease as well as a cognitive one[51] and, while Evagrius several times refers to λύπη's damage to contemplation and intellection, it is interesting that he opts to localise that damage in the brain. Thus, as Evagrius concludes in *To Eulogius*, 'Λύπη is a disease of soul and body: it leads the former captive and withers the latter on the spot.'[52] In his various discussions of λύπη, Evagrius engages both philosophical and medical conceptions of this passion to describe both how it damages the sufferer's thinking and how its operation can be recognised and countered.

Metaphorical Lexica

Before turning to Evagrius' account of 'godly λύπη', I want to pause over another of his contributions to the transformation of emotional psychology in late antiquity. I have highlighted above the function of passion-lists as affective lexica and will show briefly that Evagrius writes one of his own through the accumulation of metaphors in *On the Eight Wicked Spirits* and *On the Vices in Opposition to the Virtues*. To begin with the latter:

Λύπη: One who inhabits his loss, a companion to frustration, forerunner of exile, memory of family, the familiar of constraint, connate of despondency, incitement to exasperation, souvenir of humiliation, darkening of soul, gloominess in moral virtues, the inebriation of prudence, a sleeping drug, a cloud over one's features, *worm in the flesh* (Jud 16:17), sadness in thoughts, a captive people.[53]

As with the definitions in passion-lists, these metaphors describe both the sensation of λύπη (darkening, gloominess, a cloud, a sleeping drug, a

---

[49] As, e.g., *De loc. aff.* 10.10 (8.193 Kühn): ἐπιγίνεται δὲ ἡ τοιαύτη μελαγχολία προηγησαμέναις θερμαῖς διαθέσεσι τῆς κεφαλῆς, ἤτοι γε ἐξ ἐγκαύσεως, ἢ φλεγμονώδους ἐν αὐτῇ γενομένου πάθους, ἢ καὶ φρενίτιδος· ἐπιγίνεται δὲ καὶ φροντίσι καὶ λύπαις μετ' ἀγρυπνιῶν. So too Oribasius, *Eunap.* 4.117.10; Alexander of Tralles, *Therapeutica* 7.1, etc.
[50] Aristotle, *Sens.* 1 (436a8–10).
[51] See now Singer and Thumiger 2018b: 1–32; Boudon-Millot 2013.
[52] *Eulog.* 6.28–29 (SC 591: 296): Λύπη ψυχῆς νόσος καὶ σαρκὸς τυγχάνει καὶ τὴν μὲν αἰχμαλώτιδα αἴρει, τὴν δὲ ἐπὶ τόπῳ μαραίνει.
[53] *Vit.* 4 (SC 591: 420): Λύπη, ζημίας ἔνοικος, ἀποτυχίας δὲ συνόμιλος, ξενιτείας πρόδρομος, συγγενείας μνήμη, στενώσεως πάρεδρος, ἀκηδίας σύμφυτος, παροξυσμοῦ ἔγκλημα, ὕβρεως ὑπόμνημα, καὶ ψυχῆς σκότισμα, ἠθῶν κατήφεια, φρονήσεως μέθη, ὑπνωτικὸν ἀντίδοτον, μορφῆς νέφος, σαρκὸς σκώληξ, λογισμῶν λύπη, αἰχμαλωσίας δῆμος.

gnawing worm) and its causal circumstances (frustration, exile, memory of family, constraint, exasperation, humiliation). The 'familiar of constraint (στένωσις)' hearkens directly to Pseudo-Andronicus' definition of ὄχλησις as 'λύπη that constricts, and offers no release'. In *On the Eight Wicked Spirits* 5, Evagrius develops analogies from nosology, comparing the anaesthetic effects of λύπη with fever (5.5) and jaundice (5.25). Indeed, from its parasitic relation to other passions (discussed above), Evagrius compares λύπη's diagnostic value to a sick person's complexion, which betrays their illness even if they feign health (5.15): if one knows the event that occasioned λύπη, one can determine the attachment that it feeds on – love of the world (5.16), of money (5.17), or of glory (5.18). Through his accumulation of metaphors, Evagrius builds up a vocabulary for describing λύπη in its myriad forms, and even a diagnostic approach to its arousal.

We can begin to see Evagrius' transformation of classical discourses of λύπη in his intertwining of biblical language with philosophical. The 'worm in the flesh' is a quotation from Judith 16:17. In *On the Eight Wicked Spirits* 5, Evagrius refers to the 'worm in the heart' (echoing Prov 25:20). There he also calls λύπη 'the lion's jaw', recalling Ps 21:21, or perhaps 2 Tim 4:17 or 1 Pet 5:8 (5.2); he contrasts Jesus' words about the relative brevity of labour pains (John 16:21) with the lingering agony of λύπη (5.3). Likewise, in *On the Vices*, the 'captive people' conjures images of the Babylonian captivity, Jeremiah's Lamentations and the psalm of the rivers of Babylon (Ps 136[137]). These intertexts contribute to a cultural regime change in the discourses of pain, as Evagrius turns to Solomon and Israel for his exemplars. Each biblical metaphor sets the sensation of sadness, as a gnawing pain in the breast, within a world populated with adverse powers and humans' combat with them. The experience of λύπη now makes sense as one struggle among others with demons and thoughts, which the monk can expect throughout their ascetic career. Metaphors complement definitions in Evagrius' version of a passion-list: they provide a language for describing the experience of suffering. That language, though, is indelibly tinged with biblical allusions, pointing to scriptural exemplars and suggestive of a spiritual combat utterly foreign to philosophical and medical literature. In giving biblical expression to the experience of λύπη, Evagrius also draws it into specifically Christian, even recognizably monastic discourses.

Godly Grief and the New Script

Not only does Evagrius' reliance on scripture generate new exemplars and emotional contexts, but rather more importantly, it demands a reconsideration both of λύπη's noxiousness and of πένθος' relation to it. For Christian writers like Evagrius, there was no evading the words of Christ, nor yet Paul's rather more enigmatic ones:

Blessed are those who mourn, for they will be comforted. (Matt 5:4)

Now I rejoice, not because you were grieved, but because your λύπη led to repentance; for you felt a godly λύπη, so that you were not harmed in any way by us. For godly λύπη produces repentance that leads to salvation and brings no regret, but worldly λύπη produces death. (2 Cor 7:9–10)

Paul's notion that λύπη is 'beneficial' – let alone 'godly' – seems almost a contradiction in terms within the philosophical and medical accounts examined above. Perhaps the closest example from passion-lists is μεταμέλεια, or regret for one's past deeds. Some Stoics, at least, would see this emotion as useful, since it marks the beginning of a philosophical way of life.[54] Μεταμέλεια is not far, perhaps, from Paul's μετάνοια and the conversion it implies from one way of life to another. Evagrius goes further. We shall see that his psychology embraces 'godly λύπη' not only as an initial movement or spur to repentance, but as an ongoing practice of introspection and discernment. However, while he may set 'godly' against 'wicked' λῦπαι in valuation and ultimate outcomes, they share the same set of physical sensations and exhibit the same focalising, totalising cognitive effects. In Evagrius' account, the phenomenology of λύπη has two opposed causes and two opposing effects.

While I have reserved discussion of 'godly λύπη' to this later section, for reasons that will become clear, it is woven through Evagrius' discussion in *To Eulogius* 6, and his psychology cannot be understood without it. We have seen that 'wicked λύπη' is aroused by dwelling on unreal or uncertain possibilities, both in the past and the future, in contrast with present realities, and that its pain is caused by experiencing both at once. 'Godly λύπη' operates in the same manner, but with very different intentional objects. First, a past object: one's sins. Evagrius exhorts readers to mourning (πένθος) and to wailing (θρῆνος) – Pseudo-Andronicus makes both species of λύπη – over their failures (πταίσματα).[55] Much like μεταμέλεια, recollection of past sins and failures is cause for misery, but only beneficial if it leads to repentance and, especially, to humility.[56] Thus, Evagrius

---

[54] Such is Margaret Graver's (2008: 191–212) claim. Her argument is not, however, uncontested. Cf. Sorabji 2002: 345.

[55] *Eulog.* 13.27; 17.33–36 (SC 591: 324, 342). Other references to the good of πένθος are found at: *Eulog.* 26.18–20; 26.27–32. Evagrius calls tears (δάκρυα) a 'sword against hostile trains of thought' (*Eulog.* 8.10–12) and an aid in prayer-vigils (29.33–37).

[56] So too *Eulog.* 31.55–56.

elsewhere says that the demon of λύπη depicts past sins to the monk who has already repented and progressed beyond them.[57]

The other object of 'godly λύπη' lies in the future: death and judgement. Evagrius says, '*Godly λύπη* recalls the soul to tears, refusing to admit contrary delight and λύπη; rather, it is concerned with approaching death and judgment, and opens up little by little in expecting them.'[58] This passage needs to be unpacked. First, there is the fact that 'godly λύπη' constitutes a concern with, or even *anxiety* about, future events. Second, those events are each uncertain: when death will come and how judgement will turn out. Third, this anxiety is totalising: it refuses the entrance of its opponents, counterfeit delight, and demonic λύπη. In fact, a little earlier, Evagrius referred to 'godly λύπη' as the soul's 'ἡγεμών' or guide. This term is noteworthy because Evagrius, like most later Platonists, described the rational element of the soul in its guiding function as the 'ἡγεμονικόν', a term originally taken from the Stoics. 'Godly λύπη' functions as a guide or discerner for the soul precisely because it is so totalising: only when it is absent can either wicked λύπη or counterfeit joy enter; to the soul engaged in meditation on its own sins, on death, and judgement, those are impossible. Anxiety over sin, death, and judgement precludes attachment to family, pleasure, or glory; likewise, a focus on divine judgement after death reduces the apparent harm of physical ailments, and so these same godly meditations preclude the anxieties of 'wicked λύπη'. The psychological mechanisms that arouse λύπη do not differ between 'godly' and 'wicked' forms: both are totalising activities operative through imagining past and future uncertainties over against present realities.

Passion-lists, I have argued, not only fashion language for λύπη, but imply behavioural scripts – cultural (often poetic or tragic) exemplars of emotion in action, whose moral failures demonstrate the danger of emotional indulgence or successes clarify the importance of its subjection to reason. These figures reinforce the lesson of emotional management in accordance with Stoic or Platonic ideals of ethical virtue. Evagrius develops scripts as well, still emphasising the totalising, focalising power of λύπη, but organised within a Christian renovation of moral psychology and a context of monastic life and practice. These scripts prescribe conscious practices of

---

[57] *Mal. cog.* 36; this whole treatise is for the 'advanced', who have attained to 'ἀπάθεια', and so for them to dwell on old sins is no longer beneficial. Rather, such recollection might draw them into despair or old habits.

[58] *Eulog.* 6.19-22 (SC 591: 296): … ἡ κατὰ Θεόν λύπη τοῖς δάκρυσι τὴν ψυχὴν ἀνακαλεῖται τὴν ἀπεναντίας χαράν τε καὶ λύπην ἡ παραδεχομένη, τὸν δὲ ἐπιόντα θάνατον μεριμνᾷ καὶ κρίσιν καὶ τοῦτο κατ' ὀλίγον κέχηνε προσδεχομένη.

imagination and recollection, and we can discern three sorts in Evagrius' writings: metaphors, verses from scripture, and meditations on death.

The metaphors of *On the Vices* are designed to enthral the memory through rhetorical techniques: their vivacity, their strangeness and surprise, echoes and allusions to well-known texts, even the rhythm and rhyme of the words (e.g., 'θλίψεως ἀντίληψις, εὐχαριστίας ἐπανάληψις'). Everything in the metaphorical lexicon is meant to be *memorable*, and to join the furniture of readers' imaginations: when misfortunes befall them, for example, they can think of 'thanksgiving' rather than complaint, and so on. Evagrius uses pithy statements in gnomic texts for much the same purpose, and his most ambitious effort in mnemonic training is surely the *Antirrhetikos*. This text, which we have encountered already, is composed as a storehouse of biblical responses to possible thoughts and scenarios. Thus, Evagrius prescribes verses of scriptures which counteract those thoughts for seventy-six possible trains of thought defined by anxiety but emerging from λύπη. The *Antirrhetikos*' purpose is, like the metaphorical lexicon, to stock the memory with useful material to engage and even counteract other ways of perceiving the world. Biblical verses are keyed to the various modalities of anxiety so that, when these arise, the memory is primed to bring the scriptural passage before the imagination instead of λύπη's possible futures and irretrievable pasts. Whether through metaphors or scriptures, Evagrius is creating scripts for monastic imaginations which cultivate attitudes of joy or godly λύπη in the quotidian activities and situations of temptation common to ascetic lives.

Conclusion

Christians like Evagrius generally accepted the philosophical attitude towards λύπη as this appears in passion-lists and consolations. They emphasised the same good order, self-control, and cognitive restructuring that pervades consolatory literature. Yet in monastic literature especially, we find encomia of mourning given with vehemence equal to the condemnation of grief. In this chapter, I have shown how much had to change for Christians to praise πένθος even as they conformed to the philosophical and medical traditions of denigrating λύπη. The reason for the renovation is partly exegetical: against the weight of culturally embedded discourses must be balanced the authority of scripture. The reason may also be eschatological: Christian hope of resurrection was matched by anxiety over post-mortem judgement. The fear of death and judgement amplified the Stoic category of μεταμέλεια, or regret for past actions, and fuelled exhortations to weep and mourn for sins. All these reasons together point not merely to a new approach to ethical training, but to a new understanding of human cognition and moral psychology.

As Evagrius grappled with scriptural, philosophical, and medical heritages, carefully and deliberately *overdetermined* λύπη, such that an apparently single experience indicates two exclusive and opposed activities: the first is a passion, the second a virtue. We have seen that the distinction between godly and worldly λύπη, often encoded as a contrast between λύπη and πένθος, runs between intentional objects and the valuations they imply, but *not* between mechanisms of emotional arousal or its phenomenology. This overdetermination means that while the affective lexica of passion-lists and the diagnostic tools of Galenic nosologies feed monastic moral psychologies, they cannot suffice to direct the monastic who is gripped by λύπη, for two reasons. First, λύπη is problematic in ways previously unrecognised: it is part of a combat with demons and sin. Second, sometimes λύπη is a *good thing*. It can clarify self-perception and rectify relationships with others. But it is always a matter of 'can': it may be a worm in the heart, or it may be a golden nail, and the two are distinguished not by sensations but by the distance between salvation and damnation. It is rooted instead in the Christian configuration of the phenomenology of λύπη, of which Evagrius has served as case study. The usefulness of πένθος lies in its being a species of λύπη: the emotional response that accompanies meditation on death, judgement, and one's own sins is no less potent, and no less painful, than one following perceived loss of reputation, goods, or loved ones – but each is totally exclusive of the other, and each defines one's perception of the world. Is this, in some sense, a new and uniquely Christian mode of knowing?

This uniquely Christian overdetermination of λύπη demands a *hermeneutic* which can distinguish proper from improper, beneficial from harmful, by attention to the nuances of its experience and examination of its causes. We have seen Evagrius' approach to this, but he is only the first among many. Amma Syncletica (or her biographer) nuanced the Evagrian account in a new passion-list of the forms of λύπη: in one version she discerns four εἴδη of the godly γένος;[59] in another, she differentiates two godly and two 'corrosive'.[60] John Cassian developed Evagrius' exegetical

---

[59] *Apophth. patr.* S 10.102 (SC 474: 82) and Pseudo-Athanasius, *V. Syncl.* (PG 28: 1512A–B).
[60] Cod. Paris. Gr. 1592, 222v–223r : lines 347–54 in Abelarga 2002.

hints about the 'moth in the heart' in his *Institutiones*[61] and explored the four causes of godly tears in the *Conlationes*.[62] We see the same hermeneutical (perhaps, diagnostic) effort in the early sixth century, when an unnamed monk posed a curious question to the great elder, Barsanuphius of Gaza. He asked, 'Is the compunction which I seem to have true [εἰ ἡ κατάνυξις ἣν δοκῶ ἔχειν ἀληθής ἐστί]?' He wanted also to know how he might discern genuine from false forms of πένθος (with which κατάνυξις is intimately and constantly connected). This monk asked a question which would have been nonsensical within the parameters of philosophical and medical accounts of λύπη and its public expression, πένθος. But thanks to pioneering thinkers like Evagrius, Syncletica, and Cassian, Barsanuphius is ready with an answer: 'Brother, your current weeping and compunction are not true, but rather they come and go. For true weeping, which compunction accompanies, becomes a man's slave inseparably subjected to him.'[63] Hermeneutics – perhaps even diagnostics – of πένθος and λύπη sit uneasily alongside the passion-lists of Pseudo-Andronicus and his ilk, and run entirely counter to Plutarch's consolations and Galenic diagnoses. Here we might speak of a new organisation of knowledge. Between its effects on cognition and its demands for a hermeneutic, the overdetermination of λύπη has effected a transformation of both the knowing subject and the known object. In Christian monastic literature, one knows and is known, rightly or wrongly, through the lens of λύπη.

[61] *Inst.* 9.2–3. [62] *Conl.* 9.28.1–9.30.2. [63] *Resp.* 461 (SC 451: 554).

29 | Liturgical Modes of Knowing: Coming to Know God (and Oneself) in Sixth-Century Hymns and Homilies

SARAH GADOR-WHYTE

Introduction

This chapter is an exploration of Christian liturgy as a mode of knowing in late antiquity. My argument is based on an understanding of the rhetorical power of words and the performative power of ritual to provoke certain intellectual, sensual, and emotional responses in an audience. As Ruth Webb has argued, words are able not only to create images in the mind (turning the listener into a viewer), but also to kindle in the listener sensory and emotional responses to that scene or image.[1] By hearing the vivid description of the skilled orator, the 'listener does not simply learn facts about what happened (or may have happened) but experiences them in a quasi-physical way'.[2] In relation to liturgical language, Jean Ladrière argued for the performative power of words in this setting to create a particular affective state in listeners and performers,[3] to create a sense of group identity through plural verbs and joint actions,[4] and to make present the reality it utters for the liturgical participants.[5] In this chapter, I bring together these two theoretical understandings of how language works to explore how liturgical texts both reveal God and make him known to listeners and also help listeners come to knowledge of themselves and of what being Christian means. Audience members are brought to knowledge through listening and experiencing, feeling and sensing, so that their minds, feelings, and senses are reshaped – all (potentially) without their being conscious of it.

I investigate this liturgical mode of knowing through two contemporaneous sixth-century writers, a poet and a preacher: Romanos the Melodist, who wrote liturgical hymns; and Leontius, presbyter of Constantinople. Romanos the Melodist was a hymnographer and deacon at a suburban

---

[1] Webb 2017: 261; 2016a: 206.
[2] Webb 2016a: 213. Webb cites cognitive neurologist Marc Jeannerod, who argues that descriptions of actions or movements are able to simulate those physical actions (Jeannerod 2006: 24 and passim).
[3] Ladrière 1973: 51.   [4] Ladrière 1973: 59.   [5] Ladrière 1973: 61.

church in Constantinople dedicated to the Theotokos. We know very little with certainty about his life, but, according to later hagiographical *vitae*, he was born in Syriac-speaking Emesa and educated in Berytus before moving to Constantinople.[6] He wrote long narrative and dialogic hymns in Greek which were later called *kontakia* and of which nearly sixty survive.[7] The *kontakion* was a new genre of poetry in the fifth century which grew out of the joint traditions of Greek and Syriac poetry and homiletics.[8] Romanos did not invent the genre, although he is said to have perfected it. We know even less about Leontius, presbyter of Constantinople.[9] He was active in the mid-sixth century and was probably attached to a small non-imperial or suburban church in Constantinople.[10] Fourteen of his homilies survive.[11] Such information as one can glean from his homilies suggests that his congregation included artisans and labourers; his comments on poverty and the need to help the poor imply that poverty was not unknown to some members of his congregation.[12]

I put these two writers together not because they influenced each other (we have no evidence that they met or knew each other's work), but because they represent two attempts to engage lay communities in Constantinople in the sixth century CE. There are also many similarities in their dramatic retellings of scripture and their use of dialogue and rhetorical tropes like apostrophe. Leontius' prose homilies include many poetic passages, particularly contrasting couplets. Both play with biblical paradoxes and imagery to strengthen their arguments and both attempt to shape their audience's emotional responses to biblical events.[13]

---

[6] See Gador-Whyte 2017: 7–9; Arentzen 2017: 1–4. For the texts of the *synaxaria* which provide the hagiographic biographies of Romanos, see Grosdidier de Matons 1977: 162.

[7] According to the Oxford edition of Maas and Trypanis (1963). Throughout I use this edition for the texts of Romanos (the translations are my own), but I have also consulted the *Sources chrétiennes* edition (Grosdidier de Matons 1964–81).

[8] On the history, use, and setting of the *kontakion*, see Arentzen 2017: 6–14. On the joint Greek and Syriac heritage of this genre, see Gador-Whyte 2013b; 2017: 11–14.

[9] I have used Datema and Allen's edition (1987). For the limited biographical details and suggestions about audience composition based on comments in the homilies, see Datema and Allen 1991: 1–8. This is also the translation used for Leontius' works throughout.

[10] Datema dates homily I to the precise date of 17 December 557, which places Leontius firmly in the mid-sixth century; see Datema 1981: 348.

[11] Only homilies I to XI were attributed to him before Datema and Allen's edition. For the arguments in favour of attributing homilies XII, XIII, and XIV to Leontius, see Datema and Allen 1987: 367–79, 89–94, 407–31.

[12] Datema and Allen 1991: 5–8.

[13] On the comparable use of rhetoric in festal homilies of the fourth and fifth centuries, see Chapter 16 by Johan Leemans, this volume.

In what follows, I focus on a liturgical mode of knowledge creation operating in the *kontakia* of Romanos and the homilies of Leontius: immersion in a sensory and dramatic world which reveals God and establishes listeners in a cosmic community. This knowledge creation takes the forms of sensory and emotional transformation, and of writing listeners into the divine narrative, bringing them into deeper knowledge and experience of God and his plan of divine salvation. I will deal with this in two mutually reinforcing parts: narrative and ritual. As we will see, there are important similarities in the ways in which both Romanos and Leontius help their congregations come to knowledge of God and an understanding of what it means to be Christian. But in case this seems too neat or convenient, I want to highlight one important difference: the use of Mary as mediator of divine knowledge. Mary plays a very significant role in Romanos' hymns and hardly any role at all in Leontius' sermons. This suggests that differences in community, gender, and liturgical setting all impact the effectiveness of certain modes of knowing.

A second, seemingly obvious difference between Romanos' and Leontius' works is their mode of performance. Romanos' poems were hymns, sung by a cantor with a responsive refrain sung by the congregation. Leontius' homilies were prose, spoken aloud by Leontius alone. As I analyse their words, this difference will not be so apparent, but for the listeners and participants it could change their whole experience. Many Christians mused on the ability of music to evoke emotional responses (for good or ill) and to transport both musician and hearer into a constructed or remembered world.[14] Fear of this power of music to move people and impress ideas on their minds was the impetus for Ephrem the Syrian to write hymns (against those of Bardaisan, which were gaining popularity) and for John Chrysostom to create a night vigil of psalms and hymns (to rival that of the Arians). For Romanos, music adds depth to the emotional involvement of his compelling dialogues and dramatic situations, and enriches the imaginative world of the biblical stories into which his hymns delve. This chapter will focus particularly on Romanos' words, but it is important to remember that they were sung and that the music is an element which strengthens what the words attempt to achieve.

Throughout this chapter, I argue that Romanos and Leontius write their congregations into the wider Christian salvation narrative, showing them their position in God's story and thereby bringing them into a richer understanding of Christian identity. Both Leontius and Romanos

---

[14] See Harrison 2020. See also Harkins and Dunkle 2018: 610–24.

enhance this narrative knowledge-building by weaving Christian liturgical rituals like Eucharist, baptism, and fasting into their hymns and sermons, connecting the preaching and singing with the liturgical rites of the day. Through these rituals Christians are purified; their senses, emotions, and desires are transformed; and they are brought into communion with God. Both these means of knowledge creation require activation and redemption of the senses, and it is to that which I turn first.

Invitation and Transformation

The opportunity for crafting knowledge comes at the opening of many of the *kontakia*, when Romanos invites his listeners into the events he relates. In *On the Presentation in the Temple*, Romanos summons his congregation to witness Christ's presentation to Simeon (4.1.1–2):

Τῇ θεοτόκῳ προσδράμωμεν οἱ βουλόμενοι κατιδεῖν τὸν υἱὸν αὐτῆς
πρὸς Συμεὼν ἀπαγόμενον.

Let us hurry to the Theotokos, we who wish to see her son
brought before Simeon.

As Ruth Webb has argued in relation to *ekphrasis*, passages like this create a picture in the listener's mind; the listener becomes a witness and a participant. The main metaphor for knowledge, as throughout the Greek tradition, is sight: people come to know by coming to see. But cognition, desire, will, and action are joined together. Romanos shapes the listeners' desire and their actions (they are οἱ βουλόμενοι) as the first-century event becomes a contemporary one. The opening of the first nativity hymn is similarly an invitation to view the miracle ('let us see'), to engage emotions and beneficial desire ('we have found joy'), and to receive its blessings, translating cognition and emotion into action ('let us hurry'). Romanos brings the paradox of the incarnation vividly to life and invites listeners to be witnesses of this world-changing event, and thereby both discoverers and recipients of the joy it brings (1.1.1–3, 9–10):

Τὴν Ἐδὲμ Βηθλεὲμ   ἤνοιξε, δεῦτε ἴδωμεν·
τὴν τρυφὴν ἐν κρυφῇ   ηὕραμεν, δεῦτε λάβωμεν
τὰ τοῦ παραδείσου   ἐντὸς τοῦ σπηλαίου·
...
διὰ τοῦτο πρὸς τοῦτο ἐπειχθῶμεν, ποῦ ἐτέχθη
παιδίον νέον,   ὁ πρὸ αἰώνων Θεός.

Bethlehem has opened Eden. Come, let us see!
We have found joy in secret. Come, let us receive
the things of paradise within the cave.
...
Because of this, let us hurry to this place where has been born
a newborn child, God before all ages.

Through these calls to joint action, Romanos creates a community bound together by their harmonious reactions to divine events, and attempts to guide his listeners into communion with the divine by redemption of the senses and the will. Vision, desire, and action are all directed towards God.

Leontius likewise directs his audience's senses towards God. He argues that knowledge comes through listening to the illuminating gospels, an image that links seeing and hearing (XIV.40):

ἐνταῦθα ἀπόστολοι θείοις γράμμασι τὴν οἰκουμένην φωτίζοντες·

Here are apostles enlightening the world with their divine writings.[15]

Listening to the gospels makes them present and dramatises the illumination the audience receives. The light imagery helps vivify this passage and encourages listeners to associate hearing the gospel with illumination and the revelation of God.

Appeals for the congregation to listen pervade Leontius' homilies, as do reminders of pericopes recently heard. Listening well provides an opportunity to understand the truth (V.75–78):

Ἄκουε συνετῶς. Ἐν παντὶ πράγματι τὸν σκοπὸν ζήτει τοῦ πράγματος καὶ οὐδαμῶς τῆς ἀληθείας οὐ μὴ διαπέσῃς. Ἄκουε συνετῶς.

Listen attentively. In every affair seek the purport of the affair and you will never miss the truth. Listen attentively.[16]

Repetitive exhortations like this aim to be speech-acts, performing the action of the command by focusing the listener's attention.[17] Leontius wants to transform his audience's ears, casting them in the role of attentive participants.[18] Physical appetites can also be redeemed, according to Leontius, at least if the sustenance is a draft of the Holy Spirit, which acts like a medicine to heal the senses. In his homily XIII *On Pentecost*, Leontius says

---

[15] Datema and Allen 1991: 183.
[16] Translation slightly modified from Datema and Allen 1991: 76.
[17] On speech-acts, see Austin 1975; Searle 1969.
[18] On the ability of liturgical performative utterances to make participants take on given roles, see Schaller 1988: 415–32.

the apostles were not drunk on wine, but rather filled with the Holy Spirit (XIII.228–29). He continues (XIII.238, 244–49):

Ποθήσωμεν τοίνυν ταύτην τὴν μέθην ...
Οὐ γὰρ σωματικὸν καύσωνα παύει,
ἀλλὰ ψυχικὸν ἔρωτα πείθει·
οὐδὲ κοιλίας ὄγκον ἐγείρει,
ἀλλὰ διανοίας πόθον ὀξύνει·
οὐδὲ ψυχροποσίας βλάβην ἐντίθησιν,
ἀλλὰ θεογνωσίας κέρδος παρέχει.

Let us then imbibe this drink ...
It does not still the burning heat of the body,
but prevails on spiritual love;
nor does it rouse the heavy stomach,
but it sharpens the desire to understand;
nor does it cause harm as the drinking of cold drinks does,
but it produces the benefit of knowing God.[19]

Imbibing this drink involves listening to the inspired words of the apostles, as recorded in the New Testament and illuminated in Leontius' homily.[20] Drinking in the Holy Spirit through the scriptures transforms the mind and the will: 'sharpens the desire to understand' and 'produces the benefit of knowing God'. Human knowledge, in this scheme, is a divine gift by which the soul and body are made capable of understanding.

Romanos and Leontius enact the redemption of the listeners' senses through their performative utterances, and they invite their audience into communion with God by witnessing biblical events.[21]

Narrative Knowledge Formation

Both authors also write their audience into the wider historical and cosmic narrative of Christianity, helping listeners to come to an understanding of their place in Christian salvation history, and showing them how scripture, preaching, and liturgical ritual reveal God. Each writer makes use of liturgical time, which brings biblical events to life on the day they are celebrated

---

[19] Translation modified from Datema and Allen 1991: 164.
[20] See also XIII.154–55, where Leontius refers to the reading from the Acts of the Apostles as 'a spiritual breakfast before your eyes' (Datema and Allen 1991: 162).
[21] For similar use of the senses and embodiment in the hymns and homilies of Ambrose of Milan, see Chapter 21 by Brian Dunkle, this volume.

in the liturgical calendar. This is the 'presentification' which Ladrière identifies as the fundamental performative power of liturgical language.[22] Events happen 'today' (Romanos, 5.Pr.1; Leontius VII.278):

Ἐπεφάνης σήμερον τῇ οἰκουμένῃ ...

Today you have appeared to the inhabited world ...

Σήμερον γὰρ σταυρὸς πλέκεται καὶ Ἰὼβ στεφανοῦται ...

Today the cross is constructed, and Job is crowned ...

As we see in this last example, Leontius not only brings the New Testament event into the present but also establishes its link with the Old Testament and its importance in God's salvation history. This making present of past events transforms temporality, so that the congregation's time is embedded in salvation history. From the perspective of knowledge creation, divine action becomes immediately present to the minds of the congregation. Biblical events are not something to be known through historical investigation premised on temporal separation. Rather, they are immediately present to the intellect and physical and spiritual senses.

Such a making present of divine action is also achieved in both authors through the rhetorical techniques of dialogue and apostrophe, which bring biblical stories vividly to life and insert sixth-century audiences into the divine narrative. For example, in Romanos' *On the Marriage at Cana* he questions Mary on behalf of his congregation, and she responds (7.6.1–3; 7.7.2–3):

Σὲ δυσωποῦμεν, παρθένε σεμνή.   ἐκ ποίων ἔγνως θαυμάτων αὐτοῦ
ὡς δύναται ὁ υἱός σου σταφυλὴν μὴ τρυγήσας τὸν οἶνον χαρίζεσθαι
οὔπω θαυματουργήσας πρώην, ὡς Ἰωάννης ὁ θεσπέσιος ἔγραψεν;

We entreat you, holy virgin: did you know the nature of his miracles,
how your son was able to give wine freely, not having gathered the grapes,
not yet being a miracle-worker, as the godly John wrote?

'Ἀκούσατε,' φησίν, 'ὦ φίλοι,   συνετίσθητε πάντες καὶ γνῶτε μυστήρια·
εἶδον τὸν υἱόν μου ἤδη θαυματουργοῦντα καὶ πρὸ τούτου τοῦ θαύματος ...'

'Listen friends,' she says, 'that you might all understand and perceive the mystery.
See my son was already a miracle-worker even before this marvel ...'

Romanos and his listeners become part of this first-century event as Mary responds to their query. Once again, Romanos paints the scene with words and brings it to life with dialogue, thereby making it present for his listeners. And

---

[22] Ladrière 1973: 61. See also Day 2014: 108.

once more we see the collective action which binds the community together. Mary is familiar with them, addressing them as 'friends', and, as we saw earlier in the case of Leontius, listening is the key to knowledge and understanding. We will examine Mary's role in mediating knowledge of God shortly.

Similarly, Leontius (in his homily on mid-Pentecost, homily X) addresses the Jews, Herod, and the personifications of Passover and Synagogue. These opponents are brought vividly to life through apostrophe, exclamation, dialogue, and rhetorical questions as they object to Jesus' healing on the Sabbath, and Leontius and his blind man character counter their arguments (X.141–44, 145–46):

Ἡμῶν δὲ σιωπησάντων, ὦ Ἰουδαῖοι, λάβετε τῆς πλάνης ὑμῶν ὁδηγὸν αὐτὸν τὸν τυφλόν. Μὴ αἰσχυνθῆτε ὑπὸ τοῦ τυφλοῦ ὁδηγηθῆναι· ... ἔχει γὰρ λάμπουσαν, ἄσβεστον τὴν λαμπάδα τῆς πίστεως.

But we conclude our speech, Jews. Take this blind man as a guide in your error. Don't be ashamed to be guided by the blind man, ... for he has the shining, unquenchable light of faith.[23]

In this homily, Leontius plays with questions of light and dark, blindness and sight, knowledge and ignorance. The blind man has the light, not the Jews, despite their knowledge of scripture as displayed in this homily (e.g., X.162–68). By addressing the Jews in this way, Leontius vivifies the biblical story, as if he and his congregation themselves witnessed the Jewish indignation at Jesus' healing on the Sabbath. By his use of plural verbs, he also includes his listeners in his speech, casting them in the desired role of opponents to the Jews.

As well as bringing the biblical narratives to life and collapsing first-century events into sixth-century reality (or vice versa), both writers also emphasise participation in the cosmic liturgy and communion with God and the angels. The concept of the earthly liturgy participating in the heavenly one is not, of course, particular to Romanos and Leontius. Church building and decoration as well as the liturgy itself were all understood to reveal and participate in the divine.[24] As John Chrysostom said:

οὐ γὰρ κουρεῖον, οὐδὲ μυροπωλεῖον ἡ ἐκκλησία, ... ἀλλὰ τόπος ἀγγέλων, τόπος ἀρχαγγέλων, βασιλεία θεοῦ, αὐτὸς ὁ οὐρανός.[25]

For the church is not a barber's shop, nor a perfumery, ... but the place of angels, the place of archangels, the kingdom of God, heaven itself.

---

[23] Trans. Datema and Allen 1991: 125–26.
[24] On the revelatory power of sacred architecture, see Chapter 26 by Matthew R. Crawford, this volume.
[25] *Homilia in epistolam primam ad Corinthios* (PG 61: 313).

Through the liturgical cycle, churches also came to represent the *loca sancta* of Christ's life and embed worshippers in this divine landscape. On each feast day, the church became the place of commemoration of the event and congregants could be transported to Jerusalem to witness the crucifixion on Good Friday or to Bethlehem to the cave of the Nativity at Christmas.[26]

Church decoration was also intended to perform this change of space. As well as creating biblical scenes and positioning them to focus the viewer on ritual events and connect them to their cosmic liturgical community, mosaicists constructed their artworks to catch the light and reflect it in different ways and so make the mosaics gleam.[27] The variation in light throughout the day (or through the aid of candles) also helped to vary its appearance and give it life.[28] This play of light and colour represented heavenly glory and, by looking at these sparkling artworks, the viewer was believed to enter into an experience of the divine. Thus, sight was a key means of experiencing the divine through mosaics. The other senses likewise revealed God through the liturgy. Communicants tasted the body and blood of Christ at the Eucharist, were anointed with fragrant oils at baptism, and breathed in the scent of incense throughout the service. Relics and icons could be handled and kissed to bring the believer closer to these physical mediators with the divine. The vivid presentation of biblical narratives and the dramatic and engaging hymns and homilies of our two sixth-century writers were reinforced by this physical environment, and simultaneously shaped the congregation's understanding and experience of it.

In Romanos' *kontakion On the Multiplication of the Loaves*, angels watch and marvel at the celebration of the Eucharist, a meal which elevates humans to the divine (13.1.1–5):

Πάντες ἄγγελοι οἱ ἐν οὐρανοῖς θαυμάζουσι τὰ ἐπ[ίγεια],
ὅτι ἄνθρωποι γηγενεῖς τὰ κάτω κατοικοῦντες
ὑψ[οῦνται] τῇ διανοίᾳ καὶ φθάνουσι πρὸς τὰ ἄνω,
μέτοχοι Χ[ριστοῦ ὄν]τες τοῦ ἐσταυρωμένου.
Τὸ σῶμα γὰρ αὐτοῦ πάντε[ς] ἅμα ἐσθίουσι.

All the angels in heaven marvel at earthly events,
because humans born of earth, dwelling below,
are lifted up in thought and reach what is above,
and are partakers of Christ the crucified.
For they all together eat his body.

---

[26] On *loca sancta*, see Weitzmann 1974; MacCormack 1990; Frank 2006a.
[27] Borsook 2000: 9; Demus 1948: 35–37; James 1995: 4–5; James 2000: 42.
[28] James 2004: 528, 530–31.

The Eucharist is the moment when Romanos' congregation are most closely connected with the heavenly, as they consume the body of Christ in the eucharistic bread. Romanos emphasises communion with the divine by depicting the angels watching, as if from an upper gallery in the church. Through the Eucharist, earth comes closer to heaven and human minds are elevated to it. The ritual action transforms the mind and leads to ever clearer understanding (*dianoia*).

Leontius also reinforces that the earthly liturgy participates in the heavenly (X.1–4):

ἤδη γὰρ καὶ σήμερον ἡμῶν ἑορταζόντων ἄγγελοι μὲν ἀγάλλονται, ἀρχάγγελοι δὲ σκιρτῶσιν, καὶ πᾶσαι αἱ οὐράνιαι δυνάμεις σὺν ἡμῖν ἑορτάζουσιν.

Actually today, too, while we are celebrating, the angels are rejoicing, the archangels are exulting, and all the heavenly powers are celebrating with us.[29]

Leontius wants his listeners to feel part of a cosmic celebration; they are not alone in observing the festival but are joined together with the angelic orders as they too worship God and rejoice. For both writers, the liturgical rites are not only taking place on earth but are in tune with those in the celestial realm. The sixth-century church is lifted up and reaches what is above. All the heavenly powers worship with Leontius or Romanos, that is, their congregations are now placed in a cosmic liturgy. So what we have in the ritual is a transformation of time and space. These two changes together mean that knowledge of God is knowledge of something that can be present. The mind can see beyond surfaces to inner meaning, or, perhaps better, ordinary space and time is to be known as extraordinary to the extent that it is always capable of the sort of transformation effected in the liturgy. Members of the congregation come to know, not through a didactic transmission of information, but through an embodied understanding which goes beyond conscious reflection: listeners have their understanding elevated and reshaped through embodied participation in the liturgy.

Ritual Knowledge-Performance

These narrative techniques are interwoven with the performance of the rituals in the *kontakia* and Leontius' homilies. Romanos' *kontakia* invite congregants into the great mysteries of the faith, into the rituals which enable

---

[29] Trans. Datema and Allen 1991: 122.

knowledge of God and perform unity with God and the heavenly realm. Romanos' *kontakion On the Prodigal Son* tells the parable as a lengthy eucharistic metaphor.[30] Early on in the hymn, Romanos invites listeners to join him at the eucharistic feast (49.2.1–5):

Ἔνθεν σπουδάσωμεν νυνὶ καὶ μετασχῶμεν τοῦ δείπνου·
ἐὰν ἀξιωθῶμεν τῷ πατρὶ συνευφρανθῆναι,
συνεστιαθῶμεν τῷ βασιλεῖ τῶν ἀγγέλων·
ἄρτους παρέχει τοὺς διδόντας μακαριότητα,
πόμα δὲ δωρεῖται ἅγιον αἷμα …

Let us hurry there now and share in the meal.
If we are considered worthy to rejoice with the father,
let us feast with the king of the angels.
He offers bread which grants blessedness,
and as a drink he gives holy blood …

Here is a communal call to action: 'Let us hurry … and share.' And it is specifically a call to join the celestial sphere, where they can 'feast with the king of the angels'.

The *kontakion* was probably performed as part of a night vigil and so was not incorporated into the eucharistic liturgy.[31] But it is possible, and this *kontakion* encourages us to surmise that the vigil ended in time for the festal eucharistic liturgy and that Romanos intended his listeners to receive the Eucharist shortly after hearing his hymn. This second stanza sets up the expectation of participation in the heavenly feast. In the following stanza, Romanos establishes knowledge as the condition of joy at the feast (49.3.1–2):

Ἡ δὲ ἑστία τίς ἐστί; μάθωμεν πρῶτον τοῦ δείπνου
ἐκ τῶν εὐαγγελίων, ἵνα καὶ ἐπευφρανθῶμεν·

What is this banquet? Let us first learn about the meal
from the gospels, so that we also might rejoice.

Through the *kontakion*, Romanos' listeners learn to be participants: their emotions are shaped and their senses trained so that they are now capable not merely of earthly rejoicing, but of rejoicing with the father and feasting with the angels. They are able to receive not merely earthly food but salvation (blessedness, holy blood). Through liturgical purification of the senses

---

[30] Barkhuizen 1996.
[31] On the night vigil as the liturgical setting for the *kontakia*, see Lingas 1995: 50–52; Louth 2005: 199–200; Frank 2006b.

and emotions through the *kontakion*, Romanos' listeners grow into higher spiritual knowledge.

Romanos uses both the prodigal son and his elder brother to reshape the minds of his listeners. The prodigal son repents and is purified and forgiven by his father: stanzas 4 to 7 detail the reclothing of the son into the image of the father.[32] When the feast begins, we hear scriptural and angelic voices singing in praise of God, setting the eucharistic meal both in a long temporal domain and in the celestial sphere (49.10.1-2, 5-6, 10; 49.11.1-3):

Τῶν κεκλημένων πᾶς λοιπὸν ὁ θίασος ὡς ἐδείπνει,
καὶ πάντες εὐφρανθέντες ἐμελῴδουν θεῖον ὕμνον …
εἶτα μετὰ τοῦτο ὁ ψαλμολόγος
κρούων τὴν κιθάραν κράζει ἡδυτάτῃ φωνῇ …
καὶ μετ' αὐτὸν δὲ βοᾷ ὁ Παῦλος …
Ἄγγελοι εἴδοσαν αὐτοὺς οἱ ὑπουργοῦντες τῷ δείπνῳ
οὕτως εὐφραινομένους καὶ συντόνως μελῳδοῦντας,
καὶ ζηλοῦσι τούτους καὶ ἤρξαντο ὑμνῳδίας·

At last, the whole company of the invited, as they were feasting
and were all rejoicing, sang a godly hymn …
Then after this the psalmist,
striking the lyre, cries out with sweetest voice …
And after him Paul shouts out …
The angels who were serving at the feast saw them
as they rejoiced like this and sang earnestly,
and they emulated them and offered hymns of praise.

The congregation becomes part of this cosmic community in the celebration of the Eucharist, and their purified voice joins with those of the psalmist, Paul, and the angels.

But the elder son is not yet part of the feast and the rest of the hymn is devoted to his anger and frustration and then his change of mind. Possibly more people in the congregation would identify with the elder brother than with the prodigal son, so Romanos devotes several stanzas to his transformation too. Romanos gives voice to the elder son's apparently righteous indignation and to the father's gentle transformation of his senses, emotions, and actions into the right ones (49.18.3; 49.21.5-6):

---

[32] On clothing and nakedness imagery in the *kontakia*, see Gador-Whyte 2017: 84-88.

κλῖνον σου τὰ ὦτα καὶ ἄκουσον τοῦ πατρός σου ...[33]
ταῦτα οὖν ἀκούσας οὗτος ἐπείσθη
καὶ ἠγαλλιᾶτο μετὰ τοῦ συγγόνου αὐτοῦ καὶ ψάλλων ταῦτα ἔλεγεν ...

Incline your ears and listen to your father ...
When he heard these things, he was persuaded
and rejoiced greatly with his brother and singing said these things ...

The elder brother's hearing is purified and his emotional state transformed through persuasion from anger to joy. Only then can he too participate in the feast, joining the cosmic community.

The hymn thus provides two different models of transformation into worthy participants at the cosmic feast, and at the conclusion of the hymn Romanos draws on two other biblical exempla (the harlot and the tax-collector) as well as calling for the intercession of the Theotokos so that, by sitting in this wider Christian community, his listeners might be transformed into 'partakers at the feast' (22).[34]

Leontius likewise emphasises the cosmic nature of the eucharistic meal. In his homily XIV on the transfiguration, he begins by drawing attention to the table set for the feast (XIV.1–6):

Ἄγαν αἰδέσιμον ἡμῖν ὁ δαψιλὴς ἑστιάτωρ Χριστὸς καὶ
σήμερον προέθηκε
τράπεζαν οὐ τῇ συνηθείᾳ τιμωμένην,
    ἀλλὰ τῇ θεογνωσίᾳ γνωριζομένην·
τράπεζαν οὐ τῶν ἐπιγείων γλιχομένην,
    ἀλλὰ τῶν ἐπουρανίων ἐχομένην·

Exceedingly venerable is the table which Christ the lavish host has set before us today too –
a table which is not paid honour to by habit,
    but which is made known by the knowledge of God;
a table which does not crave things of earth
    but which clings to the things of heaven ...[35]

Once again, we see events made present through Leontius' words: Christ himself has laid the table at which congregants will communicate. The event will happen 'today too', as it has happened throughout Christian history and in the short lifetimes of his listeners. There follows a series of

---

[33] Cf. Ps 17:6.
[34] On the development of Mary's role as intercessor in late antiquity, see Cameron 1978. On Mary as intercessor in the *kontakia*, see Gador-Whyte 2013a: 83–87; Arentzen 2017: 137–40.
[35] Trans. Datema and Allen 1991: 182.

poetic couplets which contrasts earthly tables with that of the Eucharist; Leontius emphasises that the eucharistic feast is participation in the heavenly feast and that knowledge and understanding of the feast come from knowledge of God.

The following few paragraphs continue the theme of earthly and heavenly contrasts. Leontius compares Solomon's lavish table to 'the Lord's table' (XIV.20–47): Solomon's earthly table is rich and extravagant but leads to debauchery, whereas the Lord's table is eternal, incorruptible, and 'directs things earthly and heavenly' (XIV.23). Like Romanos, Leontius wants his listeners to understand what they participate in at the Eucharist. This is no earthly meal, but direct communion with God; this meal is not a gourmet extravaganza, but an opportunity to feed the soul.

Training the mind and body into a receptive state for knowledge of God is also achieved through ritual practices like fasting. Fasting is an important part of preparation for baptism and Eucharist for Leontius in his first homily on Palm Sunday (II.197–204):

διὰ τί μὲν ἡμεῖς πρὸ τοῦ βαπτίσματος νηστεύομεν ...; Ὅτι ἡμεῖς μὲν ὠγκωμένοι ταῖς ἁμαρτίαις καὶ πεφορτισμένοι τὴν ψυχικὴν γαστέρα, ἀναγκαίως πρὸ τοῦ βαπτίσματος τὴν νηστείαν ὡς θεοδώρητον ἀντίδοτον δεχόμεθα, ἵνα *καθάραντες ἑαυτοὺς ἀπὸ παντὸς μολυσμοῦ σαρκὸς καὶ πνεύματος* εἰς ὄρεξιν ἔλθωμεν τοῦ ἐπουρανίου ἄρτου.

Why do we fast before baptism ...? Because we are swollen with sins and our spiritual stomach is laden down, of necessity we receive the fast before the baptism as a God-given antidote, so that, *having cleansed ourselves from every defilement of body and spirit* (2 Cor 7.1), we may advance in appetite for the heavenly bread.[36]

Fasting is a ritual purification of both the bodily and the spiritual, which trains the catechumen to hunger for the right things and so to be ready to receive God through both baptism and Eucharist. Similarly, in homily III, Leontius refers to the feast day of Palm Sunday itself as a cleansing in preparation for Easter (III.236–41):

... προκαθάρσιον
γάρ ἐστιν αὕτη ἡ ἡμέρα.
Πρὸ ἓξ ἡμέραν τοῦ πάσχα,[37]
ἵνα προκαθαρίσῃς ἑαυτὸν ἀπὸ πάσης κηλῖδος,
ἵνα λύσῃς ἔχθραν,
ἵνα παύσῃς ὀργήν ...

---

[36] Trans. Datema and Allen 1991: 45. [37] Cf. John 12:1.

This day is a cleansing in advance.
Six days before the Passover,
so that you may cleanse yourself in advance from every blemish,
so that you may undo enmity,
so that you may put a stop to anger ...[38]

Cleansing oneself in preparation perhaps for baptism or, if already initiated, for the Easter Eucharist involves a change of mind and a reform of one's emotions. Fasting helps transform anger to allow the catechumen or communicant to be ready to receive deeper knowledge of God at the Eucharist.

Preparation for baptism is figured as enlightenment, a purification of desire and the senses as well as a bodily cleansing, in Romanos' *On the Sinful Woman* (10.5.5–11):

ἀλλοιοῦμαι πρὸς τὸν πόθον τοῦ ποθητοῦ,
καὶ ὡς θέλει φιληθῆναι, οὕτω φιλῶ τὸν ἐραστήν μου·
πενθῶ καὶ κατακάμπτομαι, τοῦτο γὰρ βούλεται·
σιγῶ καὶ περιστέλλομαι, τούτοις γὰρ τέρπεται·
ἀναχωρῶ τῶν ἀρχαίων ἵνα ἀρέσω τῷ νέῳ·
συντόμως ἀποτάσσομαι ἐμφυσῶσα
τῷ βορβόρῳ τῶν ἔργων μου.

I am changed towards desire of the desired,
and as he wishes to be loved, so I love my lover.
I groan and fall down, for this is what he wishes.
I am silent and restrained, for he delights in these things.
I withdraw from the old ones that I might satisfy the new.
In short, by blowing, I renounce
the filth of my deeds.

The harlot's desire is changed into desire for Christ; his wishes transform her love; her emotions and actions align with his desires. She rejects her old lovers in favour of Christ. At the end of this stanza, the harlot becomes an initiate, turning away from sin by the ritual blowing on Satan which formed part of the baptismal liturgy. Turning away from darkness and sin, the harlot turns towards Christ and prefigures her baptismal encounter with him (10.6.1, 6–11):

Προσέλθω οὖν πρὸς αὐτόν, φωτισθῶ, ὡς γέγραπται ...
φωτιστήριον ποιήσω τὴν οἰκίαν τοῦ Φαρισαίου·
ἐκεῖ γὰρ ἀποπλύνομαι τὰς ἁμαρτίας μου·

---

[38] Trans. Datema and Allen 1991: 57.

ἐκεῖ καὶ καθαρίζομαι τὰς ἀνομίας μου·
κλαυθμῷ, ἐλαίῳ καὶ μύρῳ κεράσω μου κολυμβήθραν
καὶ λούομαι καὶ σμήχομαι καὶ ἐκφεύγω
τοῦ βορβόρου τῶν ἔργων μου.

So I will go to him to be enlightened, as it is written …
I will make the house of the Pharisee a place of light,
for there I wash away my sins,
and there I purify myself of my offences.
With weeping, with oil and with perfume I will mix my font
and I am washed and cleansed and I flee
from the filth of my deeds.

Romanos turns the house of Simon the Pharisee into a place of light (*photisterion*).[39] Alliteration ('ph' sounds) and the symmetrical placement of 'place of light' and 'Pharisee' at either end of line 6 (original line numbering) emphasise this transformation. Words of washing and purifying are repeated, highlighting the similarities between the woman's repentance and Christ's forgiveness and the baptismal liturgy of repenting and being purified. Romanos wants the congregation to recall their own baptism and its meaning.[40] The three nouns (weeping, oil, and perfume) in line 9 are balanced by the three verbs (washed, cleansed, and flee) which bring her out of her sins in line 10. The reference to tears, oil, and perfume also recalls the biblical narrative, perhaps especially the Lucan version, in which the woman is said to wash Jesus' feet with her tears and dry them with her hair before she anoints them with expensive perfume (Luke 7:32–38).[41] Christ becomes the font (line 9) through which the woman's purification takes place, recalling the biblical imagery of Christ as source of living water (John 4:14) as well as emphasising that it is into Christ that the congregation is baptised and through him that they are purified.

Both Leontius and Romanos use their texts to animate the liturgical rites of Eucharist and baptism and ritual practices like fasting, using evocative imagery to provoke the participants' memories and imaginations. By bringing these rites to life in their hymns and homilies, they both perform the transformation of the self which takes place through these rituals. They make particular emotional responses normative and

---

[39] Lash (1995: 79 n. 9) calls it a baptistery, but Michael Peppard (2019) makes a convincing case against translating φωτιστήριον as 'baptistery'.
[40] On memory and baptism, see Frank 2013.
[41] On the repentant tears of the harlot in Ephrem and his followers, see Hunt 1998.

dramatise the purification of the mind and senses to make audience members receptive to knowledge of God. Romanos' *kontakia* and Leontius' homilies thus become ritual modes of knowing, weaving these significant rituals into their texts. Even as they do this, they prime their listeners to experience and come to know God through the upcoming liturgical rites.

Mediation of Divine Knowledge: Mary in Romanos

Thus far I have argued for very similar modes of knowing between Romanos and Leontius. There is, however, at least one mode of knowledge which was foreign to Leontius but very significant for Romanos and which was becoming increasingly important for lay devotion in Byzantium in this period: mediation of knowledge of the divine through Mary the Theotokos.[42] For Romanos (and for many preachers and hymnographers in this period and later), Mary's unique relationship with God made her the perfect mediator for humanity. Romanos uses stock phrases like 'through the intercessions of the Theotokos', which suggests a popular, if not widespread tradition, of Mary praying for the people.[43] In this chapter, however, I am interested particularly in how Romanos makes Mary a mediator of knowledge of God.

We have seen Mary play a familiar role, addressing the congregation as 'friends' in *On the Marriage at Cana*. In that passage, Mary has inside knowledge about Christ. She knows that he can perform miracles before his public ministry and miracle-working began. This is because he had already worked a miracle in the virgin conception and birth.[44] Mary knows her son's powers intimately, in a way that no other human can possibly know them.

In *On the Nativity II*, Mary is moved by the plight of her forebears, Adam and Eve, and questions her son about his plans for them (2.15.3–7).

---

[42] There is some debate in scholarship over the development of the Marian cult. Shoemaker (2008) sees evidence of the cult in the fourth century. Cameron (2004) prefers the late fourth century. Price (2004, 2008) argues that it begins after the council of Ephesus in the fifth century.

[43] On popular devotion to Mary as an intercessor, especially for women, see Limberis 1994: 104–7; Cameron 2004: 18–19. That there was a growing popular devotion to Mary is borne out by other narratives about Mary, including the dormition, which seem to give voice to an existing tradition rather than create something completely new. See Shoemaker 2007: 135.

[44] Arentzen 2017: 148.

Ἔτι, εἶπεν ἡ Μαρία,
ἐὰν λαλήσω, μὴ ὀργισθῇς μοι τῇ πηλῷ, ὦ πλαστουργέ·
ὡς γὰρ τέκνῳ παρρησιάσομαι· θαρρῶ ὡς γεννήσασα,
σὺ γάρ μοι τῷ τόκῳ σου πᾶσαν καύχησιν ἔδωκας·
ὃ μέλλεις τελεῖν τί ἔστι θέλω νῦν μαθεῖν·

'Yet', said Mary,
'If I should speak, do not be angry with me who am clay, O modeller.
For I will speak boldly since [I speak] to my child. I take courage since I bore you,
for you have given to me, your bearer, every reason to boast.
What you intend to accomplish is what I now wish to understand.'

As Thomas Arentzen has argued, Mary's role as the bearer of the Christ-child puts her in a unique position with Christ.[45] She has the right, as she says here, to boast and to question Jesus boldly. She humbly acknowledges her mortality (μοι τῇ πηλῷ) and her son's divinity (πλαστουργέ), but the unique and intimate relationship she has with him as his bearer (μοι τῷ τόκῳ) grants her a freedom to question which is not available to other mortals (in this case, Adam and Eve). Romanos uses this inimitable relationship to make Mary the means of acquiring knowledge of the divine plan of salvation.

This freedom to speak and, indeed, argue, is most prominent in Romanos' hymn *On Mary at the Cross*. In this hymn Mary weeps continuously over her son's death and begs him to explain it. She wants to know whether he is going to perform more miracles (19.1); she cannot understand how the triumphal entry into Jerusalem ended like this (19.2); she blames his friends for abandoning him (19.3). Jesus responds that he has freely accepted this suffering in order to save humanity (19.4, 6), and he repeatedly tells her to stop weeping (19.4–6). Mary wipes away her tears, but she is not finished with her argument (19.7.4–6; 19.8.1, 2–4, 7):

τί μοι λέγεις, σπλάγχνον· 'εἰ μὴ θάνω, ὁ Ἀδὰμ οὐχ ὑγιαίνει';
καὶ μὴν ἄνευ πάθους ἐθεράπευσας πολλούς·
λεπρὸν γὰρ καθῆρας καὶ οὐκ ἤλγησας οὐδέν …
Νεκροὺς ἀναστήσας νεκρὸς οὐκ ἐγένου …
… πῶς οὖν λέγεις·
'εἰ μὴ πάθω, ὁ Ἀδὰμ οὐχ ὑγιαίνει';
κέλευσον, σωτήρ μου, καὶ ἐγείρεται εὐθὺς κλίνην βαστάζων …
δουλεύει σοι πάντα ὡς πλάστῃ τῶν πάντων·

Why, beloved, do you say to me, 'Unless I die, Adam will not be cured'?
Indeed, you healed many people without suffering yourself.

---

[45] Arentzen 2017: 143–50.

> You cleansed a leper and did not feel any pain …
> You raised the dead without becoming a corpse …
> Why do you say 'Unless I suffer, Adam will not be cured'?
> Give the command, my Saviour, and at once he will get up and carry his bed …
> Everything serves you, as the Creator of all things.

Mary voices concerns about the crucifixion that may well have occurred to Romanos' congregation, but she uniquely possesses the ability to ask these questions of her divine son. Her queries throughout this hymn enable Romanos to put the explanations for the crucifixion in the mouth of Jesus himself. In response to Mary's weeping and pleading, Jesus explains the salvific necessity of the crucifixion and the hope of the approaching resurrection. Authoritative answers come from God, but they are mediated in Romanos through the virgin Mary. His congregation is admitted to an intimate knowledge of God through Jesus' mother Mary.

Mary hardly features in Leontius' homilies at all. This seems odd, given how prominent she is in his contemporary's hymns and also given that the cult of the virgin was growing apace in Constantinople in this period. Perhaps we might look to the liturgical and social setting of these two writers for an explanation. Romanos wrote hymns primarily for vigils, a liturgical rite we know to have been popular with women.[46] Other biblical women are given star roles in other *kontakia*: the Samaritan woman, the haemorrhaging woman, and the harlot all have hymns dedicated to them and each is held up as an exemplum.[47] This may suggest that Mary's prominence in the *kontakia* is partly to be explained by a deliberate attempt to connect with women in the congregation through the use of female exempla. Perhaps more significantly, the church to which Romanos was attached as deacon was dedicated to Mary the Theotokos. We might therefore propose that his congregation had a particular devotion to Mary and expected her to feature prominently in the hymns and sermons that they heard. If so, strategies of knowledge construction could be shaped by distinctive local factors, down to the level of individual congregations, even if the overarching narratives and rituals we have been discussing were shared across larger groups.

---

[46] Taft 1986: 166–87; 1998: 72–74; Krueger 2014: 30. Leontius attributes the female fondness for vigils to the fact that the women kept a vigil at the tomb of Christ (VIII.83–84).

[47] *On the Samaritan Woman* (*kontakion* 9), *On the Woman with the Issue of Blood* (12), *On the Sinful Woman* (10). Romanos also devotes a hymn to the nativity of Mary (35), two hymns to the annunciation (36 and 37), and two hymns to the parable of the ten virgins (47 and 48), all of which focus on female models of faith and piety, as well as the hymns discussed above in which Mary plays a key role.

Taking up this issue of local knowledge-building, Leontius' congregation, by contrast, seems to have been composed mainly of artisans and labourers, and it is clear from Leontius' comments about poverty that many in his audience were poor. In homily VI, *On the Betrayal of Christ*, Leontius speaks about the woman at Bethany who anointed Jesus' feet and dried them with her hair, emphasising that she is 'incomparable' (VI.153). But from the next few lines, we get the impression that the men in his congregation might not be too happy about this female model of piety (VI.157–61):

Πάντας ὑπερηκόντισεν αὕτη ἡ γυνή, οὐ μόνον γυναῖκας ἀλλὰ καὶ ἄνδρας. Καὶ μηδεὶς στυγνάσῃ τῶν παρόντων ἀνδρῶν γυναῖκα κατανοῶν προκρινομένην ἀνδρός· ἓν γὰρ τὸ κέρδος κἄν τε γυνὴ ἐγκωμιάζηται κἄν τε ἀνήρ

The woman surpassed all people – not only women, but men too. And let none of the men present glower at a woman when he realises that she is preferred above a man, for the gain is one, whether a woman be lauded or a man.[48]

This is the only time in Leontius' surviving homilies that he uses a woman as a model, and we can imagine from the reaction it seems to have received ('let none of the men present glower') that he was not keen to try it again. The composition of the audience is an important factor in deciding which modes of knowing will work. For Romanos, clearly, Mary was a useful means of disseminating knowledge of the divine, but not so for Leontius.

Conclusion

The liturgical texts of Romanos and Leontius activate narrative and ritual to train the minds, emotions, will, and senses of their listeners and to make them receptive to the divine. The liturgical texts we have surveyed shape the contours of the physical space inhabited by their congregations by imbuing it with Christian meaning. Material buildings or geographic locations are transformed into sacred spaces, and as they are transformed, the minds, wills, and bodies of the congregation are also changed so that congregation members come to know God and understand their own lives within the rituals and narratives presented by Romanos and Leontius. Both authors write their audiences into a communal narrative which crosses temporal and spatial boundaries, making biblical and salvific events present for their congregations and bringing them closer to God. While local

---

[48] Trans. Datema and Allen 1991: 85.

variables can be highly important for how different writers seek to shape the minds and bodies of their congregations, as in the case of Romanos' use of Mary as mediator of knowledge, common patterns of thought predominate. Romanos' hymns and Leontius' homilies weave liturgical rituals into their texts to explore the transformation of the self which takes place in those rites and to emphasise their revelatory power. In this context, it makes sense to speak of a liturgical and embodied mode of knowing which changes perceptions, communicates theological ideas, and alters experience of the world.

30 Prolegomena to Philosophy and the Ascetic Ordering of Knowledge

MICHAEL W. CHAMPION

Introduction

The idea that the goal of philosophy is to become like god was famously proposed by Plato in the *Theaetetus* (176a–b):

Therefore, we ought to try to escape from earth to the gods as quickly as possible; and to escape is to become like God, so far as this is possible; and to become like God is to become just and pious with wisdom.[1]

This statement may be piously improving, but it is also perplexing. The height of human perfection is to become something vaguely defined as not human. Further, since philosophers must escape from the world with all seemly haste, justice and piety have nothing to do with human affairs. It seems that the perfect Platonist is both irritatingly metaphysical and morally vapid. Julia Annas has identified a tension between the ethical Platonist (who must be just and pious) and the spiritual one (who must escape from the world).[2] Joining the two seems impossible, partly because the vision of virtue is related to different visions of God. The urge towards spiritual perfection means that humans should avoid the complexity of worldly good and evil, and try to emulate a god who is completely separated from the world; ethical perfection would have humans exercise wisdom in the world by participating in divine providential action.

Such difficulties with this view of the goal of philosophy led modern philosophers and historians of philosophy to pay it little attention.[3] But the modern neglect is inversely proportional to the ancient significance of this passage across the major philosophical schools, Christian thought, and on into Arabic philosophy. In the case of Platonism, Dirk Baltzly has traced the tradition from Plato through Alcinous' Middle Platonism to Plotinus,

---

[1] διὸ καὶ πειρᾶσθαι χρὴ ἐνθένδε ἐκεῖσε φεύγειν ὅτι τάχιστα. φυγὴ δὲ ὁμοίωσις θεῷ κατὰ τὸ δυνατόν· ὁμοίωσις δὲ δίκαιον καὶ ὅσιον μετὰ φρονήσεως γενέσθαι. Compare Chapter 8 by Peter Struck, this volume.
[2] Annas 1999: 54, 63–66, 70. The godlikeness theme recurs in other Platonic passages, for example *Resp.* 613a–b; *Tim.* 90b–d.
[3] See now Annas 1999; Sedley 1999; O'Meara 2003; Baltzly 2004; Runia 2013; Mansfeld 2020.

Porphyry, Iamblichus, and Proclus.[4] He argues that while the tension between the spiritualist and the ethicist is clear in Plotinus, by the time one reaches Proclus, Neoplatonism has the resources to unite the two. Where Plotinus sees a strict division between civic and cathartic virtues, such that achieving higher purification means leaving behind the lesser demands of civic or political virtue, Proclus' scheme makes all virtues participate in each other, so that civic and political virtues always remain (below the One) in the divine realm at the level of Soul and Intellect.[5]

This is especially so since for Proclus (unlike for Plotinus, whose sage is best imagined as a mind assimilating to an impersonal Intellect) the perfect human participates in gods who have personal characteristics and themselves display analogues to civic virtue and act providentially.[6] The sage does not aim to return to some undescended, intellectual part of ourselves (a Plotinian idea which Proclus rejects).[7] Baltzly has mounted a convincing argument that the relevant gods (even up to the level of Intellect, which humans can approach through the mediating *logoi* implanted in them) possess virtues in some (increasingly rarefied) sense.[8] Thus ascent to the gods through philosophical perfection – flight from the world – need not mean the elimination of civic virtues. As Baltzly has argued, Proclus' *Timaeus* commentary provides further support for this account. Since like is known by like, coming to know the cosmos (the 'living god' of the *Timaeus*) means becoming more like god, and since it is good, coming to know the cosmos means attaining greater goodness. Proclus particularly emphasises the importance of self-sufficiency and self-ordering. The cosmos acts on itself immediately to keep itself in order; it is arranged in a way that is revelatory of the providential Demiurge.[9] Humans participate in this providential

---

[4] Baltzly 2004. For the earlier tradition up to Neoplatonism, see also O'Meara 2003: 31–39; Russell 2004.

[5] For Plotinus on political virtues, see Smith 1999; O'Meara 2003; Baltzly 2004.

[6] But not in the One: see Proclus, *ET* 116. At *In Tim.* 3.262.6–14, 279.14–19, Proclus argues that our psychic character is determined by our 'leading gods', to whom we should try to assimilate ourselves, thus aligning ourselves to our proper place in the cosmos. See Baltzly 2004. These gods are at a considerably lower level than the heights the Plotinian sage can reach (communication with the One is demoted to participation in hypostases at the level of Soul, i.e., below Intellect). See also O'Meara 2003: 96.

[7] Baltzly 2004. See also O'Meara 2003: 96.   [8] Baltzly 2004.

[9] 'For since the universe is one living thing, it exhibits sympathy with itself with the result that all the things that have come to be are parts of the life of the universe just like a single drama. It is as if some tragic poet has created a drama in which, after the divine interventions, heroic parts and other characters [have been introduced], he assigned to those players who were willing responsibility for the words of the heroes or some other role. The poet himself, though, encompasses in a single cause all of the things that are said. It is necessary to conceive that this is how it is with the world soul' (Proclus, *In Tim.* 2.305.7–15; cited in Baltzly 2004).

action by correctly performing the actions most suited to them within the total cosmic order and thereby reveal its divinity (*In Tim.* 3.275.11–15). The administration of providence means that humans must constantly aim to assimilate themselves to their leading gods by attaining greater knowledge and by ordering their souls appropriately. And this, as Baltzly has pointed out, may well mean serious political, military, or social service.[10] Flight to the gods does not mean, for Proclus, ethically vacuous otherworldliness.

I have spent some time on Baltzly's important account of this development because, despite O'Meara's landmark study of Neoplatonic political philosophy, the godlikeness theme is still commonly considered to be equivalent to otherworldliness.[11] Objects of knowledge are ordered, in this schema, so that the more important an object of knowledge is, the more removed it is from material reality. Since coming to know things has been seen as a constitutive element of godlikeness, the knower becomes an otherworldly figure. While this may well be true of some strands of Christianity as it was for Plotinus, the asceticism represented by Dorotheus of Gaza shares with later Neoplatonism a rejection of the claim that knowledge implies otherworldliness.

In what follows, I explore late antique *Prolegomena to Philosophy* and compare their assumptions about godlikeness and knowledge with Dorotheus' ascetic *Didaskaliai*. Where others have focused on the ethical and political consequences of godlikeness, I focus on its epistemic consequences, although we will see that the ethical and epistemic are intertwined. As in the case of ethics and politics, godlikeness orders knowledge and promotes ways of knowing developed in order to bridge the gap between the politico-ethical and the spiritual, the practical and the theoretical. In the Neoplatonic case, we have seen that different ideas of God in Plotinus and Proclus generated different accounts of how to attain godlikeness. The comparison with Dorotheus distils further differences in how godlikeness affected how knowledge was conceptualised. Most importantly, in the asceticism Dorotheus represents, humility is the key epistemic virtue, which generated distinctive attitudes towards knowledge. Comparing two very different epistemic communities enables points of overlap and difference to be identified, thus enabling a clearer picture of Christian contributions to epistemology to emerge.

---

[10] Baltzly 2004.
[11] There are also advances in natural philosophy, long thought to be another area that Neoplatonists neglected on the basis of their fixation on flight from the world. See Wilberding and Horn 2012.

Philosophical Prolegomena

The *Prolegomena* to philosophy[12] – pedagogical introductions to philosophy which preface late antique commentaries on Aristotle's *Categories*[13] or Porphyry's *Isagoge*[14] – provide a fascinating window into how philosophy was defined, categorised, and conceptualised in late antiquity. They enable us to identify how knowledge was supposed to be organised and attained in philosophical education in the period, and to glimpse the sorts of intellectual habits philosophers attempted to promote.[15] I focus on the *Isagoge* introductions, since they are more expansive, treat godlikeness in greater detail, and thus enable epistemological questions to intersect with this theme. Starting with Ammonius in the fifth century, we have *Prolegomena* also from Eutocus, Olympiodorus, Elias, Stephanus of Alexandria, David, and Pseudo-Elias (Pseudo-David),[16] probably in that chronological order, although dating remains controversial, and the latest versions may be pushed back into the early seventh century.[17] Only those of Ammonius, Elias, David, and Pseudo-Elias (Pseudo-David) are extant in extended

---

[12] Westerink (1990) provides a thorough overview of these texts and associated questions.

[13] For *Prolegomena* to Aristotle's *Categories*, see Ammonius, Philoponus, Olympiodorus, Elias, and Simplicius (*CAG* 4.4; 13.1; 12.1; 18.2, 8). These texts are highly uniform, in each case treating: (1) origins of names of philosophical schools; (2) classification of Aristotle's writings; (3) priority of logic and ethics; (4) the final goal of philosophy understood as knowledge of the first cause (god); (5) attaining this goal through ethics, physics, mathematics, and theology; (6) the characteristics of a good student; (7) the characteristics of a good exegete; (8) Aristotle's style; (9) the purpose of his obscurity; (10) preliminaries for each work. Note that the *Introductions* to Aristotle argue that knowledge of God is the goal of Aristotle's philosophy and that the student of philosophy should aim towards the assimilation of his soul to the universe, congruent with Proclus' scheme of assimilation at the level of Soul and in line with the wider theme of godlikeness. See, e.g., Olympiodorus 9,28ff; 10,4ff.

[14] The *Isagoge* introductions treat definitions of philosophy and its division into theoretical and practical elements. They begin from Aristotle, *An. post.* 2.1 by asking (i) does philosophy exist? (ii) what is it? (iii) what is its nature? (iv) what is its purpose. They then consider six definitions, namely that philosophy is (1) knowledge of real beings *qua* real beings; (2) knowledge of divine and human things; (3) preparation for death; (4) godlikeness, inasmuch as that is possible; (5) the art of arts and science of sciences; (6) love of wisdom.

[15] These *Prolegomena* would have a long afterlife into Byzantium, particularly through John Damascene's *Dialectica* 3 and 66. See Duffy 2002; Louth 2004: 32–33, 38–53. For other *Nachleben*, see Roueché 1974. In the West, they would influence generations of education through Boethius (who wrote commentaries on Porphyry and the *Categories* that align with the Greek tradition), Cassiodorus (*Inst.* 2.3.9), and Isidore of Seville (*Etym.* 2.24.1–2, 9). On Boethius, see Chapter 35 by John Magee, this volume. On Cassiodorus, see Vessey 2004 and Magee in this volume. The long-standing divisions of knowledge identified by Matyáš Havrda (Chapter 5, this volume) persist but are set within a more differentiated account, in keeping with the later Platonic interest in division and hierarchy.

[16] I refer to this text as Pseudo-Elias with no confidence about attribution.

[17] See Roueché 1974, 1980, 1990; Wildberg 1990.

form.[18] Of these, the last three may have been Christian.[19] Stephanus' other works suggest acceptance of Christian authoritative sources even if he never tries to reconcile traditional philosophical claims (e.g., eternity of the world, pre-existence of the soul) with Christian doctrine.[20] David and Elias similarly cite such pagan beliefs uncontroversially.[21] Pseudo-Elias (Pseudo-David) uses language which may be biblical, but could equally be found in Platonic texts and, like David, depends at times on Stephanus' commentary.[22] Thus the dating, authorship, and religious allegiance of the authors are difficult to pin down, especially in the cases of David, Elias, and Pseudo-Elias (Pseudo-David).

What are we to make of this? One thing is certain: at this stage of the development of the tradition, the Christianity of the authors, if they were indeed Christian, does nothing to change the content of their texts.[23] The texts provide evidence over an extended period for a stable and well-resourced intellectual tradition which orders knowledge and specifies how knowledge is to be attained in ways that are unconnected with epistemological changes associated with Christianity. Thus, where there is overlap between Christian traditions and the *Prolegomena*, one may speak of a shared epistemology; where Christian traditions do not align with the *Prolegomena*, other factors become relevant for assessing epistemological change.

Godlikeness and Knowledge in the Prolegomena

How is knowledge conceptualised in these texts, and how does the godlikeness goal affect how knowledge is ordered and attained? It is sometimes argued that later Neoplatonists became 'less ambitious' about the capacities of human reason.[24] Yet the *Prolegomena* provide no evidence for a failure of nerve about human rational capacity. For the authors of the *Prolegomena*, philosophy provides complete knowledge of what exists

---

[18] Texts: CAG 4.3; 17.1; 18.2; Westerink 1967. On Ammonius, see Blank 2010. On David, see Wildberg 2018. On Elias, see Wildberg 2016. On all three, see Geertz 2018; Wildberg 1990.
[19] For scepticism about the Christianity of the later philosophers, see Wildberg 1990, 2016, 2018; Westerink 1967 and Roueché 1990 and are less sceptical.
[20] Roueché 1990; Westerink 1990.
[21] There is evidence that Stephanus is a source for David and Pseudo-Elias (but not Elias). See Roueché 1990.
[22] Westerink (1990) found references to Genesis and 1 Cor 9:24.
[23] This is not true later, for example, in the use of the *Prolegomena* by John of Damascus or middle Byzantine thinkers, for which see Duffy 2002.
[24] E.g., O'Meara 2003: 96.

(e.g., David 17,15ff.). It demonstrates that the philosopher is a 'god on earth by their knowledge of everything' (Elias 6,32–33; 12,14). Certainly, God differs from the ideal philosopher. Philosophers can hope for discursive rather than simultaneous knowledge, but that knowledge is otherwise all-encompassing. All agree that there is a hierarchy of knowledge and that philosophy stands at its apex, since it deals with real being and the fundamental nature of things. It alone provides the reasons and principles from which all the arts and sciences derive their power to investigate and change the physical world. And it can order souls and societies so that they are aligned with their proper natures. Hence philosophers have knowledge of the nature of all real beings, they know all human and divine things inasmuch as they are perishable or eternal, they know the principles of all the human arts and sciences, and they can so order their souls that knowledge is unimpeded by bodily desires and society approximates divine order.

David is perhaps the most optimistic about knowledge, but his optimism is different from the other *Prolegomena* in degree rather than kind. He repeatedly claims that the perfect philosopher knows everything. He is like a king since reason rules him (also Elias 18,35), and like a god because he has divine characteristics of goodness, knowledge, and power (David 17,1ff.). The cultural power of this description may be seen both in portraits of Neoplatonic philosophers and in imperial propaganda. The philosopher cares for the soul and society regally by bringing them to knowledge and by ordering them appropriately, he knows everything, and he desires everything within his power. When this claim is first introduced, the first two claims (philosophical goodness and knowledge) are unmodified, leaving the impression that the philosopher is only less than god with respect to power (David 17,16ff.). Unlike god, philosophers cannot reach out and touch the heavens with their fingers, since in the case of humans, desire does not imply capacity (David 17,20–22). But like god, they can be perfectly good and have knowledge of all real being.

Later in the introduction, David is more circumspect, but his optimism about kingly knowledge remains. He offers an extended discussion of how one thing can be like another (David 34,30–35,29).[25] Members of a species can be alike (all swans are white); a quality (e.g., hotness) may be greater or lesser in different species (white and black pepper); there may be various qualities in different species (pigeons and doves may be alike in different colours); and there can be likeness between an original and its image. This last case is the relevant sense in which philosophers may be like god. Such

---

[25] See also Ammonius; Elias 16,35–17,36; Pseudo-Elias (Pseudo-David) 14.

a likeness preserves the unique substance of philosopher and deity but allows likeness in characteristics. So God is consubstantial with goodness and thus is incapable of evil, unlike philosophers, who may nevertheless attain goodness; God's knowledge is simultaneous and always actual rather than potential, whereas the knowledge of philosophers is at best discursive and includes the possibility of forgetting and initial ignorance; finally, as in the earlier discussion, God's power alone is convertible with divine will.

David's optimism about human capacity for knowledge (and goodness and power) is key to his claims about godlikeness. Humans become godlike, as in the *Timaeus*, through justice, piety, and wisdom. David's account emphasises that philosophy is the location of the virtues. Justice and piety include all the virtues ordered under practical philosophy, since they are the most excellent of such virtues. Plato's claim that godlikeness is achieved through the exercise of these virtues with wisdom signals the elimination of the affections (πάθη). It therefore denotes the centrality of theoretical philosophy (which is taken to provide theoretical knowledge necessary for practical wisdom) and affirms the unity of the virtues. Only virtues performed 'with wisdom' – that is, with an understanding of the necessary connection between virtues – are truly virtuous and rational and thus truly godlike. Elias agrees, citing Plotinus: the exercise of virtue through internalised reasoning moves the knower towards godlikeness, since such reasoning means that the virtues imply one another and are not in conflict in any way, thus mirroring divine perfection.[26]

This distinction between different types of virtue on the basis of whether they are performed with rational understanding is a significant Neoplatonic claim, its significance perhaps most clearly signalled in the *Prolegomena* by a revealing misquotation (Elias 18,1–8):

Since Plato was not content with saying that philosophy is becoming like god as far as is possible for man, but also added the way of attaining likeness by saying 'one becomes like god by being pious and just with wisdom and by knowing this', let us examine the following three questions:

1. Why did he add 'justice' to 'piety'?
2. Why did he only mention two virtues, justice and wisdom, when there are four?
3. Why did he say 'and by knowing this'?[27]

---

[26] Cf. Plotinus, *Enn.* 1.3.6; 1.4.15; Plato, *Phaed.* 69b; Geertz 2018: 110. This discussion depends on the canonical Platonic hierarchy of virtues.

[27] Ἐπειδὴ μὴ ἠρκέσθη ὁ Πλάτων εἰπεῖν τὴν φιλοσοφίαν ὁμοίωσιν θεῷ κατὰ τὸ δυνατὸν ἀνθρώπῳ, ἀλλὰ καὶ τὸν τρόπον τῆς ὁμοιώσεως προσέθηκεν εἰπὼν 'ὁμοίωσις δέ ἐστι δίκαιον καὶ ὅσιον γενέσθαι μετὰ φρονήσεως καὶ ταῦτα γινώσκειν', φέρε τρία τινὰ ζητήσωμεν· πρῶτον

We may focus on the third question. For Plato, of course, did not employ the phrase 'and by knowing this' in his discussion of godlikeness.[28] In Elias' hands, this misquotation enables him to distinguish between natural virtues (which humans share with animals) and virtues that require education (παιδεία) and work (πόνος). The pairing of παιδεία and πόνος in this sense is unique to Elias (19,30–20,16). While education can be described as laborious,[29] distinguishing between education and work seems to be an innovation; the centrality of ascetic labour for knowledge may be significant. The ethical virtues, understood as inculcated through habituation (ἐκ συνηθείας), require the right teacher or parent (Elias 20,1ff.).[30] But this implies that a person may act virtuously with reason without internalising the reason: an authority figure like a parent or teacher can provide the reason for the learner and that can be sufficient to achieve the right outcome, if not the right internal state. Elias characterises such ethical virtue as 'external' (θύραθεν). The more perfect student may habituate themselves to the virtue rationally through intellectual effort and acquire internal virtue (οἴκοθεν). In this scheme (as later in Dorotheus' case), habituation is not mere mindless repetition. Habituation requires intellectual change, whereby the reason initially accepted as a matter of authority becomes internalised as a matter of rational understanding. Gaining this rational understanding requires 'work': such knowledge is effortful, not merely theoretical, on this account. Hence what separates ethical virtues from philosophical virtue is knowledge characterised as work. Throughout, this account of knowledge sits uncomfortably with the claim that knowledge is a flight from reality. Attaining virtues of this rational kind makes the learner godlike, since goodness is unified with truth rather than merely indexing conventional behaviour.

Elias goes a long way towards clarifying that godlikeness is an intellectual, ethical, political, and spiritual pursuit. Justice orders and unifies all the virtues in the soul, practical and theoretical. This orderly unification of theoretical and practical knowledge pervades each of the extant *Prolegomena*,

---

μὲν διὰ τί προσέθηκε τῷ δικαίῳ τὸ ὅσιον, δεύτερον διὰ τί τεσσάρων οὐσῶν ἀρετῶν δύο μόνων ἐμνήσθη, δικαιοσύνης καὶ φρονήσεως, τρίτον διὰ τί εἶπε 'καὶ ταῦτα γινώσκειν' (trans. Geertz 2018).

[28] I am not sure why Elias did not use Plato's 'μετὰ φρονήσεως' to do this work for him (as David comes close to doing). It may be that the addition picks up Plato's reference to γνῶσις at *Theaet.* 176c: see Geertz 2018, 110. Alternatively, it may be that he thinks he needs different terms for the virtue (φρόνησις) and the internal reasoning associated with it (γνῶσις).

[29] E.g., Lucian, *Somn.* 1.4; Libanius, *Ep.* 664.2.4; Socrates, *Hist. eccl.* 7.21.27; cf. Elias 19,31; 20,6,14.

[30] On the concept of habituation, see the essays in Sparrow and Hutchinson 2013.

and is a key way in which the philosopher can be said to be like god. For Ammonius (4,8–14), just as God has two powers, theoretical and practical (δυνάμεις, αἵ τε γνωστικαὶ καὶ αἱ πρακτικαί), so too our souls are twofold. As such, the godlike philosopher desires to order both parts of the soul in an imitation of God (τῇ πρὸς τὸν θεὸν μιμήσει). He therefore investigates the real nature of all beings and cares for his own soul and those of others by ordering them (κοσμεῖν) appropriately. Such a care for the soul requires theoretical knowledge and is itself required for attaining knowledge of intelligibles. This, says Ammonius, is why Plato defined philosophy as godlikeness.

Ammonius' scheme thus makes godlikeness crucial for both theoretical and practical philosophy.[31] The other authors of *Prolegomena* extend this argument. Philosophers move from perception (particular knowledge of something present), to imagination (particular knowledge of something absent through recollection), through irrational opinion to justified belief first of particulars and then of universals, and ultimately through discursive thinking to immediate apprehension, a form of thinking which is not distinguished from divine intellection. The philosopher attains 'infallible knowledge of universals' (David 44,17–22).[32] Knowledge moves from beings which are material in existence and conception (e.g., trees, a subject of natural science), to those which are material in existence but immaterial in thought (e.g., shapes, a mathematical subject), to beings which are immaterial in both existence and thought (e.g., angels, a theological subject). Such knowledge enables the philosopher to be likened to god. Godlikeness is an epistemic virtue. The philosopher is godlike in that he knows everything by knowing all being in an exercise of theoretical philosophy.

But the philosopher is also godlike, David argues, by creating (David 55,35–56,16). This builds on Ammonius' claim that the philosopher is godlike by ordering (κοσμεῖν) souls and aligns with Proclus' claim that godlikeness means participation in the providential and immediate ordering of the cosmos by the demiurge. This second means of godlikeness (creativity) ties divine providence to divine wisdom and makes godlikeness as central to practical philosophy as it is to theoretical philosophy. Godlikeness is ethical and political as well as epistemic. For our purposes, the key point

---

[31] See Mansfeld 2020: 102: 'it is the assimilation unto God that enables and perhaps even constrains the philosopher to join theory and praxis together'.

[32] ἐπιστήμη δέ ἐστιν ἡ τῶν καθόλου ἄπταιστος καὶ ἀμετακίνητος γνῶσις (ἀπταίστως γὰρ γινώσκει τὰ γινωσκόμενα), ἢ γνῶσις ἄπταιστος τῶν ὑποκειμένων αὐτῇ πραγμάτων, καθὸ ἔχουσι φύσεως· ὡς γὰρ ἔχουσι φύσεως καὶ οἱονεὶ τὴν φύσιν τῶν ὑποκειμένων αὐτῇ πραγμάτων γινώσκει. ταῦτα μὲν ἐν τούτοις περὶ τῆς ἐπιστήμης.

is that godlikeness in the domain of knowledge requires both theoretical understanding of fundamental principles and practical thought about correct action. As David put it, 'the perfect philosopher is not only decorated with theoretical knowledge but also glorified by practice' (71,3–4).[33]

This mutual relation is clear in David's first argument for the existence of philosophy (8,10–19). If god exists, he argues, providence exists. And since only a madman would deny god's existence, providence exists.[34] Given that providence exists, wisdom exists, since providence is the exercise of wisdom. Since all things strive for the good, and wisdom is good, there is desire for wisdom. Philosophy, understood as love of wisdom, is just such a desire, so philosophy must exist. This argument provides the grounds, in David's scheme, for claiming that godlikeness is also attained through practical, rather than merely theoretical philosophy. The good is greater than truth, he argues. Truth includes goodness, but goodness need not include truth, as in Plato's famous argument about the goodness of lying to a murderer.[35] Practical philosophy is the eradication of affections and the ordering both of the individual soul and of the wider society, and is therefore equated with striving towards the good. The soul is taken to have cognitive powers (perception, imagination, opinion, discursive thought, and immediate apprehension) and vital powers (will, choice, spirit, and appetite). Where theoretical philosophy organises the cognitive powers and thus attains godlike knowledge and truth, practical philosophy organises the vital powers and thus attains godlike goodness. The two are not entirely separate domains: character is shaped through theory and reason (including through the intellectual effort required of the higher practical virtues) and theoretical knowledge is only possible for a philosopher who has purified his soul and thereby removed its conceptual blinkers through the exercise of practical knowledge (David 74,1–6). Through the dual and interrelated work of theoretical and practical philosophy, the philosopher is lifted 'from murky and muddy life to divine and immaterial life'.[36] This is understood as a fulfilment of divinely sustained human nature: everyone loves knowing, and everyone is always active in desire for the god

---

[33] δεῖ γὰρ τὸν τέλειον φιλόσοφον μὴ μόνον τῇ θεωρίᾳ κοσμεῖσθαι, ἀλλὰ καὶ τῇ πράξει ἐγκαλλωπίζεσθαι.

[34] The Armenian text explicitly identifies Epicurus as a madman in this sense. See Geertz 2018: 289.

[35] See Plato, *Resp.* 331c–d. Dorotheus makes this an example of the logic of virtue ethics: lying even in this case remains wrong but is the correct action, so long as it is done with suitable repentance and as a genuine last resort (9.102).

[36] ἡ φιλοσοφία διὰ τὸ κοσμεῖν τὰς τῶν ἀνθρώπων ψυχὰς καὶ διὰ τὸ ἐκ τοῦ ἀχλυώδους καὶ ὑλώδους τούτου βίου μεταφέρειν τὴν ψυχὴν ἐπὶ τὰ θεῖα καὶ ἄυλα (79,2–4).

who knows everything and is always actively caring for what it knows by enlightening them (David 55, 20ff.).

The mutuality between theoretical and practical philosophy is underscored when David responds to the objection that god should be easy to see, since the divine is naturally manifest in that it autonomously preserves and communicates the light of its nature (David 46,15–26). The problem, David insists, is that like bats who cannot see the sun, our senses are unsuited to seeing the purity of the divine. The 'mist of the body' and our desire for 'pleasurable indulgences' (David 46,24–25) makes it impossible for our senses correctly to perceive divine reality. We must therefore purify our soul if we are to come to know the divine. But such purification is both a theoretical and a practical problem, as we train our intellect to move from perceptions to immediate truths and order our souls both cognitively and emotionally. To know is to see clearly by removing the impediments of embodiment and by regulating the desires of the soul.

Thus, if philosophy's goal is to enable the philosopher to become as much like god as possible, godlikeness has irreducibly theoretical and practical components. Knowledge is the practical action of the soul and reason shapes character. Godlikeness is thus political and providential: godlike philosophers act providentially by ordering individual souls and ordering society to enable individuals and communities to attain truth and goodness, and they simultaneously become more and more godlike through ever greater and more immediate knowledge of what exists, with such divine knowledge made possible through the ordering of the soul and the exercise of reason.

Throughout the *Prolegomena*, then, the concept of the divine that the later Neoplatonists are working with is central to how philosophers go about knowing and ordering knowledge. While the lectures step back from detailed investigation of theology, since the students are not yet prepared for such rarefied instruction, it is clear that assumptions about divinity help to structure Neoplatonic knowledge. The divine is both different from philosophers, the object of their desire and curiosity, and simultaneously present to their souls. Philosophical knowledge is generated from this difference and presence in key ways. The presence of the divine to the philosopher means that philosophers are highly optimistic about the possibilities of human knowledge. It also means that they 'look through' material and particular experiences in order to come to know the divinely given reasons, principles, or nature of things they perceive. Divine presence means divine providence, and it also means that philosophers know by aligning themselves with this providential concern which continues to hold things in intelligible being. This requires knowledge built on the purification of bodily senses and on the correct ordering of the soul, which must be aligned to divine order. The details of such ordering and purification are not given in the *Prolegomena*, and while something like the scheme we saw earlier in Proclus is entirely consistent with them, the details are less important for our purposes. (In affirming that philosophy's aim is the ordering of the soul – both its vital and its cognitive powers – the *Prolegomena* assume, with Proclus, that the philosopher is assimilated to the divine at the level of Soul.) Knowing requires both intellectual insight into the nature of things which are assumed to be both disclosed as reflections of divine order and difficult to discern given the nature of imperfect human senses, which the knower may nevertheless purify through intellectual, psychic, and embodied effort. This joins goodness and truth (with truth viewed as a subset of goodness, since not all good actions are truthful). Opinion and discursive thought remain important components of the epistemology of the *Prolegomena* even as the sage aims to gain immediate intellectual apprehension. The divine perspective the sage seeks to attain enables him to order himself, others, and the wider society in ways taken to be more reasonable because they are more like the divinity which guarantees the order, structure, intelligibility, and goodness of the cosmos.

Godlikeness and Knowledge in the Asceticism of Dorotheus of Gaza

Much of the structure of knowing we have seen outlined in the *Prolegomena* remains in Dorotheus' account. While to identify a 'late antique episteme' is to assume an improbably homogeneous and monocultural society,[37] it is nevertheless clear that the 'philosophy' of asceticism and the 'philosophy' of the schools share important epistemological assumptions. Such epistemic patterns support claims that asceticism is philosophy, beyond considerations of similar ways of life.[38] There are three key intersections. First, both philosophers and ascetics think that there is a mutuality between theoretical and practical knowledge, requiring both intellectual effort and purification of the senses. This includes the claim that knowing more leads to greater virtue and that greater virtue implies greater knowledge.

---

[37] Cf. Stefaniw 2018.
[38] Most productively and foundationally in Hadot 1995a, who takes Dorotheus as a prime example of philosophical patterns at the end of antiquity.

Second, both groups think that when properly known, matter, human action, and social structure disclose the divine, since the physical is never merely physical. Third, greater knowledge of the world makes the knower more godlike. Within this shared epistemological framework, Dorotheus' theological-ascetic commitments lead to distinctive contributions. Thinking of godlikeness as becoming like the incarnate Christ, together with the claim that divine transcendence is compatible with absolute presence, radically shifts the epistemic virtues and practices associated with attaining genuine knowledge.[39] Humility is prized and helps to unify Dorotheus' epistemology in a manner which, if not strictly unthinkable for a Neoplatonist, was at least actually unthought in the history of Neoplatonism. The emphasis on humility has far-reaching consequences. It results in a greater emphasis on the importance of epistemic authorities, depending on others for knowledge, divine inscrutability, and resulting mystery in knowledge of physical things, and the need for divine gift (including through sacraments) in the process of attaining knowledge.

The first of the *Didaskaliai* sets out Dorotheus' account of the divine plan of salvation, which moves from initial perfection, through the fall that takes away proper human nature, through history – from prophets, incarnation, Christ's commandments, the church's sacramental action – to the unification of humans with God in the restoration of human nature. This *Didaskalia* frames the collection by providing the theological narrative that supports the largely ascetic-ethical teachings which follow. Its account of paradise discloses the true nature of humanity. Humans were created such that, according to nature, they were endowed with secure perception and every virtue and enjoy paradise in prayer and contemplation with honour and glory (1.1).[40] Since they were created in the image of God, they naturally have immortality, freedom, and virtue. The fall means that humans now live contrary to nature, subject to passion, lacking in godlikeness, and set in a world of pervasive error (1.1). Only a few had true knowledge, and they attained it only externally, from the law they read from nature. The common lot of post-lapsarian humanity was epistemological failure leading to the false knowledge of idolatry, magic, and polytheism (1.1–3). God provides written law to 'turn people's minds' from false knowledge, correct them, and return them to their proper nature (1.2–3). The incarnation is presented as an intensification of this providential action.

---

[39] This scheme resonates with that identified in the case of Augustine by Ayres 2015a.

[40] Καὶ ἦν ἐν τρυφῇ τοῦ παραδείσου, ἐν εὐχῇ, ἐν θεωρίᾳ, ἐν πάσῃ δόξῃ καὶ τιμῇ, ἔχων σώας τὰς αἰσθήσεις καὶ ὢν ἐν τῷ κατὰ φύσιν καθὼς καὶ ἐκτίσθη (1.1.4–7).

It restores human nature and perfects the senses (1.4).[41] That is, restoration to human perfection in Christ is explicitly figured as epistemic renewal, and, in the following passage, a purification given to humanity through baptism (1.5). Humans on the way to godlikeness participate in the humility which is characteristic of the incarnation to overcome the perversion of their understanding (διάνοια) (1.5).[42] The epistemic products of humility are self-critique and mistrust of one's wisdom and will, which counteracts this perversion of mind and imagination in the wake of the fall. All 'the saints thus try to unite themselves to God through humility'.[43] This unification is cast as the purification of the soul and the mind made possible after incorporation into Christ through baptism (1.11).

This account sets out *in nuce* the key elements of Dorotheus' epistemology. The plan of salvation means that history and the physical cosmos reveal divine truth. Theoretical and practical knowledge are mutually reinforcing. Knowledge of God is impossible without spiritual and affective purification, as in the Neoplatonic case. Purification of will and intellect is coded as unification with God. The progressive purification of will and intellect results in the restoration of the true nature of humanity, the image and likeness of God. Such overlaps with the epistemic scheme set out in the *Prolegomena* can be readily multiplied. Humanity in its true nature is equipped with conscience, which Dorotheus defines as reason which illuminates the mind and enables the ethical judgement, again joining theoretical and practical understanding (3.40). An optimism about the capacity for human knowledge is justified, since nobody is without conscience (3.40). Failing to act in accordance with this reason is living the 'muddy life' to which the *Prolegomena* also refer (3.40). Errors (epistemic and ethical) quickly multiply, so one is required to pay close attention to truth, reason, and goodness in practices of self-examination (3.42). Quoting Evagrius and building on a Platonic threefold division of the soul, Dorotheus can argue that the soul is purified and returns to its original nature, which is godlike in its rational endowment with conscience, when desire is directed to virtue through well-ordered affections and the soul applies its reasoning powers to understanding created beings (17.176).[44] Ordering and directing the desires and affections of the soul and paying appropriate attention with

---

[41] ἀνανεοῖ γὰρ τὸ κατὰ φύσιν καὶ σώας πάλιν ποιεῖ τὰς αἰσθήσεις ὡς ἐξ ἀρχῆς ἐγένοντο (1.4.17–18).
[42] Dorotheus cites Gen 8:21.
[43] Τοῦτο καὶ οἱ ἅγιοι πάντες ἐπιστάμενοι, ἔσπευδον διὰ πάσης ταπεινῆς ἀγωγῆς ἑνῶσαι ἑαυτοὺς τῷ Θεῷ (1.11.1–2).
[44] τὸ μὲν ἐπιθυμητικὸν μέρος αὐτῆς τῆς ἀρετῆς ἐφίεται, τὸ δὲ θυμικὸν ὑπὲρ ταύτης ἀγωνίζεται, τὸ δὲ λογιστικὸν ἐπιβάλλει τῇ θεωρίᾳ τῶν γεγονότων (17.176.43–46).

the mind to the physical world is required for the restoration of such godlike rationality in humanity. As in the Neoplatonic case, divine knowledge exceeds the capacity of human reason. True human knowledge of created things is contrasted with God's knowledge of 'deep and hidden things, even of non-being' (17.178).[45] As in the *Prolegomena*, humans can know what exists, whereas God's knowledge extends beyond natural being. But Dorotheus makes strong claims for human conscience and rationality as a divine seed. Restoration of human nature is understood as a return to created and godlike intelligence, and goodness in this scheme means greater intellectual and ethical attention to created beings, including the practice of virtue, rather than flight from the world.

That the outline of Dorotheus' epistemology can be derived from his account of the divine plan of salvation and human restoration to their proper nature in the programmatic first *Didaskalia* is to say that his epistemology is thoroughly bound up with his view about what God is like and what it is to become like god. This generates overlaps with the knowledge schemes of the *Prolegomena*, but it is also the key to distinctive features of ascetic epistemology. The most important move is elevating humility as the primary epistemic virtue. Humility is the way to unification with God. Since mercy characterises God, and the way to mercy is humility, humility is the virtue that makes monks like God (1.11; 11.123; 14.156). Humility is the only road to salvation (5.68). Repeatedly across the *Didaskaliai*, the humble excision of one's own will brings one closer to accurate self-knowledge and apprehension of God's will for his creation. God reveals his will to those who direct their desires to him (e.g., 5.68). Such direction of desire must always be done provisionally and includes asking advice from others and knowing oneself to be under divine judgement. We can never trust our own judgement alone that we are acting well (5.62); the fall means independence of thought that leads to error (2.39). Given that monks are creatures, ascetic knowledge is always tentative and provisional, a communal activity which is always open to correction. Humility is again central to such a notion of knowledge.

Epistemic humility means, Dorotheus argues, that monks should always consider others wiser than themselves and should be constantly aware that human achievements are not their own, but God's (2.33). This makes active dependency on God an important part of Dorotheus' epistemology and differentiates his vision of godlikeness from Neoplatonism in a significant way. Dorotheus shares with Neoplatonists the view that rationality is a

---

[45] ὁ Θεὸς τὰ πάντα γινώσκει καὶ τὰ κρυπτὰ καὶ τὰ βαθέα καὶ τὰ μὴ ὄντα (17.178.13–14).

divine spark, and that the exercise of reason makes Christians godlike as they progress towards perfection. But he always insists on the gulf between humans and God. The more humans approach God, the more they realise their imperfection. Recognition of sin is the flip side of knowing the grandeur of God ever more deeply, so greater humility is generated by greater knowledge. But the converse is also true: without humility, knowledge is impossible, since the knower would not be in the appropriate state to know anything. Humility is the correct stance for the knower given that it signals an accurate understanding of humanity's place in the cosmos. It is an epistemic virtue because without humility, all actions are performed 'without knowledge' (14.152–53). Humility is thus a necessary element of any act of knowing.

This account helps to fill out the epistemic structure of humility, as Dorotheus understands it. On the one hand, humility is itself understood as, in part, a function of reason and rational knowledge. Greater knowledge of self and of God generates greater humility. Further, there are reasoned principles involved in practising and identifying humility, including the claims that good action is God's alone, divine judgement may differ from human judgement, and that the will should be subjected to others and to God (2.37). On the other hand, Dorotheus repeatedly insists that as a divine thing, humility cannot be perfectly grasped by rational thought (e.g., 2.37) even as it is essential for any act of knowing. Progression to greater knowledge in humility is always a divine gift, both in baptism and as God reveals his will to monks who are open to it. In this register, humility means that knowledge includes irreducible mystery, which is not merely a failure to know on account of one's imperfection (as in the *Prolegomena*), but the recognition that there is always more to be disclosed.

This takes us further into Dorotheus' ascetic epistemic world, as he underscores that 'nobody can express by reason what this humility is and how it grows in the soul unless he learns from experience; by reason nobody is able to learn it' (2.35).[46] Dorotheus asks, 'how then can we learn the art of arts without labours?' (8.95). This aligns with Elias' comment about the importance of *ponos* and foregrounds knowledge oriented towards practice (practical reasoning). Dorotheus' reference to the 'art of arts' claims asceticism as philosophy, which was understood, as in the *Prolegomena*, as the 'art of arts and science of sciences'. But his omission of the coordinate phrase 'science of sciences' puts the accent on practice and habituation

---

[46] Ταύτην τὴν ταπείνωσιν οὐδεὶς δύναται λόγῳ φράσαι πῶς ἐστιν ἢ πῶς ἐγγίνεται τῇ ψυχῇ, ἐὰν μὴ ἀπὸ πείρας μάθῃ αὐτὴν ἄνθρωπος· λόγῳ δὲ οὐδεὶς δύναται μαθεῖν αὐτήν.

over against more purely rational cognition in the development of ascetic perfection.[47] Continual habituation and work are necessary for humility and therefore for gaining true knowledge. The reference to work and experience makes gaining knowledge a thoroughly embodied activity.[48]

This makes ascetic labour crucial for developing humility and hence accurate understanding.[49] Like Elias, Dorotheus distinguishes between education and work, and makes both necessary for developing knowledge. Following the commandments and submitting to the authority of spiritual guides and monastic superiors inculcates humility (a divine version of Elias' submission to a teacher or parent), and, Dorotheus tells us, generates knowledge in the soul (8.92). While we have seen that philosophers could regard information accepted on the basis of external authority of the teacher as a lower form of knowledge, Dorotheus' strong emphasis on habituation makes this element of knowledge construction a much larger component of his thought than it is in philosophical sources. Since habituation can create a 'second nature', even unthinking actions have effects on souls, positive and negative. Habituation (understood as physical, affective, and intellectual) thus becomes a necessary part of Dorotheus' account of the internalisation of divine precepts. Like the philosophers, he argues that labour internalises precepts in the soul of the monk. Ascetic labour habituates humility, and thus reforms the monk's nature. This is both threat and promise. Small errors can quickly create a second nature vying with one's God-given nature; but, in the other direction, ethical and intellectual habits in accordance with the nature God intends for humanity can help to re-establish monks in the image of God (12.131, 134). Dorotheus sets out in considerable detail the sort of work required to habituate the soul to humility: practices include remembrance of death and awareness of judgement, confession, self-examination, and constant prayer – including prayer for and from those who have upset you (e.g., 4.52; 8.94–95). Discussion of remembrances of death should recall a further definition of philosophy as 'practice of death', which the *Prolegomena*, like Dorotheus, identify with the philosophical task of purifying the soul. As also in Elias, work both creates and signifies an internal state. In 'labouring and enduring' the monk 'learns the art through the help of God who sees his intention

---

[47] This includes non-rational learning from teachers within ascetic knowledge formation, where some philosophical schemes demoted it to pre-philosophical training.
[48] Dorotheus develops that point with reference to contemporary medical understanding about how souls can be affected by bodies. See further Champion 2017.
[49] Dorotheus' preferred term for ascetic labour is κόπος, arising from a favourite saying of the fathers, although he can use πόνος in a similar sense.

and his labour' (8.95).[50] Making humility the governing epistemic virtue means that knowing is always embodied and practised rather than purely intellectual.

So we should not be surprised to find that Dorotheus returns in two *Didaskaliai* to the saying that 'the way of humility is embodied labours with knowledge' (ἡ ὁδὸς τῆς ταπεινώσεώς ἐστιν οἱ κόποι οἱ σωματικοὶ ἐν γνώσει) (e.g., 2.37–39; 14.153). His treatment of the phase ἐν γνώσει, however, distinguishes him further from contemporary Neoplatonists. In the *Prolegomena*, the phrase is used to identify both the need for internalisation of rational principles in gaining knowledge and to explain that the unity of the virtues consists in the principles which connect them. In Dorotheus, however, reason is replaced by humility as the means of the unification of the virtues, which accentuates the role of practical reasoning over theoretical reasoning. Humility is the girder that binds all the virtues together; every good work is done with humility (14.152). That is, bodily labour performed with the right understanding – humility – enables the monk to act well. Reason is not what perfects a virtue; humility does, because the relevant sort of knowledge is self-understanding. Humility, in this scheme, becomes an intellectual habit, a correct intention, and mental or spiritual disposition towards the world, which should be present in all good action, including all good intellection. So one can pray, repent, confess, or examine one's conscience in ways that fall epistemically and ethically short because one fails to act with humility. Without humility, ignorance and self-deception are rife.

This radical concern about ignorance, self-deception, and error pervades Dorotheus' writings, often in the context of exploring ways in which monks can fail to act well. But the concern is not merely ethical; it is also epistemic. His account of conscience and its connections to Neoplatonism is revealing. The Neoplatonist Olympiodorus modified Plato's argument that common agreement could be taken as a criterion of truth (*Alc. maj.* 111a–c) by adopting a concept of conscience which could stand against the ignorance of the crowd. One's rational judgement may override common agreement if such agreement is an index of ignorance. Dorotheus has a very similar account of conscience: it is a divine rational seed which makes knowledge possible, and, as in Olympiodorus' argument, conscience keeps an account of actions after death. But where Olympiodorus has a high degree of confidence in the

---

[50] κοπιῶν καὶ ὑπομένων μανθάνει τὴν τέχνην, τοῦ Θεοῦ βλέποντος τὴν προαίρεσιν καὶ τὸν κόπον αὐτοῦ, καὶ συνεργοῦντος αὐτῷ. Ἡμεῖς δὲ τὴν τέχνην τῶν τεχνῶν λόγῳ θέλομεν παραλαβεῖν, μὴ ἐπιβαλλόμενοι ἔργῳ; (8.95.6–9).

impartiality and truthfulness of this rational divine element, a confidence that recalls the confidence in reason as that which makes philosophers godlike in the *Prolegomena*, Dorotheus foregrounds dangers of trusting even this epistemic guide.[51] The 'thoughts' which lead monks to sin are presented in the guise of epistemic virtues like discretion, prudence, wisdom, and knowledge (5.66). In this context, humility acts epistemically to make monks aware that error may seem reasonable. More than that, human imperfection is such that even conscience may be corrupted. Knowing accurately thus demands that monks constantly doubt their own intellectual capacity, being thrown continually back to the humble recognition of their imperfection. Like the notable provincial who feels out of place in larger towns or the imperial court, approaching God generates humility (2.34). Hence the primary philosophical metaphor of ascent to royal glory is modified by a corresponding movement to humble subjection.

This move also governs ascetic epistemic training. The demanding examination of conscience which Dorotheus repeatedly recommends is required because monks must not trust themselves (4.54; 5.66). Confession enables accurate knowledge of God's word (5.65). Salvation is made possible through much 'counsel' (5.61) and, after God and the bible, monks should seek out guides to help them understand the world and act rightly in it (5.61). In all these cases, the epistemic aim is to make sure that monks do not seek to justify their own knowledge and thereby deceive themselves that they have things properly worked out (5.62). This aligns with, but goes beyond, Neoplatonic emphasis on the authority of teachers in that it decentres the autonomy of the individual, kingly mind connecting to divine reason. The monastic knower knows that their knowledge is another's. This means that the monastic community is essential for securing knowledge. Dependence on others is required since it acts as a check on sinful autonomy. Dorotheus harnesses the image of the church as a body to argue for the co-dependence of its members, since, as Paul put it, 'we are individually members of one another' (Rom 12:5) (6.77). At its base, of course, this is a christological metaphor, and while Dorotheus does not explicitly discuss

---

[51] Olympiodorus translates the Platonic 'guiding daimon' or 'daimonion' which famously informed Socrates as 'conscience' in a move that may have been intended to connect Neoplatonic to ascetic epistemology: '[Socrates'] guiding daimon is conscience, which is the purest pinnacle of the soul, sinless within us, and an impartial judge and witness of what has happened here below before Minos and Rhadamanthys. And this is also the cause of our salvation' (δαίμονα τὸ συνειδὸς ὑπάρχειν, ὅπερ ἄκρον ἄωτόν ἐστι τῆς ψυχῆς καὶ ἀναμάρτητον ἐν ἡμῖν καὶ ἀκλινὴς δικαστὴς καὶ μάρτυς τῶν ἐνταῦθα γινομένων τῷ Μίνωϊ καὶ τῷ Ῥαδαμάνθυϊ. τοῦτο δὲ καὶ σωτηρίας ἡμῖν αἴτιον γίνεται) (Olympiodorus, *In Alc.* 23,2–5). See Westerink 1962: XVIII–XIX et par. Dorotheus' preferred term for conscience is συνείδησις.

the christology, he does argue that monks should strive 'to be at one with everyone else [in the community], for the more one is united to his neighbour, the more one is united to God' (6.77). That is, the unity of the body of Christ in the world implies that the body is conformed to divine goodness and truth. As Dorotheus puts it:

> Let us suppose that this circle is the world and God is the centre. The straight lines drawn from the circumference to the centre are the lives of men. As far as the saints, desiring to approach God, move inward, they become near God and near each other and as far as they approach each other, they approach God ... as much as we are united to our neighbour [through love] we are united to God.[52]

In this image, we have lost any sense of godlikeness as flight from the world. Ethically, love for neighbour is coterminous with love for God. The epistemic corollary is that coming closer to knowledge of God means coming to know one's neighbour more perfectly; this helps to explain Dorotheus' insistence that the soul made in the image of God seeks to know created beings (17.176). The epistemic role for the community in Dorotheus' account is distinctive. It makes knowledge a shared activity, dependent on communal practices and interactions, secured through structures of epistemic authority in the monasteries, and developed in shared desire for God.

Conclusions

There are clear epistemic connections between Dorotheus' *Didaskaliai* and the philosophical epistemology of the *Prolegomena*. The most significant connection is an account of godlikeness which demands intellectual attention to material things in the training of the mind. True knowing includes knowledge oriented towards practice and is consistent with careful investigation of the world rather than intellectual otherworldliness. This, in turn, requires ascetics like Dorotheus and contemporary Neoplatonic philosophers to imagine the world – real material being and social structures – as revelatory. It also demands a mutually reinforcing relation between theoretical and practical knowledge. Further patterns in their intellectual habits

---

[52] Τοῦτον τὸν κύκλον νομίσατέ μοι εἶναι τὸν κόσμον, αὐτὸ δὲ τὸ μέσον τοῦ κύκλου τὸν Θεόν, τὰς δὲ εὐθείας τὰς ἀπὸ τοῦ κύκλου ἐπὶ τὸ μέσον τὰς ὁδοὺς ἤτοι τὰς πολιτείας τῶν ἀνθρώπων. Ἐφ᾽ ὅσον οὖν εἰσέρχονται οἱ ἅγιοι ἐπὶ τὰ ἔσω ἐπιποθοῦντες ἐγγίσαι τῷ Θεῷ κατὰ ἀναλογίαν τῆς εἰσόδου, πλησίον γίνονται τοῦ Θεοῦ καὶ ἀλλήλων· καὶ ὅσον πλησιάζουσι τῷ Θεῷ, πλησιάζουσιν ἀλλήλοις, καὶ ὅσον πλησιάζουσιν ἀλλήλοις, πλησιάζουσι τῷ Θεῷ ... καὶ ὅσον ἑνούμεθα τῷ πλησίον, τοσοῦτον ἑνούμεθα τῷ Θεῷ (6.78.6–14,24–25).

and way of life join philosophers and ascetics, including practices of meditation and cognitive discipline through the practice or remembrance of death and the related claim that true knowledge requires spiritual and psychic purification. Such similarity goes beyond ways of life – which in any case differed markedly between philosophers and ascetics in late antiquity – to include many shared epistemic assumptions and commitments.

Nonetheless, Dorotheus' epistemology differs in decisive ways from contemporary Neoplatonism, given that different theological foundations result in a conception of godlikeness not found in the *Prolegomena*. For Dorotheus, humility becomes the governing epistemic virtue both because of the gulf which separates humanity from God and because humility characterises the God who humbles himself. Hence restoration of human nature – to accurate perception, true knowledge, and ethical freedom in the image of God – irreducibly includes humility. Since knowledge is a gift rather than something the monk can attain through his own intellectual capacity, godlikeness is revealed in humility rather than in autonomous rationality. Humility, then, replaces reason as the means of unifying virtues or as the governing criterion of true knowledge, while the possibility of genuine knowledge comes under greater pressure than it does in the epistemic world of the *Prolegomena*. This pressure generates distinctive ascetic epistemic practices designed to counter self-deception and error. Prayer, examination of conscience, remembrance of death, confession, and dependence on epistemic authorities all fit within this doubt about how trustworthy claims to knowledge can be. Yet there is also optimism. Humility includes the recognition that God and therefore his creatures have more to disclose. Hence, genuine humble knowledge includes both a motivation to seek ever greater knowledge and the recognition of the genuine otherness of the object of knowledge, even as, in love, humans are united to each other as they are united to God.

While Dorotheus does not reflect in detail on the theological foundations for such claims, Nicene theology and its concomitant anthropology supports his epistemology. God is immediately and providentially present, so history and nature, imbued as they are by narratives of faith, are revelatory. Recognition of the divine transcendent presence generates humility and codes knowledge as gift rather than achievement, revising metaphors of intellectual ascent to godlikeness to include the ever-humble created intellect. Ascetic attempts to exercise reason and order souls and communities cannot succeed without divine action and gift – hence the importance of baptism – although such effort is required in turning towards God. Dorotheus' epistemology thus resonates with contemporary philosophy while also witnessing to Christian innovations becoming embedded in ascetic culture.

31 | Bureaucratic Modes of Knowing in the Late Roman Empire

SARA AHBEL-RAPPE

Introduction: Bureaucracy in the Late Roman Empire

The epistemological function of what I will call Proclus' bureaucratic approach to ontology is the subject of my inquiry. We meet in Proclus a taxonomic approach to epistemology itself, one in which the ordering power of the mind is projected on a cosmic level, in terms that must at least remind us of the delegation of power that we see in the governmental deployment of *imperium*, the right of command. In order to pursue this line of comparison, it will be helpful to notice a prominent form of knowledge-making in the fourth through sixth centuries, appearing in the form of texts that enumerate lists, ranks, offices, and power dynamics, whether these systems are deployed for governmental agencies, metaphysical schemata, celestial realms, or ecclesiastical orders. Texts such as the *Notitia Dignitatum*, the 'List of Offices',[1] John Lydus' *On the Magistracies of Rome*[2]),[3] Proclus' *Elements of Theology*, or Book 3 of the *Platonic Theology* (which logs an elaborate system of divinities initiating causal chains) have more than a little in common. At the same time, there are contemporaneous treatises that make explicit the relationship between Roman government and the taxonomies of power that belong to the deep ontology of

---

I am grateful to Jonathan Zecher for inviting me to participate in this seminar and to all of my distinguished fellow participants. My thanks also go to Michael Champion and Matthew Crawford for their helpful comments on a previous draft. I also am grateful to Professor David Potter, University of Michigan, for his help in thinking about Roman bureaucracy and to Dr Donka Markus, University of Michigan, for her views on Proclus' theurgy. It goes without saying that all views and errors are entirely my own.

[1] *Notitia Dignitatum* (1999) is a late fourth-century to early fifth-century CE document that enumerates the administrative system of the late Roman empire, describing several thousand offices.

[2] Ioannes Lydus (1983) is a historical-personal narrative fusion written by a retired official who served forty years in the imperial service.

[3] See Kelly 2004: 14: 'After retiring from the prefecture John devoted himself to writing a history of the Empire's administration from the foundation of Rome by its first king, Romulus, to the reign of the Emperor, Justinian. It aimed not only to outline developments in government over thirteen centuries but also to argue for the continued significance of ancient Roman practices and traditions.'

the cosmos, such as Dionysius' *Ecclesiastical Hierarchy* or the anonymous Justinianic *Dialogue on Political Science* (which Cameron ascribes to the *magister officiorum* Peter the Patrician).[4] Finally, late antique treatises on virtue ethics explicitly reserve a category of *political* virtues that not only is preliminary to the contemplative virtues but also defines political life in terms of the larger ethical project of Neoplatonism, assimilation to the divine as far as possible.[5]

The parallels between bureaucratic regimes both metaphysical and political are not simply taxonomic, but also dynamic, deploying cross-over forms of discourse and textuality, surveying methods of government and systems of rank, and framing the parallel projects of metaphysics and governance in light of each other. As we know, the basic feature of bureaucratic organisation is a hierarchy of positions in the organisation. Hierarchy is a system of ranking various positions in descending scale from top to bottom of the organisation. In bureaucratic organisation, offices follow the principle of hierarchy, such that each lower office is subject to control and supervision by higher office. No office is left uncontrolled. This hierarchy, by means of the delegation of authority, entails that communication coming down or going up must pass through each successive position.

When we look at the structure of Proclean ontology, it seems obvious that such a bureaucratic model of reality is on offer. Hierarchic ranking, explicitly understood and explained by Proclus in terms of the devolution of power, results in his novel use of the term *dunamis*.[6] The notion of *archai* (offices or loci), conceived as ontologically stable but individually fungible, functions as a bureaucratic structure in his philosophy. Specific comparisons to Roman bureaucracy of the late fourth century include a geographic element, attached to the global expanse of pagan religious affiliations; a repetitive or even a superfluous deployment of sub-offices; and a technical vocabulary that specifically hails a regionally aligned or functionally determined, but nevertheless impersonal holding place in the overall taxonomy of being.

While scholars of Roman government theorise about the causes of this explosion in officialdom and scholars of Neoplatonism theorise about the causes of Proclus' expansive image of the intelligible world, we might wonder what advantage we gain by placing these proliferative world orders

---

[4] Cameron 1985: 251.
[5] On the political structure of late antique virtue theory, see O'Meara 2003: 73–138.
[6] Gersh (1973: 27–48) discusses the concept of power (*dunamis*) extensively in the philosophy of Proclus.

side by side.[7] This method may initially seem to allow, at best, a recursive analysis. We can speculate that the hierarchy of Roman imperial bureaucracy provided a perfect model for Proclus' conception of the flow of power through the stations of being, all declining from the one *archē*, the monadic principle and source of all lesser powers. In turn, we might speculate that the Roman imperial model – a hierarchy of officialdom punctuated by ceremony that is sacramental in its nomenclature and characterised by the pre-eminence of rank over the individual occupant of a given station – is informed by a Greek thought-world wherein taxonomy is everything. But rather than asking about the direction of influence, this chapter will instead seek to understand the epistemological implications of Proclus' metaphysical taxonomy.[8]

What interests me is Proclus' philosophical *oeuvre* as a whole. I want to ask if what we observe is Proclus' investment in the institutionalisation of metaphysics as an intellectual structure. In emphasising hierarchy and insisting on its prolific description, Proclus privileges soul's activity, which in the philosophy of Proclus consists in a descriptive or unfolding capacity. Therefore, by preserving a structural analysis of being, one might think that this philosophy ultimately works against the liberational aspirations of Neoplatonism as a philosophy of freedom, of helping the person detach from her limits as a particular being and allowing the stifling grasp of fate to loosen its hold on the destiny of the soul. Ultimately, Neoplatonism is devoted to the Platonic principle that the individual or particular being is not the self in the truest sense. But what we find in this bureaucracy is an epistemology where the individual soul comes to know its place in the vast edifices of a sprawling spiritual structure. Could it be that Proclus' didactic purpose is at odds with his anagogical commitments? Admittedly, there is another side of Proclus' philosophy, developed alongside the discursive branch, which celebrates the liturgical performance of theurgy as a method of recovering a lost proximity to the origin or principle of all things. Whether or not the increasingly preponderant bureaucratisation of the empire is related to this muted emphasis on freedom as the essence of the One is an open question. However, I do find that this theurgic path through consecrated

---

[7] What strikes the reader about both sets of data is the sudden and enormous increase in the sheer number of offices (*archai*). Of the later Roman bureaucracy, Smith (2007: 180) writes, 'Estimates of the total size of the bureaucracy in the mid to late fourth century, by contrast, put it at around 35,000, of whom perhaps as many as 6,000 held "upper-level" posts that presupposed senatorial status or automatically conferred it. The increase is very striking: three to four times as many posts overall, and at the upper level perhaps up to twenty times as many.'

[8] At the same time, I wish to leave room for the idea that philosophy of government is understood as part of a larger philosophical project, at least by late antique political thinkers. This is the thesis of O'Meara 2003.

activity and unitive prayer leaves aside a fundamental Platonic tenet, the insistence that the truest nature of the human self is our capacity to know.[9]

In what follows, I explore these questions, comparing and contrasting important texts that enumerate the deployment of power and at the same time offer a way of thinking about reality in the fifth and sixth centuries CE. I show that it is in the very construction of a totalising system, one that extends both horizontally in terms of expanse and vertically in terms of rank, that a bureaucratic way of knowing is realised. The ability to define, control, and locate elements within the totalising system constitutes the pinnacle of this bureaucratic epistemology, whether for the governmental official or the metaphysician. In the first section of this chapter, I survey elements of Proclus' metaphysics, the definition of knowledge in Proclus' system, and the limits of that knowledge. In the second section, I outline important similarities between, on the one hand, the literature of official lists and, on the other hand, Proclus' theological and ontological descriptions of his system in the *Elements of Theology* and *Platonic Theology*; I emphasise the elements of repetition, subordination, superfluity, and localisation. In the third section, I explore principles governing the taxonomy, especially the relationship between hierarchy and specialisation, as well as the mechanisms of bureaucratic control. In the conclusion, I discuss sixth-century developments in both Christian and polyteist discourse that constitute, despite their similarities, a possible insurgency against the Proclean system.

But first let us glimpse, however briefly, the relationship between ontology and political philosophy in the sixth century.[10] In an anonymous and fragmentary Justinianic dialogue on political science, after the end of the fifth *logos*, a table of contents announces the themes treated in the remaining parts of the dialogue. Among the chapter headings we find:

ὅτι δεῖ τὸν ὄντως βασιλέα πρὸς μίμησιν θ(εο)ῦ καὶ τῶν θείων κυβερνᾶν τὰ ἀνθρώπινα.

That the true king must govern human affairs by looking to imitate God and the divine realm.

And

πῶς ἂν γινώσκοι ἑαυτὸν καὶ θ(εὸ)ν καὶ τὰ θεῖα, καὶ γινώσκων πρὸς τὸ παράδειγμα κυβερνῴη τὴν πολιτείαν.

---

[9] For example, in *Alcibiades I*, the dialogue concerning knowledge of the 'self itself', Socrates recommends that Alcibiades introspect 'that by which he knows' as the one key to self-knowledge (*Alcibiades I* 133b6).

[10] See most importantly, Mazzucchi 1982. On the dialogue see especially Cameron 1985: 250–51, who dates the dialogue to *c.* 565 CE and sees it as expressing the viewpoint of the senatorial elite. See also O'Meara: 2002.

How if [the king] knows himself, together with God and the divine realm, he should govern in such a way that the constitution looks to the paradigm.

This political language has obvious affiliations with the *Republic*, as well as with popular political manifestoes such as the roughly contemporaneous *Mirror of Princes* by Agepetus. In a fragment discussed by O'Meara, the interlocutor Meno says:

God, providing by means of his great beneficence for the exile of the race of humankind which he ordained from their homeland above into this worldly realm, for the sake of good governance here below established and contrived a divine method, by which I mean political science, through which one might, progressing upwards through the designated cycle of the seasons, attain to the motherland above, to the merit of the immortal constitution.[11]

The long, winding ascent through the ranks and over time, the use of the political order to heal our separation from the highest god, and the conception of political science itself as a divine revelation – this kind of thinking brings the political and spiritual hierarchies in close alignment.

The other example I would like to consider is the writing of John of Lydus, who presents himself as a remote disciple – or, rather, as a member of the scholastic chain – of Proclus. In Book 3 of his *Peri Archon* (*On Magistracies*), Lydus tells the reader about his path to the imperial service, a decision about which he has come to harbour some regrets (3.25.173). He writes (3.26.173.17):

In order, however, that I might not seem to suffer the loss of the intervening time [*sc.* before his service began] I decided to frequent a philosopher's school. It was Agapius at that time, about whom the poet Christodorus in his one-volume work *On the Disciples of the Great Proclus* even says that 'Agapius is assuredly last but chief of all'. I had the good fortune to hear also some lectures on Platonic philosophy under him.

It is remarkable that Lydus draws attention to his membership in the school of Proclus and sees this affiliation as a fitting preparation for what then happened, as fortune intervened and 'thrust [John] rather into this service'. Indeed, Lydus' reflections about the illusory nature of his imagined

---

[11] My translation. Text: Mazzucchi 1982. ὡς ἄρα θεὸς διὰ πολλὴν (ἀγαθότητα προνοούμενος τῆς ἀποικίας τοῦ γένους τῶν ἀνθρώπων, ἣν ἀπὸ τῆς ἄνω πατρίδος ἐν τῷδε τοῦ παντὸς τόπῳ ἀποικισάμενος διετάξατο, τῆς τῶν τῇδε ἕνεκα εὐκοσμίας ἐμηχανήσατο θεία(ν) τινὰ μέθοδον, τὴν πολιτικήν φημι γνῶσιν, δι' ἧς ἄ(ν) δύναιτο ταῖς τεταγμέναις τῶν καιρῶν περιόδοις ἐπανιόντες τὴν ἄνω μητρόπολιν ἀπολαβεῖν, τὴν τῆς ἀθανάτου πολιτείας ἀξίαν. Discussion in O'Meara 2002.

rewards for such a long career – he says that he 'obtained nothing from it by way of consolation' (173.8) – signal for this reader, at least, an ominous foreboding to the bureaucratic way as ultimately not perhaps the most fulfilling career choice, whether in government or, even more consequentially, in one's spiritual career. Sometimes, playing it safe turns out to be dangerous. Or so I worry.

The Epistemology of Proclus

Proclus Diadochus is best known for his *Elements of Theology*,[12] an aphoristic work that sets out the basic principles of Neoplatonic metaphysics in a systematic presentation that is (arguably, at least) modelled on Euclid's *Elements*.[13] Proclus elaborates what, by comparison, is Plotinus' austere view of the unseen world (One, Intellect, Soul) into a complex and intricate series of triads that are characterised in various ways, principal among which are the intelligible triad of limit, unlimited, and mixed (with the mixed, or Being, itself the head of a triad that consists in Being, Life, and Intellect). These ontological triads are complemented and informed by the dynamic triad of procession, remaining, and reversion.

Proclus defines the One as the cause of all things, as causing that which it itself does not possess, through the doctrine according to which 'every cause properly so-called transcends its effects' (*ET*, prop. 75). For Proclus, the entire procession of effects from their original cause flows backwards towards the source in a circuit that ultimately allows the lower to function as, in some sense, the dispatch of the higher: 'every effect simultaneously proceeds, remains, and reverts to its cause'.

How then does the cause return to or revert upon its effect? In order to understand the process of reversion in greater detail, it is necessary to discuss the vertical and horizontal gradations that allow both differentiation and ranking among similar kinds of reality and distinction and hierarchy between superior and subordinate kinds of realities. For Proclus, multiplicity, the proliferation of effects from their causes, can be studied as internal and external, as uniform and heteroform procession, or as horizontal and vertical procession. Proclus refers to 'procession and multiplication as the

---

[12] Some of these summaries are taken from previous publications: Ahbel-Rappe 2010 (Prolegomenon) and Ahbel-Rappe 2014.

[13] For a critique of this simplistic frame, see Gerson and Martijn 2017.

external activity of an entity, and reversion and unification as its internal activity'.[14] At *ET* 108, Proclus sketches these two kinds of profusion:

> Every particular member of any order can participate the monad of the rank immediately superjacent in one of two ways: either through the universal of its own order, or through the particular member of the higher series which is co-ordinate with it in respect of its analogous relation to that series as a whole.

This sentence is imposing and sounds quite abstract, but a simple example illustrates these two kinds of procession. Suppose that the hypostasis Intellect proceeds horizontally into various lesser forms of intellect (the demiurgic and human intellects). Suppose further that Intellect also proceeds vertically (declines) into a lesser hypostasis, Soul, while the Soul hypostasis itself proceeds horizontally into the various members of that hypostasis.

Each member of these series can revert in each of two ways: vertically (Soul reverts to Intellect) or horizontally (Soul reverts to or within its own hypostasis, becoming in a sense most profoundly itself). Either way, Intellect's reversion to the One does not result in the disappearance of Intellect. Instead, reversion enables the effect to become most distinctively itself: it achieves its essence, its definition, its formal nature, by engaging in the internal act that is most appropriate to itself. For Proclus, reversion to the cause takes place according to the three channels or aspects of the intelligible order: Being, Life, and Intellect. Thus, reversion to the cause results in the complete realisation of, e.g., the human soul as a living, intelligent being possessed of self-knowledge and fully cognisant of its eternal source.[15]

We see then that not only does Proclus suggest that the One is the cause of all things and that every cause transcends its effects, but he also provides a 'circular' model of causation according to which, 'every effect remains in its cause, proceeds from it, and reverts upon it' (*ET*, prop. 35).[16] Yet the strength of Proclus' system is perhaps also its weakness. The terms of the procession can never be reversed, as reversion itself entails a strengthening of identity with respect to the being that reverts to the higher, receiving its good and fulfilling its nature through that very reversion. Proclus' Soul, in reverting to its ultimate source, the One, is able according to the metaphysics of Proclus, to realise a kind of unification with the divine, an act that

---

[14] Lloyd 1990: 33. Lloyd cites the example of *PT* 5.18.283–84. The demiurge addresses the younger gods and his words are described 'as the external activity of the intellect; for they "make the indivisible proceed to divisible existence"' (1990: 33).
[15] On the Soul's reversion to Intellect, see Chlup 2012: 86–87, quoting *ET* 70.8–19.
[16] The classic work is Gersh 1973; see now the excellent treatment of Chlup 2012: section 2.2.

takes place when the soul actualises its own 'centre', as Proclus calls it, but reverts to the transcendent. As he describes this process in the *In Parm.*, Proclus suggests that the formal boundaries between Soul and first principle in fact strengthen Soul in its otherness, its ontological station apart from that principle:[17]

> We must awaken the One in us in order that we might able, if it is permissible to say this, to know somehow what is like [us] with what is like [that], within the parameter of our own ontological station (*taxis*). (*In Parm.* 1081.5).[18]

Proclus emphasises the ontological distance between the One in us and the One *qua* transcendent principle. The upshot is that even this highest form of union, where the soul awakens the faculty that is most akin to the One, also at the same time recommits Soul to its identity as other than the One; as ontologically inferior and as eternally, even irremediably, belonging to a different order or rank. In *ET* 31, Proclus repeats what is essentially Plotinus' understanding of procession and reversion: procession grants existence; reversion grants essence. Proclus' metaphysics of Being emphasises a hierarchical world: Soul visits, as it were, its source in the One. It catches a glimpse of that ultimate principle but accepts its place in the cosmic chain. As Chlup describes the overall activity of the Soul, 'it is only in projecting its logoi that the soul acts as a self-moving entity, unfolding its essence step-by-step'.[19]

Because the resources of the Soul are exhausted in its relationship to the *logoi* that inform its activity, whether *in nuce* as the Soul finds them when it reverts to Intellect or fully expressed in discursive thinking as Soul acts to project the contents of Intellect in its temporal life, Soul offers at most a representation of reality, a picture of the whole that is necessarily partial and fragmentary. Proclus tells us that 'soul possesses by derivation the irradiations of the intellectual forms' (*ET* 194 corollary), which it has 'after the manner of an image' (*ET* 195).

This overview of Proclus' metaphysics leaves us, as we saw, with a certain confusion about what is at stake for the soul, for the knower. On the one hand, Proclus' larger vision of the soul's destiny clearly posits a return to its source. Primarily, we see this bias towards unity not so much through the epistemological resources of the soul, but rather in modalities that escape the intellective plane. Proclus captures the restoration of the individual self

---

[17] On the ontological boundaries of the soul in its contact with the One, see Chlup 2012: 174–84.
[18] δέον ἀνεγείρειν τὸ ἐν ἡμῖν ἕν, ἵνα τῷ ὁμοίῳ τὸ ὅμοιον, εἰ θέμις εἰπεῖν, γνῶναί πως κατὰ τὴν ἡμετέραν τάξιν δυνατοὶ γενώμεθα.
[19] Chlup 2012: 147.

from its fragmentation and isolation, a state that, as we saw, cannot be healed through knowing, in terms that are rather religious than philosophical. It is especially in Book 1 of the *Platonic Theology*, when Proclus is addressing the One, not as *archē*, as metaphysical principle, but in metaphors that might return us to Plotinus' earlier methods, that we find the idea of union with the highest god. For example, in celebrating the Henadic reality of beauty (*kallos*), the aspect of the divine that inspires longing for the divine, Proclus describes union in terms that go far beyond the bureaucratic language of hierarchy. He writes that '[beauty] peeks out from the ineffable unification with the gods and as it were floats on the light of the forms, allows the intelligible light to shine out, and reveals the secret message of goodness, which Plato describes as "luminous, brilliant, and illuminating"' (1.24.108.16–20). Here Proclus reveals that it is actually not only through wisdom, but also through faith (*pistis*) and love (*eros*) that all things are 'saved' (*sozetai*, 1.25.113.4), that is, 'joined with the primordial causes' by means of the theurgic power.[20] Insofar as Proclus relies on these extra-intellectual virtues, his philosophy suggests a powerful comparison and perhaps parallel to the Christian religion to which he referred in code as 'the prevailing ideology'.[21]

The Offices of the Later Roman Empire

So far we have seen that Proclus' philosophy cuts in two directions: he departs significantly from the Platonic commitment to the path of knowledge as the path of liberation. In return, he offers an elaborate ontology that maps the stations and transit trajectories of any being within the system, and at the same time, *celebrates* this very description as an essential dimension of Platonic philosophy. We could say that this intricate articulation resonates with earlier Platonic pathways, as, for example, in the *Sophist* or the *Philebus*,[22] but I argue that Plato's work on division in terms of linguistic and conceptual networks that derive from discursive activity does not pretend to substitute a map (or even a theological concordance) with the ascent to the Forms that is the heart of his greatest visionary works.

---

[20] Dr Donka Markus drew my attention to this passage and to Proclus' use of the metaphor of light in the *Platonic Theology*.
[21] Saffrey 1979: 553–63.
[22] Indeed, Proclus derives the divine Henads precisely from the writings of Plato in his *Platonic Theology*, as we see in Book 1, chapter 2, where Proclus explains the method that he follows (see below for a translation of this passage).

Now it is time to review some of the systems that proliferate in Proclus' works and, if possible, compare them to the lists of offices that survive from approximately the same period. Proclus describes the complexity of his hierarchy at *Platonic Theology* 3.1, in a chapter that gives an outline of the various Henads, or divine unities, that comprise Proclus' rarefied pantheon. But before we look at specific examples, it will be important to understand the project of the *Platonic Theology* as Proclus outlines it in Book 1:

Initially, this treatise will be divided in three. The first part consists of all of the general intuitions concerning the gods that Plato transmits; my aim is to collect them together and evaluate everywhere their force and soundness; the middle part will consist in an enumeration of the complete ranks of the gods together with their characteristics and their processions, following the rankings of Plato, and referring all of them back to the principles established by the theologians. And in the final part I will elaborate the gods that are scattered and celebrated throughout the writings of Plato, whether hypercosmic or encosmic, arranging this survey of the gods into the universal ranks of the gods. (1.2.9.8, my translation)

In brief, although Proclus everywhere understands the divine as ineffable and transcending reason, insisting that the rational soul cannot grasp the divine unity, his catalogue of divinities in the *Platonic Theology*, a discursive map of the divine mystery, is intrinsically puzzling.

As an example of Proclus' method in theology, we can survey the hypercosmic gods together with the hypercosmic-encosmic gods as follows:[23]

I. Hypercosmic deities:
  1. Demiurgic Triad: Zeus, Poseidon, Pluto
  2. Vitalising Triad: Artemis, Persephone, Athena
  3. Triad of Conversion: Apollo

II. Hypercosmic-encosmic deities:
  1. Demiurgic gods: Zeus, Poseidon, Hephaistos
  2. Guardian gods: Hestia, Athena, Ares
  3. Vitalising gods: Demeter, Hera, Artemis
  4. Elevating gods: Heres, Aphrodite, Apollo

Without getting into a detailed discussion of the functions of all of these gods, a few remarks are in order. Proclus has culled these names from his exegesis of Plato's dialogues and has assigned them functions in the theurgic

---

[23] Table adapted from Westerink and Saffrey 2003 in Proclus: LXVI.

technology that operates for the practitioner who relies on the levers and pulleys of divine influence to arrive, it would seem, at ever greater proximity to the ground of unity.

To explain the theurgic function of the Henadic series or *taxeis*, Proclus shows that each characteristic of a given Henad must be transmitted vertically down through the series, so that at any point in the hierarchy, the divine presence is manifest precisely through its unique nature: 'The distinctive character of any divine order travels through all the derivative existents and bestows itself upon all the inferior kinds' (*ET* 145). One of the principles of this transmission is expressed in a more general rule of Proclean bureaucracy, 'Every order originates from a monad and proceeds into a plurality which is coordinated with the monad' (*ET* 21). Moreover, the ranks of the orders that descend from the deity are held in strict subordination to the immediately superjacent rank through a principle of likeness: 'There will be likeness between the initial principles of the lower order and the last members of the higher' (*ET* 147 corollary).

At this point, it is worth noticing features of this divine bureaucracy and then, as stated earlier, comparing them with the roughly contemporaneous texts of Lydus and the *Notitia*. One obvious feature of the Henadic structure is the use of the word, *archai* (principles), referencing the stations of the various orders that descend from the gods. This word is, of course, the same word that Lydus uses in the title of his study of the imperial bureaucracy 'On Magistracies' (*Peri Archon*). In brief, it seems that Proclus is thinking of these stations as offices, staffed by administrators with decreasing roles of responsibility, a feature captured by Proclus' idea of diminishing causal efficacy of each successive rank.

Repetition of titles in inferior or transverse series is another obvious feature of Proclus' schemes, whether onto- or theo-logical. Reiterative and graduated degrees with assimilative patterning is also a prominent feature. Thus, we have 'Demiurgic Hypercosmic Zeus' and 'Demiurgic Hypercosmic-Encosmic Zeus', both of whom are paired with different deities to complete their respective triads on the different levels. Or, another example, we have Being, Vital Being, and Intelligible Being as a transverse series that anticipates the Being–Life–Intellect Triad that will be expressed lower in the series.

Another dimension of this nomenclature is the assignation of functions, as we see in the above example, elevating gods, demiurgic gods, and vitalising gods, or, in a more complicated scheme, in terms of the theurgic roles that each rank of gods performs. For example, as Majercik explains, Proclus 'conceived the noetic-noeric order as an ennead: in this case, composed of a triad of Teletarchs, a triad of Connectors, and a triad of Iynges'.[24]

This last example illustrates one more feature of Proclus' theological project, and this is its universalising scope, which we may think of as culturally appropriative or, to use jargon that keeps in mind the associations with Roman imperialism, colonising. We saw above that Proclus mines the *Chaldean Oracles* for a nomenclature that will lend a suitably theurgic colouration to his Platonising schema. In fact, Proclus wrote a lost *Commentary on the Oracles* following his teacher, Syrianus, and finds a Chaldean equivalent to every member of his triadic system.[25] This tendency to appropriate the theologies of ancient religions comes to a summit in Damascius' *Problems and Solutions*, who works out an elaborate scheme of equivalencies between Greek, Chaldean, Orphic, Egyptian, and Babylonian divine systems. All the indigenous traditions of the Roman empire turn out to be simply forms of Platonism.

Now it is time for brief comparison with the bureaucratic literature of the Roman empire. Let us consider this paragraph in Lydus' *Magistracies*:

Since the *commentarienses* themselves, whom time produced from the office of speedwriters, also happened to be two in number, as I already stated, six assistants, taken on from the body of the *augustales*, men who were unflinching and exhibited a severity befitting the law, with whom the entire might of the magistracy resided, assisted them, too, just as those before them. These men brought the examinations of criminals to the court of justice. Subalterns to them, as has already been shown, were both *applicitarii* and *clavicularii* along with a host of *lictors* who shook the court of justice with fear by their iron chains and by their assortment of punitive instruments and striking tools. By the deployment, however, of a throng of *ducenarii*, they sufficed to sober up wrongdoers even apart from the authority of the law. (3.16.159)

This paragraph could perhaps be diagrammed along the lines of a taxonomic scheme as follows:

	scriniarii (speed writers)	
	commentariensis	commentariensis
augustales assistant	*augustales* assistant	*augustales* assistant
augustales assistant	*augustales* assistant	*augustales* assistant
applicitarii clavicularii	applicitarii clavicularii	applicitarii clavicularii
lictores	lictores	lictores
ducenarii	ducenarii	ducenarii

---

[24] Majercik 2001.
[25] Majercik 2001: 266; cf. Saffrey 1992.

Also interesting in this paragraph is the philosophy of punishment and respect for the law, the administration of justice through torture combined with an officious description of this office (we might think of it as the office of torture) and the incorporation of the justice department under the larger rubric of the imperial administration.

This arrangement is strikingly familiar to us today, as modern governments also have justice departments and a federal prison system under the larger rubric of federal administration. Consider just how closely Proclus' rules for the divine bureaucracy follow the principles implied in Lydus' survey. For example, the governmental offices expressly operate through the transmission of power and authority; the same arrangement governs the procession of the *archai* in Proclus' system. Again, the progression is towards the increasingly material: under the office of justice as an abstract concept, employing the class of scribes as its head, come the throngs of enforcers who wield their material instruments of bodily torture, since the power dynamics of justice manifest in the physical world as enforced through violence. Likewise, the devolution of power in its most material terms is the very essence of the Proclean system.

Let us turn, finally, to the document known as the *Notitia Dignitatum*, composed in two phases at the end of the fourth century and beginning of the fifth. In what follows, although many obvious parallels can be noted, I would like to call attention to the necessary element of geography, since, after all, the Roman empire existed as a global network, bringing together physical regions and their peoples under an ideological system of hierarchy that nevertheless used concrete methods of exchange to deploy its control. In like manner, we might compare the entire structure of Proclus' metaphysics, which after all, functions in some sense as an explanation for the various kinds of life that flourish under the offices of a globalising theology, whose divine regents can be contacted under the titles of their provincial designations.[26]

II. THE PRETORIAN PREFECT OF THE EAST
Under the control of the illustrious praetorian prefect of the East are the dioceses below mentioned:
    of the East; of Egypt; of Asia; of Pontus; of Thrace.
Provinces:
    of [the diocese of] the East fifteen:
        Palestine; Phoenice; Syria; Cilicia; Cyprus; Arabia (also a duke and a military count); Isauria; Palaestina salutaris; Palaestina secunda; Phoenice Libani; Euphratensis; Syria salutaris; Osroena; Mesopotamia; Cilicia secunda.

---

[26] *Notitia Dignitatum* 1.2. Translation from Fairley 1899, 5–7. For the Greek edition, see Ireland 1999.

of [the diocese of] Egypt five:
  upper Libya; lower Libya; Thebais; Egypt; Arcadia.
of [the diocese of] Asia ten:
  Pamphylia; Hellespontus; Lydia; Pisidia; Lycaonia; Phrygia Pacatiana; Phrygia salutaris; Lycia; Caria; the Islands.
of [the diocese of] Pontus ten:
  Galatia; Bithynia; Honorias; Cappadocia prima; Cappadocia secunda; Pontus Polemoniacus; Helenopontus; Armenia prima; Armenia securida; Galatia salutaris.
of [the diocese of] Thrace six.
  Europa; Thracia; Heemimontus; Rhodopa; Moesia secunda, Scythia.
The staff of the illustrious praetorian prefect of the East:
  chief of staff (*princeps*)
  chief deputy (*cornicularius*)
  chief assistant (*adiutor*)
  custodian (*commentariensis*)
  keeper of the records (*ab actis*)
  receivers of taxes (*numerarii*)
  assistants (*subadiuuae*)
  a curator of correspondence (*cura epistolarum*)
  a registrar (*regerendarius*)
  secretaries (*exceptores*)
  aids (*adiutores*)
  notaries (*singularii*)

In this section of the chapter, I have demonstrated the parallel features of the kind of knowledge-making that flourished in the later Roman empire, whose fundamental mechanism was the metaphor of officialdom – of *archai* (offices) able to represent, enforce, and make accessible imperial rule. Crucial to both imperial government and Proclus' metaphysics is the communicative function, the scribal dimension that conveys the power structure to members of the order. Likewise, soul itself is assigned the task of translating or even publishing the atemporal, timeless truths of the eternal order into discursive sentences that can be communicated from individual to individual.[27]

Some Rules for Governing

We have already begun to touch on the way that power is deployed in a bureaucratic regime, with authority devolving in increasingly smaller

---

[27] See also Chapter 32 by Peter Sarris, this volume.

increments that simultaneously approach a greater degree of localisation, physicality, and concretisation. Another principle that operates in later Roman bureaucracy is the rule of remoteness, which preserves the specialisation of each office while at the same time ensuring that the higher echelons of power are inaccessible except to near peers. The chief instance of isolation is the One itself (the emperor), the first principle that deploys only through its subordinates and can, as we saw, merely be glimpsed in a brief audience by the lowest members of the spiritual taxonomy, which is to say, human souls. Again, let us recall that, according to Proclus: 'there will be likeness between the initial principles of the lower order and the last members of the higher' (*ET* 147 corollary). In other words, to communicate with a higher level one must have access, and this access is determined by sharing in the characteristic features of the higher class.

To return to the anonymous *Dialogue on Political Science*, we read that 'kingship is the foundation of political light which is communicated, by a scientific method, to the ranks subordinated to it in the state, rank after rank, so that each rank shares in knowledge of the rank above it that rules it' (27.7–15). As O'Meara comments, this fragment reflects 'a fundamental theory of Neoplatonic metaphysics, the theory of a series of terms in which the first member of the series pre-contains and produces the other members of the series', a feature we have already glimpsed in Proclus.[28]

But let us get clearer on the rule of remoteness, according to which, at least in the anonymous *Dialogue*, 'the ruler will deal only with his immediate subordinates and they will transmit his providential rule'.[29] In Proclus, we find this axiom expressed in *ET* 108: 'Every particular member of any order can participate in the monad of the rank immediately suprajacent in one of two ways: either through the universal of its own order, or through the particular member of the higher series which is co-ordinate with it'. As Chlup writes, 'a significant consequence of Proclus' model is that participation always takes place through plurality. If the level of soul is said to "participate in Intellect", it does not really participate in Monadic intellect but in its various aspects'.[30] As *ET* 98 reminds us, 'every cause which is separate from its effects is enthroned above all alike and resides in no being inferior to itself'.

---

[28] O'Meara 2002: 54.
[29] O'Meara 2002, commenting on 26.23–27.
[30] Chlup 2012: 102.

Postscript: After Proclus – Developments in the Sixth Century

As we move into the sixth century, Proclus' influence is everywhere, perhaps no more so than in the *Celestial* and *Ecclesiastical Hierarchy* of Pseudo-Dionysius, which applies the metaphysical proliferation of late antique Neoplatonism to the political and liturgical structures of the church, in a way that directly recalls the anonymous *Dialogue*.[31] As this volume concerns the taxonomies of knowledge in late antiquity, and especially the epistemological structures of Christianity in relationship to predecessor cultures, it would be remiss not to notice parallel developments in the *Ecclesiastical* and *Celestial Hierarchy* of Pseudo-Dionysius.[32] For example, in a passage that reads as if it could have been written by Proclus himself, Dionysius describes the celestial hierarchy in terms of a triad of triads (200D):

> The word of God (*theologia*) has provided nine explanatory designations for the heavenly beings, and my own divine initiator has divided these into three triadic groups. This threefold group, says my distinguished teacher, forms a single hierarchy which is truly first and whose members are of equal status. No other is more like the divine or receives more directly the first enlightenment from the Deity. The second group, he says, is made up of 'Authorities', 'Dominions', and 'Powers'; and the third, at the end of the heavenly hierarchies, is the group of angels, archangels, and principalities.[33]

Perl remarks on a feature of Dionysius' hierarchy – a term that the Christian writer actually coined – that we have already glimpsed in Proclus as follows:

> The principle that in any hierarchy the same perfection or activity is analogously present throughout all the levels is evident in Dionysius' accounts of the angelic and the ecclesiastical hierarchies. In the *Celestial Hierarchy*, he explains that the name of a higher level may be applied to a lower because 'just as the first [i.e. the higher ranks of angels] possess eminently the holy befitting properties of the lower, so the later possess those of the earlier, not in the same way, but in a lesser way'.[34] (*CH* 12.2, 293B)

One striking Proclean borrowing that we find throughout the Dionysian sacred order is the centrality of power as the fundamental character of

---

[31] O'Meara 2003.
[32] See Dylan Burns' excellent summary of scholarship, which demonstrates the clear dependence of Pseudo-Dionysius on the metaphysics of Proclus (2019). Burns cites, among other scholars, Saffrey 1990 and Beierwaltes 1997.
[33] Trans. Dillon 2014, modified.   [34] Perl 2007: 71.

the divine character that pervades it. Dionysius writes that 'the power of the hierarchic [i.e. episcopal] order pervades all the sacred totalities, and through all the sacred order effects the mysteries of its own hierarchy' (*EH* 5.1.5, 505AB). Finally, Dionysius agrees with Proclus that the epistemological divisions that delineate the diversity of beings present in the spiritual world must be transcended in the union with the divine that itself transcends knowledge:

Leave behind sense-perceptions and intellectual activities and all sensible and intelligible things and all non-beings and beings, and be lifted up unknowingly toward the union, as far as possible, of that which is above all being and knowledge; for by the irresistible and absolute ecstasy, purely, from yourself and all things, you will be led up to the ray beyond being of the divine darkness, taking away all things and being loosed from all things.[35] (*MT* 1.1, 997B–1000A)

Nor did Proclus have the last word. True, the metaphysics of bureaucracy could never be erased from the last phase of the post-Platonic academy. Nevertheless, in his *Problems and Solutions Concerning First Principles*, the last scholarch of the Academy, Damascius, takes aim at the rules of governance that undergird Proclus' entire project.[36] The spiritual circuit, the return of all to the One and especially the Soul's special function as a conduit of this return, is the crucial premise of Neoplatonism insofar as it constitutes a religion. What, after all, is the place of the human self in this cosmic drama of the One's radiance and of attaining to the goal of wisdom, which is to uncover a vision of the whole? The Soul's destiny is to return to the One, not just in the sense that the Soul will develop wisdom or knowledge but also in the sense that the Soul becomes instrumental in the completion of the spiritual circuit. Yet how the Soul accomplishes this very journey is exactly the problem entailed by the system that, as it were, underwrites it. This anxiety pervades Damascius' criticisms.

In attempting to undermine the metaphysics of Being developed by Proclus, Damascius will appear to be a David, flinging shots against the towering system of Proclus. He can sound even more scholastic, almost pointlessly refining the language of metaphysics in order to bring down a creative edifice that, after all, remains a celebration of the divine nature of Being, of the sanctity of the cosmos as a whole.

Yet, in my view, Damascius performs a crucial role in the tradition he inherits. He shifts the perspective of his metaphysics. Instead of creating

---

[35] Trans. Wear, in Wear and Dillon 2007: 96.
[36] These remarks on Damascius are adapted from Ahbel-Rappe 2014.

an objective ontology, Damascius writes ever mindful of the limitations of dialectic and of the pitfalls and snares inherent in the very structure of metaphysical discourse:

> If, in speaking about [the Ineffable], we attempt the following collocations, viz. that it is Ineffable, that it does not belong to the category of all things, and that it is not apprehensible by means of intellectual knowledge, then we ought to recognise that these constitute the language of our own labors. This language is a form of hyperactivity that stops on the threshold of the mystery without conveying anything about it at all. Rather, such language announces the subjective experiences of *aporia* and misapprehension that arise in connection with the One, and that not even clearly but by means of hints.[37] (Peri Archon 1.8.11–16)

For Damascius, like so many of his philosophical predecessors, beyond the discourse of metaphysics lies the empty ground of wisdom, rooted in the unconditioned reality that is the One. Epistemology, bureaucracy, and officialdom, together with their institutions, can only take us so far on the path to truth, it turns out. There is a surer, less labyrinthine path, that skirts the official checkpoints and name checking about which Proclus and John Lydus obsess. As Plotinus succinctly puts the matter, referencing the One, the divine nature that underlies all metaphysics and underwrites all knowledge:

> ἀλλ' ὅταν αὐτὸν εἴπῃς ἢ ἐννοηθῇς, τὰ ἄλλα πάντα ἄφες. Ἀφελὼν πάντα, καταλιπὼν δὲ μόνον αὐτόν.

> When you speak of Him, or when you conceive Him, throw away everything else! Throw away everything else and you are left with Him alone![38] (VI.8.21.26)

---

[37] Trans. Ahbel-Rappe 2010.   [38] My rather free translation.

32 | The Dissemination and Appropriation of Legal Knowledge in the Age of Justinian

PETER SARRIS

Introduction: Majesty and Tyranny

In the year 533 CE, in the imperial capital of Constantinople, the emperor Justinian promulgated his *Institutes* – an introductory legal textbook designed for those studying the law with a view to entering governmental service. In the constitution with which Justinian presented the *Institutes* to the Constantinopolitan public, the emperor set out his ambition that, in his words, 'Imperial Majesty should not only be graced with arms but also armed with laws, so that good government may prevail in time of war and peace alike.' 'The head of the Roman state', Justinian thundered, 'can then stand victorious not only over enemies in war, but also over troublemakers at home.'[1]

In his constitution on 'Imperial Majesty', we see Justinian adopting a posture of autocratic omnipotence that was meant to cow his rivals and intimidate his foes. This rhetorical stance would eventually be inverted and cast back at the emperor in the allegation of *tyranny* at the heart of the historian Procopius' contemporary critique of Justinian's *modus operandi*, as most forcefully set out in his vituperative *Secret History*.[2] And, as a result, modern scholars of the 'Age of Justinian' have sometimes had great difficulty in escaping from the impression of the regime imposed on them by these two superficially contrasting but ultimately interdependent perspectives. Thus, to the late Tony Honoré, writing in the 1970s, Justinian was a prototype Stalin, who imposed a regime of terror on contemporary Constantinople.[3] More recently, Anthony Kaldellis has referred to Justinian's 'totalitarian disposition' and has described the emperor as one whose 'tyranny was modern', whilst Kyle Harper has characterised Constantinople in the Age of Justinian as shaped by insurmountable 'centripetal force … concentrating power in the capital, the bureaucracy, the court – and at the very centre of it all, the divinely chosen figure of the emperor himself.'[4]

---

[1] *C. Imperiam Maiestatem.*   [2] Procopius, *Anecdota.*   [3] Honoré 1978: 28.
[4] Kaldellis 2004: 157; Harper 2017: 199.

In representing the Age of Justinian as an era either of tyranny or of smoothly operating imperial omnipotence, Honoré, Harper, Kaldellis, and others have, however, arguably become intellectually pinned down by the ideological crossfire between Procopius' *Secret History* and Justinian's legislation. For, as indeed both Anthony Kaldellis himself and others have emphasised, much of the final section of Procopius' *Secret History* is driven by piece-by-piece critique of a number of the emperor's laws, and, throughout, his writings are given piquancy by the hostile inversion of motifs deployed by Justinian in his own legislation to convey a positive image of the regime.[5] Hence, the motif of the 'sleepless' emperor, labouring night and day on behalf of his subjects is inverted by Procopius into the image of the sleepless demon king, haunting the palace late at night to the terror of his courtiers. So, for example, when Justinian declares of himself that 'we shun no extreme of discomfort, constantly enduring sleeplessness, fasting, and every other form of hardship for the benefit of our subjects',[6] Procopius responds in his *Secret History* by writing, 'and how could this man fail to be some wicked demon, he who never had a sufficiency of food or drink or sleep?'[7] (*Anecdota* 12.27).

The mutually interdependent rhetorical stances of 'Imperial Majesty' and imperial tyranny have tended to distract historians from the clear evidence that sixth-century Constantinople was home to a lively culture of political debate conducted through the public media of widely advertised imperial laws and, amongst other literary forms, contemporary histories, chronicles, philosophical dialogues, and *ekphrasis*. Some of our best evidence for this, perhaps ironically, is to be found in the writings of Procopius himself. We know for a fact that Procopius' multi-volume *History of the Wars*, detailing Justinian's campaigns against the Persians, Vandals, and Ostrogoths, was widely read. He tells us in the preface to Book 8 that his preceding volumes 'have already been published and have appeared in every corner of the Roman Empire'.[8] Perhaps more significantly, he would be heavily relied upon by the next generation of Byzantine historians, such as Agathias, Evagrius, and Menander Protector, who declared of Procopius 'I am not able, nor do I wish to hold up my candle before such a beam of eloquence.'[9] Yet the *History of the Wars* is replete with sometimes veiled but sometimes extremely obvious criticism of Justinian and his chief ministers, with which one could evidently get away.[10]

---

[5] Kaldellis 2004: 223; Williamson and Sarris 2007: xviii.　　[6] *J. Nov.* 30.
[7] Procopius, *Anecdota* 12.27.　　[8] Procopius, *de Bellis* 8.1.1–2.　　[9] Blockley 1985: 147.
[10] Williamson and Sarris 2007: 19.

One can trace both *pro-regime* and *anti-regime* literature being written and circulated in response to the same events, revealing the contours of what could almost be described as a pamphleteering culture in sixth-century Constantinople through which the 'culture wars' of the period were fought. For example, in 558 CE, the eastern arch supporting the dome of Justinian's great cathedral, Hagia Sophia, collapsed. As I argued over a decade ago, whilst Procopius' treatise *On Buildings* makes no explicit mention of this collapse, it can be inferred that he uses knowledge of it to satirise Justinian and his regime:[11] for, in the seemingly original, fuller recension of this work, he places enormous and quite disproportionate emphasis on the personal role of the emperor himself in designing and constructing the very arch that would collapse in 558 CE, declaring, of that arch, that 'the Emperor, in this way, enjoys a kind of testimonial from the work'.[12] The collapse of the arch and the dome arguably becomes a metaphor for the vanity and failure of the entire Justinianic project. Likewise, the repair of the dome, which was brought down by the collapse of the arch in 558 CE, is the subject of a major piece of contemporary pro-Justinianic propaganda, the *Description of Hagia Sophia* written by the aristocratic *litteraire* Paul the Silentiary.[13]

Perhaps most strikingly in certain of his laws, we see Justinian responding to his contemporary critics, including the writers of contemporary history such as Procopius. In 537 CE, for example, in a law addressed to military legal officers known as *assessores*, Justinian rounds on critics who were accusing him of sowing legal confusion by issuing too many laws:

If they scrutinised the true facts, those whose goal is truth would not lightly resort to criticism. It is probable that some may complain at the large number of laws daily being issued by us, without reflecting that it is the call of necessity that obliges us to enact laws to suit the circumstances when those already enacted cannot provide remedies for the succession of unexpected problems that arise.[14]

'Those whose goal is truth' sounds like a reference to contemporary historians, Procopius having declared in the preface to Book 1 of his *History of the Wars*, for example, that 'while cleverness is appropriate to rhetoric, and inventiveness to poetry, truth alone is appropriate to history'.[15] Procopius was himself an *assessor* at the time this law was issued and so may well have received it; he would, of course, go on to accuse Justinian of exactly the charges the emperor claimed people were levelling at him.[16]

---

[11] Williamson and Sarris 2007: xx.   [12] Procopius, *de Aedificiis* 1.1.78.   [13] Bell 2009: 189–212.
[14] *J. Nov.* 60 pr.   [15] Procopius, *de Bellis* 1.1.4–5.   [16] Procopius, *Anecdota* 6.14; 6.21–22.

Concepts of lawfulness were at the forefront of the political struggles of the age, and it is impossible to make sense of those struggles (and many of the key literary sources that they generated) without paying careful attention to the law. At the same time, as we shall see, the legal systems that were generated and sustained by the broader governmental and social system in the Age of Justinian helped to organise knowledge and associated power structures across the empire and across a wide range of social levels. Consequently, they served to bolster and underpin the institutional, structural, and social mechanisms for the transmission and sustaining of knowledge across a number of related fields – including, but not limited to, those pertaining to religious belief.

The Social Function of Law in the Age of Justinian

In order to fully appreciate the significance of the legal sources, it is important to understand the social function as well as the ideological significance of law in the Roman world. The intellectual and moral discourse of Roman law had always been fundamental to concepts of Roman self-identity. Indeed, as the late Tony Weir emphasised, legal scholars (or 'jurisconsults') had traditionally possessed almost sacerdotal status.[17]

Moreover, in late antiquity, the study of Roman law had become a core component of the intellectual training and professional formation of members of the emergent aristocracy of service who, from the fourth century onwards, began to administer and, increasingly to dominate the empire both economically and socially.[18] As is well known, this educational trend was a cause of great irritation, for example, to the rhetorician Libanius in fourth-century Antioch, who bemoaned the flight of well-born students from the schools of rhetoric to the law school of Berytus.[19] Law and legal thinking thus became engrained in the psychological *habitus* of the elite and inevitably informed the way in which they constructed the world around them and thought metaphorically about even non-legal affairs. In the early fifth century, for example, the Christian author Symeon the Mesopotamian even regarded the relationship between the study of law and a young man's associated advance up the imperial career structure (or *cursus honorum*) as an appropriate analogy for the progress of the soul towards grace.[20] Likewise,

---

[17] Weir 2006: 35–51. [18] Sarris 2006; Banaji 2007. [19] Cribiore 2007.
[20] As noted by Roueché 1998: 34. There are clear parallels with views of hierarchy in the writings of Proclus and John Lydus; see Chapter 31 by Sara Ahbel-Rappe, this volume.

Roman legal vocabulary and an awareness of Roman law would leave a deep imprint on lay documentary practice.[21]

As a result, it is probably impossible to appreciate fully how many late antique authors would have approached concepts such as 'authority' or would have regarded the written word, for example, without an appreciation of their attitude to law and the inherited legal order. The impact of the modes of thought derived from Roman law on late antique theology would, of course, be particularly significant, especially with respect to the 'institutional' literature, and the definition of orthodoxy through the councils and canons.[22] But there is also arguably discernible a close synergy and developmental relationship between legal and philosophical scholarship in late antiquity. This has been frequently noted stylistically with respect to Neoplatonic influences on imperial legislation, but the influence is also likely to have been exerted in the opposite direction too:[23] certainly, by the sixth century, we are dealing with a world in which both philosophy and jurisprudence would be conducted almost entirely through commentary.[24]

The programme of legal codification and reform in which Justinian and his law commissioners were engaged in the early 530s CE, and which would witness, alongside the *Institutes*, the promulgation of the *Codex Iustinianus* and the *Digest* (Justinian's great recasting of the inherited body of imperial constitutions and jurisprudential literature), was thus always bound to raise hackles, for reforming the law was inevitably a sensitive affair. But this fact was then further compounded by the realisation that Justinian was set upon more than simply a reordering of legal knowledge. For whilst the emperor did set out a conservative vision of restoring Roman law to its pristine glory, at the heart of his programme of legal reform was a determined effort to restore the writ of imperial law and the political authority of the emperor at the provincial grassroots of East Roman society.[25]

This would become clear in the years following 534 CE, when Justinian promulgated the second recension of his *Codex*. For, with the programme of legal codification complete, the emperor now sought to take the reformed law to the provinces. Consequently, in the legislation which ensued, he set about overhauling provincial structures and imperial courts of appeal, and cracking down on a range of abuses which Justinian deemed injurious to the state and hence to the public good, or, crucially, injurious to public morality. As a result, from 534 CE, in the legislation that would

---

[21] Sarris 2013. [22] See, for example, discussion in Maas 2003; Humfress 2007.
[23] Lanata 1984. [24] Wildberg 2005. [25] See Sarris 2006: 200–27.

subsequently be collected in his so-called *Novels* or 'new laws' (*novellae constitutiones*), we see the emperor increasingly seeking, with unprecedented fervour, to target, isolate, marginalise, and extirpate those of whom he disapproved or whom he felt threatened his regime. It was for this reason that law and legal reform were so political, with legislation being responded to positively by those who essentially approved of the ideological direction of the regime (such as the author of the *Chronicle of John Malalas*) or negatively by conservative authors who were more critical (such as Procopius or John Lydus).[26]

The 'Orthodox Republic'

Justinian's post-codificatory legislation, taken as whole, can be seen to have been driven by two overriding principles. The first was the emperor's determination to confront and confound those who challenged the authority of the government at a local level, above all by withholding the crucial tax revenues upon which the East Roman state depended. The early sixth century had witnessed the revival of warfare on a massive scale between the Eastern Roman empire and its great superpower rival, the Sasanian empire of Persia. The 530s CE would also see the empire drawn into opportunist wars of reconquest in Africa and Italy, which had been lost to Roman imperial control over the course of the fifth century.[27] Given that, even in periods of peace, it has been estimated that the Roman army received somewhere in the region of one-half to two-thirds of all tax revenues accruing to the Roman state, the revival of warfare on multiple fronts placed mounting fiscal pressure on the Roman government which Justinian addressed by overhauling provincial administration and cracking down on tax-dodging. It is instructive that the period of Justinian's main legislative focus on provincial and fiscal reform witnessed a parallel programme of internal reform in the Sasanian empire of Persia, where the *Shah* Khusro I sought to upgrade the Sasanian empire's fiscal machinery, presumably for identical reasons. A perceived shortfall in imperial tax revenues was further exacerbated in the 540s CE, when the empire found itself struck by the first known outbreak of bubonic plague in the Mediterranean world, a cataclysm which seems to have led to a dramatic diminution in taxpayers (as well as much human misery) and which necessitated a series of legislative responses, extant in the emperor's *Novels*.[28]

---

[26] See Scott 1985; Maas 1992. [27] Sarris 2011a: 125–52. [28] See especially *J. Nov.* 122.

The second great guiding principle, however, was moral rather than fiscal. Even Justinian's fiercest critics were obliged to admit that Justinian was a devout and dogmatic Christian who was determined to press ahead with the full-blown Christianisation of late Roman law and society. As Procopius declared in the preface to his treatise on *Buildings*, 'finding that the belief in God was, before his time, straying into errors and being forced to go in many directions, he [Justinian] completely destroyed all the paths leading to such errors, and brought it about that it stood on the firm foundation of a single faith'.[29] As a result, Justinian's reign would witness not just the agenda, but increasingly the tone and language of Christian homiletic literature, and of the more hard-line Christian moralists such as the fourth-century Cappadocian Fathers, increasingly shaping and determining imperial law. This development would be facilitated by the transition we see in the 530s CE from Latin to Greek as the main legislative language, which made it easier for the prose and mindset of patristic authors to inflect the Greek of the law.[30]

This tendency to infuse the law with greater scriptural solemnity and theological and moralising intent is evident even in the most purely jurisprudential or dryly administrative of the emperor's measures. So, for example, as Caroline Humfress has noted, Justinian had confirmed the promulgation of the *Digest* 'in the name of our Lord God Jesus Christ', thereby symbolically baptising it and, one might add, effectively exorcising the intellectual inheritance of the non-Christian classical jurists whose writings Justinian's law commissioners had edited and pared down.[31] In his *Novel* 8 of 535 CE, with which the emperor overhauled the system of appointment for provincial governors and set about beginning to carve out a new system of provincial administration, he can be seen to adopt a highly hymnographic register, in which the language of imperial law almost morphs into that of the ecclesiastical liturgy. 'We dedicate this law to God', Justinian declares, 'purposing that all may be able to receive their rulers as fathers, rather than as thieves and enslavers.' 'Therefore', he continues, 'let all people alike send up hymns of praise to our great God and Saviour Jesus Christ for this very law … a further reason of our enacting it is to be able to bring ourselves closer to the Lord God, and commend our reign to him … [not allowing] any unjust treatment of the people whom God has entrusted to us.'[32] Officials who failed in their duties were threatened in the same law that they would share 'the fearful judgement of our great Lord and Saviour Jesus

---

[29] Procopius, *de Aedificiis* 1.1.6. [30] Honoré 1978: 125; Millar 2006: 84–96. [31] Humfress 2005.
[32] *J. Nov.* 8 c.11.

Christ ... the lot of Judas, the leprosy of Gehazi, and the dread of Cain'.[33] In particular, in a series of laws on individual provinces, Justinian drew on the biblical language of the mighty and the humble to denounce those provincial and senatorial great landowners – the *dynatoi* – who were most responsible for tax evasion and whose flouting of imperial law in the territory of Cappadocia, for example, made him blush with shame.[34] Thereafter, this biblicised targeting of the 'mighty' would become a standard rhetorical feature of imperial legislation in the Byzantine world, prominent, for example, in the so-called 'land legislation' of the Macedonian emperors of the tenth century.[35]

Across the *Digest*, *Codex*, and the *Novels*, we arguably see the emperor Justinian engaged in a concerted programme effectively to recast the Roman empire and finally to transform it into what historians today would refer to as a 'confessional state'. The opening volume of the *Codex Iustinianus*, in marked contrast to the fifth-century *Codex Theodosianus*, had given pride of place to laws concerned with 'the most exalted Trinity and the catholic faith'. Only once the rights and concerns of the church had been addressed did the *Codex* proceed to those of the state. Crucially, Justinian sought to transform the Roman empire into a state that was officially orthodox and Christian, not only in its ideology and official pronouncements, but also in its interactions with its subjects. Hence, we see him progressively advancing the rights of those most lawful of the emperor's subjects who upheld the imperially sanctioned definition of the Christian faith, whilst curtailing and applying steady downward pressure on the rights of religious and other minorities regarded as outsiders in what Justinian described in an important law of 537 CE as the 'orthodox republic' (*orthodoxos politeia*).[36]

The emperor was thus engaged not only in a codification of law but also in a codification of faith. Indeed, under Justinian, one's rights at civil law were increasingly determined by one's officially reckoned degree of religious conformity. As a result, deliberate efforts were made to marginalise the heterodox and to treat heretics, Jews, Samaritans, and pagans as an undifferentiated mass of second-class citizens, burdened with obligations rather than bearing rights, and declaring them, as Sarah Bond has emphasised, to be *infames*, subject, as Justinian made clear in the law of 537 CE, to the same physical punishments and public degradations as members of the Roman lower classes (known as the *humiliores*), irrespective of their social status, with upper-class heretics and Jews unable to claim

---

[33] Oath appended to end of *J. Nov.* 8. [34] *J. Nov.* 30 c.5. [35] Morris 1976. [36] *J. Nov.* 45 c.1.

privileged physical protection.[37] So, for example, Justinian declared with respect to high-status Jews, heretics, and Samaritans charged with curial civic responsibilities: 'The law allows city councillors numerous privileged exemptions, such as from being beaten, produced for punishment, or deported to another province, and innumerable others; these people are to enjoy none of them ... Their status is to be one of disgrace, which is what they have desired for their souls as well.'[38] In particular, under Justinian, the imperial government sought to make it increasingly difficult for such 'outsiders' within Christian Roman society to maintain familial cohesion and religious identity by transmitting property from one generation to the next, for the emperor's legislation significantly affected their ability to make a will or inherit.

Ominously, the *Codex Iustinianus* expressly dropped the provision contained within the fifth-century Theodosian Code that had granted Judaism the status of a 'licit sect', and Justinian's *Novels* included measures aimed at sowing discord within the Jewish community and destabilising relations between its members.[39] The steps that would lead, in 630 CE, to the attempted forced baptism of Jews within the East Roman state and the contemporaneous disengagement of Jewish elites from Greco-Roman political and intellectual culture which Nicholas de Lange has delineated were effectively initiated by Justinian.[40]

Knowing the Law: Composition, Circulation, and Dissemination

As we have seen, Justinian's legislation was reflected and responded to in the writings of contemporary historians such as John Malalas, John Lydus, and Procopius. This fact is likely to have resulted in part from the fact that, along with other historians of the period, both secular and ecclesiastical (such as Agathias, Evagrius Scholasticus, and Menander Protector), Procopius and John Malalas in particular appear to have possessed legal training.[41] But the literary echoes of Justinian's legislation reverberated considerably more widely. The emperor's legislation regulating monastic institutions, for example, was reflected in contemporary spiritual literature, such as the writings of Cyril of Scythopolis or of the hermits Barsanuphius and John, eager to demonstrate their commitment and conformity

---

[37] Bond 2014.   [38] *J. Nov.* 45 pr.   [39] *Codex Theodosianus* 16.8.9; *J. Nov.* 146.
[40] de Lange 2005.   [41] Greatrex 2001.

to the imperial conception of the monastic life and its broader societal role.[42] Being seen to be regulated in accordance with imperial law may have become increasingly important for religious institutions at this time, given the apparent growing prominence within the sixth-century church of clerical legal officers known in Latin as *defensores ecclesiae*, charged with the supervision of morality, discipline, and possibly even doctrine.[43]

So how was the law known? Our best evidence for the process whereby imperial constitutions were drafted and circulated in late antiquity is found with respect to the *Novels* of Justinian referred to earlier.[44] These laws were predominantly issued in Greek, unless the legislation primarily concerned Latin-speaking provinces (in the Balkans, Africa, or Italy) or were addressed to high-ranking officials in Constantinople (such as the *quaestor*) for whom Latin was deemed more appropriate.[45] Where laws were issued in both languages, we know that the Greek text was written first. In the case of *Novel* 62 (concerned with the *Lex Falcidia*), for example, the Latin version was produced one month after the Greek. The law was not, however, officially promulgated until both versions were ready.

The major law schools of the empire at this time, we should note, operated on the basis of a carefully calibrated curriculum designed to enable Greek-speaking law students to progressively master predominantly Latin legal texts such as the *Digest*, *Institutes*, and *Codex*, or Latin-speaking students to master Greek texts such as the *Novels*. In the case of Greek speakers, this instruction initially took the form of lectures, provided in Greek, translating, summarising, and explaining the Latin texts. This part of the course was known as the *index*, after the pointing or wagging finger of the professor. There would then follow more advanced classes in which students examined, contextualised, and debated passages taken directly from the Latin texts (after the manner of 'gobbets'), and on which students would produce notes in Greek, known as *paragraphai*. Finally, the student would advance to private study of the set texts, assisted by word-for-word interlinear Greek translations, known as *kata podas* ('foot-by-foot'). With respect to Latin speakers, the process was reversed. Hence, in the so-called *Authenticum* (one of the main conduits by which Justinianic law was transmitted

---

[42] See, for example, *J. Nov.* 133; Booth 2014: 16–17.
[43] See *J. Nov* 17 c.7; *J. Nov.* 56; *J. Nov.* 59 c.1 and c.6; *J. Nov.* 74 c.4; *J. Nov.* 117 c.15; *J. Nov.* 133 c.5; *J. Edict* 13 c.10 and c.28; for their role in establishing doctrinal orthodoxy, see Underwood (forthcoming).
[44] See Miller and Sarris 2018.
[45] See, for example, *J. Nov.* 9, 11, 36, 37, 62, 75, 114, and *J. Nov. App.* 7.

to the medieval West), we possess a sixth-century *kata podas* translation of the Greek *Novels*, supplemented with legislation initially drafted in Latin.[46]

The dates attached to Justinian's *Novels* indicate that there was a regular rhythm to law-making by the sixth century, with legislation generally being written in the winter and typically issued around the middle of the month.[47] Once a law intended to be of general effect was formally promulgated, it was immediately advertised in Constantinople before being sent out to provincial governors, who were expected to advertise it throughout the cities under their charge. The law was deemed to take effect two months from its date of issue or receipt, which Justinian regarded as a 'long enough time after its notification to allow it to be published to everyone … and for our subjects to come to know about it and to observe the law'.[48] The form in which the *Novels* survive further appears to indicate that 'bundles' of new legislation were dispatched to the provinces on a six-monthly basis.[49] It is also clear that new laws were automatically notified to bishops, who were expected to advertise them in the porticoes of their churches, as well as to others (such as the professors of the law schools of Constantinople and Berytus) who needed an up-to-date knowledge of the law and who, consequently, are likely to have belonged to an official subscription list.

The emperor thus clearly expected his laws to circulate with considerable rapidity. The papyrological evidence suggests that such hopes were not entirely in vain. In 537 CE, for example, Justinian issued a law that henceforth all contracts and legal documents were to be dated according to the regnal year of the current emperor.[50] This measure formed part of a wider effort on his part to crack down on forgery by making legal documents and contracts easier to authenticate.[51] The new dating formula appears almost immediately on a papyrus document from Palestine; it is attested in Egypt in Oxyrhynchus by 539 CE; and by 540 CE, it was being used in the Hermopolite and Heracleopolite nomes, as well as appearing eventually in *formulae* on Coptic documentation.[52]

Using the Law

The papyrological evidence thus suggests that imperially promulgated legislation informed provincial practice relatively quickly, and we also know that legal practitioners were expected to be familiar with Justinian's

---

[46] See Scheltema 1970. [47] See Noailles 1912 and 1914. [48] *J. Nov.* 66 c.1.
[49] Noailles 1912: 87. [50] *J. Nov.* 47. [51] See Feissel 2010: 504–7.
[52] Feissel 2010: 510; Nowak 2015: 217.

post-codificatory legislation. Epitomes of Justinian's *Novels* would be produced in both Latin and Greek. Of the three most important such texts in Greek, two were the work of individuals (Theodore of Hermopolis and Athanasius of Emesa) bearing the title of *scholastikos*, indicating that they were primarily professional rather than academic lawyers by background.[53] The author of the Latin epitome, Julian, was one of the last great legal scholars (or *antecessores*) of the age, but he also taught the *Novels* for practical purposes. Justinian was adamant that more recent legislation should always take precedence over earlier laws.[54] As a result, provincial advocates were constantly faced with the challenge of triangulating between the facts of the case, the codified law, and more recent legislation. Accordingly, in a work known as his *Instructions for Counsel* (*Dictatum de consiliariis*), Julian provided careful advice to jobbing barristers on how to juggle and master legal texts once away from the classroom, suggesting, for example, that they pay particularly close attention to Justinian's lengthy and complicated *Novels* concerned with marriage (which clearly generated a great deal of litigation).[55]

Provincial judges presiding over courts of first instance were, of course, faced with similar challenges: what was to happen, for example, if the law relevant to a case changed between the joinder of issue (*litis contestatio*) and the judgement? Justinian vacillated on this issue. In 541 CE, for example, he decreed that litigants could only rely upon laws that were in force at the start of a trial, and that new laws or rescripts could not be introduced for consideration into proceedings once they were under way. Nor were judges permitted, he emphasised, to delay judgement in anticipation of a new law.[56] Just the following year, however, he modified that stance: when issuing judgement, judges were entitled to rely upon the law as it stood at that moment in time. Likewise, judges presiding over a court of appeal were to decide the case referred to them on the basis of the law as it stood when they came to reach their decision, rather than how the law had stood when the matter had first been adjudicated.[57] Not for nothing did Procopius accuse Justinian of causing legal confusion.[58]

Any uncertainty as to the state of the law was also informed by the emperor's willingness to respond to the pleas of petitioners from both the provinces and the capital. In 540 CE, for example, Justinian issued a law in response to an approach that had been made to him by two maritime

---

[53] Scheltema 1970: 61.   [54] *Digest* 1.4.4.   [55] See Humfress 2005: 172.   [56] *J. Nov.* 113.
[57] *J. Nov.* 115.   [58] Procopius, *Anecdota* 14.7–11.

financiers from Constantinople, asking him to give express legal form to what they asserted to be the customary arrangements by which agreements between shipowners and lenders had hitherto been framed.[59] One suspects that the financiers (named as Peter and Eulogetus) had been having the emperor on, for just seven months later, in response to counter-petitions, he abrogated the measure. Faced with the fact that 'it had already been made public in some provinces', Justinian was obliged to publicly declare that cases were to be tried 'as if the said law had, in fact, not even been laid down'.[60] Likewise, in the same year (541 CE), Justinian rescinded a right he had granted the imperial church in 530 CE, whereby its administrators had been granted permission to sue for the restitution of any illegally alienated ecclesiastical land a full one hundred years after the church had ceased to possess it.[61] Justinian was obliged to backtrack on this measure, we are told, because its consequences at a local level had been too destabilising. As the emperor declared, 'numerous cases have been launched under the licence of such legislation, and it is as if the concealed scars of ancient wounds have been reopened'.[62] Instead, the traditional period for *praescriptio longissimi temporis* was reasserted.[63]

Legal information and knowledge thus passed both ways, and we should note that the courts were capable of acting with considerable alacrity even in the most challenging of circumstances. In 544 CE, for example, Justinian responded to a petition over a disputed inheritance. A widow from Antioch by the name of Thecla had died, leaving as her immediate heir a daughter, still only a child, by the name of Sergia. Just sixteen days after the death of Thecla, however, Sergia too had died, we are told, of the plague.[64] As a result, a dispute had then arisen between Sergia's paternal uncle and her maternal aunt as to who had priority of claim over the estate. The aunt had taken legal advice, which had indicated that the law favoured her. The court in Antioch, however, though presided over by the same lawyer who had initially given the aunt such encouraging advice, had in fact decided in favour of the uncle.[65] Accordingly, the aunt had petitioned the emperor, who ultimately upheld her claim on sound legal principles.[66] But what is perhaps most striking in this instance is how little time appears to have elapsed between the death of Thecla and the emperor's decision to overturn

---

[59] *J. Nov.* 106.   [60] *J. Nov.* 110 c.1.
[61] *J. Nov.* 111, rescinding *Codex Iustinianus* 1.2.23 and *J. Nov.* 9.   [62] *J. Nov.* 111 pr.
[63] *J. Nov.* 111 c.1.   [64] *J. Nov.* 158 pr.
[65] The uncle's case rested upon *Codex Iustinianus* 6.30.18.4; the aunt's case relied upon *Codex Iustinianus* 6.30.19.
[66] *J. Nov.* 158 c.1.

the decision of the Antiochene court. The plague, which took the life of Sergia (and probably that of her mother too) is recorded to have struck Antioch in 542 CE. The period between the death of the mother and daughter in Syria, the judgement given at the court of first instance, and the hearing of the appeal in Constantinople, therefore, must have been less than two years, which would bear favourable comparison with the length of time it would take a case to reach and obtain judgement in the UK Supreme Court, even in the absence of bubonic plague.

The unfortunate Thecla and her litigious relatives probably belonged to the highest echelons of late antique landed society, and we might expect such people to have shown a keen interest in the technicalities of the law, especially as it pertained to matters of inheritance. A later constitution issued by Justinian reveals a still more complicated property dispute within a family which seemingly owned property in Constantinople, Antioch, and Italy, the origins of which went back to the technicalities of a post-mortem trust (*fideicommissum*) which had been set up by the head of the family in the late fifth century, details of whose will were placed before the emperor when he heard the case in the year 555 CE.[67]

Such people were bound to seek to assert their legal rights both against one another and also, crucially, against their social rivals and inferiors. Emperors since the fourth century, for example, had legislated on the legal status of agricultural workers known as *coloni adscripticii*. Such *coloni* were formally free (i.e., they were not slaves) but found themselves bound to the estate of their landowning employer, through whom they paid their taxes.[68] Not surprisingly, landowners were keen to take advantage of the law with respect to *adscripticii* to entrench their social and economic power on the ground. This is amply recorded, for example, with respect to the estates of the Apion family in the sixth century. The Flavii Apiones were one of the best-connected senatorial families of the Justinianic era. Fortunately, the documentary papyri enable us to reconstruct much of the reality of life and administration on a portion of their estates around the Middle Egyptian city of Oxyrhynchus from the fifth to seventh centuries.[69] One fact that comes across clearly from the Apion archive is the extent to which the family's administrators and stewards deployed the legal category of *colonus adscripticius* (or *enapographos georgos* in Greek) to control the household's workforce. Through the documentary papyri, we can see how imperial legislation on the 'colonate' was used as a weapon of social domination.[70]

---

[67] J. Nov. 159. [68] See Sirks 2008. [69] See Sarris 2006. [70] See discussion in Sarris 2011b.

Likewise, we should note how Justinian's *Novels* record landowners to have continued to lobby to have legislation with respect to *adscripticii* further honed, finessed, and clarified to serve their interests well into the sixth century. The status of the *colonus adscripticius* was hereditary. This situation was unproblematic as long as peasant families consisted of male and female *adscripticii* owned (as the law regarded them) by the same master. But what happened if a non-adscript woman gave birth to a child fathered by an *adscripticius*? Could the employer of the father claim the labour services of the child? Justinian's instinct in the *Codex* was that a child born to a non-adscript mother should inherit the mother's fully free status.[71] However, in 535 CE, in order to avoid such a situation, he ordained that male *coloni* were to be forbidden from marrying fully free women and allowed their owners to beat them if they did so.[72] In subsequent legislation, however, expressly issued in response to petitions from landowners, Justinian can be seen to have moderated his initially liberal stance, agreeing to tie such progeny to the estate.[73]

But what happened if the mother was tied to one estate and the father to another? Which estate could claim the children of any such union? Here, Justinian decided to give preference to the owner of the mother, but to divide the peasant family if there was more than one child.[74] Again, this law was issued in response to a petition from the managers of ecclesiastical estates in Syria, who wanted clarification as to the status of such offspring, whom the church evidently wished to put to work on its lands. Such petitions only make sense if imperial legislation with respect to *coloni adscripticii* was put into effect on the ground.[75] Imperial law, in other words, not only circulated, but helped to frame and determine social relations at the grassroots of East Roman society.

Memory and Appropriation

Knowledge of imperial legislation also clearly circulated beyond the administrative structures of the imperial government and the realm of private or institutional 'great estates'. The sixth-century documentary papyri that survive from the Middle Egyptian village of Aphrodito, for example, reveal how the local lawyer Dioscorus was well informed about recent imperial

---

[71] *Codex Iustinianus* 11.48.24 (533 CE).   [72] *J. Nov.* 22 c.17 pr.
[73] *J. Nov. App.* 1 and *J. Nov.* 162 c.2.   [74] *J. Nov.* 156.
[75] A point frequently contested in the secondary literature; see, for example, Grey 2007.

legislation and made use of it in his practice, even drawing upon it in the context of extra-judicial dispute resolution concerning a contested landholding.[76] But to what extent did knowledge of the law circulate beyond what we might think of as the 'propertied classes'?

Justinian's legislation sends out somewhat contradictory messages in this respect. On the one hand, in a law of 538 CE, Justinian issued a law prohibiting upper-class men from taking wives without dowries.[77] This law, as I have noted elsewhere, effectively provides a gazetteer to late antique social distinctions, differentiating between 'men of the higher ranks, at the level of the senators and most magnificent *illustres*', 'those in the upper service appointments, or in business, and in the more respectable professions', and finally those 'of the least regarded station in life, owning little property, and down to the lowest level of society ... of undistinguished soldiers under arms, or agricultural workers'. Of these, Justinian declared, 'their ignorance of public affairs and lack of desire for anything other than tilling the land or warfare is something highly desirable, and praiseworthy'.[78]

Yet some such men were clearly considerably more interested in public affairs, and especially in the law, than Justinian was willing to let on. Indeed, he had been obliged to admit as much just the previous year. In 533 CE, as we have seen, Justinian legislated that children fathered by *coloni adscripticii* but born of 'free' mothers were not to inherit adscript status. In response, the emperor informs us in a law dating from 537 CE, that a number of *coloni* had sought to assert their freedom and leave their masters, on the assumption that the law applied retrospectively.[79] This, Justinian declared, was completely illegal, and those who claimed otherwise were 'stupid or criminal', and engaged in 'schemes ... to the detriment of great landowners'.[80] It may have been such presumption on the part of *coloni* that inclined Justinian to inflect the law in favour of landowners in his measure of 539 CE. Again, however, one is struck by the rapidity with which knowledge of the law (however garbled) circulated.

Nor was this an isolated example of legal opportunism on the part of the peasantry. In an earlier law that was included in the *Codex Iustinianus*, the emperor Anastasius had decreed that *coloni adscripticii* who provided their employer with thirty years' continuous service could transfer to the new legal category of 'free' *coloni* (*coloni liberi*).[81] Such workers were no

---

[76] Gagos and Van Minnen 1994: 27. For the extensive presence of imperial law in documentary papyri from the early Byzantine period, see also Beaucamp 2007.
[77] *J. Nov.* 74.   [78] *J. Nov.* 74.   [79] *J. Nov.* 54.   [80] *J. Nov.* 54.
[81] *Codex Iustinianus* 11.48.19. See also Sirks 2008.

longer legally bound to pay any taxes to which they were liable through their employer and were granted ownership of the *peculium* or 'working capital' that they were assigned by their employer, which could include a parcel of land. Such 'free' *coloni*, however, were still obliged to reside on the estate and offer the landowner labour and other services. Revealingly, in both 530 CE and then 535 CE, we discover, Justinian was obliged to legislate to close a legal loophole that the Anastasian *lex* had opened, and of which *coloni* had seemingly taken advantage. For, by granting *coloni liberi* ownership of their *peculium*, Anastasius had inadvertently enabled long-standing *adscripticii* on church estates (such as those attested in *J. Nov.* 156) to assert ownership over ecclesiastical property, which, strictly speaking, was meant to be inalienable.[82]

Conclusion

Knowledge of imperial law in the Age of Justinian thus appears to have been capable of circulating with surprising rapidity, and across a broad spectrum of society, advertised by the government, the church, and, one might imagine, still more widely by legally informed preachers, itinerant clergy and bishops, or small-town lawyers such as Dioscorus. In such circumstances, legislation could be learned of and rights memorialised even at the level of peasant society, periodically allowing the law to become a weapon for the humble as well as the mighty. But if this was true of law and perceived legal rights, what of the other concepts, ideas, and arguments that such itinerant preachers, clergymen, and provincial lawyers may also have conveyed or upon which the law touched? It has been suggested, for example, that the private archive of Dioscorus also included a verse composition penned by the Egyptian lawyer in which he poked fun at the contemporary veneration of Christian images (or 'icons').[83] Did Dioscorus perhaps also pass on such contentious religious attitudes to his provincial clients? In terms of directions for future research, might the evidence for the circulation of legal knowledge amongst non-elite *strata* of society also provide parallels for how religious ideas, confessional identities, and attitudes to religious leadership more generally formed and became embedded across a range of provincial contexts at this time? On the basis of the legal evidence, might even doctrinal concepts (albeit in a simplified form) have

---

[82] *Codex Iustinianus* 1.2.24; *J. Nov.* 7. [83] Kuehn 1995.

circulated much more widely than has sometimes been supposed? The legal sources do not provide clear answers, but they raise intriguing possibilities, not least given the growing visibility of religious issues in sixth-century legislation and political debate. For, as we have seen, in Justinian's 'orthodox republic', law was increasingly at the forefront of religious as well as political struggles, and in such circumstances, the circulation of legal knowledge is likely to have had increasingly pronounced religious consequences. As the case of Jewish communities within the empire of Justinian might suggest, for example, rhetorically branding groups and communities as 'outsiders' or 'schismatics' may have entrenched a sense of alienation and hostility on the part of significant numbers of the emperor's subjects who found themselves so described, if the legislation criticising such groups was circulated amongst them. Knowledge of the law, one might hypothesise, could thus have served to unite the early Byzantine world at the level of institutional culture, whilst also potentially dividing it politically as the realms of law and faith became increasingly intertwined. For if perceived rights could be memorialised, so too, after all, could perceived wrongs. The dissemination and appropriation of legal knowledge in the Age of Justinian thus still has much to teach us not only about the workings of Roman law but also about the broader cultural, economic, and religious struggles that characterised the history of the East Roman empire at this time.

33 | The Ordering of Knowledge in Four Late Patristic Christological Handbooks

DIRK KRAUSMÜLLER

Introduction

Late antique Christianity was a religion not only of the Book, but also of books. While the Bible was recognised as the foundational text, it did not provide ready-made answers to crucial questions of belief. Controversies ensued during which the proponents of different views produced a great number of texts. This had already been the case in the fourth century, when the debate centred on the ontological bond between God and his Son; it was even more the case during the christological controversies of the fifth to seventh centuries, when the focus was on the relationship between the Son, who was now universally recognised as divine, and the human being Jesus whose life was recounted in the gospels. The debate started in earnest in the 420s when the patriarchs Cyril of Alexandria and Nestorius of Constantinople engaged in a publicity war, which was avidly followed by their contemporaries. In his writings, Cyril put great emphasis on the unity of the human and divine components in Christ, whereas Nestorius stressed the difference between them. In 431, Cyril engineered Nestorius' downfall at the Council of Ephesus, but this did not put an end to controversy. Twenty years later another council, this time held in the city of Chalcedon, produced a creedal formula that defined Christ's humanity and divinity as two natures but added that these two natures were united in one hypostasis. This was intended as a compromise, which sought to address the concerns of both parties. Yet it was immediately attacked by the so-called Monophysites, who claimed to defend Cyril's legacy. They defined the incarnate Word as one nature and one hypostasis, and averred that Chalcedon was heretical because it had vindicated Nestorius' teachings. The fifty years following the council saw a hardening of positions but generated surprisingly little literary output.

A change came only in the first half of the sixth century, when the two parties started to produce numerous texts. At first, the Monophysites had the upper hand, but eventually a group of Chalcedonian writers, including John of Caesarea, Leontius of Byzantium, and Heraclianus of Chalcedon, developed novel conceptual frameworks that supported their doctrinal stance. New ideas continued to be put forward until the seventh century, when Maximus the Confessor created a sophisticated theoretical edifice.[1] Yet around 550, the nature of the discourse changed. By then the discussions of the Chalcedonians with the Monophysites had produced a stock of arguments and counter-arguments, which kept being repeated without significant change. As a consequence, some authors took it upon themselves to organise this information in handbooks. These texts have an explicitly didactic character. Their target audience appears to have been non-specialists. They were told what to believe and what to reject, and how to defend their own sect and attack the other sects. Yet there is also an encyclopaedic element, a wish to be exhaustive, which leads some authors to add material that would not have been directly relevant to religious controversy. In what follows I will discuss in sequence the *Capita diversa* of Pamphilus, the *Contra Monophysitas* of Leontius of Jerusalem, the *Praeparatio* of Theodore of Raithou, and the treatise *De Sectis*, and then focus on corresponding passages in the different texts.

Authors and Works

Pamphilus, *Capita diversa*

The *Capita diversa* of Pamphilus are transmitted in two codices, where they appear in the company of other doctrinal texts.[2] The author's name is mentioned only in excerpts that were included in a seventh-century florilegium, the so-called *Doctrina Patrum*.[3] References to the Tritheist heresy, which erupted in the middle of the sixth century, establish a *terminus post quem*.[4] The most likely date of composition is the late sixth or early seventh century. Its title reads as follows:

Κεφαλαίων διαφόρων ἤτοι ἐπαπορήσεων λύσις περὶ τῆς εἰς Χριστὸν εὐσεβείας· ἐν ταὐτῷ δὲ ἔλεγχος καὶ ἀνατροπὴ τῆς κατὰ τὴν θεότητα τοῦ Χριστοῦ καὶ ἀνθρωπότητα τῶν Ἀκεφάλων ἐναντίας δοκήσεως, τῶν ἀπὸ Νεστορίου καὶ Εὐτυχοῦς τῶν δυσσεβῶν, καὶ ἀπολογία πρὸς τοὺς ἀθετοῦντας τὴν ἁγίαν σύνοδον τὴν ἐν Χαλκηδόνι, ἐκ τῆς διδασκαλίας τῶν θεοσδότων ἡμῶν ἁγίων πατέρων.[5]

Solution of different chapters or aporias concerning the correct worship of Christ, and at the same time *examination and refutation of the opposed docetism concerning the divinity and humanity of Christ*, of the Headless, which are

---

[1] On the christological discourse, see now the synthesis of Zachhuber 2020a.
[2] Pamphilus, *Capita diversa*, ed. Allen and Declerck 1989: 127–61, with an excellent introduction, esp. 85–93. On Pamphilus, see Grillmeier and Hainthaler 2002: 135–58; and dell'Osso 2010: 377–94.
[3] Allen and Declerck 1989: 94–98. [4] See Krausmüller 2017: esp. 633–36.
[5] Pamphilus, *Capita diversa* (Allen and Declerck 1989: 127.2–9).

followers of the impious *Nestorius and Eutyches*, and defence against those who dismiss the holy synod in Chalcedon, on the basis of the teaching of our God-given holy Fathers.

The italicised words are adapted from the title of Leontius of Byzantium's treatise *Contra Nestorianos et Eutychianos*.[6] This was without doubt a conscious choice. In this way, Pamphilus could signal his indebtedness to the earlier author. Indeed, quotations from Leontius' treatises *Contra Nestorianos et Eutychianos* and *Solutiones* are ubiquitous in the text.[7] It is impossible to identify Pamphilus with other contemporary bearers of the name.[8] Yet it is likely that he was a monk and lived in Palestine.[9]

The treatise comprises seventeen sections. Each section is numbered and consists of a question and its answer, indicated as such through the terms ἐρώτησις and ἀπόκρισις.[10] Other articulating features are missing, and we do not find a proem. The title suggests a bipartite structure: proposed solutions to christological problems, followed by a defence of the Council of Chalcedon. Both parts can be identified in the text. Chapters twelve to seventeen deal with criticism of the Council of Chalcedon,[11] and chapters three to eleven explain why certain doctrinal formulae should not be used or accepted by members of the Chalcedonian sect.[12] They are, however, complemented with a third part, chapters one and two, which contain definitions of the theological key terms 'substance' and 'hypostasis', without reference to the specific case of the incarnation.[13]

The last section will be discussed in greater detail later on. I will therefore make only a few remarks about the central section. There Pamphilus formulates the questions in such a way that they appear to be posed by his fellow-Chalcedonians. The eighth chapter may serve as an example:

Εἰ δυνατὸν εἰπεῖν ἐπὶ τοῦ δεσπότου Χριστοῦ οὐσίαν σύνθετον ὡς ἐπὶ τοῦ ἀνθρώπου, καθὼς καὶ ὑπόστασιν σύνθετον δοξάζομεν[14]

If it is possible to speak of a composite substance in the case of the Lord Christ, as in the case of the human being, just as we also confess a composite hypostasis.

---

[6] Leontius of Byzantium, *Contra Nestorianos et Eutychianos* (ed. Daley 2017: 124).
[7] See Richard 1938: 35–39; Declerck 1994.   [8] See Grillmeier and Hainthaler 2002: 137–39.
[9] See Pamphilus, *Capita diversa* (ed. Allen and Declerck 1989: 134.4–23), with a description of the spiritual ascent, which is typical for monastic literature.
[10] In late antiquity, questions and answers or *erotapokriseis* were an established literary genre. See the contributions in Volgers and Zamagni 2004.
[11] Pamphilus, *Capita diversa* (ed. Allen and Declerck 1989: 213–61).
[12] Pamphilus, *Capita diversa* (ed. Allen and Declerck 1989: 144–212).
[13] Pamphilus, *Capita diversa* (ed. Allen and Declerck 1989: 127–43).
[14] Pamphilus, *Capita diversa* (ed. Allen and Declerck 1989: 179.1–3).

To speak of the incarnated Word as a 'composite hypostasis', understood as the union of two – divine and human – substances, was the official Chalcedonian position.[15] By contrast, the concept of a single 'composite substance', which was employed by some Monophysites, had been condemned as heretical at the Second Council of Constantinople.[16] Yet Pamphilus' text shows that questions could still be raised. It seems that his intended readers were aware of what was being discussed in the other sects and were wondering whether the various views were correct or not. Pamphilus' answer is equally significant. He sets out patiently and at great length why such a position is untenable. Only at the end of the chapter does the tone become more aggressive. There he states that this position is held by heretics and claims that those who are not convinced by his reasoning would themselves be considered heretics.[17]

Theodore of Raithou, Praeparatio

The *Praeparatio* has come down to us in more than twenty manuscripts of varying content.[18] It was known in ninth-century Constantinople, where it was quoted by George the Monk. The lemma informs us that it was written by Theodore, priest of Raithou, an important monastic centre on the Sinai Peninsula.[19] We can be certain that it dates to the late sixth or early seventh century because it presupposes not only the Tritheist heresy, but also the orthodox reaction to it.[20] Its title reads as follows:

Προπαρασκευή τις καὶ γυμνασία τῷ βουλομένῳ μαθεῖν, τίς ὁ τρόπος τῆς θείας ἐνανθρωπήσεως καὶ οἰκονομίας, καθ' ὃν πέπρακται, καὶ τίνα τὰ πρὸς τοὺς ταύτην μὴ ὀρθῶς νοοῦντας λεγόμενα παρὰ τῶν τῆς ἐκκλησίας τροφίμων.[21]

A preparation and training for those who wish to know what is the manner of the divine inhumanation and dispensation, according to which it has been performed, and what is said by the nurselings of the church to those who do not correctly conceive of it.

---

[15] See Grillmeier and Hainthaler 2002: 468–69.
[16] See Grillmeier and Hainthaler 2002: 375–83. The Monophysites preferred to speak of a composite nature.
[17] Pamphilus, *Capita diversa* (ed. Allen and Declerck 1989: 183.139–186.203).
[18] Theodore of Raithou, *Praeparatio* (ed. Diekamp 1938: 185–222, with discussion of the manuscript tradition, 182–85). For a brief discussion of the content, see Grillmeier and Hainthaler 2002: 119–27. The article by Chase (2009–10) is highly speculative.
[19] Theodore of Raithou, *Praeparatio* (ed. Diekamp 1938: 185.1). See Grillmeier and Hainthaler 2002: 117–19.
[20] See Krausmüller 2015: 13–28.
[21] Theodore of Raithou, *Praeparatio* (ed. Diekamp 1938: 185.1–5).

This title emphasises the didactic character of the text and Theodore's indebtedness to the theological tradition. It is followed by a carefully crafted proem in which Theodore explains why he has taken up the pen. He declares that members of the Monophysite sect are equipped with arguments that allow them to define and defend their position, whereas Chalcedonians neither understand the differences between the other sects and their own nor know why their beliefs are correct.[22] Here we can see an affinity with the *Capita diversa* of Pamphilus. Yet Theodore approaches the issue in quite a different manner. In the title, two topics are mentioned, which leads one to expect an exposé of the Chalcedonian understanding of the incarnation, followed by Chalcedonian arguments against the Monophysites. This is not, however, the case. After the proem, Theodore inserts a subtitle:

Ἵνα δὲ εὔληπτα γένηται παντὶ τῷ ἐντυγχάνοντι τῷ προκειμένῳ πονήματι τὰ πρὸς τοὺς δι' ἐναντίας λεγόμενα, μικρά τινα πρὸς εἰσαγωγὴν συντάξαι ἀναγκαῖον ἐνόμισα.[23]

In order that that which is said to the adversaries become easy to comprehend for everyone who reads the present work, I have considered it necessary to put together a few brief remarks as introduction.

This introductory section, which ends with the words 'and so much about this' (καὶ ταῦτα μὲν εἰς τοσοῦτον), in fact takes up more than a third of the text.[24] In it, Theodore provides information about a number of heresies and explains the creed of Chalcedon. The remainder of the text is a discussion of theological and philosophical key terms. No information is given about how they can be applied to the specific case of the incarnation.

'Abbas Theodore', De sectis

The treatise *De sectis* has come down to us in nineteen manuscripts.[25] Excerpts are already included in the *Doctrina Patrum*.[26] No critical edition of the text has yet been published, so we must rely on Migne's *Patrologia Graeca*, where it is attributed to Leontius of Byzantium.[27] This reference, however, is not found in most manuscripts and was most likely added by a

---

[22] Theodore of Raithou, *Praeparatio* (ed. Diekamp 1938: 200.14–22).
[23] Theodore of Raithou, *Praeparatio* (ed. Diekamp 1938: 186.26–29).
[24] Theodore of Raithou, *Praeparatio* (ed. Diekamp 1938: 200.10).
[25] See Gleede 2013: esp. 180. [26] See Richard 1938: esp. 712–21.
[27] *Patrologia Graeca* 86: 1194–1268. The edition by M. Waegeman (1982) remains unpublished.

scribe who knew that Leontius had written several christological treatises.[28] The text can be dated to between 580 and 608 since it contains a list of the patriarchs of Alexandria ending with Eulogius, who held the office during these years.[29] The title reads as follows:

Σχόλια ἀπὸ φωνῆς Θεοδώρου τοῦ θεοφιλεστάτου ἀββᾶ καὶ σοφωτάτου φιλοσόφου τήν τε θείαν καὶ ἐξωτικὴν φιλοσοφήσαντος γραφήν.[30]

Notes heard from Theodore, the most God-loving abbas and most wise philosopher, who has engaged philosophically with divine and the external scripture.

It has been argued that the 'abbas Theodore' mentioned here should be identified with Theodore of Raithou, but it is impossible to substantiate this hypothesis.[31] It is, however, very likely that he lived in Alexandria. The formula σχόλια ἀπὸ φωνῆς indicates that *De sectis* is not a work of Theodore himself, but rather a student's transcript of lectures that he gave. This is frequently encountered in late antique Aristotelian commentaries. An affinity with philosophical discourse is also evident in the structure of the text. It is divided into ten sections, which are called πρᾶξις, the Neoplatonic term for lecture. The formula 'so far the lecture' (ἐν τούτοις ἡ πρᾶξις or ἐν τούτοις ἡ θεωρία) that is found at the end of most sections is also typical for Neoplatonic texts.[32] Unfortunately, we do not know whether there existed a theological 'school' in Alexandria which was organised along the lines of Neoplatonic teaching establishments. Yet a crossover is suggested by the contention that Theodore was familiar not only with theological, but also with philosophical texts.

It is difficult to summarise the content of *De sectis* because its structure is rather chaotic. Different frameworks overlap, and material that one would expect to be discussed together is distributed over several contexts, which requires frequent cross-referencing. As we have an excellent analysis by Benjamin Gleede, I will at this point limit myself to a few remarks and will then discuss selected parts in the second half of the article.[33] Despite all divergent features, one can discern a tripartite structure. In the first sentence of the text, the author declares that he intends to give an overview of the various 'sects' (αἱρέσεις). Lecture one functions as an introduction to the topic. It contains an exposition of Christian doctrine and an overview of the history of salvation. Only at the end do we find brief references to the four archetypal heresies: Arianism, Sabellianism, Nestorianism, and

---

[28] See Gleede 2013: 181–82. [29] See Lang 1998. [30] *De sectis* (PG 86: 1193).
[31] See Böhm 2000: 1418.
[32] For a full discussion of these characteristics, see Richard 1950. [33] See above note 25.

Eutychianism.[34] Lectures two to five discuss, in chronological sequence, heresies from the pre-Christian period to the time of the author.[35] Then follow four thematically organised lectures in which the author refutes different kinds of Monophysite arguments against Chalcedon and its creed.[36] In the last lecture, he returns to his main topic. He discusses in greater detail two groups of contemporary heretics, the Gaianites and the Agnoetes, which he had already mentioned in chapter five, and concludes with information about the Origenists.[37]

Despite this confusion, *De sectis* was a very popular text. One reason was no doubt the author's ability to describe doctrinal debates in a vivid, easily understood manner. The section about Tritheism may serve as an example.

Ἠπόρητο γὰρ τῇ ἐκκλησίᾳ, ὅτι εἰ δύο λέγετε φύσεις ἐν τῷ Χριστῷ, ἀνάγκη ὑμᾶς καὶ δύο ὑποστάσεις εἰπεῖν. ἡ δὲ ἐκκλησία ἀνταπεκρίνετο, ὅτι εἰ μὲν ταὐτόν ἐστι φύσις καὶ ὑπόστασις, ἀνάγκη ὑμᾶς ὁμολογῆσαι τὸ ἄτομον. εἰ δὲ ἄλλο τί ἐστι φύσις, καὶ ἄλλο ὑπόστασις, τίς ἡ ἀποκλήρωσις, λέγοντας ἡμᾶς δύο φύσεις ὁμολογῆσαι πάντως καὶ δύο ὑποστάσεις; ἀπεκρίναντο πρὸς τὴν ἐκκλησίαν οἱ αἱρετικοὶ ὅτι ναί, ταὐτόν ἐστι φύσις καὶ ὑπόστασις.[38]

The church was confronted with the following aporia: 'If you speak of two natures in Christ, you necessarily also speak of two hypostases'. The church answered: 'If nature and hypostasis are the same, you necessarily also confess the individual. But if nature is one thing and hypostasis another, what arbitrary rule is there that we who speak of two natures must on all accounts also confess two hypostases?' The heretics responded to the church: 'Yes, nature and hypostasis are the same'.

The following exchanges then show how the heretics ended up concluding that God consisted not only of three hypostases but also of three particular natures. The account is greatly simplified, but not altogether wrong.[39] In other dialogues, 'the church' is replaced by 'I' or 'we', which gives the impression of a real debate in which the author and his audience engage.[40]

Leontius of Jerusalem, Contra Monophysitas

Leontius' writings are preserved in a single manuscript.[41] From the title, we know that he was a monk and that he had links with the city of Jerusalem. Internal evidence shows that he lived in the late sixth or early seventh

---

[34] *De sectis* (PG 86: 1193–1200).   [35] *De sectis* (PG 86: 1200–33).
[36] *De sectis* (PG 86: 1233–60).   [37] *De sectis* (PG 86: 1260–68).   [38] *De sectis* (PG 86: 1233A).
[39] On this debate see Erismann 2008.   [40] See, e.g., *De sectis* (PG 86: 1205B–D).
[41] See Gray 2006: 32–36.

century.[42] The text that is relevant for our topic is part of a larger oeuvre. It was originally preceded by a refutation of arguments put forward by the Monophysites, which is now lost, and it is still followed by the lengthy treatise *Contra Nestorianos*, where passages from a Nestorian treatise are quoted and then refuted.[43] Its title reads as follows:

Ἀπορίαι πρὸς τοὺς μίαν φύσιν λέγοντας σύνθετον τὸν κύριον ἡμῶν Ἰησοῦν Χριστόν, καὶ μαρτυρίαι τῶν ἁγίων, καὶ ἀνάλυσις τοῦ δόγματος αὐτῶν.[44]

Aporias addressed to those who call our Lord Jesus Christ one composite nature, and testimonies of the saints, and refutation of their doctrine.

Analysis of the content shows that the text does indeed contain two such parts. Sixty syllogisms directed against Monophysite christology are followed by a *florilegium* of patristic texts, which is meant to show that the Chalcedonians are faithful to the teachings of earlier theologians, including Cyril of Alexandria, and that even Monophysite authors clandestinely admit this.[45] Appended to the *florilegium* is a third section, where Monophysite arguments against the validity of the Council of Chalcedon are refuted.[46] On the whole the text is rather dry. Many syllogisms are introduced by the word 'further' (ἔτι), and the quotations begin with the name of the author and the work. Yet occasionally a brief dialogue enlivens the presentation, which shows that the author had literary pretensions.

Themes

After this brief characterisation of the four texts, I will now focus on two different topics – the arsenal of counter-arguments and the history of heresies – and in each case make a comparison of the texts in which they appear.

The Arsenal of Counter-Arguments

Pamphilus' *Capita diversa* contain no comments that would guide the reader to a better understanding of the structure of the text. Yet even so, it is possible to make out discrete sections where the chapters share a common topic. This is most obvious in the third part of the text, chapters twelve

---

[42] Krausmüller 2001. Cf. Gleede 2013: 181.   [43] See Krausmüller 2005.
[44] Leontius of Jerusalem, *Contra Monophysitas* (ed. Gray 2006: 226).
[45] Leontius of Jerusalem, *Contra Monophysitas* (ed. Gray 2006: 162–224, 46–134). For reasons best known to himself, Gray has reversed the sequence in his edition.
[46] Leontius of Jerusalem, *Contra Monophysitas* (ed. Gray 2006: 134–60).

to seventeen, which respond to Monophysite criticism of the Council of Chalcedon. Such a section is also found in Leontius of Jerusalem's treatise. There, however, it is preceded by the following comment:

Ἐπεὶ γὰρ μήτε ἀποδεικτικοῖς ἐπιχειρήμασι παραστῆσαι, μήτε γραφικοῖς ἢ πατρικοῖς μαρτυρήμασι βεβαιῶσαι τὰ οἰκεῖα φρονήματα δεδύνηνται, ἐν ἐσχατολογίᾳ τῶν αἰτιῶν τῆς ἀφ' ἡμῶν ἐκφοιτήσεως, φασὶν ἔτι ὡς· Κἂν τοιάδε ὑμεῖς εὐσεβοφανῆ νῦν δογματίζετε, οὐ συνεκκλησιαζόμεθα ὑμῖν· δέχεσθε γὰρ καὶ σέβετε τὴν ἐν Χαλκηδόνι σύνοδον.[47]

Since they have been able neither to prove their own assumptions with apodictic arguments, nor to confirm them from scriptural or patristic testimonies, at the very end of the reasons for their departure from us they go on to say: 'Even though you teach now the kind of things that seem to be orthodox, we do not come together in church with you, for you accept and reverence the council of Chalcedon'.[48]

Here the defence of Chalcedon is part of an overarching framework, which consists of three parts: refutation of Monophysite syllogisms, refutation of Monophysite testimonies, and refutation of 'historical' arguments that question the validity of the Council of Chalcedon. Significantly, a similar tripartite structure is found in *De sectis*. In lecture six we read:

Μετὰ τὰ εἰρημένα, φέρε καὶ περὶ ἐπιχειρημάτων τινῶν, ἅπερ κοινῶς πρὸς τὴν ἐκκλησίαν λέγουσι πάντες οἱ διακρινόμενοι, μικρὰ διαλάβωμεν. διέλθωμεν δὲ αὐτὰ τριχῆ, ἐπειδὴ τὰ μὲν αὐτῶν ἱστορικά εἰσιν, ἐκ τῶν πραχθέντων τῇ ἐν Χαλκηδόνι συνόδῳ λαμβανόμενα, τὰ δὲ ἀπὸ συλλογισμῶν καὶ περινοίας, τὰ δὲ ἀπὸ χρήσεων.[49]

After what has been said, let us then also discourse briefly about some arguments, which all hesitators commonly say to the church. Let us consider them in three parts, since some of them are historical, taken from the acts of the synod in Chalcedon, some are from subtle syllogisms, and some are from quotations.

The marked similarities between *Contra Monophysitas* and *De sectis* leave no doubt that we are in the presence of an established pattern. Although the topics are arranged differently, it may be that the two texts are responses to a Monophysite polemical work which already had a tripartite structure. Yet this does not mean that the authors deal with the topics in the same manner.

The approach of *De sectis* is best characterised as 'scholastic'. The three topics are discussed respectively in lecture six, lecture seven, and lectures eight and nine. The transitions from one topic to the next are clearly signposted, and each topic is then further subdivided. Lecture eight may serve as an example. It begins as follows:

---

[47] Leontius of Jerusalem, *Contra Monophysitas* (ed. Gray 2006: 134).
[48] Trans. Gray 2006: 135, with modifications. [49] *De sectis* (PG 86: 1233B–C).

Ὑπόλοιπόν ἐστι περὶ τῶν ἐπιχειρημάτων ὧν ἀπὸ χρήσεων τῶν ἁγίων πατέρων παραφέρουσιν ἡμῖν, διεξελθεῖν. τούτων δὲ τὰ μέν εἰσιν, ἀφ' ὧν οὐκ εἶπεν ἡ σύνοδος, τὰ δὲ παραφέρουσι πρὸς πίστιν τοῦ οἰκείου δόγματος, τὰ δὲ ἀφ' ὧν εἶπεν.[50]

It is left to engage with the arguments that they produce on the basis of quotations from the holy fathers. Of these some are based on what the synod did not say, some are produced by them for the corroboration of their own doctrine, and some are based on what it said.

The three sections are then discussed in sequence, and the transitions are again clearly demarcated. At the end of the first section, we read 'And this is based on what it did not say, but they produce many quotations for the corroboration of their own doctrine' (καὶ ταῦτα μέν εἰσιν, ἀφ' ὧν οὐκ εἶπε, πρὸς πίστιν δὲ τοῦ οἰκείου δόγματος παραφέρουσι χρήσεις πολλάς).[51] This pattern then repeats itself within the sections. The first section begins with the statement: 'On the basis of what it did not say, they attack it from three angles' (ἀφ' ὧν μὲν οὐκ εἶπεν, ἐπιλαμβάνονται αὐτῆς ἐκ τριῶν).[52] The bone of contention is the doctrinal formulae 'union according to hypostasis', 'one incarnate nature of the Word', and 'from two natures', which Cyril used and which the Chalcedonians also accepted, but which were not mentioned in the creed of Chalcedon. The author who focuses exclusively on the first formula explains this 'oversight' in the following manner: Cyril wrote against Nestorius, who wanted to split Christ into two and therefore stressed the one hypostasis, whereas the Council of Chalcedon dealt with the diametrically opposite heresy of Eutyches and therefore focused on the two natures. Therefore one cannot say that Chalcedon deviated from Cyril's teaching.[53]

When we now turn to Leontius of Jerusalem, we first of all need to consider that the text has not come down to us in its entirety. In the extant part, Leontius presents a long series of syllogisms which target aspects of Monophysite christology. The lost part where he refuted Monophysite syllogisms preceded it. This is evident from the introductory remark: 'But having responded to their aporias, let us now respond with some aporias out of many that are directed against them' (ἀλλὰ ταῖς αὐτῶν ἀπαντήσαντες ἀπορίαις, ὀλίγα τινὰ νῦν ἐκ πλειόνων καὶ ἡμεῖς αὐτοῖς ἀνταπορήσωμεν).[54] The following discussion of the testimonies, which is preserved in its entirety, permits a comparison with *De sectis*. It begins with a question that is put into the mouth of the Monophysites, which functions as a

---

[50] *De sectis* (PG 86: 1252B).   [51] *De sectis* (PG 86: 1252D).
[52] *De sectis* (PG 86: 1252B).   [53] *De sectis* (PG 86: 1252C).
[54] Leontius of Jerusalem, *Contra Monophysitas* (ed. Gray 2006: 162).

transition from the syllogisms: 'But why', they say, 'do you push us towards your teaching, pressing us on every side' (ἀλλὰ τί ἡμᾶς, φασί, πανταχόθεν περιτρέχοντες, εἰς τὴν ὑμετέραν δόξαν συνελαύνετε).[55] They then protest that they merely follow the tradition of the fathers, whereas the creed of Chalcedon is an innovation. Leontius of Jerusalem's response is directed at these fictitious adversaries who are addressed as 'you people' (ὦ οὗτοι).[56] One example may suffice. Leontius states that different formulae can have the same meaning, in which case it does not matter whether the fathers used them or not. Then he presents several counter-arguments, which are articulated through 'first' (πρῶτον μέν), 'besides' (ἄλλως δέ), and 'but neither' (ἀλλ' οὐδέ), but are not formulated in analogous fashion.[57] The next topic is then introduced through another Monophysite objection, which begins with the phrase: 'but perhaps you would say to this' (ἀλλ' ἴσως πρὸς τάδε εἴποιτε).[58] From this summary it is evident that Leontius' text has a distinctly literary character. The Monophysite criticisms are not chopped up into small units and the refutations are also much longer. In consequence, Leontius' text would have been of much less use for somebody who sought guidance in doctrinal debates.

The texts differ not only in structure but also in content. This can be seen most clearly in the defence of the Council of Chalcedon, which is the only topic that is found in the *Capita diversa* as well. The *Capita diversa* and *De sectis* each have five arguments. In Leontius of Jerusalem's treatise the number of arguments has risen to twelve, which are conveniently summarised in an appendix to Gray's edition.[59] Yet there are not many overlaps. The accusation that Chalcedon vindicated Nestorius is found in the *Capita diversa* and in Leontius' treatise, but not in *De sectis*.[60] By contrast, the claim that the Alexandrian patriarch Dioscorus was not condemned because he was a heretic but because he did not heed the summons of the council is only found in Leontius' treatise and *De sectis*.[61] Only one topic appears in all three texts, the supposed presence of 'heretical' bishops at Chalcedon. The Monophysites complained that Theodoret of Cyrus and Ibas of Edessa took part in the council despite their known sympathies for Nestorius. In the *Capita diversa* the relevant chapter begins with the following question:

[55] Leontius of Jerusalem, *Contra Monophysitas* (ed. Gray 2006: 46).
[56] Leontius of Jerusalem, *Contra Monophysitas* (ed. Gray 2006: 46).
[57] Leontius of Jerusalem, *Contra Monophysitas* (ed. Gray 2006: 48).
[58] Leontius of Jerusalem, *Contra Monophysitas* (ed. Gray 2006: 50).
[59] Gray 2006: 231–33.
[60] Pamphilus, *Capita diversa* (ed. Allen and Declerck 1989: 213); Leontius of Jerusalem, *Contra Monophysitas* (ed. Gray 2006: 134).
[61] Leontius of Jerusalem, *Contra Monophysitas* (ed. Gray 2006: 142); *De sectis* (PG 86: 1236B).

ιβ' Ἐρώτησις. ἐπειδὴ τινὲς ἐπιμέμφονται τῇ ἐν Χαλκηδόνι συνόδῳ ὡς ἀκρίτως καὶ ἀκανονίστως δεξαμένῃ Θεοδώριτον καὶ Ἴβαν, τί δεῖ πρὸς τούτους λέγειν[62]

12. Question: Since some rebuke the synod in Chalcedon as having accepted Theodoret and Ibas in an inconsiderate and uncanonical fashion, what must one say to these?

In his answer Pamphilus then explains how 'we' must respond. He quotes from the *Acts* of the council, and from a supposed writing of Theodoret, in order to show that the two bishops anathematised Nestorius before they were permitted to take their places.

In *De sectis*, the theme is more developed. Here the refutation proceeds in two stages, considering not only the persons but also the writings of the alleged Nestorians:

Τετάρτη ἐστὶν ἀπορία (ἡ γὰρ δευτέρα εἰς δύο διαιρεῖται) ὅτι αἱρετικοὺς ἀνθρώπους ἐδέξατο ἡ ἐν Χαλκηδόνι σύνοδος. ἐδέξατο γὰρ Θεοδώρητον καὶ τὸν Ἴβαν.[63]

The fourth aporia (for the second one is divided into two) is that the synod in Chalcedon accepted heretical men. For it accepted Theodoret and Ibas.

The two cases are discussed in sequence but in exactly analogous fashion: 'we, then, say about the doctrine of Theodoret that …' (λέγομεν οὖν πρὸς μὲν τοῦ Θεοδωρήτου δόγμα ὅτι …) is followed by 'we say about that of Ibas that … (πρὸς δὲ τὸ τοῦ Ἴβα λέγομεν ὅτι …).[64] In both cases the same answer is given: They were not admitted to the council before they had anathematised Nestorius. This is then in both cases followed by the phrase 'but they confront us again with an additional aporia, that …' (ἀλλὰ πάλιν ἐπαποροῦσιν ὅτι …), which introduces further objections: why did the council not ask Theodoret to anathematise his writings against Cyril, and why did it not demand of Ibas that he anathematise his letter, which praised Theodore of Mopsuestia, Nestorius' source of inspiration? The answer is in each case: even Cyril whom the Monophysites regard as the highest authority did not demand such a thing. Then a fifth aporia is added: If the Council of Chalcedon acted properly, why did Justinian have the writings of Theodoret and Ibas condemned at the Second Council of Constantinople? Here the author explains that Justinian took this step solely in order to win over the Monophysites, but that this initiative was not crowned with success.[65]

Leontius of Jerusalem's treatise is again quite different. Here the topic is discussed under two headings: 'Yes', they say, 'there were some at the synod who were caught out as having once been sympathisers of

---

[62] Pamphilus, *Capita diversa* (ed. Allen and Declerck 1989: 235.1-4).
[63] *De sectis* (PG 86: 1236D). [64] *De sectis* (PG 86: 1236D-37A).
[65] *De sectis* (PG 86: 1237C-D).

Nestorius' (ναί, ἦσάν τινες, φησίν, ἐν τῇ συνόδῳ, οἳ ἐφωράθησαν Νεστορίῳ πάλαι προσκείμενοι),[66] and 'but if it had a part that was altogether blameworthy', he says, 'then the whole is judged to be invalid' (ἀλλ' εἰ ὅλως μέρος ἔσχε ψεκτόν, τὸ ὅλον, φησί, λοιπὸν ἀδόκιμον κρίνεται).[67] Leontius repeats Pamphilus' argument that those who had been close to Nestorius anathematised him at the Council of Chalcedon but makes no mention of writings that the Monophysites found objectionable. Indeed, even the names of Theodoret and Ibas are missing. This 'omission' has been taken as evidence that Leontius' treatise was written before Justinian's council.[68] Yet this hypothesis can no longer be upheld because other evidence shows clearly that Leontius lived several decades later.[69] Indeed, it is much more likely that he was deliberately vague. It is possible that like the author of *De sectis*, he was not happy with Justinian's religious policy. This shows that we cannot simply assume that all an author cared about was being comprehensive. Arguments may well be coloured by personal views, and there may be significant silences.

Of course, this does not mean that occasionally the three authors could not use the same arguments. One of the ways in which they sought to show that Chalcedon was valid despite a possible presence of 'Nestorians' was to draw a parallel with the universally accepted Council of Nicaea, which was attended by Arian bishops.

Contra Monophysitas:	Capita diversa:	De Sectis:
Ἦ ἀγνοεῖτε ὅτι καὶ τῶν ἐν Νικαίᾳ τιη' περὶ τοὺς δέκα καὶ ἑπτά, φόβῳ τῆς καθαιρέσεως, ὑπέγραψαν κατὰ Ἀρείου, οἳ καὶ ἐπολέμησαν δεινῶς μετὰ ταῦτα τὸν μέγαν Ἀθανάσιον, καὶ οὐ παρὰ τοῦτο ἡ σύνοδος ὅλη διαβάλλεται.[70]	Εὑρίσκομεν γὰρ καὶ τῶν ἐν Νικαίᾳ τιη' ἁγίων πατέρων περὶ ιζ' τὸν ἀριθμὸν τὰ Ἀρείου πρεσβεύσαντας, καὶ ἐπὶ τοσοῦτον, ὡς πολλὰ κακὰ κατὰ τῆς τοῦ θεοῦ ἐκκλησίας ἐπιδείξασθαι, οἵτινες φόβῳ τῆς καθαιρέσεως ὡς ἐδίδαξαν ταῦτα τῷ ὅρῳ καθυπέγραψαν, καὶ οὐ δεῖ παρὰ τοῦτο αἰτιᾶσθαι τὴν ἁγίαν ἐκείνην σύνοδον.[71]	Ἰδοὺ καὶ ἡ ἐν Νικαίᾳ σύνοδος ἐδέξατο ἑπτὰ αἱρετικοὺς καὶ πρὸ τούτου Ἀρειανοῦντας, καὶ μετὰ ταῦτα ἐπιμείναντες, καὶ ὅμως οὐ διὰ τοῦτο λέγομεν τὴν σύνοδον, τια', ἀλλὰ τιη'.[72]

---

[66] Leontius of Jerusalem, *Contra Monophysitas* (ed. Gray 2006: 136).
[67] Leontius of Jerusalem, *Contra Monophysitas* (ed. Gray 2006: 137).
[68] See Gray 2006: 36–40.   [69] See n. 50 above.
[70] Leontius of Jerusalem, *Contra Monophysitas* (ed. Gray 2006: 138).
[71] Pamphilus, *Capita diversa* (ed. Allen and Declerck 1989: 241.153–58).
[72] *De sectis* (PG 86: 1237C).

Or do you not know that out of fear of deposition about seventeen of the 318 in Nicaea signed against the decree against Arius, who even later waged a terrible war against the great Athanasius, and the entire synod is not slandered for this reason.	For we find that about seventeen of the 318 holy Fathers in Nicaea favoured the case of Arius, and so much that they showed many bad things against the church of God, who out of fear of deposition signed the definition as they had taught it, and one must not for this reason accuse that holy synod.	Behold, the synod in Nicaea, too, admitted seven heretics, who were followers of Arius before and remained so afterwards, and nevertheless we do not for this reason say about the synod 311 but 318.

In this case the versions in Leontius of Jerusalem's treatise and in the *Capita diversa* are so close that we can assume that they borrowed from the same source.[73] By contrast, the author of *De sectis* reproduced the argument but phrased it quite differently.

The History of Heresies

The sections that we have discussed so far are directly relevant to religious controversy. In some instances, the texts even provide ready-made arguments that would enable non-specialists to hold their own in discussions about faith. Yet this was not the only function of doctrinal handbooks. Two of them, *De sectis* and the *Praeparatio*, begin with an overview of the development of Christian doctrine, which not only provides information about heresies but also inculcates the notion that only the Chalcedonian sect has an impeccably orthodox pedigree.

Theodore of Raithou presents his heretics in pairs: Mani and Paul of Samosata, Apollinarius and Theodore of Mopsuestia, and Nestorius and Eutyches. The arrangement is chronological. The readers are told that Paul was a 'contemporary' (σύγχρονος) of Mani, and that Apollinarius appeared 'when not a little time had passed' (χρόνου δὲ οὐ μικροῦ προϊόντος).[74] More importantly, each pair represents two 'diametrically' (ἐκ διαμέτρου) opposite positions. Theodore declares that according to Mani Jesus was a phantom, whereas Paul of Samosata regarded him as a mere human being, and concludes with the comment:

---

[73] See the *apparatus testimoniorum* in Allen and Declerck 1989: 241.

[74] Theodore of Raithou, *Praeparatio* (ed. Diekamp 1938: 187.13, 24).

Αὗται μὲν οὖν αἱ πρῶται φυαὶ τοῦ τὴν μίαν φύσιν καὶ τὰς δύο κακῶς καὶ δυσφημῶς λέγεσθαι ἐπὶ τοῦ σωτῆρος Χριστοῦ, τὸ μὲν ἐπ' ἀναιρέσει τῆς ἀνθρωπότητος, τὸ δὲ τῆς θεότητος.[75]

These, then, are the first shoots of speaking wrongly and evilly of the one nature and the two in the case of the saviour Christ, the one so as to eliminate the humanity, and the other so as to eliminate the divinity.

The discussion of the next pair, Apollinarius and Theodore of Mopsuestia, is followed by an almost identical formula, which characterises them as 'second sprout' (δευτέρα βλάστη) of those who held the same divergent views.[76] In the next case, the notion of a genealogy of heresies is emphasised even further. We are told that Nestorius is, after Paul and Theodore of Mopsuestia, the 'third leader' (τρίτος προστάτης) of those who teach two separate natures, and that Eutyches is, after Mani and Apollinarius, the 'third defender' (τρίτος προασπιστής) of the teaching of the one nature.[77] The concatenation of names then appears two more times.[78] In the last instance, the reason for this arrangement is made obvious. The Catholic church, that is the Chalcedonian sect, 'walks on the royal highway' (ὁδῷ βασιλικῇ πορευομένη) between two equally heretical extremes, since it speaks of two natures but at the same time declares that these natures are substantially united in one hypostasis.[79] Here the influence of Leontius of Byzantium makes itself felt. Theodore claims that 'the church pushed away the deviations in either direction of the opposed docetists' (τῆς ἐκκλησίας παρωσαμένης τὰς ἐφ' ἑκάτερα τῶν ἐναντιοδοκητῶν παρατροπάς).[80] Then follows a section about the conflict between the Monophysite theologians Julian of Halicarnassus and Severus of Antioch about the corruptibility of the human aspect of Christ. Here Theodore deviates from the previous pattern, calling Severus the follower of Mani, Apollinarius, and Eutyches, and Julian an even more fervent follower of the same men.[81] This is a recognition of the fact that in the sixth century Nestorianism had been marginalised in christological discourse. Establishing a genealogy was so important for Theodore of Raithou that he spends relatively little time on the actual 'opinions' (δόξαι) of the heretics. The account he gives is highly biased. The doctrinal positions of the fifth and sixth centuries are projected back into

---

[75] Theodore of Raithou, *Praeparatio* (ed. Diekamp 1938: 187.20–22).
[76] Theodore of Raithou, *Praeparatio* (ed. Diekamp 1938: 188.25–26).
[77] Theodore of Raithou, *Praeparatio* (ed. Diekamp 1938: 189.20–21).
[78] Theodore of Raithou, *Praeparatio* (ed. Diekamp 1938: 189.24–25).
[79] Theodore of Raithou, *Praeparatio* (ed. Diekamp 1938: 190.11–17).
[80] Theodore of Raithou, *Praeparatio* (ed. Diekamp 1938: 196.4).
[81] Theodore of Raithou, *Praeparatio* (ed. Diekamp 1938: 196.5–8, 15–16).

the third century, with the result that Mani and Paul appear to be Monophysites and Nestorians *avant la lettre*. They can only be made to fit the overall pattern through misrepresentation of their views.

The treatment of the topic in *De sectis* is quite different. Its author mentions not only christological heresies but also trinitarian ones. Moreover, he starts at a much earlier point, with pre-Christian 'heresies', and he includes more recent heresies. The central part resembles the *Praeparatio* more closely. Here the same heretics appear, and they do so in the same order. Yet the content is arranged in a much less straightforward manner. The discussion begins in lecture two with the Jews and the Samaritans.[82] Yet the structuring principle is only introduced at the beginning of the third lecture.

Ἐπειδὴ περὶ Χριστιανῶν δογμάτων ὁ λόγος, ἀναγκαῖόν ἐστι τῶν χρόνων διαίρεσίν τινα ποιήσασθαι, ἵνα ἐκ τούτων γνῶμεν, τίνες διδάσκαλοι, καὶ ποῖαι αἱρέσεις.[83]

Since the treatise is about Christian doctrines, it is necessary to make some division, in order that we know from it, which teachers, and what kind of heresies there were.

The author begins by distinguishing between the time before Christ and the time after Christ. Then he divides the latter period into three parts, from Christ to the beginning of the reign of Emperor Constantine, from Emperor Constantine to the Council of Chalcedon, and from the Council of Chalcedon to his day.[84] Since he has already spoken about pre-Christian heresies, he adds the comment 'which we have already considered in the previous section' (ὧν ἤδη ἐν τοῖς προλαβοῦσιν ἐμνήσθημεν).[85] The first two Christian periods are then organised according to the pattern that the author has set out. In each case, we find a list of authorities, introduced by the formula 'there were these teachers and fathers' (ἐγένοντο διδάσκαλοι καὶ πατέρες οἵδε),[86] which is then followed by a discussion of various heresies, in the first case those of Mani and Paul of Samosata,[87] and in the second case those of Arius, Macedonius, Apollinarius, Theodore of Mopsuestia, Diodore of Tarsus, and Nestorius.[88] After the discussion of Nestorius' views, the character of the text changes markedly. Whereas up to this point the focus has been entirely on theology, and virtually no historical information has been given, the following paragraphs tell the story of the

---

[82] *De sectis* (PG 86: 1200–12).   [83] *De sectis* (PG 86: 1212C).
[84] Further subdivisions are added, but they do not play a role in the following discussion.
[85] *De sectis* (PG 86: 1212C).   [86] *De sectis* (PG 86: 1213A, 1216B–C).
[87] *De sectis* (PG 86: 1213A–1216B).   [88] *De sectis* (PG 86: 1216C–1221C).

events leading up to the Council of Chalcedon.[89] In lecture five, the historical account that had started in lecture four simply continues. The sequence of fathers and heresies is tacitly dropped. We are given information about the see of Alexandria for the years between Chalcedon and the author's own time.[90] At the very end, he adds two further comments, about the so-called Agnoetes and Tritheists, the former claiming that Christ's human nature did not have the same knowledge as his divine nature, and the latter averring that there were three natures in the divinity and not just one.[91]

The author seeks to help his readers find their way through the confusing welter of heresies by highlighting both similarities and differences between them. This can lead to awkwardness in the arrangement of the material. The problems are particularly evident in the case of Paul of Samosata. The author first explains that Paul had erroneous views about the divinity and the incarnation, claiming that only the Father was eternal whereas the Son came to be in the human being Jesus. Then he distinguishes these teachings from the positions of Nestorius and Sabellius. In the second case, he states that according to Sabellius the same being was Father, Son, and Spirit. Then he adds the remark: 'In those years there also emerged the heresy of Sabellius' (ἐν τοῖς χρόνοις δὲ τούτοις καὶ ἡ Σαβελλίου αἵρεσις ἐγένετο), as if he had not just spoken about him. Instead of offering further information, he continues with the relative clause 'about which we have spoken before' (περὶ ἧς ἐν τοῖς προλαβοῦσιν εἰρήκαμεν).[92] This is a reference to lecture one where the four archetypal heresies are briefly mentioned. In the first case, too, there is awkwardness. When the author later discusses Nestorius' views in their context, he begins with the words: 'But what the doctrine of Nestorius was, we have already said previously, and now let us go through a few things' (τί δὲ ἦν τὸ δόγμα τοῦ Νεστορίου, ἤδη μὲν ἐν τοῖς προλαβοῦσιν εἰρήκαμεν, καὶ νῦν δὲ μικρὰ διεξέλθωμεν).[93]

The two texts differ not only in structure but also in spirit. The *Praeparatio* could only give such a streamlined account because it was highly biased. By contrast, the author of *De sectis* shows himself to be scrupulously even-handed. He stresses that unlike Paul, Nestorius propounded an orthodox trinitarian theology, which is worth noting since in the *Praeparatio* Nestorius is presented as a Paul *redivivus*. In the case of Theodore and Diodore, theologians of the late fourth and early fifth centuries, he goes even further. He states that the two men had been charged with Nestorianism at

---

[89] *De sectis* (PG 86: 1221C–1228A).   [90] *De sectis* (PG 86: 1228B–1232C).
[91] *De sectis* (PG 86: 1232D–1233B).   [92] *De sectis* (PG 86: 1216A–B).
[93] *De sectis* (PG 86: 1221B).

the Second Council of Constantinople, long after their death, as having unduly emphasised the division between divinity and humanity in Christ. Yet then he adds that they were never attacked during their lifetime, and only became controversial when Nestorius built his christology on their teachings.[94]

Conclusion

Pamphilus' *Capita diversa*, Theodore of Raithou's *Praeparatio*, the treatise *De sectis*, and Leontius of Jerusalem's *Contra Monophysitas* were all written in the late sixth or early seventh century. They were produced at a time when christological discourse had begun to fossilise. Their function was to help their Chalcedonian readers to understand the doctrinal position of their own church and to be able to hold their own in debates with members of other sects, in particular with the Monophysites. Yet no two treatises are entirely alike, and there are no borrowings from one text in another. Moreover, the nature of the texts differs greatly. Leontius of Jerusalem writes a refutation with literary pretensions, that hearkens back to the treatises of John of Caesarea and Leontius of Byzantium. Pamphilus' *Capita diversa* have a very simple structure. They consist of questions and answers, and do not contain any transitions from one topic to the next. By contrast, the treatise *De sectis* and Theodore of Raithou's *Praeparatio* have a strongly didactic character. They repeatedly remind the reader of the overall structure of the text and clearly signpost where a topic ends and another begins.

---

[94] See Gleede 2013: 200–2.

34 World and Empire: Contrasting the Cosmopolitan Visions of George of Pisidia and Maximus the Confessor in Seventh-Century Byzantium

PAUL M. BLOWERS

Introduction

As Averil Cameron has demonstrated in a number of incisive studies, and especially in her landmark *Christianity and the Rhetoric of Empire* (1991), the basic hard work of framing and expanding Christian discourse, and so too publicly managing and disseminating Christian knowledge among and beyond elite audiences, was a theatre all its own in the dramatic cultural transitions of early Byzantium. Loosely speaking, it was a team effort – indeed, the prolonged labour of a broad cadre of authors, communicating in increasingly diverse literary and rhetorical genres, and with definite variations of purpose and perspective. Bishops (especially as preachers) played a crucial role, no doubt, but at the end of the day so did erudite deacons like Ephrem the Syrian, Romanos the Melodist, and in our case George of Pisidia, a deacon of Hagia Sophia who rose to fame as a panegyrist for the emperor Heraclius. Non-episcopal monastic writers also contributed in their own ways to the multifaceted 'rhetoric of empire', whether as hagiographers, authors of monastic 'histories' and sapiential texts, or, for our interests here, ascetical and doctrinal theologians like Maximus the Confessor, whose writings ultimately laid claim to a much wider readership than monks.

At stake throughout the early Byzantine era were the solicitation and authorisation of forms of knowledge and 'ways of knowing' responsive to processes of cultural upheaval and redefinition. In the fourth and fifth centuries, it had been a matter of orienting citizens to the idea of a Christian emperor and empire embodied within a cosmos whose transcendent ruler was believed by the faithful to be Christ himself.[1] Instilling confidence in the viability and destiny of such a regime entailed, as Cameron has argued, the rhetorical and epistemic shaping of a Christian 'past', and

---

[1] Cameron 1991: 123–41.

a collective public memory thereof, out of the Hellenic cultural inheritance as well as the church's antecedent experience and identification with sacred biblical history.[2] For example, beyond the writing of imperial history (Procopius, Theophylact Simocatta, et al.) and ecclesiastical history (Eusebius of Caesarea and his heirs), we see, with John Malalas in the fifth century, the beginnings of Byzantine chronography, a literary genre of maturing sophistication that aspired to date creation itself in constructing the timeline of watershed events in the Christian past.[3] Accordingly, cosmic, biblical, and imperial history were of a piece. Commitment to this project deepened rather than subsided during and after the Justinianic age, in a sustained endeavour to establish the cosmic-historical backdrop of the Christian presence and mission in the *oikoumenê*. Even Maximus the Confessor, known principally for his ascetical and theological writings, composed a work of chronography, his *Computus Ecclesiasticus* (*c.* 641 CE).[4]

By the seventh century, however, confidence in this grand imperial and 'cosmic' order was severely tested by an array of storms and stresses: residual instability in the imperial throne prior to the reign of Heraclius; drawn-out military conflict with the Persian empire on the Eastern frontier, including temporary capture of the relic of the True Cross (614 CE); abiding tensions with Slavs and Avars in the Balkans; the rapid Arab onslaught and rise of Islam; and not least of all, the emergence of an intensive new wave of christological controversy in the church, with the imperial establishment deeply involved. Heraclius (r. 610–41 CE), who had revolted against his predecessor Phocas, was technically a usurper in an already uncertain state of affairs, and, despite his dreams of recuperating the glory of Justinian, faced enormous obstacles in administrating, consolidating, and protecting his imperial domains. Into this fray stepped two of the most prolific writers of seventh-century Byzantium, George of Pisidia and Maximus the Confessor, addressing in their distinctive ways the need to sustain the imperial *mythos* in its properly Christian and cosmic dimensions – George as an imperial panegyrist, Maximus as a monastic theologian and controversialist. And yet despite their different platforms, George and Maximus, as we shall see, both resorted to a classical 'way of knowing', Platonic *theôria*, now thoroughly Christianised, in presenting their respective visions of the Byzantine cultural cosmos, wherein creation, empire, and ecclesia were projected as inextricably interconnected – historically *and eschatologically*.

---

[2] Cameron 1991: 120–54; Cameron 1992.   [3] See Jeffreys 2003; Whitby 2007.
[4] PG 19: 1217–80.

Each writer, I shall argue, articulated a 'cosmopolitan' vision to guide souls and consciences, and a tutorial in how the Christian faithful were to appropriate and sustain that vision amid severe crisis.

The Distinctive Vantage Points of George and Maximus

Even though the historical records of George's career are quite limited, they provide a relatively simple profile compared with the complex sources for Maximus. George was a deacon of Hagia Sophia under Patriarch Sergius,[5] but pre-eminently a poet laureate commissioned to eulogise the military and political exploits of Heraclius and to cultivate and amplify his imperial prestige.[6] It was a privileged position for which George actively lobbied.[7] His various panegyric poems for the emperor reveal his capacity to draw lavishly on Homeric epic and classical mythology, on Greek poetic, rhetorical, and philosophical traditions, and on biblical hero stories.[8] Among the many titles assigned to Heraclius (such as a new Hercules,[9] Perseus, Noah,[10] Moses, Elijah, David, Daniel, et al.), George's more embracing images of him as 'deliverer of the world' (κοσμορύστης),[11] as proxy of the divine Logos in saving 'the whole cosmic ship' (ἡ κοσμικὴ ἅπασα ὁλκάς) amid dangerous storms,[12] and as 'commander of cosmic rebirth' (στρατηγὸς κοσμικοῦ γενεθλίου)[13] are most significant to our interests here. At one level, certainly, these epithets are candidly political, even 'apophatically' so, as George confesses the utter inadequacy of his human verses to convey the gravitas of Heraclius as a model of piety and as the divine Word's own agent to redeem the cosmos.[14] This is the emperor purported to have vanquished the very nemesis

---

[5] On the basics of George's career, see Howard-Johnston 2010: 16–35.
[6] There is already much good scholarship on these panegyric poems, including their historical backgrounds and datings. Besides Howard-Johnston 2010, see Whitby 1994 and 1998.
[7] As noted by Lauxtermann 2003: 38–39.
[8] Many of the citations and allusions in this regard have already been identified by George's modern critical editors and commentators: Pertusi 1959; Gonnelli 1991 and 1998; Tartaglia 1997. See also Frendo 1986.
[9] E.g. *De expeditione Persica* 3, lines 349–54 (Pertusi 1959: 131); *Heraclias* 1, lines 65–79 (Pertusi 1959: 243).
[10] *Heraclias*, 1, lines 84–92 (Pertusi 1959: 244).
[11] *In Bonum patricium*, line 7 (Pertusi 1959: 163); *Heraclias* 1, line 70 (Pertusi 1959: 243); *Hexaemeron*, line 1800 (Gonnelli 1998: 238).
[12] *De expeditione Persica* 1, lines 248–52 (Pertusi 1959: 96).
[13] *Heraclias* 1, line 201 (Pertusi 1959: 249).
[14] See *In Heraclium ex Africa redeuntem*, lines 1–38, 86–89 (Pertusi 1959: 77–78, 81). On this important early panegyric and George's attention to inadequacy of language, see Frendo 1984.

of civilisation itself, Khusro II, the 'ancient serpent' *redivivus*, thereby saving the world from the disease of ignorance and irreligion.[15] But particularly in his *Hexaemeron* (*c.* 628–30 CE), which dramatises Heraclius' achievement against the background of the Creator's work in producing and preserving his creation, George moves into a discursive register that is more candidly theological.[16] This is important going forward, since it makes possible a much more engaging comparison with Maximus.

Grounding Maximus the Confessor's vision of world and empire firmly in his own career is a much more complicated affair. Potentially, it would be intriguing to contrast Maximus and George as imperial insiders, were we to take the 'official' Greek *Life* of Maximus as definitive, for by that account, Maximus was reared in Constantinople to prestigious parents who provided him an elite private education, enabling him to serve Heraclius as 'chief secretary of imperial records' until he embraced monastic life.[17] This would corroborate the image of Maximus, like George, as a well-bred loyalist and courtier. But abundant recent scholarship has cast serious doubt on the Greek *Life*, and significant attention has instead been turned to the controversial Syriac *Life* of Maximus, written by a hostile Miaphysite who considers Maximus a native of Palestine, an Origenist monk, and by default a total outsider to the imperial court.[18] Whatever his precise provenance, Maximus' letters and writings, as well as the various biographical documents connected with his trial and demise, provide ample evidence that this monastic pedagogue and disciple of Sophronius entered, during and after Heraclius' reign, a downward spiral of alienation from Constantinople. Quite unlike George, he lived much of his life as a relative migrant in voluntary – and at the last involuntary – exile.[19]

Indeed, in the deepening monenergist–monothelete controversy in Byzantium, the last major phase of the ancient christological debates, Maximus famously pitted himself, and an expanding contingent of Greek monks in Africa and Italy, against emperor and patriarch alike. As we shall see,

---

[15] *In Christi resurrectionem*, lines 64–69 (Tartaglia 1997: 254); *Heraclias*, passim.
[16] There has been lively debate about the religious and theological character of George's panegyric, notably in the *Hexaemeron*. Olster (1991) vigorously insisted that George's panegyric is purely and simply political propaganda, its religious overtones being a mere patina. Whitby (1995) countered by pointing out that religion, far from superficial, provides a crucial matrix for George's panegyric. I too have argued for the seriousness of George's theological interest (Blowers 2020).
[17] Greek *Vita* §1–5, Recension 3, in Neil and Allen 2003: 38–48.
[18] For the text of the Syriac *Life*, see Brock 1973. Booth (2014: 148–49, 153, 234, 239–41, 289–90, 324), among others, has contended for the credibility of elements of the Syriac *Life*.
[19] On the current attempts to reconstruct Maximus' career, see Blowers 2016a: 9–63.

however, the upshot of this dissent was not simple anti-imperial backlash, but calling into question the very legitimacy of a 'Christian Empire'. Maximus' 'cosmopolitan' vision is dialectical and nuanced. It is the vision of a reluctant patriot who, while acknowledging the roles of emperor and patriarch in stabilising the empire and the world at large, holds them both accountable to the mystery that is Jesus Christ, the mystery around which the whole cosmos revolves.

George and Maximus as Cosmopolitan Visionaries

Let me establish what I mean by 'visionaries'. Plato's model of spiritual vision (θεωρία) had a considerable afterlife in early Christianity. While still conveying Plato's sense of piercing beyond the ephemeral veil to 'behold' intelligible realities, *theōria* was also applied in early and medieval Christian usage to the rarefied contemplation of created nature and of scripture as economies of divine self-revelation and as keys to the Creator's purposes, with a view to the highest mystical contemplation of the Trinity.[20] As I will show, both George and Maximus found substantial inspiration in the *theōria* exemplified in all these respects by the Cappadocian fathers. Already lay *didaskaloi* like Clement and Origen inaugurated the Christian discipline of 'contemplation of nature' (θεωρία φυσική), Clement commending doctrine concerning created nature (φυσιολογία), and the consideration of the origins of the world in the light of the 'prophecy' of Gen 1, as requisite to higher *theologia*.[21] The Cappadocians Basil and Gregory of Nyssa took this up in earnest, Basil in his *Homilies on the Hexaemeron* and Gregory in his *Hexaemeron*, taking account of Greco-Roman cosmological science but pressing to a more theologically fruitful vision of the order of creation. The bishops assumed a parallel function to that of the *theoros* in ancient Greece, an intellectual ascetic and philosophical professional charged to gather metaphysical or religious insights from near and far to edify his native *polis*.[22] In his Hexaemeral sermons, Basil acts as a guide leading his audience into the 'sublime and blessed amphitheatre' of creation to be his fellow contemplatives and ascetics in exploring the Creator's wisdom in nature's grand panorama. Like Athanasius before him,

---

[20] For excellent background on θεωρία, see Bénatouïl and Bonazzi 2012.
[21] *Stromateis* 4.1.3 (SC 15: 249). On the background of θεωρία φυσική in Christian usage, see Lollar 2013: 102–20. On Clement's understanding of the role of physics in the philosophical curriculum, see Chapter 5 by Matyáš Havrda, this volume.
[22] On this role, see Nightingale 2004: 40–252.

Basil portrays the universe as an ancient *polis*, bearing its own witness to the creation and fall of humanity and the greater invisible glories still in store for the human race.[23] Elsewhere Gregory Nazianzen, in a sermon on ecclesial order needing to be recovered from chaos, first takes his audience on a tour of the cosmic order as instructive for healthy ecclesial decorum. Gregory compares himself to Moses ascending Sinai to enter more intimately into the divine presence while less worthy souls – not yet competent in this 'way of knowing', unable to endure such a vision, and inarticulate in the mysteries of *theologia* – remain below.[24] Underlying all this, meanwhile, was an admonition to trust the bishop as the church's authoritative 'seer' who mediated to the church the order and perfection of the all-wise Creator.[25] The whole church, then, was invited into θεωρία φυσική, which went well beyond pious wonderment at the beauty and majesty of creation to discern the depths and secrets of God's economy. As Gregory of Nyssa insists, Christians must seek to ascend with the apostle Paul to the vista of the 'third heaven' (2 Cor 12:2–4), passing beyond physical sense to the θεωρία of spiritual realities (τὰ νοητά).[26] Epistemically to penetrate the more sublime truths of creation, however, cannot rely on mere allegorical interpretation of the Hexaemeron;[27] it is a matter of spiritual intuition gained by an attendant asceticism of the mind (and virtuous will) that is impatient of superficiality. Maximus thoroughly concurred that it entailed an overhaul of human perception, involving reason, contemplation, and even the retrained body.[28] As I will discuss later, this heightened θεωρία was attained, for Maximus, precisely through the deeply embedded 'principles' (λόγοι) of all created things, the access points where 'nature' became ever more transparent to supernature.

In Byzantium, the function of *theoros* for the cosmic *polis* ultimately did not have to remain exclusively with bishops. It was virtually built into George of Pisidia's contract as imperial panegyrist. He was to project a vision of the emperor's mission and achievement in their widest possible extent (the whole cosmic *polis* with Constantinople at its centre), and with fervent hope for Byzantium's future flourishing. As I already noted, the whole creation in George's panegyric is the theatrical backdrop for the current outworking

---

[23] *Hom. in Hexaemeron* 6.1 (GCS NF 2: 87–88); on the cosmic *polis*, cf. Athanasius, *Contra gentes* 38, 43, 47 (Thomson 1971: 102–4, 118–20, 132). For extended analysis, see Blowers 2012a: 315–28; 2016b.

[24] *Oratio* 32.1–19 (SC 318: 82–126).   [25] *Oratio* 32.20–33 (SC 318: 126–54).

[26] *Hexaemeron* (GNO 4/1: 81).   [27] *Hexaemeron* (GNO 4/1: 83–84).

[28] See *Amb. Jo.* 10 (PG 91: 1105C–37C, esp. 1112D–16C, 1133A–37C); also the commentary of Steel 2012.

of the divine economy through the agencies of emperor and patriarch. The redundant image whereby the emperor's stabilisation of the empire is of a piece with the Creator's original and continuing work of creation is already found in the *De expeditione Persica*, where George prays that the divine 'Strategist' (Στρατηγός) of heaven and earth, to whom is beholden every creature visible and invisible, will graciously guide his earthly vice-commander, the emperor, to fulfil the holy commandments by vanquishing the wicked passions that haunt the soul and the ignoble barbarians that haunt the earth.[29] Gingerly admitting that the emperor has had foibles in the past for which his present faithfulness to the Creator will atone,[30] George still petitions for Heraclius to be revealed as a new Moses, imitating the ancient biblical sage by becoming a *theoros* in his own right, modelling the contemplative vision (θεωρία) of God while still constrained with bodily eyes (cf. Exod 33).[31]

The historic and cosmic scope of George's vision of Heraclius comes into sharp focus in a passage from the mostly lost ending of George's *Heraclias*, preserved (either as direct quotation or paraphrase) in the *Chronicle* of Theophanes the Confessor:

Now the emperor, having defeated Persia in the course of six years, made peace in the seventh and returned with great joy to Constantinople, thereby fulfilling a certain mystical allegory: for God completed all of creation in six days and called the seventh day a day of rest. So the emperor also, after undergoing many toils for six years, returned in the seventh to the City amid peace and joy, and took his rest.[32]

These are the words not just of a poet but of a *theoros*, and in George's *Hexaemeron*, this vision is carried to a whole new level. What might well have been the culmination of his major panegyrics is oddly titled, for the poem is in no sense a straightforward interpretation of the six-day creation account in Gen 1. In fact, Gen 1 is nowhere even cited in the 1,864 lines of the *Hexaemeron*, save for an oblique reference to the opening words 'in the beginning' or 'heaven and earth' (Gen 1:1), wherewith George opposes the 'great power of a few syllables' (μικρῶν συλλαβῶν κράτος μέγα) to the long-winded cosmological sophistry of the Neoplatonist Proclus.[33] George's silence on Gen 1, however, may well be golden. In a separate essay,[34] I have suggested that George was likely unaware of the ancient rabbinic tradition,

---

[29] *De expeditione Persica* 3, lines 385–410 (Pertusi 1959: 133–34).
[30] *De expeditione Persica* 3, lines 407–9 (Pertusi 1959: 133). On George's consideration of Heraclius' weaknesses, see Whitby 1998: 261–62.
[31] *De expeditione Persica* 3, lines 415–25 (Pertusi 1959: 134).
[32] §327–28, trans. Mango and Scott 1997: 457.
[33] *Hexaemeron*, lines 57–65 (Gonnelli 1998: 120). [34] See Blowers 2020.

taken over by Origen for Christian usage,[35] of reserving Gen 1, along with other privileged sacred texts, only for advanced interpreters. But he quite probably knew the rhetorical discipline, exemplified especially by Gregory Nazianzen and later Maximus, of 'honouring in silence' a particular mystery of faith, guarding its sacrosanct character.[36] And since George defers to earlier Hexaemeral commentators in espousing the intricacies of creation, Basil in particular, there is doubtless no compulsion to add to a venerable tradition of patristic interpretation, something which only Patriarch Sergius, whom George esteems as the authoritative expositor of scripture in relation to current events in Byzantium, could possibly do.[37] His silence on Gen 1, moreover, befits the larger posture of self-limitation characteristic of his entire *Hexaemeron*, as he repeatedly recurs to the inadequacy of his words to fathom the mysteries of the Creator.

In the bulk of the *Hexaemeron*, meanwhile, George opens out his cosmopolitan vision in what Mary Whitby rightly emphasises are deeply personal and religious terms,[38] prepared for a Lenten recitation.[39] George here is fully self-invested as *theoros*, exploring doxologically and philosophically the created order – from the heavenly bodies in their rhythms,[40] to the beauty of the human constitution,[41] to the wonders of the animal kingdom,[42] to the seemingly useless fruits of the earth that have medicinal and other value.[43] The panoply of creation is theophanic through and through, and yet, even in its incalculable magnificence and munificence, it can never fully disclose the Creator who commands the universe through his Logos and his imperial vicegerent. Creatures wisely know the Creator by their silence in his presence: 'How great is that mysterious knowledge of your wise creatures, which announces in unwritten words (ἀγράφοις λόγοις) the divine darkness (τὸν θεῖον γνόφον).'[44] George concedes that even if God

---

[35] Origen, *Comm. Cant.*, pr. 1.7 (SC 375: 84–86).
[36] See Maximus in *Amb. Jo.* 10 (PG 91: 1129C, 1165B); 17 (1228A); 20 (1241B); *Quaestiones ad Thalassium*, intro. (CCSG 7: 37); 21 (CCSG 7: 133); 43 (CCSG 7: 293); *Amb. Th.* 5 (CCSG 48: 31).
[37] See George's praise of the Patriarch's interpretative expertise at *Hexaemeron*, lines 24–33 (Gonnelli 1998: 116–18). Though not mentioning the Patriarch's name, George's prologue to the *Hexaemeron* is addressed directly to Sergius.
[38] Whitby 1995: 116.
[39] Whitby 1995: 125–26; Howard-Johnston 2010: 24. The Lenten occasion is signalled by a reference towards the end of the *Hexaemeron* (lines 823–24, Gonnelli 1998: 240) to Patriarch Sergius being weak-voiced from intense fasting.
[40] *Hexaemeron*, lines 81–359 (Gonnelli 1998: 120–40).
[41] *Hexaemeron*, lines 624–758 (Gonnelli 1998: 158–66).
[42] *Hexaemeron*, lines 916–1293 (Gonnelli 1998: 178–204).
[43] *Hexaemeron*, lines 1488–608 (Gonnelli 1998: 218–26). For helpful analysis of the layout of George's *Hexaemeron*, see Gonnelli 1990.
[44] *Hexaemeron*, lines 731–33 (Gonnelli 1998: 164); cf. lines 81–84 (Gonnelli 1998: 120–22).

were to grant him an ecstatic vision like Peter's (cf. Acts 10:10–16), piercing beyond the heavens to the waters above, the 'abyss from the abyss', he would merely suffer vertigo (ἴλιγξ) and have to fall back because of his creaturely constraints.[45]

Only late in the *Hexaemeron* do we discover that George's *theoria* of creation has been a long, suspenseful build-up to the poem's finale. As he brings things to a close, he first sets forth a doxology on the incarnational ministry (and miracles) of the Logos as a work of 'new creation' (νέα πλάσις), resolving the residual morass of human sin and bringing multiple graces to *all* creatures high and low.[46] George at last places a prayer on the lips of Patriarch Sergius, a bidding to the Creator, the 'Architect of such great marvels', who commands the 'upper gates' of heaven, now to open the 'lower gates' of Constantinople and allow entry for the victorious Heraclius, who is (metaphorically) ready and waiting just outside.[47] In Sergius' words,

For we call this city that you protected the gates of the universe's inhabitants. And grant that he who received power from you, the deliverer of the world (κοσμορύστης), the pursuer of Persia, or rather the one who saved even Persia, should rule all the places under the sun. Show that the earth imitates heaven with one sun ruling also the parts below. For it is fitting that the manifest Persian universe-slayer should also become universal master.[48]

Here Sergius has become the herald of Heraclius' own work of 'new creation'.[49] The theme is mirrored in the *Heraclias*, which celebrates the emperor as a new Hercules who 'choked the fury of the voracious dog [Khusro], which brought Alcestis – that is the *oikoumenê* – back to life', and by defeating the enemy has dispelled all darkness and ushered in a νεωτέρα κτίσις.[50] A new Noah, Heraclius has unfolded a whole new *oikoumenê* after the enemy flood.[51] The crown prince, Heraclius Constantine, moreover, is effectively a new 'Adam', symbolising hope for the future of this new creation.[52]

By contrast, Maximus the Confessor's 'cosmopolitan vision' of the Byzantine empire in relation to the Creator's universal purposes arises from a profoundly divergent discourse spread across an equally divergent array of writings. Here there is no poetry, no panegyric, and to a great extent no emperor except as a shadowy figure in the background of his expansive

---

[45] *Hexaemeron*, lines 1689–719 (Gonnelli 1998: 230–32).
[46] *Hexaemeron*, lines 1720–91 (Gonnelli 1998: 232–38).
[47] *Hexaemeron*, lines 1792–96 (Gonnelli 1998: 238).
[48] *Hexaemeron*, lines 1797–806 (Gonnelli 1998: 238), trans. Whitby 1995: 119.
[49] On George's proclivity for 'new creation' imagery, see Lauxtermann 2019: 31, 34.
[50] *Heraclias* 1, lines 71–84 (Pertusi 1959: 243–44).
[51] *Heraclias* 1, lines 84–92 (Pertusi 1959: 244).
[52] See *In Christi resurrectionem*, lines 64–129 (Tartaglia 1997: 254–58); also Lauxtermann 2019: 34.

θεωρία of the work of Christ the Logos – who was, is, and ever shall be the pre-eminent inaugurator of God's new creation. Lest we quickly paint Maximus as a dissident pure and simple, however, it is good to remember that this reticent patriot valued the Byzantine imperium to the extent that it had the potential not only to maintain political order but to partner with the church in propagating sound christological doctrine. Maximus famously expressed his own fears, for example, about the security of civilised peoples in the face of the Arab invasions, even expressing a quasi-apocalyptic urgency.[53] He also valued his connections with government officials, be it his correspondent John the Chamberlain or various provincial administrators, albeit at a time when some provincial officials, notably his confidant George, prefect of Africa, found themselves at odds with Constantinople. Still, Maximus' perspective on the 'stabilising' role of the empire was fatefully skewed when, around 616 CE, Heraclius and Sergius began to entertain monenergism, and much later Heraclius endorsed the formally monothelete doctrine of Sergius' *Ekthesis* (638 CE), all in a bid to lure Eastern Miaphysites back into the Chalcedonian fold and thereby secure doctrinal allegiance to Constantinople. The monastic insurgency that Maximus organised against imperial monotheletism with the ultimate help of the Roman papacy would lead to his arrest, trials, tortures, and exiles as a political prisoner.[54]

Elsewhere I have spelled out what I see as the distinctiveness of Maximus' cosmopolitan vision, deeming it a 'cosmo-politeian' vision,[55] for in Maximus the ancient and multifaceted notion of *politeia* is arguably more central than *polis*. Before its more formally political usage in Plato's *Republic*, *politeia* indicated the organising of human life for collective thriving, which in Presocratic thought was of a piece with philosophical speculation into the very order of 'nature' (φύσις) vis-à-vis the divine.[56] Over time, *politeia* could also mean citizenly demeanour, or in the ecclesial and monastic contexts of the early church, the disciplinary regimen of the moral and spiritual life. Maximus for his part takes it up christologically. Explicating Dionysius the Areopagite's controversial idea of the single 'theandric activity' (θεανδρικὴ ἐνέργεια) according to which Christ lived his earthly life (πολιτευσάμενος),[57] Maximus identifies this with Christ's unique and unprecedented *politeia*, his 'life lived according to the law of nature', which, since he dwelled in two natures, simultaneously satisfied the laws

---

[53] *Ep.* 14 (PG 91: 540A–B, 541B).
[54] For a good survey of these developments, and presentation of the documents connected with them, see Allen and Neil 2002.
[55] Blowers 2016a: esp. 130–34, 202.   [56] See Lollar 2013: 43–99.
[57] *Amb. Th.* 5 (CCSG 48: 29, lines 204–5; 30, lines 211–12), commenting on Dionysius, *Ep.* 4 (PTS 36: 161).

of humanity and divinity.[58] More, indeed, than just an exemplary earthly life, Christ's 'new' *politeia* was a function of the perfect circumincession (περιχώρησις) of his natures, manifesting the ineffable mode (τρόπος) of his recreated, deified, *eschatological* humanity (and creaturehood).[59]

What is more, Christ's unique *politeia* is intrinsically bound up with his cosmic rule and ministry as divine Logos. As universal Word, he authors three commanding laws for the world: the law of created nature, the law of scriptural revelation, and the transcending law of grace. Together they govern his creative and redemptive economy, and all have their prime focus and fulfilment in his embodiment in Jesus Christ.[60] The three laws, which are complemented by what Maximus designates as three 'incarnations' of the Logos (in/as the *logoi* of creation, in words and meanings of scripture, and in Jesus of Nazareth), serve the progressive participation of all created beings in Christ's *politeia*, at the level of their own individuated natures and modes of existence. Maximus insists that Christ's new *politeia* (≈ unique 'theandric activity') has effectively opened the way for renovating all created beings. Not only the miracle of his incarnation itself, but the miracles of his earthly ministry demonstrated his power to innovate the behaviours (τρόποι ≈ πολιτεῖαι) of created natures of all kinds.[61] All created beings are projected to a new kind of agency (moral and otherwise) in the transfigured state of creation.

Indeed, in Maximus' cosmo-politeian vision, Christ's new creation takes shape as an expanding 'cosmic liturgy' of adoration and service, an *eschatological* liturgy ingathering creatures of all ranks and vocations, from the highest heavens to the depths of the earth – a sanctuary not constrained by the boundaries of empire. Maximus draws heavily here on Dionysius the Areopagite, who envisioned divine revelation as disclosing the 'divinely delivered and theo-mimetic regimens of life' (θεοπαραδότους καὶ θεομιμήτους πολιτείας) appropriate to Christ's disciples,[62] and as setting in motion a kind of cosmic mimesis in which lower creatures imitate higher ones[63] – such as human beings imitating the angels[64] – in perpetual

---

[58] *Amb. Th.* 5 (CCSG 48: 32–33, lines 260–66).
[59] See *Disputatio cum Pyrrho* (PG 91: 345D).
[60] Cf. *Qu. Thal.* 19 (CCSG 7: 119, lines 7–30); 39 (CCSG 7: 259, lines 14–45); *Amb. Jo.* 10 (PG 91: 1128D–33A, 1149C–53C).
[61] Cf. *Amb. Jo.* 42 (PG 91: 1341D–45A); *Amb. Th.* 5 (CCSG 48: 23).
[62] *De ecclesiastica hierarchia* 3.3.4 (PTS 36: 83).
[63] Already in Dionysius, see *De caelesti hierarchia* 7.2 (PTS 36: 29); *Eccl. hier.* 2.3.6 (PTS 36: 77).
[64] See Maximus' *Capita de caritate* 3.33; 3.80; 3.94 (Ceresa-Gastaldo 1963: 158–60, 182, 188); also *Amb. Jo.* 10 (PG 91: 1168A); 20 (1241A); 41 (1305D, 1308A); 50 (1368B); *Liber asceticus* (CCSG 40: 121–23).

assimilation to the perfect divine Image, Jesus Christ. The church, not the empire, sponsors the true *politeia*, fortified by true teaching on the incarnation and by practice of the Christian virtues.[65] Christ, and derivatively the church, hosts the realisation of a new creation, as dramatised in its Divine Liturgy and sacraments.[66]

The political ramifications of Maximus' vision may be more latent than overt, but their subtlety is itself significant. In a passage in his *Ambigua to John*, Maximus reflects on how Christ's universal sovereignty has been embodied in the insignia of the cross hoisted on his shoulders (the image enshrined in the celebrated mosaic of Christ Militant in the Archiepiscopal Chapel at Ravenna). 'He was first to bear it', says Maximus, but 'afterward he gave [it] … to another to bear, indicating through these things that whoever is entrusted with governing must first lead those who are governed, by complying with all the rules of government (for only thus will his own rulings be acceptable), and then he can issue directives to those who have been entrusted to him to perform the same things'.[67] Just when we might think that Maximus was imagining Christ to have passed the symbol of his rule to emperor or patriarch, he instead indicates that he is speaking of the *ascetical* bearers of his cross, those victorious over the passions. There is no triumphalism here save the confidence accompanying disciplined participation in the *politeia* of Christ. But since that participation also entailed, in Maximus' judgement, right knowledge of the manner of Christ's incarnation (i.e. orthodox christological conviction), that same confidence was needed to motivate fellow monastic dissenters in Maximus' fateful challenge to imperial monotheletism.

Protocols and *Paideia* for Contemplating the Cosmos

Thus far we find little real compatibility in the cosmopolitan visions proper to George and Maximus. That changes, however, when we scrutinise their respective instructions for contemplating the cosmos as a 'natural' order, not just an imperial-cultural one. Both authors contributed to what Averil Cameron calls the stabilisation of knowledge in Byzantium in the face of the twin threats of doctrinal crisis from within and encroaching enemies from without. 'What mattered', she observes, 'was the achievement of a

---

[65] *Qu. Thal.* 48 (CCSG 7:339).
[66] For detailed discussion, focusing on Maximus' *Mystagogia*, see Blowers 2016a: 166–95.
[67] *Amb. Jo.* 32 (PG 91: 1284A–B).

discourse that provided for a secure sense of total order, the perception that all knowledge could be contained in one system embracing all things divine and human.'[68] And yet, I would suggest, it was not just a remastered discourse that mattered, but also the appeal to the deep *intuitions* of Christians about the world they inhabited. Even if George was writing primarily for elites in Byzantium,[69] and Maximus for monks, this did not restrict the scope and relevance of their work for a much broader Christian public. Both George and Maximus were invested in training Christians in ascetic and epistemic protocols for seeing the 'enduring reality' (μένουσα οὐσία)[70] beneath and beyond the vicissitudes of history. Both held to a providentialist account of this 'enduring reality', but differed significantly on the capacity of the empire, even when aligned with the church, sufficiently to host and sustain it.

For both George and Maximus, in part because of shared sources (namely, the Cappadocian Fathers and Dionysius the Areopagite) and their reverence for the deeply rooted ascetic and monastic traditions of their time,[71] contemplation must ever be attended by an intense asceticism. Basic to that asceticism, furthermore, is contrition and lament over the fallen state of the world and one's own implication in the 'vanity' (ματαιότης) to which creation has been punitively but redemptively subjected (cf. Eccl 1:2; Rom 8:19–23). Apart from his panegyrics, George's two meditative and sobering poems *On the Vanity of Life* and *On Human Life* bring into sharp focus the raw instability of existence that underlies and undermines humanity's attempts to secure itself. On its own terms, apart from God, human life is mere folly. We human beings are mere dirt, emerging, as it were, from an abyss and yet animated with the image of God, left to 'decry our earthly tragedies and scoff at what merely appears to be life'.[72] We pridefully and scandalously recur to the rule of Fortune (τύχη), betraying our true origins.[73] We ignore our own magnificent human nature.[74] We strive for merely material stability on a throne of our

---

[68] Cameron 1992: 271.
[69] As Lauxtermann (2003: 39) observes, George's verse is so complex and recondite that it would have been hard work even for elites to comprehend.
[70] *In Heraclium ex Africa redeuntem*, lines 72–75 (Pertusi 1959: 80).
[71] For George, even in a panegyric like the *Hexaemeron*, these are simply presupposed, as emphasised by Pertusi 1956: 408.
[72] *De vanitate vitae*, lines 53–56 (Tartaglia 1997: 430–32).
[73] *De vanitate vitae*, lines 13–21, 128–29, 142–48, 172–85 (Tartaglia 1997: 428–30, 436–38, 428–40); *De vita humana*, lines 8–14, 78–80 (Gonnelli 1991: 123–24, 129).
[74] *De vita humana*, lines 31–51 (Gonnelli 1991: 125–27); cf. *Hexaemeron*, lines 636–758 (Gonnelli 1998: 158–66).

own vain making.[75] We habitually succumb to pride, envy, greed, and all manner of passions.[76] We make of life a bad stage play:

Hence for me the shadowy glitter of a life that loves play
seems but a stage impression, as when other men
being mocked by turn and mocking in rounded theatres
seated on a throne a man with ridiculous face
resplendent in improvised cloak, yet mocked
because he thought to hide poverty with wealth not his.[77]

George goes further, depicting himself, sometimes even in his panegyric poems, as a lowly ascetic mired in passions and ignorance. He implores the God who opened the mouth of Balaam's ass (Num 22:28) to open the gates of his own reasoning and press him beyond the passions that impede his speech.[78] He requires divine aid to dispel the 'gloom' (ζόφος) that shrouds him, his failure of articulation, the 'cognitive blindness' (γνωστικῆ ἀβλεψία) and 'cloud of anxiety' (τῆς μερίμνης νέφος) and 'desolate heart' (ἐρῆμος καρδία) that encumber him.[79] Expression of profound humility, especially at the front of discourses, was a rhetorical *topos* to be sure, and one that Maximus too abundantly engaged, as when he bewails the 'cloud' or 'veil' of the flesh that frustrates contemplation and obstructs the mind's passover (διάβασις) to noetic realities.[80] But, for both George and Maximus, this is more than a rhetorical convention. The posture of docility and the confession of incapacitation necessarily precede any and all advance in contemplation.

Maximus too couches the contemplative quest in a necessary and sobering appraisal of the 'stunted' (κολοβουμένη)[81] state of human existence after the Adamic fall. Not surprisingly, his diagnosis is far more theologically nuanced than George's, but there is a compatible consciousness of the ontological vulnerability of humanity, the 'weakness' (ἀσθένεια) of our nature apart from the Creator,[82] and the post-lapsarian liability to destructive

---

[75] *De vita humana*, lines 59–64 (Gonnelli 1991: 127–28); cf. *De vanitate vitae*, lines 86–105 (Tartaglia 1997: 434).

[76] On pride, see esp. *De vanitate vitae*, lines 22–33, 242–45 and passim (Tartaglia 1997: 430, 444). On greed (ἀπληστία), see *De vanitate vitae*, lines 196–97 (Tartaglia 1997: 440); as φιλαργυρία, also *Hexaemeron*, lines 780–85 (Gonnelli 1998: 168). On envy (φθόνος), see *De vanitate vitae*, lines 192–95 (Tartaglia 1997: 440); *Epigramma* 111 (Tartaglia 1997: 504).

[77] *De vita humana*, lines 67–72 (Gonnelli 1991: 128–29), trans. Whitby 2014: 440.

[78] *De vanitate vitae*, lines 1–2 (Tartaglia 1997: 428).

[79] *Hexaemeron*, lines 5–23 (Gonnelli 1998: 116).

[80] *Amb. Jo.* 10 (PG 91: 1112A–B); cf. *Amb. Jo.* 6 (1065B–68C). For Maximus' own exemplification of this humility, see Blowers 2016a: 71–73.

[81] *Qu. Thal.* 65 (CCSG 22: 279, l. 454).

[82] Cf. *Amb. Jo.* 7 (PG 91: 1069A, 1091A–B); *Amb. Jo.* 8 (1104D, 1105A–B); *Amb. Th.* 5 (CCSG 48: 17).

passions that weigh down the entire human race.[83] Humans are subjects of a fateful dialectic of pleasure and pain that has effectively become existential law, a new normal as it were.[84] Our life is marked by an ambiguity to which only Christ, the New Adam, can bring clarity and hope.[85] In order to transcend their epistemic limitations, human beings are called to specific ascetical protocols in the quest for knowledge of God and the world.[86]

For both George and Maximus, the pursuit of a higher θεωρία φυσική requires not just contrition but a robust *self-knowledge*, a philosophical imperative deeply rooted in ancient Greek *paideia*, but more immediately modelled in the Cappadocians. Basil of Caesarea representatively outlined how the Christian ascetic must cognitively pierce through the flesh, the sinful self, to the true nature thoroughly outfitted for virtue.[87] Basil certainly lies behind George's admonition that, before rashly aspiring to the highest heights of contemplation, the Christian subject must accede to the axiomatic 'γνῶθι σαυτόν'.[88] This prefaces his long excursus on the intricacies of human nature, including the mind (νοῦς) and the 'eye of the soul' (ὄμμα τῆς ψυχῆς) in their capacity for more sublime contemplation, although George, sounding much like a monk, abruptly warns of the Devil who continuously lies in wait to assail the mind with vain thoughts (λογισμοί) and passions.[89]

Maximus for his part, we know, had thoroughly assimilated formative Eastern monastic traditions of spiritual anthropology and moral psychology in which scrupulous self-knowledge (in tandem with repentance and compunction) was instrumental to the contemplative life. For him, the soul and its faculties are themselves objects of contemplation. Self-knowledge not only serves self-mastery (ἐγκράτεια) in the ascetic sense but can release the soul's native powers to their proper performance in the spiritual life. The mind (νοῦς) can, for example, discriminate the constitutive factors in the emergence of dangerous passions: a sensible object, sense itself, and a faculty of the tripartite soul (reason, desire, or temper) that has deviated from its natural function. By a kind of intro-circumspection, then, the mind can assert its hegemony, and induce a healthy correlation between these things such that it purifies destructive passions and strengthens the soul for its true vocation.[90]

---

[83] *Qu. Thal.* 1 (CCSG 7: 47–49); 21 (CCSG 7: 127–33).
[84] See esp. *Qu. Thal.* 61 (CCSG 22: 85–97).
[85] For discussion, see Blowers 2016a: 199–224, esp. 221–24.
[86] See the substantive study of Dimitrova 2016.
[87] See his *Homilia in illud: Attende tibi ipsi*, ed. Rudberg 1962.
[88] *Hexaemeron*, lines 626ff. (Gonnelli 1998: 158).
[89] *Hexaemeron*, lines 734–58 (Gonnelli 1998: 165–66). [90] *Qu. Thal.* 16 (CCSG 7: 109).

Still another protocol for contemplation shared by George and Maximus is their *heuristic* rule. Beyond mere inquisitiveness or curiosity (πολυπραγμοσύνη), which, as Gregory of Nyssa cautioned, can either help or hinder the contemplative life,[91] the Christian is called to relentless investigation of the deep structure and mysterious frontiers of the cosmos, not for knowledge's own sake but for that of greater intimacy with the elusive Creator. It is a venture that can take the subject into dizzying heights, even to the point of speculation and pious 'conjecture' (στοχασμός) in trying to fathom the Creator's self-revelation.[92] This heuristic rule thus converges with another, the apophatic rule that the contemplative quest is interminable (and so too transformative) because the triune Creator is himself infinite and incomprehensible. Both rules necessitate models and mentors, and while they called on a variety of biblical exemplars, neither George nor Maximus (both in deference to Gregory Nazianzen and Gregory of Nyssa) could resist focusing supremely on Moses, the master of θεωρία φυσική and θεωρία μυστική alike. George desires the astute and diligent Christian to become like a new Moses:

having reverently genuflected like Moses, and having found smoke in the wind and darkness, and reaching the cleft [in the rock] that served as his spur, [such a person] shall scarcely look upon the hidden back parts of God (Exod 33:18–33), and seeing nothing more, shall desire what is hidden all the more; for the desires of lovers are rendered idle if they quickly gain what they desired. And with everyone who searches after the essence of God, the more he beholds, the more he squints his eyes. For if someone with acquisitive pupils, staring down into the deep or up at the blazing disk of the sun, dulls his pupils the more intently he gazes, what sort of all-seeing mind will endure looking on the very one who forms the light of this sun of ours?[93]

According to Maximus, Moses had already mastered natural contemplation before he ever ascended Sinai, where he worthily acquired 'knowledge embracing the genesis of time and nature', revealing it in his face (Exod 34:30–35) and in his written inheritance, and paving a way for others to follow.[94] It was altogether fitting, then, for Moses to take his place as a witness

---

[91] *De vita Moysis* II (GNO 7/1: 66–67, 87).
[92] Both George (*Hexaemeron*, line 752 (Gonnelli 1998: 166)) and Maximus (e.g., *Qu. Thal.* 55 (CCSG 7: 481–83); *Amb. Jo.* 71 (PG 91: 1412A–B)) know the principle of pious 'conjecture' from Gregory of Nyssa (e.g., *Hom. in Canticum Canticorum* (GNO 6: 37)), though it has even earlier roots in Philo.
[93] *Hexaemeron*, lines 831–72 (Gonnelli 1998: 172–74). On the 'insatiable' desire for the Creator, see also *Hexaemeron*, lines 1678–88 (Gonnelli 1998: 230).
[94] *Amb. Jo.* 10 (PG 91: 1117A–C, 1148A–49C).

on another mountain, at the Transfiguration of Christ, where the Lord illuminated not only his own incarnate face but the secrets of creation and scripture.[95]

The parallel apophaticism of George and Maximus owes much to their common reliance on Dionysius the Areopagite as well as on the two Cappadocian Gregories. George, like Maximus, revels in the paradoxically frustrating and energising game of hide-and-seek that the Creator has put in play for those who engage in contemplation of the creation in hopes of advancing to the higher mysteries of *theologia*:

> For if the abyss of reason sinks into you (God), you, being exalted at the summit [of reality] still do not wish to manifest yourself. And if our minds rise to the ultimate height, you yourself turn them back in the opposite direction toward the deepest abyss, such that neither does their length escape your depth, nor their breadth have your height as its reach. Rather, the profuse flow of infinite things toward the infinite is cut short by your own extension (παρεκτάσει), just as, need it be said, even those things not yet created depend on your intention to be brought into being. For you are present, and, being present, you are absent. You remain yet you flee, and like a pale shadow, when seized on you evade grasp.[96]

For Maximus, this divine hide-and-seek has always been the work of the immanent divine Logos, who 'plays' (παίζει) among and with his creatures, teasing them away from their infatuation with ephemeral things and goading them onward and upward to more enduring realities, even the mystical knowledge of God itself.[97] In the same vein, Maximus draws on Dionysius' image of the Creator going out of himself ecstatically, beguiled by his deep love for his creatures and desiring to draw them into gracious communion with himself.[98] The dialectic of divine absence (radical transcendence) and presence (radical immanence) – the Logos who 'in appearing conceals himself, and in hiding manifests himself'[99] – proves crucial in Maximus' understanding of θεωρία in all its contexts. The contemplation of nature, being the deep exploration of the principles (λόγοι) of all created things, opens real access to God's teleological purposes for the cosmos, but since it is the Logos (Christ) himself who indwells and who in some sense 'is' the

---

[95] *Amb. Jo.* 10 (PG 91: 1125D–33A).   [96] *Hexaemeron*, lines 1665–77 (Gonnelli 1998: 230).
[97] *Amb. Jo.* 71 (PG 91: 1413C–16A), commenting on the image of the 'playful' Logos in Gregory Nazianzen, *Poemata theologica (moralia)* 1.2.2 (PG 37: 624A–25A). See also *Amb. Jo.* 10 (PG 91: 1153B–C). For further examination of this motif, see Blowers 2012b.
[98] *Amb. Jo.* 71 (PG 91: 1413A–B), citing Dionysius, *De divinis nominibus* 4.12 (PTS 33: 159).
[99] *Amb. Jo.* 10 (PG 91: 1129B–C).

logoi,[100] the eschatological fullness of his presence in, with, and for the creation still remains elusive and mysterious. Being forever the 'forerunner of himself' (πρόδρομος ἑαυτοῦ),[101] he alone holds the key to creation's future.

Conclusion

The turbulent seventh century in Byzantium demanded its cultural commentators, a role already long filled by historians, chroniclers, scholars, and rhetors. But the labour of the *theoros* – be he a bishop, a deacon, or even an unordained monk – was an expertise all its own, one that could be altogether institutionalised and imperially sanctioned, as with the panegyrist George, or else wholly of a charismatic or prophetic character, as with Maximus. The *theoros*, as a 'seer' contemplating the foundations and architecture of the world, also projected the true stability of that world amid and beyond the fray of human events and historical circumstances, and assumed the task of integrating the past, present, and future of the cosmic *polis* into a single comprehensive vision, taking due account of Byzantium's classical and biblical legacies.

Despite the profound differences of their political dispositions and social locations, with George a professional imperial loyalist and Maximus an imperial dissident-in-the-making, there is an intriguing comparison in the way that both authors, with their contrasting discursive strategies, frame the livelihood of the Byzantine *oikoumenê* against the backdrop of the history of creation itself and the emergence of a 'new creation', a new flourishing amid the crises in the foreground of the empire and the church. Indeed, each writer aspired to articulate what we might call a *teleo-cosmology*, something more trenchant than a world-view or a narratable cosmic *mythos*, since it intended to provide a deeper ontological interpretation of the sources of instability and stability in the cosmos, and to contemplate divine providence not simply as an object of faith or an antidote to fatalism but as the cooperative outworking of divine and creaturely agencies concretely in nature and in the contingencies of history.

For George, at least in his panegyric poems, this teleo-cosmology is candidly political, and centred on the emperor as the principal human

---

[100] *Amb. Jo.* 7 (PG 91: 1077C–85A). For Maximus' actual procedure of θεωρία φυσική, which, like Clement, Origen, and Evagrius before him, he couches between 'ethical' and 'theological' *philosophia*, see esp. *Amb. Jo.* 10 (PG 91: 1133A–37C). For a detailed investigation of θεωρία φυσική, see Lollar 2013: 169–332; Steel 2012.

[101] *Amb. Jo.* 21 (PG 91: 1253D).

actor in the drama of the new and salutary order of things inaugurated by Jesus Christ. The profile, however, is not without nuance, not only because the Christian imperial aura or persona is larger than any one holder of it, including Heraclius, but also because the emperor must himself model penitence, asceticism, and contemplative devotion to Christ in order to sustain the integrity of this new creation. But for Maximus, Christ, as the Creator-Logos, perennially needs no earthly viceroy to do his bidding, even if the emperor and patriarch can serve noble ends for the orthodox faith and the vitality of the *oikoumenê*. As he confesses in a letter to John the Chamberlain, an emperor is only as good as his service to the divine will; otherwise, he puts his trust in flawed earthly advisors, makes them his minions, and instigates disorder.[102] Christ's *new* creation has been in the works literally from the beginning of the world. It was latent in the *logoi* of all created things and has now been disclosed in Christ's incarnation, passion, and resurrection, the summation of God's purposes.[103] Maximus' proto-scholastic fervency for conceptual and terminological precision in the fight against monothelete christology, which brought him to violent loggerheads with Constantinople, is explained in part as a function of his fierce defence of Christ as the singular cosmic ruler, the unique dramaturge of salvation and transformation to whom all creatures are accountable.

Still, we have found some remarkable commonalities in the ways that George and Maximus commended their respective visions to their Christian audiences. Very much in the spirit of the Cappadocian Fathers, George and Maximus expected and prompted their audiences to be fellow ascetics and contemplatives. They invited them to participate actively in a collective θεωρία of the new creation continuing to take shape in their midst, a work begun at the very inception of the world and reiterated in all manner of divine interventions in history. Discursive appeal was crucial, no doubt, but so was the appeal to Christians' religious intuition, the same intuition that was concurrently being formed and reformed in early Byzantium through the veneration of (speechless) icons and participation in the church's liturgical and sacramental mysteries.

---

[102] *Ep.* 10 (PG 91: 449A–53A).
[103] *Capita theologica et oeconomica* 1.66 (PG 90: 1108A–B); *Qu. Thal.* 60 (CCSG 22: 73–81).

35 | Boethius on the Ordering of Knowledge

JOHN MAGEE

> *Sed cum artium multa sint genera, ingenio philosophantis animi primae omnium liberales occurrunt. hae quidem omnes aut trivii aut quadruvii ratione clauduntur, et tantam dicuntur optinuisse efficaciam apud maiores qui eis diligenter institerant ut omnem aperirent lectionem, ad omnia intellectum erigerent, et omnium quaestionum quae probari possunt difficultatem sufficerent enodare.*
> John of Salisbury, *Metal.* 1.12

Artes Liberales (I)

Sometime in the 470s or 480s CE,[1] very near the year of Boethius' birth (*c.* 480), Martianus Capella composed his *De nuptiis Philologiae et Mercurii*, a bizarrely fascinating compendium of the sciences (arts), selecting seven[2] for review, assigning a separate book to each, and treating them as coordinate fields of knowledge, i.e., as unsubordinated either to one another or to any other disciplines.[3] An overarching ordering is indeed evident insofar as the three linguistic disciplines of Grammar, Dialectic, and Rhetoric (Books 3–5) precede the four mathematical ones of Geometry, Arithmetic, Astronomy, and Music (Books 6–9), with additional hints to the effect that the seven together form a 'cycle', an 'encyclopaedic' whole (*disciplinae cyclicae*) or ἐγκύκλιος παιδεία.[4] For those accustomed to Boethius' thought, however, there are two puzzling points in Martianus' ordering – the placement of Arithmetic after Geometry and of Music after Astronomy. Why not begin instead with the science of number, first absolute then relative (Arithmetic, Music), and proceed thereafter to the study of quanta, first stationary then mobile (Geometry, Astronomy)? Such a disposition would appear, at any rate, to provide more rigorous support for the notion of philosophical ascent

---

[1] Shanzer 1986: 28. [2] Excluding Medicine and Architecture (*Nupt.* 9.891).
[3] I. Hadot 1984: 137–55; Grebe 1999: 701–801 (with I. Hadot 2004).
[4] Martianus Capella, *Nupt.* 9.998; cf. Quintilian, *Inst.* 1.10.1; Pliny the Elder, *Nat.* pref. 14; Seneca, *Ep.* 88.23; Augustine, *Acad.* 3.4.7; below, n. 18.

that so obviously informs Martianus' general plan. Unsettling, in other words, is the apparent lack of internal ranking for the four mathematical sciences, which leaves uncertain their relationship to one another and the order in which they are to be studied. It looks as though Martianus has sequenced the sciences, but not ordered them in any strong sense.[5] Along with Boethius' *Institutio arithmetica*, Martianus' work became a literary and educational cornerstone of the Carolingian and subsequent eras.[6] And yet the two works cannot be construed as having charted a coherent course for the development of medieval school curricula: Boethius and Martianus were two very different minds, and at some level medieval readers would ultimately have to decide between them. The point may be illustrated with reference to a Carolingian scholium to Horace (*Ars* 306–7) which appears to furnish the first attestation for *trivium* as denoting the three linguistic arts of Grammar, Dialectic, and Rhetoric:

> *I will* also *teach what* it is that *nurtures the poet*, as in the case of Logic (sc., Grammar, Dialectic, and Rhetoric), and *what informs the poet*, as in the case of Ethics, which pertains to character, and Physics, which treats of the natures of things and embraces the Quadrivium; and the Quadrivium has the capacity to *inform* precisely because it is reached only by way of the Trivium.
>
> *et etiam* DOCEBO QUID *sit illud quod* ALAT POETAM, *ut logica, scilicet grammatica, dialectica, et rhetorica, et* QUID *sit illud quod* INFORMAT POETAM, *ut est ethica, quae ad mores pertinet, et physica, quae de naturis rerum tractat, in qua continetur quadruvium; et datur quadruvio ideo* INFORMARE *quia numquam illuc venitur nisi per trivium.*[7]

From Martianus and Cassiodorus (to whom we will turn later), Carolingian writers inherited the notion of a closed system of seven arts, so that, from the Boethian *quadruvium*, the scholiast could readily deduce and christen a trivium of linguistic arts. His use of 'Logic' is apparently influenced by Boethius' distinction between a Peripatetic sense of *logica* and a Stoic or Platonic one of *dialectica*,[8] while his broader construct harkens back to an ancient division of philosophy frequently associated with the Stoics, and before them Plato.

---

[5] See I. Hadot 1984: 149, 171–72; Boethius, *Inst. arith.*, xlvi–l (ed. Guillaumin); Grebe 1999: 733–37.
[6] I do not enter here into the possible connections between Boethius and Martianus' *De nuptiis* or Ennodius' *Paraenesis didascalica*.
[7] Zechmeister 1877: 36–37; cf. Rajna 1928.   [8] See below, n. 48.

Philosophy:
    Logic (*trivium*)
    Ethics
    Physics (*quadruvium*).[9]

If Boethius takes credit for having applied *quadruvium* to the mathematical disciplines, we have the scholiast to thank for rescuing *trivium* from the ancient streets and giving it a home in medieval schoolrooms.[10]

The notion of a unified cycle of liberal arts appears to have been Roman rather than Greek in inspiration, with speculative roots in Cicero and the New Academic tradition he represented, and drawing varying degrees of public support from the time of Julius Caesar on.[11] Sometime *c.* 100 CE, Nicomachus of Gerasa postulated, as we will see, a coherent model of the four mathematical disciplines of Arithmetic, Music, Geometry, and Astronomy,[12] a construct which was to prove a unifying theme for Calcidius' great and diffuse commentary on Plato's *Timaeus*, written sometime *c.* 325–*c.* 400.[13] Calcidius outruns Nicomachus in locating the mathematical disciplines within a taxonomy which at its highest divide separates Practical (*actus*) from Theoretical (*consideratio*) cognitive modes, as in a traditional Peripatetic method of organisation to which we will turn presently.[14] Beneath the Practical division, Calcidius situates the study of private, domestic, and public affairs, the disciplines of Ethics, Economics, and Politics, and beneath the Theoretical division, Theology, Physics, and Mathematics or possibly (also) Logic (*praestandae rationis scientia*).[15] Physics, the domain of the *Timaeus*, stands above Mathematics, and higher

---

[9] Cicero, *Acad.* 19; *Luc.* 114; *De or.* 1.68; Seneca, *Ep.* 88.24; Plutarch, *Stoic. rep.* 1035a; Apuleius, *Dogm. Plat.* 1.3; Diogenes Laertius, *Lives* 1.18; 3.56; 7.39; Sextus Empiricus, *Math.* 7.16 (Xenocrates, frag. 1 Heinze; Posidonius, frags. 87–88 Edelstein-Kidd); *SVF* 2.35–38; cf. Aristotle, *Top.* 105b19–25; Augustine, *Civ.* 8.4; Macrobius, *Somn.* 2.17.15. Alcuin similarly subordinates the four mathematical sciences (Arithmetic, Geometry, Music, Astronomy) to Physics (*Opp. didasc.* (PL 101.952b)) but augments the linguistic arts with orthography (901c–20a); and although Hrabanus Maurus obliquely distinguishes between logic (Grammar, Rhetoric, Dialectic) and mathematics (Arithmetic, Geometry, Music, Astronomy), he does not mention a trivium or quadruvium as such (*Inst. cleric.* 3.20, 542.23–24 Zimpel²). Cf. Isidore, *Etym.* 2.24.3–7: Physics (Arithmetic, Geometry, Music, Astronomy) – Ethics (Prudence, Fortitude, Temperance, Justice) – Logic (Dialectic, Rhetoric). See also Chapter 5 by Matyáš Havrda, this volume, which examines Clement of Alexandria's version of the divisions of philosophy.

[10] Cf. Bonner 1977: 116–17.

[11] E.g., Cicero, *De or.* 1.9–11, 187; cf. I. Hadot 1984: 44–61, 221–30.

[12] Excluding Stereometry (Plato, *Resp.* 528a–d; Pseudo-Plato, *Epin.* 990d).

[13] Calcidius, *In Tim.* 2, 355; cf. 32, 55; cf. Reydams-Schils 2020: 21, 25, 37.

[14] Aristotle, *Metaph.* 993b19–21; cf. 1025b18–26a28; *Top.* 145a15–18; *Eth. Nic.* 1139a26–31; *Eth. Eud.* 1214a9–15; Diogenes Laertius, *Lives* 5.28.

[15] Calcidius, *In Tim.* 264–65.

still stands Theology, the domain of the *Parmenides*.[16] Matters are complicated by the fact that Calcidius also hints at the 'Stoic' division of Philosophy (Ethics, Physics, Logic)[17] without investigating its relationship to the 'Peripatetic' one. In short, medieval readers would have been hard-pressed to extract a coherent system of sciences from Calcidius, precisely because his brief exposition of the question in the three main passages at issue (*In Tim.* 148, 264–65) suggests slightly confused reliance upon a doxographical tradition of some sort. There is, however, one point on which Calcidius consistently evinces focused intention, and that is the purpose of his commentary. For although hazy, if not confused, in his command of details, he deliberately makes the commentary an occasion for mapping out, perhaps at the request of his dedicatee Osius, a plan for a liberal education (*studia humanitatis*), a Platonising 'path' or 'method' (*via*) leading from the quadripartite mathematical προπαιδεία to a unified vision of the highest realities.[18] That either Calcidius or Osius nurtured hopes of founding a school or establishing a fixed academic curriculum cannot be determined from the evidence of the commentary, but it seems unlikely.

The first securely datable articulation of a 'cycle' of interconnected arts occurs in the second book of Augustine's *De ordine*, composed in early 387 CE.[19] Here we have the seven disciplines implicitly ordered in groups of three (Grammar, Rhetoric, Dialectic) and four (Arithmetic, Music, Geometry, Astronomy), with an unmistakable indication of the practical (*ad usum vitae*) and theoretical value (*ad cognitionem rerum contemplationemque*) of the liberal arts (*artes liberales*) – but no mention of further disciplines such as Ethics, Economics, Politics, Physics, or Theology.[20] Ilsetraut Hadot has identified Augustine's analysis as Neoplatonic in origin and reflecting an essentially Latin or Roman tradition of some sort. Although she rightly insists that the dialogue does not qualify as evidence for the existence of any institutionally based standard curricula of the period,

---

[16] Calcidius, *In Tim.* 272. Possibly echoing Iamblichus (*In Tim.* frag. 1 D illon), although Calcidius' reference to the *Parmenides* as 'epoptic' in scope evidently points in another direction (cf. *In Tim.* 127; Theon of Smyrna, *Expos.* 15.16–18).

[17] Calcidius, *In Tim.* 148.

[18] Calcidius' terminology is coherent, if slightly idiosyncratic: (a) *studia humanitatis*: *Ep.* 4; *Tim.* 20a (οὐδενὸς ἰδιώτην ὄντα ὧν λέγομεν); *In Tim.* 128 (cf. Gellius, *Noct. att.* 13.17.1; Cicero, *Arch.* 3; *De or.* 2.154; Seneca, *Ep.* 88.30). (b) *omnes eruditionis ingenuae viae*: *Tim.* 53c (τῶν κατὰ παίδευσιν ὁδῶν) ~ *In Tim.* 355, combining the notions of a liberal education and scientific method (*via* ~ μέθοδος, cf. Cicero, *Fin.* 3.18; Quintilian, *Inst.* 2.17.41 (SVF 1.72); Plato, *Resp.* 531c–d; I. Hadot 1984: 276–82; below, n. 49). (c) *educatio liberalis*: *In Tim.* 168 (cf. Cicero, *De or.* 1.11, 72; 2.162; 3.127; *Tim.* 1; Seneca, *Ep.* 88 passim; Aristotle, *Pol.* 1337b15).

[19] I. Hadot 1984: 101–36. [20] Augustine, *De ord.* 2.5.13–14, 12.35–16.44.

the circumstances of its composition are nevertheless significant: Augustine wrote it in the months immediately after his conversion, the first stages in his recovery from Manichaean and Sceptical 'hangovers' that necessitated dogmatic grounds for belief in the goodness of creation. The experiment was, however, short-lived, for early work on *De doctrina christiana* (c. 397) already betrays signs of Augustine's movement away from the liberal arts as the basis for a comprehensive educational programme.[21]

Pueriles disciplinae

This brings us to Boethius. The year 510 CE saw him balancing consular duties with the work of translating and commenting on Aristotle's *Categories*. The proem to the second book of his commentary occasions a revealing reflection on the theme of *translatio imperii, translatio studii*:

> Although the concerns attending consular office prevent me from devoting full time and attention to these studies, to instruct citizens in a subject suitable for the midnight oil seems nevertheless to be relevant to a certain concern for the state. I will not have done poorly by my fellow citizens if, now that the ancient virtue of men from other cities has transferred dominion and empire to this state alone, I at least accomplish the finishing task of instructing the character of our citizenry in the arts of Greek wisdom. And in that sense, neither is *this* work exempt from the duties of a consul, for it has always been a part of Roman custom assiduously to honour through imitation what was noble and praiseworthy throughout the world.

> *Etsi nos curae officii consularis impediunt quominus in his studiis omne otium plenamque operam consumimus, pertinere tamen videtur hoc ad aliquam rei publicae curam, elucubratae rei doctrina cives instruere. nec male de civibus meis merear si, cum prisca hominum virtus urbium ceterarum ad hanc unam rem publicam dominationem imperiumque transtulerit, ego id saltem quod reliquum est Graecae sapientiae artibus mores nostrae civitatis instruxero. quare ne hoc quidem ipsum consulis vacat officio, cum Romani semper fuerit moris, quod ubicumque gentium pulchrum esset atque laudabile, id magis ac magis imitatione honestare.*[22]

Later in the commentary, Boethius glosses the same thought, momentarily shutting down the exegetical machinery in order to comment on the cultural conditions of his day. The reflection is stirred by his account of logical correlatives, in illustration of which Aristotle adduces the case of

---

[21] Ayres 2010: 23–30, 121–33.   [22] Boethius, *In Cat.* 201b; cf. Magee 2016: 15–16.

knowledge and knowables.[23] In explaining the priority of the knowable to knowledge – that there can be no knowledge in the absence of a related object, although there can be knowable objects in the absence of any knowledge thereof, as in the cases of (say) a pre-Copernican heliocentric theory or all that we have not yet learned as children – Boethius indulges a slightly bitter observation. Of course, he notes, the absence of a knowable object precludes the possibility of any knowledge thereof, but things have now reached the point where knowledge is disappearing despite the continued existence of the subjects themselves:

Many too are the arts which we clearly see existing in their respective domains; however, neglect has removed the knowledge of them, and I myself now gravely fear that this may in utter truth be said of liberal studies as a whole.

Multae quoque sunt artes quas esse quidem in suae naturae ratione perspicimus, quarum <vero> neglectus scientiam sustulit, multumque ego ipse iam metuo ne hoc verissime de omnibus studiis liberalibus dicatur.[24]

In principle, the observation ought to be otiose, for Boethius has already explained *in abstracto* the priority of knowables to knowledge, and it cannot be explained as mere mimicry of a comment made by Porphyry in *his* commentary. What, then, is driving it? Some allowance undoubtedly has to be made for the streak of aristocratic arrogance that characterises other passages, especially Boethius' more esoteric prefaces, but in the end we probably have to take him at his word, right or wrong: education, according to him, is in decline.[25] Boethius does not elaborate here or elsewhere on the notions of *artes* or *studia liberalia*;[26] but silence obviously is not evidence of ignorance, and the question whether he has a fixed view of the liberal arts or an ἐγκύκλιος παιδεία seems well worth investigating. It will be convenient to begin with the three traditional linguistic arts of Grammar, Rhetoric, and Dialectic.

About Grammar, Boethius has little to say, although he undoubtedly received a thorough grounding in the subject and was well versed in its history and tradition. Priscian dedicated three *opuscula* to Symmachus,[27] and it seems inevitable that the library Boethius used as a child and adolescent

---

[23] Aristotle, *Cat.* 7b27–33.   [24] Boethius, *In Cat.* 230c (supplying *vero*).
[25] Cf. Simplicius, *In Epict. Ench.* 14, 257.25–32.
[26] The *bonae artes* are referenced twice at *De divis.* 877b but without elaboration. Boethius is seduced by Victorinus into rendering ἐπιστήμην (Porphyry, *Isag.* 6.16) with *vel artium* (*vel disciplinarum*) at *In Isag.* I 77.9–13 (cf. II 225.17). I know of no Boethian passage that suggests a close connection between *humanitas* and παιδεία (cf. *Inst. mus.* 1.1, 179.24; *In Isag.* I 84.4).
[27] Keil, *Gramm. Lat.* 3.405.

contained copies of his works and those of other grammarians. The adult Boethius, however, evinces no strong interest in explaining Grammar as a discrete field of study. His emphasis is rather on distinguishing the separate domains of philosophers and grammarians, a distinction which may perhaps be likened to the difference between Numismatics, the study of coins, and Economics, the study of their purchasing power:

> For the name and verb are not merely spoken sounds: just as, similarly, for a coin to be called a coin it is not merely to be stamped with a certain form but to carry the value of some item, so too verbs and names are not merely spoken sounds but ones that have been imposed for a particular signification of thoughts. For although grammarians, attending to the form of a spoken sound that signifies nothing, as in the case of 'garulus', maintain that it is a name, philosophy nevertheless will not deem it a name unless it has been imposed so as to have the capacity to signify some mental conception and, thereby, some item. For a name must necessarily be the name of something, but if a given spoken sound signifies nothing, it is the name of nothing; and so if it is the name of nothing, it will not even be called a name. Hence a spoken sound of the kind intended, i.e., a significative one, is not merely a spoken sound but is called a verb or name in the way that a coin is called, not bronze, but a coin, with a proper name to distinguish it from other bronze.

> *Non enim ... nomen et verbum voces tantum sunt: sicut nummus quoque non solum aes impressum quadam figura est ut nummus vocetur sed etiam ut alicuius rei sit pretium, eodem quoque modo verba et nomina non solum voces sunt sed positae ad quandam intellectuum significationem. vox enim quae nihil designat, ut est 'garulus', licet eam grammatici figuram vocis intuentes nomen esse contendant tamen eam nomen philosophia non putabit nisi sit posita ut designare animi aliquam conceptionem eoque modo rerum aliquid possit. etenim nomen alicuius nomen esse necesse erit, sed si vox aliqua nihil designat, nullius nomen est; quare si nullius est, ne nomen quidem esse dicetur. atque ideo huiusmodi vox, id est significativa, non vox tantum sed verbum vocatur aut nomen, quemadmodum nummus non aes sed proprio nomine nummus, quo ab alio aere discrepet, nuncupatur.*[28]

Grammarians study the 'second imposition' of words, the forms 'stamped' on them according to conventions which differ from people to people (and language to language), whereas philosophers investigate their natural power of signifying thoughts (*imaginatio significandi*) and extra-mental objects.[29] The latter, consequently, concentrate on only two of the

---

[28] Boethius, *In Perih.* II 32.12–29; cf. Ammonius, *In De int.* 22.27–23.2.

[29] On the two impositions, see Boethius, *In Cat.* 159b–c; Porphyry, *In Cat.* 57.20–59.2; Ebbesen 1990: 382–83; and on *imaginatio significandi*, Boethius, *In Perih.* II 4.26–28; 5.22–6.3; 58.3; 92.10–17; Aristotle, *De an.* 420b29–32; Themistius, *De an.* 67.8, 25; Ammonius, *In De int.* 33.30; 61.30.

eight parts of speech, names and verbs, the building blocks of scientific demonstrations, and do so with the aim of situating language in a scheme that explains the relationship between the mind and the natural world.[30] The approach is essentially Peripatetic, and Boethius shows no interest in Stoic speculations about how other parts of speech function in complex sentence structures. Conjunctions, as he rather bluntly puts it, may be disregarded as mere *locutiones* (as opposed to *interpretationes*) with no per se signification, and names in their oblique inflections may similarly be disregarded, since they do not combine with predicates to form assertoric statements.[31] Boethius' general approach *eo ipso* precludes discussion of Grammar as a form of literary instruction in the *scholae liberales*,[32] and that not out of any hostility, as the finely wrought artistry of his own *Consolatio* implicitly demonstrates many times over,[33] but because it simply was not what he set out to do. In the end, the grammarian belongs to the same *res publica litterarum* as the dialectician, mathematician, and natural philosopher do; each sheds independent light on shared objects of investigation and none competes with the others, although some are indeed either elevated or subordinated by the very nature of their investigations.[34] Of course, personal aptitudes and inclinations also play a role, and Boethius for his part abjures taking up the *pueriles disciplinae* for exposition.[35]

Rhetoric involves similar considerations insofar as Boethius does not treat it as a discrete and independent discipline but instead strives, especially in the fourth book of *De topicis differentiis* (c. 522–23), to explain it as a branch of Dialectic, the more universal and hence more philosophical of the two disciplines. More precisely, his aim is to reclaim Topical method

---

[30] Boethius, *In Perih.* I 32.11–21; II 14.23–15.5; cf. Ammonius, *In De int.* 11.1–12.15.
[31] Boethius, *In Perih.* II 5.16–6.15; 63.14–65.22.   [32] On which see Kaster 1988: 32–95.
[33] So too, presumably, his lost *Carmen bucolicum* (Usener 1877: 4.16).
[34] Boethius, *Introd. syllog. cat.* 762c; cf. Ebbesen 2003: 257–58. This is a theoretical consequence of Boethius' view (articulated later) that different levels of knowledge reflect differences between the cognitive powers of knowing subjects rather than the natures of known objects (*Cons.* 5.4.24–39). Reason, for example, can form a universal definition of spheres in a way that Imagination cannot, but cannot itself grasp pure spherical form in the way that Intelligence does. At the same time, there are indeed differences between the cognitive *objects*: an individual *material sphere*, in the case of Sense-Perception; its perceptible *shape*, in the case of Imagination; the *geometrical form* it shares with all other spheres, in the case of Reason; and its *transcendent form*, in the case of Intelligence. And as we will see, Boethius also maintains a Neoplatonic view of the ontological transformations experienced by the human soul in connection with the objects of its contemplation.
[35] Cf. Boethius, *Syllog. cat.* 793d.

(*omnis rationis disserendi pars inveniendi*)[36] for Aristotle by subordinating it to Dialectic.[37] He remarks on the novelty of the project:

> I think it time now to give very brief consideration to the discipline as a whole. It is a great and difficult task, for the question of the internal relationships binding the rhetorical art together cannot easily be brought under examination, and it is barely the case even that it can be grasped once heard, and still less that it is easy to discover. Now, concerning the tradition of this subject we have received nothing from the ancient teachers, for they offer instruction in particulars without endeavouring to explain what they have in common. We should take this missing piece of doctrine in hand to the extent possible.

> *Nunc paulisper mihi videtur de tota admodum breviter facultate tractandum. magnum opus atque difficile, quanta enim sibimet ars rhetorica cognatione iungatur non facile considerari potest vixque est etiam ut auditu animadverti queat, nedum sit facile repertu. de cuius quidem rei traditione nihil ab antiquis praeceptoribus accepimus, de unoquoque enim praecipiunt nihil de communi laborantes. quam partem doctrinae vacuam, ut possumus, aggrediamur.*[38]

And indeed, *De topicis differentiis* is one of Boethius' most original and fascinating works, one which alongside *De divisione* enjoyed a rich *Fortleben* in the medieval schools. Most original of all is its systematic harmonisation of Cicero's *Topics* (and related rhetorical works) with Themistius' lost paraphrase of Aristotle's *Topics*, a work otherwise known only from citations in Averroes. *De topicis differentiis* is Boethius' monument to two philosopher-orators, one Roman and the other Greek, and like his commentary on Cicero's *Topics* (*c.* 520–23) it shows him grappling, no doubt with a sober eye to his own political experience, with the relationship between Rhetoric and Philosophy. In the Cicero commentary, he is determined to repair the damage done by Victorinus' obtuse confusion of the two domains, a concern that dates back already to his first commentary on Porphyry's *Isagoge* (*c.* 504–9).[39] Otherwise, for more detailed points of theory, Boethius refers readers to unspecified rhetorical manuals which presumably informed his own development as a public orator.[40] Although no speech of his has survived, the 'apology' at *Consolatio* 1.4 is constructed as one long, self-indulgent rush of Ciceronian grandiloquence for which Philosophia immediately brings him up short.[41] Moreover, the first half

---

[36] See below, n. 47.
[37] Magnano 2017: lxx–lxxi, 279, 321; cf. Aristotle, *Rhet.* 1354a1; 1356a30–31.
[38] Boethius, *Top. diff.* 4.1.15–17; cf. Aristotle, *Soph. elench.* 184a10–b4.
[39] Boethius, *In Isag.* I 34.12–35.6 (cf. 36.22–37.1); *In Cic. Top.* 1099d–1100a; 1156b; cf. Courcelle 1969: 280–81; Magee 2016: 16.
[40] Boethius, *Top. diff.* 4.7.30 (cf. 9).   [41] Boethius, *Cons.* 1.5.2.

of the *Consolatio* skilfully plays off of commonplace themes with roots in the declamatory tradition (the fickleness of fortune, the downfall of the mighty, contempt for death, the insignificance of empires, etc.), while the fourth book gives rise to an interesting, if clumsy, imitation of Socrates' ironic praise of orators (Rhetoric) in Plato's *Gorgias*.[42]

Dialectic, or Logic (on which more presently), is a different matter insofar as most of what we have from Boethius, including even the theological tractates, intersects with it in one way or another. As to its place in the ordering of knowledge, Boethius does indeed have something to say, and in the first instance it comes down to the question of whether Logic is a part or instrument of Philosophy, i.e., whether its subject matter is intrinsically philosophical, as the Stoics (unnamed) maintained, or merely serves the pursuit of truth in other more strictly philosophical domains, as the Peripatetics (also unnamed) held.[43] The work at issue is the second *Isagoge* commentary (*c*. 511–12), in which Boethius strategically sits on the fence, likening Logic to a hand or eye which serves but is also a part of the human body, i.e., which both functions as and is a bodily organ (hence 'Organon').[44] With a particularly subtle, if not actually question-begging, manipulation of terminology, Boethius states the Stoic case in such a way as to imply that the Ethics-Physics branches (*moralis, naturalis*) of the division of Philosophy traditionally associated with them[45] map directly onto the Practical–Theoretical split (*activa, speculativa*) at the head of the 'Peripatetic' taxonomy mentioned earlier, which otherwise has no fixed place for Logic; insofar as Ammonius and others similarly divide the Aristotelian corpus into Theoretical (θεωρητικά), Practical (πρακτικά), and 'Instrumental' or Logical (ὀργανικά) treatises, Boethius is obviously working within an established tradition.[46] The most detailed discussion appears in the commentary on Cicero's *Topics*, where he introduces Logic as a branch of Philosophy coordinate with Physics and Ethics (*naturalia, moralia*, the 'Stoic' division), lays out its two broad divisions, and explores the relationship between them. The first division is tripartite, comprising Definition, Enumeration, and Argumentation, with the latter then subdivided into

---

[42] Boethius, *Cons.* 4.4.38–40; Plato, *Gorg.* 480a–81b; cf. Magee 2014: 24.
[43] Cf. Moraux 1973: 77–78; P. Hadot: 1990.
[44] Boethius, *In Isag. II* 140.13–43.7; cf. *I* 10.2–5; Moraux 1973: 77, nn. 61–64 (evidence for Alexander, Ammonius, Philoponus, Olympiodorus).
[45] See above, n. 9; also Boethius, *In Cat.* 161b; *In Perih. II* 79.18–20; *In Cic. Top.* 1044c–d; *Top. diff.* 1.5.50.
[46] Ammonius, *In Cat.* 4.28–5.8; Philoponus, *In Cat.* 4.23–30; Olympiodorus, *Proleg.* 7.24–28; cf. Moraux 1973: 71–78.

Demonstration, Dialectic, and Sophistic; the second is bipartite, comprising the Topical and Dialectical methods (*pars inveniendi, pars iudicandi*), which are related to one another as matter is to form, i.e., with dialectical argumentation 'supervening' on topical 'material'.[47] Boethius associates the term *logica* with Aristotle, a usage evidently unattested before Alexander of Aphrodisias, and *dialectica* with Plato; the latter, he explains following Cicero, was adopted by the Stoics, who eschewed Topical method altogether.[48] These two commentaries show Boethius reflecting on the 'Peripatetic' and 'Stoic' taxonomies over the course of a decade or more, implicitly harmonising them but without actually addressing the question of their relationship to one another. In the end, his allegiance is with the Peripatetics rather than Stoics, and in that he was undoubtedly influenced by Porphyry.

Quadruvium

It seems quite clear that if Boethius had any views on Grammar, Rhetoric, and Dialectic as a coherent body of linguistic disciplines, he was as unconcerned to elaborate upon them as he was to lay out a unified system of *artes liberales* in general. The situation differs dramatically, however, with his exposition of the four mathematical sciences. As is well known, it is to the *Institutio arithmetica* (*c.* 500–6) that we owe the description of Arithmetic, Music, Geometry, and Astronomy as a *quadruvium*, a 'fourfold path' or 'intersection of four roads', Boethius' metaphorical take on what Nicomachus terms the 'four methods' (τέσσαρες μέθοδοι), which too, of course, captures the notion of a 'path' or 'way' (ὁδός).[49] The system elaborated by each both subordinates and coordinates the four disciplines. The subordinating principle is a division of Being (*essentia*, τὰ ὄντα) into Multitude (*multitudo*, πλῆθος), the discrete and infinitely multipliable, and Magnitude (*magnitudo*, μέγεθος), the continuous and infinitely divisible, a fundamental distinction also discussed by Boethius in the *Categories* commentary.[50] Arithmetic and Music are the coordinate sciences of absolute and relative Multitudes, and Geometry and Astronomy those of stationary and

---

[47] Boethius, *In Cic. Top.* 1044c–48a; cf. *Top. diff.* 1.1.1; Magnano 2017: lxxvi–xci. The matter-form distinction appears in a scholium, probably Boethius, to *An. pr.* 52b38 (*Arist. Lat. III.4* 330; cf. Philoponus, *In An. pr.* 387.9–11; 388.3–5).
[48] Boethius, *In Cic. Top.* 1045a–b; 1047c–d; Cicero, *Top.* 6; cf. *Fat.* 1.
[49] Boethius, *Inst. arith.* 1.1.1, 7; Nicomachus, *Introd. arith.* 1.4.1; cf. above, n. 18.
[50] Boethius, *In Cat.* 201c–204b; Aristotle, *Cat.* 4b20–37.

mobile Magnitudes, respectively.[51] The two pairs are themselves ranked, for Arithmetic-Music is prior to Geometry-Astronomy insofar as Multitude is prior to Magnitude; and each is internally ranked, for Arithmetic is prior to Music insofar as the absolute is prior to the relative, while Geometry is prior to Astronomy insofar as rest is prior to motion.[52] Together, however, these disciplines form the unified 'path' or 'steps' which the mind must ascend in order to reach the incorporeal certainties of Intellect. They are, in other words, the first stages of Philosophy *stricto sensu*.[53] This is a thoroughly Platonic, or 'Pythagorean',[54] construct which in its cosmological implications neither presupposes nor entails a fixed arts curriculum or associated institutional structure:

From this it follows, since there are four mathematical disciplines, that the other [three share with Music] the task of searching for truth, whereas Music is associated not only with theoretical speculation, but also with morality. For nothing is as characteristic of human nature as to be soothed by pleasant modes and disturbed by their opposites. This is not restricted to either particular pursuits or particular ages; rather, [Music] suffuses all pursuits, and infants, youths, and indeed the elderly are so naturally attuned to musical modes by a kind of voluntary affection that there is no period of life at all which is excluded from the charm of sweet song. Hence what Plato to good effect has said can likewise be understood (*Tim.* 34b–36b): the World Soul was joined together in musical harmony. For when we hear what is properly and harmoniously united in sounds in conjunction with that which is harmoniously coupled and joined together within us, and are attracted to it, we recognise that we ourselves are also constructed in its likeness. For likeness attracts, whereas unlikeness disgusts and repels, and it is from this that radical transformations in character also arise.

Unde fit ut, cum sint quattuor matheseos disciplinae, ceterae quidem in investigatione veritatis laborent, musica vero non modo speculationi verum etiam moralitati coniuncta sit. nihil est enim tam proprium humanitatis quam remitti dulcibus modis, adstringi contrariis. idque non sese in singulis vel studiis vel aetatibus tenet, verum per cuncta diffunditur studia et infantes ac iuvenes nec non etiam senes ita naturaliter affectu quodam spontaneo modis musicis adiunguntur ut nulla omnino sit aetas quae a cantilenae dulcis delectatione seiuncta sit. hinc etiam internosci potest quod non frustra a Platone dictum sit, mundi animam musica convenientia fuisse coniunctam. cum enim eo quod in nobis est iunctum convenienterque coaptatum

---

[51] Boethius, *Inst. arith.* 1.1.1–12; *Inst. mus.* 2.3; Nicomachus, *Introd. arith.* 1.1.1–5.3.
[52] Cf. Boethius, *Inst. arith.* xlvi–l (ed. Guillaumin).
[53] Boethius, *Inst. arith.* 1.1.7; cf. Crialesi 2020: 109.
[54] Boethius, *Inst. arith.* 1.1.1 (*Pythagora duce*); Nicomachus, *Introd. arith.* 1.1.1 (κατάρξαντος Πυθαγόρου).

illud excipimus, quod in sonis apte convenienterque coniunctum est eoque delectamur, nos quoque ipsos eadem similitudine compactos esse cognoscimus; amica est enim similutudo, dissimilitudo odiosa atque contraria, hinc etiam morum quoque maximae permutationes fiunt.[55]

The mathematical sciences, to put it another way, form part of the connective tissue that binds together individual human beings and the world, Microcosm and Macrocosm, and indeed, the Theoretical and Practical domains.[56]

In 507 CE, Cassiodorus drafted for Theoderic a letter praising Boethius, still in his twenties but ostensibly holding the title of Patrician, in the following terms:

We understand that your knowledge [of sundials and water-clocks] is packed with such erudition that arts which [the Burgundians] ply with the ignorance of commoners you have imbibed at the very fount of disciplines. For you have entered the Athenian schools from afar and blended the toga in among cloaked troupes in such a way as to turn Greek *dogmata* into Roman *doctrina*. You understand the depth involved in contemplating theoretical doctrine and its parts, the reasoning involved in learning practical doctrine and its branches. All of this, while bringing back to Roman senators all that the Athenians have uniquely produced in the world. For in your translations Pythagoras and Ptolemy, musician and astronomer, are read while Nicomachus and Euclid, arithmetician and geometer, are heard as natives of Italy; Plato and Aristotle, theologian and logician, dispute with Roman voice; the mechanician Archimedes too, now a native of Latium, you have restored to the people of Sicily. And all of the disciplines and arts which eloquent Greece has brought forth through individual men Rome on your sole initiative has adopted in its native language. And you have brought them back shining with such verbal splendour and notable for such linguistic propriety that even they would have been able to regard yours as the preferred work, had they known both. Through the fourfold gateway of knowledge, you have gained entrance to the above-mentioned art which becomes known because of the noble disciplines.

Hoc te multa eruditione saginatum ita nosse didicimus ut artes quas exercent vulgariter nescientes in ipso disiplinarum fonte potaveris; sic enim Atheniensium scholas longe positus introisi, sic palliatorum choris miscuisti togam, ut Graecorum dogmata doctrinam feceris esse Romanam. didicisti enim qua profunditate cum partibus speculativa cogitetur, qua ratione activa cum sua divisione discatur, deducens ad

---

[55] Boethius, *Inst. mus.* 1.1 (trans. Bower, modified and reading *sonis* at 180.7); cf. 1.2; *Inst. arith.* 1.2.1; 2.2.1, 32.3, 46.1; *In Cic. Top.* 1092d; *Cons.* 3.m9.10–17, m12.20–39; I. Hadot 1984: 68–69, 206; Vogel 2019: 35–36.

[56] Cf. *Inst. arith.* 2.45, in which Boethius reflects, independently of Nicomachus (but in a Pythagorean vein), on correspondences between types of political constitution and the arithmetic, harmonic, and geometric means.

Romuleos senatores quicquid Cecropidae mundo fecerant singulare. translationibus enim tuis Pythagoras musicus Ptolemaeus astronomus leguntur Itali, Nicomachus arithmeticus geometricus Euclides audiuntur Ausonii, Plato theologus Aristoteles logicus Quirinali voce disceptant, mechanicum etiam Archimedem Latialem Siculis reddidisti, et quascumque disciplinas vel artes facunda Graecia per singulos viros edidit te uno auctore patrio sermone Roma suscepit. quos tanta verborum luculentia reddidisti claros, tanta linguae proprietate conspicuos, ut potuissent et illi opus tuum praeferre si utrumque didicissent. tu artem praedictam ex disciplinis nobilibus notam per quadrifarias mathesis ianuas introisti.[57]

The point of the letter is to cast Boethius as a new Archimedes, engineering a water-clock and sundial to support Theoderic's efforts to ease relations with Gundobad; another one was issued at about the same time, petitioning Boethius' recommendation of a harpist for Clovis.[58] The fawning bombast reflects the political context of the letter and obfuscates details concerning Boethius' actual progress with the project. The reference to Plato breeds pointed scepticism, and any translations of Aristotle's logical works that may have existed in 507 can only have been draft versions at best.[59] And, as to the mathematical works, are we to understand the closing metaphor (*per quadrifarias mathesis ianuas*)[60] as a nod to, or as a sign of ignorance of, the Boethian *quadruvium*? The *Institutio arithmetica*, of course, survives intact, with a rich manuscript tradition that includes an ancient fragment possibly used for instruction at Bobbio in the early Middle Ages.[61] It undoubtedly is the work denoted by *Nicomachus arithmeticus*,[62] but as Boethius himself points out, it is not a translation in any strict sense of the word.[63] Similarly, *Pythagoras musicus*: the *Institutio musica* (c. 506–9?) survives nearly intact[64] and almost certainly is the targeted treatise,[65] although it cannot be described as a translation of any single Greek source, and certainly not of Pythagoras.[66] Evidence for a Boethian translation of Euclid's *Elements*

---

[57] Cassiodorus, *Var.* 1.45.3–4.
[58] Cassiodorus, *Var.* 2.40.17. On these two letters generally, see Bjornlie 2013: 171–78.
[59] The second book of the *Categories* commentary dates to 510 (see above, n. 22), when Boethius was still testing methods of translation, and the second *Isagoge* commentary, which opens with a pronouncement on the question (*In Isag. II* 135.5–13), to c. 511–12. Hence among the extant works, the *Institutio arithmetica* (c. 500–6) and first *Isagoge* commentary (c. 504–9, based on Victorinus' translation) may have been the only ones completed by 507.
[60] Cf. Cassiodorus, *Inst.* 2.3.19 (*ut quasi quibusdam ianuis apertis*).
[61] Turin, Bibl. Naz. e Univ. F.IV.1. fasc. 3 (sixth–seventh century).
[62] Cf. Cassiodorus, *Inst.* 2.4.7. [63] Boethius, *Inst. arith.* pref. 3.
[64] The final eleven chapters are missing.
[65] Mutianus is the only translator of Vivarian musical texts actually mentioned by Cassiodorus (*Inst.* 2.5.1, cf. 10).
[66] Boethius clearly makes use of Nicomachus and Ptolemy, but other sources too are in play.

comes down to two sources, passages interpolated in the Δ-recension of Cassiodorus' *Institutiones* and an ancient fragment which may originally have belonged to Boethius himself.[67] Was there, or were there plans for, a separate *Institutio geometrica*?[68] Finally, although Cassiodorus specifies no translator for the copy of Ptolemy in the Vivarium library, Gerbert of Aurillac saw what may have been a Boethian *Institutio astronomica* at Bobbio in 983.[69] Such are the accidents of survival that condition our reliance upon the *Institutio arithmetica* and *Institutio musica* for an understanding of Boethius' ordering of the mathematical sciences. Since neither work situates the quadrivium in a full taxonomy of philosophical disciplines, we must turn to the first commentary on Porphyry's *Isagoge*, *De trinitate*, and the *Consolatio* for further elucidation.

Philosophia

We have touched on Boethius' effort in the second *Isagoge* commentary to elide differences between the 'Stoic' division of Philosophy (Logic, Physics, Ethics) and a 'Peripatetic' one that orders the sciences under Practical and Theoretical branches. The latter will be most familiar to readers from the description of Philosophia's gown at the beginning of the *Consolatio* (524/525), where an embroidered Π and Θ, connected by steps leading from the former to the latter, symbolise an ascent from the Practical to the Theoretical domain.[70] Moreover, parts of the gown are described as having been torn away by Epicureans and Stoics, philosophical 'heretics' or 'schismatics' who, in the manner of Numenian Maenads, snatch away pieces believing that they possess the whole.[71] Now, ascent and unity are themes that run parallel through the *Consolatio* before finally intersecting with one another. The theme of unity gradually unfolds as a moral and metaphysical concern, more precisely, in a diagnosis of human suffering as the failure to connect the multiplicity of phenomenal goods with one transcendent Good.[72] The theme of ascent, by contrast, emerges in the form of a medical

---

[67] Verona, Bibl. Capit. XL (38) (fifth–sixth century); cf. Bohlin 2016; Troncarelli 2017: 1–6, 35–45. Like the *Institutio arithmetica*, it was evidently dedicated to Symmachus (Usener 1877: 47). The so-called *Geometrie I–II* are later compilations which may preserve some Boethian material.
[68] Cf. Cassiodorus, *Inst.* 2.6.3; *Expos. psalm.* I 29.86–88; *XCV.13* 869.331–33.
[69] Cassiodorus, *Inst.* 2.7.3; cf. *Expos. psalm. CXLVIII.14* 1321.261–63 (with *Inst.* 2.7.2); Boethius, *Cons.* 2.7.4 (*sicut Ptolemaeo probante didicisti*); Boethius, *Inst. arith.* xxviii (ed. Guillaumin); Gruber 2011: 24.
[70] Boethius, *Cons.* 1.1.4.   [71] Boethius, *Cons.* 1.1.5, 3.7; Numenius, frag. 24.71–73 des Places.
[72] Boethius, *Cons.* 3.9.4, 16.

or therapeutic metaphor. 'Boethius' (the interlocutor) is suffering from a mental disturbance which, at the end of Book 1, is described in terms of the four canonical passions of pleasure, fear, appetite, and distress: a false ordering of the practical and theoretical concerns of life finds him caught, as a result, in the fatal crossfire between politics and philosophy.[73] One of the first therapeutic moments passes almost imperceptibly, in a poem whose final lines no doubt stirred Dante's imagination. There, Philosophia strives to reintegrate for him the Love that governs the natural order of sea, land, and sky (2.m8.5–15) with the Love that presides over the human bonds of the individual, family, and state – in essence, over the practical spheres of Ethics, Economics, and Politics (22–27):

[Love] also holds peoples
Joined by a hallowed pact,
It binds the sacred rite
Of matrimony in chaste affection,
And prescribes its laws
For faithful companions.

Hic sancto populos quoque
iunctos foedere continet,
hic et coniugii sacrum
castis nectit amoribus,
hic fidis etiam sua
dictat iura sodalibus.[74]

From agonising over the vicissitudes of Fortune (Books 1–2) to reaffirmation of the supreme Good (Book 3) and its implications for human suffering and freedom (Books 4–5) – from beginning to end, in other words, the *Consolatio* pursues a course for reintegration of the Practical and Theoretical, of Goodness and Truth, and indeed, of the Human and Divine.[75] Against this background, Philosophia symbolises the possibility of ascent from the phenomenal multiplicity of this world to the transcendent unity of the one above, from *res publica* to *patria*.[76]

The tripartite division of Practical philosophy harkens back to Boethius' first commentary on Porphyry's *Isagoge* (c. 504–9). There,

---

[73] Boethius, *Cons.* 1.m7.25–28 (*gaudium, timor, spes, dolor* ~ ἡδονή, φόβος, ἐπιθυμία, λύπη); cf. 1.1.9; Magee 2005: 353–55; *SVF* 3.378–94 (65A–B Long–Sedley).
[74] The poem is in two evenly divided sections of fifteen verses (the natural and human orders), each punctuated by *amor* (2.m8.15, 29).
[75] Cf. Boethius, *Cons.* 5.3.29–36 (with 4.m6.34–48).   [76] Cf. Boethius, *Cons.* 1.4.5, 5.3–4.

the principles uniting and separating Ethics (*sui cura*), Economics (*familiaris rei officium*), and Politics (*rei publicae cura*) are briefly articulated, with further subdivisions alluded to but not specified.[77] Ammonius explores subdivisions in the regulative and corrective branches of each, adapting a distinction from Plato's *Gorgias* which Boethius obliquely acknowledges in the *Consolatio,* but not the commentary;[78] in the latter, he points instead in the direction of the four cardinal virtues, Macrobius' exposition of which he certainly knew, possibly Porphyry's as well.[79] Alongside the Practical branch there of course stands the Theoretical one,[80] which also embraces three subdivisions. Here a certain intellectual immaturity or uncritical reliance upon some source emerges. For although Boethius dutifully lays out the separate domains of Physics (*physiologia*) and Metaphysics (θεολογία), the investigation of natural and 'intellectible' objects, respectively, his focus flags in discussion of the intermediate science, where a concern for the transience of 'intelligibles' completely eclipses Mathematics.[81] More sober impulses inform *De trinitate* (*c.* 520–21), where Mathematics (*mathematica*) and mathematical method come back into view. The mathematical sciences consider form as abstracted from matter by the mind,[82] proceeding according to scientific discipline (*disciplinaliter*) or the different boundaries of what manifests itself in the mind as discrete fields of investigation, analysing arithmetic ratios in the case of Music, employing axioms, corollaries, and proofs in the case of Geometry, and calculations of movement based on observational evidence in the case of Astronomy.[83]

Looking now to the *Institutio arithmetica*, *Institutio musica*, first *Isagoge* commentary, *De trinitate*, and *Consolatio*, we may reconstruct the full 'Peripatetic' taxonomy of sciences discussed by Boethius:

Philosophy:
    Theoretical:
        Theology

---

[77] Boethius, *In Isag.* I 9.13–22; cf. Ammonius, *In Isag.* 15.1–16.16; *In Cat.* 5.5–6; Philoponus, *In Cat.* 5.6–7; Olympiodorus, *Proleg.* 7.34–8.3.
[78] Ammonius, *In Isag.* 15.11–16.4; Plato, *Gorg.* 464b–c; Boethius, *Cons.* 4.7.3.
[79] Boethius, *In Isag.* I 9.18–19 (*suae prudentiae* [*providentiae*, Brandt] ... *iustitiae* ... *fortitudinis* ... *temperantiae*; cf. *Top. diff.* 2.7.10, *iustitia, fortitudo, moderatio, atque prudentia*); Macrobius, *Somn.* 1.8.4 (Boethius, *In Isag.* I 31.22–32.1); Porphyry, *Sent.* 32.
[80] Cf. above, n. 14. [81] Boethius, *In Isag.* I 8.6–9.12.
[82] Cf. Boethius, *In Isag.* II 164.16–65.18. [83] Boethius, *Trin.* 2, 73–79.

             Mathematics
          Multitude:
                Arithmetic
                Music
                    Cosmic
                    Human
                    Instrumental[84]
          Magnitude:
                Geometry
                Astronomy
          Physics
   Practical:
       Politics
       Economics
       Ethics

Although its origins and development remain obscure, there is little evidence to support the view (maintained by some) that the system reaches back in its entirety to Andronicus of Rhodes in the first century BCE.[85]

Finally, what does Boethius have to say about Philosophy itself – or *herself*? It will be convenient to begin with the *Institutio arithmetica*, *Institutio musica*, and first *Isagoge* commentary, early works influenced by a widespread ancient tradition that traced the word φιλοσοφία, and philosophy itself, back to Pythagoras.[86] The etymological connection is intimated in the *Institutio arithmetica*, but explicitly stated in the *Institutio musica*, and in each case the driving consideration is one that has been discussed above: Mathematics is a lower branch of Philosophy.[87] Both treatises betray a note of scholastic routine in their handling of the ancient attribution, probably owing to Nicomachus' influence. The *Isagoge* commentary takes a slightly different approach:

First we must consider what *philosophia* itself is: *philo-sophia* is the *love* or *pursuit of* – a *friendship*, we might say, *with* – *wisdom*,[88] not the wisdom employed in particular arts or any branch of practical craftsmanship and knowledge, but the wisdom which is completely self-sufficient, life-giving mind or the sole primeval guiding principle of things. This *love of wisdom*, moreover, is an illumination of the thinking mind by that wisdom in its purity, its drawing or summoning, as it were, the mind back to itself, such that the *pursuit of wisdom* evidently is a pursuit of divinity and a *friendship with* that mind in its purity. And so this wisdom indeed

---

[84] Boethius, *Inst. mus.* 1.2.
[85] Cf. Tarán 2001: 501–8; Barnes 1997: 28–66; but also Ptolemy, *Harm.* 3.6.
[86] Cicero, *Tusc.* 5.8–9; Diogenes Laertius, *Lives* 1.12; 8.8.
[87] Boethius, *Inst. arith.* 1.1.1, 5; *Inst. mus.* 2.2–3.
[88] Cf. Boethius, *Cons.* 1.4.5 (*studiosi sapientiae*); Cicero, *Tusc.* 1.1 (*studio sapientiae, quae philosophia dicitur*); Seneca, *Ep.* 89.4 (*philosophia sapientiae amor est et affectatio*).

imposes the obligation of its own divinity on souls of every kind in leading them back to the power and purity proper to its nature. From it arises the truth in theoretical speculation and the sacrosanct and pure goodness of action.

Et prius quid sit ipsa philosophia considerandum est. est enim philosophia amor et studium et amicitia quodammodo sapientiae, sapientiae vero non huius quae in artibus quibusdam et in aliqua fabrili scientia notitiaque versatur sed illius sapientiae quae nullius indigens, vivax mens et sola rerum primaeva ratio est. est autem hic amor sapientiae intellegentis animi ab illa pura sapientia illuminatio et quodammodo ad se ipsam retractio atque advocatio, ut videatur studium sapientiae studium divinitatis et purae mentis illius amicitia. haec igitur sapientia cuncto equidem animarum generi meritum suae divinitatis imponit et ad propriam naturae vim puritatemque reducit. hinc nascitur speculationum cogitationumque veritas et sancta puraque actuum castimonia.[89]

Pythagoras is sidelined, but the etymology itself given more focused attention. Now, Ammonius began his course of lectures on the *Isagoge*, of which our extant text is a *reportatio*, with a lengthy introduction to Philosophy, expounding its subject matter and purpose, its various definitions, and its taxonomy.[90] The last of his definitions is in fact a version of the one discussed by Boethius in the passage above.[91] The contrast is striking: Ammonius lecturing students who may well be imagined as struggling against tedium, wondering what will be on the quiz, and Boethius distilling[92] in consideration of his literary genre (philosophical dialogue) while breathing the same arid air of the ancient classroom, glossing the etymology in an effort to restore what is lost in translation.

This brings us to the *Consolatio* and the figure of Philosophia, whose gown has been touched on above. The language describing her initial appearance vividly recalls – indeed, virtually translates – Plato's description of a dream vision experienced by Socrates in prison.[93] 'Boethius' is to be imagined as having drifted off while taking dictation from the Muses.[94] The following detail is of particular interest:

… her stature wavered and was difficult to ascertain; for she confined herself to ordinary human dimensions at one moment, but could be seen striking the sky with the crown of her forehead at the next, and raising her head higher she would even penetrate the sky itself, evading the gaze of human onlookers.

---

[89] Boethius, *In Isag.* I 7.11–23.   [90] Ammonius, *In Isag.* 1.18–16.16.
[91] Ammonius, *In Isag.* 9.7–23.
[92] Assuming, of course, that he is drawing from a tradition related to the one from which Ammonius is.
[93] Boethius, *Cons.* 1.1.1; Plato, *Cri.* 44a–b; cf. Cicero, *Div.* 1.52; Calcidius, *In Tim.* 254.
[94] Boethius, *Cons.* 1.1.7.

> ... *statura discretionis ambiguae; nam nunc quidem ad communem sese hominum mensuram cohibebat, nunc vero pulsare caelum summi verticis cacumine videbatur, quae cum altius caput extulisset, ipsum etiam caelum penetrabat respicientiumque hominum frustrabatur intuitum.*[95]

With it may be compared 4.4.28–29:

> Just see what the eternal law ordains: conform your mind to better things and there is no need of a judge to confer rewards, for on your own you have joined yourself to things of a higher order; turn aside to worse things but do not look abroad for one to exact retribution, for on your own you have thrust yourself down among things of a lower order – as though by shifting your gaze between the sordid ground and the sky, with all other external factors out of the way, just by reason of your gazing you were to appear to be in the mud at one moment and amidst the stars at the next.

> *Vide autem quid aeterna lex sanciat: melioribus animum conformaveris, nihil opus est iudice praemium deferente, tu te ipse excellentioribus addidisti; studium ad peiora deflexeris, extra ne quaesieris ultorem, tu te ipse in deteriora trusisti – veluti, si vicibus sordidam humum caelumque respicias, cunctis extra cessantibus ipsa cernendi ratione nunc caeno nunc sideribus interesse videaris.*

Philosophia, in other words, is in one sense a figure for the human soul and its movement between divinity and animality.[96] Which brings us back to a passage of the first *Isagoge* commentary discussed earlier:

> The second part [of Theoretical Philosophy] is the Intelligible, which through thought and understanding grasps the first or Intellectible one. And it includes all celestial works of heavenly divinity, whatever shares in the more blessed mind and purer substance of the sublunary sphere, and at the lowest level human souls. Although all of them would have belonged to the first substance, or Intellectible, through bodily contagion they have degenerated from Intellectibles to Intelligibles, so that they are themselves objects of understanding only to the extent that they *exercise* understanding, and exist in a more blessed state of pure understanding whenever they apply themselves to the Intellectibles.

> *Secunda vero est pars intellegibilis, quae primam intellectibilem cogitatione atque intellegentia comprehendit. quae est omnium caelestium supernae divinitatis operum et quicquid sub lunari globo beatiore animo atque puriore substantia valet et postremo humanarum animarum. quae omnia cum prioris illius intellectibilis substantiae fuissent, corporum tactu ab intellectibilibus ad intelligibilia degenerarunt, ut non magis ipsa intellegantur quam intellegant et intellegentiae puritate tunc beatiora sint quotiens sese intellectibilibus applicarint.*[97]

---

[95] Boethius, *Cons.* 1.1.1–2.   [96] Boethius, *Cons.* 3.10.22–26; 4.3.8–21.
[97] Boethius, *In Isag. I* 8.19–9.6 (*est* at 8.21 *pace* Boethius, *In Isag.* lxxxiv (ed. Brandt)).

The human soul *becomes what it thinks*, undergoing transformations which are real despite the abiding state of its embodiment: tyrants harbour the very same part of soul as accounts for the ferocity of lions, and cowards, the part that accounts for the timidity of deer.[98] The soul suffers contagion, oblivion, and enslavement in descending into a human body,[99] but it does not enter into either animal or other human bodies after separation (death). Boethius systematically avoids hints of transmigration and metempsychosis, leaving Philosophia to address the questions of this life, and an unspecified *divini speculator* to ponder questions about providential order and the afterlife.[100] Boethius appears, moreover, to have shaped the figure of Philosophia with an eye to Plato's *Symposium* (204b), where Love is described as a 'friend of wisdom' or philosopher moving between ignorance and understanding: *igitur quisquis vera requirit / neutro est habitu*.[101] The pursuit of truth involves a dialectical process which is described in language obviously meant to recall the first appearance of Philosophia herself (5.m4.22–23): *nunc summis caput inserit, / nunc decedit in infima*. Philosophia ultimately represents the supreme unifying and ordering principle of human knowledge; the human *pursuit* of philosophy, however, is a necessary but insufficient condition for perfect happiness, a state which involves an ineffable leap of the mind as aided by prayer and *divina gratia*.[102]

It may be an accident of history that the work which most comprehensively maps out the four mathematical sciences at the bottom of the philosophical taxonomy is Boethius' earliest known one (*Institutio arithmetica*),[103] whereas the one which restricts attention to the Practical–Theoretical division at its summit is his final one (*Consolatio*). There is a certain irony, moreover, in the fact that the *Consolatio*, with its insistence on the unity of Philosophy, leaves us to assemble the various components of the taxonomy from an array of works scattered across two decades or more. Did Boethius have a comprehensive vision from the start or did his conception of it develop over time? And if the latter, is it necessary to assume that he integrated the pieces as we have done for him here? If we look to c. 500–9, i.e., to the *Institutio arithmetica*, *Institutio musica* and first *Isagoge* commentary, what leaps out is the precision with which Boethius, aided by Nicomachus, expounds the mathematical sciences in the two monographs but omits mention of them in the commentary, for which there is no firmly

---

[98] Boethius, *Cons.* 4.m3.29–39 (inverting Homer, *Od.* 10.237–40).
[99] Boethius, *Cons.* 3.12.1; 5.2.8–9.
[100] Boethius, *Cons.* 4.4.8–9, 22–23, 6.53–54; 5.6.25; cf. *Fid. Cath.* 234–43.
[101] Boethius, *Cons.* 5.m3.11–31; cf. Plato, *Men.* 80d; *Theaet.* 198b–199b; Augustine, *Conf.* 10.18.27.
[102] Boethius, *Cons.* 5.3.33–35, 6.46.   [103] Boethius, *Inst. arith.* pref. 4 (*laboris mei primitias*).

identified source. Looking back from 524/525, on the other hand, we note the clarity with which *Consolatio* 2.m8.22–27 recalls the tripartite division of Practical disciplines laid out much earlier in the commentary. The first *Isagoge* commentary is, in several respects, a failed experiment, one which drove Boethius to reconsider. His discovery of the flaws in Victorinus' command of philosophical Greek prompted him to devise translations of his own, first of the *Categories* (in several passes) and then of the *Isagoge*, the second commentary on which opens with a general statement of policy on translation.[104] In addition, he set aside the (clumsily handled) literary genre of the philosophical dialogue without showing any further interest in it until his final days. And, of course, his exposition of the Theoretical branches of Philosophy left an omission which had to be remedied in *De trinitate*, and yet the doctrine which displaces Mathematics is clearly linked, as we have seen, with certain passages of the *Consolatio*. Between the first *Isagoge* commentary and *De trinitate* stands the second *Isagoge* commentary, where, as we have seen, Boethius experiments with possibilities for enabling Logic to straddle the traditional 'Stoic' and 'Peripatetic' divisions of Philosophy. Boethius undoubtedly grasped the basic structure of the taxonomy from the start and held on to it until the end; along the way, it seems, he refined his understanding of its internal components.

Corpus aristotelicum

Before concluding, we must touch briefly on a lost monograph of direct relevance to our concerns, *De ordine Peripateticae disciplinae*.[105] In his two earliest logical commentaries, Boethius systematically expounds the six propaedeutic *didascalica* regarded by commentators of the day as having to be addressed before approaching an ancient philosophical text, and included among them is the question of the order (*ordo*, τάξις) in which Aristotle's works are to be taken up for study.[106] With the second *Isagoge* and the two *De interpretatione* commentaries (c. 513–16), however, Boethius adopts a more selective approach, variously addressing the questions of title, scope, authorship, and utility and leaving more fluid boundaries between them.[107] Moreover, in the advanced edition of the *De interpretatione* commentary, he speaks of plans for

---

[104] See above, n. 59.
[105] Boethius, *De divis.* 877b, 6.15; cf. Boethius, *De divis.* xxviii–xxix (ed. Magee).
[106] Boethius, *In Isag.* I 4.14–15.21; *In Cat.* 159a–163c.
[107] Boethius, *In Isag.* II 143.8–47.3; *In Perih.* I 32.7–34.28; II 4.15–13.24; cf. Magee 2010: 27–30. See also Chapter 30 by Michael Champion, this volume.

ordering the Aristotelian corpus, from which we may provisionally conclude that *De ordine Peripateticae disciplinae* post-dated *c.* 516:

> My firm intention, assuming the divine power's sanction, is the following. Although there have been illustrious talents whose toil and study have given much to the Latin language concerning the subjects which I too am now treating, nevertheless they did not produce any ordering, any thread or steps, as it were, in the disposition of disciplines. Hence, after translating every work of Aristotle I can get my hands on for a Roman readership, I will write full commentaries in Latin on them all: after setting each of Aristotle's contributions to the subtlety of the logical art, the gravity of moral understanding, and the insight into natural truth in order, I will translate it in its entirety and shed the light, as it were, of commentary on it; and I will bring all of Plato's dialogues into Latin form by translating and commenting on them. Once those tasks have been accomplished, I will not shrink from restoring the doctrines of Aristotle and Plato to a unified concord, so to speak, and I will demonstrate that the two men are not in complete disagreement, as so many are, but concur on many points, and those the ones of greatest philosophical import.
>
> *Mihi autem si potentior divinitatis adnuerit favor, haec fixa sententia est, ut, quamquam fuerint praeclara ingenia quorum labor ac studium multa de his quae nunc quoque tractamus Latinae linguae contulerit, non tamen quendam quodammodo ordinem filumque et dispositione disciplinarum gradus ediderunt, ego omne Aristotelis opus quodcumque in manus venerit in Romanum stilum vertens eorum omnium commenta Latina oratione perscribam, ut, si quid ex logicae artis subtilitate, ex moralis gravitate peritiae, ex naturalis acumine veritatis ab Aristotele conscriptum sit, id omne ordinatum transferam atque etiam quodam lumine commentationis inlustrem omnesque Platonis dialogos vertendo vel etiam commentando in Latinam redigam formam. his peractis non equidem contempserim Aristotelis Platonisque sententias in unam quodammodo revocare concordiam eosque non ut plerique dissentire in omnibus sed in plerisque, et his in philosophia maximis, consentire demonstrem.*[108]

This passage has several important implications. First, there is the ordering of Aristotelian treatises according to the 'Stoic' categories of Logic, Ethics, and Physics (*logica ars, moralis peritia, naturalis veritas*), which also reflects a systematic 'disposition of disciplines'. As we have seen, Boethius in the second *Isagoge* commentary attempts to elide differences between the 'Stoic' and 'Peripatetic' divisions of Philosophy, and he may here be intimating an intention to adopt the Theoretical–Practical–Instrumental division familiar from other commentators of the period. Second, Boethius did not yet have a complete set of Aristotelian texts to hand (*quodcumque in manus venerit*). How much are we entitled to assume he did have and how fully developed was his plan at the

---

[108] Boethius, *In Perih.* II 79.9–80.6.

time of writing? Finally, Boethius says nothing about ordering the Platonic dialogues, whether thematically, into tetralogies, or otherwise. Either that was not part of the plan or it had not yet taken shape in Boethius' mind.

Artes liberales (II)

Boethius' aspirations collapsed in 524/525, leaving the body of his work, completed and in-progress, subject to the vicissitudes of fortune thereafter. Although the *Fortleben* of his corpus is enshrouded in obscurity for the decade between his death and the outbreak of war, the years 535–36 clearly involved some consolidation in connection with plans laid by Cassiodorus and Agapetus I for the founding of a Christian university and library near the Caelian Hill in Rome.[109] The project generated funds but was almost immediately abandoned due to the outbreak of war and Agapetus' death.[110] In *c.* 540, Cassiodorus withdrew to Constantinople, destined to return permanently to his Calabrian estates in *c.* 554. Whether any of the books originally assembled for the library in Rome ever reached Vivarium is an open question, but that there had been losses, as well as renewed collecting and consolidation in Constantinople, is certain.[111]

The taxonomy of Philosophy laid out in Cassiodorus' *Institutiones* is essentially the 'Peripatetic' one reconstructed for Boethius above:

Philosophy:
    Theoretical:
        Theology
        Mathematics
            Arithmetic
            Music
            Geometry
            Astronomy
        Physics
    Practical:
        Politics
        Economics
        Ethics.[112]

---

[109] The Δ-recension of the second book of the *Institutiones* probably represents a body of material, Boethian texts included, gathered for the library in those years (Troncarelli 1998: 7–19). Cf. Courcelle 1969: 334–35, 361–409; O'Donnell 1979: 179–85; Giuliani–Pavolini 1999.
[110] Cf. Cassiodorus, *Inst.* 1 pref. 1.   [111] Cf. Cassiodorus, *Inst.* 2.5.10; Troncarelli 2008–9.
[112] Cassiodorus, *Inst.* 2.3.4–7; cf. I. Hadot 1984: 191–206.

However, two significant differences, both related to context, must be borne in mind. First, Cassiodorus' overarching concern, extending beyond Philosophy proper, is for a closed system of seven liberal arts and sciences[113] embracing first Grammar, Rhetoric, and Dialectic (*Inst.* 2.1–3) and then Arithmetic, Music, Geometry, and Astronomy (2.4–7).[114] The latter four observe the Boethian order, but with a flattening effect due to their silence about the superordinate principles of Multitude and Magnitude and their internal rankings.[115] Hence a mathematical ordering coordinately sequenced with a linguistic one,[116] which suits the practical aim of charting a course of study for monks, but deprives Boethius' analysis of its theoretical depth.[117] The second difference is in the institutional setting itself, the *monasterium Vivariense*,[118] an outgrowth of administrative aspirations dating back to the mid-530s[119] and something for which there is no parallel in Boethius' known activities or extant writings. Cassiodorus' administrative impulses, to sum up these two considerations, condition curricular concerns which form a very different context for the philosophical taxonomy.

What are the implications of Cassiodorus' disposition of the liberal arts for our understanding of instruction at Vivarium? For one thing, it downgrades Philosophy to the level of a link in the curricular chain, stripped, as noted, of its hierarchical depth; at the same time, it restricts its disciplinary breadth, narrowing Philosophy down to the study of Dialectic (Logic) and the quadrivium. In practical terms, Boethius' philosophical taxonomy had served as a functional component of what gradually evolved into a comprehensive research project, a systematic ordering, rooted in an established exegetical tradition, that informed his pursuit of individual translations, commentaries, and monographs; the project had pedagogical implications,

---

[113] Cassiodorus, *Inst.* 2 pref. 1 (*aliis septem titulis saecularium lectionum*); cf. 1 pref. 6 (*de artibus ac disciplinis liberalium litterarum*); 2.3.19 (*de liberalibus ... artibus ... ad ingressum disciplinarum*); *Var.* 1.45.4 (*disciplinas vel artes*). Grammar and Rhetoric are *artes*, while Arithmetic, Music, Geometry, and Astronomy are *disciplinae* (*Inst.* 1.27.1); Dialectic is both, straddling probability and truth (2.2.17; cf. 2.3.20, 22; Ammonius, *In Isag.* 6.28–7.5). Cassiodorus was unable to obtain a copy of Martianus' *De nuptiis* for the Vivarium library (*Inst.* 2.3.20; cf. 2.2.17).
[114] Cf. Cassiodorus, *Inst.* 1.27.1; 2 pref. 5 (Music, Geometry reversed at 4); 2.3.6, 21.
[115] The primacy of Arithmetic is, however, acknowledged at *Inst.* 2.4.1; cf. *Var.* 9.21.3–4 on Grammar.
[116] Although the point is left vague, the 'table of contents' at *Inst.* 2 pref. 5 (Ω-recension) presumably is not intended to imply full mastery of the linguistic arts as a stringent prerequisite to the study of mathematics.
[117] Cf. Klinkenberg 1959: 8–13.   [118] Cassiodorus, *Inst.* 1.29.1, 3.
[119] Note, in addition to his work with Agapetus, Cassiodorus' concern as prefect (*c.* 533) for instructors in the *scholae liberalium litterarum* at Rome (*Var.* 9.21.1–5; cf. 8.31.6).

of course, which, however, remained incomplete and unrealised in 524/525. Cassiodorus' was perforce an ordering after the fact, the assembling and cataloguing of Boethian works for use by monks whose appointed goal was to develop a command of scripture. He and the disciples with whom he collaborated had an imperfect grasp of the texts to hand, evincing signs of confusion that reach right down to the level of their misunderstanding of authorship.[120] And since the *Institutiones* restricts attention to works furnished for the course of study, any provisions for higher-order philosophical study at Vivarium inevitably remain a matter of conjecture. Aristotle's *Ethics*, *Politics*, *De anima*, *Physics*, and *Metaphysics* – to say nothing of Plato's dialogues – are conspicuously absent, eclipsed by the *artes liberales*.

To judge from a series of diagrams and images created for the archetype of the *Institutiones*, instruction at Vivarium emphasised mastery of the complex divisions and subdivisions of material treated in the works available for study. Thirty-four of the thirty-seven illustrations are concentrated in Book 2 and serve as visual *aides-mémoires* to study of the seven liberal arts and sciences, the offshoots of 'seeds' of 'spiritual wisdom'.[121] The philosophical taxonomy discussed above is a case in point (*Inst.* 2.3.4–7): a plant (Philosophy), depicted as sprouting forth from a vase, sends arching off to the left a Theoretical branch (*inspectiva*) from which the three shoots of Physics (*naturalis*), Mathematics (*doctrinalis*), and Theology (*divinalis*) issue, with Mathematics then sending out Arithmetic, Music, Geometry, and Astronomy; similarly, a Practical branch (*activa*) arching off to the right sends out the three shoots of Ethics (*moralis*), Economics (*dispensativa*), and Politics (*civilis*). The ten Aristotelian Categories too are depicted as offshoots of a plant, whereas the five Porphyrian Predicables descend from the hooves and torso of a lamb, and so on. The ornamentation may appear obscure or irrelevant at first glance,[122] but closer scrutiny reveals a subtle system of mnemonics designed to guide readers through some densely forested taxonomies.[123]

We have come a long way from Boethius, and although it may be tempting to construct a narrative of decline by connecting him with Cassiodorus as two dots on a matrix, with one standing for scientific progress and the other for pedagogical retrenchment, to do so would seriously distort both fact and intention. Boethius and Cassiodorus were individuals who

---

[120] Cassiodorus, *Inst.* 2.3.18 (ΦΔ- /Ω-recensions divided between Boethius and Victorinus, respectively).
[121] Cassiodorus, *Inst.* 1 pref. 6.   [122] Cassiodorus, *Inst.* xxiii (ed. Mynors).
[123] Troncarelli 2020: 15–64.

differed *toto caelo*, with a relationship that was fraught from the moment Cassiodorus replaced Boethius as Master of the Offices, if not earlier. In the event, however, a symbiotic bond developed between them, one that left Boethius dependent on Cassiodorus for the preservation of his *Nachlass*, and Cassiodorus on Boethius for intellectual material with which to fuel an educational project. Boethius' professional disinterest in Grammar probably arose from a personal disinclination to teaching, schools, and the liberal arts generally.[124] He evidently distinguished between introducing material (*introducere*) and actually teaching it (*docere*),[125] a distinction which obviously included writing elementary philosophical commentaries and monographs but just as obviously excluded any professional engagement with elementary subjects such as Grammar. Cassiodorus, who had a natural instinct for institution building and had evolved from statesman to monk in midlife, founded a school long after his hopes for a university had vanished, and he understood the necessity of training young monks in Grammar – not to mention orthography.[126] At the same time, he gathered what Boethius had left behind and repurposed it for an arts-based Christian education. So when the sun set on Vivarium sometime *c.* 598 CE, Philosophy indeed entered into what was destined to prove a long period of decline, but not because *Cassiodorus* had condemned it. And when the lights finally came back on, it was possible for our Carolingian scholiast to christen a trivium to complement the quadrivium within the full suite of liberal arts precisely because he could seek guidance from Cassiodorus as well as from Boethius.

---

[124] Cf. above, n. 55.   [125] Boethius, *Syllog. cat.* 809c.
[126] Cassiodorus, *Inst.* 1.30; Keil, *Gramm. Lat.* 7.143–216.

36 | Ordering Emotional Communities: Modes of Knowing in Gregory the Great

BRONWEN NEIL

Introduction

Gregory I, monk and bishop of Rome (590–604 CE), had a greater impact as an author than any other Western writer of the sixth to seventh centuries. His prolific output featured many genres of patristic writing, including homilies and commentaries on scripture, an encyclopaedia of Italian hagiography, over 850 letters of many types, and a manual of instruction for clerics. All this came from a relatively short pontificate of fifteen years in one of the most troubled periods of Rome's history. It is difficult to know whether Gregory's prolific output was a deliberate programme of ordering spiritual, administrative, and ecclesiastical knowledge for posterity, or a lucky accident of literary survival, or indeed both. If there is one thing that stands out as a constant across his oeuvre, it is the coupling of spiritual and intellectual knowledge for the benefit of all levels of society. This insight has been explored in almost every modern biography of Gregory I.[1]

This study of the modes of knowing that are threaded through different genres in Gregory's oeuvre will assess how his ordering of knowledge reflected various levels of social organisation, from emotional communities within the local church of Rome to the larger organisational structures of power and knowledge that governed the Roman empire at the end of late antiquity. Michel Foucault was the first to suggest that the strategies used to collect and organise knowledge were constitutive of larger power structures in classical and late antiquity, even of the Roman empire itself.[2] Jason König and Tim Whitmarsh have also argued that the organisational strategies of Greco-Roman technical manuals, compilations, and miscellanies can tell us much about the larger organisational structures of power and knowledge across the Roman empire.[3] Such literary works tell us what the hierarchies of power were interested in and how the leaders of an empire that stretched from Spain to the Black Sea understood themselves and their project of government. Gregory the Great brought to bear spiritual and

---

[1] Homes Dudden 1905, followed by Battifol 1928; Straw 1991; Markus 1997; Müller 2009.
[2] Hodkinson 2009: 157.   [3] König and Whitmarsh 2007a.

emotional knowledge in his interactions with the ecclesial and imperial power structures of his day, and by his writings he shaped lay and clerical communities in ways that were significantly different from the classical intellectual ideal of the Roman leader.

Gregory's many works reveal three main avenues to knowledge: the exegetical, the emotional, and the social. These modes of knowing – nurtured through appeals to the passions, rational thought, and the paradoxes at the heart of the church and its faith – bind the sum of Gregory's worldly knowledge and his sharing of divine wisdom in an indivisible corpus. C. M. Chin and Moulie Vidas sum up the mutual influence of epistemography and the praxis of late antique historians as follows: 'the process of knowing influenced a variety of historical actions in late antiquity and in turn … a variety of historical actions and circumstances produced what became the content and practice of knowing'.[4] The same mutual influence can be ascribed to Gregory's epistemography and his praxis as a spiritual thinker and teacher. The process of knowing influenced Gregory's actions and beliefs as a monk and bishop of Rome, and those actions and contexts informed what he considered to be the content and practice of Christian wisdom. Gregory treated the ordering of knowledge as fundamental to a well-ordered Christian society, and as inseparable from his ecclesiology and his duties as a bishop of Rome. He approached knowing as a spiritual process rather than as the mastery or delivery of content, even while he strove to deliver these as well.

In the first section of this chapter, I examine the ordering of exegetical knowledge in Gregory's homilies and commentaries on Job,[5] Ezekiel,[6] the Song of Songs,[7] and the gospels.[8] The second section analyses his appeal to emotional knowledge in preaching spiritual truths to clerics and laypeople. Its subjects are Gregory's manual for clerics on the application of spiritual and practical knowledge for the care of souls (*Pastoral Rule*), and his collection of Italian hagiography (*Dialogues in Four Books*). The third section, on Gregory's vast collection of letters (*Registrum*), shows how Gregory engaged with women of influence outside Rome and their knowledge of ecclesiastical and imperial hierarchies to further his interventions. His epistolography affords a rare opportunity to explore the value of gendered knowledge to a bishop far from the centre of power at the Constantinopolitan court. His letters also convey the value of material gifts with ritual power, such as contact relics, in reinforcing papal authority *ex officio*.

---

[4] Chin and Vidas 2015b: 1.   [5] Greg. Mag. *Moralia in Iob* (Adriaen 1979–85).
[6] Greg. Mag. *Homiliae in Hiezekielem* (Adriaen 1971).
[7] Greg. Mag. *In cantica canticorum* (Verbraken 1963).
[8] Greg. Mag. *Homiliae XL in euangelia* (Étaix, Morel, and Judic 2005–8).

Ordering Exegetical Knowledge

First, let us look at how Gregory communicated his knowledge of scripture in an extended commentary on the book of Job, the *Moralia*, and in homilies on the book of the prophet Ezekiel and the gospels.[9] In the fifth century, Vincent of Lérins advised his clerical readers that 'we must, with the Lord's help, fortify our belief in two ways: first, by the authority of divine law, and then by the tradition of the Catholic Church'.[10] He meant that faith was dependent on two types of knowledge: scripture (divine law) and the body of thought written down by church fathers and canon law-makers up to his day. To Gregory's mind also, truth was buttressed by two pillars: first, scripture and second, tradition. The divine law or scripture was above earthly law but also determined and underpinned imperial rule by divine providence:[11] this was a given in Gregory's hierarchical ordering of the world and its knowledge. The rule for the right understanding of prophetic and apostolic scriptures was conformity to the 'standard of ecclesiastical and catholic interpretation'.[12]

Gregory's knowledge of scripture was vast, allowing him to supplement his exegetical commentary with many similar verses from other books of the Bible. This in itself was not new. More innovative was his use of the genre of biblical commentary as a vehicle for a running commentary on his times. By combining an elaborate exposition of Job – an amoral tale from the Hebraic tradition that challenged Roman values of honour, virtue, and their just reward – with an indictment of sixth-century Italian society, Gregory gave his moral viewpoint a status that would perhaps have been lacking in any other literary context. Self-revealing prose was not part of the project of knowing oneself or the getting of wisdom in the sixth century. However, when that revelation accompanied the tale of another mortal who plumbed the depths of the human condition, namely Job, it seems that self-revelation was perfectly acceptable. As in the *Pastoral Rule*, the *Moralia* demonstrate Gregory's understanding that knowledge needs to be tailored to suit the audience. In *Book* 30, on preaching the gospel, he writes,

For if holy men were to choose to preach to us those things which they hear, when they are intoxicated with heavenly contemplation, and did not rather

---

[9] Greg. Mag. *Hom. in ev.* (Étaix, Morel, and Judic 2005–8).
[10] Vinc. Ler. *Comm.* 2.4 (Demeulenaere 1985: 150). Composed in 434 CE.
[11] Straw 2019: 357.   [12] Vinc. Ler. *Comm.* 2.5 (Demeulenaere 1985: 150).

temper their knowledge with some moderation and sobriety, who could receive those streams of the heavenly font, in the still contracted channel of his understanding?[13]

In the first book of his homilies on Ezekiel, Gregory deals with the important hermeneutical question of whether literal or allegorical interpretations of scripture are better. He answers that neither is superior; the first is suitable for the weak, by which we understand the ordinary person, and the second for the strong or educated.[14] Like the *Moralia* on Job, the homilies on Ezekiel reveal an awareness of different kinds of knowledge as suitable for different kinds of people. Gregory also allows that he is better able to understand the interior meaning of the text 'when in the company of my brothers'.[15] This deeper understanding of the prophet Ezekiel's meaning is a gift to the monastic community to which he belonged. Knowledge-seeking was a communal endeavour and, in Gregory's age, an institutional one. True knowledge was not just for a small elite but for the whole community of believers. This is another significant departure from traditional Roman intellectual values.

The third departure from secular Roman epistemology is Gregory's humble acceptance of his limited knowledge.[16] Gregory compares his sufferings to the trials suffered by Job and is able to come to terms with them, and with his imperfect knowledge of God's economy of salvation, through his reflection on Job's journey to acceptance. Gregory's linking of individual suffering with the death throes of the world in the end times is another unusual feature of this work. Hester argues that Gregory believes that Christ the Judge uses redemptive pain to bring individuals to recognise their own sinfulness and to focus on their salvation.[17] This theology of the body, linking the pain of the dying world with individual pain, is perhaps unique in Western patristic literature up to his day.[18] The third-century Alexandrian, Origen, came to a similar conclusion: that since the body is required to experience pain, the body is implicated in the process of redemptive knowing.[19] The limited popularity of Gregory's teaching on this subject in the West may be judged by the relatively small number

---

[13] Greg. Mag. *Mor.* 30.48. [14] Greg. Mag. *Hom. in Ezek.* 1.9.30–31 (Moorhead 2005: 50–51).
[15] Greg. Mag. *Hom. in Ezek.* 2.2.1 (Moorhead 2005: 51).
[16] On humility as an epistemological ideal, see also Chapter 30 by Michael Champion, this volume.
[17] Hester 2007.
[18] On physical pain as an instrument of positive knowledge and purification, see Chapter 38 by Zachary Guiliano, this volume.
[19] On Origen's scriptural exegesis and the influence of the body of the church on it, see Chapter 6 by Peter Martens, this volume.

of surviving Latin manuscripts of the *Moralia*.[20] The communication of emotional knowledge is most obvious in Gregory's biographies of saints, to which we now turn.

Communicating Emotional Knowledge

A great deal of Gregory's appeal and influence must be attributed to his ordering of emotional knowledge, which was based on his understanding of the operation of the virtues and vices on ordinary human lives. In his handbook for clergy on pastoral care, Gregory communicated to priests how to tailor pastoral responses to the various types of people in their care, whether laypeople or clerics. Laity or clergy is just one binary distinction out of thirty-five that he identifies in Book 3 of the *Regula pastoralis*.[21] Other distinctions are made in the admonishments suitable for men and women, young and old, married and unmarried, servant and master, rich and poor, healthy and sick, and fortunate and unfortunate. Some of Gregory's divisions are based on human passions: lacking in shame or sensitive; arrogant or timid; impatient or patient. His taxonomic description of seventy kinds of Christian is aimed at enabling clerics to judge what is required to care for each parishioner's soul according to their different personality types and circumstances, as he says in the prologue to the work.[22] Discretion is as important for successful pastoral care as it is for making correct legal judgements.

In the four books of *Dialogues*, Gregory took a different approach to the communication of spiritual knowledge. The *Dialogues* were almost certainly written by Gregory while he was bishop of Rome (590–604 CE). Despite one scholar's protracted attempt to dispute the work's authenticity, claiming that the text was constructed from archival papal documents *c.* 670–680,[23] most scholars now accept their attribution to Gregory or a contemporary who knew his works well.[24] The four books of the *Dialogues* between Gregory and his deacon and close friend, Peter of Triacola, were intended to supply the conspicuous lack of edifying tales of Italian saints. These stories, although perhaps as difficult for late antique audiences to believe as they

---

[20] Unlike the *Dialogues*, the thirty-five books of the *Moralia* were not translated into any other language in the Middle Ages.
[21] *Reg. past.* 3.2–15 (Moorhead 2005: 96–125).   [22] *Reg. past.* 1.1 (Straw 2019: 363).
[23] Clark (1987) argued that the author of the commentaries on Job, Ezekiel, and the gospels could not have indulged in such lowbrow literary fantasy.
[24] Dal Santo 2013; Demacopoulos 2013: 135, 145.

are for the modern reader, were meant to evoke the passions of fear and wonder. Wonder held an important place in popular Christian literature of late antiquity, when miracle stories, or as Marnie Hughes-Warrington calls them, 'ecclesiastical paradoxology', first gained traction.[25] Gregory did not consider such miraculous testaments to the working of divine power in the material world as lowbrow or unsuitable for an educated audience. He also cited miracles around the tombs of saints in his correspondence with the empress Constantina, discussed in the final section of this chapter.

The *Dialogues* are written in question-and-answer format, where Peter asks the questions and Gregory supplies the answers, as he had heard them from revered elders who relayed the stories of holy men and women's miraculous deeds, prophecies, curses, and healings from their personal experience. The format suited the broad audience for which the *Dialogues* were intended, with Peter representing the common reader with his disingenuous questions. Peter's naïve acceptance of the miraculous content encourages the credulous reader. The question-and-answer technique, or Socratic method, was used to similar effect by Augustine in his work *The Teacher*, ostensibly a dialogue with his son, Adeodatus.[26] The *Dialogues* do not seem to have circulated widely in the seventh century but enjoyed widespread popularity in the Middle Ages in various vernacular versions.[27] They are strongly infused, as were most of Gregory's works, with a sense of fearful expectation of the last judgement.[28] Fear was a powerful motivator for conformity: one should approach the just Judge with genuine contrition while he could still be swayed towards mercy. Gregory describes a vision received by Redemptus, bishop of Ferenti, that warned of the approaching end of the world during the reign of Pope John III (561–574) when the Lombard invaders first appeared in Italy.[29] Gregory played to the human passion of fear of the end, but he probably did not expect the day of judgement to come within his lifetime.[30]

In the miraculous economy of the *Dialogues*, we can see how Gregory spiritualised political conflict to make Rome's enemies, the Lombards – who were Christians of the Homoean or Arian persuasion – synonymous with devil worshippers and the Antichrist, signalling the end of the world. Here we can see how imperial and ecclesial hierarchies overlapped implicitly to produce the conclusion that Rome's enemies were in league with evil forces. The Devil was, for Gregory, the 'ancient enemy of mankind'

---

[25] Hughes-Warrington 2018: 23.   [26] Aug. *De mag.* (Deferrari 1968: 7–61).
[27] E.g., Old English, Old French, and Middle Dutch: Mews and Renkin 2013: 316.
[28] Greg. Mag. *Reg.* 3.29; 3.61; 4.23; 7.26; 10.20; 13.33.
[29] Greg. Mag. *Dial.* 3.28, my translation.
[30] Greg. Mag. *Reg.* 11.37 (Norberg 1982: 2.931; Baun 2013: 175).

(*Dial.* 2.8), and one of the ways that 'the master of deceit' plagued unsuspecting humans was to send false dreams or illusions.[31] While other writers in the Neoplatonic tradition, such as Origen and Synesius of Cyrene, insisted that only virtue allowed the wise man to distinguish true, revelatory dreams from false, misleading ones, in Gregory's *Dialogues* even sinners could have revelatory or prophetic dreams. Likewise, both saints and sinners could perceive the interaction of demons in the everyday lives of monastics, bishops, and laypeople. Sinful monks received visions of divine punishment for their particular passions. For example, a greedy nun was possessed by a demon after eating a lettuce leaf straight out of the garden.[32] In her haste, she had failed to notice the leaf had a demon sitting on it. Her ignorance of invisible malevolent powers seems to be associated with the sin of gluttony. Fortunately, she was able to avert this punishment by contrition and the demon was cast out under protest.

The devil and his angels appeared not only to bishops, monks, and nuns but also to ordinary people. A memorable instance is a father's vision of his five-year-old son being escorted to hell because he repeatedly sinned by blasphemy in emulation of his parent.[33] These memorable stories of visions appearing to ordinary folk are meant to be understood literally, not figuratively. Respect for the episcopal hierarchy was reinforced by the story of a couple who entertained a stranger as a guest in their home and listened avidly while he slandered their bishop. The parents then watched in horror as their young son fell into the hearth and burned to death before their eyes. This accident is construed as a punishment for their secret sin against their bishop (*Dial.* 4.18). Arcane spiritual knowledge was useful for reinforcing the ecclesial hierarchies of power and for keeping the laity obedient. The emphasis in the *Dialogues* on divine retribution is probably a product of the apocalyptic context in which Gregory wrote, having lived through several decades of warfare in Italy, first Justinian's Gothic wars and then the Lombard invasions of the 560s onwards.

Inscribing Social Order and Tradition

The correspondence of Pope Gregory I shows a bishop who thrived at the centre of a vast information network, one that advanced his career as

---

[31] Cf. Sir 34:7; Lev 19:26.   [32] Greg. Mag. *Dial.* 1.4.
[33] Greg. Mag. *Dial.* 4.19 (de Vogüé and Antin 1978–80: 2.72–74). See also *Dial.* 4.35 and 4.36. On Christian theories of vision as a conduit for spiritual knowledge, especially in Augustine, see the discussion in Chapter 25 by Robin Jensen, this volume.

an *apocrisiarius* or papal representative in Constantinople and eventually elevated him to the head of the apostolic see. His letters to four imperial consorts illustrate a range of persuasive strategies, the most basic of which was to access male power through the women most closely associated with the emperor. Gregory wrote several times to Empress Constantina with the expectation that she would take up his petitions with her husband Maurice. His interventions included a plea on behalf of the oppressed inhabitants of the islands Sardinia, Sicily, and Corsica, who were facing debilitating levels of taxation from Constantinople. On the same day, Gregory appealed to the empress concerning John the Faster's bid to claim the title of universal patriarch for himself.[34] Gregory's concept of the Roman church covered both the orthodox believers of the city of Rome and, in a broader sense, the universal imperial church governed from Constantinople. Both were aspects of the emotional community of believers to which he belonged.[35]

In a letter of unusual boldness, Gregory refused the empress's request for some of Rome's holiest relics, the head or other bones of St Paul, offering contact relics (*brandea*) instead: filings from the chains that bound St Peter.[36] To justify disappointing her, he told how others before him had dropped dead after presuming to touch the sarcophagi of important Roman saints, including Peter and Lawrence. He suspects that she did not think of this request herself but was prompted by men who intended to stir up strife between them by making an impossible demand. The real possibility that the letters written by imperial women might reflect not their own wishes but those of men in the background should make us wary of assumptions about apparently gendered content in their letters.

Gregory's letters to women of the imperial court reveal that this form of knowledge exchange was to some extent gendered. The women to whom he wrote were keepers of a particularly valuable form of knowledge: inside information. As König and Whitmarsh have observed, 'Epistemology cannot be divorced from particular social relations and situations. It is not some abstract activity, practised from a position of detachment; rather it is enacted within all institutions of social encounter'.[37] Information needs context to be translated into knowledge by the user or receiver. In Foucauldian terms, we might say that papal power was inextricably bound up

---

[34] Greg. Mag. *Reg.* 5.38 and 39, both dated 1 June 595; see Booth 2013: 113–15 and Demacopoulos 2015: 41–43.

[35] Rosenwein 2006: 80 coined the phrase 'emotional communities' in reference to the early medieval West.

[36] Greg. Mag. *Reg.* 4.30.   [37] König and Whitmarsh 2007a: 6.

with the ordering of knowledge, and that imperial power could not exist without social and ecclesial networks of mediation.

Women were assumed to have social and emotional knowledge that could be brought to bear on resolving differences in matters of faith as well as on practical problems such as over-taxation.[38] By approaching women who could petition their male relations, Gregory used an indirect approach to networks of power. Writing to Constantina, he asked her to advise her husband to accept papal authority and follow his advice. It is not clear whether she was expected to translate his appeals into a different form or simply to wave Gregory's letters under the emperor's nose. In a letter to Maurice's sister Theoctista, who was entrusted with caring for the royal princes, Gregory begged her to take care of the princes' moral training and to make sure that the eunuchs who helped educate them would foster unity between the brothers and clemency towards their subjects.[39] Gregory seems to have been worried that any enmity between them would become public and threaten the security of the Byzantine empire.[40] Gregory's use of his friendships with Byzantine women like Constantina and Theoctista to further his influence over the powerful men in their sphere reflects a wider currency of knowledge exchange between bishops and their aristocratic female networks in the East.

Gregory was not above using women to spy on other women in the imperial court. He writes to Theoctista requesting a report on the spiritual health of her mistress Constantina.[41] Knowledge of imperial women's business was highly gendered and could only be obtained by the agency of another woman in service to the empress. The letter is also nominally addressed to Andrew, the imperial children's teacher, but its content concerns Theoctista alone. The seriousness of Gregory's request is underlined by the valuable gift that accompanied it: one of St Peter's precious keys. Knowledge was power in the imperial court, and Gregory knew he would have to pay to get it. Again, the ritual power of the gifted object served to reinforce the spiritual power of the giver and writer of the letter. Gregory's doctrinal knowledge gave him formidable bargaining power and made him a successful arbiter of worldly affairs.

---

[38] On the gendered nature of certain topics in ancient philosophy, see Chapter 19 by Dawn LaValle Norman, this volume.
[39] Greg. Mag. *Reg.* 7.23 (Norberg 1982: 476). The letter is also addressed to the princes' tutor Andrew.
[40] Dal Santo 2013: 62.
[41] Greg. Mag. *Reg.* 7.23, written in 597 CE. Gregory also wrote to her in his first year as bishop of Rome: *Reg.* 1.5.

When writing to Theoctista, Gregory assumed the duty of pastoral caregiver, assuring her that she is like the sons of Israel, who walked a dry path through the Red Sea (Exod 15:19), so untouched is she by the worldly tumult that surrounds her:[42]

For you breathe in the odour of sweetness and hence love the Bridegroom of your soul with such ardour that you can say to him, along with the heavenly Bride, *Draw me. After you shall we run in the odour of your ointments.* (Song 1:3)

His allusion to the Song of Songs seems to be particularly suited to a woman of the royal court. Gregory chided her for omitting to tell him what her mistress Constantina was reading in the way of religious texts and whether they moved her to contrition. Theoctista's presence should recall her mistress's mind to the love of the heavenly kingdom; she should ask her mistress to examine whether her contrition was caused by fear or love.[43] Gregory went on to give a mini-homily on the contrition caused by fear and the superiority of the contrition caused by love. Again, this sort of emotional knowledge seems aptly conveyed to women involved in the intrigues and conspiracies of the Eastern court.

In a letter from the same period, Gregory mentioned briefly that he wrote to Maurice's sister Gordia, later wife of the general Philippikos, who was accused of conspiring against the emperor shortly before Maurice's death in 602, according to Theophanes.[44] In response to the count Narses, a 'religious man', who had asked him to give some spiritual advice to Theoctista, her mother Gordia, and their respective husbands, Gregory confessed that he had written only to Gordia, due to the difficulty of getting his letters translated into good Greek.[45] In the same letter, he offered spiritual advice to Narses' daughter Domenica, who was head of a convent, that she should collect other women's souls by moving them to contrition for their sins.[46] This is another instance of Gregory playing on human passions within emotional communities to reinforce a rule of obedience. To the query of Gregoria, lady-in-waiting to the empress Constantina, as to whether her

---

[42] Greg. Mag. *Reg.* 7.23 (Norberg 1982: 474–75; trans. DelCogliano 2012: 245).

[43] Greg. Mag. *Reg.* 7.23 (Martyn 2004: 2.475). See also the discussion of the difference between godly and worldly sadness in Chapter 28 by Jonathan Zecher, this volume.

[44] Theoph. Conf. *Chron.* AM 6089 (de Boor 1883–85: 1.285).

[45] Greg. Mag. *Reg.* 7.27 (Martyn 2004: 2.482). Narses is also the recipient of *Reg.* 1.6; 3.63; 5.46; 6.14.

[46] Greg. Mag. *Reg.* 7.27 (Martyn 2004: 2.482). Gregory here identified Gordia's husband as Marinus, not Philippikos. On the epistolary evidence for two Theoctistas, one the emperor's sister and the other his sister Gordia's daughter, see Martyn 2004: 2.482 n. 166. Maurice also had a daughter named Theoctista, who died *c.* 605.

sins had been forgiven, he regretted that he could not respond because he was unworthy of receiving such a revelation.[47]

In a later letter of 601, the year before Phocas came to power, Gregory sought to console Theoctista, his 'most charming and most excellent daughter', when she became the subject of slanderous gossip in the Eastern court.[48] The reason for the accusations remains a mystery – could she have been accused of spying for Rome? – but Gregory likened her to Job, who knew that his conscience was clean, even though his friends abused him (Job 16:19).[49] Constantina, loyal to her late husband to the end, left Constantinople in 602 and was executed *c.* 605 along with her three daughters in Chalcedon for conspiring against the usurper Phocas.[50] The new emperor Phocas used torture to gain the knowledge he needed – the names of the former empress's conspirators – and they too were executed.

The indirect approach also characterised Gregory's letters to women of the Lombard and Frankish courts and correlates with contemporary evidence for the nurturing of Christian faith through the women of royal households in the early medieval period. His letters to women of influence such as Theodelinda, wife of the Lombard king Agilulf, and the Frankish queen Brunhilde covered disciplinary problems in the church like simony in clerical office and schismatic priests.[51] Such female correspondents were charged with the conversion of their husbands and with raising their royal children in the correct knowledge of the faith. Bishops like Gregory wrote to women who could exercise influence in their households for the preservation of Christian knowledge and practices.

To Brunhilde (r. *c.* 567–613 CE), Gregory wrote ten times on various civil and religious matters. Brunhilde outlived her son Childebert II (575–96 CE) by seventeen years and acted as regent for her grandsons when they assumed the throne. Gregory requested her continued support for the mission to the Anglo-Saxons[52] and her foundation of three monasteries and convents.[53] He also wrote five times to the Catholic queen Theodelinda.[54]

---

[47] Greg. Mag. *Reg.* 7.22 (Martyn 2004: 2.473).
[48] Greg. Mag. *Reg.* 11.27 (Martyn 2004: 3.766). Written in February 601, this is the longest extant letter to an individual in the collection of over 850 letters: Dal Santo 2013: 62. The closing reference to her bringing up the 'little lordships' indicates that its addressee is the nurse Theoctista, recipient of *Reg.* 7.23.
[49] Greg. Mag. *Reg.* 11.27 (Martyn 2004: 3.763).
[50] Theoph. Conf. *Chron.* AM 6099 (de Boor 1883–85: 1.294–95).
[51] Greg. Mag. *Reg.* 11.46 (schismatic priests); 11.49 (council on simony).
[52] Greg. Mag. *Reg.* 6.5; 6.58; 6.60; 8.4; 9.213; 9.214; 11.46; 11.48; 11.49; 13.5. See Ricci 2013: 43–49.
[53] Greg. Mag. *Reg.* 13.9; 13.10; 13.11.
[54] Greg. Mag. *Reg.* 4.4; 4.33; 5.52; 9.68; 14.12. See Ricci 2013: 39–41.

The last of these letters, written shortly before his death while he was bedridden from gout and stomach pains, congratulated Theodelinda on the birth of a son, Adaloald.[55] Accompanying the letter were two amulets: a miniature crucifix made of wood from the Holy Cross and a text from a holy gospel enclosed in a Persian case for the new baby prince. The immense ritual power of such objects reinforced Gregory's claim of superior spiritual knowledge and authority. Powerful spiritual knowledge and material power went hand in hand. Gregory promised that, when his health improved, he would reply at length to the letter from Abbot Secundus, which concerned the Three Chapters controversy. In the meantime, he could only send a copy of the *Acts* of the Fifth Ecumenical Council of 553 CE and ask Theodelinda to bring them to the attention of Secundus so that, in rereading the text, he might recognise its truth:

> God forbid that we should accept the interpretation of any sort of heretic or should deviate at all from the *Tome* of our predecessor Leo, of holy memory! But we accept whatever was decided by the four holy synods, and we condemn whatever was rejected.[56]

Since the first four holy synods had been accepted by his predecessors, the fifth should also be accepted by all Western abbots and bishops as it had been by Rome.

Gregory seems to have believed that empresses shared their husband's responsibility for just rule. He offered the following praise to Leontia, wife of Phocas, who murdered Maurice and his heirs, including Gregory's godson Theodosius, to clear his own path to imperial power:[57]

> (L)et God himself be the guardian of your empire, let him be your protector on earth and let him intercede for you in heaven, so that through the fact that you make the subjects of your empire rejoice by relieving their harsh burdens, you may yourself rejoice in the heavenly kingdom after many years.[58]

Gregory's judgements on temporal matters stretched beyond royal family members, courtiers, clerics, and Christian laity to embrace to non-citizen slaves and Jews.[59] Generally, he afforded Jewish citizens all the protections of Roman law, including freedom of worship in their synagogues.[60] Debts to Jews were to be repaid; however, Jews were not to possess Christian slaves, for fear of forced conversions to Judaism.[61]

---

[55] Greg. Mag. *Reg.* 14.12.   [56] Greg. Mag. *Reg.* 14.12 (Martyn 2004: 3.878).
[57] Greg. Mag. *Reg.* 13.40, from July 603.
[58] Greg. Mag. *Reg.* 13.40 (Gregory I 1982: 2.1044; trans. Martyn 2004: 3.855 (modified)).
[59] Straw 2019: 375–77.   [60] Greg. Mag. *Reg.* 8.25.   [61] Greg. Mag. *Reg.* 1.42, 2.45, and 3.37.

Several other letters offer his interpretations of the law regarding slaves and other forms of property. The church could manumit slaves to allow them to enter monastic life, but their owners had to be compensated unless those owners were Jews.[62] He once sent a young slave boy as a gift to his friend Narses in Constantinople, 'so that in this world he might live in servitude to a man through whom he can reach his freedom in heaven'.[63] Gregory's engagement in the traditional Roman gift economy, combined with social networking and imparting spiritual knowledge, was aimed at inscribing social order not just in the Roman West but also in Constantinople. As Carol Straw put it, 'The judgements in Gregory's letters are those of an active pope serving the church in the world.'[64]

Conclusion

Papal knowledge was not like any other kind of knowledge of the first millennium. It was essentially both ecumenical and totalising. The see of Rome's incumbents inherited along with the office a corpus of knowledge, based on scripture and tradition, that was portrayed as solid and invariable over time. Its custodians were not open to challenge; it was not just a monolith, but the rock on which the church itself was built. It was thus able to create and sustain hierarchies of power. When Gregory asked Theodelinda to thank her husband, the Lombard king Agilulf, for having made peace and to keep calling his mind to peace, 'so that among your many good deeds, you may find a reward in the sight of God for an innocent people, who might perish through inducement to sin',[65] it is very likely that she would have complied.

In this brief survey of knowledge-ordering in Gregory's oeuvre, I focused first on the ordering of exegetical knowledge in his homilies and biblical commentaries, in which he drew allegorical, rational, and emotional readings from the divine law of scripture. Second, I discussed Gregory's taxonomies of emotional knowledge in the *Pastoral Rule*, which taught priests how to target a specific audience, whether in their preaching or pastoral care. His focus on the kinds of knowledge or guidance that were

---

[62] On Boethius's attempt to reorder the social institution of Roman citizenship through philosophical wisdom, see Chapter 35 by John Magee, this volume.
[63] Greg. Mag. *Reg.* 7.27 (Martyn 2004: 2.483).   [64] Straw 2019: 376.
[65] Greg. Mag. *Reg.* 14.12 (Martyn 2004: 3.879).

appropriate to different classes of person shows subtlety and an unusual awareness of the responsibilities of those who were trusted with caring for souls. In his *Dialogues* on the miracles of Italian saints, appeals to negative emotions like fear were used to inspire contrition. Gregory's metaphysics is at times strange and confusing, but its ultimate goal was to encourage the gifts of discernment and compunction to flower in the earthly garden that was no longer Eden.

Gregory's epistolography proved a rich source for the inscribing of social order. His letters to women of influence in the Byzantine court reveal a strategy of indirect petitioning on issues of church doctrine and governance which correlates with what is already well attested in the late antique West: the handing down of orthodox Christian faith was a gendered practice. Like their Frankish and Lombard counterparts, the mothers and sisters of Byzantine emperors were expected to work on the conversion and conformity of their husbands, brothers, and children in matters of faith. Gregory's letters signal a wider cultural phenomenon of women sustaining members of their social network, especially their family, in the faith in ways not expected of their male peers. Gifts like the filings from the iron chains that bound Rome's founding apostle, Peter, served to reinforce the weight of spiritual advice offered in the pope's letters, and to bind the correspondent to him and his 'universal' church.

The organisational strategies of these texts have much to tell us about the larger organisational structures of power and knowledge across the Roman empire at the end of late antiquity. As Chin and Vidas comment regarding late antique historiography, the process of knowing contributed to historical outcomes, just as historical contexts shaped the project of knowledge and its organisation.[66] If Hellenistic philosophy's goal was unifying knowledge into a whole that was more than the sum of its separate strands, in what König and Whitmarsh called a 'totalising gesture',[67] the way this knowledge was organised fundamentally shaped the structures of power in late antiquity, especially in the Roman church. Emotional control over spiritual and earthly subjects was the privilege of those who held imperial and ecclesial power. This predominantly male power was to some extent shared with leading women in imperial families and other emotional communities, such as female monasteries. Gregory, like other bishops of his day, was heavily reliant on the spiritual and the supernatural as means of shaping what lay Christians knew about their world

---

[66] Chin and Vidas 2015b: 1–2; see n. 4 above.   [67] König and Whitmarsh 2007b: 9.

from their imaginations and feelings, as well as their minds. Fear of the imminent end times was a prominent theme in all genres of Gregory's oeuvre examined here, as was the idea that the Lord put worldly rulers into place and could just as easily remove them. His knowledge of hidden things, including people's secret passions, allowed him to govern the emotional community to which he belonged, the Roman church. These strategies and skills helped Gregory pursue his twin goals, self-mastery and the discipline and organisation of the church, which were the true purpose of knowledge.

37 Creating Knowledge and Knowing Creation in Theological and Scientific Writing in Late Antique Western Christendom

HELEN FOXHALL FORBES

Introduction

In the second half of the eighth century CE, a scribe in Freising compiled a volume bringing together scriptural commentaries and writing on the natural world. The book, now Munich, clm 6302, opens with a copy of *De ordine creaturarum*, a seventh-century cosmological text by an Irish author (although long attributed to Isidore), and includes commentaries on Mark and parts of Genesis, as well as exegetical dialogues.[1] As a collection, the volume may have been intended at least partly for the study of creation, since the natural world, both visible and invisible, is the subject of a substantial proportion of the material it contains. Late antique authors relied both on 'scientific' knowledge and on theological interpretation of scripture to understand and explain the natural world. The Freising manuscript could be thus considered as a kind of microcosm of contemporary scholarly investigation into creation. This chapter offers a preliminary examination of the methods and processes of inquiry used by late antique scholars in their attempts to uncover knowledge, focusing on the topic of creation.

For studying the created world, an important facet of the process was the combination of aspects of what are now two different disciplines, science and theology. Late antique writers did not distinguish these as separate disciplines, as modern scholars do; indeed, in late antiquity there was no fixed terminology for referring to either of the subjects now termed theology and science.[2] Previous scholarship discussing the process of seeking knowledge in general, and the investigation of science and theology in particular, has often centred on the issues of innovation and derivativeness. For centuries, following ideas developed during the Renaissance and 'Enlightenment', it was held that the fall of the Western Roman empire heralded a 'Dark Age', in which there was little intellectual development and scholarship was almost entirely derivative. More recently scholars have argued instead that there was innovation in this period, at least to some degree.

---

[1] Bischoff 1966; Gorman 1997. [2] See, e.g., Wallis 2006; Lazaris 2020; Zachhuber 2020b.

Both for the history of science and for the history of theology, modern studies which take a long view from the ancient world to modernity still sometimes present the period from about the fifth century to about the eleventh as one of limited interest.[3] Such overviews suggest that in this period there was a lack of innovation, particularly with regard to scientific and theological thinking, so that modes of knowledge, thinking, and inquiring were primarily derivative. Even in many (otherwise good) works which aim to explore how science or theology (or aspects of them) changed over the *longue durée*, the period is either barely mentioned or treated in only a limited way.[4] Late antiquity and the early Middle Ages, perhaps as a result of being transitional periods between 'antiquity' and the '(later) Middle Ages', often simply get short shrift.[5] Scholarship on the history of science or theology from the twelfth century onwards frequently retains a perception of the period from the fifth century to the eleventh as one of little interest.[6] Unsurprisingly, scholars of late antiquity and the early Middle Ages are much less dismissive of the scientific and theological endeavours of late antique and early medieval writers, and an increasing body of work demonstrates the vibrance and interest of scientific and theological writing in this period.[7]

One of the issues is the concept of authority: theological writers of late antiquity and the early Middle Ages often introduced their works by noting their indebtedness to past authorities and stress that they have not

---

[3] Late antiquity and the early Middle Ages overlap to some extent, but they are unfixed and depend to some degree on geography (and they are in any case Eurocentric). Late antiquity is often defined as starting *c.* 300 or 400 CE and ending *c.* 700 or 800 CE; the early Middle Ages can begin as early as *c.* 400 CE and may end as early as *c.* 950 CE or as late as *c.* 1100 CE.

[4] Lindberg, for example, argues that the early Middle Ages was a period of the transmission of knowledge but that new knowledge was not created (2010: 155–58). In contrast, Johnston jumps straight from Augustine to Aquinas (2009), giving the impression that no theology of note occurred in the intervening centuries. Alister McGrath (2012) includes virtually nothing about early medieval theology, and again jumps from Augustine to the late Middle Ages.

[5] In the *Cambridge History of Science*, for example, the period 400–800 CE falls uneasily between Ancient Science (Vol. I: Jones and Taub 2018) and Medieval Science (Vol. II: Lindberg and Shank 2013). There is one chapter (out of thirty) on late antiquity in volume I; in volume II, there are three (out of twenty-seven) chapters which discuss the early Middle Ages, in whole or in part.

[6] This too is perhaps sometimes an issue of periodisation, though not always. In his otherwise excellent *Introduction to Medieval Theology* (2012), Rik van Nieuwenhove discusses only two theologians in the section on the early Middle Ages and then leaps from the ninth century to the eleventh. By far the bulk of the book (pp. 64–284) is focused on the high and late Middle Ages. An egregious example in relation to the study of one theological concept is Walker Bynum 2017, which claims to cover over a millennium of thought but in fact has one section on 'The Patristic Background' (200–*c.* 400) before leaping straight to the twelfth century.

[7] Examples include Wallis 2010, 2020; Phelan 2014; Ramirez-Weaver 2017.

introduced anything new in relation to theology. There was good reason for this, since sometimes the accusation of novelty could lead to charges of heresy or heterodoxy: the Carolingian scholar Amalarius of Metz (d. 850 CE) was condemned at the Council of Quierzy (839 CE) because, in answer to the question of what he had read to produce his substantial exposition of the liturgy, he had replied that he had read it in the spirit.[8] Even the Northumbrian monk Bede (d. 735 CE), who was accepted as an authority in his own lifetime, was accused of heresy when he recalculated the date of the world as part of his work on time.[9] These examples demonstrate both that innovation existed and that it was not always prized: originality certainly did occur even within an intellectual milieu in which novelty was not usually as highly valued as authority. However, it is also clear from contemporary writers that even if originality was not usually important, creativity was, and that scholars were concerned to use their creative abilities to further knowledge.

Recent work has demonstrated that even where late antique authors relied heavily on earlier works, they exercised choice, agency, and creativity in the process. It has also been shown that some late antique and early medieval writers were genuinely innovative, at least for a certain value of innovation.[10] This research has been hugely important for disrupting traditional narratives, but this chapter seeks to disrupt those narratives further by shifting the focus away from the dichotomy between innovation and tradition. I instead investigate what late antique authors thought they were doing and how they did it. My argument is that seeing late antique writers as either derivative or innovative, or even somewhere in between, is fundamentally unhelpful, since these are modern categories which make little sense in relation to how these authors saw themselves and understood their tasks as Christian scholars in their own times. It is well known that late antique writers did not value innovation and originality in the way that modern academics do. It is certainly important to note that authors in the period *c.* 400–800 CE did not simply pass on information without questioning it, and that scholars in late antiquity and the early Middle Ages did not have such respect for earlier authorities that they only attempted to address questions which had already been asked and answered.

---

[8] *Flori relatio de concilio Carisiacensi*, III–VI (MGH, *Leges. Concilia* 2.2, 57C); cf. Chazelle 2001: 158–59.
[9] Wallis 1988: xxx–xxxi, 253–54, 358, 361 (with translation of Bede's *Letter to Plegwin*, in which he defends himself against the accusation of heresy, at Appendix 3.1).
[10] See, e.g., the articles in DeGregorio 2006a, as well as Belén Sánchez Prieto 2016; Sowerby 2016: 20–34.

But searching for evidence that late antique authors were innovative simply because that is what modernity prizes, and because it enables these authors to be rescued from the label of derivative, is problematic since it is abundantly clear that neither of these terms would be meaningful for the way that those authors themselves thought.

Instead, I suggest, late antique authors must be viewed as engaging both individually and collectively in an endeavour to advance knowledge: contemporary scholars affirmed what was already known about God and creation but also sought to uncover more information and to address questions that arose in their own times. The changing contexts of study in late antiquity are significant. The premise that God is rational – which underpinned Christian study of the created world – is quite different from many ancient Mediterranean or Near Eastern beliefs in which gods were not believed to behave rationally even though the natural world itself was understood to operate along rational lines. Late antique Christians studying creation relied on a rational approach requiring proofs and assumed that information about creation could be reasoned out by careful thought with appropriate use of evidence and with established methodological approaches. Sometimes it was enough to record and note what previous authorities had said, but late antique scholars also asked and addressed new questions which arose in their own times. Sometimes writers offered original solutions and sometimes they did not, but originality was not central to the task. More importantly, their aim as part of a Christian mission of learning was that of advancing knowledge of God and of his ordered creation through a series of rational approaches. I examine how late antique writers approached and analysed their evidence in their attempts to further knowledge, and I centre the creative process and the aims and interests of the authors rather than evaluating the innovative (or otherwise) nature of the finished product. I do not argue that the authors considered here were not derivative or that they were necessarily innovative; examples of both derivativeness and innovation are discussed here. But by moving away from this dichotomy and focusing instead on the *process* of scholarly inquiry, it is possible to understand these writers and their texts on their own terms, and to see a more nuanced and more interesting picture of Western late antique scientific and theological writing and modes of knowing.

Knowing Creation

Although scripture provided an account of creation and discussion of the created world, writers could also make observations and judgements based on experience. For both of these modes of thinking, scholars – i.e., those who were involved in academic study of theology, science, or other matters – undertook investigative study via an evidence-based approach.[11] The resources for understanding creation in Western Christendom between the fifth century and the eighth were primarily classical authorities and exegetical commentary. Classical scientific works drawing on ancient Greek and Roman learning were significant, although the availability of these was variable depending on chronology and geography. Library resources in eighth-century Britain or Ireland, for example, were substantially different from those available to Augustine in early fifth-century North Africa or Italy.[12] In his multiple discussions of Genesis, Augustine refers to the opinions of the 'philosophers', seeking to reconcile their statements with scripture.[13] Even by the early seventh century, when Isidore of Seville wrote the first known Christian treatise on the natural world, earlier works of natural philosophy were much less easily obtainable and the Roman educational curriculum had been transformed into a system which focused on learning for Christian religious purposes.[14] Some Roman works, such as Pliny's *Historia naturalis*, were available and influential throughout late antiquity, but other ancient scientific knowledge gradually became more difficult to obtain. Exegetical texts became increasingly important for the study of creation and the created world, especially commentaries on Genesis.

As a result of these developments, the study of the natural world which had once been the realm of philosophers became the province of Christian scholars, who could present their discussions either 'scientifically' or 'theologically'. Different genres could be used depending on the kind of inquiry undertaken, and information was presented and analysed according to each genre and its purposes: more 'scientific' inquiry might occur through treatises on nature or the created world, while more 'theological' study of creation often involved scriptural exegesis, particularly of Genesis. This meant that 'scientific' and 'theological' modes of thinking were not completely distinct, but they were distinguishable, even though the lines between the approaches and evidence used in these were often blurred. Bede composed 'scientific' treatises on time and nature but also wrote a commentary on

---

[11] Occasionally, wisdom was reported to have been granted to the unlearned directly by revelation, but this was not (though this hardly needs saying) the normal way by which late antique Christians expected to find answers to their questions. In Cassian's *De institutis coenobiorum* (5.33), written *c.* 420 CE, Abbot Theodore received an answer to a tricky question not by reading and learning, since he was uneducated, but after constant prayer for seven days and seven nights.
[12] Lapidge 2006; Contreni 2014.   [13] E.g., Augustine, *Gen. litt.* 7.13–15; *Conf.* 5.3.
[14] Inglebert 2001; Wallis 2020; see Chapter 35 by John Magee, this volume.

Genesis. Across these texts he uses much of the same information but the way that he presents his material and the specific details that he identifies for discussion vary, often significantly, because his purposes for each type of text were substantially different.[15]

Late antique guides to exegesis explained how to approach the process of studying and explaining scripture, and outlined a number of investigative methods. The most influential was Augustine's *De doctrina christiana*: Augustine stresses the importance of knowledge of scripture but also argues that scriptural study requires understanding, including searching for the full meanings in the text.[16] Augustine's text is particularly significant because attitudes to novelty in theological texts changed over the course of late antiquity: although Augustine aimed to build on earlier authorities, he does not seem to have felt that originality was a danger in quite the way that writers from around the mid sixth century and later often did. The Christian-focused educational system which developed from about the sixth century onwards influenced how writers approached the task of scholarship and, as a result, both the purposes and processes of study were altered to some degree. However, Augustine's *De doctrina christiana* recommended methods originating from the secular classical curriculum which were maintained in a Christian context. He advocated that teachers who want to clarify doubtful points must do so using both reasoning and proof, and his approach highlights the perceived importance of uncovering what was currently unknown, as a way to increase knowledge of God and his purposes.[17] Augustine often included multiple possible interpretations, allowing the reader to choose what seems most fitting; he recommended that if better interpretations were found in future they should be accepted.[18] In avoiding making dogmatic pronouncements on every line of scripture, and instead allowing multiple interpretations and the potential for new ones, Augustine set an important precedent for subsequent writers. This was also one way that late antique authors visibly engaged in the process of advancing knowledge and with a community of both past and future readers who made their own choices about what constituted the best interpretation.

Two other Latin exegetical guides were produced in the mid sixth century, both of which demonstrate the changes in education which had occurred since Augustine's time. In Constantinople the Quaestor of the Sacred Palace, Junillus, produced his *Instituta regularia divinae legis*

---

[15] Wallis 2010. [16] *Doctr. chr.* 1.1; 2.7, 9; 4.8–9.
[17] *Doctr. chr.* 2.18, 27–42; and esp. 4.4. [18] *Doctr. chr.* 2.12–13.

probably during the 540s; in southern Italy, Cassiodorus began putting together some form of his *Institutiones divinarum et humanarum lectionum* perhaps in the 550s, and recommended both Augustine and Junillus as guides to the practice of exegesis.[19] Junillus' *Instituta* follow the principle of introducing students first to the literal meaning of scripture and then to more advanced study in order to understand the purpose and arrangement of the principles of Divine Law.[20] The *Instituta* are arranged in the form of a dialogue between teacher and pupil, posing and asking questions about how the scriptures are presented, and how to study them; the work was influential and widely used by later authors.[21] Cassiodorus' *Institutiones* take a different approach, offering a kind of handbook of the most useful reference works for explaining and interpreting scripture. Cassiodorus noted that secular teaching was still available but that he aimed to remedy the lack of teaching of scripture: he suggests that through these introductory books the reader may come to know more both about the salvation of the soul and about secular learning.[22] He emphasised that Latin learning of all kinds could be brought to bear on biblical study, recommending a range of different authors on topics such as geography and medicine.[23] Assessments of the influence of the *Institutiones* have been mixed, and it is worth noting that later users tended to separate the first book, on divine learning, from the second, on the liberal arts.[24] Importantly, all these guides indicate that the work of interpreting scripture was perceived to be incomplete: students needed to be trained both as future teachers and as scholars who could uncover the still hidden meanings of the biblical text. Christians were supposed to be continually engaged in the process of growing closer to God through knowing him. For learned Christians, that meant study of scripture and God's ordered creation, as well as careful scrutiny of the works of earlier authorities.[25]

As classical authorities became increasingly less available, and as Christianity flourished in places far from its original homeland, the principle of combining sacred and secular disciplines to study scripture became more significant. Later authors can be found employing precisely the kind of dialogue between sacred and secular learning that Cassiodorus expounds in his *Institutiones* and demonstrates in his *Expositio in Psalmos*, in which the

---

[19] Maas 2003: 13–15; Vessey 2004: 4, 15, 23–42.
[20] Junillus, *Preface*, ed. and trans. in Maas 2003: 118–12; cf. Maas 1996.
[21] Laistner 1947.   [22] Cassiodorus, *Inst.* 1.1.   [23] Cassiodorus, *Inst.* 1.25, 31; Brown 2013: 150.
[24] Vessey 2004: 94–95. On Cassiodorus and the liberal arts, see also Chapter 35 by Magee, this volume.
[25] Cf. Chapter 34 by Paul Blowers, this volume.

Psalter is presented as containing all aspects of the liberal arts. One example is discussions of flora and fauna mentioned in scripture which were unfamiliar to writers in northern Europe. Bede notes in the introduction to his commentary on the Song of Songs that he will explain the nature of trees and plants mentioned in the text, in accordance with what he has learned in the books of the ancients, because for him and his readers in Britain, places like Arabia and India, Judaea and Egypt are unknown except through written works.[26] For example, he drew on texts like Pliny's *Historia naturalis* and Isidore's *Origines* to explain the significance of plants such as cane and cinnamon, interpreting them allegorically on the basis of the physical descriptions he found in his sources.[27] Explanation of the physical environments described in scripture was a particular issue as Christianity moved west and north: writers needed not only to explain the natural world in relation to cosmology and the origins of the universe, but also to elucidate descriptions of nature rooted in the unknown and unfamiliar environment of the Near East. Seventh- and eighth-century northern European writers could not always find relevant explanatory information in earlier authorities on scripture, such as Augustine or Gregory the Great, who were themselves products of Mediterranean environments and for whom many, even if not all, of the plants and animals described in biblical texts were more familiar. The continuing spread of Christianity throughout Europe was thus one means through which modes of knowing and the means of understanding scripture started to change.

Creating Knowledge

Throughout late antiquity and the early Middle Ages, new works relating to creation and cosmology were produced, indicating that the available works inherited from earlier generations of scholars did not always meet contemporaries' needs. The question of why and how new works were created is significant in understanding the purposes and aims of late antique scholars, and relates closely to the methods which they used to advance knowledge and to discover new information. Although late antique writers of theological and scientific texts often claimed to be simply handing on the wisdom of ancient authorities, it is also clear that they did not see this as their only task, even if that did form part of their efforts. A common method of producing new texts was by abbreviating and excerpting the

---

[26] Bede, *In cantica canticorum allegorica expositio*, pr., lines 508–10 (ed. Hurst 1983b).
[27] Cf. *Libri quattuor in principium Genesis*, 2.12b (ed. Jones 1967).

opinions of earlier scholars, with variable amounts of additional material joining these together, to create a kind of focused florilegium. This could, in some cases, lead to the production of new texts based substantially on earlier writers, a kind of patchwork of quotations; however, as recent scholars have pointed out, this process required creativity and intelligence in the selection and arrangement of material. Moreover, the decision to create such new texts rather than to rely on copies of earlier authoritative texts demonstrates a perceived need for something different.

An interesting example of a new work based heavily on those of earlier writers is the commentary on Genesis by Wigbod, part of his *Commentary on the Octateuch*, which he composed for Charlemagne probably between 775 and 800 CE, perhaps at Lorsch.[28] While his other commentaries closely reproduce Isidore's allegorical exegesis, Wigbod's *Commentary on Genesis* combines excerpts from Isidore, Augustine and Augustinian florilegia, Junillus, Jerome, and Prudentius, as well as from Paterius' commentary on the Bible compiled from Gregory I's writings.[29] The effort which Wigbod put into compiling and adapting excerpts from earlier authorities for the commentary on Genesis indicates that his initial intention was to produce a work synthesising current knowledge; it is likely that his original aim was to provide a comprehensive commentary on the Pentateuch at least, and perhaps even on the whole Bible, but that when it became clear that this ambition was simply unrealisable he instead edited Isidore's texts lightly to create his own commentary.[30] Nonetheless, it seems that Wigbod's commentaries were produced in response to a particular need: existing texts, either as whole works or as passages scattered across multiple texts and manuscripts, were felt to be inadequate.

The availability and accessibility of material was an important consideration in the production of new works. Bede noted in the letter to Bishop Acca of Hexham (d. 740 CE), which prefaces his commentary on Genesis, written perhaps between 717 and 720 CE, that he had produced a new commentary because so many volumes treat Genesis that they cannot be acquired except by those who are very wealthy, and because the subject matter of Genesis is so profound that it is difficult for those who are not already extremely learned to study it.[31] Therefore, Bede explained, he selected and arranged passages from earlier texts to instruct readers who are still inexperienced, and also by which scholars might advance to more

---

[28] Gorman 1982: 175, 192–95. [29] Gorman 1982: 178–79. [30] Gorman 1982: 180–81, 187.
[31] Bede, *Libri quattuor in principium Genesis*, pr., lines 18–24 (ed. Jones 1967); cf. Kendall 2008: 40–53.

complex readings.[32] (Interestingly, Wigbod seems not to have used Bede's commentary on Genesis and may not have had access to it, an important reminder that both the availability of earlier writings and the lack of them could result in a perceived need for a new work.[33]) Bede's comments should, at some level, be understood both as part of a conventional modesty topos and as an appeal to authority, since his commentary on Genesis is much more than a simple selection and arrangement of material; he also often paraphrased and abbreviated earlier authorities (as indeed he noted in his prefatory letter), and he included his own opinions at times.[34] Other authors, too, noted that Genesis was the territory of relatively advanced scholars rather than beginners: Cassiodorus remarked that the Psalms are the entry point to scripture for novices rather than Genesis or the gospels; Augustine also noted the difficulty of interpreting Genesis, especially in a literal sense.[35] Bede's commentary is genuinely relatively accessible and clearly filled a perceived need for a new work on the topic, which brought together the best opinions that Bede could find in order to advance knowledge of God and his creation.

By the time Isidore of Seville (d. 636 CE) was writing in the early seventh century, the classical Roman system of schooling in the West had transformed into a Christian educational programme centred around monastic needs and interests. An important effect of this transformation was what counted as evidence and how it was used. Earlier authors who had discussed the natural world in exegetical contexts, such as Augustine or his teacher Ambrose in the West, or Basil of Caesarea in the East, had referred to contemporary scientific knowledge taught as secular learning and generally tried to present this as concordant with information drawn from scripture, so far as possible. Scripture was thus used as a form of evidence which complemented other evidence and information drawn from natural philosophy. Isidore read earlier works discussing the natural world such as Lucretius, Vegetius, and Pliny, but he also accessed older scientific knowledge indirectly through the works of patristic commentators, a process which has been described as 'reverse engineering'.[36] For Isidore, patristic commentaries themselves became a form of evidence as well as interpretation. Where he felt it appropriate, Isidore also borrowed material from

---

[32] Bede, *Libri quattuor in principium Genesis*, pr., lines 24–32 (ed. Jones 1967).
[33] Gorman 1982: 179–92.
[34] Bede, *Libri quattuor in principium Genesis*, pr., lines 24–32 (ed. Jones 1967).
[35] Cassiodorus, *Explanation of the Psalms*, pr., ca. 16, lines 38–41 (ed. Adriaen 1958); Augustine, *Gen. litt.* 1.38–41; *Retract.*, 1.18.
[36] Kendall and Wallis 2016: 12.

poets such as Vergil, and so brought all kinds of inherited learning together with scripture, as Cassiodorus (for example) had advised. Isidore's methods and modes of inquiry were widely available as models for later authors because his texts were transmitted and rapidly became influential. Significantly, although appeals to earlier authorities were once seen as confirming that late antique authors were unimaginative, their reliance on older works stemmed partly from a desire to demonstrate that their assertions were based on evidence as an essential part of rational inquiry.

The changing circumstances of Christian education and learning led Isidore to create a new genre, the Christian treatise on the natural world. He composed his *De natura rerum* (perhaps c. 613 CE) and dedicated it to King Sisebut, stating that his aim was to provide a treatise suitable for the king to learn about 'the nature and causes of things', since no such appropriate single work then existed.[37] Isidore modelled his treatise on earlier cosmological works but drew on Christian scripture and exegesis as well as on scientific traditions for its explanations: he stated that he relied on 'scholars of antiquity', and especially on 'catholic authors', but emphasised that the study of nature is not 'superstitious', suggesting instead that it had an important place within a Christian context.[38] Isidore set the pattern for one line of inquiry into the natural world and his text was hugely influential: not only was it widely copied, but it served as a model for subsequent texts, such as Bede's works on cosmology and time-reckoning (*De natura rerum, De temporibus, De temporum ratione*).[39] Like Isidore, Bede was not content to rely on copies of earlier authors but compiled his own treatises which were more appropriate for his own purposes and which also included updated information.

Late antique scholars studying creation and the created world were faced with contradictory bodies of evidence that did not agree. Discord between scripture and ancient non-Christian authors was often resolved by the assumption that ancient authors were wrong. Isidore notes that 'most authorities assert that Sancus, king of the Sabines, first divided the year into months' and counters this by noting that scripture shows that 'the twelve months of the year existed even before the flood'.[40] Less often, disagreement could be explained through allegorical interpretation of scripture. Often, where patristic works offered multiple opinions the situation was

---

[37] Isidore, *De natura rerum*, pr., 1 (ed. Fontaine 1960); for the date, see Fontaine 1960: 3–6.
[38] Isidore, *De natura rerum*, pr., 2 (ed. Fontaine 1960); cf. Kendall and Wallis 2016: 13–14.
[39] Wallis 1988: xxii–xxiv; Kendall and Wallis 2010: 12–20; Kendall and Wallis 2016: 56–57.
[40] Isidore, *De natura rerum*, 4.5 (ed. Fontaine 1960).

considered uncertain. Importantly, however, late antique scholars did not simply acknowledge that something was unknown but saw this as an invitation to future scholars to seek out more certain interpretations and, in so doing, to further knowledge. As already noted, Augustine often included multiple interpretations and encouraged the reader to choose among them. The anonymous seventh-century Irish author of *De ordine creaturarum* built on this, advising that first the reader should examine what was best supported by scripture and, if this was inconclusive, follow the opinion expressed by most catholic believers.[41] He advised too that where different catholic writers presented views which were conflicting but potentially acceptable, the matter should be left undecided.[42] Still other subjects, particularly those which were more complex (such as paradise), led some authors to declare that they were unable to offer a definite opinion.[43] A slightly earlier seventh-century Irish author, known now as 'Augustinus Hibernicus' (the 'Irish Augustine'), explained in his work on the miracles within scripture that he did not know enough to offer a definite opinion on the origins of the waters of the flood, and so he offered multiple interpretations from 'masters', presenting them as of equal authority and leaving the reader to choose between them.[44] Bede, whose approach to exegesis is profoundly Augustinian, indicates clearly how he intended readers to treat multiple authoritative opinions recorded in his works. Probably in about 715 CE, he replied to a series of questions about the Book of Kings which had been sent to him by Nothhelm, a priest in London who subsequently became archbishop of Canterbury. In his prefatory letter, Bede stated that it 'could very easily happen' that Nothhelm might find better explanations to answer his questions and, if so, that he should send them quickly to him.[45] Bede quickly became established as an authority on scripture and, like Augustine, he assumed that scriptural study required constantly searching for better interpretations and the discovery of new knowledge; he clearly believed that he and his contemporaries were engaged in this task both individually and collectively.

As a methodological enterprise, the most well-known work to encourage the resolution of contradictory statements was Abelard's *Sic et non*, written

---

[41] *De ordine creaturarum*, 5.11 (ed. Díaz y Díaz 1972).

[42] *De ordine creaturarum*, 5.11 (ed. Díaz y Díaz 1972).

[43] Some authors considered certain topics problematic for detailed scrutiny. See, for example, Julian Pomerius, who suggests that the nature of the future life is a topic that one should believe in rather than discuss (*Contempl.* 1.2); see also Augustine, *Doctr. chr.* 4.9.

[44] *De mirabilibus sacrae scripturae* 6 (ed. MacGinty 1971: 2.23–28).

[45] Bede, *In regum librum xxx questiones*, pr. (ed. Hurst 1962); cf. Meyvaert 1999.

long after late antiquity in the early twelfth century.[46] Abelard posed a series of theological questions and included conflicting opinions from the church fathers which related to them, although the contradictions were left for the reader to resolve. This method is often seen as characteristic of new scholastic approaches used by theologians from the late eleventh century onwards but, in essence, occurs frequently in late antique texts. The author of *De ordine creaturarum* asserted that he could not determine which was the best explanation of the firmament but presented several opinions and invited readers to make their own judgements on the matter. In his *De natura rerum*, Bede's discussion of the heavenly waters resolves the conflict between an interpretation drawn from *De ordine creaturarum* with the opinions of Ambrose and Jerome.[47] At times earlier authorities could be corrected without being named, or their opinions presented as commonly held, to avoid the embarrassment of having to identify an authority as holding an incorrect opinion. Bede states in his treatise on nature that the Milky Way is commonly and erroneously said to shine because of the sun, although he seems to be referring to a statement in Isidore's *Etymologies* rather than genuinely to popular opinion.[48]

The extent of the reasoning that such resolution of contradictory opinions might involve is visible in the *Reference Bible*, written probably in the first half of the eighth century, perhaps by an Irish (or Irish-influenced) author.[49] This text examines passages from scripture and addresses problems by excerpting from authorities such as Jerome, Augustine, Junillus, and Isidore.[50] In treating the statement that God made man 'in his own image' ('ad imaginem'; Gen 1:26), the author cites passages which lead him to consider the origin of the soul, concluding with his own opinion: 'we do not believe that souls, as Isidore and Ambrose and Augustine say, we do not believe souls are created before the body is created.'[51] He follows this with a quotation attributed to Augustine (though seemingly not from Augustine's works) which seems to contradict this – 'the souls of men play in heaven before they receive their bodies' – but he resolves this with reference to a different time frame, noting that 'this is not contrary, because he is speaking about the souls of the saints, who are in heaven before they receive their body in the resurrection'.[52] Abelard's decision to present

---

[46] Brittain Bouchard 2003: 36–40.   [47] Bede, *De natura rerum* 8 (ed. Jones 1975).
[48] Bede, *De natura rerum* 18 (ed. Jones 1975); cf. McCready 1995: 52.
[49] Bischoff 1966: 1.88, 97–102; MacGinty 2000: x–xi.   [50] MacGinty 1999.
[51] *Pauca problemata* 151, lines 5–7: 'Tamen nos credimus animas, ut Isidorus et Ambrosius et Agustinus dicunt, animas non credimus creari antequam corpus creatur' (ed. MacGinty 2000).
[52] *Pauca problemata*, 151, lines 7–10: 'Agustinus dicit: Anime hominum ludunt in caelo antequam caelo recipient; sed tamen non est contrarium, quia de animabus sanctorum dicit, que sunt in caelo antequam corpus in resurrectione suscipiant' (ed. MacGinty 2000).

conflicting opinions as an exercise for students may have been new as a type of text in its own right, but as a method for approaching theology this was long-established and was used frequently by late antique and early medieval authors.

Most importantly, the efforts of late antique authors to uncover knowledge about the created world are visible in the questions that they posed and attempted to answer. Sometimes the answers (and sometimes the questions, too) included material excerpted from earlier texts, but this was often not the case. As the world which had produced the scientific knowledge of antiquity slipped further into the past, and as Christianity spread into different geographical areas, successive generations of scholars posed and encountered new questions which had not been addressed by previous authorities. The practice of raising and answering questions was a routine and important part of late antique efforts to further knowledge in multiple contexts, and questions were addressed through a range of methodologies, including reasoning. Sometimes questions were posed and answered in the context of treatises or exegesis; sometimes writers shaped their work using the dialogue form, which had a long history in philosophical and scientific works from antiquity extending into late antiquity and the early Middle Ages before ultimately becoming a key part of the scholastic method.[53] Late antique questions and answers about creation are significant because they reveal the ways that contemporary authors investigated the topic, and they also demonstrate the intellectual curiosity and creativity which formed part of a collective and individual effort to advance knowledge and to find out information which was not previously known. Since (as university tutors and students know) it is usually much more difficult to ask interesting questions than to answer them, late antique questions about creation are particularly important for understanding how and why contemporary authors approached the topic as they did, and how they perceived their intellectual task.

The purposes and contexts of late antique works affected how precisely questions were posed and addressed. Works written for publication, such as complete commentaries, usually assert interpretations more certainly than works which were not intended for wide circulation. Bede's commentary on Genesis, intended for students and to prepare readers for further study, raises questions throughout. Some are clearly rhetorical, but many of the questions he raises or addresses (even without posing them directly)

---

[53] On Christian use of dialogue forms, see Leinsle 1995: 9–15; Cooper and Dal Santo 2008; Rigolio 2019.

relate to passages of scripture which leave something unsaid or unclear. Bede notes in his discussion of Adam's naming of the animals and birds that scripture says nothing about the fish brought to Adam; he reasons that, as different types of fish became known, they received a variety of names in accordance with the variety of peoples.[54] Elsewhere he raises the question of how humankind was made immortal but still took earthly nourishment like mortal animals.[55] His answer draws on Augustine to note the difference between the immortality of God's first creation and the immortality of resurrected souls, and he reasons based on evidence from scripture that souls will ultimately be like angels and so not require corporeal food, which will not exist anyway in the spiritual life. Bede's efforts to find out more certain knowledge about the created world and how it came to be, as well as what this means for future salvation, were intrinsic to his purposes as a scholar.

Interesting questions could prompt whole works, particularly those which were not intended as systematic scriptural commentaries. A particularly good example is the seventh-century *De mirabilibus sacrae scripturae*, long thought to be by Augustine of Hippo, now attributed to 'Augustinus Hibernicus' ('the Irish Augustine').[56] *De mirabilibus* centres around the question of how to explain scriptural miracles which apparently involved the creation of new matter, and aims to show that it is always possible to demonstrate that God did not create anything new after the first six days of creation. The author argues instead that even when something seemingly required the creation of new matter, in fact God simply ordered in a particular way the universe which he created in the first six days.[57] 'Augustinus Hibernicus' was clearly conscious that his work was different from previous writings, even though he relies at times on earlier interpretations. Throughout the work his aim is to relate the visible world of his 'now' to the historic creation of the universe and to reason through the implications of the text of scripture.[58] Like other writers, 'Augustinus Hibernicus' clearly saw himself engaging in an individual and collective attempt to further knowledge and to clarify the unknown: the answers and interpretations given in response to his scrutiny of the Bible, as well as the questions he raised, show the effort put into explaining the created world with critical reasoning based on evidence.

---

[54] Bede, *Libri quattuor in principium Genesis* 1.2, lines 1749–65 (ed. Jones 1967).
[55] Bede, *Libri quattuor in principium Genesis* 1.1, lines 907–9 (ed. Jones 1967).
[56] See MacGinty 1971; MacGinty 1987.
[57] *De mirabilibus sacrae scripturae* 1 (ed. MacGinty 1971: 6–10).
[58] *De mirabilibus sacrae scripturae*, pr. (ed. MacGinty 1971: 1–4).

Works intended for circulation were, at least in some sense, intended to be authoritative in themselves, and their authors may therefore have been sensitive to the possibility of accusations of impropriety. Relatively few surviving texts offer insight into the informal exposition of scripture in the context of classroom teaching, but those that do offer an important insight into how contemporary scholars undertook exegesis.[59] The scriptural commentaries connected with the late seventh-century Canterbury school, where the teachers were Archbishop Theodore (from Tarsus) and Abbot Hadrian (from North Africa), seem to have originated as student notes.[60] The interpretations show clear knowledge of patristic works and include references to earlier authorities, particularly those of the Greek tradition such as Basil of Caesarea and John Chrysostom, but their words do not dominate: unlike commentaries intended for written circulation, these notes present something close to ex *tempore* discussion and do not include substantial extracts from earlier writers. Instead, they show a combination of the citation of authorities, reasoning, and observation, and offer both figurative and literal interpretations; sometimes they include scientific knowledge or observation, or grammatical and linguistic comments. These texts offer an important and rare glimpse into the process by which students learned to explore scripture and to interpret its words.

Throughout the notes on Genesis, the question of whether there was rain before the flood appears. It is unclear whether this was particularly interesting to the student note-taker or to Theodore or Hadrian, but the question arose because after the statement that 'God had not yet rained upon the earth' (Gen 2:5), there is no mention of rain until the description of the flood. In explanation, the commentary first mentions scientific knowledge, stating that without the sun there could be no rain, and concludes by noting that 'scripture does not say whether there was rain before the flood or not'.[61] In the interpretation of Gen 5:29, 'on the earth which God has cursed', the text discusses the earth's barrenness, noting again that scripture reveals little about rain before the flood, but it also observes that rain is certainly attested after the flood in the announcement of the rainbow.[62] Commenting on the rainbow in

---

[59] A much later example is some of the commentaries included in the *Glossa Ordinaria*, which may be derived from the teaching of Anselm of Laon (d. 1117): see Smalley 1983: 49–51; Smith 2009: 17–38; Clanchy and Smith 2010: 14; Andrée 2011.

[60] Bischoff and Lapidge 1994: 1–5, 243–74.

[61] *First Commentary on the Pentateuch* 33 (ed. Bischoff and Lapidge 1994: 308): 'Non dicit scriptura pluuiam ante diluuium si esset an non.'

[62] *First Commentary on the Pentateuch* 65 (ed. Bischoff and Lapidge 1994: 316). Unusually, this section also suggests that the rainbow is a sign that rain will come, a point which is not raised in the editors' commentary to the text.

Gen 9:14, the text states that 'the rainbow signifies the mercy of rain, which previously was sparse if there was any at all'; where Noah is described tilling the earth and planting a vineyard (Gen 9:20), the same information reappears.[63] It is tempting to assume that this issue particularly bothered two scholars from hot, arid climates working in the damp atmosphere of south-east England but, whatever prompted this interest, someone evidently devoted considerable thought to it. These statements are scattered through the commentary rather than brought together because of the text's form and context of production, but they show how interpreters of scripture might focus in on particular issues and offer an insight into the process of learning and thinking which could precede the composition of a more formal commentary. Additionally, they demonstrate the role that discussion and 'live' interpretation played in transmitting information and advancing knowledge.

Other texts which are perhaps less formal also offer insight into the process of reasoning, which can otherwise be difficult to see. The commentary on Genesis in Munich, clm 6302, probably written in the late seventh or early eighth century in an Irish milieu, includes an extended discussion of the appearance of the rainbow.[64] Like 'Augustinus Hibernicus', this author was concerned by the possibility of creation occurring outwith the first six days. He notes that:

> It should be considered if there was a (rain)bow in the sky before the flood. On the one hand, if it was there, how is it called 'a sign', when it was there before? But on the other hand, if it was not there before the flood, and it was a new thing, that is difficult, because it says 'The Lord rested from all his works', and [the rainbow] not only was not there in the first week, but it was not before the flood.[65]

This section draws on no known source and shows the author reasoning through the problem occasioned by apparently contradictory evidence. He attempted to address the problem both through reasoning and through contemporary scientific knowledge, stating his argument first: the rainbow 'did not exist before and is not a new thing for the reason that they did not exist much previously before the flood, but afterwards they existed in abundance'.[66]

---

[63] *First Commentary on the Pentateuch* 83–84 (ed. Bischoff and Lapidge 1994: 318–20).

[64] For the date, see Gorman 1997: 206–7; on the Irish milieu of the commentary, see Wright 2000.

[65] Munich, clm 6302, fol. 58v: 'interrogandum est si arcus in caelo ante diluuium fuit. Si autem fuit quomodo dicitur signum dum primus fuit. Si autem non fuit ante diluuium res noua quod deficile est. Quia dicitur requieuit dominus ab omnibus operibus suis et non solum non fuit in prima ebdomata sed ante diluuium non fuit'. An edition of the text is printed in Gorman 1997: 212–33, but unfortunately this contains numerous errors and problems.

[66] Munich, clm 6302, fol. 58v: 'Respondimus non fuit prius et non res noua ideo quia nuper non multe fuerunt ante diluuium sed postea habundabant.'

This leads him to discuss the formation of the rainbow, and he explains that 'with wind driving water from the earth into clouds, when rain threatens, if the sun begins to shine over the earth and a cloud repels [it], the outer part of the sun which is not repelled …' – at which point there is a lacuna in the text.[67] It looks like the author was trying to explain the relationship between the watery clouds and the sun, and that the shape of the rainbow is formed by the outer part of the (round) sun in relation to the clouds. This is similar in some ways to explanations of the rainbow in earlier works, such as Isidore's *De natura rerum*,[68] but the author has framed it in a way which is entirely his own, and it is likely that this part of the commentary is the author's original explanation, since there is no obvious source. Although he draws on established learning, for example in stating that the rainbow only occurs before sun, and in the allegorical explanation of the rainbow's colours, he does not simply repeat earlier scholars in attempting to explain the appearance of the rainbow. This is particularly striking since substantial chunks of the commentary *are* excerpted from the works of earlier scholars. His resolution of the problem is reminiscent of 'Augustinus Hibernicus' (who neither comments on the sudden appearance of the rainbow nor questions whether it was a new creation), since he concludes ultimately that 'the rainbow does not appear except before rain; it is for this reason that it is said that there was no rainbow before the flood, and it is not a new thing and not created: the sun and the rains were separate in the works of the six days'.[69] His reasoning seems to be that the rainbow must have existed *in potentia* but the appropriate conditions for creating a rainbow simply did not occur before the flood, since sun and rain did not appear together. This explanation resolves a problem of apparent contradiction within scripture but also created knowledge, which was then available for future readers to accept or improve as they saw fit. This passage is significant because it shows how an author perceived a problem and attempted to address it to advance knowledge and to reconcile contradictory evidence. He may not have tried to be innovative, even if his answer was original, but evidently he did care to explain what was unknown or uncertain, and to reason through the questions which occurred to him in his reading of scripture.

---

[67] Munich, clm 6302, fols 58v–59r: 'Vento cogente aquam de terra in nubes. cum autem inminet pluuia. super terram si sol luciscerit. et nubes defenderit; / medium eius extrema pars solis quae non defenditur. ….'. Gorman has not apparently noticed the lacuna.

[68] Isidore, *De natura rerum* 31 (ed. Fontaine 1960).

[69] Munich, clm 6302, fol. 59r: 'Arcus non ostenditur nisi ante pluuia; Ideo autem dicitur arcus ante diluuium non fuit et non res noua et non creatura. Seorsum sol et pluuia in operibus sex dierum fuerunt.' A vague reference to this idea, but without the full explanation is found also in *De mirabilibus sacrae scripturae* 6 (ed. MacGinty 1971: 23–28).

Alongside reasoning, late antique authors wove observations into discussions of the created world as one of multiple types of evidence.[70] Late antique authors were certainly capable of making detailed and accurate observations of natural phenomena. The observations of the stars in a text usually known now as *De cursu stellarum* were precise enough, for example, that it is possible to identify that they were made in northern Gaul near the end of the sixth century and so have enabled the identification of the author of the treatise as Gregory of Tours, even though the text is ascribed to him in only one of the eight surviving manuscripts.[71] An anonymous Genesis commentary preserved uniquely in St Gallen, Stiftsbibliothek, MS 908, includes observation as one of multiple types of evidence used in the explanation of the day on which the discs, or wheels (*rotae*), of the sun, moon, and stars were made. The manuscript was written probably in northern Italy, perhaps in the late eighth century, but it seems likely that the commentary on the first three chapters of Genesis was composed in an earlier eighth-century Insular milieu.[72] The discussion of the discs of the sun, moon, and stars is puzzling from a modern scientific perspective because the author distinguishes between the discs of the heavenly bodies and the heavenly bodies themselves. He explains that for the sun and stars the light comes from their discs but that the moon is lit by the sun, and, as a result, he states, the question of which day saw the creation of the sun, moon, and stars has a two-part answer. He notes that some scholars suggest that the discs were created on the second day with the firmament and left ready for the creation of the heavenly bodies themselves to be inserted into them on the fourth day, at which point they were illuminated. He likens this to when goldsmiths leave spaces for gems in their works, and then put the gems themselves in only afterwards when they are ready. However, he critiques this explanation by observing that this cannot be correct since, if the sun and moon were fixed, the day and night would always be of equal length: he notes that 'because we see unequal days and nights, and the sun and moon do their setting and rising variably, we do not believe that they are fixed in heaven'.[73] This may be at least partly drawn from other texts,

---

[70] Again, this is sometimes suggested to be a feature which appears (or reappears from classical writings) in the context of scholastic learning; see, e.g., Park 2011.
[71] McCluskey 1990: 18; James 1993: 47.   [72] Wright 1987.
[73] St Gallen 908, 18–20: 'Diximus quod de aqua fecit deus rotam solis et lune et stillarum. unde sol lumen acciperit et luna. contentio est alii dicunt ex claritate diuinitatis. alii de splendore angelorum et non est conueniens. non enim legimus deum. nisi in ade specie spiritum inflasse. nec legimus angelos habere consortium cum alia creatura nisi [19] cum anima. Inde aptius credimus solem et stillas igne rote caelestis inluminatos. luna uero a sole inluminari sanctissimi christiani fideliter confirmant in figuram ecclesie a christo inluminata. Sed quali

such as Isidore's *De natura rerum* which also (following Hyginus) comments on the unequal lengths of days; much of the evidence used to discuss the heavenly bodies and to reason through the questions can be found in some form in earlier scientific and other works.[74] Nonetheless, the author has made this discussion his own, and it is difficult to read the passage as one where the information comes *only* from earlier sources; that is, the author surely observed the unequal lengths of days and nights, and the rising and setting of the sun and moon, even if he also found this information confirmed by book-learning.

Differences in climate and environment between northern Europe and the Mediterranean are important in making visible other instances of observation relating to local environmental information. When 'Augustinus Hibernicus' considered what happened during the flood to animals which lived both in the water and on land, he mentioned otters and seals, commenting – probably from his own experiential knowledge – that they find food in the waters but breed and sleep on land.[75] He probably also drew on his own observations to assert that rainbows can sometimes be seen in the brightness of the moon: the lunar rainbow is not well attested in earlier scientific writings, but where it is mentioned its existence is often denied, for example by both Pliny and Ambrose.[76] Since monks were often awake during the night for prayers, moving between the dormitory and the church, it is possible, as Marina Smyth notes, that 'Augustinus Hibernicus' saw the lunar rainbow and used this observation to refute earlier scholars.[77] Perhaps most famously, Bede's works relatively often contain

die creatae sunt rote solis et lune et siderum bipertitae est. Hic intellegentia sapientium. quidam autem adfirmant quod secunda feria cum firmamento simul create fuissent. Fixas rota[s] solis et lune et stillarum. quomodo aurifices locum gemmarum praeparant In operibus suis et postea quando uolunt in locis preparatis mittunt gemmas sic et deus ut ipsi dicunt rotas cum firmamento naturaliter fixas et preparatas in secunda feria. quando uero dixit in quarta feria fiant luminaria inluminari tantum tunc rotas fecit. Sed hoc ex parte possibile est et ex parte non. Nam si ita esset ut essent fixas consequens essent dies et noctes omnes semper aequales esse. Necesse enim esset ut sol semper in eodem loco occidere et in unum locum semper omni tempore orire. Sed quia inaequales aspicimus dies et noctes et diuersos ortus et occasus faciunt. sol et luna fixas esse in caelo non credimus. quanta de stillis credimus possibile esse nec hoc de omnibus stillis fatemur stille enim septem. [20] quae greci planete latinae uero erraticae nominantur hieronimus dicit non quod ipse errant sed quod nos errare faciunt iste septem stille sua natura negat fixas esse in caelo. hoc autem aptius credimus esse rotas istas non fixas sed liberas cursus suos per se domino obediendo perficiunt ut dicit salomon girans girando. pergit spiritus et in circulos suus regreditur.'

[74] Isidore, *De natura rerum* 17 (ed. Fontaine 1960).
[75] *De mirabilibus sacrae scripturae* 5 (ed. MacGinty 1971: 22–23).
[76] *De mirabilibus sacrae scripturae* 6 (ed. MacGinty 1971: 27); cf. Smyth 1996: 204.
[77] Smyth 1996: 206–7.

his own observations and, interestingly, he also includes thought experiments which relate the visible to the theoretical. Like the author of the St Gallen 908 commentary, Bede discusses the inequality of the days, but he also makes specific reference to his situation – 'we who are placed in the north' – explaining that northern regions see much less daylight in the winter than southern regions do, and vice versa in the summer.[78] He notes, too, that not only in Britain but also in Italy it is not possible to see the brightest star, Canopus, explaining that this is not because the light of the stars is withdrawn by fading gradually, but because the mass of the earth is in the way and prevents it being visible: he says that 'all these things can be proved easily by any especially large mountain surrounded by settlements'.[79] His most famous thought-experiment relates to the question of why the moon sometimes appears to be above the sun, even though it is actually beneath it. In order to give an example of how viewpoint affects the way that objects in different places are perceived, he invites his reader to imagine that:

at night-time, you go into a very large hall, or better, a church, immense in its length, breadth and height, and ablaze with countless lamps burning in honour of a martyr's feast-day. Amongst these are two very large lamps of marvellous workmanship, hanging by chains from the ceiling, but the one which is nearer to you when you enter is also closer to the floor. However, the hall is so vast, and the height of these distant lamps so great, that with your night vision you can make out the light and rays of flame more than you can the vessel itself which contains the fire. Now indeed, as you start to advance towards the lamps, looking straight at them, and beyond them towards the ceiling or opposite walls, the lamp which is nearer appears higher to you. The closer you approach, the higher up will be the one which is lower appear to you, until, by a more evident truth, you see where they are all positioned. So likewise we, situated beneath the two great luminaries of heaven, see them both at the meridian in such a way that the one which is lower, in rising further and further to the north, seems ever higher and higher, and as we train our eyes upon them and through them to the heavens, the one which, by obvious reason, is patently riding lower down appears to be higher than the other.[80]

Bede's explanation suggests that he had made detailed observations of the heavenly bodies, and that he had thought long and hard about how these moved and existed within the ordered universe. But even though Bede is remarkable in many ways, and his scientific acumen and perceptive

---

[78] Bede, *De temporum ratione* 32 (ed. Jones 1977): 'nos qui ad septentrionem positi'.
[79] Bede, *De temporum ratione* 32 (ed. Jones 1977): 'Quae cuncta de monte quolibet pergrandi undique circum habitato ualent facillime probari.'
[80] Bede, *De temporum ratione* 28 (ed. Jones 1977; trans. Wallis 1988: 78).

comments bear witness to his extraordinary learning and intelligence, it is also clear that he was not the only late antique writer to make and record observations and to bring observational evidence into his interpretation of the created world. Most importantly, it is clear that Bede was not alone in his attempt to further knowledge of the natural world but saw himself as part of a scholarly community engaged in the task of continually considering anew how they understood God's creation and pushing at the boundaries of knowledge.

Conclusion

Many of the questions posed in late antique theological and scientific texts can look arcane to modern readers, and this is partly why it is essential that these writings are not judged primarily in terms of innovation or derivativeness, or in relation to a narrative of progress which presents a straightforward linear development from the ancient world to the present day. For late antique Christian writers, investigation of God's created world was focused on understanding the rationality of God's intentions and how these related to his (soteriological and other) purposes for humankind. This makes sense in a world where much was unknown and where the intellectual context required that learning was primarily directed towards growing closer to God. Questions might therefore focus on the details of why certain things happened as they did, according to the scriptures. For example, in his questions relating to the flood, 'Augustinus Hibernicus' asks why land animals rather than water animals were wiped out when their sins were no more numerous; why God did not curse the waters when he cursed Adam and the earth after the fall; and (as already noted) what happened to animals which live both in the water and on the land.[81] The anonymous author of the Genesis commentary in St Gallen 908 asked why waters were placed above the firmament where there was no human need for them, such as drinking or washing; the question about rain before the flood which was raised repeatedly in seventh-century Canterbury appears also – surely independently – in *De mirabilibus sacrae scripturae*.[82] Several scholars considered how Moses, traditionally held to be the author of the Pentateuch, knew of the events described in Genesis, but the answers were variable. The *Commemoratio Geneseos*, a seventh- or eighth-century commentary on Genesis

---

[81] *De mirabilibus sacrae scripturae* 4–5 (ed. MacGinty 1971: 19–23).
[82] St Gallen, 908, 16: 'pro quali utilitate posuit deus aquas supra firmamentum. ubi non est humanus usus nec ad bibendum neque ad lauandum'; *De mirabilibus sacrae scriptuarae* 6 (ed. MacGinty 1971: 23–28).

(up to Gen 9:7) whose two surviving manuscripts were both copied in northern Italy, notes simply that 'it is asked how Moses knew all this' and answers that this was 'certainly through the Holy Spirit by which the three types of prophecy are generated', thus drawing on a stock of patristic learning.[83] The author of the Genesis commentary in Munich, clm 6302, asks more specifically, 'How did Moses know what happened before writing?', thus highlighting the importance of written texts in establishing knowledge of former times.[84] His answer also asserts spiritual revelation, but in a way which differs from standard treatments of the subject: he suggests that the knowledge came from 'the spirit about which it is said, "and the spirit of God came upon the waters"', thus implying that Moses received the direct witness of the spirit.[85] The examples considered here and above show intellectual curiosity and a sense of wonder at the created world: late antique ancient authors posed questions and tried to address them to find out what was not known, to refine how the created world was understood, and to consider the nature of contemporary knowledge about creation and how this knowledge was established.

Late antique scholars themselves were aware of the limitations of their knowledge and recognised that many questions had uncertain answers or could not be answered effectively. They negotiated the tension between authority and the advancement of knowledge in multiple ways, acknowledging the existence of previous opinions and deferring to past authorities at times, but this did not mean that they did not question received opinions, or the workings of the created universe in which they lived. Authors like Augustine sought to apply the perceived rationality of the created world which they inherited from antiquity to God himself and to his nature, and also to his creation. Investigations of the created world utilised recognised and established approaches which were rational and evidence-based, even if the parameters of those investigations and the premises on which the discussion was based are not those of modern, or even ancient or later medieval, thinking. Ultimately modern scholars must find ways to reconcile late antique authors' assertions of reliance on authority with their demonstrable intention to find new information, and these must make

---

[83] The text is found in two manuscripts probably written in Verona: Paris, Bibliothèque nationale de France, lat. 10457, fols. 2r–159v (dated c. 800) and Verona, Biblioteca capitolare, XXVII, fols. 99r–138v (s. ix²). Paris, lat. 10457, fol. 3r: 'Sed queritur unde moyses hoc nouerit. certe per spiritum sanctum a quo trea prophetiae genera fiunt.' For the three types of prophecy, see, e.g., Augustine, *Civ.* 17.3.

[84] Munich, clm 6302, fol. 49r: 'unde scit Moysin quod factum est ante littera[m]'.

[85] Munich, clm 6302, fol. 49r: 'id [est] spiritum de quo dictum est et spiritus dei superferebatur super aquas'.

sense in relation to late antique writers' aims and purposes. It is clear that late antique scholars writing about creation aimed neither to be innovative and so to contradict authority, nor to be derivative and simply repeat established opinions, since the purpose of writing new works was to fulfil the needs of their own times and circumstances, and to ascertain the most accurate information available about the created world. Viewing their works as either derivative or innovative, with the implicit value judgements that these terms entail, is hugely unhelpful: for one thing, in simple terms, most of these works are both, in that they sometimes borrow directly from earlier scholars and sometimes present new ideas and interpretations. Instead, it is more important to recognise the ways in which Christian scholars, even working as individuals, were drawn into a collective attempt to uncover the mysteries of the created world, in which scholars past, present, and future were linked by their desire to uncover the unknown. Despite their professed reliance on authority, late antique scholars certainly did create knowledge, but more significant for those authors themselves was that in their attention to exploring the natural world they as individuals, and the intellectual community of Christians collectively, might ultimately come to know creation and, through it, God himself.

38 | Hierarchies of Knowledge in the Works of Bede

ZACHARY GUILIANO

Introduction

The ordering of knowledge is central to Bede's writings and has at least two emphases: scholarly and experiential. He articulated an epistemology focused on the interpretation of sacred scripture. Yet he thought every part of life was ordered towards the knowledge of God in Christ, while particular experiences and dispositions, bodily practices, institutional settings, and states of life provided more intense forms of that knowledge: granting glimpses of the divine nature, the mind of Christ, or the life of the world to come. In commenting on these, I hope to move beyond a traditional emphasis on Bede's scholarship,[1] describing instead his understanding of Christian life and work, along with the potential transformations wrought by ascetic life in a particular kind of intellectual community and economy.[2]

Bede's ordering of knowledge is deeply hierarchical. A particular class emerges as an ideal: the 'perfect', who bore heightened responsibility for the welfare of the church, in line with their greater wisdom and material privileges.[3] The framework for this epistemology grew out of the context of the Northumbrian church, its elite institutions and leaders, and their material limitations and advantages. Bede sought to reform and influence all of them through his writing, teaching, and preaching, which formed the substance of his many works. These were distributed widely and in later generations became part of the standard collections of patristic writings studied, preached, or recited in varied communal, educational, and liturgical settings.[4] In this way, his epistemology and his justification of

---

My thanks to Eoghan Ahern, Robert Evans, Conor O'Brien, and Joseph Lear for their comments on this chapter. Remaining errors are, of course, mine.

[1] See, e.g., Brown 1996; Ray 1997; Thacker 2006.
[2] I am guided here by, e.g., Foucault's *History of Sexuality* and his later attendance to 'governmentality' and pastoral practice; cf. Brown 1988; Hadot 1995b. See Guiliano 2015: 78–79, 90–91.
[3] For comments on Bede's class milieu, see Mayr-Harting 1976; Thacker 1983: 39–44.
[4] For assessments of Bede's legacy, see Rollason 2010; Rowley 2010; Westgard 2010; for the reception of his homilies, see Guiliano 2021.

a particular kind of knowledge economy (both intellectual and material) influenced the Latin-speaking churches for centuries.

Bede's context was in some ways unique, and its influence on his thought justifies some comment, here and throughout this chapter.[5] He was born in 673 CE, a year before the monastery of St Peter's, Wearmouth, was founded. King Ecgfrith of Northumbria granted land to Benedict Biscop to found St Peter's, and the land where Bede was born and spent his early years became part of the monastery's territory.[6] Bede entered the monastery at age seven and ended his life there or at its twin house, St Paul's, Jarrow, which was founded in 681 CE. He travelled on occasion and had extensive contacts, but we have little reason to think he ventured further than Hexham, York, or Lindisfarne, all within eighty-five miles of his birthplace. During his life, the monasteries in Wearmouth and Jarrow grew quickly, and acquired varied resources.

The twin monasteries were part of the great monastic expansion that took place in Anglo-Saxon England during the seventh and early eighth centuries, as kings and nobles (among other lesser donors) handed over vast swathes of land, along with significant wealth, for the founding of monasteries or *mynsters*.[7] The conversion of the Anglo-Saxons involved a material and cultural revolution. The landscape and economy came to be centred on ecclesiastical sites and their activities.[8] Among these, Wearmouth-Jarrow was not the absolute wealthiest, but was far above average: with several nobles among its monks, multiple connections to the Northumbrian royal family, and landholdings ten times the size of many monastic foundations. It was 'an immensely, and almost extravagantly expensive enterprise', sustaining 600 brethren by the year 716 CE and with abbots controlling wealth on a high aristocratic level.[9] Bede was forty-three then, already an established priest and a scholar of note.

---

[5] O'Brien 2015: 23–27 and 183–206 sets the context especially well; see also Ahern 2020 and Ahern (forthcoming).

[6] See Wood 2010, though some believed the land was not originally royal but possibly a monastery drawn from the land of Biscop's family. Grocock and Wood 2013 expands these suggestions.

[7] For broader European contexts, see Wood 2013: 52–57.

[8] Classically stated in Wormald 2004: 135–36. Argued with further reference to developing archaeological knowledge: Blair 2005: 50–51, 203–5, 208–9, and esp. 246–90. See also Wood 2008: 13–14; Wood 2013: 72–73.

[9] Campbell 2003: 17. Wearmouth-Jarrow had over 150 hides of land, enough to sustain 150 *familiae*, while the average monastery might have had ten to twelve. In comparison, the typical well-equipped soldier or *thegn* might have needed land and income equivalent to five hides. For a sense of the average size of land held by *thegns* or by monasteries, see Bede, *Hist. eccl.* 3.24; Blair 2005: 72–73, 87–91; Jones 1995; Faith 2020: 112. For the size and character of Wearmouth-Jarrow, we rely on Bede's *Hist. eccl.* (esp. chs. 4, 7, 9, 15, and 17) and the anonymous *Vita Ceolfridi* (esp. 7–8, 11, and 20). On the monastery's royal connections, see Wood 2008: 24–25; Wood 2009: 93–100; Grocock and Wood 2013.

Like other foundations, Wearmouth-Jarrow's landed wealth and resources had a purpose: to foster the intellectual and spiritual vitality of Northumbria.[10] Its initial foundation was partly to house the books of the monastery's founder, Benedict Biscop.[11] By the end of Bede's life, Wearmouth-Jarrow possessed the greatest library assembled in England before the Norman conquest, and possibly the most extensive in Europe.[12] As part of 'the tradition of learned, contemplative reading', it 'represented a prodigious investment of money', to use Peter Brown's description.

Each copy of the Gospels alone cost as much as a marble sarcophagus. The setting up of a library stocked with texts of the holy scriptures and with their commentaries (not to mention other Christian writings) left a footprint of real wealth. It was an act of monumentalization that was as costly as the building or redecoration of a villa.[13]

Meanwhile, Biscop was simultaneously creating an economic and productive zone comparable to some late Roman estates. He built up the monastic library, buildings, and territories over the course of six treasure-gathering trips to Rome, with supplies sourced from other European locations along the way – no small outlay of money, time, and planning.[14] 'He strove to labour in so many ways', said Bede, 'that no necessity of our labouring would remain. He went away to so many places across the sea so that we would be plentifully supplied with all sorts of nourishment of saving knowledge.'[15] Biscop's acquisitions were the foundation of the libraries. His successor, Ceolfrith, 'doubled' them during his long tenure as abbot.[16] Its holdings were varied for the time. Descriptions recount 'a huge quantity of holy books' and 'a countless number of books of every sort'.[17] Source studies have revealed significant patristic, historical, hagiographic, and classical sources, along with texts of Old English law, king-lists, genealogies, and many biblical and liturgical texts: at least 200 books across both monastic sites or as a result of Bede's networks.[18]

In Bede's education and work, these basic resources – books, money, stability of life – took their place alongside teaching and conversation with others at Wearmouth-Jarrow and further abroad. He was prone to describing his conditions in negative terms, citing at one point 'the countless chains of monastic service' as a hindrance to completing a

---

[10] Wormald 2004: 136.   [11] Bede, *Hist. eccl.* A. 4.
[12] Laistner 1935; Lapidge 2006: 193–228 within Appendix E, providing references to some 255 works cited by Bede; Love 2011.
[13] Brown 2012: 275.   [14] Wood 1995: 15–19.   [15] Bede, *Hom.* 1.13.185–90.
[16] Bede, *Hist. eccl.* 15.   [17] Bede, *Hist. eccl.* 4, 6, 9, and 15.
[18] Love 2011: 631; Shaw 2018: 121–24; Ahern 2020: 5–7.

commission from his bishop.[19] But they were both hindrance and help. His work was driven by others' thoughts and requests, whether they were patrons, brothers, or 'lewd rustics in their cups'.[20] In several instances, Wearmouth-Jarrow's monks and Bede's broader contacts received more varied formation than him. Some studied or were formed as monks or priests in various parts of England, Ireland, Francia, and Italy.[21] Some were trained by John, the Archcantor of Rome and Abbot of Tours, when he visited England at Benedict Biscop's behest. Some may have studied at the Canterbury school founded by Archbishop Theodore and Abbot Hadrian, who had international formations and connections across the Christian world, East and West.[22] Bede also benefited throughout his life from ongoing contact with others who had been educated like him, such as Bishop Acca of Hexham, the priest Nothhelm of London, and Abbot Albinus of Canterbury.[23]

Wearmouth-Jarrow was of course a monastery, not a modern research institute, college, or university.[24] Study focused on practical elements ordered to the knowledge of God, the reading of holy scripture, and the proclamation of the Christian faith. The simplest literate monk in Bede's time needed the basics of Latin pronunciation, grammar, and rhetoric, alongside the memorisation of set texts and musical settings: the Psalter, the Pauline Epistles, and many series of antiphons, responsories, hymns,

---

[19] Bede, *Luc.*, pr. 95. All quotations from *in Lucam* are my translation. At times, I modify the translations of his other works cited in the bibliography.

[20] Patrons: see, e.g., the prologues to Bede, *in Gen., Expos. Act. Apos., Luc.*, among many others. 'Brothers' and 'lewd rustics' in Bp. Wilfrid's entourage: *Epist. Pleg.* 1.1; 1.6.; 1.17. Two 'brothers' with questions about *computus*: *Epist. Helm.* with *De temporum ratione* 38–39; *Epist. VVichth.* 1. A 'brother' in his monastery, Hwaetberht/Eusebius: prologues to *De temporum ratione, Expos. Apoc.*; a 'sister': *De Hab.*

[21] E.g., Biscop at 'seventeen ancient monasteries', of which only Rome, Vienne, and Lérins are named by Bede; the anonymous writer says he travelled to 'Gaul, Italy, and the Islands'; Eddius Stephanus describes a stop in Lyons with Wilfrid (Bede, *Hist. eccl.* 2, 4, 11; Anonymous, *Vita Ceolfridi* 6; Eddius Stephanus, *Vita Wilfridi* 3). Ceolfrith was formed at Trumhere's Gilling, Wilfrid's Ripon, Botulph's Iken, as well as Kent. He later went to Rome with Biscop and perhaps Tours (*Vita Ceolfridi* 2–3, 10). Hwaetberht was homegrown at Wearmouth-Jarrow but also travelled to Rome for study (*Hist. eccl.* 18). See O'Brien 2017: 307, 313–16 on his formation and differences of training in the monasteries.

[22] For Theodore, Hadrian, and their school, see Bischoff and Lapidge 1994; Lapidge 1995. Alas, for the remarkable monk 'Witmer', Bede only provides the tantalising detail that he was 'a man well versed in every branch of secular learning, as well as in the scriptures' (*Hist. eccl.* 15).

[23] Whitelock 1976.

[24] I might seem to differ here from the characterisation of Wearmouth-Jarrow in Thacker 2006: 42. But see 52: 'I am arguing ... that by the 720s Bede viewed his oeuvre as an interconnected program for a monastic education.' What Thacker sees as the goal of Bede in the 720s CE may always have been the environment of Wearmouth-Jarrow, given Biscop's focus on forging the right *regula* for monastic life out of his experience of many other institutions. But see O'Brien 2017.

and other elements of chant.[25] Further investigation of biblical or patristic texts required specialised learning for interpreting rare words, unfamiliar objects and settings, natural and supernatural phenomena, and the significance of biblical numbers, among other things. The real labour involved in attaining monastic proficiency is illustrated in contemporary sources.[26] Descriptions of Bede faithfully reproduce this liturgical and pastoral ordering of knowledge and effort, too. In a letter commissioning Bede's commentary *in Lucam*, Bishop Acca of Hexham applied to him the words of Psalm 1:2: 'you who meditate on the law of the Lord day and night without any rest'.[27] At the end of his *Historia ecclesiastica gentis Anglorum*, Bede said of himself: 'I have spent all my life in this monastery, applying myself entirely to the study of the scripture; and, amid the observance of the discipline of the Rule and the daily task of singing in the church, it has always been my delight to learn or to teach or to write.'[28]

Textual criticism was also a specialty at Wearmouth-Jarrow,[29] and Bede practised it, working with his brothers on the copying of weighty pandect Bibles and showing in his commentaries a knowledge of several Latin translations and some competence in Greek.[30] Finally, as a priest, Bede's responsibilities required further mastery of ritual actions and texts, as well as preaching.[31] Had Bede never written a book, his duties at Wearmouth-Jarrow would have required a significant education and implied an epistemology ordered around monastic transformation and the word of God: its study, transmission, and proclamation. He was, however, a gifted writer, commissioned to produce some works, while he made others of his own accord. His writing encompassed many fields: rhetoric, orthography, poetry, *computus*, cosmology and cosmography, history, hagiography, and hymnography – alongside his

---

[25] A useful contrast between Bede's setting and that of earlier authors in late antiquity (e.g., grammatical schools, philosophical schools) may be seen in Chapter 6 by Peter Martens and Chapter 30 by Michael Champion (this volume).
[26] E.g., Bede, *Hist. eccl.* 7; *Vita Ceolfridi* 11.   [27] Acca's letter to Bede: *Luc.*, pr. 60–61.
[28] Bede, *Hist. eccl.* 5.24.
[29] The Codex Amiatinus (Florence, Biblioteca Medicea Laurenziana, Amiatino 1) remains among the finest complete examples of Jerome's Vulgate. See Bruce-Mitford 1967; Gameson 1992; Marsden 1995: 107–201.
[30] For Bede's contribution to Amiatinus and Bible manuscripts: Meyvaert 1996; Marsden 1998. Bede's knowledge of multiple Latin translations is implied by his participation in the pandect Bible efforts, but he evinces knowledge of many differing texts throughout his commentaries. For this and his knowledge of Greek and textual criticism, see Laistner 1957; Dionisotti 1982; Marsden 1995: 72–75; Marsden 1998: 190–201. Chazelle 2019 and Hawkes and Boulton 2019 came to my attention too late for this contribution.
[31] For Bede's reference to rites and sacraments (even altar cloths and other details), see Carroll 1946: 80–84, 99–115, 131–37; for a picture of a later period of Anglo-Saxon priesthood and its resources, see Dyson 2019.

homilies, biblical commentaries, an Augustinian florilegium on the Pauline Epistles, and a small number of significant letters.[32] It is to these works that I now turn to consider Bede's understanding of Christian knowledge.

'Clay Hardened in the Fire': Embracing Pain

The experience of pain is a human universal. Contemporary writing, whether scientific or personal, usually focuses on its deleterious effects. Pain impairs cognition (including memory, attention, and decision-making), whether the pain is short-term or chronic.[33] In early years, it can stunt physical and emotional development or deteriorate a sense of agency and selfhood, and stress is increasingly seen as a condition with considerable physical impacts.[34] Attention has been given to various methods for healing the psyche or sense of self in the wake of traumatic events, and allowing sufferers to reinhabit their bodies.[35] In the light of these explorations, Bede's emphasis on the positive epistemic value of pain may surprise.[36] For him, pain is a feature of 'the cursed earth' after the fall into sin: ranging from women's 'pain and sorrow of childbirth' to the universal 'labour of needful suffering' by which we bring forth food from the earth until death.[37] In line with Augustine, Bede believed the world produced food abundantly and 'without the support of human effort' while humanity was in Eden, and all work took place with 'no distress ... but a delight of the will'.[38] Now, an unstable and dangerous world marked by pain, work, and exile puts 'the crime of human sin always before men's eyes'; 'men are mocked' by poisonous plants, barren trees, and thorns springing up, both in the world around and, mystically, in their spirit and flesh.[39] To take care of the needs of the flesh, to endure 'the body of death', is a burden, a condemnation, a form of slavery.[40] This is the human plight.

---

[32] For a useful survey of Bede's work, see Brown 2009: 17–101. His letters, save two, are prefaces to his works. We have likely lost others. Compare this 'curriculum' and range of writing with Martens' contribution on Origen's teaching and setting (Chapter 6, this volume).

[33] Low 2013; Moriarty et al. 2017.   [34] van der Kolk 2014: 105–68.

[35] van der Kolk 2014: 203–346.

[36] Bronwen Neil suggests the unique influence of Gregory on the idea and value of 'redemptive pain' (Chapter 36, this volume).

[37] Bede, *Gen.* 1.3.2135 (*dolor et gemitus parientis*), 1.3.2204 (*per laborem necessariae adflictionis*). Ahern (2020: 78–83) outlines some of Bede's understanding of the post-lapsarian transformation of the world, including the effect of the flood.

[38] Bede, *Gen.* 1.2.1607, quoting Augustine, *Gen. litt.* 8.8; 8.10: *Non enim erat laboris adflictio sed exhilaratio uoluntatis.*

[39] Bede, *Cant.* 1.1.207–14; *Gen.* 1.3.2175–201.   [40] Bede, *Gen.* 1.2.1592–605; 1.3.2175–201.

For the elect, however, pain and suffering can become a means of positive knowledge and transformation, through being conformed to the experience of the suffering Christ and 'the righteous who have always suffered'.[41] 'It is only through the sadness of the passing world and afflictions that one can reach eternal joys', Bede says.[42] 'Return to the heavenly fatherland ... lies open to us through the discipline of heavenly knowledge and the labour of temporal afflictions.'[43] One learns and becomes prepared for further knowledge of the divine through painful experience. This is a particular theme of Bede's commentaries *in Genesim* and *in epistulas catholicas septem*, but it pervades his work and is a particular feature of his celebration of the saints, among whom martyrs are pre-eminent.[44] 'Blood has a great voice', he says.[45]

To suffer while doing right: 'this is a gift from God' (*haec est gratia apud Deum*).[46] Such experiences allow the faithful to be 'imitators of our Lord's passion',[47] whether sufferings come 'through insulting words ... through losses of our temporal goods, [or] through bodily afflictions' brought on by others.[48] The martyrs exhibit this truth, and 'blessed Peter wants us always to imitate the mind of such persons'. Suffering (*patiens*) may be put on like clothing even 'when the Church is at peace', making it possible to avoid sin and subdue 'all human desires' to the divine will.[49] Bede also considers

---

[41] Bede, *Epist. Cath.* 2.5.100–6 (1 Peter 5:9). See also *tab.* 2.438–42: believers must choose 'to be conformed to the likeness of the Lord's death as far as they are able, by living continently and suffering for his sake' (*in quantum ualet similitudini mortis domini continenter uiuendo ac patiendo pro illo assimilari*).

[42] Bede, *Epist. Cath.* 2.1.101–5 (1 Peter 1:6). Cf. *Cant.* 1.1.732–44, my trans.: the Lord 'arranges for her [the Church] to be trained by repeated tribulations at present, by which, being purer, she may attain to eternal joys' (*ipse crebris eam in praesenti tribulationibus exerceri disponit quo mundior ad perpetua bona perveniat*).

[43] *Gen.* 1.3.2298–304: *per disciplinam nobis scientiae celestis et per laborem afflictionum temporalium reditus ad supernam patriam patet.*

[44] Martyrs, with celibates and those who have renounced possessions, are literally the top of 'the heap' of the faithful: see *Cant.* 4.7.130–39. Bede's liturgical calendar of saints' days, the foundation of the Roman Martyrology, lovingly memorialises eighty martyrs and the details of their suffering, alongside other saints.

[45] *Gen.* 2.4.161–63: 'Blood has a great voice, not only Abel's but also that of all those who are killed for the Lord. For the voice of their blood is the very firmness of faith, the very fervour of charity, through which they deserved to suffer for the Lord' (*Magnam vocem habet sanguis, non solum abel sed et omnium interfectorum pro domino. Vox est enim sanguinis eorum ipsa fidei constantia, ipse feruor caritatis per quem pati pro domino meruere*).

[46] 1 Peter 2.20: *Haec est gratia apud Deum.*   [47] Bede, *Epist. Cath.* 2.2.325–27 (1 Peter 2:20).

[48] Bede, *Epist. Cath.* 2.3.70 (1 Peter 3:13).

[49] Bede, *Epist. Cath.* 2.4.24–41 (1 Peter 4:3). Cf. *tab.* 1.243–62, and Bede's language of putting on 'the habit of penitence and lamentation' (*cum habitum paenitentiae ac luctus induimus*), alongside being bathed in the blood of Christ and awaiting the spiritual body of the future.

the experience of bodily weakness and sickness as a form of 'blessed' (*felix*) purgation. The lesson may have been driven home vividly in his teens. Many of the monks of Jarrow and the abbot Eosterwine died of plague in the year 686 CE, and he watched the abbots Sicgfrith and Benedict Biscop slowly die from drawn-out illnesses in 690 CE.[50] Around the same time (687 CE), St Cuthbert died from a long illness.[51]

What makes the transformation wrought by pain possible, let alone bearable? Partly, practices of meditation, whether on the Lord's passion or on scripture, particularly its allegorical meaning.[52] Partly, the grace of baptism and the other sacraments,[53] allied with the decision 'to follow the Lord', rather than a simple choice to accept what is burdensome or renounce the world.[54] Bede described not a single decision but a practice, a form of life, an ongoing conversion of the mind into something like the mind of Christ and the saints. The suffering Christian, 'trained by long struggles', becomes like 'clay hardened in fire', like gold purified 'by the flames of sufferings', or like linen harvested green from the earth, before being dried, pounded, bleached, baked, and twisted to become fine and white.[55] Along with patience amid temptation and other exterior afflictions, Bede envisaged chosen dispositions and bodily practices that allow the Christian to become 'crucified and suffering', particularly in the absence of persecution or martyrdom.[56] These are 'laborious works of righteousness at which the elect toil and sweat',[57] such as aspiring to heavenly life,[58] trampling 'every delight and luxury of the age' and renouncing possessions,[59] desiring spiritual things alone like 'tears, hunger, and poverty' and 'the more perfect life',[60] avoiding entertainment or earthly

---

[50] See Bede's *Hist. eccl.* 11, 13, 14. On Biscop's end (ch. 14): 'And so that holy soul, refined and tested by the prolonged flames of blessed tribulation, left behind the oven of clay, that is the flesh, and flew off in freedom to the glory of the blessed life above.'

[51] Bede, *Vit. Cuth.* 37 on preparation for eternal bliss 'by the fires of internal pain'.

[52] For the passion, see, e.g., *Cant.* 1.1.596–609, 2.4.170–91; for scriptural meditation as empowerment for holiness, see *Prov.* 1.3.185–99; *Cant.* 1.1.713–44; *Marcum* 1.667–72; *Hom.* 1.12.79–113, 1.12.219–21; and more generally *Hom.* 1.16; 2.2. Cf. Guiliano 2018: 292–94, 297–99, 301.

[53] Bede, *Hom.* 1.12.234.

[54] If the latter were true, according to Bede, the renunciations of pagan philosophers might have counted for something. Bede, *Hom.* 1.13.7–13.

[55] Post-baptismal life as 'training': *Hom.* 1.49–54. Hardened clay: *tem.* 2.1240–50. Gold: Bede, *Epist. Cath.* 2.1.112–21 (1 Peter 1:7). Fine linen: see, esp. *tab.* 2.135–42: Linen 'designates bodies that are gleaming with the beauty of chastity' (*corpora designat castitatis nitida*). For Bede, the commonly cited interpretive key is Rev 19:7–8.

[56] Bede, *Epist. Cath.* 2.4.24–41 (1 Peter 4:3); *Cant.* 1.1.713–44: When 'holy church takes her rest' from violent persecution, her members are free to pursue spiritual delights.

[57] *tem.* 2.1269–75: *laboriosis iustitiae operibus quibus … insudant electi.*   [58] *tab.* 1.277–302.

[59] *Luc.* 5.1344: *omnes saeculi delicias luxusque calcauerit.*

[60] *Luc.* 2.1530: *Qui … fletus esuriem papertatemque pati desiderat beatus est*; cf. *tab.* 1.746.

honours,[61] 'eating simply',[62] 'humiliation',[63] 'fasts and vigils ... prayers and readings',[64] and sexual continence, either celibacy or chaste widowhood.

The descriptions of continence are particularly revealing. Celibacy is surpassed only by the 'martyr enduring torture',[65] while the suffering of a lonely widow accustomed to earthly comfort and companionship is precisely what makes his or her state of life meritorious in Bede's eyes. 'They are placed in confinement and tribulation ... for the more the will of a [sexually] experienced person suffers in abstaining from sin, the greater the reward.'[66] Discussions of sexual continence as unusual suffering and self-denial are frequent in Bede's work. He describes asceticism as 'bitterness' for 'a healthy, growing body' (*sanum corpus ... ac uegetum*) amid 'material abundance' (*rerum copia*).[67] Bede places the practice of general works of mercy like preaching, hospitality, and almsgiving under this rubric of intensified suffering, too. They are more meritorious when undertaken for neighbours who wrong, annoy, or kill.[68] These are unique experiences of pain – self-inflicted mortifications to subdue the flesh, allied with love – that change the mind, purifying it and preparing it for the final cessation of suffering and the pleasurable vision of God.[69] Some are experienced by all. But others are experienced only by the Christian or chosen by those committed to an intense observation of Christian discipline, as a form of 'perfection'.

'Taste and See': Practising Future Pleasures in the Present

After reading such things, we might think Bede believed the present life to be marked only by pain and suffering, and pleasure deferred until the end. We would be wrong. For Bede, only residents of hell can 'lack all pleasures' (*cunctis carentes uoluptatibus*).[70] Life began in Eden, a 'place of pleasure'

---

[61] Bede, *Epist. Cath.* 1.4.9 (James 4:1); 4.2.162–90 (1 John 2:16).
[62] Bede, *Epist. Cath.* 4.5.277–79 (1 John 5:17), my translation.
[63] Bede, *Epist. Cath.* 2.5.70 (1 Peter 5:6): undertaken in times of peace for God and neighbour by 'those more perfect' (*perfectioribus*).
[64] *tab.* 2.135–42; 2.762–76, where fasts are characterised as one of a number of pious and bodily 'chastisements'.
[65] *tab.* 2.666–83.
[66] *Luc.* 3.439–47; *De temporum ratione* 1.1, citing Jerome's *Jov.* 1 and its symbolic interpretation of hand calculation: *in angustia et tribulatione sint positae ... maior est difficultas expertae quondam uoluptatis inlecebris abstinere tanto maius et praemium.*
[67] See also *Cant.* 3.4.901–13.   [68] Bede, *tem.* 1.1701–20.
[69] Bede, *Epist. Cath.* 4.4.164–203 (1 John 4:12), drawing on Augustine's *Ep.* 147 (*De videndo Deo*).
[70] Bede, *Epist. Cath.* 2.2.228–30 (1 Peter 2:11). As Ahern (2020: 187–94) points out, Bede's conception of hell is mostly a place of lack: no light, no hope, no comfort, no happiness – only torment, an overwhelming stench, and excessive heat or cold.

(*locum voluptatis*), where humans enjoyed 'the most blessed and holy delights of the flesh and the soul'.[71] And God has retained earthly comforts in the present world for the necessities of life, through which his goodness may be known. One of Bede's examples is the good of created light; another is the human use of animals and animal flesh for food, clothing, labour, and travel.[72] There are many others. Through pleasures, divine benevolence is known in body and soul.

Bede follows and modifies an ascetic tradition that focuses on 'trampling' on or 'passing over' many ordinary, bodily, or worldly desires, in favour of spiritual joys.[73] Greater pleasure is to be found in abstinence and continence.[74] Bede names food, drink, and sex, as part of the 'yearnings and delights of the body', primordial sources of temptation that, if enjoyed without any regard for the heavenly life, are sinful.[75] They are temporary and will pass away in the coming age. But the pleasures of the body are not in themselves sinful, if ordered well, and may be part of the things of the world that are to be 'used' for human need, so long as they are not 'loved' or desired.[76] Bede even transmitted ancient medical advice on the married man's proper management of pleasures according to the seasons of the year – not least, when to enjoy sex and wine or eat varied foods (sweet, smelly, bitter, hot, cold) – in line with ancient theories about the humours.[77]

This distinction of pleasures, temporal and spiritual, does not fully capture Bede's thought. When he urges asceticism or, say, scriptural reading as an ecstatic pleasure, he uses the language of earthly gratification in all its specificity: the caress of a lover; the beauty of nature; the satisfaction of a meal; the taste, aroma, and warming qualities of wine, even its intoxicating effects. 'There is a constant play … between the temporal and the eternal, the false and the true, the fleshly and the spiritual, which cannot banish the

---

[71] *Gen.* 1.2.1501 and 2.4.586. Bede believed Eden still existed in his time, though its location was unknown. See Ahern 2020: 74–77 for notes on Bede's distinctive thinking.

[72] *Gen.* 1.1.166, 1.1.874–86; *Expos. Act. Apost.* 17.37–49: *munera lucis et vitae*.

[73] E.g., Cassian, *Inst.* 5.14.4: *Nequaquam enim poterimus escarum praesentium spernere uoluptates, nisi mens contemplationi diuinae defixa amore uirtutum potius et pulchritudine caelestium delectetur.* ('We cannot possibly scorn the pleasures brought on by the present food unless the mind is fixed on the contemplation of divine things, and is more powerfully delighted by the love of virtue and the beauty of celestial things.')

[74] See *Luc.* 5.1358–72, drawing in particular on John Cassian's *Conlationes* 24.26.

[75] Bede, *Epist. Cath.* 1.4.20–26 (James 4:3); 2.3.168–84 (1 John 2:16).

[76] See Bede, *Epist. Cath.* 4.2.149–60 (1 John 2:15–16); *Luc.* 4.2127–29. The married in particular may 'enjoy this world' (*fruuntur hoc mundo*), so long as they do not forget to show mercy to others: *Cant.* 4.6.103–10.

[77] See *De temporum ratione* 30. Bede transmits Pseudo-Hippocrates, *Ad antigonum regem* 8–9.

memory and experience of the former pleasures too swiftly. It depends on them.'[78] We might wonder if this is a result of Bede's aristocratic context: some of his brothers and others in his audience knew worldly pleasures all too well.

As an example, consider one of Bede's constant examples: taste.[79] Many of the admirable figures he mentions in his historical writings practised various forms of fasting and abstinence.[80] He speaks of feasting as an opportunity for sin, partly due to the practices that surround feasts.[81] Still, taste and consumption of good things – fresh loaves, fine wine, tender meat, apples, raisins, pomegranates, milk, butter – regularly serve as a cipher for the enjoyment of God in the sacraments and a variety of Christian practices.[82] *Gustate et uidete quoniam suauis est dominus* ('Taste and see that the Lord is sweet', Ps. 34:8 (33:9)). This verse recurs in Bede's exegesis and is applied in a variety of ways.[83] One of the most common is in relation to scripture and sacramental participation: whether it is by listening attentively to readings in church, learning from a teacher's preaching or writing, or receiving the Eucharist, God's goodness may be received as 'living bread' and 'the sweetness from on high'.[84] By faith in the redeemer's incarnation and passion, the enjoyment of God's goodness is a 'sweetness' impelling members of the church to heaven,[85] preventing them from participating in evil,[86] or filling them with joy as 'the sweetest light' in the contemplative life (*theoricae vitae dulcissima lux*).[87]

---

[78] Guiliano 2018: 301.

[79] Like Origen and others, Bede does not seem to have had a full theory of how spiritual 'taste' or other senses integrate bodily experience into spiritual knowledge. See Chapter 2 by Jane Heath and Chapter 25 by Robin Jensen (this volume) on spiritual senses and sense perception.

[80] Cuthbert fasted until Nones on every Friday and always from alcohol, even as a bishop (*Vita Cuth.* 5, 6, 26) – though his fast from alcohol once led to water being changed into wine (*Vita Cuth.* 35). Aidan fasted until Nones on Wednesday and Friday and ate little when the king called him to feasts (*Hist. eccl.* 3.5); he blessed King Oswald for giving away a feast and silver dishes to the poor (*Hist. eccl.* 3.6). Abbot Eosterwine of Wearmouth always ate the same food as his monks (*Hist. eccl.* 8), while Abbot Ceolfrith exhibited 'frugality respecting food and drink and a use of clothing unusual among those who rule' (*Hist. eccl.* 16, my translation).

[81] Like too much talking (*loquacitas*): see *Luc.* 5.325–34, quoting Gregory the Great, *Hom. ev.* 2.40.207; 2.40.210–17. Compare Chapter 27 by Jeanne-Nicole Mellon Saint-Laurent (this volume) on monastic gluttony.

[82] E.g., *Gen.* 4.18.673–750 (bread, butter, milk, tender calf); *Cant.* 1.2.173–92 (apples and pomegranates); 2.4.170–93 (pomegranates with description). Some of the foods he mentions in these passages and elsewhere are exotic, perhaps pointing to the unique access he and others enjoyed to international trade.

[83] He may have learned from Augustine, who cites the verse dozens of times in his writings, particularly his *Enarrat. Ps.*

[84] Bede, *Epist. Cath.* 2.2.1–28 (1 Peter 2:1–3); cf. *Prov.* 1.3.185–99.   [85] *Cant.* 1.1.164–80.

[86] *Luc.* 5.19.1725–35; *Epist. Cath.* 4.3.126–30 (1 John 3:6).   [87] *Sam.* 1.7.2021.

However, the importance of this Psalm verse and of the present taste of 'sweetness' comes in their consistent eschatological meaning: the Christian tastes something of the future, but not its whole reality.[88] Present pleasures, even holy ones, are partial and temporary.[89] Desire for them is inconstant, and the body and mind are often too weak for continual pleasure in God, whether it is experienced through right use of ordinary pleasures, through the sacramental gifts given to the church, or through direct illumination. The present 'taste' of God points towards the final beatific vision, and an enjoyment that cannot be fully described or known now. In the present, only angels 'hold nothing sweet' except God,[90] though a human being may 'gasp for eternal desires' if they are 'perfect'.[91] As with the discussion of pain, a higher order of Christian emerges here in Bede's writing.

A longing for spiritual desire as exhibited by the poor and perfect marks Bede's thought on the knowledge brought by pleasure. Bede holds out hope that human capacities and the desire for divine wisdom may grow over the course of life through the disciplined pursuit of godly joys. This comes out in his comments on 1 Peter 1:12.[92] He begins by describing angelic life and desire. Angels long to see God, and they are continually satisfied by the beatific vision: 'The contemplation of the divine presence makes the citizens of the heavenly fatherland blessed in such a way (*ita ... beatificat*) that, in an ordering to us ineffable, they are always satisfied at seeing his glory and they always hunger insatiably after his sweetness as if it were new.'[93] This dynamic of constant hunger and satisfaction, desire and taste empowered by divine blessing, allows angels to hold God perfectly in sight. Bede believes the pursuit of spiritual pleasures in the present may allow the human being to enter this dynamic of desire: 'Spiritual pleasures increase desire in the mind while they satisfy, because the more greatly their flavour is sensed, the more it is known that it may be loved more.'[94] A human, including one among the class of the poor and perfect, may not attain to the constancy of the beatific vision in this life, but they might make progress towards it. A life 'like the angels' may be led in part on earth – provided that one enters something like the monastic or clerical state: unmarried,

---

[88] See Darby 2012 on pervasive eschatological themes in Bede's writing, particularly from 716 CE onwards.
[89] On the fleeting character of contemplation, see DeGregorio 1999: 24–25, 30–32.
[90] *Epist. Cath.* 4.2.390–97 (1 John 2:29), quoting Augustine, *Tract. ep. Jo.* 4.3.
[91] *Luc.* 4.2123–25.
[92] Bede, *Epist. Cath.* 2.1.182 (1 Pet 1:12), referring to Gregory the Great, *Hom. ev.* 2.36.1.
[93] Bede, *Epist. Cath.* 2.1.177–81 (1 Pet 1:12).
[94] Bede, *Epist. Cath.* 2.1.190 (1 Pet 1:12).

focused on shunning vices, embracing sanctified delight, and living in love and purity towards all neighbours.[95]

Angelic living cannot be attained fully before death and resurrection, for the mortal mind remains marked by sin and weighed down by a corruptible body. Perfect knowledge of God requires perfect righteousness, as is clear in many passages of Bede's writing. 'Blessed are those who hunger and thirst for righteousness' (Matt 5:6; Luke 6:21). Bede comments: 'The blessed should … love or, rather, burn for the daily progress of justice' because their own justice will never be sufficient. 'The Psalmist, set on fire, shows that perfect satisfaction cannot come forth in this age but in the future. He said: "And I will appear with justice in your sight. I will be satisfied when your glory is made manifest."'[96] Or, as Bede says in his comments on 1 John 2:29, quoting Augustine:

It will be perfected in you when it will delight you to do nothing else, when death will be swallowed up in victory, when no concupiscence rouses you, when there will be no struggle against flesh and blood, when there will be the crown of victory and triumph over the enemy, then there will be perfect righteousness.[97]

Here we see the difference between the enjoyment of bodily pleasures for their own sake in contrast with the experience of spiritual pleasures for the sake of divine knowledge, as well as a link to Bede's eschatology. There is greater continuity between the final beatific vision and the spiritual pleasures enjoyed in the present, particularly by 'the poor and perfect'. Activities like scriptural reading, psalm-singing, sacramental participation, and the pursuit of righteousness have God as their object and goal. They are divinely ordained and pleasurable means to the knowledge of God. But the enjoyment of ordinary food and sex, honour and power, or even music and art carry, for Bede, the potential for distraction from the goal of knowing and loving God. They must be used 'in passing … just as a traveller uses a stable or traveling money', but not desired as 'the highest good'.[98] Bede's account of poverty rests on a similar distinction between use and desire.

---

[95] On the angelic or heavenly life in the present, see Bede, *tab.* 2.632–45; 2.1102; *tem.* 1.647–57; 1.1498; *Hom.* 1.3.56–71; 1.4.12; 1.13.199. But see *tab.* 1.277–317 on the accessibility of angelic life for all.

[96] *Luc.* 2.1501–4, citing Ps. 16:15: *Cuius perfectam saturitatem non in hoc saeculo sed in futuro posse prouenire supernorum desiderio psalmista flagrans ostendit qui ait: Ego autem cum iustitia apparebo in conspectu tuo satiabor dum manifestabitur gloria tua.*

[97] Bede, *Epist. Cath.* 4.2.401–3 (1 John 2.29), citing Augustine, *Tract. ep. Jo.* 4.3.

[98] Bede, *Gen.* 2.4.540–44.

'Blessed Are the Poor': Bede on the Knowledge of Poverty

The holiness and blessedness of poverty is, for Bede, rooted in God's character and in the material circumstances and spiritual stance of Jesus and the apostles. The Word of God 'chose' the poor most visibly, 'when he created poor parents for himself' and entered 'the general state of poverty' in childhood, including a form of 'slavery' when rendering taxes to Caesar.[99] As an adult, Christ chose 'such great poverty' that he lacked normal shelter,[100] and he received food and clothing from women of means, 'to give an example' of contentment to others.[101] The apostles followed in Christ's footsteps, refusing to gather riches as they led the early church, save for the purpose of feeding the poor.[102] Their impoverishment meant they needed gifts to survive.[103] Bede insists in his commentary *in Lucam* that this was the apostles' 'right' or 'power' (*potestas*), drawing language from St Paul to describe the exercise of apostolic ministry in every age: 'Those who preach the Gospel must live from the Gospel' (1 Cor 9:14). But the apostles did not always choose to be sustained by others and sometimes laboured to support their ministry.[104]

We might expect Bede to urge the imitation of Jesus and the apostles in the freedom and dependence of holy poverty, thereby entering their experience or possessing first-hand knowledge of their state of life. This is how he treats pain and suffering, after all. Bede primarily urges such action when addressing a monastic or clerical audience.[105] His understanding of the blessedness of poverty is complicated and does not require literal material deprivation, which he describes as a state of wretchedness.[106] (Not surprising, given Bede's wealthy, yet ascetic context.) The poor man Lazarus was blessed by God in the afterlife, Bede writes, because he was tried by life's circumstances and found worthy, unlike the rich man dressed in purple, 'tortured among the dead' for his neglect of the poor.[107]

---

[99] *Epist. Cath.* 1.2.31–40 (James 2:5); *Hom.* 1.6.127–42; 1.6.263–68; cf. *Hom.* 1.18.48: Christ not only 'deigned to become human ... but he also deigned to become poor for us'.

[100] *Luc.* 3.1830–32, quoting Jerome, *Comm. Matt.* 1.1154 (Matt 8:20): *tantae sim paupertatis ut ne hospitiolum quidem habeam et non meo utar tecto.*

[101] *Luc.* 3.286–95, quoting Jerome, *Comm. Matt.* 27:55. Bede and Jerome see these examples as primarily for teachers of the gospel.

[102] *Expos. Act. Apost.* 3.23–32.   [103] *Expos. Act. Apost.* 11.34.40.

[104] *Luc.* 3.1142–52, quoting selections from Augustine, *Cons.* 2.30.71–75 on Matt 10:10 and Luke 9:3.

[105] E.g., speaking to his monastic brethren on the Feast of Benedict Biscop in *Hom.* 1.13.

[106] *Luc.* 2.1494–96.

[107] *Luc.* 5.251: *apud inferos tortum*. This example of Lazarus and the rich man recurs at least ten times in Bede's exegesis of various biblical books: *Gen.* 2.4.515; *Prov.* 1.1.373–79; 1.3.248; 2.13.21; 2.20.113; *Epist. Cath.* 1.1.106; 1.1.137; 1.5.12; *Expos. Apoc.* 1.8.6.17; 2.24.14.10.

The blessedness of Lazarus comes not from poverty alone, but virtue proved in poverty.[108] In contrast, the unvirtuous poor, those who are greedy of heart, 'are counted in the number of the rich, even if they were unable to gain riches'.[109]

Poverty emerges largely as a state of mind, a lack of improper desire for riches. The materially rich can become the blessed poor 'to whom the kingdom of heaven belongs' (Luke 6:20), so long as they consider their wealth as nothing (*pro nihilo*). Abraham, David, and 'so many rich people' in the Old Testament are Bede's examples, along with 'Matthew, Zacchaeus, and Joseph in the Gospel': all entered the kingdom of heaven, not all gave up their riches.[110] Here, Bede shows himself the heir of Ambrose and Augustine, and only distantly the heir of Jerome, whom he contradicts by insisting that the wealthy may retain their wealth.[111] 'There is no little distance between having wealth and loving wealth', Bede says.

> For many having love not, many not having do love. Again, some both have and love; others rejoice that they neither have nor love the riches of the world, whose status is safe, while they say with the apostle: to us 'the world is crucified' and us 'to the world'.[112]

Without the proper attitude towards wealth, it is not possible to be a Christian.[113] Renunciation is necessary, conversion 'from the desire for temporal things to the love of eternal things', as in Bede's account of bodily and spiritual pleasures.[114] Bede makes an important distinction while commenting on Luke 14:33: 'Every one of you who does not give up everything which he possesses cannot be my disciple.' The Greek original has a form of *apōtassō*, which ranges in meaning from 'bid farewell' and 'renounce' to 'give up', 'put away', or 'relinquish'. In Greek monastic contexts, it would be used to describe the monk's formal separation from the world and possessions. However, Jerome's Vulgate has *renuntiare*, not *relinquere* or

---

[108] Cf. *Epist. Cath.* 1.1.137 (James 1:11): Lazarus was received because he was 'humble and innocent'.
[109] *Luc.* 5.1312–13: *omnes qui diuitias amant etiam si adipisci nequeant in diuitum numero deputari.* See Ryan 2016: 91–92.
[110] *Luc.* 5.1287–90, ed. Hurst 1960: 328. In his comments on James 1:11 and 1:15, Bede refers again to Abraham and Job as examples of the virtuous rich.
[111] See Brown 2012: 313–14, 342–52; Colish 2005.
[112] *Luc.* 5.1270–75, quoting Gal 6:14: *Sed inter pecunias habere et pecunias amare non nulla distantia est. Multi enim habentes non amant, multi non habentes amant. Item alii et habent et amant, alii nec habere nec amare se diuitias saeculi gaudent quorum tutior status est cum apostolo dicentium: Nobis mundus crucifixus est et nos mundo.*
[113] Ryan 2016: 96.
[114] *Luc.* 5.1319–20, quoting Augustine, *Quaest. ev.* 2. Q. 47.19: *a cupiditate temporalium ad caritatem aeternorum.*

something similar.[115] Bede, declaring a 'great difference' between *renuntiare* and *relinquere*, concludes:

> It is for every one of the faithful 'to renounce everything which he possesses', that is, so to hold those things of the world, that they might not be held in the world through them, to hold the temporal thing in use, the eternal in desire, thus conducting earthly affairs so that – still – with the whole mind they stretch towards the celestial.[116]

Holding without being held, using without desiring: this is a state of mind all must learn, in order to become the blessed poor, entering the experience of Christ and the apostles. Bede does not claim the attitude is acquired easily. The wealthy are tempted to pride, to oppressing others, to caring only for the present.[117] Riches 'tear' and 'strangle the throat of the mind', harassing it with anxiety over preserving riches, not to mention the freedom wealth brings to fulfil evil desires.[118] The spiritual poverty of the rich requires constant humility.[119] It entails, too, a certain management of goods and property, as well as a commitment to constant almsgiving: supporting dependents and anyone in need, to the highest degree possible; and supporting holy preachers.[120] In Bede's discussion of the latter, we begin to move beyond the general contours of blessed poverty, entering instead its foothills and peaks. As always, Bede's thought involves a hierarchy of possibilities.

In holy preachers, poverty reaches its pinnacle. They ought to possess 'perfection of mind' and no desire for earthly things.[121] Their will and state of life are truly free, set apart from the cares of the world. For they are the faithful who have renounced *and* relinquished all things; they 'neither have *nor* love the riches of this world'; and theirs is the power both to demand support from others *and* to support themselves and others through work.

---

[115] See *apōtasso* in Danker 2001: 123; Lampe 1961: 216.
[116] *Luc.* 4.2125–29: *Cunctorum autem fidelium est renuntiare omnibus quae possident, hoc est sic tenere quae mundi sunt ut tamen per ea non teneantur in mundo, habere rem temporalem in usu aeternam in desiderio sic terrena gerere ut tamen tota mente ad caelestia tendant.*
[117] *Epist. Cath.* 1.1.88–110.
[118] *Luc.* 3.401–4, quoting Gregory the Great, *Hom. in ev.* 1.15.1.12–20.
[119] Bede, *Epist. Cath.* 1.1.114–45 (James 1:11).
[120] Ryan 2016: 94. See, e.g., Bede, *tem.* 1.1685–721; 2.131–52; *Ezr.* 255–70; *Cant.* 4.6.103–10; *Epist. Cath.* 1.1.343–1.2.14 (James 1:27–2:1), 1.2.144–233 (James 2:18–21); 1.5.5–50 (James 5:3–5); 4.3.258–74 (1 John 3:17–18); 6.40–54 (3 John 8); *Hom.* 1.13.41–47. Bede notably places limits on giving, such as 'bodily frailty' and 'timely opportunity', but no limits on the love that motivates such giving: *Epist. Cath.* 2.4.78–103 (1 Peter 4:8). For a brief survey of Bede on almsgiving, see Carroll 1946: 220–23.
[121] Bede, *Luc.* 3.352, quoting Gregory the Great, *Hom. in Hiez. proph.* 2.6.414.

They surpass all in virtue and knowledge. 'It is more blessed to give than to receive', Jesus said. Bede comments:

> He does not value the rich, even if they give alms, more highly than those who have 'left all things' and followed the Lord. Rather, he extols most highly those who have given up at once everything they had, and who nevertheless labour, 'working with their hands at what is good in order to have something to give to one who is suffering need.' (Eph 4:28)[122]

Those pursuing such labours constitute a higher class of the faithful, distinguished in this life and the next, because of their higher state of mind. In the present they rule the church and are chosen to 'cut down' the rich and proud by their words;[123] in the future they will join the Lord in judging the whole world.[124] Bede calls them many names: *perfecti* or *rectores*. He finds them hidden in the symbols of scripture, such as the eyes, teeth, or breasts of the Beloved in the Song of Songs, the golden crown upon the altar placed in the tabernacle of Moses, the capitals of the pillars in the temple of Solomon, its builders and its incense. These are Bede's teachers and preachers.

'The Very Wealthy and Very Learned': Bede's Preachers and Teachers

In recent years, scholars have drawn our attention to Bede's preoccupation with a particular class within Anglo-Saxon society: *doctores* and *praedicatores*, whose responsibility it is to pass on the faith, interpret scripture, and govern others within the churches, all while leading a life of self-denial. It was his own class, and he was concerned to reform its failures and excesses.[125] The basic task of teachers was to hand on the faith that leads to eternal salvation, whether through preaching or writing. It was open to any person properly 'imbued' with Christian doctrine, however limited their understanding of more complicated matters.[126] Clerics and monks, however, with greater wisdom and virtue than the average Christian and

---

[122] Bede, *Expos. Act. Apost.* 20.95–101, combining reference to Jesus' teaching around the rich young ruler and Paul's teaching about manual labour.

[123] Bede, *tem.* 1.102–9.   [124] Bede, *Hom.* 1.13.23–26.

[125] See O'Brien 2015: 113–28 for a synthesis and advance on prior discussions of Bede's pastoral and reform concerns and Matis 2019: 42–58 on Bede's interpretation of the Song as a text about the church's ministry and reform, with subsequent chapters showing the pervasive influence of Bede's views on later generations, particularly Carolingian *doctores*. Classic statements occur in Thacker 1983; DeGregorio 2002; DeGregorio 2004; DeGregorio 2006b; Thacker 2006.

[126] Bede, *Cant.* 5.8.496–512.

with the advantage of time, had higher responsibilities. They must travel if necessary to fulfil their obligations to preach to the people in their pastoral charge;[127] they must never tire of 'the time-consuming task of frequent catechising'.[128] They could proffer their teaching through plain exhortations or by explaining difficult passages of scripture, a process Bede compares to offering 'cups' or 'loaves' to the faithful: the cup may be drunk immediately, the bread must be torn and chewed through 'laborious explanation'.[129] A particularly clear statement on teaching comes in Bede's *Hom.* 2.2 on John 6:1–14 (the feeding of the five thousand). Like most patristic interpreters, Bede sees this miracle as a sign of Christ's ability to open the scriptures to his followers, breaking them open and multiplying their meaning.

> The five loaves of bread with which he satisfied the multitude of people are the five books of Moses. If they are opened by spiritual understanding, and then multiplied by [penetration of] their deeper meaning, they daily refresh the hearts of the believers who hear them ... The two fishes which he added not inappropriately signify the writings of the psalmists and prophets.[130]

Although Christ revealed the spiritual meaning of scripture in his teaching and the mystery of his life, this task was left unfinished for the apostles and those who followed them as teachers to continue. Just as the apostles gathered up the broken fragments of bread that remained after the crowds had dispersed, so some in each age must apply themselves to passages of scripture that 'those less learned are unable to assimilate, but which they are able to understand once they are explained by teachers' in oral or written instruction.[131] This task continues always and everywhere.

> This is what the apostles themselves and the evangelists did, by including quite a number of mystical sayings of the law and the prophets in their works, with the addition of their own interpretation. This is what a large number of their followers, guides of the Church throughout the entire world, have done by scrutinising complete books of both testaments of the scriptures in very diligent explanations.[132]

How is this 'laborious' multiplication of meaning accomplished? Bede alludes to meditation and study throughout his works. However, in closer analysis of his method of writing, we can see his vision of the highest teachers and their knowledge. Some of his commentaries provide particularly

---

[127] *Epistle to Egbert* 7.   [128] *Sam.* 2.2254–67.
[129] *Cant.* 4.7.143–80. A frequent distinction in Bede, likely drawn from Gregory the Great, *Mor.*, 1.21.29: 'Sacred scripture is sometimes food and sometimes drink for us. It is food in its obscure passages, for it is broken in exposition, as it were, chewed, and swallowed. It is drink, however, in its easier passages, for it is assimilated just as it is found.'
[130] Bede, *Hom.* 2.2.118–22.   [131] Bede, *Hom.* 2.2.177–82.   [132] Bede, *Hom.* 2.2.193–98.

clear images of his working methods. The prologue to *in Lucam* describes to his bishop a process of canvassing the patristic inheritance.

> Once the little works of the fathers were gathered here, like the most famous and most worthy craftsmen for so great an office, I set out diligently to consider what Ambrose, what Augustine, what Gregory ... what Jerome ... and what other fathers had sensed in the words of blessed Luke, and what they had said [about them]; and I laid out the commission in a continual sequence of little sheets, as you had ordered, either in their words – or in my phrases, when a reason for abbreviation appeared.[133]

Bede presents his work humbly here and in other places, as if he were a compiler of notebooks, and to some extent the description fits his *Expositio Apocalypseos* and portions of *in Genesim*, *in Cantica Canticum*, and *in Lucam*. We should remember, however, that even the act of compilation implied a long process: gathering materials, sifting them, and selecting statements, often reworking the material thoroughly, in order to create a coherent commentary.[134] Bede might draw primarily on a single patristic text to illuminate a pericope, as in his comments on the rich man and Lazarus.[135] More often, he drew on several. His comments on the rich young ruler show him using at least four separate patristic texts, sometimes quoting them at length, but more often weaving them together with his own contributions and new citations of scripture.[136] The same is true for his discussion of Luke's opening verses,[137] and his interpretation of Luke 9:10–17, among others.[138] However, the description of Bede as a compiler

---

[133] *Luc.*, pr. 96–105: *Aggregatisque hinc inde quasi insignissimis ac dignissimis tanti muneris artificibus, opusculis patrum, quid beatus Ambrosius, quid Augustinus, quid denique Gregorius uigilantissimus iuxta suum nomen nostrae gentis apostolus, quid Hieronymus sacrae interpres historiae, quid caeteri patres in beati Lucae uerbis senserint, quid dixerint, diligentius inspicere sategi, mandatumque continuo schedulis ut iussisti, uel ipsis eorum syllabis uel certe meis breuiandi causa sermonibus, ut uidebatur edidi.*

[134] Note a similar process in Paul the Deacon's composition of his homiliary and Florus of Lyons in his Augustinian compilations. See Boodts 2017; Guiliano 2021: 91–118.

[135] For Luke 16:19–31, see Bede, *Luc.* 5.241–461 which draws almost exclusively on the literal exposition in Gregory the Great's *Hom. ev.* 2.40, often omitting repetitions or, in one instance, Gregory's sense of the temptations and 'agitations' Lazarus suffered as he lay near the gate of the rich man. Even in this section of his commentary, however, Bede sneaks in short quotations from other sources: Augustine's definition of the 'bosom of Abraham' from *Quaest. ev.* 38; Isidore's description of the making of linen and purple in *Etym.* 19.27.4; 19.28.2,4.

[136] Bede, *Luc.* 5.1218–373 draws on Jerome's *Comm. Matt.*, Augustine's *Quaest. ev.*, John Cassian's *Conlationes*, and Gregory the Great's *Moralia*. Ahern (2020: 55–84) shows a similar use of various patristic, classical, and contemporary Irish resources in Bede's cosmographical writing.

[137] Most likely: Ambrose, *Exp. Luc.*; Augustine, *Haer.*; Jerome, *Comm. Matt.*; *Pelag.*

[138] Ambrose, *Exp. Luc.*; Jerome, *Comm. Matt.*; *Nom. hebr.*; Augustine, *Tract. ev. Jo.*; Gregory, *Moral.*; and Cassian, *Conlationes* or Jerome, *Jov.*

is wholly misleading when applied to most of his exegetical works, as many have noted, particularly his commentaries on the Old Testament and the Catholic Epistles, where he had fewer sources.[139]

Compilation and commentary were tasks for few. They required 'profound leisure, hard work, and much money', as Jerome said to Pope Damasus.[140] Bede put it similarly in his prologue to *in Genesim*. Noting that 'many persons had said many things' about the book, including Basil, Ambrose, and Augustine, he added: 'these [works] are so copious and so deep that so many volumes can scarcely be acquired except by the very wealthy and such profound matters can scarcely be studied except by the very learned'.[141] For that reason, his bishop, Acca, asked him to make a single commentary containing excerpts of 'those things which would seem sufficient for the weak'.[142] Here, Bede's takes his place as the first among preachers and teachers of his time, a guide to the churches. His erudition and access to wealth were not incidental to this status.

We do not know whether Bede gathered his sources from Wearmouth-Jarrow alone, or whether he borrowed and copied works from other places (his statements suggest the latter without ruling out the former). In either case, the highest calibre of teacher in the Bedan model needs certain material conditions: access to a library or libraries, time for study, parchments and inks for writing, a space to work in, as well as assistance from others. If patristic texts needed acquiring or copying, we must imagine time, travel, hospitality, and money. Not just any priest or monk could do it. An exceptionally resourced institution was required, and an exceptionally intelligent teacher, with both institution and teacher ordered towards scriptural education and teaching. Only then would the church be enriched with flowers 'from the most delightful fields of [the] widely blooming paradise', i.e., the extensive works of the fathers.[143] What was needed in Anglo-Saxon England for a *doctor* or *praedicator* like Bede to attain the knowledge necessary to transform self and society? A Wearmouth-Jarrow with all its wealth,

---

[139] See Brown 2009: 33–71; DeGregorio 2006c; DeGregorio 2019: 19–38. For his engagement with sources in his cosmological works, see Ahern 2020: esp. 31–61.

[140] Jerome, Prologue to *Orig. Hom. Cant.*, quoted in Brown 2012: 260.

[141] *Gen.*, pr. 1–23: *haec tam copiosa tam sunt alta ut uix nisi a locupletioribus tot uolumina adquiri, uix tam profunda nisi ab eruditioribus ualeant perscrutari*. Bede omits mentioning most of his early medieval and classical sources; see Ahern 2020: 84.

[142] *Gen.*, pr. 24.

[143] Bede, *Gen.* pr. 24–28. Bede mentions reading through Basil's *Homiliae in Hexaemeron* in Latin translation, Ambrose's *Hex.*, and Augustine's *Gen. litt.*, *Gen. Man.*, *Leg.*, and *Conf.*, but he draws on more than twenty other patristic texts throughout his commentary, along with numerous cosmographical works.

personnel, and connections, and thus an entire society and economy prepared to support such monasteries and people.

'If You Want to Be Perfect': Bede's Self-Image and the Christian Knowledge Economy

As I have argued, a set of ideal figures emerges regularly from Bede's writing, no matter the topic: those at the apex of Christian society, working to rule and guide it through teaching.[144] They heard Jesus' words – *si vis perfectus esse* ('if you want to be perfect', Matt 19:21) – and sought to meet the challenge.[145] Their position at the height of the church was mirrored by their access to Christian knowledge and experience. Everyone feels pain; they choose to be crucified with Jesus. God has made pleasures available to all, but truly exquisite delights, ecstasies of the Spirit, are reserved for those who know how to lead the life of the angels, the life of the resurrection. The faithful Christian must embrace poverty of spirit, expressed in the right use of wealth and almsgiving; but only the perfect are 'safe', who have renounced the world while continuing to labour for their neighbours' good and salvation. All must speak of God's ways and impart saving knowledge to their neighbour, but those desiring perfection are capable of grasping mysteries far beyond the ken of ordinary mortals. Christian understanding is ordered towards the knowledge of God in Christ in every part of life, but the quality of life is different for the perfect: sharper, more vivid, charged with beauty, glory, and pleasure. The trajectory of Bede's thought runs continually in this direction, and it shows how he believed a society ordered around the transmission of Christian teaching and scriptural knowledge would be riven with inequalities of experience and understanding. It is a spiritual vision of the elite, for the elite – a hierarchy of the Spirit, buttressed by material advantages and securities.[146] As noted above, Bede and others of his class enjoyed a material quality of life that was not available to most

---

[144] O'Brien 2015: 123–29.

[145] Bede directly cites Matt 19:21 (or its parallel Luke 18:22) at least fifteen times in eight of his commentaries: *Gen.* 2.6.1157; *tab.* 1.752; *tem.* 2.1340; *in Ezr.* 1.711, 1.1140; *Prov.* 1.3.179, 3.31.298; *Cant.* 3.4.486, 3.4.718, 5.7.473; *Marc.* 2.8.1657; 3.10.737; 3.10.740; *Luc.* 5.18.1252; 5.19.1586. Notably, in the last example, he brings the story into a discussion of the wealth of Zacchaeus, when he has already dealt with the rich young ruler at length in 5.1218–373. See also *Hom.* 1.14 (Matt 19:21–29 for the Feast of Benedict Biscop); *Hom.* 2.2 (John 6:1–14 in Lent); *Hist. eccl.* 1.

[146] Ryan 2016: 98. For Bede's 'immediate audience' for his histories, see Gunn 2009: esp. chs. 1 and 3; for his teaching, see McClure 1985.

of their contemporaries, built off revenue-producing lands and the work of others. In describing Bede's acceptance and support for this organisation of society, including some of its most strongly hierarchical elements, I suggest we adopt a term from the social scientist Thomas Piketty: Bede enjoyed and elaborated a whole *inequality regime*, 'a set of discourses and institutional arrangements intended to justify and structure the economic, social, and political inequalities of a given society'.[147] Bede inherited many of these structures and presumably some of their justifications through his entry into monastic life in Northumbria. It, too, was a milieu in touch with broader currents in the Latin West and further abroad. But these facts do not explain why his writings are filled with comments on property, inequality, and the management or enjoyment of goods and experiences, both material and spiritual. He chose, or felt compelled, to address such topics again and again, as he wrote to and for his class and those who supported them. And he subtly transformed and moulded the patristic and monastic inheritance as he did so. Given the popularity of his writing in the Middle Ages, historians must reckon with the influence of his views on the shape of the church, its ministry, and its justifications of various inequalities. Ian Wood has estimated that somewhere between a fifth and a third of land in Western Europe was handed over to the church in the early Middle Ages.[148] The precise proportion of its holdings fluctuated and shifted hands many times, but this early estimate is comparable to the amount of church land held as late as the eighteenth and nineteenth centuries.[149] A social hierarchy built around imparting Christian knowledge had practical consequences for over a millennium.

Not all elites were created equal, of course; and Bede stood for a reformed elite that renounced many privileges and comforts, working for the good of others.[150] Just as Wearmouth-Jarrow's character and resources stood out among church institutions, Bede stood atop the vast pyramid of expertise he constructed in his writing. He was a font of Latin Christian culture, 'following the footsteps of the fathers' in his time and place.[151] He did not declaim his status as baldly as Jerome had in the late fourth and early fifth centuries. Humility and discretion were among Bede's watchwords. But how else are we to take his words, when he describes himself as among 'the

---

[147] Piketty 2020: 2. The term is not inherently negative in Piketty's construction: every society justifies its inequalities in one way or another. Bede did so.throughout all his work.
[148] Wood 2013.   [149] Piketty 2020: 89–93.
[150] On distinctions among *praedicatores* and *perfecti*, namely, renunciation of property and sex, see O'Brien 2015: 126–27; cf. O'Brien 2017.
[151] See Ray 2006.

strong' who labour for the weak, those otherwise unable to bring themselves and others to saving knowledge? It might be their lack of resources, intelligence, or resolve. But Bede lacked none of these. In his eyes, he was an instrument of Christ, a successor to the apostles and evangelists.[152] So when he saw the church faltering, he wrote, taught, and preached for its welfare.

Bede reserved his sharpest criticism for members of his class who took advantage of their privileged state and failed to fulfil their obligations to pass on saving knowledge. They had not listened properly to the call of Jesus to lead a 'stricter form of devout life'.[153] They included clerical drunkards, too enamoured with the delights of the table to study and avoid heresy. They were bishops, taking in tithes without travelling widely to visit their flock or ordaining enough priests to ensure the availability of preaching and baptism. They were noblemen converted to the ascetic life, yet too proud and too devoted to a classical version of *otium* ('leisure') to take up teaching. They loved the world too much. Here we see Bede and his ideals in a dark mirror.

This is not to claim for Bede or his community a level of sanctity and flawlessness he would disavow.[154] His exegesis and preaching make it clear that his brethren fell short of the ideal in all sorts of ways. Bede sometimes included himself among the weak, the ignorant, and the sinful, and his vision of 'perfection' for himself and his community is less than literal. 'It is evident to everyone that there is no one who can live on earth without corruption and sorrow,' he says. 'But what ... a teacher of souls or some extraordinary purifier of his body cannot do on earth, that the Lord will do in heaven.'[155] Still, in his Northumbria and with consequences for later generations, Bede articulated an ideal of self and society, ordered around many forms of Christian knowledge, and his place was at the top.

---

[152] Thacker 2006: 44–45. I differ from Thacker's interpretation of Bede's comments on 1 Samuel ('with my help') as a directly personal statement of Bede, made in his own voice, but consider it significant when taken within the whole pattern of Bede's thought about the ministry of apostolic teachers.
[153] *Hom.* 2.2, trans. Hurst 1955: 15. See O'Brien 2015: 130–31, 153–54.
[154] See O'Brien 2015: 127–28, with citations to sections of Bede's work.
[155] Bede, *Hom.* 1.24.134–38.

39 | Epilogue

TERESA MORGAN

By tradition, an epilogue sums up or draws together the threads of a composition, often setting it in a wider context (like the well-known chorus which concludes five of Euripides' plays) or pointing to a future beyond the text (like the memorable epilogue of *Harry Potter and the Deathly Hallows*).[1] In some ways, this exercise seems doubtfully suited to an essay collection, which is intentionally diverse and already suggests multiple further lines of inquiry. This collection has explored a dazzling range of Christian appropriations of classical discourses of knowledge – Greek, Roman, biblical, and Near Eastern – exceeding even the spectrum of literary discourses and social practices the editors originally had in mind, to investigate visual imagery, sense perception, tabular organisation, the genderedness of perspective, and the role of multi-dimensional experience in early Christian knowing. In the process, it has demonstrated how varied the process of appropriation can be: sometimes aspirational, occasionally adversarial, often involving a great deal of anxiety and debate.

One question prompted by these essays is how far modes of knowing are also modes of doing and being. When Christians talk about worship, education, socialisation, physical or mental health, church hierarchy, or the rulership of Christ, they are often, if not always, talking about the nature of life in the community of the faithful as much as about ways of thinking. That community, moreover, sees itself as a full-scale society: the people of God, redefined by the Christ event, in every aspect of its present and hoped-for existence.[2] (Ironically, it is partly the thoroughgoing Jewishness of this idea of the *ekklēsia*, at its roots, that makes it receptive to so many aspects of gentile culture.) One of the ways in which this volume points beyond itself is by inviting us to think further about the relationship between how early Christians, or any group, know and how they act.

---

[1] This chorus appears in *Alcestis*, *Andromache*, *Helen*, and *Bacchae*, and in almost the same form in *Medea*: 'Many are the forms of divinities, and the gods accomplish much that is unexpected; what we expect does not happen, and the god finds a way for the unexpected. That is how this matter has turned out.'

[2] Morgan 2020: 169–74.

The collection could have gone on expanding, incorporating topics from etymology to the organisation of urban space, but essay collections are also incomplete, by design as much as by nature. They offer readers not the grand edifice of a single world-view, which we are invited to enter and inhabit, but a field scattered with polished building blocks, which we are invited to arrange as we think most interesting and appropriate. Readers who take up this invitation may add further blocks of their own, and encouraging this is also one of the collection's aims. Since the focus of this volume, moreover, is Christian appropriations of existing discourses, it does not discuss discourses with which early Christians had a limited and often negative relationship (such as mathematics), areas in which Christians arguably created new discourses (such as the validation and anathematisation of beliefs by an institutional hierarchy), or whether Christian discourses sometimes influenced non-Christian discourses (such as, perhaps, in the field of late antique law). These are left to readers, with an implicit invitation to get busy with their own hammer and chisel.

The authors of these essays share a concern, widespread in recent historiography, to show the continuities in historical change, and the deep entanglement of the most innovative cultures with their contexts. There are particular reasons to emphasise the continuity of Christianity with its contexts, since even considering the question of innovation raises the spectres of supersessionism and competitive religious truth claims. Showing the continuity in change, however, also makes us wonder about the change in continuity and invites further thought and the excavation of more building blocks.

Another traditional, but rather different function of the epilogue is to break the 'fourth wall', turning from the internal world of a novel or a play, which has steadfastly ignored its audience even while playing to it, to address it directly – as, for instance, Puck does at the end of *A Midsummer Night's Dream*. In academic writing, the fourth wall is the convention that a topic is presented for its own interest, as objectively and impartially as possible, without either author or audience taking into account whether its subject matter, style of argument, or conclusions have any relevance to the world in which they are living. Like the fourth wall in the theatre, this is an elegant convention as far as it goes but, if it is never broken, what is presented becomes little more than light entertainment or escapism. Just as many playwrights and actors, however, want not only to entertain, but also to move their audiences and make them think, so do many scholars.

In the spirit of breaking the fourth wall here, two questions suggest themselves. The first, which we have already begun to consider, is what kind of discourse of knowledge an essay collection is. The second – given that the discourses explored in this volume are understood by those who write about them in the ancient world as important, even existentially significant – is what kind of claim a collection like this might make for itself in its own world. Do the arguments of this volume matter beyond the proscenium arch of the book boards and dust jacket, as the arguments discussed in it mattered to those who made them, and, if so, how?

There is nothing in the ancient world quite like the modern academic essay collection. Perhaps the nearest equivalent, together with late antique and early medieval collections of mathematical and technical treatises, is the Hippocratic corpus: a group of treatises on different topics by practitioners who are all independent thinkers, but who share some principles and aims of investigation, and see themselves, in some respects, as being in a common tradition. (They distinguish, for instance, medicine from healing by the gods and the care of the body from that of the soul, and share a commitment to observation and to inductive reasoning in diagnosis.) The Hippocratic corpus is less obviously curated than a modern essay collection is, the authors wrote over several centuries, and the treatises are very diverse, but the collection is curated up to a point, and all the contributions share some practical and ethical common ground.

We might see a modern essay collection in similar terms, as an initiative by its editor(s) to create a field of some significance, without claiming to map it definitively or exhaustively, to offer some approaches to it, by means of a deliberately multivocal group of writings which share some principles and aims of investigation, and implicitly to invite further contributions. This broad definition reminds us why essay collections tend to arise from conferences and workshops: they are written expressions of a scholarly recognition that knowledge is temporally, geographically, and culturally contextual, partial, and provisional, together with a scholarly commitment to diversity of opinion, debate, and intellectual evolution. As such, essay collections are among the most significant discourses of knowledge in contemporary humanities (and other) disciplines. In a world which is often all too ready to accept and inhabit the grand edifices of big ideas or monolithic assumptions, academic productions which refuse to see knowledge as complete, objective, or incontestable, and actively demonstrate the opposite, perform much needed acts of intellectual resistance, and make an essential contribution to the way we think.

The editors and contributors of this volume do not make this claim explicitly (and I did not check with them whether they would approve of it). The fourth wall remains in place throughout these chapters. But it is tempting to make some claims on their behalf. A volume like this seeks to serve scholarship by careful, deeply informed, discerning investigation of its material. Through careful scholarship, it challenges readers to think better, both about its own subject matter and more generally. By extension, it informs and challenges wider society. We can go further and argue that a volume like this may aspire to make as significant a contribution to wider society as did any of its subjects.

One of the grand edifices of the contemporary world is Christianity itself, so these chapters, most obviously, make their contribution in a field which is as significant to many people today as it was to the writers and artists they discuss. By resisting, through historical examples, any simplistic view of the relationship between Christianity and the world around it, they show how even groups and traditions which see themselves as unique or highly distinctive are liable to be interwoven with the world around them on every level, from the kind of buildings they construct to the way they experience distress. They remind us that any group or tradition is characterised as often by what it accepts without question, or with minimal adaptation, as what it defines itself against or how it innovates.

The topics of these essays raise a wealth of questions which are as relevant, and as provocative, to twenty-first century societies as they were to the world of the Roman empire. Is power self-justifying, or must it answer to justice, truth, or love? How do we negotiate the relationship between authority and reason? How is what we validate as knowledge or understanding shaped by immersion in particular environments – physical, intellectual, social, or ritual? Do people of different genders (or, we might add, sexualities, colours, or social backgrounds) know differently? Can we borrow other people's ideas without being shaped by their values? When are arguments and controversies not really about what we think they are about – and what, then, are they really about? What is the relationship between physical and psychological or spiritual health? The subjects of these chapters offer their own answers to these, and other equally topical questions. They ask us to consider whether their answers make sense in our world, and, if not, to ponder our own.

One of the most powerful movements of recent years, throughout the Western world including in the academy, has been that which demands justice and equality for people of every colour. The way the language of colour is used in different cultures might be described as a discourse of aesthetics and ethics rather than knowledge, which would put it outside the scope of this volume (though definition comes into it, so it has an epistemological aspect), but these chapters also offer ways to think about it. Early

Christians derived their discourse of light and dark, black and white, like many others, from the wider Mediterranean and Near Eastern worlds, but they adopted it much less critically than they did many others. But what makes a society or culture adopt one idea with little or no modification, while it resists or substantially reworks others that do not seem obviously more or less significant? Historians often assume that emergent societies or cultures, including religious cults, are likely to retain characteristics of their host cultures unless they have a reason not to. In contrast, historians of Christianity, especially if they also have a confessional interest in it, often assume that emergent Christianity is likely to be distinctive unless it has a reason not to be. The chapters in this volume take a non-confessional perspective, but they show how subtle and complicated Christianity's relationship with its host cultures is and suggest that it involves much more than a general tendency to do one thing rather than another except in special circumstances. They prompt us to think again about why early Christians thought about colour as they did, how earlier affects later thinking, and the implications for us now.

In modern Western democracies and their academies, it can be easy to forget how much is at stake in scholarship in general, and the study of history in particular. But we only have to remember the persecution of scholars by totalitarian regimes of the past century, around the globe, to be reminded how threatening scholarship is to tyrannies. Persecution is the measure of scholarship's power to capture hearts, change minds, and inspire action. History, at its simplest, is powerful because it remembers that the past was different from the present, and therefore that things do not have to be the way they are. Modern historiography tends to see processes of historical change as highly complex, and never under the control of any one personal or impersonal force, so the present is only one of many possible outcomes of the past, multiple futures are possible from here, and any number of factors may influence what emerges. Though society and identity are strongly shaped by present circumstances, moreover, they are also shaped by past experience and the imaginability of a different future. Reading the past therefore liberates us from the straitjacket of the material present, and encourages us to ask not only, 'Who are we?' or 'What are we?' but 'Who could we be? What could we be? Who or what should we be?'

In addition, as essay collections make especially clear, studying history heightens our consciousness that there is always more than one interesting topic to discuss, more than one way to define and approach it, and more than one argument to be made about it. Though there may be better or worse approaches – better or worse reasoned, or more or less productive – there is never one indisputably right one. What is more, because we have choices about what we study and how, scholars' own interests, attitudes, and assumptions are always implicated in the topics we choose, the ways we approach them, and the arguments we frame.

When we study any topic in history, therefore, we do so knowing that the topic we choose may make a difference to our view of the past, how the present evolved from it, and where we might go from here. There will be multiple ways to define and approach a topic, and more than one argument to be made about it, and our own attitudes and assumptions will be implicated in every choice we make. The whole process will therefore be highly risky, both because of the uncertainties involved and because what we say may affect how we and others think and act in the future. But we have to make choices and commit to them, because if we do not, we will be stuck in intellectual and practical *aporia*.

These intellectual and ethical risks are not only thought-provoking for historians; they mirror the risks that arise in all kinds of everyday situations, from the personal and individual to the communal and global. Whether we are making a new friend, closing a deal, debating laws, or practising diplomacy, the way we decide what we want to do, how to approach situations or people, what claims or arguments to accept, what conclusions to draw from a situation as we see it, and how to go forward, involve all the ways of looking, analysing, debating, and making decisions which preoccupy historians. A volume like this, and all the disciplines and practices that form it, therefore reflects the discourses of knowledge that shape our lives and that help us reflect on them. It reminds us that, whether or not we share the particular religious commitments of the writers, artists, ritual practitioners, legislators, and others whose productions are discussed here, what we claim to know, and how, and how we enact our knowing are as significant for us, our society, and our future as any discourse of knowledge was to early Christians. It invites us to take that responsibility as seriously in our world as the subjects of these chapters did in theirs.

Bibliography

Acta Proconsularia

von Hartel, W. (ed.) (1868) *Acta proconsularia*. CSEL 3.1. Vienna.

Acts of the Scillitan Martyrs

Musurillo, H. (ed. and trans.) (1872) 'Acts of the Scillitan Martyrs', in *The Acts of the Christian Martyrs*. Oxford: 86–89.

Aëtius

Mansfeld, J., and D. T. Runia (eds.) (2020) *Aëtiana V: An Edition of the Reconstructed Text of the Placita with a Commentary and a Collection of Related Texts*. PhA 153. Leiden.

Alcinous

Dillon, J. (trans.) (1993) *The Handbook of Platonism*. Clarendon Later Ancient Philosophers. Oxford.

Alexander of Tralles

Puschmann, T. (ed.) (1879) *Therapeutica: Original-Text und Übersetzung nebst einer einleitenden Abhandlung. Ein Beitrag zur Geschichte der Medicin*. 2 vols. Vienna.

Ambrose of Milan

Banterle, G., G. Biffi, I. Biffi, and L. Migliavacca (eds.) (1994) *Opere poetiche e frammenti*. Sancti Ambrosii Episcopi Mediolanensis opera 22. Milan.
Faller, O. (ed.) (1962) *De fide ad Gratianum Augustum*. CSEL 78. Vienna.
Faller, O. (ed.) (1964) *De incarnationis dominicae sacramento*. CSEL 79. Vienna: 223–81.
Faller, O., and M. Zelzer (ed.) (1968–90) *Epistulae*. CSEL 82.1-3. Vienna.
Fontaine, J., et al. (ed. and trans.) (1992) *Hymnes*. Patrimoines Christianisme. Paris. Repr. 2008.
Petschenig, M. (ed.) (1919) *Explanatio super psalmos XII*. CSEL 64. Vienna.
Schenkl, K. (ed.) (1896–97) *Hexameron*. CSEL 32.1. Berlin.
Schenkl, K. (ed.) (1902) *In Lucam*. CSEL. 32.4. Berlin.
Tissot, G. (ed. and trans.) (1958) *Expositio euangelii secundum Lucam*. SC 52.1-2. Paris.

Ammonius

Busse, A. (ed.) (1891) *In Porphyrii Isagogen sive V Voces*. CAG 4.3. Berlin.
Busse, A. (ed.) (1895) *In Aristotelis Categorias*. CAG 4.4. Berlin.
Busse, A. (ed.) (1897) *De interpretatione commentarii*. CAG. 4.5. Berlin.
Wallies, M. (ed.) (1899) *In Aristotelis Analyticorum priorum librum I commentarium*. CAG 4.6. Berlin.

Amphilochius of Iconium

Datema, C. (ed.) (1978) *Opera*. CCSG 3. Turnhout.

Analecta Sacra

Pitra, J.-B. (ed.) (1876) *Analecta sacra spicilegio Solesmensi parata*. 8 vols. Paris.

Anastasius of Sinai

Uthemann, K.-H. (ed.) (1985) *Sermones duo in constitutionem hominis secundum imaginem Dei necnon opuscula adversus monotheletas*. CCSG 12. Brepols.

Anonymous Dialogue on Political Science

Mazzucchi, C. (ed.) (1982) *Menae patricii cum Thoma referendario de Scientia politica dialogus.* Scienze filologiche e letteratura 23. Milan.

Anonymous Prolegomena

Westerink, L. G. (ed.) (1962) *Anonymous Prolegomena to Platonic Philosophy.* Platonic Texts and Translations 5. Amsterdam.

Antisthenes of Athens

Kennedy, W. J. (2017) Antisthenes' Literary Fragments: Edited with Introduction, Translation and Commentary. PhD diss., University of Sydney.
Prince, S. (ed.) (2015) *Antisthenes of Athens: Texts, Translations and Commentary.* Ann Arbor.

Apophthegmata Patrum

Guy, J.-C. (ed. and trans.) (1993–2005) *Les apophtegmes des pères: Collections systématique.* 3 vols. SC 387, 474, 498. Paris.

Apostolic Constitutions

Metzger, M. (ed. and trans.) (1985–87) *Les constitutions apostoliques.* 3 vols. SC 320, 329, 336. Paris.

Aristotle

Halliwell, S. (ed. and trans.) (1995) *Poetics.* LCL 199. Cambridge.
Ross, W. D. (ed.) (1955) *Parva naturalia: A Revised Text with Introduction and Commentary.* Oxford.
Ross, W. D. (ed.) (1961) *De anima.* Oxford.
Shields, C. (trans.) (2016) *De anima.* Clarendon Aristotle Series. Oxford.

Asterius of Amasea

Datema, C. (ed.) (1970) *Homilies I–XIV*. Leiden.

Athanasius of Alexandria

Bright, W. (ed.) (1884) *The Orations of St Athanasius against the Arians*, 2nd edn. Oxford.
Hansen, D. U., K. Metzler, and K. Savvidis (eds.) (1996) *Epistula ad episcopos Aegypti et Libyae, in Athanasius Werke*, Vol. I: *Die Dogmatischen Schriften, Part 1*. Berlin: 39–64.
Meijering, E. P. (trans.) (1984) *Contra Gentes: Introduction, Translation, and Commentary*. Philosophia Patrum 7. Leiden.
Metzler, K., D. U. Hansen, and K. Savvidis (eds.) (1998) *Oratio I contra arianos, in Athanasius: Werke*, Vol. I: *Die Dogmatischen Schriften, Part 1, lfg.* 2. Berlin: 109–75.
Migne, J.-P. (ed.) (1857) *De sabbatis et circumcisione*. PG 28. Paris.
Optiz, H.-G. (ed.) (1935) *De Synodis Arimini in Italia et Seleuciae in Isauria, in Athanasius Werke*, Vol. II.1 Berlin: 231–78.
Radde-Gallwitz, A. (trans.) (2017) 'On the Synods at Ariminum and Seleucia', in *The Cambridge Edition of Early Christian Writings*, Vol. I: *God*. Cambridge: 134–49.
Thomson, R. (ed. and trans.) (1971) *Contra gentes and De incarnatione*. OECT. Oxford.

Athenagoras of Athens

Marcovich, M. (ed.) (1990) *Legatio pro Christianis*. PTS 31. Berlin.

Augustine of Hippo

Agaësse, P. (ed. and trans.) (1994) *In epistulam Johannis ad Parthos tractatus decem*, 4th edn. SC 75. Paris.
Agaësse, P., and A. Solignac (eds. and trans.) (1972) *La Genèse au sens littéral en douze livres*. 2 vols. BAug 48–49. Paris.
Chadwick, H. (trans.) (1991) *Confessions: A New Translation*. Oxford.
Daur, K.-D. (ed.) (1985) *Contra aduersarium legis et prophetarum*. CCSL 49. Turnhout.
Deferrari, R. J. (trans.) (1968) *The Teacher, The Free Choice of the Will, Grace and Free Will*. FC 59. Washington.

Di Giovanni, A., A. Penna, and L. Carrozzi (eds.) (1988) *De Genesi adversus Manichaeos*. NBA 9.1. Rome.
Fuhrer, T., and S. Adam (eds.) (2017) *Contra academicos, De beata vita, De ordine*. BSGRT. Berlin.
Goldbacher, A. (ed.) (1895–1923) *Epistulae*. 5 vols. CSEL 34.1–2; 44; 57–58. Vienna.
Green, R. P. (ed.) (1996) *De doctrina christiana*. OECT. Oxford.
Hill, E. (trans.) (1994) *Sermons*. WSA 3.8. Hyde Park.
Migne, J.-P. (ed.) (1845) *Sermones*. PL 38. Paris.
Mutzenbecher, A. (ed.) (1980) *Quaestiones evangeliorum*. CCSL 44B. Turnhout.
Petschenig, M. (ed.) (1963) *Traités anti-Donatistes*. BAug 28. Turnhout: 150–91.
Schlapbach, K. (ed.) (2003) *Contra academicos (vel De academicis), Buch I: Einleitung und Kommentar*. PTS 58. Berlin.
Schopp, L. (trans.) (1948) *The Happy Life; Answer to Sceptics; Divine Providence and the Problem of Evil, Soliloquies*. FC 5. Washington.
Tarulli, V., P. de Luis, and F. Monteverde (eds.) (1996) *De consensu euangelistarum*. NBA 10.1. Rome.
Taylor, J. H. (trans.) (1982) *The Literal Meaning of Genesis*. 2 vols. ACW 42. New York.
Teske, R. (trans.) (1997) *The Predestination of the Saints*. WSA 1.26. Hyde Park.
Teske, R. (trans.) (2006) *The Catholic Way of Life and the Manichean Way of Life*. WSA 1.19. Hyde Park.
Vander Plaetse, R., and C. Beukers (eds.) (1969) *De haeresibus ad Quodvultdeum*. CCSL 46. Turnhout.
Verheijen, L. (ed.) (1981) *Confessionum libri tredecim*. CCSL 27. Turnhout.
Walsh, P. G. (trans.) (2009) *The City of God Book V*. Aris and Phillips Classical Texts. Liverpool.
Willems, R. (ed.) (1954) *In Johannis Evangelium tractatus*. CCSL 36. Turnhout.
Zycha, J. (ed.) (1894) *De Genesi ad litteram*. CSEL 28.1. Paris.

Ausonius

Green, R. P. (ed.) (1999) *Opera*. OCT. Oxford.

Bardaisan

Drijvers, H. J. W. (ed. and trans.) (1965) *The Book of the Laws of Countries: Dialogue on Fate of Bardaisan of Edessa*. Assen.
Poirier, P.-H., and É. Crégheur (2020) *Le livre des lois des pays: un traité syriaque sur le destin de l' "école" de Bardesane*. Bibliothèque de l'Orient chrétien 6. Paris.

Basil and Eustathius

Amand de Mendieta, E., and S. Y. Rudberg (eds.) (1958) *Ancienne version latine des neuf homélies sur l'Hexaéméron de Basile de Césarée*. TU 66. Berlin.

Basil of Caesarea

Courtonne, Y. (ed. and trans.) (2003) *Correspondance,* Vol. II: *Lettres CI–CCXVIII*, 2nd edn. Paris.
Deferrari, R. (ed. and trans.) (1928) *Epistulae*. LCL 215. Cambridge.
Giet, S. (ed. and trans.) (1968) *Homilia VIII in Hexaemeron*, 2nd edn. SC 26bis. Paris.
Holman, S. R., and M. DelCogliano (trans.) (2013) *On Fasting and Feasts*. Popular Patristics. Crestwood.
Migne, J.-P. (ed.) (1857) *De baptismo libri duo*. PG 31. Paris: 1513–628.
Migne, J.-P. (ed.) (1857) *In Gordium*. PG 31. Paris: 491.
Radde-Gallwitz, A. (trans.) (2017) 'Canonical Letters', in *The Cambridge Edition of Early Christian Writings,* Vol. II: *Practice*, ed. E. Muehlberger. Cambridge: 143–67.
Rudberg, S. (ed.) (1962) *L'homélie de Basile de Césarée sur le mot 'Observe-toi toi-même': Édition critique du texte grec et étude sur la tradition manuscrite*. Studia Graeca Stockholmensia 2. Stockholm.
Way, A. C. (trans.) (1963) *Exegetic Homilies*. FC 46. Washington.

Bede

Colgrave, B. (ed. and trans.) (1940) *Two Lives of St Cuthbert*. Cambridge.
Colgrave, B., and R. A. B. Mynors (eds. and trans.) (1969) *Bede's Ecclesiastical History of the English People*. Oxford Medieval Texts. Oxford.
Conolly, S., and J. O'Reilly (trans.) (1995) *On the Temple*. TTH 21. Liverpool.
De Maeyer, N. (ed.) (2022) *Collectio Bedae presbyteri ex opusculis sancti Augustini in Epistulas Pauli Apostoli*. 2 vols. CCSL 121B, 121C. Turnhout.
Dubois, J., and G. Remaud (1976) *Édition pratique des martyrologes de Bède, de l'anonyme lyonnais et de Florus*. Paris.
Grocock, C., and I. N. Wood (2013) *Abbots of Wearmouth and Jarrow*. Oxford Medieval Texts. Oxford.
Gryson, R. (ed.) (2001) *Expositio Apocalypseos*. CCSL 121A. Turnhout.
Holder, A. G. (trans.) (1994) *On the Tabernacle*. TTH 18. Liverpool.
Hurst, D. (ed.) (1955) *Homeliae euangelii*. CCSL 122. Turnhout.

Hurst, D. (ed.) (1960) *In Lucae euangelium expositio; In Marci euangelium expositio*. CCSL 120 Turnhout.
Hurst, D. (ed.) (1962) *In primam partem Samuhelis*. CCSL 119. Turnhout.
Hurst, D. (ed.) (1969) *De tabernaculo; De templo*. CCSL 119A. Turnhout.
Hurst, D. (ed.) (1983a) *In epistolas VII catholicas*. CCSL 121. Turnhout.
Hurst, D. (ed.) (1983b) *In Tobiam; In Proverbia; In Cantica canticorum; In Habacuc*. CCSL 119B. Turnhout.
Hurst, D. (trans.) (1985) *Commentary on the Seven Catholic Epistles*. CSS 82. Kalamazoo.
Hurst, D. (trans.) (1999) *Excerpts from the Works of Saint Augustine on the Letters of the Blessed Apostle*. CSS 183. Kalamazoo.
Jones, C. W. (ed.) (1967) *Libri quattuor in principium Genesis usque ad natiuitatem et eiectionem Ismahelis adnotationum*. CCSL 118A. Turnhout.
Jones, C. W. (ed.) (1975) *De natura rerum*. CCSL 123A. Turnhout.
Jones, C. W. (ed.) (1977) *De temporibus; De temporum ratione*. CCSL 123B. Turnhout.
Jones, C. W. (ed.) (1980) *Epistola ad Pleguinam*. CCSL 123C. Turnhout.
Kendall, C. (2008) *On Genesis*. TTH 48. Liverpool.
Kendall, C., and F. Wallis (2010) *'On the Nature of Things' and 'On Times'*. TTH 56. Liverpool.
Laistner, M. L. W. (ed.) (1983) *Expositio Actuum Apostolorum*. CCSL 121. Turnhout.
Lifshitz, F. (trans.) (2001) 'Martyrologium', in *Medieval Hagiography: An Anthology*, ed. T. Head. New York: 179–97.
Martin, L. T. (trans.) (1989) *Commentary on the Acts of the Apostles*. CSS 117. Kalamazoo.
Martin, L. T., and D. Hurst (trans.) (1989–91) *Homilies on the Gospels*. 2 vols. CSS 110 and 111. Kalamazoo.
McClure, J., and R. Collins (trans.) (1999) *The Ecclesiastical History of the English People; The Greater Chronicle; Bede's Letter to Egbert*. Oxford World Classics. Oxford.
Wallis, F. (trans.) (1999) *The Reckoning of Time*. TTH 29. Liverpool.
Wallis, F. (trans.) (2013) *Commentary on Revelation*. TTH 58. Liverpool.

Boethius

Brandt, S. (ed.) (1906) *In Isagogen Porphyrii commenta*. CSEL 48. Vienna.
Friedlein, G. (ed.) (1867) *De institutione arithmetica libri duo, De institutione musica libri quinque. Accedit geometria quae fertur Boetii*. BSGRT. Leipzig.
Guillaumin, J.-Y. (ed.) (1995) *Institution arithmétique*. Budé. Paris.
Magee, J. (ed.) (1998) *De divisione liber*. PhA 77. Leiden.

Meiser, C. (ed.) (1877–80) *Commentarii in librum Aristotelis* ΠΕΡΙ ΕΡΜΗΝΕΙΑΣ *partes prior et posterior.* BSGRT. Leipzig.

Migne, J.-P. (ed.) (1891) *In Categorias Aristotelis libri quatuor, In Topica Ciceronis commentariorum libri sex.* PL 64. Paris.

Moreschini, C. (ed.) (2005) *De consolatione philosophiae; Opuscula theologica,* 2nd edn. BSGRT. Munich.

Nikitas, D. Z. (1990) *Boethius' 'De topicis differentiis' und die byzantinische Rezeption dieses Werkes.* Corpus philosophorum medii aevi 5. Paris.

Thörnqvist, C. T. (ed.) (2008) *De syllogismo categorico, Introductio ad syllogismos categoricos.* Studia Graeca et Latina Gothoburgensia 68–69. Gothenburg.

Cassiodorus

Adriaen, M. (ed.) (1958) *Expositio psalmorum.* CCSL 97–98. Turnhout.

Fridh, A. J. (ed.) (1973) *Variarum libri XII.* CCSL 96. Turnhout.

Halporn, J. W. (trans.) (2004) *Institutions of Divine and Secular Learning and On the Soul.* TTH 42. Liverpool.

Mynors, R. A. B. (ed.) (1937) *Institutiones.* Oxford.

Cicero

Kumaniecki, K. (ed.) (1995) *De oratore.* BSGRT. Leipzig.

Sutton, E. W., and H. Rackham (eds. and trans.) (1942) *On the Orator: Books 1–2.* LCL 348. Cambridge.

Codex Theodosianus

Mommsen, T., and P. M. Meyer (eds.) (1905) *Theodosiani libri XVI cum Constitutionibus Sirmondianis et leges novellae ad Theodosianum pertinentes.* 2 vols. Berlin.

Council of Constantinople

Mansi, J. D. (ed.) (1759) *Sacrorum conciliorum nova et amplissima collectio.* Florence, Venice, and Paris.

Council of Nicaea

DelCogliano, M. (trans.) (2017) 'Creed of the Council of Nicaea', in *The Cambridge Edition of Early Christian Writings*, Vol. I: *God*, ed. A. Radde-Gallwitz. Cambridge: 114–15.

Dossetti, G. (ed.) (1967) *Il simbolo di Nicea e di Constantinopoli: Edizione critica*. Testi e ricerche di scienze religiose Bologna 2. Rome.

Cyprian of Carthage

Bévenot, M. (trans.) (1957) *The Lapsed; The Unity of the Catholic Church*. ACW 25. Mahwah.

Bévenot, M. (ed.) (1972) *De lapsis*. CCSL 3. Turnhout.

Clarke, G. (trans.) (1984–89) *The Letters of St Cyprian of Carthage*. 4 vols. ACW 43–44, 46–47. Mahwah.

Diercks, G. F. (ed.) (1994) *Epistulae 1–57*. CCSL 3B. Turnhout.

Diercks, G. F. (ed.) (1996) *Epistulae 58–81*. CCSL 3C. Turnhout.

Molager, J. (ed. and trans.) (1982) *À Donat et La vertu de patience*. SC 291. Paris.

Moreschini, C. (ed.) (1976) *De dominica oratione*. CCSL 3A. Turnhout.

Réveillaud, M. (ed. and trans.) (1964) *L'oraison dominicale*. Études d'histoire et de philosophie religieuses 58. Paris.

Simonetti, M. (ed.) (1976) *Ad Demetrianum*. CCSL 3A. Turnhout.

Simonetti, M. (ed.) (1976) *Ad Donatum*. CCSL 3A. Turnhout.

Simonetti, M. (ed.) (1976) *De opere et eleemosynis*. CCSL 3A. Turnhout.

Weber, R. (ed.) (1972) *Ad Fortunatum; Ad Quirinum*. CCSL 3. Turnhout.

Cyril of Alexandria

Crawford, M. (trans.) (2022) 'Cyril of Alexandria: *Third Letter to Nestorius*', in *The Cambridge Edition of Early Christian Writings*, Vol. III: *Christ: Through the Nestorian Controversy*, ed. M. DelCogliano. Cambridge: 623–36.

Riedweg, C., and W. Kinzig (eds.) (2015) *Kyrill von Alexandrien I: Gegen Julian*. Part I, Books 1–5. GCS NF 20. Berlin.

Schwartz, E. (ed.) (1927) *Epistula tertia ad Nestorium in Concilium universale Ephesenum*. ACO 1.1.1. Berlin: 33–42.

Damascius

Ahbel-Rappe, S. (trans.) (2010) *Problems and Solutions Concerning First Principles*. AAR Religion in Translation. New York.

Westerink, L. G. (ed.) and J. Combès (trans.) (1987) *Traité des premiers principes*. 3 vols. Budé. Paris.

David

Busse, A. (ed.) (1904) *Prolegomena et in Porphyrii Isagogen commentarium*. CAG 18.2. Berlin.
Muradyan, G. (ed. and trans.) (2015) *Commentary on Porphyry's Isagoge*. PhA 137. Leiden.

De mirabilibus sacrae Scripturae

MacGinty, G. (1971) 'The treatise *De mirabilibus sacrae Scripturae*: Critical Edition, with Introduction, English Translation of the Long Recension and Some Notes'. 2 vols. PhD diss., National University of Ireland.

De ordine creaturarum

Díaz y Díaz, Manuel, C. (ed.) (1972) *Liber de ordine creaturarum. Un anónimo irlandés del siglo VII*. Monografías de la Universidad de Santiago de Compostela 10. Santiago de Compostela.

Didymus of Alexandria

Migne, J.-P. (1845) *Liber de Spiritu Sancto secundum translationem quam fecit Hieronymus*. PL 23. Paris: 109–62.

Diogenes Laertius

Hicks, R. D. (ed. and trans.) (1925) *Lives of Eminent Philosophers*. 2 vols. LCL 184–85. Cambridge.

Dorotheus

Regnault, L., and J. de Préville (ed. and trans.) (2001) *Oeuvres spirituelles.* SC 92bis. Paris.

Doxographers

Diels, H. (ed.) (1879) *Doxographi graeci: Collegit recensuit prolegomenis indicibusque instruxit*. Berlin.

Elias

Busse, A. (ed.) (1900) *In Porphyrii Isagogen et Aristotelis Categorias Commentaria*. CAG 18.1. Berlin.

Ephrem of Nisibis

Assemani, J. S. (ed.) (1732) *Opera omnia quae exstant Graece, Syriace, Latine, in sex tomos distribute*. 6 vols. Rome.
Beck, E. (1951) 'Ephraems Hymnen über das Paradies: Übersetzung und Kommentar', *SA* 26: xii–174.
Beck, E. (ed.) (1962) *Hymnen de Virginitate*. CSCO 223. Louvain.
Beck, E. (ed.) (1966) *Sermo de Domino nostro*. CSCO 270. Louvain.
Beck, E. (ed.) (1970a) *Sermones I*. 2 vols. CSCO 305–6. Louvain.
Beck, E. (ed.) (1970b) *Sermones II*. CSCO 311. Louvain.
Beck, E. (ed.) (1972a) *Hymnen auf Abraham Kidunaya und Julianos Saba*. 2 vols. CSCO 322–23. Louvain.
Beck, E. (ed.) (1972b) *Sermones III*. 2 vols. CSCO 320–21. Louvain.
Beck, E. (ed.) (1973) *Sermones IV*. 2 vols. CSCO 334–35. Louvain.
Beck, E. (ed.) (1979) *Sermones in Hebdomadam Sanctam*. CSCO 413. Louvain.
Lamy, T. J. (ed.) (1882) *Hymni et sermones quos e codicibus Londinensibus, Parisiensibus et Oxoniensibus descriptos edidit, Latinitate donavit, variis lectionibus instruxit, notis et prolegomenis illustravit*. 4 vols. Mechliniae.
Ruani, F. (ed. and trans.) (2018) *Hymnes contre les hérésies*. Bibliothèque de l'Orient chrétien 4. Paris.

Epictetus

Schenkl, H. (ed.) (1898) *Dissertationes ab Arriano digestae*. BSGRT. Leipzig.

Epiphanius of Salamis

Holl, K. (ed.) (1915) *Ancoratus*. GCS 25. Leipzig.

Kim, Y. R. (trans.) (2014) *Epiphanius: Ancoratus*. FC 128. Washington.

Eusebius of Caesarea

Cameron, A., and S. Hall (trans.) (1999) *Life of Constantine*. Oxford.
Gifford, E. H. (ed. and trans.) (1903) *Evangelicae praeparationis libri XV*. Oxford.
Klostermann, E. (ed.) (1904) *Das Onomastikon der biblischen Ortsnamen*. GCS. Eusebius Werke 11.1. Leipzig.
McGiffert, A. C. (trans.) (1995) *Eusebius: Church History from AD 1–324*. In *The Church History of Eusebius: Translated with Prolegomena and Notes*. NPNF², Vol. I. Peabody, MA.
Mras, K. (ed.) (1982–83) *Eusebius Werke 8: Praeparatio Evangelica*, 2nd edn. 2 vols. GCS 43/1–43/2. Berlin.
Opitz, H.-G. (ed.) (1935) 'Eusebius' Letter to His Diocese', in *Athanasius Werke*, Vol. II.1: *De decretis*. Berlin.
Winkelmann, F. (ed.) (1975) *Eusebius Werke 1.1: Über das Leben des Kaisers Konstantins*. GCS. Eusebius Werke 1.1. Berlin.

Evagrius of Pontus

Brakke, D. (trans.) (2009) *Talking Back: A Monastic Handbook for Combating Demons*. CSS 229. Collegeville.
Fogielman, C.-A. (ed.) (2017) *À Euloge: Les vices opposés aux vertus*. SC 591. Paris.
Frankenberg, W. (ed.) (1912) *Euagrius Ponticus: Antirrhetikos*. AKGWG.PHK N.F. 13.2. Berlin.
Géhin, P., C. Guillaumont, and A. Guillaumont (eds.) (1998) *Sur les pensées*. SC 438. Paris.
Guillaumont, C., and A. Guillaumont (eds.) (1971) *Traité pratique ou Le moine*. 2 vols. SC 170–71. Paris.
Migne, J.-P. (ed.) (1865) *De octo spiritibus malorum*. PG 79. Paris: 1146–66.
Sinkewicz, R. (trans.) (2006) 'On the Eight Thoughts', in *Evagrius of Pontus: The Greek Ascetic Corpus*. OECS: 66–90

Galen of Pergamum

de Boer, W. (ed.) (1937) *De propriorum animi cuiuslibet affectuum dignotione et curatione*. CMG 5.4.1.1. Leipzig and Berlin.
Helmreich, G. (ed.) (1904) *De temperamentis libri iii*. BSGRT. Leipzig.
Koch, K. (ed.) (1923) *De sanitate tuende*. CMG 5.4.2. Leipzig.

Kühn, C. G. (ed.) (1821–25) *Opera omnia.* 10 vols. Leipzig. Repr. Hildesheim.
Nutton, V. (ed.) (1979) *De praecognitione.* CMG 5.8.1. Berlin.

George of Pisidia

Gonnelli, F. (ed.) (1991) 'Il *De vita humana* di Georgio Pisida', *Bollettino dei Classici* 3.12: 118–38.
Gonnelli, F. (ed. and trans.) (1998) *Esamerone.* Pisa.
Pertusi, A. (ed. and trans.) (1959) *Poemi, I. Panegirici Epici.* Studia patristica et byzantina 7. Ettal.
Tartaglia, L. (ed.) (1997) *Carmi di Giorgio di Pisidia.* Classici greci. Turin.

Grammarians

Keil, H. (ed.) (1857–80) *Grammatici latini.* 8 vols. Repr. Hildesheim, 1961.

Gregory of Nazianzen

Mossay, J., and G. Lafontaine (eds.) (1981) *In laudem S. Cypriani.* SC 284. Paris: 40–85.

Gregory of Nyssa

Daniélou, J., SJ (ed. and trans.) (1968) *La vie de Moïse ou traité de la perfection en matière de vertu*, 3rd edn. SC 1. Paris.
Heil, G., J. P. Cavarnos, and O. Lendle (eds.) (1990) *Sermones, pars II.* GNO 10.1. Leiden.
Malherbe, A. J., and E. Ferguson (trans.) (1978) *The Life of Moses: Translation, Introduction and Notes.* CSS 31. New York.
Maraval, P. (ed. and trans.) (1990) *Grégoire de Nysse: Lettres.* SC 363. Paris.
Muhlenberg, E. (ed.) (2008) *Epistula Canonica ad Letoium* in *Epistula Canonica.* GNO 3.5. Leiden.
Musurillo, H. (ed.) (1964) *De vita Moysis.* GNO 7.1. Leiden.
Radde-Gallwitz, A. (trans.) (2017) 'Epistula Canonical ad Letoium', in *The Cambridge Edition of Early Christian Writings*, Vol. II: *Practice*, ed. E. Muehlberger. Cambridge: 168–77.
Roth, C. P. (trans.) (2002) *The Soul and the Resurrection.* Crestwood.
Spira, A. (ed.) (2014) *De anima et resurrection.* GNO 3.3 Leiden.

Gregory the Great

Adriaen, M. (ed.) (1971) *Homiliae in Hiezechielem prophetam*. CCSL 142. Turnhout.
Adriaen, M. (ed.) (1979–85) *Moralia in Iob*. 3 vols. CCSL 143, 143A, and 143B. Turnhout.
de Vogüé, A. (ed.), and P. Antin (trans.) (1978–80) *Dialogues*. 3 vols. SC 251, 260, 265. Paris.
DelCogliano, M. (trans.) (2012) *On Song of Songs*. CSS 244. Collegeville.
Étaix, R. (ed.) *Homiliae in Evangelia*. CCSL 141. Turnhout.
Étaix, R. (ed.), C. Morel, and B. Judic (trans.) (2005–8) *Homélies sur l'Évangile: Texte latin, introduction, traduction et notes*. 2 vols. SC 485, 522. Paris.
Hurst, D. (trans.) (1990) *Forty Gospel Homilies*. CSS 123. Kalamazoo.
Kerns, B. (trans.) (2014–19) *Moral Reflections in the Book of Job*. 5 vols. CSS 256–60. Collegeville.
Martyn, J. R. C. (trans.) (2004) *The Letters of Gregory the Great*. 3 vols. Mediaeval Sources in Translation 40. Toronto.
Norberg, D. (ed.) (1982) *Epistularum libri I–XIV*. 2 vols. CCSL 140 and 140A. Turnhout.
Rommel, F. (ed.), and C. Morel (trans.) (1992) *Règle Pastorale*. 2 vols. SC 381–82. Paris.
Tomkinson, T. (trans.) (2008) *Homilies on the Book of the Prophet Ezekiel*, 2nd edn. Etna.
Verbraken, P. (ed.) (1963) *Expositio in Canticum Canticorum*. CCSL 144. Turnhout.

Hellenistic Philosophers

Long, A. A., and D. N. Sedley (ed. and trans.) (1987) *The Hellenistic Philosophers*. 2 vols. Cambridge.

Hermias

Hanson, R. P. C., and D. Joussot (eds.) (1993) *Satire des philosophes païens*. SC 388. Paris.

Hesychius

Hansen, P. A. (ed.) (2005) *Lexicon*, Vol. III: Π–Σ. SGLG 11.3. Berlin.

Hilary of Poitiers

Feder, A. (ed.) (1916) *Hymni III e codice Aretino*. CSEL 65. Vienna: 209–16.

Migne, J.-P. (ed.) (1844) *Commentarius in evangelium Matthaei*. PL 9. Paris.
Smulders, P. (ed.) (1979–80) *De trinitate*. 2 vols. CCSL 62, 62A. Turnhout.

Hippolytus

Stewart-Sykes, A. (ed. and trans.) (2001) *On the Apostolic Tradition*. Popular Patristics. Crestwood.

Iamblichus

Clarke, E. C., J. M. Dillon, and J. P. Hershbell (ed. and trans.) (2003) *On the Mysteries*. WGRW 4. Atlanta.
des Places, É. (ed.) (1966) *Les mystères d'Égypte*. Budé. Paris.
Deubner, L., and U. Klein (eds.) (1975) *De vita Pythagorica liber*. BSGRT. Leipzig.

Inscriptions

Breytenbach, C., and Julien M. Ogereau (eds.) (2019) *Inscriptiones Christianae Graecae*. Edition Topoi. DOI: 10.17171/1-8.

Irenaeus of Lyon

Harvey, W. (ed.) (1857) *Libros Quinque Adversus Haereses*. Cambridge.
Rousseau, A. (ed. and trans.) (1965–82) *Contre les hérésies*. SC 100.1–2, 152–53, 210–11, 263–64, 293–94. Paris.
Rousseau, A. (ed. and trans.) (1995) *Démonstration de la prédication apostolique*. SC 406. Paris.
Smith, J. (trans.) (1952) *Proof of the Apostolic Preaching*. London.
Ter-Mekerttschian, K., and S. G. Wilson (ed.) (1919) 'S. Irenaeus, Εἰς ἐπίδειξιν τοῦ ἀποστολικοῦ κηρύγματος, The Proof of the Apostolic Preaching with Seven Fragments, Armenian version', PO 12: 655–746. Turnhout.

Irish Reference Bible (*Pauca problesmata de enigmatis ex tomis canonicis*)

MacGinty, G. (ed.) (2000) *Pauca problesmata de enigmatis ex tomis canonicis*. CCCM 173. Turnhout.

Isaac of Antioch

Bedjan, P. (ed.) (1903) *Homiliae*. Paris.

Isidore of Seville

Fontaine, J. (ed.) (1960) *Traité de la nature*. Bibliothèque de l'école des hautes études hispaniques 28. Bordeaux.
Kendall, C., and F. Wallis (trans.) (2016) *On the Nature of Things*. TTH 66. Liverpool.
Lindsay, W. M. (ed.) (1911) *Etymologiarum sive originum libri xx*. OCT. Oxford.

Jacob of Serugh

Amar, J. (ed. and trans.) (1995) *A Metrical Homily on Holy Mar Ephrem by Mar Jacob of Sarug*. PO 47.1, no. 209. Turnhout.
Bedjan, P. (ed.) (1905) *Homiliae selectae*. 5 vols. Leipzig.

Jerome of Stridon

Herding, W. (ed.) (1879) *De viris inlustribus liber*. Leipzig.
Hurst, D., and M. Adriaen (eds.) (1969) *Commentariorum in Matheum libri IV*. CCSL 77. Turnhout.
Migne, J.-P. (ed.) (1845) *Adversus Iovianianum*. PL 23. Paris: 205–338A.
Migne, J.-P. (ed.) (1845) *De viris illustribus*. PL 23. Paris.
Migne, J.-P. (ed.) (1845) *Homiliae II Origenis in Canticum canticorum Latine redditae*. PL 23. Paris: 1117–44.
Moreschini, C. (ed.) (1990) *Adversus Pelagianos*. CCSL 80. Turnhout.
Raspanti, G. (ed.) (2006) *Commentarii in epistulam Pauli apostoli ad Galatas*. CCSL 77A. Turnhout.

John Cassian

Guy, J.-C. (ed. and trans.) (1965) *Institutiones coenobiorum*. SC 109. Paris.
Petschenig, M. (ed.) (1886) *Opera*. 2 vols. CSEL 13 (*Conlationes*); 17 (*Institutiones*). Vienna.
Pichery, E. (ed. and trans.) (1955–59) *Conférences*. 3 vols. SC 42, 54, 65. Paris.

Ramsey, B. (trans.) (1997) *The Conferences*. ACW 57. New York.
Ramsey, B. (trans.) (2000) *The Institutes*. ACW 58. New York.

John Chrysostom

Brottier, L. (ed.) (1998) *Sermons sur la Génèse*. SC 433. Paris.
Hill, R. C. (trans.) (2004) *Eight Sermons on the Book of Genesis*. Boston.

John Lydus

Bandy, A. C. (ed. and trans.) (1983) *On Powers or The Magistracies of the Roman State*. Memoirs of the American Philosophical Society 149. Philadelphia.

John of Damascus

Brennecke, H. C., and B. Kotter (ed.) (1969) *Institutio elementaris: Capita philosophica (dialectica)*. PTS 7. Berlin.

Julius Africanus

Wallraff, M., C. Scardino, L. Mecella, C. Guignard, and W. Adler (eds.) (2012) *Julius Africanus: Cesti: The Extant Fragments*. GCS 18. Berlin.
Wallraff, M., U. Roberto, K. Pinggéra, and W. Adler (eds.) (2007) *Julius Africanus: Chronographiae: The Extant Fragments*. GCS 15. Berlin.

Julius Pollux

Bethe, E. (ed.) (1900–31) *Onomasticon*. 2 vols. Lexicographi graeci 9.1–2. Leipzig.

Justin of Rome

Bobichon, P. (ed.) (2003) *Dialogue avec Tryphon*. 2 vols. Paradosis 47.1–2. Fribourg.
Minns, D., and P. Parvis (eds. and trans.) (2009) *Justin, Philosopher and Martyr: Apologies*. OECT. Oxford.

Justinian

Krüger, P. (ed.) (1877) *Codex Iustinianus*. Berlin.
Krüger, P., and T. Mommsen (eds.) (1928) *Corpus Iuris Civilis: Institutiones, Digesta*. Berlin.
Miller, D., and P. Sarris (2018) *The Novels of Justinian: A Complete Annotated English Translation*. Cambridge.
Schöll, R., and G. Kroll (eds.) (1928) *Novellae*, 6th edn. Berlin.

Juvencus

Marold, K. (ed.) (1886) *Evangeliorum libri quattuor*. Leipzig.
McGill, S. (trans.) (2016) *Juvencus' Four Books of the Gospels*. London.

Lactantius

Lactantius (1890) *Divinae institutiones*, ed. Samuel Brandt. CSEL 19. Vienna.

Leontius of Byzantium

Daley, B. (ed. and trans.) (2017) 'Contra Nestorianos et Eutychianos', in *Leontius of Byzantium: Complete Works*. OECT. Oxford.
Datema, C., and P. Allen (eds.) (1987) *Homiliae*. CCSG 17. Turnhout.
Datema, C., and P. Allen (trans.) (1991) *Fourteen Homilies*. Byzantina australiensia 9. Brisbane.

Leontius of Jerusalem

Waegeman, M. (1982) 'He traktat de sectis (Ps. Leontius Byzantinus)'. PhD diss., University of Ghent.
Gray, P. T. R. (ed. and trans.) (2006) *Against the Monophysites: Testimonies of the Saints and Aporiae*. OECT. Oxford.

Life of Ephrem of Nisibis

Amar, J. (ed. and trans.) (2011) *The Syriac Vita Tradition of Ephrem the Syrian*. 2 vols. CSCO 629–30. Louvain.

Life of Maximus Confessor

Brock, S. (1973) 'An Early Syriac Life of Maximus the Confessor', *AnBoll* 91: 299–364.

Neil, B., and P. Allen (eds. and trans.) (2003) *Life of Maximus the Confessor: Recension 3*. Strathfield.

Lucian of Samosata

MacLeod, M. D. (ed.) (1980) *Opera III*. Oxford Classical Texts. Oxford.

Marcus Aurelius

Farquharson, A. S. L. (ed.) (1944) *The Meditations of the Emperor Marcus Aurelius*, Vol. I. Oxford.

Maximus Confessor

Allen, P., and B. Neil (eds. and trans.) (2002) *Maximus the Confessor and His Companions: Documents from Exile*. OECT. Oxford.

Ceresa-Gastaldo, A. (ed.) (1963) *Capitoli sulla carità*. Verba seniorum 3. Rome.

Musonius Rufus

Lutz, C. E. (ed.) (1947) 'Musonius Rufus: "The Roman Socrates"', *Yale Classical Studies* 10: 3–147.

Nemesius of Emesa

Morani, M. (ed.) (1987) *De natura hominis*. BSGRT. Leipzig.

Sharples, R. W., and P. J. van der Eijk (trans.) (2008) *On the Nature of Man*. TTH 49. Liverpool.

Nichomachus

Hoche, R. (ed.) (1866) *Introductionis arithmeticae libri II*. Leipzig.

Notitia Dignitatum

Fairley, W. (ed. and trans.) (1899) '*Notitia Dignitatum* or Register of Dignitaries', in *Translations and Reprints from Original Sources of European History*, vol. 6.4. Philadelphia.

Ireland, R. (ed.) (1999) *Notitia dignitatum*. BSGRT. Leipzig.

Olympiodorus

Busse, A. (ed.) (1902) *Prolegomena et in Categorias commentarium*. CAG 12.1. Berlin.

Griffin, M. (ed. and trans.) (2015) *Life of Plato and on Plato First Alcibiades 1–9*. London.

Oribasius

Raeder, J. (ed.) (1926) *Libri ad Eunapium*. CMG 6.3. Leipzig.

Origen of Alexandria

Borret, M. (ed. and trans.) (1967–69) *Contre Celse*. 5 vols. SC 132, 136, 147, 150, 227. Paris.

Borret, M., L. Brésard, and H. Crouzel (eds. and trans.) (1991) *Commentaire sur le Cantique des Cantiques*. SC 205, 375. Paris.

Butterworth, G. W. (trans.) (1973) *On First Principles*. Gloucester.

Chadwick, H. (trans.) (1953) *Contra Celsum*. Cambridge.

Crouzel, H., F. Fournier, and P. Périchon (eds. and trans.) (1962) *Homélies sur s. Luc*. SC 87. Paris.

Field, F. (ed.) (1875) *Hexaplorum quae supersunt*. Oxford.

Fürst, A., and H. Strutwolf (eds. and trans.) (2016) *Der Kommentar zum Hohelied*. OW 9.1. Berlin.

Lawson, R. P. (trans.) (1957) *The Song of Songs: Commentary and Homilies*. ACW 26. New York.
Lewis, G. (trans.) (1911) *The Philocalia of Origen*. Edinburgh.
Nautin, P. (ed. and trans.) (1976) *Homélies sur Jérémie, t. 1, Homélies I–XI*. SC 232. Paris.
Scheck, T. P. (trans.) (2009) *Homilies on Numbers*. ACT. Downers Grove.
Trigg, J. W. (trans.) (1998) *Origen*. London.

Palladius Ratiarensis

Gryson, R. (ed.) (1982) *Scholia Ariana in concilium Aquileiense*. CCSL 87. Turnhout: 172–95.

Passion of Perpetua and Felicity

Heffernan, T. J. (ed. and trans.) (2012) *The Passion of Perpetua and Felicity*. Oxford.

Paulinus of Milan

Pellegrino, M. (ed. and trans.) (1961) *Vita di S. Ambrogio: Introduzione, testo critico e note*. Verba seniorum 1. Rome.

Philo of Alexandria

Colson, F. H., J. W. Earp, R. Marcus, and G. H. Whitaker (eds. and trans.) (1929–62) *Philo in Ten Volumes (and Two Supplementary Volumes)*. LCL 226–27, 247, 261, 275, 289, 320, 341, 363, 379–80, 401. Cambridge.
Petit, F. (ed. and trans.) (1978) *Quaestiones in Genesim et in Exodum: Fragmenta graeca*. Les Œuvres de Philon d'Alexandrie 33. Paris.

Philogelos

Thierfelder, A. (ed.) (1968) *Philogelos: Der Lachfreund von Hierokles und Philagrios*. Sammlung Tusculum. Munich.

Philoponus

Busse, A. (ed.) (1898) *In Aristotelis Categorias commentarium*. CAG 13.1. Berlin.
Wallies, M. (ed.) (1905) *In Aristotelis Analytica priora commentaria*. CAG 13.2. Berlin.

Philoxenos of Mabbug

Budge, E. A. W. (ed.) (1893) *The Discourses of Philoxenus, Bishop of Mabbôgh, A.D. 485–519*/ ܫܪܒܐ ܕܝܠܗ ܕܡܪܝ ܐܟܣܢܝܐ ܡܡܠܠܐ ܡܛܠ ܗܘܦܟܐ ܕܕܘܒܪܐ ܕܥܢܘܝܘܬܐ. London.
de Halleux, A. (ed. and trans.) (1963) *Lettre aux moines de Senoun*. CSCO 231. Louvain.
Graffin, F. (ed.) (1982) *Dissertationes decem de Uno e sancta Trinitate incorporato et passo* (Philoxenus Mabbugensis). PO 41.1. Turnhout.
Kitchen, R. A. (trans.) (2013) *The Discourses of Philoxenos of Mabbug: A New Translation and Introduction*. CSS 235. Collegeville.

Plato of Athens

Burnet, J. (ed.) (1900) *Opera*. Oxford Classical Texts. Oxford.
Grube, G. M. A. (trans.) (1980) *Meno*, 2nd edn. Indianapolis.

Plotinus

Gerson, L. P. (ed.), G. Boys-Stones, et al. (trans.) (2018) *The Enneads*. Cambridge.

Plutarch of Chaeronea

Sieveking, W. (ed.) (1929) *De exilio* in *Plutarchi moralia*, Vol. III. BSGRT. Leipzig: 512–32.
Mau, J. (ed.) (1971) *Moralia*. BSGRT. Leipzig.

Pontius

Bastiaensen, A. A. R. (ed.) (1997) *Vita di Cipriano, Vita di Ambrogio, Vita di Agostino*, 4th edn. Vita dei Santi 3. Milan.

Porphyry of Tyre

Armstrong, A. H. (ed. and trans.) (1989) 'Life of Plotinus', in *Plotinus*. LCL 440. Cambridge.
Becker, M. (ed.) (2016) *Contra Christianos: Neue Sammlung der Fragmente, Testimonien und Dubia mit Einleitung, Übersetzung und Anmerkungen*. Texte und Kommentare 52. Berlin.
Busse, A. (ed.) (1887) *In Aristotelis Categorias commentarium*. CAG 4.1. Berlin.
Lamberton, R. (trans.) (1983) *On the Cave of the Nymphs*. Barrytown.
Nauck, A. (1860) *Opuscula tria*. Leipzig.
Smith, A. (ed.) (1993) *Fragmenta*. BSGRT. Leipzig.

Posidonius

Edelstein, L., and I. G. Kidd (eds. and trans.) (1972) *Fragments*. 3 vols. Cambridge Classical Texts and Commentaries. Cambridge.

Proclus of Constantinople

Baltzly, D., D. Runia, M. Share, and H. Tarrant (eds. and trans.) (2007–13) *Commentary on Plato's Timaeus*. 5 vols. Cambridge.
Barkhuizen, J. H. (trans.) (2001) *Homilies on the Life of Christ*. Early Christian Studies 1. Brisbane.
Diehl, E. (ed.) (1903–6) *In Platonis Timaeum Commentaria*, Vol. I. BSGRT. Leipzig.
Dodds, E. R. (ed.) (1963) *The Elements of Theology*, 2nd edn. Oxford.
Steel, C. (ed.) (2007) *In Platonis Parmenidem commentaria*. Oxford.
Westerink, L. G. (ed.), and H. D. Saffrey (trans.) (2003) *Théologie platonicienne*. 6 vols. Budé. Paris.

Procopius of Caesarea

Dewing, H. B., and G. Downey (trans.) (1914–40) *Buildings; History of the Wars; Secret History*. 7 vols. LCL 48, 81, 107, 173, 217, 290, 343. Cambridge.
Haury, J., and G. Wirth (eds.) (1962–64) *Opera omnia*. 4 vols. BSGRT. Leipzig.
Williamson, G., and P. Sarris (trans.) (2007) *The Secret History*. Penguin Classics. London.

Progymnasmata

Kennedy, G. A. (ed. and trans.) (2003) *Progymnasmata: Greek Textbooks in Prose Composition and Rhetoric.* WGRW 10. Atlanta.

Prudentius

Lavarenne, M. (ed. and trans.) (1943–51) *Prudence.* 4 vols. Budé. Paris.
Pelttari, A. (ed.) (2019) *The Psychomachia of Prudentius: Text, Commentary, and Glossary.* Norman.
Thomson, H. J. (ed. and trans.) (1949–54) *Prudentius.* 2 vols. LCL 387, 398. New York.

Pseudo-Andronicus

Wachsmuth, K. (ed.) (1884) *Andronici qui fertur libelli ΠΕΡΙ ΠΑΘΩΝ pars prior de affectibus.* Heidelberg.

Pseudo-Athanasius

Abelarga, L. (ed.) (2002) *The Life of Saint Syncletica: Introduction–Critical Text–Commentary.* Byzantine Texts and Studies 31. Thessalonica: 183–264.
Migne, J.-P. (ed.) (1857) *De sabbatis et circumcisione.* PG 28. Paris: 133–42.
Migne, J.-P. (ed.) (1857) *Vita Syncleticae.* PG 28. Paris.

Pseudo-Elias

Westerink, L. G. (ed.) (1967) *Lectures on Porphyry's Isagoge.* Amsterdam.

Pseudo-Gregory the Great

Clark, F. W. (ed. and trans.) (1987) *The Pseudo-Gregorian Dialogues.* 2 vols. Leiden.

Pseudo-Justin of Rome

D'Anna, A. (ed.) (2001) *Sulla resurrezione: discorso cristiano del II secolo.* Letteratura cristiana antica: Testi. Brescia.

Heimgarten, M. (ed.) (2001) *Über die Auferstehung: Text und Studie.* PTS 53. Berlin.

Marcovich, M. (ed.) (1990) *Cohortatio ad Graecos, De Monarchia, Oratio ad Graecos.* PTS 32. Berlin.

Riedweg, C. (ed.) (1994) *Ps.-Justin (Markell von Ankyra?) Ad Graecos de vera religione (bisher 'Cohortatio ad Graecos'): Einleitung und Kommentar.* 2 vols. Schweizerische Beiträge zur Altertumswissenschaft 25. Basel.

Pseudo-Plutarch

Lachenaud, G. (ed. and trans.) (1993) *Œuvres morales, tome XII/2: Opinions des philosophes.* Budé. Paris.

Mansfeld, J., and D. T. Runia (eds.) (2020) *Aëtiana V: An Edition of the Reconstructed Text of the Placita with a Commentary and a Collection of Related Texts.* PhA 153. Leiden.

Mau, J. (ed.) (1971) *Moralia.* BSGRT. Leipzig.

Pseudo-Zonaras

Tittmann, J. A. H. (ed.) (1967) *Lexicon ex tribus codicibus manuscriptis.* 2 vols. Amsterdam.

Quintilian

Russell, D. A. (ed. and trans.) (2002) *The Orator's Education,* Vol. V: Books 11–12. LCL 494. Cambridge.

Romanos the Melodist

Maas, P., and K. Trypanis (eds.) (1963) *Cantica genuina.* Oxford.

Grosdidier de Matons, J. (ed. and trans.) (1964–81) *Hymnes.* 5 vols. SC 99, 110, 114, 128, 283. Paris.

Scholia Vindobonensia

Zechmeister, J. (ed.) (1877) *Scholia Vindobonensia ad Horatii Artem poeticam*. Vienna.

Seneca the Younger

Hense, O. (ed.) (1938) *Epistulae morales ad Lucilium*. BSGRT. Leipzig.

Sentences of Sextus

Wilson, W. T. (ed. and trans.) (2012) *The Sentences of Sextus*. Wisdom Literature from the Ancient World 1. Atlanta.

Simplicius

Hadot, I. (ed. and trans.) (1996) *Commentaire sur le 'Manuel' d'Épictète*. PhA 66. Leiden.

Soranus of Ephesus

Burguière, P., D. Gourevitch, and Y. Malinas (eds. and trans.) (1988–90) *Maladies des femmes*. 4 vols. Budé. Paris.

Stobaeus

Wachsmuth, K. (ed.) (1884) *Anthologii libri duo priores*. 2 vols. Berlin.

Stoics

von Arnim, H. F. A. (ed.) (1903–24) *Stoicorum veterum fragmenta*. 4 vols. BSGRT. Leipzig.

Tatian the Assyrian

Nesselrath, H.-G. (ed.) (2016) *Gegen falsche Götter und falsche Bildung: Tatian, Rede an die Griechen*. SAPERE 28. Tübingen.
Trelenberg, J. (ed.) (2012) *Oratio ad Graecos. Rede an die Griechen*. BHT 165. Tübingen.

Tertullian of Carthage

Borleffs, J. W. P. (ed.) (1954) *De paenitentia*. CCSL 1. Turnhout.
Refoulé, R. F. (ed.) (1954) *De praescriptione haereticorum*. CCSL 1. Turnhout.

Themistius

Heinze, R. (ed.) (1899) *In libros Aristotelis De anima paraphrasis*. CAG 5.3. Berlin.

Theodore and Hadrian

Bischoff, B., and M. Lapidge (eds. and trans.) (1994) *Biblical Commentaries from the Canterbury School of Theodore and Hadrian*. Cambridge Studies in Anglo-Saxon England 10. Cambridge.

Theodoret of Cyr

Fernández Marcos, N., and A. Sáenz-Badillos (eds.) (1979) *Quaestiones in Octateuchum*. Textos y estudios 'Cardenal Cisneros' 17. Madrid.
Halton, T. (trans.) (2013) *A Cure for Pagan Maladies*. ACW 67. New York.
Parmentier, L., and F. Scheidweiler (eds.) (1954) *Kirchengeschichte*, 2nd edn. GCS 44. Berlin.
Petruccione, J. F. (ed.) (2007) *The Questions on the 'Octateuch'*, Volume 2: *On Leviticus, Numbers, Deuteronomy, Joshua, Judges, and Ruth*. Library of Early Christianity 2. Washington.
Raeder, J. (ed.) (1904) *Graecarum affectionum curatio*. BSGRT. Leipzig. Repr. Stuttgart 1969.

Theon of Smyrna

Hiller, E. (ed.) (1878) *Expositio rerum mathematicarum ad legendum Platonem utilium*. BSGRT. Leipzig.

Theophanes the Confessor

de Boor, C. (ed.) (1883–85) *Chronographia*. 2 vols. BSGRT. Leipzig.
Mango, C., and R. Scott (eds.) (1997) *The Chronicle of Theophanes Confessor: Byzantine and Near Eastern History, AD 284–813*. Oxford.

Various

Allen, P., and J. H. Declerck (eds.) (1989) *Diversorum Postchalcedonensium Auctorum Collectanea*, Vol. I: *Pamphili Theologi opus*, ed. José H. Declerck; *Eustathii Monachi opus*, ed. Pauline Allen. CCSG 19. Turnhout.
Diekamp, F. (ed.) (1938) *Analecta Patristica: Texte und Abhandlungen zur griechischen Patristik*. OCA 117. Rome.
Lauxtermann, M. (ed. and trans.) (2003) *Byzantine Poetry from Pisides to Geometres: Texts and Contexts*, Vol. I. Vienna.
Lauxtermann, M. (ed. and trans.) (2019) *Byzantine Poetry from Pisides to Geometres: Texts and Contexts*, Vol. II. Vienna.
Leemans, J., W. Mayer, B. Dehandschutter, and P. Allen (eds. and trans.) (2003) *'Let Us Die that We May Live': Greek Homilies on Christian Martyrs from Asia Minor, Palestine and Syria, c. 350–c. 450 AD*. London.
Opitz, H.-G. (ed.) (1935) *Urkunden zur Geschichte des arianischen Streites, 318–28* in *Athanasius Werke 3.1*. Berlin.

Vincent of Lérins

Demeulenaere, R. (ed.) (1985) *Commonitorium* in *Scriptores minores Galliae s. IV–V: Foebadius, Victricius, Leporius, Vincentius, Evagrius, Ruricius*. CCSL 64. Turnhout: 147–95.

Xenocrates

Heinze, R. (ed.) (1892) *Xenocrates*. BSGRT. Stuttgart. Repr. Hildesheim, 1965.

Secondary Literature

Abraham, W. J. (2012) 'Analytic Philosophers of Religion', in Gavrilyuk and Coakley 2012a: 275–90.
Adam, A. (1953–54) 'Grundbegriffe des Mönchtums in sprachlicher Sicht', *ZKG* 65: 209–39.

Adams, J. N. (1993) 'The Generic Use of "Mula" and the Status and Employment of Female Mules in the Roman World', *Rheinisches Museum für Philologie* 136: 35–61.

Adamson, P., H. Baltussen, and M. W. F. Stone (eds.) (2004) *Philosophy, Science and Exegesis in Greek, Arabic and Latin Commentaries*. London.

Adler, W. (2017) 'The Creation of Christian Elite Culture in Roman Syria and the Near East', in *The Oxford Handbook of the Second Sophistic*, ed. D. S. Richter and W. A. Johnson. Oxford: 655–67.

Agosti, G. (2016) 'Epigrafia metrica tardoantica e democratizzazione della cultura', in *Forme di accesso al sapere in età tardoantica*, ed. L. Cristante and V. Veronesi. Trieste: 131–47.

Ahbel-Rappe, S. (2014) 'Metaphysics: The Origins of Becoming and the Resolution of Ignorance', in Slaveva-Griffin and Reemes 2014: 161–81.

Ahern, E. (2020) *Bede and the Cosmos: Theology and Nature in the Eighth Century*. New York.

Ahern, E. (forthcoming) 'Bede on "The Nature of Things"', in *Bede the Scholar*, ed. M. MacCarron and P. Darby. Manchester.

Alexander, L. (2004) 'Paul and Hellenistic Schools: Evidence of Galen', in *Paul in His Hellenistic Context*, ed. T. Engberg-Pederson. London: 60–83.

Alexandre, M. (1986) 'L'épée de flamme (Gen 3,24): Textes chrétiens et traditions juives', in *Hellenica et Judaica: Hommages à V. Nikiprowetsky*, ed. A. Caquot, M. Hadas-Lebel, and J. Riaud. Leuven: 403–41.

Alexis-Baker, A. (2009) '*Ad Quirinum* Book Three and Cyprian's Catechumenate', *JECS* 17: 357–80.

Alexopoulos, T. (2006) 'Das unendliche Sichausstrecken (*Epektasis*) zum Guten bei Gregor von Nyssa und Plotin: Eine vergleichende Untersuchung', *ZAC* 10: 302–12.

Alison, J. (1996) *Raising Abel: The Recovery of Eschatological Imagination*. New York.

Allen, J. S. (2008) *The Despoliation of Egypt in Pre-Rabbinic, Rabbinic and Patristic Traditions*. Leiden.

Allen, P. (1996) 'The Homilist and the Congregation: A Case Study of Chrysostom's Homilies on Hebrews', *Aug* 36: 397–421.

Allen, P. (1997) 'John Chrysostom's Homilies on I and II Thessalonians: The Preacher and His Audience', *StPatr* 31: 3–21.

Allen, P., and B. Neil (eds.) (2002) *Maximus the Confessor and His Companions: Documents from Exile*. Oxford.

Allen, P., and W. Mayer (1994) 'Chrysostom and the Preaching of Homilies in Series: A New Approach to the Twelve Homilies *In epistulam ad Colossenses* (CPG 4433)', *OCP* 60: 21–39.

Allen, P., and W. Mayer (1995) 'Chrysostom and the Preaching of Homilies in Series: A New Approach to the Fifteen Homilies *In epistulam ad Philippenses* (CPG 4432)', *VC* 49: 270–89.

Allison, D. (1987) 'The Eye is the Lamp of the Body (Matthew 6.22–23 = Luke 11.34–36)', *NTS* 33: 61–83.

Amar, J. P. (1990) 'Hermits and Desert Dwellers', in *Ascetic Behavior in Greco-Roman Antiquity: A Sourcebook*, ed. V. L. Wimbush. Minneapolis: 66–89.

Amidon, P. R., SJ (1983) 'The Procedure of St Cyprian's Synods', *VC* 37: 328–39.

Amidon, P. R., SJ (2002) 'Paulinus' Subscription to the *Tomus ad Antiochenos*', *JTS* 53: 53–74.

Amirkhanian, R. (2008) 'Les tables de canons arméniennes et le thème iconographique de la Jérusalem céleste', *Revue des études arméniennes* 31: 181–232.

Amsler, M. (2019) 'Affectus in Medieval Grammar', in *Before Emotion: The Language of Feeling, 400–800*, ed. M. Champion, J. Feros Ruys, and K. Essary. London: 26–37.

Amundsen, D. W. (1995) 'Tatian's Rejection of Medicine in the Second Century', in *Ancient Medicine in its Socio-Cultural Context*, ed. P. J. van der Eijk, H. F. J. Horstmanshoff, and P. H. Schrijvers. 2 vols. Amsterdam: 2.377–92.

Anatolios, K. (2011) *Retrieving Nicaea: The Development and Meaning of Trinitarian Doctrine*. Grand Rapids.

Ando, C. (2008) *The Matter of the Gods: Religion and the Roman Empire*. Berkeley.

Ando, C. (2012) 'Narrating the Decline and Fall', in *A Companion to Late Antiquity*, ed. P. Rousseau. Chichester: 59–76.

Andrade, N. (2020) 'Bardaisan's Disciples and Ethnographic Knowledge in the Roman Empire', in *Literature and Culture in the Roman Empire, 96–235: Cross-Cultural Interactions*, ed. A. König, R. Langlands, and J. Uden. Cambridge: 291–308.

Andrée, A. (2011) 'Anselm of Laon Unveiled: The *Glosae super Iohannem* and the Origins of the *Glossa Ordinaria* on the Bible', *MS* 73: 217–60.

Annas, J. (1999) *Platonic Ethics, Old and New*. Ithaca.

Apostolos-Cappadona, D. (2008) 'Dove', *RPP* 4: 176–77.

Aquino, F. D. (2012) 'Maximus the Confessor', in Gavrilyuk and Coakley 2012a: 104–20.

Archambault, P. J. (1986) 'Shifts of Narrative Level in Saint Augustine's Confessions', *AugStud* 17: 109–17.

Arentzen, T. (2017) *The Virgin in Song: Mary and the Poetry of Romanos the Melodist*. Philadelphia.

Arnhold, M., H. O. Maier, and J. Rüpke (eds.) (2018) *Seeing the God: Image, Space, Performance, and Vision in the Religion of the Roman Empire*. Tübingen.

Arnold, E. (1879) *The Light of Asia, or The Great Renunciation*. London.

Arnold, E. (1893) *The Light of the World, or The Great Consummation*. London.

Ashwin-Siejkowski, P. (2008) *Clement of Alexandria: A Project of Christian Perfection*. London.

Asper, M. (2007) *Griechische Wissenschaftstexte: Formen, Funktionen, Differenzierungsgeschichten*. Stuttgart.

Aubineau, M. (1956) 'Incorruptibilité et divinisation selon saint Irénée', *RSR* 44: 25–52.

Audet, Th-André. (1943) 'Orientations théologiques chez Saint Irénée: Le contexte mental d'une ΓΝΩΣΙΣ ΑΛΗθΗΣ', *Traditio* 1: 15–54.

Aune, D. E. (1997) *Revelation 1–5*. Dallas.

Austin, J. L. (1975) *How to Do Things with Words*, 2nd edn. Oxford.

Ayres, L. (2004a) 'Athanasius' Initial Defense of the Term Ὁμοούσιος: Rereading the *De decretis*', *JECS* 12: 337–59.

Ayres, L. (2004b) *Nicaea and Its Legacy: An Approach to Fourth-Century Trinitarian Theology*. Oxford.

Ayres, L. (2010) *Augustine and the Trinity*. Cambridge.

Ayres, L. (2015a) 'God', in *Late Ancient Knowing: Explorations in Intellectual History*, ed. C. M. Chin and M. Vidas. Berkeley: 134–51.

Ayres, L. (2015b) 'Irenaeus vs. the Valentinians: Toward a Rethinking of Patristic Exegetical Origins', *JECS* 23: 153–87.

Ayres, L. (2020) 'Irenaeus and the "Rule of Truth": A Reconsideration', in Ayres and Ward 2020: 145–64.

Ayres, L., and H. C. Ward (eds.) (2020) *The Rise of the Christian Intellectual*. Berlin.

Bäbler, B., and H.-G. Nesselrath (eds.) (2018) *Origenes der Christ und Origenes der Platoniker*. Tübingen.

Bacq, P. (1978) *De l'ancienne à la nouvelle alliance selon S. Irénée: Unité du livre IV de l'Adversus haereses*. Paris.

Bakirtzis, C., E. Kourkoutidou-Nikolaidou, and C. Mauropoulou-Tsioumi (2012) *Mosaics of Thessaloniki, 4th–14th Century*, trans. A. Doumas. Athens.

Baltussen, H. (2008) *Philosophy and Exegesis in Simplicius: The Methodology of a Commentator*. London.

Balty, J. (1995) *Mosaïques antiques du proche-orient: Chronologie, iconographie, interprétation*. Paris.

Balty, J., and F. Briquel Chatonnet (2000) *Nouvelles mosaïques inscrites d'Osrhoène*. Paris.

Baltzly, D. (2004) 'The Virtues and "Becoming like God": Alcinous to Proclus', *Oxford Studies in Ancient Philosophy* 26: 297–321.

Banaji, J. (2007) *Agrarian Change in Late Antiquity*. Oxford.

Bandmann, G. (1966) 'Beobachtung zum Etschmiadzin-Evangeliar', in *Tortulae: Studien zu altchristlichen und byzantinischen Monumenten*, ed. W. N. Schumacher. Rome: 11–29.

Banterle, G., G. Biffi, I. Biffi, and L. Migliavacca (eds.) (1994) *Ambrogio: Opere poetiche e frammenti*. Milan.

Bardy, G. (1932) 'La littérature patristique des "quaestiones et responsiones" sur l'écriture sainte', *RB* 41: 224–27.

Bardy, G. (1937) 'Aux origins de l'école d'Alexandrie', *RSR* 27: 65–90.

Barkhuizen, J. H. (1996) 'The Parable of the Prodigal Son as a Eucharistic Metaphor in Romanos Melodos' *Kontakion* 49 (Oxf.)', *Acta Classica* 39: 39–54.

Barkman, H. (2014) 'The Church of the Martyrs in Egypt and North Africa: A Comparison of the Melitian and Donatist Schisms', *JCSCS* 6: 41–51.
Barnes, J. (1997) 'Roman Aristotle', in *Philosophia Togata II: Plato and Aristotle at Rome*, ed. J. Barnes and M. Griffin. Oxford: 1–69.
Barnes, T. D. (1973) 'Lactantius and Constantine', *JRS* 63: 29–46.
Barnes, T. D. (1981) *Constantine and Eusebius*. Cambridge.
Barnes, T. D. (1982) *The New Empire of Diocletian and Constantine*. Cambridge.
Barnes, T. D. (1989) 'The Date of the Council of Gangra', *JTS* 40: 121–24.
Barnes, T. D. (1993) *Athanasius and Constantius*. Cambridge.
Barthes, R. (2002) *A Lover's Discourse*. London.
Barton, T. S. (2002) *Power and Knowledge: Astrology, Physiognomics, and Medicine under the Roman Empire*. Ann Arbor.
Baskin, J. R. (1983) 'Origen on Balaam: The Dilemma of the Unworthy Prophet', *VC* 37: 22–35.
Batiffol, P. (1911) *Primitive Catholicism*, trans. H. I. Brianceau. London.
Batiffol, P. (1928) *Saint Grégoire le Grand*. Paris.
Baumstark, A. (1922) *Geschichte der syrischen Literatur, mit Ausschluß der christlich-palästinensischen Texte*. Bonn.
Baun, J. (2013) 'Gregory's Eschatology', in Neil and Dal Santo 2013: 157–76.
Bausi, A., C. Brockmann, M. Friedrich, and S. Kienitz (eds.) (2018) *Manuscripts and Archives: Comparative Views on Record-Keeping*. Berlin.
Beard, M. (1986) 'Cicero and Divination: The Formation of a Latin Discourse', *JRS* 76: 33–46.
Beard, M., J. A. North, and S. R. F. Price (1998) *Religions of Rome*. 2 vols. Cambridge.
Beatrice, P. F. (1998) 'Ascetical Fasting and Original Sin in the Early Christian Writers', in *Prayer and Spirituality in the Early Church*, ed. P. Allen, R. Canning, L. Cross, B. J. Caiger, and P. F. Beatrice. Everton Park: 211–28.
Beaucamp, J. (2007) 'Byzantine Egypt and Imperial Law', in *Egypt in the Byzantine World*, ed. R. Bagnall. Cambridge: 271–87.
Beck, E. (1956) 'Ein Beitrag zur Terminologie des ältesten syrischen Mönchtums', *SA* 38: 254–67.
Beck, E. (1958) 'Asketentum und Mönchtum bei Ephraem', *OrChrAn* 153: 341–62.
Beck, E. (1975) *Nachträge zu Ephraem Syrus*. Louvain.
Becker, A. (2006) *The Fear of God and the Beginning of Wisdom: The School of Nisibis and the Development of Scholastic Culture in Late Antique Mesopotamia*. Philadelphia.
Beekers, D., and D. Kloss (eds.) (2017) *Straying from the Straight Path: How Senses of Failure Invigorate Lived Religion*. New York.
Beer, M. (2010) *Taste or Taboo: Dietary Choices in Antiquity*. Totnes.
Behr, J. (1993) 'Irenaeus *AH* 3.23.5 and the Ascetic Ideal', *SVTQ* 37: 305–13.
Behr, J. (1997) *St Irenaeus of Lyons: On the Apostolic Preaching*. Crestwood.
Behr, J. (2000) *Asceticism and Anthropology in Irenaeus and Clement*. Oxford.

Behr, J. (2013) *Irenaeus of Lyons: Identifying Christianity*. Oxford.

Beirwaltes, W. (1997) 'Dionysius Areopagites: Ein christlicher Proklos?' in *Platon in der abendländischen Geistesgeschichte. Neue Forschungen zum Platonismus*, ed. T. Kobusch and B. Mojsisch. Darmstadt: 44–84.

Belén Sánchez Prieto, A. (2016) 'Authority and Authorship, Tradition and Invention, Reading and Writing in Early Medieval Compilation Genres: The Case of Hrabanus Maurus' *De institutione clericorum*', *De Medio Aevo* 10: 179–240.

Bell, P. (2009) *Three Political Voices from the Age of Justinian*. Liverpool.

Bénatouïl, T., and M. Bonazzi (eds.) (2012) *Theoria, Praxis and the Contemplative Life after Plato and Aristotle*. Leiden.

Bendinelli, G. (1997) *Il commentario a Matteo di Origene: L'ambito della metodologia scolastica dell'antichità*. Rome.

Berchman, R. M. (2005) *Porphyry against the Christians*. Studies in Platonism, Neoplatonism, and the Platonic tradition. Leiden.

Bernabò, M. (2008) *Il Tetravangelo di Rabbula: Firenze, Biblioteca medicea laurenziana, Plut. 1.56: L'illustrazione del Nuovo Testamento nella Siria del VI secolo*. Folia Picta 1. Rome.

Bernabò, M. (2014) 'The Miniatures in the Rabbula Gospels: Postscripta to a Recent Book', *DOP* 68: 343–58.

Bernardi, J. (1968) *La prédication des pères cappadociens: Le prédicateur et son auditoire*. Paris.

Berthouzoz, R. (1980) *Liberté et grâce suivant la théologie d'Irénée de Lyon: Le débat avec la gnose aux origines de la théologie chrétienne*. Paris.

Betz, H. D. (1979) 'Matthew VI.22f. and Ancient Greek Theories of Vision', in *Text and Interpretation: Studies in the New Testament Presented to Matthew Black*, ed. E. Best and R. M. Wilson. Cambridge: 43–56.

Betz, H. D. (ed.) (2007–13) *Religion Past and Present: Encyclopedia of Theology and Religion*. Leiden.

Bévenot, M. (1979) '"Sacerdos" as Understood by Cyprian', *JTS* 30: 413–29.

Biddle, M. (1999) *The Tomb of Christ*. Stroud.

Biffi, N. (2011) 'Ciò che Bardesane venne a sapere sull'India', *Classica et Christiana* 6: 305–35.

Bischoff, B. (1966) 'Wendepunkte in der Geschichte der lateinischen Exegese im Frühmittelalter', in *Mittelalterliche Studien*. 3 vols. Stuttgart: 1.205–73.

Bischoff, B., and M. Lapidge (1994) *Biblical Commentaries from the Canterbury School of Theodore and Hadrian*. Cambridge.

Bjornlie, M. S. (2013) *Politics and Tradition between Rome, Ravenna and Constantinople: A Study of Cassiodorus and the 'Variae', 527–554*. Cambridge.

Blackburn Griffith, S. (2016) 'Ambrose the Appropriator: Borrowed Texts in a New Context in the Commentary on Luke', in *Commentaries, Catenae and Biblical Tradition*, ed. H. Houghton. Piscataway: 199–225.

Blair, J. (2005) *The Church in Anglo-Saxon Society*. Oxford.

Blanchard, Y.-M. (1993) *Aux sources du canon, le témoignage d'Irénée*. Paris.
Blank, D. L. (2010) 'Ammonius Hermeiou and His School', in *The Cambridge History of Philosophy in Late Antiquity*, ed. L. Gerson. Cambridge: 654–66.
Blockley, R. C. (1985) *The History of Menander the Guardsman*. Cambridge.
Blowers, P. (1997) 'The *regula fidei* and the Narrative Character of Early Christian Faith', *Pro Ecclesia* 6: 199–228.
Blowers, P. (2012a) *Drama of the Divine Economy: Creator and Creation in Early Christian Theology and Piety*. Oxford.
Blowers, P. (2012b) 'On the "Play" of Divine Providence in Gregory Nazianzen and Maximus the Confessor', in *Re-Reading Gregory of Nazianzus: Essays on History, Theology, and Culture*, ed. C. Beeley. Washington: 183–201.
Blowers, P. (2016a) *Maximus the Confessor: Jesus Christ and the Transfiguration of the World*. Oxford.
Blowers, P. (2016b) 'Beauty, Tragedy, and New Creation: Theology and Contemplation in Cappadocian Cosmology', *IJST* 18: 7–29.
Blowers, P. (2020) 'George of Pisidia among the Hexaemeral Commentators', in *Receptions of the Bible in Byzantium: Texts, Manuscripts, and Their Readers*, ed. R. Ceulemans and B. Crostini. Uppsala: 63–77.
Blumenthal, H. J., and A. C. Lloyd (eds.) (1982) *Soul and the Structure of Being in Late Neoplatonism: Syrianus, Proclus, and Simplicius: Papers and Discussions of a Colloquium Held at Liverpool, 15–16 April 1982*. Liverpool.
Bobertz, C. A. (1992) 'An Analysis of *Vita Cypriani* 3, 6–10 and the Attribution of *Ad Quirinum* to Cyprian of Carthage', *VC* 46: 112–28.
Bockmuehl, M. N. A. (1988) 'Das Verb φανερόω im Neuen Testament: Versuch einer Neuauswertung', *BZ* 32: 87–99.
Boersma, H. (2013) *Embodiment and Virtue in Gregory of Nyssa: An Anagogical Approach*. Oxford.
Bogdanović, J. (2017) *The Framing of Sacred Space: The Canopy and the Byzantine Church*. Oxford.
Bohlin, E. (2016) 'On the *Euclides Latinus* in MS Verona, Biblioteca Capitolare XL (38), as a Witness to the Greek Text of the *Elements*', *CQ* 66: 724–41.
Böhm, T. (1996) *Theoria – Unendlichkeit – Aufstieg: Philosophische Implikationen zu De vita Moysis von Gregor von Nyssa*. Leiden.
Böhm, T. (2000) 'Theodoros', *LTK* 9: 1418.
Böhm, T. (2002) 'Origenes, Theologe und (Neu-)Platoniker? Oder: Wem soll man mistrauen: Eusebius oder Porphyrius?', *Adamantius* 8: 7–23.
Bonazzi, M., and F. M. Petrucci (2020) 'Definition und philosophische Systemstelle der platonischen Ethik', in *Die philosophische Lehre des Platonismus: Die Ethik im antiken Platonismus der Kaiserzeit*, ed. C. Pietsch. Stuttgart: 151–78.
Bond, S. (2014) 'Altering Infamy: Status, Violence and Civic Exclusion in Late Antiquity', *ClAnt* 33: 1–30.
Bonner, S. F. (1977) *Education in Ancient Rome: From the Elder Cato to the Younger Pliny*. Berkeley.

Bonwetsch, G. N. (1891) *Methodius von Olympus*. Leipzig.
Boodts, S. (2017) 'Les sermons d'Augustin dans la bibliothèque de Florus: Perspectives comparatistes avec la Collectio ex dictis XII Patrum', in *Les douze compilations pauliniennes de Florus de Lyon: Un carrefour des traditions patristiques au IXe siècle*, ed. P. Chambert-Protat, F. Dolveck, and C. Gerzaguet. Rome: 197–211.
Booth, P. (2013) 'Gregory and the Greek East', in Neil and Dal Santo 2013: 109–32.
Booth, P. (2014) *Crisis of Empire: Doctrine and Dissent at the End of Late Antiquity*. Berkeley.
Borsook, E. (2000) 'Rhetoric or Reality: Mosaics as an Expression of a Metaphysical Idea', *Mitteilungen des Kunsthistorischen Institutes in Florenz* 44: 2–18.
Botner, M. (2015) 'How Do the Seeds Land? A Note on ΕΙΣ ΑΥΤΟΝ in Mark 1:10', *JTS* 66: 547–52.
Boudalis, G. (2018) *The Codex and Crafts in Late Antiquity*. Chicago.
Boudon-Millot, V. (2013) 'What Is a Mental Illness, and How Can It Be Treated? Galen's Reply as a Doctor and Philosopher', in Harris 2013: 129–45.
Boudon-Millot, V. (2019) 'Galien de Pergame ou le médecin qui voulait se faire philosophe', in *Médecins et philosophes: Une histoire*, ed. C. Crignon and D. Lefebvre. Paris: 109–28.
Boulogne, J. (1996) 'Plutarque et la medicine', *ANRW* 2.37.3: 2762–92.
Bourdieu, P. (1977) *Outline of a Theory of Practice*. Cambridge.
Bourdieu, P. (1985) 'The Market of Symbolic Goods', *Poetics* 14: 13–44.
Bourdieu, P. (1993) *The Field of Cultural Production*. Cambridge.
Bourdieu, P. (2000) *Pascalian Meditations*, trans. R. Nice. Stanford.
Bouton-Touboulic, A.-I. (2007) 'Le *De divination daemonum* de saint Augustin: Le pouvoir des démons en question', in *Fictions du diable: Démonologie et literature de saint Augustine à Léo Taxil*, ed. F. Lavocat, P. Kapitaniak, and M. Closson. Geneva: 15–34.
Boys-Stones, G. R. (2001) *Post-Hellenic Philosophy: A Study of Its Development from the Stoics to Origen*. Oxford.
Boys-Stones, G. R. (2018) *Platonist Philosophy 80 BC to 250 AD: An Introduction and Collection of Sources in Translation*. Cambridge.
Bracht, K. (1999) *Vollkommenheit und Vollendung: Zur Anthropologie des Methodius von Olympus*. Tübingen.
Bradshaw, P. F. (1999) 'The Gospel and the Catechumenate in the Third Century', *JTS* 50: 143–52.
Bradshaw, P. F. (2002) *The Search for the Origins of Christian Worship: Sources and Methods for the Study of Early Liturgy*. Oxford.
Bradshaw, P. F. (2012) 'The Status of Jesus in Early Christian Prayer Texts', in *Portraits of Jesus*, ed. S. E. Myers. Tübingen: 249–60.
Brakke, D. (1995) *Athanasius and the Politics of Asceticism*. Oxford.
Brakke, D. (2006) *Demons and the Making of the Monk: Spiritual Combat in Early Christianity*. Cambridge.

Brakke, D. (2008) 'From Temple to Cell, from Gods to Demons: Pagan Temples in the Monastic Topography of Fourth-Century Egypt', in *From Temple to Church: Destruction and Renewal of Local Cultic Topography in Late Antiquity*, ed. J. Hahn, S. Emmel, and U. Gotter. Leiden: 92–113.

Brakke, D. (2009) 'Introduction', in *Talking Back: A Monastic Handbook for Combating Demons*. Collegeville: 1–44.

Brand, M. (2020) 'In the Footsteps of the Apostles of Light: Persecution and the Manichaean Discourse on Suffering', in *Heirs of Roman Persecution: Studies on a Christian and Para-Christian Discourse in Late Antiquity*, ed. É. Fournier and W. Mayer. New York: 112–34.

Bremmer, J. N. (2007) 'Peregrinus' Christian Career', in *Flores Florentino: Dead Sea Scrolls and Other Early Jewish Studies in Honour of Florentino Garcia Martinez*, ed. A. Hilhorst, É. Puech, and E. Tigchelaar. Leiden: 729–47.

Bremmer, J. N. (2021) 'Roman Judge vs. Christian Bishop: The Trial of Phileas during the Great Persecution', in Maier and Waldner 2021: 81–117.

Brennan, P. (1998) 'The User's Guide to the "Notitia Dignitatum": The Case of the "Dux Armeniae" ("ND Or." 38)', *Antichthon* 32: 34–49.

Brennecke, H. C. (1993) 'Lucian von Antiochien in der Geschichte des arianischen Streites', in *Logos: Festschrift für Luise Abramowski*, ed. H. C. Brennecke, E. L. Grasmuck, and C. Markschies. Berlin: 170–92.

Brent, A. (2010) *Cyprian and Roman Carthage*. Cambridge.

Breytenbach, C. (ed.) (2007) *Frühchristliches Thessaloniki*. Tübingen.

Breytenbach, C. (2012) 'Psalms^{LXX} and the Christian Definition of Space: Examples Based on Inscriptions from Central Asia Minor', in *Text-Critical and Hermeneutical Studies in the Septuagint*, ed. J. Cook and H.-J. Stipp. Leiden: 381–94.

Breytenbach, C. (2014) 'The Early Christians and Their Greek Bible: Quotations from the Psalms and Isaiah in Inscriptions from Asia Minor', in *Die Septuaginta – Text, Wirkung, Rezeption. 4. Internationale Fachtagung veranstaltet von Septuaginta Deutsch (LXX.D), Wuppertal 19.–22. Juli 2012*, ed. W. Kraus and S. Kreuzer. Tübingen: 759–74.

Breytenbach, C. (2015) '"Metaphorical" Redefinition of Church Space through LXX Texts on Christian Monuments from Asia Minor', in *The Metaphorical Use of Language in Deuterocanonical and Cognate Literature*, ed. M. Witte and S. Behnke. Berlin: 473–74.

Breytenbach, C., and C. Zimmermann (2018) *Early Christianity in Lycaonia and Adjacent Areas: From Paul to Amphilochius of Iconium*. Leiden.

Breytenbach, C., and E. Tzavella (2023) *Early Christianity in Athens, Attica, and Adjacent Areas: From Paul to Justinian I (1st–6th cent. AD)*. Early Christianity in Greece 1. Leiden.

Breytenbach, C., K. Hallof, et al. (2019) *Inscriptiones christianae graecae*. Edition Topoi. Berlin. DOI: 10.17171/1-8. http://repository.edition-topoi.org/collection/ICG.

Briggman, A. (2012) *Irenaeus of Lyons and the Theology of the Holy Spirit*. Oxford.

Briggman, A. (2013) 'Irenaeus' Christology of Mixture', *JTS* 64: 516–55.

Briggman, A. (2015) 'Literary and Rhetorical Theory in Irenaeus, Part 1', *VC* 69: 500–27.
Briggman, A. (2017) 'Theological Speculation in Irenaeus: Perils and Possibilities', *VC* 71: 175–98.
Briggman, A. (2019) *God and Christ in Irenaeus*. Oxford.
Briquel-Chatonnet, F., and M. Debié (2017). *Le monde syriaque: Sur les routes d'un christianisme ignoré*. Paris.
Brisson, L., S. O'Neill, and A. Timotin (eds.) (2018) *Neoplatonic Demons and Angels*. Leiden.
Brittain Bouchard, C. (2003) *'Every Valley Shall Be Exalted': The Discourse of Opposites in Twelfth-Century Thought*. Ithaca.
Brock, S. P. (1971) 'Notes and Studies: Didymus the Blind on Bardaisan', *JTS* 22: 530–31.
Brock, S. P. (1979) 'Aspects of Translation Technique in Antiquity', *GRBS* 20: 69–87.
Brock, S. P. (1982) 'Clothing Metaphors as a Means of Theological Expression in Syriac Tradition', in *Typus, Symbol, Allegorie bei den östlichen Vätern und ihren Parallelen im Mittelalter: Internationales Kolloquium*, ed. M. Schmidt and C.-F. Geyer. Regensburg: 11–40.
Brock, S. P. (1987) *The Syriac Fathers on Prayer and the Spiritual Life*. Kalamazoo.
Brock, S. P. (1990) 'The Holy Spirit as Feminine in Early Syriac Literature', in *After Eve*, ed. J. M. Soskice. London: 73–88.
Brock, S. P. (1992) 'Eusebius and Syriac Christianity', in *Eusebius, Christianity, and Judaism*, ed. H. W. Attridge and G. Hata. Detroit: 212–34.
Brock, S. P. (1997) 'Transmission of Ephrem's *Madrashe* in the Syriac Liturgical Tradition', StPatr 33: 490–505.
Brock, S. P. (1999) 'St Ephrem in the Eyes of Later Syriac Liturgical Tradition', *Hug* 2: 5–25.
Brock, S. P. (2004) 'Without Mushe of Nisibis, Where Would We Be? Some Reflections on the Transmission of Syriac Literature', *Journal of Eastern Christian Studies* 56: 15–24.
Brock, S. P. (2007a) 'A Brief Guide to the Main Editions and Translations of the Works of Saint Ephrem', in *Saint Éphrem: Un poète pour notre temps: Patrimoine Syriaque XI, Actes du Colloque XI*. Antélias: 281–338.
Brock, S. P. (2007b) 'In Search of Saint Ephrem', in *Saint Ephrem: Un poète pour Notre temps: Patrimoine Syriaque XI, Actes du Colloque XI*. Antélias: 11–25.
Brock, S. P. (2016) 'Ephremiana in Manuscript *Sinai Syr. 10*', *Mus* 129: 285–322.
Brock, S. P., A. M. Butts, G. A. Kiraz, and L. van Rompay (eds.) (2011) *The Gorgias Encyclopedic Dictionary of the Syriac Heritage*. Piscataway.
Broilo, F. (2016) 'A Dome for the Water: Canopied Fountains and Cypress Trees in Byzantine and Early Ottoman Constantinople', in *Fountains and Water Culture in Byzantium*, ed. B. Shilling and P. Stephenson. Cambridge: 314–23.
Brown, G. H. (1996) *Bede the Educator*. Jarrow.
Brown, G. H. (2009) *A Companion to Bede*. Woodbridge.

Brown, P. (1988) *The Body and Society: Men, Women and Sexual Renunciation in Early Christianity*. Columbia.

Brown, P. (2012) *Through the Eye of a Needle: Wealth, the Fall of Rome, and the Making of Christianity in the West, 350–550 AD*. Princeton.

Brown, P. (2013) *The Rise of Western Christendom: Triumph and Diversity, AD 200–1000*, rev. ed. Chichester.

Brown, P. (2015) *The Cult of the Saints: Its Rise and Function in Latin Christianity*, 2nd edn. Chicago.

Brown, P. (2018) 'Review of Muriel Debié, *L'écriture de l'histoire en syriaque*', *Al-'Usur Al-Wusta* 26: 225–31.

Brown Hughes, A. (2016) 'The Legacy of the Feminine in the Christology of Origen of Alexandria, Methodius of Olympus, and Gregory of Nyssa', *VC* 70: 51–76.

Brubaker, L. (2008) 'Critical Approaches to Art History', in *The Oxford Handbook of Byzantine Studies*, ed. R. Cormack, J. F. Haldon, and E. Jeffreys. Oxford: 59–66.

Bruce-Mitford, R. L. S. (1967) *The Art of the Codex Amiatinus*. Jarrow.

Bryen, A. Z. (2008) 'Visibility and Violence in Petitions from Roman Egypt', *GRBS* 48: 181–200.

Bucur, B. G. (2006) 'The Other Clement: Cosmic Hierarchy and Interiorized Apocalypticism', *VC* 60: 251–68.

Bucur, B. G. (2009) *Angelomorphic Pneumatology: Clement of Alexandria and Other Early Christian Witnesses*. Leiden.

Bucur, B. G. (2018) '"God Never Appeared to Moses": Eusebius of Caesarea's Peculiar Exegesis of the Burning Bush Theophany', *JBRec* 5: 235–57.

Bucur, B. G. (2019) *Scripture Re-Envisioned: Christophanic Exegesis and the Making of a Christian Bible*. Leiden.

Buell, D. K. (1999) *Making Christians: Clement of Alexandria and His Rhetoric of Legitimacy*. Princeton.

Burgess, R., and M. Kulikowski (2013) *Mosaics of Time: The Latin Chronicle Traditions from the First Century BC to the Sixth Century AD*. Turnhout.

Burkitt, F. (1901) *S. Ephraim's Quotations from the Gospel*. Cambridge.

Burn, A. E. (1899) *An Introduction to the Creeds and to the Te Deum*. London.

Burns, D. (2019) 'Proclus and the Theurgic Liturgy of Pseudo-Dionysius', in *Platonism and Christian Thought in Late Antiquity*, ed. P. G. Pavlos, L. F. Janby, E. K. Emilsson, and T. T. Tollefsen. London: 151–80.

Burrus, V. (1991) 'The Heretical Woman as Symbol in Alexander, Athanasius, Epiphanius, and Jerome', *HTR* 84: 229–48.

Burrus, V. (2005) 'Is Macrina a Woman? Gregory of Nyssa's *Dialogue on the Soul and Resurrection*', in *The Blackwell Companion to Postmodern Theology*, ed. G. Ward. Oxford: 249–64.

Burton-Christie, B. (2009) 'Evagrius on Sadness: Sadness and Christian Spirituality', *Cistercian Studies Quarterly* 44: 395–409.

Butcher, K. (2003) *Roman Syria and the Near East*. Los Angeles.

Butler, S. (2015) *The Ancient Phonograph*. New York.

Butts, A. (2017) 'Manuscript Transmission as Reception History: The Case of Ephrem the Syrian (d. 373)', *JECS* 25: 281–306.
Caillet, J.-P. (2014) 'Eusèbe de Césarée face aux images: Vers une interprétation plus positive – et moins incertain – de ses attitudes?' *Antiquité tardive* 22: 137–42.
Cameron, A. (1978) 'The Theotokos in Sixth-Century Constantinople', *JTS* 29: 79–108.
Cameron, A. (1985) *Procopius and the Sixth Century*. London.
Cameron, A. (1991) *Christianity and the Rhetoric of Empire: The Development of Christian Discourse*. Berkeley.
Cameron, A. (1992) 'Byzantium and the Past in the Seventh Century: The Search for Redefinition', in *The Seventh Century: Change and Continuity*, ed. J. Fontaine and J. N. Hillgarth. London: 250–76.
Cameron, A. (1994) *Christianity and the Rhetoric of Empire: The Development of Christian Discourse*. Berkeley.
Cameron, A. (2004) 'The Cult of the Virgin in Late Antiquity: Religious Development and Myth-Making', in *The Church and Mary*, ed. R. N. Swanson. Woodbridge: 1–21.
Cameron, A. (2010) *The Last Pagans of Rome*. Oxford.
Cameron, A. (2014) *Dialoguing in Late Antiquity*. Washington.
Cameron, A., and S. Hall (trans.) (1999) *Eusebius: Life of Constantine*. Oxford.
Campbell, C. R. (2012) *Paul and Union with Christ: An Exegetical and Theological Study*. Grand Rapids.
Campbell, J. (2003) 'Production and Distribution in Early and Middle Anglo-Saxon England', in *Markets in Early Medieval Europe: Trading and 'Productive' Sites, 650–850*, ed. T. Pestell and K. Ulmschneider. Oxford: 12–19.
Campbell, S. D. (1995) 'The Peaceful Kingdom: A Liturgical Interpretation', in *Fifth International Colloquium on Ancient Mosaics*, ed. R. Ling. Ann Arbor: 125–34.
Campbell, S. D. (1998) *Mosaics of Anemurium*. Toronto.
Camplani, A. (1998a) 'Note Bardesanitiche', *Miscellanea Marciana* 12: 11–43.
Camplani, A. (1998b) 'Rivisitando Bardesane: Note sulle fonti siriache del bardesanismo e sulla sua collocazione storico–religiosa', *CNS* 19: 519–96.
Camplani, A. (2003) 'Bardesane et les Bardesanites', *École pratique des hautes études, Section des sciences religieuses: Annuaire* 12: 29–50.
Camplani, A. (2009) 'Traditions of Christian Foundation in Edessa between Myth and History', *SMSR* 75: 251–78.
Caner, D. F. (1997) 'The Practice and Prohibition of Self-Castration in Early Christianity', *VC* 51: 396–415.
Carlson, M. L. (1948) 'Pagan Examples of Fortitude in the Latin Christian Apologists', *CP* 43: 93–104.
Carr, D. M. (2005) *Writing on the Tablet of the Heart: Origins of Scripture and Literature*. New York.
Carriker, A. (2003) *The Library of Eusebius of Caesarea*. Leiden.
Carroll, M. T. A. (1946) *The Venerable Bede: His Spiritual Teachings*. Washington.

Carruthers, M. (1990) *The Book of Memory: A Study of Memory in Medieval Culture.* Cambridge.
Carruthers, M. (1998) *The Craft of Thought: Meditation, Rhetoric, and the Making of Images, 400–1200.* Cambridge.
Carter, J. (ed.) (2003) *Understanding Religious Sacrifice: A Reader.* London.
Cartwright, S. (2012) 'The Image of God in Irenaeus, Marcellus, and Eustathius', in *Irenaeus: Life, Scripture. Legacy*, ed. S. Parvis and P. Foster. Minneapolis: 199–208.
Cartwright, S. (2015) *The Theological Anthropology of Eustathius of Antioch.* OECS Oxford.
Cary, P. (1998) 'What Licentius Learned: A Narrative Reading of the Cassiciacum Dialogues', *AugStud* 29: 141–63.
Caspari, C. P. (ed.) (1866–75) *Ungedruckte, unbeachtete, und wenig beachtete Quellen zur Geschichte des Taufsymbols und der Glaubensregel.* 3 vols. Christiania.
Castagno, A. M. (2014) 'Contesto liturgico e cronologia della predicazione origeniana alla luce delle nuove *Omelie sui Salmi*', *Adamantius* 20: 238–55.
Castelli, E. (2004) *Martyrdom and Memory: Early Christian Culture Making.* New York.
Catapano, G. (1986–) 'Ratio', in *Augustinus-Lexikon*, ed. C. Mayer, E. Feldmann, K.-H. Chelius, A. E. J Grote, R. Dodaro, C. Müller, et al. 5 vols. Basel: 1069–84.
Cavarero, A. (2005) *For More than One Voice: Towards a Philosophy of Vocal Expression.* Stanford.
Černušková, V., J. L. Kovacs, and J. Plátová (eds.) (2017) *Clement's Biblical Exegesis: Proceedings of the Second Colloquium on Clement of Alexandria (Olomouc, May 29–31, 2014).* Leiden.
Chadwick, H. (1999) 'Philosophical Tradition and the Self', in *Late Antiquity: A Guide to the Postclassical World*, ed. G. W. Bowersock, P. Brown, and O. Grabar. Cambridge: 60–81.
Champion, M. (2014) 'Grief and Desire, Body and Soul in Gregory of Nyssa's *Life of Saint Macrina*', in *Conjunctions of Mind, Soul and Body from Plato to the Enlightenment*, ed. D. Kambraskovic. Dordrecht: 99–118.
Champion, M. (2017) 'Paideia as Humility and Becoming Godlike in Dorotheos of Gaza', *JECS* 25: 441–69.
Charalabopoulos, N. (2012) *Platonic Drama and Its Ancient Reception.* Cambridge.
Charlet, J. (1988) 'Richesse spirituelle d'une hymne d'Ambroise: Aeterne rerum conditor', *La Maison-Dieu* 173: 61–69.
Chase, M. (2009–2010) 'La subsistence néoplatonicienne: De Porphyre à Théodore de Raithu', *Chora: Revue des études anciennes et médiévales* 7–8: 37–52.
Chazelle, C. (2001) *The Crucified God in the Carolingian Era: Theology and Art of Christ's Passion.* Cambridge.
Chazelle, C. (2019) *The Codex Amiatinus and Its 'Sister' Bibles: Scripture, Liturgy, and Art in the Milieu of the Venerable Bede.* Leiden.
Chiaradonna, R. (2017) 'Théologie et époptique aristotéliciennes dans le médio-platonisme: La réception de *Métaphysique* Λ', in *Réceptions de la théologie*

aristotélicienne d'Aristote à Michel d'Éphèse, ed. F. Baghdassarian and G. Guyomarc'h. Louvain-la-neuve: 143–57.

Chin, C. M. (2008) *Grammar and Christianity in the Late Roman World*. Philadelphia.

Chin, C. M., and M. Vidas (2015a) *Late Ancient Knowing: Explorations in Intellectual History*. Oakland.

Chin, C. M., and M. Vidas (2015b) 'Introduction', in Chin and Vidas 2015a: 1–16.

Chlup, R. (2012) *Proclus: An Introduction*. Cambridge.

Choufrine, A. (2002) *Gnosis, Theophany, Theiosis: Studies in Clement of Alexandria's Appropriation of his Background*. New York.

Chwe, M. S.-Y. (2001) *Rational Ritual: Culture, Coordination, and Common Knowledge*. Princeton.

Cipriani, N. (1994) 'Le fonti cristiane della dottrina trinitaria nei primi Dialoghi di S. Agostino', *Aug* 34: 253–312.

Clanchy, M., and L. Smith (2010) 'Abelard's Description of the School of Laon: What Might It Tell Us about Early Scholastic Teaching?', *Nottingham Medieval Studies* 54: 1–34.

Clark, E. (1998) 'The Lady Vanishes: Dilemmas of a Feminist Historian after the "Linguistic Turn"', *CH* 67: 1–31.

Clarke, E. C., J. M. Dillon, and J. P. Hershbell (2003) 'Introduction', in *Iamblichus: De mysteriis*. Atlanta: xxi–xxiii.

Clarke, J. (2012) 'Constructing the Spaces of Epiphany in Ancient Greek and Roman Culture', in *Text, Image, and Christians in the Greco-Roman World*, ed. A. Cissé Niang and C. Osiek. Princeton: 257–79.

Coakley, S. (2000) 'The Eschatological Body: Gender, Transformation, and God', *Modern Theology* 16: 61–73.

Coakley, S. (2011) 'In Defense of Sacrifice: Gender, Selfhood, and the Binding of Isaac', in *Feminism, Sexuality, and the Return of Religion*, ed. L. Martín Alcoff and J. D. Caputo. Bloomington: 17–38.

Coakley, S. (2012) 'Gregory of Nyssa', in Gavrilyuk and Coakley 2012a: 36–55.

Cobb, S. (2016) *Divine Deliverance: Pain and Painlessness in Early Christian Martyr Texts*. Berkeley.

Colish, M. (2005) *Ambrose's Patriarchs: Ethics for the Common Man*. Notre Dame.

Conant, J. (2020) 'Memories of Trauma and the Formation of a Christian Identity', in *Memories of Utopia: The Revision of Histories and Landscapes in Late Antiquity*, ed. B. Neil and K. Simic. London: 36–56.

Congar, Y., OP (2004) *The Meaning of Tradition*, trans. A. N. Woodrow. San Francisco. Originally publ. in French, Paris 1963.

Constas, N. (2003) *Proclus of Constantinople and the Cult of the Virgin in Late Antiquity*. Supplements to Vigiliae Christianae 66. Leiden.

Contreni, J. J. (2014) 'Learning for God: Education in the Carolingian Age', *JML* 24: 90–100.

Conybeare, C. (2002) 'The Ambiguous Laughter of Saint Laurence', *JECS* 10: 175–202.

Conybeare, C. (2006) *The Irrational Augustine*. Oxford.

Coogan, J. (2017) 'Mapping the Fourfold Gospel: Textual Geography in the Eusebian Apparatus', *JECS* 25: 337–57.

Coogan, J. (2018) 'Divine Truth, Presence, and Power: Christian Books in Roman North Africa', *JLA* 11: 375–95.

Coogan, J. (2020) 'Transmission and Transformation of the Eusebian Gospel Apparatus in Medieval Greek Manuscripts', in *Canones: The Art of Harmony: The Canon Tables of the Four Gospels*, ed. A. Bausi, B. Reudenbach, and H. Wimmer. Berlin: 29–46.

Coogan, J. (2021) 'Gospel as Recipe Book: Nonlinear Reading and Practical Texts in Late Antiquity', *EC* 12: 40–60.

Coogan, J. (2023) 'Reading (in) a Quadriform Cosmos: Gospel Books in the Early Christian Bibliographic Imagination', *JECS* 31: 85–103.

Coolman, B. T. (2012a) 'Alexander of Hales', in Gavrilyuk and Coakley 2012a: 121–39.

Coolman, B. T. (2012b) 'Thomas Gallus', in Gavrilyuk and Coakley 2012a: 140–58.

Coolman, B. T. (2016) *Knowing God by Experience: The Spiritual Senses in the Theology of William of Auxerre*. Washington.

Cooper, J. M. (2012) *Pursuits of Wisdom: Six Ways of Life in Ancient Philosophy from Socrates to Plotinus*. Princeton.

Cooper, K., and M. Dal Santo (2008) 'Boethius, Gregory the Great and the Christian "Afterlife" of Classical Dialogue', in *The End of Dialogue in Antiquity*, ed. S. Goldhill. Cambridge: 173–90.

Copeland, R., and I. Sluiter (2009) *Medieval Grammar and Rhetoric: Language Arts and Literary Theory, AD 300–1475*. Oxford.

Corke-Webster, J. (2012) 'Author and Authority: Literary Representations of Moral Authority in Eusebius of Caesarea's "The Martyrs of Palestine"', in *Christian Martyrdom in Late Antiquity: History and Discourse, Tradition and Religious Identity*, ed. P. Gemeinhardt and J. Leemans. Berlin: 51–77.

Corke-Webster, J. (2019) *Eusebius and Empire: Constructing Church and Rome in the Ecclesiastical History*. Cambridge.

Corrigan, K. (2009) *Evagrius and Gregory: Mind, Soul and Body in the 4th Century*. Aldershot.

Courcelle, P. (1950) 'Plotin et Saint Ambroise', *RevPhil* 76: 29–56.

Courcelle, P. (1969) *Late Latin Writers and Their Greek Sources*, trans. H. E. Wedeck. Cambridge.

Crawford, M. R. (2015a) 'Reading the Diatessaron with Ephrem: The Word and the Light, the Voice and the Star', *VC* 69: 70–95.

Crawford, M. R. (2015b) 'Ammonius of Alexandria, Eusebius of Caesarea and the Origins of Gospels Scholarship', *NTS* 61: 1–29.

Crawford, M. R. (2015c) '"Reordering the Confusion": Tatian, the Second Sophistic, and the so-called *Diatessaron*', *ZAC* 19: 209–36.

Crawford, M. R. (2016) 'The *Problemata* of Tatian: Recovering the Fragments of a Second-Century Christian Intellectual', *JTS* 67: 542–75.

Crawford, M. R. (2019) *The Eusebian Canon Tables: Ordering Textual Knowledge in Late Antiquity*. Oxford.
Crawford, M. R. (2020) 'Do the Eusebian Canon Tables Represent the Closure or the Opening of the Biblical Text? Considering the Case of Codex Fuldensis', in *Canones: The Art of Harmony: The Canon Tables of the Four Gospels*, ed. A. Bausi, B. Reudenbach, and H. Wimmer. Berlin: 17–28.
Crawford, M. R. (2021) '"The Hostile Devices of the Demented Demons": Tatian on Astrology and Pharmacology', *JECS* 29: 31–60.
Crialesi, C. V. (2020) 'The Status of Mathematics in Boethius: Remarks in the Light of His Commentaries on the *Isagoge*', in *The Sustainability of Thought: An Itinerary Through the History of Philosophy*, ed. L. Giovannetti. Naples: 95–124.
Cribiore, R. (2001) *Gymnastics of the Mind*. Princeton.
Cribiore, R. (2007) *The School of Libanius in Late Antique Antioch*. Princeton.
Crislip, A. (2023) 'The Ascetic Construction of Emotions: *Lupe* and *Akedia* in the Works of Evagrios of Pontos', in *Managing Emotions in Byzantium: Passions, Affects and Imaginings*, ed. S. Ashbrook Harvey and M. Mullett. Studies in Byzantine Cultural History. New York: 240–65.
Crosignani, C. (2017) 'The Influence of Demons on the Human Mind According to Athenagoras and Tatian', in *Demons and Illness from Antiquity to the Early-Modern Period*, ed. S. Bhayro and C. Rider. Leiden: 175–91.
Cross, R. (2012) 'Thomas Aquinas', in Gavrilyuk and Coakley 2012a: 174–89.
Crouzel, H. (1970) 'L'école d'Origène à Césarée', *BLE* 71: 15–27.
Cunningham, M. B., and P. Allen (ed.) (1998) *Preacher and Audience: Studies in Early Christian and Byzantine Homiletics*. Leiden.
Dal Santo, M. (2013) 'Gregory the Great, the Empire and the Emperor', in Neil and Dal Santo 2013: 57–81.
Daly, R. (1978) *Christian Sacrifice: The Judaeo-Christian Background before Origen*. Washington.
Damgaard, F. (2013) *Recasting Moses: The Memory of Moses in Biographical and Autobiographical Narratives in Ancient Judaism and 4th-Century Christianity*. Frankfurt am Main.
D'Ancona Costa, C. (2002) 'Commenting on Aristotle: From Late Antiquity to the Arab Aristotelianism', in *Der Kommentar in Antike und Mittelater: Beiträge zu einer Erforschung*, ed. W. Geerlings and C. Schulze. Leiden: 201–49.
Daniélou, J. (1977) *A History of Early Christian Doctrine Before the Council of Nicaea*. Vol. III: *The Origins of Latin Christianity*, trans. D. Smith and J. A. Baker. London.
Danker, F. W. (2001) *A Greek–English Lexicon of the New Testament and Other Early Christian Literature*, 3rd edn. Chicago.
Darby, P. (2012) *Bede and the End of Time*. Farnham.
Datema, C. (1981) 'When Did Leontius, Presbyter of Constantinople, Preach?', *VC* 35: 346–51.

Daunton-Fear, A. (2009) *Healing in the Early Church: The Church's Ministry of Healing and Exorcism from the First to the Fifth Century*. Eugene.
Davis, P. (2008) *Translation and the Poet's Life*. Oxford.
Davis, S. (2001) *The Cult of Saint Thecla: A Tradition of Women's Piety in Late Antiquity*. Oxford.
Day, J. J. (2014) *Reading the Liturgy: An Exploration of Texts in Christian Worship*. London.
De Andia, Y. (1986) *Homo vivens: Incorruptibilité et divinisation de l'homme chez Irénée de Lyon*. Paris.
De Ghellinck, J. (1948) 'Un aspect de l'opposition entre hellénisme et christianisme: L'attitude vis-à-vis de la dialectique dans les débats trinitaires', *Patristique et moyen age* 3: 245–310.
De Halleux, A. (1963) *Philoxène de Mabbog: Sa vie, ses écrits, sa théologie*. Louvain.
De Halleux, A. (1972) 'Une clé pour les hymnes d'Ephrem dans le ms. Sinaï syr. 10', *Mus* 85: 171–99.
De Lange, N. (2005) 'Jews in the Age of Justinian', in *The Cambridge Companion to the Age of Justinian*, ed. M. Maas. Cambridge: 401–26.
De Vegvar, C. N. (2006) 'Remembering Jerusalem: Architecture and Meaning in Insular Canon Table Arcades', in *Making and Meaning in Insular Art*, ed. R. Moss. Dublin: 242–56.
De Vicente García, J. L. (2001) 'San Agustin, San Gregorio y San Isidori ante el problema de las esterellas: Fundamentos para el rechazo frontal de la astrologia', *Revista espanola de filosofia medieval* 8: 187–203.
Debié, M. (2000) 'Record Keeping and Chronicle Writing in Antioch and Edessa', *Aram* 12: 409–17.
Debié, M. (2015) *L'écriture de l'histoire en syriaque: Transmissions interculturelles et constructions identitaires entre hellénisme et islam*. Leuven.
Declerck, J. H. (1994) 'Encore une fois Léonce et Pamphile', in *Philohistôr: Miscellanea in honorem Caroli Laga septuagenarii*, ed. A. Schoors and P. Van Deun. Leuven: 199–216.
DeGregorio, S. (1999) 'The Venerable Bede on Prayer and Contemplation', *Traditio* 54: 1–39.
DeGregorio, S. (2002) '"Nostrorum socordiam temporum": The Reforming Impulse of Bede's Later Exegesis', *Early Medieval Europe* 11: 107–22.
DeGregorio, S. (2004) 'Bede's *In Ezram et Neemiam* and the Reform of the Northumbrian Church', *Spec* 79: 1–25.
DeGregorio, S. (ed.) (2006a) *Innovation and Tradition in the Writings of the Venerable Bede*. Morgantown.
DeGregorio, S. (2006b) 'Introduction: The New Bede', in DeGregorio 2006a: 1–10.
DeGregorio, S. (2006c) 'Footsteps of His Own: Bede's Commentary on Ezra-Nehemiah', in DeGregorio 2006a: 143–68.
DeGregorio, S. (ed.) (2010) *The Cambridge Companion to Bede*. Cambridge.
DeGregorio, S. (2019) *Bede: On First Samuel*. Liverpool.

DelCogliano, M. (2006) 'Eusebian Theologies of the Son as the Image of God before 341', *JECS* 14: 458–84.
dell'Osso, C. (2010) *Cristo e Logos: Il Calcedonismo del VI secolo in Oriente*. Rome.
Demacopoulos, G. E. (2013) *The Invention of Peter: Apostolic Discourse and Papal Authority in Late Antiquity*. Philadelphia.
Demacopoulos, G. E. (2015) *Gregory the Great: Ascetic, Pastor, and First Man of Rome*. Notre Dame.
Demus, O. (1948) *Byzantine Mosaic Decoration: Aspects of Monumental Art in Byzantium*. London.
den Boeft, J. (1996–2002a) '*Daemon(es)*', in *Augustinus-Lexicon II*, ed. C. Mayer. Basel: 213–22.
den Boeft, J. (1996–2002b) '*Divinatione Daemonum (De)*', in *Augustinus-Lexicon II*, ed. C. Mayer. Basel: 519–24.
den Boeft, J. (2003) 'Aeterne rerum conditor: Ambrose's Poem about "Time"', in *Jerusalem, Alexandria, Rome: Studies in Ancient Cultural Interaction in Honour of A. Hilhorst*, ed. F. García Martínez and G. P. Luttikhuizen. Leiden: 27–40.
den Boeft, J. (2008) 'Delight and Imagination: Ambrose's Hymns', *VC* 62: 425–40.
den Dulk, M. (2018) 'Justin Martyr and the Authorship of the Earliest Anti-Heretical Treatise', *VC* 72: 471–83.
Denecker, T., and G. Partoens (2014) '*De uoce et uerbo*: Augustine's Exegesis of John 1:1–3 and 23 in *Sermons* 288 and 293A auct. (Dolbeau 3)', *ASE* 31: 91–114.
Denzinger, H. (ed.) (1854) *Enchiridion symbolorum et definitiorum: quae de rebus fidei et morum a conciliis oecumenicis et summis pontificibus emanarunt*. Wireburgi.
Detienne, M., and J. P. Vernant (1989) *The Cuisine of Sacrifice among the Greeks*. Chicago.
DeVore, M. (2017) '*Catechumeni*, Not "New Converts": Revisiting the *Passio Perpetuae et Felicitatis*', StPatr 91: 237–47.
Dibelius, M. (1910) 'Wer Ohren hat zu hören, der höre', *TSK* 83: 461–71.
Dickey, E. (2015) 'Columnar Translation: An Ancient Interpretive Tool that the Romans Gave the Greeks', *CQ* 65: 807–21.
Diels, H. (1879) *Doxographi graeci*. Berlin. 4th unaltered repr. 1976.
Digeser, E. D. (2018) 'Collaboration and Identity in the Aftermath of Persecution: Religious Conflict and Legacy', in *Reconceiving Religious Conflict: New Views from the Formative Centuries of Christianity*, ed. W. Mayer and C. L. de Wet. London: 261–81.
Dijkstra, R. (2016) *The Apostles in Early Christian Art and Poetry*. Leiden.
Dillon, J. (1986) 'Noêstis Aisthêtê: A Doctrine of the Spiritual Senses in Origen and in Plotinus', in *Hellenica et Judaica: Hommage à Valentin Nikiprowetzky*, ed. A. Caquot, M. Hadas-Lebel, and J. Riaud. Leuven: 443–55.
Dillon, J. (1996) *The Middle Platonists: 80 BC to AD 220*, rev. ed. Ithaca.
Dillon, J. (2014) 'Dionysius the Areopagite', in *Interpreting Proclus: From Antiquity to the Renaissance*, ed. S. Gersh. Cambridge: 111–34.
Dimitrova, N. (2016) *Human Knowledge According to St Maximus the Confessor*. Eugene.

Dionisotti, A. C. (1982) 'On Bede, Grammars, and Greek', *RBén* 92: 111–41.
Dobell, B. (2009) *Augustine's Intellectual Conversion: The Journey from Platonism to Christianity.* Cambridge.
Dodds, E. R. (1951) 'Appendix II, Theurgy', in *The Greeks and the Irrational.* Berkeley: 283–312.
Doignon, J. (1986) 'La praxis de l'*admonitio* dans les Dialogues de Cassiciacum de saint Augustin', *Vetera christianorum* 23: 21–37.
Dolar, M. (2006) *A Voice and Nothing More.* Cambridge.
Dorival, G. (2004) 'Est-il légitime d'éclairer le *Discours* de remerciement par la *Lettre à Grégoire* et réciproquement? Ou la tentation de Pasolini', in *La biografia di Origene fra storia e agiografia: Atti del VI convegno di studi del gruppo italiano di ricerca su Origene e la tradizione alessandrina, Torino, 11–13 settembre 2002*, ed. A. M. Castagno. Villa Verucchio: 9–26.
Dresken-Weiland, J. (2010) *Bild, Grab und Wort: Untersuchungen zu Jenseitsvorstellungen von Christen des 3. und 4. Jahrhunderts.* Regensburg.
Dreyer, O. (1968–69) 'Lyseis', *KlPauly* 3.16–17: 832–33.
Drijvers, H. J. W. (1966) *Bardaisan of Edessa.* Assen.
Drijvers, H. J. W. (1980) *Cults and Beliefs at Edessa.* Leiden.
Drijvers, H. J. W. (1984a) *East of Antioch: Studies in Early Syriac Christianity.* London.
Drijvers, H. J. W. (1984b) 'Edessa und das jüdische Christentum', in Drijvers 1984a: §2.
Drijvers, H. J. W., and J. F. Healey (eds.) (1999) *The Old Syriac Inscriptions of Edessa and Osrhoene: Texts, Translations, and Commentary.* Leiden.
DuBois, P. (1988) *Sowing the Body: Psychoanalysis and the Ancient Representations of Women.* Women in Culture and Society. Chicago.
du Roy, O. (1966) *L'intelligence de la foi en la Trinité selon Saint Augustin: Genèse de sa théologie trinitaire jusqu'en 391.* Paris.
Duffy, J. (2002) 'Hellenic Philosophy in Byzantium and the Lonely Mission of Michael Psellos', in *Byzantine Philosophy and Its Ancient Sources*, ed. K. Ierodiakonou. Oxford: 139–56.
Dujarier, M. (1979) *A History of the Catechumenate: The First Six Centuries*, trans. E. J. Hassl. New York.
Dungan, D. L. (2006) *Constantine's Bible: Politics and the Making of the Canon.* Minneapolis.
Dunkle, B. (2016) *Enchantment and Creed in the Hymns of Ambrose of Milan.* Oxford.
Dupont, A., and D. Finn (2019) 'Preaching Adam in John Chrysostom and Augustine of Hippo', *VC* 73: 190–217.
Dutsch, Dorota M. (2020) *Pythagorean Women Philosophers: Between Belief and Suspicion. Pythagorean Women Philosophers.* Oxford Studies in Classical Literature and Gender Theory. Oxford.
Dyson, G. P. (2019) *Priests and Their Books in Late Anglo-Saxon England.* Woodbridge.

Ebbesen, S. (1990) 'Boethius as an Aristotelian Commentator', in *Aristotle Transformed: The Ancient Commentators and their Influence*, ed. R. Sorabji. Ithaca: 373–91.

Ebbesen, S. (2003) 'Boethius on the Metaphysics of Words', in *Boèce ou la chaîne des savoirs: Actes du colloque international de la fondation Singer-Polignac, Paris, 8–12 juin 1999*, ed. A. Galonnier. Louvain: 257–75.

Edwards, C. (2007) *Death in Ancient Rome*. New Haven.

Edwards, M. J. (2012) 'Alexander of Alexandria and Homoousion', *VC* 66: 482–502.

Edwards, M. J. (2013a) *Image, Word and God in the Early Christian Centuries*. Farnham.

Edwards, M. J. (2013b) 'Why Did Constantine Label Arius a Porphyrian?' *L'antiquité classique* 82: 239–47.

Edwards, M. J. (2015a) 'One Origen or Two? The *Status Quaestionis*', *SO* 89: 81–103.

Edwards, M. J. (2015b) *Religions of the Constantinian Empire*. Oxford.

Edwards, M. J. (2019) *Aristotle and Early Christian Thought*. London.

Ehlers, B. (1966) *Eine vorplatonische Deutung des sokratischen Eros: Der Dialog Aspasia des sokratikers Aischines*. Munich.

Ehlers, B. (1970) 'Bardesanes von Edessa: Ein syrischer Gnostiker: Bemerkungen aus Anlaß des Buches von H. J. W. Drijvers, *Bardaisan of Edessa*', *ZKG* 81: 334–51.

Eleuteri, P. (1993) *I manoscritti greci della Biblioteca palatina di Parma*. Milan.

Elliot, M. (2013) 'Wisdom of Solomon, Canon and Authority', StPatr 53: 3–16.

Elm, S. (2004) *Virgins of God: The Making of Asceticism in Late Antiquity*. Oxford.

Elsner, J. (1995) *Art and the Roman Viewer: The Transformation of Art from the Pagan World to Christianity*. Cambridge.

Elsner, J. (2007) *Roman Eyes: Visuality & Subjectivity in Art & Text*. Princeton.

Elsner, J. (2012) 'Iconoclasm as Discourse: From Antiquity to Byzantium', *Art Bulletin* 94: 369–95.

Elsner, J. (2020a) 'Beyond Eusebius: Prefatory Images and the Early Book', in *Canones: The Art of Harmony: The Canon Tables of the Four Gospels*, ed. A. Bausi, B. Reudenbach, and H. Wimmer. Berlin: 99–132.

Elsner, J. (2020b) *Empires of Faith in Late Antiquity: Histories of Art and Religion from India to Ireland*. Cambridge.

Emerton, J. (1956) 'The Purpose of the Second Column of the Hexapla', *JTS* 7: 79–87.

Emerton, J. (1970) 'Were Greek Transliterations of the Hebrew Old Testament Used by Jews before the Time of Origen?', *JTS* 21: 17–31.

Emerton, J. (1971) 'A Further Consideration of the Purpose of the Second Column of the Hexapla', *JTS* 22: 15–28.

Emilsson, E. K. (1988) *Plotinus on Sense Perception*. Cambridge.

Engberg, J. (2012) 'The Education and (Self-)Affirmation of (Recent or Potential) Converts: The Case of Cyprian and the *Ad Donatum*', *ZAC* 16: 129–44.

Enroth, A.-M. (1990) 'The Hearing Formula in the Book of Revelation', *NTS* 36: 598–608.

Enterline, L. (2015) 'Rhetoric and Gender in the 16th Century', in *The Oxford Handbook of Rhetorical Studies*, ed. M. MacDonald. Oxford.

Erismann, C. (2008) 'The Trinity, Universals, and Particular Substances: Philoponus and Roscelin', *Traditio* 63: 277–305.

Eshleman, K. (2012) *The Social World of the Intellectuals in the Roman Empire: Sophists, Philosophers, and Christians*. Cambridge.

Evans, G. R. (1990) *Augustine on Evil*. Cambridge.

Évieux, P. (1967) 'La théologie de l'accoutumance chez saint Irénée', *RSR* 55: 5–54.

Fagerberg, D. (2004) *Theologia Prima: What Is Liturgical Theology?* Chicago.

Fahey, M. A. (1971) *Cyprian and the Bible: A Study in Third-Century Exegesis*. Tübingen.

Fairweather, J. (1973) 'The Death of Heraclitus', *GRBS* 13: 233–39.

Faith, R. (2020) *The Moral Economy of the Countryside: Anglo-Saxon to Anglo-Norman England*. Cambridge.

Fantino, J. (1986) *L'homme image de Dieu chez saint Irénée de Lyon*. Paris.

Fantino, J. (1994) *La théologie d'Irénée: Lecture des écritures en réponse à l'exégèse gnostique – une approche trinitaire*. Paris.

Feissel, D. (2010) *Documents, droit, diplomatique dans l'empire romain tardif*. Paris.

Felle, A. E. (2006) *Biblia epigraphica: La sacra scrittura nella documentazione epigrafica dell'orbis christianus antiquus, iii–viii secolo*. Bari.

Ferguson, E. (1980) 'Spiritual Sacrifice in Early Christianity and Its Environment', *ANRW* 2.23.2: 1152–90.

Ferguson, E. (2001) 'Catechesis and Initiation', in *The Origins of Christendom in the West*, ed. A. Kreider. Edinburgh: 229–68.

Ferguson, E. (2011) 'Angels of the Churches in Revelation 1–3: *Status Quaestionis* and Another Proposal', *BBR* 21: 371–86.

Ferngren, G. B. (2009) *Medicine & Health Care in Early Christianity*. Baltimore.

Ferrari, L. C. (1977) 'Augustine and Astrology', *LTP* 33: 241–51.

Festugière, A. J. (1969) 'L'ordre de lecture des dialogues de Platon aux Ve/VIe siècles', *MH* 26: 281–96.

Fialon, S. (2018) *Mens Immobilis: Recherches sur le corpus latin des actes et des passions d'Afrique romaine (IIe–VIe siècles)*. Paris.

Fichtner, G. (1982) 'Christus als Arzt: Ursprünge und Wirkungen eines Motivs', *FMSt* 16: 1–18.

Fiedrowicz, M. (2005) 'Introduction to "Demonic Divination (*De divinatione daemonum*)"', in *On Christian Belief*, trans. M. Connell, ed. B. Ramsay. New York: 197–202.

Field, F. (1875) *Origenis Hexaplorum quae supersunt*. Oxford.

Filoramo, G. (2014) 'Eschatology', in *Encyclopedia of Ancient Christianity*, Vol. I: *A–E*, ed. A. Di Berardino, T. C. Oden, and J.C. Elowsky. Downers Grove: 837–40.

Finn, R. (2009) *Asceticism in the Graeco-Roman World*. Cambridge.

Finney, P. C. (1994) *The Invisible God: The Earliest Christians on Art*. Oxford.

Flemming, R. (2000) 'The Physicians at the Feast: The Place of Medical Knowledge at Athenaeus' Dinner-Table', in *Athenaeus and His World: Reading Greek Culture in the Roman Empire*, ed. D. Braund and J. Wilkins. Exeter: 476–82.

Flemming, R. (2005) 'Suicide, Euthanasia and Medicine: Reflections Ancient and Modern', *Economy and Society* 33: 295–321.

Föllinger, S., and G. M. Müller (eds.) (2013) *Der Dialog in der Antike: Formen und Funktionen einer literarischen Gattung zwischen Philosophie, Wissensvermittlung und dramatischer Inszenierung*. Berlin.

Fontaine, J. (1976) 'Prose et poésie: L'interférence des genres et des styles dans la création littéraire d'Ambroise de Milan', in *Ambrosius Episcopus: Atti del Congresso internazionale di studi ambrosiani nel XVI centenario della elevazione di sant'Ambrogio alla cattedra episcopale, Milano, 2–7 dicembre 1974*, ed. G. Lazzati. Milan: 124–70.

Fontaine, J. (1981) *Naissance de la poésie dans l'occident chrétien: Esquisse d'une histoire de la poésie latine chrétienne du IIIe au vie siècle*. Paris.

Formisano, M. (2001) *Tecnica e scrittura: Le letterature tecnico-scientifiche nello spazio letterario tardolatino*. Rome.

Formisano, M. (2013) 'Late Latin Encyclopaedism: Towards a New Paradigm of Practical Knowledge', in *Encyclopaedism from Antiquity to the Renaissance*, ed. J. König and G. Woolf. Cambridge: 197–215.

Formisano, M. (2018) 'Literature of Knowledge', in *A Companion to Late Antique Literature*, ed. S. McGill and E. J. Watts. London: 492–504.

Formisano, M., and P. van der Eijk (eds.) (2017) *Knowledge, Text and Practice in Ancient Technical Writing*. Cambridge.

Foucault, M. (1966) *Les mots et les choses*. Paris. (= Foucault 1973)

Foucault, M. (1969) *L'archéologie du savoir*. Paris. (= Foucault 1972)

Foucault, M. (1972) *The Archaeology of Knowledge*, trans. A. Sheridan. New York.

Foucault, M. (1973) *The Order of Things*, trans. A. Sheridan. New York.

Foucault, M. (1978–2021) *The History of Sexuality*, trans. R. Hurley. 4 vols. New York.

Foucault, M. (2005) *The Hermeneutics of the Subject: Lectures at the Collège de France, 1981–1982*. New York.

Fournier, É. (2020) 'The Christian Discourse of Persecution in Late Antiquity: An Introduction', in *Heirs of Roman Persecution: Studies on a Christian and Para-Christian Discourse in Late Antiquity*, ed. É. Fournier and W. Mayer. New York: 1–22.

Fowden, G. (1982) 'The Pagan Holy Man in Late Antique Society', *JHS* 102: 33–59.

Fowl, S. E. (2011) 'The Primacy of the Witness of the Body to Martyrdom in Paul', in *Witness of the Body: The Past, Present and Future of Christian Martyrdom*. Grand Rapids: 43–60.

Francis, J. (2003) 'Living Icons: Tracing a Motif in Verbal and Visual Representation from the Second to the Fourth Centuries CE', *AJP* 124: 575–600.

Francis, J. (2009) 'Verbal and Visual Representation: Art and Text, Culture and Power in Late Antiquity', in *A Companion to Late Antiquity*, ed. P. Rousseau. Oxford: 285–305.

Francis, J. (2020) 'Classical Conceptions of Visuality and Representation in John of Damascus' *Definition of Holy Images*', *SLA* 4: 281–308.

Frank, G. (2000a) 'Macrina's Scar: Homeric Allusion and Heroic Identity in Gregory of Nyssa's *Life of Macrina*', *JECS* 8: 511–30.

Frank, G. (2000b) *The Memory of the Eyes: Pilgrims to Living Saints in Christian Late Antiquity*. Berkeley.

Frank, G. (2001) '"Taste and See": The Eucharist and the Eyes of Faith in the Fourth Century', *CH* 70: 619–43.

Frank, G. (2006a) '*Loca Sancta* Souvenirs and the Art of Memory', in *Pèlerinages et lieux saints dans l'Antiquité et le Moyen Âge: Mélanges offerts à Pierre Maraval*, ed. B. Caseau, J.-C. Cheynet, and V. Déroche. Paris: 193–201.

Frank, G. (2006b) 'Romanos and the Night Vigil in the Sixth Century', in *Byzantine Christianity*, ed. D. Krueger. A People's History of Christianity. Minneapolis: 59–78.

Frank, G. (2013) 'Memory and Forgetting in Romanos the Melodist's *On the Newly Baptized*', in *Between Personal and Institutional Religion: Self, Doctrine, and Practice in Late Antique Eastern Christianity*, ed. B. Bitton-Ashkelony and L. Perrone. Turnhout: 37–55.

Frank, H. (1971) 'Die Vorrangstellung der Taufe Jesu in der altmailändischen Epiphanieliturgie und die Frage nach dem Dichter des Epiphaniehymnus *Inluminans altissimus*', *Archiv für Liturgiewissenschaft* 13: 115–32.

Frank, K. S. (1978) 'Maleachi 1, 10ff. in der frühen Väterdeutung: Ein Beitrag zu Opferterminologie und Opferverständnis in der alten Kirche', *TP* 53: 70–78.

Frankfurter, D. (2008) 'Iconoclasm and Christianization in Late Antique Egypt: Church Treatments in Time and Space', in *From Temple to Church: Destruction and Renewal of Local Cultic Topography in Late Antiquity*, ed. J. Hahn, S. Emmel, and U. Gotter. Leiden: 136–60.

Frede, M. (1983) 'The Stoics and Skeptics on Clear and Distinct Impressions', in *The Skeptical Tradition*, ed. M. Burnyeat. Berkeley: 65–93.

Fredouille, J.-C. (2010) 'L'humanité vue d'en haut (Cyprien, *Ad Donatum*, 6–13)', *VC* 64: 445–55.

Freisenbruch, A. (2007) 'Back to Fronto: Doctor and Patient in His Correspondence with an Emperor', in *Ancient Letters: Classical and Late Antique Epistolography*, ed. R. Morello and A. D. Morrison. Oxford: 235–55.

Frend, W. C. (1972) *The Rise of the Monophysite Movement*. Cambridge.

Frendo, J. D. C. (1984) 'The Poetic Achievement of George of Pisidia', in *Maistor: Classical, Byzantine and Renaissance Studies for Robert Browning*, ed. A. Moffatt. Canberra: 159–87.

Frendo, J. D. C. (1986) 'Classical and Christian Influences on the *Heracliad* of George of Pisidia', *Classical Bulletin* 62: 53–62.

Fürst, A. (2011) 'Origen: Exegesis and Philosophy in Early Christian Alexandria', in *Interpreting the Bible and Aristotle in Late Antiquity: The Alexandrian Commentary Tradition Between Rome and Baghdad*, ed. J. Lössl and J. W. Watt. Farnham: 13–32.

Fürst, A. (2017) *Origenes: Grieche und Christ in römischer Zeit*. Stuttgart.

Gador-Whyte, S. (2013a) 'Changing Conceptions of Mary in Sixth-Century Byzantium: The Kontakia of Romanos the Melodist', in *Questions of Gender in Byzantine Society*, ed. B. Neil and L. Garland. Farnham: 77–92.

Gador-Whyte, S. (2013b) 'Playing with Genre: Romanos the Melodist and His Kontakion', in *Approaches to Genre in the Ancient World*, ed. M. Borg and G. Miles. Newcastle: 159–75.

Gador-Whyte, S. (2017) *Theology and Poetry in Early Byzantium: The Kontakia of Romanos the Melodist*. Cambridge.

Gager, J. (1999) *Curse Tablets and Binding Spells from the Ancient World*. Oxford.

Gagos, T., and P. van Minnen (1994) *Settling a Dispute: Towards a Legal Anthropology of Late Antique Egypt*. Ann Arbor.

Gameson, R. (1992) 'The Cost of the Codex Amiatinus', *Notes and Queries* 39: 2–9.

Gao, F. F. (2002) *Vergil and Biblical Exegesis in Early Christian Latin Epic*. Berkeley.

Gasparini, V., M. Patzelt, R. Raja, A.-K. Rieger, J. Rüpke, and E. Urcivoli (2020) 'Pursuing Lived Ancient Religion', in *Lived Religion in the Ancient Mediterranean World: Approaching Religious Transformation from Archaeology, History and Classics*, ed. V. Gasparini, M. Patzelt, R. Raja, A.-K. Rieger, J. Rüpke, and E. Urcivoli. Berlin: 1–9.

Gasquet, A. T. (ed.) (1914) *Codex Vercellensis*. Rome.

Gassman, M. (2017) 'The Conversion of Cyprian's Rhetoric? Towards a New Reading of *Ad Donatum*', StPatr 94: 247–57.

Gassman, M. (2019) 'Cyprian's Early Career in the Church of Carthage', *JEH* 70: 1–17.

Gavrilyuk, P. L. (2007) *Histoire du catéchuménat dans l'église ancienne*. Paris.

Gavrilyuk, P. L. (2012) 'Pseudo-Dionysius the Areopagite', in Gavrilyuk and Coakley 2012a: 86–103.

Gavrilyuk, P. L., and S. Coakley (eds.) (2012a) *The Spiritual Senses: Perceiving God in Western Christianity*. Cambridge.

Gavrilyuk, P. L., and S. Coakley (2012b) 'Introduction', in Gavrilyuk and Coakley 2012a: 1–19.

Gee, E. (2013) *Aratus and the Astronomical Tradition*. Oxford.

Geerard, M. (ed.) (1974–87) *Clavis Patrum Graecorum*. 5 vols. Turnhout.

Geertz, C. (1980) *Negara: The Theatre State in Nineteenth-Century Bali*. Princeton.

Geertz, C. (2000) 'Common Sense as a Cultural System', in *Local Knowledge: Further Essays in Interpretive Anthropology*. New York: 73–93.

Geertz, S. (2018) 'Introduction', in *Elias, David: Introductions to Philosophy and Olympiodorus: Introduction to Logic*, trans. S. Geertz. London: 11–31.

Geljon, A. C. (2002) *Philonic Exegesis in Gregory of Nyssa's de vita Moysis*. Providence.

Geljon, A.-K. (2005) 'Divine Infinity in Gregory of Nyssa and Philo of Alexandria', *VC* 59: 152–77.

Gemeinhardt, P. (2016) 'Men of Letters or Fishermen? The Education of Bishops and Clerics in Late Antiquity', in *Teachers in Late Antique Christianity*, ed. P. Gemeinhardt, O. Lorgeoux, and M. Munkholt Christensen. Tübingen: 32–55.

Georges, T. (2012) 'Justin's School in Rome: Reflections on Early Christian "Schools"', *ZAC* 16: 75–87.

Gersh, S. (1973) *Κίνησις ἀκίνητος: A Study of Spiritual Motion in the Philosophy of Proclus*. Philosophia Antiqua 26. Leiden.

Gerson, L., and M. Martijn (2017) 'Proclus's System', in *All from One: A Guide to Proclus*, ed. P. d'Hoine and M. Martijn. Oxford.

Gerzaguet, C. (2018) 'Ambrosius Mediolensis', in *Preaching in the Patristic Era: Sermons, Preachers, and Audiences in the Latin West*, ed. A. Dupont, S. Boodts, G. Partoens, and J. Leemans. Leiden: 159–67.

Giannantoni, G. (1991) *Socratis et Socraticorum Reliquiae*. Naples.

Gibbon, E. (1914–19) *History of the Decline and Fall of the Roman Empire*, ed. J. B. Bury. 7 vols. London. Original publication: 1776–79.

Gibbons, K. (2015) 'Passions, Pleasures, and Perceptions: Rethinking Evagrius Ponticus on Mental Representation', *ZAC* 19: 297–330.

Gibson, C. A. (2013) 'Doctors in Ancient Greek and Roman Rhetorical Education', *Journal of the History of Medicine and Allied Sciences* 68: 529–50.

Giddens, A. (1984) *The Constitution of Society: Outline of a Theory of Structuration*. Berkeley.

Gignac, F. T. (1975) *A Grammar of the Greek Papyri of the Roman and Byzantine Periods*, Vol. I: *Phonology*. Milan.

Gilhus, I. S. (2006) *Animals, Gods and Humans: Changing Attitudes to Animals in Greek, Roman and Early Christian Thought*. London.

Gill, C. (2006) *The Structured Self in Hellenistic and Roman Thought*. Oxford.

Gill, C. (2010) *Naturalistic Psychology in Galen and Stoicism*. Oxford.

Gill, C. (2018) 'Philosophical Psychological Therapy: Did It Have Any Impact on Medical Practice?' in Singer and Thumiger 2018a: 365–80.

Gilson, E. (1946) 'Egypte ou Grèce?', *MS* 8: 43–52.

Giuliani, E., and C. Pavolini (1999) 'La "Biblioteca di Agapito" e la Basilica di S. Agnese', in *The Transformations of 'Urbs Roma' in Late Antiquity*, ed. W. V. Harris. Portsmouth: 85–107.

Gjesdal, K. (2015) 'Bildung', in *The Oxford Handbook of German Philosophy in the Nineteenth Century*, ed. M. N. Forster and K. Gjesdal. Oxford: 695–719.

Gleede, B. (2013) 'Der Traktat *De sectis* des Abbas Theodor: Eine unvollendete Handreichung zur Widerlegung der διακρινόμενοι', in *Christliches Ägypten in der spätantiken Zeit. Akten der 2. Tübinger Tagung zum Christlichen Orient (7.–8. Dezember 2007)*, ed. D. Bumazhnov. Tübingen: 179–216.

Gnilka, C. (1984) *Der Begriff des 'rechten Gebrauchs'*. Basel.

Gnisci, J. (2020) 'An Ethiopian Miniature of the Tempietto in the Metropolitan Museum of Art: Its Relatives and Symbolism', in *Canones: The Art of Harmony: The Canon Tables of the Four Gospels*, ed. A. Bausi, B. Reudenbach, and H. Wimmer. Berlin: 67–98.

Goldhill, S. (1995) *Foucault's Virginity: Ancient Erotic Fiction and the History of Sexuality*. Cambridge.

Goldhill, S. (2008) *The End of Dialogue in Antiquity*. Cambridge.
Goldhill, S. (2010) 'The Seductions of the Gaze: Socrates and His Girlfriends', in *Oxford Readings in Classical Studies: Xenophon*, ed. V. Grey. Oxford: 167–91.
Gonnelli, F. (1990) 'Le parole del cosmo: Osservazioni sull'*Esamerone* di Giorgio Pisidia', *ByzZ* 83: 411–22.
Gonnelli, F. (ed.) (1991) 'Il *De vita humana* di Georgio Pisida', *Bollettino dei Classici* 3.12: 118–38.
Gordon, R. L. (2020) '(Re)Modeling Religious Experience: Some Experiments with Hymnic Form in the Imperial Period', in *Lived Religion in the Ancient Mediterranean World: Approaching Religious Transformation from Archaeology, History and Classics*, ed. V. Gasparini, M. Patzelt, R. Raja, A.-K. Rieger, J. Rüpke, and E. Urciuoli. Berlin: 23–48.
Gorman, M. (1982) 'The Encyclopedic Commentary on Genesis Prepared for Charlemagne by Wigbod', *RA* 17: 173–201.
Gorman, M. (1997) 'A Critique of Bischoff's Theory of Irish Exegesis: The *Commentary on Genesis* in Munich clm 6302 (*Wendepunkte* 2)', *JML* 7: 178–233.
Gourevitch, D. (1969) 'Suicide among the Sick in Classical Antiquity', *Bulletin of the History of Medicine* 43: 501–18.
Grafton, A., and M. H. Williams (2006) *Christianity and the Transformation of the Book: Origen, Eusebius, and the Library of Caesarea*. Cambridge.
Graham, S. (2001) 'Structure and Purpose of Irenaeus' *Epideixis*', StPatr 36: 210–21.
Grant, R. M. (1980) *Eusebius as a Church Historian*. Oxford.
Grant, R. M. (1986) *Gods and the One God*. Philadelphia.
Graumann, T. (1994) *Christus Interpres: Die Einheit von Auslegung und Verkündigung in der Lukaserklärung des Ambrosius von Mailand*. Berlin.
Graver, M. (2008) *Stoicism and Emotions*. Chicago.
Gray, P. T. R. (2006) *Leontius of Jerusalem: Against the Monophysites – Testimonies of the Saints and Aporiae*. Oxford.
Greatrex, G. (2001) 'Lawyers and Historians in Late Antiquity', in *Law, Society and Authority in Late Antiquity*, ed. R. W. Mathisen. Oxford: 148–61.
Grebe, S. (1999) *Martianus Capella, 'De nuptiis Philologiae et Mercurii': Darstellung der sieben freien Künste und ihrer Beziehungen zueinander*. Stuttgart.
Green, G. W. (2012) 'Nicholas of Cusa', in Gavrilyuk and Coakley 2012a: 210–23.
Green, R. P. (1991) *The Works of Ausonius, with Introduction and Commentary*. Oxford.
Green, R. P. (1993) 'The Christianity of Ausonius', StPatr 28: 39–48.
Green, R. P. (2006) *Latin Epics of the New Testament*. Oxford.
Gregg, R. C., and D. Groh (1981) *Early Arianism: A View of Salvation*. Philadelphia.
Grey, C. (2007) 'Contextualising *colonatus*: The *origo* of the Late Roman Empire', *JRS* 97: 15–75.
Griffith, S. (1995) 'Asceticism in the Church of Syria: The Hermeneutics of Early Syrian Monasticism', in *Asceticism*, ed. V. L. Wimbush and R. Valantasis. New York: 220–48.

Grigg, R. (1977) 'Constantine the Great and the Cult without Images', *Viator* 8: 1–32.

Grigoryan, G. (2014) 'The Roots of *Tempietto* and Its Symbolism in Armenian Gospels', *Iconographica* 13: 11–24.

Grillmeier, A., and T. Hainthaler (2002) *Jesus der Christus im Glauben der Kirche, 2/3: Die Kirchen von Jerusalem und Antiochien*. Freiburg.

Grimm, V. E. (2010) *From Feasting to Fasting, The Evolution of a Sin: Attitudes to Food in Late Antiquity*. London.

Grosdidier de Matons, J. (1977) *Romanos le Mélode et les origines de la poésie religieuse à Byzance*. Paris.

Gruber, J. (2011) *Boethius: Eine Einführung*. Stuttgart.

Gudeman, A. (1927) 'Λύσεις', *PW* 1.13.2: 2511–29.

Guffy, A. (2014) 'Motivations for Encratite Practices in Early Christian Literature', *JTS* 65: 515–49.

Guiliano, Z. (2015) 'Patristic Allegorical Preaching as a Mimetic Technology of the Self: An Exploration and Proposal', in *Preaching and the Theological Imagination*, ed. Z. Guiliano and C. Partridge. New York: 77–104.

Guiliano, Z. (2018) 'Holy Gluttons: Bede and the Carolingians on the Pleasures of Reading', in *Pleasure in the Middle Ages*, ed. N. Cohen-Hanegbi and P. Nagy. Turnhout: 281–308.

Guiliano, Z. (2021) *The Homiliary of Paul the Deacon: Religious and Cultural Reform in Carolingian Europe*. Turnhout.

Gulácsi, Z. (2015) *Mani's Pictures: The Didactic Images of Manichaeans from Sasanian Mesopotamia to Uygur Central Asia and Tang-Ming China*. Leiden.

Gulácsi, Z. (2018) 'Visual Catechism in Third-Century Mesopotamia: Reassessing the Pictorial Program of the Dura-Europas Synagogue in Light of Mani's *Book of Pictures*', *JAJ* 9: 201–29.

Gunn, V. (2009) *Bede's Historiae: Genre, Rhetoric and the Construction of Anglo-Saxon Church History*. Woodbridge.

Gwynn, D. M. (2007a) *The Eusebians: The Polemic of Athanasius and the Construction of the Arian Controversy*. Oxford.

Gwynn, D. M. (2007b) 'From Iconoclasm to Arianism: The Construction of Christian Tradition in the Iconoclast Controversy', *GRBS* 47: 226–51.

Habicht, C. (1987) 'Neue Inschriften aus Demetrias: Tafel xxii–xxx', in *Demetrias V*, ed. S. C. Bakuizen et al. Bonn: 52–55.

Hadot, I. (1978) *Le problèm du néoplatonisme alexandrin: Hiéroclès et Simplicius*. Paris.

Hadot, I. (1984) *Arts libéraux et philosophie dans la pensée antique*. Paris.

Hadot, I. (1987) 'Les introductions aux commentaires exégétiques chez les auteurs néoplatoniciens et les auteurs chrétiens', in *Les règles de l'interprétation*, ed. M. Tardieu. Paris: 99–122.

Hadot, I. (2003) 'Der philosophische Unterrichtsbetrieb in der römischen Kaiserzeit', *Rheinisches Museum für Philologie* 146: 49–71.

Hadot, I. (2004) Review of Grebe 1999, in *Gnomon* 76: 125–36.

Hadot, P. (1956) 'Platon et Plotin dans trois sermons de saint Ambroise', *Revue des études latines* 34: 202–20.
Hadot, P. (1960) 'Citations de Porphyre (à propos d'un ouvrage récent)', *REAug* 2: 204–44.
Hadot, P. (1974) 'Exercices spirituels', *École pratique des hautes études, Section des sciences religieuses* 84: 25–70.
Hadot, P. (1982) 'Die Einteilung der Philosophie im Altertum', *Zeitschrift für philosophische Forschung* 36: 422–44.
Hadot, P. (1990) 'La logique, partie ou instrument de la philosophie?' in *Simplicius: Commentaire sur les 'Catégories'*, ed. I. Hadot. Leiden: 183–88.
Hadot, P. (1993) *Plotinus, or The Simplicity of Vision*, trans. Michael Chase. Chicago.
Hadot, P. (1995a) *Qu'est-ce que la philosophie antique?* Paris. (= Hadot 2002)
Hadot, P. (1995b) *Philosophy as a Way of Life: Spiritual Exercises from Socrates to Foucault*, trans. A. Davidson. Malden.
Hadot, P. (2002) *What is Ancient Philosophy?*, trans. M. Chase. Cambridge. (= Hadot 1995a)
Hadot, P. (2020) 'The Divisions of the Parts of Philosophy in Antiquity', in *The Selected Writings of Pierre Hadot: Philosophy as Practice*, trans. M. Sharpe and F. Testa. London: 105–32.
Hagendahl, H. (1958) *Latin Fathers and the Classics: A Study on the Apologists, Jerome and Other Christian Writers*. Gothenburg.
Hagendahl, H. (1967) *Augustine and the Latin Classics*. 2 vols. Gothenburg.
Hahn, A. (ed.) (1842) *Bibliothek der Symbole und Glaubensregeln der apostolisch-katholischen Kirche*. Breslau.
Hahn, A. (ed.) (1857) *Lehrbuch des christlichen Glaubens*. 2 vols. Leipzig.
Hahn, J. (1989) *Der Philosoph und die Gesellschaft: Selbstverständnis, öffentliches Auftreten und populäre Erwartungen in der hohen Kaiserzeit*. Stuttgart.
Hall, S. (2007) 'Patristic Divergences about the Image of God in Man', in *Discipline and Diversity: Papers Read at the 2005 Summer Meeting and the 2006 Winter Meeting of the Ecclesiastical History Society*, ed. K. Cooper and J. Gregory. Woodbridge: 69–76.
Halperin, D. (1990) 'Why Is Diotima a Woman? Platonic Eros and the Figuration of Gender', in *Before Sexuality: The Construction of Erotic Experience in the Ancient Greek World*, ed. D. M. Halperin, J. J. Winkler, and F. I. Zeitlin. Princeton: 257–308. Expanded version: 'Why Is Diotima a Woman?' in *One Hundred Years of Homosexuality and Other Essays on Greek Love* (Routledge 1990): 113–51.
Hamman, A.-G. (1991) 'Le rythme de la prière chrétienne ancienne', in *Études patristiques: Méthodologie, liturgie, histoire, théologie*, ed. A.-G. Hamman. Paris: 159–81.
Hammerstaedt, J., and P. Terbuycken (1996) 'Improvisation', *RAC* 17: 1212–84.
Hanaghan, M. P. (2019) *Reading Sidonius' Epistles*. Cambridge.

Hankinson, R. J. (2003) 'Philosophy and Science', in *The Cambridge Companion to Greek and Roman Philosophy*, ed. D. Sedley. Cambridge: 271–99.

Hanson, R. (2005, 1st edn. Edinburgh 1988) *The Search for the Christian Doctrine of God: The Arian Controversy 318–381*. Grand Rapids.

Hardie, P. (2017) 'How Prudentian is Virgil's *Aeneid*?', *Dictynna* 14. DOI: 10.4000/dictynna.1431.

Hardie, P. (2019) *Classicism and Christianity in Late Antique Latin Poetry*. Cambridge.

Hardy, B. C. (1968) 'The Emperor Julian and His School Law', *CH* 37: 131–43.

Harkins, A. K., and B. P. Dunkle (2018) 'Hymns and Psalmody', in *The Oxford Handbook of Early Christian Ritual*, ed. R. Uro, J. J. Day, R. Roitto, and R. E. DeMaris. Oxford: 610–24.

Harl, M. (1987) 'Les trois livres de *Salomon* et les trois parties de la philosophie dans les prologues des commentaires sur le *Cantique des Cantiques* (d'Origène aux chaînes exégétiques grecques)', in *Texte und Textkritik: Eine Aufsatzsammlung*, ed. J. Dummer and J. Irmscher. Berlin: 249–69.

Harl, M. (2009) '*Agalma* in Philo, Origen, Eusebius, and Methodius', *Semitica et classica* 2: 51–71.

Harl, M. (2014) *Voix de louange: Les cantiques bibliques dans la liturgie chrétienne*. Paris.

Harmless, W. (2014) *Augustine and the Catechumenate*, rev. edn. Collegeville.

Harmon, A. M. (2017) 'History and Virtue: Contextualizing Exemplarity in Ambrose', *JECS* 25: 201–29.

Harmon, T. (2019) 'The Few, the Many, and the Universal Way of Salvation: Augustine's Point of Engagement with Platonic Political Thought', in *Augustine's Political Thought*, ed. R. Dougherty. Rochester: 129–51.

Harper, K. (2017) *The Fate of Rome: Climate, Disease, and the End of Empire*. Princeton.

Harpham, G. (1987) *The Ascetic Imperative in Culture and Criticism*. Chicago.

Harpham, G. (2008) 'Trading Pain for Knowledge, or, How the West Was Won', *Social Research* 75: 485–510.

Harris, W. V. (ed.) (2013) *Mental Disorders in the Classical World*. Leiden.

Harrison, C. (2006) *Rethinking Augustine's Early Theology: An Argument for Continuity*. Oxford.

Harrison, C. (2019a) 'Mellifluous Music in Early Western Christianity', in *God's Song and Music's Meanings: Theology, Liturgy, and Musicology in Dialogue*, ed. J. Hawkey, B. Quash, and V. White. London: 3–18.

Harrison, C. (2019b) *On Music, Sense, Affect and Voice*. New York.

Harrison, C. (2020) 'Resilience and Music in the Early Church', in *Biblical and Theological Visions of Resilience: Pastoral and Clinical Insights*, ed. N. H. White and C. C. H. Cook. Abingdon: 113–23.

Harrison, Verna E. (1990) 'Male and Female in Cappadocian Theology,' *JTS* 14: 441–71.

Hartung, B. (2018) 'The Authorship and Dating of the Syriac Corpus Attributed to Ephrem of Nisibis: A Reassessment', *ZAC* 22: 296–321.

Harvey, S. A. (2004) 'Feminine Imagery for the Divine: The Holy Spirit, the Odes of Solomon, and Early Syriac Tradition', *SVTQ* 37: 1–29.

Harvey, S. A. (2005) 'On Mary's Voice', in *The Cultural Turn in Late Ancient Studies*, ed. D. Martin and P. C. Miller. Durham: 63–86.

Hasler, V. E. (1953) *Gesetz und Evangelium in der alten Kirche bis Origenes*. Zürich and Frankfurt.

Hass, C. (1997) *Alexandria in Late Antiquity: Topography and Social Conflict*. Baltimore.

Hauerwas, S. (2011) *War and the American Difference: Theological Reflections on Violence and National Identity*. Grand Rapids.

Hausherr, I. (1944) *Penthos: La doctrine de la compunction dans l'orient chrétien*. Rome.

Havrda, M. (2011) 'Grace and Free Will According to Clement of Alexandria', *JECS* 19: 21–48.

Havrda, M. (2012) 'Demonstrative Method in *Stromateis* VII: Context, Principles, and Purpose', in Havrda, Hušek, and Plátová 2012: 261–75.

Havrda, M. (2016) *The So-Called Eighth Stromateus by Clement of Alexandria: Early Christian Reception of Greek Scientific Methodology*. Leiden.

Havrda, M. (2019) 'Two Projects of Christian Ethics: Clement, *Paed.* I 1 and *Strom.* II 2, 4–6', *VC* 73: 121–37.

Havrda, M. (2021) 'Clement of Alexandria', in *The Routledge Handbook of Early Christian Philosophy*, ed. M. J. Edwards. Abingdon: 357–71.

Havrda, M., V. Hušek, and J. Plátová (eds.) (2012) *The Seventh Book of the Stromateis*. Leiden.

Hawkes, J., and M. Boulton (eds.) (2019) *All Roads Lead to Rome: The Context and Transmission of the Codex Amiatinus*. Turnhout.

Hawley, R. (1994) 'The Problem of Women Philosophers in Ancient Greece', in *Women in Ancient Societies: 'An Illusion of the Night'*, ed. L. Archer, S. Fischler, and M. Wyke. Basingstoke: 70–87.

Hayes, A. (2012) 'The Rhetoric and Themes of the Madrāšâ Cycle in Praise of Abraham Qidunāyâ Attributed to Ephrem the Syrian'. PhD diss. Washington.

Hayward, R., and A. Louth (1999) 'Sanctus', *TRE* 30: 20–29.

Healey, J. F. (2011) 'The Edessan Milieu and the Birth of Syriac', *Hug* 10: 115–27.

Heath, J. (2016) 'Sight and Christianity: Early Christian Attitudes to Seeing', in *Sight and the Ancient Senses*, ed. M. Squire. London: 220–36.

Heath, J. (2018) '"Textual Communities": Brian Stock's Concept and Recent Scholarship on Antiquity', in *Scriptural Interpretation at the Interface between Education and Religion: In Memory of Hans Conzelmann*, ed. F. Wilk. Leiden: 5–35.

Hebing, J. (1922) 'Ueber *conscientia* und *conservatio* im philosophischen Sinne bei den Römern von Cicero bis Hieronymus', *Philosophisches Jahrbuch* 35: 215–31.

Hegedus, T. (2007) *Early Christianity and Ancient Astrology*. New York.

Heil, U. (2002) '... bloß nicht wie die Manichäer! Ein Vorschlag zu Hintergründen des arianischen Streits', *ZAC* 6: 299–319.

Heil, U. (2010) 'Markell von Ankyra und das Romanum', in *Von Arius zum Athanasium: Studien zur Edition der 'Athanasius Werke'*, ed. A. von Stockhausen and H. C. Brennecke. Berlin: 85–104.

Heim, M. S. (2006) *Saved from Sacrifice: A Theology of the Cross*. Grand Rapids.

Heimgartner, M. (ed.) (2001) *Über die Auferstehung: Text und Studie*. Berlin.

Heine, R. E. (1993) 'Three Allusions to Book 20 of Origen's *Commentary on John* in Gregory Thaumaturgus' *Panegyric to Origen*', StPatr 26: 261–66.

Heine, R. E. (2010) *Origen: Scholarship in Service of the Church*. Oxford.

Heldman, M., S. C. Munro-Hay, and R. Grierson (1993) *Africa Zion: The Sacred Art of Ethiopia*. New Haven.

Helmig, C. (2012) *Forms and Concepts: Concept Formation in the Platonic Tradition*. Berlin.

Helmig, C. (2017) 'Proclus on Epistemology, Language, and Logic', in *All from One: A Guide to Proclus*, ed. P. d'Hoine and M. Martijn. Oxford.

Henry, M. (1995) *Prisoner of History: Aspasia of Miletus and Her Biographical Tradition*. Oxford.

Herrero de Jáuregui, M. (2010) *Orphism and Christianity in Late Antiquity*. Berlin.

Hess, H. (2002) *The Early Development of Canon Law and the Council of Serdica*. Oxford.

Hester, K. (2007) *Eschatology and Pain in St Gregory the Great*. Milton Keynes.

Heurtley, C. A. (ed.) (1858) *Harmonia symbolica: A Collection of Creeds Belonging to the Ancient Western Church, and to the Mediaeval English Church Arranged in Chronological Order, and after the Manner of a Harmony*. Oxford.

Hijmans, B. L. (1959) *Askesis: Notes on Epictetus' Educational System*. Assen.

Hinds, S. (1998) *Allusion and Intertext: Dynamics of Appropriation in Roman Poetry*. Cambridge.

Hirsch-Luipold, R. (2017) *Gott Wahrnehmen: Die Sinne im Johannesevangelium*. Tübingen.

Hock, R. F. (2001) 'Homer in Greco-Roman Education', in *Mimesis and Intertextuality in Antiquity and Christianity*, ed. D. MacDonald. Harrisburg: 56–77.

Hodkinson, O. (2009) Review of König and Whitmarsh 2007b, *Classical Review* 59: 157–59.

Holl, K. (1904) *Amphilochius von Ikonium in seinem Verhältnis zu den grossen Kappadoziern*. Tübingen.

Holmes, B. (2013a) 'Disturbing Connections, Sympathetic Affections, Mental Disorder, and the Elusive Soul in Galen', in Harris 2013: 147–76.

Holmes, B. (2013b) 'Causality, Agency, and the Limits of Medicine', *Apeiron* 46: 302–26.

Holte, R. (1962) *Béatitude et sagesse: St Augustin et le problème de le fin de l'homme dans la philosophie ancienne*. Paris.

Homes Dudden, F. (1905) *Gregory the Great, His Place in History and Thought.* 2 vols. London.
Honoré, A. M. (1978) *Tribonian.* London.
Hornschuh, M. (1960) 'Das Leben des Origenes und die Entstehung der alexandrinischen Schule', *ZKG* 71: 1–25, 193–214.
Hort, F. J. A. (1876) *Two Dissertations.* Cambridge.
Howard, G. (1981) *The Teaching of Addai.* Texts and Translations 16. Chico, CA.
Howard-Johnston, J. (2010) *Witnesses to a World in Crisis: Historians and Histories of the Middle East in the Seventh Century.* Oxford.
Howley, J. A. (2017) 'Book-Burning and the Uses of Writing in Ancient Rome: Destructive Practice Between Literature and Document', *JRS* 107: 1–24.
Hughes-Warrington, M. (2018) *History as Wonder: Beginning with Historiography.* London.
Humfress, C. (2005) 'Law and Legal Practice in the Age of Justinian', in *The Cambridge Companion to the Age of Justinian*, ed. M. Maas. Cambridge: 161–84.
Humfress, C. (2007) *Orthodoxy and the Courts in Late Antiquity.* Oxford.
Hunink, V. (2011) 'Singing Together in Church: Augustine's Psalm against the Donatists', in *Sacred Words: Orality, Literacy and Religion*, ed. A. Lardinois, J. Blok, and M. van der Poel. Leiden: 389–403.
Hunt, E. J. (2003) *Christianity in the Second Century: The Case of Tatian.* London.
Hunt, H. M. (1998) 'The Tears of the Sinful Woman: A Theology of Redemption in the Homilies of St Ephraim and His Followers', *Hug* 1: 165–84.
Hunt, H. M. (2004) *Joy-Bearing Grief: Tears of Contrition in the Writings of Early Syrian and Byzantine Fathers.* Leiden.
Hupsch, P. H. (2016) 'Mystagogical Theology in Gregory of Nyssa's Epiphany Sermon', in *Seeing through the Eyes of Faith: New Approaches to the Mystagogy of the Church Fathers*, ed. P. van Geest. Leuven: 125–36.
Inglebert, H. (2001) *Interpretatio Christiana: Les mutations des savoirs (cosmographie, géographie, ethnographie, histoire) dans l'Antiquité chrétienne (30–630 après J.-C.).* Paris.
Inowlocki, S. (2006) *Eusebius and the Jewish Authors: His Citation Technique in an Apologetic Context.* Ancient Judaism and Early Christianity 64. Leiden.
Inwood, B. (1985) *Ethics and Human Action in Early Stoicism.* Oxford.
Israelowich, I. (2015) *Patients and Healers in the High Roman Empire.* Baltimore.
Jaeger, W. (1954) *Two Rediscovered Works of Ancient Christian Literature: Gregory of Nyssa and Macarius.* Leiden.
Jaeger, W. (1961) *Early Christianity and Greek Paideia.* Cambridge.
James, E. (1993) 'A Sense of Wonder: Gregory of Tours, Medicine and Science', in *The Culture of Christendom: Essays in Medieval History in Commemoration of Denis L. T. Bethell*, ed. M. A. Meyer. London.
James, L. (1995) *Light and Colour in Byzantine Art.* New York.
James, L. (2000) 'What Colours Were Byzantine Mosaics?' in *Medieval Mosaics: Light, Colour, Materials*, ed. E. Borsook, F. G. Superbi, and G. Pagliarulo. Milan: 35–46.

James, L. (2004) 'Senses and Sensibility in Byzantium', *Art History* 27: 522–37.
James, L. (2007) *Art and Text in Byzantine Culture*. Cambridge.
James, L., and R. Webb (1991) '"To Understand Ultimate Things and Enter Secret Places": *Ekphrasis* and Art in Byzantium', *Art History* 14: 1–17.
Jansma, T. (1959) 'L'Hexaeméron de Jacques de Sarug', *OrSyr* 4: 3–42, 129–62, 253–84.
Jauss, H. (1982) *Towards an Aesthetic of Reception*. Minneapolis.
Jay, N. B. (1992) *Throughout Your Generations Forever: Sacrifice, Religion, and Paternity*. Chicago.
Jeannerod, M. (2006) *Motor Cognition: What Actions Tell the Self*. Oxford.
Jefferson, L. M. (2014) *Christ the Miracle Worker in Early Christian Art*. Minneapolis.
Jeffreys, E. (2003) 'The Beginning of Byzantine Chronography: John Malalas', in *Greek and Roman Historiography in Late Antiquity*, ed. G. Marasco. Leiden: 497–527.
Jellicoe, S. (1978) *The Septuagint and Modern Study*. Winona Lake.
Jensen, R. M. (2005) *Face to Face: Portraits of the Divine in Early Christianity*. Minneapolis.
Jensen, R. M. (2008) '*Mater Ecclesia* and *Fons Aeterna*: The Church and Her Womb in Ancient Christian Tradition', in *A Feminist Companion to Patristic Literature*, ed. A.-J. Levine and M. M. Robbins. London: 137–55.
Jensen, R. M. (2011) *Living Water: Images, Symbols, and Settings of Early Christian Baptism*. Leiden.
Jensen, R. M. (2012a) *Baptismal Imagery in Early Christianity: Ritual, Visual, and Theological Dimensions*. Grand Rapids.
Jensen, R. M. (2012b) 'Nudity in Early Christian Art', in *Text, Image and Christians in the Graeco-Roman World: A Festschrift in Honor of David Lee Balch*, ed. A. Cissé Niang and C. Osiek. Eugene: 296–319.
Jensen, R. M. (2013) 'Visuality', in *The Cambridge Companion to Ancient Mediterranean Religion*, ed. B. Stanley Spaeth. Cambridge: 309–43.
Jeremiah, E. (2018) 'Statistical Explorations of the *Placita* of Aëtius', in Mansfeld and Runia 2018: 279–373.
Johnson, A. P. (2006a) 'Eusebius' *Praeparatio evangelica* as Literary Experiment', in *Greek Literature in Late Antiquity: Dynamism, Didacticism, Classicism*, ed. S. F. Johnson. Aldershot: 67–89.
Johnson, A. P. (2006b) *Ethnicity and Argumentation in Eusebius' Praeparatio evangelica*. Oxford.
Johnson, A. P. (2013) *Religion and Identity in Porphyry of Tyre: The Limits of Hellenism in Late Antiquity*. Cambridge.
Johnson, A. P. (2014) *Eusebius*. London.
Johnson, A. P., and J. Schott (eds.) (2013) *Eusebius of Caesarea: Tradition and Innovation*. Cambridge.
Johnson, S. F. (2006) *The Life and Miracles of Thekla: A Literary Study*. Washington.
Johnson, S. F. (2007) 'Review of Grafton and Williams 2006: *Christianity and the Transformation of the Book: Origen, Eusebius, and the Library*

of Caesarea, Cambridge, MA', *BMCR* 2007.06.41: https://bmcr.brynmawr.edu/2007/2007.06.41.

Johnson, S. F. (2016) *Literary Territories: Cartographical Thinking in Late Antiquity*. Oxford.

Johnson, S. F. (2021) 'Syriac Hymnography before Ephrem', in *Hymns, Homilies, and Hermeneutics in Byzantium*, ed. S. Gador-Whyte and A. Mellas. Leiden: 193–215.

Johnston, D. (2009) *A Brief History of Theology: From the New Testament to Feminist Theology*. London.

Jones, A. H. M. (1964) *The Later Roman Empire 284–602: A Social, Economic and Administrative Survey*. 2 vols. Norman.

Jones, A., and L. Taub (eds.) (2018) *The Cambridge History of Science*, Vol. I: *Ancient Science*. Cambridge.

Jones, C. P. (1986) *Culture and Society in Lucian*. Cambridge.

Jones, G. R. J. (1995) 'Some Donations to Bishop Wilfrid in Northern England', *Northern History* 31: 22–38.

Joosen, J. C., and J. H. Waszink (1950) 'Allegorese', *RAC* 1: 283–93.

Jouanna, J. (2012) 'Dietetics in Hippocratic Medicine: Definition, Main Problems, Discussion', in *Greek Medicine from Hippocrates to Galen: Selected Papers*. Leiden: 137–53.

Jouéjati, R. (2012) 'L'église de Temanaa', *Syria* 89: 235–58.

Junod, É. (1994) 'Wodurch unterscheiden sich die Homilien des Origenes von seinen Kommentaren?' in *Predigt in der alten Kirche*, ed. E. Mühlenberg and J. van Oort. Kampen: 50–81.

Kahlos, M. (2016) *Debate and Dialogue: Christian and Pagan Cultures c. 360–430*. London.

Kaldellis, A. (2004) *Procopius of Caesarea: Tyranny, History, and Philosophy at the End of Antiquity*. Philadelphia.

Kantzer Komline, H. (2014) 'Grace, Free Will, and the Lord's Prayer: Cyprian's Importance for the "Augustinian" Doctrine of Grace', *AugStud* 45: 247–79.

Karavites, P. (1990) 'Gnome's Nuances: From Its Beginning to the End of the Fifth Century', *Classical Bulletin* 66: 9–34.

Kaster, R. A. (1988) *Guardians of Language: The Grammarian and Society in Late Antiquity*. Berkeley.

Kattenbusch, F. (1894) *Das apostolische Symbol: Seine Entstehung, sein geschichtlicher Sinn, seine ursprüngliche Stellung im Kultus und in der Theologie der Kirche. Ein Beitrag zur Symbolik und Dogmengeschichte*, Vol. I: *Die Grundgestalt des Taufsymbols*. Leipzig.

Kelly, C. (2004) *Ruling the Later Roman Empire*. Cambridge, MA.

Kelly, C. (2006) 'Bureaucracy and Government', in *The Cambridge Companion to the Age of Constantine*, ed. N. Lenski. Cambridge: 183–204.

Kelly, J. N. D. (1972) *Early Christian Creeds*, 3rd edn. New York.

Kendall, C. (2008) *Bede: On Genesis*. TTH. Liverpool.

Kendall, C., and F. Wallis (2016) *Isidore of Seville: On the Nature of Things*. TTH. Liverpool.

Kennedy, G. A. (2003) *Progymnasmata: Greek Textbooks in Prose Composition and Rhetoric*. Atlanta.

Kennedy, W. J. (2017) 'Antisthenes' Literary Fragments: Edited with Introduction, Translation and Commentary', PhD diss., University of Sydney.

Kenyon, E. (2018) *Augustine and the Dialogue*. Cambridge.

Kiilerich, B., and H. Torp (2017) *The Rotunda in Thessaloniki and Its Mosaics*. Athens.

King, D. (2011) 'Origenism in Sixth-Century Syria: The Case of a Syriac Manuscript of Pagan Philosophy', in *Origenes und sein Erbe in Orient und Okzident*, ed. A. Fürst. Münster: 179–212.

King, K. (2010) 'Which Ancient Christianity?' in *The Oxford Handbook of Early Christian Studies*, ed. S. Ashbrook Harvey and D. G. Hunter. Oxford: 66–84.

King, P. (2005) 'Augustine's Encounter with Neoplatonism', *The Modern Schoolman* 82: 213–26.

Kinzig, W. (1999) '"… natum et passum etc.": Zur Geschichte der Tauffragen in der lateinischen Kirche bis zu Luther', in Kinzig, Markschies, and Vinzent 1999: 75–184.

Kinzig, W. (2017) *Faith in Formulae*. 4 vols. OECT. Oxford.

Kinzig, W., and M. Vinzent (1999) 'Recent Research on the Origin of the Creed', *JTS* 50: 535–59.

Kinzig, W., C. Markschies, and M. Vinzent (eds.) (1999) *Tauffragen und Bekenntnis: Studien zur sogenannten 'Traditio Apostolica' zu den 'Interrogationes de fide' und zum 'Römischen Glaubensbekenntnis'*. Berlin.

Kitchen, R. A. (2010) 'The Lust of the Belly Is the Beginning of All Sin: A Practical Theology of Asceticism in the Discourses of Philoxenos of Mabbug', *Hug* 13: 49–63.

Kitchen, R. A. (2013) 'Introduction to the *Discourses* of Philoxenos of Mabbug', in *The Discourses of Philoxenos of Mabbug: A New Translation and Introduction*, trans. R. A. Kitchen. Collegeville: xiii–lxxix.

Klauser, T. (1961) 'Das Ciborium in der älteren christlichen Buchmalerei', *NAWG* 7: 191–207.

Klawans, J. (2006) *Purity, Sacrifice, and the Temple: Symbolism and Supercessionism in the Study of Ancient Judaism*. New York.

Klemm, E. (1972) 'Die Kanontafeln der armenischen Handschrift Cod. 697 im Wiener Mechitaristenkloster', *ZKunstG* 35: 69–99.

Klinkenberg, H. M. (1959) 'Der Verfall des Quadriviums im frühen Mittelalter', in *'Artes Liberales' von der antiken Bildung zur Wissenschaft des Mittelalters*, ed. J. Koch. Leiden: 1–32.

Klock, C. (1987) *Untersuchungen zu Stil und Rhythmus bei Gregor von Nyssa. Ein Beitrag zum Rhetorikverständnis der griechischen Väter*. Frankfurt am Main.

Klostermann, E. (1947) 'Formen der exegetischen Arbeiten des Origenes', *TLZ* 72: 203–8.

Knauber, A. (1968) 'Das Anliegen der Schule des Origenes zu Cäsarea', *MTZ* 19: 182–203.

Knight, J. (2012) 'The Origin and Significance of the Angelomorphic Christology in the *Ascension of Isaiah*', *JTS* 63: 66–105.

Knipfing, J. R. (1923) 'The Libelli of the Decian Persecution', *HTR* 16: 345–90.
Kobusch, T. (2006) *Christliche Philosophie: Die Entdeckung der Subjektivität*. Darmstadt.
Koch, H. (1932) *Pronoia und Paideusis: Studien über Origenes und sein Verhältniss zum Platonismus*. Berlin.
Köckert, C. (2016) 'Augustine and Nebridius (Augustine, *epp.* 3–14): Two Christian Intellectuals and Their Project of a Philosophical Life', *REAug* 62: 235–62.
Koerner, J. L. (2004) *The Reformation of the Image*. Chicago and London.
Kofsky, A. (2002) *Eusebius of Caesarea Against Paganism*. Leiden.
König, J. (2012) *Saints and Symposiasts: The Literature of Food and the Symposium in Greco-Roman and Early Christian Culture*. Cambridge.
König, J., and T. Whitmarsh (2007a) 'Ordering Knowledge', in König and Whitmarsh 2007b: 3–40.
König, J., and T. Whitmarsh (eds.) (2007b) *Ordering Knowledge in the Roman Empire*. Cambridge.
Korsmeyer, C., and A. Smith (2004) 'Visceral Values: Aurel Kolnai on Disgust', in *On Disgust*, ed. C. Korsmeyer and A. Smith. Chicago: 1–25.
Kovacs, J. L. (2017) 'Clement as Scriptural Exegete: Overview of History and Research', in Černušková, Kovacs, and Plátová 2017: 1–37.
Kraemer, R. (2010) *Unreliable Witnesses: Religion, Gender, and History in the Greco-Roman Mediterranean*. Oxford.
Krausmüller, D. (2001) 'Leontius of Jerusalem, a Theologian of the 7th Century', *JTS* 52: 637–57.
Krausmüller, D. (2005) 'Conflicting Anthropologies in the Christological Discourse at the End of Late Antiquity: The Case of Leontius of Jerusalem's Nestorian Adversary', *JTS* 56: 413–47.
Krausmüller, D. (2015) 'Responding to John Philoponus: Hypostases, Particular Substances and *Perichoresis* in the Trinity', *JLARC* 9: 13–28.
Krausmüller, D. (2017) 'Under the Spell of John Philoponus: How Chalcedonian Theologians of the Late Patristic Period Attempted to Safeguard the Oneness of God', *JTS* 68: 625–49.
Krautheimer, R. (1969) 'Introduction to an "Iconography of Medieval Architecture"', in *Studies in Early Christian, Medieval, and Renaissance Art*. New York: 115–50.
Krautheimer, R. (1975) *Early Christian and Byzantine Architecture*. Harmondsworth.
Kreider, A. (2016) *The Patient Ferment of the Early Church*. Grand Rapids.
Kristensen, T. M. (2013) *Making and Breaking the Gods: Christian Responses to Pagan Sculpture in Late Antiquity*. Aarhus.
Krolikowski, J. (2010) 'Paideia', in *The Brill Dictionary of Gregory of Nyssa*, ed. L. F. Mateo-Seco and G. Maspero. Leiden: 568–75.
Krueger, D. (1996) *Symeon the Holy Fool: Leontius's Life and the Late Antique City*. Berkeley.
Krueger, D. (2000) 'Writing and the Liturgy of Memory in Gregory of Nyssa's *Life of Macrina*', *JECS* 8: 483–510.

Krueger, D. (2014) *Liturgical Subjects: Christian Ritual, Biblical Narrative, and the Formation of the Self in Byzantium*. Philadelphia.

Krulak, T. C. (2011) '"Invisible Things on Visible Forms": Pedagogy and Anagogy in Porphyry's Περί ἀγαλμάτων', *JLA* 4: 343–64.

Kuehn, C. A. (1995) *Channels of Imperishable Fire: The Beginnings of Christian Mystical Poetry and Dioscorus of Aphrodito*. New York.

Kühn, K. (2004) 'Augustins Schrift *De divinatione daemonum*', *Augustiniana* 47: 291–337.

L'Huillier, P. (1976) 'Origenes et developpement de l'ancienne collection canonique grecque', *Messager de l'Exarchat du patriarchat russe en Europe occidentale* 93–96: 53–66.

L'Huillier, P. (1997) 'The Making of Written Law in the Church', *Studia canonica* 31: 117–46.

Ladrière, J. (1973) 'The Performativity of Liturgical Language', trans. J. Griffiths, *Concilium* 9: 50–62.

Lahire, B. (2003) 'From the Habitus to an Individual Heritage of Dispositions: Towards a Sociology at the Level of the Individual', *Poetics* 31: 329–55.

Laird, A. W. (1996) 'Ut figura poesis', in *Art and Text in Roman Culture*, ed. J. Elsner. Cambridge: 75–102.

Laird, R. (2012) *Mindset, Moral Choice and Sin in the Anthropology of John Chrysostom*. Strathfield.

Laistner, M. L. W. (1935) 'The Library of the Venerable Bede', in *Bede: His Life, Times, and Writings – Essays in Commemoration of the Twelfth Centenary of His Death*, ed. A. H. Thompson. Oxford: 237–66.

Laistner, M. L. W. (1947) 'Antiochene Exegesis in Western Europe during the Middle Ages', *HTR* 40: 24–26.

Laistner, M. L. W. (1957) 'The Latin Versions of Acts known to the Venerable Bede', in *The Intellectual Heritage of the Early Middle Ages: Selected Essays by M. L. W. Laistner*, ed. C. G. Starr. Ithaca: 150–64.

Lamberton, R. (2001) 'The Schools of Platonic Philosophy of the Roman Empire: The Evidence of the Biographies', in *Education in Greek and Roman Antiquity*, ed. Y. L. Too. Leiden: 433–58.

Lampe, G. W. H. (ed.) (1961) *A Patristic Greek Lexicon*. Oxford.

Lanata, G. (1984) *Legislazione e natura nelle novelle Giustinianee*. Naples.

Lanéry, C. (2008) *Ambroise de Milan hagiographe*. Paris.

Lang, U. M. (1998) 'The Date of the Treatise *De sectis* Revisited', *OLP* 29: 89–98.

Lapidge, M. (1995) *Archbishop Theodore: Commemorative Studies on His Life and Influence*. Cambridge.

Lapidge, M. (2006) *The Anglo-Saxon Library*. Oxford.

Larchet, J.-C. (2000) *Thérapeutique des maladies spirituelles*. Paris.

Larisa Culture Index, 'Βασιλική στο Βαρόσι': http://larisa.culture.gr/index.php/component/phocagallery/60-enotita-9/detail/324-tmnma-psnfidwtou-dapedoume-epigrafn-tns-afierwtrias-marias-basilikn-sto-barosi-elassova?tmpl=component&Itemid=1 (accessed on 3 April 2020).

Lash, E. (1995) *On the Life of Christ: Kontakia*. San Francisco.
Lauxtermann, M. (2003) *Byzantine Poetry from Pisides to Geometres: Texts and Contexts*, Vol. I. Vienna.
Lauxtermann, M. (2019) *Byzantine Poetry from Pisides to Geometres: Texts and Contexts*, Vol. II. Vienna.
LaValle Norman, D. (2019) *The Aesthetics of Hope in Late Imperial Greek Literature: Methodius of Olympus' Symposium and the Crisis of the Third Century*. Greek Culture in the Roman World. Cambridge.
LaValle Norman, D. (2022) *Early Christian Women*. Elements on the History of Women in Philosophy. Cambridge.
Law, T. M. (2008) 'Origen's Parallel Bible: Textual Criticism, Apologetics, or Exegesis?', *JTS* 59: 1–21.
Lazaris, S. (2020) 'Introduction', in *A Companion to Byzantine Science*, ed. S. Lazaris. Leiden: 3–9.
Le Boulluec, A. (1987) 'Pour qui, pourquoi, comment? Les *"Stromates"* de Clément d'Alexandrie', in Le Boulluec 2006: 95–108.
Le Boulluec, A. (1989) 'Clément d'Alexandrie et la conversion du "parler grec"', in Le Boulluec 2006: 63–79.
Le Boulluec, A. (2006) *Alexandrie antique et chrétienne: Clément et Origène*. Paris.
Le Boulluec, A. (2012) 'Comment Clément applique-t-il dans le *Stromate* VII, à l'intention des philosophes, la méthode définie dans le prologue (1–3)?' in Havrda, Hušek, and Plátová 2012: 39–62.
Le Boulluec, A. (2019) 'Clément d'Alexandrie', in *L'abeille et l'acier: Clément d'Alexandrie et Origène*, ed. G. Dorival and A. Le Boulluec. Paris: 13–163.
Le Boulluec, A. (2021) 'Les recours polémiques des pères grecs aux écrits hérétiques, d'Irénée à Épiphane', *REAug* 67: 33–49.
Leatherbury, S. V. (2020) *Inscribing Faith in Late Antiquity: Between Reading and Seeing*. Abingdon.
Leemans, J. (2005) 'Style and Meaning in Gregory of Nyssa's Panegyrics on Martyrs', *ETL* 81: 109–29.
Leemans, J. (2008) 'Job et les autres: L'usage de l'écriture dans les panégyriques sur les martyrs de Grégoire de Nysse: Cinq exemples', in *Grégoire de Nysse: La Bible dans la construction de son discours*, ed. M. Cassin and H. Grélier. Paris: 227–44.
Leemans, J. (2009) 'Communicating Truth in Gregory of Nyssa's Sermons: Preaching Orthodoxy, Constructing Heresy', in *Orthodoxy, Process and Product*, ed. M. Lamberigts, L. Boeve, and T. Merrigan. Leuven: 61–83.
Leemans, J. (2012) 'Flexibele Heiligkeit: Der Beitrag der Märtyrer zur Identitätskonstitution christlicher Gemeinden im griechischen Osten im 4. Jahrhundert', in *Heilige, Heiliges und Heiligkeit in spätantiken Religionskulturen*, ed. P. Gemeinhardt and K. Heyde. Berlin: 205–27.
Leemans, J. (2016a) 'Bible, Rhetoric and Theology: Some Examples of Mystagogical Strategies in Gregory of Nyssa's Sermons', in *Seeing through the Eyes of Faith:*

New Approaches to the Mystagogy of the Church Fathers, ed. P. van Geest. Leuven: 105–24.

Leemans, J. (2016b) 'The Relative Routine of Preaching: Pneumatomachians in Greek Patristic Sermons on Pentecost', in *Preaching after Easter: Mid-Pentecost, Ascension and Pentecost in Late Antiquity*, ed. J. Leemans et al. Supplements to Vigiliae Christianae 136. Leiden: 269–93.

Leemans, J., and H. Tamas (2022) 'Retrieving Information on Liturgical Readings from Sermons: Examples from Asia Minor', in *Liturgische Bibelrezeption: Dimensionen und Perspektiven interdisziplinärer Forschung/Liturgical Reception of the Bible: Dimensions and Perspectives of Interdisciplinary Research*, ed. H. Buchinger and C. Leonhard, Göttingen: 69–85.

Leinsle, U. G. (1995) *Die Einführung in die scholastische Theologie*. Paderborn.

Leitao, D. D. (2012) *The Pregnant Male as Myth and Metaphor in Classical Greek Literature*. Cambridge.

Lenox-Conyngham, A. (1993) 'Ambrose and Philosophy', in *Christian Faith and Greek Philosophy in Late Antiquity: Essays in Tribute to George Christopher Stead, Ely Professor of Divinity, University of Cambridge (1971–1980), in Celebration of His Eightieth Birthday, 9th April 1993*, ed. L. Wickham and C. Hammond Bammel. Leiden: 112–28.

Leonhard, C. (2015) 'Morning *salutationes* and the Decline of Sympotic Eucharists in the Third Century', *ZAC* 18: 420–42.

Lepage, C., and J. Mercier (2012) 'Un tétraévangile illustré éthiopien à cycle long du XVe siècle – Codicologie et iconographie', *Cahiers archéologiques* 54: 99–174.

Leroy, J. (1962) 'Recherches sur la tradition iconographique des canons d'Eusèbe en Éthiopie', *Cahiers archéologiques* 12: 173–204.

Leuenberger-Wenger, S. (2008) *Ethik und christliche Identität bei Gregor von Nyssa*. Tübingen.

Lietzmann, H. (1906) *Symbole der alten Kirche*, 1st edn. Bonn.

Lietzmann, H. (1922) 'Symbolstudien', *ZNW* 21: 1–34.

Lilla, S. R. C. (1971) *Clement of Alexandria: A Study in Christian Platonism and Gnosticism*. Oxford.

Limberis, V. (1994) *Divine Heiress: The Virgin Mary and the Creation of Christian Constantinople*. London.

Limberis, V. (2011) *Architects of Piety: The Cappadocian Fathers and the Cult of the Martyrs*. New York.

Limonata, R. (2017) 'Cite una più del diavolo: Divinazione, prescienza e futuri contingenti nel *De divinatione daemonum* di Agostino d'Ippona', *Dianoia* 24: 3–14.

Lindberg, D. C. (2010) *The Beginnings of Western Science: The European Scientific Tradition in Philosophical, Religious and Institutional Context, Prehistory to AD 1450*, 2nd edn. Chicago.

Lindberg, D. C., and M. H. Shank (eds.) (2013) *The Cambridge History of Science*, Vol. II: *Medieval Science*. Cambridge.

Lingas, A. (1995) 'The Liturgical Place of the Kontakion in Constantinople', in *Liturgy, Architecture and Art of the Byzantine World: Papers of the XVIII International Byzantine Congress (Moscow, 8–15 August 1991) and Other Essays Dedicated to the Memory of Fr. John Meyendorff*, ed. C. C. Akentiev. St Petersburg: 50–57.

Lloyd, A. C. (1990) *The Anatomy of Neoplatonism*. Oxford.

Löhr, W. (2006a) 'Arius Reconsidered (Part 1)', *ZAC* 9: 524–60.

Löhr, W. (2006b) 'Arius Reconsidered (Part 2)', *ZAC* 10: 121–57.

Lollar, J. (2013) *To See into the Life of Things: The Contemplation of Nature in Maximus the Confessor and His Predecessors*. Turnhout.

Long, A. A. (1986) *Hellenistic Philosophy: Stoics, Epicureans, Sceptics*, 2nd edn. London.

Lorenz, R. (1979) *Arius judaizans? Untersuchungen zur dogmengeschichtlichen Einordung des Arius*. Göttingen.

Louth, A. (2004) *St John Damascene: Tradition and Originality in Byzantine Theology*. Oxford.

Louth, A. (2005) 'Christian Hymnography from Romanos the Melodist to John Damascene', *Journal of Eastern Christian Studies* 57: 195–206.

Louth, A. (2007) *Greek East and Latin West: The Church AD 681–1071*. Crestwood.

Love, R. (2011) 'The Library of the Venerable Bede', in *The History of the Book in Britain*, Vol. I, ed. R. Gameson. Cambridge: 606–32.

Low, L. A. (2013) 'The Impact of Pain upon Cognition: What Have Rodent Studies Told Us?', *Pain* 154: 2603–5.

Lowden, J. (1999) 'The Beginnings of Biblical Illustration', in *Imaging the Early Medieval Bible*, ed. J. Williams. University Park: 9–59.

Ludlow, M. (2009) 'Science and Theology in Gregory of Nyssa's *De anima et resurrectione*: Astronomy and Automata', *JTS* NS 60: 467–89.

Ludlow, M. (2013) *Gregory of Nyssa: Ancient and (Post)Modern*. Oxford.

Ludlow, M. (2014) 'Texts, Teachers and Pupils in the Writings of Gregory of Nyssa', in *Literature and Society in the Fourth Century AD: Performing Paideia, Constructing the Present, Presenting the Self*, ed. L. van Hoof and P. Van Nuffelen. Leiden: 83–102.

Ludlow, M., and S. Lunn-Rockliffe (2019) 'Education and Pleasure in the Early Church: Perspectives from East and West', in *SCH 55: Churches and Education*, ed. M. Ludlow, C. Methuen, and A. Spicer. Cambridge: 6–34.

Lütcke, K.-H. (1968) *'Auctoritas' bei Augustin*. Stuttgart.

Lütcke, K.-H. (1986–94) 'Auctoritas', in *Augustinus-Lexikon*, Vol. I, ed. C. P. Mayer. Basel: cols. 498–510.

Lutz, C. E. (1947) 'Musonius Rufus, "The Roman Socrates"', *YCS* 10: 3–147.

Lyman, R. (1989) 'Arians and Manichees on Christ', *JTS* 40: 493–503.

Lyman, R. (2010) 'Arius and Arians', in *The Oxford Handbook of Early Christian Studies*, ed. S. Ashbrook Harvey and D. G. Hunter. Oxford: 237–57.

Lyman, R. (2021) 'Arius and Arianism: The Origins of the Alexandrian Controversy', in *The Cambridge Companion to the Council of Nicaea*, ed. Y. Kim. Cambridge.

Maas, M. (1992) *John Lydus and the Roman Past*. New York.

Maas, M. (1996) 'Junillus Africanus' "Instituta Regularia Divinae Legis" in its Justinianic Context', in *The Sixth Century: End or Beginning?*, ed. P. Allen and E. M. Jeffreys. Brisbane: 131–44.

Maas, M. (2003) *Exegesis and Empire in the Early Byzantine Mediterranean: Junillus Africanus and the Instituta Regularia Divinae Legis*. Tübingen.

Macaskill, G. (2013) *Union with Christ in the New Testament*. Oxford.

MacCormack, S. (1990) 'Loca Sancta: The Organisation of Sacred Topography in Late Antiquity', in *The Blessings of Pilgrimage*, ed. R. Ousterhout. Urbana: 7–40.

MacGinty, G. (1987) 'The Irish Augustine: *De mirabilibus Sacrae Scripturae*', in *Ireland and Christendom: The Bible and the Missions*, ed. P. Ní Chatháin and M. Richter. Stuttgart: 70–83.

MacGinty, G. (1999) 'The Pentateuch of the *Reference Bible*: The Problem Concerning Its Sources', in *The Scriptures and Early Medieval Ireland*, ed. T. O'Loughlin. Turnhout: 163–77.

MacGinty, G. (2000) 'Introduction', in *Pauca problesmata de enigmatis ex tomis canonicis*. Turnhout.

Mack, B. L. (2000) *Thomas Gray: A Life*. New Haven.

Madec, G. (1974) *Saint Ambroise et la philosophie*. Paris.

Magee, J. (2005) 'Boethius' *Consolatio* and the Theme of Roman Liberty', *Phoenix* 59: 348–64.

Magee, J. (2010) 'On the Composition and Sources of Boethius' Second *Peri Hermeneias* Commentary', *Vivarium* 48: 7–54.

Magee, J. (2014) 'Boethius' *Consolatio* and Plato's *Gorgias*', in *Boethius as a Paradigm of Late Ancient Thought*, ed. T. Böhm, T. Jürgasch, and A. Kirchner. Berlin: 13–29.

Magee, J. (2016) 'Boethius: Last of the Romans', in *Vernacular Traditions of Boethius's* De consolatione philosophiae, ed. N. H. Kaylor and P. E. Phillips. Kalamazoo: 3–22.

Magnano, F. (2017) *Boethius:* On Topical Differences. Barcelona.

Magny, A. (2014) *Porphyry in Fragments*. Farnham.

Maguire, H. (1987) *Earth and Ocean: The Terrestrial World in Early Byzantine Art*. University Park, PA.

Maguire, H. (2008) 'Art and Text', in *The Oxford Handbook of Byzantine Studies*, ed. R. Cormack, J. F. Haldon, and E. Jeffreys. Oxford: 721–30.

Maguire, H. (2016) 'Where Did the Waters of Paradise Go after Iconoclasm?' in *Fountains and Water Culture in Byzantium*, ed. B. Shilling and P. Stephenson. Cambridge: 229–45.

Mahmood, S. (2005) *Politics of Piety: The Islamic Revival and the Feminist Subject*. Princeton.

Maier, H. O., and K. Waldner (eds.) (2021) *Desiring Martyrs: Locating Martyrs in Space and Time*. Berlin.

Majercik, R. (2001) 'Chaldean Triads in Neoplatonic Exegesis: Some Reconsiderations', *CQ* 51: 265–96.

Maldonado Rivera, D. (2017) 'Encyclopedic Trends and the Making of Heresy in Late Ancient Christianity 360–460 CE', PhD diss., Indiana University.

Mandouze, A. (1968) *Saint Augustin: L'aventure de la raison et de la grâce*. Paris.

Manent, P. (2013) *Metamorphoses of the City*, trans. M. LePain. Cambridge.

Mansfeld, J. (1988) 'Philosophy in the Service of Scripture: Philo's Exegetical Strategies', in *The Question of 'Eclecticism': Studies in Later Greek Philosophy*, ed. J. M. Dillon and A. A. Long. Berkeley: 70–102.

Mansfeld, J. (1990) 'Doxography and Dialectic: The *Sitz im Leben* of the *Placita*', in *ANRW* 2.36.4: 3056–229.

Mansfeld, J. (1994) *Prolegomena: Questions to be Settled before the Study of an Author, or a Text*. Leiden.

Mansfeld, J. (2012) 'Doxography of Ancient Philosophy', in *Stanford Encyclopedia of Philosophy*: http://plato.stanford.edu/entries/doxography-ancient (accessed 6 July 2020).

Mansfeld, J. (2013) 'Detheologization: Aëtian Chapters and Their Peripatetic Background', *Rhizomata* 1: 330–62.

Mansfeld, J. (2016) 'Theodoret of Cyrrhus' *Therapy of Greek Diseases* as a Source for the Aëtian *Placita*', in *SPhiloA 28: Studies in Philo in Honor of David Runia*, ed. G. E. Sterling. Atlanta: 151–68.

Mansfeld, J. (2020) 'The Complete Philosopher', in *Introduction générale à la philosophie chez les commentateurs néoplatoniciens*, ed. M.-J. Huh. Turnhout: 97–121.

Mansfeld, J., and D. T. Runia (1997) *Aëtiana IV: Papers of the Melbourne Colloquium on Ancient Doxography*. Philosophia Antiqua 148, Vol. I: *The Sources*. Leiden.

Mansfeld, J., and D. T. Runia (2009) *Aëtiana: The Method and Intellectual Context of a Doxographer*, Vol. II: *The Compendium*, Part I: *Macrostructure and Microcontext*, Part II, *Aëtius Book II: Specimen Reconstructionis*. Leiden.

Mansfeld, J., and D. T. Runia (2010) *Aëtiana: The Method and Intellectual Context of a Doxographer*, Vol. III: *Studies in the Doxographical Traditions of Greek Philosophy*. Leiden.

Mansfeld, J., and D. T. Runia (eds.) (2018) Aëtiana IV: Towards an Edition of the Aëtian Placita: Papers of the Melbourne Conference *1–3 December 2015*. Leiden.

Mansfeld, J., and D. T. Runia (2020) *Aëtiana V: An Edition of the Reconstructed Text of the* Placita *with a Commentary and a Collection of Related Texts*. 4 parts. Leiden.

Margoni-Kögler, M. (2010) *Die Perikopen im Gottesdienst bei Augustinus: Ein Beitrag zur Erforschung der liturgischen Schriftlesung in der frühen Kirche*. Vienna.

Markschies, C. (1995a) *Ambrosius von Mailand und die Trinitätstheologie: Kirchen- und theologiegeschichtliche Studien zu Antiarianismus und Neunizänismus bei Ambrosius und im lateinischen Westen (364–381 n.Chr.)*. Tübingen.

Markschies, C. (1995b) 'War der Bischof Ambrosius von Mailand ein schlechter Theologe?', *Jahrbuch der Akademie der Wissenschaften in Göttingen* 1994: 63–66.

Markschies, C. (1999) 'Wer schrieb die sogenannte Traditio Apostolica? Neue Beobachtungen und Hypothesen zu einer kaum lösbaren Frage aus der altkirchlichen Literaturgeschichte', in Kinzig, Markschies, and Vinzent 1999: 1–74.

Markschies, C. (2013) 'On Classifying Creeds the Classical German Way: "Privat-Bekenntnisse" ('Private Creeds')', StPatr 63: 259–71.

Markschies, C. (2015) *Christian Theology and Its Institutions in the Early Roman Empire: Prolegomena to a History of Early Christian Theology*, trans. W. Coppins. Waco.

Markschies, C. (2019) *God's Body: Jewish, Christian, and Pagan Images of God*, trans. A. J. Edmonds. Waco.

Markus, R. A. (1997) *Gregory the Great and His World*. Cambridge.

Marrou, H. I. (1938) *Saint Augustin et la fin de la culture antique*. Paris.

Marrou, H. I. (1964) *A History of Education in Antiquity*, trans. G. Lamb. New York.

Marsden, R. (1995) *The Text of the Old Testament in Anglo-Saxon England*. Cambridge.

Marsden, R. (1998) '*Manus Bedae*: Bede's Contribution to Ceolfrith's Bibles', *Anglo-Saxon England* 27: 65–85.

Martens, P. W. (2012) *Origen and Scripture: Contours of the Exegetical Life*. Oxford.

Martens, P. W. (2013) 'Origen's Doctrine of Pre-Existence and the Opening Chapters of Genesis', *ZAC* 16: 516–49.

Martens, P. W. (2015) 'Embodiment, Heresy and the Hellenization of Christianity: The Descent of the Soul in Plato and Origen', *HTR* 108: 594–620.

Martens, P. W. (2022) 'Classifying Early Christian Writings: Boundaries, Arrangements, and Latent Dynamics', *EC* 12: 431–46.

Martin, M. (2004) 'Origen's Theory of Language and the First Two Columns of the Hexapla', *HTR* 97: 99–106.

Mateo-Seco, L. F. (2010) 'Epektasis', in *The Brill Dictionary of Gregory of Nyssa*, ed. L. F. Mateo-Seco and G. Maspero. Leiden: 263–68.

Matis, H. (2019) *The Song of Songs in the Early Middle Ages*. Leiden.

Mattern, S. P. (2008) *Galen and the Rhetoric of Healing*. Baltimore.

Mattern, S. P. (2016) 'Galen's Anxious Patients: Lypē as Anxiety Disorder', in Petridou and Thumiger 2016: 203–23.

Mayoral, J. A., and A. Ballesteros (2001) 'Prosōpopoeia', in *Encyclopedia of Rhetoric*, ed. T. Sloane. Oxford.

Mayr-Harting, H. (1976) *The Venerable Bede, the Rule of St Benedict, and Social Class*. Jarrow.

Mazzini, I. (2001) 'La medicina in Frontone e Marco Aurelio', in *Docente natura: Mélanges de médecine ancienne et médiévale offerts à Guy Sabbah*, ed. A. Debru, N. Palmieri, and B. Jacquinod. Saint-Étienne: 193–207.

McClure, J. (1985) 'Bede's *Notes on Genesis* and the Training of the Anglo-Saxon Clergy', in *The Bible in the Medieval World: Essays in Memory of Beryl Smalley*, ed. K. Walsh and D. Wood. Oxford: 17–30.

McCluskey, S. C. (1990) 'Gregory of Tours, Monastic Time-Keeping, and Early Christian Attitudes to Astronomy', *Isis* 81: 9–22.

McClymond, K. (2008) *Beyond Sacred Violence: A Comparative Study of Sacrifice*. Baltimore.

McCready, W. D. (1995) 'Bede and the Isidorian Legacy', *MS* 57: 41–73.

McGinn, B. (2012) 'Late Medieval Mystics', in Gavrilyuk and Coakley 2012a: 190–209.

McGowan, A. B. (1999) *Ascetic Eucharists: Food and Drink in Early Christian Ritual Meals*. Oxford.

McGowan, A. B. (2004) 'Rethinking Agape and Eucharist in Early North African Christianity', *Studia Liturgica* 34: 165–76.

McGowan, A. B. (2012) 'Eucharist and Sacrifice: Cultic Tradition and Transformation in Early Christian Ritual Meals', in *Mahl und religiöse Identität im frühen Christentum*, ed. M. Klinghardt and H. Taussig. Tübingen: 191–206.

McGowan, A. B. (2014) 'Rehashing the Leftovers of Idols: Cyprian and Early Christian Constructions of Sacrifice', in *Religious Competition in the Third Century CE: Jews, Christians, and the Greco-Roman World*, ed. J. D. Rosenblum, N. DesRosiers, and L. Vuong. Göttingen: 69–77.

McGrath, A. E. (2012) *Historical Theology: An Introduction to the History of Christian Thought*, 2nd edn. Chichester.

McInroy, M. (2012) 'Origen of Alexandria', in Gavrilyuk and Coakley 2012a: 20–35.

McInroy, M. (2014) *Balthasar on the Spiritual Senses: Perceiving Splendour*. Oxford.

McKenzie, J. (2007) *The Architecture of Alexandria and Egypt 300 BC to AD 700*. New Haven.

McKenzie, J., and F. Watson (2016) *The Garima Gospels: Early Illuminated Gospel Books from Ethiopia*. Oxford (Manar al-Athar).

McLynn, N. (2014) 'Julian and the Christian Professors', in *Being Christian in Late Antiquity: A Festschrift for Gillian Clark*, ed. C. Harrison, C. Humfress, and I. Sandwell. Oxford: 120–34.

Méhat, A. (1966) *Étude sur les 'Stromates' de Clément d'Alexandrie*. Paris.

Meijering, R. (1987) *Literary and Rhetorical Theories in Greek Scholia*. Groningen.

Melki, J. (1983) 'Saint Ephrem le syrien: Un bilan de l'edition critique', *ParOr* 11: 3–88.

Mercier, J. (ed.) (2000) *L'arche éthiopienne: Art chrétien d'Éthiopie*. Paris.

Merki, H. (1952) Ὁμοίωσις θεῷ: *Von der platonischen Angleichung an Gott zur Gottähnlichkeit bei Gregor von Nyssa*. Freiburg.

Meulenbroek, B. L. (1947) 'The Historical Character of Augustine's Cassiciacum Dialogues', *Mnemosyne* 13: 203–29.

Mews, C., and Renkin, C. (2013) 'The Legacy of Gregory the Great in the Latin West', in Neil and Dal Santo 2013: 315–42.

Meyvaert, P. (1996) 'Bede, Cassiodorus, and the Codex Amiatinus', *Spec* 71: 827–83.

Meyvaert, P. (1999) '"In the Footsteps of the Fathers": The Date of Bede's *Thirty Questions on the Books of Kings* to Nothelm', in *The Limits of Ancient*

Christianity: Essays in Late Antique Thought and Culture in Honor of R. A. Markus, ed. M. Vessey and W. Klingshirn. Ann Arbor: 267–86.

Michaud, D. A. (2017) *Reason Turned into Sense: John Smith on Spiritual Sensation*. Leuven.

Michelson, D. (2011a) 'Introduction: A Double Issue on Philoxenos of Mabbug', *Hug* 13: 1–8.

Michelson, D. (2011b) 'Philoxenos of Mabbug', in *Gorgias Encyclopedic Dictionary of the Syriac Heritage: Electronic Edition*, ed. S. P. Brock, A. M. Butts, G. A. Kiraz, and L. van Rompay. Piscataway: https://gedesh.bethmardutho.org/Philoxenus-of-Mabbug.

Michelson, D. (2014) *The Practical Christology of Philoxenos of Mabbug*. Oxford.

Miles, G. (2015) 'Stones, Wood and Woven Papyrus', *JHS* 135: 78–94.

Miles, R. (2008) 'Let's (Not) Talk About It: Augustine and the Control of Epistolary Dialogue', in *The End of Dialogue in Antiquity*, ed. S. Goldhill. Cambridge: 135–48.

Millar, F. (1993) *The Roman Near East, 31 BC–AD 337*. Cambridge.

Millar, F. (2006) *A Greek Roman Empire*. Berkeley.

Miller, D., and P. Sarris (2018) *The Novels of Justinian: A Complete Annotated English Translation*. Cambridge.

Miskjian, Hovhannes (1966) *Manuale lexicon armeno-latinum: Ad usum scholarum*. Louvain.

Mitchell, C. W. (ed.) (1912–21) *S. Ephraim's Prose Refutations of Mani, Marcion, and Bardaisan: Of Which the Greater Part Has Been Transcribed from the Palimpsest B.M. Add. 14623 and Is Now First Published*. 2 vols. London.

Mitchell, S. (1991) 'The Cult of Theos Hypsistos between Pagans, Jews, and Christians', in *Pagan Monotheism in Late Antiquity*, ed. P. Athanassiadi and M. Frede. Oxford: 81–148.

Moorhead, J. (1999) *Ambrose: Church and Society in the Late Roman World*. London.

Moorhead, J. (2005) *Gregory the Great*. London.

Moorhead, J. (2010) 'Ambrose and Augustine on Hymns', *DRev* 128: 79–92.

Moraux, P. (1973) *Der Aristotelismus bei den Griechen von Andronikos bis Alexander von Aphrodisias: Erster Band: Die Renaissance des Aristotelismus im I. Jh. v. Chr*. Berlin.

Morgan, T. (1998) *Literate Education in the Hellenistic and Roman Worlds*. Cambridge.

Morgan, T. (2020) *Being 'in Christ' in the Letters of Paul: Saved through Christ and in His Hands*. Tübingen.

Moriarty, O., N. Ruane, D. O'Gorman, C. H. Maharaj, C. Mitchell, K. M. Sarma, et al. (2017) 'Cognitive Impairment in Patients with Chronic Neuropathic or Radicular Pain: An Interaction of Pain and Age', *Frontiers in Behavioural Neuroscience* 11, article 100: 1–13.

Morlet, S. (2011) 'Eusebius' Polemic Against Porphyry: A Reassessment', in *Reconsidering Eusebius: Collected Papers on Literary, Historical, and Theological Issues*, ed. S. Inowlocki and C. Zamagni. Supplements to Vigiliae Christianae 107. Leiden: 119–50.

Morlet, S. (2019) *Symphonia: La concorde des textes et des doctrines dans la littérature grecque jusqu'à Origène*. Paris.

Morris, R. (1976) 'The Powerful and the Poor in Tenth-Century Byzantium: Law and Reality', *P&P* 73: 3–27.

Mortley, Raoul (1973) 'The Theme of Silence in Clement of Alexandria', *Journal of Theological Studies* 24, no. 1: 197–202.

Moss, C. R. (2010) *The Other Christs: Imitation of Jesus in Ancient Christian Ideologies of Martyrdom*. Oxford.

Moss, J. (2012) *Aristotle on the Apparent Good: Perception, Phantasia, Thought and Desire*. Oxford.

Mossmann, J. (2005) 'Plutarch on Animals: Rhetorical Strategies in *De sollertia animalium*', *Herm* 179: 141–63.

Muehlberger, E. (2015) 'On Authors, Fathers, and Holy Men'. https://marginalia.lareviewofbooks.org/on-authors-fathers-and-holy-men-by-ellen-muehlberger/.

Muehlberger, E. (trans.) (2017) *The Cambridge Edition of Early Christian Writings*, Vol. II: *Practice*. Cambridge.

Mühlenberg, E. (2006) *Altchristliche Lebensführung zwischen Bibel und Tugendlehre: Ethik bei den griechischen Philosophen und den frühen Christen*. Göttingen.

Müller, B. (2000) *Der Weg des Weinens*. Göttingen.

Müller, B. (2009) *Führung im Denken und Handeln Gregors des Grossen*. Tübingen.

Murphy-O'Connor, J. (2012) 'Restoration and Discovery: Bringing to Light the Original Holy Sepulchre Church', in *Keys to Jerusalem: Collected Essays*. Oxford: 193–218.

Murphy, E. (2014a) '"As Far as My Poor Memory Suggested": Cyprian's Compilation of *Ad Quirinum*', *VC* 68: 533–50.

Murphy, E. (2014b) 'Divine Ordinances and Life-Giving Remedies: Galatians in the Writings of Cyprian of Carthage', *JTI* 8: 81–101.

Murphy, E. (2016) 'Cyprian, Paul, and Care for the Poor and Captive: Offering Sacrifices and Ransoming Temples', *ZAC* 20: 418–36.

Murphy, E. (2017) 'Widows, Welfare and the Wayward: *1 Timothy* 5 in Cyprian's *Ad Quirinum*', StPatr 94: 67–74.

Murphy, E. (2018a) 'Imitating the Devil: Cyprian on Jealousy and Envy', *Scrinium* 14: 75–91.

Murphy, E. (2018b) *The Bishop and the Apostle: Cyprian's Pastoral Exegesis of Paul*. Berlin.

Murphy, E. (2020) 'Cyprian, Parenthood, and the Hebrew Bible: Modelling Munificence and Martyrdom', StPatr 100: 123–31.

Nasrallah, L. S. (2005) 'Empire and Apocalypse in Thessaloniki: Interpreting the Early Christian Rotunda', *JECS* 13: 465–508.

Nasrallah, L. S. (2010) *Christian Responses to Roman Art and Architecture: The Second Century Church Amid the Space of Empire*. New York.

Nasrallah, L. S. (2019) *Archaeology and the Letters of Paul*. Oxford.

Nauck, A. (1860) *Porphyrii philosophi platonici opuscula tria.* Leipzig.
Nauroy, G. (1989) 'Le martyre de Laurent dans l'hymnodie et la predication des IVe et Ve siècles et l'authenticité ambrosienne de l'hymne *Apostolorum supparem*', *REAug* 35: 44–82.
Nautin, P. (1976) 'La fin des *Stromates* et les *Hypotyposes* de Clément d'Alexandrie', *VC* 30: 268–302.
Nautin, P. (1977) *Origène: Sa vie et son oeuvre.* Paris.
Nawar, T. (2014) 'The Stoic Account of Apprehension', *Philosopher's Imprint* 14: 1–21.
Neil, B., and M. Dal Santo (eds.) (2013) *A Companion to Gregory the Great.* Leiden.
Neis, R. (2012) 'Eyeing Idols: Rabbinic Viewing Practices in Late Antiquity', *JQR* 102: 533–60.
Neis, R. (2013) *The Sense of Sight in Rabbinic Culture: Jewish Ways of Seeing in Late Antiquity.* Cambridge.
Neis, R. (2015) 'Religious Lives of Image-Things, *Avodah Zarah*, and Rabbis in Late Antique Palestine', *AfR* 17: 91–121.
Nethercut, J. S. (2018) 'The Alexandrian Footnote in Lucretius' *De Rerum Natura*', *Mnemosyne* 71: 75–99.
Neuschäfer, B. (1987) *Origenes als Philologe.* 2 vols. Basel.
Newman, J. H. (1979) *An Essay in Aid of a Grammar of Assent.* Notre Dame.
Newman, R. J. (1989) '*Cotidie meditare*: Theory and Practice of *meditatio* in Imperial Stoicism', *ANRW* 2.36.3: 1473–517.
Niculescu, M. V. (2007) 'Spiritual Leavening: The Communication and Reception of the Good News in Origen's Biblical Exegesis and Transformative Pedagogy', *JECS* 15: 447–81.
Nightingale, A. (1995) *Genres in Dialogue: Plato and the Construct of Philosophy.* Cambridge.
Nightingale, A. (2004) *Spectacles of Truth in Classical Greek Philosophy: Theoria in Its Cultural Context.* Cambridge.
Nightingale, A. (2016) 'Sight and the Philosophy of Vision in Classical Greece', in *Sight and the Ancient Senses*, ed. M. Squire. London.
Noailles, P. (1912 and 1914) *Les collections de novelles de l'empereur Justinien.* Paris.
Nodes, D. (2009) 'The Organization of Augustine's *Psalmus contra Partem Donati*', *VC* 63: 390–408.
Nongbri, B. (2013) *Before Religion: A History of a Modern Concept.* New Haven.
Nongbri, B. (2018) *God's Library: The Archaeology of the Earliest Christian Manuscripts.* New Haven.
Nordenfalk, C. (1938) *Die spätantiken Kanontafeln.* 2 vols. Gothenburg.
Nordenfalk, C. (1951) 'The Beginning of Book Decoration', in *Beiträge für Georg Swarzenski, zum 11. Januar 1951.* Berlin: 9–20.
Norris, R. A. (1980) 'Irenaeus and Plotinus Answer the Gnostics: A Note on the Relation Between Christian Thought and Platonism', *USQR* 36: 13–24.
Norton, G. (1998) 'Observations on the First Two Columns of the Hexapla', in *Origen's Hexapla and Fragments*, ed. A. Salvesen. Tübingen: 103–24.

Nowak, M. (2015) *Wills in the Roman Empire: A Documentary Approach.* Warsaw.

Nugent, G. (1990) 'Ausonius' Late-Antique Poetics and Post-Modern Literary Theory', *Ramus* 19: 26–50.

Nussbaum, M. (2001) *The Fragility of Goodness: Luck and Ethics in Greek Tragedy and Philosophy.* Cambridge.

Nutton, V. (1985) 'Murders and Miracle Cures: Lay Attitudes towards Medicine in Antiquity', in *Patients and Practitioners*, ed. R. Porter. Cambridge: 23–53.

Nutton, V. (1992) 'Healers in the Medical Market Place: Towards a Social History of Graeco-Roman Medicine', in *Medicine in Society: Historical Essays*, ed. A. Wear. Cambridge: 15–58.

Nutton, V. (2013) *Ancient Medicine*, 2nd edn. London.

Nuzzo, G. (2006) '*Vix sibi credere*: Appunti per la storia di un *Topos*', *Sileno: Rivista semestrale di studi classici e cristiani fondata da Quintino Cataudella* 32: 135–52.

O'Brien, C. (2015) *Bede's Temple: An Image and Its Interpretation.* Oxford.

O'Brien, C. (2017) 'The Reforming of Wearmouth and Jarrow', *Early Medieval Europe* 25: 301–19.

O'Connell, R. (1968) *St Augustine's Early Theory of Man, AD 386–391.* Cambridge.

O'Daly, G. (1987) *Augustine's Philosophy of Mind.* Berkeley.

O'Donnell, J. J. (1979) *Cassiodorus.* Berkeley.

O'Keefe, J. J., and R. R. Reno (2005) *Sanctified Vision: An Introduction to Early Christian Interpretation of the Bible.* Baltimore.

O'Loughlin, T. (1992) 'The Libri philosophorum and Augustine's Conversions', in *The Relationship between Neoplatonism and Christianity*, ed. T. Finan and V. Twomey. Dublin: 101–25.

O'Loughlin, T. (1999) 'The Development of Augustine the Bishop's Critique of Astrology', *AugStud* 30: 83–103.

O'Meara, D. J. (2002) 'The Justinianic Dialogue *On Political Science* and Its Neoplatonic Sources', in *Byzantine Philosophy and Its Ancient Sources*, ed. K. Ierodiakonou. Oxford: 49–62.

O'Meara, D. J. (2003) *Platonopolis: Platonic Political Philosophy in Late Antiquity.* Oxford.

O'Meara, J. (1951) 'St Augustine's View of Authority and Reason in AD 386', *ITQ* 18: 338–46.

O'Meara, J. (1969) '"Philosophy from Oracles" in Eusebius of Caesarea and Augustine's Cassiciacum Dialogues', *RA* 6: 105–38.

O'Neill, S. (2011) '"You have been in Afghanistan, I perceive": Demonic Agency in Augustine', *Dionysius* 29: 9–27.

O'Neill, S. (2017) 'The Demonic Body: Demonic Ontology and the Domicile of the Demons in Apuleius and Augustine', in *Philosophical Approaches to Demonology*, ed. B. W. McCraw and R. Arp. New York: 39–58.

O'Sullivan, T. M. (2007) 'Walking with Odysseus: The Portico Frame of the Odyssey Landscapes', *AJP* 128: 497–532.

Öhler, M. (2014) 'Cultic Meals in Associations and the Early Christian Eucharist', *EC* 5: 475–502.

Olivar, A. (1991) *La predicacion cristiana antigua*. Barcelona.

Olster, D. (1991) 'The Date of George of Pisidia's *Hexaemeron*', *DOP* 45: 159–72.

Orbe, A. (1969) *Antropología de San Ireneo*. Madrid.

Orbe, A. (1985) *Teología de San Ireneo: Comentario al libro V del Adversus Haereses*. Madrid.

Orlinsky, H. (1936) 'The Columnar Order of the Hexapla', *JQR* 27: 137–49.

Osborn, E. F. (1989) 'Reason and the Rule of Faith in the Second Century AD', in *The Making of Orthodoxy: Essays in Honour of Henry Chadwick*, ed. R. Williams. Cambridge; New York: 40–61.

Osborn, E. F. (1993) *The Emergence of Christian Theology*. Cambridge.

Osborn, E. F. (2005) *Clement of Alexandria*. Cambridge.

Otto, A. (1890) *Die Sprichwörter und sprichwörtlichen Redensarten der Römer, gesammelt und erklärt*. Leipzig.

Ousterhout, R. (1990) 'The Temple, the Sepulchre, and the Martyrion of the Savior', *Gesta* 29: 44–53.

Ousterhout, R. (2010) 'New Temples and New Solomons: The Rhetoric of Byzantine Architecture', in *The Old Testament in Byzantium*, ed. P. Magdalino and R. Nelson. Washington: 223–53.

Palmer, A.-M. (1989) *Prudentius on the Martyrs*. Oxford.

Papanikola-Bakirtzi, D. (ed.) (2002) *Everyday Life in Byzantium*. Athens.

Park, K. (2011) 'Observation in the Margins, 500–1500', in *Histories of Scientific Observation*, ed. L. Daston and E. Lunbeck. Chicago: 15–44.

Parker, D. C. (2010) *Codex Sinaiticus: The Story of the World's Oldest Bible*. London.

Parvis, S. (2006) *Marcellus of Ancyra and the Lost Years of the Arian Controversy, 325–345*. OECS. Oxford.

Parvis, S. (2007) 'Justin Martyr and the Apologetic Tradition', in *Justin Martyr and His Worlds*, ed. S. Parvis and P. Foster. Minneapolis: 115–27.

Pearson, L. (1952) '*Prophasis* and *Aitia*', *TAPA* 83: 205–23.

Pelekanidis, S. M., A. W. Carr, P. C. Christou, C. Tsioumis, and S. N. Kadas (1975) *The Treasures of Mount Athos: Illuminated Manuscripts*, Vol. II: *The Monasteries of Iveron, St. Panteleimon, Esphigmenon and Chilandari*. Athens.

Pelikan, J. (1993) *Christianity and Classical Culture: The Metamorphosis of Natural Theology in the Christian Encounter with Hellenism*. New Haven.

Pelikan, J., and V. Hotchkiss. (eds.) (2003) *Creeds and Confessions of Faith in the Christian Tradition*. 3 vols. New Haven.

Pellò, C. (2022) *Pythagorean Women*. Cambridge Elements: Women in the History of Philosophy. Cambridge.

Pelttari, A. (2014) *The Space that Remains: Reading Latin Poetry in Late Antiquity*. Ithaca.

Pelttari, A. (2019) *The* Psychomachia *of Prudentius: Text, Commentary, and Glossary*. Norman.

Pender, E. (1992) 'Spiritual Pregnancy in Plato's *Symposium*', *CQ* 42: 72–86.

Penniman, J. D. (2015a) '"The Health-Giving Cup": Cyprian's Ep. 63 and the Medicinal Power of Eucharistic Wine', *JECS* 23: 189–211.

Penniman, J. D. (2015b) 'Fed to Perfection: Mother's Milk, Roman Family Values, and the Transformation of the Soul in Gregory of Nyssa', *CH* 84: 495–530.

Penniman, J. D. (2017) *Raised on Christian Milk: Food and the Formation of the Soul in Early Christianity*. New Haven.

Pépin, J. (1977) *'Ex platonicorum persona': Études sur les lectures philosophiques des saint Augustin*. Amsterdam.

Pépin, J. (1999) 'Augustine sur la divination, les démons et les signes', in *Signum: IX Colloquio internaztionale, Roma, 8–10 gennaio 1998*, ed. M. L. Bianchi. Florence: 67–78.

Peppard, M. (2013) 'Archived Portraits of Jesus: Unorthodox Christological Images in John and Athanasius', in *Portraits of Jesus*, ed. S. E. Myers. Tübingen: 393–409.

Peppard, M. (2015) 'Was the Presence of Christ in Statues? The Challenge of Divine Media for a Jewish Roman God', in *The Art of Empire: Christian Art in its Imperial Context*, ed. L. M. Jefferson and R. M. Jensen. Minneapolis: 225–68.

Peppard, M. (2019) 'The Photisterion in Late Antiquity: Reconsidering Terminology for Sites and Rites of Initiation', *JEH* 71: 463–83.

Perkams, M. (2015) 'Die Ursprünge des spätantiken philosophischen Curriculums im kaiserzeitlichen Aristotelismus', *Elenchos* 36: 149–63.

Perl, E. (2007) *Theophany: The Neoplatonic Philosophy of Dionysius the Areopagite*. Albany.

Perrone, L. (1994) '*Quaestiones et responsiones* in Origene: Prospettive di un'analisi formale dell'argomentazione esegetico-teologica', *CNS* 15: 1–50.

Perrone, L. (1995) 'Perspectives sur Origène et la littérature patristique des *quaestiones et responsiones*', in *Origeniana sexta: Origène et la Bible/Origen and the Bible*, ed. G. Dorival and A. Le Boulluec. Leuven: 151–64.

Perrone, L. (2011) *La preghiera secondo Origene: L'impossibilità donate*. Brescia.

Perrone, L. (2013) '*Origenes rediuiuus*: La découverte des *Homélies sur les Psaumes* dans le *Cod. Gr.* 314 de Munich', *REAug* 59: 55–94.

Pertusi, A. (1956) 'Dei poemi perduti di Giorgio di Pisidia', *Aev* 30, fasc. 5/6: 395–427.

Petrey, T. G. (2016) *Resurrecting Parts: Early Christians on Desire, Reproduction, and Sexual Difference*. London.

Petridou, G., and C. Thumiger (eds.) (2016) *Homo Patiens: Approaches to the Patient in the Ancient World*. Leiden.

Petruccione, J. F. (ed.) (2007) *Theodoret of Cyrus: The Questions on the 'Octateuch'*, Vol. II: *On Leviticus, Numbers, Deuteronomy, Joshua, Judges, and Ruth*. Washington.

Pevarello, D. (2018) 'Pythagorean Traditions in Christian Asceticism', in *Monastic Education in Late Antiquity: The Transformation of Classical Paideia*, ed. L. Larsen and S. Rubenson. Cambridge: 256–77.

Phelan, O. (2014) *The Formation of Christian Europe: Baptism, the Carolingians and the Imperium Christianium*. Oxford.

Pigeaud, J. (2006) *La maladie de l'âme: Étude sur la relation de l'âme et du corps dans la tradition médico-philosophique antique*, 3rd edn. Paris.

Piketty, T. (2020) *Capital and Ideology*. Cambridge.

Pinault, J. R. (1992) 'The Medical Case for Virginity in the Early Second Century CE: Soranus of Ephesus, *Gynecology* 1.32', *Helios* 19: 123–39.

Pingree, D. (1986–94) 'Astrologia, Astronomia', in *Augustinus-Lexicon II*, ed. C. Mayer. Basel: 482–90.

Platt, V. (2009) 'Virtual Visions: Phantasia and the Perception of the Divine in the *Life of Apollonius of Tyana*', in *Philostratus*, ed. E. Bowie and J. Elsner. Cambridge: 131–54.

Platt, V. (2011) *Facing the Gods: Epiphany and Representation in Graeco-Roman Art, Literature and Religion*. Cambridge.

Platt, V., and M. Squire (eds.) (2017) *The Frame in Classical Art: A Cultural History*. Cambridge.

Poeschke, J. (1968) 'Taube', in *Lexikon der christlichen Ikonographie*. 8 vols. Freiburg: 4.241–44.

Poirier, P.-H. (2002) 'Faith and Persuasion in the Book of the Laws of the Countries: A Note on Bardaisan's Epistemology', *JCSSS* 2: 21–28.

Pongratz-Leisten, B., and K. Sonik (2015) 'Between Cognition and Culture: Theorizing the Materiality of Divine Agency in Cross-Cultural Perspective', in *The Materiality of Divine Agency*, ed. B. Pongratz-Leisten and K. Sonik. Boston: 3–69.

Possekel, U. (1999) *Evidence of Greek Philosophical Concepts in the Writings of Ephrem the Syrian*. Leuven.

Possekel, U. (2007) 'Bardaisan of Edessa: Philosopher or Theologian?', *ZAC* 10: 442–61.

Possekel, U. (2012) 'Bardaisan and Origen on Fate and the Power of the Stars', *JECS* 20: 515–41.

Possekel, U. (2016) 'Friendship with Rome: Edessan Politics and Culture in the Time of King Abgar VIII', *Aram* 28: 453–61.

Possekel, U. (2018) 'Bardaisan's Influence on Late Antique Christianity', *Hug* 21: 81–125.

Poster, C. (2001) 'A Conversation Halved: Epistolary Theory in Graeco-Roman Antiquities', in *Letter Writing Manuals and Instruction from Antiquity to the Present: Historical and Bibliographical Studies*, ed. C. Poster and L. Mitchell. Columbia.

Pouderon, B. (1998) 'Réflexions sur la formation d'une élite intellectuelle chrétienne au IIe siècle: Les 'écoles' d'Athènes, de Rome et d'Alexandrie', in *Les apologistes chrétiens et la culture grecque*, ed. B. Pouderon and J. Doré. Paris: 238–69.

Poulain, A. (1910) *The Graces of Interior Prayer: A Treatise on Mystical Theology*, trans. L. L. Yorke Smith, preface by Daniel Considine. London.

Praechter, K. (1909) 'Die griechischen Aristoteleskommentare', *ByzZ* 18: 516–38.

Price, R. M. (2004) 'Marian Piety and Nestorian Controversy', in *The Church and Mary*, ed. R. N. Swanson. Woodbridge: 31–38.

Price, R. M. (2008) 'The Theotokos and the Council of Ephesus', in *The Origins of the Cult of the Virgin Mary*, ed. C. Maunder. London: 89–103.

Prince, S. (2015) *Antisthenes of Athens: Texts, Translations and Commentary*. Ann Arbor.

Pucci, J. (1991) 'Prudentius' Readings of Horace in the *Cathemerinon*', *Latomus* 50: 677–90.

Puchner, M. (2010) *The Drama of Ideas: Platonic Provocations in Theatre and Philosophy*. Oxford.

Rabbow, P. (1954) *Seelenführung: Methodik der Exerzitien in der Antike*. Munich.

Radde-Gallwitz, A. (2016) 'Private Creeds and Their Troubled Authors', *JECS* 24: 465–90.

Radde-Gallwitz, A. (2018) *Gregory of Nyssa's Doctrinal Works: A Literary Study*. Oxford.

Rahner, K. (1932) 'Le début d'une doctrine des cinq sens spirituels chez Origène', *Revue d'Asceticisme et de la Mystique* 13: 113–45. German: 'Die "geistlichen Sinne" nach Origenes', *Schriften zur Theologie* XII, ed. K. H. Neufeld, SJ. Zürich 1975: 113–36. English: 'The "Spiritual Senses" According to Origen', *Theological Investigations*, Vol. XVI: Experience of the Spirit: Source of Theology, trans. D. Morland. London 1979: 81–103.

Räisänen, H. (1973) *Die Parabeltheorie im Markusevangelium*. Helsinki.

Rajna, P. (1928) 'Le denominazioni *Trivium* e *Quadrivium* (con un singolare accessario)', *Studi medievali* 1: 4–36.

Ramelli, I. L. E. (2009a) *Bardaisan of Edessa: A Reassessment of the Evidence and a New Interpretation*. Piscataway.

Ramelli, I. L. E. (2009b) Bardesane di Edessa: *Contro il fato = Kata heimarmenes*. Rome and Bologna.

Ramelli, I. L. E. (2009c) 'Origen, Patristic Philosophy, and Christian Platonism: Re-Thinking the Christianisation of Hellenism', *VC* 63: 217–63.

Ramelli, I. L. E. (2013) 'Origen in Augustine: A Paradoxical Reception', *Numen* 60: 280–307.

Ramelli, I. L. E. (2017a) 'The Mysteries of Scripture: Allegorical Exegesis and the Heritage of Stoicism, Philo, and Pantaenus', in Černušková, Kovacs, and Plátová 2017: 80–110.

Ramelli, I. L. E. (2017b) 'Prophecy in Origen: Between Scripture and Philosophy', *JECH* 7: 17–39.

Ramirez-Weaver, E. (2017) *A Saving Science: Capturing the Heavens in Carolingian Manuscripts*. Philadelphia.

Rand, E. K. (1920) 'Prudentius and Christian Humanism', *TAPA* 51: 71–83.

Rankin, H. D. (1964) *Plato and the Individual*. London.

Rasmussen, A. D. P. (2014) 'Basil of Caesarea's Uses of Origen in His Polemic against Astrology', *ZAC* 18: 471–85.
Ray, R. (1997) 'Rhetoric and Christian Latin Culture'. Jarrow Lecture. Jarrow.
Ray, R. (2006) 'Who Did Bede Think He Was?' in DeGregorio 2006a: 11–35.
Rebillard, É. (2012) *Christians and Their Many Identities in Late Antiquity, North Africa, 200–450 CE.* Ithaca.
Reudenbach, B. (2009) 'Der Codex als heiliger Raum: Überlegungen zur Bildausstattung früher Evangelienbücher', in *Codex und Raum*, ed. S. Müller, L. E. Saurma-Jeltsch, and P. Strohschneider. Wiesbaden: 59–84.
Reuss, J. (1966) *Johannes-Kommentare aus der griechischen Kirche*. Berlin.
Reydams-Schils, G. (2020) *Calcidius on Plato's 'Timaeus': Greek Philosophy, Latin Reception, and Christian Contexts*. Cambridge.
Reynders, B. (1954) *Lexique comparé du texte grec et des versions latine, arménienne et syriaque de l'"Adversus haereses" de Saint Irénée, Index des mots latins*. Louvain.
Ricci, C. (2013) 'Gregory's Missions to the Barbarians', in Neil and Dal Santo 2013: 29–56.
Richard, M. (1938) 'Léonce et Pamphile', *RSPT* 27: 27–52.
Richard, M. (1950) 'Ἀπὸ φωνῆς', *Byzantion* 20: 191–221.
Ridings, D. (1995) *The Attic Moses: The Dependency Theme in Some Early Christian Writers*. Gothenburg.
Riedinger, U. (1956) *Die Heilige Schrift im Kampf der griechischen Kirche gegen die Astrologie von Origenes bis Johannes von Damaskos*. Innsbruck.
Riedweg, C., C. Horn, and D. Wyrwa (eds.) (2018) *Die Philosophie der Antike 5/1*. Basel.
Riggsby, A. (2018) 'Cognitive Aspects of Information Technology in the Roman World', in *History of Distributed Cognition*, ed. D. Cairns. Edinburgh: 57–70.
Riggsby, A. (2019) *Mosaics of Knowledge: Representing Information in the Roman World*. Oxford.
Riginos, A. S. (1976) *Platonica: The Anecdotes Concerning the Life and Writings of Plato*. Leiden.
Rigolio, A. (2019) *Christians in Conversation: A Guide to Late Antique Dialogues in Greek and Syriac*. Oxford.
Ritter, A. M. (1991) 'Creeds', in *Early Christianity: Origins and Evolution to AD 600 in Honour of W. H. C. Frend*, ed. I. Hazlett. London: 92–100.
Rives, J. B. (1999) 'The Decree of Decius and the Religion of Empire', *JRS* 89: 135–54.
Rizzerio, L. (1996) *Clemente di Alessandria e la 'physiologia veramente gnostica': Saggio sulle origini e le implicazioni di un'epistemologia e di un'ontologia 'cristiane'*. Leuven.
Robbins, F. E. (1912) *The Hexameral Literature: A Study of the Greek and Latin Commentaries on Genesis*. Chicago.
Roberts, M. (1989) *The Jeweled Style: Poetry and Poetics in Late Antiquity*. Ithaca.

Robertson, J. (2007) *Christ as Mediator: The Study of the Theologies of Eusebius of Caesarea, Marcellus of Ancyra, and Athanasius of Alexandria*. Oxford Theological Monographs. Oxford.

Rockem, F. (2010) *Philosophers and Thespians: Thinking Performance*. Stanford.

Rollason, D. (2010) 'The Cult of Bede', in DeGregorio 2010: 193–200.

Rondeau, M.-J. (1960) 'Le commentaire sur les Psaumes d'Évagre le Pontique', *OCP* 27: 307–48.

Rosen, R., and M. Horstmanshoff (2003) 'The Andreia of the Hippocratic Physician and the Problem of Incurables', in *Andreia: Studies in Manliness and Courage in Classical Antiquity*, ed. R. Rosen and I. Sluiter. Leiden: 95–113.

Rosenwein, B. H. (2006) *Emotional Communities in the Early Middle Ages*. Ithaca.

Ross, S. K. (2001) *Roman Edessa: Politics and Culture on the Eastern Fringes of the Roman Empire, 114–242 CE*. London.

Roth, C. P. (1992) 'Platonic and Pauline Elements in the Ascent of the Soul in Gregory of Nyssa's *Dialogue on the Soul and Resurrection*', *VC* 46: 20–30.

Roueché, M. (1974) 'Byzantine Philosophical Texts of the Seventh Century', *JÖB* 23: 61–76.

Roueché, M. (1980) 'A Middle Byzantine Handbook of Logic Terminology', *JÖB* 29: 71–98.

Roueché, M. (1990) 'The Definitions of Philosophy and a New Fragment of Stephanus the Philosopher', *JÖB* 40: 107–28.

Roueché, M. (1998) 'The Functions of the Governor in Late Antiquity', *Antiquité tardive* 6: 31–36.

Rouwhorst, G. (2013) 'The Bible in Liturgy', in *The New Cambridge History of the Bible*, Vol. I: *From the Beginnings to 600*, ed. J. Carleton Paget and J. Schaper. Cambridge: 822–42.

Rouwhorst, G. (2019) 'Initiation by Circumcision and Water Baptism in Early Judaism and Early Christianity', in *Ritual Dynamics in Jewish and Christian Contexts: Between Bible and Liturgy*, ed. C. Bergmann and B. Kranemann. Leiden: 165–89.

Rowe, C. K. (2016) *One True Life: The Stoics and Early Christians as Rival Traditions*. New Haven.

Rowley, S. (2010) 'Bede in Later Anglo-Saxon England', in DeGregorio 2010: 216–28.

Runia, D. T. (1981) 'Philo's *De aeternitate mundi*: The Problem of its Interpretation', *VC* 35: 105–51.

Runia, D. T. (1993) *Philo in Early Christian Literature: A Survey*. Assen.

Runia, D. T. (2008) 'Philo and Hellenistic Doxography', in *Philo of Alexandria and Post-Aristotelian Philosophy*, ed. F. Alesse. Leiden: 13–52.

Runia, D. T. (2013) 'The Theme of Becoming like God in Plato's *Republic*', in *Dialogues on Plato's Politeia*, ed. L. Brisson and N. Notomi. Sankt Augustin: 288–93.

Russell, D. (2004) 'Virtue as "Likeness to God" in Plato and Seneca', *Journal of the History of Philosophy* 42: 241–60.

Russell, J. (1980) 'Excavations at Anemurium (Eski Anamur) 1976', *Türk Arkeoloji Dergisi* 25: 263–90.

Russell, J. (1987) *Mosaic Inscriptions of Anemurium*. Vienna.
Ryan, M. J. (2016) '"To Mistake Gold for Wealth": The Venerable Bede and the Fate of Northumbria', in *Making Early Medieval Societies: Conflict and Belonging in the Latin West, 300–1200*, ed. K. Cooper and C. Leyser. Cambridge: 80–103.
Saffrey, H. D. (1979) 'Allusions antichrétiennes chez Proclus: Le diadoque platonicien', *RSPT* 59: 553–63.
Saffrey, H. D. (1990) 'Un lien objectif entre le Pseudo-Denys et Proclus', in *Recherches sur le néoplatonisme après Plotin*, ed. H. D. Saffrey. Paris: 239–52.
Saffrey, H. D. (1992) 'Accorder entre elles les traditions théologiques: Une charactéristique du néoplatonisme athénien', in *On Proclus and His Influence in Medieval Philosophy*, ed. E. P. Bos and P. A. Meijer. Leiden: 35–50.
Sage, M. M. (1975) *Cyprian*. Philadelphia.
Sahlins, M. (1985) *Islands of History*. Chicago.
Saieg, P. (2016) 'Irenaeus Philosophicus and the Stoic *praemeditatio malorum*', StPatr 74: 71–88.
Saieg, P. (2019) 'Lived Theology: Economy, Asceticism, and Spirit in Irenaeus and His Readers', *VC* 73: 297–332.
Samama, É. (2003) *Les médecins dans le monde grec: Sources épigraphiques sur la naissance d'une corps medical*. Hautes études du monde gréco-romain 31. Geneva.
Sanday, W. (1899) 'Recent Research on the Origin of the Creed', *JTS* 1: 3–22.
Sandnes, K. O. (2016) *Early Christian Discourses on Jesus' Prayer at Gethsemane: Courageous, Committed, Cowardly?* Leiden.
Sarris, P. (2006) *Economy and Society in the Age of Justinian*. Cambridge.
Sarris, P. (2011a) *Empires of Faith: The Fall of Rome to the Rise of Islam*. Oxford.
Sarris, P. (2011b) 'Aristocrats, Peasants and the State in the Later Roman Empire', in *Der wiederkehrende Leviathan: Staatlichkeit und Staatswerdung in Spätantike und Früher Neuzeit*, ed. P. Eich, S. Schmidt-Hofner, and C. Wieland. Heidelberg: 377–94.
Sarris, P. (2013) 'Lay Archives in the Late Antique and Byzantine East: The Implications of the Documentary Papyri', in *Documentary Culture and the Laity in the Early Middle Ages*, ed. W. Brown, M. Costambeys, M. Innes, and A. J. Kosto. Cambridge: 17–35.
Satterlee, C. (2000) *Ambrose of Milan's Method of Mystagogical Preaching*. Collegeville.
Savon, H. (1977) *Saint Ambroise devant l'exégèse de Philon le Juif*. Paris.
Savon, H. (1999) 'Ambroise prédicateur', *Connaissance des pères de l'église* 74: 33–45.
Savvidis, K., and M. Dorn (eds.) (1999–2014) *Lexicon Gregorianum: Wörterbuch zu den Schriften Gregors von Nyssa*. 10 vols. Leiden.
Scarborough, J. (1971) 'Galen and the Gladiators', *Episteme* 5: 98–111.
Schaller, J. J. (1988) 'Performative Language Theory: An Exercise in the Analysis of Ritual', *Worship* 62: 415–32.
Schelkle, K. H. (1959) *Paulus Lehrer der Väter: Die altkirchliche Auslegung von Römer 1–11*, 2nd edn. Düsseldorf.
Scheltema, H. J. (1970) *L'enseignement de droit des antécesseurs*. Leiden.

Schironi, F. (2015) 'P. Grenf. 1.5, Origen, and the Scriptorium of Caesarea', *BASP* 52: 181–233.

Schlapbach, K. (2005) 'Divination, Wissen und Autorität in Augustins Cassiciacum-Dialogen', *MH* 62: 84–98.

Schlapbach, K. (2013) 'De divinatione daemonum', in *The Oxford Guide to the Historical Reception of Augustine*, Vol. I, ed. K. Pollmann. Oxford: 132–34.

Schmid, K., and J. Schröter (2019) *Die Entstehung der Bibel: Von den ersten Texten zu den heiligen Schriften*. Munich.

Schoedel, W. R. (1972) *Athenagoras* Legatio *and* De Resurrectione. Oxford.

Schofield, M. (1986) 'Cicero for and against Divination', *JRS* 76: 47–65.

Scholten, C. (1995) 'Die alexandrinische Katechetenschule', *JbAC* 38: 16–37.

Scholten, C. (2015) *Theodoret de graecarum affectionum curatione / Heilung der griechischen Krankheiten*. Leiden.

Schott, J. M. (2011) 'Eusebius' *Panegyric on the Building of Churches* (H.e. 10.4.2–72): Aesthetics and the Politics of Christian Architecture', in *Reconsidering Eusebius: Collected Papers on Literary, Historical, and Theological Issues*, ed. S. Inowlocki and C. Zamagni. Supplements to Vigiliae Christianae 107. Leiden: 177–97.

Schroeder, S. (2010) 'A Tale of Two Problems: Wittgenstein's Discussion of Aspect Perception', in *Mind, Method, and Morality: Essays in Honour of Anthony Kenny*, ed. J. Cottingham and P. Hacker. Oxford: 352–71.

Schubart, W. (1952) *Religion und Eros*. Munich.

Schwartz, E. (1960, original 1936) 'Die Kanonessammlungen der alten Reichskirche', in *Gesammelte Schriften*, Vol. IV. Berlin: 159–275.

Scott, M. S. (2018) *The Idea of Nicaea in the Early Church Councils, AD 431–451*. OECS. Oxford.

Scott, R. (1985) 'Malalas, the *Secret History*, and Justinian's Propaganda', *DOP* 39: 99–109.

Seagraves, R. (1993) *Pascentes cum disciplina: A Lexical Study of the Clergy in the Cyprianic Correspondence*. Fribourg.

Searle, J. R. (1969) *Speech Acts: An Essay in the Philosophy of Language*. Cambridge.

Secord, J. (2018) 'The Celibate Athlete: Athletic Metaphors, Medical Thought, and Sexual Abstinence in the Second and Third Centuries CE', *SLA* 2: 464–90.

Secord, J. (2020) *Christian Intellectuals and the Roman Empire: From Justin Martyr to Origen*. College Park.

Sedley, D. (1999) 'The Ideal of Godlikeness', in *Plato 2: Ethics, Politics, Religion, and the Soul*, ed. G. Fine. Oxford: 309–28.

Segal, J. B. (1970) *Edessa 'the Blessed City'*. Oxford.

Segal, J. B. (1982) 'Abgar', *EIr* 1: 210–13.

Selby, A. (2020) *Ambrose of Milan's* On the Holy Spirit: *Rhetoric, Theology, and Sources*. Piscataway.

Serrati, J. (2015) 'The Rise of Rome to 264 BC', in *A Companion to the Punic Wars*, ed. D. Hoyos. Oxford: 9–27.

Sewell, W., Jr. (1992) 'A Theory of Structure: Duality, Agency, and Transformation', *American Journal of Sociology* 98: 1–29.

Sewell, W., Jr. (2005) *Logics of History: Social Theory and Social Transformation*. Chicago.

Shanzer, D. (1986) *A Philosophical and Literary Commentary on Martianus Capella's* De nuptiis Philologiae et Mercurii *Book 1*. Berkeley.

Shaw, R. (2018) *The Gregorian Mission to Kent in Bede's* Ecclesiastical History: *Methodology and Sources*. Abingdon.

Shaw, T. M. (1998) *The Burden of the Flesh: Fasting and Sexuality in Early Christianity*. Minneapolis.

Shepardson, C. (2014) *Controlling Contested Places. Late Antique Antioch and the Spatial Politics of Religious Controversy*. Berkeley.

Sheppard, A. (2007) 'Porphyry's Views on Phantasia', in *Studies on Porphyry*, ed. G. E. Karamanolis and A. Sheppard. London: 71–76.

Shilling, B. (2016) 'Fountains of Paradise in Early Byzantine Art, Homilies and Hymns', in *Fountains and Water Culture in Byzantium*, ed. B. Shilling and P. Stephenson. Cambridge: 208–28.

Shoemaker, S. J. (2007) 'Marian Liturgies and Devotion in Early Christianity', in *Mary: The Complete Resource*, ed. S. J. Boss. London: 130–48.

Shoemaker, S. J. (2008) 'The Cult of the Virgin in the Fourth Century: A Fresh Look at Some Old and New Sources', in *The Origins of the Cult of the Virgin Mary*, ed. C. Maunder. London: 71–87.

Silvas, A. (2008) *Macrina the Younger, Philosopher of God*. Turnhout.

Silverman, A. (1991) 'Plato on "Phantasia"', *ClAnt* 10: 123–47.

Singer, P. N. (2018) 'Galen's Pathological Soul: Diagnosis and Therapy in Ethical and Medical Texts and Contexts', in Singer and Thumiger 2018a: 381–420.

Singer, P. N., and C. Thumiger (eds.) (2018a) *Mental Illness in Ancient Medicine: From Celsus to Paul of Aegina*. Leiden.

Singer, P. N., and C. Thumiger (2018b) 'Introduction: Disease Classification and Mental Illness: Ancient and Modern Perspectives', in Singer and Thumiger 2018a: 1–32.

Sirks, A. J. B. (2008) 'The Colonate in Justinian's Reign', *JRS* 98: 120–43.

Skjaervø, P. O. (1988) 'Bardesanes', *EIr* 3: 780–85.

Skutsch, O. (1985) *Annals of Quintus Ennius*. Oxford.

Slaveva-Griffin, S., and P. Reemes (2014) *The Routledge Handbook of Neoplatonism*. London.

Small, J. P. (2003) *The Parallel Worlds of Classical Art and Text*. Cambridge.

Smalley, B. (1983) *The Study of the Bible in the Middle Ages*, 3rd edn. Oxford.

Smit, P.-B. (2011) 'The Reception of the Truth at Baptism and the Church as Epistemological Principle in the Work of Irenaeus of Lyons', *Ecclesiology* 7: 354–73.

Smit, P.-B. (2013) *Paradigms of Being in Christ: A Study of the Epistle to the Philippians*. London.

Smith, A. (1999) 'The Significance of Practical Ethics for Plotinus', in *Traditions of Platonism: Essays in Honour of John Dillon*, ed. J. Cleary. Aldershot: 227–36.

Smith, A. (2000) 'Porphyry and the Platonic Theology of Proclus', in *Proclus et la théologie platonicienne: Actes du Colloque international de Louvain, 13–16 mai 1998: En l'honneur de H. D. Saffrey et L. G. Westerink*, ed. A.-P. Segonds and C. Steele. Paris: 177–88.

Smith, C. (1989) 'Christian Rhetoric in Eusebius' Panegyric at Tyre', *VC* 43: 226–47.

Smith, G. (2017) 'Augustine on Demons' Bodies', StPatr 72: 7–32.

Smith, J. W. (2001) 'Macrina: Tamer of Horses and Healer of Souls: Grief and the Therapy of Hope in Gregory of Nyssa's *De Anima et Resurrectione*', *JTS* 52: 37–60.

Smith, J. W. (2004a) 'A Just and Reasonable Grief: The Death and Function of a Holy Woman in Gregory of Nyssa's *Life of Macrina*', *JECS* 12: 57–84.

Smith, J. W. (2004b) *Passion and Paradise: Human and Divine Emotion in the Thought of Gregory of Nyssa*. New York.

Smith, L. (2009) *The 'Glossa Ordinaria': The Making of a Medieval Bible Commentary*. Leiden.

Smith, N. (2003) *The Poems of Andrew Marvell*. Harlow.

Smith, R. (2007) 'The Imperial Court of the Late Roman Empire, c. AD 300–c. AD 450', in *The Court and Court Society in Ancient Monarchies*, ed. A. J. S. Spawforth. Cambridge: 157–233.

Smith, W. (2011) *Christian Grace and Pagan Virtue: The Theological Foundation of Ambrose's Ethics*. Oxford.

Smyth, M. (1996) *Understanding the Universe in Seventh-Century Ireland*. Woodbridge.

Snyder, H. G. (2000) *Teachers and Texts in the Ancient World*. London.

Solheid, J. (2020) 'The Word in the City: Biblical Scholarship and Reading Culture in Origen's *Psalm Homilies* from the Codex monacensis Graecus 314.' PhD thesis, University of St Michael's College Faculty of Theology.

Somos, R. (2015) *Logic and Argumentation in Origen*. Münster.

Sorabji, R. (2002) *Emotion and Peace of Mind: From Stoic Agitation to Christian Temptation*, 2nd rev. edn. Oxford.

Sorabji, R. (2004) *The Philosophy of the Commentators 200–600 AD: A Sourcebook*. Vols. I–III. London.

Sorabji, R. (ed.) (2019) *Aristotle Transformed: The Ancient Commentators and their Influence*, 2nd edn. London.

Sorensen, E. (2002) *Possession and Exorcism in the New Testament and Early Christianity*. Tübingen.

Sowerby, R. (2016) *Angels in Early Medieval England*. Oxford.

Sparrow, T., and A. Hutchinson (eds.) (2013) *A History of Habit from Aristotle to Bourdieu*. Lanham.

Speyer, W. (1986) 'Asterios von Amaseia', in *RAC Suppl.* 4. Stuttgart: 626–39.

Spieser, J.-M. (2014) 'En suivant Eusèbe au Saint-Sépulcre', *Antiquité tardive* 22: 95–103.

Springer, C. (1991) 'Ambrose's "Veni Redemptor Gentium": The Aesthetics of Antiphony', *JbAC* 34: 76–87.

Springer, C. (1995) 'The Concinnity of Ambrose's Illuminans Altissimus', in *Panchaia: Festschrift für Professor Klaus Thraede*, ed. M. Wacht. Münster: 228–37.

Springer, C. (2014) 'Of Roosters and *Repetitio*: Ambrose's *Aeterne rerum conditor*', *VC* 68: 155–77.

Squire, M. (2009) *Image and Text in Graeco-Roman Antiquity*. Cambridge.

Squire, M. (2011) *The Iliad in a Nutshell: Visualizing Epic on the Tabulae Iliacae*. Oxford.

Squire, M. (2015) 'Ecphrasis: Visual and Verbal Interactions in Ancient Greek and Latin Literature', Oxford Handbooks Online. DOI: 10.1093/oxfordhb/9780199935390.013.58.

Squire, M. (2016) '"How to Read a Roman Portrait"? Optatian Porfyry, Constantine and the *Vultus Augusti*', *Papers of the British School at Rome* 84: 179–240.

Stead, C. (1983) 'The Freedom of the Will and the Arian Controversy', in *Platonismus und Christentum: Festschrift für Heinrich Dörrie*, ed. Horst-Dieter Blume and Friedhelm Mann. Jahrbuch für Antike und Christentum Erganzungsband 10. Münster: 245–57.

Steel, C. (2012) 'Maximus Confessor on *Theory* and *Praxis*: A Commentary on *Ambigua ad Johannem* VI (10) 1–19', in Bénatouïl and Bonazzi 2012: 229–57.

Stefaniw, B. (2018) 'Knowledge in Late Antiquity: What Is It Made of and What Does It Make?', *SLA* 2: 266–93.

Steiner, D. T. (2003) *Images in Mind: Statues in Archaic and Classical Greek Literature and Thought*. Princeton.

Stenger, J. R. (2022) *Education in Late Antiquity: Challenges, Dynamism, and Reinterpretation, 300–550 CE*. Oxford.

Stenger, J. R. (forthcoming) 'Christian Education and Classical *Paideia*', in *The Edinburgh Critical History of Christian Theology*, Vol. I, ed. M. J. Edwards. Edinburgh.

Stephens, C. W. B. (2015) *Canon Law and Episcopal Authority: The Canons of Antioch and Serdica*. Oxford Theology and Religion Monographs. Oxford.

Stewart-Sykes, A. (2003) 'Catechumenate and Contra-Culture: The Social Process of Catechumenate in Third-Century Africa and Its Development', *SVTQ* 47: 289–306.

Stewart, C. (2005) 'Evagrius Ponticus and the "Eight Generic *Logismoi*"', in *In the Garden of Evil: The Vices and Culture in the Middle Ages*, ed. R. Newhauser. Toronto: 3–34.

Stewart, P. (2003) *Statues in Roman Society: Representation and Response*. Oxford.

Stock, B. (1983) *The Implications of Literacy: Written Language and Models of Interpretation in the 11th and 12th Centuries*. Princeton.

Stock, B. (1996) *Augustine the Reader: Meditation, Self-Knowledge, and the Ethics of Interpretation*. Cambridge.

Stock, B. (2010) *Augustine's Inner Dialogue: The Philosophical Soliloquy in Late Antiquity*. Cambridge.
Stowers, S. K. (2011) 'The Religion of Plant and Animal Offerings versus the Religion of Meanings, Essences, and Textual Mysteries', in *Ancient Mediterranean Sacrifice*, ed. J. W. Knust and Z. Varhelyi. New York: 35–56.
Straw, C. (1991) *Gregory the Great: Perfection in Imperfection*. Los Angeles.
Straw, C. (2019) 'Gregory the Great', in *Great Jurists and Legal Collections in the First Millennium*, ed. P. Reynolds. Cambridge: 353–80.
Striker, G. (1996) 'Κριτήριον τῆς ἀληθείας', in *Essays on Hellenistic Epistemology and Ethics*. Cambridge: 22–76.
Strøm-Olsen, R. (2018) 'The Propylaic Function of the Eusebian Canon Tables in Late Antiquity', *JECS* 26: 403–31.
Stroumsa, G. (2016) *The Scriptural Universe of Ancient Christianity*. Cambridge.
Struck, P. T. (2001) 'Pagan and Christian Theurgies: Iamblichus, Pseudo-Dionysius, Religion and Magic in Late Antiquity', *Ancient World* 32: 25–38.
Struck, P. T. (2004) *Birth of the Symbol: Ancient Readers at the Limits of Their Texts*. Princeton.
Struck, P. T. (2016) *Divination and Human Nature: A Cognitive History of Intuition in Antiquity*. Princeton.
Swift, L. J. (1981) 'Basil and Ambrose on the Six Days of Creation', *Aug* 21: 317–28.
Taft, R. F. (1986) *The Liturgy of the Hours in East and West: The Origins of the Divine Office and Its Meaning for Today*. Collegeville: 166–87.
Taft, R. F. (1996) 'Prayer to or for the Saints? A Note on the Sanctoral Intercessions / Commemorations in the Anaphora', in *Ab Oriente et Occidente (Mt 8,11): Kirche aus Ost und West: Gedankschrift für Willhelm Nyssen*. St Ottilien: 439–55.
Taft, R. F. (1998) 'Women at Church in Byzantium: Where, When – and Why?', *DOP* 52: 27–87.
Tannous, J. (2018) *The Making of the Medieval Middle East: Religion, Society, and Simple Believers*. Princeton.
Tarán, L. (2001) 'Aristotelianism in the First Century BC', in *Collected Papers (1962–1999)*. Leiden: 479–524.
Taylor, J. E. (2006) *Jewish Women Philosophers of First-Century Alexandria: Philo's 'Therapeutae' Reconsidered*. Oxford.
Teixidor, J. (1992) *Bardesane d'Edesse: La première philosophie syriaque*. Paris.
Temkin, O. (1991) *Hippocrates in a World of Pagans and Christians*. Baltimore.
ten Napel, E. (1987) 'Some Remarks on the Hexaemeral Literature in Syriac', in *IV Symposium Syriacum 1984: Literary Genres in Syriac Literature*, ed. H. J. W. Drijvers et al. Rome: 57–69.
Teske, R. (1994) 'St Augustine and the Vision of God', in *Augustine: Mystic and Mystagogue*. New York.
Tester, J. (1987) *A History of Western Astrology*. Woodbridge.

Thacker, A. (1983) 'Bede's Ideal of Reform', in *Ideal and Reality in Frankish and Anglo-Saxon Society: Studies Presented to J. M. Wallace-Hadrill*, ed. P. Wormald. Oxford: 130–53.

Thacker, A. (2006) 'Bede and the Ordering of Understanding', in DeGregorio 2006a: 37–63.

Theiler, W. (1933) *Porphyrios und Augustin*. Halle.

Tomlinson, M. (2010) 'The Influence of Pagan Sacrificial Thought on Christian Martyr-Soteriology'. DPhil thesis, University of Oxford.

Tonstad, L. M. (2016) *God and Difference: The Trinity, Sexuality, and the Transformation of Finitude*. New York.

Topping, R. (2012) *Happiness and Wisdom: Augustine's Early Theology of Education*. Washington.

Toynbee, A. J. (1979) *A Study of History*, Vol. VI: *The Disintegration of Civilisations (continued)*. Oxford.

Trapp, M. (2017) 'Philosophical Authority in the Imperial Period', in *Authority and Expertise in Ancient Scientific Culture*, ed. J. König and G. Woolf. Cambridge: 27–57.

Trelenburg, J. (2009) *Augustins Schrift De ordine: Einführung, Kommentar, Ergebnisse*. Tübingen.

Troiano, M. S. (1987) 'L'omelia XXIII In Mamantem martyrem di Basilio di Cesarea', *Vetera christianorum* 24: 147–57.

Troncarelli, F. (1998) *Vivarium: I libri, il destino*. Turnhout.

Troncarelli, F. (2008–2009) 'Boezio a Costantinopoli: testi, contesti, edizioni', *Litterae caelestes* 3: 191–225.

Troncarelli, F. (2017) *L'antica fiamma: Boezio e la memoria del sapere antico nell'Alto Medioevo*. Rome.

Troncarelli, F. (2020) *La lettera rubata: Segni speciali e immagini simboliche nei codici di Cassiodoro*. Rome.

Tschiedel, H. J. (1986) '*Hic Abdera*. Gedanken zur Narrheit eines Gemeinwesens im Altertum – oder: Wie dumm waren die Abderiten?' in *Concentus hexachordus: Beiträge zum 10. Symposion der bayerischen Hochschullehrer für klassische Philologie in Eichstätt*, ed. P. Krafft and H. J. Tschiedel. Regensburg: 169–95.

Turner, C. H. (1910) *The History and Use of Creeds and Anathemas in the Early Centuries of the Church*, 2nd edn. London.

Twelftree, G. H. (2007) *In the Name of Jesus: Exorcism among Early Christians*. Grand Rapids.

Ullucci, D. C. (2012) *The Christian Rejection of Animal Sacrifice*. New York.

Ulrich, J. (2009) 'The Reception of Greek Christian Apologetics in Theodoretus' *Graecarum affectionum curatio*', in *Continuity and Discontinuity in Early Christian Apologetics*, ed. J. Ulrich, A.-C. Jacobsen, and M. Kahlos. Frankfurt.

Ulrich, J. (2012) 'What Do We Know about Justin's "School" in Rome?', *ZAC* 16: 62–73.

Underwood, N. (forthcoming) 'Lawyers and Inquisitors: Reassessing the Role of the *Defensor Ecclesiae* in Late Antiquity', *SLA*.

Underwood, P. A. (1950) 'The Fountain of Life in Manuscripts of the Gospels', *DOP* 5: 41–138.

Urbano, A. P. (2013) *The Philosophical Life: Biography and the Crafting of Intellectual Identity in Late Antiquity*. Washington.

Usener, H. (1877) *Anecdoton Holderi: Ein Beitrag zur Geschichte Roms in ostgothischer Zeit*. Bonn.

Vaggione, R. (1989) '"Arius: Heresy and Tradition" by Rowan Williams: A Review Article', *TJT* 5: 63–87.

Vaggione, R. (2000) *Eunomius of Cyzicus and the Nicene Revolution*. Oxford.

van den Broek, R. (1995) 'The Christian "School" of Alexandria in the Second and Third Centuries', in *Centres of Learning: Learning and Location in Pre-Modern Europe and the Near East*, ed. J. W. Drijvers and A. A. MacDonald. Leiden: 39–47.

van den Hoek, A. (1988) *Clement of Alexandria and His Use of Philo in the Stromateis: An Early Christian Reshaping of a Jewish Model*. Leiden.

van den Hoek, A. (1997) 'The "Catechetical" School of Early Christian Alexandria and Its Philonic Heritage', *HTR* 90: 59–87.

van der Horst, P. W. (1996) 'Maximus of Tyre on Prayer: An Annotated Translation of Εἰ δεῖ εὔχεσθαι (*Dissertatio* 5)', in *Geschichte – Tradition – Reflexion: Festschrift für Martin Hengel zum 70. Geburtstag*, ed. H. Cancik, H. Lichtenberger, and P. Schäfer. 3 vols. Tübingen: 2.323–38.

van der Horst, P. W. (2014) 'Biblical Quotations in Judeo-Greek Inscriptions', in *Studies in Ancient Judaism and Early Christianity*. Leiden: 66–79.

van der Kolk, B. A. (2014) *The Body Keeps the Score: Brain, Mind, and Body in the Healing of Trauma*. New York. Penguin Books.

van der Louw, A. W. (2007) *Transformations in the Septuagint: Towards an Interaction of Septuagint Studies and Translation Studies*. Leuven.

van Fleteren, F. (1973) 'Authority and Reason, Faith and Understanding in the Thought of St Augustine', *AugStud* 4: 33–71.

van Fleteren, F. (1977) 'Augustine and the Possibility of the Vision of God in this Life', *Studies in Medieval Culture* 11: 9–16.

van Lengerich, H.-G. (1994) Πίστις καὶ παιδεία καὶ μόρφωσις: *Ein ideengeschichtlicher Beitrag zur Einschmelzung antiker Philosopheme und christlicher Spekulationen zur Zeit der Hochpatristik. Untersucht am Beispiel der Schriften* De professione christiana, De perfectione *und* De virginitate *des Kappadokiers Gregor von Nyssa*. PhD diss., Universität Münster.

van Nieuwenhove, R. (2012) *An Introduction to Medieval Theology*. Cambridge.

van Nuffelen, P. (2011) 'The Rhetoric of Rules and the Rhetoric of Consensus', in *Episcopal Elections in Late Antiquity*, ed. J. Leemans, P. Van Nuffelen, S. W. J. Keough, and C. Nicolaye. Boston: 243–58.

van Nuffelen, P. (2013) '*The Life of Constantine*: The Image of an Image', in Johnson and Schott 2013: 133–49.

van Reyn, G. (2015) 'Hippo's Got Talent: Augustine's *Psalmus Contra Partem Donati* as a Pop(ular) Song', in *The Uniquely African Controversy: Interdisciplinary Studies on Donatist Christianity*, ed. A. Dupont, M. Gaumer, M. Lamberigts, N. de Maeyer, and B. van Egmond. Leuven: 251–68.

van Rompay, L. (2005) 'Society and Community in the Christian East', in *The Cambridge Companion to the Age of Justinian*, ed. M. Maas. Cambridge: 239–66.

van Rompay, L. (2007) '*Mallpānā Dilan Suryāyâ*: Ephrem in the Works of Philoxenus of Mabbog: Respect and Distance', *Hug* 7: 86–94.

van Unnik, W. C. (1976) 'Two Notes on Irenaeus', *VC* 30: 201–13.

Vanhaelen, M. (2013) 'Marsilio Ficino and the Irrational', in *Renaissance Studies in Honor of Joseph Connors*, ed. M. Israëls and L. A. Waldman. 2 vols. Cambridge: 2.438–44.

Vannier, M.-A. (2016) *Creatio–conversio–formatio chez saint Augustin*. Fribourg.

Verdoner, M. (2011) *Narrated Reality: The Historia ecclesiastica of Eusebius of Caesarea*. Berlin.

Vermes, G. (2013) *Christian Beginnings: From Nazareth to Nicaea*. New Haven.

Vessey, M. (2004) 'Introduction', in *Cassiodorus: Institutions of Divine and Secular Learning and On the Soul*, ed. J. W. Halporn and M. Vessey. TTH. Liverpool.

Vinzent, M. (1993) *Asterius von Kappadokien: Die theologischen Fragmente*. Leiden.

Vinzent, M. (1999) 'Die Entstehung des "Römischen Glaubensbekenntnisses"', in Kinzig, Markschies, and Vinzent 1999: 185–409.

Vinzent, M. (2016) 'Embodied Early and Medieval Christianity: Challenging its "Canonical" and "Institutional" Origins', *RRE* 2: 103–24.

Vinzent, M., and W. Kinzig (1999) 'Recent Research on the Origin of the Creed', *JTS* 50: 535–59.

Visonà, G. (2004) *Cronologia Ambrosiana / Bibliografia Ambrosiana (1900–2000)*. Milan.

Vivian, T. (1988) *Peter of Alexandria: Bishop and Martyr*. Philadelphia.

Vogel, C. (2019) 'Boethius – Lehrer ohne Schüler?', *Working Paper des SFB 980 'Episteme in Bewegung', Freie Universität Berlin* 16: 1–43.

Volgers, A., and C. Zamagni (eds.) (2004) *Erotapokriseis: Early Christian Question-and-Answer Literature in Context*. Leuven.

von Harnack, A. (1896) 'Apostolisches Symbolum', in *Realencyclopädie für protestantische Theologie und Kirche*, 3rd edn., ed. J. Herzog and A. Hauck. 24 vols. Leipzig: 1.741–55.

von Humboldt, W. (1903) *Wilhelm von Humboldts Gesammelte Schriften*, Vol. I: *Erste Abteilung: Werke I. Wilhelm von Humboldts Werke*, Vol. 1: *1785–1795*, ed. A. Leitzmann. Berlin.

von Staden, H. (1990) 'Incurability and Hopelessness: The Hippocratic Corpus', in *La maladie et les maladies dans la collection hippocratique*, ed. P. Potter, G. Maloney, and J. Desautels. Québec: 75–112.

Vööbus, A. (1958) *Literary Critical and Historical Studies in Ephrem the Syrian*. Stockholm.

Vopřada, D. (2016) *La mistagogia del commento al Salmo 118 di Sant-Ambrogio*. Rome.
Wainwright, W. J. (2012) 'Jonathan Edwards and his Puritan Predecessors', in Gavrilyuk and Coakley 2012a: 224–40.
Waithe, M. E. (ed.) (1987) *A History of Women Philosophers*, Vol. I: *600BC–500AD*. Dordrecht.
Walch, J. G. F. (ed.) (1770) *Bibliotecha symbolica vetus: Ex monimentis quinque priorum seculorum maxime collecta et observationibus historicis ac criticis illustrata*. Lemgovia.
Walker Bynum, C. (2017) *The Resurrection of the Body in Western Christianity, 200–1336*, 2nd edn. New York.
Wallis, F. (1988) *Bede: The Reckoning of Time*. TTH. Liverpool.
Wallis, F. (2006) 'Si naturam quaeras: Reframing Bede's "Science"', in DeGregorio 2006a: 61–94.
Wallis, F. (2010) 'Bede's "Science"', in *The Cambridge Companion to Bede*, ed. S. DeGregorio. Cambridge: 113–26.
Wallis, F. (2020) 'Isidore of Seville and Science', in *A Companion to Isidore of Seville*, ed. A. Fear and J. Wood. Leiden: 182–221.
Wallner, C. (2011) *Die Inschriften des Museums in Yozgat*. Vienna.
Wallraff, M. (2013) 'The Canon Tables of the Psalms: An Unknown Work of Eusebius of Caesarea', *DOP* 67: 1–14.
Walsh, P. G. (1988) 'The Rights and Wrongs of Curiosity (Plutarch to Augustine)', *GR* 35: 73–85.
Wang, K.-H. (2017) *Sense Perception and Testimony in the Gospel According to John*. Tübingen.
Ward, G. (2005) *Christ and Culture*. Oxford.
Watson, F. (2016) *The Fourfold Gospel: A Theological Reading of the New Testament Portraits of Jesus*. Grand Rapids.
Watson, F. (2021) '"The House of God": Text, Image and Sacred Space', in *Beyond Canon: Early Christianity and the Ethiopic Textual Tradition*, ed. M. T. Gebreananaye, L. Williams, and F. Watson. London: 145–61.
Watson, G. (1988) *Phantasia in Classical Thought*. Galway.
Watts, E. J. (2006) *City and School in Late Antique Athens and Alexandria*. Berkeley.
Watts, E. J. (2012) 'Education: Speaking, Thinking, and Socializing', in *The Oxford Handbook of Late Antiquity*, ed. S. F. Johnson. Oxford: 567–86.
Wear, S. K., and J. Dillon (2007) *Dionysius the Areopagite and the Neoplatonist Tradition: Despoiling the Hellenes*. Aldershot.
Webb, R. (1999) 'The Aesthetics of Sacred Space: Narrative, Metaphor, and Motion in Ekphraseis of Church Buildings', *DOP* 53: 59–74.
Webb, R. (2009) *Ekphrasis, Imagination and Persuasion in Ancient Rhetorical Theory and Practice*. Farnham. Repr. as Webb 2016b.
Webb, R. (2016a) 'Sight and Insight: Theorizing Vision, Emotion and Imagination in Ancient Rhetoric', in *Sight and the Ancient Senses*, ed. M. Squire. Milton Park: 205–19.

Webb, R. (2016b) *Ekphrasis, Imagination and Persuasion in Ancient Rhetorical Theory and Practice*. New York.

Webb, R. (2017) 'Virtual Sensations and Inner Visions: Words and the Senses in Late Antiquity and Byzantium', in *Knowing Bodies, Passionate Souls: Sense Perceptions in Byzantium*, ed. S. Ashbrook Harvey and M. Mullett. Washington: 261–69.

Weir, A. (2006) 'Two Great Legislators', *Tulane European and Civil Law Forum* 21: 35–51.

Weitzman, M. (1999) *The Syriac Version of the Old Testament: An Introduction*. Cambridge.

Weitzmann, K. (1935) *Die byzantinische Buchmalerei des 9. und 10. Jahrhunderts*. Berlin.

Weitzmann, K. (1959) *Ancient Book Illumination*. Cambridge.

Weitzmann, K. (1970) *Illustrations in Roll and Codex: A Study of the Origin and Method of Text Illustration*. Princeton.

Weitzmann, K. (1974) '"Loca Sancta" and the Representational Arts of Palestine', *DOP* 28: 31–55.

Wendt, H. (2016) *At the Temple Gates: The Religion of Freelance Experts in the Roman Empire*. Oxford.

Wessel, K. (1978) 'Kanontafeln', in *Reallexikon zur byzantinischen Kunst*. Stuttgart: 927–68.

Wessel, S. (2010) 'Memory and Individuality in Gregory of Nyssa's *Dialogus de anima et resurrectione*', *JECS* 18: 369–92.

Westerink, L. G. (1990) 'The Alexandrian Commentators and the Introductions to Their Commentaries', in *Aristotle Transformed: The Ancient Commentators and Their Influence*, ed. R. Sorabji. Ithaca: 325–48.

Westgard, J. A. (2010) 'Bede and the Continent in the Carolingian Age and Beyond', in DeGregorio 2010: 201–15.

Whitby, M. (1994) 'A New Image for a New Age: George of Pisidia on the Emperor Heraclius', in *The Roman and Byzantine Army in the East*, ed. E. Dabrowa. Krakow: 197–225.

Whitby, M. (1995) 'The Devil in Disguise: The End of George of Pisidia's *Hexaemeron* Reconsidered', *JHS* 115: 115–29.

Whitby, M. (1998) 'Defender of the Cross: George of Pisidia on the Emperor Heraclius and His Deputies', in *The Propaganda of Power: The Role of Panegyric in Late Antiquity*, ed. M. Whitby. Leiden: 247–73.

Whitby, M. (2007) 'The Biblical Past in John Malalas and the *Paschal Chronicle*', in *From Rome to Constantinople: Studies in Honour of Averil Cameron*, ed. H. Amirav and B. ter Haar Romeny. Leuven: 279–302.

Whitby, M. (2014) 'A Learned Spiritual Ladder? Toward an Interpretation of George of Pisidia's Hexameter Poem *On Human Life*', in *Nonnus of Panopolis in Context: Poetry and Cultural Milieu in Late Antiquity with a Section on Nonnus and the Modern World*, ed. K. Spanoudakis. Berlin: 435–58.

White, L. M. (1990) *The Social Origins of Christian Architecture*. 2 vols. Valley Forge: Trinity Press.

White, R. (1991) *The Middle Ground: Indians, Empires and Republics in the Great Lakes Region, 1650–1815.* New York.

Whitelock, D. (1976) 'Bede and His Teachers and Friends', in *Famulus Christi: Essays in Commemoration of the Thirteenth Centenary of the Birth of the Venerable Bede*, ed. G. Bonner. London: 19–39.

Wickes, J. (2019) *Bible and Poetry in Late Antique Mesopotamia: Ephrem's Hymns on Faith.* Berkeley.

Wiebe, G. (2014) 'Augustine and The Devil's Two Bodies', paper presented at the annual meeting of the North American Patristics Society, Chicago: www.academia.edu/7173678/Augustine_and_the_Devils_Two_Bodies (accessed 13 June 2018).

Wilberding, J., and C. Horn (eds.) (2012) *Neoplatonism and the Philosophy of Nature.* Oxford.

Wildberg, C. (1990) 'Three Neoplatonic Introductions to Philosophy: Ammonius, David, Elias', *Herm* 149: 33–51.

Wildberg, C. (2005) 'Philosophy in the Age of Justinian', in *The Cambridge Companion to the Age of Justinian*, ed. M. Maas. Cambridge: 316–42.

Wildberg, C. (2016) 'Elias', in *The Stanford Encyclopedia of Philosophy* (Fall 2016 Edition), ed. E. N. Zalta. https://plato.stanford.edu/archives/fall2016/entries/elias/.

Wildberg, C. (2018) 'David', in *The Stanford Encyclopedia of Philosophy* (Summer 2018 Edition), ed. E. N. Zalta. https://plato.stanford.edu/archives/sum2018/entries/david/.

Wiles, M. (1996) *Archetypal Heresy: Arianism Through the Centuries.* Oxford.

Wiles, M. (1999) 'The Journal of Theological Studies: Centenary Reflections', *JTS* 50: 491–514.

Wilhite, D. E. (2010) 'Cyprian's Scriptural Hermeneutic of Identity: The Laxist "Heresy"', *HBT* 32: 58–98.

Wilken, R. L. (1967) 'The Homeric *Cento* in Irenaeus, "Adversus Haereses" I, 9,4', *VC* 21: 25–33.

Wilken, R. L. (1992) *The Land Called Holy: Palestine in Christian History and Thought.* New Haven.

Williams, M. (2013) 'Hymns as Acclamations: The Case of Ambrose of Milan', *JLA* 6: 108–34.

Williams, R. D. (1982) *Eucharistic Sacrifice: The Roots of a Metaphor.* Nottingham.

Williams, R. D. (1987) *Arius: Heresy and Tradition.* London. Rev. edn. 2001.

Williams, R. D. (1993) 'Macrina's Deathbed Revisited: Gregory of Nyssa on Mind and Passion', in *Christian Faith and Greek Philosophy in Late Antiquity: Essays in Tribute to George Christopher Stead, Ely Professor of Divinity, University of Cambridge (1971–1980), in Celebration of His Eightieth Birthday, 9th April 1993*, ed. L. Wickham and C. Hammond Bammel. Leiden: 227–46.

Williams, R. D. (2014) *The Edge of Words: God and the Habits of Language.* London.

Wilson, N. G. (1975) *St Basil on the Value of Greek Literature.* London.

Winter, F. (1999) *Bardesanes von Edessa über Indien: Ein früher syrischer Theologe schreibt über ein fremdes Land.* Thaur.

Wissowa, G., and W. Kroll (eds.) (1894–1980) *Paulys Real-Encyclopädie der classischen Altertumswissenschaft*. Stuttgart.

Witakowski, W. (1984) 'Chronicles of Edessa', *Orientalia Suecana* 33–35: 487–98.

Wood, I. (1995) 'Northumbrians and Franks in the Age of Wilfrid', *Northern History* 31: 10–21.

Wood, I. (2008) 'Monasteries and the Geography of Power in the Age of Bede', *Northern History* 45: 11–25.

Wood, I. (2009) 'The Gifts of Wearmouth and Jarrow', in *The Languages of Gift in the Early Middle Ages*, ed. W. Davies and P. J. Fouracre. Cambridge: 89–115.

Wood, I. (2010) 'The Foundation of Bede's Wearmouth-Jarrow', in DeGregorio 2010: 84–96.

Wood, I. (2013) 'Entrusting Western Europe to the Church, 400–750', *Transactions of the Royal Historical Society* 23: 37–73.

Wormald, P. (2004) 'Bede and the Conversion of England: The Charter Evidence'. Jarrow Lecture 1984. Jarrow. Repr. in *The Times of Bede: Studies in Early English Christian Society and Its Historian*, ed. S. Baxter. Malden: 135–66.

Wright, C. D. (1987) 'Apocryphal Lore and Insular Tradition in St Gall, Stiftsbibliothek MS 908', in *Ireland and Christendom: The Bible and the Missions*, ed. P. Ní Chatháin and M. Richter. Stuttgart: 124–45.

Wright, C. D. (2000) 'Bischoff's Theory of Irish Exegesis and the Genesis Commentary in Munich clm 6302: A Critique of a Critique', *JML* 10: 145–73.

Wright, S., O. A. Jäger, and J. Leroy (1961) *Ethiopia: Illuminated Manuscripts*. New York.

Wright, W. (1870–72) *Catalogue of Syriac Manuscripts in the British Museum Acquired Since the Year 1838*. 3 vols. London.

Wulf, C. (2003) 'Perfecting the Individual: Wilhelm von Humboldt's Concept of Anthropology, Bildung and Mimesis', *Educational Philosophy and Theory* 35: 241–49.

Wyrwa, D. (1983) *Die christliche Platonaneignung in den Stromateis des Clemens von Alexandrien*. Arbeiten zur Kirchengeschichte 53. Berlin.

Wyrwa, D. (2005) 'Religiöses Lernen im zweiten Jahrhundert und die Anfänge der alexandrinischen Katechetenschule', in *Religiöses Lernen in der biblischen, frühjüdischen und frühchristlichen Überlieferung*, ed. B. Ego and H. Merkel. WUNT 180. Tübingen: 271–306.

Yarshater, E. (ed.) (1982–) *Encyclopaedia Iranica*. London.

Yasin, A. M. (2009) *Saints and Church Spaces in the Late Antique Mediterranean: Architecture, Cult and Community*. Cambridge.

Yates, F. A. (1966) *The Art of Memory*. London.

Young, F. M. (1979) *The Use of Sacrificial Ideas in Greek Christian Writers from the New Testament to John Chrysostom*. Cambridge.

Young, F. M. (1990) *The Art of Performance: Towards a Theology of Holy Scripture*. London.

Young, F. M. (2011) 'God's Image: "The Elephant in the Room" in the Fourth Century', *StPatr* 50: 57–71.

Young, R. D. (2011) 'The Influence of Evagrius of Pontus', in *'To Train His Soul in Books': Essays on Syrian Asceticism in Honor of Sidney H. Griffith*, ed. R. D. Young and M. Blanchard. Washington: 157–75.

Zachhuber, J. (2020a) *The Rise of Christian Theology and the End of Ancient Metaphysics: Patristic Philosophy from the Cappadocian Fathers to John of Damascus*. Oxford.

Zachhuber, J. (2020b) 'Philosophy and Theology in Late Antiquity: Some Reflections on Concepts and Terminologies', in *Eastern Christianity and Late Antique Philosophy*, ed. E. Anagnostou-Laoutides and K. Parry. Texts and Studies in Eastern Christianity 18. Leiden: 52–77.

Zaqzuq, A.-R. and M. Piccirillo (1999) 'The Mosaic Floor of the Church of the Holy Martyrs at Tayibat al-Imam – Hamas, in Central Syria', *Liber Annuus* 49: 443–64.

Zecher, J. L. (2018) 'The Reception of Evagrian Psychology in the Ladder of Divine Ascent: John Cassian and Gregory Nazianzen as Sources and Conversation Partners', *JTS* 69: 674–713.

Zerfass, Z. (2008) *Mysterium mirabile: Poesie, Theologie und Liturgie in den Hymnen des Ambrosius von Mailand zu den Christusfesten des Kirchenjahres*. Tübingen.

Index Locorum

Manuscripts

Adishi Gospels, 489, 496, 498

Codex Amiatinus, 733
Codex Bobiensis, 372
Codex Vercellensis, 372

Garima Gospels, 489, 497
Geʻez gospel-books, 489
Godescalc Gospel Lectionary, 491

Heidelberg, Biblioteca Palatina, gr. 5, 491
Hiera Monē tou Megalou Spēlaiou gospel-book, 486

Iviron Monastery, ms. 27, 486

London, British Library
   Add. Ms. 14,592, 261
   Add. Ms. 14,658, 122

Munich, clm 6302, 705, 721, 722, 727

papyri
   BKT 9.150, 193
   O.Max. 356, 193
   P.Laur. 4.147, 193
   P.Lund. 1.5, 193
   P.Mich. 2458, 193
   P.Oxy.
      33.2660, 193
      33.2660a, 193
      46.3315, 193
      49.3452, 193

Paris, Bibliothèque nationale de France
   gr. 1592, 546
   lat. 10457, 727

Rabbula Gospels, 489–91
Rossano Gospels, 490

Saint-Médard de Soissons Gospels, 490, 491
St Gallen, Stiftsbibliothek, MS 908, 723, 726
Stauronikita ms. 13, 486
Stutt. HB VII 64, 372

Turin, Bibl. Naz. e Univ. F.IV.1, 676

Vatican Library
   Codex Vaticanus, 322, 323, 325
   gr. 354, 488
   Vatican Vergil (lat. 3225), 512
Verona, Biblioteca capitolare
   XL, 677
   XXVII, 727

Biblical Passages

Genesis
   1, 648, 650
   1:1, 650
   1:14, 108
   1:26, 467
   2:5, 720
   2:8–9, 109
   2:21–22, 110
   3:6, 23, 518
   3:19, 316, 323
   3:21, 111
   3:24, 300
   5:29, 720
   8:21, 582
   9:7, 727
   9:14, 721
   9:20, 721
   15:11, 203
   21:31, 313
   28:10, 202
   28:12, 313, 346
   30:37, 477
   39:8, 289
   49, 179

Exodus
- 2:11, 335
- 2:16–22, 342
- 3:21–22, 337
- 4:19–27, 342
- 4:21, 109
- 14, 317
- 14:21–31, 315
- 14:27–28, 322
- 14:30, 315
- 14–15, 326
- 15:4, 322
- 15:8, 323
- 15:21, 322
- 20:7, 268
- 33, 650
- 33:13, 203
- 33:18–33, 659
- 34:30–35, 659

Numbers
- 7:20, 176
- 11:3, 71
- 11:14, 109
- 19:13, 158
- 19:26, 696
- 22:28, 657

Joshua
- 4:22–23, 315
- 5:1, 315
- 5:2, 316
- 5:9, 315, 316, 326
- 6:9, 326
- 6:13, 74
- 9:2d–e, 315
- 19:15, 391

Judges 14:5–9, 289
Job 16:19, 700
Psalms
- 1:1–2, 71, 72
- 1:2, 163, 733
- 3:9, 309
- 16:15, 741
- 17:6, 560
- 21:7, 325
- 21:21, 542
- 22 [23]:5, 180
- 26:1, 308
- 27:9, 468
- 28:3, 325
- 31:1, 308
- 32:3, 322
- 33:9, 24
- 33:9, 6, 308
- 41:2, 468
- 42:4, 306
- 51:10, 322
- 53:6, 306
- 61 [62], 382
- 69:6, 306
- 74:10, 101
- 75:21, 91
- 77 [78], 109
- 78:9, 306
- 84:9, 24
- 91:13, 322
- 93:18, 306
- 96:11, 308
- 103:24, 291
- 108:26, 306
- 109:1, 290, 291
- 117:20, 306, 325
- 117:24, 323, 324
- 118:86, 117, 306
- 128:8, 309
- 136 [137], 542
- 140:2, 322

Proverbs
- 2:3–7, 31
- 2:5, 22, 23, 30, 31, 37, 43
- 3:5–12, 94
- 3:23, 31
- 9, 179
- 10:6, 11, 309
- 25:20, 542
- 30:15, 521

Ecclesiastes 1:2, 656
Song of Songs
- 1:3, 699
- 1:8, 107

Isaiah
- 1:10, 44
- 1:16–18, 307
- 1:18, 325
- 6, 295
- 6:1–10, 295
- 6:3, 318, 325
- 7:9, 82
- 10b–c, 308
- 11:6, 8–9, 319
- 11:6, 319, 326
- 11:6b, 319
- 11:6–9, 319
- 25:6–7a, 308
- 28:16, 324

35:1–7, 503
35:6, 7, 504
53:7, 325
58:7, 157
61:1a, 308
63:2, 179
Jeremiah
  2:4, 44
  2:22, 44
Ezekiel
  6:3, 44
  16:35, 44
  21:3, 44
Amos 7:16, 44
Habakkuk 2:4–5, 521
Malachi 3:20, 325
3 Maccabees 6:8, 320
4 Maccabees
  6:27–28, 183
  17:22, 183
Judith 16:17, 541, 542
Sirach 34:7, 696
Wisdom
  7:17–20, 94
  7:21, 94
  9:1–18, 74
  9:6, 74
  13:1, 382
  13:1–9, 205
Mark
  1:10, 32
  4:39, 370
  11:1–11, 312, 326
  11:9, 310
  11:9–10, 323
Matthew
  3:16, 32
  3:17, 468
  4:8, 109
  4:10, 74
  5:4, 543
  5:6, 741
  5:8, 468
  5:33, 268
  6:22, 475
  6:22–23, 466
  6:24, 74
  7:13–14, 370
  8:20, 742
  10:10, 742
  10:16, 310
  10:25, 157
  10:26, 164
  11:27, 2
  12:38–40, 326
  12:39, 41, 326
  12:39–40, 320
  13:8, 377
  13:31, 325
  17:5, 468
  18:16, 391
  18:19–20, 157
  19:21, 749
  19:21–29, 749
  21:9, 42, 323
  23:39, 323
  25:14–30, 377
  25:31–46, 160
  25:41, 370
  28:19–20, 303
Luke
  1:1–2, 468
  2:8–20, 391
  2:32, 369
  3:22, 32
  6:21, 741
  9:3, 742
  9:10–17, 747
  11:34, 475
  13:35, 323
  14:33, 743
  16:19–31, 287, 747
  18:22, 749
  19:8, 70
  19:38, 323
  20:17, 323
  23:43, 300
John
  1:1–3, 467
  1:2, 373
  1:5, 32
  1:9, 324
  1:11, 382
  1:14, 418
  1:18, 41
  1:32, 32, 41
  1:51, 313, 317
  2, 41
  2:1–12, 379
  3:13, 313
  4:14, 563
  5:19, 505
  5:19–20, 41
  6:1–14, 746, 749

John (cont.)
   6:33, 22
   9:39–41, 41
   10:7, 324
   10:11, 324
   10:32, 383
   11–12, 42
   12:13, 323
   12:21, 562
   12:49–50, 41
   14:6, 324
   14:8–9, 253
   14:8–11, 41
   14:9, 468
   14:19–21, 41
   15:12–13, 157
   16:21, 542
   19:25, 383
   20, 42
   20:22, 41
   20:29, 42
Acts
   2:2, 295
   2:13–15, 294
   2:38, 316
   4:32, 157
   5:4, 295
   5:27, 382
   7:22, 334
   7:55, 470
   9:3, 468
   10:10–16, 652
   17:27, 24
   28, 295
Romans
   1, 474
   1:18–19, 467
   1:20, 470
   1:20–25, 205
   1:28, 38
   2:29, 315–17
   3:2, 72
   3:8, 155
   3:20, 38
   3:30, 315
   4:1, 23–24, 326
   5:14, 326
   6:5, 316
   6:17, 326
   8:5, 72, 86
   8:19–23, 656
   8:31, 323
   10:2, 38

   10:17, 466
   12:5, 587
   12:16, 74
   14:1, 373
   15:8, 315
1 Corinthians
   2:8, 382
   2:9, 31
   3:1–3, 344
   3:15, 370
   3:18–23, 388
   3:19, 206
   6:9–11, 158
   6:18, 158
   6:19, 255
   9:1, 468
   9:14, 742
   9:24, 573
   10:1–2, 322
   10:1–5, 315
   10:6, 315, 326
   10:15–21, 169
   11:23, 179
   12:11, 295
   13:12, 38, 468, 479
   15:1–2, 303
   15:2, 326
   15:3–4, 320
   15:8, 468
   15:40, 430
   15:48, 323
   15:52, 430
   16:22, 239, 309
2 Corinthians
   1:3, 307
   1:13, 38
   2:15, 22
   2:18, 24
   3:18, 24, 468, 479
   5:17, 322
   6:9, 323
   7:9–10, 543
   12:2–4, 649
Galatians
   1:6–9, 181
   1:8, 239
   5:17, 19–24, 158
   5:18, 158
   6:14, 743
Ephesians
   1:3, 307
   1:17, 38
   1:18, 24

2:20, 324
4:13, 38, 74
4:17–20, 381
4:28, 745
6:14, 60
Philippians
  1:4–10, 38
  1:6–8, 38
  1:8, 38, 39
  1:8–9, 45
  1:9, 37
  1:10–11, 38
  1:12–18, 39, 41
  1:13, 39
  1:17, 39
  1:20, 39
  1:30, 40
  2:6, 382
  2:6–11, 40
  2:17, 39
  3:10–11, 20, 40
  3:13, 333
  4:9, 40
  4:12, 40
Colossians
  1:15, 467
  2:8a, 153
  2:11, 316, 317
  2:11–12, 315
  3:9, 316
  4:2, 163
1 Thessalonians
  4:17, 323
  5:8, 60
1 Timothy
  3:16, 213
  4:13, 305
  5:8, 157
  6:16, 467
2 Timothy
  3:16, 290, 321
  4:17, 542
Titus 3:5, 316
Hebrews
  1:3, 467
  5:14, 23, 37, 40
  8:5, 326
  13:6, 323
James
  1:11, 743, 744
  1:15, 743
  1:27–2:1, 744
  2:5, 742
  2:18–21, 744
  4:1, 737
  4:3, 738
  5:3–5, 744
1 Peter
  1:3, 307
  1:6, 735
  1:7, 736
  1:12, 740
  1:23, 316
  2:1–3, 739
  2:4, 7, 324
  2:11, 737
  2:20, 735
  3:13, 735
  3:18–19, 381
  4:3, 735, 736
  4:8, 744
  5:6, 737
  5:8, 542
  5:9, 735
2 Peter 2:22, 523
1 John
  1:1, 22
  1:1–3, 468
  2:15–16, 738
  2:16, 737, 738
  2:29, 740, 741
  3:2, 468
  3:6, 739
  3:17–18, 744
  4:12, 737
  5:17, 737
3 John 8, 744
Revelation
  1:3, 44
  1:8, 381
  1:10–12, 44
  2–3, 43–44, 45
  2:7, 11, 17, 29, 43
  3:6, 13, 22, 43
  4:8, 318
  5:6, 317
  5:8, 326
  19:7–8, 736
  22:13, 318

Other Ancient Sources

Acts of the Scillitan Martyrs 9–10, 164
Aelius Donatus, *Ars Maior* 1.1, 404
Aelius Theon, *Prog.* 7, 501

Aëtius, *Placita*
- 1. proem.1.1–3, 200
- 1.proem.1.2, 200
- 1. proem. 3.13–14, 200
- 1.1.1.2–3, 200
- 1.2.1.11, 201
- 1.3, 200, 206, 209, 211, 214, 215, 218
- 1.3.1.4–5, 200
- 1.3.2.19, 201
- 1.3.3.27, 201
- 1.4–5, 204
- 1.6, 205, 215
- 1.7, 201, 204, 209, 214, 215
- 1.7.1.27, 206
- 1.7.1.35, 201
- 1.7.2.59, 205
- 1.8.2.4–6, 205
- 1.9, 204
- 1.10, 204
- 1.25–28, 212
- 2.1, 204
- 2.1.3, 206
- 2.1–4, 215
- 2.3, 210, 215
- 2.4 tit., 202
- 2.6.5, 206
- 2.21, 218
- 2.25.13, 200
- 2.28.1, 200
- 2.29.2, 200
- 4.2, 213
- 4.2–7, 206
- 4.3, 213
- 4.6, 211
- 4.12, 213

Alcinous
- *Didaskalikos*
  - 1, 106
  - 1.2–3, 112

Alcuin, *Opp. didasc.* (PL 101.952b), 665

Alexander of Tralles, *Therapeutica* 7.1, 541

Ambrose of Milan
- *De fide* 3.15.125, 230
- *Ennarat. Ps.* 36.28, 389
- *Epistulae*
  - 7.36.5–7, 391
  - 10.77, 390
  - 75a.34, 392
- *Expositio evangelii secundum Lucam*
  - 2.43, 394
  - 2.45, 395
  - 2.49, 394
  - 2.51, 391
  - 2.83, 393
  - 6.84, 398
  - 6.85, 396
  - 6.87, 396
- *Fid. Grat.*
  - 1.5.42, 388, 391
  - 1.8, 391
  - 1.13, 391
- *Hexaemeron*
  - 4.4.14, 431
  - 4.5.20, 428
- Hymn 1, 401
- Hymn 2, 401
- *Incarn.* 9.89, 391
- *Myst.*
  - 7.34, 308
  - 9.53, 392
- *Praescr.* 7.6, 391

Ammianus Marcellinus
- *Res Gestae* 20.10.7, 374

Ammonius of Alexandria
- *In Aristotelis Categorias commentarius*
  - 4.28–5.8, 672
- *In Aristotelis de interpretatione commentariis*
  - 11.1–12.15, 670
  - 22.27–23.2, 669
- *In Porphyrii Isagogen*
  - 1.18–16.16, 681
  - 6.28–7.5, 687
  - 9.7–23, 681
  - 15.1–16.16, 679
  - 15.11–16.4, 679
- *Prolegomena* 4,8–14, 577

Amphilochius of Iconium
- *De recens baptizatis*
  - 45–46, 322
  - 56–57, 322
  - 57–59, 322
  - 60–63, 323
  - 63–68, 323
  - 68–71, 323
  - 78–81, 324
  - 82–84, 324
  - 91–93, 324
  - 95–97, 324
  - 160, 127, 130, 142, 150–51, 324
- *In occursum Domini* 257–58, 324

Aphthonius, *Progym.*
- 12, 501
- 13, 77

Apophthegmata patrum S 10.102, 546

Index Locorum

Apostolic Constitutions
    5.7.12, 320
    8.13, 310
Apostolic Tradition 17.1, 160
Apuleius
    De deo Socratis
        3.8, 440
        4.7, 440
        6.2–3, 438
        6.3, 426
        11.2–4, 438
        12, 439
        13.3, 438
    De dogmate Platonis 1.3, 665
Aretaeus, *Cur. acut.* 2.5, 47
Aristophanes, *Nubes* 3.20, 215
Aristotle
    Analytica posteriora
        2.1, 572
        2.19 (100a), 81
    Categories. See also Porphyry
        4b20–37, 673
        7b27–33, 668
    De anima
        1.1.403a30, 538
        2.7, 476
        420b29–32, 669
        420b32–35, 410
    De generatione et corruptione 2.10, 75
    De sensu
        1, 541
        2, 476
    Ethica Eudemia 1214a9–15, 665
    Ethica Nicomachea 1139a26–31, 665
    Metaphysica
        1.1–2 (980a), 81
        993b19–21, 665
        1025b18–26a28, 665
    Poetica 25, 109
    Politica
        7.17, 74
        1337b15, 666
    Prophesying by Dreams 462b12–14, 137
    Rhetorica
        1354a1, 671
        1356a30–31, 671
    Sophistici elenchi 184a10–b4, 671
    Topica
        105b19–25, 665
        132b2, 447
        145a15–1, 665
Arius Didymus
    Epitome of Peripatetic Ethics 128.21–22, 70
    Epitome of Stoic Ethics 5b24, 70
Arnobius, *Contra* 1.42, 260
Athanasius of Alexandria
    Contra arianos
        1.1, 388
        1.5, 254, 258
        1.22, 257
        1.35, 257
        2.18, 257
        3.5, 259
    Contra gentes
        2.34, 471
        19–21, 259
        30, 259
        38, 43, 47, 649
        46, 259
    De decretis
        15, 254
        20.3, 257
        33.5, 231
    De incarnatione
        14.1–2, 470
        14.4–6, 470
        14.8, 470
        16.3–5, 470
    De sabbatis et circumcisione 39–53, 316
    De synodis
        1, 238, 229
        5, 229
        6, 229
        7, 238
        8, 233
        14, 238
        21, 233
        23, 239
        25, 237, 238
        26.2, 237
        27, 237
    Epistula ad episcopos Aegypti et Libyae
        1, 388
    Epistula ad Marcellinum 9, 307
    Vita Antonii
        21, 28, 65, 439
        72–80, 340
Athenaeus, *Deipnosophistae* 8.341E, 58
Athenagoras
    Legatio pro Christianis
        4.2, 205
        4.2–5.1, 204
        7.2, 204, 205
        16.1, 205
        23.3, 205
        23.4, 205

Augustine of Hippo
  Confessiones
    1.8.13, 407
    4.3, 433
    4.3.4, 426
    4.3.4–6, 428
    5.3, 709
    6.8.13, 477
    7, 456
    7.6.8, 433
    7.6.8–10, 433
    7.6.9–10, 435
    7.6.10, 433
    7.9.13, 439
    7.9.15, 439
    7.17.23, 479
    7.17.24, 479
    8.6.14–15, 439
    9.7, 392
    10, 423
    10.8.13, 474, 479
    10.11.18, 474
    10.17–11.18, 474
    10.18.27, 683
    10.35.51, 477
    10.35.54, 478
    11.5.7, 475
    12, 419
    12.29.40, 413
  Cons.
    2.30.71–75, 742
  Contra academicos
    1.1.1, 445
    1.2.5, 447
    1.3.7, 445
    1.3.9, 445, 447
    1.4.1, 447
    1.4.12, 447
    1.7.20, 446
    1.8.23, 447
    1.9.24, 445, 447
    2.6.14, 445
    2.10.24, 445
    2.13.29, 445
    3.4.7, 663
    3.7.14, 445
    3.18.41, 445
    3.19.42, 445, 456, 460, 464
    3.20.43, 445, 464
  Contra Julianum
    4.65, 423
    4.66, 423
    4.69, 423
    4.73, 423
    5.14.51, 477
    5.23, 424
  De beata vita
    1.1.1, 448
    1.4, 445
    35, 452, 453
  De civitate Dei (City of God)
    5.2, 434, 435
    5.2.4, 434
    5.2–4, 435
    5.5, 435
    8.4, 665
    8.12, 439
    8.14, 438
    8.16, 439
    10, 456
    22.8, 421, 422
    22.29, 480
  De divinatione daemonum
    1.1–2.6, 437
    2.6, 437
    3.7, 427, 436, 439
    5.9, 440
  De doctrina christiana
    1.1, 710
    2.1.2–2.3.4, 408
    2.7, 710
    2.9, 710
    2.12–1, 710
    2.18, 27–42, 710
    2.20.31, 441
    2.22.33, 435
    2.22.34, 441
    2.23.33, 434
    2.23.34, 434
    2.23.36, 426, 435, 436
    2.40.60, 343
    2.40.60–42.63, 337
    4.4, 710
    4.9, 716
  De Genesi ad litteram
    1.4.9, 417
    1.5.10, 417, 418
    1.38–41, 714
    7.13–15, 709
    8.8, 734
    12.6.15–16, 478
    12.11.22, 478
    12.13.38, 427
    25.26–34, 434

De musica 6.1.1, 458
De ordine
    1.1.2, 445
    1.2.4, 447
    1.8.24, 452, 453
    1.8.25, 446
    1.11.31, 347
    1.24, 448
    2.5.13–14, 666
    2.5.14, 457
    2.5.15, 450
    2.5.16, 444, 449, 456, 462
    2.7.24, 446, 458
    2.8.25, 455
    2.9.26, 444–46, 449, 453, 458, 462
    2.9.27, 445, 456, 459, 460
    2.11.30, 446, 447
    2.11.31, 446, 447
    2.15.16, 456, 459–61
    2.15.43, 458
    2.16.44, 458
    2.19.49, 446
    2.19.51, 452, 455
    5.16, 448
    7.22, 446
    12.35–16.44, 666
De trinitate
    8.4, 475
    11.1, 475, 478
    11.2–6, 477
    11.15, 477
    13, 418
    13.1–4, 418
    13.5, 418
    13.12, 418
    13.26, 419
    15.22, 419
    15.24, 420
    15.25, 420
De vera religione 7.12, 465
Div. quaest. Simpl.
    1 Q.2.14, 480
Enarrationes in Psalmos
    4, 408
    99.3, 408
    99.4, 410
Epistulae
    9.2, 436, 437
    9.3, 436, 437, 440
    55.20, 426
    101.4, 422
    102.18, 427
    147, 480, 481, 737
    Adv. Ar. I.50, 463
Leg.
    1.8.11–9.12, 413
Mag.
    11.38, 430
Mor. 1.17.30, 459
On the One Baptism, 14.23–24, 383
Praed.
    2.5, 454
Psalmus contra partem Donati
    v. 1, 402
    vv. 8–9, 402
    vv. 47–48, 402
Quaestiones evangeliorum
    2. Q. 47.19, 743
    38, 747
Retractationes
    1.2.1, 452
    1.3.2, 449
    1.3.2–3, 452
    1.18, 714
    1.20, 401
    2.30, 438
Sermones
    51.1–2, 478
    57.1–2, 163
    57.8, 163
    112A.3, 436
    277.10, 476
    288.2, 408, 409
    288.3, 409
    289.3, 410
    293A (Dolbeau 3), 411, 416
    293A.4, 409
    293A.5, 411
    293A.7, 409, 411
    293A.8, 411
    293A.10, 412
    316.5, 483
    341.5, 408
Solil.
    1.6.12, 453
Tract. ev. Jo.
    1, 419
    4.3, 740, 741
    7.12.2, 426
    24.1, 480
    24.2, 481
Aulus Gellius, *Noctes atticae* 13.17.1, 666
Ausonius of Bordeaux
    Cupido cruciatus (*Cupid Crucified*)

Ausonius of Bordeaux (cont.)
    47, 51–54, 382
    59–64, 382
    79–98, 384
    80–85, 383

Bardaisan, *Book of the Laws of the Countries*
    r. 218–22, 122
Basil of Caesarea
    Ad adolescentes de legendes libris gentilium
        7.6–13, 341
    De baptismo 2.1, 394
    Epistles
        38.8, 473
        113, 241
        125, 233, 241
    Exhortatio ad baptismum 2, 301
    Hexaemeron
        6.1, 649
        6.5, 430
        6.5–7, 430
        8.2, 300
    Homily on Gordius 1, 289
    Homily on Mamas 1, 298
    Homily on Psalm 114 1, 297
    Regula brevis tractatae 13, 308
Bede
    De natura rerum
        8, 717
        18, 717
    De temporum ratione
        1.1, 737
        28, 725
        30, 738
        32, 725
        38–39, 732
    Epist. Pleg.
        1.1; 1.6, 732
    Epist. VVichth. 1. A, 732
    Epistle to Egbert
        7, 746
    Expos. Act. Apost.
        3.23–32, 742
        11.34.40, 742
        17.37–49, 738
        20.95–101, 745
    Expositio Apocalypseos
        1.8.6.17, 742
        2.24.14.10, 742
    Historia ecclesiastica gens Anglorum
        1, 749
        2, 4, 11, 732

3.5, 739
3.24, 730
4, 731
4, 6, 9, and 15, 731
5.24, 733
7, 733
8, 739
11, 13, 14, 736
15, 731, 732
16, 739
18, 732
Homilies
    1.3.56–71, 741
    1.4.12, 741
    1.6.127–42, 742
    1.6.263–68, 742
    1.12.79–113, 1.12.219–21, 736
    1.12.234, 736
    1.13, 742
    1.13.7–13, 736
    1.13.23–26, 745
    1.13.41–47, 744
    1.13.185–90, 731
    1.13.199, 741
    1.14, 749
    1.16, 736
    1.18.48, 742
    1.24.134–3, 751
    1.49–54, 736
    2.2, 746, 749, 751
    2.2.118–22, 746
    2.2.177–82, 746
    2.2.193–98, 746
In cantica canticorum allegorica expositio
    pr., lines. 508–10, 712
    1.1.164–80, 739
    1.1.207–14, 734
    1.1.596–609, 2.4.170–191, 736
    1.1.713–44, 736
    1.1.732–44, 735
    1.2.173–92, 739
    2.4.170–93, 739
    3.4.486, 749
    3.4.718, 749
    3.4.901–13, 737
    4.6.103–10, 738, 744
    4.7.130–39, 735
    4.7.143–80, 746
    5.7.473, 749
    5.8.496–512, 745
In epistulas catholicas septem
    1.1.88–110, 744

1.1.106, 742
1.1.114–45, 744
1.1.137, 742, 743
1.1.343–1.2, 744
1.2.31–40, 742
1.2.144–233, 744
1.4.9, 737
1.4.20–26, 738
1.5.5–50, 744
1.5.12, 742
2.1.101–5, 735
2.1.112–21, 736
2.1.177–81, 740
2.1.182, 740
2.1.190, 740
2.2.1–28, 739
2.2.228–30, 737
2.2.325–27, 735
2.3.70, 735
2.3.168–84, 738
2.4.24–41, 735, 736
2.4.78–103, 744
2.5.70, 737
2.5.100–106, 735
4.2.149–60, 738
4.2.162–90, 737
4.2.390–97, 740
4.2.401–3, 741
4.3.126–30, 739
4.3.258–74, 744
4.4.164–203, 737
4.5.277–79, 737
6.40–54, 744

In Ezr.
1.711, 1.1140, 749
255–70, 744

In Genesim
pr. 1–23, 748
pr. 24, 748
pr. 24–28, 748
1.1.166, 1.1.874–86, 738
1.2.1501, 738
1.2.1592–1605, 734
1.2.1607, 734
1.3.2135, 734
1.3.2175–2201, 734
1.3.2204, 734
1.3.2298–2304, 735
2.4.161–63, 735
2.4.515, 742
2.4.540–44, 741
2.4.586, 738

2.6.1157, 749
4.18.673–750, 739

In Lucam
pr. 60–61, 733
pr. 95, 732
pr. 96–105, 747
2.1494–96, 742
2.1501–4, 741
2.1530, 736
3.286–95, 742
3.352, 744
3.401–4, 744
3.439–4, 737
3.1142–52, 742
3.1830–32, 742
4.2123–25, 740
4.2125–29, 744
4.2127–29, 738
5.241–461, 747
5.1218–1373, 747, 749
5.1270–75, 743
5.1287–90, 743
5.1312–13, 743
5.1319–20, 743
5.1344, 736
5.1358–72, 738
5.18.1252, 749
5.19.1586, 749
5.19.1725–35, 739
5.25, 742
5.325–34, 739

In regum librum xxx questiones
pr., 716

Libri quattuor in principium Genesis
pr., lines 18–24, 713
pr., lines 24–32, 714
1.1, lines 907–909, 719
1.2, lines 1749–65, 719
2.12b, 712

Marcum
1.667–72, 736
2.8.1657, 749
3.10.737, 749
3.10.740, 749

Prov.
1.1.373–79, 742
1.3.179, 749
1.3.185–99, 736, 739
1.3.248, 742
2.13.21, 742
2.20.113, 742
3.31.298, 749

Bede (cont.)
   Sam.
      1.7.2021, 739
      2.2254–67, 746
   tab.
      1.243–262, 735
      1.277–302, 736
      1.277–317, 741
      1.746, 736
      1.752, 749
      2.135–42, 736, 737
      2.438–42, 735
      2.632–45, 741
      2.666–83, 737
      2.1102, 741
   tem.
      1.102–9, 745
      1.647–57, 741
      1.1498, 741
      1.1685–1721, 744
      1.1701–20, 737
      2.131–52, 744
      2.1240–50, 736
      2.1269–75, 736
      2.1340, 749
   Vita Cuthberti
      5, 6, 26, 739
      35, 739
      37, 736
Boethius
   De consolatione philosophiae
      1.1.1, 681
      1.1.1–2, 682
      1.1.4, 677
      1.1.5, 677
      1.1.7, 681
      1.1.9, 678
      1.4, 671
      1.4.5, 680
      1.4.5, 5.3–4, 678
      1.5.2, 671
      1.m7.25–28, 678
      2.7.4, 677
      2.m8.5–15, 678
      2.m8.15, 29, 678
      2.m8.22–27, 684
      3.7, 677
      3.9.4, 16, 677
      3.m9.10–17, m12.20–39, 675
      3.10.22–26, 682
      3.12.1, 683
      4.4.28–29, 682
      4.4.38–40, 672
      4.7.3, 679
      4.m3.29–39, 683
      4.m6.34–48, 678
      4.4.8–9, 683
      4.4.22–23, 683
      4.6.53–54, 683
      5.3.29–36, 678
      5.3.33–35, 6.46, 683
      5.m3.11–31, 683
      5.4.24–39, 670
      5.m4.22–23, 683
      5.6.25, 683
   De divisione
      877b, 668
      877b, 6.15, 684
      xxviii–xxix, 684
   Fid. Cath.
      234–43, 683
   In Cat.
      5.5–6, 679
      159a–163c, 684
      159b–c, 669
      161b, 672
      201b, 667
      201c–204b, 673
      230c, 668
   In Cic. Top.
      1044c–48a, 673
      1044c–d, 672
      1045a–b, 673
      1047c–d, 673
      1092d, 675
      1099d–1100a, 671
   In Isag. I
      4.14–15.21, 684
      7.11–23, 681
      8.6–9.12, 679
      8.19–9.6, 682
      9.13–22, 679
      9.18–19, 679
      10.2–5, 672
      31.22–32.1, 679
      34.12–35.6 (cf. 36.22–37.1), 671
      77.9–13, 668
      84.4, 668
   In Isag. II
      135.5–13, 676
      140.13–43.7, 672
      143.8–47, 684
      164.16–65.18, 679
      225.17, 668
   In Perih. I
      32.7–34.28, 684
      32.11–21, 670

In Perih. II
    4.26–28, 669
    5.16–6.15, 670
    5.22–6.3, 669
    32.12–29, 669
    58.3, 669
    79.9–80.6, 685
    79.18–20, 672
Institutio arithmetica
    pref. 3, 676
    pref. 4, 683
    1.1.1, 674
    1.1.1, 5, 680
    1.1.1, 7, 673
    1.1.1–12, 674
    1.1.7, 674
    1.2.1, 675
    2.2.1, 675
    2.45, 675
    32.3, 675
    46.1, 675
    xlvi–l, 664, 674
    xxviii, 677
Institutio musica
    1.1, 675
    1.1, 179.24, 668
    1.2, 675, 680
    2.2–3, 680
    2.3, 674
Syllog. cat.
    762c, 670
    793d, 670
    809c, 689
Top. diff.
    1.1.1, 673
    1.5.50, 672
    2.7.10, 679
    4.1.15–17, 671
    4.7.30, 671
Trin. 2, 73–79, 679

Caesar, *Civil War* 3.69, 384
Calcidius
    Epistula 4, 666
    In Tim.
        2, 355, 665
        127, 666
        128, 666
        148, 666
        168, 666
        254, 681
        264–65, 665
        272, 666
        355, 666

Cassiodorus
    Expositio in Psalmos
        pr., ca. 16, lines 38–41, 714
        I 29.86–88, 677
        XCV.13 869.331–33, 677
        CXLVIII.14 1321.261–63, 677
    Institutiones
        pref. 5, 687
        1, 711
        1 pref. 1, 686
        1 pref. 6, 687, 688
        1.25, 31, 711
        1.27.1, 687
        1.29.1, 3, 687
        1.30, 689
        2 pref. 1, 687
        2 pref. 5, 687
        2.1–3, 687
        2.2.17, 687
        2.3.4–7, 686, 688
        2.3.6, 21, 687
        2.3.9, 572
        2.3.18, 688
        2.3.19, 676
        2.3.20, 687
        2.4.1, 687
        2.4.7, 676
        2.4–7, 687
        2.5.1, cf. 10, 676
        2.5.10, 686
        2.6.3, 677
        2.7.2, 677
        2.7.3, 677
        xxiii, 688
    Variae
        1.45.3–4, 676
        1.45.4, 687
        2.40.17, 676
        9.21.1–5, 687
        9.21.3–4, 687
Celsus, *On Medicine*, praef. 9, 48
Chrysippus, frags. 395, 396, 397, 538
Cicero
    Academicae quaestiones 19, 665
    De divinatione
        1.52, 681
        2.19–21, 437
        2.22, 436
        2.28.61, 436
        2.90, 435
        2.91, 429
    De finibus
        3.18, 666

Cicero (cont.)
    3.33, 79
    3.44, 80
    4.65, 440
De lege agraria 2.29, 187
De officiis 2.25, 106
De oratore
    1.9–11, 187, 665
    1.11, 666
    1.68, 665
    1.72, 666
    2.86–88, 158
    2.154, 666
    2.157–58, 388
    2.162, 666
Epistulae ad familiares 5.12, 366
Lucullus
    7, 21, 447
    114, 665
Pro Archia 3, 666
Topica 6, 673
Tusculanae disputationes
    1.1, 680
    5.8–9, 680
1 Clement 8:4, 308
Clement of Alexandria
    Excerpta Theodoti
        10.5, 31
        80.3, 96
    Paedagogus
        prologue, 96
        1.1.1.1–2.1, 97
        1.1.1.4, 97
        1.1.2.1, 99
        1.1.3.3, 96
        1.3.7.2, 33
        1.4.37.1, 31
        1.6, 31
        1.6.28.1, 32
        1.6.37.1, 34
        2.2.36.2, 96
        2.12.129.4, 31
        29.4, 33
    Protrepticus
        10.94.4, 31
    Quis dives salvetur
        23.3, 31
        39.4–5, 308
    Stromateis
        1.18.176, 92
        1.18.176.1, 3, 91
        1.23.153, 334
        1.25.165, 341

        1.28.176, 90, 92
        1.28.176.1–2, 91
        1.28.177.1, 91
        1.4, 31
        1.4.27.2, 30
        1.5.31, 106
        1.5.31.5, 96
        1.6.35.2, 97
        2, 95
        2.1.1.1, 94
        2.1.1.2, 94
        2.18.78.1, 95
        2.18.87.1, 96
        2.19.97.1, 95
        2.2.4.1–6.4, 93
        2.2.4.2–4, 94
        2.2.5.3, 94
        2.2.7–77, 95
        2.4.15.3, 31
        2.4.15–17, 217
        2.20.104.3, 95
        2.21.127–22.136, 95
        3–4, 95
        4.1.1.1–2.3, 93
        4.1.2.2, 93
        4.1.3, 648
        4.1.3.1, 98
        4.1.3.2–3, 96
        4.18.114.1, 31
        4.22.135.3, 31
        4.25.161.2–162, 96
        4.25.162.2, 96
        4.8.58.3, 97
        4.9.70–73, 96
        5.4.25.4, 31
        5.6.40.1, 31
        5.11.67.4, 34
        5.11.71.2, 96
        5.11.73.2, 96
        6.8.68.1, 31
        6.13.106.2, 95
        7.6.33.6, 61
        7.11.67.1, 96
        7.14.88.7, 95
        7.15.90.1–2, 96
        7.88.5, 74
        62.4, 97
        67.1, 97
        69.4, 97
Codex Theodosianus
    13.3.5, 374
    16.8.9, 616
Columella, *De re rustica* 6.6.1, 440

Cyprian of Carthage
  Ad Quirinum (Test.)
    1.pr., 154, 156, 157, 159, 161
    1, 159
    1.24, 308
    2.30, 160
    3, 159, 162, 163
    3.pr., 159
    3.1, 158, 160, 162
    3.2, 158
    3.3, 157
    3.25–27, 97, 114, 116, 119, 156
    3.39, 162
    3.63, 158
    3.64, 158
    3.65, 158
    3.75, 157
    3.80, 158
    3.81, 158
    3.98, 154, 155
    3.120, 163
  De lapsis
    2, 173
    4, 173
    5–6, 173
    7, 173
    8, 164, 173, 175
    10, 175
    11–12, 175
    15, 176
    16, 176
    25, 176
    26, 176
  Demetr. 26, 155
  Dom. orat.
    1, 154
    7, 163
    23–24, 32, 164
    28, 153, 155, 163
    31, 163
    34, 164
    35, 164
    35–36, 164
  Don.
    3–4, 154
    15, 161, 165
  Eleemosyna 16, 164
  Epistulae
    1.2.1, 160
    11.5.1, 163
    29, 160
    41, 175
    55.14.1, 161
    55.16.1, 153
    63, 172
    63.1, 179
    63.4, 179
    63.14, 178
    63.17, 181
    64.5, 383
    69.15.2, 161
    73.3.2, 160
    73.22.1–2, 156
  Fort. pr.3, 157, 161, 162
Cyril of Alexandria
  Contra Julianum
    1.4.5–13, 214
    1.4.7, 214
    1.4.10, 214
    1.20.12, 215
    1.20.27, 216
    1.38, 214
    1.39, 215
    1.39.11, 215
    1.40.18–21, 215
    2.14.9, 215
    2.14–15, 215
    2.16, 215
    2.16.2, 215
    2.16.13, 215
    2.20, 215
    2.20.4, 216
    2.20.22, 216
    2.21.7, 216
    2.22.7, 216
    2.22.8, 215
    7.17, 1
  Third Letter to Nestorius 12, 244
Cyril of Jerusalem
  Catecheses 14.18, 320

Damascius
  Problems and Solutions Concerning First Principles
    1.8.11–16, 607
David, *Prolegomena*
    8,10–19, 578
    17,1ff., 574
    17,15ff., 574
    17,16ff., 574
    17,20–22, 574
    34,30–35,29, 574
    44,17–22, 577
    46,15–26, 579
    46,24–25, 579
    55,20ff., 579

David, *Prolegomena* (cont.)
   55,35–56,16, 577
   71,3–4, 578
   74,1–6, 578
   79,2–4, 578
De mirabilibus sacrae scripturae
   pr., 719
   1, 719
   4–5, 726
   5, 724
   6, 716, 724
De ordine creaturarum
   5.11, 716
De sectis
   PG 86: 1193, 631
   PG 86: 1193–1200, 632
   PG 86: 1200–12, 641
   PG 86: 1200–33, 632
   PG 86: 1205B–D, 632
   PG 86: 1212C, 641
   PG 86: 1213AB–C, 641
   PG 86: 1213A–1216B, 641
   PG 86: 1216A–B, 642
   PG 86: 1216C–1221C, 641
   PG 86: 1221B, 642
   PG 86: 1221C–1228A, 642
   PG 86: 1228B–1232C, 642
   PG 86: 1232D–1233B, 642
   PG 86: 1233–60, 632
   PG 86: 1233A, 632
   PG 86: 1233B–C, 634
   PG 86: 1236B, 636
   PG 86: 1236D, 637
   PG 86: 1236D–37A, 637
   PG 86: 1237C, 638
   PG 86: 1237C–D, 637
   PG 86: 1252B, 635
   PG 86: 1252C, 635
   PG 86: 1252D, 635
   PG 86: 1260–68, 632
Dialogue on Political Science 27.7–15, 604
Didache 1, 68
Didymus Caecus, *Fragmenta in Joanneum*
   1, 313
Diogenes Laertius, *Lives*
   1.12, 680
   1.18, 665
   3.56, 665
   5.28, 665
   6.23, 58
   6.76, 58
   7.39, 665
   7.53 (SVF 2.87), 79
   7.112, 533, 534
   7.113, 538
   8.8, 680
Dionysius the Areopagite. *See* Pseudo-Dionysius
Donatus, *Ars Maior* 652.5–6, 405
Dorotheus of Gaza, *Didaskaliai*
   1.1, 581
   1.1–3, 581
   1.2–3, 581
   1.4, 582
   1.4.17–18, 582
   1.5, 582
   1.11, 582, 583
   1.11.1–2, 582
   2.33, 583
   2.34, 587
   2.35, 584
   2.37, 584
   2.37–39, 586
   2.39, 583
   3.40, 582
   3.42, 582
   4.52, 585
   4.54, 587
   5.61, 587
   5.62, 583, 587
   5.65, 587
   5.66, 587
   5.68, 583
   6.77, 587
   6.78.6–14,24–25, 588
   8.92, 585
   8.94–95, 585
   8.95, 584, 586
   8.95.6–9, 586
   9.102, 578
   11.123, 583
   12.131, 134, 585
   14.152, 586
   14.152–153, 584
   14.153, 586
   14.156, 583
   17.176, 582, 588
   17.176.43–46, 582
   17.178, 583
   17.178.13–14, 583

Eddius Stephanus, *Vita Wilfridi* 3, 732
Elias, *Prolegomena*
   6,32–33, 574
   12,14, 574
   16,35–17,36, 574

18,1–8, 575
18,35, 574
19,30–20,16, 576
19,31, 576
20,1ff, 576
20,6,14, 576
Ephrem the Syrian
   Madrashe Against Heresies 40, 263
   Madrashe on Abraham Qidunaya 7–15, 269
   Madrashe on Faith 49, 263
   Madrashe on Nisibis
      2, 263
      15.9, 278
      73.4, 275
   Madrashe on Paradise
      2.3–5, 275
      7.8, 275
      14.10, 275
      14.13, 275
   Madrashe on Virginity 7.15, 261
   Sermo de Domino nostro 4.4, 521
Epictetus, *Diatribe*
   3.12, 67
   3.21.1–3, 71
   3.23.30, 51
Epicurus, *Epistula ad Menoeceum* 135, 71
Epiphanius of Salamis
   Ancoratus
      118, 242
      119, 242
      119.1–2, 243
      119.5–6, 242
      119.12, 242
   Panarion
      64.3.5–7, 191
      64.3.12–13, 53
      67.3–4, 252
Epistula Barnabae
   2.1–3, 69
   18–20, 68
Eunapius, *Lives of the Philosophers and Sophists* 466–471, 348
Eusebius of Caesarea
   Commentary on Isaiah 62, 319
   De Laudibus Constantini
      9.15, 505
      11–18, 500
   Demonstratio evangelica
      1.6.21–22, 248
      10.8, 257
   Historia ecclesiastica
      3.24.7, 42
      5.19, 25, 231

6.2.12–3.3, 100
6.2.15–3.1, 102
6.3.1, 102
6.3.3, 102
6.3.7, 104
6.3.8–9, 102
6.3.9–13, 103, 112
6.3.13, 104
6.8.1, 53
6.15, 103
6.15.1, 97
6.18.2, 104
6.18.2–3, 103
6.19.5–8, 103
6.19.8, 110
6.19.12–14, 104
7.18, 248
8.3–4, 248
8.45, 248
8.69, 248
9.10.7–11, 253
10.4.3, 503, 504
10.4.14–16, 503
10.4.20, 503
10.4.25, 505
10.4.26, 506
10.4.28–32, 503
10.4.32, 504
10.4.38–45, 506
10.4.39–40, 507
10.4.45, 507
10.4.46–55, 503
10.4.55, 506
10.4.63, 508
10.4.63–6, 506
10.4.64, 508
10.4.70, 503
10.5.1–14, 253
Life of Constantine
   3.6–14, 231
   3.13, 231
Praeparatio evangelica
   1.1.12, 207
   1.7.16, 208
   1.8, 208
   3, 513
   3.7.1, 514
   3.7–10, 258
   6.11, 431
   7.11, 208
   7.12.1, 209
   11–13, 208
   13.21.14, 208

870 Index Locorum

Eusebius of Caesarea (cont.)
    14, 208
    14.1.2, 208
    14.3, 208
    14.5.3, 508
    14.13.9, 209
    14.14, 209
    14.16, 209
    14.16.6, 209
    15.22.68, 209, 210
    15.34, 210
    15.61.11, 210
    15.62.1–6, 210
  Theophania 3.44, 257
  Vita Constantini
    2.46, 253
    3.1, 493
    3.29–40, 500
    4.36, 372
    4.45, 501
    4.46, 500
    11–18, 500
Evagrius of Pontus
  Antirhêtikos
    4.1–7, 12, 27–28, 30, 46, 50–52, 57, 59, 66, 68–69, 71, 72, 539
    4.8–11, 13–21, 23, 26, 32–34, 38–39, 45, 47–49, 53–54, 56, 58, 62–65, 72, 539
    4.25, 37, 43, 64, 68–69, 74, 76, 539
    4.29, 31, 539
    4.35–36, 41, 539
    4.40, 44, 539
    4.42, 539
    4.50, 68–69, 74, 76, 539
    4.55, 73, 539
    4.60, 68, 539
    4.61, 67, 539
    54, 520
    54–55, 520
    57, 520
    58, 520
    61, 520
    63, 520
  Capita practica ad Anatolium
    10, 538
    10.2–10, 538
    10.10–12, 540
    11, 538
    22, 537
    23, 538
  De malignis cogitationibus
    1, 537
    12.9–14, 540
    17, 537
    28.15–22, 539
    36, 544
  De passionibus 1.2.1, 534
  On the Eight Thoughts
    66–90, 519
    73, 517
    74, 520
  On the Eight Wicked Spirits
    5, 542
    5.1, 530, 537, 538
    5.2, 542
    5.3, 542
    5.5, 542
    5.9–11, 538
    5.15, 542
    5.16, 542
    5.17, 542
    5.18, 542
  Scal. 7.1, 530
  To Eulogius
    6, 543
    6.5–9, 538
    6.16–19, 540
    6.19–22, 544
    6.28–29, 541
    6.30–31, 540
    8.10–12, 543
    9.12–16, 538
    13.27, 543
    26.18–20, 543
    29.33–37, 543
    31.55–56, 543
  Vita
    prol. 24–25, 538
    4, 541
Firmicus Maternus, *De errore profanarum religionum*
  21, 377
  22.1, 383
  24.2, 381
  26, 377
Galen
  Affections and Errors 1.6, 58
  Ars Medicinalis 24, 534
  De alimentorum facultatibus 1.19, 518
  De Animi Cuiuslibet Peccatorum Dignotione et Curatione
    1.7.2, 535
    5.14.9–10, 74
  De locis affectis
    6.6, 53

10.10, 541
De Methodo Medendi
  8.2, 534
  10.4, 534
  10.6, 534
De Praegnotione ad Epigenem (Praen.)
  6, 534
De Sanitate Tuenda
  1.5, 534
  1.8, 534
De temperamentis 2.6, 534
Simple Drugs 10.23, 58
George Cedrenus, *Compendium historiarum*
  314, 493
George of Pisidia
  De expeditione Persica
    l, lines 248–52, 646
    3, lines 349–5, 646
    3, lines 385–410, 650
    3, lines 407–409, 650
    3, lines 415–25, 650
  De vanitate vitae
    lines 1–2, 657
    lines 13–21, 656
    lines 22–33, 657
    lines 53–56, 656
    lines 86–105, 657
    lines 128–29, 656
    lines 142–48, 656
    lines 172–85, 656
    lines 192–95, 657
    lines 196–97, 657
    lines 242–45 et passim, 657
  De vita humana
    lines 8–14, 656
    lines 31–51, 656
    lines 59–64, 657
    lines 67–72, 657
    lines 78–80, 656
  Epigramma 111, 657
  Heraclias
    1, lines 65–79, 646
    1, l. 70, 646
    1, lines 71–84, 652
    1, lines 84–92, 646, 652
    1, l. 201, 646
  Hexaemeron
    lines 5–23, 657
    lines 24–33, 651
    lines 57–65, 650
    lines 81–359, 651
    lines 624–758, 651
    lines 626ff, 658
    lines 636–758, 656
    lines 731–33, 651
    lines 734–58, 658
    l. 752, 659
    lines 780–85, 657
    lines 823–24, 651
    lines 831–7, 659
    lines 916–1293, 651
    lines 1488–1608, 651
    lines 1665–77, 660
    lines 1678–88, 659
    lines 1689–171, 652
    lines 1720–91, 652
    lines 1792–96, 652
    lines 1797–1806, 652
    l. 1800, 646
  In Bonum patricium l. 7, 646
  In Christi resurrectionem
    lines 64–69, 647
    lines 64–129, 652
  In Heraclium ex Africa redeuntem
    lines 1–38, 646
    lines.72–75, 656
    lines 86–89, 646
Gesta Concilii Toletani 4.13, 400
Gospel of Truth 30.17–30, 34
Gregory I the Great (pope)
  Dialogues in Four Books
    1.4, 696
    2.8, 695
    3.28, 695
    4.18, 696
    4.19, 696
    4.35, 696
    4.36, 696
  Homiliae in evangelia
    1.15.1.12–20, 744
    2.36.1, 740
    2.40, 747
    2.40.207, 739
    2.40.210–17, 739
  Homilies on Ezekiel
    1.9.30–31, 693
    2.2.1, 693
    2.6.414, 744
  Moralia
    1.21.29, 746
    30.48, 693
  Pastoral Rule
    1.1, 694
    3.2–15, 694
  Registrum (letters)
    1.5, 698

Gregory I the Great (pope) (cont.)
   1.6, 699
   1.42, 701
   2.45, 701
   3.29, 695
   3.37, 701
   3.61, 695
   3.63, 699
   4.4, 700
   4.23, 695
   4.30, 697
   4.33, 700
   5.38, 697
   5.39, 697
   5.46, 699
   5.52, 700
   6.5, 700
   6.14, 699
   6.58, 700
   6.60, 700
   7.2, 698
   7.22, 700
   7.23, 698–700
   7.26, 695
   7.27, 699, 702
   8.4, 700
   8.25, 701
   9.68, 700
   9.213, 700
   9.214, 700
   10.20, 695
   11.27, 700
   11.37, 695
   11.46, 700
   11.48, 700
   11.49, 700
   13.5, 700
   13.9, 700
   13.10, 700
   13.11, 700
   13.33, 695
   13.40, 701
   14.12, 700–702
Gregory Nazianzen
  Oratio
    4, 328
    11.4, 307
    14.37, 308
    32.1–19, 649
    32.20–33, 649
  Poemata theologica (*moralia*) 1.2.2, 660
Gregory of Nyssa
  De anima
    1.6 (12M), 354

    1.8 (12M), 361
    1.9 (12M), 361
    1.10 (12M), 361
    2.1 (12M), 354
    2.3-8 (12–13M), 361
    2.10–12 (12–13M), 361
    4.1 (16M), 354
    5.8 (17M), 354
    7.3–7 (20M), 362
    33.13–17 (51–52M), 363
    38.10–14 (56M), 363
  De hom. opif. 5.1–2, 473
  De perfectione et qualem oporteat esse Christianum
    256 M., 332
    260 M., 332
    269–72 M., 332
    285 M., 333
  De professione Christiana
    244 M, 332
    244–45 M, 332
  De vita Gregorii Thaumaturgi
    900–901 M., 345
    901 M, 334, 346
  De vita Moysis
    1.1, 329
    1.2–3, 329
    1.5–8, 333
    1.10, 333
    1.14, 329, 344
    1.14–15, 330
    1.18, 334, 335
    1.19, 22, 342
    2.7–8, 336
    2.10, 344
    2.12, 340
    2.13, 339
    2.14, 340
    2.17, 343
    2.37, 342
    2.39, 343
    2.44, 332
    2.45, 330
    2.105, 330
    2.112–16, 337
    2.115, 336, 342
    2.116, 337
    2.157–58, 332
    2.221–23, 330
    2.225, 333
    2.227, 346
    2.251, 330
    2.313–15, 333
    2.318, 332

2.319, 328
II, 659
Epistula canonica, Canon 6, 235
Epistulae
   5, 244
   5.8, 244
Hexaemeron
   GNO 4/1: 81, 649
   GNO 4/1: 83–84, 649
Homiliae in Canticum Cantorum
   8, 333
In Christi resurrectionem oratio I PG
   46:604B, 320
In laudem Basilii fratris
   789 M, 334
   808–809 M, 334, 340, 344
   809 M., 334, 341
In xl martyres
   Ia, 288
   Ib, 300
Life of Macrina
   3.2, 354
Oratio catechetica
   8, 332
   15, 332
Gregory Thaumaturgus
   Panegyric 1.3, 104
   Sermo in omnes sanctus 1201.28–40, 313

Hermas, *Mandata pastoris* 6.2 (36), 85
Hermias, *Ridicule of the Outside Philosophers*
   1, 206
   4, 206
   15, 206
   18, 206
Hesiod, *Theogony* 27–28, 369
Hesychius, *Lexicon* Π.1399, 535
Hilary of Poitiers
   Commentary on Matthew 5.1, 163
   De trinitate 1.13, 388
Homer, *Odyssey* 10.237–40, 683
Horace
   Ars poetica 306–7, 664
   Carmina
      3.30, 369
      4.9.25, 384
Hrabanus Maurus, *De institutione clericorum*
   3.20, 542.23–24, 665

Iamblichus
   De mysteriis
      3, 145
      3.1, 147
      3.3.25, 146

      3.4.2, 146
      3.6, 148, 149
      3.7, 148
      3.7.3, 147
      3.8.3, 146
      3.10.2, 146
      3.12, 148
      3.15, 150
      3.17.51, 146
      3.26.23, 146
      3.27.2, 146
      3.27.6, 9, 12, 37, 45, 56, 146
      9.3.33, 146
      9.5.19, 146
      10.4.1, 146
      10.5.2, 146
      10.8.2, 146
   De vita pythagorica
      15.65, 535
      36.267, 348
   In Timaeum frag. 1 D, 666
Ignatius of Antioch, *Epistle to the Magnesians*
   8.2, 382
Irenaeus of Lyons
   Adversus haereses
      1.pr.1, 76
      1.6–7, 82
      1.8.1, 78
      1.9.2, 77
      1.9.4, 78, 83
      1.28.1, 61, 67
      1.29.3, 75
      1.30–31, 75
      2.6.1, 75, 84
      2.13.1, 84
      2.13.2, 84
      2.18.1, 85
      2.18.2, 85
      2.25.1, 77, 78
      2.25.2, 77
      2.25.3, 75
      2.25.4, 77
      2.26.1, 77
      2.27.1, 67, 72, 73, 75, 77
      2.27.1–2, 73
      2.28.1, 78
      2.28.1–3, 82
      2.28.3, 75
      2.29.3, 82, 84
      2.33.4, 81
      2.33–34, 75
      2.34.2, 75
      3.9.3, 75
      3.20.1, 82

Irenaeus of Lyons (cont.)
    3.20.2, 82
    3.23.4, 73, 79, 82
    3.23.4–5, 85
    3.23.5, 69, 70, 72, 79, 80, 86
    3.25.1, 66
    4.9–11, 66
    4.11.2, 74, 83
    4.12, 83
    4.12.2, 83
    4.12.5, 70
    4.13.1, 70
    4.13.1–3, 70
    4.13.2, 70, 71
    4.13.4, 70
    4.15.1, 70
    4.16.3, 70
    4.16.5, 70
    4.18.2, 73
    4.18.3, 79
    4.20.5, 254
    4.27.2, 381
    4.30.2, 87
    4.36.6, 80
    4.37.1, 66, 81, 85, 86
    4.37.5, 85
    4.37.6, 80, 81
    4.37.6–7, 81
    4.37.7, 70, 73, 80, 87
    4.38.1, 66, 74, 75
    4.38.2, 76, 79
    4.38.3, 67, 75
    4.38.4, 66
    4.39.1, 68, 69, 76, 77, 79, 80, 84
    4.39.2, 81, 82
    4.39.2–3, 82, 83
    4.40.2–3, 87
    5.1.3, 81, 86
    5.2.3, 76, 77, 79, 82
    5.2.3–3.1, 82
    5.3.1, 69, 82
    5.5.2, 320
    5.6.1, 67, 81
    5.8.1, 66, 67, 81
    5.8.2, 70, 72, 86
    5.8.2–3, 71
    5.8.3, 71–73
    5.9.1, 72
    5.9.2, 86
    5.9.3, 67
    5.10.1, 67, 72, 73, 86, 87
    5.10.1–2, 87
    5.11.1, 86
    5.20.1, 73
    5.20.1–2, 77
    5.20–22, 73
    5.21–22.1, 74
    5.22.2, 74
    5.28.1, 68
    5.31.1, 320
    5.36.1, 75
    Epideixis
        1–2, 68, 72
        2, 68, 69, 71
        3b, 78, 82, 83
        6, 77, 78, 83
        8, 82
        12, 72
        12–14, 80, 85
        14, 87
        87, 84
Isidore of Seville
    De natura rerum
        pr., 1, 715
        pr., 2, 715
        4.5, 715
        17, 724
        31, 722
    Etymologies
        1.14, 407
        2.24.1–2, 9, 572
        2.24.3–7, 665
        19.27.4, 747
        19.28.2, 4, 747

Jerome
    Commentary on Galatians 2.3, 400, 402
    Commentary on Matthew
        1.1154, 742
        27:55, 742
    De viris illustribus
        68, 154
        84, 367
    Jov. 1, 737
    Orig. Hom. Cant., prologue, 748
Joannes Stobaeus, *Florilegium*
    2.7.10, 532
John Cassian
    Conf. 5.11: 199, 519
    Conlationes
        9.28.1–9.30.2, 547
        24.26, 738
    De institutis coenobiorum 5.33, 709
    Institutiones
        5.14.4, 738
        9.2–3, 547
John Damascene, *Dialectica* 3 and 66, 572

John Lydus
    On the Magistracies of Rome
        3.16.159, 601
        3.25.173.8, 595
        3.25.173.17, 594
John of Salisbury, *Metal.* 1.12, 663
Josephus, *Antiquities* 9.213, 320
Julian Pomerius, *De Vita Contemplativa* 1.2, 716
Julius Africanus
    Chronographiae T88, 120
    Kesti F12.20.35–47, 120
Justin Martyr
    Dialogue with Trypho
        2.4–5, 51
        18.2, 308
        44.4, 308
        46.7, 51
        69.3, 51
        69.7, 52
        107, 320
    First Apology (1 Apol.)
        1.1, 53
        2.2, 53
        3.1, 52
        26.8, 55
        31.7, 51
        42a, 212
        44.3, 308
        48.1, 51
        54.10, 51
        57.2, 54
        61.7, 308
    Second Apology (2 Apol.)
        2.1–20, 53
        2.15–20, 54
        2.16, 53
        3.1, 54
        5.6, 52
        12.1, 54
        29.2–3, 52
Justinian
    Codex Iustinianus
        1.2.23, 620
        1.2.24, 624
        6.30.18.4, 620
        6.30.19, 620
        11.48.19, 623
        11.48.24, 622
    Digest 1.4.4, 619
    Edict
        13 c.10, 617
        13 c.28, 617
    Novels
        7, 624
        8, 615
        8 c.11, 614
        9, 617, 620
        11, 617
        17 c.7, 617
        22 c.17 p, 622
        30, 609
        30 c.5, 615
        36, 617
        37, 617
        45 c.1, 615
        45 pr, 616
        47, 618
        54, 623
        56, 617
        59 c.1, 617
        59 c.6, 617
        60 pr, 610
        62, 617
        66 c.1, 618
        74, 623
        74 c.4, 617
        75, 617
        106, 620
        110 c.1, 620
        111, 620
        111 c.1, 620
        111 pr., 620
        113, 619
        114, 617
        115, 619
        117 c.15, 617
        122, 613
        133, 617
        133 c.5, 617
        146, 616
        156, 622
        158 c.1, 620
        158 pr., 620
        159, 621
        162 c.2, 622
        App. 1, 622
        App. 7, 617
Juvenal, *Satires* 13.64, 436
Juvencus
    Libri Evangeliorum Quattuor
        1.210, 369
        1.588–89, 370
        1.679–89, 370
        2.25–38, 370
        4.284–87, 370
        4.805–11, 371
        4.808, 367
        Preface 6–10, 368

Juvencus (cont.)
  Preface 15–20, 369
  Preface 21–24, 369
Lactantius, *Divine Institutes*
  2.2, 260
  4.6.1–2, 252
  7.24, 377
Leontius (presbyter of Constantinople), *Homilies*
  II.197–204, 561
  III.236–41, 561
  V.75–78, 552
  VI.153, 567
  VI.157–61, 567
  VII.278, 554
  VIII.83–84, 566
  X.1–4, 557
  X.10.141–44, 145–46, 555
  X.162–68, 555
  XIII.154–55, 553
  XIII.228–229, 553
  XIII.238, 244–49, 553
  XIV.1–6, 560
  XIV.20–47, 561
  XIV.23, 561
  XIV.40, 552
Lex Irnitana 91, 187
Libanius, *Epistulae* 664.2.4, 576
Livy, 5.18.4, 440
Lucian of Samosata
  Abdicatus 2, 62
  Peregrinus
    44, 54
    45, 54, 55
  Somnium 1.4, 576
  Vitarum auctio 10, 58
Lucretius, *De rerum natura*
  4.379, 430
  5.1, 369

Macrobius, *Somnium Scipionis*
  1.8.4, 679
  2.17.15, 665
Manilius, *Astronomica* 1.57, 429
Marcus Aurelius, *Meditationes*
  3.4.3, 54
  10.36, 54
  46.7, 52
Martianus Capella, *De nuptis Philologiae et Mercurii* 9.998, 663
Martyrdom of Perpetua and Felicitas
  2, 160
  3, 164
  4, 161
  13, 160

Maximus of Tyre, *Dissertations* 18, 351
Maximus the Confessor
  Ambigua to John
    6, 657
    7, 657, 661
    8, 657
    10, 649, 651, 654, 657, 659–61
    17, 651
    20, 651, 654
    21, 661
    32, 655
    41, 654
    42, 654
    71, 659, 660
  Ambigua to Thessalonians 5, 651, 653, 654, 657
  Capita de caritate
    3.33, 654
    3.80, 654
    3.94, 654
  Capita theologica et oeconomica
    1.66, 662
  Epistulae
    10, 662
    14, 653
  Quaestiones ad Thalassium
    intro., 651
    1, 658
    16, 658
    19, 654
    21, 651, 658
    43, 651
    48, 655
    55, 659
    60, 662
    61, 658
    65, 657
  Vita (Greek) §1–5, 647
Menander, *Epit.* fr. 2, 1
Methodius of Olympus
  On the Resurrection 2.25.8–9, 320
  Symposium
    2.6–7, 249
    3.7–8, 249
    6.2, 249
    6.3.139, 356
    8.2, 249
    8.11, 249
    8.17.230, 356
    8.231, 357
    10.2, 249
    Epilogue 295–96, 355
    Epilogue 301, 356
Minucius Felix, *Octavius* 32.4, 467

Musonius Rufus
  Discourses
    3.7, 48
    4.2, 48
    6, 67
    6.1, 74
    16.8, 48
    18b.1, 58

Nemesius of Emesa, *De natura hominis* 19, 535
    17.9–10, 213
    17.10–14, 213
Nicolaus, *Prog.* 11, 501
Nicomachus, *Introduction to arithmetic*
    1.1.1, 674
    1.1.1–5.3, 674
    1.4.1, 673
Notitia Dignitatum 2.1, 602–603
Numenius, frag. 24.71–73 des Places, 677

Olympiodorus
  In Platonis Alcibiadem commentarii
    11, 514
    23,2–5, 587
  Prolegomena
    7.24–2, 672
    7.34–8.3, 679
    9.28ff, 572
Oribasius, *Eunap.* 4.117.10, 541
Origen
  Commentary on Genesis pref. 4, 108
  Commentary on John, 102
    1.8.44–45, 42
    5.8, 101, 115
    6.14, 107
    20.47, 254
    20.157–59, 253
  Commentary on Matthew 15.4–19.18, 196
  Commentary on Psalms 1–25 pref. 4, 105
  Commentary on Romans
    pr. 2, 107, 111
    8.8, 114
  Commentary on the Song of Songs
    pr. 1.7, 651
    pr. 3.1–2, 89
    pr. 3.2, 90
    pr. 3.4, 107
    pr. 3.8, 107
    pr. 3.14, 107
    2.5.22–23, 107
  Contra Celsum
    1.28, 383
    1.32, 383
    1.41, 21

    1.43–48, 21
    1.48, 22, 23, 27
    2.43, 381
    3.23, 110
    3.58, 104, 111
    3.72, 106
    4, 139
    4.17, 110
    4.30, 107
    4.38, 110
    4.40, 111
    4.48, 110
    4.49, 113
    4.51, 110
    4.92, 140, 439
    4.98, 141
    6.42, 110
    6.49, 114
    6.63–65, 255
    7, 139, 141
    7.3, 141
    7.4, 142
    7.33–34, 22
    7.39, 254
    7.44, 254
    7.48, 53
    8.17–18, 255
  De oratione 5–7, 107
  De Principiis
    pr., 113
    pr. 3, 111
    pr. 5, 107
    pr. 8–9, 107
    1.1.8–9, 254
    1.1.9, 27
    1.2.8, 473
    3.1.8–14, 109
    3.6.1, 113
    4.2.1, 319
    4.2.7, 106
    4.3.1–5, 109
  Dial. 15, 101
  Exp. Prov. 1.6, 111
  Fr. Luc. 186.40–45, 23
  Fr. Ps. ad Ps 134:15–18, 23
  Homilia 1 in Ps. 77
    sect. 1, 114
    sect. 5, 109
    sect. 6, 114
  Homilia 2 in Ps. 77 sect. 4, 114, 115
  Homilia 7 in Ps. 77 sect. 4, 115
  Homilia in Ps. 74, sect. 6, 100, 101
  Homiliae in Exodum 13.3, 115
  Homiliae in Ezechielis 2.2, 114

Origen (cont.)
  Homiliae in Genesim
    10, 114
    10.1, 115
    10.5, 115
    12.5, 115
    13.3, 114, 115
  Homiliae in Isa. 7.3, 114
  Homiliae in Jer.
    5.13.2, 116
    5.14.1, 114
    8.2, 106
    14.3.1, 114
    14.3.2, 116
    15.5.2, 114
    16.10.1, 114
  Homiliae in Jos.
    1.7, 115
    7.6, 9.8, 114
  Homiliae in Judic. 1.1, 114
  Homiliae in Lev.
    1.1, 114
    1.1.4–6, 114
    1.1.5, 114
    7.1.1, 114
    10.1, 101
  Homiliae in Lucam 16.6, 101, 114
  Homiliae in Num.
    9.1.1–7, 114
    14.1.1, 114
  Letter to Gregory
    1–3, 337
    2.1, 105
  Philocalia
    23.6, 431
    23.17, 431, 435
Ovid
  Amores 1.1.1–16, 368
  Fasti 5.451–80, 378
  Metamorphoses
    10.503–504, 382
    11.1–43, 380
    15.871–79, 369

Pamphilus, *Capita diversa*
  127.2–9, 627
  127–43, 628
  134.4–23, 628
  144–212, 628
  179.1–3, 628
  183.139–186.203, 629
  213, 636
  213–61, 628
  235.1–4, 637
  241.153–58, 638
Pauca problesmata 151, lines 7–10, 717
Paulinus of Milan, *Vita Ambrosii* 13.3, 392
Paulinus of Nola, *Carmina* 27.542, 483
Philo of Alexandria
  Congr.
    79–80, 106
    145, 104
  De aeternitate mundi
    3, 202
    19, 204
  De vita contemplativa 3.28, 110
  Ebr. 193–202, 203
  Her.
    243–48, 203
    246, 206
    247, 204
    248, 203
  On the Life of Moses
    1.5, 20–24, 334
    1.140–42, 337
  Opif. 7, 205
  Post. 18, 94
  Quaestiones in Exodum frag. 4, 203
  Somn.
    1.21–32, 203
    1.205, 336
Philogelos
  110, 55
Philoponus
  In An. pr. 387.9–11, 673
  In Cat.
    4.23–30, 672
    5.6–7, 679
Philoxenos of Mabbug
  Faith, 53 (ET), 70 (Syr.), 518
  Letter to the Monks of Senun 89–90, 518, 525
  On Gluttony
    276 (ET), 353 (Syr.), 517, 520
    276 (ET), 354 (Syr.), 522
    277 (ET), 355 (Syr.), 523
    277 (ET), 356 (Syr.), 520
    279 (ET), 359 (Syr.), 523
    281 (ET), 360 (Syr.), 527
    281–82 (ET), 361–62 (Syr.), 520
    282 (ET), 362 (Syr.), 521, 524
    283 (ET), 363 (Syr.), 519
    283 (ET), 364 (Syr.), 522, 526
    284 (ET), 365 (Syr.), 523
    285 (ET), 366 (Syr.), 523, 524

    287 (ET), 368 (Syr.), 525
    287 (ET), 369 (Syr.), 525
    288 (ET), 369 (Syr.), 525
    288 (ET), 370 (Syr.), 525
    288–89, (ET), 369–72, (Syr.), 522
    294 (ET), 377 (Syr.), 527
    295–96 (ET), 380 (Syr.), 526
    296 (ET), 380 (Syr.), 526
    296 (ET), 381 (Syr.), 526
    297 (ET), 381 (Syr.), 527
    297 (ET), 382 (Syr.), 522, 525, 526
    298 (ET), 382 (Syr.), 527
    299 (ET), 384 (Syr.), 524
    300 (ET), 385 (Syr), 525, 526
    300 (ET), 386 (Syr.), 526
    301 (ET), 387 (Syr.), 524
    301–302 (ET), 387–88 (Syr.), 524
    302 (ET), 388 (Syr.), 525
    303 (ET), 390 (Syr), 523
    303 (ET), 389 (Syr.), 522
    318–19 (ET), 409–10 (Syr.), 522
    section 29, 521
Placita. See Aëtius
Plato
  Alcibiades I, 513
    111a–c, 586
    133b6, 593
  Apologia
    25b, 448
    36d, 40a–b, 140
  Crito 44a–b, 681
  Euthyphro 3e, 140
  Gorgias
    464b–c, 679
    480a–81b, 672
  Menexenus 237c, 352
  Meno
    80d, 683
    80e, 454
  Phaedo
    60a, 359
    67e, 47
    69b, 575
    116b, 360
    117c, 360
    117c–e, 360
    117d–e, 359
  Phaedrus 242b–d, 140
  Republic, 448
    1.331c–d, 578
    2.377c–383c, 469
    2.595a–608b, 469
    5.461, 547
    5.475b, 106
    6, 143
    6–7, 476
    6.493e–494a, 448
    6.496c, 140
    6.500c, 332
    6.509d–520e, 449
    7.528a–d, 665
    7.531c–d, 666
    10.595, 386
    10.601c, 469
    10.613a, 332
    10.613a–b, 569
  Symposium
    201d, 350
    202e, 426
    204b, 683
    211c, 469
  Theaetetus
    150a–151b, 204
    176a–b, 332, 569
    176b, 113
    198b–199b, 683
  Timaeus
    1, 666
    20a, 666
    44d–47e, 469
    45b–46a, 476
    48e4, 415
    53c, 666
    90b–d, 569
Pliny the Elder, *Historia naturalis* pref. 1, 663
Plotinus
  Enneads
    1.3.6, 575
    1.4.15, 575
    1.6, 452
    2.9, 146
    4.3.1, 472
    4.5.7.24, 476
    5.3, 472
    5.5.7.24, 476
    5.5.12, 471
    5.8, 472
    5.8.1, 471
    5.8.9, 471
    6.8.21.26, 607
Plutarch
  De esu 995C–D, 58
  De exilio 1, 599B–C, 535
  Life of Pericles 24.2–3, 351

880 Index Locorum

Plutarch (cont.)
   Soll. an. 962C–D, 439
   Stoic. rep. 1035a, 665
Polycarp, *Epistle to the Philippians* 1.2, 381
Pontius, *Vita Cypriani*
   2, 154, 156
   3, 162
   4, 160
Porphyry
   De abstinentia
      3.16, 439
      3.23, 439
   De antro nympharum 4, 7, 502
   De simulac. frag. 351, 514
   In Cat. 57.20–59.2, 669
   Isagoge 6.16, 668
   Sent. 32, 679
   Vita Plotini 24–26, 90
Posidonius, frags. 87–88 Edelstein–Kidd, 665
Priscian, *Institutiones grammaticae*
   1.1, 406
   3:91.3–4, 406
   20:20.4, 406
Proclus Diadochus
   Elements of Theology
      21, 600
      31, 597
      35, 596
      70.8–19, 596
      75, 595
      108, 596, 604
      116, 570
      145, 600
      147 corollary, 600
      194 corollary, 597
      195, 597
   In Timaeus
      2.305.7–15, 570
      3.262.6–14, 570
      3.275.11–15, 571
      3.279.14–19, 570
   Platonic Theology
      1.2, 598
      1.2.9.8, 599
      1.24.108.16, 598
      1.25.113.4, 598
      3.1, 599
      5.18.283–84, 596
Proclus of Constantinople, *Homilia* 16, 293
Procopius
   Anecdota (Secret History)
      6.14, 610
      12.27, 609
      14.7–11, 619
   De aedificiis
      1.1.6, 614
      1.1.78, 610
   De bellis
      1.1.4–5, 610
      8.1.1–2, 609
Propertius, *Elegies* 3.1.1–12, 368
Prudentius
   Apotheosis 712, 378
   Cathemerinon
      1.163–64, 376
      2.25, 377
      3.101–102, 376
      3.126–27, 376
      6.140–45, 376
      7.220, 377
      11.91–92, 376
   Peristephanon
      2, 378
      2.9–16, 378
      2.45–167, 378
      2.142, 378
   Psychomachia 583, 378
Pseudo-Andronicus, *De passionibus* 1.2, 533
Pseudo-Athanasius, *De sabbatis et circumcisione* 23–53, 316
Pseudo-Clementine, *Recognitiones* 10.9, 428
Pseudo-Dionysius
   Celestial Hierarchy
      7.2, 654
      12.2, 293B, 605
      200D, 605
   De divinis nominibus 4.12, 660
   Ecclesiastical Hierarchy
      2.3.6, 654
      3.3.4, 654
      5.1.5, 505AB, 606
   Epistulae 4, 653
   Mystical Theology
      1.1, 606
      997B–1000A, 606
Pseudo-Elias (Pseudo-David) 14, 574
Pseudo-Hermogenes, *Progymnasmata*
   10, 501
   11.24, 77
   11.25, 77
Pseudo-Hippocrates, *Ad antigonum regem* 8–9, 738
Pseudo-Hippolytus, *Refutation of All Heresies*, 5.8.40, 53
Pseudo-Justin
   Cohortatio ad Graecos

3.2–4.1, 211
6.1, 211
7.1, 212
31, 206
35.2, 212
36.1–2, 212
37, 212
On the Resurrection
3.1–2, 61
3.4–12, 61
3.14, 62
3.15, 62
10.14, 63
10.17, 63
Pseudo-Plato, *Epin.* 990d, 665
Pseudo-Plutarch
Epitome 15.60–61, 218
Plac. philos
911B, 58
Plac. Philos.
1.pr.3.3, 74
Ptolemy
Tetrabiblos
1.3, 429
3.2, 429
3.3, 429

Quintilian, *Institutes*
1.10.1, 663
2.7.3–4, 158
2.17.41, 666

Romanos the Melodist
5.Pr. 1, 554
On Mary at the Cross
19.1, 565
19.2, 565
19.4, 6, 565
19.4–6, 565
19.7.4–6, 565
19.8.1, 2–4, 7, 565
On the Marriage at Cana
7.6.1–3, 554
7.7.2–3, 554
On the Multiplication of the Loaves
3.1.1–5, 556
On the Presentation in the Temple
1.1.1–3, 9–10, 551
4.1.1–2, 551
On the Prodigal Son
49.2.1–5, 558
49.3.1–2, 558
49.10.1–2, 5–6, 10, 559
49.11.1–3, 559

49.18.3, 559
49.21.5–6, 559
On the Sinful Woman
10.5.5–11, 562
10.6.1, 6–11, 562

Scribonius Largus, *Compounds* ep. 4–5, 47
Seneca
Controversiae 4.5, 62
Dial. 2.6.8, 74
Epistulae
16.1, 71
84.5–7, 71
88 passim, 666
88.23, 663
88.24, 665
88.25–28, 104
88.30, 666
88.34, 107
89.4, 106, 680
89.5, 106
90.28, 440
108, 61
113.18, 86
Epistulae morales ad Lucilium 45.5, 388
Hercules furens frag. 653, 440
Naturales quaestiones 1.3.7, 440
Sentences of Sextus 240, 519
Severianus, *In dictum apostoli* 669 (PG 4203), 313
Sextus Empiricus
Adversus mathematikos
6.52–54, 430
7.16, 665
7.248, 76
7.257–58, 76
9.13, 106
9.153, 70
Pyrrhōneioi hypotypōseis 2, 25, 447
Simplicius, *Enchiridion of Epictetus* 14, 257.25–32, 668
Socrates Scholasticus, *Historia ecclesiastica*
2.18, 238
7.15, 348
7.21.27, 576
Soranus, *Gynaeceia*, 1.32.1, 62
Statius, *Thebaid* 1.85, 370
Suetonius
Domitianus 18.1, 440
Galba 4, 436
Nero 51, 440
Synesius, *Dio* 15, 351

Tacitus, *Annales*
   15.63–64, 47
   15.69, 47
Tatian
  Oratio ad Graecos
    2.1, 58
    3.2, 58
    7, 57
    8.2, 57, 61
    11.1, 60
    12.5, 57
    12.10, 57
    15.7, 60
    16.3, 59
    16.7, 60
    16.8, 60
    17.5, 59, 60
    18.1, 60
    18.4, 59
    18.5, 59
    18.6, 57
    19.2, 61
    20.1, 59
    23.1, 61
    23.5, 61
    25.1, 58
    32.2, 61
    33.1, 57, 61
    33. 5, 61
Tertullian
  Adversus Hermogenem 11, 319
  Adversus Praxeam 5, 373
  Adversus Valentinianos 5.1, 50
  De baptismo
    1.1, 34
    9.1, 322
  De corona militis 3, 178
  De paenitentio 6.16–17, 155
  De praescritione haereticorum
    7.9, 340
  De resurrectione
    32, 320
    58.8–10, 320
  De testimonio animae 17, 469
Themistius, *De anima* 67.8, 25, 669
Theodore of Raithou, *Praeparatio*
    185.1, 629
    185.1–5, 629
    186.26–29, 630
    187.13, 24, 639
    187.20–22, 640
    188.25–26, 640
    189.20–21, 640
    189.24–25, 640
    190.11–17, 640
    196.4, 640
    196.5–8, 15–16, 640
    200.10, 630
    200.14–22, 630
Theodoret of Cyrrhus
  Healing of the Hellenic Illnesses
    pr. 16–17, 216
    1.62, 217
    1.63, 217
    1.96, 218
    1.97, 217
    1.99, 218
    2.95, 216
    4.15, 217
    4.22, 217
    4.31, 216
    5.15, 217
    5.16, 216
    5.19, 217
    5.44–47, 218
    5.49–50, 218
  Historia ecclesiastica
    1.7.15, 230
    1.7.16, 231
    1.8.1–5, 230
    1.8.3, 230
  Quaestiones in Octateuchum
    274.18–21, 317
    276.8–10, 317
  Question on Joshua
    3, 316
    4, 317
Theon (Aelius Theon), *Progymnasmata* 11, 77
Theon of Smyrna, *Expos.* 15.16–18, 666
Theophanes the Confessor, *Chronicle*
    §327–28, 650
    AM 6089, 699
    AM 6099, 700

Valerius, *Argonautica*
    2.192, 370
Vergil
  Aeneid
    2, 376
    2.57–58, 370
    2.205–31, 376
    2.380, 376
    2.471–75, 376
    2.576, 376
    5.80–84, 376
    5.273–75, 376

    6, 380
    8.435–38, 376
Eclogues
    2.25–37, 430
    3.93, 376
    4, 372, 382
    6, 368
    6.1–5, 368
Georgics
    1.53, 376
    2.458, 384
    3.4–6, 368
    3.314–19, 376
    4.459, 376
    4.563–66, 371
Vincent of Lérins, *Commonitory*
    2.4, 692
    2.5, 692
Virgil. *See* Vergil
Vita Ceolfridi
    6, 732
    11, 733

Xenocrates, frag. 1 Heinze, 665
Xenophon
    Memorabilia
        1.1.11–16, 210
        2.2.7–9, 359
        2.6.36, 352
        3.11, 352
        4.27–29, 217
    Oeconomicus 3.14, 352
    Symposium 2.10, 359

General Index

Abba Poemen, 531
Abelard, *Sic et non*, 716, 717
Abgar V Ukkama (king of Edessa), 120
Abgar VIII (king of Edessa), 118, 119, 124, 127, 130, 133
Abraham, W. J., 29
Abraham Qidunaya, 261–81, 275
Acca of Hexham, 713, 732, 733, 748
Acta of Abraham, 269
Acts of Thomas, 43, 121, 125
Adeodatus (son of Augustine), 695
adoration of the Magi, Ambrose of Milan on, 394–95
Aelius Aristides, 57
Aenesidemus, 203
Aeschines
    Aesop, 192
    Aspasia, 351
    female characters in dialogues of, 351
Aesop
    bilingual texts of, 192
Aëtius *Placita*, 9, 198–220
    Athenagoras and, 204–5
    Cyril on, 214–16
    dialectical methodology of, 201
    doxography genre and, 198–99
    Eusebius and, 207–11
    Hellenic tradition, reliance on, 200
    Hermias and, 205–6
    lost text, reconstruction of, 198
    Nemesius and, 212–13
    ordering of knowledge in, 199–202, 219
    Philo and, 202–4
    on philosophy, 200, 201
    physics, focus on, 200
    Pseudo-Justin and, 211
    'secular' attitude towards discussions of Deity, 201
    Theodoret of Cyrrhus and, 198, 216–19
affective lexica, 531, 536, 541
Agapetus, 686
    Mirror of Princes, 594
Agapius, 594

Agathias, 609, 616
Agilulf (Lombard king), 700, 702
Agnes (martyr), 390
Agnoetes, 632, 642
Agosti, G., 373
Ahbel-Rappe, Sara, 18, 590, 611
akrasia, Irenaeus on, 70, 84–87
Albinus (abbot, Canterbury), 732
Alcinous
    Didaskalikos, 112
    on godlikeness as goal of philosophy, 569
Alexander
    in Arian conflict, 247, 249, 251, 256
    church building by, 252
    on divine nature, 253
Alexander of Hales, on spiritual senses, 28
Alexander Romance, 132
Alexander the Great, 119
Alexandria, Arian conflict in. *See* Arius and Arians
Alexis-Baker, Andy, 157
allegory
    Gregory of Nyssa on use of, 330, 333
    Origen on, 109–11
    resolution of discord between ancient non-Christian authors and scripture, 715
Amalarius of Metz, 707
Ambrose of Milan
    on astrology, 428
    astrology, critique of, 431, 442
    Bede and, 717, 743, 748
    De Fide (On the Faith), 388, 391
    De mysteriis, 392
    De officiis, 390
    De uirginibus, 390
    dialectic, hostility towards, 388
    Explanation of the Psalms, 389
    Expositio evangelii secundum Lucam, 747
    Hexaemeron, 428, 748
    On the Holy Spirit, 389
    on lunar rainbow, 724

in *Reference Bible*, 717
On the Sacrament of the Lord's Incarnation, 389
secular and exegetical knowledge, compatibility of, 714
Ambrose of Milan, hymns of, 7, 388–403
   on adoration of the Magi, 394–95
   'Aeterne rerum conditor', 390
   Agnes, hymn to, 390
   Augustine compared, 401–2
   on baptism of Christ, 393–94
   basilica crisis (386), 392
   'building up [the] faith' as aim of, 390
   epistemology of, 388
   exempla, use of, 391
   Hilary of Poitiers compared, 400–1
   homilies of Ambrose and, 390–93
   'Iam surgit hora tertia', 390
   'Illuminans Altissimus' and miracles of Christ in *Expositio on Luke*, 389–91, 393–400
   on miracle of the loaves and fishes/wedding at Cana, 396–98
   Newman on real assent and, 388, 389, 403
   stylistic features, 392
   Victor, Nabor, and Felix, hymn to, 390
Amidon, Philip, 229
Amma Syncletica, 546
Ammianus Marcellinus, 374
Ammonius of Alexandria, 490
   Aristotelian corpus, classification of, 672
   Diatessaron, 190, 265
   lectures on *Isagoge*, 681
   prolegomena of, 572, 577
Ammonius Saccas, 90, 103, 138
Amphilochius of Iconium, 235, 321
   biblical narratives disseminated via sermons of, 303, 315, 321–25
   Contra Haereticus, 322
   De recens baptizatis, 322
   homilies of, 287
   Iambi ad Seleucum, 321
   Pater si possible est, 322
ampullae (pilgrims' flasks), and *tholos* image in Eusebian Canon Tables, 497
Amsler, Mark, 405
Ananias (Hanan), 120
Anastasius (emperor), 623
Anastasius of Sinai, 354
anathemas, conciliar, 229, 230, 235

anathemas, creedal, 221, 228, 231, 236–44
Anaxagoras, 201, 206, 209, 215
Anaximander, 201, 214
Anaximenes, 201, 206
Ando, Clifford, 254
Andrade, Nathanael, 123
Andreas (Christian harper), 309
angels, Bede on, 740
animals, and divination, 141, 438
Annas, Julia, 569
Anselm of Laon, 720
Antioch, creed associated with, 228, 232, 238–40
Antioch, Dedication Council of (341), 232, 237, 240
antirrhetic *meletē*, 73
Antisthenes, 351
antithetical construction, 286
Aphrahat, 271
Aphrodito papyri, 622, 624
Apion family, 621
Apollinarius, 375, 639, 640, 641
Apostles' Creed, 222, 224
Apostolic Constitutions, 225
Apuleius
   Augustine and, 436, 437
   De deo Socratis, 437
   demonology of, 437
Aquileia, Council of, 388
Aquino, Frederick, 40
Aratus, 366
   Phaenomena, 132
Arentzen, Thomas, 565
Aristides, 385
Aristobulus, 110
Aristocles, 207
Aristotle
   Categories, 572, 667
   Homeric Problems, 108
   Protrepticus, 455
   Topics, 671
Aristotle and Aristotelianism
   asceticism in, 69
   Athenagoras on, 205
   Boethius on ordering of Aristotelian corpus, 684–86
   Celsus and, 139
   classification of Aristotelian corpus, 672
   Cyril on, 215
   on divination, 137, 141, 146, 148
   on language, 410

Aristotle and Aristotelianism (cont.)
  ordering of philosophical knowledge by
    commentators on, 8
  Origen and, 139, 141
  on passions/emotions, 531
  rhetoric, as branch of dialectic of, 671
  translation of Aristotle through
    commentary tradition, 9
  vision, theory of, 476
  on wisdom, 98
arithmetic. *See* quadrivium
Arius and Arians, 19, 246–60
  agency of Arius in Alexandria, 251
  anathematisation of, at Nicaea, 229
  basilica crisis (386), 392
  creeds, 223, 225, 232, 240
  De sectis on, 631, 641
  on divine nature, 253, 256
  Great Persecution, as consequence of,
    246, 249
  imperially sponsored tolerance,
    adjustment to, 247
  lived religion in Alexandria and, 250–56
  Lombards, as Arians, 695
  material culture of, 252
  material images, nature of, 254
  monotheism and image in texts of, 248,
    249
  mutability and images, problem of,
    256–60
  on visuality and divine nature, 254
Arius Didymus, 207, 535
Arnold, Sir Edwin, 373
Ascension of Isaiah, 252
asceticism. *See also* Evagrius of Pontus, on
    λύπη; Philoxenos of Mabbug,
    on gluttony
  contemplation and, 656
  contemplative life, 655–61
  Ephrem the Syrian and, 271–74
  godlikeness and knowledge, Dorotheus of
    Gaza on, 571, 580–88
  Great Persecution shaping, 246
  health, medicine, and philosophy
    impacting, 56, 60
  Irenaeus' framework for, 66
  knowledge of God, as way towards, 528
  ordering of knowledge and, 8
  Platonic-Aristotelian pattern of, 69
  virginity, pre-monastic valuation of, 272
Asclepius
  Justin Martyr on Christ and, 51
  laudatory speeches offered to, 57

Aspasia (mistress of Pericles), 348, 350–52
Aspasius, 90, 160
Asterius of Amaseia
  creed of, 232
  homilies of, 285, 287, 297
astronomy/astrology. *See also* quadrivium
  Augustine's critique of, 426, 432–36
  Bardaisan and, 123, 125, 126
  tables, use of, 197
  taboos associated with practice of, 428
Atargatis (deity), 124, 130, 131
Athanasius of Alexandria
  Arian debates preserved by, 249
  Augustine and, 480
  Contra arianos, 257
  Contra gentes, 248, 258, 259
  on council of Jerusalem, 232
  De decretis, 231, 241
  De incarnatione, 248, 470
  De synodis, 228, 233, 234, 238, 240
  on image, vision, and materiality, 259
  Life of Anthony, 340, 439
  on *mimesis* and *theosis*, 257
Athanasius of Emesa, 619
Athenagoras, 49, 215
  Aëtian *Placita* and, 204–5
  An Embassy on Behalf of the Christians,
    204, 217
Atticus (T. Pomponius)
  Liber annalis, 196
  polemics on Aristotle, 207
Auden, W. H., 385
Augustine of Hippo
  on artistic works, 481
  Bede and, 719, 734, 741, 743, 748
  classical *paideia*, proper engagement
    with, 345
  Confessiones, 392, 407, 413, 433, 436, 443,
    473, 748
  Contra academicos, 443, 453, 460, 461
  Contra adversarium legis et prophetarum,
    412
  Contra Julianum, 422
  De beata vita, 443
  De civitate Dei (*City of God*), 434, 437, 479
  De divinatione daemonum, 437
  De doctrina christiana, 407, 434, 667, 710
  De Genesi ad litteram, 416, 748
  De magistro, 459
  De musica, 422
  De ordine, 347, 443, 457, 461, 666
  De trinitate, 476
  De vera religione, 459, 465

Gen. Man., 748
Genesis, on study of, 714
Haer., 747
on images, 6
Leg., 748
on liberal arts, 666
library resources available to, 709
on Lord's Prayer, 163
Manicheans, involvement with, 444, 667
mother Monica as character in dialogue of, 347
multiple interpretations, tendency to note, 716
official note-takers, use of, 347
Psalmus contra partem Donati, 401–2
Quaestiones evangeliorum, 747
in *Reference Bible*, 717
Response to Simplician, 480
Retractationes, 443
secular and exegetical knowledge, compatibility of, 714, 727
on spiritual seeing, 479–81
on spiritual senses, 29
The Teacher, 695
theory of sight, 475–79
Tract. ev. Jo., 747
on vision, as mode of knowing, 473–83
Wigbod's *Commentary on Genesis* and, 713
Augustine of Hippo, Cassiciacum dialogues, 14, 443–65
on aerial beings, 436
authority and reason, on relationship between, 443
defining authority and reason, 445–48
education and pedagogy, priorities of authority and reason in, 453–54
epistemology of, 444
fortuna in, 449
on ideal liberal arts curriculum, 457–61
on integration of authority and reason, 461–63
interrelated nature of *duplex via* of authority and reason, 448–53
location and dating of, 443
modern scholarship on, 443, 448
on moral purification, 455–57
Nicaea, appealing to, 463
pedagogical christology in, 459
Augustine of Hippo, on language, 14, 404–25
ambivalence of Augustine's relationship with language, 407
christological view of, 416–21
creation of world from formless matter, 412–16
John the Baptist and Christ, as voice and word, 408–12
on *jubilus* or belch, 415
meaning, words versus sound as means of conveying, 404–8
music, hymns, and singing, 421–24
theological significance of affective interjections, 406
Augustine of Hippo, on pagan divination, 14, 426–42
astrological divination, critique of, 426, 432–36
Cicero, influence of, 435, 438, 441
deceit and trickery, divination's dependence on, 440
demonic divination, critique of, 426, 436–40
on divination, 138
earlier critiques of astrology influencing, 428–32
limits of human autopsy as basis for critique, 427, 437, 440
mischaracterisations of opponents, 428
modern scholars on, 427
Augustinus Hibernicus, 716, 719, 721, 722, 726
Ausonius of Bordeaux, 379–85, 387
Christian identity of, 379
Cupido cruciatuis (Cupid Crucified), 380–85, 387
Gryphus Ternarii Numeri, 379
Paschal Verses, 379
authority, faith, and reason. *See* Augustine of Hippo, Cassiciacum dialogues
authority, in late antique scholarship, 706, 720, 727
Averroes, 671
Ayres, Lewis, x, 1, 246, 457, 463

Bakirtzis, Charalambos, 495
Baltzly, Dirk, 569–71
Bandmann, Günter, 497
baptism
Ambrose of Milan on Christ's baptism, 393–94
Amphilocius of Iconium on, 322
biblical narratives as types for, 316, 326
circumcision as biblical typology for, 316
creeds and, 232
Cyprian on, 154
homilies on, 289

baptism (cont.)
  Romanos the Melodist, liturgical hymns of, 562
  spiritual senses and, 30–34
Bar Jamma, 128
Bardaisan, *Book of the Laws of the Countries*, 9, 118–33
  Christianity of, 125, 127
  contents of, 122–25
  as ethnography, 123
  on free will/determinism, 123, 125, 127–32
  life of Bardaisan, 119, 120
  metaphysics of, 125, 133
  public archive of Edessa, 120
  purpose of structure of, 132–33
  Roman takeover of Osrhoene and Edessa, 119
  writings of Bardaisan, 121
Bardy, Gustave, 108
Barlaam and Joasaph, 132
Barnes, Timothy, 257
Barsanuphius and John (hermits), 616
Barsanuphius of Gaza, 547
Basil of Ancyra, 241
Basil of Caesarea
  Address to the Young, 328, 341
  anathemas collected by, 236
  astrology, critique of, 430, 442
  Bede and, 748
  canons collected by, 235
  Canterbury school commentaries and, 720
  classical *paideia*, proper engagement with, 328, 343, 345, 375
  death of, Gregory of Nyssa's dialogue with Macrina on, 361
  On Detachment, 300
  Eighth Homily on the Hexaemeron, 299
  Epistles, 241
  Gregory of Nyssa on, 328, 334, 337, 341
  Hexaemeron, 430, 648, 748
  Homilia in illud: Attende tibi ipsi, 658
  homilies of, 287
  Homily on Gordius, 289
  Homily on Julitta, 297
  Homily on Mamas, 298
  Homily on Psalm 114, 297
  on Nicene Creed as test of orthodoxy, 241
  Quod rebus mundanis adhaerendum non sit, 300
  secular and exegetical knowledge, compatibility of, 714
  on self-knowledge, 658
  on vision, as mode of knowing, 473

basilica crisis (386), 392
Baumstark, Anton, 264, 266
Beck, Edmund, 261, 264, 267–78, 281
Bede, 19, 729–51
  accused of heresy for recalculating date of the world, 707
  as both scientific and theological scholar, 709
  In cantica canticorum allegorica expositio, 712, 747
  De natura rerum, 715, 717
  De temporibus, 715
  De temporum ratione, 715
  in epistulas catholicas septem, 735
  Expositio Apocalypseos, 747
  In Genesim, 713, 718, 735, 747, 748
  Historia ecclesiastica gens Anglorum, 730, 733
  inequality regime, acceptance of/ expectations for, 749–51
  Letter to Plegwin, 707
  library at Wearmouth-Jarrow available to, 731, 748
  life, career, and context, 730–34
  In Lucam, 733, 742, 747
  on multiple authoritative opinions, 716
  multiple Latin versions of Bible, knowledge of, 733
  observational evidence, use of, 724–26
  ordering of knowledge by, 729
  on pain, 734–37
  on poverty, 742–45
  preachers and teachers, focus on, 745–49
  on taste, 739
  on temporal and spiritual pleasure, 737–41
Benedict Biscop, 730, 731, 736, 742, 749
Bernard of Clairvaux, 40
Bernhard Neuschäfer, 100
Berosus, 200
Bible. *See also* Origen, biblical exegesis of; Septuagint
  access of fourth-century readers to New Testament, 372
  Bede's knowledge of multiple Latin versions of, 733
  catechumenate and, 161
  creation and the created world, exegetical resources for studying, 708–12, 714
  Cyprian's *Ad Quirinum*, summarising divine truths of, 156–62
  Evagrius of Pontus, on λύπη, intertwining biblical and philosophical language, 542

flora and fauna mentioned in scripture, guides to, 712
Genesis, reserved for advanced scholars, 651, 714
gospel-books in late antiquity, 485
Gregory the Great, ordering of exegetical knowledge by, 692–94
homiletic use of, 287–91
memorisation of scriptures, Cyprian on, 159–60
modelling Christian life on characters from, 162, 288
Origen's text-critical approach to, in *Hexapla*, 196
prophets and prophecy in, 141, 142
rain before the flood, interest in question of, 720, 726
resolution of discord between ancient non-Christian authors and, 715
sacred and secular disciplines used to study, 711
secular and exegetical knowledge, compatibility of, 714
on seeing God, 468
shaping thought and practice of Christians, 165
biblical narratives, 14, 303–27
baptism, biblical types for, 316, 326
dissemination, means of, 303
homilies, dissemination through, 303, 315, 316, 321–25
inscriptions alluding to/citing, 19, 304–7
ekphrasis, 312–17
ekphrasis, use of, 326
Jonah and the Son of Man, 319
liturgical phrases, 309
liturgical phrases, use of, 325
paradisiac peace from Isaiah, 319
sermons of Amphilocius of Iconium and, 323
in south-east Phrygia, 307–8
symbols, use of, 310
in Thessaly, 308–18
trisagion from Isaiah and lamb from Revelation, combination of, 317
widespread use of, 317
naming as means of disseminating, 325
Bibliotheca symbolica (Walch), 222
Bibliothek der Symbole und Glaubensregeln der apostolisch-katholischen Kirche (Hahn), 222
bilingual texts and tablular organisation, 191–97

bishops, creeds for, 227, 245
Blowers, Paul M., 15, 644
body. *See* embodiment
Boersma, Gerald, 14, 443
Boethius
Aristotle's *Categories*, commentary on, 667, 673
Carmen bucolicum (now lost), 670
Christian university and library, plans for founding, 686
De consolatione philosophiae 22–27, 678
Progelomena influencing, 572
Boethius, on ordering of knowledge, 8, 663–89
basic knowledge of citizens, concerns about, 667–68
Cassiodorus' *Institutiones*, taxonomy of philosophy in, 686–89
Cicero's *Topics*, commentary on, 671
Consolatio, 677, 679, 681–84
De divisione, 671
De interpretatione commentaries, 684
De ordine Peripateticae disciplina, on ordering of Aristotelian corpus, 684–86
De topicis differentiis, 670
De trinitate, 677, 679, 684
first *Isagoge* commentary, 677, 678, 680, 682, 684
Institutio arithmetica, 664, 673, 676, 679, 680
Institutio musica, 676, 679, 680
Martianus Capella compared, 663
philosophy, taxonomic ordering of, 677–84
priority of knowables to knowledge, 667–68
quadrivium (mathematical sciences), 673–77
second *Isagoge* commentary, 672, 677, 684
seven liberal arts, closed system of, 663–67
trivium (grammar, rhetoric, logic), 668–73
Bonaventure, on spiritual senses, 29
Bond, Sarah, 615
book culture in late antiquity, 306, 366
The Book of Pictures, 252
Bourdieu, Pierre, 12, 170
Bradshaw, Paul, 155
Brent, Allen, 171, 174
Breytenbach, Cilliers, 14, 19, 303
Britten, Benjamin, 385
Brock, Sebastian, 191, 279
Brooks, Thomas, 37
Brown, Peter, 278

Brunhilde (Frankish queen), 700
bubonic plague, 613, 736
bureaucratic modes of knowing, 18, 590–607
    defined, 590
    lists of offices compared to Proclus' divine bureaucracy, 598–603
    metaphysical and political regimes of, 591, 593–95
    Neoplatonism and, 592
    remoteness, rule of, 603–4
    texts making use of, 590
    totalising systems and, 593
Burgess, R., 189
Burkitt, Francis, 265
Burns, A. E., 223

Caecilianus, 160
Calcidius, commentary on *Timaeus*, 665
Callimachus, 368
Cameron, Averil, 153, 501, 591, 644, 655
Canterbury school, 720, 732
Carneades, 123
Carr, D. M., 159
Carruthers, Mary, 485
Cary, Philip, 457
Cassiodorus
    Boethius and, 675, 686
    Expositio in Psalmos, 711
    Institutiones, 677, 686, 688, 711
    ordering of knowledge and, 8
    philosophy, taxonomy of, 686–89
    reserving study of Genesis for advanced students, 714
    secular and exegetical knowledge, compatibility of, 715
castration, 52, 124
Catacomb of Saints Marcellinus and Peter, baptismal fresco, 34
catechumenate. *See also* Cyprian of Carthage, *testimonia* collections of
    biblical narratives, dissemination of, 303
    creeds for, 227, 245
    goal of, 164
    in North Africa, 160
    Origen and, 102
    structures for transmitting knowledge via, 160–62
Cato, 80
Catullus, 368, 375
Cavarero, Adriana, 414
Celsus, on divination, 139
Ceolfrith (abbot of Wearmouth-Jarrow), 731
Chadwick, Henry, 22

Chalcedon, Council of (451)
    canons of, 235
    christological debates at, 626
    christological handbooks and, 638
    De sectis on, 632, 634
    Leontius of Jerusalem on, 633, 634, 636
    Nicaea, christological handbooks drawing parallels with, 638
    Pamphilus on, 628, 634, 636
    Philoxenos of Mabbug and, 516
    Theodore of Raithou on, 630
Chalcedonians, 626
Chaldean Oracles, 601
Champion, Michael, x, 1, 8, 569
Charlemagne, 713
Childebert II (Frankish king), 700
Chin, C. M., 3, 691, 703
Chlup, R., 597, 604
Choufrine, A., 32
Christ
    Agbar of Edessa, correspondence with, 120
    antirrhetic *meletē* and temptation of, 73
    Asclepius compared, 51
    Augustine on language and, 408–12
    pagan memorial statue of, in Caesarea Philippi, 248
    politeia of, 654
    poverty of, Bede on, 742
    universal sovereignty of, 655, 662
    visible incarnation of, as image and word, 467–68, 470
Christianity
    divination and prophecy, influence on thought about, 134
    exclusivity of ritual practice sought by, 177
    Justinianic legal reforms and, 613–16
    prolegomena to philosophy and, 573
    relationship to world, 755
    transformation of lives as goal of, 153
Christianity and the Rhetoric of Empire (Cameron), 644
Christianity and the Transformation of the Book (Grafton and Williams), 185
Christodorus, *On the Disciples of the Great Proclus*, 594
christological handbooks, 11, 626–43
    controversies over christological positions and, 626–27
    counter-arguments, providing arsenal of, 633–39
    De sectis, 627, 630–32, 634–36, 638, 641–43
    didactic character and audience, 627

history of heresies presented by, 639–43
Leontius of Jerusalem, *Contra Monophysitas*, 627, 632–35, 637, 638
Pamphilus, *Capita diversa*, 627–29, 633, 636, 638
syllogisms in, 635
Theodore of Raithou, *Praeparatio*, 627, 629–30, 639–41
christology
Augustine on language and, 416–21
Augustine's pedagogical christology, 459
debates and controversies over, 626–27, 645, 647
Philoxenos of Mabbug on gluttony and, 525
Chronicle of Edessa to 540, 120
chronography, as genre, 645
Chrysippus, 110, 535
church
alienated land, right to sue for, 620
amount of land held by, 750
clerical legal officers within, 617
papal knowledge, nature of, 702
Chwe, Michael, 166, 168
Cicero
astrology, critique of, 429, 435
Augustine on authority/reason and, 445, 455
Augustine's critique of astrology and, 435, 441
Augustine's critique of demons and, 438
bilingual texts of, 192
Counsels (now lost), 424
De divinatione, 429, 435, 438, 441
De fato 1, 673
Hortensius, 455
liberal arts and, 665
Topica 6, 671, 672
Cipriani, Nello, 463
circumcision
baptism, as typology for, 316
Gregory of Nyssa on, 343
Clarke, Graeme, 160, 180
cledonomancy, 140
Clement of Alexandria
contemplation of nature by, 648
divination and, 138
John the Evangelist and, 42
material images and, 255
Paedagogus, 92, 97, 99
Protrepticus, 92
spiritual senses for, 5, 30–34
Stromateis, 92, 97, 98

Clement of Alexandria, order of education and knowledge in, 8, 89–99
adaptation of EPHE scheme to programme of Christian instruction, 93–95
EPHE scheme, familiarity with, 90–92
order of knowledge differing from order of education, 96–98
physics, 96
programme of Christian education central to, 92, 98
theology, 96
virtues of truth, treatment of, 95–96
Clovis (king of the Franks), 676
Coakley, Sarah, 24, 25, 27, 45, 360
codex, innovation of, 305, 485, 498, 515
Codex Theodosianus, 615, 616
Colish, Marcia, 392
Collectanea Antiariana Parisina, 234
coloni adscriptici, 621, 623
colour, discourse and language of, 755
columnar tables. *See* tables and tabular organisation
Commemoratio Geneseos, 726
concreation, 412
confession, Dorotheus of Gaza on, 587
Congar, Yves, 245
conscience, concept of, 586
Constans (emperor), 238
Constantina (empress), 697, 698, 700
Constantine, *Coet. sanct.* 19–21, 377
Constantine I the Great (emperor), 231, 259, 371, 377, 492, 496, 500
Oration to the Saints, 372
Constantinople
culture of political debate in, 609
Hagia Sophia, collapse and repair of, 610
Constantinople, Council of (381)
anathemas, collection of, 236
canons of, 235, 243
creeds, evolution of, 224, 242
Constantinople, Council of (553), 629, 701
Constantius II (emperor), 234, 240
contemplation, George of Pisidia and Maximus the Confessor on, 655–61
Coogan, Jeremiah, 372
Cosmas Indicopleustes, *Christian Topography*, 132
cosmologies of George of Pisidia and Maximus the Confessor, 15, 644–62
contemplation, 655–61

cosmologies of George (cont.)
  cosmopolitan visionaries, George and Maximus as, 648–55
  instabilities of late antiquity and, 645, 655
  life and career of George of Pisidia, 646
  life and career of Maximus the Confessor, 647
  Platonic *theoria*, resorting to, 645, 648
  rhetoric of empire, framing and sustaining, 644–46
  self-knowledge, importance of, 658
  teleo-cosmology, articulation of, 661
  unity of creation, empire, and ecclesia, 645
Crawford, Matthew R., x, 1, 6, 19, 190, 484
creatio ex nihilo, Arian emphasis on, 248, 250
creation and the created world, 15, 705–28
  Augustine, on creation of world from formless matter, 412–16
  authority in late antique scholarship and knowledge of, 706, 720, 727
  cosmopolitan visionaries (*theoroi*), George and Maximus as, 648–55, 661
  innovation and derivativeness, issues of, 705–8, 726
  new works and genres, late antique and early medieval production of, 712–26
  observation of, 723–26
  questions posed by late antique authors about, 726
  rain before the flood, interest in question of, 720, 726
  reasoning through problems of, 721
  resolution of discord between ancient non-Christian authors and scripture, 715
  resources for studying, 708–12
  scientific and theological knowledge used to apprehend, 705–6, 709
creeds, 10, 221–45
  anathemas as part of, 221, 227, 228, 231, 236–44
  anthologies or libraries of, 221–28
  Antiochene creed, 228, 238
  Apostles' Creed, 222, 224
  Asterius', 232
  authoritative status of Nicaea, 240
  for catechumenate versus bishops, 227, 245
  collection of, 234–36
  Dated Creed, 233
  disciplinary canons compared, 228–36, 240
  Eunomianism and, 224
  internal frame, 227
  lost 'O' text, efforts to reconstruct, 223, 224
  Macrostich Creed, 237
  Nicene anathema, 236–44
  Nicene-Constantinopolitan Creed, 242
  Nicene Creed, 223, 224, 227, 233
  Nicene profession, 236
  ordering of knowledge regarding, 227
  procedures for producing, 228–32
  profession of faith, 227
  publication of, 233–34
  Roman Creed, 224
  Second Creed, Dedication Council of Antioch, 232, 239, 240
  signatures, 227, 233
  Sirmium, Creed of First Synod of, 237, 239
  Theophronius', 232
  Third Creed, Dedication Council of Antioch, 237
  typology of, 223, 225, 226
  variations of form in, 223
Crescens, 61
Crislip, Andrew, 530
cultural production, concept of, 170
Cyprian of Carthage
  Ad Donatum, 154
  De dominica oratione, 162
  De lapsis, 171–77, 182
  Felicissimus and, 175
  Gregory Nazianzen's festal sermon for, 299
  life of, 153, 154, 160
  Pontius, *Vita Cypriani*, 154
  on sacrifice, 171–83
  on use of water versus wine at Eucharist, 177–82
Cyprian of Carthage, *testimonia* collections of, 10, 153–65
  Ad Donatum, on process of conversion, 154–56, 165
  Ad Fortunatum, 162, 165
  Ad Quirinum, summarising divine truths, 154, 156–62, 165
  De dominica oratione, commenting on Lord's Prayer, 154, 162–165
  memorisation of scriptures, 159–60
  modelling Christian life on biblical figures, 162
  ordering of knowledge in, 156–59

scripture as means of shaping thought and practice of Christians in, 165
Cyril of Alexandria
    Aëtian *Placita* and, 214–16
    anathemas written by, 236
    christological debates of, 626, 635
    Contra Julianum, 214–16
    Second Letter to Nestorius, 243
    Third Letter to Nestorius, 243
Cyril of Jerusalem
    Catecheses, 243
    creed of, 242
Cyril of Scythopolis, 616

daemones. *See* demons
Damascius
    Problems and Solutions Concerning First Principles, 601, 606
Damasus (pope), 748
Dante Alighieri, 678
Dated Creed, 233
David, prolegomena of, 572, 574, 578
De cursu stellarum, 723
de Lange, Nicholas, 616
De mirabilibus sacrae scripturae, 719
De ordine creaturarum, 705, 716
De sectis, 627, 630–32, 634–36, 638, 641–43
De Vegvar, C. N., 493
death
    Evagrius of Pontus, on λύπη, 544
    female characters in dialogues on, 349, 352
    gluttony linked to, 520
    Justin Martyr's focus on Christian approach to, 53
Decian decree of universal sacrifice (Decian persecution), 172–78, 183
Decius (emperor), 164, 172
declarative creeds. *See* creeds
DelCogliano, Mark, 238
Delphi, oracle at, 135, 141, 142, 145
Democritus, 209, 214
demons
    Augustine on demonic divination, 427, 436–40
    Evagrius of Pontus, on λύπη, 538, 539
    Iamblichus on, 149
    Origen on, 139
    in Platonism, 140
    Tatian on, 57, 59, 60
Denzinger, Heinrich, 222, 224, 245
derivativeness and innovation in late antiquity, 705–8, 726

determinism/free will, Bardaisan on, 123, 125, 127–32
dialectic
    Boethius on study of, 672
    rhetoric described by Boethius as branch of, 670
dialogue genre. *See* female characters in dialogues
Dialogue on Political Science, 591, 593, 604
Diatessaron
    Ammonius, 190
    Tatian, 265, 367, 373
Dickey, Eleanor, 192, 193
Diels, Herman, 198
Dillon, John, 27, 104, 106
Diodore of Tarsus, 641
Diodorus Siculus, 211
Diogenes Laertius, 533, 534, 536
Diogenes the Cynic, 58, 435
Diomedes (grammarian), 405
Dionysius Periegetes, 132
Diotima (priestess), 350–52, 358
disciplinary canons, creeds compared, 228–36, 240
discourse, 13, 16
distress. *See* Evagrius of Pontus, on λύπη
divination and prophecy, 134–52. *See also* Augustine of Hippo, on pagan divination
    Christian influences on, 134
    defined, 135
    in Greek and Roman thought, 135–38
    Iamblichus on, 143–52
    as mode of knowing, 5, 137
    Origen on, 138–43, 151
    theurgy and, 144
dixit-placet, 233
Dobell, Brian, 443, 448
Doctrina Addai, 120, 121
Doctrina Patrum, 627, 630
Dolar, Mladen, 406, 413, 415
Domenica (daughter of count Narses), 699
Donatists
    Augustine's misrepresentations of, 428
    Augustine's *Psalmus contra partem Donati*, 401–2
Donatus (grammarian), on sound versus words, 404–6, 410, 414
Dorotheus of Gaza
    on confession, 587
    Didaskaliai, 571, 581
    epistemological assumptions of, 8
    humility, importance of, 581–84, 586, 589

Dorotheus of Gaza (cont.)
  on godlikeness as goal of philosophy, 571, 580–88
  ignorance, self-deception, and error, radical concern about, 586
Doxographi graeci (Diels), 198
doxographies, 198–99
Drijvers, H. J. W., 129, 130
du Roy, Olivier, 443, 448
Dunkle, Brian, 7, 388, 418, 517, 529

Early Christian Creeds (Kelly), 224
Ecgfrith (king of Northumbria), 730
education and pedagogy. *See also* Gregory of Nyssa, pedagogy of; *paideia*
  Augustine on priorities of authority and reason in, 453–54. *See also* Boethius, on ordering of knowledge
  Bede's focus on teachers and preachers, 745–49
  bilingual texts, tabular organisation of, 191–97
  book culture in late antiquity and, 366
  Christian repurposing of, 709, 710, 714
  exegetical guides, 710
  homilies, educational mission of, 114
  Irenaeus of Lyons, ascetic training of, 66
  Julian's interdict on Christian teaching of pagan literature, 339, 374
  law schools in Justinianic era, 617
  ordering schemes in, 7
  Origen's biblical exegesis shaped by educational institutions, 100–2
  sacred and secular disciplines, combining, 711
  seven liberal arts, development of closed system of, 663–67
  wisdom in, 98
Edward VI (king of England), 224
Edwards, Mark, 14, 366
egkrateia, 69, 70
Ehlers, Barbara, 351
ekphrasis, 260, 501
  Eusebius on Constantine's building projects as, 501, 509
  in homilies, 286
  inscriptions disseminating biblical narratives, 312–17, 326
Elagabalus (emperor), 121, 122
'Elegy in a Country Churchyard' (Gray), 384
Elias, prolegomena of, 572, 576, 584
Elsner, Jaś, 254, 498, 513
Elysian mysteries, 303

embodiment
  female characters in dialogues on, 349, 364
  Gregory the Great's theology of the body, 693
  Irenaeus' physics of, 81
  pain and suffering, Bede on experience of, 734–37
  pleasure, temporal and spiritual, Bede on, 737–41
Emerton, J., 194
emotional knowledge, Gregory the Great on, 694–96
emotions. *See* passions
Empedocles, on vision, 475
Enchiridion symbolorum et definitionum (Denzinger), 222
Ennodius, *Paraenesis didascalica*, 664
Eosterwine (abbot of Jarrow), 736
EPHE educational scheme (ethics, physics, and epoptics)
  familiarity of Clement and Origen with, 90–92
Ephesus, Council of (431), 216, 626
Ephrem the Syrian, 15
  asceticism and, 271–74
  authorship and authenticity, questions about, 261–62, 268–69, 272, 278
  Bardaisan and, 121, 126, 127, 129
  Beck on, 261, 264, 267–78, 281
  biographical and literary traditions about, 262–64
  Christian discourse, role in framing and expanding, 644
  Commentary on Genesis, 270
  eschatology of, 274
  'On the fear of God and the end', 275
  fragmentary works, study of, 279
  historical frameworks constructed by Beck around, 276
  historical references in work attributed to, 263
  historiography of scholarship on, 264–67
  Hymns against Heresies, 121
  on gluttony of Sheol, 521
  'On the Ihidaye and Desert Dwellers', 269
  internal canon, Beck's development of, 270–71
  literary genius, constructed by Beck as, 276
  Madrasha on the Church, 263
  Madrashe on Abraham Qidunaya, 261, 276
  Madrashe on Faith, 275
  Madrashe on Julian Saba, 275
  Madrashe on Paradise, 270

Memra on the End, 263
Memra on the Ihidaye and the Mourners, 272
metres and melodies of, 279
modern Western reception of, 264–67
Peshitta and, 265
Philoxenos on, 265, 266
post-Beck scholarship on, 278
Prose Refutations, 121, 270
'On Repentance', 276, 280
'On Reproof', 270, 277
sanctity, poetics of, 275
'On the Sinful Woman', 277
'On Solitaries and Mourners', 276
stylistic analysis of, 269–70
'On the Word which Qohelet Spoke', 275, 277
works ascribed to authors other than Ephrem, 280
Epicureans
  Boethius on, 677
  Hermias on, 206
  psychological holism of, 82
Epiphanius of Salamis
  Ancoratus, 242
  on Bardaisan, 121
  on Nicene Creed, 242
epistemology in late antique world, 1–2, 752–57
  architectural imagery, as mode of knowing, 512–15
  continuities in historical development of, 753
  discourse and, 13
  doing and being, modes of knowing as modes of, 752
  innovation and derivativeness in late antiquity, 705–8, 726
  institutions and, 16–18
  Irenaeus and, 81
  materiality and, 18–20
  modes of, 5–7
  Newman's real assent, 388
  ordering, 7–11
  significance of, 1–5, 753–57
  structures of, 11–13
eschatology
  Bede and, 740
  Ephrem the Syrian and, 274
Eucharist
  comparability to sacrifice in late antique world, 169, 170
  Cyprian on, 171
  gluttony, as remedy for, 517, 527
  morning versus evening rituals, 178

pagan theurgy, influence of, 134
Romanos the Melodist, liturgical hymns of, 556, 559, 562
use of water versus wine for, Cyprian's *Ep.* 63 on, 177–82
Euclid's *Elements*, 595, 676
Eulogius (patriarch of Alexandria), 631
Eunomianism, and creeds, 224
Euripides, 752
Eusebius of Caesarea. *See also tholos* image in Eusebian Canon Tables
  Aëtian *Placita* and, 207–11
  Canon Tables, 185, 187, 189, 190, 196, 484
  Chronicle, 185, 189
  Church History, 231, 234, 248
  creed of, 223
  Cyril's familiarity with, 214
  De laudibus Constantini, 500
  Demonstratio evangelica, 247
  Edessa, access to archive at, 120
  gospel portraits of, 490
  Great Persecution shaping theology of, 246
  Letter to Carpianus, 186, 190, 492, 498
  Letter to Constantia, 248
  Letter to His Diocese, 231, 236
  Life of Constantine, 231, 500
  Martyrs of Palestine, 248
  material images, on, 255
  imperial history, composition of, 645
  Onomasticon, 313
  Origen and, 100, 102, 104
  Pinax of the Psalms, 185, 187
  Praeparatio evangelica, 207–11, 218, 247, 258
  tables, use of, 10, 185, 186, 189, 190
  Tyre, dedication of Paulinus' church at, 502–12
Eusebius of Nicomedia, 230, 231, 247, 248, 253
Eustathius of Antioch, 230, 231, 233, 255
Eustathius of Sebasteia, 241
Eutocus, 572
Eutychianism
  De sectis on, 632, 635
  Theodore of Raithou on, 640
Euzoius (Homoian bishop of Antioch), 234
Evagrius of Pontus
  Antirrhētikos, 520
  De malignis cogitationibus 25, 537

Evagrius of Pontus (cont.)
  gluttony and, 517, 519
  Philoxenos influenced by, 519
Evagrius of Pontus, on λύπη, 19, 530–47
  affective lexica, passion lists creating, 531, 536, 541
  Antirrhêtikos, 538, 545
  behavioural scripts, passion lists generating, 531, 544
  biblical and philosophical language, intertwining, 542
  Christian passion lists, 536, 545
  complex/multivalent analysis of, 537–40, 546
  De malignis cogitationibus, 538
  distress/grief/mourning, defining and characterising, 530
  eight thoughts of wickedness, 536
  On the Eight Wicked Spirits, 537, 541
  To Eulogius, 537, 540
  godly or beneficial λύπη, 542–46
  Hellenistic lists of passions/emotions, λύπη in, 531–36
  influence of, 546
  metaphorical lexica, development of, 541–42, 545
  physiological and psychological dimensions of, 540
  Praktikos, 538, 540
  vice and virtue, bifurcation of λύπη as, 530, 546
  On the Vices in Opposition to the Virtues, 541, 542, 545
Evagrius Scholasticus, 609, 616
exegesis. *See* Bible
eyesight. *See* vision, as mode of knowing

faenus ('interest'), Prudentius' use of, 377
Fagerberg, David, 283
faith
  authority and reason, relationship between. *See* Augustine of Hippo, Cassiciacum dialogues
  doxographical tradition and concept of, 218
  Irenaeus on action arising from, 82
Faith in Formulae (Kinzig), 225
Felicissimus, 175
Felix (martyr), 390
female characters in dialogues, 14, 347–65
  Augustine's *De ordine*, 347
  body, women as experts on, 349, 364
  Christian innovation of, 348, 349, 353

  classical philosophical dialogues, 348, 350–53
  Gregory of Nyssa using, 348
  Gregory of Nyssa, *De anima* (*On the Soul and the Resurrection*), 354, 358–64
  late imperial Christian dialogues, 353–55
  Methodius of Olympus using, 348
  Plato's *Phaedo* and Gregory's *De anima*, 358–60, 364
  segregation versus mixing of genders, 358
  Methodius, *Symposium*, 354–58
feminist theory, 166
Ferguson, Everett, 156
Ferrara-Florence, Council of (1438–45), 222
Ficino, Marsilio, 145
Firmicus Maternus, 372, 377
Firminus (friend of Augustine), 432
First Commentary on the Pentateuch (Canterbury school)
  33, 720
  65, 720
  83–84, 721
Florus of Lyons, 747
For More Than One Voice (Cavarero), 414
Foucault, Michel, 3, 690, 729
Foxhall Forbes, Helen, 15, 705
Frank, Georgia, 512
free will/determinism, Bardaisan on, 123, 125, 127–32
Frevert, Ute, 530

Gador-Whyte, Sarah, 7, 19, 548
Gaianites, 632
Galen, 48, 53, 58, 64, 115, 211, 534–36, 547
  De Methodo Medendi
    10.2, 534
Gassman, Mattias, 156
Gavrilyuk, Paul, 24, 25, 27, 34, 45
Geertz, Clifford, 16, 168
gender. *See also* female characters in dialogues; women
  Gregory the Great's engagement with women of influence, 691, 696–702
  Holy Spirit, Syriac shift from feminine to masculine term for, 268
  philosophy, as male activity, 348
  Pythagoreans, female members of, 348
geometry. *See* quadrivium
George Cedrenus, 493
George of Pisidia. *See also* cosmologies of George of Pisidia and Maximus the Confessor
  De expeditione Persica, 650

Heraclias, 650, 652
Hexaemeron, 647, 650, 651
On Human Life, 656
life and career, 646
On the Vanity of Life, 656
George the Monk, 629
Gerbert of Aurillac, 677
Gervasius (martyr), 390
Geschichte der syrischen Literatur (Baumstark), 266
Gibbon, Edward, 385
Giddens, Anthony, 12
gift economy, 702
Gill, C., 82
Girard, Rene, 166
Glossa Ordinaria, 720
gluttony. *See also* Philoxenos of Mabbug, on gluttony
  Adam and Eve linked to, 518
  death, linked to, 520
  defined, 520
  Evagrius on, 517
  medical and philosophical writings on, 58
Godescalc Gospel Lectionary, 486
godlikeness and the ordering of knowledge, 569–89
  comparison of Dorotheus and Prolegomena, 588–89
  concept of the divine, 579, 583
  in Dorotheus of Gaza's asceticism, 571, 580–88
  Plato on goal of philosophy to become like god, 569–71
  in *Prolegomena to Philosophy*, 571–80
Goldhill, Simon, 356
good, Irenaeus of Lyons on choosing, 79–81
Gordia (sister of emperor Maurice), 699
gospel-books in late antiquity, 485
Gospel of Mary, 43
Gospel of Thomas, 43
Gospel of Truth
  as baptismal homily, 34
  spiritual senses, doctrine of, 36
Grafton, Anthony, 185, 189, 190, 196
grammar, Boethius on study of, 668–70
A Grammar of Assent (Newman), 388
Gratian (emperor), 379
Graumann, Thomas, 390
Gray, Thomas, 'Elegy in a Country Churchyard', 384
Great Persecution, 246, 249, 260, 503
Green, Roger, 367, 370, 381

Gregoria (court lady of empress Constantina), 699
Gregory I the Great (pope), 14, 690–704
  commentaries by Gregory, 691
  coupling of intellectual and spiritual knowledge, 690
  Dialogues in Four Books (hagiography collection), 691, 694, 703
  emotional knowledge, 691, 694–96
  exegetical knowledge, ordering, 691–94
  homilies of, 691–93
  on Jews and Judaism, 701
  life and career, 690
  on limits of human knowledge, 693
  Moralia (Commentary on Job), 692–94, 747
  mutual influence of epistemography and praxis on, 691
  papal knowledge, nature of, 702
  Pastoral Rule, 691, 692, 694, 702
  Paterius, commentary on the Bible, 713
  power organisation in Roman empire, reflecting, 690, 703
  Registrum (letter collection), 691, 696–702
  on slaves and slavery, 702
  social order and tradition, 691, 696–702
  on spiritual senses, 29
  theology of the body, 693
  women of influence, engagement with, 691, 696–702
Gregory Nazianzen
  classical *paideia*, proper engagement with, 328
  on cosmic order, 649
  In laudem S. Cypriani, 299
  on Moses, 659
  mysteries of faith, 'honouring in silence', 651
  Oration in Praise of Cyprian, 299
Gregory of Nyssa
  To Ablabius, 244
  Against Eunomius, 333
  Against Those Who Deal with Rebukes Difficultly, 299
  On Ascension, 289
  Canonical Letter to Letoius, 235
  Catechetical Oration, 243
  Christmas Homily, 299
  creed of, 244
  De anima (On the Soul and the Resurrection), 328, 350, 354, 358–64
  De instituto Christiano, 331

Gregory of Nyssa (cont.)
　De pauperibus amandis I, 286
　De perfectione, 331, 332
　In diem luminum 235, 308
　ekphrasis on martyrium of St Theodore by, 506
　female characters in dialogues of, 348
　First Homily on Stephen the Protomartyr, 285
　First Homily on the Martyrs of Sebaste, 288, 299, 300
　Hexaemeron, 648
　Homilia in Canticum Canticorum, 659
　homilies of, 285, 287
　Homily on the Day of Lights, 289
　Life of Gregory Thaumaturgus, 328, 334, 336, 346
　Life of Macrina, 328, 360
　On the Making of Man, 473
　Methodius' *Symposium*, familiarity with, 354
　Moses as contemplative master, 659
　On Pentecost, 289
　The Person Who Commits Impurity Sins against His Own Body, 289
　on spiritual senses, 28
　on vision, as mode of knowing, 473
Gregory of Nyssa, pedagogy of, 15, 328–46
　allegory and negotiation of otherness, 330, 333
　on classical *paideia*, 328, 331, 334, 336, 338–45
　human perfection, theory of, 329, 331–33, 345
　Life of Moses, on Moses as paradigm of educated Christian, 328, 333–45
　morphosis at heart of, 330, 331
　otherness, negotiation of, 329, 346
Gregory of Tours, 723
Gregory Thaumaturgus
　Gregory of Nyssa on, 328, 336, 345, 346
　Panegyric, 104
grief. See Evagrius of Pontus, on λύπη
Grigoryan, Gohar, 497
Guiliano, Zachary, 19, 729
Gundobad (Burgundian ruler), 676
Gurya (martyr), 263

habituation, ethical virtues inculcated through, 576
Hadot, Ilsetraut, 666
Hadot, Pierre, 3, 90, 98, 99, 111, 112

Hadrian (abbot, Canterbury), 720, 732
Hagia Sophia, Constantinople, collapse and repair of, 610
hagiography
　Gregory the Great's *Dialogues in Four Books*, 691, 694, 703
　Philoxenos of Mabbug on gluttony as inverted hagiographic narrative, 521–27
Hahn, August, 222, 224
Hall, S., 501
Hanaghan, Michael, 14, 426
Hanan (Ananias), 120
hapax legomena, 269
Harl, Marguerite, 255
Harmless, W., 164
Harmonia Symbolica (Heurtley), 222
Harper, Kyle, 608
Harrison, Carol, 13, 19, 404, 449, 457
Hartung, Blake, 279
Hauerwas, Stanley, 167
Havrda, Matyáš, 8, 89
Hawley, Richard, 365
health, medicine, and philosophy in School of Justin Martyr, 47–65
　Christian engagement with medicine, 48
　competition between pagan philosophers and physicians, 47–48
　death, Justin's focus on Christian approach to, 53
　defining 'School of Justin Martyr', 49
　Justin's self-presentation as philosopher and, 49, 50–56
　Pseudo-Justin, 49, 61–64
　Tatian, 49, 56–61
Heath, Jane, 5, 21
Henry, Madeleine, 348
Heraclas, 103
Heraclianus of Chalcedon, 626
Heraclitus, 58, 108, 110
Heraclius (emperor), 645–47, 652, 653, 662
heresies. See also *specific heresies*
　Bede accused of heresy for recalculating date of world, 707
　christological handbooks presenting histories of, 639–43
Hermias
　Aëtian *Placita* and, 205–6
　Ridicule of the Outside Philosophers, 205
Herodotus, 196
Herrero de Jáuregui, Miguel, 381
Hesiod, 110, 305
Hess, H., 233

Hester, K., 693
Hesychius, 535
Heurtley, Charles A., 222–24
Hieracas, 251
Hilary of Poitiers
　commentary on Matthew, 163
　De synodis, 234
　hymns compared to Ambrose of Milan, 400–2
Hill, Geoffrey, 385
Hippocratic corpus, 754
Hirsch-Luipold, Rainer, 41
History of Asceticism in the Syrian Orient (Vööbus), 267
Holl, Karl, 321
Holmes, Brooke, 48
holy fools, 523
Holy Sepulchre, Jerusalem
　celestial Jerusalem, viewed by Eusebius as, 503
　tholos image in Eusebian Canon Tables and, 486, 492, 496, 500–2
Holy Spirit, Syriac shift from feminine to masculine term for, 268
Homer
　on demons, 139
　in inscriptions, 305
　Irenaeus on the Homeric cento, 78
　Porphyry on cave of the nymphs in, 501, 513, 514
　problems and solutions in study of, 108
　Vergil and, 370
homilies
　Ambrose's hymns and preaching, 390–93
　Bede's focus on teachers and preachers, 745–49
　biblical narratives, dissemination of, 303, 315, 316, 321–25
　educational function of, 114
　of Gregory the Great, 691–93
　in illud sermons, 287
　Philoxenos of Mabbug on gluttony using rhetorical devices of, 521–27
homilies, as modes of knowing, 7, 282–302
　discursive power of commentary and, 14
　festal sermons, focus on, 283
　improvisation, use of, 298
　in intellectual world of Christian late antiquity, 282
　liturgy and, 288–91
　negotiating space between temporal and eternal, 291–96

preacher/congregant dynamic, 296–301
　rhetoric and, 284–86
　scriptures, homiletic use of, 287–91
Homoiousians and Nicene Creed, 241
Honoré, Tony, 608
Horace, 371, 375, 377
Hughes-Warrington, Marnie, 695
Humboldt, William von, 330
Humfress, Caroline, 614
humility, Dorotheus of Gaza on, 581–84, 586, 589
Huxley, Aldous, 385
Hyginus, 724
hymns and singing. *See also* Ambrose of Milan, hymns of
　Augustine on, 421–24
　Boethius, *Institutio musica*, 679
　Hilary of Poitiers, hymns of, 400–2
Hypatia of Alexandria, 348

Iamblichus
　De mysteriis, 144
　on demons, 149
　on divination and prophecy, 5, 143–52
　on godlikeness as goal of philosophy, 570
　Julian the Apostate and, 145
　Plato's *Alcibiades* and, 514
Ibas of Edessa, 636, 638
Iconium, inscriptions from, 304
'iconoclash', 248
Ignatius of Antioch, *Letter to the Romans*, 381
ihidaya, 271
in illud sermons, 287
illustrated manuscripts in late antiquity, 511, 514
images. *See* Arius and Arians; vision, as mode of knowing
imago Dei, 332, 467, 581
imperium, 590
inequality regime, Bede's acceptance of/expectations for, 749–51
innovation and derivativeness in late antiquity, 705–708, 726
inscriptions, biblical narratives in. *See* biblical narratives
institutions and epistemology, 16–18, 100
Irenaeus of Lyons, 19, 66–88
　action and change, psychology of, 82–84
　Against Heresies, 76
　akrasia, on, 70, 84–87
　Arian theology and, 254
　ascetic framework developed by, 66

Irenaeus of Lyons (cont.)
  body, holiness for, 69–70
  Demonstration of the Apostolic Preaching, 68, 157
  Epideixis, 68, 82
  epistemology of, 81
  faith, on action arising from, 82
  good, on choosing, 79–81
  growth in knowledge, on, 74–75
  holiness, on, 67–69
  Homeric cento and, 78
  image and likeness of God, as goal of human existence, 66
  learning through experience, on, 76–77
  maturity, on, 67, 74, 76, 81, 86
  ordering the self and, 81–82
  psychological holism of, 82
  sexual licence attributed to heresiologists by, 61
  soul, composition of, 81
  soul, holiness of the, 71–74
  truth, on perception of, 76–79
Isidore of Seville
  Bible as form of evidence for, 714
  classical sources on natural history, access to, 709
  De natura rerum, 715, 722, 724
  Etymologiae, 2, 717
  Origines, 712
  in *Reference Bible*, 717
  resolution of discord between ancient non-Christian authors and scripture, 715
  Wigbod's *Commentary on Genesis* compared, 713
Islam, 263, 645, 653

Jacob of Serugh, 269
  Memra on Ephrem, 263
Jaeger, Werner, 330
Jarrow and Wearmouth monasteries, Northumbria, Britain, 730–34
Jay, Nancy, 171
Jeannerod, Marc, 548
Jellicoe, S., 194
Jensen, Robin M., 6, 19, 466, 696
Jerome
  Bede and, 717, 743
  classical *paideia*, proper engagement with, 345
  Commentary on Matthew, 747
  Hilary of Poitiers and, 402
  Jov., 747
  Juvencus and, 367
  Letter to Damasus, 748
  Nom. hebr., 747
  Pelag., 747
  in *Reference Bible*, 717
  Wigbod's *Commentary of Genesis* and, 713
Jerusalem, Council of, 232
Jerusalem, Council of (335), 240
Jesus. See Christ
Jews and Judaism
  Bardaisan on, 124, 131, 133
  dietary avoidance of wine, purposes of, 178
  ekklesia, idea of, 752
  exclusivity of ritual practice of, 177
  Gregory the Great on, 701
  inscriptions citing Bible, 304
  Justinianic Code and, 616
Joannes Stobaeus, 198, 214, 532
John III (pope), 695
John (Archcantor of Rome and Abbot of Tours), 732
John Cassian
  classical *paideia*, proper engagement with, 345
  Conlationes, 547, 747
  on gluttony, 519
  Institutiones, 547
John Chrysostom
  Canterbury school commentaries and, 720
  classical *paideia*, proper engagement with, 345
  On Eutropius, 298, 299
  Homilia in epistolam primam ad Corinthios, 555
  inattention of congregants addressed by, 282
  liturgy and, 555
  sermons of, 283, 284, 287, 297
John Climacus, on mourning, 530
John Damascene
  list of passions/emotions, 536
  on ordering of philosophical knowledge, 8
  Prolegomena, use of, 573
John, Gospel of, spiritual senses in, 41–43
John Lydus
  Justinianic legal regime and, 613, 616
  On the Magistracies of Rome, 590, 594, 600
  Proclus compared, 600

John Malalas
- *Chronicle*, 613
- chronography, as genre, 645
- legal knowledge of, 616

John the Baptist, 408–12, 418
John the Chamberlain, 653, 662
John the Faster, 697
Johnson, Scott Fitzgerald, 9, 118, 196
Johnston, D., 706
Journal of Theological Studies, 224
Judaism. *See* Jews and Judaism
Julian (emperor), 145, 214, 263, 328, 339, 374, 421, 422
Julian (legal scholar), *Instructions for Counsel*, 619
Julian of Halicarnassus, 640
Julian Saba, 274, 275
Julitta (martyr), 297
Julius Africanus, on Bardaisan and Edessa, 119, 127
Junillus, *Institutio regularia divinae legis*, 710, 713, 717
Justin Martyr. *See also* health, medicine, and philosophy in School of Justin Martyr
- *Dialogue with Trypho*, 51

Justina (empress), 392
Justinian (emperor). *See also* law and legal knowledge in Justinianic era
- christological handbooks and, 638
- *Codex Iustinianus*, 612, 615–17, 622, 623
- constitution on 'Imperial Majesty', 608
- *Digest*, 612, 614, 617
- epitomes of legal works of, 619
- imperial majesty versus imperial tyranny of, 608–11
- *Institutes*, 608, 612, 617
- *Novels*, 613, 615–19, 622
- rescindment of laws by, 619

Justinianic plague, 613
Juvenal, *Satires*, 377
Juvencus, 367–74
- Christ as proper poetic topic for, 369–70
- Lazarus, on raising of, 374
- *Libri Evangeliorum Quattuor*, 367
- motives of, 371–74, 385
- *recusatio*, use of, 367
- Vergil and, 370, 373, 374, 385

Kaldellis, Anthony, 608
Kantzer Komline, Han-luen, 163
katalepsis, 76, 83

Kattenbusch, F., 232
Kelly, J. N. D., 224
kenosis, 166, 260
Khusro I (Sasanian ruler), 613
Khusro II (Sasanian ruler), 647
King, Daniel, 122
Kinzig, Wolfram, 223, 225, 226
Klauser, Theodore, 496, 498
Klemm, Elisabeth, 497
knowledge. *See* epistemology in late antique world
König, J., 697, 703
Krausmüller, Dirk, 11, 529, 626
Krautheimer, R., 507
Kreider, A., 157, 162
Kristeva, Julia, 415
Krolikowski, J., 339
Kulikowski, M., 189

L'Huillier, Peter, 235
Lactantius, 252, 377
- *Divine Institutes*, 372

Ladrière, Jean, 548, 554
language. *See also* Augustine of Hippo, on language
- Greek, laws primarily issued in, 617
- vision/images compared to, 466

late antiquity. *See* epistemology in late antique world
late antique period, dating of, 706
Latin Christian poetry, 14, 366–87
- Ausonius of Bordeaux, 379–85, 387. *See also* Ausonius of Bordeaux
- Christian identity of poets, determining, 379
- Juvencus, 367–74
- Prudentius, 374–79, 386
- purposes of, 366, 385–87

Lawrence (martyr), 378, 390, 697
Law, T. M., 192
law and legal knowledge in Justinianic era, 17, 608–25
- circulation and dissemination of, 616–18
- codification and reform programme, 612
- *coloni adscriptici*, status of, 621, 623
- dating of legal documents by regnal year, 618
- epitomes of Justinianic legal works, 619
- Greek, laws primarily issued in, 617
- imperial majesty versus imperial tyranny of, 608–11
- implementation of, 618–22
- inheritance disputes, 620

law and legal knowledge (cont.)
  orthodox Christian state, transformation of Roman empire into, 613–16
  philosophical knowledge and, 612
  political culture of Constantinople and, 609
  rescindment of laws, 619
  social class and legal knowledge, 622–24
  social function of, 611–13
  tax revenues, maintaining and controlling, 613
Leemans, Johan, 7, 14, 282, 517
Lemuria, 378
Leo I the Great (pope), *Tome*, 701
Leontius (presbyter of Constantinople)
  Homilies, 7
  knowledge-creation, liturgical mode of, 550–51
  life and career, 549
  Mary not featuring in sermons of, 566
  narrative knowledge formation in works of, 553–57
  On Pentecost, 552
  ritual knowledge-performance and, 557–64
  Romanos the Melodist compared, 549
  senses of congregants, engaging, 552–53
Leontius of Byzantium, 626
  Contra Nestorianos et Eutychianos, 628
  De sectis attributed to, 630
  Solutiones, 628
  Theodore of Raithou influenced by, 640
Leontius of Jerusalem, *Contra Monophysitas*, 627, 632–35, 637, 638
Libanius, 611
liberal arts, systems or cycles of, 663–67
Licinius (emperor), 247
Lietzmann, Hans, 223
The Light of Asia (Arnold), 373
Limberis, Vasiliki, 506
Lindberg, D. C., 706
Lipsius, 382
'List of Offices', 590
Literary, Critical, and Historical Studies in Ephrem (Vööbus), 267
liturgical modes of knowing, 7
liturgy, 548–68. *See also* Romanos the Melodist
  biblical inscriptions taken from, 309, 325
  church decoration and transformation of space, 556
  homilies and, 288–91

  knowledge-creation, liturgical mode of, 550–51
  Mary in Romanos' hymns, 550, 554, 564–67
  mode of knowing, as, 548
  narrative knowledge formation, 553–57
  Origen's biblical exegesis and, 113–16
  plural verbs, inclusion of congregation through use of, 555
  ritual knowledge-performance, as, 557–64
  senses of congregants, engaging, 551–53
logic, Boethius on study of, 672
Löhr, Winrich, 249
Lord's Prayer
  Ausonius' *Cupido cruciatus* and, 384
  Cyprian on, 162–64
Louth, Andrew, 245
Lucian of Antioch, 247
Lucian of Samosata, 385
  How to Write History, 366
  Peregrinus, 54
Lucretius, 375, 714
lunar rainbow, 724
Lyman, Rebecca, 19, 246

Macedonius, 641
Macrina
  as female character in philosophical dialogue, 354, 358–64
  Gregory of Nyssa on, 328, 360
  Thecla as secret family name for, 354
Macrobius, 679
Macrostich Creed, 237
Madec, Goulven, 389
Magee, John, 8, 663, 702
magic and divination, 136
Manent, Pierre, 450
Mani and Manichaeans
  Arian theology and, 251
  Augustine speaking against, on creation, 412
  Augustine's involvement with, 444, 667
  Bardaisan and, 126
  Bardaisan treatise used by, 121
  creatio ex nihilo and, 248
  De sectis on, 641
  images and, 248
  Nemesius on, 213
  Theodore of Raithou on, 639
Mansfeld, Jaap, 198
Marcellina (sister of Ambrose), 390
Marcellus of Ancyra, 211, 224, 225, 255, 257
Marcion and Marcionites, Bardaisan's treatise against, 121, 125, 128

Marcus Aurelius (emperor), 51, 53, 121, 204
Marius Victorinus (emperor), 379
Martens, Peter, 16, 734
Martianus Capella, *De nuptiis Philologiae et Mercurii*, 663, 687
Martin, M., 194
Martyrdom of Perpetua and Felicitas, 161
martyrs and martyrdom
    Bede on, 737
    Cappadocian festal sermons on, 292
    Great Persecution shaping cult of, 246
    Manicheans and, 252
Marvell, Andrew, 380
Mary (mother of Jesus)
    development of cult of, 564
    Leontius' sermons, not featuring in, 566
    as mediator of divine knowledge, 564–67
    in Romanos' hymns, 550, 554, 564–67
materiality, 18–20
Mattern, Susan, 534
Maurice (emperor), 697, 699
Maximus of Tyre, 107
Maximus the Confessor. *See also* cosmologies of George of Pisidia and Maximus the Confessor
    Ambigua to John, 654, 655
    christology of, 627, 647
    Computus Ecclesiasticus, 645
    Disputatio cum Pyrrho, 654
    Greek and Syriac *Lives* of, 647
    Liber asceticus, 654
    life and career, 647
    list of passions/emotions, 536
    politeia, centrality of, 653
    on spiritual senses, 28, 40
McGill, Scott, 374, 386
McGowan, Andrew, 16, 166
McGrath, Alister, 706
McInroy, Mark, 26–28
McKenzie, Judith, 494
medicine. *See* health, medicine, and philosophy in School of Justin Martyr
meletē, 71–73, 83
Meletius of Antioch, 235
Melissus, 206
Memorius (father of emperor Julian), 422
Menander Protector, 609, 616
Meno's Paradox, 454
Methodius of Olympus
    Arius' refutation of eternal generation and, 249
    De lepra, 358
    on direct creation of body and soul, 258
    familiarity of Gregory of Nyssa with *Symposium* of, 354
    female characters in dialogues of, 348
    on material images, 255
    Symposium, 249, 350, 354–58, 362
    virginity, valuation of, 272
Miaphysites, 516, 529, 653
Michelson, David, 516
Middle Ages, dating of, 706
Milan, Edict of (313), 247
Milky Way, Bede on, 717
Milton, John, 380
Minucius Felix, 467
monenergist-monothelete controversy, 647, 653
Monica (mother of Augustine), 347
Monophysites, 626. *See also* christological handbooks
Morgan, Teresa, 16, 752
Moses. *See also* Gregory of Nyssa; Philo of Alexandria
    as contemplative master, 659–60
    Gregory Nazianzen on, 659
    knowledge of events in Genesis, questions about, 726
Moses of Khoren, 120, 121
Moss, Candida, 257
mother church imagery, in Clement of Alexandria, 35
mourning. *See* Evagrius of Pontus, on λύπη
Murphy, Edwina, 10, 153, 390
music. *See* hymns and singing
music, as discipline. *See* quadrivium
Musonius Rufus, 58

Nabor (martyr), 390
Naevius, 374
Narses (count), 699, 702
natural world. *See* creation and created world
Nautin, Pierre, 113, 116
Neil, Bronwen, 14, 19, 690, 734
Nemesius of Emesa, 212–13, 535, 536
Neoplatonism. *See also* Plato and Platonism
    architectural imagery, as mode of knowing, 513
    Augustine's Cassiciacum dialogues and, 455, 460
    bureaucratic modes of knowing and, 592
    capacities of human reason in, 573
    Christianity and, 134
    conscience, concept of, 586
    De sectis and, 631

Neoplatonism (cont.)
    divination in, 137, 138
    divine, concept of, 579
    epistemological assumptions of, 8
    godlikeness as goal of philosophy in, 570, 582, 583, 588
    law/legal knowledge and, 612
    liberal arts, cycle of, 666
    Licinius and, 247
    liturgical practice as mode of knowing in, 5
    Plotinus as founder of, 143
    vision, as mode of knowing for, 471–73
Nero (emperor), 47
Nestorianism, *De sectis* on, 631
Nestorius of Constantinople
    christological debates of, 626, 635, 636, 638
    De sectis on, 641, 642
    Theodore of Raithou on, 640
Newman, John Henry, 388, 403
Nicaea, Council of (325)
    accounts of proceedings at, 230–32
    Augustine appealing to, 463
    Chalcedon, christological handbooks drawing parallels with, 638
    creeds, evolution of, 223, 228
    Hilary's use of Nicene language, 401
Nicene Creed, 223, 224, 227, 233, 236–44
Nicene-Constantinopolitan Creed, 242
Nicholas of Cusa, on spiritual senses, 28
Nicomachus arithmeticus, 676
Nicomachus of Gerasa, 665, 673
Nordenfalk, Carl, 489, 492, 493, 496, 498
Norman, Dawn LaValle, 14, 347
Nothhelm of London, 716, 732
Notitia Dignitatum, 590, 600, 602
Numenius, 110

O'Connell, Robert, 443, 448, 450, 451
O'Keefe, John, 157
O'Meara, John, 443, 446, 448, 571, 594, 604
O'Sullivan, Timothy, 499
Olympiodorus, 513, 572, 586
One True Life (Rowe), 153
Optatianus Porfirius, 371
Optatus, 160
ordering of knowledge. *See also* Boethius, on ordering of knowledge; epistemology in late antique world

    in Aëtian *Placita*, 199–202, 219
    Augustine's Cassiciacum dialogues, on ideal order of liberal arts curriculum, 457–61
    concept of order, 2
    in creeds, 227
    Cyprian of Carthage, *testimonia* collections of, 156–59
    Irenaeus on ordering of activity, 86
    Irenaeus on ordering the self, 81–82
    Martianus Capella, *De nuptiis Philologiae et Mercurii*, 663
Origen
    Arian theology and, 254
    on castration, 52
    Commentary on Psalms 1–25, 105
    Commentary on the Song of Songs, 89, 91, 107, 381
    contemplation of nature by, 648
    Contra Celsum, 21–23, 110, 111, 138
    divination and theurgy, criticism of, 6, 138–43, 151
    EPHE scheme, familiarity with, 90–92
    On First Principles, 102, 103, 105
    on Genesis 1, 651
    as grammarian, 100, 102–5
    Gregory of Nyssa compared, 337, 342
    Hexapla, 10, 185, 189, 191–97
    Homilies on Luke, 398
    Homilies on Numbers, 138
    Homilies on the Psalms, 116
    Iamblichus on divination compared, 151
    on John the Evangelist, 42
    Letter to Gregory, 104, 105, 111
    life and career, 101, 103
    on material images, 255
    ordination and delivery of homilies by, 113
    philosophical schools, association with, 101–5
    philosophy, tripartite division of, 8
    On Prayer, 107
    on spiritual senses, 5, 21–30
    Stromata, 102
    tables, use of, 10, 191–97
    text-critical approach of, 196
    on theology of the body, 693
    virginity, valuation of, 272
    vision as mode of knowing for, 472
Origen, biblical exegesis of, 16, 100–16
    allegory, 109–11

educational institutions configuring, 100–2
grammatical and philosophical schools associated with Origen and, 102–5
homilies and commentaries, relationship between, 113
ideal readers for, 111–13
liturgy and, 113–16
problems and solutions, identifying and proposing, 108–9
scripture and the philosophical classroom, 105–13
wisdom, as subject matter of scripture, 105–8
Origenists, 122, 632
Orlinsky, H., 194
Osborn, Eric, 18
Ousterhout, R., 505, 510
Ovid, 368, 378, 385
　Metamorphoses, 369, 382

paideia, 162, 282, 328, 331, 334, 336, 338–45, 658. *See also* education and pedagogy
pain and suffering; Evagrius of Pontus, on λύπη
　Bede on experience of, 734–37
Palladius of Ratiaria, 388
Pamphilus, 247
　Capita diversa, 627–29, 633, 636, 638
Pantaenus, 103
papal knowledge, nature of, 702
Parian Chronicle, 196
Parmenides, 206
Parthia, Osrhoene as buffer between Rome and, 119
Passio sanctorum Montani et Lucii, 159
Passions. *See also* Evagrius of Pontus, on λύπη; gluttony; sex/sexuality
　Bede on temporal and spiritual pleasure, 737–41
　lower desires, Plato on use of, 356
Paterius, commentary on the Bible, 713
Paul and Pauline writings. *See also specific epistles in biblical index*
　codices, use of, 305
　relics of St Paul, empress Constantina requesting, 697
　on spiritual senses, 5, 37–40
　visual appearance of Christ to, after death, 470
Paul of Samosata
　De sectis on, 641, 642
　Theodore of Raithou on, 639
Paul the Deacon, 747
Paul the Silentiary, *Description of Hagia Sophia*, 610
Paulinus of Nola
　on images, 6, 483
Pausanias, Bardaisan compared, 132
pedagogy. *See* education and pedagogy
Pender, Elizabeth, 351
Peregrinus, Lucian on, 54
Perkams, Matthias, 90
Perl, E., 605
Perpetua (martyr), 160. *See also Martyrdom of Perpetua and Felicitas*
Peshitta, Ephrem the Syrian and, 265, 268
Peter of Triacola, 694
Peter the Patrician, 591
Petilian, 159
Pherecydes, 110
Phidias, 471
Philebus, 598
Philippikos (general), 699
Philo of Alexandria
　Aëtian *Placita* and, 202–4
　De aeternitate mundi, 202, 204
　on four parts of Moses' philosophy, 91
　Hebrew Bible, prioritisation of, 8
　on material images, 255
　on Moses, 333, 334, 336
　Origen's familiarity with, 110
　problems/solutions format, use of, 108
　Quaestiones in Exodum, 203
Philogelos, 55
Philosophy. *See also* godlikeness and the ordering of knowledge; health, medicine, and philosophy in School of Justin Martyr
　Aëtian *Placita* and, 200, 201
　Boethius' taxonomic ordering of, 677–84
　Cassiodorus' taxonomy of, 686–89
　competition between physicians and philosophers, 47–48
　dietary avoidance of wine, purposes of, 178
　law/legal knowledge and, 612
　as love of wisdom, Boethius on, 680

Philosophy (cont.)
   as male activity, 348
   Origen's association with philosophical schools, 101–5
   purpose of threefold division of, 99
   scripture in the philosophical classroom, 105–13
   threefold division of, 8, 98
   as way of life, 3
Philoxenos of Mabbug
   Discourses, 518
   on Ephrem the Syrian, 265, 266
   Evagrian theology of, 519
   life and career, 518
   Memra against Habbib, 265
Philoxenos of Mabbug, on gluttony, 19, 516–29
   communal life, threat to, 523
   dangers to divine knowledge posed by gluttony, 517–21
   death, gluttony linked to, 520
   definition of gluttony, 520
   Eucharist as remedy for gluttony, 517, 527
   On Gluttony, 517, 518, 521
   inverted hagiographic narrative structure of text, 517, 521–27
Phocas (emperor), 645, 700
Piketty, Thomas, 19, 750
pilgrimage, development of, 512
pilgrims' flasks (*ampullae*), and *tholos* image in Eusebian Canon Tables, 494, 497
Pingree, D., 427
Pistis Sophia, 43
Pius IX (pope), 224
placuit, 233
Plato
   female characters in dialogues, 350
   gluttony attributed by Tatian to, 58
   Gorgias, 672, 679
   Menexenus, 350–52, 360
   Parmenides, 666
   Phaedo, 352, 358–60, 364
   Republic, 594, 653
   Symposium, 350, 352, 355, 358, 360, 364, 452, 683
   Timaeus, 132, 133, 137, 146, 415, 570, 665
Plato and Platonism. *See also* Neoplatonism
   Aëtian *Placita* and, 201
   on *akrasia*, 84
   asceticism in, 69
   Athenagoras on, 205
   Augustine and, 445, 448–57, 464, 474

   Bardaisan and, 122, 125
   Boethius and, 674
   chora, on, 415
   cosmologies of late antiquity resorting to *theoria* of, 645, 648
   on demons, 140
   on divination, 137, 146, 148
   EPHE scheme and, 90, 91
   Eusebius on, 208
   the few and the many, distinction between, 448–53, 464
   godlikeness, as goal of philosophy, 569–71, 575
   Gregory of Nyssa on human perfectibility and, 332
   Hermias on, 206
   lower desires, on use of, 356
   on passions/emotions, 531, 533
   Proclus' diversion from, 598
   soul, composition of, 82
   spiritual senses, Christian doctrine of, 36
   vision, disparagement of, 466, 469
   vision, theory of, 476
   women's expertise on birth, death, and sexuality in, 349
pleasure, temporal and spiritual, Bede on, 737–41
Pliny, *Historia naturalis*, 709, 712, 714, 724
Plotinus, 18
   Ammonius Saccas, as student of, 138
   Augustine's Cassiciacum dialogues and, 464
   Enneads, 90
   godlikeness as goal of philosophy for, 569, 571
   Iamblichus as follower of, 143
   metaphysics of, 143
   Proclus compared, 595, 597, 598, 607
   vision as mode of knowing for, 471–73, 475, 476
Plutarch
   consolations of, 547
   Cyril on, 215, 216
   passions/emotions and, 535
   Stromateis attributed to, 207, 208
poetry, Latin Christian. *See* Latin Christian poetry
politeia, 653
Pontius, *Vita Cypriani*, 154
Porphyry
   Against the Christians, 103, 144
   Arians and, 252
   Boethius influenced by, 673

Christianity critiqued by, 138
divination and theory, criticism of, 5
godlikeness as goal of philosophy for, 570
Homer's cave of the nymphs and, 501, 513, 514
Iamblichus as student of, 143
Iamblichus' *De mysteriis* responding to, 144
On Images, 258, 501, 513
Isagoge, 572
lectures of Ammonius on *Isagoge* of, 681
Life of Plotinus, 103
Origen critiqued by, 110
On Philosophy from Oracles, 501
on priority of knowables to knowledge, 668
problems/solutions format, use of, 108
On Statues, 513
Possekel, U., 127
Poulain, Augustin, 27
poverty, Bede on, 742–45
prayer, Christian life marked by rhythms of, 164
preachers and preaching. *See* homilies
Priscian (grammarian), on sound versus words, 406, 410, 414
Proclus Diadochus
  cosmological sophistry of, 650
  on demons, 139
  on godlikeness as goal of philosophy, 570
  In Parmenides 1081.5, 597
  Timaeus, commentary on, 570
Proclus Diadochus' bureaucratic approach to ontology, 590–93
  Commentary on the Oracles, 601
  dunamis, novel use of, 591
  Elements of Theology, 590, 593, 595
  hypercosmic and hypercosmic-encosmic gods, comparison of, 599
  John Lydus on, 594
  lists of offices compared to, 598–603
  In Parmenides, 597
  Platonic ends, diversion from, 598
  Platonic Theology, 590, 593, 598
  rule of remoteness in bureaucratic systems and, 603–4
  sixth-century repercussions of, 605–7
  survey of Proclus' metaphysics, 595–98
Proclus of Constantinople, 18
  homilies of, 283, 285
  Homily on the Incarnation and on the Lampstand of Zechariah, 290

  Pentecost sermon of, 293–96
Procopius
  On Buildings, 610, 614
  critique of Justinianic regime by, 609–10, 613
  History of the Wars, 609, 610
  imperial history, composition of, 645
  legal knowledge of, 616
  Secret History, 608
Prodicus, 'Choice of Heracles', 370
progymnasmata, 501
Prolegomena. *See* godlikeness and the ordering of knowledge
Propertius, 368
prophecy. *See* divination and prophecy
prosopopoeia, 521
Protasius (martyr), 390
Prudentius, 374–79, 386
  Apotheosis, 375, 377
  Cathemerinon, 375
  Contra Symmachum, 375, 387
  Hamartigenia, 375
  Peristephanon, 375, 378
  Psychomachia, 375, 378, 386
  Wigbod's *Commentary of Genesis* and, 713
Pseudo-Andronicus, 534, 535, 542, 543, 547
Pseudo-Athanasius
  baptismal homily of, 316
  Vita Syncleticae, 546
Pseudo-Dionysius
  Celestial Hierarchy, 605
  Ecclesiastical Hierarchy, 591, 605
  George of Pisidia/Maximus the Confessor and, 660
  Neoplatonism and, 134
  Proclus and, 605
  on spiritual senses, 28, 34
  theandric activity of, 653
Pseudo-Elias (Pseudo-David), 572
Pseudo-Hippolytus, on castration, 53
Pseudo-Justin
  Cohortatio ad Graecos, 211
  Cyril's familiarity with, 214
  on health, medicine, and philosophy, 49, 61–64
  identified with Athenagoras, 49
Pseudo-Plutarch, 58
  Epitome, 198, 202, 207, 209, 210, 212, 214, 216
Pseudo-Zonaras, *Lexicon*, 535

psychological holism, 82
Ptolemy
　　astrology, critique of, 428
　　Boethius and, 677
　　Tetrabiblos, 429
Pythagoras musicus, 676
Pythagoreans
　　Boethius and, 674
　　ekphrasis, 501
　　female members of, 348
　　on gluttony, 519
　　Hermias on, 206
　　on silence, 34
Pythia. *See* Delphi, oracle at

quadrivium, 664, 673–77
Quierzy, Council of (839), 707

Radde-Gallwitz, Andrew, 10, 15, 221
Rahner, Karl, 23, 25, 28, 45
rainbows, 720–22, 724
Ramelli, I. L. E., 127
reason, faith, and authority. *See* Augustine of Hippo, Cassiciacum dialogues
recusatio, 367
Redemptus, bishop of Ferenti, 695
Reference Bible, 717
Reno, Russell, 157
Reudenbach, Bruno, 498
Réveillaud, M., 163
Revelation, on spiritual senses, 43–44
rhetoric
　　Boethius on study of, 670–72
　　homilies, as modes of knowing, and, 284–86
Riedweg, Christoph, 211
Riggsby, Andrew, 10, 185
Rimini, Council of, 229, 234
Roman Creed, 224
Romanos the Melodist, 7
　　Christian discourse, role in framing and expanding, 644
　　knowledge-creation, liturgical mode of, 550–51
　　kontakia of, 285, 549
　　Leontius compared, 549
　　life and career, 548
　　On the Marriage at Cana, 564
　　On Mary at the Cross, 565
　　Mary in hymns of, 550, 554, 564–67
　　narrative knowledge formation in works of, 553–57
　　On the Nativity, 564

On the Presentation in the Temple, 551–52
　　ritual knowledge-performance and, 557–64
　　On the Samaritan Woman, 566
　　On the Sinful Woman, 566
　　On the Woman with the Issue of Blood, 566
Romulus and Remus, 378
Rowe, Kavin, 153
Rufinus
　　Commentary on the Apostles' Creed, 222
　　on creeds, 224
Runia, David T., 9, 198

Sabellianism, *De sectis* on, 631, 642
sacrifice, 16, 166–84
　　in classical world, 168–69
　　cultural production, as, 169–71
　　Cyprian of Carthage on, 171–83
　　Decian persecution, Cyprian's *De lapsis* on aftermath of, 173–77
　　defined, 166
　　magic and, 136
　　mode of knowing, as, 166, 169, 177, 182
　　modern versus late antique concepts of, 167, 183
　　use of water versus wine at Eucharist, Cyprian's *Ep.* 63 on, 177–82
Sahlins, Marshall, 12
Saieg, Paul, 19, 66, 517
Saint-Laurent, Jeanne-Nicole Mellon, 19, 516, 739
Sancus (king of the Sabines), 715
Sanday, W., 224
Sarris, Peter, 17, 608
Sasanian empire
　　cosmic order of empire affected by conflict with, 645
　　Justinianic warfare with, 613
Saturus, 161
scaffolding, 190
Scholten, Clemens, 216, 219
Schott, Jeremy, 512
Schwartz, Eduard, 235
scientific and theological knowledge used to apprehend creation, 705–6, 709
Scribonius Largus, medical formulary of, 186
scripture. *See* Bible
Second Sophistic, rhetoric of, 284
Secord, Jared, 47

Secundus (abbot), on Three Chapters controversy, 701
Seleucia, Council of (359), 229, 234
Seleucus I Nicator (Seleucid ruler), 119
Seneca
  on health and medicine, 64
  on philosophy as love and pursuit of wisdom, 106
  suicide of, 47
senses. *See also* spiritual senses; vision, as mode of knowing
  Bede on taste, 739
  liturgy engaging, 551–53
  as reliable mode of knowing, 5
Sentences of Sextus, 519
Septimius Severus (emperor), 119
Septuagint
  Apollinarius' classical versification of, 375
  Proverbs in, 43
Sergius (patriarch of Constantinople), 646, 651–53
  Ekthesis, 653
Sergius of Resh'ayna, 122
sermons. *See* homilies
Servius (grammarian), 405
Severian of Gabala, homilies of, 283
Severus of Antioch, 640
Sewell, William, 13
sex/sexuality. *See also* virginity
  Bede on continence, 737
  Bede on temporal pleasure of, 738
  castration as means of sexual continence, 52
  female characters in dialogues on, 349, 351, 353
  holiness of the body, Irenaeus on, 69–70
  oracle at Delphi and, 142
  Pseudo-Justin on, 61
  self-castration by worshippers of Atargatis, 124
  Tatian on, 61
Sextus Empiricus
  on *egkrateia*, 70
  on philosophy as cultivation of wisdom, 106
Shemashgram, 128
Shmona (martyr), 263
Sicgfrith (abbot of Jarrow), 736
sight. *See* vision, as mode of knowing
Sirmium, First Synod of (351), 237, 239
Sisebut (Visigothic ruler), 715
slaves and slavery
  coloni adscripticii, status of, 621, 623
  Gregory the Great on, 702
Small, J. P., 511

Smith, C., 510
Smith, Warren, 392
Smyth, Marina, 724
Socrates, 47, 204, 212, 215, 351, 353, 357–59, 681
Socratic method, 695
song and singing. *See* hymns and singing
Sophia of Jesus Christ, 43
Sophist, 598
Sophronius, 647
Soranus, 62
Sosipatra, 348
soul
  Irenaeus on composition of, 81
  Irenaeus on holiness for, 71–74
spiritual senses, 5, 6, 21–46
  Augustine on spiritual seeing, 479–81
  baptism and, 30–34
  Bede on, 739
  christological nature of concept of, 30, 45
  Clement of Alexandria on, 5, 30–34
  John's Gospel on, 41–43
  metaphor and analogy, distinguishing, 26
  modern discussions of, 23–30
  Origen on, 5, 21–30
  Paul's letter to the Philippians on, 37–40
  Revelation on, 43–44
Squire, Michael, 511
Statius Annaeus, 47
Stenger, Jan R., 15, 328
Stephanus of Alexandria, 572
Stephen protomartyr, 470, 482
Stewart-Sykes, Alistair, 155, 163
Stobaeus. *See* Joannes Stobaeus
Stock, Brian, 2
Stoics and Stoicism
  Athenagoras on, 205
  Bardaisan and, 130
  on contraction, 540
  Cyril on, 215
  death, contemplation of, 54
  divination, on, 137, 146
  human decision-making for, 109
  logic, on, 672
  passions/emotions for, 531–33, 536, 543
  philosophy, on divisions of, 666, 677
  psychological holism of, 82
  Rowe's *One True Life* on, 153
  wisdom, on, 98, 106
Stowers, Stanley, 170
Straw, Carol, 702
Strøm-Olsen, R., 502, 510
Stroumsa, Guy, 19, 306

Struck, Peter T., 5, 134, 426
Suetonius, *Life of Lucan*, 47
syllogisms, in christological handbooks, 635
Symeon the Mesopotamian, 611
Symeon the New Theologian, 531
synchronism, 189
Syriac world. *See* Ephrem the Syrian; Bardaisan, *Book of the Laws of the Countries*
Syrianus, 601

tables and tabular organisation, 10, 185–97
    Ammonius, *Diatessaron*, 190
    astronomical tables, 197
    authorising cross-reference, 187
    bilingual texts, 191–97
    Cicero's *Leg. Agr.*, 187
    defined, 187
    Eusebius' use of, 10, 185, 186, 189, 190
    in late antique world, 186–91
    Lex Irnitana 91, 187
    obligatory cross-reference, 187
    Origen's use of, 10, 185, 189, 191–97
    rarity of, in classical world, 188
    reader expectations about, 195
    as scaffolding, 190
    Scribonius Largus, medical formulary of, 186
    synchronism and, 189
Tabula Cebetis, 370
Tatian
    Diatessaron, 367, 373
    on health, medicine, and philosophy, 49, 56–61
    Oratio ad Graecos, 2
    problems/solutions format, use of, 108
Tertullian
    on baptism, 34
    De oratione, 163
    De paenitentia, 155
    on divination, 138
    on Greco-Roman culture versus Christian faith, 340
    on Justin Martyr, 50
    sensory experience, disparagement of, 469
testimonia. *See* Cyprian of Carthage, *testimonia* collections of
textual community, concept of, 2
Thacker, A., 751
Thales
    Aëtian *Placita* and, 201, 209
    Athenagoras on, 205
    Cyril on, 214
    on Deity, 214
    Eusebius on, 209
Thalia, 250, 253, 259
Thecla (saint)
    cult of, 354
    as family name for Macrina, 354
    in Methodius' *Symposium*, 354
Thecla (widow), disputed inheritance of, 620
Themistius, 671
Theoctista (sister of emperor Maurice), 698–700
Theoctistus (bishop of Caesarea), 113
Theodelinda (queen to Lombard king Agilulf), 700, 702
Theoderic I the Great (emperor), 675
Theodore (archbishop of Canterbury), 720, 732
Theodore of Hermopolis, 619
Theodore of Mopsuestia, 637, 640, 641
Theodore of Raithou
    'abbas Theodore' in *De sectis* identified with, 631
    De sectis compared to *Praeparatio* of, 642
    Praeparatio, 627, 629–30, 639–41
Theodoret of Cyrrhus
    Aëtian *Placita* and, 198, 216–19
    at Chalcedon, 636, 638
    Church History, 230
    Healing of the Hellenic Illnesses, 216–19
Theodote (*hetaera*), 351, 353, 357, 358
theological and scientific knowledge used to apprehend creation, 705–6, 709
Theophanes the Confessor, *Chronicle*, 650
Theophronius, creed of, 232
Theophylact Simocatta, 645
Theophylactus, 252
theoria, 15
theoroi, 648–55, 661
theosis, 2
theurgy. *See* divination and prophecy
    concept of, 144
tholos image in Eusebian Canon Tables, 6, 484–515
    catalogue of surviving examples, 485–92
    church architecture, late antique approach to, 486, 500
    definition of, 485
    Holy Sepulchre, Jerusalem, and, 486, 492, 496, 500–2

iconography of, 485, 496–99
illustrated manuscripts in late antiquity and, 511, 514
indeterminacy/polyvalence of image, 498
late antique *comparanda* for, 492–96
mode of knowing, architectural imagery as, 512–15
origins of, 492
Tyre, church of Paulinus at, 486, 502–11
Thomas Aquinas
 on analogy versus metaphor, 27
 on spiritual senses, 29
Thomas Gallus, on spiritual senses, 29
Three Chapters controversy, 701
Thucydides, historiographical tables discussed by, 196
Timon, *Silloi*, 210
titulus, 376
Tomlinson, Mark, 378
Topping, Ryan, 458, 462
Tritheism, 632, 642
trivium, 664, 668–73
True Cross relic, 645
Turner, C. H., 227, 245
Tyre, *tholos* image in Eusebian Canon Tables and church of Paulinus at, 486, 502–11

Ullucci, Daniel, 169, 172
Ulrich, Jörg, 219
Underwood, Paul, 489, 496
Urbano, Arthur, 104, 341
Ussher, James, 224

Vaggione, Richard, 246
van Bavel, Tarcisius, 459
van Fleteren, F., 451
van Nieuwenhove, Rik, 706
Vaughan, Henry, 381
vegetarianism, 61
Vegetius, 714
Verecundus (friend of Augustine), 443
Vergil
 Aeneid, 368, 373
 bilingual texts of, 192
 Georgics, 368
 Isidore's use of, 715
 Juvencus and, 370, 373, 374, 385
 Prudentius and, 375–77

Victor (martyr), 390
Victorinus, 463, 668, 676
Vidas, Moulie, 3, 691, 703
Vincent of Lérins, 692
Vinzent, Markus, 225, 257
virginity
 as perfect image of humanity, 249
 pre-monastic valuation of, 272
vision, as mode of knowing, 6, 466–83
 ancient critiques of sensory/visual perception, 468–71
 ancient theories of seeing, 475–79
 artistic works, 481
 Augustine on, 473–83
 Augustine's critique of demonic divination and, 440
 Bible, on seeing God, 468
 in Christian thought generally, 467–68
 eye-witnesses to life of Christ, authority of, 468
 God, utter invisibility of, 467
 imago Dei, concept of, 467
 incarnation of Christ, as image and word, 467–68, 470
 language compared, 466
 metaphor for knowledge, sight as, 551
 Plotinus and Neoplatonists on, 471–73
 witnessing Christ's actions in the world, Athanasius on, 470
Vita Ceolfridi, 730
Vivarium, study of philosophy at, 686–89
Vologese (bishop), 278
Vööbus, Arthur, 264, 267

Walch, J. G. F., 222
Wearmouth-Jarrow monasteries, Northumbria, Britain, 730–34
Webb, Ruth, 548, 551
Weir, Tony, 611
Weitzmann, Kurt, 511
Wesley, John, 28
Wessel, Klaus, 497
Whiston, William, 224
Whitby, Mary, 651
White, Richard, 247
Whitmarsh, T., 697, 703
Wickes, Jeffrey, 15, 261
Wigbod, *Commentary on Genesis*, 713, 714
Wiles, Maurice, 224
William of St-Thierry, 40

Williams, Megan, 185, 189, 190, 196
Williams, Rowan, 362, 405
wisdom, as primary subject of scripture, 105
women. *See also* female characters in dialogues; gender; Mary (mother of Jesus)
   feminist theory, 166
   mother church imagery, in Clement of Alexandria, 35
Wood, Ian, 750

Xanthippe (wife of Socrates), 359
Xenophon
   female characters in dialogues of, 351, 352
   Memorabilia, 357, 360, 364
   women's expertise in birth, death, and sexuality for, 349

Yeats, William Butler, 16

Zecher, Jonathan, 19, 530, 699
Zeno, on Homeric problems, 108